Personal Property Law

Personal Property Law

Text, Cases and Materials

SARAH WORTHINGTON

• HART •
PUBLISHING
OXFORD – PORTLAND OREGON
2000

Hart Publishing
Oxford and Portland, Oregon

Published in North America (US and Canada) by
Hart Publishing c/o
International Specialized Book Services
5804 NE Hassalo Street
Portland, Oregon
97213-3644
USA

Distributed in the Netherlands, Belgium and Luxembourg by
Intersentia, Churchillaan 108
B2900 Schoten
Antwerpen
Belgium

Hart Publishing Ltd is a specialist legal publisher based in Oxford, England.
To order further copies of this book or to request a list of other publications please write to:

Hart Publishing Ltd, Salter's Boatyard, Oxford OX1 4LB
Telephone: +44 (0)1865 245533 or Fax: +44 (0)1865 794882
e-mail: mail@hartpub.co.uk
www.hartpub.co.uk

British Library Cataloguing in Publication Data
Data Available
ISBN 1 901362–43–4 HBK
ISBN 1 901362–44–2 PBK

Typeset by Hope Services (Abingdon) Ltd.
Printed in Great Britain on acid-free paper
by Biddles Ltd, www.biddles.co.uk

Preface

Personal property law is a fascinating and challenging subject. Its importance to everyday commercial and social interaction is obvious. Many transactions, whether elementary or elaborate, stand or fall by the rules of the law of personal property. Despite this, personal property law is one of the most neglected and least understood aspects of English law. This book seeks to turn the tide. It aims to provide a stimulating and accessible, but also challenging, introduction to the fundamental principles of the law of personal property. The book is intended for students and their teachers, although others may also find it engaging. A word of warning is necessary, however. Although the relevant principles are fundamental, they are not simple, nor are they uncontested. This is perhaps to be expected when the law at issue has to deal with everything from minor gift-giving to multi-party international secured commercial transactions. Moreover, the assets subjected to these dealings can be tangibles, such as bottles of wine or barrels of oil, or intangibles, such as shares or debts. As well, the interests at stake can be legal or equitable, and designed to confer either ownership or merely security. To make matters still more complicated, money has some special rules of its own.

From all this diversity, it is necessary to cull the underlying principles and determine their limits. Only then can the law be properly utilised, either to resolve disputes or to permit new and more inventive dealings. More importantly, only then can the law be evaluated, and its functions and consequences defensibly criticised or supported. There is no shortcut from knowledge to understanding, and from there to analysis, synthesis and evaluation. The text and materials in this book are intended simply to provide a route map for embarking on the journey.

Some of the features of this book need explaining. Measured in pages, the bulk of the material in the book is devoted to elucidating the significant principles within the law of personal property. This weighting is necessary because the principles themselves are often complicated and rather obscure; it follows that their limits have to be teased out with some particularity. Nevertheless, the overriding aim is to inspire the reader to assess and evaluate the different legal principles and their structural coherence. There is, it is hoped, sufficient guidance within the text, the questions at the end of readings, and certain selected materials within the Chapters themselves, especially within Chapters 1 and 8, to direct and stimulate a formal appraisal of the substantive issues. The trick is to keep asking "Why?" and "What follows from that?".

A second feature of the book is that the selected extracts tend to be quite long. Some of the most engrossing debates within the law of personal property can only be properly appreciated by resort to the materials generating the debate, whether sourced in judicial pronouncements or in academic comment. Moreover, it is not enough simply to read the concluding views of the different proponents. The arguments and counter-arguments, the process of reasoning and evaluation, the relevance of context, are all important in conveying a true sense of both the cogency and the limitations inherent in the matters under discussion. The extracts aim to convey the authentic flavour of the debates. Of course, readers familiar with the subject are sure to find that some of their favourites have been omitted. However, the objective is simply to encourage reflection, not to cover every inch of the territory. Within each Chapter, the intention is to provide enough diversity to enable an enquiring reader to sift through the analyses advocated by different authors, pausing often to assess whether the arguments are both coherent and compelling. At the end of this process, the challenge is to advance a rational view of the boundaries of a particular legal principle and its potential ramifications.

This process of definition and evaluation is not for novices alone. The more one delves into this area of the law searching for the ultimate truth, the more shadowy that figure seems to become. Matters held to be absolute truths one year become qualified the next. The law of personal property has serious and wide-ranging functions to perform. Its remit is vast and conceptually difficult. Its foundation principles need to be secure, but, beyond that, continuous assessment and re-assessment is vital if the basic framework is to be properly and effectively developed, refined and improved. While this book may fairly represent the modern state of play, the nuances will no doubt change over time.

In the course of collecting materials and ideas, and writing a book such as this, the debts to various people multiply. Not all can be thanked personally: too many colleagues and students have been party to discussions of these issues over the years. However, a few deserve to be singled out. Len Sealy supervised the doctorate which marked the beginnings of my fascination with personal property. Roy Goode is, still, my most challenging and stimulating critic on issues relating to personal property. He kindly read and commented on the manuscript. With characteristic good humour, he is sure to disagree with certain explanations within these pages. However, he must also notice how often his views are comprehensively adopted to account for difficult issues. Many friends and colleagues at the LSE, but especially Niki Lacey, James Penner and Hugh Collins, have all provided legal argument and laughter in appropriate doses. Sinead Agnew did much of the preliminary research for this book, and in the process became a friend and colleague. Last, but certainly not least, I owe a huge debt to my husband and children: notwithstanding their own busy lives, they bear the tribulations and disruptions of authorship with unfailing good humour and unending encouragement.

The idea for this book began as a joint project with Paul Eden. In the end, other matters took up his time far more profitably: a new wife, a new job and a new house. He would have approached matters quite differently, and I look forward to his future writings in the area. Richard Hart was associated with the project from the start. His enthusiasm, good humour and efficiency are legendary. Hannah Young steered the book through the editorial process and John Jeffries did a superb job on the index. I thank them all.

Finally, I would like to dedicate this book to my parents. I have them to thank for the firm conviction that personal relationships, not personal property, deserve our real energies. I hope they see in this book an effort to stimulate people, not to define things.

Sarah Worthington
London

August 2000

Table of Contents

PART III: TRANSFERS OF INTERESTS IN PERSONAL PROPERTY

4 CONSENSUAL TRANSFERS OF INTERESTS IN PROPERTY

5 TRANSFERS OF INTERESTS IN PROPERTY BY OPERATION OF LAW

Acknowledgements

The author and publisher gratefully acknowledge all the authors and publishers of extract material which appears in this book, and in particular thank the following for permission to quote the following extracts from the sources indicated:

LLP Professional Publishing:

Corporate and Commercial Law: Modern Developments published by LLP Professional Publishing, 69-77 Paul Street, London, EC2A 4LQ, Tel: +44 (0) 20 7553 1000 Fax: +44 (0) 20 7553 1107

Sweet and Maxwell:

Journal of Business Law, A Boyle " TheValidity of Automatic Crystallisation Clauses (1979) JBL 231, pp. 234, 236-7; S Worthington, "Sorting out Ownership Interests in a Bulk: Gifts Sales & Trust (1999) JBL 1, pp. 7-13;
Insolvency Lawyer, S. Worthington, "Backdoor Security Devices" (1991) Insolvency Lawyer 153, pp. 157-9
Law Quarterly Review, P J Millett "The Quistclose Trust: Who Can Enforce It?" (1985), 101, LQR 269, pp. 284-91; R Goode "Ownership & Obligation in Commercial Transactions (1987), 103 LQR 433, pp. 433-5; S. Worthington "Fixed Charges over Book Debts and Other Receivables (1997) 113 LQR 562, pp. 565-6; S Kurshid and P Matthews "Tracing Confusion" 95 LQR, 78, pp. 79-83.
W T Murphy and S Roberts, Understanding Property Law, 3rd edn, pp1-5.
R Goode, Principles of Corporate Insolvency Law, 2nd edn, pp. 35-52.
J R Bradgate, "Reservation of Title Ten Year On", The Conveyancer, (1987) 51 Conv., 434, pp. 443-6

Butterworths:

K Gray – Elements of Land Law,

Thomson Legal & Regulatory Group

J W Gough, "The Floating Charge: Traditional Themes and New Directions (1987) pp. 247-8 in "Equity and Commercial Relationships" edited by P D Finn.

The Cambridge Law Journal:

K Gray, "Property in Thin Air" [1991] CLJ 252, pp. 292-9, 301-3, 307, 264-9.

The SPTL:

W J Swadling "A New Role for Resulting Trusts" (1996) 16 Legal Studies 110, pp. 130-1

Blackwell Publishers:

Goodhart and Jones " The infiltration of equitable doctrine into English commercial law", Modern Law Review, (1980), vol 43.
Pennington "The Genesis of the Floating Charge" , Modern Law Review, (1960) vol 23.

Oxford University Press:

M. Bridge, "The Quistclose Trust", 20 (1992) Oxford Journal of Legal Studies, pp. 334-342.

Table of Cases

Table of Legislation

Part I

Introduction

1

Defining Personal Property

1.1 Introduction

Everyone is familiar with personal property. Everyone owns, buys, borrows and hires things. Everyone uses money. But not everyone knows about the ways in which the law supports those dealings. This is the remit of the law of personal property. This book describes the fundamental aspects of that law.

Some boundaries must be recognised, however, otherwise the law of personal property would swallow whole much of every other category of the law. Large parts of the law of obligations, criminal law and public law are concerned with *obligations* imposed on parties in relation to their use of personal property. Here the focus is much narrower. It is on the *rights* which the law entitles a party to exercise in relation to personal property, and on the factors which determine when those rights will arise.

In any discussion of personal property, it is impossible to avoid the disjunction between property as a 'thing' and property as a 'right', or, more accurately, a bundle of rights.[1] Even in the preceding paragraphs, there is an evident, if subliminal, tension between the 'thing' that is dealt with, and the 'rights' that are obtained or conferred in dealing with the thing. That tension continues to be evident in what follows. 'Personal' property is distinguished from 'real' property by looking at the nature of the 'thing'. Yet, once that is done, the real preoccupation is with the consequences of such a classification—then the focus is on the 'rights' associated with the thing. It is the unusual features of those rights which mark property as special.

[1] This view of property as a 'bundle of rights' is the dominant one, but it has its critics: see J E Penner, 'The "Bundle of Rights" Picture of Property' (1996) 43 *UCLA Law Review* 711–820. Certainly the 'bundle of rights' view has taken over from the 'property as thing' view: see K J Vandevelde, 'The New Property of the Nineteenth Century: The Development of the Modern Concept of Property' (1980) 29 *Buffalo Law Review* 325.

1.2 Types of property

1.2.1 Real and personal property

The common law distinguishes between 'real' and 'personal' property. Generally speaking, real property is land and everything attached to land. Personal property is everything else—it is a residual category. The reason for the distinction is historical. In the Middle Ages, an owner of real property who was wrongfully dispossessed could recover the land *in specie* (in what was termed a *real* action); an owner of personal property in similar circumstances could only recover damages (in a *personal* action). This distinction lives on, although courts now have a discretion to order specific re-delivery of personal property in appropriate circumstances.[2]

This different treatment of real and personal property has been explained on the basis that real property is immovable, permanent, readily split into multiple interests, and primarily acquired for use rather than for circulation in the course of trade. Personal property, on the other hand, is usually moveable, of relatively short lifespan, not amenable to division into multiple interests, but possessed of a value readily measurable in money and therefore easily tradeable.[3]

Question:

Are these distinctions between real and personal property still accurate? If they are not, should the law take any cognisance of the fact?

1.2.2 Types of personal property

The diagram below (Fig. 1) indicates the sub-classification of personal property into its different types. This classification is based on the characteristics of the underlying 'thing'. The terminology is specialist, but it is necessary to come to grips with it. It provides an essential shorthand for the discussion which follows. As the diagram indicates, sometimes different expressions are used to indicate the same class of property. This book is concerned exclusively with chattels personal, both tangible and intangible, although it does not attempt to deal with the specialist subject of intellectual property rights (such as copyright, patents and trademarks). For practical purposes, chattels real are treated as part of the law of real property. The subdivisions indicated in the diagram are largely self-explanatory. The distinction between tangibles and intangibles reflects a readily recognisable physical difference between these two types of property. Computers and cars are 'tangible' assets; cheques, shares and debts are 'intangible' assets. However, something more needs to

[2] Torts (Interference with Goods) Act 1977 s 3.

[3] R Goode, *Commercial Law* (2nd edn, 1995, Penguin: Harmondsworth) pp 33–5.

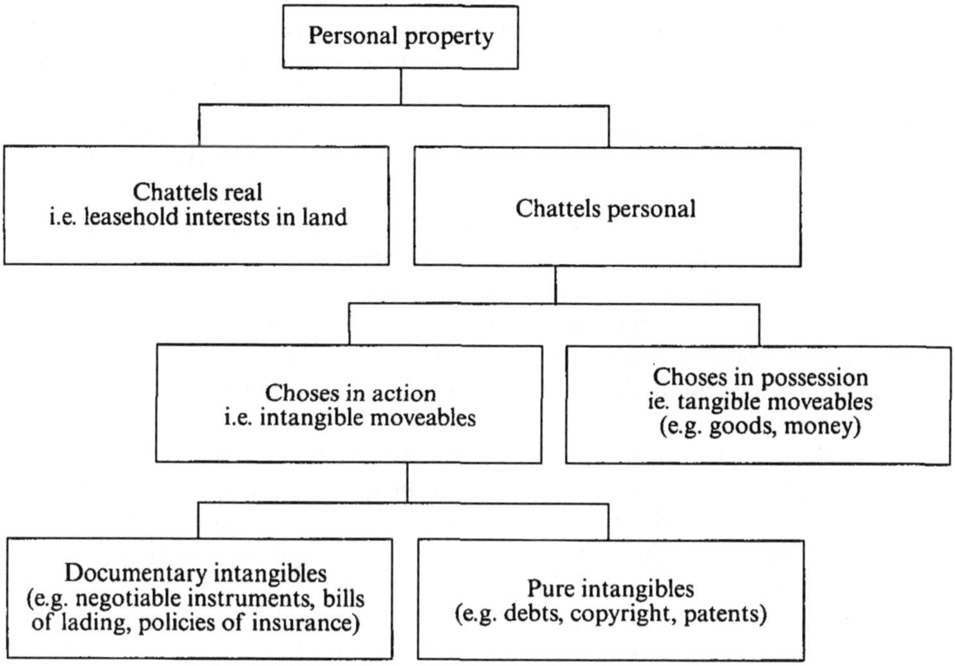

Fig. 1. *Types of personal property.*

be said about the next sub-classification into pure and documentary intangibles. Documentary intangibles are documents that the law regards as able to stand for the property itself: they represent the underlying right to money, goods or securities, and, importantly, they allow that right (the 'property') to be transferred by delivery of the document, supported by any necessary indorsements.

One further distinction is not represented in the diagram. This has to do with *legal* property and *equitable* property. The distinction must be made carefully. It is important, for example, in determining which rules govern the transfer of the property. Note that the focus is still on the *nature* of the underlying asset.[4] The common law recognises all choses in possession as property. It follows that all these choses are legal property and will have a legal owner. Choses in action, on the other hand, can be either legal or equitable property. Choses in action are personal property rights which can only be claimed or enforced by action, not by taking physical possession. Legal choses in action are those which, historically, could be enforced in a common law court: debts, bills of exchange, insurance policies and company shares

[4] To anticipate what will come later, *legal* property (classified as such because of the nature of the underlying asset) can have both a *legal* and a beneficial (or *equitable*) owner. Third parties may also have *legal* or *equitable* security interests in the property. In short, different parties can have either legal or equitable interests in the 'legal' property. These legal and equitable interests may then themselves be classified as legal and equitable property, respectively. Note, however, that *equitable* property (classified as such because of the nature of the underlying asset) can only have an equitable owner (not a legal one, since by definition the common law does not recognise the asset as property), and, similarly, third parties can have only equitable security interests in the property.

are all examples. Like choses in possession, these choses in action are legal property and will all have a legal owner. Equitable choses in action, such as the beneficiaries' rights to a share in the trust estate, are those which, historically, could only be enforced in the Court of Chancery. These choses are not recognised at law. They are not legal property, but equitable property. They cannot be owned at law, only in equity; it follows that they cannot have legal owners, only equitable owners.

As already noted, personal property is a residual category: anything that *is* property, but not real property, is personal property; anything that is not property is merely a *personal* right (rather than a real, or proprietary, right). So what is property? The question is important, because property and property rights receive special protection not reserved for personal rights. This means that there is some pressure to have new rights classified as property (or property rights), not merely as personal rights.

The issue can be put into sharp relief by an example. From what has already been said, it is clear that a debt is classified as a chose in action: it is a personal right given to a creditor to sue the debtor to recover the sum owed. By analogy, it might seem that *any* right under a contract could be regarded as a chose in action: it gives the contracting party a right to sue the counter-party to enforce the contract or to obtain damages for breach of contract. But debts are regarded as property, whereas in general rights under contracts are not property rights, but personal rights. What does this distinction reflect? The next section examines the issues.

1.3 What is property?

[101] K Gray, *Elements of Land Law* (1st edn, 1987, Butterworths: London), pp 8–14:

'THE MEANING OF PROPERTY

It is important at the outset to dispel one common lay notion concerning 'property'. Non-lawyers (and sometimes lawyers) speak loosely of property as the *thing* which is owned. While this usage is harmless enough in day-to-day speech, it has the effect of obscuring certain salient features of property as a legal phenomenon, for semantically 'property' is the condition of being 'proper' to (or belonging to) a particular person.

(1) Property is not a 'thing' but a 'relationship'

It was the philosopher, Jeremy Bentham, who had to remind lawyers that property is not a thing but a relationship. Bentham pointed out that 'in common speech in the phrase *the object of a man's property*, the words *the object of* are commonly left out; and by an ellipsis, which, violent as it is, is now become more familiar than the phrase at length, they have made that part of it which consists of the words *a man's property* perform the office of the whole.' More recently Professor Macpherson has drawn attention to the way in which, in the transition from the pre-capitalist world to the world of the exchange economy, the distinction between a right to a thing (ie the legal relation) and the thing itself, became blurred. 'The thing itself became, in common parlance, the property'.

(a) Potential multiplicity of competing users

At one level of analysis, then, 'property' is a relation between the owner and the thing (ie between a 'subject' and an 'object'). However, as has already been suggested, it is unreal to think simply in terms of 'the' owner of any particular thing. It is possible for conflicting claims to be brought by two or more 'subjects' in respect of the same 'object', and therefore the property lawyer is almost always concerned with the relative merits of different claims. In order to establish what belongs to, or is 'proper' to, any particular 'subject', he must first analyse the legal relations between a number of competing subjects vis à vis the same object. A further level of complexity arises because any particular 'object' of property may itself be capable of sustaining a wide variety of different (but not necessarily conflicting) claims. This is demonstrated most clearly in the case of land. Land may, for instance, be the object of a multiplicity of claims made simultaneously by an owner-occupier, a tenant, a building society, a neighbour who enjoys a right of way or restrictive covenant, or even by a spouse who has certain rights not to be evicted from the property.

(b) A network of 'property' relationships

In the ultimate analysis the law of property is concerned with entire networks of legal relationship existing between individuals in respect of things. 'Property' is thus the name given to the bundles of mutual rights and obligations which prevail between 'subjects' in respect of certain 'objects', and the study of property law accordingly becomes an inquiry into a variety of socially defined relationships and morally conditioned obligations. This relational view highlights certain characteristics of property which are essential to any real understanding of land law [and personal property law].

Professor Bruce Ackerman has spoken of the need to disabuse law students of their primitive lay notions regarding ownership. In the words of Ackerman, 'only the ignorant think it meaningful to talk about owning things free and clear of further obligation'. Instead of defining the relationship between a person and 'his' things, property law considers the 'way rights to use things may be parcelled out amongst a host of competing resource users'. Ackerman points out that each resource user is conceived as holding 'a bundle of rights vis à vis other potential users' and that the ways in which user rights may be legally packaged and distributed are 'wondrously diverse'. Ackerman concludes that

> it is probably never true that the law assigns to any single person the right to use any thing in absolutely *any* way he pleases. Hence, it risks serious confusion to identity any single individual as *the* owner of any particular thing. At best, this locution may sometimes serve as identifying the holder of that bundle of rights which contains a range of entitlements more numerous or more valuable than the bundle held by any other person with respect to the thing in question. Yet, like all shorthands, talk about 'the' property owner invites the fallacy of misplaced concreteness, of reification. Once one begins to think sloppily, it is all too easy to start thinking that 'the' property owner, by virtue of being 'the' property owner, must *necessarily* own a particular bundle of rights over a thing. And this is to commit the error that separates layman from lawyer. For the fact (or is it the law?) of the matter is that property is not a thing, but a set of legal relations between persons governing the use of things.

(2) Property is a dynamic relationship

If property is a relationship, it is a dynamic relationship; the content of the relationship is liable to change. The 'subjects' of property may differ from one social era to another. The 'objects' of property are likewise liable to fluctuate with the passage of time and the emergence of new economic conditions. Above all, the ideology of property is profoundly influenced by changing factors of social, political and economic philosophy.

(a) The changing 'subjects' of property
An element of social control is exercised over the property relation in every society, in that each social group to a greater or lesser extent determines for itself the categories of person who may be recognised as the potential 'subjects' of property. In some societies of the past various classes of labourer or serf (eg slaves) were excluded from legal competence as potential 'subjects' of property. Even until relatively recently in England, the married woman was deprived of capacity to hold a legal title in her own name. However, the present century has seen the 'emergence of a property-owning, particularly a real-property-mortgaged-to-a-building-society-owning, democracy.' The years of greater affluence following the World Wars brought about, in the words of Lord Wilberforce, 'the extension, beyond the paterfamilias, of rights of ownership, itself following from the diffusion of property and earning capacity.' Less obviously this diffusion of ownership rights has accentuated the demand that other kinds of right should be recognised as 'proprietary' rights on behalf of less advantaged social groups. Those, for instance, who are not owners of the homes in which they live may wish to assert that their occupation rights (eg as tenants) represent a proprietary status equivalent to that of the owner-occupier.

(b) The changing 'objects' of property
If the 'objects' of property are those resources to which social or economic value is generally attached, it is inevitable that over time variations of social interest and concern should alter the emphasis of the property relationship. There was, for instance, an age in which both wives and slaves were regarded as appropriate 'objects' of property. In medieval England the husband was viewed as enjoying proprietary rights in relation to his wife, her domestic services and her productive capacity. Much of the concern which generated this assessment of the spousal relationship was itself brought about by the supposed paramountcy of the need to ensure the devolution of property within a dynastic line of legitimate issue. However, the 'objects' of property are continually redefined by the prevalent social ethic, and today it is no longer acceptable that either wives or certain classes of labourer should be regarded as the 'objects' of a proprietary relation.

(i) *Transformation of material wealth* The 'objects' of property can, however, change in more subtle degrees. For centuries the most highly prized 'object' of property in the common law world was land. In the 19th century and early 20th century the phenomenon of the company share came close to dislodging land as the pre-eminent 'object' of commercial value, at a time when the bulk of ordinary men and women owned little of value other than perhaps the clothes which they wore. In the modern post-industrial society, however, with the diffusion of ownership amongst classes never before entitled, the traditional concept of a man's wealth has undergone yet another transformation. Nowadays a person's material substance is no longer related particularly to the ownership of tangible assets designed for enjoyment and consumption; it is more readily expressed in terms of intangible, non-assignable, and often non-survivable, claims of a largely personal nature. The things which today are of real value to the man in the street are assets like his job, his pension, and the right to undisturbed possession of his home. On the fringes of these new categories of property lie certain less well defined rights such as the right to education, the right to health and the right to a wholesome environment.

(ii) *The 'new property'* The changing concept of wealth in the modern world was classically described by Professor Charles Reich in a seminal law review article in 1964. Reich drew attention to the dramatic changes taking place in the nature and forms of wealth in industrial democratic societies. In particular, he pointed to the way in which government has begun to operate today as a major distributor of wealth in the form of welfare payments, salaries for those in public service, pensions for those who have retired from employment, and many other forms of licence, franchise, subsidy and fiscal benefit. As Reich inicated, 'today's distribution of largesse is on a vast, imperial scale.' Reich went on to argue that the principal forms of wealth for most people in our society are comprised in their employment or profession (and in various work-related benefits such as pensions) or in their dependency claims upon government (in the guise of social security payments). These forms of wealth, which for Reich were concerned essentially with income security, have become in fact the 'new property', and Reich's major thesis was that this 'new property' should be accorded the same standard of legal protection as had been accorded in the past to more traditional entitlements of private property. In his view, the goal of future development in this area must be to 'try to build an economic basis for liberty today—a Homestead Act for rootless twentieth century man. We must create a new property.'

The call for legal recognition of and protection for the 'new property' has intensified during the two decades since the publication of Reigh's major article. In 1970, in its fundamentally significant decision in *Goldberg v Kelly*, the Supreme Court of the United States acknowledged the 'new property' to be deserving of constitutional protection. In the years following this decision, the prominence of the 'new property' has been accentuated by developments in other fields of law.

(iii) *The changing balance of family, work and government* The emergence of the 'new property' can also be placed in the historical context of a more general shift in the relative importance of family, work and government as determinants of social status and as sources of economic security. Today, in an age of liberal divorce and increasingly attenuated family ties, the primary source of economic security for the individual is no longer the family but rather the individual's employment or his dependency relationship with government. . . .

. . . .

(iv) *Residential security* The jurisprudence of the 'new property' has emerged largely in the context of the individual's rights in the fields of employment and social security. However, an object which lies more immediately within the ambit of a 'Homestead Act for rootless twentieth century man' is the general provision of security in the enjoyment of residential accommodation. . . .

(c) The contemporary redefinition of 'property'

During the present century claims of social welfare have been increasingly recognised through interventionist legislation in the fields of social security, housing and employment protection. By according legal force to various kinds of 'security claim', this legislation has already gone some distance towards ensuring a more equitable distribution of the 'goods of life'. The security claims recognised in these areas broadly cover the kinds of interest which are comprised within the 'new property'. Thus the claim to security in employment is recognised, at least to some extent, by legislation which protects the individual employee from 'unfair dismissal'; the claim to residential security, by the Rent and Housing Acts and other statutory means; the claim to income security, by the vast range of legislation which underpins the social security system. Inherent in all these measures is a significant return to the idea of a 'status'. The individual receives the benefits of protective legislation, not because he has in any sense contracted or bargained to receive them, but because he enjoys a defined 'status' which entitles him to some appropriate form of 'security'.

All these developments tend to suggest that, by operating effectively as an agent of distributive justice, the 'new property' has initiated a redefinition of the ideology of property. In the conventional analysis, the concept of property is essentially negative and exclusory: the traditional concept of a property right comprises the right to exclude all others from the use or enjoyment of some thing. The 'new property' comprises by contrast various kinds of claim *not* to be excluded from the use or enjoyment of some thing. Indeed it has been said that the idea of property is gradually being broadened to include a 'right to a kind of society or set of power relations which will enable the individual to live a fully human life.' At least in some incipient form, this perspective may indicate an intellectual shift away from the idea that property is a private right to exclude from personally owned resources, and may point instead towards a reappraisal of property as a public right of access to socially valued resources.'

Questions:

To a lawyer, is property a thing? Can two or more people have property in one thing? What features indicate that certain bundles of rights can be labelled as 'property'? For example, the fact that a debt is personal property has already been noted, but can a person's rights in relation to confidential information be classified as 'property'?[5]

[102] *National Provincial Bank Ltd v Ainsworth* [1965] AC 1175 (HL), 1247–8 *per* Lord Wilberforce:

[This case concerns real property, not personal property, but the few lines below have become a classic statement of general relevance. A deserted wife remained in occupation of the family home. The house belonged to the husband, and, after leaving his wife, he mortgaged the house to the bank. When he later defaulted on his repayments, the bank sought repossession. The wife unsuccessfully sought to allege that she had some sort of property interest in the house.]

'. . . . Before a right or an interest can be admitted into the category of property, or of a right affecting property, it must be definable, identifiable by third parties, capable in its nature of assumption by third parties, and have some degree of permanence or stability. The wife's right has none of these qualities, it is characterized by the reverse of them. . . .'

[5] In land law, similar questions arise: why is a lease an interest in property, but a licence is not?

Question:

As will become evident later, this will not do as a *definition* of property. It is both too wide and too narrow. It is too wide because, in its terms, it is capable of encompassing rights which are personal, not proprietary. It is too narrow, because it would exclude rights which are clearly proprietary, but which do not meet all the conditions apparently imposed. What familiar examples of personal and proprietary rights illustrate this assessment of Lord Wilberforce's statement?

[103] K Gray, 'Property in Thin Air' [1991] *CLJ* 252, 292–9, 301–3, 307:
[Footnotes in the original are omitted.]

'And so continues our search for the inner mystery of "property". Let us look back and see how far we have got since we started. There is no real likelihood that we have arrived at our destination, for the quest for the essential nature of "property" has beguiled thinkers for many centuries. The essence of "property" is indeed elusive. That is why, in a sense, we have tried to catch the concept by surprise by asking not "What is property?" but rather "What is not property?" We have started from the other end of the earth—both geographically and conceptually—and we have deliberately come by the direction which seemed least probable. But along the way we may have discovered something of value. We may have discovered the irreducible conditions which underlie any claim of "property".

The classic common law criteria of "property" have tended to rest a twin emphasis on the assignability of the benefits inherent in a resource and on the relative permanence of those benefits if unassigned. Before a right can be admitted within the category of "property" it must, according to Lord Wilberforce in *National Provincial Bank Ltd. v. Ainsworth* [[1965] AC 1175, 1247–8] be "definable, identifiable by third parties, capable in its nature of assumption by third parties, and have some degree of permanence or stability". This preoccupation with assignability of benefit and enforceability of burden doubtless owes much to the fact that the formative phases of the common law concept of property coincided with a remarkable culture of bargain and exchange. Non-transferable rights or rights which failed on transfer were simply not "property". Within the crucible of transfer lawyers affected to demarcate rights of "property" from rights founded in contract and tort or, for that matter, from human rights and civil liberties. Only brief reflection is required in order to perceive the horrible circularity of such hallmarks of "property". If naively we ask which rights are proprietary, we are told that they are those rights which are assignable to and enforceable against third parties. When we then ask which rights these may be, we are told that they comprise, of course, the rights which are traditionally identified as "proprietary". "Property" is "property" because it is "property": property status and proprietary consequence confuse each other in a deadening embrace of cause and effect.

Nor have the philosophers given significantly greater assistance in explaining the phenomenon of "property". Perhaps inevitably lawyers have concentrated their attention on locating the *ownership* of "property", this task of identification assuming vial significance in a legal culture dominated by transfer and conveyance. By contrast philosophers have directed their efforts principally towards rationalising the *institution* of "property". While lawyers discuss who owns what, philosophers ask why anyone can legitimately claim to own anything. Justificatory theories of "property" range diversely from appeals to the investment of labour or the existence of a social contract to arguments based upon first occupancy, utility or personhood. A pervasive influence in all philosophical thinking on "property" is still the brooding omnipresence of John Locke. But Locke's concentration on original acquisition ill suits legal discourse in a modern world which is based on derivative acquisition and in which original acquisition (except perhaps in the area of intellectual property) is now virtually impossible. Even Locke himself cannot have believed that in late 17th century England the "Commons" still contained many unappropriated acorns yet to be "pickt up under an Oak" or apples to be "gathered from the Trees in the Wood", even if he did think that "property" in such things was "fixed" by the labour invested in their "first gathering". As Walton Hamilton noted much later, Locke's natural state is "a curious affair, peopled with the Indians of North America and run by the scientific principles of his friend Sir Isaac Newton".

In their respective preoccupations with resource allocation and institutional justification, lawyers and philosophers alike have largely failed to identify the characteristic hallmark of the common law notion of "property". If our own travels in search of "property" have indicated one thing, it is that the criterion of "excludability" gets us much closer to the core of "property" than does the conventional legal emphasis on the assignability or enforceability of benefits. For "property" resides not in consumption of benefits but in control over benefits. "Property" is not about *enjoyment of access* but about *control over access*. "Property" is the power-relation constituted by the state's endorsement of private claims to regulate the access of strangers to the benefits of particular resources. If, in respect of a given claimant and a given resource, the exercise of such regulatory control is physically impracticable or legally abortive or morally or socially undesirable, we say that such a claimant can assert no "property" in that resource and for that matter can lose no "property" in it either. Herein lies an important key to the "propertiness" of property.

. . . .

The concept of excludability thus takes us some way towards discovering a rationally defensible content in the term "property". The differentiation of excludable and non-excludable resources points up the irreducible elements which lie at the core of the "property" notion. But these irreducibles, once isolated and identified, leave little if anything of value to be gathered from the traditional indicia of "property". The concept of excludability does not, of course, resolve entirely the issue of justice in holdings; it merely demarcates the categories of resource in which it is possible to claim "property". It sets outer limits on claims of "property", but provides no criteria for justifying such claims on behalf of particular individuals—except to the extent that we accept the initially unpalatable (but historically attested) proposition that the sustained assertion of effective control over access to the benefits of a resource tends ultimately to be constitutive of "property" in that resource. The precise allocation of "property" in excludable resources is left to be determined—is indeed constantly formulated and reformulated—by various kinds of social and moral consensus over legitimate modes of acquisition and the relative priority of competing claims. This consensus is reinforced by a machinery of legal recognition and enforcement which thus adds or withholds the legitimacy of state sanction in relation to individual assertions of "property".

V. Conclusions

If "property" is a power-relation constituted by legally sanctioned control over access to the benefits of excludable resources, certain conclusions follow.

A. "Property" is a Relative Concept

Since the physical, legal and moral conditions of excludability may vary according to time and circumstance, it becomes clear that the notion of "property" in a resource is not absolute, but relative. The concept of "property" is not static, but dynamic. I may have "property" in a resource today, but not tomorrow. I may have "property" in a resource for one purpose but not for another. I may have "property" in a resource as against X but not necessarily as against Y or Z. It may be that P and Q can both claim "property" in the same resource although their respective interests are mutually opposed. It is not even inevitable that there should be a quantum step between having "property" in a resource and not having "property" in it. Propertiness is represented by a continuum along which varying kinds of "property" status may shade finely into each other.

B. "Property" has Moral Limits

The essential relativity of "property" emerges perhaps most clearly in the proposition, discussed earlier in this paper, that claims of "property" may be abridged in order to further more highly rated social objectives. "Property" is not a value-neutral phenomenon. "Property" in a resource stops where the infringement of more basic human rights and freedoms begins. There are distinct moral limits to the concept of "property". As the Supreme Court of New Jersey observed in *State v. Shack*, "[p]roperty rights serve human values. They are recognised to that end, and are limited by it." The same Court confirmed that "an owner must expect to find the absoluteness of his property rights curtailed by the organs of society, for the promotion of the best interests of others for whom these organs also operate as protective agencies".

Quite profound—although as yet barely acknowledged—consequences flow from this recognition of the moral limits of "property". The moral qualification has, of course, a major significance for those who endorse the rhetoric of stewardship and the communitarian theory that the earth's resources are effectively held on trust for a number of social and environmental interests. Thin air, for instance, may not be made thick with pollutants. Land in particular takes on the character of a social commodity—a realisation which impacts just as keenly on patterns of land use and development as it now does on the increasingly contentious issue of recreational access to wild country.

In some deeper and broader sense it is the collectively defined moral baselines of the property concept which alone secure the foundations for cultural development, personal fulfilment and the enjoyment of a civilised and dignified way of life. Vast areas of human resource and human capacity are excluded from the reach of private property, and are indeed excluded so effectively that we rarely pause to reflect either that it might have been otherwise or, more ominously, that some day it may yet be.

In most societies, for instance, there is a general consensus that no attempt should be made to propertise certain ranges of humane, intellectual or sensory experience. There is no "property" in the right to listen to Chopin nocturnes; or to play the saxophone; or to engage in sexual intercourse; or to reproduce children. Nobody can assert that he (or some restrictively defined group of "owners") has an exclusive right to determine who may read novels or paint pictures or go to the theatre or climb mountains. There is no such phenomenon as "property" in the game of golf or in the right to play chess. (Even William Webb Ellis, who in 1823 first lifted the ball and ran with it, claimed no "property" in the resulting game of rugby football.) For the most part no one "owns" the right to consume certain kinds of food or drink. Nowadays at least there is no "property" in the right to vote or to be eligible for public office, and every democratic society is ultimately underpinned by the denial that there can be any "property" in political thought. But it is salutary to reflect that none of this need be so.

The current range of the world's propertised resources is indeed much more limited than we might imagine. Only a relatively small part of the total field of economic facility and human capacity is at present permitted to be the subject of private claims of "property". Amongst the challenges of the 21st century will be the question whether such "property" claims are to be allowed in relation to a wider group of assets and resources. The ambit of eligibles will include resources which range variously from human body parts and cells to fecundity, reproductive capacity and live babies; from the exploitable aspects of the human persona to the asset of commercial product goodwill; from leisure options to the eventual cure for AIDS and cancer; from Antarctica to outer space. It is at this point that we will really test the proposition that there are moral limits to the notion of "property".

C. "Property" is a Term of Wide Signification

Leaving aside for a moment the issue of moral limitation, it is clear that the perspective of excludability has an otherwise liberating impact on the identification of "property". An extensive frame of reference is created by the notion that "property" consists primarily in control over access. Much of our false thinking about property stems from the residual perception that "property" is itself a thing or resource rather than a legally endorsed concentration of power over things and resources. If "property" is not a thing but a power-relationship, the range of resources in which "property" can be claimed is significantly larger than is usually conceded by orthodox legal doctrine. (This is indeed the source of both the greatest challenge and the greatest danger confronting the law of property in the 21st century.) The limits on "property" are fixed, not by the "thinglikeness" of particular resources but by the physical, legal and moral criteria of excludability. By lending the support of the state to the assertion of control over access to the benefits of particular resources, the courts have it in their power to create "property". But of critical importance in this definitional process is obviously the care with which the courts determine which resources are recognisably non-excludable.

. . . .

D. "Property" is Definable Otherwise than in Terms of Proprietary Consequence

The adoption of excludability as the constitutive criterion of "property" brings about the further result that the legal concept of "property" need no longer be defined tautologously in terms of legal consequence. Whether X has or has not "property" in a given resource should not depend on whether his rights are assignable to Y or are binding upon Z, any more than the transferability or enforceability of X's rights should turn on some obscure characterisation of those rights as "property". Both formulae exhibit a similar infirmity in so far as each tends to link property status incenstuously with proprietary consequence.

The attribution of property status is instantly rescued from such circularity of argument if "property" is defined, not by reference to the traditional indicia of assignability and enforceability, but rather by independent reference to the free-standing criterion of excludability. This substitution is easily defensible on the ground that the notion of excludability offers an immeasurably more convincing explanation of the legal phenomena of assignability of benefit and enforceability of burden. Assignment (whether voluntary or involuntary) constitutes the ultimate release or abnegation of control over the access of strangers to the benefits of an excludable resource. In the absence of such assignment, "property" in an excludable resource can be vindicated against third parties precisely because the resource is excludable.

E. "Property" is Assimilable within Consensual Theory

In conventional legal doctrine much energy is devoted to patrolling the frontier between property and contract. Property lawyers keep especially vigilant watch for those fugitive varieties of contractual right which threaten to cross the frontier and settle in property territory. Much fuss is made whenever the conceptual border is realigned and rights of "contract" are brought within the province of "property". . . .

No quantum step differentiates contract from "property", for "property" has no clear threshold. There exists instead a spectrum of "propertiness" in which obligations which derive their moral force from discrete acts of affirmative consent shade gradually and almost imperceptibly into obligations whose social persuasiveness rests upon the collective acceptance of sustained acts of assertive control.

. . . .

In the end the "property" notion, in all its conceptual fragility, is but a shadow of the individual and collective human response to a world of limited resources and attenuated altruism.'

Question:

In seeking the characteristics which define 'property', some analyses emphasise alienability. The previous extract emphasises excludability. What are the potential consequences of this altered focus in defining rights as proprietary?

Clearly one of the attributes of property is that it is assignable—it is not just wealth, it is *usable* wealth. Without this attribute, a right is unlikely to be classed as property, notwithstanding its value. For example, a job is clearly valuable. It generates wealth. But the job-holder cannot deal with the job; the job cannot be sold to a third party for cash. If a right which was previously non-assignable is somehow made assignable, the ultimate effect may be to create a new form of property.[6]

Equity has contributed to this process—it has permitted the assignment of things which historically were not assignable at law. As already noted, personal property can be classified according to the characteristics of the underlying asset. On this basis, choses in possession are different from choses in action (see Section 1.2.2 above). Historically the common law considered it impossible to assign (or transfer) choses in action, even if the chose was a legal one. However, equity regarded this distinction between choses in action and choses in possession as somewhat absurd, and, from the start, both legal and equitable choses in action were freely assignable in equity. This difference in approach is significant. Equity regarded choses in action as *property* which could be assigned to third parties and would then warrant protection against the world (or at least a segment of it). The common law, on the other

[6] Assignability is not the only attribute required of property, so re-classification would not be automatic.

hand, regarded the rights as purely personal, enforceable only between the parties concerned, not assignable and not meriting protection against the world (or even a section of it). Equity thus had a different perception of which forms of wealth, or which rights, should be treated as property and which should not.[7] The common law had a more limited vision of what constitutes property—the focus was on tangible assets. Predictably, the common law view had to change, if only because much of modern wealth is tied up in intangibles. Now assignment of choses in action is possible using either the common law statutory route[8] or the older equitable route.

FURTHER READING:

J Waldron, *The Right to Private Property* (1988, Clarendon: Oxford).
J E Penner, 'The "Bundle of Rights" Picture of Property' (1996) 43 *UCLA Law Review* 711.
K Gray, 'Equitable Property' (1994) 47 *CLP* 157.
S Munzer, *A Theory of Property* (1990, Cambridge University Press: Cambridge).
C Reich, 'The New Property' (1964) 73 *Yale Law Journal* 733.
F S Cohen, 'Dialogue on Private Property' (1954) 9 *Rutgers Law Review* 357.

1.4 Types of property rights: interests in property

The preceding extracts suggest that the law finds it difficult to distinguish between rights which are 'proprietary' and rights which are 'personal'. At root, the debate often centres on whether the right-holder has, and should have, all the benefits normally associated with *ownership*[9]—the ability to deal with the rights and extract value from them, perhaps by conferring positive benefits on third parties, perhaps by excluding them from access or interference. Does a right-holder 'own' a car, a debt, or a right to see a spectacle? The answers are not always easy. Sometimes the law concludes that certain rights cannot be 'owned' in this way.

In fact, ownership is not the only form of property right, or *interest* in property. 'Interest' is preferred to 'right' for two reasons. It is a word which recognises that there is not simply one single right marking out 'ownership', but a bundle of rights.[10] Moreover, the individual rights within the bundle can be altered and amended without denying the right-holder's ownership. In short, people with ownership interests do not necessarily have precisely the same rights as each other. The various different types of property interests are considered in detail in Chapters 2 and 3. Here it is sufficient to note that the common law recognises two different *interests* in property: ownership and possession. These two 'bundles of rights', or interests, can be used in numerous different ways for personal or commercial bene-

[7] It seems this attitude was directed at preventing unconscionable behaviour in relation to both common law and equitable rights, and prevention was enforced via equitable proprietary rights.
[8] Law of Property Act 1925 s 136: see **[405]** below. See Chapter 4 generally.
[9] See Chapter 2.
[10] Although see note 1 above.

fit. For example, possession can be given to another for a limited time or for limited purposes: goods can be hired, or deposited for repair, or deposited as security against performance of another obligation. None of these possibilities removes 'ownership' from the owner. Ownership can be enjoyed to the exclusion of others, or shared, or given away, or sold.

Equity, too, has its own forms of property rights—*or equitable interests* in property. Equity recognises equitable ownership, equitable charges and liens,[11] and a mortgagor's equity of redemption.[12] Under an express trust, for example, the beneficiary has equitable ownership of the trust property,[13] the trustee has legal ownership.

In addition, equity also recognises 'mere equities'. These are *personal* rights (not proprietary rights) the exercise of which will deliver a proprietary interest in the assets of another. For example, A may sell a car to B under a contract which A is entitled to rescind for fraud or undue influence. Before rescission, B is the legal and beneficial owner of the car. After rescission, however, the car will re-vest (at law or in equity)[14] in A. This feature—the ability to deliver proprietary interests—makes mere equities more valuable that other personal rights.

The *general* rule is that all these different interests in personal property are both assignable and enforceable against third parties. These two characteristics traditionally mark rights as proprietary. However, as will become evident in later chapters, this is a general rule with numerous exceptions. Constraints on transfer can be imposed; enforcement against third parties can be denied.

1.5 The legal significance of property

The legal significance of property lies in the special attributes of proprietary rights. This requires careful explanation. Lawyers commonly classify rights as proprietary (*in rem*) or personal (*in personam*). The fundamental distinction is very simple. Proprietary rights ('real rights'[15]) describe the relationship between a person and a thing. The particular nature of the relationship determines what rights the person has to deal with the thing. Proprietary rights include ownership, possession and

[11] These are security interests (see Chapter 3), both providing similar rights, distinguished by the fact that the first arises by agreement between parties, the second by operation of law.

[12] This is not considered in this book. Texts on land law describe the interest in detail.

[13] In practice, matters are rarely quite so simple. There are often several beneficiaries with different interests. Moreover, the trust may be discretionary, so that the beneficiaries have no immediate proprietary interest in the trust property and no guarantee that any particular individual will ever necessarily acquire such an interest.

[14] This depends upon both the nature of the asset and the nature of the flaw permitting rescission. Certain assets cannot immediately re-vest at law, because, as with shares, the location of legal title depends upon compliance with appropriate registration formalities. Furthermore, if the 'flaw' permitting rescission is only recognised in equity, and not in law, then revesting can only occur in equity.

[15] Do not confuse the different uses of 'real'. Real and personal *property* refers to the distinction between land and other forms of property. Real and personal *rights* refers to the distinction between rights in property (both real and personal property) and other rights.

various security interests, and each of these can be specifically tailored to meet particular needs. So, for example, ownership of a ship is a proprietary right. It is shorthand way of indicating the rights the owner has to deal with the ship. Personal rights, on the other hand, describe a relationship between a person and another person. Again, the particular terms of the relationship indicate the rights one person has against the other. For example, if the relationship between two parties is one of a contract of sale, then the intending purchaser is entitled to assert particular personal rights against the vendor, and vice versa.

However, at another very fundamental level *both* proprietary and personal rights have to do with the relationship between persons. The proprietary right of ownership does not just describe the relationship between the owner and the property owned. It also indicates the constraints placed on all those other than the owner in dealing with the property. In this sense, proprietary (or real) relations are distinguishable from personal relations because of the number of persons affected by the relationship. Ownership of a ship, given earlier as an example, entitles the owner to assert certain rights (proprietary rights) against the whole world. Anyone who interferes with those rights can be sued. Personal relations, on the other hand, usually affect only two parties, the right holder and the obligor. Under a contract for sale, for example, the only person an intending purchaser can exercise (personal) rights against if the sale falls through is the nominated vendor. It is this distinction between proprietary and personal rights which marks out one of the more significant and valuable attributes of proprietary rights—proprietary rights operate against 'the world'.

Of course, not all the examples which can be imagined are quite so clearcut. Sometimes a relationship with a thing will affect not the whole world, but only those people who know, or ought to know, about the relationship—or the right—and are therefore said in legal terminology to have 'notice' of it. This explains why there are registers of so many property rights, such as rights in land, shares, patents, and so forth. Note that sometimes—especially when there are registers, but in other circumstances too—the right affects not only those who actually know about it, but also those who could and should know about it (and so are said to have 'constructive notice' of the right). These limitations mean that the underlying rights are not good against the whole world, but only against a more limited class. Nonetheless, all these rights in relation to things, whether they affect the whole world or only those who have actual or constructive notice of the right, are classed as proprietary rights, or rights *in rem*.

In summary, *if* a right is proprietary then it is enforceable against the world, or at least against a section of the world (perhaps only those with notice of the right). This is the first significant attribute of proprietary rights. Admittedly that just brings the problem full circle: *which* rights are proprietary? The earlier extracts considered the issue from a theoretical perspective. But take the practical example of a debt. If X is owed money by Y, then X can enforce that obligation against Y, but not of course against anyone else. Looked at from this perspective, X's right is a *personal* right against Y entitling X to sue Y for repayment of the debt should that become necessary. But it is also true that debts can be sold, and that they can be used as security for a loan (receivables financing). In this respect a debt looks like a real right. Other contractual (personal) rights operate in the same way. Consider the right to royalties, or the right to dividend or interest payments. In all these instances it might seem that there is no clear line between a personal right and a real right. As already noted, at the margins the answers are unclear. At root there is a policy decision at stake: which rights *ought* to be enforceable against the world, rather than simply between consenting parties? Much of the debate over whether certain *assets* are *property*, or, in legal terms, whether certain *rights* are *proprietary*, is concerned to answer this policy question.

The second significant attribute of proprietary rights arises *because* these rights give their holder claims to property which are good against the world (or a defined section of it). This combination of features can deliver significant advantages over rights which are purely personal. These advantages are critical in several contexts, but they are thrown into sharpest relief when the person against whom the rights are claimed becomes insolvent. It is a fundamental rule of insolvency law that the only assets which can be distributed to the insolvent's creditors to repay outstanding debts are assets which belong beneficially to the insolvent. A claimant with a proprietary interest in assets in the insolvent's hands can withdraw those assets (to the extent permitted by the particular proprietary interest), and other third party creditors of the insolvent cannot complain that this diminishes the pool of assets available to pay them. Parties with proprietary interests are therefore in a more favourable position than parties with only personal rights.

An example will illustrate the difference. Suppose A has agreed to purchase a work of art from B, and B becomes insolvent after taking payment but before delivering the painting. Ideally A will want delivery of the painting notwithstanding B's insolvency. *If* the contract of sale made A the owner of the painting before B became insolvent (perhaps when the price was paid, or when the contract was made), then A can demand the painting.[16] A will then not lose anything on the sale despite B's insolvency. On the other hand, if the contract did not deliver ownership to A prior to B's insolvency, then A is simply a purchaser with personal rights exercisable against B, but with no real rights in any property. A can then frame her personal claim against B in two ways, claiming either damages for breach of contract, or restitution of the purchase price. In either case, however, the money claim will rank alongside all the other claims made by B's general creditors, and A, along with all these other creditors, will simply be paid a *pro rata* sum which will depend upon the size of B's estate available for distribution. A is unlikely to recover in full. This distinction between the effect of proprietary and personal rights on a defendant's insolvency is another reason for the push to have rights classified as proprietary.

This protection which proprietary rights can deliver to a claimant on a defendant's insolvency merits further comment. In the illustration given in the previous paragraph the purchaser was protected if she could claim a proprietary interest in the painting rather than relying on any personal rights to money remedies. But the picture is not quite so simple. Three points should be noted. They will be developed later. First, the fact that A is the legal owner of the painting does not necessarily give her the right to demand that it be delivered up to her. This may seem surprising. However, as noted at the outset, English law adopted one rule in relation to real property and another in relation to personal property. With personal property, the

[16] This is not quite as simple as is made out here: see the next paragraph and Section 7.2.3.

defendant can elect whether to return the property in specie or pay damages for its conversion.[17] Secondly, if B no longer has the painting—say it had been destroyed by fire—then, even if A owns the painting, her ownership cannot possibly deliver her proprietary advantages; she can only claim entitlement to a personal remedy of money damages. In these circumstances she will have no special privileges on the defendant's insolvency. Finally, if the facts were altered so that A was the *equitable* owner and B the legal owner of the painting, then, in most cases, A *would* be able to demand specific delivery of the asset. In this respect equitable ownership appears more advantageous than its legal counterpart. These three points might be summarised by saying that proprietary rights do not inevitably deliver proprietary remedies, although when they do the advantages to the right-holder can be dramatic.

[104] R Goode, 'Ownership and Obligation in Commercial Transactions' (1987) 103 *LQR* 433, 433–5, 436–41:

[Footnotes in the original are omitted. The latter part of the extract highlights an important debate which resurfaces later: see especially Chapters 5 and 6.]

'In common with other legal systems, English law sharply distinguishes property rights from mere personal rights to the delivery or transfer of an asset. I *own* property; I am *owed* performance of a transfer obligation. Ownership attracts several advantages, and some disadvantages, in law, and is frequently a condition precedent to the assertion of contractual rights. If I own an asset in the possession of another who becomes bankrupt, I can withdraw it from the reach of his creditors; if I am owed a purely personal obligation to transfer the asset to me I have no right to remove it from the common pool. As owner of a chattel I am entitled to a remedy in tort for negligence if it is carelessly damaged or destroyed by another. Ownership also carries with it a right to possession, where no one else has a better right, and is protected by the law of torts, in particular the tort of conversion. If I own goods, I bear the burden of accidental loss or damage.

. . .

II. Ownership in Insolvency

(i) Practical importance of the question

In the commercial world the distinction between ownership of an asset and a purely personal right to acquire an asset, *e.g.* under a contract, is usually of little significance so long as the debtor is traceable and solvent, for the interest of a commercial creditor in the performance of a transfer undertaking is usually monetary rather than in ownership for its own sake, and if the debtor (using this term in the broad sense of an obligor) fails to deliver then the creditor can simply obtain what is due to him, either in cash or in kind, by suing for it and enforcing any resulting judgment.

It is upon the debtor's insolvency that the distinction between ownership and a personal right to an asset becomes of crucial significance, for it is a basic policy of insol-

[17] Although the court has a discretion to order specific restitution: Torts (Interference with Goods) Act 1977 s 3. In addition, it seems that a defendant who has the goods in his or her possession cannot elect to pay damages and keep the goods unless the damages are paid in full. This means that *if* the defendant still has the goods, then the claimant is protected on the defendant's insolvency, at least in money terms, even if the asset itself is not recovered; the damages claim will not rank with all the other claims of unsecured creditors.

vency law to adopt the non-bankruptcy ordering of rights and thus to respect proprietary rights held by another prior to the debtor's bankruptcy. Hence in principle the estate available for distribution among the general body of creditors is limited to the debtor's own assets. Owners and secured creditors can withdraw from the pool the assets they own or over which they have security, whilst unsecured creditors are left to prove in competition with each other for such crumbs as remain after proprietary rights, the expenses of the insolvency proceedings and the claims of preferential creditors have been satisfied.

It follows that the degree in which the law is willing to recognise rights as proprietary rather than merely personal is of great moment to unsecured creditors, for every extension of the concept of ownership erodes the debtor's estate and thus reduces the significance of the hallowed principle of pari passu distribution. Conversely, every condition precedent attached by the law to the acquisition of ownership represents a pitfall for the would-be investor and the would-be secured creditor who lays out his money in the expectation of receiving in exchange some proprietary interest in the debtor's patrimony.

One might, then, expect our law to have determined and made explicit the policy considerations underlying the recognition of proprietary rights in insolvency. In particular, one might have supposed that a relevant factor would be the satisfaction of reasonable expectations engendered in the minds of investors and creditors by the type of transaction under consideration and the circumstances in which it was made. Instead, our insolvency law has for the most part been content to adopt as operative on insolvency technical rules for the acquisition of proprietary rights applicable prior to bankruptcy.

. . .

(iii) The growth of equitable property rights

Property and obligation at law

The common law (in its narrow sense) sharply distinguished transfers of property from mere personal undertakings. A transfer from A to B had to relate to an existing asset in which A had a subsisting interest, and the transfer itself had to be in proper form. Except in the case of a contract for the sale of existing goods, where the agreement was effective by itself to transfer title, an agreement for transfer conferred no proprietary rights on the intended transferee even if he had parted with his money. A purported transfer by A to B of A's after-acquired property was at best a contract and could not of itself operate to vest the property in B even after A had acquired it; a new act of transfer was necessary after the acquisition. Similarly, a transfer by A to C to hold on trust for B conferred no interest on B, for the conveyance was not made to him.

These common law rules still apply in relation to the transfer of a legal title, save for the special case of contracts of sale of goods, in relation to which the Sale of Goods Act prescribes the automatic transfer of title to future goods upon their acquisition by the seller, if the parties so agree.

Property and obligation in equity

Under the influence of equity the distinction between property rights *in* an asset and personal rights *to* an asset became blurred. Acting on the basis that equity treats as done that which ought to be done, courts of equity came to regard an unperfected agreement to assign as an assignment which became perfected by payment of the consideration; they upheld the assignment of future property as effective on acquisition by the debtor without the need for any new act of transfer; they recognised the interest of the beneficiary under a passive trust as a proprietary interest; and they accorded proprietary status to the right of an owner of an asset to trace the products and proceeds of dispositions by the owner's bailee.

Even after all this the ingenuity of the equity lawyers was not exhausted. A person might succeed to a claim by assignment or by subrogation. Equity also came to recognise the existence of proprietary rights not in a specific asset but in a shifting fund of assets, as exemplified by the interest of the beneficiary under an active trust and of a debenture holder under a floating charge, and these interests became included in the category of proprietary rights having priority over the claims of unsecured creditors.

The development of the resulting trust and the constructive trust led to the recognition of proprietary rights in a variety of situations in which one person improperly held assets or benefits to which another had a better right. Among the events that have been held to attract these forms of trust are the payment of money for a purpose which has failed, the payment of money under a mistake of fact and the acquisition of an asset by the defendant from a third party, or the retention of such an asset, in breach of the defendant's fiduciary duty to the plaintiff.

Finally, even a "mere equity," such as a right to rescind (*e.g.* for fraud or misrepresentation) a contract under which the bankrupt acquired an asset can be asserted against his trustee, thus removing the asset from the general body of creditors even after the commencement of bankruptcy.

The result of this equitable development is that most obligations owed by B to A to transfer an asset to A are proprietary in nature rather than merely personal, though often A has a personal right to the asset running concurrently with his proprietary interest in it. It is unusual to find a situation in which B has a duty to make over to A an asset still in B's hands without A thereby enjoying equitable ownership of the asset. In equity, the obligation to transfer, whatever its source, is itself a transfer provided that the obligation is not merely contingent, the subject-matter is identifiable and the consideration is in due course paid. The one outstanding exception to this rule is the contract of sale of goods, where the buyer either acquires legal title or acquires nothing beyond a mere contract right. This exception reflects not only the universality of the contract of sale of goods, which makes it undesirable to complicate the contract by equitable ownership, but the fact that under a contract of sale title passes by agreement, and except where this is reserved to secure payment a seller who has not reached the stage of passing legal title usually intends to reserve a right to dispose of the goods elsewhere.

(iv) The fairness of equitable ownership in insolvency

All these equitable proprietary rights diminish the debtor's apparent estate. Some of them are bargained for expressly, others arise as a matter of implied agreement, whilst some are purely the result of the imposition of equitable obligation and make no pretence to a consensual foundation. Apart from consensual security interests, none of these equitable proprietary rights is registrable, hence none of them is visible to the bankrupt's general creditors, who may well be induced to believe that the bankrupt is himself the beneficial owner.

Small wonder, then, that complaint has been made of the unfairness of these equitable rules to unsecured creditors. Why should a mistaken double payment be impressed with a trust in favour of the payer when a payment made under a contract in the mistaken belief that the recipient will perform his part of the bargain is recoverable only by a personal action? Is it fair that the owner of goods which are wrongfully sold by his bailee should have a preferential right to the proceeds of sale? Why does a failure of the consideration for B's payment as the buyer of goods leave him an unsecured creditor when a failure of the purpose for which a payment is earmarked entitles the payer to recover it as held on a constructive trust? Why should the seller of goods who was induced to sell them by the buyer's misrepresentation be able to rescind the contract as against the buyer's trustee in bankruptcy, and recover his goods, when a seller who delivers goods against the buyer's promise of payment is left to rank as an unsecured creditor if the buyer becomes bankrupt without paying? Is it not true that in their zeal to provide equitable proprietary remedies the courts have ignored the fact that the real loser is not the wrongdoer but his unsecured creditors?

At first sight these objections to the recognition of equitable proprietary rights in bankruptcy seem compelling. However, further analysis suggests that in general the argument is not so convincing after all. The factor that is common to all the forms of equitable proprietary right is that at no time was the debtor ever entitled to a beneficial interest in the asset. A debtor receiving a mistaken double payment clearly has no right to retain it; a bailee receiving the proceeds of his principal's goods under a duty to account (either because his disposition was unlawful or because the agreement between them imposed an accounting duty) manifestly cannot claim the proceeds as his own. A party receiving money to be applied exclusively for a designated purpose cannot be allowed, if the purpose fails, to disregard the trust and hold the money for some other, unauthorised purpose but must return the payment to the party from whom he received it. In all these cases the bankrupt never enjoyed beneficial ownership of the asset, and it would unjustly enrich his general creditors to treat the asset as part of his estate.

. . .

Up to this point there seems little reason for unsecured creditors to complain of equitable proprietary rights, for the recognition of these simply reflects the fact that the asset claimed, far from being thereby unfairly removed from the debtor's estate, was never part of it in the first place. Much more disputable is the contention advanced by some judges and textbook writers that where the defendant has received a benefit from acting in breach of fiduciary duty to the plaintiff and is personally accountable for the benefit so received equity will impose a constructive trust or charge on that benefit or on other assets in the hands of the defendant even though the benefit or other assets cannot be identified as constituting or derived from the plaintiff's property. In other words, the court can (so the argument goes) make an order which will ensure that a personal duty to account is satisfied by a proprietary remedy against the defendant's own unincumbered assets.'

1.6 The political and social significance of property

The next three extracts summarise the key issues involved in accepting and protecting property as an institution. Read them carefully to assess the different implications of the various arguments presented.

[105] C M Rose, 'Property as the Keystone Right?' (1996) 71 *Notre Dame Law Review* 329, 329–33, 364:

[The footnotes in the original are omitted.]

'But property rights have a somewhat uneasy place in a constitutional ordering. There are of course substantial libertarian arguments for property rights as an element of personal autonomy, but on the whole, the post-socialist enthusiasm for property seems to have been overwhelmingly economic: the allure of property is that it enhances wealth, both personal and social. Constitutions, on the other hand, are concerned classically and fundamentally with *political* ordering. While property is often included among constitutionally protected rights, it seems less central to the political core of constitutional government than the rights most critical to self-governance—primarily voting, speech, and assembly. On the other hand, property's central role in *economic* (or "merely economic") ordering would seem to be peripheral to the political order, or to the individual rights that support democratic governance.

One of the classic property theorists was Jeremy Bentham, and it is easy to extract from his work the idea that property serves essentially economic ends rather than political ones. Bentham argued powerfully for the economic benefits of property, but he regarded property not as a right but as a creature of law, and indeed as "nothing but a basis of expectation." The security of property is vitally important, he said, not because property is a right with a political role, but because a society that safeguards property is *wealthy*. Being wealthy, that society can satisfy more individual preferences than a society in which property is at risk (and hence poor).

Bentham is one of many authors who have contributed to a very standard story about property as a wealth-creating institution. The point of origin is John Locke's observation that resources only become valuable if people work on developing them. But people will not work much without some inducement, and if there is no such inducement to labor, resources lie undeveloped and total wealth remains low.

What induces people to labor? Property does. Let people have secure property, and they will learn to invest their labor on the things that they own, because they themselves will take the rewards. They will plan carefully and prudently, because if they do not, they will bear the losses. Moreover, they will organize trades, because property is a signalling device, telling everyone which things belong to whom and allowing people to bargain with one another instead of just taking things or (worse yet, and even more wasteful) fighting over them. Once able to trade, they will invest even more in socially useful activities, because the whole world becomes the market for their efforts. Finally, they will monitor the behavior of others, because if others transgress, they themselves will lose the fruits of their investment, prudence, and planning; thus to a considerable degree, a property regime enlists the self-interest of individuals to become a self-policing system.

By way of contrast, when ownership is insecure, we see something like the turmoil of recent Russia or indeed of any place undergoing social revolution. Investment and effort in trade or business may be dampened when "Mafia" thugs threaten the successful, or when vaguely-authorized officials siphon off the fruits of one's efforts. Valuable natural resources—forests, fisheries, minerals, waters—may be treated as unmanaged commons, where everyone takes and no one replenishes and the resources themselves dwindle to nothing. And indeed, the gains of the toughest takers dwindle too, since they may dissipate their proceeds in an effort to guard them from everyone else. The lesson is clear: we are better off with secure property rights, which induce us to invest, trade, and gently monitor each other in ways that make us all better off.

But suppose all this is true: from the perspective of constitutional ordering, the obvious question is, "So what?" Even supposing that the security of property brings greater wealth, why should a constitution aim at wealth? Should it not rather aim at orderly processes of governance and the individual rights that support those processes? . . .

How different from these slights to property, then, are the startlingly bold observations of Adam Smith, not on the mere *importance* of property as a political matter, but on its *centrality* to governance. Here are his words in his *Lectures on Jurisprudence*, given in the 1760s, and somewhat unartfully passed on to us through his note-takers:

> The first and chief design of every system of government is to maintain justice; to prevent the members of a society from incroaching [sic] on one anothers [sic] property, or siezing [sic] what is not their own. The design here is to give each one the secure and peacable [sic] possession of his own property. The end proposed by justice is the maintaining [of] men in what are called their perfect rights.

Each of these three sentences essentially repeats the same message: three times over, Smith tells us that justice means protecting people in what is theirs. Note that this is not simply *an* object of government, but rather "the first and chief" one—a sort of Benthamite program for the security of property, but with the name "justice" tacked on.

An even more pointed comment on property's centrality was made by an American contemporary of Smith's, Arthur Lee, according to whom property is "the guardian of every other right." A modern legal historian, James Ely, has titled his history of property with Lee's line, and he has used it to argue that property rights are equal in status to all other constitutional rights.

To be sure, property may be *an* important right, but what is most interesting in Smith's and Lee's remarks is a much headier suggestion: that property rights are not simply *equally* important to other rights, but are the *most* important of all rights. Their remarks locate property as the linchpin, the pivot, the central right on which all the others turn, the "guardian of every other right."

As it turns out, this quite remarkable claim has had a number of permutations, old and new. All of them clearly look to property to do considerably more for a constitutional order than "merely" to secure economic prosperity. My purpose in this paper is to explore seven of those permutations, along with the caveats and critiques that they raise—caveats and critiques that at a minimum leave the political implications of property rights in an ambiguous state, though not without considerable residual force. Beneath the ambiguity, and complementing its "merely" economic role, I will conclude that property's most serious *political* claim is as an almost invisible educational institution.

There are many reasons why one might say that property is *an* important right. But why would anyone say that property is the keystone right, the central right on which all others rest? Here are seven answers.

. . .

[Carol Rose then presents seven arguments, each suggesting that property may be the key to all other rights:

1. the priority argument: property is prior to politics, and hence is the basis upon which all other rights rest;
2. the power-spreading argument: property diffuses power;
3. the independence argument: property makes individuals independent and thus capable of self-government;
4. the symbolic argument: property symbolises all other rights;
5. the civilising argument: the acquisition and management of property inculcates the moral and civil behaviour on which rights depend (this is extracted at **[809]** below);
6. the distraction argument: the pursuit of property makes politics seem boring; and
7. the luxury-good argument: property protects all other rights precisely by fulfilling its economic function, and making society wealthier.]

Perhaps property could protect other rights by its own force *if only it were easy to safeguard*; but instead, property is itself a delicate institutuion.

Still, property does bounce back constantly, in spite of the jolts it takes from predation. Why? The answer might lie in whatever truth there is in the Civilizing Argument. That is, property regimes may tend to regenerate endogenously, as it were, because given the slightest elbow room, they induce the very qualities of cooperation, attentiveness to others, responsibility, and self-restraint that themselves are the prerequisites to the successful handling and trade of property. In societies where people can cultivate those traits, property regimes generally reward them in a very simple way: the societies get richer. It should be noted that when property rewards cooperative traits, it also rewards the very qualities of "self-interest rightly understood" that helps democratic government to function. And the depradations to property are educational too, if only in a cautionary way; a few of the strong may become very much wealthier, but only temporarily, because everyone else becomes very much poorer.

All this suggests at most a rather modest claim for property as a keystone right, that is, as an educative institution. On that conception, property would play a central role not as the fierce bulldog guardian of autonomous individual rights, but rather as the gentle and somewhat fragile persuader, rewarding the character traits needed not only for commerce but also for self-government.'

[106] J W Harris, *Property and Justice* (1996, Clarendon: Oxford) pp 3–4, 6–7, 146–7, 149–51, 155:

[The following excerpts are taken from Chapter 1 ('Introduction') and Chapter 9 ('What Property Is'). Most of the footnotes in the original have been omitted.]

'Property is a legal and social institution governing the use of most things and the allocation of some items of social wealth. 'Social wealth' comprises all those things and services for which there is a greater potential total demand than there is a supply.

As an institution, property is a complex organizing idea. Through social learning and interaction, it is made available to the individual as a point of reference intervening between the brute facts of his situation, on the one hand, and his claims, desires, projects, and plans, on the other hand. Its complexity is twofold. It resides partly in the fact that the institutuion comprises many elements, from determinate prescriptive or permissive rules to open-ended principles of exclusive use and allocation. Its complexity resides also in the fact that the package of elements it contains varies enormously in time and place and is nowhere static for long.

Despite its complexity, property, as an organizing idea, is very old and is now worldwide. The oldest written records attest to it. Few primitive peoples, whose societies have been researched by anthropologists, have turned out to lack any conception of it. In the modern world, any normal person will have heard of it, from childhood up.

In the modern world, the institution of property is everywhere embodied in law. That is to say, the various organs of government deploy it, officially, as part of the mechanism for controlling the use of things and as part of the mechanism for supervising or directing the allocation of wealth. The role played by property in forwarding these endeavours varies according to the cultural and ideological backgrounds of different political communities. At a minimum, the use of chattels of small value (which are numerically most of the tangible 'things' that there are) and the spending of residual income are governed by rules and principles of property law. In most jurisdictions, the compass of property is much more extensive, reaching to the use of most valuable things, such as houses and factories, and to the allocation of a substantial part of social wealth.

Nowhere is property the only mechanism for controlling the use of things or the exclusive device for wealth-allocation. There are commonly laws controlling abuse of the atmosphere, but the air, above a certain height, is not parcelled out into thing-like units subject to the institution of property. A considerable proportion of social wealth is allocated *in specie* through the form of public services, such as education and health-care, without benefit of property.

Property is a social institution as well as a legal institution. Members of societies make assumptions and claims, and defer to the claims of others, against a background in which the institution of property is taken for granted. They have done so throughout recorded history. The historical origins of property, like those of other major social institutions such as marriage, kinship, contractual bargains, and criminal responsibility, are not recoverable from our primeval past. When property becomes a legal as well as a social institution depends on whatever heuristic conditions we care to stipulate for the emergence of legal systems. If there is no 'law' until the emergence of official agencies prefiguring those of the modern State, like courts and legislatures, then property was merely a social institution before such agencies came into being to give official recognition to property rules and principles. In any event, the social dimensions of property continued, and continue, alongside its legal dimensions. Countless assumptions and claims are informed by the idea of property without reference to official agencies of the law. Furthermore, the open-ended nature of many proprietary principles entails that, even when embodied in law, their official interpretation and implementation often interact with current social understandings of them.

Property has a dual function, since it governs both the use of things and the allocation of items of social wealth. It is in this duality of function that its controversiality principally resides. It is one thing to say that a society ought to afford to an individual the use of some resource. It is another to say that the individual should be armed with power over others by virtue of a capacity to dictate the use of the resource. 'Property' encompasses both.

. . .

Property is ubiquitous and complex, socially important and controversial. Yet any general notion of property is notoriously elusive. Political philosophers who have dealt with it are not obviously discussing the same thing, and what lawyers mean by it seems to be something different again.

One tradition of political philosophy sought to explicate that relationship between a person and a thing (conceived of as paradigmatic of property) and to explore its moral foundations—property as rights to things. Today political philosophers ask whether unequal distributions of property can be justified—property as wealth. Does anything unite these senses of property, the one which begins with the individual and some feature of the physical environment, and the other which conceives of property as a social cake capable of being sliced up in different ways? A third tradition explored the connections between property and independence within civil society. Does that enquiry have in mind property in things, or holdings of property (including money), or both? To add to the problem, political philosophers have always contrasted private property with common property, and sometimes with State property. Anthropologists and historians have added notions of collective property, group property, tribal property, and communal property. Is there anything in the term 'property' which makes all these expressions branches of a common conceptual tree?

Further mystifications arise when, in pursuit of a variety of theoretical projects, 'property' is extended beyond the sphere of resource-holdings. Philosophers have for centuries advised us that we have property in our own bodies. Social theorists of our day insist that welfare entitlements and jobs are in some sense 'property'. The literature of modern economics includes references to 'property' wherein propertization is a function of internalizing externalities into the decisions of economic actors. Is there anything, could there be anything, which constitutes an essence of propertiness underlying all these uses?

The practising lawyer is not concerned with these problems. She consults legal materials and advises her clients about property transactions. If she looks to English textbooks and manuals, she will usually find that they deal with property piecemeal—real property, personal property, intellectual property, and so forth. . . .

For all this elusiveness of the idea of property, all of us (philosophers, lawyers, and ordinary folk) seem to share an intuitive sense of what property is. We get by in daily life with a range of conventional property talk which has no problems in 'knowing' who owns a particular book or a car or a house or a £10 note. Otherwise we could not borrow or lend or sell, or use things without consulting other people's preferences.

. . .

(a) Economic analysis of property rights

. . .

How has the tendency to property-concept expansion come about? There is, as we shall see, an important argument for property institutions which derives from their use-channelling and use-policing advantages as compared with non-property allocations of resource-use. That argument can be framed in the terminology of economic analysis as follows. The use which any person makes of a resource will often have effects (good or bad) on others. How should the problem of these 'externalities' be met in order that all resources are put to uses which all involved value most (that is, to achieve the 'efficient' or 'pareto-optimal' solution)? If there is a free-for-all the problem can only be solved by inter-personal transactions. They will need to involve all those affected, to avoid 'free-loader' problems. They will be difficult to achieve because of transaction costs and because of 'hold-outs'. They will be expensive to police. If, instead of a free-for-all, we substitute ownership interests over the resource—that is, open-ended use-privileges, control-powers, and powers of transmission—the efficient solution to the externalities problem is much easier to achieve. Anyone wishing to share in beneficial externalities must bargain with resource-owners. Owners themselves will do most of the policing. Owners can be called to account, by suitable property-limitation rules, for harmful externalities. In sum, property solutions are to be preferred to non-property solutions because they facilitate the internalization of externalities.

Nothing in the foregoing argument requires any departure from conventional notions of property. However, some economic analysts have supposed that similar considerations are in play in the case of each and every right to use a resource provided the right is one I might bargain not to exercise—and that proviso could, in principle, be fulfilled for any right. Hence, if society favours me with a right over any resource (including all my bodily and mental resources) then, so long as it has not prohibited me from agreeing with another not to exercise the right, it has already adopted a 'property' solution in relation to the right and the right therefore comes within the category of 'property rights'. Strictly speaking, we should not speak of ownership interests over resources at all, but only of a muiltiplicity of individuated property rights.

The drift from economic analysis of 'property' in the conventional sense to a specialist economic conception of 'property' may be illustrated from two papers written by Harold Demsetz. In 'Toward a Theory of Property Rights',[12] Demsetz advances the above-cited argument, in terms of internalizing externalities, for private ownership interests (property in the ordinary sense). He proffers it as an explanation for the historical emergence of 'ownership of land'. In passing, he suggests that a similar analysis

[12] (1967) 57 *American Economic Review* 347.

could be applied to other possible rights. For example, if instead of there being a compulsory military draft, either the State had to buy citizens into (or citizens had to buy themselves out of) military service, in either case externalities would be internalized. In a subsequent paper, written with Armen Alchian,[14] the same argument is rehearsed, but this time it is prefaced with a general conceptual claim: although in common speech we frequently refer to someone owning resources, we would do better to speak of owning rights to use resources, 'including one's body and mind'. 'What are owned are socially recognized rights of action.' 'Property' rights include, for example, 'the right to advocate particular political doctrines'.

This conceptual shift relies, terminologically, on one of the red herrings we identified at the end of Chapter 5—the conflation of 'owning' and 'ownership'. As we saw there, it is one thing to say that a person is vested with ('owns') either a right or a bundle of rights; it is another to say that what he is vested with is that particular set of open-ended privileges and powers over a resource which counts as an ownership interest.

. . .

What we have called 'cashable rights' (bank accounts, shares, and so forth) are conventionally described as 'property' because expropriation and appropriation rules apply to them—they pass into a bankrupt's estate and they can be inherited. The same would not be true of the following rights: (1) X's claim that the State should provide his children with free education; (2) X's liberty to take a shower when it suits him; (3) X's power to enter into a contract to have his hair cut; (4) X's immunity from compulsory military service. Within the genre of economic analysis just discussed, all the foregoing would be 'property' rights provided, first, that X is free to contract not only to exercise any of them (Alchian and Demsetz), and, secondly, that infraction of them is not remediable only in damages (Calabresi and Mellamed [See further reading.]). Cashable rights are the subject of real markets. These analysts seek an extended definition which will enable the effects of notional markets to be explored in terms of transaction costs, efficiency, and distribution considerations, and effects on externalities.

By all means let rights of all kinds be analysed in these terms. Calling all rights 'property rights' is, however, anything but an aid to clarity for the enterprises at hand since both the analyst and the reader must constantly remind themselves that they are not talking about 'property' as ordinarily understood. More importantly, if we wish to confront and contrast economic with non-economic justifications for property institutions, we cannot employ an extended definition fashioned solely for the use of economic analysis.

(b) Reich's 'New Property'

When the boundaries of the concept of property are discussed in modern Anglo-American theory, reference is frequently made to an article written by Charles Reich, published in 1964, which is entitled 'The New Property'.[28] Reich seeks to show that the wealth-allocation function of property institutions is, in modern societies, of diminishing relative importance because of the growth of 'government largesse'. Wealth is increasingly allocated through welfare benefits, government jobs, occupational licences, State franchises, contracts, and subsidies, and access to State-owned resources and to governmental services. Allocation takes place in accordance with the assessment by various governmental agencies of what would best serve the public interest. In the past, Reich contends, holdings of wealth in the form of private property had the great merit

[14] Armen A. Alchian and Harold Demsetz, 'The Property Rights Paradigm' (1973) 33 *Journal of Economic History* 16.

[28] Charles A. Reich, 'The New Property' (1964) 73 *YLJ* 733.

of securing independence from the State. However, it also had the great demerit that holders of wealth were increasingly able to dominate the lives of others, especially as wealth became consolidated in the form of large corporate holdings. The 'public interest State' has evolved as a counter to this domination-potential of private property holdings, as well as a vehicle for performing many functions which modern societies expect their governments to discharge. But with it has come the loss of independence which private property once secured.

. . .

He advocates measures which will, so far as possible, ensure that the wealth which results from government largesse confers upon its recipients an independence equivalent to that which private property provides. Discretionary receipts should be replaced, where possible, with entitlements held as of right. Substantive restraints should be imposed so that discretion cannot be exercised on improper grounds—especially so as to prevent rights guaranteed by the constitution being indirectly infringed. All withholding or cancellation of government largesse should be subjected to procedural due process.

. . .

(c) Constitutional Theory

The doctrine of separation of powers, which is a cornerstone of constitutional theory in modern liberal-democratic societies, calls on lawyers and judges to answer the following questions (among others). In what circumstances, and by reference to what criteria, should courts undertake the responsibility of deciding on the validity of measures adopted by legislators, deputy legislators, or agents of the executive? In practice such theorizing is usually piecemeal rather than holistic, but in either case it is likely to announce respect for individuated citizen rights (whether political, welfarist, familial, or personal). By virtue either of constitutional instruments or of principles emerging from case-law doctrine, the constitutional theory may separate out property rights as one species of constitutionally protected right. In the view of some commentators, property rights can find their place within an acceptable constitutional theory only if 'property' is understood in a sense wider than that suggested by the stipulation at the beginning of this Chapter.

As we have seen, *ad hoc* reasons may always be advanced for giving references to 'property' or 'proprietary interest' a wide interpretation in the context of particular rules. Given the range of political considerations typically in play, interpretative strategies directed towards 'property' rules in a constitutional context may be thought to license even greater flexibility. If a constitutional text protects 'property', and there is to hand a good case for saying that some personal or political right merits that kind of protection, then perhaps the concept of property should be extended, for that particular constitutional context, to include the favoured right.

. . .

(d) MacPherson's Political Property-Rhetoric

An advocate of a particular right—political or personal—may invoke 'property' as part of a frankly rhetorical strategy. He may suppose that 'property', in the conventional sense, has a certain prestige in his society. He may not share the assumptions upon which this prestige has been built. Nevertheless, he may seek to cash in on it by proclaiming, for example, that welfare rights, or rights to jobs, or the right to participate in political decision-making, or the right to pursue a lifestyle reflecting personal sexual preferences, are (all or any of them) facets of a person's 'property'.

It is, in the end, to such a rhetorical strategy that appeal is made in the most sustained case for a change in the concept of property that has been advanced in recent years—that of C. B. MacPherson.[54] We have already noted that MacPherson considered that using 'property' to refer to things was a misusage peculiar to laymen and that it was unlikely to survive beyond this century. He recognized, however, that the existing paradigm of a property right is the exclusive right to something (what has here been called an ownership, or quasi-ownership, interest). This, he maintained, should be changed. We should conceive of a property right as an enforceable claim to the use or benefit of something, of which the paradigm is a right not to be excluded whilst the right to exclude others is merely a special case. Armed with this conceptual shift, we will then be able to extend the idea of property to encompass, not merely rights to welfare payments and services, rights to jobs, and rights to a decent environment, but also rights of access to the means of production, equal rights to share in social produce, rights to share in political power, and finally, rights to a truly free and democratic society. 'Property will . . . increasingly have to become a right to a set of social relations, a right to a kind of society.' '

[107] J Waldron, *The Right to Private Property* (1988, Clarendon: Oxford), pp 6–10, 12–14, 22–3:

[Footnotes in the original have been omitted.]

. . .

[On utilitarian arguments.]

Many of the most familiar arguments in favour of private property and against socialism are utilitarian arguments. They purport to show that the total or average happiness of society will be greater, or that the general welfare (under some other utilitarian conception) will be better served, if material resources and in particular the main material means of production are owned and controlled by private individuals and firms rather than by the state or the community as a whole.

Early examples of such arguments are found in Book Two of Aristotle's *Politics*. 'What is the proper system of property for citizens who are to live under an ideal constitution?' Aristotle asks, 'Is it a system of communism or one of private property?' He points out some difficulties in systems of common ownership, in particular common ownership of land. If those who own also work the land, then quarrels are likely to break out continually about the proportion between work and recompense: 'Those who do more work and get less recompense will be bound to raise complaints against those who get a large recompense and do little work.' Such social disharmony will be avoided, Aristotle suggests, if each person is the exclusive owner of the plot that he works upon. To this he adds the suggestion that the net product of privately owned land is likely to be greater than that of commonly owned land: 'When everyone has his own separate sphere of interest, there will not be the same ground for quarrels; and the amount of interest will increase, because each man will feel he is applying himself to what is his own.' The latter suggestion is discussed in more detail earlier in Book Two:

> What is common to the greatest number gets the least amount of care. Men pay most attention to what is their own: they care less for what is common; or, at any rate, they care for it only to the extent to which each is individually concerned. Even when

[54] C. B. MacPherson, *Property: Mainstream and Critical Positions* (Basil Blackwell, 1978), chs. 1 and 12; 'Capitalism and the Changing Concept of Property', in E. Kamenka and R. S. Neale (eds.), *Feudalism, Capitalism and Beyond* (Edward Arnold, 1975).

> there is no other cause for inattention, men are more prone to neglect their duty when they think another is attending to it: this is exactly what happens in domestic service, where many attendants are sometimes of less assistance than a few.

But although he makes out these arguments for private ownership, Aristotle is in favour of the communal *use* of resources. The property of each should be made 'to serve the use of all, in the spirit of the proverb which says "Friends' goods are goods in common' ". (In this regard, his position is not so distant from Plato's. Plato believes that in an ideal state land will be owned privately by farmers; the farmers will provide produce to the Guardians as a class and it will be consumed by them in common). But Aristotle does not think this should be one of the rules of property. Virtue not legal compulsion should lead men to share their wealth. Certainly, he thinks it the function of the legislator 'to ensure that men shall be good men, to consider what practices will make them so, and what is the end or aim of the best life'. But this function is fulfilled, not by the direct legislative prescription of morally good acts, but by the constitution of a society in which moral virtue is nurtured and encouraged. (Here Aristotle differs from Plato, who calls explicitly for legislation to govern the Guardians' common mode of consumption.) This combination, then, of private ownership and communal virtue is more conducive to prosperity and social harmony, on Aristotle's account, than any other arrangement for the ownership and use of material resources.

Aristotle's second argument—that individuals are likely to care more for what is their own—has been taken up by some modern defenders of private property.

According to Harold Demsetz, the 'primary function of property rights is that of guiding incentives to achieve a greater internalization of externalities'. If land, for instance, is held in common, it is likely each user will not feel the full impact, in terms of the benefits but particularly the costs of his use. When, for example, many individuals hunt in the same territory, no one has any incentive to increase or maintain the stock of game, since the benefits of *his* doing so will redound to others as well as himself whether the others are also conservationists or not. Unless the benefits exceed the costs of his action by a huge amount, he is unlikely to find conservation personally advantageous. (This rests, of course, on controversial assumptions about human motivation: Demsetz is working within a tradition which regards such assumptions as axiomatic.) The result is that over intensive hunting is likely to occur. The cost of each hunter's activity in terms of the depleted game stock will be felt not only by him but by his fellow hunters and by the generations of hunters who follow. Thus when individual hunting decisions are made, the full benefits but only some of the costs of a decision to hunt will be taken into account, and, in the aggregate, a level of hunting may be maintained which is in fact against the long-term interests of all. The more this happens (i.e. the greater the level of costs not taken into account in individual decision-making about hunting), the more defensible a scheme of private property rights over game and territory will begin to seem in utilitarian terms, and (on Demsetz's view) the more likely it is that such a scheme of property will emerge. A communal form of ownership 'fails to concentrate the costs associated with any person's exercise of his common right on that person'. A scheme of private ownership, on the other hand,

> will internalize many of the external costs associated with communal ownership, for now an owner, by virtue of his power to exclude others, can generally count on realizing the rewards associated with husbanding the game and increasing the fertility of his land. This concentration of benefits and costs on owners creates incentives to utilize resources more efficiently.

Of course, owners-in-common, perceiving the tendency of their over-exploitation of resources, could get together and agree to limit their use. But Demsetz suggests that the transaction costs involved in securing such an agreement together with the costs (and the assurance problem) involved in its policing might be prohibitive. An advantage of private property rights is that they reduce transaction costs, at least in resolving subsequent problems of externalities.

Another utilitarian argument for private property concerns the role of markets in promoting productive efficiency and social prosperity. It is now accepted that a centralized command economy, in which all productive decisions were taken on the basis of the central allocation of scarce resources, would lead, in the conditions of modern industry, to radically inefficient and perhaps catastrophic results.

The *locus classicus* of this argument is in the work of Ludwig von Mises. Socialist planners, von Mises points out, face two problems: first, the problem of what to produce and, secondly, the problem of how to produce it. It is conceivable that socialist planners might solve the first problem, particularly if they adhered to some 'objective' theory of human and social 'need' which was not dependent on the interplay of the subjective preferences of actual consumers. But the second problem, he claims, will be intractable as a problem of planning. How will a planner know where a given quantity of (say) coal or iron ore is best applied, or to what purposes certain machine parts should be devoted? The use of what are called 'production goods' is not related directly to the need for specified consumption goods, since each of the former could go through any one of a series of stages in contributing to the production of the latter.

Von Mises' suggestion is that the only way through this decisional morass is via a system of prices, fixed by the interaction of a plurality of entrepreneurs, each risking the capital commodities under his control in production or exchange, and adjusting his activity to his perception of the similarly adjusted activity of others: in other words, a system of market prices. A market economy has powerful tendencies in the direction of efficient resource allocation. But a centrally planned economy will have no grip on these processes at all—nowhere to start and no idea of which direction to go.

. . .

3. NON-UTILITARIAN THEORIES

The idea of a non-utilitarian argument is apt to seem at first bewildering to a layman, a politician, or an economist. What, they will ask, could possibly count in favour of or against an institution like private property except its effects on the welfare of everyone in the society, assessed in a roughly aggregative way?

But the situation is quite different in moral and political philosophy. Philosophers have never been more aware than they are today of the grave ethical defects (as well as the technical difficulties) of utilitarian argument. Two points in particular may be mentioned. First, utilitarianism is criticized for the fact that it takes human interests and desires as given: in utilitarian theory, the satisfaction of any preference and the fulfilment of any interest is taken to have a positive value in itself no matter what it is a preference for or an interest in. So when one section of the population takes pleasure in persecuting another, that satisfaction may conceivably be taken as decisive in justifying on utilitarian grounds a decision not to extend social protection to the persecuted group. Secondly, quite apart from the question of the quality of desires and interests, there is the more general problem of distribution. A utilitarian concerned to maximize the sum of happiness or satisfaction in a society cares little about the distribution of that sum: the slightly greater happiness of many, over the long term, is capable of outweighing, in a utilitarian calculation, the intense suffering and abject deprivation of a few. This leaves no room in social decision-making for considerations of justice and equality, except perhaps as subordinate maxims. But ethical thinking about social and political issues has always been informed by a conviction that justice and equality are independent values, co-ordinate with if not superior to considerations of aggregate utility.

Can the theories known as rule- or indirect utilitarianism provide adequate utilitarian solutions to these problems? I have my doubts. Either they cease to be utilitarian, and take on a commitment to rules and moral institutions for their own sake; or, if they remain utilitarian, they produce at best rules and institutions which, in their foundations and justification, continue to evince a commitment to the very aspects of utilitarian theory that have been found objectionable. Their sophistication gives us a reason perhaps to believe that utilitarians can have *a* theory of justice and rights; but it does not give us any confidence that the principles of that theory will have anything in common with the principles underlying our fundamental 'intuitive' misgivings about utilitarianism. It therefore does nothing to allay the widespread suspicion that the difficulties in utilitarian theory are very deep-set, reflecting a failure of that theory to take seriously the moral significance of certain fundamental individual interests in security, autonomy, and independence.

The decline of confidence in utilitarian argument has been accompanied by a growth in moral and political theories of a non-utilitarian kind. Explicitly or implicitly, the dominant idea in recent non-utilitarian thought has been that of *rights*: the idea that people have certain key interests (in specific freedoms or in specific aspects of their material well-being) which they are not to be required to sacrifice, and which therefore may not be overridden, for the sake of the collective welfare or other goals of their society.

For example, many liberal philosophers argue that each person has a right to life, and a right to at least the minimum amount of negative liberty necessary for his development as an autonomous moral agent. Some argue also that each person has a right to certain conditions of positive liberty, such as the material conditions which make his negative freedom worth exercising and the spiritual conditions (like education and the support of secure human relationships) which make its exercise humanly fulfilling. These, it is said, are morally crucial interests for each person, and they are not to be sacrificed merely for the sake of the greatest happiness or prosperity of society in general. As this sort of argument becomes more common, it is interesting to see whether the individual interest in having private property can plausibly be regarded in the same sort of way.

Often accounts of human rights have not gone beyond a list of these crucial interests and the bare assertion that they are to be accorded special respect. Since the mid-1970s, however, moral and political philosophy has seen a growing interest in systematic theories of rights. Philosophers have become interested in the foundations of the idea that certain individual interests are worthy of special respect, and there have been several impressive attempts to work out systematically the sort of theory that is needed to connect the surface rhetoric of rights-assertions, so common in political life, with the deep values and assumptions about morality and human nature that we find in moral philosophy.

. . .

(iv) The General Right to have Private Property

It is sometimes said that the ownership of private property has a great moralizing effect on the individual owner. It promotes virtues like responsibility, prudence, and self-reliance; it gives him a place to stand in the world, a place where he can be confident that his freedom will be recognized and respected; and it affords him control of at least a minimum of those natural resources access to which is a necessary condition of his agency. (Often indeed it is said that private ownership has such moralizing effects that only those who own property are fit to be citizens in a republic.)

We find an early version of this kind of argument in Aristotle's *Politics*, alongside the utilitarian arguments we have already mentioned. Like many of the ancients, Aristotle treats the moral issues of monogamy and private property as on a par. Both, he suggests, promote individual virtue, and in both cases important forms of moral goodness are liable to be destroyed by the socialization of the relations in question:

> The first of these [forms of goodness] is temperance in the matter of sexual relations (it is an act of moral value to refrain from loving the wife of another in the strength of temperance): the second is liberality in the use of property. In a state which is excessively unified no man can show himself liberal, or do a liberal act; for the function of liberality consists in the proper use which is made of private property.

We may not find this argument particularly convincing: other modes of liberality (and sexual restraint!) may be available even in a communist state. But it provides the prototype of a category of argument that becomes very important in the ideology of private property in the nineteenth century and which remains influential in conservative ideology today. . . .

The connection between private property and moral virtue is not always seen as a matter of individual right. (Often this approach may be seen as a duty-based rather than as a right-based argument for private property.) But increasingly philosophers are prepared to argue that individuals have a right to the conditions necessary for the full development of their autonomy, their ethical personality, and their capacity for responsible agency. Mere negative freedom is not enough: we must look, at least in the abstract, at the quality of choice which it is open to individuals to exercise, otherwise we risk attracting the accusation that we do not after all take the issue of human freedom seriously. Since this position is increasingly common, and since it has been argued that private property is a necessary element in the ethical development of individual choice, it seems appropriate to consider claims of this sort as a fourth category of interpretations of the statement that property is one of the rights of man.'

Questions:

1. Are there any immutable themes in these analyses?
2. How might these ideas influence the development of the law of personal property?
3. Most of these writings suggest that property ownership provides a benefit to the owner (and to others). An alternative view sees ownership as a burden, not just a privilege.[18] On this view, the legal and social institution of property satisfies a need to make someone ultimately responsible for the care and control of property and for the harm that may flow from it. Even in socialist legal systems there must be some concept of property and

[18] A Tay and E Kamenka, 'Introduction: Some Theses on Property' (1988) 11 *University of New South Wales Law Review* 1, 3.

property ownership. If this view of property were the dominant paradigm, would it have different consequences for the development of personal property law and the assessment of which rights are proprietary and which are not?

FURTHER READING:

C A Reich, 'The New Property' (1964) 73 *Yale Law Journal* 733.

H Demsetz, 'Towards a Theory of Property Rights' (1967) 57 *American Economic Review* 347.

G Calabresi and A D Melamed, 'Property Rules, Liability Rules, and Inalienability: One View of the Cathedral' (1972) 85 *Harvard Law Review* 1089.

C B Macpherson (ed), *Property: Mainstream and Critical Positions* (1978, Basil Blackwell: Oxford); and 'Capitalism and the Changing Concept of Property' in E Kamenka and R S Neale (eds), *Feudalism, Capitalism and Beyond* (1975, Edward Arnold: Canberra).

B A Ackerman, *Private Property and the Constitution* (1977, Yale University Press: New Haven).

R A Posner, *Economic Analysis of Law* (4th edn, 1992, Little Brown & Co: Boston) (see **[807]** below).

J Wolff, *An Introduction to Political Philosophy* (1996, OUP: Oxford) ch 5 ('The Distribution of Property').

J W Harris, *Property and Justice* (1996, Clarendon: Oxford).

J E Penner, *The Idea of Property in Law* (1997, Clarendon: Oxford).

Also see the readings extracted in Chapter 8.

Part II

Interests in Personal Property

2

Ownership and Possession

2.1 Introduction

Three fundamental concepts in the law of property are ownership, possession and title.[1] This chapter examines these concepts. The fourth concept—security—is considered in the next chapter. Certain aspects are already familiar. For example, it is common knowledge that certain assets—such as cars and books—can be both owned and possessed. Moreover, ownership and possession can be in different people. The owner of a car can hire it to another, thereby splitting the rights to ownership and possession. Other assets, such as debts, copyrights and patents, cannot be possessed. Money has its own special rules. In order to understand how rights of ownership and possession may be used, it is necessary to understand the concepts themselves and how they interact. It is then possible to contemplate the various different legal relationships which can be created in dealings with personal property. Some of these relationships, such as hire and bailment, are noted at the end of this chapter. Others, such as security, gift and sale, are considered in detail later in the book.

2.2 Ownership

2.2.1 Legal ownership

Honoré defines ownership as 'the greatest possible interest in a thing which a mature legal system recognises'.[2] He then describes the standard incidents of

[1] Ownership and possession are different types of *interests* in property. It is also possible to have security interests in property (see chapter 3). An interest holder's ability to defend his interest against third parties asserting conflicting interests depends upon the holder's *title* to his interest: see Section 2.4 below.

[2] A M Honoré, 'Ownership' in A G Guest (ed), *Oxford Essays in Jurisprudence* (1961, OUP: Oxford), p 107.

ownership—some rights and some obligations—as 'the right to possess, the right to use, the right to manage, the right to the income of the thing, the right to the capital, the right to security, the rights or incidents of transmissibility and absence of term, the prohibition of harmful use, liability to execution, and the incident of residuarity'.[3]

Taken at face value, this description disguises the fact that a person can be an 'owner' without all these listed incidents of ownership. For example, an owner remains 'the owner' even after granting rights of possession to a third party (whether on terms of hire, or gratuitous loan, or pledge[4]). The different residuary rights which remain in the owner in these circumstances are still described as 'ownership'.[5]

The other point to notice about legal ownership of personal property is that there is no equivalent of the real property doctrine of estates. That doctrine allows the legal ownership of real property to be divided along a time line. For example, real property can be owned (and presently enjoyed) by someone who has only a life interest and, on that person's death, the enjoyment of the property will pass to the person with the interest in remainder. Death is not the only possible marker along the time line. An owner of real property can have a conditional interest, which will end (or determine) when the particular condition, whatever it is, is met. The enjoyment of the property will then pass to the person nominated to take in default. The point about the doctrine of estates is that the current 'owner' of the real property *and* the other parties taking later along the time line all have present (ie '*vested*') ownership interests in the property; it is only their enjoyment of those interests which is deferred. The same approach is not adopted with personal property.

Nevertheless, it must be said that this lack of a doctrine of estates has little real impact. Precisely the same effects can be achieved by using equitable doctrines. Successive interests under a trust are possible, even where the trust property is personal rather than real. A beneficiary under a trust can have a life interest, or an interest in remainder, for example. In addition, the practical arrangements delivered by the doctrine of estates can be mimicked by the use of contracts. The critical difference, however, is that a contract will not give the intended later owners any present *legal* ownership interest; they will simply have a contractual right to obtain that interest when the stated conditions are met.[6]

Lawson and Rudden[7] suggest that the doctrine of estates was not extended to personal property because this form of property was not sufficiently permanent to warrant it. That may have been true when dealings in personal property were largely concerned with sheep, or grain, or candle wax. Now it is no longer true—consider the lifespan of company shares or industrial patents. However, the use of trusts to achieve the desired ends is now so deeply entrenched that the common law rules are unlikely to change.

[3] A M Honoré, 'Ownership' in A G Guest (ed), *Oxford Essays in Jurisprudence* (1961, OUP: Oxford), p 113.

[4] See Section 3.1.2.

[5] Note 3 above, pp. 125–8.

[6] Such a contract may, however, give the intended later owner an *equitable* ownership interest (if the contract is specifically enforceable—see Chapter 4) or, alternatively, a mere equity (see Section 2.2.4 below).

[7] F H Lawson and B Rudden, *The Law of Property* (2nd edn, 1982, Clarendon: Oxford) p 95.

Question:

All of this makes the concept of 'ownership' seem quite simple. But care is needed. For example, if someone owns a share in a company what, precisely, does that person 'own'? (See *Borland's Trustee v Steel Bros & Co Ltd* [1901] 1 Ch 279, 288.)

The next extract, too, is designed to dispel the notion that ownership is a simple concept. Its focus is on the nature of the 'things' which can be owned, and on the potential for external controls to be imposed on 'ownership'.

[201] A M Honoré, 'Ownership' in A G Guest (ed), *Oxford Essays in Jurisprudence* (1961, OUP: Oxford), p 107, 128–32, 144–7:
[Footnotes in the original are omitted]

' 'To own' is transitive; the object of ownership is always spoken of as a 'thing' in the legal sense, a *res*. There is, clearly, a close connexion between the idea of ownership and the idea of things owned, as is shown by the use of words such as 'property' to designate both. We ought, apparently, to be able to throw some light on ownership by investigating 'things'.

Outside the law, external material objects arc thought of as the prime examples of things and, in this sense, things are contrasted with persons. But, in a wide sense, any object of discourse may be called a thing—events, states, emotions, actions, processes are all things. The extra-legal use of 'thing' is therefore not likely to help us in finding out what can be owned.

In the law we find the following position. As regards external material objects, it is natural to speak of ownership. A person 'owns' a book, house or car. The terminology of ownership is also extended to some things other than material objects. A person may 'own' a copyright, leasehold property, goodwill, a business, patent rights. In these cases the analogy with the incidents of the ownership of external material objects is a close one.

In other cases the holder of a right is said to 'have' rather than own the interest in question. Thus, one 'has' an easement or a chose in action or a reputation. Here the analogy with the ownership of material objects is less strong or, as in the case of easements, the alternative expression is adopted to avoid confusion with the ownership of the material object to which the right relates.

In other cases again, we speak not of 'having' a thing but of 'having a right' to or in something. Thus, a person does not either 'own' or 'have' his body or liberty. He has a right to bodily security or liberty. Here the analogy with the ownership of a thing is tenuous; thus, these rights are inalienable. Finally, there are interests which the law refuses to recognize: one does not own, have or have a right to them. An example in English law is privacy.

In any viable society we shall expect certain interests (having a house, clothes, food, preserving one's body from harm) to be protected, but, as regards many other interests, (copyright, reputation, privacy, shares) there will be nothing absurd in a system which does not protect them, though it may be an inconvenient system. There will be no way of telling, apart from knowing the details of a system, whether such interests are protected and, *a fortiori*, no way of telling whether they are conceived as consisting in the ownership of things. Apart from the basic interests mentioned, protection of an interest is not merely the recognition of a social necessity. The meaning of the words 'right' or 'thing' will not help one to guess what the decision has been or is likely to be.

Much the same may be said of the difference between simple rights and interests conceived in terms of ownership. A person is not, in most systems, regarded as owning his body, reputation, skill, honour or dignity. At most he has a simple right to these things, which are therefore not legally 'things'. By a 'simple right', I mean one which is protected by law but is not alienable or transmissible. Now it may be that the doctrine that one does not own one's body, etc. is influenced by the linguistic fact that such aspects of one's person do not fall within the prime class of things, external material objects. But a more likely explanation is simply that it has been thought undesirable that a person should alienate his body, skill or reputation, as this would be to interfere with human freedom. When human beings were regarded as alienable and ownable they were, of course, also regarded as being legally things: and it is quite easy to conceive arrangements under which one could, for instance, lease one's reputation or one's skill for a term of years, so that the lessee could sue for infringements of the lessor's good name or for the fruits of his work. It may, indeed, be argued that contracts for the assignment of goodwill and contracts of service are examples of at least partial alienations of these interests.

However that may be, it is clear that to stare at the meaning of the word 'thing' will not tell us which protected interests are conceived in terms of ownership. When the legislature or courts think that an interest should be alienable and transmissible they will *rei*-fy it and say that it can be owned, that it is property. They will not say that it can be owned and is a *res* because of a prior conviction that it falls within the appropriate definition of 'thing'. The investigation of 'things' seems to peter out in a false trail.

A more promising approach is to try to classify the things that can be owned. An obvious classification is into material objects and things that are not material objects (incorporeals). According to one school of thought, this division is so important that only corporeals can really be owned; according to another, it is so unimportant that we ought always to speak of owning rights over material objects, never of owning the objects themselves; in this way we shall keep in mind the parallel with the ownership of incorporeal rights.

Both schools propose a departure from lay and legal usage which stands in need of justification. The former has little to commend it. Consider the difference between 'owning' land and 'owning' (having) an easement over land. The first counts as the ownership of a material object, the second of an incorporeal. Yet their incidents are in every way similar and, in both cases, include the right to exclude others from interfering with or obstructing a particular physical thing, a right which at first sight might seem to differentiate the ownership of material objects from the ownership of incorporeals. It is true that, when we come to consider claims, we find cases in which either there is no right to exclude others or no right to exclude them from a particular physical thing.

Copyright is an example of one type of claim. It involves the right to prevent others publishing, etc. one's written work without consent, and hence a sort of right to exclude others; but this right does not relate to a particular physical thing, a particular book. It relates to all material objects which have certain characteristics, *viz.* that they are copies of the work in question. Again, it is not clear that the incident of prohibition of harmful use applies in a straightforward way to copyrights: on the other hand convincing analogues of the other standard incidents are to be found. Thus it may be said that the notion of ownership applies to copyrights in an extended and somewhat weaker sense than that in which it applies to material objects and interests in them.

Debts due and other choses in action present an example of another type of claim. Here the claim is to the performance of some positive act. No right to exclude others is involved, and, as in the case of copyrights, no question of harmful use arises. On the other hand, incidents such as alienability (nowadays) and transmissibility do apply to choses in action. Hence the ownership of choses in action is to be understood in a still weaker sense than that of copyrights.

. . .

IV. SOCIAL CONTROL

'Absolute' is perhaps the most ambiguous word met in discussions of ownership. Sometimes it is used to deny the 'temporary' (intransmissible or determinate) character of an interest, sometimes to deny its defeasible character (liable to be divested by another, liable to escheat or forfeiture), sometimes to emphasize its exemption from social control.

In the last sense, ownership has never been absolute. Even in the most individualistic ages of Rome and the United States, it has had a social aspect. This has usually been expressed in such incidents of ownership as the prohibition of harmful use, liability to execution for debt, to taxation and to expropriation by the public authority.

Emphasis on the social aspect of ownership has, however, varied from age to age. Those 'sacred and inviolable' rights, which, according to the *Declaration of the Rights of Man*, no one could be forced to cede except for *public necessity* have become, in French law, liable to expropriation on grounds of *public utility* and subject to a general doctrine forbidding 'abuse'. According to the liberal conception of ownership, there is a sharp distinction between government and ownership, *imperium* and *dominium*. Though, in a loose sense, the state may be said to have an 'eminent domain' over at least the land comprising its territory, this does not carry with it rights to possess, enjoy or alienate it, so that the sense in which the state is owner is very loose indeed. The interest of the state, according to this conception, is confined to powers of expropriation and a minimum of restrictive regulation, together with the expectancy of acquiring property as *bona vacantia* or by escheat in a few rather remote contingencies.

Socialism has led to a revised view of the relation between government and ownership, at least as regards some important types of property, such as land and businesses. This means, in practice, that the owner's privileges of using and powers of managing a thing as he wishes have been curtailed and that the social interest in the productive use of things has been affirmed by legislation. Negatively, this process has meant that, in the interests of health and comfort, many substances cannot be used at all or can only be used in certain ways. The sale of drugs is minutely controlled, only smokeless fuel may be used in certain areas, garden hoses may not be used at certain periods. Such instances, multiplied a thousand fold, have come to seem so natural that we hardly realize that the social interest in the use of things, the conservation of resources and in the details of manufacturing processes is a modern, though it is also a primitive, conception.

Positive control by the state shades into prohibition. The positive duty to exploit one's property in a socially beneficial way, as opposed to the prohibition of a harmful exploitation, has not been generally imposed or its implications fully worked out. The British Agriculture Act imposed an obligation on farmers to observe the rules of good husbandry; the owners of patents can in certain cases be compelled to allow their exploitation. According to the Russian civil law book of 1944, the state has a general right to order forfeiture of property in case of mismanagement; there is also a general prohibition on the use of property to exploit others.

A different form of state control is exercised by drawing a distinction between different types of ownership. In Russia the ownership of collective farmers, of handicraftsmen and of the Government are all treated as differing from 'personal ownership' and from one another. The difference lies, of course, in the right of officials to interfere in the management of the former categories and in state regulation of income rights deriving from the property; also in differing rules about alienation. In this way the sphere of operation of ownership in the liberal sense is narrowed and a form of state participation in management substituted in the remaining sphere.

A third form of social control consists in the exercise by officials of the management of things in the 'private' ownership of the state. Such arrangements present the form but not the substance of ownership in the liberal sense. Management and enjoyment are split, and political control, directly or indirectly, is exercised over the allocation of resources and the uses to which the thing owned is put. The nationalized industries in the United Kingdom follow this pattern of control.

Fourthly, social control may be exercised by a restriction on the type of thing that is subject to ownership by persons other than the state, as in the Russian building lease, where the building is owned by a private individual, the land remaining in state ownership. In effect, this restricts the privileges of the building owner in the general interest.

It remains to be seen which combination of these techniques will prove most effective and most acceptable to the people who have to operate them. So far, they have not, singly or together, reached the point in any country at which they could be said to have displaced the liberal conception of ownership and replaced it by a social conception. In practice the two overlap, and operate side by side, together with various types of split ownership and ownership of funds which diverge, to a greater or less extent, from the standard instances depicted in the first Section. The final picture is that of a set of related institutions of great complexity which are best studied against the background of the basic model—a single human being owning, in the full liberal sense, a single material thing.'

Question:

How should the law—or society—decide which things it should be possible to own, and what controls should be imposed on that ownership?

2.2.2 Equitable ownership

Ownership may be legal or equitable. So far the discussion has considered only legal ownership, and it has been assumed, without making the fact explicit, that the legal owner has 'full legal and beneficial ownership'—in short, that the sum of legal and equitable ownership are vested in the same person (although it is seen as incorrect to speak of two separate interests in this context[8]). But it is also possible for legal ownership to be vested in one person and equitable ownership in another. For example, under a trust, the legal owner (the trustee) is under a duty to hold the legal title to property on trust for the benefit and enjoyment of the beneficiary (the equitable owner). With most *express* trusts (ie trusts intentionally created for the bene-

[8] See the comments in the further issues addressed at the end of this sub-section.

fit of certain individuals, as distinct from trusts imposed by operation of law[9]), the trustee also has duties to *manage* the trust property to the greater advantage of the beneficiary.

The common law's approach to this situation is unique. Civilian jurisdictions have not adopted the concept of a 'trust', where 'legal ownership' resides in one person and 'equitable ownership' in another.

[202] F H Lawson and B Rudden, *The Law of Property* (2nd edn, 1982, Clarendon: Oxford), p 102:

> 'It would have been possible to say either that the trustee owns the property but is under a duty to manage it for the benefit of the beneficiary, who has nothing more than a correlative personal right against the trustee, or on the contrary that the beneficiary owns the property but gives full powers of management to the trustee, who stands in no direct relation to the property but acts merely by delegation of property rights vested in the beneficiary. English law has taken neither course, but has in effect said that both trustee and beneficiary own the property in different ways, or, more accurately, that neither owns the property in the strict Roman sense of the term ownership, but each owns a different estate in it, called respectively the legal estate and the equitable interest. It says that to ask in such a situation who owns the physical object is an improper question, just as it would be improper to ask whether a tenant for life or a person entitled to the land after his death owned the land itself.'

Even in common law jurisdictions, it was some time before the personal obligations imposed upon the trustee were seen as giving rise to proprietary interests in the beneficiary.[10] Originally equity's jurisdiction was seen as being in relation to persons rather than property. The Court of Chancery acted upon the defendant's conscience and could compel the defendant to act in certain ways. The rights which the claimant acquired as a result of such an order were personal rights to have the defendant meet the remedy ordered; they were not proprietary rights in specific property. This was true even when the remedy was an order that the defendant hold specific property for the benefit of the claimant: the claimant's rights were specific to the named defendant; they did not follow the property. This is no longer true. Since the fifteenth century, Chancellors have enforced certain equitable rights not only against the person originally bound, but also against strangers who took the relevant property either as donees or as purchasers but with notice of the claimant's claim. The end result is that equitable rights to property[11] are enforceable against anyone other than a person purchasing the property in good faith and on the assumption that no-one had conflicting rights (see Section 6.2.5 below).

This concept of equitable rights as proprietary interests is thus a remarkable and somewhat strange invention of the common law (or, more specifically, of Equity as a branch of the common law). It prompts the obvious question, when will such equitable interests arise? Given the origins of the jurisdiction, it is clear that equitable ownership will only arise in situations where the law regards it as unconscionable for a legal owner of property to be permitted to keep the property for

[9] These trusts—resulting and constructive trusts—are discussed in Chapters 5 and 6 (Section 6.5).

[10] See *Baker v Archer-Shee* [1927] AC 844 (HL).

[11] But not other equitable rights.

himself. This is not very informative, but for the moment it will do. Equity, acting on the conscience of the legal owner, will then compel him to hold the property for the benefit of others. Equitable ownership interests are not the only equitable proprietary interests to arise in this way. A similar analysis gives rise to equitable security interests (see Sections 3.5 and 3.6 below). The difference depends upon the *way* in which the defendant is required to hold the property for the claimant beneficiary. This defines the package of rights to which the claimant is entitled—in short, it defines the nature of the claimant's proprietary interest. Express trusts and equitable charges illustrate the jurisdiction in operation in relation to consensual arrangements between parties. It is also possible for similar interests to arise by operation of law—ie to be imposed notwithstanding the express arrangements between the parties—if the circumstances warrant such a response (see Chapter 5 below, especially Sections 5.4 ff). The detail can wait until later. However, it ought to be clear even at this introductory stage that not all equitable ownership interests (or equitable security interests) come packaged in the same way. The obligations which equity sees fit to impose on the defendant will depend upon what constraints are necessary to prevent the defendant acting unconscionably. This will circumscribe both the proprietary and the personal rights imposed in equity. In particular, it may be appropriate to subject some defendants—such as express trustees—to onerous collateral personal duties of management and investment; with others—such as volunteers— it may not. Such differentiation seems to follow as a matter of course from the jurisdiction being exercised, yet the issue remains controversial (see, for example, Sections 6.5.3, 7.4.2, 7.4.3 and 8.2.1). This is notwithstanding the long history of the jurisdiction and the practical importance of the issue to the claimant.

Three further issues need to be addressed at this stage. They are left as open-ended questions, since the answers remain controversial.

(i) Legal ownership and the ability to deal with equitable ownership interests

The first issue relates to the point, noted earlier, that the absolute legal owner of property is not regarded as having both legal and equitable ownership of the property. Legal ownership itself encompasses all the relevant rights. As Lord Browne-Wilkinson said in *Westdeutsche Landesbank Girozentrale v Islington London Borough Council* [1996] AC 669 (HL) (see **[518]** below), at p 706:[12]

> 'A person solely entitled to the full beneficial ownership of money or property, both at law and in equity, does not enjoy an equitable interest in that property. The legal title carries with it all rights. Unless and until there is a separation of the legal and equitable estates, there is no separate equitable title. Therefore to talk about the [legal owner] "retaining" its equitable interest is meaningless. The only question is whether the circumstances under which the money was paid were such as, in equity, to impose a trust on the [recipient of the funds]. If so, an equitable interest arose for the first time under that trust.'

[12] Also see *Vandervell v Inland Revenue Commissioners* [1967] 2 AC 291, 311 *per* Lord Upjohn, and 317 *per* Lord Donovan; *Commissioner of Stamp Duties (Queensland) v Livingston* [1965] AC 694, 712.

If regard is had to the way in which equitable ownership arises, then the statement makes a lot of sense. It would be ridiculous to see the legal owner as bound in conscience to hold the property for the benefit of himself, and able to sue himself for any breaches of that equitable obligation.

However, how that position should govern the legal owner's ability to deal with the property is not so clear. Because there is no distinct equitable title until the legal and equitable interests are separated, it follows, so it is said, that the legal owner cannot '*retain*' the equitable interest in property and transfer legal title to another. The transaction has to be effected by full transfer of legal and beneficial ownership to the other who must then re-transfer the equitable interest to the donor. The practical implications of this compulsory two-step process can be harsh for the original transferor: see *Westdeutsche Landesbank Girozentrale v Islington London Borough Council* [1996] AC 669 (**[504]** and **[518]** below); and *Re Bond Worth* [1980] 1 Ch 228 (**[306]** below). Note that this two-step process makes it plain that the legal and beneficial owner can *transfer* the equitable interest to another without any difficulty. This is what happens when a person declares himself to be a trustee of property for another. How can this distinction between 'retaining' and 'transferring' an equitable interest be justified? If it has to do with the legitimacy of imposing obligations on the legal owner to hold the property for the benefit of the beneficiary, should the analysis depend upon whether the beneficiary asserts that the relationship arose consensually or was imposed by operation of law?

(ii) Locating the equitable ownership interest

This next issue is related to the previous one. Consider a person who is not the absolute legal owner, but a legal owner who is subject to restrictions in dealing with particular property. The question is whether this feature indicates that equitable ownership of the property must necessarily lie in someone else's hands. The courts have held that it does not. All depends upon the form of the restriction imposed on the legal owner.

[203] ***Commissioner of Stamp Duties (Qld) v Livingston*** **[1965] AC 694 (PC), 712** ***per*** **Viscount Radcliffe:**

[The case concerned the interest of a beneficiary in one-third of the residue of an unadministered estate. The Judicial Committee held that, during the course of the administration, the beneficiary had no proprietary interest in any particular asset in the estate. Her only right was to compel the personal representative to administer the estate properly. However, this right was a chose in action which was transmissible by will. The focus here is not on her rights, but on the nature of the personal representative's legal ownership.]

> 'Where, it is asked, is the beneficial interest in [the assets of an unadministered estate] during the period of administration? It is not, ex hypothesi, in the executor: where else can it be but in the residuary legatee? This dilemma is founded on a fallacy, for it assumes mistakenly that for all purposes and at every moment of time the law requires the separate existence of two different kinds of estate or interest in property, the legal and the equitable. There is no need to make this assumption. When the whole right of property is in a person, as it is in an executor, there is no need to distinguish between the

legal and equitable interest in that property, any more than there is for the property of a full beneficial owner. What matters is that the court will control the executor in the use of his rights over assets that come to him in that capacity; but it will do it by the enforcement of remedies which do not involve the admission or recognition of equitable rights of property in those assets. Equity in fact calls into existence and protects equitable rights and interests in property only where their recognition has been found to be required in order to give effect to its doctrines.

Criticisms of this kind arise from the fact that the terminology of our legal system has not produced a sufficient variety of words to represent the various meanings which can be conveyed by the words "interest" and "property." Thus propositions are advanced or rebutted by the employment of terms that have not in themselves a common basis of definition. For instance, there are two passages quoted by the Chief Justice in his dissenting judgment in this case which illustrate the confusion. There is the remark of Jordan C.J. in *McCaughey's* case (46 S.R.(N.S.W.) 192, 204), "The idea that beneficiaries in an unadministered or partially administered estate have no beneficial interest in the items which go to make up the estate is repugnant to elementary and fundamental principles of equity." If "by beneficial interest in the items" it is intended to suggest that such beneficiaries have any property right at all in any of those items, the proposition cannot be accepted as either elementary or fundamental. It is, as has been shown, contrary to the principles of equity. But, on the other hand, if the meaning is only that such beneficiaries are not without legal remedy during the course of administration to secure that the assets are properly dealt with and the rights that they hope will accrue to them in the future are safeguarded, the proposition is no doubt correct. They can be said, therefore, to have an interest in respect of the assets, or even a beneficial interest in the assets, so long as it is understood in what sense the word "interest" is used in such a context. . . .'

This case decided that the executor was the legal owner of the assets comprising the deceased's estate, and that the beneficiaries were not the equitable owners. Importantly, it did *not* decide that the executor must therefore be the equitable owner of these assets. This final point is often of great practical importance. In many taxing statutes, for example, liability is imposed on the 'beneficial owner' of assets. These statutes are construed strictly according to their terms, so generalisations are dangerous. But the courts often conduct a detailed examination of the rights remaining to the legal owner. They then decide whether these are sufficiently expansive to conclude that the legal owner is also the beneficial owner of the asset.[13]

Question:

Does this mean that it is possible to have assets without any beneficial owner? Consider the position with assets held on a discretionary trust: see *Gartside v IRC* [1968] AC 553.

[13] See, eg, *Ayerst v C & K Constructions Ltd* [1976] AC 168.

(iii) Is the right to claim possession an equitable interest?

In all the discussion so far, the focus has been on equitable ownership. It has never been considered possible to have 'equitable possession'. Why not? Does Sir Nicolas Browne-Wilkinson VC in *Bristol Airport plc v Powdrill* [1990] Ch 744, 759 (**[303]** below) base his decision on something akin to 'equitable possession', or does he provide a more legitimate basis? Also see *Melluish (Inspector of Taxes) v BMI (No 3) Ltd* [1996] AC 454, 473–5 *per* Lord Browne-Wilkinson (HL).

2.2.3 Co-ownership

Two or more people can be the co-owners of property either at law or in equity. Co-ownership of personal property operates in much the same way as co-ownership of real property. As with real property, the co-owners may be either joint tenants or tenants in common. Joint tenants share the four unities of possession, interest, title and time of commencement of the interest. Tenants in common, on the other hand, share unity of possession, but they have a distinct title to their shares.[14]

This 'unity of possession' means that the co-owners have a contemporaneous right to possession of the whole property. It follows that, ordinarily, one co-owner cannot maintain an action against the others for possession of the property. However, if one co-owner destroys or gives away the property without the authority of the others, the others may bring an action in conversion.[15]

In addition, and probably most importantly, joint ownership is associated with a right of survivorship. This means that if one of the joint tenants dies, the deceased's share passes to the other joint tenants in *pro rata* shares. With ownership in common, there is no such right. The deceased's share forms part of his or her estate, and will pass under the deceased's will or on an intestacy.

It is quite common to have legal ownership in common of goods and other choses in possession. For example, a silo of wheat may be owned by several co-owners. This ownership in common can arise by express or implied agreement between the parties concerned,[16] or it can arise under statute.[17] Interestingly, it is not possible to have legal ownership in common of choses in action; at law, these assets can only be owned jointly. This is because section 136(1) of the Law of Property Act 1925 (**[405]** below) does not enable a joint owner to effect a legal severance of joint ownership of a chose in action by assigning his or her interest at law.[18] In equity, however, either form of co-ownership is possible, although, if the form is not made clear, then there is a presumption in favour of ownership in common. Why would this be?

[14] If a co-owner owns more than half of a chattel in undivided shares, he may apply to the court for division of the chattels, according to a valuation or some other method: Law of Property Act 1925 s 188(1).

[15] Torts (Interference with Goods) Act 1977 s 10(1)(a). See Section 7.2.3 below.

[16] See *Re Stapylton Fletcher Ltd* [1994] 1 WLR 1181 (**[422]** below); *Mercer v Craven Grain Storage Ltd* [1994] CLC 328 (HL) (see Section 2.5 below).

[17] Sale of Goods Act 1979 s 20A, 20B: see **[421]** below.

[18] *Re McKerrell, McKerrell v Gowans* [1912] 2 Ch 648, 653.

Lawson and Rudden explain the utility of joint ownership as opposed to ownership in common:[19]

> 'The right of survivorship at first sight gives such unfair results that it is difficult to see how anybody should want to give property in joint tenancy or joint ownership. A moment's reflection will, however, show that joint tenancy or joint ownership is an extremely convenient form of ownership for trustees. For the ownership of trustees is for the purpose of management and not enjoyment. Now it is only where a number of persons have concurrent rights to enjoy a thing that the right of survivorship produces unfair results; on the other hand, it is very convenient that the interest of one of a number of managers should not devolve on those who succeed him on death, but should vest automatically in all the survivors. If one looks on the trustees as a committee, all that has happened is that a member of the committee has disappeared, and the others carry on as if he were still there, taking steps to add to their number if it becomes too small. Thus, joint tenancy or joint ownership is appropriate to management, tenancy or ownership in common to beneficial enjoyment of property.'

For different reasons, joint ownership rather than ownership in common is also the preferred form in domestic relationships. Why should this be so?

2.2.4 'Mere equities'

The idea of a 'mere equity' has already been noted (see Section 1.4). Mere equities are *not* proprietary interests, so it might be thought that they should have no place in this discussion. However, although they are *personal* rights, their exercise will[20] deliver a proprietary interest to their holder. That makes them important in the context of personal property. It is necessary to know when mere equities arise, and how to distinguish them from fully fledged proprietary interests.

In Chapter 1, the right to rescind a contract of sale was used as an example of a mere equity. Before rescission, the right holder has no proprietary interest in the sale property which he wants to recover; after rescission, provided the property is identifiable in the hands of the transferee, its ownership will revest in the transferor (at law or in equity).[21]

Also see:

Latec Investments Ltd v Hotel Terrigal Pty Ltd (1965) 113 CLR 265 (Aust HCt), especially 289–91 *per* Menzies J (**[607]** below).

[19] F H Lawson and B Rudden, *The Law of Property* (2nd edn, 1982, Clarendon: Oxford), at pp. 83–4.

[20] 'Mere equity' is not a term of art, but in this book the expression is used *only* to refer to rights the exercise of which will deliver a proprietary interest to their holder. If, contrary to this, all equitable rights were to be called 'mere equities', then the expression would have no value as a definition. However, see *National Provincial Bank v Ainsworth* [1965] AC 1175, where Lord Upjohn uses the expression in an all-embracing sense.

[21] As noted in Section 1.4, this depends upon both the nature of the asset and the nature of the flaw permitting rescission. Certain assets *cannot* immediately re-vest at law; certain 'flaws' permitting rescission are only recognised in equity—in either case, revesting can only occur in equity.

2.3 Possession

2.3.1 The concept of a possessory interest

The layman's definition of possession is based on the notion of intentional physical control of an asset. The law's definition is not quite the same. The law distinguishes between the right to possess a thing physically and the package of advantages or rights which the law gives to possessors. This package of rights defines the possessory interest in property.

[204] F H Lawson and B Rudden, *The Law of Property* (2nd edn, 1982, Clarendon: Oxford), pp 42–4:

'Now in certain circumstances, although a person's possession passes the ordinary tests applied by the average layman, a judge may think it improper to accord such rights to a person whom an average layman would not regard as a possessor; or again he may wish to vary the concept depending on the function it is to fulfil. Thus if money and heroin are slipped into someone's handbag unawares, the owner certainly has possession of the money as against a thief, but not of the drug so as to incur criminal liability.

The proper way to express this divergence between the use of the term 'possession' by laymen and by lawyers is to say that when lawyers use the term they have in mind the legal consequences of certain states of fact which, though they tend to conform to the ordinary layman's notion of possession, often depart from it; and where possession is relevant to the law of property it really means the collection of possessory rights which are collectively known as the 'right of possession'.

In what ensues we shall have to deal with this legal concept of possession and not with possession as it is regarded by the ordinary layman.

Certain persons who have physical control of a thing are held not to possess but merely to have custody of it on behalf of someone else. Thus, although a servant possesses what he has taken on his master's behalf, whether from a third party or from nobody at all, the answer to the question whether he possesses something he has received from his master or, on the contrary, his master continues to possess it through him, depends on the circumstances; he does not possess, for instance, his master's silver when he has cleaned it, but he may possess his master's luggage if he is travelling overland to meet him when he steps down from an aircraft. Other difficulties arise with regard to lodgers and tenants; the law governing the attribution to them of possession of furnished or unfurnished rooms is both complicated and doubtful. Further, the merely temporary control that a guest has, for instance, over the cutlery he is using at a dinner party is not treated as possession. His host possesses it through him. But, generally speaking, physical control does imply possession, and so tenants of land or houses, and borrowers, pledgees, or other bailees of goods possess what they have under their control; though for certain purposes the landlord and, in certain cases, the lender or other bailor are also held to possess at the same time.

Although these principles do not amount to a very neat doctrine, they afford answers to all the obvious problems which are likely to arise except one. Difficulties have arisen particularly where one person has found something in or on land possessed by another person, and the presence of the thing was hitherto unknown to the latter. Does his possession of the land or house carry with it possession of all its contents? Or if the possessor must intend to acquire possession of the contents in addition to acquiring possession of the land or house, will a general intention to acquire the contents suffice, or must he have directed his mind to each specific object, or at least to such specific objects as would not ordinarily be expected to be there? Again, does it matter whether the object in question is on or embedded in the land or again whether it was in or on the land when he took possession of the latter or, on the other hand, came on to it later without his knowledge? The few decisions on this topic are not easy to reconcile with each other and do not tell a very clear story. Some at least seem to turn on the special facts of the case. Perhaps some of them are unsound.

Thus a Viking ship was held to be possessed by the possessor of the land in which it had been buried centuries before, and rings found imbedded in a reservoir were held to be possessed by the owner of the reservoir. But a shopkeeper was not held to possess a five-pound note dropped by someone on the part of the floor of the shop open to the public; and the possessor of a house which had subsequently been requisitioned by the military authorities was held not to possess a brooch which was afterwards found on a ledge at the top of a window (though the true reason for the decision may be that, whatever might have been the correct view as between the finder and the military authorities, the person who, as former possessor, brought the action against the finder, had never actually taken possession of the house before it was requisitioned).

For the general purposes of property law, however, the concept of *possession* is useful as a contrast with *ownership*. Thus if A borrows B's book it is sufficient for most purposes to say that A has possession and B ownership.'

[205] F Pollock and R S Wright, *An Essay on Possession in the Common Law* (1888, Clarendon: Oxford), pp 26–8:

'The Nature of Possession

Throughtout our inquiry we have to bear in mind that the following elements are quite distinct in conception, and, though very often found in combination, are also separable and often separated in practice. They are

i. Physical control, detention, or *de facto* possession. This, as an actual relation between a person and a thing, is a matter of fact. Nevertheless questions which the Court must decide as matter of law arise as to the proof of the facts.

ii. Legal possession, the state of being a possessor in the eye of the law.

This is a definite legal relation of the possessor to the thing possessed. In its most normal and obvious form, it coexists with the fact of physical control, and with other facts making the exercise of that control rightful. But it may exist with or without detention, and wither with or without a rightful origin.

A tailor sends to JS's house a coat which JS has ordered. JS puts on the coat, and then has both physical control and rightful possession in law.

JS takes off the coat and gives it to a servant to take back to the tailor for some alterations. Now the servant has physical control (in this connexion generally called "custody" by our authorities) and JS still has the possession in law.

While the servant is going on his errand, Z assaults him and robs him of the coat. Z is not only physically master of the coat, but, so soon as he has complete control of it, he has possession in law, though a wrongful possession. To see what is left to JS we must look to the next head.

iii. Right to possess or to have legal possession. This includes the right to physical possession. It can exist apart from both physical and legal possession; it is, for example, that which remains to a rightful possessor immediately after he has been wrongfully dispossessed. It is a normal incident of ownership or property, and the name of 'property' if often given to it. Unlike possession itself, it is not necessarily exclusive. A may have the right to possess a thing as against B and every one else, while B has at the same time a right to possess it as against every one except A. So joint tenants have both single possession and a single joint right to possess, but tenants in common have a single possession with several rights to possess. When a person having right to possess a thing acquires the physical control of it, he necessarily acquires legal possession also.

Right to possess, when separated from possession, is often called 'constructive possession'. The correct use of the term would seem to be coextensive with and limited to those cases where a person entitled to possess is (or was) allowed the same remedies as if he had really been in possession. But it is also sometimes specially applied to the cases where the legal possession is with one person and the custody with his servant, or some other person for the time being in a like position; and sometimes it is extended to other cases where legal possession is separated from detention.

'Actual possession' as opposed to 'constructive possession' is in the same way an ambiguous term. It is most commonly used to signify physical control, with or without possession in law. 'Bare possession' is sometimes used with the same meaning. 'Lawful possession' means a legal possession which is also rightful or at least excusable; this may be consistent with a superior right to possess in some other person.

The whole terminology of the subject, however, is still very loose and unsettled in the books, and the reader cannot be too strongly warned that careful attention must in every case be paid to the context.'

The preceding extracts make it clear that legal possession is not necessarily the same as physical possession. Moreover, what constitutes legal possession depends upon the context. For example, different statutory provisions may rely upon different definitions of the term: the nature of possession for the purpose of a drugs offence may differ from the nature of possession in the context of the sale of goods legislation. Usually, however, legal possession involves two features: the intention to possess, and sufficient control over the property to prevent strangers from interfering with it.

Even this statement of the features of legal possession only serves to reinforce the fact that legal possession and physical possession need not coincide. When this is the case, the legal possessor is sometimes said to have 'constructive possession'.[22] This disjunction between legal and physical possession can create difficulties. Legal liabilities and legal rights may depend upon legal possession. It is then important to identify accurately the person with legal possession, as distinct from physical possession. The extracts which follow address these difficulties.

[206] *The Tubantia* [1924] P 78, 89–91 *per* Duke P:

[This case considers the element of 'control' necessary to constitute possession. In 1922 the claimants went on an expedition to salvage cargo from the wreck of a Dutch steamship which had sunk in over 100 feet of water in the North Sea. The cargo was estimated to be worth over £2m in 1922. The claimants worked at the scene of the wreck whenever weather and tides permitted during the summer of 1922 and between April and July 1923. During that time they cut a hole in the hold,

[22] 'Constructive' is a word much favoured by the law. In this context it means that the person does not have (physical) possession, but nevertheless will be treated by the law as if he had. Similar usage is seen with 'constructive' notice and 'constructive' trust and, most problematically, 'constructive' trustee (see Sections 7.2.4 and 7.4.2).

buoyed the wreck and extracted some cargo, all at a cost of over £40,000. In July 1923, the defendants sent down their own divers and tried to secure possession of the wreck and cargo to prevent further work by the claimants or to lay their own claim as concurrent occupiers of the wreck. It was held that the claimants were sufficiently in occupation of the wreck to exclude third parties from interfering with the property and that an injunction should be ordered to prevent the defendants from committing further trespass (also see Sections 7.2.2 and 7.6.2).]

'On the question whether in the state of facts I have described the plaintiffs could be found to have had possession of the *Tubantia* when the defendants appeared on the scene, counsel on both sides cited largely from Sir Frederick Pollock's well-known treatise on possession: Pollock and Wright, Possession in the Common Law. The questions suggested in this way I have sought to apply. They involve inquiries such as these: what are the kinds of physical control and use of which the things in question were practically capable? Could physical control be applied to the res as a whole? Was there a complete taking? Had the plaintiffs occupation sufficient for practical purposes to exclude strangers from interfering with the property? Was there the animus possidendi? I have also taken this to be a true proposition in English law: A thing taken by a person of his own motion and for himself, and subject in his hands, or under his control, to the uses of which it is capable, is in that person's possession. "Omnia ut dominum gessisse" is, Sir Frederick Pollock says, a good working synonym for "in possessione esse," and I cannot doubt that if the owners of the *Tubantia* in 1916 had put themselves, in 1923, in the position in which the plaintiffs put themselves they would be held to have been in actual possession. It would not be safe, though, to rely on this, for there is a presumption in law which aids the operative effect of the possessory acts of an owner. To illustrate my meaning, I am told that the Trinity House commonly holds possession of the wreck of a ship by mooring on it a single buoy. I had the advantage of the assistance of the Elder Brethren at the hearing, and I have consulted them as to the practical aspects of the matters in question. They advise me that by reason of the great depth at which the wreck lies the difficulties involved in the work of the plaintiffs are formidable, but that, if I accept the plaintiffs' evidence, they were in effective control of the wreck as a whole; that they were in a position to prevent any useful work by new-comers; and that, while the plaintiffs' people remained in the position they claimed to have taken up, no new-comer could, without violence, have exercised upon the wreck the kind of control the plaintiffs had, or could have made any valuable use of the wreck. They advise me that what the plaintiffs did upon the wreck was what a prudent owner would probably have done, assuming he did not know how the holds of the *Tubantia* were stowed and desired to inform himself fully as to the situation on the wreck before employing larger graft or more powerful appliances than the plaintiffs were employing. These opinions entirely commend themselves to my judgment, and I have come to certain conclusions which I will now state.

There was animus possidendi in the plaintiffs. There was the use and occupation of which the subject matter was capable. There was power to exclude strangers from interfering if the plaintiffs did not use unlawful force. The plaintiffs did with the wreck what a purchaser would prudently have done. Unwieldy as the wreck was, they were dealing with it as a whole. The fact on the other side which is outstanding is the difficulty of possessing things which lie in very deep water and can only be entered upon by workmen in fine weather and for short periods of time. Must it be said that, because the work of the plaintiffs' divers was that of only one pair at a time, in short spells with long interruptions, and because access to the holds of the *Tubantia* was often prevented altogether by stress of weather, therefore the vessel, and her cargo, were incapable of possession? To my mind this would be an unfortunate conclusion, very discouraging to salvage enterprise at a time when salvage, by means of bold and costly work, is of great public importance. I do not feel bound to come to it. I hold that the plaintiffs had in July, 1923, the possession of the *Tubantia* and her cargo, which they allege.'

The next two extracts illustrate that rights and liabilities associated with possession lie with the person who has legal possession, even if someone else has physical possession.

[207] *Chabbra Corporation Pte Ltd v Jag Shakti (Owners) (The Jag Shakti)* [1986] 1 AC 337 (PC), 345–6 *per* Lord Brandon:

[The sellers shipped a cargo of salt on the defendant shipowners' vessel. The buyers had financed the purchase by pledging the bills of lading to the claimant. (This is a pledge of a documentary intangible: see Sections 1.2.2 and 3.1.2.) When the ship arrived with its cargo, the buyers persuaded the shipowners to deliver the salt to them (in return for a bank indemnity in the shipowners' favour) even though they could not produce the bills of lading. The buyers then refused to redeem their pledge with the claimant. The claimant therefore sued the shipowners in conversion for their wrongful release of the cargo. The Privy Council considered the measure of damages.]

'[I]t is not in dispute that the pledgee of a bill of lading is entitled, on presentation of it to the ship at the port of discharge, to the possession of the goods represented by it. It has further, in their Lordships' opinion, been established, by authority of long standing, that where one person, A, who has or is entitled to have the possession of goods, is deprived of such possession by the tortious conduct of another person, B, whether such conduct consists in conversion or negligence, the proper measure in law of the damages recoverable by A from B is the full market value of the goods at the time when and the place where possession of them should have been given. For this purpose it is irrelevant whether A has the general property in the goods as the outright owner of them, or only a special property in them as pledgee, or only possession or a right to possession of them as a bailee. Furthermore the circumstance that, if A recovers the full market value of the goods from B, he may be liable to account for the whole or part of what he has recovered to a third party, C, is also irrelevant, as being res inter alios acta.

The only exception to the general principle just stated is when B has one or more cross-claims against A arising out of the same or some connected transaction. In that case B may be entitled to set-off or deduct the amount of any such cross-claim or cross-claims from the full market value of the goods in arriving at the amount of the damages recoverable from him by A: see *McGregor on Damages*, 14th. ed. (1980), paras. 1075–1080. . . .'

Note:

A bill of lading is a documentary intangible (see Section 1.2.2). This makes is quite different from other 'documents of title' to goods—which are usually simply invoices or receipts for the goods. The holder of a bill of lading has constructive (or symbolic) possession of the goods represented by the document. The holder of other documents which relate to the goods does not. Whether or not these other parties have possession or constructive possession depends upon the normal rules relating to possession of goods. This is important, because remedies for interference with goods are only available to those with a possessory interest in the goods.

Question:

Does the previous extract suggest that a claimant claiming damages for conversion can recover more than his or her actual loss?

Also see:

The Winkfield [1902] P 42 (CA) (**[719]** below).

[208] ***Towers & Co Ltd v Gray* [1961] 2 QB 351 (CA), 361–2, 365 *per* Lord Parker CJ:** [A farmer supplied the appellant company with frozen chickens, each wrapped in a cellophane bag and marked with its weight. The appellant company stored these chickens in another company's cold store. When an inspector of weights and measures weighed the chickens, he found that some weighed less than their marked weights. The appellant company was charged with having in its possession for the purpose of trade 39 chickens to which a false trade description applied contrary to the Merchandise Marks Act 1887, as amended. The Court of Appeal held that, even though the cold storage company was in physical possession of the chickens, the appellant company was in constructive possession of them and so could be properly convicted and fined.]

> 'The justices came to the conclusion on the facts of this case that although the chickens were in the physical possession, if I may use that word, of the cold storage company, they were immediately available on demand to the appellant company and that the appellant company were in constructive possession of them for the purposes of its trade. Alternatively, they found, if they were wrong on that, that at the time when the inspector of weights and measures came and weighed the chickens, those chickens were at that point of time in the possession of the appellant company.
>
> The term "possession" is always giving rise to trouble. As Earl Jowitt said in *United States of America and Republic of France v. Dollfus Mieg et Cie. S.A. and Bank of England* ([1952] A.C. 582, 605): "The person having the right to immediate possession is, however, frequently referred to in English law as being the 'possessor'—in truth the English law has never worked out a completely logical and exhaustive definition of 'possession.' "
>
> For my part I approach this case on the basis that the meaning of "possession" depends upon the context in which it is used. Thus its meaning was dealt with in connection with the Bills of Sale Act, 1854, in *Ancona v. Rogers* ((1876) 1 Ex.D. 285, C.A). Again, in *United States of America and Republic of France v. Dollfus Mieg et Cie. S.A. and Bank of England*, to which I have referred, the meaning of "possession" was dealt with in connection with the law of foreign sovereign immunity. In each case it must depend, in my judgment, on the context in which it is used. In some contexts, no doubt, a bailment for reward subject to a lien, and where perhaps some period of notice has to be given before the goods can be removed, could be of such a nature that the only possession that there

could be said to be would be possession in the bailee. In other cases it may well be that the nature of the bailment is such that the owner of the goods who has parted with the physical possession of them can truly be said still to be in possession.

In the present case we are dealing with a penal statute dealing with the sellers of goods, and it is to be observed that at any rate possession in the eyes of the commercial community is a word perfectly apt to cover an owner of goods who has those goods warehoused or in the hands of some third person. That appears from the judgment of Branson J. in *City Fur Manufacturing Co. Ltd. v. Fureenbond (Brokers) London Ltd* ([1937] 1 All E.R. 799). The facts of the case do not matter. The question was what was meant by "possession" in the Sale of Goods Act, 1893, s. 25. Branson J. in that case refers to the fact that the Factors Act, 1889, had defined "possession" as including possession by another person on behalf of the person whose possession was material. He took the view that in dealing with the Sale of Goods Act, 1893, there was no reason why the same meaning should not be given to the word "possession." He said this (at p. 802): "Possession by an agent, possession by a warehouseman or mercantile agent, is a perfectly well known form of possession in the business world, and I can see no reason for confining the meaning of it to personal possession or actual possession of the person who has sold the goods." There one has a meaning put on the word "possession" that is common in the commercial world.

. . .

It seems to me that in the present case in the context in which it appears, both looked at from the point of view of the criminal law and from the point of view of the commercial community, "possession" in its popular sense would cover a case such as this, where the goods are held to the order of the seller on terms on which he can get them back at once. . . .'

The next extract indicates that legal possession may be transferred without any change in the physical circumstances. The goods need not be relocated, nor need the identity of their custodian change. Goods stored in warehouses are often subjected to changes in possession in this way: the warehouseman 'attorns', usually to the new owner, who thereby acquires possession ('constructive possession') as well as ownership of the goods in question.

[209] *Charlesworth v Mills* [1892] AC 231 (HL), 236, 238 *per* Lord Halsbury LC: [The owner of goods that had been seized under a fi. fa., agreed with the defendant that the defendant should pay out the sheriff, that the goods should be pledged to the defendant as security for his advance, and that the sheriff's officer should hold the goods on behalf of the defendant. It was held that before the agreement the sheriff's officer held the goods for the sheriff, but that after the agreement he held them for the defendant.]

'Now let us see what the transaction here is. . . . The transaction here is a very plain one. The debtor has an execution in his house, the sheriff takes possession (upon what the effect and quality of that possession is, I will say a word presently), the debtor is under the impression that he can raise sufficient money upon the security of the goods of which the sheriff has taken possession to satisfy him, and also perhaps to leave a surplus for himself. For that purpose it is necessary that the execution should be paid out; the sheriff will not relinquish possession, and for his own security cannot relinquish possession until he has been paid the money. Accordingly the debtor goes to the appellant, Mr. Charlesworth, and invites him to lend him the money upon the security of the

> goods which at that moment are in the possession of the sheriff. Mr. Charlesworth agrees to do so, but he bargains and makes it a necessary part of the transaction without which he will not advance his money, that he shall get possession of the goods. That is agreed to. . . . That was a bargain that the possession should be changed from the person to whom the money was being advanced to the person lending it. . . .
>
> . . .
>
> My Lords, under these circumstances, what is the problem which your Lordships are called upon to solve? We have the fact that the debtor has given a perfectly good mandate. . . . the man says, "I hand over these goods to you," in the only sense in which goods that are distributed over a house are capable of being handed over, "in consideration of your paying money to the sheriff and getting them out of the hands of the sheriff"; and then he draws up a document in which he says, "Now keep this possession for me, and sell the goods for what they will fetch by auction"; and of course after he has done that the person to whom they are handed holds them with this kind of trust attached to them, and when they are realized, if there is anything remaining beyond the amount of £62 which he has advanced upon them, he holds that money to the order of the person who has given him the mandate. . . .'

This final extract indicates the potential for dealing with possessory interests by contract.

[210] ***Re Cosslett (Contractors) Ltd*** **[1998] Ch 495 (CA), 506–8** ***per*** **Millett LJ:**
[A coal washing plant was brought onto a county council site by a contractor for use in a land reclamation scheme. The contract between the site owner and the contractor deemed all plant on the site to be the property of the site owner (clause 53(2)). A further clause (clause 63(1)) provided that if the contractor went into liquidation or abandoned the contract the council could enter the site, expel the contractor, retain possession of the plant and use it to complete the works, and then sell it and apply the proceeds of sale towards whatever sums might be or become due from the company under the contract. When the council sought to rely on these clauses, the contractor's administrator unsuccessfully applied under section 234 of the Insolvency Act 1986 for delivery up of the washing plant or payment for its use.]

> 'As appears therefrom, by the present proceedings the administrator of the company claims the delivery up of certain plant as property of the company together with damages for its wrongful retention. The council has refused delivery up in reliance on its contractual rights under the standard form of contract issued by the Institution of Civil Engineers. Clause 63(1) of this contract grants the council two distinct rights in the event of the company being expelled from the site. One is the right to retain possession of the plant and use it to complete the works without further payment to the company. The other is the right to sell plant on completion of the works as well as plant not required to complete the works and to apply the proceeds of sale towards whatever sums might be or become due from the company under the contract. The administrator contends that these rights constitute a floating charge which is void against him for want of registration under section 395 of the Companies Act 1985. . . .
>
> [506] In my judgment the two rights on which the council relies are distinct rights and must be considered separately. At the date when the writ was issued the works were not complete, and accordingly the council's right to retain possession of the plant and use it to complete the works, if valid, is sufficient to defeat the administrator's claim in the action. The works have, however, now been completed, so that to justify its continued

retention of the plant the council must rely on its power of sale. We have been asked to indicate our view whether this power is void as against the administrator, even if this is not strictly necessary for the disposal of the appeal, so that future disputes can be avoided.

In my judgment the following questions arise for decision. (1) Whether clause 53(2) of the contract has the effect of transferring the legal property in the plant to the council. If it does then (i) it was still the property of the council when delivery up was demanded; and (ii) there can be no question of the council's rights in respect of the plant constituting a charge on its own property. (2) If it does not, whether the council's right to retain possession of the plant and use it to complete the works constitutes an equitable charge. . . . [The three further questions raised by Millett LJ are noted at **[328]** below.]

(1) Does clause 53(2) transfer legal property in the plant to the council?

This depends on the terms of the contract and is a pure question of construction: see *In re Fox; Ex parte Oundle and Thrapston Rural District Council v. The Trustee* [1948] Ch. 407, 419. The authorities show that it may turn on fine distinctions. Where the contract provides that plant and materials brought onto the site "shall be and become" the property of the employer the words are given literal effect and the contract is treated as passing legal title to the employer: *Reeves v. Barlow*, 12 Q.B.D. 436, 442; *Bennett White (Calgary) Ltd. v. Municipal District of Sugar City No. 5* [1951] A.C. 786. Where, however, as in the present case the contract provides only that the plant and materials "shall be deemed" or "shall be considered" to be the property of the employer, the words are regarded as ambiguous. In such a case other provisions of the contract may be taken into account in order to decide whether the contract has the effect of passing the legal property in the plant and materials to the employer or whether, as the prima facie meaning of the words suggests, it does not have this effect but merely entitles the employer to act as if the property in the plant and materials had passed to him: see *Brown v. Bateman*, L.R. 2 C.P. 272; *In re Winter; Ex parte Bolland* (1878) 8 Ch.D. 225; *Milnes v. Mayor of Huddersfield* (1883) 12 Q.B.D. 443, 449; *In re Keen & Keen; Ex parte Collins* [1902] 1 K.B. 555.

Not all the cases are consistent. In *In re Weibking; Ex parte Ward* [1902] 1 K.B. 713 a provision that plant and materials brought onto the site should "be deemed to be annexed to the freehold" was held by Wright J. to pass legal title to the employer, but the case was said in *In re Fox; Ex parte Oundle and Thrapston Rural District Council v. The Trustee* [1948] Ch. 407 to turn on its own particular facts; while in *Hart v. Porthgain Harbour Co. Ltd.* [1903] 1 Ch. 690 Farwell J. seems to have [507] thought it immaterial which form of words was used. I cannot think that this is correct. Of course the contract must be construed as a whole, but given that it is susceptible of two possible meanings the actual words of the clause relied on to pass the title must be of great importance.

In the present case there are several indicia that the legal ownership of plant and materials brought onto the site does not pass to the council. Such plant and materials are described throughout as "plant and materials which have been deemed to become the property" of the council, a circumlocution which might well have been dispensed with if they had become the actual property of the council. The company is prohibited by clause 53(6) from removing plant or materials from the site without the consent of the engineer (a similar clause was said in *In re Keen & Keen; Ex parte Collins* [1902] 1 K.B. 555 to be unnecessary if the plant and materials belonged to the council). Finally, clause

53(9) exempts the council from liability for loss of or injury to plant or materials brought onto the site (a provision which was also said in *In re Keen & Keen; Ex parte Collins* to be inconsistent with the property having passed to the council).

I do not find this last consideration persuasive in view of the fact that the contract in the present case, unlike that in *In re Keen & Keen; Ex parte Collins* [1902] 1 K.B. 555, contains a revesting provision (clause 53(7)). For its part the council relies on the provisions of clause 53(6) by which the company is granted permission to use the plant to complete the work and clause 53(7) by which the plant and materials revest in the company on completion of the works or previous removal from the site. The council submits that neither provision would be necessary unless legal title had passed to the council under clause 53(2). In my judgment there is no substance in this point. The company would need permission to make use of the plant whether legal ownership had actually passed to the council or had only been deemed to pass to it; while clause 53(7) is carefully drawn to provide for a deemed revesting, and merely "undeems" that which is previously deemed.

If there were nothing more I would hold that clause 53(2) is merely a deeming provision which does not have the effect of passing legal title. But the last sentence of clause 53(2) puts the matter beyond argument. It applies the clause indiscriminately both to plant belonging to the company and to plant belonging to its controlled subsidiaries. These are not parties to the contract. In relation to plant which belongs to a subsidiary, the clause is effective in equity as a deeming provision, for the court could order specific performance of the contract by requiring the company to exercise its powers of control over the subsidiary and thus procure compliance with its own contractual obligations. But the clause cannot possibly operate at law to pass title to property owned by a company not a party to the contract.

Accordingly I agree with the judge that clause 53(2) of the contract does not pass legal ownership in the plant to the council.

(2) Does the council's right to retain possession of the plant and use it to complete the works constitute an equitable charge?

In my judgment the council's right to retain possession of the plant and use it to complete the works does not constitute an equitable charge [508] because (i) it does not give the council a proprietary interest in the plant but only rights of possession and use and (ii) it is not by way of security.

It is of the essence of a charge that a particular asset or class of assets is appropriated to the satisfaction of a debt or other obligation of the chargor or a third party, so that the chargee is entitled to look to the asset and its proceeds for the discharge of the liability. This right creates a transmissible interest in the asset. A mere right to retain possession of an asset and to make use of it for a particular purpose does not create such an interest and does not constitute a charge.

But there is an even more fundamental reason why this right of the council in the present case does not constitute a charge. This is that it does not constitute any kind of security interest, since it is not given to the council by way of security. It does not secure the performance of the contract by the company, but merely enables the council to perform the contract in its place. It does not, therefore, secure the discharge of any debt or other legal obligation of the company or of any third party, whether to complete the works or to pay damages for its failure to do so. Completion of the works by the council does not discharge either of these obligations.

This is sufficient to dispose of the administrator's claim in the action. . . .'

[See **[328]** for the analysis of the other issues.]

Question:

Does this analysis suggest that a possessory interest is not proprietary?

FURTHER READING:

N Palmer, 'Possessory Title' in N Palmer and E McKendrick (eds), *Interests in Goods* (2nd edn, 1998, Lloyd's of London Press: London) ch 3.

D R Harris, 'The Concept of Possession in English Law' in A G Guest (ed) *Oxford Essays in Jurisprudence* (1961, OUP: Oxford) p 69.

2.3.2 Finders' and occupiers' possessory interests

As noted in **[204]** above, the law of property has faced particular difficulties in assessing the legitimate rights of people who find things. However, the law now seems more settled than it was when that piece was written. It is now clear that a finder cannot assert possessory rights against the true owner of the property. Moreover, as between two parties, neither being the true owner but both claiming a possessory interest, the rule seems to be that the first to take legal possession can maintain it as against the other. The next two extracts illustrate these rules.

[211] ***Moffatt v Kazana*** **[1969] 2 QB 152, 156–7** ***per*** **Wrangham J:**
[R purchased a bungalow in 1950 and lived there with his wife until 1961, when he sold it to the defendant. In 1964, some bricks were dislodged from the kitchen chimney and a biscuit tin full of £1 notes fell down from above. R sued the defendant for the money and after R's death his executors carried on the proceedings. It was held that on the evidence the money had belonged to R. R's wife testified that she saw him put the biscuit tin into the roof in 1950. R's son-in-law testified that when R offered to lend him some money, he disappeared into the roof and re-appeared with £98 in £1 notes. R never lost the ownership of the notes and so his title to the money was unassailable.]

> 'It is clear therefore that in the existing authorities there is an implication at least from the language in which the judgments are expressed that the true owner of a chattel found on land has a title superior to that of anybody else. Accordingly, having disposed of the authorities in that way, Mr. Appleby on behalf of the plaintiffs was able to say that the plaintiffs are, as representatives of Mr. Russell, the true owners of this money and they must be held to remain the true owners of the money unless they or Mr. Russell had divested himself or themselves of the ownership by one of the recognised methods, abandonment, gift or sale. Abandonment is not suggested. One does not abandon property merely because one has forgotten where one put it. Gift is not suggested.

There remains only sale. That sale can only be the conveyance of No. 19 Northcliffe Avenue and Mr. Heald was obliged at the outset of his argument boldly to face the difficulty that section 62 of the Law of Property Act, 1925, provides in effect that a conveyance of land does not include a conveyance of chattels. In this conveyance there is no reference to chattels, so it would appear on the face of it that that section wholly excludes any possible argument based upon the conveyance.

Having mentioned that difficulty, Mr. Heald looked it in the face and passed on; and he passed on in this way. He said that the law must be held to imply a conveyance of lost property in circumstances of this kind, because if it did not a complete impasse might easily be reached. The nature of the impasse could be shown by imagining that the parties in this case had taken a rather different course to that which they did take. Suppose that the defendant had himself discovered the tin box in the flue and suppose that he had said to the plaintiffs, "I do not claim this tin box at all, it is not mine; I dare say it is yours, but in no circumstances am I going to allow you upon my land. Still less am I going to allow you to burrow about in the false flue of the bungalow, possibly damaging the flue, and in those circumstances the tin box remains where it is."

Mr. Heald said that would be an absurdity, because the result would be that there was property admittedly belonging to the plaintiffs which could not be reached by the plaintiffs, because the plaintiffs could have no right to trespass on the defendant's land and the defendant could be under no duty to bother himself to move the biscuit tin to the edge of his land. Why should he do anything? Still less could he be expected to incur the risk of perhaps some damage to the flue if by any chance the biscuit tin had become in some way attached to the flue by the effluxion of time.

I am bound to say that Mr. Heald's argument did seem to me to raise difficulties which Mr. Appleby was never able wholly satisfactorily to answer to me. I am reduced in the circumstances to saying this. Whatever the answer to Mr. Heald's difficulties may be, that answer will have to be sought in some case in which the difficulties themselves actually arise.

I am content to ground my judgment on this, that the conveyance itself, in view of the language of section 62, cannot be said to have transferred the ownership of these £1 notes from Mr. Russell to the defendant and that there is no other way in which it is even suggested that the ownership of these notes could have been transferred from Mr. Russell to the defendant. If Mr. Russell never got rid of the notes, that is to say, never got rid of the ownership of the notes, he continued to be the owner of them and, if he continued to be the owner of them, he had a title to those notes which nobody else, whether the owner of the land in which they were found, or the finders, or anybody else would have.

In those circumstances, it seems to me that this biscuit tin and the contents of the biscuit tin remain the property of the plaintiffs and the defendant had no right to put into his bank account the £1,987 which he admittedly received from the police as part or whole of the contents of the biscuit tin and that he had no right to refuse re-delivery of those notes, as he did, to the plaintiffs. He did not refuse re-delivery on the ground that they were there available for the plaintiffs, but the plaintiffs were not allowed to go and find them, so that the impasse suggested never arose. On the contrary, those notes were put by those acting for him into his own bank account.

It follows that, in my judgment, the plaintiffs succeed and should have judgment for £1,987. . . .'

Question:

How should the 'impasse' noted by Wrangham J be resolved?

[212] ***Parker v British Airways Board*** **[1982] QB 1004, 1008–19** ***per*** **Donaldson LJ:** [A passenger found a gold bracelet on the floor of the defendant airline's international executive lounge. He handed it to one of the defendant's employees and requested that if the owner did not claim the bracelet it should be returned to him. No one claimed it. The defendant sold it for £850 and retained the proceeds. The claimant successfully sued in conversion (see Section 7.2.3 below) for £850 as damages and £50 as interest. The dispute turned on which party had the better right to possession.]

> '[1008] It is astonishing that there should be any doubt as to who is right. But there is. Indeed, it seems that the academics have been debating this problem for years. In 1971 the Law Reform Committee reported that it was by no means clear who had the better claim to lost property when the protagonists were the finder and the occupier of the premises where the property was found. . . . The committee recommended legislative action but, as is not uncommon, nothing has been done. The rights of the parties thus depend upon the common law.
>
> As a matter of legal theory, the common law has a ready made solution for every problem and it is only for the judges, as legal technicians, to find it. The reality is somewhat different. Take the present case. The conflicting rights of finder and occupier have indeed been considered by various courts in the past. But under the rules of English jurisprudence, none of their decisions binds this court. We therefore have both the right and the duty to extend and adapt the common law in the light of established principles and the current needs of the community. This is not to say that we start with a clean sheet. In doing so, we should draw from the experience of the past as revealed by the previous decisions of the courts. . . .
>
> Neither the plaintiff nor the defendants lay any claim to the bracelet either as owner of it or as one who derives title from that owner. The plaintiff's claim is founded upon the ancient common law rule that the act of finding a chattel which has been lost and taking control of it gives the finder rights with respect to that chattel. The defendants' claim has a different basis. They cannot and do not claim to have found the bracelet when it was handed to them by the plaintiff. At that stage it was no longer lost and they received and accepted the bracelet from the plaintiff on terms that it would be returned to him if the owner could not be found. They must and do claim on the basis that they had rights in relation to the bracelet immediately before the plaintiff found it and that these rights are superior to the plaintiff's. The defendants' claim is based upon the proposition that at common law an occupier of land has such rights over all lost chattels which are on that land, whether or not the occupier knows of their existence.
>
> The common law right asserted by the plaintiff has been recognised for centuries. In its simplest form it was asserted by the chimney sweep's boy who, in 1722, found a jewel and offered it to a jeweller for sale. The [1009] jeweller refused either to pay a price acceptable to the boy or to return it and the boy sued the jeweller for its value: *Armory v. Delamirie* (1722) 1 Stra. 505. Pratt C.J. ruled:

> "That the finder of a jewel, though he does not by such finding acquire an absolute property or ownership, yet he has such a property as will enable him to keep it against all but the rightful owner, and consequently may maintain trover."

In the case the jeweller clearly had no rights in relation to the jewel immediately before the boy found it and any rights which he acquired when he received it from the boy stemmed from the boy himself. The jeweller could only have succeeded if the fact of finding and taking control of the jewel conferred no rights upon the boy. The court would then have been faced with two claimants, neither of which had any legal right, but one had de facto possession. The rule as stated by Pratt C.J. must be right as a general proposition, for otherwise lost property would be subject to a free-for-all in which the physically weakest would go to the wall.

Pratt C.J.'s ruling is, however, only a general proposition which requires definition. Thus one who "finds" a lost chattel in the sense of becoming aware of its presence, but who does no more, is not a "finder" for this purpose and does not, as such, acquire any rights.

Some qualification has also to be made in the case of the trespassing finder. The person vis à vis whom he is a trespasser has a better title. The fundamental basis of this is clearly public policy. Wrongdoers should not benefit from their wrongdoing. This requirement would be met if the trespassing finder acquired no rights. That would, however, produce the free-for-all situation to which I have already referred, in that anyone could take the article from the trespassing finder. Accordingly, the common law has been obliged to give rights to someone else, the owner ex hypothesi being unknown. The obvious candidate is the occupier of the property upon which the finder was trespassing.

Curiously enough, it is difficult to find any case in which the rule is stated in this simple form, but I have no doubt that this is the law. It is reflected in the judgment of Chitty J. in *Elwes v. Brigg Gas Co.* (1886) 33 Ch.D. 562, 568, although the chattel concerned was beneath the surface of the soil and so subject to different considerations. It is also reflected in the judgment of Lord Goddard C.J. in *Hibbert v. McKiernan* [1948] 2 K.B. 142, 149. That was a criminal case concerning the theft of "lost" golf balls on the private land of a club. The only issue was whether for the purposes of the criminal law property in the golf balls could be laid in someone other than the alleged thief. The indictment named the members of the club, who were occupiers of the land, as having property in the balls, and it is clear that at the time when the balls were taken the members were very clearly asserting such a right, even to the extent of mounting a police patrol to warn off trespassers seeking to harvest lost balls.

. . .

One might have expected there to be decisions clearly qualifying the general rule where the circumstances are that someone finds a chattel and thereupon forms the dishonest intention of keeping it regardless of the rights of the true owner or of anyone else. But that is not the case. There could be a number of reasons. Dishonest finders will often be trespassers. They are unlikely to risk invoking the law, particularly against another subsequent dishonest taker, and a subsequent honest taker is likely to have a superior title: see, for example, *Buckley v. Gross* (1863) 3 B. & S. 566. However, he probably has some title, albeit a frail one because of the need to avoid a free-for-all. This seems to be the law in Ontario, Canada: *Bird v. Fort Frances* [1949] 2 D.L.R. 791.

In the interests of clearing the ground and identifying the problem, let me now turn to another situation in respect of which the law is reasonably clear. This is that of chattels which are attached to realty (land or buildings) when they are found. If the finder is not a wrongdoer, he may have some rights, but the occupier of the land or building will have a better title. The rationale of this rule is probably either that the chattel is to be treated as an integral part of the realty as against all but the true owner and so incapable of being lost or that the "finder" has to do something to the realty in order to get at or detach the chattel and, if he is not thereby to become a trespasser, will have to justify his actions by reference to some form of licence from the occupier. In all likely circumstances that licence will give the occupier a superior right to that of the finder.

Authority for this view of the law is to be found in *South Staffordshire Water Co. v. Sharman* [1896] 2 Q.B. 44 where the defendant was employed by the occupier of land to remove mud from the bottom of a pond. He found two gold rings embedded in the mud. The plaintiff occupier was held to be entitled to the rings. Dicta of Lord Russell of Killowen C.J., with whom Wills J. agreed, not only support the law as I have stated it, but go further and may support the defendants' contention that an occupier of a building has a claim to articles found in that building as opposed to being found attached to or forming part of it. However, it is more convenient to consider these dicta hereafter. . . .

. . .

I must now return to the respective claims of the plaintiff and the defendants. Mr. Brown, for the plaintiff, relies heavily upon the decision of Patteson J. and Wightman J., sitting in banc in *Bridges v. Hawkesworth* (1851) 21 L.J.Q.B. 75; 15 Jur. 1079. It was an appeal from the county court by case stated. The relevant facts, as found, were as follows. Mr. Bridges was a commercial traveller and in the course of his business he called upon the defendant at his shop. As he was leaving the shop, he picked up a small parcel which was lying on the floor, showed it to the shopman and, upon opening it in his presence, found that it contained £65 in notes. Mr. Hawkesworth was called and Mr. Bridges asked him to keep the notes until the owner claimed them. Mr. Hawkesworth advertised for the true owner, but no claimant came forward. Three years later Mr. Bridges asked for the money and offered to indemnify Mr. Hawkesworth in respect of the expenses which he had incurred in advertising for the owner. Mr. Hawkesworth refused to pay over the money and Mr. Bridges sued for it. The county court judge dismissed his claim and he appealed.

Patteson J. gave the judgment of the court. The decision is sufficiently important, and the judgment sufficiently short and difficult to find, for me to feel justified in reproducing it in full. In so doing, I take the text of the report in the *Jurist*, 15 Jur. 1079, 1082 but refer to the *Law Journal* version, 21 L.J. Q.B. 75, 77–78, in square brackets where they differ. It reads:

> "The notes which are the subject of this action were incidentally ['evidently'] dropped, by mere accident, in the shop of the defendant, by the owner of them. The facts do not warrant the supposition that they had been deposited there intentionally, nor has the case been put at all upon that ground. The plaintiff found them on the floor, they being manifestly lost by some one. The general right of the finder to any article which has been lost, as against all the world, except the true owner, was established in . . . *Armory v. Delamirie*, 1 Stra. 505, which has never been disputed. This right would clearly have accrued to the plaintiff had the notes been picked up by him outside the shop of the defendant; and if he once had the right, the case finds that he did not intend, by delivering the notes to the defendant, to waive the title (if any) which he had to them, but they [1012] were handed to the

defendant merely for the purpose of delivering them to the owner, should he appear. Nothing that was done afterwards has altered the state of things; the advertisements inserted ['indeed'] in the newspaper, referring to the defendant, had the same object; the plaintiff has tendered the expense of those advertisements to the defendant, and offered him an indemnity against any claim to be made by the real owner, and has demanded the notes. The case, therefore, resolves itself into the single point on which it appears that the learned judge decided it, namely, whether the circumstance of the notes being found inside [word emphasised in *Law Journal*] the defendant's shop gives him, the defendant, the right to have them as against the plaintiff, who found them. There is no authority in our law to be found directly in point. Perhaps the nearest case is that of *Merry v. Green* (1841) 7 M. & W. 623, but it differs in many respects from the present. We were referred, in the course of the argument, to the learned work of *Von Savigny*, edited by Perry C.J.; but even this work, full as it is of subtle distinctions and nice reasonings, does not afford a solution of the present question. It was well asked, on the argument, if the defendant has the right, when did it accrue to him? If at all, it must have been antecedent to the finding by the plaintiff, for that finding could not give the defendant any right. If the notes had been accidentally kicked into the shop ['the street' in *Law Journal*, which must be right], and there found by someone passing by, could it be contended that the defendant was entitled to them from the mere fact of their being originally dropped in his shop? If the discovery had never ['not'] been communicated to the defendant, could the real owner have had any cause of action against him because they were found in his house? Certainly not. The notes never were in the custody of the defendant, nor within the protection of his house, before they were found, as they would have been had they been intentionally deposited there; and the defendant has come under no responsibility, except from the communication made to him by the plaintiff, the finder, and the steps taken by way of advertisement. These steps were really taken by the defendant as the agent of the plaintiff, and he has been offered an indemnity, the sufficiency of which is not disputed. We find, therefore, no circumstances in this case to take it out of the general rule of law, that the finder of a lost article is entitled to it as against all persons except the real owner, and we think that that rule must prevail, and that the learned judge was mistaken in holding that the place in which they were found makes any legal difference. Our judgment, therefore, is, that the plaintiff is entitled to these notes as against the defendant; that the judgment of the court below must be reversed, and judgment given for the plaintiff for £50."

The ratio of this decision seems to me to be solely that the unknown presence of the notes on the premises occupied by Mr. Hawkesworth could not without more, give him any rights or impose any duty upon him in relation to the notes.

Mr. Desch, for the defendants, submits that *Bridges v. Hawkesworth*, [1013] 15 Jur. 1079, can be distinguished and he referred us to the judgment of Lord Russell of Killowen C.J., with which Wills J. agreed, in *South Staffordshire Water Co. v. Sharman* [1896] 2 Q.B. 44. *Sharman's* case itself is readily distinguishable, either upon the ground that the rings were in the mud and thus part of the realty or upon the ground that the finders were employed by the plaintiff to remove the mud and had a clear right to direct how the mud and anything in it should be disposed of, or upon both grounds. However, Lord Russell of Killowen C.J. in distinguishing *Bridges v. Hawkesworth* expressed views which, in Mr. Desch's submission, point to the defendants having a superior claim to that of the plaintiff on the facts of the instant case. Lord Russell of Killowen C.J. said, at pp. 46–47:

"The principle on which this case must be decided, and the distinction which must be drawn between this case and that of *Bridges v. Hawkesworth*, is to be found in a passage in Pollock and Wright, . . . *Possession in the Common Law*, p. 41: 'The possession of land carries with it in general, by our law, possession of everything which is attached to or under that land, and, in the absence of a better title elsewhere, the right to possess it also. And it makes no difference that the possessor is not aware of the thing's existence. . . . It is free to anyone who requires a specific intention as part of a de facto possession to treat this as a positive rule of law. But it seems preferable to say that the legal possession rests on a real de facto possession, constituted by the occupier's general power and intent to exclude unauthorised interference.' That is the ground on which I prefer to base my judgment. . . . It is somewhat strange that there is no more direct authority on the question; but the general principle seems to me to be that where a person has possession of house or land, with a manifest intention to exercise control over it and the things which may be upon or in it, then, if something is found on that land, whether by an employee of the owner or by a stranger, the presumption is that the possession of that thing is in the owner of the *locus in quo*."

[1014] For my part, I can find no trace in the report of *Bridges v. Hawkesworth*, 21 L.J.Q.B. 75, of any reliance by Patteson J. upon the fact that the notes were found in what may be described as the public part of the shop. . . .

However, I would accept Lord Russell of Killowen C.J.'s statement of the general principle in *South Staffordshire Water Co. v. Sharman* [1896] 2 Q.B. 44, 46–47, provided that the occupier's intention to exercise control over anything which might be on the premises was manifest. But it is impossible to go further and to hold that the mere right of an occupier to exercise such control is sufficient to give him rights in relation to lost property on his premises without overruling *Bridges v. Hawkesworth*, 21 L.J.Q.B. 75. Mr. Hawkesworth undoubtedly had a right to exercise such control, but his defence failed.

South Staffordshire Water Co. v. Sharman was followed and applied by McNair J. in *City of London Corporation v. Appleyard* [1963] 1 W.L.R. 982. There workmen demolishing a building found money in a safe which was recessed in one of the walls. The lease from the corporation to the building owners preserved the corporation's right to any article of value found upon any remains of former buildings and the workmen were employed by contractors working for the building owners. McNair J. upheld the corporation's claim. The workmen claimed as finders, but it is clear law that a servant or agent who finds in the course of his employment or agency is obliged to account to his employer or principal. The contractor similarly was bound to account to the building owner and the building owner, who was the occupier, was contractually bound to account to the corporation. The principal interest of the decision lies in the comment of McNair J., at p. 987, that he did not understand Lord Russell of Killowen C.J. as intending to qualify or extend the principle stated in Pollock and Wright, *Possession in the Common Law* (1888), p. 41, that possession of land carries with it possession of everything which is attached to or under that land when the Chief Justice restated the principle [1896] 2 Q.B. 44, 47:

". . . where a person has possession of house or land, *with a manifest intention to exercise control over it and the things which may be upon or in it*, then, if something is found on that land, whether by an employee of the owner or by a stranger, the presumption is that the possession of that thing is in the owner of the locus in quo." (My emphasis).

. . . .

[1017] One of the great merits of the common law is that it is usually sufficiently flexible to take account of the changing needs of a continually changing society. Accordingly, Mr. Desch rightly directed our attention to the need to have common law rules which will facilitate rather than hinder the ascertainment of the true owner of a lost chattel and a reunion between the two. In his submission the law should confer rights upon the occupier of the land where a lost chattel was found which were superior to those of the finder, since the loser is more likely to make inquiries at the place of loss. I see the force of this submission. However, I think that it is also true that if this were the rule and finders had no prospect of any reward, they would be tempted to pass by without taking any action or to become concealed keepers of articles which they found. Furthermore, if a finder is under a duty to take reasonable steps to reunite the true owner with his lost property, this will usually involve an obligation to inform the occupier of the land of the fact that the article has been found and where it is to be kept.

In a dispute of this nature there are two quite separate problems. The first is to determine the general principles or rules of law which are applicable. The second, which is often the more troublesome, is to apply those principles or rules to the factual situation. I propose to confront those two problems separately.

Rights and obligations of the finder

1. The finder of a chattel acquires no rights over it unless (a) it has been abandoned or lost and (b) he takes it into his care and control.

2. The finder of a chattel acquires very limited rights over it if he takes it into his care and control with dishonest intent or in the course of trespassing.

3. Subject to the foregoing and to point 4 below, a finder of a chattel, whilst not acquiring any absolute property or ownership in the chattel, acquires a right to keep it against all but the true owner or those in a position to claim through the true owner or one who can assert a prior right to keep the chattel which was subsisting at the time when the finder took the chattel into his care and control.

4. Unless otherwise agreed, any servant or agent who finds a chattel in the course of his employment or agency and not wholly incidentally or collaterally thereto and who takes it into his care and control does so on behalf of his employer or principal who acquires a finder's rights to the exclusion of those of the actual finder.

5. A person having a finder's rights has an obligation to take such measures as in all the circumstances are reasonable to acquaint the true owner of the finding and present whereabouts of the chattel and to care for it meanwhile

Rights and liabilities of an occupier

1. An occupier of land has rights superior to those of a finder over chattels in or attached to that land and an occupier of a building has [1018] similar rights in respect of chattels attached to that building, whether in either case the occupier is aware of the presence of the chattel.

2. An occupier of a building has rights superior to those of a finder over chattels upon or in, but not attached to, that building if, but only if, before the chattel is found, he has manifested an intention to exercise control over the building and the things which may be upon it or in it.

3. An occupier who manifests an intention to exercise control over a building and the things which may be upon or in it so as to acquire rights superior to those of a finder is under an obligation to take such measures as in all the circumstances are reasonable to ensure that lost chattels are found and, upon their being found, whether by him or by a third party, to acquaint the true owner of the finding and to care for the chattels meanwhile. The manifestation of intention may be express or implied from the circumstances including, in particular, the circumstance that the occupier manifestly accepts or is obliged by law to accept liability for chattels lost upon his "premises," e.g. an innkeeper or carrier's liability.

4. An "occupier" of a chattel, e.g. a ship, motor car, caravan or aircraft, is to be treated as if he were the occupier of a building for the purposes of the foregoing rules.

Application to the instant case

The plaintiff was not a trespasser in the executive lounge and, in taking the bracelet into his care and control, he was acting with obvious honesty. Prima facie, therefore, he had a full finder's rights and obligations. He in fact discharged those obligations by handing the bracelet to an official of the defendants' although he could equally have done so by handing the bracelet to the police or in other ways such as informing the police of the find and himself caring for the bracelet.

The plaintiff's prima facie entitlement to a finder's rights was not displaced in favour of an employer or principal. There is no evidence that he was in the executive lounge in the course of any employment or agency and, if he was, the finding of the bracelet was quite clearly collateral thereto. The position would have been otherwise in the case of most or perhaps all the defendants' employees.

The defendants, for their part, cannot assert any title to the bracelet based upon the rights of an occupier over chattels attached to a building. The bracelet was lying loose on the floor. Their claim must, on my view of the law, be based upon a manifest intention to exercise control over the lounge and all things which might be in it. The evidence is that they claimed the right to decide who should and who should not be permitted to enter and use the lounge, but their control was in general exercised upon the basis of classes or categories of user and the availability of the lounge in the light of the need to clean and maintain it. I do not doubt that they also claimed the right to exclude individual undesirables, such as drunks, and specific types of chattels such as guns and bombs. But this control has no real relevance to a manifest intention to assert custody and control over lost articles. There was no evidence that they searched for such articles regularly or at all.

[1019] Evidence was given of staff instructions which govern the action to be taken by employees of the defendants if they found lost articles or lost chattels were handed to them. But these instructions were not published to users of the lounge and in any event I think that they were intended to do no more than instruct the staff on how they were to act in the course of their employment.

It was suggested in argument that in some circumstances the intention of the occupier to assert control over articles lost on his premises speaks for itself. I think that this is right. If a bank manager saw fit to show me round a vault containing safe deposits and I found a gold bracelet on the floor, I should have no doubt that the bank had a better title than I, and the reason is the manifest intention to exercise a very high degree of control. At the other extreme is the park to which the public has unrestricted access during daylight hours. During those hours there is no manifest intention to exercise any such control. In between these extremes are the forecourts of petrol filling stations, unfenced front gardens of private houses, the public parts of shops and supermarkets as part of an almost infinite variety of land, premises and circumstances.

This lounge is in the middle band and in my judgment, on the evidence available, there was no sufficient manifestation of any intention to exercise control over lost property before it was found such as would give the defendants a right superior to that of the plaintiff or indeed any right over the bracelet. As the true owner has never come forward, it is a case of "finders keepers." . . .'

Also see:

Waverley Borough Council v Fletcher [1996] QB 334 (CA).

Questions:

How can the rules on finders be summarised? Does a finder ever become the legal *owner* of property?

2.3.3 Treasure trove

The common law doctrine of treasure trove gives the Crown title to any gold or silver which is found, provided that the true owner is unknown and it could be shown that the property had been deliberately concealed in a private place with the intention that it be recovered later. By its own terms, the doctrine is quite narrow. The next extract outlines the history and changing purposes of the doctrine of treasure trove.

[213] *Webb v Ireland* [1988] IR 353 (Irish SCt), 381–2 *per* Finlay CJ:
[The facts are immaterial.]

'Treasure trove as we know it, is a creature of the common law. It is part of the more general right of *bona vacantia* which in the common law of England belonged to the Crown. The general purpose of the vesting of the property in *bona vacantia* in the Crown is usually stated to have been to prevent the strife and contention to which title by occupancy might otherwise give rise in relation to goods, land or rights to which no one can make a lawful claim.

With regard to the prerogative of treasure trove, however, it would seem clear that, historically, it also had the major purpose of being a source of revenue for the Royal Mint.

It applied only to valuable chattels which it could be established were concealed for the purpose of protecting them and with the intention of subsequently recovering them on the part of the person who hid them and which were made of the precious metals of silver or gold, a combination of them or an alloy containing a substantial ingredient of either or both of them. The right of the Crown to the possession and ownership of such treasure trove was subject always to the obligation to restore it or its value to the "true owner" if he could be found.

It would appear obvious that the confining according to the common law of the right of treasure trove to gold and silver objects or objects substantially made of either or both of those metals was directly associated with the purpose of enriching the Royal Mint, and it is stated in most of the textbooks concerning this topic that in early days treasure trove when recovered by the Crown was frequently melted down into coin.

It would appear that since the accession of George III the right to treasure trove vested in the Crown has been part of the surrendered revenue of the Crown, surrendered by each succeeding monarch to the Treasury for his lifetime in return for the provision of the Civil List.

It would appear that from the earliest times the right to treasure trove was enforced on the one hand by penalties imposed on the finders of such treasure trove who failed to reveal to the appropriate authorities the find and failed to yield them to the Crown, and on the other hand by the giving of rewards to those who did reveal their finds and yielded them to the Crown.

By the nineteenth century it is quite clear that the prerogative of treasure trove in England and in Ireland continued to be exercised on behalf of the Crown by the Government of Great Britain and Ireland but for a purpose wholly different from that which had been its historical origin. Its purpose now clearly was the retention by the State, for the common good, of antiquarian objects of interest and value, which formed part of the heritage of the People.

Thus, during this period it would appear, for example, that internal arrangements were made by the Treasury of the British Government, dealing with the scale and measure of rewards for the finding of treasure trove which were quite inconsistent with the possibility of the acquisition by the State of the objects of treasure trove for the purpose of profit. Furthermore, the right or franchise of treasure trove in Ireland was apparently *de facto* exercised on behalf of the State by the Royal Irish Academy who received a grant from the Treasury for the purpose of providing rewards and who do not appear to have had any obligation to account in any way to the State for the value of what they might have acquired under this right.

In general terms, it would appear that at common law the payment of a reward to the finder of treasure trove was an act of grace and the finding and giving up of treasure trove to the State or its agent was not considered to confer on the finder any right enforceable at law to the payment of any particular reward or of a reward at all.

. . .

It would, I think, now be universally accepted, certainly by the People of Ireland, and by the people of most modern states, that one of the most important national assets belonging to the people is their heritage and knowledge of its true origins and the buildings and objects which constitute keys to their ancient history. If this be so, then it would appear to me to follow that a necessary ingredient of sovereignty in a modern state and certainly in this State, having regard to the terms of the Constitution, with an emphasis on its historical origins and a constant concern for the common good is and should be an ownership by the State of objects which constitute antiquities of importance which are discovered and which have no known owner. It would appear to me to be inconsistent with the framework of the society sought to be created and sought to be protected by the Constitution that such objects should become the exclusive property of those who by chance may find them.

The existence of such a general ingredient of the sovereignty of the State, does, however, seem to me to lead to the conclusion that the much more limited right of the prerogative of treasure trove known to the common law should be upheld not as a right derived from the Crown but rather as an inherent attribute of the sovereignty of the State which was recognised and declared by article 11 of the 1922 Constitution.'

The difficulty with the common law doctrine of treasure trove is that it excludes any antiquities not made of gold or silver, with the result that many collections of archaeological significance end up being divided—anything made of gold or silver goes to the Crown; everything else is subject to the usual rules relating to finders. Moreover, even if the article is made of gold or silver, it will not be classed as 'treasure trove' unless the true owner hid it with the intention of later retrieving it. This can be difficult to prove.

FURTHER READING:

N Palmer, 'Treasure Trove and Title to Discovered Antiquities' in N Palmer and E McKendrick (eds), *Interests in Goods* (1st edn, 1993, Lloyd's of London Press: London) ch 12, especially pp 307–12.

Not surprisingly, the common law doctrine of treasure trove has now been replaced by a new regime under the Treasure Act 1996. This Act provides that any treasure now found,[23] wherever and in whatever circumstances, vests, subject to prior interests and rights, in the franchisee, if there is one, or otherwise in the Crown.[24] 'Treasure' includes objects which, before the commencement of the Act, would have constituted treasure trove, but also extends to include a much wider range of objects, and the Secretary of State has the power to order still further widening of the definition (see **[214]** below).[25] A person must notify the coroner within 14 days if he finds an object which he has reasonable grounds for believing is treasure.[26] The coroner retains jurisdiction to hold inquests into treasure,[27] but it seems he has no power to make legal determinations as to title between the finder, the occupier and the landowner; such issues must be determined by the courts.[28] The Secretary of State has the power to transfer, dispose of, or disclaim title to treasure.[29] If treasure is transferred to a museum, the Secretary of State has the power to determine whether the museum should pay a reward, and to whom, and in what amount.[30]

[214] Treasure Act 1996, ss 1–3:

'**1.**—(1) Treasure is—

(a) any object at least 300 years old when found which—

(i) is not a coin but has metallic content of which at least 10 per cent by weight is precious metal;

[23] On or after 24 September 1997.
[24] Treasure Act 1996 s 4.
[25] *Ibid* ss 1–3.
[26] *Ibid* s 8.
[27] *Ibid* s 7.
[28] *AG v Moore* [1893] 1 Ch 676.
[29] Treasure Act 1996 s 6.
[30] *Ibid* s 10, but note s 10(6), which provides that payment of the reward is not enforceable against either the museum or the Secretary of State.

(ii) when found, is one of at least two coins in the same find which are at least 300 years old at that time and have that percentage of precious metal; or

(iii) when found, is one of at least ten coins in the same find which are at least 300 years old at that time;

(b) any object at least 200 years old when found which belongs to a class designated under section 2(1);

(c) any object which would have been treasure trove if found before the commencement of section 4;

(d) any object which, when found, is part of the same find as—

(i) an object within paragraph (a), (b) or (c) found at the same time or earlier; or

(ii) an object found earlier which would be within paragraph (a) or (b) if it had been found at the same time.

(2) Treasure does not include objects which are—

(a) unworked natural objects, or

(b) minerals as extracted from a natural deposit,

or which belong to a class designated under section 2(2).

2.—(1) The Secretary of State may by order, for the purposes of section 1(1)(b), designate any class of object which he considers to be of outstanding historical, archaeological or cultural importance.

(2) The Secretary of State may by order, for the purposes of section 1(2), designate any class of object which (apart from the order) would be treasure.

(3) An order under this section shall be made by statutory instrument.

(4) No order is to be made under this section unless a draft of the order has been laid before Parliament and approved by a resolution of each House.

3.—(1) This section supplements section 1.

(2) "Coin" includes any metal token which was, or can reasonably be assumed to have been, used or intended for use as or instead of money.

(3) "Precious metal" means gold or silver.

(4) When an object is found, it is part of the same find as another object if—

(a) they are found together,

(b) the other object was found earlier in the same place where they had been left together,

(c) the other object was found earlier in a different place, but they had been left together and had become separated before being found.

(5) If the circumstances in which objects are found can reasonably be taken to indicate that they were together at some time before being found, the objects are to be presumed to have been left together, unless shown not to have been.

(6) An object which can reasonably be taken to be at least a particular age is to be presumed to be at least that age, unless shown not to be.

(7) An object is not treasure if it is wreck within the meaning of Part IX of the Merchant Shipping Act 1995.'

2.3.4 Are possessory interests proprietary in nature?

At first sight this is a strange question. Certainly the assumption so far has been that interests in possession are proprietary interests. Recall from Chapter 1 that if a right is proprietary it will bind third parties: its effect will extend beyond the grantor and grantee of the right, although it may not necessarily affect the whole world. For example, if P purchases property from O, then P can assert rights of ownership against the world, not simply against O. Often this is the real value of proprietary rights, and the reason for their extensive study.

It has been suggested that, in this respect, interests in possession are not the same as ownership interests. In particular, if H hires property from O, rather than purchasing it, then H's interests are not proprietary.[31] This must be doubted, although the question is of enormous significance and warrants some attention here. If the suggestion is correct, then H's rights as hirer of the property lie in contract only, and not in property.[32] If those rights are interfered with, H's remedies lie against O in contract. Any claims against third parties are limited to claims in tort for knowing interference with H's contractual rights, not for any proprietary torts. This would severely restrict the value of something we have so far called an interest (meaning a *proprietary* interest) in possession.

Take the simplest case, where the contracts of sale and hire used as illustrations in the preceding paragraphs are entered into properly and effectively by the true owner of the property. Possession is not the same as ownership, so H's possessory interest as a hirer is fundamentally different from P's ownership interest as a purchaser. But the difference does not appear to go to the proprietary nature of their respective interests. The hirer can assert possessory rights against all the world. The hirer's answer to a competing claim to possession of the property is that the hirer has *title* to the possessory interest[33] derived from the true owner. This is the best claim to possession—*even as against the true owner.*[34] As the extracts earlier in this section (especially Section 2.3.1) illustrate, claims by H to any rights associated with having a possessory interest do not depend upon H being in physical possession of the asset. The law is interested in the location of the possessory interest, not the physical siting of the property. These earlier extracts would all suggest that interests in possession are proprietary.

The difficulty seems to arise not with the assertion of interests in possession against all the world, but with their assertion against one particular party in very specific circumstances. Imagine the following scenario. O hires property to H. O then sells the same property to P before the period of hire is over. Can H assert his possessory interest, as hirer, against P, the new owner? One point should be noted

[31] W Swadling, 'The Proprietary Effect of a Hire of Goods' in N Palmer and E McKendrick (eds), *Interests in Goods* (2nd edn, 1998, Lloyd's of London Press: London) ch 20.

[32] On the other hand, if H's rights were proprietary, H would be able to take advantage of *both* the contractual and property aspects of the relationship with O.

[33] See Section 2.4 below.

[34] Of course, the possessory interest is defined by its terms. If O hires property to H under a hire which is expressly or impliedly determinable at will, then H's claim to possession against O will fail, but this is because H's possessory interest is thereby determined, not because, while it existed, it was not proprietary.

at the outset. Even if H cannot assert his possessory interest in these circumstances, that would not be sufficient to deny proprietary status to possessory interests. Ownership interests, too, even legal ones, are not invariably good against all the world.[35]

But what is the answer to the problem? If H's interest is *not* proprietary, then H will have no proprietary claims against P, nor any contractual claims (there being no privity or consideration between the two parties). He may have a claim against P in respect of the tort of knowing interference with H's contractual rights, but that requires proof of special facts. Otherwise H's claims will all be in contract against O. On the other hand, if H's interest *is* proprietary, the dispute between H and P will have to be resolved according to the rules on title conflicts (see Section 6.2 below). H will not necessarily win, although the general rule is *nemo dat quod non habet*: no one can give what he does not have. In particular, no one can give a better title than he has to give. This should mean that O cannot give (or sell) to P a title to an interest in property which conflicts with the possessory interest already given to H. H's interest should prevail against P's. P may have a possessory interest—P may even have physical possession—but P will not have the best *title* to possession. But this rule concerning priorities in title conflicts is a rule of law. It admits of exceptions. Those exceptions are based on policy considerations relevant to the dispute in hand (see Section 6.2). The rule and its exceptions do not deny the proprietary nature of the underlying rights being disputed, but are concerned to administer justice between competing claimants.[36]

There are difficult questions in this area, but the one just posed ought not to be one of them. Two further and more difficult questions stand out. First, if O contracts to hire specific property to H in the future, and then, before the time for hire arrives, O sells the property to P, can H assert any proprietary claims against P? The answer seems to be no. In reaching that conclusion it is necessary to consider the effect, in equity, of the contract of hire being specifically enforceable.[37] That aspect had no relevance to the simpler problem posed earlier.[38] Secondly, if O contracts with X to *use* property in a particular manner (or to allow X to use the property in a particular way), but without giving X any proprietary interest in the property in question, and O then sells the property to P, is P equally bound by the restriction in favour of X? For example, O may contract with X, promising that he will exercise the voting rights attached to shares in a particular manner; or that he will not grant security (or other proprietary) interests in certain property to third parties. These promises do not give X any proprietary interests in the shares or the

[35] See Chapter 6.

[36] Also see R Goode, *Hire Purchase Law and Practice* (2nd edn, 1970, Butterworths: London), pp. 34–6.

[37] Although it does not alter the answer: an enforceable promise to deliver ownership can give rise equitable *ownership*, but an enforceable promise to deliver possession has no equitable counterpart of equitable *possession*: see Sections 4.10–4.12 below.

[38] The answer would seem to be as follows. Even if the contract of hire were specifically enforceable, it would not give H an equitable proprietary interest in advance of the legal possessory interest. This is because there is no such thing as an equitable possessory interest, and the contract does not promise H an ownership interest. At most, H has a mere equity. Provided P takes the property as a *bona fide* purchaser for value without notice of H's interest, P will therefore take free of H's interest. This argument is really only intelligible after digesting the material in Chapter 4 and Section 6.2.

nominated property. Nevertheless, are there circumstances in which X could enforce the promised restriction against P, a purchaser of the property in question? If the answer is yes, then the basis seems to require resort to the uncertain principles derived from *De Mattos v Gibson*[39] and succeeding cases.

All of this is difficult, but it does indicate the scope of the debates associated with proprietary interests.

Question:

Even if H, the hirer of property, has a proprietary interest in the hired property, does it afford him any protection on the owner's insolvency?

FURTHER READING:

Bristol Airport plc v Powdrill [1990] Ch 744, 759 (**[303]** below).

W Swadling, 'The Proprietary Effect of a Hire of Goods' in N Palmer and E McKendrick (eds), *Interests in Goods* (2nd edn, 1998, Lloyd's of London Press: London) ch 20.

S Worthington, *Proprietary Interests in Commercial Transactions* (1996, Clarendon: Oxford) ch 5 (on *De Mattos v Gibson*).[40]

2.4 Interests in property and title to property

So far the discussion has centred on *interests* in property—ownership interests and possessory interests. The next chapter considers security interests (both legal and equitable). A person's interest in an asset measures the *quality* of the rights which can be exercised over the asset. An ownership interest entitles the owner to exercise certain quite extensive rights over the asset. A possessory interest describes an entitlement to a different bundle of rights. As will become evident from the next chapter, security interests (and there are several different types) describe still different bundles of rights. To say that a person has an interest by way of charge over the property, for example, is a shorthand way of describing the total bundle of rights and obligations which that person has in respect of the asset.

But talk of *title* to property is also common. A person's title to an asset measures the *strength* of the interest in the asset as against other parties asserting conflicting interests. For example, a person in possession of an asset has a possessory interest. He can assert that interest against all who might try to take possession of the asset

39 (1858) 4 De G & J 276, 45 ER 108.

40 Parts of this chapter in *Proprietary Interests in Commercial Transactions* suggest that a hire of goods confers no proprietary interest on the hirer. It would have been better to specify that no *ownership* or *security* interests are conferred. The debate in this section concerns conferral of *possessory* interests—the answer then, it seems, is different.

from him, at least until he is confronted by someone with a better *title* to that possessory interest. *Parker v British Airways Board* ([212] above) provides a simple illustration: in that case the finder of an asset was entitled to assert his possessory interest against all the world other than the true owner (or someone to whom the true owner had given a possessory interest). The resolution of these disputes between parties asserting conflicting interests in property is considered in Section 6.2 below.

The true owner has an absolute and indefeasible title to the asset. The true owner may of course carve out of that title other *titles*: he may, for example, give a third party a possessory title for a limited term, thereby reducing the bundle of rights which the owner is entitled to exercise. This does not alter the assessment that the true owner has title to the ownership interest in the asset. However, for the specified term, the chosen third party will have title to the possessory interest. Each will be able to assert their respective titles against all others claiming inconsistent ownership or possessory interests.

The person with possessory title to an asset is commonly assumed to be the true owner, although it takes little in the way of evidence to displace the assumption. The converse also holds true. A person who is the true owner of an asset is assumed to have possessory title to the asset, unless the contrary is proved to be the case.[41]

2.5 Bailment

So far the discussion has ranged over interests in property, and title to those interests. It is commonly the case that ownership and possessory interests in property (and titles to those interests) are held by the same person. Then it is customary to describe the total package of rights as ownership rights, and not to bother about the component parts. However, these two interests, and titles, are not always held by the same party. When goods are hired or lent or pledged, then the owner retains the title to the ownership interest, but the hirer or borrower or pledgee obtains the title to the possessory interest. In these circumstances it is sometimes said that the owner has the 'general property' in the asset, while the other party has a 'special property' in it. This split between the title to the ownership interest and title to the possessory interest—or between the 'general' and the 'special' property—is termed a bailment. It is irrelevant why the split arises,[42] or whether it is for reward. The special significance of bailment is outlined below.

2.5.1 Elements of bailment

The essence of bailment is that the owner of an asset (the bailor) gives possession of the asset to a bailee for a limited period of time and, at the end of that period,

[41] *Ramsay v Margrett* [1894] 2 QB 18 (CA), 25 *per* Lord Esher MR.

[42] Although a thief would not be described as a bailee: a thief may have physical possession, but not *title* to the legal interest in possession.

the bailee returns the asset to the owner. Clearly an asset which cannot be possessed cannot be bailed. Many different practical arrangements between two parties will constitute bailments at law. For example, an owner who leaves goods[43] with another for safe custody, or for repair, or for transport to another place will effectively constitute himself a bailor of the goods, and the other party a bailee. So, too, a hire of goods will constitute the owner a bailor and the hirer a bailee. Similarly, a pledge[44] of goods as security for a loan will constitute the owner a bailor and the pledgee a bailee.

The importance of bailment lies in the duties which the law imposes on bailees. While the goods are in the possession of the bailee, the bailee has a duty to take care of them. At the end of the bailment, the bailee has a duty to return the goods. The former duty is analogous to a duty of care in negligence, although it pre-dates *Donoghue v Stevenson*.[45] The latter duty raises the possibility of an action analogous to an action in conversion.[46] However, in bailment the onus of proof is reversed: if the asset is lost or damaged while it is in the bailee's hands, then the onus of proof is on the *bailee* to show either that all reasonable care was taken, or that the loss would have occurred in any event.

There are several approaches which aim to explain how the rights and obligations associated with bailment arise. On one assessment, these rights and duties are *sui generis*. The hallmark of bailment is possession, and it is this possession itself which gives rise to a new source of common law obligations, which cannot be classified as obligations in contract, tort or unjust enrichment. Other assessments of bailment take a contrary approach. They regard the practical situation of a bailment as simply providing the context in which familiar obligations in contract or in tort will arise. However, the cases suggest that it would be hard to defend the notion that bailment obligations are contractual: the obligations are imposed without regard to issues of privity or consideration. The problems are less pronounced in seeing bailment obligations as tortious. The principal difficulty then is to explain bailment's reversal of the onus of proof.

The most significant recent case on bailment is *The Pioneer Container*[47] (see **[218]** below). This is a Privy Council decision, but it may be taken as modifying the law of bailment, although it has not changed its fundamentals. The case suggests that the essential elements of a bailment are that the bailee has possession of the assets, and has voluntarily assumed that possession knowing that the assets belong to someone else.[48] The owner's consent to the bailment is not essential. Moreover, this case also makes it plain that it is possible for the duties of a bailee to be attenuated if the owner gives express, implied or even ostensible consent to any limitation in the terms of the bailment (see Section 7.5 below).

[43] Or other choses in possession.

[44] See Section 3.1.2 below.

[45] [1932] AC 562 (HL).

[46] See Section 7.2.3 below.

[47] [1994] 2 AC 324 (PC).

[48] So, eg, a bailment will not arise if goods are left on A's premises without A's knowledge or consent. Nor will a bailment arise if A reasonably believes that the goods belong to A, not to some third party.

The extracts which follow illustrate these essential elements of a bailment and the duties imposed on bailees. The first case illustrates the fundamental point that there can be no bailment unless the bailee is given possession of the goods.

[215] *Ashby v Tolhurst* [1937] 2 KB 242, 249–50 *per* Sir Wilfred Greene MR, 255–6 *per* Romer LJ:

[The owner of a car left it on a private parking ground, and, on payment of 1s, received from the attendant a ticket headed 'Seaway Car Park, Car Park Ticket', containing a receipt for 1s, followed by the provision: 'The proprietors do not take any responsibility for the safe custody of any cars or articles therein nor for any damage to the cars or articles however caused. . . . all cars being left in all respects entirely at their owners' risk.' When the owner returned for his car, the attendant told him he had just given it to the owner's friend. The man who had taken the car had neither the parking ticket nor the keys to the car (which was locked), but he was nevertheless able to start the car and drive it away. The car was never recovered, and the owner unsuccessfully sued the proprietors of the car park for damages.]

Sir Wilfred Greene MR:

'It seems to me that reading the document [the car parking ticket] as a whole, including its own description of itself, namely "Car park ticket," it really means no more than this: the holder of this ticket is entitled to park his car in the Seaway Car Park, but this does not mean that the proprietors are going to be responsible for it. If that be the true construction of the document, and I think it is, the argument that the presence of these exempting conditions points to the view that they are inserted in order to remove a contractual liability which would otherwise be there disappears and, in my opinion, the argument, when applied to a document of this kind, is of no real weight. If that be the true view, the relationship was a relationship of licensor and licensee alone, and that relationship in itself would carry no obligations on the part of the licensor towards the licensee in relation to the chattel left there, no obligation to provide anybody to look after it, no liability for any negligent act of any person in the employment of the licensor who happened to be there.

[250] There is one other way I think of testing the position, and that is to consider in whom possession of this car was at the relevant time. In doing that, of course, one has to be careful to see that one is not unconsciously begging the whole question; but it would be a surprising result I think if the effect of the relationship between these parties was that when the car was left on this piece of ground possession of the car in the legal sense became vested in the owners of the park. It would involve the consequence that the owners of the park could maintain an action of trespass to the car, and an action of conversion if their special property in the car was interfered with. As I say, that argument must not be used in such a way as to beg the question; but it would be rather a surprising result if, when a man left his car on land like this and paid 1s for the privilege of doing so, possession passed in a way in which it certainly would not pass if he left it in a public park in a square in London and paid the attendant 6d for the ticket. In such a case possession, it seems to me, clearly would not pass; I quite fail to see why possession should pass in a case such as this. That, as I say, is merely a way of looking at the matter and is not, of course, a conclusive argument.

It is said, contrary to that view, and I must deal with this branch of the argument, that the true relationship of the parties was that of bailor and bailee, but that the obligations which that contract would normally impose upon a bailee are cut down to the extent, and only to the extent, that the conditions prescribe. I find difficulty myself in seeing, when the conditions are truly construed, what there is left of the obligations arising under a contract of bailment when the obligations are cut out of it to which these conditions refer. But, assuming that there is the ghost, so to speak, of a contract of bailment left here one has to see what the conditions mean. . . .'

[Sir Wilfred Greene concluded that in any event the condition would be effective to protect the defendant.]

Romer LJ:
'This much, at any rate, emerges .... quite clearly: in order that there shall be a bailment there must be a delivery by the bailor, that is to say, he must part with his possession of the chattel in question. In the present case there is no evidence whatever of any delivery in fact of the motor-car to the attendant on behalf of the defendants. All that the plaintiff did was to leave his car on the car park, paying the sum of 1s for the privilege of doing so. It is true that, if the car had been left there for any particular purpose that required that the defendants should have possession of the car a delivery would rightly be inferred. If, for instance, the car had been left at the car park for the purpose of being sold or by way of pledge or for the purposes of being driven to some other place or indeed for the purposes of safe custody, delivery of the car, although not actually made, would readily be inferred. But it is perfectly plain in this case that the car was not delivered to the defendants for safe custody. You cannot infer a contract by A to perform a certain act out of circumstances in which A has made it perfectly plain that he declines to be under any contractual liability to perform that act. The defendants made it as clear as writing can make it in the ticket which was delivered to the plaintiff [256] that they would not take any responsibility for the safe custody of any car. One cannot infer, therefore, in those circumstances that the car was left in the car park for the purpose of being in the custody of the defendants. It is also plain that the car was not left there for any other purpose. That being so it is impossible, as it seems to me, to find that the car was delivered to the defendants or that there was any contract of bailment. In these circumstances I need not deal further with the numerous authorities, not all of them very easily reconcilable, in which the Court has had to consider to what extent and in what circumstances a bailee is entitled to defend himself by a stipulation purporting to exonerate him from all damage or loss to the article which has been delivered to him as bailee. There being no contract of bailment here, because there was no delivery and no evidence of any undertaking on the part of the defendants to take the car into their custody, I do not have to consider the particular circumstances, as I say, in which a bailee is entitled to exonerate himself. But further than that, inasmuch as there was no delivery of the car to the defendants, one cannot infer a contract between the defendants and the plaintiff that the defendants would only redeliver the car on production of the ticket. . . .'

The next extract is often taken as suggesting that an arrangement cannot be a bailment unless the bailor is intended to recover the very goods bailed. However, it is perhaps better read as indicating that an arrangement cannot be a bailment unless the bailor retains ownership of the bailed goods (see the note which follows this extract).

[216] *The South Australian Insurance Co v Randell* (1869) LR 3 PC 101 (PC), 108, 110, 113–14 *per* Sir Joseph Napier:
[A farmer deposited corn with a miller. The miller was entitled to consume the corn in his business and to mix it with other corn deposited for the same purposes, but

subject to the farmer's right to reclaim an equal quantity of corn of similar quality or, in lieu, a sum representing the market price on that day. A small general charge was levied by the miller. The Privy Council held that the transaction was a sale, not a bailment. The miller was therefore entitled to claim for the corn on an insurance policy taken out against the risk of fire on his own property.]

> 'A bailment on trust implies, that there is reserved to the Bailor the right to claim a redelivery of the property deposited in bailment. . . .
>
> The law seems to be concisely and accurately stated by Sir William Jones in the passages cited by Mr. Mellish from his treatise on *Bailments*, pp. 64 and 102 [3rd Ed.]. Wherever there is a delivery of property on a contract for an equivalent in money or some other valuable commodity, and not for the return of his identical subject matter in its original or an altered form, this is a transfer of property for value—it is a sale and not a bailment.
>
> . . . .
>
> An indelible incident of trust property is that a Trustee can never make use of it for his own benefit. An incident of property, that is in bailment, is that the Bailor may require its restoration. This right of recalling the deposit is relied on by Lord Cottenham [in *Foley v Hill* (1848) 2 HLC 28, a case concerning money deposited with a banker] (p. 39), as a test to try the principle on which the fiduciary relation was sought to be maintained. But in this case, no right seems to exist on the part of the Depositor to get back either his identical wheat, or a share of the specific bulk in which his wheat was mixed with his consent; there is no such right on the one side, while, on the other, there is the power in the Miller of doing what he liked with the wheat after it became part of his current stock. This is an inverted order of right that is wholly inconsistent with the relation of Trustee and cestui que trust that is contended for in this case.
>
> . . . .
>
> It appears to their Lordships, that this is not the case of a possession given subject to a trust, but that it is the case of a property transferred for value, at the time of delivery, upon special terms of settlement.
>
> . . . . It comes to this, that where goods are delivered upon a contract for a valuable consideration, whether in money or money's worth, then the property passes. It is a sale and not a bailment. In the case of mixture by consent, the identity of the specific property of each who consents is no longer ascertainable, and the mixed property belongs to all in common. It may perhaps be regarded, under special circumstances, as the case of persons having a common property, and if they all concur in a bailment of this property, all may require a redelivery of what they have so put in bailment. It may be that in such a case each might claim separately to have an aliquot part of the whole restored to him; but here the current stock was, from its very nature, liable to be changed from day to day, both in quantity and quality. The delivery was not for the peculiar or primary purpose of storage simpliciter, as in the case of a bailment of property to be returned to one Bailor, or of any part to one or more of several joint Bailors; but the wheat was delivered by each Farmer independently, to be stored and used as part of the current stock or capital of the Miller's trade. There seems to be no ground upon which a Banker is held not to be a Trustee, or a Banker's current capital not to be trust property, that is not applicable in principle to the case of the Miller and his current stock of wheat, which is his trading capital.'

Also see:

Mercer v Craven Grain Storage Ltd [1994] CLC 328 (HL). This case illustrates the alternative analysis postulated at the end of the previous extract. The House of Lords here considered that there was a bailment between the growers and a grain storage company notwithstanding that grain delivered by one particular grower was intermixed with and indistinguishable from the grain delivered by other growers, and that re-delivery could not possibly return the original grains to the grower. However, the arrangement between the growers was held to constitute them co-owners of the bulk, so that the bailee owed duties to them all as co-owners. This analysis does not alter the fundamental principles of bailment; it merely adopts a more sophisticated approach to defining the 'bailor'.

FURTHER READING:

L D Smith, 'Bailment with Authority to Mix—and Substitute' (1995) 111 *LQR* 10.

The previous extracts concerned arrangements made directly between the owner (the bailor) and the bailee. It is also possible for goods to be sub-bailed, and the sub-bailee will then owe duties directly to the owner, notwithstanding that the two parties may never have met or dealt with each other. The next extract illustrates this, and also indicates the duties imposed on bailees.

[217] *Morris v CW Martin & Sons Ltd* [1966] 1 QB 716 (CA), 726, 728–9 *per* Lord Denning MR, 731–2 *per* Diplock LJ:
[The claimant sent a mink stole to a furrier to be cleaned. The furrier, with the claimant's consent, delivered the fur to the defendants, who were specialist cleaners, to be cleaned by them for reward. The contract between the furrier and the defendants contained an exclusion clause upon which the defendants sought to rely when the fur was stolen by one of their employees and never recovered. The Court of Appeal held that the defendants owed the claimant duties as a bailee for reward to take reasonable care of the fur and not to convert it. On the facts, the exclusion clause was too narrow to protect the defendants. It was therefore unnecessary for the court to consider whether such a clause could affect the relationship between the owner and the defendants, notwithstanding the absence of privity (although see the obiter remarks of Lord Denning MR at **[720]** below).]

> ***Lord Denning MR:***
> '*Bailment for reward.* Once a man has taken charge of goods as a bailee for reward, it is his duty to take reasonable care to keep them safe: and he cannot escape that duty by delegating it to his servant. If the goods are lost or damaged, whilst they are in his possession, he is liable unless he can show—and the burden is on him to show—that the loss or damage occurred without any neglect or default or misconduct of himself or of any of the servants to whom he delegated his duty. This is clearly established by *Reeve v. Palmer* ((1858) 5 C.B.N.S. 84), *Coldman v. Hill* ([1919] 1 K.B. 443 (CA)) and *Building and Civil Engineering Holidays Scheme Management Ltd. v. Post Office* [1966] 1 Q.B. 247 (CA), 260). . . . If he shows that he took due care to employ trustworthy servants, and that he and his servants exercised all diligence, and yet the goods were stolen, he will be excused: but not otherwise. Take a case where a cleaner hands a fur to one of his ser-

vants for cleaning, and it is stolen. If the master can prove that thieves came in from outside and stole it without the fault of any of his servants, the master is not liable. But if it appears that the servant to whom he entrusted it was negligent in leaving the door unlocked—or collaborated with the thieves—or stole the fur himself, then the master is liable: see *Southcote's* case ((1601) 4 Co. Rep. 83b), *United Africa Co. Ltd. v. Saka Owoade* ([1955] A.C. 130) and *Reg. v. Levy Bros. Co. Ltd.* ([1961] S.C.R. 189; 26 D.L.R. (2d) 760).

. . .

So far I have been dealing with the cases where the owner himself has entrusted the goods to the defendant. But here it was not the owner, the plaintiff, who entrusted the fur to the cleaners. She handed it to Beder, who was a bailee for reward. He in turn, with her authority, handed it to the cleaners who were sub-bailees for reward. Mr. Beder could clearly himself sue the cleaners for loss of the fur and recover the whole value, see *The Winkfield* case ([1902] P. 42; 18 T.L.R. 178, C.A), unless the cleaners were protected by some exempting conditions. But can the plaintiff sue the cleaners direct for the misappropriation by their servant? And if she does, can she ignore the exempting conditions?

These are questions of the first importance. At one time the owner of goods who bailed them to another could not sue a third person who had wrongfully lost or damaged or detained the goods. He could only sue the bailee; and the bailee could sue the third person. See the history of the matter fully discussed in Holmes: *The Common Law* (1881), pp. 164–180. But now an action does lie by the owner direct against the wrongdoer if he has the right to immediate possession: see *Kahler v. Midland Bank Ltd.* ([1950] A.C. 24, 33, 56 (HL)). Even if he has no right to immediate possession, he can sue for any permanent injury to, or loss of, the goods by a wrongful act of the defendant: see *Mears v. London & South Western Railway Co.* ((1862) 11 C.B.N.S. 850). But what is a wrongful act as between the owner and the sub-bailee? What is the duty of the sub-bailee to the owner? Is the sub-bailee liable for misappropriation by his servant? There is very little authority on this point. Pollock and Wright on Possession (1888), p. 169, say: "If the bailee of a thing sub-bails it by authority . . . and there is no direct privity of contract between the third person and the owner . . . it would seem that both the owner and the first bailee have concurrently the rights of a bailor against the third person according to the nature of the sub-bailment." By which I take it that if the sub-bailment is for reward, the sub-bailee owes to the owner all the duties of a bailee for reward: and the owner can sue the sub-bailee direct for loss of or damage to the goods; and the sub-bailee (unless he is protected by any exempting conditions) is liable unless he can prove that the loss or damage occurred without his fault or that of his servants. So the plaintiff can sue the defendants direct for the loss of the goods by the misappropriation by their servant, and the cleaners are liable unless they are protected by the exempting conditions. . . .'

Diplock LJ:

'Duties at common law are owed by one person to another only if there exists a relationship between them which the common law recognises as giving rise to such duty. One of such recognised relationships is created by the voluntary taking into custody of goods which are the property of another. By voluntarily accepting from Beder the custody of a fur which they knew to be the property of a customer of his, they brought into existence between the plaintiff and themselves the relationship of bailor and bailee by sub-bailment. The legal relationship of bailor and bailee of a chattel can exist independently of any contract, for the legal concept of bailment as creating a relationship which gives rise to duties owed by a bailee to a bailor is derived from Roman law and is older in our common law than the legal concept of parol contract as giving rise to legal duties owed by one party to the other party thereto. The nature of those legal duties, in particular as to the degree of care which the bailee is bound to exercise in the custody of the goods and as to his duty to redeliver them, varies according to the circumstances in which and purposes for which the goods are delivered to the bailee. But we are concerned here with conversion. This is a breach of a particular duty common to all classes of bailment. While most cases of bailment today are accompanied by a contractual relationship between bailee and bailor which may modify or extend the common law duties of the parties that would otherwise arise from the mere fact of bailment, this is not necessarily so—as witness gratuitous bailment or bailment by finding In the present case Beder was authorised by the plaintiff to hand over the custody of her fur to the defendants for them to do work on it, i.e., to create between her and them the common law relationship of bailee for reward to do work upon the fur. That this relationship was created by sub-bailment, although it might affect a claim by the plaintiff in detinue (see *Kahler v. Midland Bank Ltd.* [1950] A.C. 24), is irrelevant to claim for conversion of or damage to the goods (see *Meux v. Great Eastern Railway Co.* [1895] 2 K.B. 387 (CA)). Whether Beder had authority also to create a contractual relationship between the defendants and the plaintiff is immaterial, for it is found as a fact that he did not do so. But the mere existence of the common law relationship of bailor and bailee for reward gave rise to common law duties owed by the defendants to the plaintiff in respect of their custody of her fur and the work to be done by them upon it as well as to common law rights enforceable against her (cf. *Tappenden v. Artus* ([1964] 2 Q.B. 185)).

One of the common law duties owed by a bailee of goods to his bailor is not to convert them, i.e., not to do intentionally in relation to the goods an act inconsistent with the bailor's right of property therein. (See *Caxton Publishing Co. Ltd. v. Sutherland Publishing Co.* ([1939] A.C. 178 (HL)), *per* Lord Porter (at p. 202). This duty, which is common to all bailments as well as to other relationships which do not amount to bailment, is independent of and additional to the other common law duty of a bailee for reward to take reasonable care of his bailor's goods. Stealing goods is the simplest example of conversion . . . some confusion has, I think, arisen in later cases through failure to recognise the co-existence of the two duties of a bailee for reward; to take reasonable care of his bailor's goods and not to convert them—even by stealing. . . .'

The previous extracts indicate there can be a bailment either by direct dealing between the bailor and bailee, or by sub-bailment. The next issue, particularly in relation to sub-bailment, is whether there can be a bailment without the knowledge or consent of the bailor.

[218] ***The Pioneer Container* [1994] 2 AC 324 (PC), 341–2 *per* Lord Goff:**
[The facts are not material here, but are summarised at **[721]** below.]

'In truth, at the root of this question lies a doctrinal dispute of a fundamental nature, which is epitomised in the question: is it a prerequisite of a bailment that the bailor should have consented to the bailee's possession of the goods? An affirmative answer to this question (which is the answer given by *Bell, Modern Law of Personal Property in England and Ireland*, at pp. 88–89) leads to the conclusion that, if the owner seeks to hold a sub-bailee responsible to him as bailee, he has to accept all the terms of the sub-bailment, warts and all; for either he will have consented to the sub-bailment on those terms or, if not, he will (by holding the sub-bailee liable to him as bailee) be held to have ratified all the terms of the sub-bailment. A negative answer to the question is however supported by other writers, notably by *Palmer, Bailment*, at pp. 31 et seq., where Professor Palmer cites a number of examples of [342] bailment without the consent of the owner, and by Professor Tay in her article "The Essence of Bailment: Contract, Agreement or Possession?" (1966) 5 Sydney Law Review 239. On this approach, a person who voluntarily takes another person's goods into his custody holds them as bailee of that person (the owner); and he can only invoke, for example, terms of a sub-bailment under which he received the goods from an intermediate bailee as qualifying or otherwise affecting his responsibility to the owner if the owner consented to them. It is the latter approach which, as their Lordships have explained, has been adopted by English law and, with English law, the law of Hong Kong.

Their Lordships wish to add that this conclusion, which flows from the decisions in *Morris v. C. W. Martin & Sons Ltd.* [1966] 1 Q.B. 716 and the *Gilchrist Watt* case [1970] 1 W.L.R. 1262, produces a result which in their opinion is both principled and just. They incline to the opinion that a sub-bailee can only be said for these purposes to have voluntarily taken into his possession the goods of another if he has sufficient notice that a person other than the bailee is interested in the goods so that it can properly be said that (in addition to his duties to the bailee) he has, by taking the goods into his custody, assumed towards that other person the responsibility for the goods which is characteristic of a bailee. This they believe to be the underlying principle. Moreover, their Lordships do not consider this principle to impose obligations on the sub-bailee which are onerous or unfair, once it is recognised that he can invoke against the owner terms of the sub-bailment which the owner has actually (expressly or impliedly) or even ostensibly authorised. In the last resort the sub-bailee may, if necessary and appropriate, be able to invoke against the bailee the principle of warranty of authority. . . .'

Question:

Is the knowledge and consent of the owner necessary? What is necessary?

2.5.2 The duty of care

The final issue is to determine what duty of care is owed by the bailor to the bailee.

[219] *Sanderson v Collins* [1904] 1 KB 628 (CA), 630–2 *per* Collins MR:
[The facts appear from the judgment.]

Collins MR:
'This case no doubt raises a question of some interest, but the decision at which we ought to arrive is clear when we get back to the principles by which the law of bailments is governed.

The question arises on this state of facts: the defendant owned a carriage which he entrusted to the plaintiff, who was a carriage-builder, to repair, and the plaintiff sent another carriage to the defendant during such time as his own carriage should be under repair. The bailment was for mutual consideration, and was not gratuitous or voluntary, and the degree of the obligation on the bailee in such a case is well settled, that the bailee must use reasonable care, which has been described as ordinary care, in the custody of the article bailed. That proposition was not seriously contested on behalf of the plaintiff.

What happened was, as appears by the findings of the county court judge, that the defendant used the carriage between three and five o'clock on the day on which it was injured. The proper place for the key of the coach-house was said to be a drawer in the hall of the house, and the defendant said that the [631] last time that he saw the key was at three o'clock—that is, as I gather, at the time it was taken out by the coachman for the afternoon drive. The carriage was used for two hours, and after that it became the duty of the coachman to put it back in the coach-house. After the carriage came back, and at some time later in the day, it was taken out by the coachman absolutely for his own purposes, and on a frolic of his own. He took some friends with him and drove about to see the illuminations. They all appear to have got drunk, and a collision with a tramcar occurred, and the carriage was injured. It was afterwards returned to the plaintiff in a damaged condition, and he has brought this action claiming the cost of putting the carriage into repair.

. . .

To begin with, as I have said, the obligation on the defendant as bailee was only to take reasonable care, and so far as the act of his servant was to be taken as the act of the defendant he would be bound by it; and if the servant in the course of his employment and acting within the scope of his authority did not use reasonable care in the custody of the carriage, the master would be responsible. On the other hand, it is clear law that such a bailee as the defendant was is not responsible for the acts of persons who are not his servants in respect of particular acts—that is, who are not acting within the scope of their employment in doing those acts. If a burglar broke into the coach-house and took away the carriage and caused damage to it and brought it back, no liability would attach to the bailee, because the act would not be his, and he would not be responsible for the acts of a person between whom and himself there was no connection. But while not responsible in such a case, yet if his servant whose duty it was to keep the [632] carriage safely had been negligent in leaving the coach-house open, and the carriage were taken away, the master would be liable, because of the negligence of a person for whom he is responsible. That, I think, illustrates the distinction between the two cases. Burglary is perhaps an extreme instance of something not done under any mandate from the master, but any other act outside the scope of the authority given by him would equally relieve the master. If the servant in doing any act breaks the connection of service between himself and his master, the act done under those circumstances is not that of the master. The county court judge has by his judgment acquitted the defendant of negligence in employing as coachman the man who caused the mischief, and that ground of action does not exist. It seems to me that a satisfactory answer to the question raised on this appeal only involves a careful analysis of the facts, and when that is done it appears that there is no legal liability on the defendant. . .'

Also see:

Morris v CW Martin & Sons Ltd [1966] 1 QB 716 (CA), 726, 728–9 *per* Lord Denning MR, at **[217]** above.

Question:

When will a bailee be liable for the theft of the bailed goods?

[220] *Houghland v RR Low (Luxury Coaches) Ltd* [1962] 1 QB 694 (CA), 698 *per* Ormerod LJ:

[The case concerned a gratuitous bailment of the claimant's suitcase, deposited with the coach driver of one of the defendant's coaches and stowed in the boot of the coach. The coach later broke down and the passengers and their luggage were transferred to another coach. On arrival at their destination, the claimant's suitcase could not be found. The Court of Appeal denied that liability depended upon proof of gross negligence. The onus of proof was on the defendant to show that the loss was not caused by their negligence.]

> '[I]t appears to me that the standard of care required in a case of bailment, or any other type of case, is the standard demanded by the circumstances of that particular case. It seems to me that to try and put a bailment, for instance, in a watertight compartment—such as a gratuitous bailment on the one hand, and bailment for reward on the other—is to overlook the fact that there might well be an infinite variety of cases, which might come into one or the other category. The question that we have to consider in a case of this kind, if it is necessary to consider negligence, is whether in the circumstances of the particular case a sufficient standard of care has been observed by the defendants or their servants. . . .'

Also see:

Port Swettenham Authority v T G Wu & Co Sdn Bhd [1979] AC 580 (PC).
China-Pacific SA v Food Corpn of India, The Winson [1982] AC 939 (HL), especially p 960 *per* Lord Diplock.

Both of these cases suggest that a lower standard of care is imposed on a gratuitous bailee.

Question:

What standard of care should be owed by an involuntary bailee?

FURTHER READING:

A Bell, 'The Place of Bailment in the Modern Law of Obligations' in N Palmer and E McKendrick, *Interests in Goods* (2nd edn, 1998, Lloyd's of London Press: London) ch. 19.
N Palmer, *Bailment* (2nd edn, 1991, Sweet & Maxwell: London).

The remedies which are available to the bailor against the bailee are discussed in Section 7.5 below.

2.6 Acquisition of ownership and possessory interests

It is commonly said that personal property is never without an owner. The statement is meant to indicate that title to both the ownership interest and the possessory interest (if the property is a chose in possession, and so is capable of being possessed) always rest in someone. Ownership in this sense may be acquired in different ways. When an asset is first created, its creator generally assumes ownership. For example, an author owns the copyright in her written work; a sculptor owns his sculpture. The author has title to the ownership interest; the sculptor has title to both ownership and possessory interests. So too, when one asset is produced from another by natural means, the owner of primary asset generally acquires ownership of the produce (although see **[221]** below). A sheep-owner owns the lambs delivered; an orchard-owner owns the fruit produced; a share-owner owns the dividends paid out. In each of these cases, 'ownership' encompasses title to both the ownership interest and the possessory interest where both exist. These methods of acquiring ownership are termed 'original modes of acquisition'.

Questions:

Can an asset be created for someone else, so that the creator never for an instant owns the new creation, or is a two step process required, so that the new asset belongs initially to its creator and must then be transferred by a separate transaction to the intended recipient? Is the rule the same at law and in equity? When might the answer be important? (See Sections 3.8.4 and 4.12 below.)

The position is more complicated if the creator of the 'new' asset does not simply use his own property in the creation, but uses the property of another, perhaps alone or perhaps combined with his own property. Who then owns the creation? The trite examples are of a person using another's grapes to make wine, or flour to make bread. But the illustrations need not be so homely. A manufacturer may use another's petroleum to make plastics, or paper to print magazines. The *prima facie* rule that the creator owns the creation must be attenuated to accommodate the express or implied agreement between the parties as to the ownership of the product,[49] or, where there is no agreement as to the use of the product's components, it must accommodate the mechanisms the law has developed to preserve the proprietary interests of any non-consenting party whose property has been consumed without approval. These are difficult issues. They are addressed later.[50]

[49] The extent to which this is possible is not clear: see the dicta in *Clough Mill Ltd v Martin* [1985] 1 WLR 111 (CA), at **[331]** below.

[50] See Sections 3.8 and 6.4 below. Equity's resolution of the problem is not necessarily the same as the common law's: see Sections 5.5, 5.10 and 6.5 below.

More usually, however, a person acquires title by succession to the title of a previous owner. Gifts, sales and dispositions under a will or on an intestacy all provide mechanisms for the transfer of title to the ownership interest in an asset from one person to another. These interests can also be transferred by operation of law, sometimes regardless of the intention of the parties concerned. These various mechanisms for the transfer of ownership interests in personal property are examined in detail later in the book: see Chapters 4 and 5.

Similarly, possessory interests in personal property can be acquired by succession to the title of the previous owner. An owner (with both the ownership and possessory interests in the property) can part with possession voluntarily, giving the possessory interest in the asset to another by pledging, lending, hiring out or bailment of the property. Where the arrangement is consensual, the new possessor has title (perhaps only for a limited term) to the possessory interest. An owner may also part with possession involuntarily, as when property is stolen or lost. In these circumstances others may acquire possessory interests in the property, but they will not have the best title to those interests; the owner will retain that. In both cases, the owner will retain title to the ownership interest, even though the property is not in his or her possession.

[221] *Tucker v Farm and General Investment Trust Ltd* [1966] 2 QB 421 (CA), 429–30 *per* Harman LJ:

[A farmer acquired 84 ewes on hire-purchase from the defendant, a finance company. The farmer had the ewes served during the term of hire, and, after they had lambed, he sold the ewes and their lambs to the claimant, although all the animals remained on his farm. The defendants repossessed the ewes and lambs. The claimant successfully sued the defendant for wrongful conversion of the lambs, but not the ewes, on the basis that they belonged to him.]

> 'If I were the owner of an apple orchard and let it at a rent to John Doe for a term of five years, nobody would doubt that John Doe, as the apples ripened, could pick and sell them and that the value which he received was his. That is a familiar transaction in England and has been for centuries. It was a surprise to me that livestock were also the subject of lettings, but it evidently has been so for centuries now.
>
> There is, as my Lord has said, in *Wood v. Ash and Foster* (Owen 139) a direct authority upon the subject. The fact that this is not only a letting but a purchase, that is to say, a hire-purchase agreement, in my view makes not the least difference. It is merely a letting with an option to purchase at the end of the term, like thousands of agreements in the past where the lessee has had such an option. Therefore, the case becomes a tolerably simple one. It is merely a case of the lessee taking the fruit which falls from the subject-matter of the demise during the terms of years created by that document. This includes in this case the fleeces and the lambs, and those went to the lessee because there was nothing expressed to prevent them.
>
> The law seems to me to be tolerably plain. I need not, I think, go back into the Roman law or bother about Roman-Dutch law or authorities from Cape Province. There is a perfectly good English authority, and the analogy with an ordinary letting of farmland is quite clear. In the court below the matter was bedevilled by the fact that it was taken that there was a presumption in English law that the offspring of an animal belonged to the owner of its dam, and that no doubt is true (except for swans) as between the owner

of the dam and the owner of the sire. But that has nothing to do with the law between landlord and tenant [or owner and hirer] . . . .'

2.7 Utilising interests in property

At first sight it might seem that there are very few proprietary interests—even with the addition of security interests, discussed in the next chapter[51]—and the use to which they may be put might therefore seem inevitably limited. This is not the case. These few interests can be combined in numerous ways to provide very different commercial and domestic outcomes. A thorough understanding of the basic principles, combined with a subtle imagination, is all that is required.

Much of this book is concerned with ownership and security interests, not with possessory interests. Before moving on to those particular aspects of personal property, it is worth illustrating the possibilities for inventiveness with a simple and familiar example. Hire purchase agreements are common consumer transactions, so common that their cleverness is usually forgotten. A hire purchase agreement is essentially a contract of bailment under which goods are hired out by the owner for a fixed term; at the end of the term, the hirer has a contractual option to purchase the goods. The owner parts with possession of the goods in return for hire payments. If the hirer does not exercise the option to purchase at the end of the term, the goods must be returned to the owner.

The genius of these agreements lies in the protection they provide to the seller/hirer. In effect, these transactions are arrangements for the purchase of goods by instalments, with the added advantage that the buyer can take possession before paying the price. The intention of the hirer/buyer is to acquire ownership; the 'hire charge' is calculated to reflect this. However, if the transaction operated as an outright sale, the buyer would become the owner of the goods at the outset, free to deal with them at will, thus leaving the seller with nothing by way of security to ensure payment of the full purchase price. This security problem could be addressed by giving the buyer possession but delaying the transfer of title until the full price had been paid, but then the buyer would be classed as a 'buyer in possession' under the Sale of Goods Act 1979,[52] with the statutory power to pass good title to third party purchasers. In the end, this too would leave the seller without adequate security. Finally, if the seller transferred title at the outset, but forced the buyer to reconvey ownership to the seller as security for full payment of the purchase price, the transaction would need to be registered as a bill of sale, thus increasing the cost and complexity of the deal. All this is avoided by the hire-purchase structure: the seller remains the owner of the property; the 'buyer' is never classed as such until the option to purchase is exercised at the end of the period of hire; in the interim, he is simply a bailee of the goods for a hiring fee.[53] The scheme effectively avoids what,

[51] See Chapter 3.
[52] Section 25(2). See Section 4.2.2 below.
[53] With all the associated liabilities of a bailee, as amended by the contract of hire.

to the seller, was the undesirable operation of the Sale of Goods Act 1979 and the Bills of Sale Acts.[54]

[222] *Warman v Southern Counties Car Finance Corpn Ltd* [1949] 2 KB 576, 582–3 *per* Finnemore J:

[The claimant agreed to purchase a car on hire-purchase. During the term of the hire, evidence revealed that the hirer/seller was not the owner of the car. The buyer successfully claimed return of all the instalments paid. The seller unsuccessfully counterclaimed for hire of the car for the 7 months period of use.]

> 'A hire-purchase agreement is in law, an agreement in two parts. It is an agreement to rent a particular chattel for a certain length of time. If during the period or at the end of the period the hirer does not wish to buy the chattel he is not bound to do so. On the other hand, the essential part of the agreement is that the hirer has the option of purchase, and it is common knowledge—and I suppose, common sense—that when people enter into a hire-purchase agreement they enter into it not so much for the purpose of hiring, but for the purpose of purchasing, by a certain method, by what is, in effect, deferred payments, and that is done by this special kind of agreement known as a hire-purchase agreement, the whole object of which is to acquire the option to purchase the chattel when certain payments have been made.
>
> Now, I think it might well be right to say if at any stage the option to purchase goes, the whole value of the agreement to the hirer has gone with it. If he wanted to make an agreement merely to hire a car he would make it, but he enters into a hire-purchase agreement because he wants to have the right to purchase the car; that is the whole basis of the agreement, the very foundation of it. I should have thought, even on that broad principle, that if the defendants break the contract or are unable to carry it out they are not entitled to claim on a sort of quantum meruit and say "Anyhow, although I could not carry out the agreement and could not give you the title to this car, you had the use of it for six or seven months, and you must pay the hiring charges for those months."
>
> I think there is another way of looking at it: This car was not, at any time, the property of the defendants. I do not think that the plaintiff in any circumstances could be called on to pay to the defendants hiring money for a car which belonged to somebody else. I should have thought it was quite plain that if A. purports to hire a car to B., and in fact delivers to B. a car which belonged not to himself but to C., to which he had no right whatever in law, and during the currency of the agreement C. intervenes and asserts his right to the car, and if, in those circumstances, B. does not pay the hiring charges, A. would have no possible claim for them, because it is impossible to see how he would ever frame his case. I do not think he could come into court and say: "I claim money arising out of hiring charges from B., for C.'s car, to which, it would appear, I had no right." I cannot think that any court would direct B. to pay A. money for the use of somebody else's car. I do not see here how the defendants, because they delivered to the plaintiff somebody else's car, can claim any kind of money from him for the use of that car. That is, it seems to me, in plain English, what the claim comes to.
>
> As I say, it is an interesting point, and I think that must be the answer to it and it seems to me it must be the final answer to the defendants' counterclaim. I therefore take the view, that it is not open to the defendants to claim, either by way of set-off or counterclaim, money which is expressed in this hire-purchase agreement to be for monthly

[54] Bills of Sale Act 1878 and Bills of Sale Act (1878) Amendment Act 1882 (as amended).

rentals for the months during which the plaintiff had the use of a car which was not the defendant's car at all. Therefore, I think that quite plainly there has been a breach of this agreement and the plaintiff is entitled to recover damages. I think those damages amount to the sum of £294 17s 3d as claimed by him. . . .'

FURTHER GENERAL READING:

R Goode, *Commercial Law* (2nd edn, 1995, Penguin: Harmondsworth), ch 2.

M G Bridge, *Personal Property Law* (2nd edn, 1996, Blackstone Press: London).

A P Bell, *Modern Law of Personal Property in England and Ireland* (1989, Butterworths: London).

F H Lawson and B Rudden, *The Law of Property* (2nd edn, 1982, Clarendon: Oxford).

3

Security Interests

3.1 Introduction

This chapter is concerned with security interests in personal property.[1] These interests are more limited than ownership interests (whether legal or equitable) or interests in possession, all of which were dealt with in the previous chapter. The idea of a security interest is simple. If A is under some personal obligation to B (normally a debt), then A may *secure* that obligation by giving rights over some or all of A's property to B. The proprietary interest acquired by B is termed a *security interest*. There are several different types of consensual security interest. Each type gives B a different package of rights over A's property, although none gives B rights amounting to full ownership or possession. This chapter looks at the different forms of security which are available to parties, and at the rights which attach to each different form.[2] It also looks at certain other devices which the parties might use to obtain similar advantages to those generated by taking security.

The advantages which accrue to a person who takes security are plain. If A is unable to satisfy the personal obligation (eg unable to pay the debt), then B can exercise the proprietary rights given by the security. This often (but not always) entitles B to sell the secured property and use the proceeds to compensate B for the unperformed personal obligation (eg B can use the proceeds to pay off the outstanding debt). If the proceeds are insufficient, then A remains personally liable to B to the extent of the shortfall. In this chapter it will generally be assumed—for ease of description—that the security interest is granted to secure a debt. Reference is therefore made throughout to a *debtor* (eg the borrower in a loan transaction, or the

[1] Perhaps confusingly, this use of the term 'securities' must be distinguished from use of the same term to refer to marketable interests—'securities'—bought and sold on the Stock Exchange (and so referring to shares and bonds). In these different contexts the words have quite different meanings.

[2] However, this should not be taken to suggest that all security interests are created consensually, by agreement between the parties. Most are, but it is also possible for one form of security interest—an equitable lien—to arise by operation of law. An equitable lien gives a party rights which mirror those granted consensually by an equitable charge, but the details of equitable liens will be left until Chapter 5.

purchaser in a contract for the provision of goods or services) granting some sort of security interest to a *creditor* (eg the lender in a loan transaction, or the supplier in a contract for the provision of goods and services) to secure the debtor's personal obligation to repay the debt. However, security can be used to secure *any* personal obligation, not merely one requiring the payment of money.

These security arrangements also have advantages for A. They increase A's bargaining power, making it easier for A to persuade B to enter into the arrangement. Anyone who has needed a bank loan to purchase a house appreciates this. Almost by definition, though, once A has granted security to B, A will have more limited rights over the secured property than previously. Economic analyses of law are often used—not always satisfactorily—to help explain why a debtor would be prepared to make these sacrifices in order to persuade a creditor to contract.

[301] M Bridge, 'The Quistclose Trust in a World of Secured Transactions' (1992) 12 *OJLS* 333, 334–342:

[Footnotes in the original are omitted. Retention of title clauses and *Quistclose* trusts are dealt with at the end of this chapter: see Sections 3.8 and 3.9 respectively.]

> '*What Do We Mean by 'Security'?*
> Security in its strict legal sense is classified under the possessory heads of pledge and lien and the non-possessory heads of mortgage and charge. Apart from lien, created by operation of law (except where a special lien is swollen by contract to a general lien), these all arise where the debtor makes a grant in favour of the creditor. None is created by unilateral taking or retention on the part of the creditor. Hire purchase agreements, chattel leases and title retention clauses therefore fall outside the recognized heads of security despite the business sense of regarding an unpaid seller's reservation of the general property in goods as in substance the taking of security. Nor would legal resistance to the treatment of title retention as security crumble in the face of the realisation that it is better than conventional security: it functions as a purchase-money form of security, ranking ahead of prior charges and mortgages, and it does not have to be registered. The payer of the money under a *Quistclose* trust may therefore be regarded as having an advanced priority comparable to that of a purchase money financier.
>
> We owe it to the American realists for the insight, translated into legislative form by Article 9 of the Uniform Commercial Code, that title retention should be dealt with according to what it accomplishes rather than what it purports to be. This conclusion, firmly adopted also by the Crowther Committee and by Professor Diamond in his report to the Department of Trade and Industry, has already been accepted in part by legislation. Administrators of a company, appointed under Part II of the Insolvency Act 1986, have certain powers of interference with the rights of secured creditors that are explicitly extended to hire purchase, chattel leases and title retention agreements, though not to money received by a company under a *Quistclose* trust.
>
> There are also stirrings in the recent case law indicative of a growing judicial impatience with a law of security that elevates form over function. In *Re Curtain Dream Plc*, a sale and resale agreement concerning stock-in-trade between a trading company and a financier was treated as an artificial transaction by a court that was prepared to look at the substance of the matter and recognize the lineaments of a mortgage wrapped up in the terminology of sale. What use, after all, could a financier have for large quantities of curtain fabric unless it had to look to it for security if the trading company defaulted on its 'repurchase' obligations? If this approach is typical of future decision-making, it poses a severe threat to unregistered sale and leaseback arrangements. An

understandable judicial reluctance to disturb settled practice may nevertheless point to future restraint in handling what after all are infinitely variable issues of construction. One can predict that the enquiry: Does this transaction give rise to an equity of redemption? will play a significant question-begging role in the disposition of future cases.

. . .

Why do Creditors take Security?

In the last dozen or so years, a major debate has been conducted in the United States about the reasons underlying the giving and taking of security. What appears to have prompted the debate is the facility with which security can be taken under Article 9 and the reaction this has prompted that nothing is left for distribution to the unsecured creditors. In this respect, the English counterpart to the Article 9 security interest is the all-embracing floating charge, together with its confederates, the fixed charge on present and future book debts and the legal charge on a company's land and premises. A lay commentator has recently remarked that '[t]he final liquidation ceremony often resembles an inversion of the miracle of the loaves and the fishes'. The phenomenon is hardly new. Lord Macnaghten drew attention to it in famous language a hundred years ago. In 1982, the Cork Committee recommended that 10 *per cent* of the net proceeds of the assets subject to a floating charge should be set aside for the debtor's unsecured creditors, but this recommendation was not enacted in ensuing insolvency legislation. Unsecured creditors cannot in modern conditions look for satisfaction to uncalled share capital and it is not a common practice for companies to set aside a reserve liability for distribution only upon insolvency. Given the present spate of business failures, it seems an odd time to be asking why creditors take security.

Empirical observation would suggest that companies will only give security if they have to, preferring to exhaust first of all the possibilities of unsecured credit. Blue chip companies will be more successful than others in warding off or delaying the giving of security. It has nevertheless been argued that a willingness to give security has a 'signalling' function: it demonstrates the company's conviction that credit can safely be extended to it. As Schwartz explains it: 'Security interests restrict future borrowing opportunities, give secured creditors greater leverage over firm behaviour, and make it more difficult for a firm to reschedule debts in the event of hard times. A firm willing to encumber its assets is, thus,"signalling" that, in its view, its prospects justify those potential costs.' Kripke has convincingly argued, however, that the notorious unwillingness of companies to borrow on a secured basis when unsecured sources remain available sends 'an involuntary signal of the opposite kind, namely that the debtor cannot borrow unsecured because creditors think the risk is too great'. Banks, especially in recent decades, have shown an avid appetite for security even though prudent bankers would not lend at all if they felt there was a significant risk that the security would have to be called in, an attitude expressed in the adage that the best security is no security. In medium- and long-term financing, there is a very strong likelihood that the creditor will take security. It should be understood for present purposes that even short-term or current assets, such a book debts and stock-in-trade, can be secured on a revolving, long-term basis. This overwhelming preference for secured credit, coupled with the general reluctance of borrowers to give it, would therefore leave no room for the operation of a signalling device in the way described by Schwartz.

The American literature shows a clear tendency to ask why a debtor should wish to give security. In view especially of the chronic shortage of finance for small firms, it might be more appropriate to ask why a creditor should wish to take it. Looking through the debtor's lens, nevertheless, permits the issue to be framed in terms that are an adaptation of the Modigliani-Miller theory of stratification. According to this theory, in perfect capital markets a firm's value will not be affected by the mix of debt and equity in its capital structure. As extended to the field of credit, the theory holds that the mix of secured and unsecured credit will not affect the overall cost of credit to the firm. Any savings flowing from the reduction in the cost of credit from a creditor taking security is balanced, as though on a seesaw basis, by the higher interest demanded by unsecured creditors whose lending has become more risky as a result of their being subordinated to secured creditors. There may even be transaction costs if the firm decides to grant secured credit, though in many instances, simple title retention being perhaps the best example, transaction costs will be negligible.

Naturally, there is no such thing as a perfect and properly informed credit market. In any event, some creditors are more risk averse than others, so that not all creditors would charge the same for unsecured credit in the same conditions. Consequently, there is no 'precise mathematical relationship between yield and risk' across the field of credit. Certain unsecured creditors lending to an unencumbered debtor might not anticipate the probability or inevitability of secured credit later being granted, while others might assume this and load their interest charges accordingly. Alternatively, they might incorporate negative pledge clauses of variable effectiveness demanding an equal and rateable security if the debtor later grants a security to another creditor. Furthermore, the interposition of preferential creditors between secured and unsecured creditors upsets any simple seesaw comparison between the latter two groups. What a secured creditor fails to take may go to a preferential creditor instead. The risk of insolvency cannot therefore be dissipated within a simple interest rate spread. In the absence of a perfect credit market, a creditor will thus want to take security to avoid the insolvency risk that comes with lining up alongside unsecured creditors.

Additional benefits to the secured creditor will include the ability to exercise self-help without having to wait for judicial process, particularly potent in the case of a demand loan, and the *in terrorem* incentive, in consumer cases especially, arising out of the debtor's fear of losing needed possessions. The security that includes the power to appoint a receiver may also be useful in keeping a debtor's unsecured creditors in line. Further, there is the control or 'leverage' that security sometimes allows over the business of the debtor, though the attractions of this might pale somewhat today for those secured creditors fearful of being branded as shadow directors privy to acts of wrongful trading. Taking security may also, in a number of instances, be a cheaper alternative to an expensive credit enquiry. It may have monitoring consequences too.

Monitoring may be defined as the post-lending appraisal of the debtor's conduct to avoid misbehaviour prejudicial to the creditor's investment. It ranges from the particular investigation of a loan, dedicated to an agreed narrow purpose, being in fact so applied, to the more general and long-term scrutiny associated with broadly-based loans. In the latter case, the debtor's conduct is vetted for the due observance of proper business standards as reinforced by the terms of the loan agreement. The fondness of creditors for security hardly seems consistent with the insight that security is the mark of an inefficient monitor. A creditor with a narrow security may be content to leave to unsecured and other creditors the task of general monitoring: one with a floating security has the incentive and the opportunity to conduct general monitoring and may in the process reassure other creditors that the debtor's behaviour is being properly monitored. In some cases, trade creditors, who tend to be unsecured, will be better general monitors since they are often better placed to detect signs of a debtor's incipient decline. Monitoring will be more or less effective according to the particular form in which the security is cast. An example of effective monitoring would occur with a fixed, as opposed to a floating, charge over book debts (and that includes factoring for present purposes) with its concomitant accounting controls over the proceeds of such debts.

Why Does the Law Allow Security?

The law of security sets against each other two fundamental principles of credit and insolvency law. First, a creditor has freedom of contract to bargain for a security that will advance his priority position at the expense of other creditors of the debtor. Secondly, once insolvency supervenes, the assets of the insolvent debtor must be distributed among his creditors on a rateable (or *pari passu*) basis and, perhaps more importantly, the law will not allow any contracting out of the insolvency distribution scheme. It is no satisfactory answer in the face of the conflicting thrust of these two principles to deny any logical contradiction between the two, on the ground that the former principle operates before insolvency to define what goes into the insolvency process, while the latter only comes into play once insolvency supervenes. Freedom of contract is permitted to empty the content of an insolvent's estate. This sharp conflict between the two principles is blurred, admittedly, by provisions in the Insolvency Act 1986 striking down transactions at an undervalue, unlawful preferences and certain late floating charges where the debtor is unable to pay his debts at the relevant time and insolvency later occurs, but it seems that relatively few secured transactions have ever been, or are ever likely to be, struck down on the above grounds. It is certainly very difficult to imagine any circumstances in which a *Quistclose* trust bringing in late value would be vulnerable to such an attack. The discordancy of the two principles seems particularly marked in the case of after-acquired assets falling into the maw of the security during the course of liquidation itself. When secured creditors are able to eviscerate an insolvent's estate prior to its vesting in the liquidator, one has to ask just how fundamental is the *pari passu* principle, so important that in corporate insolvencies one looks for it in the Insolvency Rules and not in the body of the Act itself. It seems powerful enough, however, to prevent any contracting out of the insolvency set off rules, given the law's interest in the orderly distribution of insolvents' estates. Moreover, the House of Lords invoked it in the mid-70s to strike down a clearing house arrangement, a result inconvenient enough for financial markets that in their case it was reversed by recent companies legislation.

The stark contrast between the freedom of contract and *pari passu* principles has persuaded some North American writers to describe the grant of security as the issue of insolvency rights, though one ought not to lose sight of the other, non-insolvency advantages of security, discussed above. One author has been so struck with the metaphor as to remonstrate with unsecured creditors for demanding insolvency distribution rights for which they have not paid, though he is on firmer ground in asking how unsecured creditors can claim to have been misled when it is notorious that nothing is left for distribution to them once secured and preferential creditors (and receivers for their expenses and remuneration) have been paid off. Even here, however, one can sympathize with unsecured trade creditors for whom security is not a realistic possibility and who do not have genuine freedom or opportunity to police and screen rigorously all of their trading partners. Trade credit certainly has its price even if sometimes this price is dressed up as the loss of a discount for early payment. Not all trade credit, however, will consistently carry interest charges of one kind or another and, as we saw above, there is no stable relationship between the risk of a loan and its yield and thus no common currency between the two.

It has forcefully been argued by one writer, with a very lengthy history of involvement in the practical and academic aspects of credit, that the system of secured credit has been responsible for the phenomenal growth of the distribution economy. In the case of purchase money financing, 'the effect of security is enormous in keeping the sale primarily a commercial transaction and not a banking event'. On the supplier's side, the 'discovery' of revolving assets, such as stock-in-trade and book debts, as collateral for a loan has extended the availability of business credit. Valuable as this may be as a *post hoc* insight, it is unlikely to have actuated courts that have desisted from placing obstacles in the way of secured credit though it might have persuaded legislatures not to interfere in a widespread business practice.

...

In the present climate of opinion, there is little prospect of any attempt to overthrow the system of secured credit, despite the opinion of certain insolvency practitioners that security sometimes impedes corporate rescues. Consequently, the debate among American writers over the efficiency or otherwise of secured credit seems somewhat academic, though one's view of this might change if the empirical work called for by one of these writers to demonstrate various working hypotheses is ever accomplished. Should this come to pass, it would raise an interesting evidentiary problem. Is the *pari passu* principle so strong that the burden of proving efficiency rests upon those who support secured credit, or is freedom of contract paramount so that the burden falls upon those who oppose security? One American writer has plausibly argued that the abolition of security would lead to bilateral subordination arrangements between unsecured creditors tending to replicate the abolished secured credit system, as well as to the rediscovery of evasive devices such as title retention and discounting that in substance amount to security. The history of forms of lending in this country is quite supportive of this speculative line.'

FURTHER READING:

R Posner, *The Economic Analysis of Law* (4th ed, 1992, Little Brown & Co: Boston).
A Kronman and R Posner, *The Economics of Contract Law* (1979, Little Brown & Co: Boston).

Question:

Do other theories of contract law also offer adequate—or better—explanations for the existence of security? (Also see Section 3.10 below.)

3.1.1 The legal incidents of security

As already noted, the advantage of a security interest is that it provides the creditor (the security holder) with a proprietary interest to back up the performance of a personal obligation. This has two important consequences. The first is that the creditor's proprietary interest may persist in the secured property notwithstanding a change in ownership of the asset.[3] The second—and more vital—consequence arises on the insolvency of the debtor. A fundamental principle of insolvency law is that of *pari passu* distribution: all the insolvent's creditors share and share alike in

[3] Although there are limits to this: see Chapter 6. For example, the security interest will not persist if the new owner of the asset is a *bona fide* purchaser for value of the *legal* title who does not have notice of the security holder's *equitable* security interest, if such it is.

the distribution of the insolvent's estate. They shoulder the losses in proportion to the amounts owed to them by the insolvent debtor.[4] However, this principle applies only to the distribution of assets which belong beneficially to the debtor. Insolvency law respects pre-insolvency property rights. To the extent that third parties can assert ownership or security interests in assets which are in the debtor's possession, those assets do not belong beneficially to the debtor and are not available for distribution to the debtor's creditors. The more extensive these third party rights are, the smaller is the estate which is available for distribution and the smaller will be the dividend paid out to the debtor's unsecured creditors. Because of this, there are widely voiced concerns that the expansion of real rights—and the associated benefits to the few creditors in a position to claim them—has to be kept in check.[5]

A creditor who has no security simply has a right in common with all the other creditors of the insolvent to lodge a claim in the bankruptcy (of an individual) or the liquidation (of a company) and, when the assets of the insolvent have been realised, to receive a *pro rata* dividend. However, if a creditor holds security over a particular asset, then the creditor can withdraw that asset from the pool available to the general body of creditors and satisfy the outstanding debt (as far as possible) out of that asset notwithstanding that this might render it impossible for the unsecured creditors to be paid in full (or at all). This right to act outside the *pari passu* insolvency rules is a result of the right being classified as a security—a proprietary interest—so classification becomes very important.

3.1.2 Different forms of security interest

As noted earlier, the essence of a security interest is that the debtor grants the creditor some form of limited proprietary interest in the debtor's assets in order to secure the debt (or other obligation). There are four different forms of legal security device (although they can be put together in quite imaginative combinations). Two are *possessory securities*, where the effectiveness of the device depends upon the security-holder having possession of the secured asset. The other two are *non-possessory securities*, where such possession is not necessary. In outline, the four different forms are:

1. **Pledges**: these are possessory securities. They are created by the debtor assigning certain rights in the pledged asset to the creditor as security for repayment of the debt. The debtor (the pledgor) does not part with the full armoury of ownership rights, only with possession. To give a pledge, the debtor must therefore have the right of possession to give away, and the asset must be one where transfer of possession is possible (either actually, constructively or symbolically). This means that goods can be pledged, and so too can documentary intangibles (eg bills of lading and negotiable instruments). The creditor (the pledgee) has the right to retain possession of the pledged asset until the debtor discharges the underlying debt. The

[4] Subject to the insolvency rules, which specify that certain creditors are to be either preferred or deferred in the distribution of the insolvent's assets: Insolvency Act 1986 ss 40, 175, 74.

[5] See, eg, R Goode, 'Proprietary Rights and Unsecured Creditors' in BAK Rider (ed), *The Realm of Company Law* (1998, Kluwer: London) p 183 and the references cited.

creditor is not entitled to use the asset,[6] and the risk of damage lies with the creditor (who is classed as a bailee[7]). The creditor can, however, sell or make a gift of his or her limited interest as pledgee. Finally, and most importantly, the creditor can sell the pledged asset on default in payment by the debtor. Of course, the creditor is only entitled to use the sale proceeds to recoup the outstanding debt; the debtor is entitled to any surplus.

The business of local pawnbrokers is founded on the law of pledges. In addition, pledges (usually of documentary intangibles) are also an essential part of many much larger business transactions. Nevertheless, pledges provide a fairly crude security device. Since the debtor has to relinquish possession of the pledged asset, it is in practice impossible to pledge assets which are essential to the continuing operation of the debtor's social or business life. This limitation, inherent in all possessory securities, severely restricts their utility.

2. **Possessory (common law, statutory and contractual) liens**:[8] these possessory securities arise by custom, statute, or contract, respectively. Typically the debtor transfers possession of an asset to the creditor for particular purposes other than the creation of a security interest. For example, goods might be left for repair, or documents might be handed to a solicitor to enable legal work to be done. In certain circumstances (defined by custom, statute or contract), the creditor is entitled to detain possession of the debtor's property until the debtor's outstanding obligation has been met. It follows that a creditor who has already returned possession of the property to the debtor cannot assert this type of legal lien. Moreover, such liens do not generally[9] entitle the creditor to sell the asset to meet the debtor's obligation. This form of security therefore has severe limitations, whether seen from the creditor's or the debtor's perspective. The principal impact of these liens is to provide an additional means of exerting pressure on the debtor to pay up.
3. **Mortgages (*stricto sensu*[10])**: these are non-possessory securities.[11] They involve the assignment of legal title from the debtor (the mortgagor) to the creditor (the mortgagee), but the debtor usually retains possession. The creditor, as legal owner, has the ultimate right to possession, but the circumstances in which this right can be exercised are governed by the terms of the security agreement between the debtor and creditor. In addition to any limited right to possession, the debtor has an 'equity of redemption'—

[6] *The Odessa* [1916] 1 AC 145 (PC), 159.

[7] See Section 2.5 above.

[8] These securities must be distinguished from *equitable* liens, which are created by operation of law not by agreement between the parties: see Section 5.7 below.

[9] Although particular statutory provisions or contract terms might provide otherwise.

[10] Note that most real property 'mortgages' in the UK are not mortgages in the strict sense. They are legal charges permitted by the Law of Property Act 1925 Part III, which gives the 'mortgagor' all the rights associated with a strict mortgage without the need to transfer legal title to the mortgagee. This statutory change to real property securities has the advantage of making title to real property easier to trace because the legal owner does not change each time the property is subject to a 'mortgage'.

[11] Although of course the morgagor could bargain to have possession in addition to the legal incidents of a mortage.

a right to recover the legal title to the property on repayment of the debt. This equity of redemption is carefully protected. Equity has ensured that it can sometimes persist even when a debtor has breached time stipulations in the contract governing the repayment of the loan so that, on a strict reading, the creditor would be entitled to assert unencumbered ownership of the mortgaged asset. However, this protection has its limits; ultimately a breach of the underlying contract by the debtor will entitle the creditor to 'foreclose'—to demand unencumbered legal title to the mortgaged asset (ie title unencumbered by the debtor's equity of redemption).

4. **Charges**: these are non-possessory securities.[12] They differ from other security interests in that they involve the *creation of new proprietary rights* in the creditor. They are perhaps the most sophisticated form of security. The essence of a charge is that the secured property is made liable for the payment of a debt without there being *any* transfer of ownership or possession from the debtor (the chargor) to the creditor (the chargee). The debtor retains both ownership and possession of the asset; the creditor obtains neither. Instead the creditor obtains a new form of proprietary interest, a *charge*, over the secured property. Upon default by the debtor, the creditor is generally entitled by the terms of the security agreement to assume possession of the secured asset, sell it, and recoup the outstanding debt from the proceeds of sale (with any excess being returned to the debtor). Charges, unless they are created under a statute,[13] are always *equitable* charges.[14] These equitable charges can be either *fixed* or *floating*. The distinction turns on the rights of the debtor to use or deal with the charged assets during the term of the charge. The classification has important practical consequences for the effectiveness of the security, and is discussed later in this chapter.

In many respects this list of security devices proceeds from the simplest to the most sophisticated. Interestingly, the proprietary rights of *both* the debtor and the creditor are of greater personal benefit to each if the debtor's obligation is secured by a charge rather than by a pledge. Interestingly, too, the transition from pledge to charge represents an increasing level of theorising about property rights: pledges depend upon possession, a very tangible attribute of property; charges depend upon rights which are defined by contract and require no concurrent transfer of either title or possession. Because of their prevalence and utility, the focus of this chapter is on charges.

[12] Again, the chargee could bargain for possession, too, should this be necessary.

[13] See, eg, footnote 10.

[14] The difference between an equitable *charge* and an equitable *lien* is that the former is created by agreement between the parties and the latter by operation of law, although this distinction is not always recognised in judicial and non-judicial writings.

3.2 Pledges

3.2.1 The basic incidents of a pledge

[302] *The Odessa* [1916] 1 AC 145 (PC), 159:

> 'If the pledgee sells he does so by virtue of and to the extent of the pledgor's ownership, and not with a new title of his own. He must appropriate the proceeds of the sale to the payment of the pledgor's debt, for the money resulting from the sale is the pledgor's money to be so applied. The pledgee must account to the pledgor for any surplus after paying the debt. He must take care that the sale is a provident sale, and if the goods are in bulk he must not sell more than is reasonably sufficient to pay off the debt, for he only holds possession for the purpose of securing himself the advance which he has made. He cannot use the goods as his own. These considerations show that the right of sale is exercisable by virtue of an implied authority from the pledgor and for the benefit of both parties.'

FURTHER READING:

N Palmer and A Hudson, 'Pledge' in N Palmer and E McKendrick (eds), *Interests in Goods* (2nd edn, 1998, LLP: London), ch 24.

3.3 Possessory liens

3.3.1 Common law liens

The pledge, discussed above, is a possessory security which arises by agreement. Similar but more limited possessory securities arise by operation of law, and are known as common law possessory liens. Unless there has been statutory interference, such liens are dependent upon possession and give the creditor (the lienee) the right to detain possession of the asset only until the underlying obligation has been satisfied. They do not give the creditor the right of sale.

Possessory liens can be divided into general and particular liens. A general lien entitles the holder to detain the asset as security for payment of the full indebtedness of the owner, no matter on what account it may be due. A particular, or special, lien only entitles the holder to detain the asset as security for the payment of any charges which have been incurred in relation to the asset itself.

General liens are the exception rather than the rule, but the law recognises a general lien in favour of solicitors, banker, factors, stockbrokers and insurance brokers, as well as certain other parties. Particular liens, on the other hand, are intended to secure payment for services rendered in connection with particular chattels, whether it be cartage or storage, repair or improvement. The law then often implies a possessory lien, allowing the service-provider to detain possession of the chattel until the services delivered in connection with that chattel (and that chattel only) have been paid for.

It is an essential element of possessory liens that the creditor has physical or legal possession of the property. Moreover, possession must have been acquired legitimately (ie it cannot have been obtained by fraud or without authority) and with the consent of the debtor. The lien is lost if the creditor gives up possession to the debtor (or his or her agent), unless there is an express reservation of rights by the lienee. A possessory lien ceases to have effect when the debtor tenders the amount due.

3.3.2 Statutory liens

Liens granted by statute may duplicate common law liens in the rights that they deliver to the creditor, but grant those rights in circumstances where custom would not see a possessory lien as arising. If this is the import of the statute, then there are few concerns about drawing parallels between statutory and possessory liens, especially as they operate on the insolvency of the debtor. Insolvency is a critical time in this context because it throws into sharp relief the competition between different claimants to the debtor's property.

However, statutes are free to package security rights in different ways. It can then be more difficult to assess their proper impact on insolvency.

[303] *Bristol Airport plc v Powdrill* [1990] 1 Ch 744 (CA), 758–61 *per* Sir Nicolas Browne-Wilkinson V-C:

[An insolvent charter airline was operating leased aircraft under an administration order. The applicants, two airline operators, were unsecured creditors. They detained two of the airline's aircraft, purporting to act in accordance with the Civil Aviation Act 1982 section 88. Under the Insolvency Act 1986 section 11(3)(c), a creditor intending to enforce a 'lien or other security' over the company's 'property' required either the administrator's or the court's consent. The Court of Appeal held that the statutory right of detention was a 'lien or other security', even though it did not give the applicants any legal right to possession, and that it was over the company's 'property', notwithstanding that the company itself was only the lessee of the property in question.]

> '*The approach to the construction of the [Insolvency] Act of 1986*
>
> Before dealing with the issues summarised above, it may be helpful to state what, in my opinion, is the correct approach to the construction of the provisions dealing with administrators contained in Part II of the Act. The judge was very much influenced in his construction by the manifest statutory purpose of Part II of the Act. I agree with this approach. The provisions of Part II themselves, coupled with the mischief identified in the Cork Report, show that the statutory purpose is to install an administrator, as an officer of the court, to carry on the business of the company as a going concern with a view to achieving one or other of the statutory objectives mentioned in section 8(3). It is of the essence of administration under Part II of the Act that the business will continue to be carried on by the administrator. Such continuation of the business by the

administrator requires that there should be available to him the right to use the property of the company, free from interference by creditors and others during the, usually short, period during which such administration continues. Hence the restrictions on the rights of creditors and others introduced by sections 10 and 11 of the Act. In my judgment in construing Part II of the Act it is legitimate and necessary to bear in mind the statutory objective with a view to ensuring, if the words permit, that the administrator has the powers necessary to carry out the statutory objectives, including the power to use the company's property.

On the other hand, however desirable it may be to construe the Act in a way calculated to carry out the parliamentary purpose, it is not legitimate to distort the meaning of the words Parliament has chosen to use in order to achieve that result. Only if the words used by Parliament are fairly capable of bearing more than one meaning is it legitimate to adopt the meaning which gives effect to, rather than frustrates, the statutory purpose.

A. The issues under [Insolvency Act 1986] section 11(3)(c)

(1) Were the aircraft "property" of the company?

Mr. Lightman, for the airports, submits that because the aircraft were only held by Paramount under chattel-leases they are not "property." The aircraft, he submits, were the property of the ultimate lessor: Paramount has only contractual rights.

"Property" is defined by section 436 [of the Insolvency Act] as follows:

> " 'Property' includes money, goods, things in action, land and every description of property wherever situated and also obligations and every description of interest, whether present or future or vested or contingent, arising out of, or incidental to, property."

It is hard to think of a wider definition of property.

In my judgment, the interest of Paramount under a lease of the aircraft is plainly property within that definition. It is true that, to date, concepts of concurrent interests in personal property have not been developed in the same way as they have over the centuries in relation to real property. But modern commercial methods have introduced chattel-leasing. The Act of 1986 refers expressly to such leases: see section 10(4). Although a chattel lease is a contract, it does not follow that no property interest is created in the chattel. The basic equitable principle is that if, under a contract, A has certain rights over property as against the legal owner, which rights are specifically enforceable in equity, A has an equitable interest in such property. I have no doubt that a court would order specific performance of a contract to lease an aircraft, since each aircraft has unique features peculiar to itself. Accordingly in my judgment the "lessee" has at least an equitable right of some kind in that aircraft which falls within the statutory definition as being some "description of interest . . . arising out of, or incidental to" that aircraft.

(2) Is the statutory right of detention a "security over the company's property?"

Section 248 of the Act of 1986 defines "security" as including a "lien or other security." There was some discussion in the course of argument whether the statutory right of detention is strictly to be described as a "lien." It has many of the features of a lien. It is a right of retention of chattels enjoyed by a creditor against the payment of his charges for services rendered in relation to those chattels, similar to the rights enjoyed by, for example, repairers of goods. The fact that the right is conferred by statute is not inconsistent with it being a lien: see *Halsbury's Laws of England*, 4th ed., vol. 28 (1979), p. 223, para. 506. However, it is not a possessory lien of the classic type, since (as will appear hereafter) in my judgment the statutory right of detention conferred by section 88 does not give the airport legal possession of the aircraft whilst it is being detained. But there are many species of lien which do not depend on possession, for example certain equitable liens: p. 222, para. 503. In *Channel Airways Ltd. v. Manchester Corporation* [1974] 1 Ll.R. 456, Forbes J. held that a right very similar to the statutory right of detention but conferred by a Private Act was not strictly a lien.

Whether or not the statutory right of detention is strictly to be regarded as a lien, in my judgment apart from any special context it would certainly fall within the description "other security." Mr. Crystal, for the administrators, submitted the following description of a security: "Security is created where a person ('the creditor') to whom an obligation is owed by another ('the debtor') by statute or contract, in addition to the personal promise of the debtor to discharge the obligation, obtains rights exercisable against some property in which the debtor has an interest in order to enforce the discharge of the debtor's obligation to the creditor."

Whilst not holding that that is a comprehensive definition of "security," in my judgment it is certainly no wider than the ordinary meaning of the word. The statutory right of detention confers on the airport (as creditor) the right to detain and, with the leave of the court, sell the aircraft for the purpose of discharging debts incurred to that airport by the operator or by previous operators. In my judgment it is plainly a security.

I did not understand Mr. Lightman to take issue with those propositions in general. His submission was that the statutory right of detention has special features which make it sui generis and therefore the word "security" in sections 11 and 248 of the Act of 1986 should be construed so as to exclude this very special statutory right. He pointed out that the statutory right of detention extends to debts owed otherwise than by the person operating the aircraft at the time of detention; that a sale under section 88 can only take place with the leave of the court and operates to divest, not only the debtor's interests in the aircraft, but all other interests such as those of mortgagees and the ultimate owner. Moreover section 88(6) establishes its own order of priorities in the application of proceeds of sale of the aircraft.

Whilst accepting the force of these submissions, they do not persuade me that the words "other security" in the Act of 1986 ought to be given anything other than their natural meaning. The statutory right of detention in section 88, although unusual, is not unique. Parliament has conferred on port authorities similar rights in relation to the enforcement of the payment of port dues: see section 75 of the Port of London (Consolidation) Act 1920, quoted in *The Queen of the South* [1968] P. 449, 457. We were not referred to any case in which a specific statutory right has been held to fall completely outside the statutory framework laid down for dealing with insolvent companies. Moreover, to construe the Act of 1986 so as to exclude the statutory right of detention from its ambit would run counter to the purposes of the administration procedure since it would leave airports and those enjoying similar rights free to take action to enforce payment of their debts, thereby preventing or hindering continuation of the business by the administrator. In my judgment it would not be right to give the general words "other security" a narrower meaning than they would normally bear since that would tend to frustrate the purposes of Part II of the Act of 1986.

I therefore hold that the statutory right of detention is a "lien or other security" within the meaning of sections 11 and 248 of the Act of 1986. . . .'

Question:

Did Sir Nicolas Browne-Wilkinson V-C decide that a lien need not involve assignment of a right to possession to the creditor? *Could* the airline have assigned a right to possession of the aircraft?

Also see:

R M Goode, *Principles of Corporate Insolvency Law* (2nd edn, 1997, Sweet & Maxwell: London), p. 304

3.3.3 Contractual liens

As the name suggests, these liens arise by force of contract between the debtor and the creditor. Parties are free to enter into such contracts, but the courts are careful to look to the substance of the arrangement, not its form, to determine whether the security claimed is in fact a lien. The label given by the parties is not conclusive. The court's decision can have important consequences for the validity of the security. A possessory lien does not need to be registered; possession by the creditor rather than the debtor is considered sufficient notice to third parties. However, if the agreement is deemed to create a charge rather than a possessory lien, then matters are different. Many charges do require registration, and failure to register results in the charge being void as against the liquidator and other creditors.[15]

[304] ***George Barker (Transport) Ltd v Eynon*** **[1974] 1 WLR 462, 465–70, *per* Edmund Davies LJ:**
[The facts appear from the judgment.]

> 'The plaintiffs are transport contractors who from the autumn of 1970 had done regular business with Alderley Meats (U.K.) Ltd. (hereinafter called "the company"), who are meat importers. They collected the company's meat at the docks, and thence delivered it in their refrigerated trailers to the various customers of the company. It is common ground that all transport orders given by the company were accepted by the plaintiffs subject to the Conditions of Carriage of the Road Haulage Association Ltd. (revised April 1967). Condition 13 thereof is in the following terms:
>
> > "General Lien. The carrier shall have a general lien against the owner of any goods for any moneys whatsoever due from such owner to the carrier. If any lien is not satisfied within a reasonable time the carrier may at his absolute discretion sell the goods as agents for the owner and apply the proceeds towards the moneys due and the expenses of the sale, and shall upon accounting to the trader for the balance remaining, if any, be discharged from all liability whatsoever in respect of the goods."
>
> The practice followed was for the company to pay the plaintiffs' charges between four and six weeks after delivery of the consignments. The last payment before the events

[15] Companies Act 1985 s 395.

later giving rise to this litigation was made on August 5, 1971, and this covered transport charges incurred down to June 23.

Unknown to the plaintiffs, on February 5, 1970, that is, before they started doing business with Alderley Meats (U.K.) Ltd., the company had by a mortgage debenture charged its property to Westminster Bank Ltd. as a continuing security for the payment of all sums which at any time might become due to the bank as

> ". . . a floating security but so that the company is not to be at liberty to create any mortgage or charge in priority to or pari passu with the charge hereby created . . . or to deal with its book or other debts or securities for money otherwise than by getting in and realising the same in the ordinary course of business."

In accordance with their practice, the company sent to the plaintiffs on August 23, 1971, a transport order to collect from the "English Star, P. L.A. London," 649 cartons of New Zealand meat (roughly equivalent to 17 tons) and deliver them to consignees at Gravesend. By that date the company owed the plaintiffs £3,233.70 in respect of transport charges which they had incurred since June 23. As the consignment had been stored in two different parts of the vessel, the transport order was accompanied on this occasion by two delivery orders of the same date from the company, addressed to the superintendent of the Port of London Authority and requesting him to deliver to the plaintiffs (a) 333 cartons under order No. 3949, and (b) 316 cartons under order No. 3950.

. . .

[as events transpired, a receiver was appointed before this second delivery occurred.]

. . . The receiver was naturally anxious to achieve prompt delivery of the meat to Gravesend, so as to avoid its deterioration, and on September there were several discussions between him and the plaintiffs. Their effect was that, as Mocatta J. found [1973] 1 W.L.R. 1461, 1465:

> "it was orally agreed that the plaintiffs would deliver the 316 cartons to the consignees at Gravesend without prejudice to any general lien they might have upon the goods, that the receiver would in any event pay the plaintiffs' charges, which were £58. 40, for the delivery of the 316 cartons and, if the plaintiffs could thereafter establish they were entitled to refuse to deliver the cartons pursuant to their claimed general lien, the receiver would pay the plaintiffs the sum owed them by the company."

Following upon the making of this agreement, the plaintiffs duly delivered the 316 cartons at Gravesend the next day. Thereafter they wrote claiming their entitlement to payment of the sum of £3,335.30 on the aforementioned grounds, while the receiver repudiated all liability save in the sum of £58.40.

In dismissing the claim, Mocatta J. said, at p. 1468, that the real issue was

> "whether the appointment of the defendant as receiver on August 31, 1971, when the plaintiffs were not in possession of the 316 cartons, prevented the operation of condition 13 of the contract so as to allow the creation of a general lien subsequent to the plaintiffs' obtaining possession of the goods on September 2."

He expressed his conclusion in this way, at p. 1471:

> "At the date of the appointment of the receiver here the plaintiffs possessed no lien on any cartons of meat: they merely had a contractual right which, in certain circumstances, would give them a general lien. Before those circumstances arose, however, the receiver had been appointed."

This chronology constituted, so Mocatta J. considered, "a vital distinction" between the present case and such reported authorities as *In re Keever, A Bankrupt, Ex parte Trustee of the Property of the Bankrupt v. Midland Bank Ltd.* [1967] Ch. 182 where a lien was held to have come into existence before any receiving order was made. He concluded by saying, at p. 1472:

> "On the principles followed and applied in all the cases, the nonexistence of possession of goods before the appointment of a receiver is, in my judgment, fatal to reliance upon a lien dependent upon such possession, even though the extent of such a lien, had it arisen, would have been greatly enlarged beyond that available at common law by reason of a pre-appointment contract between the company and the party seeking to rely upon the lien against the receiver."

The judgment turned, accordingly, solely upon timing, Mocatta J., at p. 1470, regarding "the contractual right to exercise a general lien on coming into possession of goods in futuro" as having merely what he described as an "inchoate character" the realisation of which was defeated by the defendant's appointment as receiver before the plaintiffs ever gained physical possession.

The zeal of counsel, to whom the court is greatly indebted, led them to cite for our consideration some 32 reported decisions. At times we seemed in danger of never emerging from the thicket of authorities. And, when the receiver's counsel dilated upon the consternation which would be caused were we to reverse Mocatta J., it seemed almost preferable never to emerge from its umbrageous depths. But emerge we must, and describe what we at least think we saw within, and what in the end it all seems to come to. That I now proceed to do.

[After describing the relationship between the company and its receiver, Edmund Davies LJ continued:]

One consequence of the receiver's appointment by the debenture holders was that the incomplete assignment constituted by the 1970 deed became converted into a completed equitable assignment to them of the assets charged and of the company's rights. . . . Another was that, both by reason of clause 6 of the deed and under the ordinary law, the receiver became, on August 31, 1971, the agent of the company and not of the debenture holders. The company continued to deal with its assets under the receiver's direction and control. His duty being to carry on the business so as to preserve the goodwill, he must fulfil company trading contracts entered into before his appointment or render it liable in damages if he unwarrantably declined: see the authorities conveniently collected in *Buckley on the Companies Acts*, 13th ed. (1957), p. 244. And, as the assignment of the company's rights was subject to rights already given by the company to outside parties under ordinary trading contracts, neither the receiver nor the debenture holders were in any way relieved by the former's appointment from the obligations which by such pre-appointment contracts the company had undertaken.

. . .

2. The plaintiffs' contract.

I have already set out the terms of the transport contract made between the plaintiffs and the company on August 23, 1971, eight days before the appointment of the defendant as receiver. It had been entered into by the company in the ordinary course of business, and it was accordingly one which the company were perfectly free to enter into notwithstanding the 1970 debenture. And, as such, it remained in force notwithstanding the appointment of the receiver on August 31: *Parsons v. Sovereign Bank of Canada* [1913] A.C. 160. Assuming that the proper interpretation of what occurred between the parties on September 2 was that the defendant sought to repudiate the transport contract of August 23, it is nevertheless clear that the plaintiffs refused to accept that repudiation and insisted on fulfilling their part of the contract. This they were entitled to do—see *Avery v. Bowden* (1855) 5 E. & B. 714, *Denmark Productions Ltd. v. Boscobel Productions Ltd.* [1969] 1 Q.B. 699, 731 and *White and Carter (Councils) Ltd. v. McGregor* [1962] A.C. 413, 430—and it was greatly to their advantage, for thereby they stood to recompense themselves in full, as opposed to becoming merely one of the general body of unsecured creditors. It meant that under their general lien they could refuse to deliver up, either at Gravesend or anywhere else, the 316 cartons having a value of £4,755, until their claim for £3,335.30 was met and, furthermore, if payment was refused they were empowered by their contract to sell the meat and recoup themselves out of the proceeds of sale. If that be right, as I think it is, it follows that, delivery at Gravesend having been completed, the plaintiffs are entitled to succeed in the present appeal. The fact that the greater part of the 25 mile journey—that is, from Barking Depot onwards—was made after the "without prejudice" arrangement of September 3 does not, in my judgment, disentitle the plaintiffs (who had acquired possession strictly in accordance with their contract and pursuant to the authority so to do conferred on them by the company) to assert their general lien any more than the carrier in *Wiltshire Iron Co. Ltd. v. Great Western Railway Co.* (1871) L.R. 6 Q.B. 776 would have been had he carried out his contract.

But such a conclusion was vigorously contested by Mr. Phillips on a number of grounds. His submission that it was not open, either on the pleadings or on the notice of appeal, for the plaintiffs to approach the matter in this way is not, I think, well founded. It is furthermore clear from the judgment of Mocatta J. (see [1973] 1 W.L.R. 1461, 1470) that this was Mr. Tugendhat's primary submission below, there is nothing to indicate that his entitlement to make it was then challenged, and if it had been the challenge must surely have been dismissed.

More formidable points were, however, taken by Mr. Phillips, and they found acceptance in the lower court. He submitted that the making of the August 23 contract is irrelevant; that all it conferred on the plaintiffs was a right to a lien in certain events, the most important of them being the plaintiffs acquiring physical possession of the 316 cartons; that until this occurred they had no lien (see *Great Eastern Railway Co. v. Lord's Trustee* [1909] A.C. 109); that in fact they did not acquire possession until September 2 and that, as by then the receiver had already been appointed, the debenture holder's charge took precedence over the lien and entitled the receiver to demand the delivering up of the 316 cartons on payment simply of the £54.80 transport charges incurred in respect of that particular consignment.

One way in which Mr. Tugendhat sought before us to meet his opponent's submission that this is a contest relating to the priority of securities was to claim that the plaintiffs had been in constructive possession of the 316 cartons since August 23, that their lien therefore came into existence on that date and it accordingly preceded the defendant's appointment as receiver. The basis of this submission was that the company's transport order was accompanied, as I have already described, by two delivery orders addressed to the Port of London Authority, and thereby the company had done all it could to make delivery of the cartons of meat on that day to the plaintiffs. In this context, we were referred to the cases on constructive delivery of pawned chattels cited in *Halsbury's Laws of England*, 3rd ed. (1960), vol. 29, p. 214, and to *In re Keever, A Bankrupt* [1967] Ch. 182. This point had not been relied upon before Mocatta J. or raised in the plaintiff's notice of appeal. But, with the concurrence of defendant's counsel, we permitted the plaintiffs to amend their notice so as to raise the new point, subject to one important qualification which Mr. Phillips satisfied us we should in justice impose. This was that it would not be open to the plaintiffs to allege that the Port of London Authority had attorned to the plaintiffs before August 31. Such attornment was vital to the plaintiffs' claim to constructive possession before that date (see *Official Assignee of Madras v. Mercantile Bank of India Ltd.* [1935] A.C. 53, per Lord Wright, at pp. 58, 59), and, there being no evidence thereof and the plaintiffs being precluded from submitting that it had occurred, the case falls to be dealt with on the basis that they acquired no possession of the 316 cartons before September 2.

In these circumstances, stress was laid by defendant's counsel on what Mocatta J. described [1973] 1 W.L.R. 1461, 1468 as the "classic statement" of Romer J. in *Robson v. Smith* [1895] 2 Ch. 118, 124, that any dealing with company property in the ordinary course of business "will be binding on the debenture holders, provided that the dealing be completed before the debentures cease to be merely a floating security." On the grounds previously stated, Mr. Phillips submits that the "dealing" here with the company's 316 cartons had not been "completed" before August 31, in the sense that no lien, particular or general, had been acquired by them and he sought to distinguish the set off cases, ranging from *Collins v. Jones* (1830) 10 B. & C. 777 to *Rother Iron Works Ltd. v. Canterbury Precision Engineers Ltd.* [1973] 2 W.L.R. 281, to which we were referred, on the ground that whenever a right to set off had been successfully claimed the right had already accrued.

Despite the length of this judgment, I have in its course by no means explored again all the paths up which counsel on one side or the other took us and, with all respect to them, I do not propose doing so. In his peroration Mr. Phillips reminded us that the courts dislike general liens, which can unfairly favour one unsecured creditor out of the general body of such creditors, and ended by saying (and I quote his ipsissima verba),

> "The consequences of a decision against the receiver in this case would involve a grave inroad on the security of debenture holders, an unnecessary complication of receiverships and windings up, a scramble for possession in the days immediately after the appointment of a receiver, and detriment to the general body of creditors."

Well, we cannot say that nobody warned us. Nevertheless, at the end of the day, I have come to the conclusion that this case ultimately turns upon the question of whether the company could simply shrug off the contract it had entered into on August 23, 1971. Indeed, if the defendant is right, it would have been open to the receiver to require the plaintiffs to carry the 316 cartons of meat to Gravesend and, this having been done, he could then demand their delivery up without first paying even the £58.40 transport charge for that particular journey, leaving the plaintiffs merely to prove, with other unsecured creditors, for that and the rest of his much larger claims if a liquidation supervened. As Stamp L.J. pointed out during counsel's submission, it is difficult to reconcile that state of affairs with such decisions as *Parsons v. Sovereign Bank of Canada* [1913] A.C. 160 and *Rother Iron Works Ltd. v. Canterbury Precision Engineers Ltd.* [1973] 2 W.L.R. 281. My conclusion, in the light of those cases, is that the debenture holders could assert their position as assignees of the company's property and contractual rights in the meat only by themselves recognising and giving effect to the pre-appointment contractual rights of the plaintiffs. These included a general lien, and that became exercisable when the plaintiffs acquired actual possession on September 2, and this nonetheless because three days earlier the defendant had been appointed receiver. I find myself therefore unable to accept as correct the "vital factor" which Mocatta J. regarded as distinguishing *Rother's* case from the present one. On the contrary, the two cases appear to call for the same approach and should, mutatis mutandis, have led to similar conclusions.

In the result, I would be for allowing this appeal and granting the relief sought by the plaintiffs.

[Stamp LJ and Sir Gordon Wilmer delivered concurring judgments.]

Question:

Does this mean that a creditor with a contractual lien can have proprietary rights in the asset as soon as there is an agreement for a lien, *before* possession of the asset is transferred to the creditor? What are the defining characteristics of a possessory lien?

[305] *In Re Welsh Irish Ferries Ltd* [1986] Ch 471, 477–9 *per* Nourse J:
[A ferry company chartered a vessel from ship-owners. Hire was payable half-monthly in advance. The contract gave the owners a lien upon all sub-freights for any amounts due under the charter. The court held that this created an equitable charge on the company's book debts (the sub-freights), which was registrable according to the clear wording of what is now Companies Act 1985 section 396. Since the lien was not registered, the bank's subsequent fixed charge took priority. This conclusion was reached reluctantly since it was settled commercial practice—for good commercial reasons—not to register contractual liens of this kind. However, that could not be persuasive in the face of the clear language of the statute.]

'I now come to the first question [ie whether the lien creates an equitable charge]. It is established by the decision of the Court of Appeal in *Tagart, Beaton Co. v. James Fisher & Sons* [1903] 1 K.B. 391 that a lien on sub-freights can only be enforced by the shipowner before the shipper has made payment to the charterer. It confers no right to follow the money after it has been paid. Although it is not easy to get at the facts of that case, counsel are agreed that they were correctly understood by Greer J. in *Molthes Rederi Aktieselskabet v. Ellerman's Wilson Line Ltd.* [1927] 1 K.B. 710, 716–717, where he described it as one in which the bill of lading had been made out to the charterers. In other words, the substance of the contractual relationship between shippers, charterers and owners was the same as it is in the present case. The owners' right to payment of freight existed only under their lien.

What then is the legal effect of the lien? It is clearly not, as is the shipowner's lien on cargoes, a possessory lien. Nor, although this is really only a question of terminology, do I think that it can properly be described as an equitable lien. That admittedly is something which exists independently of possession and gives rise to a charge, but it arises by operation of law out of the relationship between the parties and not out of an express contract; for example, a vendor's lien for unpaid purchase money or a trustee's lien for expenses. The lien on sub-freights is the creature of an express contract. Its effect is to give the shipowner a limited right to require payment from the shipper of money which is owed by the shipper to the charterer. The charterer has a chose in action against the shipper. The limited right to that chose can only, as it seems to me, be acquired by the shipowner by virtue of some assignment, necessarily equitable, made by the charterer. That was how it was put in argument by Mr. Oliver for the bank and the logic of it is unanswerable.

Then, it must be asked, what sort of an equitable assignment is it? Having been given for any amounts due under the charter, it obviously cannot be an out-and-out assignment. It can only be an assignment by way of security for what is owed by the charterer to the shipowner. It is established law that an equitable assignment of a chose in action by way of security creates an equitable charge on the chose: see, e.g., *In re Kent & Sussex Sawmills Ltd.* [1947] Ch. 177 which, as it happens, was a case where the charge was held to be void for non-registration under the predecessor of section 95; and see also *Walter & Sullivan Ltd. v. J. Murphy & Sons Ltd.* [1955] 2 Q.B. 584. Accordingly, it would seem clear on analysis that the lien creates an equitable charge on the sub-freights, but I must now consider an argument to the contrary and such assistance on the point as is to be found in the authorities.

Mr. Millett, for the owners, submitted that the shipowner's inability to follow the sub-freight into the hands of the charterer demonstrates that the lien gives the shipowner no proprietary right in the sub-freight, with the result that an essential element of a charge is missing. I think that that submission proceeds on a confusion between the nature of the right and the event which defeats it. If, for example, the shipper were to make payment not to the charterer but to some third party who had notice of the lien, it could not be doubted that the shipowner could follow the money into the hands of the third party. The reason why he cannot follow it into the hands of the charterer is because it is the very event of payment to him which defeats the right. The assignment is, as Mr. Oliver described it, defeasible in that event. But, until defeated, it is nonetheless an assignment by way of security . . .'

Also see:

Care Shipping v Itex Itagrani Exports, The Cebu [1993] 3 WLR 609.

FURTHER READING:

For an alternative analysis, see F Oditah, 'The Juridical Nature of a Lien on Sub-Freights' [1989] *LMCLQ* 191, who argues that the lien is a personal right, *sui generis*, to intercept freight before payment.

3.4 Mortgages

3.4.1 The nature of a mortgage

[306] *Re Bond Worth* [1980] 1 Ch 228 (ChD), 248–9, 253 *per* Slade J, applying *Re George Inglefield Ltd* [1933] Ch 1 (CA), 27–8 *per* Romer LJ:

[Monsanto supplied man-made yarn to Bond Worth Ltd, a carpet-manufacturing company. In part, the supply contract purported to retain 'equitable and beneficial title' to the yarn in Monsanto until full payment for the goods had been received from Bond Worth. Litigation centred on interpreting this term. If the term created a charge in favour of Monsanto, then the charge would be void for non-registration under the equivalent of the Companies Act 1985 section 395. If it created some other form of security, then it might afford protection to Monsanto. A longer part of this judgment is extracted at **[313]** below.]

> 'In my judgment, any contract which, by way of security for the payment of a debt, confers an interest in property defeasible or destructible upon payment of such debt, or appropriates such property for the discharge of the debt, must necessarily be regarded as creating a mortgage or charge, as the case may be. The existence of the equity of redemption is quite inconsistent with the existence of a bare trustee-beneficiary relationship.
>
> The fact that all the characteristics of a mortgage or charge are to be found present in the retention of title clause [with which this case is concerned] is borne out by a passage from the judgment of Romer L.J. in *In re George Inglefield Ltd.* [1933] Ch. 1. There he summarises the essential characteristics of a mortgage, at pp. 27–28:
>
> > "In a transaction of sale the vendor is not entitled to get back the subject matter of the sale by returning to the purchaser the money that has passed between them. In the case of a mortgage or charge, the mortgagor is entitled, until he has been foreclosed, to get back the subject matter of the mortgage or charge by returning to the mortgagee the money that has passed between them. The second essential difference is that if the mortgagee realises the subject matter of the mortgage for a sum more than sufficient to repay him, with interest and the costs, the money that has passed between him and the mortgagor he has to account to the mortgagor for the surplus. If the purchaser sells the subject matter of the purchase, and realises a profit, of course he has not got to account to the vendor for the profit. Thirdly, if the mortgagee realises the mortgage property for a sum that is insufficient to repay him the money that he has paid to the mortgagor, together with interest and costs, then the mortgagee is entitled to recover from the mortgagor the balance of the money, either because there is a covenant by the mortgagor to repay the money advanced by the mortgagee, or because of the existence of the simple contract debt which is created by the mere fact of the advance having been made."
>
> Mutatis mutandis all these three features of a charge are present in this case. Bond Worth was entitled to redeem the charge in favour of Monsanto by paying to it the outstanding debt due under the relevant order. If Monsanto, in exercise of the rights conferred on it by the retention of title clause, were to compel a sale of the relevant assets for a sum more than sufficient to pay this debt, the parties' intention was surely that Bond Worth, rather than Monsanto, would be entitled to receive the surplus. In contrast, if such last-mentioned sale were to produce a sum less than the outstanding debt, they surely intended that Monsanto would remain entitled to recover the balance from Bond Worth as a simple contract debt.
>
> [And later, to explain why it was the debtor who had granted the security and not the supplier/creditor who had 'reserved' an interest in the yarn, Slade J continued:]
>
> A concept familiar to conveyancers is that, on a grant of land, it is possible for the grantor to except out of that which is granted something which is actually in existence at the time of the grant, such as mines and minerals. The effect of such exception is not to include in the grant that which is excepted; and, correspondingly, it will take effect even though the grantee has not executed the relevant instrument. However, no authority has been cited which satisfies me that on the transfer of the legal property in land or chattels, it is competent to a vendor expressly to except from the grant in favour of

himself an equitable mortgage or charge thereon to secure the unpaid purchase price (in addition to or in substitution for any lien which may arise by operation of law), in such manner that the exception will take effect without any express or implied grant back of a mortgage or charge in the vendor's favour by the purchaser. In my judgment, as a matter of conveyancing in the case of land, the proper course is to follow that actually adopted by the conveyancers in *Capital Finance Co. Ltd. v. Stokes* [1969] 1 Ch. 261 and described by Harman L.J. at p. 277 as "the ordinary conveyancing practice"; this is for the documentation to contain an express grant of the entire legal and beneficial title, followed by an immediate grant back of the requisite mortgage or charge. In the case of either land or personal property, an express or implied grant back in favour of the original grantor is in my judgment required to create such mortgage or charge. If the court is satisfied that both parties to a transaction of sale have contracted that the vendor shall have defined rights by way of mortgage or charge over the subject matter of the sale, no doubt it will be prepared to imply the necessary grant back of such rights by the purchaser, even though inappropriate words, for example words by way of purported exception, may have been used; equity will regard as done that which ought to be done. This does not, however, remove the theoretical necessity of a grant back.'

Question:

Has the 'grant and grant back' thesis adopted by Slade J survived the decision of the House of Lords in *Abbey National Building Society v Cann* [1991] 1 AC 56? Does the answer to this question affect the validity of the outcome in the *Bond Worth* case?

3.4.2 Distinction between a mortgage, an equitable mortgage and an equitable charge

[307] *Swiss Bank Corp v Lloyds Bank* [1982] AC 584, 594–8 *per* Buckley LJ in the CA (confirmed by the House of Lords):

[One of the defendants had borrowed foreign currency to purchase foreign securities. The borrower had covenanted to observe all the conditions attached to the Bank of England consent which had been required for the transaction. The conditions included a requirement that the securities be held in a separate account, and that the loan be repaid from the proceeds of the sale of the securities. The claimant lender unsuccessfully argued before both the Court of Appeal and the House of Lords that these terms constituted the lender a chargee or an equitable mortgagee, with a security interest which therefore had priority over an equitable charge which had been subsequently granted to Lloyds Bank by the purchaser. This conclusion turned on a finding that the Bank of England terms were not intended to operate as a security, and so the contract requiring their performance was not specifically enforceable. The lender therefore acquired no proprietary interest in the securities or their proceeds.]

'The first question for consideration is whether the judge was right in holding that the loan agreement gave rise to an equitable charge in favour of the plaintiff. The way in which the plaintiff puts its claim to be entitled to such charge is this. By clause 3 (b) of the loan agreement I.F.T. covenanted that all conditions of all necessary consents and authorisations for the service, maintenance and repayment of the loan would be observed by I.F.T. during the continuance of the agreement. The final paragraph of the conditions required that, in view of the terms of sub-paragraphs (iv) and (vi) of the conditions, the securities acquired with the foreign currency borrowing would be kept on a separate account to distinguish them from any other foreign currency securities owned by the borrower. Condition (vi) required interest and other charges in respect of the borrowing and management expenses to be paid out of the income arising from the foreign currency securities acquired, and condition (vii), which I have already read, required the loan to be repaid out of the proceeds of the foreign currency securities in question or, in the event of a shortfall and subject to Bank of England permission, with "investment currency." So, the plaintiff contends, the loan agreement contractually bound I.F.T. to keep the F.I.B.I. securities and any capital moneys arising from them and any investments of such capital moneys (which I shall call comprehensively "the fruits of the borrowing") segregated as a separate fund, to service the loan out of the income and capital of that fund and to repay the loan primarily out of it. Mr. Parker, for the plaintiff, accepts that as between I.F.T. and the Bank of England the Bank of England conditions imposed no positive obligations on I.F.T. They imposed restrictions on I.F.T. in their use of the fruits of the loan if in the event I.F.T. took up the loan. Condition (vii) was a prohibition against repaying the loan in any manner not thereby authorised. But Mr. Parker contends that, as between I.F.T. and the plaintiff, condition (vii) in conjunction with clause 3 (b) gave rise to a positive contractual obligation on the part of I.F.T. to repay the loan primarily out of the fruits of the loan. Relying mainly on *In re Nanwa Gold Mines Ltd.* [1955] 1 W.L.R. 1080, Mr. Parker says that the consequence of this is that that contractual obligation was specifically enforceable by the court and consequently gave rise to an equitable interest in the plaintiff of a proprietary nature in the fruits of the loan, which, since it was created by way of security only, is properly described as an equitable charge.

We are not concerned here with a charge on an equitable interest in property but with an equitable charge upon property in the legal ownership of the party creating the charge.

An equitable charge may, it is said, take the form either of an equitable mortgage or of an equitable charge not by way of mortgage. An equitable mortgage is created when the legal owner of the property constituting the security enters into some instrument or does some act which, though insufficient to confer a legal estate or title in the subject matter upon the mortgagee, nevertheless demonstrates a binding intention to create a security in favour of the mortgagee, or in other words evidences a contract to do so: see *Fisher and Lightwood's Law of Mortgage*, 9th ed. (1977), p. 13. An equitable charge which is not an equitable mortgage is said to be created when property is expressly or constructively made liable, or specially appropriated, to the discharge of a debt or some other obligation, and confers on the chargee a right of realisation by judicial process, that is to say, by the appointment of a receiver or an order for sale: see *Fisher and Lightwood*, p. 14. It is not, I think, necessary to determine in the present case in what circumstances there is a true distinction between these two types of charge or precisely where it lies. From the way in which the judge dealt with the matter in his judgment it is, I think, clear that he was applying his mind to the question whether the circumstances of the case gave rise to an equitable charge by way of mortgage. The argument in this court has also proceeded upon the same lines, but I must not overlook the possibility of the existence of an equitable charge which is not of the nature of a mortgage.

The essence of any transaction by way of mortgage is that a debtor confers upon his creditor a proprietary interest in property of the debtor, or undertakes in a binding manner to do so, by the realisation or appropriation of which the creditor can procure the discharge of the debtor's liability to him, and that the proprietary interest is redeemable, or the obligation to create it is defeasible, in the event of the debtor discharging his liability. If there has been no legal transfer of a proprietary interest but merely a binding undertaking to confer such an interest, that obligation, if specifically enforceable, will confer a proprietary interest in the subject matter in equity. The obligation will be specifically enforceable if it is an obligation for the breach of which damages would be an inadequate remedy. A contract to mortgage property, real or personal, will, normally at least, be specifically enforceable, for a mere claim to damages or repayment is obviously less valuable than a security in the event of the debtor's insolvency. If it is specifically enforceable, the obligation to confer the proprietary interest will give rise to an equitable charge upon the subject matter by way of mortgage.

It follows that whether a particular transaction gives rise to an equitable charge of this nature must depend upon the intention of the parties ascertained from what they have done in the then existing circumstances. The intention may be expressed or it may be inferred. If the debtor undertakes to segregate a particular fund or asset and to pay the debt out of that fund or asset, the inference may be drawn, in the absence of any contra indication, that the parties' intention is that the creditor should have such a proprietary interest in the segregated fund or asset as will enable him to realise out of it the amount owed to him by the debtor: compare *In re Nanwa Gold Mines Ltd.* [1955] 1 W.L.R. 1080 and contrast *Moseley v. Cressey's Co.* (1865) L.R. 1 Eq. 405 where there was no obligation to segregate the deposits. But notwithstanding that the matter depends upon the intention of the parties, if upon the true construction of the relevant documents in the light of any admissible evidence as to surrounding circumstances the parties have entered into a transaction the legal effect of which is to give rise to an equitable charge in favour of one of them over property of the other, the fact that they may not have realised this consequence will not mean that there is no charge. They must be presumed to intend the consequence of their acts.

In the present case the loan agreement contained no express requirement that I.F.T. should charge the F.I.B.I. securities or the fruits of the borrowing by way of mortgage to secure repayment of the loan. Such intention must be found, if at all, by implication.

A binding obligation that a particular fund shall be applied in a particular manner may found no more than an injunction to restrain its application in another way, but if the obligation be to pay out of the fund a debt due by one party to the transaction to the other, the fund belonging to or being due to the debtor, this amounts to an equitable assignment pro tanto of the fund: see *Rodick v. Gandell* (1852) 1 De G.M. & G. 763, 777 and *Palmer v. Carey* [1926] A.C. 703, 706–707:

> "This is but an instance of a familiar doctrine of equity that a contract for valuable consideration to transfer or charge a subject matter passes a beneficial interest by way of property in that subject matter if the contract is one of which a court of equity will decree specific performance."

With this in mind I address myself to the construction and effect of clause 3 (b) of the loan agreement.

. . .

The covenant is, in my opinion, in substance a negative one, viz. not to do anything which might invalidate the bargain between the parties; but, although some argument was addressed to us based upon this negative quality, it is not that which weighs with me. What is to my mind important is that there is here no obligation to repay the loan out of the fruits of the borrowing in any event; the covenant merely requires I.F.T. to repay the loan in a manner approved by the Bank of England. No doubt the plaintiff could have objected to repayment in any manner not so approved and could have obtained an injunction restraining such repayment, if this would have served any useful purpose; but the covenant does not, in my judgment, confer upon the plaintiff any specifically enforceable right to have the loan repaid out of the F.I.B.T. securities or out of any other fruits of the borrowing. It consequently did not, in my judgment, give rise to an equitable charge by way of mortgage.

Nor, in my opinion, can it have given rise to a charge of a kind to which the remedies of a mortgagee would not have attached but which would have been enforceable by the appointment of a receiver or an order for sale. In *National Provincial and Union Bank of England v. Charnley* [1924] 1 K.B. 431 it seems that Atkin L.J. may have had a charge of this nature in mind. He said, at pp. 449–450:

> "... I think there can be no doubt that where in a transaction for value both parties evince an intention that property, existing or future, shall be made available as security for the payment of a debt, and that the creditor shall have a present right to have it made available, there is a charge, even though the present legal right which is contemplated can only be enforced at some future date, and though the creditor gets no legal right of property, either absolute or special, or any legal right to possession, but only gets a right to have the security made available by an order of the court."

In the present case I do not consider that it can properly be said that the parties evinced an intention that the F.I.B.I. securities or any other fruits of the borrowing should be made available as security for repayment of the loan. The only intention which they evinced was that the loan should be repaid in a manner approved by the Bank of England.

Accordingly, in my judgment, the loan agreement did not give rise to any equitable charge in favour of the plaintiff. ...'

Note:

What does Slade J, in *Re Bond Worth* (**[306]** above), see as the essential difference between a mortgage and a charge? His elision of mortgages (at least equitable mortgages) and charges is repeated in other judicial statements. Nevertheless, there is a fundamental difference between the two forms of security. This is true even though many fact situations enable the parties to choose freely between the two forms, each serving the same purpose and providing much the same level of protection. To create a mortgage, the debtor must *transfer ownership* of the mortgaged property (either legal or equitable ownership) to the creditor *for the purpose of* providing security for some underlying personal obligation. Moreover, the *Swiss Bank case* (**[307]** above) shows that even before the necessary transfer of ownership takes place, a creditor who has advanced funds on the basis of an *agreement* to create a mortgage will have security. This follows because the agreement to grant a security is a specifically enforceable obligation: damages would provide an inadequate remedy. If an agreement is specifically enforceable, then equity treats as done that which ought to be done—equity regards the parties as already in the position they will be in once the agreement is performed. The creditor is said to have an *equitable mortgage*.[16] With both legal and equitable mortgages, then, the underlying transaction involves a transfer of ownership for the purposes of providing security. It is this which distinguishes mortgages from charges, which are discussed below.

3.5 Equitable charges

3.5.1 General features of charges

As already noted, an equitable charge is different from the other forms of security so far discussed. It involves the creation of a new proprietary interest in the secured creditor; the debtor does not give up legal or equitable ownership or, necessarily, the right to possession of the charged asset. This makes a charge an amenable form of security from the debtor's perspective. A charge can be created very easily: the debtor (the 'chargor') simply agrees with the creditor (the 'chargee') the certain assets (the 'charged assets') will be appropriated to the discharge of a debt or other obligation. The charge, and the creditor's proprietary interest in the charged asset, lasts only as long as the secured obligation remains unperformed. The creditor's rights may be enforced by a sale of the charged property, if necessary by a court order although most security documents provide for such sale without recourse to the courts. The creditor (or the court) normally exercises these powers of sale (and any other powers given to the creditor) by the appointment of a *receiver* to look after the creditor's interests.

A charge can be created over any identified property,[17] either present or future. The need for the property to be adequately identified is obvious: both parties must know which assets are subject to the security. An agreement to create a charge over *present* property (property already owned by the debtor) gives the creditor an immediate proprietary interest in the charged property even though the creditor has no immediate right of sale (and may never acquire such rights if the underlying debt or other obligation is satisfied). An agreement granting a charge over *future* property (property not yet owned by the debtor), if it is made for valuable consideration, is specifically enforceable once the property comes into the debtor's hands. The effect of such an agreement is therefore that a charge is deemed to come into existence as soon as the property is acquired by the debtor: *Holroyd v Marshall* (1862) 10 HL Cas 191 (see **[432]** below). Until the debtor acquires the property, the creditor has no proprietary interest (there is no property in which such an interest can be claimed). When the debtor does acquire the property, however, it is immediately

[16] Perhaps confusingly, the creditor is also sometimes said to have an equitable charge by way of mortgage, presumably to acknowledge the fact that the creditor does not have legal title to the mortgaged asset. However, it must be true that the creditor has *equitable* title by way of mortgage security—and so is simply an equitable mortgagee. To use different terminology is simply confusing. As will be seen later, with specifically enforceable contracts to confer legal title (not by way of security), we simply say that the purchaser has equitable *ownership*.

[17] Although see the discussion in Section 3.6.5 below.

burdened with the creditor's equitable security interest—there is no need for the debtor specifically to appropriate the property to the security. The debtor never for an instant has unencumbered title to the charged asset.

The next extract indicates that a charge will only arise if the parties intend the creditor to have a *present* right to have the charged property made available as security for a debt. The charged property may include assets currently owned by the debtor and also assets which will be acquired in the future.

[308] *National Provincial Bank v Charnley* [1924] 1 KB 431 (CA), 449–50 *per* Atkin LJ:

[The facts are immaterial.]

> 'It is not necessary to give a formal definition of a charge, but I think there can be no doubt that where in a transaction for value both parties evince an intention that property, existing or future, shall be made available as security for the payment of a debt, and that the creditor shall have a present right to have it made available, there is a charge, even though the present legal right which is contemplated can only be enforced at some future date, and though the creditor gets no legal right of property, either absolute or special, or any legal right to possession, but only gets a right to have the security made available by an order of the Court. If those conditions exist I think there is a charge. If, on the other hand, the parties do not intend that there should be a present right to have the security made available, but only that there should be a right in the future by agreement, such as a licence, to seize the goods, there will be no charge. . . .'

Also see:

Swiss Bank Corporation v Lloyds Bank Ltd [1982] AC 584 (CA and HL), **[307]** above.

3.5.2 Fixed and floating charges

Charges, whether over present or future property, can be either fixed or floating. A *fixed* (or 'specific') charge is one which restricts the debtor's power to dispose of or otherwise deal with the charged property without first obtaining the creditor's consent. A *floating* charge, on the other hand, permits the debtor the freedom to deal with the charged property in the ordinary course of business without recourse to the creditor. This liberty to deal with the charged assets continues until the floating charge *crystallises* into a fixed charge. The parties can nominate in the charge document when this will happen, and in any event the charge will crystallise by operation of law if the debtor company ceases to carry on business for any reason. A floating charge thus allows the debtor to give security over assets which need to be turned over in order to conduct the debtor's business. These include assets such as stock in trade, raw materials and book debts. These assets often represent a significant part of the value of the debtor's business and may provide the only worthwhile form of security. It is said that only a company can grant a floating charge, and that this form of security is not available to individual borrowers.[18]

[18] L S Sealy, *Cases and Materials in Company Law* (6th edn, 1996, Butterworths: London), p 424. However, it is not clear why this should be so.

Categorisation of a charge as fixed or floating is based on the substance of the arrangement between the parties, not on the label they attach to their arrangement.[19] The cases extracted below indicate the process adopted by the courts in making their determinations. The distinction has important consequences. Fixed and floating charge holders are treated differently, both during receivership and on the insolvency of the debtor. For example:

1. the holder of a floating (but not a fixed) charge over all or substantially all of the company's assets can block the appointment of an administrator, and so deny a company the benefit of a moratorium period during which a rescue plan can be implemented: Insolvency Act 1986 sections 9(3), 11(1);
2. the holder of a floating charge (but not a fixed charge) is deferred in the distribution of the proceeds of realisation of the security to the company's preferential creditors in a receivership or a winding up: Insolvency Act 1986 sections 40, 175;
3. floating charges are subject to specific invalidating provisions which do not apply to fixed charges: eg Insolvency Act 1986 section 245 (re floating charges granted for no new consideration).

The only other point which needs to be noted specifically is that a charge, whether fixed or floating, is an equitable proprietary interest created by contract. It follows that the rights of the creditor depend upon there being a valid contract and, even more importantly, those rights may only be created for consideration (see *Re Earl of Lucan* (1890) 45 Ch D 470).

3.5.3 Limitations on dealing with assets subject to a fixed charge

[309] *Siebe Gorman & Co Ltd v Barclays Bank Ltd* [1979] 2 Lloyd's Rep 142 (Ch D), 159 *per* Slade J:

[The debtor company executed a debenture in favour of Barclays Bank which, by its terms, included a 'first fixed charge [on] all book debts[20] and other debts now and from time to time due or owing to the Company'. The debenture further provided that '[d]uring the continuance of this security the Company . . . shall pay into the Company's account with the Bank [Barclays] all monies which it may receive in respect of the book debts and other debts hereby charged and shall not without the prior consent of the Bank in writing purport to charge or assign the same in favour of any other person and shall if called upon to do so by the Bank execute a legal assignment of such book debts and other debts to the Bank'. Slade J held that a fixed charge had be created, even though the company had the right to collect the book debts.]

[19] Eg *Re Armagh Shoes Ltd* [1984] BCLC 405 *per* Hutton J, holding that the charge was floating even though stated to be fixed. Although there was no provision for crystallisation, this did not matter: the charge would crystallise on the winding up of the company or the appointment of a receiver (pp. 408–11, 419). Also see *Re Brightlife Ltd* [1987] Ch 200, 209 *per* Hoffmann J (see **[323]** below).

[20] Also termed 'receivables'.

'If the debenture on its true construction had given the bank no rights whatsoever, at a time when the account of R. H. McDonald Ltd. was in credit, to prevent the company from spending in the ordinary course of business all or any of the proceeds of book debts paid into its account, I would have been inclined to regard the charge, for all the wording of the debenture, as doing no more than "hovering over and so to speak floating with" the book debts, within the words of Lord Macnaghten [see **[311]** below]. Such I would conceive, is the effect of a charge on future book debts in the form more usually employed. Commonly it is intended, by both creditor and debtor, that the debtor shall have the free disposal of the proceeds of future book debts which may come into his hands, so long as the creditor takes no steps to enforce his security, or the charge has not otherwise crystallised.

In my judgment, however, it is perfectly possible in law for a mortgagor, by way of continuing security for future advances, to grant to a mortgagee a charge on future book debts in a form which creates in equity a specific charge on the proceeds of such debts as soon as they are received and consequently prevents the mortgagor from disposing of an unencumbered title to the subject matter of such charge without the mortgagee's consent, even before the mortgagee has taken steps to enforce its security: (compare *Evans Coleman and Evans Ltd. v. R. A. Nelson Construction Ltd.*, 16 D.L.R. 123). This in my judgment was the effect of the debenture in the present case. I see no reason why the Court should not give effect to the intention of the parties, as stated in cl. 3(d), that the charge should be a first fixed charge on book debts. I do not accept the argument that the provisions of cl. 5(c) negative the existence of a specific charge. All that they do, in my judgment, is to reinforce the specific charge given by cl. 3. The mere fact that there may exist certain forms of dealing with book debts which are not specifically prohibited by cl. 5(c) does not in my judgment turn the specific charge into a floating charge.

This conclusion that the charge is a specific charge involves the further conclusion that, during the continuance of the security, the bank would have the right, if it chose, to assert its lien under the charge on the proceeds of the book debts, even at a time when the particular account into which they were paid was temporarily in credit. However, I see nothing surprising in this conclusion, bearing in mind that the charge afforded continuing security to the bank not only in respect of any indebtedness on that particular account but also in respect of any other indebtedness of R. H. McDonald Ltd. to the bank. The bank's lien would, after all, continue only during the subsistence of the debenture, which the debtor would at all times have the right to redeem.

For these reasons, I conclude that the debenture on its true construction conferred on the bank a specific charge in equity on all future book debts owed to R. H. McDonald Ltd. and that, subject to any rights of Siebe Gorman as assignee of the relevant bills, the rights of the bank, as specific chargee, attached in equity to their proceeds as soon as they were paid.'

Question:

Was the debtor *in fact* restricted in its dealings with the proceeds, or could it use them at will after it had paid them into the nominated account? Does this feature weaken the conclusions reached in this case? (See the discussion of floating charges, below.)

Note:

If the creditor is a bank, then it is relatively easy to restrict the debtor's dealings with the proceeds of any sales of the charged assets. It is more difficult for other creditors. However, in *Re Cimex Tissues Ltd* [1994] BCC 626, [1995] 1 BCLC 409, a charge over plant and machinery was held to be a fixed charge notwithstanding that it was contemplated that some of the charged items might be repaired and even replaced over time as they wore out.

3.6 Floating charges

3.6.1 Classic definitions of the floating charge

[310] *Re Yorkshire Woolcombers Association* [1903] 2 Ch 284 (CA), 295 *per* Romer LJ:

[The facts are immaterial.]

> 'I certainly do not intend to attempt to give an exact definition of the term 'floating charge', nor am I prepared to say that there will not be a floating charge, within the meaning of the [Companies] Act, which does not contain all three characteristics which I am about to mention, but I certainly think that if a charge has the three characteristics that I am about to mention it is a floating charge. (1) If it is a charge on a class of assets of a company present and future; (2) if that class is one which, in the ordinary course of the business of the company, would be changing from time to time; and (3) if you find that by the charge it is contemplated that, until some future step is taken by or on behalf of those interested in the charge, the company may carry on its business in the ordinary way as far as concerns the particular class of assets I am dealing with.'

[311] *Illingworth v Houldsworth* [1904] AC 355 (HL), 357 *per* Earl of Halsbury LC, and 358 *per* Lord Macnaghten:

[This is the appeal to the House of Lords of the decision in *Re Yorkshire Woolcombers Association*, **[310]** above.]

> ***Earl of Halsbury LC:***
> 'In the first place you have that which in a sense I suppose must be an element in the definition of a floating security, that it is something which is to float, not to be put into immediate operation, but such that the company is to be allowed to carry on its business. It contemplates not only that it [the security] should carry with it the book debts [the charged assets] which were then existing, but it contemplates also the possibility of those book debts being extinguished by a payment to the company, and that other book debts should come in and take the place of those that had disappeared. That . . . seems to me to be an essential characteristic of what is properly called a floating security. . . .'
>
> ***Lord Macnaghten:***
> 'I should have thought there was not much difficulty in defining what a floating charge is in contrast to what is called a specific charge. A specific charge, I think, is one that without more fastens on ascertained and definite property or property capable of being ascertained and defined; a floating charge, on the other hand, is ambulatory and shift-

ing in its nature, hovering over and so to speak floating with the property which it is intended to affect until some event occurs or some act is done which causes it to settle and fasten on the subject of the charge within its reach and grasp . . .'.

[312] ***Evans v British Granite Quarries Ltd*** **[1910] 2 KB 979 (CA), 999** ***per*** **Buckley LJ:**
[The facts are immaterial.]

'A floating charge is not a future security; it is a present security which presently affects all the assets of the company expressed to be included in it. . . . A floating security is not a specific mortgage of the assets plus a licence to the mortgagor to dispose of them in the course of his business, but it is a floating mortgage applying to every item comprised in the security, but not specifically affecting any item until some act or event occurs or some act on the part of the mortgagee is done which causes it to crystallise into a fixed security. . . .'

[313] ***Re Bond Worth*** **[1980] 1 Ch. 228, 266–8** ***per*** **Slade J:**
[The case concerned an unsuccessful attempt to give a supplier of goods the benefit of a retention of title clause (discussed in Section 3.8 below). Monsanto supplied Bond Worth with 'Acrilan' fibre for use in the manufacture of carpets. The sale agreement provided that 'equitable and beneficial ownership' of the fibre should remain with the sellers until the purchase price was received 'or until prior resale, in which case our beneficial ownership shall attach to the proceeds of resale'. Another clause stipulated that the suppliers should have 'the equitable and beneficial ownership' of any products made out of the fibre. Slade J held that this arrangement created a floating charge over the fibre, its products and any resale proceeds, and that as such it was void for non-registration.]

[See the extract at **[306]** above. Slade J then continued.]

'There is, however, one type of charge (and I think one type only) which, by its very nature, leaves a company at liberty to deal with the assets charged in the ordinary course of its business, without regard to the charge, until stopped by a winding up or by the appointment of a receiver or the happening of some other agreed event. I refer to what is commonly known as a "floating charge": see for example *Wheatley v. Silkstone and Haigh Moor Coal Co.* (1885) 29 Ch.D. 715, 724 per North J. and *George Barker (Transport) Ltd. v. Eynon* [1974] 1 W.L.R. 462, 467 per Edmund Davies L.J. Such a charge remains unattached to any particular property and leaves the company with a licence to deal with, and even sell, the assets falling within its ambit in the ordinary course of business, as if the charge had not been given, until it is stopped by one or other of the events to which I have referred, when it is said to "crystallise"; it then becomes effectively fixed to the assets within its scope.

[Slade J then cited Romer LJ in *In re Yorkshire Woolcombers Association Ltd* (see **[310]** above) before continuing.]

This description of a floating charge shows that it need not extend to all the assets of the company. It may cover assets merely of a specified category or categories. The third characteristic mentioned by Romer L.J. is clearly present in relation to each of the four categories of charged assets in the present case [those four categories being (i) the unused fibre (ii) any proceeds from re-sale of the fibre (iii) any products manufactured using the fibre, and (iv) any proceeds from the re-sale of those manufactured products];

it was clearly contemplated that until some future step was taken by or on behalf of Monsanto, Bond Worth might carry on its business in the ordinary way in relation to each of these four categories. The second characteristic mentioned by him is likewise clearly present at least in relation to each of the second, third and fourth categories of charged assets; these are ex hypothesi classes of assets which in the ordinary course of business will be changing from time to time.

This much could be said against the existence of floating charges in the present case. As regards the first characteristic mentioned by Romer L.J., the charge on the first category of charged assets is exclusively a charge on present assets of the company, while the charges on the other three categories of charged assets are exclusively charges on future assets of the company. If the charges are looked at separately, they do not comprise classes of mixed present and future assets. Furthermore, the second characteristic mentioned by him is present in relation to the first category of charged assets (the raw fibre) only in the sense that the assets comprised in this category may diminish by being used for the purposes of manufacture or sale; they cannot be increased. I do not, however, think that these points of possible distinction prevent all or any of the four relevant charges from being floating charges within the ordinary meaning of legal terminology. Romer L.J. himself disclaimed any intention of saying that there could not be a floating charge within the meaning of the Companies Acts which did not contain all the three characteristics that he mentioned.

The critical distinction in my judgment is that between a specific charge on the one hand and a floating charge on the other. Vaughan Williams L.J. pointed out in the *Woolcombers* case [1903] 2 Ch. 284 that it is quite inconsistent with the nature of a specific charge, though not of a floating charge, that the mortgagor is at liberty to deal with the relevant property as he pleases. He said, at p. 294:

> "I do not think that for a 'specific security' you need have a security of a subject matter which is then in existence. I mean by 'then' at the time of the execution of the security; but what you do require to make a specific security is that the security whenever it has once come into existence, and been identified or appropriated as a security, shall never thereafter at the will of the mortgagor cease to be a security. If at the will of the mortgagor he can dispose of it and prevent its being any longer a security, although something else may be substituted more or less for it, that is not a 'specific security'."

When that case went on appeal to the House of Lords, under the name *Illingworth v. Houldsworth* [1904] A.C. 355, Lord Macnaghten drew the distinction between a specific charge and a floating charge in the following terms, at p. 358. . . .

[See **[311]** above.]

In the present case, in my judgment, the respective charges on each of the four categories of charged assets were ambulatory and shifting in their nature, and were intended to hover over them until the happening of an event which caused them to crystallise. The assets comprised in each of the four categories were of a fluctuating class, albeit in the case of the first category liable to fluctuate only by diminution. Until a crystallising event occurred, it was clearly not intended that any restriction should be placed on Bond Worth to deal with them in the ordinary course of its business.

Accordingly in the end I answer question (c) above by saying that in my judgment the effect of the retention of title clause was to create floating equitable charges over the four categories of charged assets, for the purpose of securing payment of the purchase prices due under the relevant orders, and to constitute Bond Worth a trustee of such assets for the purpose of such security, but for no other purpose. The mere likelihood that evidentiary difficulties would in the event have presented Monsanto with formidable, if not insuperable, obstacles in obtaining effective remedies by way of enforcement of such charges did not, in my judgment, render them void ab initio. Nor in my judgment were they rendered void ab initio by the somewhat misleading and inadequate form of their drafting, which purported to disguise what was in essence a floating charge as a bare trust and failed to specify either the rights of the chargee or the events which would cause the charge to crystallise. I can, however, see no footing upon which Monsanto can have obtained, by virtue of the clause, proprietary rights of a nature known to the law, save by way of equitable floating charge. . .'

3.6.2 Does the floating charge holder have an immediate proprietary interest in the charged assets?

A *fixed* charge holder certainly has a proprietary interest in the charged assets. It is an interest which is not as extensive as the rights of ownership or possession, and it is an interest which is equitable rather than legal, but it *is* nevertheless proprietary—with all the benefits which flow from that fact. The holder of a floating charge *once the charge has crystallised* has precisely this type of interest too: when a floating charge crystallises, it crystallises into a fixed charge. But it remains unclear whether a floating charge holder, while the charge floats, has any proprietary interest in the charged assets. This uncertainty reflects a more fundamental problem. There is still no commonly accepted view of the theoretical basis for the floating charge. This is notwithstanding that the device has been in use for over 100 years and that difficult priority disputes turn on the nature of the charge holder's interest in the charged assets. Various theories have been advanced to explain the proper basis for floating charges, each with different consequences for the proprietary interest of the floating charge holder. Some of these theories are described below.

[314] *Wallace v Evershed* [1899] 1 Ch 891, 894 per Cozens-Hardy J:
[The facts are immaterial.]

> '[A floating charge] does not mean that there is not to be a charge, and an immediate charge, on the property, but merely that, notwithstanding the existence of the charge on all the property, including the real property, of the company, power is reserved to dispose of the property if in the ordinary course of carrying on the company's business it becomes necessary to do so. . . .'

[315] *Cretanor Maritime Co Ltd v Irish Marine Management Ltd* [1978] 1 WLR 966 (CA), 978 *per* Buckley LJ:
[The facts are immaterial.]

> '[The debenture] created an immediate equitable charge upon the assets of the charterers [the debtor], wherever situated, subject to a power in the charterers, so long as the charge continued to float to deal with their assets in the course of their business . . . while the charge continued to float, third parties dealing with the charterers in the course of their business could ignore it. This, however, does not mean that as between the charterers and the debenture holder [the creditor] the charge did not exist or had no

> operative effect. The appointment of the receiver merely crystallised the existing charge, that is to say, it put an end to the power under which, until that time, the charterers were able to deal with their assets in the course of their business as if no charge existed. The equitable assignment thereupon for the first time took complete and unqualified effect ... the debenture holder then became entitled to a fixed charge upon the deposited fund in this country, being one of the charterer's assets at that time, but subject to the necessity of getting the injunction discharged so as to enable the receiver to remove that asset from this jurisdiction....'

But also see:

Evans v British Granite Quarries Ltd [1910] 2 KB 979, 999 *per* Buckley LJ, at **[312]** above.

(i) The 'mortgage of future assets' theory:

This theory sees the floating charge as having only contractual effect, conferring no proprietary interest on the creditor prior to crystallisation.

[316] J W Gough, 'The Floating Charge: Traditional Themes and New Directions' in P D Finn (ed), *Equity and Commercial Relationships* (1987, Law Book Co: Sydney), 239, at pp 247–8:

[The footnotes in the original are omitted.]

> '*Execution possible because no equitable interest under floating charge.* The execution cases provide a good illustration of the proposition that until crystallisation the chargee acquires no equitable proprietary interest. The invariable general rule in regard to execution, well-established by decisions prior to these cases, is that an execution creditor takes subject to previous legal and equitable interests in the property of the debtor, regardless of whether the execution creditor has notice of the previous interest. Estoppel is irrelevant, since a previous equitable interest will not be postponed to an execution creditor, even if nothing has been done to remove the appearance of unencumbered ownership by the debtor. The fact, therefore, that the court was prepared to permit an execution creditor to proceed against assets subject to a floating charge prior to crystallisation clearly demonstrated that the floating chargee obtained no proprietary interest in equity prior to crystallisation. Otherwise, execution would have been precluded by the mere existence of the floating charge, with all other questions being irrelevant.
>
> *Equitable interests in future property.* This view of the floating charge was fully consistent with the general rules of property law regarding the transfer of legal and equitable interests in both present and future assets, which became fully developed during the 19th century. As regards future property, the common law view was that an owner could not dispose of future property (whether absolutely by way of sale or conditionally by way of security), because he could not convey something that did not exist and which he therefore could not own. All that the law would contemplate was that, after the future property came into present ownership, either through subsequent manufacture or acquisition, a legal interest might then be transferred by some further dispositive act, such as the execution of a bill of sale, actual delivery by the transferor or mortgagor, or seizure pursuant to a licence previously conferred. This was the so-called "new act" doctrine, long since identified in an exception contained in Bacon's Maxim stating the gen-

eral prohibition. Equity, however, progressively during the 19th century developed the doctrine that there could be a present transfer of future properly, operating initially as a contract to transfer, which would cause equitable title to vest in the transferee immediately upon legal acquisition by the transferor of the asset subject to transfer, without necessity for any further "new act" by the transferor. The only essential requirement for the subsequent transfer of equitable title to occur was that the property should be capable of identification and ascertainment upon subsequent acquisition, so as to correspond with the description of the future property contained in the terms of the contract relating to the transfer.

Equitable mortgages over future property. This doctrine was applied equally to equitable mortgages over future property as to absolute dispositions. When the future property came into the present legal ownership of the mortgagor, the mortgagee immediately acquired an equitable title, subject to the equity of redemption. In other words, there could be a "present contract" or "present security" without the mortgagee acquiring an immediate equitable title. This meant simply that, upon the mortgaged future property being subsequently identified and ascertained at the time of legal acquisition by the mortgagor, then without any further "new" dispositive act being required from the mortgagor, the mortgagee immediately acquired an equitable interest. In other words, in equity, unlike the law, the "new act" doctrine did not apply.

The appropriation test to pass title. The necessity for identification or ascertainment of future property to permit the passage of equitable title merely reflected the wider principle, formulated during the 19th century and operating both at law and in equity, that even in regard to present property no title can pass until assets are appropriated to the contract by mutual agreement. At common law, appropriation occurred in respect of sale or mortgage effected by formal deed by specific identification in the bill of sale. Otherwise, in the case of sale under informal agreement, title would pass, in the case of specific goods, immediately upon the making of the contract and, in the case of unascertained goods sold by description, when goods were appropriated to the contract, generally by means of actual delivery. . . . The same requirement for appropriation through identification and ascertainment existed in equity. In respect of present property, an equitable mortgage could arise immediately upon agreement in respect of specific goods, but not unascertained goods. In respect of future property, which was capable of being "presently" assigned so long as it was capable of being subsequently identified and ascertained in accordance with the contract description, equitable title passed when it was subsequently ascertained through the action of the mortgagor in acquiring property corresponding with the contract description.

No appropriation under floating charge. The appropriation test was referred to by the court in identifying the difference between a specific and floating charge. It was explained from an early stage that under a specific charge the chargor cannot deal with the charged property without the consent of the chargee. A specific charge has to relate to specific or ascertained property. Under a specific charge, the chargor appropriates property to the charge and cannot thereafter at his own will appropriate it in favour of a third party for some other purpose. This, of course, the chargor can do under a floating charge. Under a floating charge over the present and future assets for the time being, the charged property answering the contract description is only finally ascertained on crystallisation, being the present assets of the chargor at that time. The chargor cannot thereafter appropriate these assets for purposes other than the charge without the chargee's consent. A specific equitable proprietary interest, therefore, vests in the chargee only upon crystallisation. This reference by the court to the appropriation test should not be surprising. It made the explanation of the difference between the specific and floating charge in the context of the law of mortgage fully consistent with the fundamental principles of the law of property generally in relation to transfer of title.'

FURTHER READING:

W J Gough, *Company Charges* (2nd edn, 1991, Butterworths: London) ch 13.

(ii) The 'licence' theory:

This theory sees the floating charge as creating an equitable proprietary interest in the creditor from its inception, linked with a licence to the debtor to deal with the assets in the ordinary course of business. However, the proprietary interest enjoyed by the floating charge holder prior to crystallisation is something less than the interest which a fixed charge holder enjoys, and its precise incidents remain unclear.

[317] R R Pennington, 'The Genesis of the Floating Charge' **(1960) 23 MLR 630, 644–6:**

[Professor Pennington is not an advocate of this theory, but he describes it well. Footnotes in the original are omitted.]

'It was inevitable that in the early cases the court should conceive the floating charge to be one which attached to the property of the company for the time being, but which could not be realised until the company was wound up or the court saw fit to appoint a receiver. Every new item of property which the company acquired became subject to the charge, but ceased to be subject to it when the company disposed of it. Thus, by a complicated process of addition and subtraction it was possible to arrive at the assets of the company at the date when the charge crystallised and became enforceable. It was an easy transition from this conception of the floating charge for the court to envisage the company's right to manage its affairs and dispose of its property until crystallisation as a licence given to it by the debenture holders. This idea may have originated from the passage in Jessel M.R.'s judgment quoted above, but it received a more concrete expression in later cases. On the other hand, three cases at least have rejected the idea of a licence, and have explained the nature of the floating charge in words such as those of Buckley L.J [see **[312]** above]:

> A floating charge is not a specific mortgage of the assets, plus a licence to the mortgagor to dispose of them in the course of his business, but is a floating mortgage applying to every item comprised in the security, but not specifically affecting any item until some event occurs or some act on the part of the mortgagee is done which causes it to crystallise into a fixed security.

The difference of judicial opinion as to whether there is an implied licence given to the company is not a merely metaphysical one. It can result in different answers to problems concerning the rights of debenture holders. For example, if it is accepted that there is an implied licence, it must be subject to some limits, so that if the company proposes to dispose of its assets *ultra vires* or so as to destroy the debenture holders' security, the licence will be exceeded and the debenture holders may obtain an injunction to restrain the disposition. On the other hand, if Buckley L.J.'s opinion quoted above is correct, the debenture holders may intervene only when they have obtained a specific charge on the company's assets, and so their only remedy is to seek the appointment of a receiver by the court, whereupon their floating charge will crystallise. Again, if the theory of an implied licence is accepted, the licence will terminate on the company being wound up, and even though the debentures provide that the debenture debt shall not become due nor the security become enforceable if the winding up is merely for the purpose of amalgamation or reconstruction, the court will appoint a receiver in that event. On the other hand, if the concept of the licence is rejected, the court may allow the parties to make their own bargain about the events which shall cause the floating charge to crystallise and become enforceable. Finally, if the theory of an implied licence is accepted, the licence cannot extend to dispositions of the company's assets except in the ordinary course of its business, and since seizures of its assets by its judgment creditors cannot be of that nature, judgment creditors' claims must always be deferred to those of the debenture holders. On the other hand, if there is no implied licence, judgment creditors who have completed their executions before the floating charge crystallises will have priority for payment out of the proceeds of the property they have seized simply because at the date of the executions the debenture holders could not have interfered to prevent them.

The licence theory introduces an unnecessary complication into the law relating to floating charges, and is best rejected. If Buckley L.J.'s opinion quoted above is correct, it seems that the floating charge today occupies a position midway between the traditional mortgage and the Roman *hypotheca*. Unlike the traditional mortgage, it is not a specific charge on the assets of the company at the date of its creation and on the assets later added thereto, subject to a licence of somewhat indeterminate extent for the company to dispose of such assets. On the other hand, unlike the Roman *hypotheca*, a floating charge does not merely create a right to take possession of assets which are ascertained on the occurrence of a specified future event. In practice, however, the difference between the floating charge and the *hypotheca* are minute, and probably amount to no more than that a debenture holder secured by a floating charge has an immediate proprietary interest in the property owned by the company from time to time, whereas the rights of a lender secured by an *hypotheca* are basically contractual, and although he may recover possession of the property subject to the *hypotheca*, he will acquire a proprietary interest therein only by foreclosing.'

FURTHER READING:

Both these commentators favour the licence theory.

E Ferran, 'Floating Charges—The Nature of the Security' [1988] *CLJ* 213.

J H Farrar, 'World Economic Stagnation Puts the Floating Charge on Trial' (1980) 1 *Coy Lawyer* 83.

(iii) The 'defeasible charge' theory:

This theory sees the floating charge as, in essence, a charge which is defeasible when the charged assets are dealt with in accordance with the permitted licence to deal. It follows that the floating creditor, prior to crystallisation, has precisely the same type of proprietary interest in the charged assets as a fixed charge holder, but with the risk that the debtor will legitimately remove assets from the ambit of the security by dealing with them in permitted ways.

[318] S Worthington, *Proprietary Interests in Commercial Transactions* (1996, Clarendon Press: Oxford), ch 4, pp 79–86:
[Footnotes in the original are omitted.]

'Logic suggests that there are only three alternatives which might usefully describe the floating chargee's interest prior to crystallization. These alternatives span the spectrum of recognized proprietary interests. First, the chargee might have *no proprietary interest* at all in the charged assets; according to this theory, the floating charge is viewed simply as an agreement to grant a charge at some time in the future (when the floating charge 'crystallizes'). This theory is known as the 'mortgage of future assets theory'. An intermediate position is to regard the chargee as having a *new type of proprietary interest*, one with characteristics which are undeniably proprietary, but to a lesser degree than the proprietary interest of a chargee under a fixed charge. The precise nature of the interest has never been explained. This theory is known as the 'licence theory'. The name derives from the fact that the charge is coupled with a licence to the chargor to deal with the charged assets without recourse to the chargee (in contrast to fixed charges), although only in the ordinary course of business. Finally, the chargee might have the same quality of proprietary interest as is recognized in the context of a fixed charge, but one which is defeasible when the chargor deals with the assets in any of the ways permitted by the charge agreement. This last interest is perhaps best described as a *defeasible charge interest*. This description is intended to indicate that, prior to crystallization, a floating chargee has precisely the same quality of proprietary interest as a fixed chargee, although the interest is much more precarious since it is liable to disappear—defease—if the chargor engages in permitted dealings with the charged assets.

'Defeasible' proprietary interests are already familiar, although not generally labelled as such. Under a retention of title agreement, for example, the vendor's legal ownership is genuine legal ownership, and measured as such in any priority dispute with third parties, notwithstanding that the interest is liable to be lost when the purchaser uses or resells the sale property or pays the purchase price. Similarly, a lender's equitable ownership under a *Quistclose* trust 'defeases' when the borrower uses the funds for the nominated purposes. In both cases it is readily accepted that there is no need to reclassify the identified proprietary interest (legal or equitable ownership) simply because the interest is liable to be lost as soon as the other party deals with the underlying asset.

Before attempting to justify adoption of one of these options in preference to the others, one point must be stressed. None of the postulated theories in any measure denies the distinction between fixed and floating charges and the statutory incidents which flow from that distinction. Whichever theory is adopted, a charge will be classified as either fixed or floating in the manner described earlier. The relevant legislative provisions will then apply accordingly.

This point probably needs greatest emphasis in relation to the defeasible charge theory. With this theory, it is all too easy to assume that what is postulated is 'a fixed charge plus a licence to deal', and therefore to assume that the charge should be classified as fixed. This is not the case. In fact, the view advanced here is that a security interest described as a fixed charge with a licence to deal is unequivocally floating charge. The defeasible charge theory simply postulates that a charge classified as floating nevertheless gives the chargee the same quality of proprietary interest as a chargee with a fixed equitable charge, except that the floating interest is defeasible while the fixed one is not.

Any theory describing the floating chargee's proprietary interest prior to crystallization of the charge simply enables the rational resolution of a separate problem, the priority disputes between competing proprietary interest holders. Which theory is preferable?

. . .

There are, it seems, three reasons why the defeasible charge theory is to be preferred to its alternatives. First, the theory is based on an analysis which parallels that used in the context of other proprietary interests, and such conceptual consistency is valuable; secondly, the theory is derived directly from an analysis of the similarities and differences between fixed and floating charges, and so maintains a cohesion between the two; and, finally, it has practical benefits: since it exposes familiar fundamental concepts, it should simplify the drafting of floating charges and the resolution of disputes involving them. Each of these reasons merits amplification.

As already noted, the defeasible charge theory has obvious parallels with principles already encountered in the operation of *Romalpa* clauses and *Quistclose* trusts. All three situations might usefully be considered as instances where the agreement between the parties provides for a defeasible proprietary interest. The difference between the three lies simply in the nature of that defeasible interest: it may be legal or equitable ownership or an equitable charge.

Secondly, the defeasible charge theory is derived directly from an analysis of the similarities and differences between fixed and floating charges. With both fixed and floating charges there is an element of potentiality in the security: the chargee cannot intervene to enforce the security until there has been a default in the agreed licence conditions; until then the chargee's rights are partly suspended. Secondly, with both fixed and floating charges, future assets may be included within the ambit of the charge: in other words, it is possible to add more assets to the security. Finally, with both fixed and floating charges the chargor may deal with the assets only with the consent of the chargee: the difference is that, in general, the chargee does not give permission to deal when the charge is fixed but does when the charge is floating.

'Floating charge' is thus a general term used to describe those securities where assets may be 'lost' from the security by permitted dealings; 'fixed charge' describes those securities where assets remain forever within the ambit of the security. Put this way, the terms are really only crude linguistic generalizations: given the appropriate consent, assets may be lost from a fixed charge security; with the appropriate restrictions, assets may have to be retained in floating charge securities. This highlights the crucial role played by the agreement between the parties: fixed and floating charges are not terms of art. In fact, distinguishing between the two forms can be very difficult.

In many ways, then, fixed and floating charges are similar. As far as possible, the law should recognize these similarities in describing the fundamental attributes of both types of security. The defeasible charge theory focuses on these similarities and elects for the simplest means of accounting for the differences. This is why it postulates that fixed and floating chargees have the same type of proprietary interest in the charged assets from the inception of the charge, with the same equitable rights to protect those interests. The difference between the two types of charges is simply that the floating charge only gives the chargee a defeasible interest: if the chargor deals with the charged assets within the terms of the licence to deal as agreed between the parties, then the chargee's interest will, to that extent, be extinguished.

It is true that the practical advantages of the theory can really only be surmised. Clearly, though, the law is hampered by terminology: a 'floating' charge becomes 'fixed' upon 'crystallization'. Practitioners routinely draft clauses pronouncing a charge to be 'fixed not floating' or vice versa. The defeasible charge theory attempts to avoid some of these difficulties. It postulates that 'floating' means simply that a charge is subject to defeasance when charged assets are dealt with by the chargor in accordance with the permitted licence to deal. 'Crystallization' means that the chargor's licence to deal with the charged property has been revoked. The theory thus clarifies the impact of the agreed licence to deal and the termination of that licence (the 'crystallization' provisions). In doing this, it might simplify the drafting of floating charges.

This approach can also simplify the resolution of priority disputes between parties. This is best demonstrated by indicating how the theory would have managed the resolution of disputes arising in familiar cases. This has the advantage of amplifying the theoretical aspects of the proposal while testing its practical usefulness.'

3.6.3 Distinguishing between fixed and floating charges

As noted earlier, a *fixed* charge restricts the debtor's power to dispose of or otherwise deal with the charged property without first obtaining the creditor's consent. By contrast, a *floating* charge leaves the debtor freed to deal with the charged property in the ordinary course of business without recourse to the creditor. This, and nothing else, is the critical distinction between fixed and floating charges. Moreover, it is the substance of the arrangement which matters, not its form: the courts will look to the parties' acts, not their words.

Put like this, the next case, extracted at **[319]** below, is a rather extraordinary example. The Court of Appeal seems to have been influenced almost exclusively by the fact that the charged *property* was 'specific', rather than 'ambulatory and shifting', and concluded that therefore the *charge* was also 'specific' or 'fixed' rather than 'ambulatory or floating'. As a Court of Appeal decision, it needs to be accorded due weight, but it does suggest some surprising consequences.

This particular case and the next one also reflect the fact that some of the greatest problems in categorising charges as either fixed or floating have arisen with charges granted over a debtor's 'receivables' or 'book debts' (the terms are interchangeable). 'Receivables' or 'book debts' represent the sums due to a debtor but not yet paid. They are often worth a considerable sum. It is hardly surprising, therefore, that creditors seeking security have identified their potential. Difficulties in the classification of charges over book debts appear to arise because sometimes book debts are treated as assets entirely distinct from their collected proceeds, whereas at other times they are treated as if the paper debt and the cash proceeds from its repayment comprise a unified and indivisible asset. Read the following extracts to determine which, if either, is the more appropriate approach.

[319] *Re Atlantic Computer Systems plc* [1992] Ch 505 (CA), 534 *per* Nicholls LJ: [Rental moneys payable to the debtor company under existing, identified computer leasing agreements were assigned by way of charge. The charge was held to be a fixed charge.]

[... after citing from *In re Yorkshire Woolcombers Association Ltd* **[310]** and *Illingworth v Houldsworth* **[311]**]

'In the light of these observations we cannot accept Mr. Heslop's submissions. The notable feature of the present case is that the charges were not ambulatory. The property assigned by the company was confined to rights to which the company was entitled under specific, existing contracts. The assignments consisted of the company's rights "under or by virtue of" subleases each of which was already in existence at the time of the assignments and each of which was specifically identified in the relevant deeds of assignment. In each case the payments due to the company under a specific sublease were charged as security for the payments due by the company under the headlease relating to the same equipment. The company's right to receive future instalments from end users in due course pursuant to the terms of these subleases was as much a present asset of the company, within Romer L.J.'s reference to "present and future" assets of a company, as a right to receive payment of a sum which was immediately due. Romer L.J.'s reference to future assets was a reference to assets of which, when the charge was created, the company was not the owner. That was the position in that case. That is not the position in this case.

We have in mind that in practice sums payable by the end users under these subleases were paid to the company and utilised by it in the ordinary course of business. In so far as this is relevant, it may well be that this was what the parties intended should happen. The company was to be at liberty to receive and use the instalments until A.I.B. chose to intervene. We are unpersuaded that this results in these charges, on existing and defined property, become floating charges. A mortgage of land does not become a floating charge by reason of the mortgagor being permitted to remain in possession and enjoy the fruits of the property charged for the time being. This is so even if the land is leasehold and the term is very short, and as such the asset charged is of a wasting character. So here: the mere fact that for the time being the company could continue to receive and use the instalments does not suffice to negative the fixed character of the charge. This apart, we have seen nothing to lend any support to the administrators' contention. In particular, we have seen nothing to suggest that after the assignment the company was to be at liberty to deal with its rights under the subleases without the consent of A.I.B. . . .'

[320] *Re New Bullas Trading Ltd* [1994] 1 BCLC 485; [1994] BCC 36 (CA), 38–42 *per* Nourse LJ (the other members of the CA concurring):

[The debtor purported to create a fixed charge over book debts so long as they remained uncollected, but once collected and paid into a designated bank account the moneys were deemed released from the fixed charge and became subject to a floating charge (unless written instructions to the contrary were given by the creditor). At first instance Knox J held that the charge was a floating charge throughout, but the Court of Appeal reversed this, agreeing with the designation given by the parties. As a consequence, the preferential creditors were not entitled in the receivership to priority under the Insolvency Act 1986 section 40.]

'The condition on which the outcome of this case mainly depends is condition 12, to which the marginal note is "Book debts". I set it out in full, adding numbers for the three parts into which para. (A) is divided:

"During the continuance of this security the company shall:
(A) [(i)] pay into a current account or a separate designated account (as 3i may require) of the company with the bank all moneys which it may receive in respect of the book debts and other debts hereby charged and (subject to any rights of the bank in respect thereof) pay or otherwise deal with such moneys standing in such account in accordance with any directions from time to time given in writing by 3i; [(ii)] prior to any demand being made under condition 8 hereof or to the provisions

> of condition 9 hereof becoming operative in the absence of any directions from 3i any moneys received by the company and paid into such account in respect of the book debts and other debts hereby charged shall upon such payment in stand released from the fixed charge on such debts hereinbefore by this debenture created and shall stand subject to the floating charge hereinbefore by this debenture created over the other property and assets of the company;
> [(iii)] any such release shall in no respects derogate from the subsistence and continuance of the said fixed charge on all other book and other debts of the company for the time being outstanding:
> (B) if called upon to do so by 3i execute a legal assignment of such book debts and other debts to 3i in such terms as 3i may require and give notice thereof to the debtors from whom the debts are owing or incurred and take such other steps as 3i may require to perfect such legal assignment:
> (C) deal with such book debts and other debts in accordance with any directions from time to time given in writing by 3i (subject to any rights of the bank in respect thereof) and in default of and subject to any such directions deal with the same only in the ordinary course of getting in and realising the same (but not sell assign factor or discount the same in any way):
> (D) permit the bank to furnish directly to 3i from time to time upon request full statements and particulars of all the company's accounts with the bank and such other financial statements and information respecting the assets and liabilities of the company as are from time to time available to the bank."

The references in para. (A)(i) and (C) to the rights of the bank are evidently references to its rights under its own debenture.

The principal activities of the company were to act as agents for commissioning and consultant engineers to major oil companies and the supply of personnel to carry out non-destructive testing services. No directions were ever given by 3i pursuant to either of para. (A)(i) or (C) of condition 12. On 6 November 1991 the applicants, Mr Roger Murray Griffiths and Mr Andrew George Pearce, two partners in Ernst & Young, were appointed by the bank to be joint administrative receivers of the company. On 12 November 1991, pursuant to powers contained in the debenture, they were appointed by 3i to act in the like capacity. Those appointments brought into play s. 40 of the Insolvency Act 1986 which, so far as material, provides:

> "(1) The following applies, in the case of a company, where a receiver is appointed on behalf of the holders of any debentures of the company secured by a charge which, as created, was a floating charge.
> (2) If the company is not at the time in course of being wound up, its preferential debts ... shall be paid out of the assets coming to the hands of the receiver in priority to any claims for principal or interest in respect of the debentures."

. . .

Doubts having arisen as to whether the charge over book debts was, as created, a fixed or a floating charge, on 28 October 1992 the administrative receivers issued an originating application in the Companies Court for the determination of that question. The respondents were 3i, the Inland Revenue, the Customs and Excise and the Departments of Employment and Social Security. By an order of the registrar, the Inland Revenue were appointed to represent the interests of the respondents other than 3i. He also directed that no notice of the application need be given to any other preferential creditors, i.e. the employees. The application came before Knox J who, on 11 February 1993, held that the charge was a floating charge. 3i now appeals to this court.

Knox J's judgment is reported at [1993] BCC 251. Having considered the provisions of the debenture and several of the previous authorities, including *Re Yorkshire Woolcombers Association Ltd, Siebe Gorman & Co Ltd v Barclays Bank Ltd* and *Re Brightlife Ltd*, the judge reached the conclusion that the case fell on the floating charge side of the line, in that the company's ability to deal with book debts was, at the creation of the charge, not subject to any greater fetters than Hoffmann J had held to be inadequate in *Re Brightlife Ltd.* He continued, at p. 265F:

> "Absent a direction from 3i there was a freedom of action conferred upon the company which was in my judgment inconsistent with the existence of a specific charge."

In this court there has been much common ground. It is agreed that the question depends on the intention of the parties, to be ascertained from the terms of the debenture; legal impossibility apart, that there are no considerations of public policy which prevented them from making whatever contract they chose; that it was possible for them to create a fixed equitable charge over future as well as present book debts; that their declared intention was to create such a charge; but that that intention was nevertheless defeated if the other provisions of the debenture are inconsistent with it.

Mr Sumption QC, for 3i, has made two main submissions, whose import can be summarised as follows: first, on the footing that condition 12 treated, or must be taken to have treated, book debts indivisibly, the charge created over them by the debenture was, as it was expressed to be, a fixed charge; secondly and in the alternative, the effect of condition 12 was to create a fixed charge over book debts while they were uncollected and a floating charge over their proceeds, there being no legal objection to their being treated in that fashion. It seems that in the court below it was the first of these submissions that was primarily, if not exclusively, relied on. Certainly it was by Knox J's rejection of it that the case was decided as it was. No trace of the second submission can be found in the judge's careful judgment. In this court it has assumed great prominence. Logically, as it seems to me, it deserves to be considered first.

The question depends in the first instance on the true construction of condition 12. In order to trace the fate, actual or potential, of one of the company's book debts, it is necessary to start with condition 12(C), whose effect, in the absence of any written directions by 3i, is to require the company to get in the debt in the ordinary course by demanding payment from the debtor in full. On payment being made, condition 12(A)(i) requires it to be paid into a specified account of the company with the bank, where it must be paid or otherwise dealt with in accordance with any written directions given by 3i. Condition 12(A)(ii), which is in substance, though not in form, a proviso to condition 12(A)(i), then provides that, prior to crystallisation of the security under either of conditions 8 and 9 and in the absence of any written directions by 3i, the sum paid in shall be released from the fixed charge and become subject to the floating charge. Condition 12(A)(iii), in substance a further proviso, provides that the release of the sum paid in from the fixed charge shall not derogate from its continuation in relation to all other outstanding book debts of the company.

The judge held, and the parties are agreed, that when condition 12(A)(i) and (ii) are read together, it is seen that any directions given by 3i cannot have retrospective effect on any sums paid into the account beforehand. With that point out of the way, it is very clear, as Mr Henderson, for the Inland Revenue, accepts, that the parties intended to create a fixed charge over book debts while they were uncollected (and also, if there was any interval between collection and payment in, over the proceeds) and a floating charge over the proceeds once they had been paid into the specified account. So the decisive question is whether the law allowed the parties to make an agreement to that effect.

Mr Henderson has submitted that the distinction drawn between the book debts before collection and after realisation is unrealistic and artificial because a debt is worth nothing unless and until it is turned into money. He says that it is of the essence of a fixed charge that the asset is appropriated to the charge from the beginning and that it cannot be released from it without the consent of the chargee. He relies strongly on a passage in the judgement of Vaughan Williams LJ in *Re Yorkshire Woolcombers Association Ltd* [1903] 2 Ch at p. 294, where he said:

> ". . . what you do require to make a specific security is that the security whenever it has once come into existence, and been identified or appropriated as a security, shall never thereafter at the will of the mortgagor cease to be a security."

The short answer to these submissions is that here the asset does not cease to be subject to the fixed charge at the will of the company. It ceases to be such because both parties, not the company alone, have determined that if the proceeds of a book debt are paid into the specified account at a time when no directions have been given it shall thereupon be released. The matter is governed by a clear agreement of the parties. Unless there is some authority or principle of law which prevented them from agreeing what they have agreed, their agreement must prevail.

An equitable assignment, whether it takes effect as an out-and-out assignment or, as here, by way of charge, is a creature of exceptional versatility, malleable to the intention of its creators, adaptable to the subject-matter assigned. Provided it is in writing, made for value and the intention is clear, it requires no formalities of expression; it may take effect over property real or personal, and over estates or interests legal or equitable, vested or contingent or, as in the case of future book debts, mere expectancies.

In *Tailby v Official Receiver* (1888) 13 App Cas 523, the case in which it was decided by the House of Lords that an equitable charge over future book debts could validly be created, Lord Macnaghten said at p. 543:

> "It has long been settled that future property, possibilities and expectancies are assignable in equity for value. The mode or form of assignment is absolutely immaterial provided the intention of the parties is clear. To effectuate the intention an assignment for value, in terms present and immediate, has always been regarded in equity as a contract binding on the conscience of the assignor and so binding the subject-matter of the contract when it comes into existence, if it is of such a nature and so described as to be capable of being ascertained and identified."

Having referred to the proposition that an assignment of future book debts not limited to a specified business was too vague to have any effect, and having found that it was unsupported by authority, Lord Macnaghten dealt with it as a matter of principle. At p. 545, he said:

> "It was admitted by the learned counsel for the respondent, that a trader may assign his future book debts in a specified business. Why should the line be drawn there? Between men of full age and competent understanding ought there to be any limit to the freedom of contract but that imposed by positive law or dictated by considerations of morality or public policy? The limit proposed is purely arbitrary, and I think meaningless and unreasonable."

These observations support the view that, just as it is open to contracting parties to provide for a fixed charge on future book debts, so it is open to them to provide that they shall be subject to a fixed charge while they are uncollected and a floating charge on realisation. No authority to the contrary has been cited and, the principle being as spacious as it has been expressed to be, no objection is on that account sustainable. For these reasons, I would accept Mr Sumption's second main submission and hold that the charge over book debts of the company, as created by the debenture, was, unless and until their proceeds were paid into the specified account, a valid fixed charge. . . .'

FURTHER READING:

For further comments on these decisions, see:

R Goode, 'Charges Over Book Debts: A Missed Opportunity' (1994) 110 *LQR* 592 (critical of the approach); and

A Berg, 'Charges Over Book Debts: A Reply' [1995] *JBL* 433 (in support).

[321] S Worthington, 'Fixed Charges Over Book Debts and Other Receivables' (1997) 113 *LQR* 562, 565–6:

[This note on *Royal Trust Bank v National Westminster Bank plc* [1996] BCC 316 (CA) summarises and attempts to resolve the debate. The case concerned a purported 'first legal charge' granted by the debtor company to RTB over hiring agreements deposited with RTB. Income from the deposited agreements was paid by the debtor into an account with Natwest. The charge documentation provided that the debtor, until otherwise directed by RTB, was to collect as agent for RTB all sums due under the agreements. The debtor, if so required by RTB at any time, had to open a 'rental income account' with RTB and pay into it all such moneys received by the debtor. No such account was required to be opened. Before the Court of Appeal, Natwest conceded that this charge was a fixed, not a floating, charge, but argued that neither the agency provision nor any other aspect of the arrangement between the debtor and RTB was sufficient to constitute the debtor a trustee of the sums collected. It followed that Natwest could not be a constructive trustee of such sums, notwithstanding its alleged knowledge of the arrangement. The Court of Appeal accepted this argument. Only Millett LJ pursued the point that, notwithstanding the concession by Natwest, the charge was in fact a floating charge. In his view the contractual right of the debtor to collect the proceeds and pay them into its own bank account for use in the ordinary course of its own business was a badge of a floating charge and inconsistent with the charge being fixed (*ibid* p 619).]

'At the outset, one confusion must be laid to rest. In common parlance, a floating charge is described as 'ambulatory'—it floats. This image of 'wandering' has led to suggestions that a charge must be floating if the charged property can change over time to include any replacements, renewals and substitutions for the original property. This is not the true determinant. The current perception of a floating charge is simple and explicit: if the arrangements contemplate that the charged assets may be dealt with on the chargor's own account and without reference to the chargee, then the charge will be classified as a floating charge; if not, then it will be a fixed charge. The focus is thus on whether charged assets may be *removed* from the ambit of the charge by the chargor and for the chargor's benefit, not on whether they may be *added* (see *Siebe Gorman & Co Ltd v Barclays Bank Ltd* [1979] 2 Lloyd's Rep 142; *Re Brightlife Ltd* [1987] Ch 200; R Goode, 'Charges Over Book Debts: A Missed Opportunity' (1994) 110 *LQR* 592).

Of course, context is important. *Holroyd v Marshall* (1862) 10 HL Cas 191, [1861–73] All ER Rep 414 (HL) makes it clear that not every power to deal with the charged assets will render the charge floating. There the charge was over machinery and the chargor had the power (under the Bills of Sale Acts (1978) Amendment Act 1882 ss 5 and 6) to substitute new machinery for old without the particular consent of the chargee. Notwithstanding this, the charge is rightly categorised as fixed. Similarly, charge documents commonly require the chargor to repair and maintain the charged asset: this power to deal with the asset does not necessarily render the charge floating. Notwithstanding such examples, it is still important not to take too expansive a view of the dicta in *Re Cimex Tissues Ltd* [1995] 1 BCLC 409 (again concerning a charge over machinery). This dicta suggested that a *limited*, but quite general, power to release parts of the charged property from the scope of the charge was not necessarily inconsistent with the charge being fixed (see p 423). Except in special circumstances, as already indicated, the weight of authority is the other way (see, eg, *Re Yorkshire Woolcombers' Association* [1903] 2 Ch 284, 294; *Re Bond Worth* [1980] Ch 228, 266; *Re Armagh Shoes Ltd* [1984] BCLC 405, 415).

Where, as in the *Royal Trust Bank* case, the charge is over receivables, the above description indicates that the charge will be fixed only if the chargor cannot deal with the receivables—and so remove them from the ambit of the charge—without the consent of the chargee. This limitation can be achieved in only two ways: either the chargor must be prevented from any further handling of the receivables, including collecting the proceeds as they fall due (an impractical response), or the collected proceeds must be paid to or held for the chargee (a more practical response). This follows simply from the nature of a receivable: mere *collection* of the receivable effects a removal of the asset from the ambit of the charge; if this collection can take place at the will of the chargor, then the charge on the receivables must be a floating charge; if it cannot—either because no collection is permitted or because, although permitted, the proceeds are held solely for the chargee—then the charge is fixed. It follows that a charge over receivables can only be fixed *and* commercially practical if the collected proceeds are also subject to a fixed charge.

This conclusion must not be taken too far. It certainly does not follow that uncollected receivables and their collected proceeds must inevitably be charged in the same manner for the charge over the receivables themselves to be effective. This is in fact *only* the case when the parties wish to create a fixed charge over the receivables. Otherwise, the two assets—uncollected receivables and collected proceeds—can be treated as quite distinct. The parties may, for example, create a floating charge over the receivables. Such a charge leaves the chargor free to deal with the asset in the ordinary course of business, removing the asset from the ambit of the security by collecting the proceeds at will. Obviously characterisation of such a charge is possible without regard to potential restrictions on dealing with the proceeds themselves. Theoretically, the collected proceeds may then be subjected quite independently to either a fixed or a floating charge, or to no charge at all. In practice, of course, a fixed charge is unlikely: it would prevent the chargor using the collected funds for the business (although see, eg, *Re CCG International Enterprises Ltd* [1993] BCC 580). A floating charge or no charge at all (as with a shipowner's lien on sub-freights) is a more sensible commercial option. . . .'

Questions:

Which arguments are more defensible from (i) a doctrinal perspective? (ii) the perspective of commercial utility? (iii) the perspective of the policy underpinning insolvency law? So which approach ought to be adopted?

3.6.4 Crystallisation of floating charges

Crystallisation marks a transition point. It marks the time when the debtor's liberty to deal with the charged assets ceases and the floating charge becomes fixed. Since a floating charge is a creature of contract, it seems to follow that this aspect too can be determined by contract. However, there are policy concerns that the power to effect automatic crystallisation in pre-defined circumstances might be used as a means of avoiding insolvency priority rules (see the extracts below). Even if the parties do not expressly provide for crystallisation of their security, a floating charge will crystallise by operation of law when the debtor's business ceases to be run 'in the ordinary course'. This may happen because of a decision voluntarily taken by the debtor (see **[322]** below); more often it happens involuntarily, on the appointment of a receiver or liquidator to the debtor company.

[322] ***Re Woodroffes (Musical Instruments) Ltd*** **[1986] Ch 366 (CA), 377–8** ***per*** **Nourse LJ:**
[The facts are immaterial.]

> 'Mr. Jarvis started with Lord Macnaghten's description of a floating charge in *Governments Stock and Other Securities Investment Co. Ltd. v. Manila Railway Co. Ltd.* [1897] A.C. 81, where he said, at p. 86:
>
> > "It is of the essence of such a charge that it remains dormant until the undertaking charged ceases to be a going concern, or until the person in whose favour the charge is created intervenes."
>
> In *Illingworth v. Houldsworth* [1904] A.C. 355, 358, Lord Macnaghten returned to the subject and spoke of a floating charge as being:
>
> > "ambulatory and shifting in its nature, hovering over and, so to speak, floating with the property which it is intended to affect until some event occurs or some act is done which causes it to settle and fasten on the subject of the charge within its reach and grasp."
>
> Mr. Jarvis and Mr. Marks submit that if the company ceased business before 1 September that was an event which caused the bank's charge to settle and fasten on all the assets of the company.
>
> I was referred to the following further authorities on this question. . . . It is unnecessary for me to examine any of those cases in detail, or to quote extracts from the judgments of the many judges who decided them. They all, to a greater or lesser extent, assume that crystallisation takes place on a cessation of business. Perhaps the assumption appears most authoritatively in the judgment of Fletcher Moulton L.J. in *Evans v. Rival Granite Quarries Ltd.* [1910] 2 K.B. 979, 993. That was one of the latest of the cases to which I was referred. I would think that by that time the assumption had become well established.
>
> Although the general body of informed opinion is of the view that automatic crystallisation is undesirable (see in particular the Report of the Review Committee on Insolvency Law and Practice (Cmnd 8558) 30 April 1981, paras. 1570–1582) I have not been referred to any case in which the assumption in favour of automatic crystallisation on cessation of business has been questioned. On that state of the authorities it would

be very difficult for me to question it, even if I could see a good ground for doing so. On the contrary, it seems to me that it is in accordance with the essential nature of a floating charge. The thinking behind the creation of such charges has always been a recognition that a fixed charge on the whole undertaking and assets of the company would paralyse it and prevent it from carrying on its business: see, e.g. *In re Florence Land and Public Works Co., Ex parte Moor* (1878) 10 Ch.D. 530, 541, per Sir George Jessel M.R. On the other hand it is a mistake to think that the chargee has no remedy while the charge is still floating. He can always intervene and obtain an injunction to prevent the company from dealing with its assets otherwise than in the ordinary course of its business. That no doubt is one reason why it is preferable to describe the charge as "hovering," a word which can bear an undertone of menace, rather than as "dormant." A cessation of business necessarily puts an end to the company's dealings with its assets. That which kept the charge hovering has now been released and the force of gravity causes it to settle and fasten on the subject of the charge within its reach and grasp. The paralysis, while it may still be unwelcome, can no longer be resisted. For a more concise statement of this analysis I am indebted to Professor R. M. Goode in his collected lectures, *Legal Problems of Credit and Security*, 1st ed. (1982), p. 57. I hold that the assumption correctly represents the law. Accordingly, if the company in fact ceased business on 27 August, or some other date before 1 September, the bank's charge crystallised then and not on 1 September. . . .'

[323] *Re Brightlife Ltd* [1987] Ch 200, 212–15 *per* Hoffmann J:

[A debenture purported to create a first specific charge over all debts, including book debts, owing to the debtor company. It also created a first floating charge over the undertaking and all property of the company with a right to convert this charge into a specific charge at any time (ie a right to crystallise the charge at will). The court held that on its true construction the debenture created a floating charge and not a fixed charge, but that since the notices converted the floating charge into a fixed charge (ie the notices *crystallising* the charge) had been given prior to the passing of a resolution for the voluntary winding up of the company, the debt secured by the debenture had priority over the preferential debtors. This aspect of the law relating to priorities has now been changed so that all charges *created* as floating charges continue to be treated as floating charges for the purposes of assessment of priority of payments of debts on insolvency: see Insolvency Act 1986 section 251. The part of the judgment extracted below relates solely to the right of a creditor to effect automatic crystallisation of a floating charge.]

'The argument Mr. Mummery actually advanced before me was far more radical. He said that the events of crystallisation were fixed by law and not by the agreement of the parties. Those events were (1) winding up, (2) appointment of a receiver, and (3) ceasing to carry on business. These three events and only these three would cause crystallisation notwithstanding any agreement to the contrary. Their common features were that in each case the business of the company would cease, or at any rate cease to be conducted by the directors.

Mr. Mummery referred to a number of cases in support of this submission. First, there were cases in which it was held that crystallisation had taken place on one or other of the three events notwithstanding the absence of an express provision to that effect. For example, in *In re Crompton Co. Ltd.* [1914] 1 Ch. 954, Warrington J. held that a floating charge crystallised on a winding up for the purposes of reconstruction notwithstanding that event being excluded from a clause containing the events of default which made the loan immediately repayable. At p. 964 Warrington J. described winding up as an event "which by law independently of stipulation would make the debenture realisable." It must be observed that Warrington J. said "independently of stipulation" and not "notwithstanding any stipulation to the contrary." In a later passage he said, at p. 965: "the parties . . . have not provided as a matter of bargaining that, notwithstanding the general law, the other events shall not crystallise the security."

In my judgment, when Warrington J. said that crystallisation on winding up was a matter of general law, he meant only that such a consequence was an implied term of a floating charge in the sense described by Lord Tucker in *Lister v. Romford Ice and Cold Storage Co. Ltd.* [1957] A.C. 555, when he said, at p. 594:

> "Some contractual terms may be implied by general rules of law. These general rules, some of which are now statutory, for example, Sale of Goods Act, Bills of Exchange Act etc., derive in the main from the common law by which they have become attached in the course of time to certain classes of contractual relationships, for example, landlord and tenant, innkeeper and guest, contracts of guarantee and contracts of personal service."

The existence of such rules of law by which terms are implied in a floating charge is not inconsistent with the transaction being wholly consensual and the implied terms liable to exclusion by contrary agreement.

Secondly, Mr. Mummery relied upon a number of cases in which courts have rejected a submission that an event of default, not being one of his three, has caused an automatic crystallisation. The most famous of these is the decision of the House of Lords in *Governments Stock and Other Securities Investment Co. Ltd. v. Manila Railway Co. Ltd.* [1897] A.C. 81. Mr. Mummery said that these cases showed that such events could not as a matter of law cause crystallisation.

In my view, however, the speeches in the *Manila Railway* case make it clear that the House of Lords regarded the question as being one of construction alone. They give rise to a plain inference that a sufficiently explicit provision for automatic crystallisation on default would have been given effect. It is true that the commercial inconvenience of automatic crystallisation gives rise to a strong presumption that it was not intended by the parties. Very clear language will be required. But that does not mean that it is excluded by a rule of law.

The nearest any judge in this country has come to asserting such a rule of law is in *Edward Nelson Co. Ltd. v. Faber Co.* [1903] 2 K.B. 367, where Joyce J., after citing various judicial descriptions of the standard characteristics of a floating charge, said, at p. 376:

> "It follows, I think, from these and other cases that such a debenture as this in the present case does not cease to be a floating security . . . until the company has been wound up, or stops business, or a receiver has been appointed at the instance of the debenture-holders . . ."

Taken by itself, that remark may appear to lend support to Mr. Mummery's tripartite rule of law. But I think that a fair reading of the whole judgment shows that Joyce J. also accepted that his enumeration was subject to contrary agreement.

Thirdly, Mr. Mummery cited several authoritative statements of the standard characteristics of a floating charge, particularly those of Lord Macnaghten in the *Manila Railway* case [1897] A.C. 81 and *Illingworth v. Houldsworth* [1904] A.C. 355, 358, and Romer L.J. in the latter case in the Court of Appeal, *In re Yorkshire Woolcombers*

Association Ltd. [1903] 2 Ch. 284, 295. For example, in the *Manila Railway* case [1897] A.C. 81, 86, Lord Macnaghten said that it was of the essence of a floating charge that it remained dormant "until the undertaking charged ceases to be a going concern, or until the person in whose favour the charge is created intervenes." Mr. Mummery said that this formulation appeared to rule out automatic crystallisation without any act on the part of the debenture-holder. To this Mr. Sheldon replied that he was not asserting automatic crystallisation: both of the notices upon which he relied were acts of intervention by the party entitled to the charge.

There is force in this answer but in my judgment there is a more fundamental objection to the use Mr. Mummery seeks to make of the authorities. In *Illingworth v. Houldsworth* [1904] A.C. 355, 358, Lord Macnaghten was at pains to point out that he had not attempted in the *Manila Railway* case [1897] A.C. 81, to propound a "definition" of a floating charge. He had only offered a "description." In making this distinction, it seems to me that what Lord Macnaghten had in mind was that a floating charge, like many other legal concepts, was not susceptible of being defined by the enumeration of an exhaustive set of necessary and sufficient conditions. All that can be done is to enumerate its standard characteristics. It does not follow that the absence of one or more of those features or the presence of others will prevent the charge from being categorised as "floating." There are bound to be penumbral cases in which it may be difficult to say whether the degree of deviation from the standard case is enough to make it inappropriate to use such a term. But the rights and duties which the law may or may not categorise as a floating charge are wholly derived from the agreement of the parties, supplemented by the terms implied by law. It seems to me fallacious to argue that once the parties have agreed on some terms which are thought sufficient to identify the transaction as a floating charge, they are then precluded from agreeing to any other terms which are not present in the standard case.

Fourthly, Mr. Mummery said that the courts should take a lead from Parliament, which in the Preferential Payments in Bankruptcy Amendment Act 1897 and subsequent company legislation apparently assumed that it need provide for only two possible events of crystallisation, namely the appointment of a receiver and a winding up. Even on Mr. Mummery's own submission this means that Parliament failed to consider his third event, cessation of business. It is true that *In re Woodroffes (Musical Instruments) Ltd.* [1986] Ch. 366, [see **[322]** above] was the first case in which a court expressly decided that cessation of business had crystallised a floating charge. But, as Nourse J. pointed out, this had been generally assumed for about a century. Furthermore, if Parliament is to provide any guidance, it is of some interest that section 7(1)(iv) of the Agricultural Credits Act 1928 creates a statutory floating charge which can be crystallised without appointment of a receiver or winding up by a notice not dissimilar from that given under clause 3(B) in this case. I therefore do not think that I can draw any inferences about the nature of a floating charge from the way in which it has been treated in legislation.

Fifthly, Mr. Mummery said that public policy required restrictions upon what the parties could stipulate as crystallising events. A winding up or the appointment of a receiver would have to be noted on the register. But a notice under clause 3(B) need not be registered and a provision for automatic crystallisation might take effect without the knowledge of either the company or the debenture-holder. The result might be prejudicial to third parties who gave credit to the company. Considerations of this kind impressed Berger J. in the Canadian case of *Reg. in right of British Columbia v. Consolidated Churchill Copper Corporation Ltd.* [1978] 5 W.W.R 652 where the concept of "self-generating crystallisation" was rejected.

I do not think that it is open to the courts to restrict the contractual freedom of parties to a floating charge on such grounds. The floating charge was invented by Victorian lawyers to enable manufacturing and trading companies to raise loan capital on debentures. It could offer the security of a charge over the whole of the company's undertaking without inhibiting its ability to trade. But the mirror image of these advantages was the potential prejudice to the general body of creditors, who might know nothing of the floating charge but find that all the company's assets, including the very goods which they had just delivered on credit, had been swept up by the debenture-holder. The public interest requires a balancing of the advantages to the economy of facilitating the borrowing of money against the possibility of injustice to unsecured creditors. These arguments for and against the floating charge are matters for Parliament rather than the courts and have been the subject of public debate in and out of Parliament for more than a century.

Parliament has responded, first, by restricting the rights of the holder of a floating charge and secondly, by requiring public notice of the existence and enforcement of the charge. For example, priority was given to preferential debts in 1897 and the Companies Act 1907 invalidated floating charges created within three months before the commencement of the winding up. This period has since been extended and is now one year. The registration of floating and other charges was introduced by the Companies Act 1900. The Companies Act 1907 required registration of the appointment of a receiver and the Companies Act 1927 required notice of such appointment to be given on the company's letters and invoices.

These limited and pragmatic interventions by the legislature make it in my judgment wholly inappropriate for the courts to impose additional restrictive rules on grounds of public policy. It is certainly not for a judge of first instance to proclaim a new head of public policy which no appellate court has even hinted at before. I would therefore respectfully prefer the decision of the New Zealand Supreme Court in *In re Manurewa Transport Ltd.* [1971] N.Z.L.R. 909, recognising the validity of a provision for automatic crystallisation, to the contrary dicta in the Canadian case I have cited. For present purposes, however, it is not necessary to decide any questions about automatic crystallisation. The notices under clauses 3(B) and 13 constitute intervention by the debenture-holder and there is in my judgment no conceptual reason why they should not crystallise the floating charge if the terms of the charge upon their true construction have this effect. . . .'

Note:

The Cork Committee (1982, Cmnd 8558, paras 1578–9) considered that automatic crystallisation was 'not merely inconvenient', but that there was 'no place for it in a modern insolvency law'. The Committee recommended that the circumstances in which a floating charge could crystallise should be defined exclusively by statute, but this recommendation has never been taken up. Nor has the recommendation that crystallisation should be ineffective until registration gives third parties notice that the event has occurred.

[324] A J Boyle, 'The Validity of Automatic Crystallisation Clauses' [1979] *JBL* 231, pp 234, 236–7:

'The root objection to automatic crystallisation is that any security is more than a contractual bond between debtor and creditor. It inevitably affects the rights of third parties in the event of liquidation and that indeed is its *raison d'être*. This is true of any change in the rules governing a particular type of security which alters its priority in relation to other creditors. It is a commonplace of English legal history that a new type of proprietary interest, at the time of its origin and early development, will be conceptualised primarily in terms of the bond or obligation between the parties primarily concerned (*e.g.* the use or the restrictive covenant). However, in the course of time the courts, in working out the implications of a new institution (say the use, or the restrictive covenant), have had to determine its impact on the rights of third parties. In so doing, its essentially proprietary character was more fully delineated. As part of this process the legitimate interests of various third parties was properly assessed and the policy issues involved at least tacitly influenced the solutions adopted to particular problems. The same has been true in the case of the origin and evolution of the floating charge. As the case law has developed the judicially determined character of this peculiar type of security has been imposed upon what was originally a company draftsman's device. The courts have in the course of time become more aware of the policy implications of allowing the draftsman a free hand. In refusing to adopt a wholly permissive attitude it may be surmised that the courts have to some extent been schooled by the restrictions that Parliament has seen fit to impose so as to curtail the abuses to which the floating charge had given rise *(e.g.* the provision as to preferential creditors and as to avoiding certain charges).

It may be argued that the whole system of priorities in insolvent liquidation unfairly favours the secured creditor at the necessary expense of the general creditors. Automatic crystallisation simply increases that unfairness by catching by surprise those who give unsecured credit to a company where all they know or should know is that they are subject to the usual peril of a valid floating charge. Without any means of warning or real opportunity of discovery at the time credit is extended, they later discover that the assets which they purchased, or whose existence they relied on as justifying the extension of credit, were in fact subject to a fixed charge—*i.e.* crystallised floating charge.'

FURTHER READING:

J H Farrar, 'The Crystallisation of a Floating Charge' [1976] 40 *Conv.* 397 (although note that parts of this are now out of date, in that they do not reflect the current statutory provisions).

3.6.5 Are there limitations on the types of assets which can be made subject to a floating charge?

It seems clear from what has gone before that if the debtor has a proprietary interest (whether legal or equitable) in some asset, then that asset can be charged with the repayment of a debt (or the performance of some other obligation). Moreover, many of the cases already considered in this chapter are cases where the debtor has given security over book debts. Book debts are personal rights in the debtor/chargor entitling the debtor to receive sums of money from certain third parties. Nevertheless, debts are considered to be a species of personal property. Debts can be assigned: a creditor can assign to a third party the right to be paid by the debtor. Debts can also be charged. In none of the cases considered earlier was it ever considered material that the underlying 'property' being charged was merely a personal obligation owed to the debtor.

However, where the debt being charged is a debt owed to the debtor *by the creditor who is taking the security*, does the analysis need to change? The issue commonly arises with banks attempting to enlarge the security they take from their borrowing customers. Fixed and floating charges enable banks to take security over all a customer's fixed assets and stock-in-trade. These customers may also have substantial sums of money in the bank. Put in contractual terms, these are sums of money that the bank owes to the customer. The customer 'owns' a debt owed by the bank. Can the bank take a charge over this asset to secure a loan it might make to its customer? The issue has now been resolved in favour of this form of security, but the earlier counter-arguments merit consideration. Contrast the following two extracts.

[325] *Re Charge Card Services Ltd* [1987] Ch 150, 175–6 *per* Millett J (confirmed on appeal [1989] Ch 497 (CA)):
[The facts are immaterial.]

> 'If the right of retention constitutes a charge, there is no doubt that it is a charge on book debts and is a charge created by the company. But is it a charge at all? The sum due from Commercial Credit to the company under the agreement is, of course, a book debt of the company which the company can charge to a third party. In my judgment, however, it cannot be charged in favour of Commercial Credit itself, for the simple reason that a charge in favour of a debtor of his own indebtedness to the chargor is conceptually impossible.
>
> Counsel for the company conceded that a debt cannot be assigned in whole or in part to the debtor, since such an assignment operates wholly or partially as a release. Likewise, it was conceded, it cannot be made the subject of a legal or equitable mortgage in favour of the debtor, since this requires a conveyance or assignment by way of security, and this operates as a conditional release. But, it was submitted, an equitable charge need involve no conveyance or assignment of property, so that any objection on this ground falls away.
>
> The locus classicus for the requirements of an equitable charge is the following passage in *Palmer v. Carey* [1926] A.C. 703, 706:
>
>> "The law as to equitable assignment, as stated by Lord Truro L.C. in *Rodick v. Gandell* (1851) 1 De M. & G. 763, 777, 778, is this: 'the extent of the principle to be deduced from them is, that an agreement between a debtor and a creditor that the debt owing shall be paid out of a specific fund coming to the debtor, or an order given by a debtor to his creditor upon a person owing money or holding funds belonging to the giver of the order, directing such person to pay such funds to the creditor, will create a valid equitable charge upon such fund, in other words, will operate as an equitable assignment of the debts or funds to which the order refers.'
>>
>> An agreement for valuable consideration that a fund shall be applied in a particular way may found an injunction to restrain its application in another way. But if there be nothing more, such a stipulation will not amount to an equitable assignment. It is necessary to find, further, that an obligation has been imposed in favour of the creditor to pay the debt out of the fund. This is but an instance of a familiar doctrine of equity that a contract for valuable consideration to transfer or charge a subject matter passes a beneficial interest by way of property in that

> subject matter if the contract is one of which a court of equity will decree specific performance."

Similar definitions of equitable charge are to be found in *National Provincial and Union Bank of England v. Charnley* [1924] 1 K.B. 431. It is sufficient to cite the language of Atkin L.J., at p. 449:

> "It is not necessary to give a formal definition of a charge, but I think there can be no doubt that where in a transaction for value both parties evince an intention that property, existing or future, shall be made available as security for the payment of a debt, and that the creditor shall have a present right to have it made available, there is a charge, even though the present legal right which is contemplated can only be enforced at some future date, and though the creditor gets no legal right of property, either absolute or special, or any legal right to possession, but only gets a right to have the security made available by an order of the court."

Thus the essence of an equitable charge is that, without any conveyance or assignment to the chargee, specific property of the chargor is expressly or constructively appropriated to or made answerable for payment of a debt, and the chargee is given the right to resort to the property for the purpose of having it realised and applied in or towards payment of the debt. The availability of equitable remedies has the effect of giving the chargee a proprietary interest by way of security in the property charged.

It is true, therefore, that no conveyance or assignment is involved in the creation of an equitable charge, but in my judgment the benefit of a debt can no more be appropriated or made available to the debtor than it can be conveyed or assigned to him. The objection to a charge in these circumstances is not to the process by which it is created, but to the result. A debt is a chose in action; it is the right to sue the debtor. This can be assigned or made available to a third party, but not to the debtor, who cannot sue himself. Once any assignment or appropriation to the debtor becomes unconditional, the debt is wholly or partially released. The debtor cannot, and does not need to, resort to the creditor's claim against him in order to obtain the benefit of the security; his own liability to the creditor is automatically discharged or reduced.

In *Halesowen Presswork Assemblies Ltd. v. National Westminster Bank Ltd.* [1971] 1 Q.B. 1, 46 Buckley L.J., in a passage subsequently approved in the House of Lords [1972] A.C. 785 by Viscount Dilhorne, at p. 802, Lord Simon of Glaisdale at p. 808, and Lord Cross of Chelsea, at p. 810, stated that he could not understand how it could be said with any kind of accuracy that the bank had a lien upon its own indebtedness to its customer. It is true that this comment was made in relation to a lien rather than a charge, and a lien unlike a charge can only attach to tangible property. But the reason why it was said that the bank did not have a lien on the credit balance in its customer's current account was clearly based on the identity of the parties rather than the particular character of the security given. . . .'

[326] ***Re Bank of Credit and Commerce International SA (No 8)*** **[1998] AC 214 (HL), 225–8** ***per*** **Lord Hoffmann:**

[The facts are immaterial. What are extracted below are *dicta* supporting the idea that a person can take a charge over his or her own indebtedness. Note too the comments on whether such a charge would be registrable.]

> 'The doctrine of conceptual impossibility was first propounded by Millett J. in *In re Charge Card Services Ltd.* [1987] Ch. 150, 175–176 and affirmed, after more extensive

discussion, by the Court of Appeal in this case. It has excited a good deal of heat and controversy in banking circles; the Legal Risk Review Committee, set up in 1991 by the Bank of England to identify areas of obscurity and uncertainty in the law affecting financial markets and propose solutions, said that a very large number of submissions from interested parties expressed disquiet about this ruling. It seems clear that documents purporting to create such charges have been used by banks for many years. The point does not previously appear to have been expressly addressed by any court in this country. Supporters of the doctrine rely on the judgments of Buckley L.J. (in the Court of Appeal) and Viscount Dilhorne and Lord Cross of Chelsea (in the House of Lords) in *Halesowen Presswork Assemblies Ltd. v. Westminster Bank Ltd.* [1971] 1 Q.B. 1; [1972] A.C. 785. The passages in question certainly say that it is a misuse of language to speak of a bank having a lien over its own indebtedness to a customer. But I think that these observations were directed to the use of the word "lien", which is a right to retain possession, rather than to the question of whether the bank could have any kind of proprietary interest. Opponents of the doctrine rely upon some 19th century cases, of which it can at least be said that the possibility of a charge over a debt owed by the chargee caused no judicial surprise.

The reason given by the Court of Appeal [1996] Ch. 245, 258 was that "a man cannot have a proprietary interest in a debt or other obligation which he owes another." In order to test this proposition, I think one needs to identify the normal characteristics of an equitable charge and then ask to what extent they would be inconsistent with a situation in which the property charged consisted of a debt owed by the beneficiary of the charge. There are several well known descriptions of an equitable charge (see, for example, that of Atkin L.J. in *National Provincial and Union Bank of England v. Charnley* [1924] 1 K.B. 431, 449–450) but none of them purports to be exhaustive. Nor do I intend to provide one. An equitable charge is a species of charge, which is a proprietary interest granted by way of security. Proprietary interests confer rights in rem which, subject to questions of registration and the equitable doctrine of purchaser for value without notice, will be binding upon third parties and unaffected by the insolvency of the owner of the property charged. A proprietary interest provided by way of security entitles the holder to resort to the property only for the purpose of satisfying some liability due to him (whether from the person providing the security or a third party) and, whatever the form of the transaction, the owner of the property retains an equity of redemption to have the property restored to him when the liability has been discharged. The method by which the holder of the security will resort to the property will ordinarily involve its sale or, more rarely, the extinction of the equity of redemption by foreclosure. A charge is a security interest created without any transfer of title or possession to the beneficiary. An equitable charge can be created by an informal transaction for value (legal charges may require a deed or registration or both) and over any kind of property (equitable as well as legal) but is subject to the doctrine of purchaser for value without notice applicable to all equitable interests.

The depositor's right to claim payment of his deposit is a chose in action which the law has always recognised as property. There is no dispute that a charge over such a chose in action can validly be granted to a third party. In which respects would the fact that the beneficiary of the charge was the debtor himself be inconsistent with the transaction having some or all of the various features which I have enumerated? The method by which the property would be realised would differ slightly: instead of the beneficiary of the charge having to claim payment from the debtor, the realisation would take the form of a book entry. In no other respect, as it seems to me, would the transaction have any consequences different from those which would attach to a charge given to a third party. It would be a proprietary interest in the sense that, subject to questions of registration and purchaser for value without notice, it would be binding upon assignees and a liquidator or trustee in bankruptcy. The depositor would retain an equity of redemption and all the rights which that implies. There would be no merger of interests because the depositor would retain title to the deposit subject only to the bank's charge. The creation of the charge would be consensual and not require any formal assignment or vesting of title in the bank. If all these features can exist despite the fact that the beneficiary of the charge is the debtor, I cannot see why it cannot properly be said that the debtor has a proprietary interest by way of charge over the debt.

The Court of Appeal said that the bank could obtain effective security in other ways. If the deposit was made by the principal debtor, it could rely upon contractual rights of set-off or combining accounts or rules of bankruptcy set-off under provisions such as rule 4.90. If the deposit was made by a third party, it could enter into contractual arrangements such as the limitation on the right to withdraw the deposit in this case, thereby making the deposit a "flawed asset." All this is true. It may well be that the security provided in these ways will in most cases be just as good as that provided by a proprietary interest. But that seems to me no reason for preventing banks and their customers from creating charges over deposits if, for reasons of their own, they want to do so. The submissions to the Legal Risk Review Committee made it clear that they do.

If such charges are granted by companies over their "book debts" they will be registrable under section 395 and 396(1)(e) of the Companies Act 1985. There is a suggestion in the judgment of the Court of Appeal that the banking community has been insufficiently grateful for being spared the necessity of registering such charges. In my view, this is a matter on which banks are entitled to make up their own minds and take their own advice on whether the deposit charged is a "book debt" or not. I express no view on the point, but the judgment of my noble and learned friend, Lord Hutton, in *Northern Bank Ltd. v. Ross* [1990] B.C.C. 883 suggests that, in the case of deposits with banks, an obligation to register is unlikely to arise.

Since the decision in *In re Charge Card Services Ltd.* [1987] Ch. 150 statutes have been passed in several offshore banking jurisdictions to reverse its effect. A typical example is section 15A of the Hong Kong Law Amendment and Reform (Consolidation) Ordinance (c. 23), which I have already mentioned. It reads:

> "For the avoidance of doubt, it is hereby declared that a person ('the first person') is able to create, and always has been able to create, in favour of another person ('the second person') a legal or equitable charge or mortgage over all or any of the first person's interest in a chose in action enforceable by the first person against the second person, and any charge or mortgage so created shall operate neither to merge the interest thereby created with, nor to extinguish or release, that chose in action."

There is similar legislation in Singapore (section 9A of the Civil Law Act (c. 43)); Bermuda (the Charge and Security (Special Provisions) Act 1990 (c. 53)) and the Cayman Islands (the Property (Miscellaneous Provisions) Law 1994 (No. 7 of 1994)). The striking feature about all these provisions is that none of them amend or repeal any rule of common law which would be inconsistent with the existence of a charge over a debt owed by the chargee. They simply say that such a charge can be granted. If the trick can be done as easily as this, it is hard to see where the conceptual impossibility is to be found.

In a case in which there is no threat to the consistency of the law or objection of public policy, I think that the courts should be very slow to declare a practice of the commercial community to be conceptually impossible. Rules of law must obviously be consistent and not self-contradictory; thus in *Rye v. Rye* [1962] A.C. 496, 505, Viscount Simonds demonstrated that the notion of a person granting a lease to himself was inconsistent with every feature of a lease, both as a contract and as an estate in land. But the law is fashioned to suit the practicalities of life and legal concepts like "proprietary interest" and "charge" are no more than labels given to clusters of related and self-consistent rules of law. Such concepts do not have a life of their own from which the rules are inexorably derived. It follows that in my view the letter was effective to do what it purported to do, namely to create a charge over the deposit in favour of B.C.C.I. . . .'

Questions:

1. Which of these analyses is more persuasive?
2. Even if Lord Hoffmann is correct that a debt at a bank is not a book debt, and so the charge does not require registration under that head, is the charge nevertheless a floating charge, so requiring registration in any event? What could the bank do to avoid this conclusion? (See Companies Act 1985 sections 395, 396, extracted at **[603]** below.)

FURTHER READING:

R Calnan, 'Fashioning the Law to Suit the Practicalities of Life' (1998) 114 *LQR* 174.

3.6.6 Effectiveness of floating charges

All of the matters covered so far have concerned the *nature* of a floating charge. However, the *effectiveness* of a floating charge as a security device depends upon how it stands up in competition with other security holders (ie its strength in *priority* disputes) and even against claims from unsecured creditors of the debtor. The general issues are discussed in more detail in Chapter 6. For the moment it is sufficient to recognise that it is of the nature of a floating charge that the secured assets will be dealt with by the debtor in the ordinary course of the debtor's business. These dealings may often involve the creation of proprietary rights in the assets in favour third parties, and those rights can generally be granted by the debtor free of the encumbrance of the floating security.

In general, a debtor who has granted a floating charge over certain assets can, notwithstanding the charge, deal with those assets so as to:

(i) sell the assets in the ordinary course of business to third party purchasers who will acquire unencumbered legal title. It is this characteristic of a floating charge which gives it its commercial value. It enables the debtor to continue to operate a business which uses the charged assets.
(ii) grant a subsequent *fixed* charge over the same assets so as to give priority to the fixed charge holder over the earlier floating charge holder: *Wheatley v Silkstone and Haigh Moor Coal Co* (1885) 29 Ch D 715. In an attempt to

avoid this possibility, floating charge holders usually insert 'negative pledge' clauses in their charges. These are clauses that restrict the debtor's ability to create subsequent charges which rank ahead of or equally with the floating charge. However, these clauses are only effective to protect the floating charge holder if the subsequent chargee has actual (not just constructive) notice[21] of the existence of the clause itself (not just the earlier floating charge): *English & Scottish Mercantile Investment Co Ltd v Brunton* [1892] 2 QB 700 (CA). Since negative pledges are not part of the registrable particulars of a charge, third parties are not affected by constructive notice of their existence. However, a third party with actual notice will take the charged property subject to the equities (ie subject to the rights of the earlier floating charge holder); and

(iii) grant a subsequent *floating* charge over *part* of the secured assets so as to give priority to the second floating charge holder, but only provided the power to do so is reserved in the original charge: *Re Benjamin Cope & Sons Ltd* [1914] 1 Ch 800 and *Re Automatic Bottle Makers Ltd* [1926] Ch 412 (CA).

As the next extract illustrates, the debtor's other dealings with the charged property can have an adverse impact on the creditor's security.

[327] ***George Barker Ltd v Eynon*** **[1974] 1 WLR 462 (CA), 472–3** ***per*** **Stamp LJ:** [The case concerned a priority dispute between the holder of a contractual lien and the holder of a floating charge. The claimants had a contractual lien over the goods of a meat importing company whose indebtedness to a bank was secured by a mortgage debenture creating a floating charge. The debenture holder's rights crystallised on the appointment of a receiver, but the Court of Appeal held that the lien took priority because the contractual rights arose even earlier, before the appointment of the receiver and so before crystallisation of the charge. This was notwithstanding that the claimants did not acquire actual possession of the goods until three days after the receiver's appointment.]

[Also re-read the judgment of Edmund-Davies LJ at pp 468–70, at **[304]** above.]

> 'Shorn of the arguments supporting it, the receiver's contention before this court was that this is a case of priorities. The lien was a possessory lien which did not come into existence until the carriers were in possession of the goods. Before the carriers came into possession of the goods the charge in favour of the debenture holder crystallised by the effect of the appointment of the receiver. The goods had become the subject of an equitable assignment to the debenture holder and the lien could not come into existence as against the debenture holder.
>
> These submissions are not, in my judgment, well founded. What is in law described under the convenient label of a "lien" is in relation to a carrier the right to hold the goods which have been carried in respect of the costs of the carriage or, as in this case, the contractual right to hold the goods which have been carried in respect of the debt for the carriage and in respect of the debts of the same character previously contracted. The duty of the carriers here was to carry the goods and deliver them, or they might say

[21] *Siebe Gorman & Co Ltd v Barclays Bank Ltd* [1979] 2 Lloyd's Rep 142.

after they had carried them, "We will hold these goods in exercise of the right to do so conferred by the contract of carriage until we have been paid," and they might say, "Moreover, we will, unless we are paid within a reasonable time, in exercise of our right under the contract, sell the goods and pay ourselves out of the proceeds. These are the terms upon which we carried the goods." In my judgment, these rights did not arise or come into existence at the time the carriers took possession of the goods. Nor clearly did they become exercisable at that time. The rights were rights created by the contract which became exercisable at the moment of time when the goods had been carried. The rights which were conferred on the carriers by condition 13 of the contract are conveniently and accurately described as a "lien," but you do not by so describing them alter their character. They are conveniently described as "a possessory lien," because it is only if the carriers have possession that they can be exercised. But to say that a lien, because it is so described, does not come into existence until possession is assumed is to reason falsely. Contractual rights come into existence at the time of the contract creating them notwithstanding that they may not be exercisable except upon the happening of a future event. Here the fact of obtaining possession of the goods was a preliminary to the exercise of the right claimed, but still the rights were not exercisable until the carriers had carried the goods. The contractual "lien" to which the carriers were entitled under the contract was not a legal "thing" or "chose in action" arising by the effect of possession, but no more than a description of the bundle of rights belonging to the carriers under condition 13 and which the company had contracted they should have.

There was nothing remarkable about the contract. It was simply a contract for the carriage of goods incorporating the Conditions of Carriage of the Road Haulage Association. It was, in my judgment, clearly a contract into which, so long as the charge created by the debenture was a floating charge, the company could, consistently with the terms of the debenture, properly enter into. It was, as I have indicated, a contract which was not determined by the effect of the appointment of the receiver. The receiver might, so I will assume, have repudiated it before the carriers started the journey, so preventing the carriers obtaining possession of the goods and carrying out their obligations under it. He did not do so. How then could the receiver or the debenture holder as assignee of the goods and of the rights of the company under the contract be in any better position than would the company have been to insist at the end of the journey that the goods be handed over without making the payments for which condition 13 provided? In my judgment, Mr. Tugendhat was right in his contention that the assignment to the debenture holder brought about by the appointment of the receiver was subject to the rights already given by the company to other persons under ordinary trading contracts. As against the company, the carriers on arriving at the door of the consignees at Gravesend could have withheld the goods against payment, and in my judgment, the debenture holder as assignee from the company can be in no better position. The debenture holder as assignee of the company's rights under the contract can be in no better position than any other assignee of the company's rights under the contract. . . .'

3.6.7 Summarising the issues

The next extract provides useful summary of the steps necessary in analysing a security arrangement suspected of being a floating charge.

[328] ***Re Cosslett (Contractors) Ltd*** **[1998] Ch 495 (CA), 506, 508–11** ***per*** **Millett LJ:**
[The facts are outlined at **[210]** above.]

'In my judgment the following questions arise for decision. . . . (3) Whether the council's power of sale arises by way of equitable charge or possessory lien. (4) If either right arises by way of charge, whether the charge is a fixed or floating charge. (5) If so, what are the consequences of the company's failure to register it?

[See **[210]** above for Millett LJ's analysis of the earlier questions.]

(3) Does the council's power of sale arise by way of equitable charge?
By contrast the council's power to sell the plant and apply the proceeds in or towards discharge of whatever sums might be or become due from the company by reason of its failure to complete the works clearly is a security interest. The council contends that its rights constitute a possessory lien with a power of sale and not an equitable charge, and cites *Great Eastern Railway Co. v. Lord's Trustee* [1909] A.C. 109 in support.

This proposition cannot be accepted. In the *Great Eastern Railway* case there was no dispute that the railway company's power of sale was attached to its lien. The question which divided the House of Lords was whether the lien was contractual or possessory. The majority held that its carrier's lien was not extinguished until the goods were unconditionally delivered up to the consignee and that accordingly it did not need to rely upon any contractual right of possession.

There are only four kinds of consensual security known to English law: (i) pledge; (ii) contractual lien; (iii) equitable charge and (iv) mortgage. A pledge and a contractual lien both depend on the delivery of possession to the creditor. The difference between them is that in the case of a pledge the owner delivers possession to the creditor as security, whereas in the case of a lien the creditor retains possession of goods previously delivered to him for some other purpose. Neither a mortgage nor a charge depends on the delivery of possession. The difference between them is that a mortgage involves a transfer of legal or equitable ownership to the creditor, whereas an equitable charge does not.

In the present case the council's rights in relation to the plant and materials are exclusively contractual, and are not attributable to any delivery of possession by the company. When the company brings plant and materials onto the site they remain in the possession of the company to enable it to use them in the completion of the works. There is no question of the company delivering possession at that stage, either by way of security (i.e. as a pledge) or otherwise (i.e. by way of lien). The council comes into possession of the plant and materials when it expels the company from the site leaving the plant and materials behind. But this does not amount to a voluntary delivery of possession by the company to the council. It is rather the exercise by the council of a contractual right to take possession of the plant and materials against the will of the company.

In my judgment, therefore, the council's rights are derived from contract not possession and, in so far as they are conferred by way of security, constitute an equitable charge.

(4) Is the charge a fixed or floating charge?
In my judgment the three characteristics of a floating charge which were identified by Romer L.J. in *In re Yorkshire Woolcombers Association Ltd.; Houldsworth v. Yorkshire Woolcombers Association Ltd.* [1903] 2 Ch. 284, 295 are all present. There is no difficulty in regard to the first two characteristics. Plant and materials become subject to the charge as they are brought onto the site and cease to be subject to it as they are removed from the site. Accordingly the charge is a charge on present and future assets of the

company which, in the ordinary course of the business of the company, would be changing from time to time. The dispute has centred on the third characteristic. The administrator submits that, until the council takes steps under clause 63(1) to enter upon the site and expel the company therefrom, the company is free to carry on its business in the ordinary way with the plant and materials on the site. The judge accepted the council's submission that this was not so, because of the council's absolute right under clause 53(6) to refuse to permit the company to remove from the site plant and materials immediately required to complete the works, and its qualified right to refuse permission for the removal of plant and materials not immediately required for this purpose provided only that it acts reasonably. I am unable to agree with him.

The judge held that it is of the essence of a floating charge that until the charge crystallises the chargor should retain an unfettered freedom to carry on his business in the ordinary way. He relied for this purpose on two passages, one in the judgment of Vaughan Williams L.J. in the *Yorkshire Woolcombers* case, at p. 294, and the other in the judgment of Slade J. in *In re Bond Worth Ltd.* [1980] Ch. 228, 266. The first passage reads as follows:

> "If *at the will of the mortgagor* he can dispose of [the asset] and prevent its being any longer a security, although something else may be substituted more or less for it, that is not a 'specific security.'" (My emphasis.)

The second passage reads:

> "It is in my judgment quite incompatible with the existence of an effective trust by way of specific charge in equity over specific assets that *the alleged trustee* should be free to use them as he pleases for his own business in the course of his own business." (My emphasis.)

But with respect the converse does not follow. The chargor's unfettered freedom to deal with the assets in the ordinary course of his business free from the charge is obviously inconsistent with the nature of a fixed charge; but it does not follow that his unfettered freedom to deal with the charged assets is essential to the existence of a floating charge. It plainly is not, for any well drawn floating charge prohibits the chargor from creating further charges having priority to the floating charge; and a prohibition against factoring debts is not sufficient to convert what would otherwise be a floating charge on book debts into a fixed charge: see in *In re Brightlife Ltd.* [1987] Ch. 200, 209, per Hoffmann J.

The essence of a floating charge is that it is a charge, not on any particular asset, but on a fluctuating body of assets which remain under the management and control of the chargor, and which the chargor has the right to withdraw from the security despite the existence of the charge. The essence of a fixed charge is that the charge is on a particular asset or class of assets which the chargor cannot deal with free from the charge without the consent of the chargee. The question is not whether the chargor has complete freedom to carry on his business as he chooses, but whether the chargee is in control of the charged assets.

The business of the company was to carry out works of civil engineering. In the ordinary course of that business it entered into the contract with the council. In bringing plant and materials onto the site and carrying out the works for the council it was carrying on the ordinary course of its business. It is not to be supposed that its business was confined to the performance of its contract with the council; and if it wished to remove plant or materials from the site and deploy them elsewhere this too would be in the ordinary course of its business. In forbidding the company from removing from the site plant or materials required, whether immediately or not, for the completion of the works, the council was, therefore, placing a restriction on the way in which the company carried on business.

Thus far I agree with the judge. Where I part company from him is that I do not regard this restriction as having any relation to the council's security. The council's purpose in imposing the restriction was not to protect its security but to ensure that the company would give proper priority to the completion of the works. A similar restriction would have been appropriate even if the council had not taken any security interest.

In a case where the plant or materials are not immediately required, the engineer's consent is not to be unreasonably withheld. As Evans L.J. pointed out in argument, the fact that the decision is left to the engineer shows that it is to be made on operational grounds. If completion of the works will not be prejudiced or delayed by the removal of an item of plant or materials, then consent to its removal must be given; consent cannot be withheld on the ground that the remaining plant and materials would be insufficient security if the company were in default.

In the course of argument it was pointed out that the council must give seven days' notice before expelling the company from the site, and it was suggested that once such notice has been given and while it has not yet expired the engineer may properly refuse his consent on the ground that the remaining security is insufficient. I do not agree with this; but even if I did it would make no difference. If the council's right to prevent removal on security and non-operational grounds arises only upon notice of expulsion, then in my judgment the effect of giving such notice is to crystallise the charge.

Accordingly, and in disagreement with the judge, I hold the charge to be a floating charge.

What are the consequences of the want of registration?

Of all the contractual rights which the council enjoys only one, the power of sale, constitutes a charge of a kind which is registrable under section 395 of the Companies Act 1985. The section provides that the failure to register a charge makes the charge (that is to say the registrable charge) void as a security against a liquidator or administrator of the company. The effect of this is to entitle the liquidator or administrator to deal with the company's assets free from the security created by the charge in question.

In my judgment, therefore, the failure to register the charge renders the security created by the power of sale void as against the administrator, but does not affect any other right of the council which is not a security and which does not require registration. In particular, it does not invalidate the council's contractual right to retain possession of plant and materials and use them to complete the works. But after the completion of the works the council's right to continue in possession is referable to a security which is void against the administrator and cannot prevail against him.

In reaching this conclusion I have derived much assistance from the illuminating judgment of Brinsden J. in *Young v. Matthew Hall Mechanical & Electrical Engineers Pty. Ltd.* (1988) 13 A.C.L.R. 399 with which I am in full agreement.'

3.6.8 Policy arguments for eliminating the floating charge as a security device

[329] R Goode, 'The Exodus of the Floating Charge' in D Feldman and F Meisel (eds), *Corporate and Commercial Law: Modern Developments* (1996, Lloyd's of London Press: London) ch 10, pp 201–3:
[Footnotes in the original are omitted.]

'SHOULD ENGLISH LAW PRESERVE THE FLOATING CHARGE?

There is no doubt that the floating charge has made a major contribution to the ability of companies to raise secured finance. Its attractions are considerable. Like the Article 9 security interest it can provide global security over existing and future assets to secure present and future indebtedness. It can be created by a single security agreement and perfected by a single filing. It provides the creditor with an inchoate security while leaving the debtor company free to deal with its assets in the ordinary course of business. Its principal weakness, the risk of subordination to subsequent secured and execution creditors, can be largely (though not entirely) overcome by negative pledge clauses noted on the register and by provision for automatic crystallisation of the charge as regards those assets against which an execution is initiated.

But despite all these advantages the floating charge is now an anachronism. The fundamental problem lies not so much in the floating charge itself but in the fact that English personal property security law consists mainly of an aggregation of judicial artefacts which have evolved over the centuries, each with its own distinctive legal characteristics, its own mode of creation, its own rules of perfection and priorities. It is true that in formulating the rules the courts have been as responsive to policy considerations as they feel judicial lawmaking will allow. But principles and rules extracted with effort from a huge body of case law are no substitute for a modern personal property security statute in which all transactions intended to serve a security function are brought together in a uniform system of regulation, with rules of attachment, perfection and priorities being determined by legislative policy rather than by conceptual reasoning. It is the lack of this integrated framework which is at the root of our present troubles.

This can readily be demonstrated. The existence of the floating charge as a distinct security device makes it necessary to lay down criteria for distinguishing it from a fixed charge. The importance of the distinction lies in the different priority rules for fixed and floating charges and in the subordination of floating, but not fixed, charges to preferential claims on a winding-up or the appointment of a receiver. It is therefore essential to have clear criteria for differentiating the two types of security. But in relation to charges on book debts and their proceeds the law is now in a state of confusion which can only be resolved by the House of Lords or by legislation. A secured creditor cannot appoint an administrative receiver unless his security consists of or includes a floating charge, but there is no requirement that the assets covered by the floating charge should have a significant value in relation to the whole. So if a creditor takes a fixed charge only, the fact that this covers 99 per cent of the debtor's assets does not entitle him to appoint a receiver. Again, the Insolvency Act contains special provisions for the avoidance of floating charges given by an insolvent company otherwise than for new value of a specified kind. The underlying policy, carried over from earlier legislation, is presumably to prevent unsecured creditors from being excessively disadvantaged by the broad sweep of the floating charge. Yet most of the debtor's assets are capable of being tied up by a fixed charge which is not subject to these special provisions.

The sweep of the floating charge and its impact on other creditors have been matters of criticism and concern almost from the time of its creation. Judges have complained that it is unfair to execution creditors, who see the fruits of their diligence slip away from them as the result of crystallisation; government committees, such as the Loreburn Committee in 1906 and the Cork Committee in 1982, have been urged to recommend its total abolition; the Cork Committee itself, though not going so far, advocated that 10 per cent of net realisations of assets subject to a floating charge should be set aside to create a fund for distribution among ordinary unsecured creditors. A further ground of criticism is that crystallisation of the floating charge, which has potential implications for subsequent creditors, is not required to be registered, so that third parties subsequently dealing with the company may be misled.

Article 9 avoids all these complications by permitting immediate attachment of the security interest, even where the debtor is given power to deal with its assets in the ordinary course of business, and by using priority rules based on considerations of policy to determine in what circumstances that interest will be overreached by a subsequent dealing or execution against assets. It is arguable that the priority rules in Article 9 are weighted too heavily in favour of the secured creditor, but that is a policy issue which can be addressed by modifying the rules and does not affect the fundamental point that a unified concept of security interests in which rules of attachment, perfection and priority are clearly laid out and are designed to produce results that are fair in the typical case is greatly preferable to the uncodified and unsystematised collocation of rules we have painfully developed in this country over the past century.

Nearly 30 years ago Professor Jim Gower and I argued that Article 9 was eminently suitable for importation into England. Three years later the same conclusion was reached by the Crowther Committee, which recommended legislation along similar lines, a conclusion supported by evidence submitted to the Insolvency Law Review Committee in 1982 and by the Diamond Report in 1989. So far, nothing has been done in this direction, nor is there any indication that it will be.

The result has been all too predictable: the extensive use of non- registrable retention of title clauses in sale agreements, followed by a great amount of litigation on the validity of claims to proceeds on the buyer's liquidation; a bevy of cases which have left the distinction between fixed and floating charges in a state of confusion; and an outcome of priority disputes which owes more to judicial precedent and conceptual reasoning than to considerations of policy or commercial practicality. The fault lies not with the judges, who have struggled valiantly, and to remarkably good effect, to produce a coherent pattern of security rights, but with the government and Parliament for failing to appreciate the huge waste of time and expense caused by our failure to modernise our personal property security law.

I shall mourn the passing of the floating charge, which has done so much to facilitate large-scale secured financing and, in the process, to enrich English doctrine and jurisprudence. English law can take pride in having fashioned through the ingenuity of its equity judges an instrument of great power and even greater mystery. But the world moves on, and we must move with it. As we enter the next millennium it is time for the unified personal property security interest to take hold in these islands.'

3.7 Practical security arrangements

All of the preceding sections of this chapter have concerned *legal* securities. However, there are other *practical* routes open to creditors who wish to have protection in the event of their debtor's insolvency. All these practical devices are designed to allow the creditor to claw back specific assets in the event that the debtor seems to be unable to meet his or her personal obligations. Some of these devices are very familiar. For example, hire purchase arrangements operate on the basis that the hirer/purchaser is given the right to possess and use certain goods during the period of hire and the right to purchase those goods at the end of hiring period. The protective element arises because the seller/hirer retains legal ownership of the goods until their eventual purchase, so that if in the interim the customer cannot maintain the agreed repayments the seller/hirer can simply reclaim the asset as its own (subject to the terms of the agreement and the equitable rules on penalties). Other devices are less familiar. The rest of this chapter looks at two particular options open to creditors: retention of title agreements (or *Romalpa* clauses) and *Quistclose* trusts. These devices depend for their effectiveness upon the creditor's ability to assert legal or equitable title (respectively) to property which is in the hands of the debtor, and so to claim that property to the exclusion of any other creditors, secured or unsecured. Both of these devices thus put assets outside the *pari passu* insolvency distribution rules and also outside the reach of parties with legal security.

3.8 Retention of title (*Romalpa*) clauses

A bank lending to a corporate business will usually secure its loan by an all-assets floating charge. In the event of the company's insolvency, the bank is then likely to claim all that the company has.[22] The ordinary trade creditors will be left with little or nothing. The injustice seems particularly stark when goods supplied to the company on credit are immediately captured by the floating charge, notwithstanding that the credit has been advanced by the supplier, not the bank. Retention of title clauses are devices aimed at protecting such suppliers. They are commonly inserted into contracts for the sale of goods. At their most basic, they provide for goods to be sold and delivered to the purchaser, but for legal title to the goods to remain with the seller until the full purchase price for the goods has been paid. The effect is evident: the goods are isolated from the corporate debtor's dominion; they cannot feed the floating charge nor satisfy the claims of other unsecured creditors.

The attraction of effective retention of title clauses is that they secure the supplier's position in the event of the buyer's insolvency, and they do this without the

[22] Subject to the rights of preferred creditors to have access to the assets subject to a floating charge: Insolvency Act 1986 ss 40, 175.

need for registration of the agreement. This is because the Companies Act 1985 Part XII contains a very restrictive definition of registrable securities. A retention of title clause does not give the supplier a legal security interest—although it certainly provides functional security.

The doctrinal basis for retention of title clauses is very simple. In a contract for the sale of unascertained goods, legal title usually passes to the buyer when the goods are unconditionally appropriated to the contract (see the Sale of Goods Act 1979 section 18, Rule 5(1)). According to this rule, delivery of the goods to the buyer would certainly be sufficient to effect a transfer of legal title. However, the Sale of Goods Act 1979 section 19(1) permits the seller to impose conditions on the passing of legal title:

> 'the seller may, by the terms of the contract or appropriation, reserve the right of disposal of the goods until certain conditions are fulfilled; and in such a case, notwithstanding the delivery of the goods to the buyer . . . the property in the goods does not pass to the buyer until the conditions imposed by the seller are fulfilled.'

This provision is the basis for *simple retention of title clauses* (securing the payment of the purchase price of the goods) and also for *'all-moneys' retention of title clauses* (securing the payment of all moneys owed by the buyer to the seller, or even all moneys owed by the buyer and any associated companies to the seller and its associated companies). On the plain reading of the Sale of Goods Act 1979 section 19(1), there seems to be no limit to the nature of the condition which may be imposed to restrict the transfer of title to goods from the seller to the buyer, although the matter has been the subject of debate: see **[337]** below. As the cases extracted below indicate, simple retention of title clauses and all moneys clauses are routinely upheld by the courts.[23]

However, in the typical scenario both parties anticipate that the goods supplied will be either sold by the buyer or used in some manufacturing process *before* the price is fully paid—ie before the imposed condition is met. This activity is the source of the buyer's income from which to pay the price, and is normally expressly consented to by the seller.[24] Clearly use or disposal of the goods themselves defeats the efficacy of the supplier's practical security device. More sophisticated variations of the simple retention of title clause therefore attempt to give the seller full or partial ownership of the proceeds of any sale of the goods ('*proceeds clauses*') or of the products derived from them ('*products clauses*'). As will be seen below, such clauses are generally unsuccessful because they are construed as registrable but unregistered charges.

[23] The difficulties are generally practical, not legal: the clause must be incorporated as a term of the contract; the goods claimed by the seller must be those supplied under the contract; and the amount secured by the retention of title clause must be wholly or partly unpaid.

[24] And even if it were not, a sale by the buyer to a third party would nevertheless deliver full legal title to the third party: the Sale of Goods Act 1979 ss 21(1), 25(1).

3.8.1 Simple retention of title clauses

[330] ***Aluminium Industrie Vaassen BV v Romalpa Aluminium Ltd*** **[1976] 1 WLR 676 (Mocatta J and CA), 680–3** ***per*** **Mocatta J and 689–90** ***per*** **Roskill LJ:**
[The defendants (a Dutch company) supplied the claimants with aluminium foil for processing. The contract of sale stipulated that ownership of the foil would not pass until the price had been paid in full; that products made from the foil should be kept by the buyers as 'fiduciary owners' separately from other stock, and on the supplier's behalf, as 'surety' for the outstanding price; and that the buyers should have the power to sell the manufactured articles in the ordinary course of business, but as the supplier's agent. Mocatta J, whose judgment was affirmed by the Court of Appeal, held that the suppliers could trace the price due to them into the proceeds of sales of the unused foil, ahead of the buyer's secured and unsecured creditors. This conclusion was reached on the basis that the retention of title clause, read as a whole, indicated an intention to create a fiduciary relationship between the supplier and the buyer.]

Mocatta J:

'In the first place, it is admitted that the plaintiffs are the owners of the remaining unsold aluminium foil held by the receiver, and that they are entitled to an order for its delivery up to them. The real contest arose in relation to the plaintiffs' right to a charge on the receiver's account with the Hume Corporation to the extent of £35,152.66 representing, as certified by the receiver, the sum recovered by him from customers of the defendants as a result of A.I.V. materials supplied to the defendants by the plaintiffs. This right the plaintiffs claim on the basis of the principle established in *In re Hallett's Estate*, 13 Ch.D. 696 [see **[627]** below] entitling them to trace the proceeds of the sale of their property sold by the plaintiffs into the receiver's bank account. It is common ground that the effect of clause 13 is that, while money was owing by the defendants to the plaintiffs, any aluminium foil delivered by the plaintiffs to the defendants, while still in their possession, was held by them as bailees.

It is further common ground that the clause must be read subject to the necessary implication that the defendants were entitled to sell the foil to sub-purchasers. It is curious that this is not said about sales of unmixed foil whilst it is said in the last sentence of the clause about foil mixed with other material. In respect of this, it is to be noted that the defendants were, if required, to assign to the plaintiffs their rights against sub-purchasers in respect of the mixed materials sold to them. Notwithstanding the generally far-reaching and somewhat elaborate provisions in clause 13, reserving the plaintiff's right of ownership in the goods until nothing was owing from the purchasers, and the admission that the clause had the effect of making the defendants bailees of the goods while in their possession until all money owing had been paid, the argument for the defendants was that once foil had been sold to bona fide purchasers, the relationship between the plaintiffs and the defendants was purely one of debtor and creditor. As against this, the plaintiffs argued that a fiduciary relationship stemming from the bailment continued after sales to third parties, and that in consequence equitable remedies applied, including the right to trace proceeds of the sub-sales. It was not necessary, said the plaintiffs, to find as a prerequisite to the right to trace an express or constructive trust. The equitable proprietary remedy followed as a consequence of the finding that the defendants were bailees.

Having indicated the general nature of the competing arguments, I can go straight to the judgment of Sir George Jessel M.R. in *In re Hallett's Estate*, 13 Ch.D. 696.

Although in that case there had been breaches of express trust, it is clear from the passages I am about to read that the reasoning was not founded on this, and that the principle stated applied to much wider circumstances. It is necessary to make certain fairly extensive quotations. Sir George Jessel M.R. said, at p. 708:

> "The modern doctrine of equity as regards property disposed of by persons in a fiduciary position is a very clear and well-established doctrine. You can, if the sale was rightful, take the proceeds of the sale, if you can identify them. If the sale was wrongful, you can still take the proceeds of the sale, in a sense adopting the sale for the purpose of taking the proceeds, if you can identify them. There is no distinction, therefore, between a rightful and a wrongful disposition of the property, so far as regards the right of the beneficial owner to follow the proceeds. . . ."

Pausing there for a moment, it is not, of course, suggested here that there was a wrongful disposition of the plaintiff's property when the defendants sold the foil to bona fide sub-purchasers. The latter would get a good title pursuant to section 25 of the Sale of Goods Act 1893. As between the plaintiffs and defendants, however, property had never passed to the defendants. I continue with the quotation, at p. 709:

> "But it very often happens that you cannot identify the proceeds. The proceeds may have been invested together with money belonging to the person in a fiduciary position, in a purchase. He may have bought land with it, for instance, or he may have bought chattels with it. Now, what is the position of the beneficial owner as regards such purchases? I will, first of all, take his position when the purchase is clearly made with what I will call, for shortness, the trust money, although it is not confined, as I will shew presently, to express trusts. In that case, according to the now well-established doctrine of equity, the beneficial owner has a right to elect either to take the property purchased, or to hold it as a security for the amount of the trust money laid out in the purchase; or, as we generally express it, he is entitled at his election either to take the property, or to have a charge on the property for the amount of the trust money. But in the second case, where a trustee has mixed the money with his own, there is this distinction, that the cestui que trust, or beneficial owner, can no longer elect to take the property, because it is no longer bought with the trust money simply and purely, but with a mixed fund. He is, however, still entitled to a charge on the property purchased, for the amount of the trust money laid out in the purchase; and that charge is quite independent of the fact of the amount laid out by the trustee. The moment you get a substantial portion of it furnished by the trustee, using the word 'trustee' in the sense I have mentioned, as including all persons in a fiduciary relation, the right to the charge follows. That is the modern doctrine of equity . . ."

There then follows this passage showing the width of the application of the principle:

> "Has it ever been suggested, until very recently, that there is any distinction between an express trustee, or an agent, or a bailee, or a collector of rents, or anybody else in a fiduciary position? I have never heard, until quite recently, such a distinction suggested. It cannot, as far as I am aware (and since this court sat last to hear this case, I have taken the trouble to look for authority), be found in any reported case even suggested, except in the recent decision of Fry J. [*Ex parte Dale & Co.* (1879) 11 Ch.D. 772,] to which I shall draw attention presently. It can have no foundation in principle, because the beneficial ownership is the same, wherever the legal ownership may be."

There is the following short passage, at p. 710:

"Now that being the established doctrine of equity on this point, I will take the case of the pure bailee. If the bailee sells the goods bailed, the bailor can in equity follow the proceeds, and can follow the proceeds wherever they can be distinguished, either being actually kept separate, or being mixed up with other moneys."

Finally, this sentence, at p. 711:

"Therefore, there is no difficulty in following out the rules of equity and deciding that in a case of a mere bailee, as Fry J. has decided, you can follow the money."

These passages are clearly most apposite, since they refer to the position of a mere bailee, and were strongly relied upon by Mr. Lincoln. Mr. Pickering sought to avoid them by saying that they were obiter or had in some way been modified in *In re Diplock* [1948] Ch. 465 and that it was necessary that there should be some express or constructive trust before the equitable doctrine could apply. My attention was not drawn to any passage in *In re Diplock* criticising or modifying, in any way, the statements of principle which I have quoted. Although I fully recognise that in considering this problem I find myself in a most unfamiliar field, I feel it my duty to follow and apply those statements. Mr. Pickering drew my attention to two authorities as illustrating the simple debtor/creditor relationship, namely, *King v. Hutton* [1900] 2 Q.B. 504 and *Henry v. Hammond* [1913] 2 K.B. 515. It is unnecessary to refer to these in detail, save to say that the former makes it clear that the special facts of each case are crucial in determining whether there is a simple debtor/creditor relationship, although the intention of the parties as ascertained from the terms of their contract shows that some kind of fiduciary relationship exists. The preservation of ownership clause contains unusual and fairly elaborate provisions departing substantially from the debtor/creditor relationship and shows, in my view, the intention to create a fiduciary relationship to which the principle stated in *In re Hallett's Estate*, 13 Ch. D. 696 applies. A further point made by Mr. Pickering was that if the plaintiffs were to succeed in their tracing claim this would, in effect, be a method available against a liquidator to a creditor of avoiding the provisions establishing the need to register charges on book debts: see section 95 (1) (2) (e) of the Companies Act 1948 [now see Companies Act 1985 ss 395, 396]. He used this only as an argument against the effect of clause 13 contended for by Mr. Lincoln. As to this, I think Mr. Lincoln's answer was well founded, namely, that if property in the foil never passed to the defendants with the result that the proceeds of sub-sales belonged in equity to the plaintiffs, section 95 (1) had no application. . . .'

[The Court of Appeal confirmed this analysis, and in the extract below Roskill LJ notes that the fact that the buyers are granted a period of credit is not sufficient to negate the conclusion that, in entering into sub-sales of the foil, the buyer acts as fiduciary for the supplier.]

***Roskill LJ*:**
'It was common ground at the trial and during argument in this court that some implication had to be made into the first part of clause 13 [which retained title in the unused foil in the suppliers]; since otherwise the defendants could not lawfully sell the unmanufactured goods in their possession, at least until they were paid for—for, as already pointed out, they were the plaintiffs' and not the defendants' goods. To hold otherwise, as I think both parties accepted, would be to stultify the whole business purpose of these transactions. What (if any) implication is to be made beyond that? The first part of clause 13 is silent not only as to the power of sale but as to the dealing with any proceeds of the goods lawfully so sold by the defendants. Is the admitted power of sale (if I may respectfully borrow Goff L.J.'s phrase during the argument) fettered or

unfettered? If it is fettered, is the fetter that, so long as any indebtedness remained outstanding in any respect from the defendants to the plaintiffs, the defendants after a sub-sale remained accountable to the plaintiffs for all proceeds of sub-sales—not even, as Mr. Price pointed out in argument, being able to retain for themselves the profit upon any such sales?

Mr. Price relied much upon the 75-days' credit—though, as I have already ventured to point out, the problem is the same whatever the length of the credit. But the longer the period it can fairly be said the greater the business, if not the legal, force of this part of Mr. Price's argument. If the plaintiffs were right, Mr. Price argued, then whenever sub-purchasers paid the defendants before the 75 days' credit had expired the defendants could not use those proceeds in their business for any purposes whatever save for paying their creditors, the plaintiffs: they must always retain those proceeds specifically for the plaintiffs' account and pay them over to the plaintiffs unless and until the entirety of outstanding indebtedness was discharged. This, he said, would deprive the defendants of all day-to-day finance and, so far from according with business efficacy, would produce precisely the opposite result, for it would cause acute cash-flow problems and make conduct of the defendants' business impossible. This is a formidable argument if one looks at the matter solely from the point of view of the defendants. But this matter has to be regarded in the light of the contractual provisions agreed upon by both parties, and the question of business efficacy, in relation to which there are here obvious competing business considerations, must be answered in the light of what both parties expressly agreed upon and therefore must be taken also impliedly to have agreed upon, and not unilaterally from the point of view of one party only.

Now, the crucial facts to my mind are two: first, that the defendants were selling goods which the plaintiffs owned at all material times; and secondly, that clause 13 as a whole is obviously designed to protect the plaintiffs, in the event of later insolvency, against the consequences of having parted with possession of, though not with legal title to, these goods before payment was received, 75 days' credit being allowed. When, therefore, one is considering what, if any, additional implication has to be made to the undoubted implied power of sale in the first part of clause 13, one must ask what, if any, additional implication is necessary to make effective the obvious purpose of giving the requisite security to the plaintiffs? One is, I think, entitled to look at the second part of clause 13 to answer this; for it would be strange if the first part were to afford no relevant security when the second part is (as I think) elaborately drawn to give such security in relation to manufactured or mixed goods.

I see no difficulty in the contractual concept that, as between the defendants and their sub-purchasers, the defendants sold as principals, but that, as between themselves and the plaintiffs, those goods which they were selling as principals within their implied authority from the plaintiffs were the plaintiffs' goods which they were selling as agents for the plaintiffs to whom they remained fully accountable. If an agent lawfully sells his principal's goods, he stands in a fiduciary relationship to his principal and remains accountable to his principal for those goods and their proceeds. A bailee is in like position in relation to his bailor's goods. What, then, is there here to relieve the defendants from their obligation to account to the plaintiffs for those goods of the plaintiffs which they lawfully sell to sub-purchasers? The fact that they so sold them as principals does not, as I think, affect their relationship with the plaintiffs; nor (as at present advised) do I think—contrary to Mr. Price' s argument—that the sub-purchasers could on this analysis have sued the plaintiffs upon the sub-contracts as undisclosed principals for, say, breach of warranty of quality.

It seems to me clear (and so far from helping Mr. Price I think the second part of clause 13, properly construed, helps Mr. Lincoln) that to give effect to what I regard as the obvious purpose of clause 13 one must imply into the first part of the clause not only the power to sell but also the obligation to account in accordance with the normal fiduciary relationship of principal and agent, bailor and bailee. Accordingly, like the judge I find no difficulty in holding that the principles in *Hallett's* case, 13 Ch.D. 696 are of immediate application, and I think that the plaintiffs are entitled to trace these proceeds of sale and to recover them, as Mocatta J. has held by his judgment.

Mr. Price relied upon the conduct of the parties after the defendants took over from the partnership, pointing out (as was the fact) that the defendants were never required to account to the plaintiffs in the way I think, as a matter of law, the plaintiffs were entitled to require them to account. As a matter of business I would not have expected the plaintiffs so to have required the defendants to account. But, as Mr. Lincoln forcefully replied on this point, clause 13 is directed to a state of insolvency, not to what he described as to the halcyon days of solvency; and it is only upon insolvency that the question of what the powers are under clause 13 comes into play. . . .'

Note:

This case goes further than subsequent cases in allowing the supplier's claim to the proceeds. In doing this, the court seemed to regard it as vital that there was an express bailment of the goods (the buyer was the 'fiduciary owner'), both the goods and their proceeds had to be kept separate and identifiable, and that there was a fiduciary relationship between the parties (an essential prerequisite for tracing). The first and last of these points were conceded, and the possibility of charge was not seriously argued; 'products', 'proceeds' and 'all monies' clauses were not in issue. All of this rather weakens the impact of the case.

[331] *Clough Mill Ltd v Martin* [1985] 1 WLR 111 (CA), 113, 115–21 *per* Robert Goff LJ:

[A simple retention of title clause was upheld as effective against the crystallised floating charge taken by a bank. The clause entitled the seller to repossess unused yarn which had been supplied to a fabric manufacturer but not paid for.]

'This appeal is concerned with what is sometimes called a "retention of title clause," but more frequently nowadays a "Romalpa clause." The plaintiff, Clough Mill Ltd, carry on business as spinners of yarn. Under four contracts entered into between December 1979 and March 1980, it contracted to supply yarn to the buyer, a company called Heatherdale Fabrics Ltd, which carried on business as a manufacturer of fabric. When the plaintiff entered into these contracts, it knew that the yarn to be supplied under them was to be used by the buyer for such manufacture. Each of the contracts incorporated the plaintiff's standard conditions. These included a condition (condition 12) entitled "Passing of Title"; this is the Romalpa clause, with the construction and effect of which this case is concerned. It is convenient that I should immediately set out the terms of condition 12. It is a continuous clause, but I will, for convenience of reference, segregate the four sentences of which the condition is comprised into separate paragraphs. It provides:

"However, the ownership of the material shall remain with the seller, which reserves the right to dispose of the material until payment in full for all the material has been received by it in accordance with the terms of this contract or until such time as the buyer sells the material to its customers by way of bona fide sale at full market value.

> "If such payment is overdue in whole or in part the seller may (without prejudice to any of its other rights) recover or resell the material or any of it and may enter upon the buyer's premises by its servants or agents for that purpose.
> "Such payment shall become due immediately upon the commencement of any act or proceeding in which the buyer's solvency is involved.
> "If any of the material is incorporated in or used as material for other goods before such payment the property in the whole of such goods shall be and remain with the seller until such payment has been made, or the other goods have been sold as aforesaid, and all the seller's rights hereunder in the material shall extend to those other goods."

There are certain other conditions to which, though of less importance, I ought to refer for the sake of completeness. . . .

We have to construe condition 12 as a whole, and in its contractual context; but it is convenient to start with the opening sentence of the condition, upon which the plaintiff particularly relies. In that sentence, it is provided:

> "the ownership of the material shall remain with the seller, which reserves the right to dispose of the material until payment in full for all the material has been received by it in accordance with the terms of this contract or until such time as the buyer sells the material to its customers by way of bona fide sale at full market value."

Now there are various points to notice about this sentence. The first is that what is reserved by the seller is the ownership of the material, the material being (see condition 1(a)(ii)) the material supplied under the particular contract. Prime facie, in a commercial document such as this, ownership means, quite simply, the property in the goods. The second point is that the reservation of the right to dispose of the material is expressed to be until a certain event, viz until payment in full for all the material received by the buyer or until resale by the buyer. This shows the purpose for which the right of disposal is reserved, which is to provide the seller with security for any unpaid and overdue purchase price payable under the contract. It is obvious from the third sentence that the possibility of insolvency is a matter which is particularly in contemplation. It also appears from the first sentence that the buyer has power to sell the material to his customers; and we know from the last sentence that it is also contemplated that the buyer has power to consume the material in the manufacture of goods, mixing it with other material in the process, the function of the last sentence being to provide for the rights of the seller in and in respect of any such manufactured goods. The second sentence empowers the seller to recover or resell the material or any of it, and to enter on the buyer's premises for that purpose.

The submission of Mr Henry, for the plaintiff, as to the nature of the plaintiff's retention of title under the first sentence of the condition, was extremely simple. Under the Sale of Goods Act 1979, a seller of goods is fully entitled, after delivery of the goods to the buyer, to retain title in the goods until he has been paid: see section 19(1) of the Act of 1979. That is precisely what the plaintiff has done by condition 12. The plaintiff's title did not derive from the contract; on the contrary, it was simply retained by them, though under the contract power was conferred on the buyer both to sell the goods and to use them in manufacturing other goods. As the buyer never acquired any title to the unused yarn in question, it could not charge the yarn to the plaintiff. So the plaintiff was, quite simply, the owner of the yarn; and there was no question of there being any charge on the yarn in its favour, which was void if unregistered.

This attractively simple approach was challenged by Mr Blackburne for the defendant. He submitted, first of all, that, if the first sentence is read literally, as Mr Henry suggested it should be read, the buyer can only have had possession of the yarn in a fiduciary capacity, whether as bailee or as fiduciary agent. But, he said, the power conferred on the buyer under the contract, not merely to sell the material but also to mix it with other materials in the manufacture of goods, was inconsistent with the existence of any fiduciary capacity in the buyer, or indeed with the plaintiff's unqualified ownership of the yarn. In support of this submission, he relied in particular on a proposition derived from the judgment of Slade J in *In re Bond Worth Ltd* [1980] Ch 228, 261 [see **[332]** below]:

> "where an alleged trustee has the right to mix tangible assets or moneys with his own assets or moneys and to deal with them as he pleases, this is incompatible with the existence of a presently subsisting fiduciary relationship in regard to such particular assets or moneys."

Now this is a submission which I am unable to accept. In every case, we have to look at the relevant documents and other communications which have passed between the parties, and to consider them in the light of the relevant surrounding circumstances, in order to ascertain the rights and duties of the parties inter se, always paying particular regard to the practical effect of any conclusion concerning the nature of those rights and duties. In performing this task, concepts such as bailment and fiduciary duty must not be allowed to be our masters, but must rather be regarded as the tools of our trade. I for my part can see nothing objectionable in an agreement between parties under which A, the owner of goods, gives possession of those goods to B, at the same time conferring on B a power of sale and a power to consume the goods in manufacture, though A will remain the owner of the goods until they are either sold or consumed. I do not see why the relationship between A and B, pending sale or consumption, should not be the relationship of bailor and bailee, even though A has no right to trace the property in his goods into the proceeds of sale. If that is what the parties have agreed should happen, I can see no reason why the law should not give effect to that intention. I am happy to find that both Staughton J and Peter Gibson J have adopted a similar approach in the recently reported cases of *Hendy Lennox (Industrial Engines) Ltd v. Grahame Puttick Ltd* [1984] 1 WLR 485 and *In re Andrabell Ltd* [1984] 3 All ER 407.

Even so, it is necessary to examine Mr Henry's construction in a little more detail. If, under this condition, retention of title applied only to goods not yet paid for, I can see that his construction could be given effect to without any problem. But the difficulty with the present condition is that the retention of title applies to material, delivered and retained by the buyer, until payment in full for all material delivered under the contract has been received by the seller. The effect is therefore that the seller may retain his title in material still held by the buyer, even if part of that material has been paid for. Furthermore, if in such circumstances the seller decides to exercise his rights and resell the material, questions can arise as to (1) whether account must be taken of the part payment already received in deciding how much the seller should be entitled to sell, and (2) whether, if he does resell, he is accountable to the buyer either in respect of the part payment already received, or in respect of any profit made on the resale by reason of a rise in the market value of the material.

Let me highlight these problems by taking a hypothetical example. Suppose that the seller agrees to sell 1,000 tons of material to the buyer at £10 a ton. He delivers 500 tons. Of those 500 tons, only 250 tons are paid for by the buyer: so £2,500 have been paid, and another £2,500 are due and outstanding. The buyer becomes insolvent, and is unable further to perform the contract. The seller accepts the repudiation. Of the 500 tons delivered, 300 tons are still at the buyer's premises, unsold and unused, now worth £4,000 instead of £3,000 as they were at the time of the contract of sale. Can the seller resell the whole 300 tons? And, if he can and does so, does he have to account to the buyer for that part of the price already paid which cannot be appropriated to the 200 tons already used by the buyer in manufacture and so must be appropriated to part of the 300 tons, ie, £500? And must the seller account to the buyer for the profit element of £1,000 obtainable on the resale, no doubt allowing for any expenses of the sale?

Now, if the contract was still subsisting instead of having been determined by the seller's acceptance of the buyer's repudiation, it would be perfectly possible to conclude, on the basis of an implied term in the contract, that the seller could only resell so much of the material as was necessary to pay the outstanding part of the purchase price, the rest to remain available to the buyer for the purposes of the contract, and that if, contrary to that term, the seller were to sell more than was necessary to pay off the balance of the price, he must account for the surplus to the buyer. On that basis, any part payment would be taken into account, and there would be no question of the seller retaining any profits obtained on a resale. But, if the contract has been determined, such term could not be given effect to, unless it were to be held, on a true construction of the contract, that the term survived the determination of the contract upon the seller's accepting the buyer's repudiation, for which I can see no basis as a matter of construction. So the situation would simply be that the property in the 300 tons belonged to the seller who could exercise his rights as owner uninhibited by any contractual restrictions He could therefore sell the material for his own account; though he would, I consider, be bound to repay any part of the purchase price already paid by the buyer which must be appropriated to the goods so sold, because such sum would be recoverable by the buyer on the ground of failure of consideration.

There is another possible solution to this problem. This is that the seller should be held to retain the title to the material as trustee, upon trust to sell the goods and apply the proceeds of sale, first in discharge of the outstanding balance of the purchase price, and then as to any surplus upon trust for the buyer. On that basis the seller, in my hypothetical example, would on selling the 300 tons hold the balance realised on the resale over and above the outstanding purchase price on trust for the buyer.

To me, the answer to these questions lies in giving effect to the condition in accordance with its terms, and on that approach I can discern no intention to create a trust. The condition provides that the plaintiff retains his ownership in the material. He therefore remains owner; but, during the subsistence of the contract, he can only exercise his powers as owner consistently with the terms, express and implied, of the contract. On that basis, in my judgment, he can during the subsistence of the contract only resell such amount of the material as is needed to discharge the balance of the outstanding purchase price; and if he sells more, he is accountable to the buyer for the surplus. However, once the contract has been determined, as it will be if the buyer repudiates the contract and the seller accepts the repudiation, the seller will have his rights as owner (including, of course, his right to sell the goods) uninhibited by any contractual restrictions; though any part of the purchase price received by him and attributable to the material so resold will be recoverable by the buyer on the ground of failure of consideration, subject to any set off arising from a cross-claim by the plaintiff for damages for the buyer's repudiation.

This approach to the first sentence of condition 12 is, I consider, consistent with the view expressed by Templeman LJ in *Borden (UK) Ltd v. Scottish Timber Products Ltd* [1981] Ch 25 [see **[334]** below] of the Romalpa clause considered by the court in that case. The relevant part of that clause read:

> "Property in goods supplied hereunder will pass to the customer when: (a) the goods the subject of this contract; and (b) all other goods the subject of any other contract between the company and the customer which, at the time of payment of the full price of the goods sold under this contract, have been delivered to the customer but not paid for in full, have been paid for in full."

Of that clause, Templeman LJ said, at p. 44:

> "In my judgment, when resin was sold and delivered the property in the resin could be retained by the plaintiffs, and was retained only as security for the payment of the purchase price and other debts incurred, and to be incurred, by the defendants to the plaintiffs in respect of supplies of resin. If the defendants repudiated one contract the plaintiffs could accept that repudiation and recover possession of the resin. If the plaintiffs did not accept repudiation, or if the defendants failed to make payment due under any other contract, the plaintiffs could enforce their security by selling the resin, for which purpose they had reserved the title to themselves."

The opinion so expressed by Templeman LJ on the clause before him appears to me to be consistent with the view which I have just expressed about the first sentence of the Romalpa clause now before this court.

Furthermore, if this approach is right, I can see no reason why the retention of title in the first sentence of condition 12 should be construed as giving rise to a charge on the unused material in favour of the plaintiff. In the course of his argument, Mr Blackburne prayed in aid another proposition culled from the judgment of Slade J in *In re Bond Worth Ltd* [1980] Ch 228, 248:

> "In my judgment, any contract which, by way of security for the payment of a debt, confers an interest in property defeasible or destructible upon payment of such debt, or appropriates such property for the discharge of the debt, must necessarily be regarded as creating a mortgage or charge, as the case may be. The existence of the equity of redemption is quite inconsistent with the existence of a bare trustee-beneficiary relationship."

However, so far as the retention of title in unused materials is concerned, I see no difficulty in distinguishing the present case from that envisaged by Slade J. Under the first sentence of the condition, the buyer does not, by way of security, confer on the plaintiff an interest in property defeasible upon the payment of the debt so secured. On the contrary, the plaintiff retains the legal property in the material.

There is however one further point which I must consider. Mr Blackburne relied, in support of his argument, on the last sentence of the condition. It will be remembered that this reads:

> "If any of the material is incorporated in or used as material for other goods before such payment the property in the whole of such goods shall be and remain with the seller until such payment has been made, or the other goods have been sold as aforesaid, and all the seller's rights hereunder in the material shall extend to those other goods."

The submission of Mr Blackburne was that the effect of this provision is to confer on the plaintiff an interest in the buyer's property and so must have been to create a charge; and he further submitted that, having regard to the evident intention that the plaintiff's rights in goods in which the material provided by it has been incorporated shall be the same as its rights in unused material, the plaintiff's rights in unused material should likewise be construed as creating a charge.

Now it is no doubt true that, where A's material is lawfully used by B to create new goods, whether or not B incorporates other material of his own, the property in the new goods will generally vest in B, at least where the goods are not reducible to the original materials: see *Blackstone's Commentaries*, 17th ed (1830), vol 2, pp. 404–405. But it is difficult to see why, if the parties agree that the property in the goods shall vest in A, that agreement should not be given effect to. On this analysis, under the last sentence of the condition as under the first, the buyer does not confer on the seller an interest in property defeasible upon the payment of the debt; on the contrary, when the new goods come into existence the property in them ipso facto vests in the plaintiff, and the plaintiff thereafter retains its ownership in them, in the same way and on the same terms as the plaintiff retains its ownership in the unused material. However, in considering the fourth sentence, we have to take into account not only the possibility that the buyer may have paid part of the price for the material, but also that he will have borne the cost of manufacture of the new goods, and may also have provided other materials for incorporation into those goods; and the condition is silent, not only about repaying such part of the price for the material as has already been paid by the buyer, but also about any allowance to be made by the plaintiff to the buyer for the cost of manufacture of the new goods, or for any other material incorporated by the buyer into the new goods. Now, no injustice need arise from the exercise of the plaintiff's power to resell such goods provided that, having applied the price received from the resale in satisfaction of the outstanding balance of the price owed to the plaintiff by the buyer, the plaintiff is bound to account for the remainder to the buyer. But the difficulty of construing the fourth sentence as simply giving rise to a retention by the plaintiff of title to the new goods is that it would lead to the result that, upon the determination of the contract under which the original material was sold to the buyer, the ownership of the plaintiff in the new goods would be retained by the plaintiff, uninhibited by any terms of the contract which had then ceased to apply; and I find it impossible to believe that it was the intention of the parties that the plaintiff would thereby gain the windfall of the full value of the new product, deriving as it may well do not merely from the labour of the buyer but also from materials that were the buyer's without any duty to account to the buyer for any surplus of the proceeds of sale above the outstanding balance of the price due by the buyer to the plaintiff. It follows that the last sentence must be read as creating either a trust or a charge. In my judgment, however, it cannot have been intended to create a trust. Those who insert *Romalpa* clauses in their contracts of sale must be aware that other suppliers might do the same; and the prospect of two lots of material, supplied by different sellers, each subject to a *Romalpa* clause which vests in the seller the legal title in a product manufactured from both lots of material, is not at all sensible. Accordingly, consistent with the approach of Vinelott J to a similar provision in *In re Peachdart Ltd* [1984] 1 Ch 131, I have come to the conclusion that, although it does indeed do violence to the language of the fourth sentence of the condition, that sentence must be read as giving rise to a charge on the new goods in favour of the seller.

Even so, I do not see why the presence of the last sentence in the condition should prevent us from giving effect to the first sentence in accordance with its terms. The fact that I feel driven to do violence to the language of the last sentence of the condition is not of itself enough to persuade me that further violence must be done to the language of the first. The provision in the first sentence is perfectly clear. The concept of retention of title—or reservation of the right of disposal—pending payment of the price is, and has for very many years been, well known in commerce, as section 19(1) of the Sale of Goods Act 1979 clearly demonstrates. For my part I cannot see why, if the law should require that the last sentence, expressed to be a retention of title, must nevertheless take effect as a charge, we should be required to impose a meaning on the first sentence which conflicts with the natural and ordinary meaning of the words there used.

I recognise that, on the view which I have formed of the retention of title in the first sentence of condition 12 in this case, its effect is very similar to that of a charge on goods by the buyer in favour of the plaintiff. But the simple fact is that, under the first sentence of the condition, the buyer does not in fact confer a charge on his goods in favour of the seller: on the contrary, the seller retains his title in his goods, for the purpose of providing himself with security. I can see no reason in law why a seller of goods should not adopt this course, and if the relevant contractual term is effective to achieve that result, I can see no reason why the law should not give effect to it in accordance with its terms. We were treated in argument to what I understand to be the common form appeal to the merits in cases of this kind, Mr Henry describing the unfortunate plight of suppliers of goods to manufacturers who, if in a poor financial position, are kept going by the suppliers for the benefit of debenture holders, usually banks, and Mr Blackburne describing the difficulties of liquidators grappling with incomprehensible *Romalpa* clauses. I sympathise with both; though I am tempted to observe that the mechanism of the floating charge, upon which secured creditors are content to rely, is perhaps as much open to criticism as the mechanism of the retention of title clause, at which they now express their dismay. Be that as it may, my conclusion in the present case derives not from sympathy, but from an analysis of the clause.'

Even a simple retention of title clause has some element of flexibility in its operation. For example, in *Hendy Lennox (Industrial Engines) Ltd v Grahame Puttick Ltd* [1984] 1 WLR 485, Staughton J allowed the sellers to repossess a diesel engine delivered under a retention of title clause notwithstanding that the engine had already been incorporated by the buyer into a generator and its removal would require several hours' work. In addition, minor changes to the supplied goods will not bar the operation of a simple retention of title clause: in *Armour v Thyssen Edelstahlwerke AG*, **[333]** below, steel strip sold subject to an all monies retention of title clause had been cut into sheets; the unpaid seller was permitted to take possession of the sheets, which were considered substantially to represent the original goods delivered, not some manufactured product. These instances should be contrasted with the cases on products retention of title clauses, considered below.

3.8.2 Attempts to retain equitable rather than legal title render the clause ineffective

In the cases considered so far, the seller has expressly reserved *legal* title to the goods being supplied. Such clauses, at least to the extent that they relate to the goods themselves rather than their products or proceeds, are successful. By contrast, a clause where the seller purports to retain equitable or benefical title will not work. The following extract provides the analysis.

[332] ***Re Bond Worth*** **[1980] 1 Ch 228, 246–67** ***per*** **Slade J:**
[Bond Worth purchased man-made fibre from Monsanto which it spun, dyed and wove into carpets. The fibre was sold under conditions of sale which, from July 1, 1976, included a "retention of title clause" which provided: "(a) . . . equitable and beneficial ownership shall remain with us [the sellers] until full payment has been received . . . or until prior resale, in which case our beneficial entitlement shall attach to the proceeds of resale or to the claim for such proceeds. (b) Should the goods become constituents of or be converted into other products while subject to our equitable and beneficial ownership we shall have the equitable and beneficial ownership in such other products as if they were solely and simply the goods. . . .". On 16 August 1977, Bond Worth went into receivership. At that date some £529,000

was owing to the Monsanto under 29 contracts which incorporated the retention of title clause. The seller immediately notified the receiver of its claim. Slade J held that, given the express terms of the contract of sale and the retention of title clause, the legal property in the fibre passed to the buyer on delivery and it was free to sell or deal with the fibre in the ordinary course of its business. Given these extensive powers in the buyer, it was impossible to construe the retention of title clause as creating a bare trust for the seller, even though the clause referred to 'equitable and beneficial ownership'. Moreover, the seller could not by its agreement *retain* a proprietary interest by way of charge in the nominated assets. The law relating to equitable property demanded that the seller first transfer full legal (including beneficial) title to the buyer, and that the buyer then *grant back* to the seller an interest by way of charge. On this basis, the *buyer* had granted a floating charge in favour of the seller as security for the purchase price. This floating charge covered the raw fibre, the proceeds of its resale and any products manufactured from the fibre. Since this charge was a registrable but unregistered floating charge, it was void against the receivers. The extract at **[306]** is repeated here in its proper context.]

'Thus far, the position would seem to me reasonably clear. The real difficulty arises concerning the meaning and legal effect, if any, of the provisions in the retention of title clause concerning "equitable and beneficial ownership." If the contracts embody something more than a mere sale, what is this additional feature? What is the nature of the relationship beyond a mere vendor-purchaser relationship between Monsanto and Bond Worth that comes into existence by virtue of the provisions relating to "equitable and beneficial ownership?"

In *Aluminium Industrie Vaassen BV v. Romalpa Aluminium Ltd.* [1976] 1 W.L.R. 676 [[**330** above], to which I shall have to refer in greater detail later, it was expressly admitted that the retention of title clause had the effect of making the defendants bailees of the relevant goods while in their possession until all money owing had been paid: see per Mocatta J. at p. 680H. On the different facts of the present case, however, there can be no question of a bailor-bailee relationship, since it is common ground that the property in the Acrilan fibre passed to Bond Worth at latest when it was delivered, while it is of the essence of a bailment that the general property in the goods concerned remains in the bailor, while only a special property passes to the bailee, which entitles him to exercise certain possessory remedies. Nor can the relationship be one of agency, since the documents contain no suggestion that Bond Worth is to be regarded as an agent and the rights which by necessary implication are given it to deal with the goods on its own behalf are quite inconsistent with a principal-agent relationship.

In these circumstances, I think it plain that, if the retention of title clause operated to create any effective rights at all for the benefit of Monsanto, such rights can only have been rights either (i) by way of a trust under which Monsanto was the sole beneficiary or (ii) by way of a trust under which Monsanto had a charge in equity over the relevant assets to secure payment of the unpaid purchase price. No possible third alternative has occurred to me. Mr. Sears, in contending for the first of these two alternatives on behalf of Monsanto, submitted that the retention of title clause, in the context of each of the relevant contracts, had the effect of creating a trust, under which the legal title to the Acrilan fibre delivered to it passed to Bond Worth, but the entire beneficial interest therein remained in Monsanto, until it was paid in full for all the goods comprised in the relevant order from Bond Worth. The terms of the trust, he accepted, were such that Bond Worth would have the right to sell the Acrilan even before it had made full payment; but in such event, he submitted, the trust would be transferred and attach to the proceeds of sale, until payment in full had been made. It was not in the least inconsistent with the existence of a trust that Bond Worth should be given the authority to sell the Acrilan before payment since, even in the absence of an express authority so to do, it would have had the power to pass the property in the goods to a third party during this interim period under section 25 of the Sale of Goods Act 1893. The ordinary law of trusts, he submitted, would itself produce the result that the proceeds of Acrilan sold during this period would themselves be held in trust for Monsanto as sole beneficiary, unless and until the relevant payment was made in full. Furthermore, he accepted and affirmed that the terms of the trust were such that, even during this interim period, Bond Worth would be at liberty to use the Acrilan for the purposes of manufacture and thus to mix it with other goods of which it was the absolute owner—but only in his submission on terms that the products of which the Acrilan thus became a constituent, or into which it was converted, would themselves be held by Bond Worth in trust for Monsanto as sole beneficiary, unless and until the relevant payment was made in full. The retention of title clause, he submitted, may be an unusual one, but there is no good reason why effect should not be given to it in accordance with the express terms of the agreement into which the parties entered. Since they have chosen to adopt a clause which expressly leaves the entire "equitable and beneficial ownership" with Monsanto until a specified event occurs, the court in his submission is entitled and bound to give effect to that clause according to its terms: see, for example, the passage from Lord Watson's speech in *McEntire v. Crossley Brothers Ltd.* [1895] A.C. 457, 467. The mere fact that it might be necessary for a court of equity to grant a remedy by way of equitable charge as the only effective means of enabling Monsanto to enforce its rights under the clause, does not of itself, it was contended, convert Monsanto's full equitable and beneficial ownership into a right by way of a mere mortgage or charge; right and remedy must not be confused.

I readily accept that the court is not entitled to discard the plain ordinary meaning of the phrase "equitable and beneficial ownership" unless there can be found in the relevant contracts other language and stipulations which necessarily deprive it of its ordinary meaning. The court, however, is entitled and indeed bound to look at the substance of the transactions as appearing from the wording of the whole of the retention of title clause, and indeed the other provisions of the relevant contracts of sale, for the purpose of deciding whether the essence of the transactions which the clause embodied was on the one hand a bare trust or on the other hand a trust by way of equitable mortgage or charge: see *In re George Inglefield Ltd.* [1933] Ch. 1, per Lord Hanworth M.R. at p. 17, per Lawrence L.J. at p. 23 and per Romer L.J. at p. 27. Mr. Sears accepted, as I think he had to accept, that the whole purpose of the retention of title clause was to afford Monsanto security for the payment of the purchase price under each relevant order. I have come to the clear conclusion that, if contrary to the submissions of other counsel, the clause operated so as to give any legally enforceable rights at all to Monsanto, such rights must necessarily have been rights by way of mortgage or charge. In my judgment, any contract which, by way of security for the payment of a debt, confers an interest in property defeasible or destructible upon payment of such debt, or appropriates such property for the discharge of the debt, must necessarily be regarded as creating a mortgage or charge, as the case may be. The existence of the equity of redemption is quite inconsistent with the existence of a bare trustee-beneficiary relationship.

The fact that all the characteristics of a mortgage or charge are to be found present in the retention of title clause is borne out by a passage from the judgment of Romer L.J.

in *In re George Inglefield Ltd.* [1933] Ch. 1. There he summarises the essential characteristics of a mortgage, at pp. 27–28:

> "In a transaction of sale the vendor is not entitled to get back the subject matter of the sale by returning to the purchaser the money that has passed between them. In the case of a mortgage or charge, the mortgagor is entitled, until he has been foreclosed, to get back the subject matter of the mortgage or charge by returning to the mortgagee the money that has passed between them. The second essential difference is that if the mortgagee realises the subject matter of the mortgage for a sum more than sufficient to repay him, with interest and the costs, the money that has passed between him and the mortgagor he has to account to the mortgagor for the surplus. If the purchaser sells the subject matter of the purchase, and realises a profit, of course he has not got to account to the vendor for the profit. Thirdly, if the mortgagee realises the mortgage property for a sum that is insufficient to repay him the money that he has paid to the mortgagor, together with interest and costs, then the mortgagee is entitled to recover from the mortgagor the balance of the money, either because there is a covenant by the mortgagor to repay the money advanced by the mortgagee, or because of the existence of the simple contract debt which is created by the mere fact of the advance having been made."

Mutatis mutandis all these three features of a charge are present in this case. Bond Worth was entitled to redeem the charge in favour of Monsanto by paying to it the outstanding debt due under the relevant order. If Monsanto, in exercise of the rights conferred on it by the retention of title clause, were to compel a sale of the relevant assets for a sum more than sufficient to pay this debt, the parties' intention was surely that Bond Worth, rather than Monsanto, would be entitled to receive the surplus. In contrast, if such last-mentioned sale were to produce a sum less than the outstanding debt, they surely intended that Monsanto would remain entitled to recover the balance from Bond Worth as a simple contract debt.

Thus in my judgment there are to be found within the retention of tide clause itself other language and stipulations which necessarily deprive the phrase "equitable and beneficial ownership" of its primary meaning. In my judgment, the clause, when properly construed, purported to create equitable charges in favour of Monsanto over four separate categories of assets, namely: (a) the raw Acrilan which was the original subject matter of the original sale; (b) the proceeds of sale of any such raw Acrilan which might be sold; (c) any products of which any part of the raw Acrilan might become a constituent or into which it might be converted; (d) the proceeds of sale of any such products which might be sold. I shall for brevity, from time to time hereafter, refer respectively to these four categories as the first, second, third and fourth categories of charged assets.

. . . .

Mr. Sears, who was concerned to argue that the charges (if any) involved in the present case should not be treated as having been "created" by Bond Worth for the purpose of section 95 (1) of the Companies Act 1948, submitted in effect that there are two alternative methods by which, on a sale, a charge can be created in favour of the vendor to secure the purchase price. It may be created by means of a grant back in favour of the vendor as was done in *Capital Finance Co. Ltd. v. Stokes* [1969] 1 Ch. 261. Alternatively, he suggested, it may be created by the vendor reserving or excepting to himself a charge over the relevant property and simply disposing of the equity of redemption. The latter, he submitted, if a charge was created at all, was precisely what happened in the present case. The terms of the retention of title clause themselves, he suggested, made it plain that the "equitable and beneficial ownership" of the goods was to "remain" in Monsanto until it had been paid in full for the relevant order and correspondingly that no part of the beneficial ownership, beyond at most a mere equity of redemption, passed to Bond Worth on the sale, even for a moment of time. In this context, he relied particularly on the decision of the Court of Appeal in *In re Connolly Bros. Ltd. (No. 2)* [1912] 2 Ch. 25. In that case, a company had issued debentures creating a floating charge upon all its present and future property, one of the conditions of the debenture being that the company should not be at liberty to create any other mortgage or charge in priority to the debenture. Subsequently, it wanted to purchase certain property, but had not the necessary money and applied to a Mrs. O'Reilly to lend it the sum of £1,000. It agreed to give her a charge on the property to secure this loan. She advanced the money on these terms. The company then concluded a contract to buy the property from the owner (who was not Mrs. O'Reilly) for £1,100 and paid a deposit of £150. Mrs. O'Reilly duly gave the company a cheque for £1,000, which was paid into its banking account. It then drew a cheque for £950, which was cashed, the cash being paid over to the vendor. A week later, the company executed in favour of Mrs. O'Reilly a memorandum of equitable charge on the property, for the express purpose of securing the £1,000 debt. The question then arose whether the security acquired by her took priority over the debentures. The Court of Appeal held that it did, on the grounds that, before the purchase was completed, a contract had been concluded between her and the company under the terms of which, on completion of the purchase, she was to have a first charge and the company was only to get the property subject thereto. Accordingly, as Cozens-Hardy M.R. said, at p. 31: ". . . all the company in equity obtained was the equity of redemption in the property subject to Mrs. O'Reilly's charge of £1,000."

Correspondingly, it was submitted on behalf of Monsanto in the present case, even if, contrary to its primary submission, the retention of title clause operated to confer on it a mere charge, this was a charge created by Monsanto in favour of itself, by way of exception out of the entirety of the beneficial interest in the property; Bond Worth, it was suggested, never acquired in equity, even for a moment in time, more than the equity of redemption in the Acrilan, subject to Monsanto's interest by way of charge. Though this argument has some superficial attraction, I do not think that the *Connolly* decision, when properly analysed, is of any assistance to Monsanto. As will have appeared, that was a case where A, the purchaser of the relevant property from B, had, before completion, entered into a contract for good consideration, to grant a charge over the property in favour of C. Accordingly, the very moment that A acquired the legal estate in the property, A held it in trust to give effect in equity to C's rights, by virtue of the pre-existing contract between A and C. In the face of this contract, it could not therefore have been successfully claimed that the purchaser A, even for a moment, acquired more than an equity of redemption in the property, (though it may be observed that the relevant charge, even in that case, was undeniably created by A, rather than the vendor, B). The case did not even touch the question whether it would have been conceptually possible for the vendor B to except to himself a mortgage in such manner that the subject matter of the sale, as between A and B, was a mere equity of redemption, so that the transaction involved no express or implied grant back by A in favour of B. Notwithstanding the arrangements made between A and C, the transaction as between A and B in the *Connolly* case remain throughout one for the sale of the entire legal and beneficial interest in the property. This case was, as Harman L.J. pointed out in *Capital Finance Co. Ltd. v. Stokes* [1969] 1 Ch. 261, 277, merely one where the Court of Appeal was considering equitable priorities.

A concept familiar to conveyancers is that, on a grant of land, it is possible for the grantor to except out of that which is granted something which is actually in existence at the time of the grant, such as mines and minerals. The effect of such exception is not to include in the grant that which is excepted; and, correspondingly, it will take effect even though the grantee has not executed the relevant instrument. However, no authority has been cited which satisfies me that on the transfer of the legal property in land or chattels, it is competent to a vendor expressly to except from the grant in favour of himself an equitable mortgage or charge thereon to secure the unpaid purchase price (in addition to or in substitution for any lien which may arise by operation of law), in such manner that the exception will take effect without any express or implied grant back of a mortgage or charge in the vendor's favour by the purchaser. In my judgment, as a matter of conveyancing in the case of land, the proper course is to follow that actually adopted by the conveyancers in *Capital Finance Co. Ltd. v. Stokes* [1969] 1 Ch. 261 and described by Harman L.J. at p. 277 as "the ordinary conveyancing practice"; this is for the documentation to contain an express grant of the entire legal and beneficial title, followed by an immediate grant back of the requisite mortgage or charge. In the case of either land or personal property, an express or implied grant back in favour of the original grantor is in my judgment required to create such mortgage or charge. If the court is satisfied that both parties to a transaction of sale have contracted that the vendor shall have defined rights by way of mortgage or charge over the subject matter of the sale, no doubt it will be prepared to imply the necessary grant back of such rights by the purchaser, even though inappropriate words, for example words by way of purported exception, may have been used; equity will regard as done that which ought to be done. This does not, however, remove the theoretical necessity of a grant back.

Support for the view that in such a case an express or implied grant back of rights by the purchaser to the vendor is in principle necessary is to be found in the decision in *Coburn v. Collins* (1887) 35 Ch.D. 373, as explained by Lord Herschell L.C. in *McEntire v. Crossley Brothers Ltd.* [1895] A.C. 457.

[Slade J then discussed these two cases.]

Applying similar reasoning, I conclude that the proper manner of construing the retention of title clause, together with all the other relevant provisions of the contracts of sale read as a whole, is to regard them as effecting a sale in which the entire property in the Acrilan passes to Bond Worth followed by a security, *eo instanti*, given back by Bond Worth to the vendor, Monsanto. In my judgment, therefore, Bond Worth rather than Monsanto must be regarded as creator of the relevant charge in relation to the first category of charged assets. A fortiori it must be so regarded in relation to the second, third and fourth categories, since the third and fourth categories, at least, might include or represent, inter alia, property for which Monsanto had never at any time been the owner (for example, materials belonging to Bond Worth other than Acrilan, with which Acrilan had been mixed). Charges over these categories could not possibly have been created except by grant made by Bond Worth. This, in my judgment, would be a powerful reason in itself for concluding that Bond Worth should be treated as having been the grantor and creator of the charges over all the categories of assets comprised in the retention of title clause even if, contrary to my view, it had been theoretically possible for charges on the first and second categories to have been created without the need for any express or implied grant by Bond Worth.

Up to this point, therefore, my prima facie conclusion is that the effect of the incorporation of the retention of title clause in each of the 29 contracts, concluded by the acceptance by Bond Worth of Acrilan, when delivered to it, was to give rise to the creation by it in favour of Monsanto of equitable charges over such Acrilan and the other three related categories of charged assets, by way of implied grant in favour of Monsanto.

Mr. Harman, on behalf of the applicants, and Mr. Morritt, on behalf of the bank, however, each made strong attacks on the essential validity of the retention of title clause, on grounds which have not yet been mentioned. They submitted in effect that, while in principle it may be possible, subject to the provisions of the Bills of Sale Act 1878, for a purchaser of chattels to declare himself a trustee thereof for the purpose of a charge in favour of the vendor to secure the purchase price, no such trust and charge, having any legal effect, exist at all on the facts of the present case. For, it was pointed out, the contracts of sales in the present case have special features of crucial importance. They do not embody chattels which are, by their very nature, likely to retain their identity (such as, for example, a grand piano). Nor do they impose any obligation on the purchaser to keep them safely and to preserve their identity, for the better safeguarding of the vendor's security. No express obligation was imposed on Bond Worth by the clause to keep the unpaid-for raw Acrilan separate from its other stores of raw Acrilan; and it is not suggested by Monsanto that the introduction of this clause in June 1976 placed Bond Worth under any implied obligation of this nature. On the contrary, Bond Worth was free to deal with the unpaid-for fibre, together with the other products and book debts referred to in the clause, just as if they were its own property. Without committing any breach of the alleged trust, it could mix the raw fibre with its other goods, sell it on such terms as to price and otherwise as it pleased, spin it into yarn and use it for all the purposes of its carpet manufacture. Likewise, without committing any such breach, it could deal with the book debts, to which the clause purported to attach, for its own purposes and for its own benefit. These facts, which were not disputed by Monsanto in argument, led to two separate allied lines of attack on the validity of the retention of title clause.

[Slade then dismissed the idea that such a trust was void for uncertainty of subject matter.]

A second, allied line of attack was made on the validity of the alleged trusts. It is quite inconsistent with the concept of a trust or fiduciary relationship, it was submitted, that Bond Worth should be free to use the Acrilan fibre and other categories of assets subject to the retention of title clause for the purposes of its own business and manufacturing processes, in the manner which I have described. Four authorities, in particular, were relied on in this context.

[Slade J then proceeded to discuss these.]

Subject to the recent decision of the Court of Appeal in *Aluminium Industrie Vaassen B.V. v. Romalpa Aluminium Ltd.* [1976] 1 W.L.R. 676, these four last-mentioned authorities seem to me clear authority for the proposition that, where an alleged trustee has the right to mix tangible assets or moneys with his own other assets or moneys and to deal with them as he pleases, this is incompatible with the existence of a presently subsisting fiduciary relationship in regard to such particular assets or moneys. It is, however, necessary to consider whether any qualification needs to be placed on that proposition in the light of the *Romalpa* case [1976] 1 W.L.R. 676, the facts of which are as follows.

. . . .

The facts of the *Romalpa* case have this much in common with those of the present case: in each instance the relevant clause, by necessary implication, left the purchaser at liberty both to sell the relevant goods and to use them unrestrictedly for the purposes of manufacture, at least in the ordinary course of business. For the purposes of my present decision therefore, it is perhaps unfortunate that the decisions in *In re Nevill; Ex parte White*, 6 Ch.App. 397; *Foley v. Hill*, 2 H.L.Cas. 28 and *South Australian Insurance Co. v. Randell*, L.R. 3 P.C. 101 do not appear to have been cited in argument before either court in the *Romalpa* case. If they had been cited, the judgments of those courts would no doubt have explained specifically why the principles exemplified in these three earlier decisions presented no obstacle to the crucial conclusion that at all material times, up to and including sale, a presently subsisting fiduciary relationship existed between vendor and purchaser in regard to the goods or their proceeds.

The reasons for this conclusion, however, are not in my judgment hard to seek. In the *Romalpa* case, unlike the present, the full legal ownership of the material sold was expressly reserved by the relevant clause to the vendors, until the purchasers had paid all that was owing to the vendors. In these circumstances the court was not prevented (as it would be prevented in the present case) from finding a bailor-bailee relationship between the parties by any previous finding that the property in the goods had passed to the purchasers. In fact, as had already been stated, the defendants in the *Romalpa* case expressly admitted that the clause had the effect of making it a bailee of the goods, while in possession, until all money owing had been paid. This was a concession of crucial importance, the like of which has not of course been made here; it may well have been influenced by the fact that in that case the relevant clause placed the purchaser under an express obligation to store the material, if so required by the plaintiffs, in such a way that it was clearly the plaintiffs' property. Similarly, it was there expressly agreed that, if the purchaser should make new objects from the material or mix it with other objects or it should become a constituent part of new objects, the purchaser should, if required, store such objects in such a way that they could be recognised as such. Furthermore, there was in that case no difficulty in ascertaining the moneys (if any) in respect of which the defendant was liable to account. The receiver received the relevant moneys after he had entered into his receivership from sales made by the defendant to sub-purchasers before that date. He duly kept them separate and they never became mixed with other moneys: see per Roskill L.J. at p. 687D. Further light as to the intentions of the parties was thrown in that case by the second limb of the relevant clause, which expressly described the purchaser as keeping the objects there referred to "in his capacity of fiduciary owner" until the moment of full payment.

In the face of the many special features of the *Romalpa* case to which I have referred, but which are not present in the case before me, it is scarcely surprising, if I may respectfully say so, that the courts in that case found little difficulty in importing to the first part of the relevant clause "not only the power to sell but also the obligation to account in accordance with the normal fiduciary relationship of principal and agent, bailor and bailee": see per Roskill L.J. at p. 690F. However, as Goff L.J. commented at p. 691F, the part of the *Romalpa* case now under discussion ultimately resolved itself to a short question of construction of the relevant clause. In the end, I think, the decision only provides very limited assistance or guidance on the facts of the present case.

. . . .

The implicit authority and freedom of Bond Worth to employ the relevant raw materials, products and other moneys as it pleased and for its own purposes during the subsistence of the operation of the retention of title clause were in my judgment quite incompatible with the existence of a relationship of Bond Worth as trustee and

Monsanto as beneficiary solely and absolutely entitled to such assets, which is the relationship asserted.

I have, however, already indicated that this is not my own view of the effect, if any, of the retention of title clause when properly construed, but that such effect, if any, is a declaration of trust by Bond Worth in respect of the relevant assets by way of equitable charge to secure repayment of the moneys from time to time owing in respect of the relevant order. Does the authority and freedom of Bond Worth, to which I have last referred, by itself negative the existence of a valid trust by way of equitable charge? In my judgment, in so far as it might be suggested that the clause operated to create in this manner an immediate specific charge, the answer to this question must be "yes." It is in my judgment quite incompatible with the existence of an effective trust by way of specific charge in equity over specific assets that the alleged trustee should be free to use them as he pleases for his own benefit in the course of his own business.

There is, however, one type of charge (and I think one type only) which, by its very nature, leaves a company at liberty to deal with the assets charged in the ordinary course of its business, without regard to the charge, until stopped by a winding up or by the appointment of a receiver or the happening of some other agreed event. I refer to what is commonly known as a "floating charge": see for example *Wheatley v. Silkstone and Haigh Moor Coal Co.* (1885) 29 Ch.D. 715, 724 per North J. and *George Barker (Transport) Ltd. v. Eynon* [1974] 1 W.L.R. 462, 467 per Edmund Davies L.J. Such a charge remains unattached to any particular property and leaves the company with a licence to deal with, and even sell, the assets falling within its ambit in the ordinary course of business, as if the charge had not been given, until it is stopped by one or other of the events to which I have referred, when it is said to "crystallise"; it then becomes effectively fixed to the assets within its scope.

. . . .

The critical distinction in my judgment is that between a specific charge on the one hand and a floating charge on the other. Vaughan Williams L.J. pointed out in the *Woolcombers* case [1903] 2 Ch. 284 [see **[310]**] that it is quite inconsistent with the nature of a specific charge, though not of a floating charge, that the mortgagor is at liberty to deal with the relevant property as he pleases.'

Questions:

1. Is the reasoning of Slade J in relation to the existence of a bare trust persuasive? Why are the buyer's powers to deal with the assets inconsistent with the seller's assertion of *equitable* title (a trust), but not inconsistent with the assertion of continuing *legal* title?
2. To repeat the question posed earlier, is the reasoning of Slade J in relation to the creation of an equitable charge by 'grant and grant back' weakened by the subsequent decision of the House of Lords in *Abbey National Building Society v Cann* [1991] 1 AC 56?
3. Also see the extract from Lawson and Rudden, at **[202]** above, and the comments and questions which follow it. Does this case help to resolve those issues?

3.8.3 All moneys retention of title clauses

The next extract explains why title to the goods supplied by the seller can be retained until the buyer meets conditions which are far more demanding than mere payment of the purchase price for the goods themselves.

[333] ***Armour v Thyssen Edelstahlwerke AG*** **[1991] 2 AC 339 (HL), 340, 352–3** ***per*** **Lord Keith (with whom the other Law Lords concurred):**
[The facts appear from the judgment.]

> 'My Lords, the appellants are a company carrying on business in West Germany as manufacturers and suppliers of steel. The respondents are the joint receivers on the assets of Carron Co. Ltd. ("Carron"), appointed on 3 August 1982 under powers contained in a floating charge in favour of two banks. Carron carried on business at Falkirk as manufacturers of metal, plastic and general engineering products.
>
> For a considerable period prior to 3 August 1982 the appellants and Carron engaged in a course of dealing under which the appellants sold and supplied to Carron steel strip for use in its manufacturing processes. The contracts of sale between them were expressed as being subject to the appellants' General Conditions of Delivery and Payment. At the time of the respondents' appointment as receivers there were lying in Carron's works at Falkirk some 67,423 kilograms of steel strip which had been delivered in pursuance of such contracts. Part of the steel had been cut into sheets and a further part was in course of being so cut, but most of it was in the state in which it had been delivered. The invoice price of the 67,423 kilograms was £71,769, no part of which had been paid.
>
> Clause I.3(1) of the appellants' General Conditions of Delivery and Payment provided, according to an agreed translation from the German:
>
> > "All goods delivered by us remain our property (goods remaining in our ownership) until all debts owed to us including any balances existing at relevant times—due to us on any legal grounds—are settled. This also holds good if payments are made for the purpose of settlement of specially designated claims. Debts owed to companies, being members of our combine, are deemed to be such debts."
>
> Following the respondents' appointment as receivers, a dispute arose between them and the appellants as to whether the 67,423 kilograms of steel strip remained the property of the latter, by reason of clause I.3(1), or whether they formed part of the assets of Carron available to its preferred or other creditors.
>
> . . . .
>
> Section 17 of the Sale of Goods Act 1979 provides:
>
> > "(1) Where there is a contract for the sale of specific or ascertained goods the property in them is transferred to the buyer at such time as the parties to the contract intend it to be transferred. (2) For the purpose of ascertaining the intention of the parties regard shall be had to the terms of the contract, the conduct of the parties and the circumstances of the case."
>
> In the present case the parties in the contract of sale clearly expressed their intention that the property in the steel strip should not pass to Carron until all debts due by it to the appellants had been paid. In my opinion there are no grounds for refusing to give effect to that intention.

Further, section 19(1) of the same Act provides:

> "Where there is a contract for the sale of specific goods or where goods are subsequently appropriated to the contract, the seller may, by the terms of the contract or appropriation, reserve the right of disposal of the goods until certain conditions are fulfilled; and in such a case, notwithstanding the delivery of the goods to the buyer, or to a carrier or other bailee or custodier for the purpose of transmission to the buyer, the property in the goods does not pass to the buyer until the conditions imposed by the seller are fulfilled."

Here the appellants, by the terms of the contract of sale, have in effect reserved the right of disposal of the steel strip until fulfilment of the condition that all debts due to them by Carron have been paid. By virtue of this enactment, that has the effect that the property in the goods did not pass to Carron until that condition had been fulfilled. Counsel for Carron argued that the word "conditions" in section 19(1) must be read as excluding any condition which has the effect of creating a right of security over the goods. I am, however, unable to regard a provision reserving title to the seller until payment of all debts due to him by the buyer as amounting to the creation by the buyer of a right of security in favour of the seller. Such a provision does in a sense give the seller security for the unpaid debts of the buyer. But it does so by way of a legitimate retention of title, not by virtue of any right over his own property conferred by the buyer.

In all cases where a right of security is conferred the debtor retains an ultimate right over the subject matter in question. The creditor, having realised out of that subject matter a sufficient sum to meet the debt, is obliged to account to the debtor for any surplus. Where, however, the seller of goods retains title until some condition has been satisfied, and on failure of such satisfaction repossesses them, then he is not obliged to account to the buyer for any part of the value of the goods. Where the condition is to the effect that the price of the goods shall have been paid and it has not been paid, then in the situation where the market price of the goods has risen, so that they are worth more than the contract price, the extra value belongs to the unpaid seller. That is clearly the position where the condition relates to payment of the price of the actual goods, and goes to show that the retention of title provision is not one creating a right of security forming an exception to the general rule requiring possession by the creditor. The same is true, in my opinion, where the provision covers not only the price of the very goods which are the subject of the particular contract of sale, but also debts due to the seller under other contracts.

In *Clough Mill Ltd. v. Martin* [1985] 1 W.L.R. 111 [**[331]** above] it was held that a retention of title provision in a contract for the sale of goods did not constitute the creation of a charge conferring a security over the property of the purchasing company such as required to be registered under what was then section 95 of the Companies Act 1948. The judgments of the Court of Appeal contain interesting discussions of the problems which might arise where the goods the subject matter of the contract of sale had been partially paid for before being repossessed by the seller. In that case the court did not find it necessary to form a concluded view as to the solution of these problems, nor is it necessary in this case.'

Question:

Is this analysis persuasive? What is the material distinction between all moneys clauses and proceeds and products clauses (discussed below)?

3.8.4 Products retention of title clauses

The parties may expressly provide for the seller to have an interest in any products manufactured from the delivered goods. Alternatively, their agreement may be silent but, after a default, the seller may attempt to use the equitable rules of tracing to trace the delivered goods into their products and then assert an interest in the products. Neither route has met with much success. Note, however, that the two routes are quite distinct and their respective failures depend upon different arguments.

Re-read:

Clough Mill Ltd v Martin [1985] 1 WLR 111 (extracted at **[331]** above), which deals with the impact of an express products clause.

Note:

Notwithstanding this analysis, it seems that contractual provision for the supplier to have ownership of the product will be given effect to if it does not represent a windfall gain to the supplier: see, eg, *Pongakawa Sawmill Ltd v New Zealand Forest Products Ltd* [1992] 3 NZLR 304, 308–9, where logs supplied by the seller had been sawn into timber but nevertheless the seller was allowed to repossess the sawn timber. Arguably the fact that there is no windfall gain to the seller is important not for itself, but because it suggests that the *form* of the parties' contract is not inconsistent with its intended *substance*. But contrast *Re Peachdart Ltd* [1984] Ch 131 (Vinelott J), where leather was supplied for the manufacture of handbags; the supplier's claim to the uncompleted handbags and the proceeds of sale of the completed bags failed.

[334] *Borden (UK) Ltd v Scottish Timber Products Ltd* [1981] Ch 25, 38–42 *per* Bridge LJ:

[This extract discusses the possibility of tracing the goods into their products. Resin was sold subject to a retention of title clause which retained title until all the goods supplied by Borden had been paid for in full. Permission was granted to use the goods in the manufacture of chipboard, and it was clearly contemplated that the resin would be used in this fashion before it had been paid for. The court held that the resin was not traceable into the end-product.]

> 'It seems to me that there are certain very clear distinctions between that case [the *Romalpa* case: see **[330]** above] and this. First, it was conceded throughout in that case that the defendants were bailees of the aluminium foil for the plaintiffs; secondly, on the facts on which the decision turns there had been no admixture of the foil with any other material; if there had been, it would have been covered by the express terms of the second part of condition 13, but all that was in issue was a claim to trace the foil into the proceeds of sale of the foil. Thirdly, the case turned on the construction of the particular clause and on what was to be implied in the first part of the clause as to the terms on which the defendants were entitled to sell aluminium foil. Here, by contrast, first, as I have said, in my judgment there clearly was no bailment of the resin; secondly, there was an admixture of the goods of the plaintiffs with other materials of the defendants,

producing a wholly new substance. Thirdly, we are not here concerned with any sale of the resin; it is not suggested by either party that the terms of sale here contemplated that the defendants should be at liberty to sell the resin as such; all that was contemplated was that they should be a liberty to use it in their own process of manufacture.

But to my mind the most important distinction is that the essence of the decision in *Romalpa* was that on the facts found or admitted Romalpa were selling the plaintiffs' material, the aluminium foil, as agents for the plaintiffs. It seems to me quite impossible to say here that in using the plaintiffs' resin in their own manufacturing process to manufacture their own chipboard, the defendants could possibly be described as acting in any sense as agents for the plaintiffs. I do not in any way question the correctness of the decision in *Romalpa*, but for my own part I really do not find that it throws any significant light on the questions which we have to decide.

The only argument derived from the consideration of *Romalpa* which is worthy of attention is that it is said here, as it was said in *Romalpa*, that the intention of the clause under consideration must have been to give the plaintiffs an effective security as unpaid purchaser for the purchase price of any resin, and their security would not be effective unless the tracing remedy claimed on behalf of the plaintiffs is an effective remedy. For my part, I am wholly unimpressed by that argument. I accept that in stipulating for condition 2 in their conditions of sale, it was a pious hope on the part of the plaintiffs that they were creating for themselves an effective security for the payment of any unpaid purchase price due to them at any time; but the mere fact that they hoped that that would be so and intended that it should be so, is quite insufficient to carry the day if the language they used in relation to the agreed facts and the legal relationship which they created, whatever it may have been, is insufficient to make their intention an effective one.

I come to what, to my mind, is really the heart of the matter: Can the tracing remedy here claimed be supported in the application, by analogy, of the well-known principles of tracing expounded so clearly in the judgment of Sir George Jessel M.R. in *In re Hallett's Estate*, 13 Ch.D. 696, 708–711 [**[627]** below, and cited in **[330]** above]? He says:

> "The modern doctrine of equity as regards property disposed of by persons in a fiduciary position is a very clear and well-established doctrine. You can, if the sale was rightful, take the proceeds of the sale, if you can identify them. If the sale was wrongful, you can still take the proceeds of the sale, in a sense adopting the sale for the purpose of taking the proceeds, if you can identify them. There is no distinction, therefore, between a rightful and a wrongful disposition of the property, so far as regards the right of the beneficial owner to follow the proceeds. But it very often happens that you cannot identify the proceeds. The proceeds may have been invested together with money belonging to the person in a fiduciary position, in a purchase. He may have bought land with it, for instance, or he may have bought chattels with it. Now, what is the position of the beneficial owner as regards such purchases? I will, first of all, take his position when the purchase is clearly made with what I will call, for shortness, the trust money, although it is not confined, as I will show presently, to express trusts. In that case, according to the now well-established doctrine of equity, the beneficial owner has a right to elect either to take the property purchased, or to hold it as a security for the amount of the trust money laid out in the purchase; or, as we generally express it, he is entitled at his election either to take the property, or to have a charge on the property for the amount of the trust money. But in the second case, where a trustee has mixed the money with his own, there is this distinction, that the cestui que trust, or beneficial

> owner, can no longer elect to take the property, because it is no longer bought with the trust-money simply and purely, but with a mixed fund. He is, however, still entitled to a charge on the property purchased, for the amount of the trust-money laid out in the purchase; and that charge is quite independent of the fact of the amount laid out by the trustee. The moment you get a substantial portion of it furnished by the trustee, using the word 'trustee' in the sense I have mentioned. as including all persons in a fiduciary relation, the right to the charge follows. That is the modern doctrine of equity. Has it ever been suggested, until very recently, that there is any distinction between an express trustee, or an agent, or a bailee, or a collector of rents, or anybody else in a fiduciary position? I have never heard, until quite recently, such a distinction suggested. It cannot, as far as I am aware (and since this court sat last to hear this case, I have taken the trouble to look for authority), be found in any reported case even suggested, except in the recent decision of Fry J., to which I shall draw attention presently. It can have no foundation in principle, because the beneficial ownership is the same, wherever the legal ownership may be. If you have goods bargained and sold to a man upon trust to sell and hand over the net proceeds to another, that other is the beneficial owner; but if instead of being bargained and sold, so as to vest the legal ownership in the trustee, they are deposited with him to sell as agent, so that the legal ownership remains in the beneficial owner, can it be supposed, in a Court of Equity, that the rights of the beneficial owner are different, he being entire beneficial owner in both cases? I say on principle it is impossible to imagine there can be any difference. In practice we know there is no difference, because the moment you get into a Court of Equity, where a principal can sue an agent as well as a cestui que trust can sue a trustee, no such distinction was ever suggested, as far as I am aware. Therefore, the moment you establish the fiduciary relation, the modern rules of equity, as regards following trust money, apply. . . .
>
> "Now that being the established doctrine of equity on this point, I will take the case of the pure bailee. If the bailee sells the goods bailed, the bailor can in equity follow the proceeds, and can follow the proceeds wherever they can be distinguished, either being actually kept separate, or being mixed up with other moneys. I have only to advert to one other point, and that is this—supposing, instead of being invested in the purchase of land or goods, the moneys were simply mixed with other moneys of the trustee, using the term again in its full sense as including every person in a fiduciary relation, does it make any difference according to the modern doctrine of equity? I say none. It would be very remarkable if it were to do so. Supposing the trust money was 1,000 sovereigns, and the trustee put a them into a bag, and by mistake, or accident, or otherwise, dropped a sovereign of his own into the bag. Could anybody suppose that a judge in equity would find any difficulty in saying that the cestui que trust has a right to take 1,000 sovereigns out of that bag? I do not like to call it a charge of 1,000 sovereigns on the 1,001 sovereigns, but that is the effect of it. I have no doubt of it. It would make no difference if, instead of one sovereign, it was another 1,000 sovereigns; but if instead of putting it into his bag, or after putting it into his bag, he carries the bag to his bankers, what then? According to law, the bankers are his debtors for the total amount; but if you lend the trust money to a third person, you can follow it."

What are the salient features of the doctrine that Sir George Jessel M.R. there expounds? First, it will be observed that in all cases the party entitled to trace is referred to as the beneficial owner of the property, be it money or goods, which the "trustee," in the broad sense in which Sir George Jessel M.R. uses that word, including all fiduciary relationships, has disposed of. In the instant case, even if I assume that so long as the resin remained resin the beneficial ownership of the resin remained in the plaintiffs, I do not see how the concept of the beneficial ownership remaining in the plaintiffs after use in manufacture can here possibly be reconciled with the liberty which the plaintiffs gave to the defendants to use that resin in the manufacturing process for the defendants' benefit, producing their own chipboard and in the process destroying the very existence of the resin.

Secondly, the doctrine expounded by Sir George Jessel M.R. contemplates the tracing of goods into money and money into goods. In the latter case it matters not that the moneys represent a mixed fund of which a part only is impressed with the relevant trust. The cestui que trust has a charge on the mixed fund or the property into which it has passed for the amount of the trust moneys. It is at the heart of Mr. Mowbray's argument to submit that the same applies to a mixture of goods with goods, relying in particular on Sir George Jessel M.R.'s illustration of the mixed bag of sovereigns. Now I can well see the force of that argument if the goods mixed are all of a homogenous character. Supposing I deposit a ton of my corn with a corn factor as bailee, who does not store it separately but mixes it with corn of his own. This, I apprehend, would leave unaffected my rights as bailor, including the right to trace. But a mixture of heterogeneous goods in a manufacturing process wherein the original goods lose their character and what emerges is a wholly new product, is in my judgment something entirely different.

Some extreme examples were canvassed in argument. Suppose cattle cake is sold to a farmer, or fuel to a steel manufacturer, in each case with a reservation of title clause, but on terms which permit the farmer to feed the cattle cake to his herd and the steelmaker to fuel his furnaces, before paying the purchase price. Mr. Mowbray concedes that in these cases the seller cannot trace into the cattle or the steel. He says that the difference is that the goods have been consumed. But once this concession is made, I find it impossible to draw an intelligible line of distinction in principle which would give the plaintiffs a right to trace the resin into the chipboard in the instant case. What has happened in the manufacturing process is much more akin to the process of consumption than to any simple process of admixture of goods. To put the point in another way, if the contribution that the resin has made to the chipboard gives rise to a tracing remedy, I find it difficult to see any good reason why, in the steelmaking example, the essential contribution made by the fuel to the steel manufacturing process should not do likewise.

These are the principal considerations which have led me to the conclusion that the plaintiffs are not entitled to the tracing remedy which they claim. But I am fortified in that conclusion by the further consideration that if the remedy were available in such cases, a most intractable problem could, and in many cases would, arise in quantifying the proportion of the value of the manufactured product which the tracer could claim as properly attributable to his ingredient. In the instant case, a breakdown of the actual costings of chipboard over a period of seven months to July 29, 1977, has been agreed, attributing 17 per cent. of the total cost to the cost of resin, subject to a reservation with respect to wastage and over-usage. But one can well see that in many cases where the cost of materials and labour involved in a particular production process were constantly fluctuating, it might be quite impossible to assign a proportion of the total cost properly attributable to one particular ingredient with any certainty at all.

The lesson to be learned from these conclusions is a simple one. If a seller of goods to a manufacturer, who knows that his goods are to be used in the manufacturing process before they are paid for, wishes to reserve to himself an effective security for the payment of the price, he cannot rely on a simple reservation of title clause such as that relied upon by the plaintiffs. If he wishes to acquire rights over the finished product, he can only do so by express contractual stipulation. We have seen an elaborate, and presumably effective, example of such a stipulation in *Aluminium Industrie Vaassen B. V. v. Romalpa Aluminium Ltd.* [1976] 1 W.L.R. 676. An attempt to acquire rights over the finished product by a stipulation which proved ineffective for want of registration under section 95 of the Companies Act 1948 is to be seen in the decision of Slade J. in *In re Bond Worth Ltd.* [1980] Ch. 228 to which in the course of argument we were helpfully referred.'

3.8.5 Proceeds retention of title clauses

The extracts which follow indicate that the courts tend to base any right to the proceeds on the express terms of the agreement between the parties, not on some independent tracing right. Moreover, they generally construe that express right as creating a charge, one which is usually void for failure to register.

[335] ***Pfeiffer Weinkellerei-Weineinkauf GmbH & Co v Arbuthnot Factors Ltd*** **[1988] 1 WLR 150, 153, 155–61** ***per*** **Phillips J:**
[The facts appear from the judgment.]

'The plaintiff is a German company which carries on business as an exporter of wines. The plaintiff supplied the wine to an English importer, Springfield Wine Importers Ltd. ("Springfield") on terms that included a reservation of title clause. Springfield sub-sold the wine to sub-purchasers on credit terms. Springfield then entered into a factoring agreement pursuant to which Springfield assigned to the defendant debts owed to Springfield by sub-purchasers. In accordance with these assignments the sub-purchasers proceeded to pay the defendant. The plaintiff claims to enjoy a title to the moneys so paid superior to that of the defendant and, in these proceedings, calls upon the defendant to account for and pay over these moneys.

...

Did the plaintiff's alleged conditions of payment and delivery have the effect in law of creating a charge requiring registration under section 95 of the Companies Act 1948?

Mr. Hapgood contended that the correct legal analysis of the facts of this case is as follows. Under clause 5 the plaintiff, while unpaid, retained both legal and equitable title in the wine up to the moment that Springfield sold it to sub-purchasers. During this period Springfield held the wine as fiduciary for the plaintiff. In these circumstances, in the absence of any express agreement to the contrary, upon sub-sale by Springfield of the plaintiff's wine, the plaintiff would automatically become beneficially entitled to the proceeds. Clause 5 did not constitute an agreement to the contrary, but on its true construction confirmed that the plaintiff was to be beneficially entitled to all proceeds of sub-sales. Section 95 of the Companies Act 1948 had no application for two reasons. First, the plaintiff's equitable interest did not constitute a charge over property owned by Springfield. It was an absolute beneficial interest in the proceeds of sale, albeit that the plaintiff would come under an implied contractual duty to account to Springfield to the extent that proceeds of sale ultimately recovered by the plaintiff exceeded the debts owed by Springfield to it. Secondly, the plaintiff's beneficial interest was not created by Springfield. It arose by operation of law as a consequence of sale by Springfield of property owned by the plaintiff. Clause 5 did not create the right—it merely recognised and confirmed its existence.

In support of his submissions, Mr. Hapgood relied on the decision of the Court of Appeal in *Aluminium Industrie Vaassen B.V. v. Romalpa Aluminium Ltd.* [1976] 1 WLR 676. Because that decision formed the cornerstone of the plaintiff's case, I must examine it in a little detail.

. . .

It seems to me inappropriate to describe the relationship of a seller and a buyer in possession to whom title has not yet passed as that of bailor/bailee, for it will not normally have the same incidents as the classic bailment relationship. The relationship of a buyer and a seller is inevitably the creature of contract. Where the seller retains title by way of security prior to sub-sale, but the contract expressly or impliedly authorises the buyer to effect sub-sales, I do not consider that any prima facie implication arises that sub-sales are to be effected by the buyer as agent for and for the account of the seller. On the contrary, I consider that the normal implication that arises from the relationship of buyer and seller is that if the buyer is permitted to sub-sell in the normal course of his business, he will do so for his own account. I consider that the conclusions of the Court of Appeal in *Aluminium Industrie Vaassen B.V. v. Romalpa Aluminium Ltd.* [1976] 1 WLR 676 as to the fiduciary relationship of the plaintiffs and the defendants turned on the particular wording of clause 13 and on the concession that the relationship of the parties was that of bailor/bailee.

I turn then to the all-important matter, the wording of clause 5 in the present case. Mr. Hapgood, in the course of an attractive argument, submitted that the provisions of clause 5 are very similar to the provisions of clause 13 in the *Romalpa* case and that, if anything, clause 5 indicates more clearly that any sales made by Springfield were to be for the account of the plaintiff.

. . .

Clause 5 in the present case makes express provisions in respect of the proceeds of sub-sale of wine, both in respect of credit sales and in respect of cash sales. The former provisions are the more important, although it is relevant also to consider the latter when examining the nature of the relationship between the plaintiff and Springfield. Lines 12 to 18 provide:

> "The buyer is only allowed to dispose of the goods or to sell them in business operations carried out in due order and as long as there is no delay in payment. All claims that he gets from the sale or due to another legal reason regarding our goods, with all rights including his profit amounting to his obligations towards us, will be passed on to us. On demand the buyer is obliged to notify the assignment of the claim to give us in written [sic] all necessary information concerning the assertion of our claims and to deliver us all necessary documents."

In my view these provisions cannot properly be read as conferring mere ancillary security rights. They comprehensively set out the nature of such interest as the plaintiff is to have by way of security in respect of debts created by sub-sales. Mr. Potts, for the defendant, submitted that these provisions were, for a number of reasons, inconsistent with a fiduciary relationship of the kind contended for by the plaintiff. I agree with him in this.

First and foremost, the claims to be "passed on" are qualified by the words "amounting to his obligations towards us." This must mean that claims are to be passed on only up to the amount of Springfield's outstanding obligations to the plaintiff. This is not consistent with the proposition that Springfield was only authorised to sell wine for the account of the plaintiff, so as to vest the beneficial interest to all proceeds in the plaintiff. Mr. Hapgood contended that the plaintiff was beneficially entitled to all the proceeds and that, as Springfield "encashed" debts owed to it, Springfield was obliged to hold all the proceeds for the plaintiff in a separate account, regardless of the amount of Springfield's indebtedness to the plaintiff. The plaintiff was beneficially entitled to call for all the proceeds but would be under a contractual duty to repay any surplus to Springfield. I cannot accept this analysis. Not merely would such an arrangement be uncommercial, it is not one which can be reconciled with the express wording of the clause.

Secondly, the language used is essentially that of assignment or cession by Springfield of rights owned by Springfield. I have particularly in mind the reference to "claims . . . he gets . . .including his profit," the obligation on demand "to notify the assignment" and the right "to encash ceded obligations." I accept that provisions in relation to cash sales to be found in lines 26 to 28 of clause 5 are more consistent with the legal analysis for which Mr. Hapgood contends, but reading these provisions in the context of the clause as a whole I think that they do no more than provide that cash received is to be held for the plaintiff up to the amount of Springfield's outstanding indebtedness to it.

In summary I find that lines 12 to 18 of clause 5 constitute an agreement by Springfield to assign to the plaintiff future choses in action, namely future debts owed by sub-purchasers to Springfield up to the amount of any outstanding indebtedness on the part of Springfield to the plaintiff. In so far as debts came into existence falling within that agreement, the agreement created an equitable assignment of the debts. The agreement was plainly by way of security, and the assignments under it were capable of being redeemed by payment by Springfield of the outstanding indebtedness. It follows that by agreeing to the provisions of clause 5 Springfield created a charge by way of security over Springfield's property, namely book debts, which being unregistered was rendered void as against Springfield's creditors by section 95(1) and (2)(e) of the Companies Act 1948 [now Companies Act 1985 section 395].'

[336] *Compaq Computer Ltd v The Abercorn Group Ltd* [1991] BCC 484, 494–7 *per* Mummery J:

[Mummery J was required to determine, as a preliminary issue of law, whether the unpaid supplier of computer equipment to a buyer who subsequently went into liquidation had a better claim, by virtue of a retention of title clause, to the proceeds of sale of such products to sub-purchasers, than an assignee from the buyer under an invoice discounting agreement. Compaq supplied computer equipment to the first defendant, Abercorn, under an all monies retention of title clause (dating from July 1987) which reserved title in Compaq products to Compaq until payment of the price of those products and any other sums owing by Abercorn to Compaq. Later, Abercorn entered into a written invoice discounting agreement with the second defendant, Kellock. Later still, Abercorn executed debentures in favour of Kellock containing a fixed charge on Abercorn's book and other debts and a floating charge over its undertaking, property and assets. When Abercorn went into receivership, it owed Compaq £702,868 in respect of Compaq products.]

'[I]t was submitted on behalf of Compaq that, if Abercorn disposed of Compaq products at a time when the price of those products had not been paid to Compaq or when there were any other sums owing by Abercorn to Compaq, Abercorn became legally entitled to the proceeds of disposal but at the same moment Compaq automatically became beneficially entitled to the entire proceeds.

That entitlement rested on Compaq's retention of the full legal and beneficial title to the Compaq products while they were unsold and unpaid for in Abercorn's hands, on

Compaq's retention of entitlement in equity to those proceeds under cl. 8.3.2 of the dealer agreement, and on the application of the principles in the *Romalpa* case.

Central to this submission was the argument that, being described as "bailee or agent" of Compaq in the express terms of cl. 8.3.2 of the dealer agreement, Abercorn stood in a fiduciary relationship with Compaq in relation to both the unsold Compaq products and the proceeds of sale. As Abercorn owed fiduciary obligations to Compaq in respect of the products and the proceeds of sale, Abercorn never had any beneficial interest in the proceeds of sale of Compaq products at a time when the price of those products had not been paid to Compaq or when there were other sums owing to Compaq. On a subsale of the Compaq products, Abercorn acquired a legal title to the proceeds of sale paid or payable by the subpurchaser, but no beneficial interest to the proceeds vested in or passed through Abercorn. There was more than a contractual obligation on the part of Abercorn to assign to Compaq its rights against the subpurchaser: there was a fiduciary obligation to account strictly for all the proceeds of sale of goods which belonged to Compaq and were sold by Abercorn as fiduciary, with the consequence that those proceeds were beneficially the property of Compaq. There could not, therefore, be any question of Abercorn creating a charge over the proceeds of sale in favour of Compaq; it had no beneficial interest either in the Compaq products or in the proceeds of sale which entitled it to create such a charge.

Kellock accepted that, if the proceeds of sale were the beneficial property of Compaq, Abercorn could not have created a charge over them. Kellock also accepted that any charge arising on the application of the principle in *Re Hallett's Estate* (1880) 13 ChD 696 to a fund in which the proceeds of sale beneficially belonging to Compaq have been mixed with other moneys of Abercorn, would not be a charge "created" by Abercorn and would not therefore be registrable under sec. 395 of the Companies Act 1985.

As to the practical mechanics of dealing with the proceeds of subsales of Compaq products by Abercorn, it was submitted on behalf of Compaq that the position was as follows. Abercorn could make full title to the Compaq products in favour of subpurchasers, but it was bound to pay the proceeds of sale into a separate bank account which, by reason of the fiduciary obligation, should be an interest-bearing account. If that account was in the name of Abercorn, Abercorn could only draw on it for the purpose of paying sums of money to Compaq, so long as the price of the Compaq products remained unpaid and other sums remained owing to Compaq. Abercorn could not use the moneys in the account for its own trading purposes so long as that state of affairs continued. The entire fund in the account belonged beneficially to Compaq. The practical consequences would be the same if the proceeds of sale were directly paid by Abercorn into an account in the name of Compaq. In that case Compaq could draw on the account so long as the price of the Compaq products and other sums owing remained unpaid.

It was, however, accepted that, as cl. 8.3.2 is qualified by the preceding provisions of cl. 8.3, Compaq's beneficial interest in the proceeds of sale, whether in an account in the name of Abercorn or in its own name, was determinable on payment to Compaq of the unpaid price of the Compaq products and the other sums owing. In that event, Abercorn would be entitled to the balance in the account. If the account was in Abercorn's name, Abercorn could then use the balance for its own trading purposes. If the account was maintained in Compaq's name, it was accepted that Compaq would be bound to hand over the balance in that account to Abercorn. Thus, when the relevant contractual debts in respect of the various supply contracts of Compaq products were paid, the beneficial interest of Compaq in the proceeds of sale would determine and Abercorn's trading profit would be freed to it for its own use.

It was forcefully argued on behalf of Compaq that to treat this arrangement as constituting a charge on the proceeds of sale by Abercorn in favour of Compaq would be to impose on the parties to the dealer agreement a different transaction than they had in fact agreed upon: see *Lloyds and Scottish Finance Ltd v Cyril Lord Carpet Sales Ltd* (1979) 129 NLJ 366 at p. 372. Although it was accepted that the purpose of retention of a determinable beneficial interest in the proceeds of sale in Compaq was to provide it with a continuing security for money owing to it, that did not necessarily make the transaction a charge if, on the true analysis, Abercorn never did acquire any beneficial interest in the proceeds of sale which it could charge. The retention of the beneficial interest in the proceeds of sale in Compaq was the result of fiduciary obligations arising from the terms of the agreement and no charge was created by Abercorn.

In my judgment, this is not the correct analysis of the true legal relationship between the parties or of the transaction under consideration. Once it is accepted that the beneficial interest in the proceeds of sale was determinable on the payment of debts, Compaq is faced with the difficulty that the rights and obligations of the parties were in reality and in substance characteristic of those of the parties to a charge and not of those in a trustee/beneficiary or other fiduciary relationship. As Slade J observed *in Re Bond Worth* at p. 248E:

> "In my judgment, any contract which, by way of security for the payment of a debt, confers an interest in property defeasible or destructible upon payment of such debt, or appropriates such property for the discharge of the debt, must necessarily be regarded as creating a mortgage or charge, as the case may be."

In my judgment that is the position here. Abercorn was entitled to redeem the charge in favour of Compaq by payment of the outstanding debts. Compaq was not entitled to retain out of the proceeds a sum more than sufficient to pay those debts. If the proceeds were insufficient for that purpose, Compaq could sue Abercorn for the balance as a contract debt.

On its true construction the dealer agreement operated in the following manner in relation to the Compaq products and the proceeds of sale.

(1) While the Compaq products remained unsold in the hands of Abercorn, Compaq retained full legal and beneficial ownership of those products, subject to contractual terms. Abercorn was bailee or agent of the unsold products. Abercorn did not confer a charge on the products in favour of Compaq; it could not do so because the products had remained the property of Compaq.

(2) It was expressly contemplated that Abercorn need not pay for the goods immediately. It had interest-free credit for 30 days under cl. 8.2. It was also expressly provided that Abercorn was authorised to dispose of Compaq products which it had not paid for to Abercorn's customers in the ordinary course of Abercorn's business and in accordance with the provisions of the agreement—see cl. 8.3.1.

(3) When Abercorn sold Compaq products which it had not paid for to subpurchasers it did not sell as bailee, agent, fiduciary or trustee. It did not sell in breach of any fiduciary obligation. Abercorn sold the Compaq products lawfully on its own account, vesting full legal and beneficial title in the Compaq products in its subpurchasers. It sold the Compaq products without reference to Compaq, when it liked, at what prices it liked and on what terms it liked, in the hope of making a profit for itself. It is not suggested that Abercorn sold the products otherwise than in the ordinary course of its business.

(4) As against the subpurchasers Abercorn was legally and beneficially entitled to the full proceeds of sale of the Compaq products. It is accepted that, as against Compaq, Abercorn was legally entitled to the proceeds of sale. In my judgment, Abercorn was also, as against Compaq, beneficially entitled to those proceeds. It was not under any

trust or fiduciary obligation in respect of them. There was a contractual obligation in cl. 8.3.2 to account for the full proceeds "as the seller's bailee or agent" and to "keep a separate account of all such proceeds or moneys for such purpose". It is true that the references to "account", "bailee" and "agent" and to the keeping of a separate account of the proceeds may indicate a fiduciary relationship, but the obligation here was not, in my view, fiduciary or apt to operate as a retention or a vesting of the beneficial interest in the entire proceeds automatically in Compaq.

It is implicit in Compaq's acceptance of the defeasible nature of its interest that Abercorn had even on that analysis a residual interest in the proceeds of sale surplus to Compaq's claims for the unpaid purchase price of the Compaq products and other sums owing to it. Abercorn's interest in the proceeds of sale in excess of the debts owing to Compaq is, in my view, more consistent with the existence of a charge over the proceeds created by Abercorn in favour of Compaq than with a fiduciary obligation on the part of Abercorn operating as a retention or vesting of the absolute interest in all the proceeds automatically in Compaq. Compaq had a limited interest in those proceeds by way of security for outstanding debts rather than by way of bare trust. Subject to compliance with the appropriate statutory requirements, that charge would be effective to protect Compaq's interest in the proceeds and, at the same time, would enable Abercorn to make use in its own business of the profits earned on the subsales. The keeping of a separate account would serve to identify thè subject-matter of that charge.

In my judgment, the answers to the points of law on the charge point in the schedule are as follows.

(1) Yes. Compaq's standard terms and conditions had the effect of creating a charge over the proceeds of sale.

(2) Yes. The charge required registration as it was a charge created by Abercorn to which sec. 395 and 396 of the Companies Act 1985 applied.

(2A) The consequence of failure to register such charge is that the charge is void as against Kellock, a creditor of Abercorn, as well as against the liquidators of Abercorn.

(4) Yes. Kellock has priority over the rights of Compaq created by virtue of the debenture of 26 July 1989, because that debenture was registered whereas the charge created by the agreement of 29 July 1987 was not registered.

(5) Yes. Kellock has priority over the rights of Compaq by virtue of the further debenture dated 4 August 1989 because that debenture was registered and the charge created by the agreement of 29 July 1987 was not registered.'

Again, the difficulty with these proceeds clauses is that they are construed as involving the *buyer* creating a new and defeasible right in the seller, a right which gives the seller an interest in the *buyer's* assets. Such a right is easily categorised as a charge, and a floating charge at that. Simple retention of title clauses, on the other hand, even when they incorporate 'all moneys' clauses, involve retention by the *supplier* of the property which was always the supplier's.

Question:

Is there any way the supplier can avoid this conclusion that there is a floating charge and instead claim an *ownership* interest in the products or proceeds? Is the analysis in the Australian case, *Associated Alloys Pty Ltd v ACN 001 452 106 Pty Ltd* [2000] HCA 25, (2000) 74 ALJR 862 (Aust HCt) persuasive?

3.8.6 Public policy issues

[337] W Goodhart and G Jones, 'The Infiltration of Equitable Doctrine into English Commercial Law' (1980) 43 *MLR* 489, 506–10:
[Footnotes in the original are omitted.]

> 'As a result of these three cases [*Romalpa*, *Bond Worth* and *Borden*], the status of reservation of title clauses is distinctly confused. A number of questions arise. The most fundamental is whether it is possible to reconcile *Romalpa* with *Re Bond Worth* and *Borden*. It might be possible to reconcile *Romalpa* with *Borden*, on the ground that the objections to the recognition of a proprietary claim where goods have been mixed in the process of manufacture, in particular that the identity of the goods has disappeared, do not apply to a right to trace into the proceeds of sale of goods resold in an unaltered state. It seems impossible, however, to reconcile *Romalpa* with *Re Bond Worth*. The passage in Slade J.'s judgment in the latter case in which he seeks to distinguish the two cases is the least satisfactory part of what is otherwise a formidable judgment. It is true that in *Romalpa* the legal and beneficial property in the goods was reserved, while in *Re Bond Worth* Monsanto had reserved only the "equitable and beneficial" interest. But in *Romalpa*, the decision turned on the fact that there was held to be a fiduciary relationship between Romalpa, as possessors of the foil, and A.I.V. The fact that Bond Worth had *legal* title to the Acrilan while Monsanto claimed to have retained the beneficial interest must, if anything, strengthen the argument that there was a fiduciary relationship between Bond Worth and Monsanto. The conditions of sale used by Monsanto certainly appear to have constituted Bond Worth an express trustee for Monsanto; in contrast the relationship of A.I.V. and Romalpa does not fit at all easily into the recognised category of bailor and bailee or of principal and agent.
>
> But if Slade J.'s attempt to distinguish *Re Bond Worth* from *Romalpa* is unsatisfactory, his reasons why a reservation of title clause must, in relation to the proceeds of sale of the goods supplied, normally create a charge rather than a beneficial trust interest seem wholly convincing. Although the conditions of sale in *Romalpa* contained a clause which enabled A.I.V. to insist on the foil being kept separate until use or resale, there was no clause requiring the proceeds of sale to be similarly segregated. Consequently it would have been perfectly consistent to have concluded that, although there was a trust of the foil, there was no trust of the proceeds of sale. It is not a convincing justification to say (as Goff L.J. did in the passage from *Romalpa* previously quoted) that "in practice, so long as all went well the plaintiffs would allow the defendants to use the proceeds of sale in their business." This treats the right to use the proceeds of sale as a matter of mere concession by A.I.V. It seems highly unlikely, however, that this can be regarded as merely an *ex post facto* concession, on the contrary, it must be virtually certain that A.I.V. assumed all along that Romalpa would use the proceeds of sale for its own purposes and indeed that it was commercially necessary for them to do so—hence the 75 days' credit clause. In the absence of any express or implied obligation on the customer to segregate the proceeds of sale, it seems, in the light of the authorities referred to by Slade J., impossible to treat the proceeds of sale as being subject to a trust. It is therefore necessary that any reservation of title clause which is to extend to the proceeds of sale should include an obligation to segregate those proceeds. But even if the customer is obliged to segregate the proceeds of sale, the supplier would not necessarily be entitled to the whole of those proceeds but only to an amount equal to the undischarged balance of the debts owed to him by the customer—and, as analysed by Slade J., a right of that kind normally constitutes a charge.

If the reasoning of *Re Bond Worth* and *Borden is* subsequently affirmed, it seems that *Romalpa* may well be relegated to that limbo of cases treated as decided on "special facts" and therefore to be ignored. Moreover, similar reasoning suggests that there is a distinction between reservation of title clauses which reserve title only until the payment of the purchase price for the goods in question and clauses which (as in *Romalpa* and *Borden*) reserve title until not only that price but debts due from the customer to the supplier in respect of other sales have also been discharged. There are strong grounds for arguing that a clause of the latter kind must be intended to operate by way of security. If a true beneficial interest is reserved in goods supplied, it must follow that if after payment of the full purchase price of those goods the supplier recovers possession of them because of non-discharge of some other liability the supplier must refund the purchase price to the customer on the ground of total failure of consideration. But this would defeat the object of the clause, as it will almost always be the intention of the supplier that he should be entitled to recover the goods and resell them elsewhere without having to refund the purchase price. This, surely, can only be done if the clause is construed as creating a security for payment of the customer's debts to the supplier and not as a condition postponing the transfer of the beneficial interest. Unfortunately, this argument, which is inconsistent with the decision of the Court of Appeal in *Romalpa*, does not appear to have been raised in that case.

Does that leave any effective role for a reservation of title clause? In our view such clauses may still be of some value to suppliers, albeit of more limited value than seemed likely in the immediate aftermath of *Romalpa*.

In the first place, any charge created by a reservation of title clause is only void if unregistered, so that it would be possible to protect the charge by registration. In practice, the right to protect a "suppliers' charge" by registration may not be of much use. It appears that each contract of sale would give rise to a separate charge requiring separate registration. This problem could perhaps be overcome by the supplier requiring the customer to give a floating charge (either general or over some specified class of assets) to secure all sums from time to time due from the customer to the supplier, much as banks take floating charges to secure the sums owing on overdraft. But any such floating charge taken by the supplier may well prove to be of little value, ranking as it does behind the claims of prior chargees and preferential creditors.

Secondly it seems clear that a suitably drafted reservation of title clause embodying an obligation to keep the seller's materials separate from other materials will give the supplier effective protection up to the point at which the goods are either resold or used in manufacture by the customer. Section 19(1) of the Sale of Goods Act 1979 permits the supplier to retain the property in goods notwithstanding that the customer is in possession of them. If goods are sold on condition that the property in them does not pass until the price is paid in full but the customer has a right in the meanwhile to use or resell the goods in the normal course of business, the Sale of Goods Act produces a result which is in its practical consequences almost identical to the result in *Quistclose*. The goods are delivered into the possession of the customer for the primary purpose of being used or resold in the course of his business. If that purpose fails because the customer goes into liquidation (and therefore ceases to have a business, or at most has a business being carried on only with a view to termination or disposal) the supplier gets his goods back and is free to treat them as his own, retaining any profit on resale and refunding any part payment for the goods as money paid for a consideration which has failed. The real problems relating to the effectiveness of reservation of title clauses arise only when the supplier has to rely on a tracing claim against the proceeds of sale or products into which the goods supplied have been incorporated or when title is reserved until not only the purchase price of the goods in question but other debts due from the customer have been discharged.

It is true that in *Re Bond Worth* Slade J. held that the reservation of title clause created merely an equitable charge over raw Acrilan in the possession of Bond Worth. It seems clear, however, that the arguments in that case were on an "all or nothing" basis and it was not argued that Monsanto retained a proprietary interest in the raw Acrilan even if it only had a charge over materials being processed or over the proceeds of sale. In any event, it may be that as a matter of construction the reservation of title clause adopted in that case—which contemplated that Monsanto's interest in processed goods and the proceeds of sale would be of the same nature as its interest in unworked Acrilan—could not properly be held to confer an interest in the raw Acrilan of a nature quite different from the interest created in processed goods or the proceeds of sale. In *Borden*, Templeman L.J. expressed the view that the rights acquired by Borden under the reservation of title clause could operate only by way of charge and that Borden would have been entitled to a return of its resin only in the event of a repudiation of the contract by S.T.P. However, neither the Sale of Goods Act nor *Quistclose* were referred to in the judgments and, if Templeman L.J. meant to say that a retention of title clause could *never* operate except by way of charge, it is suggested that this statement goes too far.'

[338] J R Bradgate, 'Reservation of Title Ten Years On' (1987) 51 *Conv* 434, 443–6: [Footnotes in the original are omitted.]

'VII. Policy Considerations

Of course, academic quibbles should not prevent the law responding to changing commercial practices in a commercially and socially desirable way. However, it is by no means clear that the recognition of reservation of title is desirable. First, it must be said that this is not a question simply of "freedom of contract." In practice there will be no real consensus between seller and buyer. Most sales will be on the seller's terms. Often all sellers in a particular trade will employ similar terms. If the buyer objects or seeks to introduce his own terms a battle of the forms will result (unless the buyer is in an unusually strong bargaining position.) The seller is best placed to fire the last shot which will normally win the battle. In fact the buyer will, in all probability, pay no attention to a reservation of title clause which will normally only bite if he becomes insolvent. The issue then is not one of contract between buyer and seller. The rights claimed by the seller disturb the prescribed order for the distribution of insolvent estates, and therefore affect third parties. Normally the courts will refuse to give effect to a contract term which purports to oust or alter that order.

In fact the principal objection to reservation of title is that it exists outside the framework of insolvency priorities and the systems for disclosure of incumbrances created by section 395 of the Companies Act 1985 and the Bills of Sale Acts, even though it seems to be squarely within the mischief of those systems. Moreover, it is not merely an undisclosed but a positively hidden security. In *Clough Mill*, Robert Goff L.J. was "tempted to observe that the mechanism of the floating charge upon which secured creditors are content to rely is perhaps as much open to criticism as the mechanism of the retention of title clause, at which they now express their dismay."

However, the floating charge must be registered to be effective. Other potential creditors may then search and, discovering its existence, take a *calculated* risk as to whether to advance credit, refuse to supply or take out insurance against bad debts. Reservation of title, on the other hand, presents the impression that the buyer of goods is their unencumbered owner, an impression reinforced by the accounting treatment of the transaction. Significantly, although the Sale of Goods Act expressly protects the unpaid seller against his buyer's insolvency, statutory protection ends once the goods enter the buyer's possession—only now to creep in by the back door in the guise of "conditional sale." As Kruse has observed, "the unpaid vendor who had been denied preference in the buyer's bankruptcy by the rule denying his right of pursuit would thus regain it by an underhand method."

The buyer has no similar protection against his seller's insolvency. If he orders and pays for goods from bulk but, before his goods have become ascertained, his seller becomes insolvent, he ranks as an unsecured creditor. In *re Wait* Atkin L.J. observed that the positions of buyer and seller were thus assimilated: "In both cases credit is given to the debtor and the buyer and the seller respectively take the well known risk of the insolvency of their customer."

Reservation of title destroys that symmetry. The buyer must insure against his seller's insolvency; the seller has no need to do the same. If the seller insures against bad debts, his prices will reflect the cost of premiums so that the risk of business failure is spread throughout the community. By reserving title to the goods he supplies, the materials supplier can leapfrog the statutory order for distribution of insolvent estates at the expense of other creditors. Not all unsecured creditors will be similarly favoured. Reservation of title is of no use to the supplier of services, nor even to the supplier of goods if they have been wholly consumed or resold before the buyer's insolvency.

The increasing use of reservation of title might also affect secured creditors, for if it were to reduce the funds available to them to satisfy their floating charge, the response of banks would presumably be to reduce the availability of credit to business, with a consequent impact on business and the economy generally and to err on the side of safety by appointing receivers at an earlier stage. If the floating charge is to be abolished as an effective security, abolition ought to be undertaken by parliament.

Of course, banks themselves could take advantage of reservation of title. Suppose that, instead of granting overdraft facilities secured by a floating charge, the bank was to arrange that its customer should place all orders through the bank, which would then purchase goods and raw materials on the customer's behalf. The bank would pay the supplier immediately and then resell the goods to its client subject to reservation of title, avoiding the need for registration and all priority problems. Even if impracticable for regular trading at present, such arrangements could be used for large, single transactions, or by a second financier to gain priority over a prior charge. Furthermore, they may well become more practicable with the growing computerisation of banking and business transactions and the linking of computer networks.'

3.9 *Quistclose* trusts

Quistclose trusts usually arise in the context of loans advanced to effect the rescue of an ailing company (although they need not be so restricted). The loan is advanced expressly on the condition that it be used only for specific and nominated purposes. The courts have read into this stipulation an implied term that if those purposes cannot be effected, then the funds should be returned in specie to the lender; and, further, that this implied term has the effect that the money continues to belong in equity, although not in law, to the lender until those purposes are carried out.[25] Again, the effect is to insulate the loan funds from the claims of the borrower's other creditors, both secured and unsecured.

[25] Or at least that it belongs in equity to the lender if the purposes *cannot* be carried out. There are various theories on the operation of *Quistclose* trusts: see below.

[339] ***Barclays Bank Ltd v Quistclose Investments Ltd*** **[1970] AC 567 (HL), 579–82** ***per*** **Lord Wilberforce:**

[Quistclose lent Rolls Razor a sum of money to cover a dividend that Rolls Razor had already legally declared. Rolls Razor was on the brink of insolvency. The advance was made on terms, known to Rolls Razor's bank, that it would be deposited in a separate account with the bank and used only to pay the dividend. But before the dividend was paid Rolls Razor went into voluntary liquidation. The bank unsuccessfully claimed to be allowed to use the money to set-off Rolls Razor's indebtedness to it.]

> 'Two questions arise, both of which must be answered favorably to the respondents if they are to recover the money from the bank. The first is whether as between the respondents and Rolls Razor Ltd. the terms upon which the loan was made were such as to impress upon the sum of £209,719 8s 6d [the sum lent to pay the dividend] a trust in their favour in the event of the dividend not being paid. The second is whether, in that event, the bank had such notice of the trust or of the circumstances giving rise to it as to make the trust binding upon them.
>
> It is not difficult to establish precisely upon what terms the money was advanced by the respondents to Rolls Razor Ltd. There is no doubt that the loan was made specifically in order to enable Rolls Razor Ltd. to pay the dividend. There is equally, in my opinion, no doubt that the loan was made only so as to enable Rolls Razor Ltd. to pay the dividend and for no other purpose. This follows quite clearly from the terms of the letter of Rolls Razor Ltd. to the bank of July 15, 1964, which letter, before transmission to the bank, was sent to the respondents under open cover in order that the cheque might be (as it was) enclosed in it. The mutual intention of the respondents and of Rolls Razor Ltd., and the essence of the bargain, was that the sum advanced should not become part of the assets of Rolls Razor Ltd., but should be used exclusively for payment of a particular class of its creditors, namely, those entitled to the dividend. A necessary consequence from this, by process simply of interpretation, must be that if, for any reason, the dividend could not be paid, the money was to be returned to the respondents: the word "only" or "exclusively" can have no other meaning or effect.
>
> That arrangements of this character for the payment of a person's creditors by a third person, give rise to a relationship of a fiduciary character or trust, in favour, as a primary trust, of the creditors, and secondarily, if the primary trust fails, of the third person, has been recognised in a series of cases over some 150 years.
>
> In *Toovey v. Milne* (1819) 2 B. & A. 683 part of the money advanced was, on the failure of the purpose for which it was lent (viz, to pay certain debts), repaid by the bankrupt to the person who had advanced it. On action being brought by the assignee of the bankrupt to recover it, the plaintiff was non suited and the non suit was upheld on a motion for a retrial. In his judgment Abbott C.J. said, at p. 684:
>
>> "I thought at the trial, and still think, that the fair inference from the facts proved was that this money was advanced for a special purpose, and that being so clothed with a specific trust, no property in it passed to the assignee of the bankrupt. Then the purpose having failed, there is an implied stipulation that the money shall be repaid. That has been done in the present case; and I am of opinion that that repayment was lawful, and that the non suit was right."
>
> The basis for the decision was thus clearly stated, viz., that the money advanced for the specific purpose did not become part of the bankrupt's estate. This case has been repeat-

edly followed and applied: see *Edwards v. Glynn* (1859) 2 E. & E. 29; *In re Rogers, Ex parte Holland and Hannen* (1891) 8 Morr. 243; *In re Drucker (No. 1)* [1902] 2 K.B. 237; *In re Hooley, Ex parte Trustee* [1915] H.B.R. 181. *In re Rogers*, 8 Morr. 243 was a decision of a strong Court of Appeal. In that case, the money provided by the third party had been paid to the creditors before the bankruptcy. Afterwards the trustee in bankruptcy sought to recover it. It was held that the money was advanced to the bankrupt for the special purpose of enabling his creditors to be paid, was impressed with a trust for the purpose and never became the property of the bankrupt. Lindley L.J. decided the case on principle but said (at p. 248) that if authority was needed it would be found in *Toovey v. Milne*, 2 B. & A. 683 and other cases. Bowen L.J. said (8 Morr. 243, 248) that the money came to the bankrupt's hands impressed with a trust and did not become the property of the bankrupt divisible amongst his creditors, and the judgment of Kay L.J., at p. 249, was to a similar effect.

These cases have the support of longevity, authority, consistency and, I would add, good sense. But they are not binding on your Lordships and it is necessary to consider such arguments as have been put why they should be departed from or distinguished.

It is said, first, that the line of authorities mentioned above stands on its own and is inconsistent with other, more modern, decisions. Those are cases in which money has been paid to a company for the purpose of obtaining an allotment of shares (see *Moseley v. Cressey's Co.* (1865) L.R. 1 Eq. 405; *Stewart v. Austin* (1866) L.R. 3 Eq. 299; *In re Nanwa Gold Mines Ltd.* [1955] 1 W.L.R. 1080). I do not think it necessary to examine these cases in detail, nor to comment on them, for I am satisfied that they do not affect the principle on which this appeal should be decided. They are merely examples which show that, in the absence of some special arrangement creating a trust (as was shown to exist in *In re Nanwa Gold Mines Ltd.*), payments of this kind are made upon the basis that they are to be included in the company's assets. They do not negative the proposition that a trust may exist where the mutual intention is that they should not.

The second, and main, argument for the appellant was of a more sophisticated character. The transaction, it was said, between the respondents and Rolls Razor Ltd., was one of loan, giving rise to a legal action of debt. This necessarily excluded the implication of any trust, enforceable in equity, in the respondents' favour: a transaction may attract one action or the other, it could not admit of both.

My Lords, I must say that I find this argument unattractive. Let us see what it involves. It means that the law does not permit an arrangement to be made by which one person agrees to advance money to another, on terms that the money is to be used exclusively to pay debts of the latter, and if, and so far as not so used, rather than becoming a general asset of the latter available to his creditors at large, is to be returned to the lender. The lender is obliged, in such a case, because he is a lender, to accept, whatever the mutual wishes of lender and borrower may be, that the money he was willing to make available for one purpose only shall be freely available for others of the borrower's creditors for whom he has not the slightest desire to provide.

I should be surprised if an argument of this kind—so conceptualist in character—had ever been accepted. In truth it has plainly been rejected by the eminent judges who from 1819 onwards have permitted arrangements of this type to be enforced, and have approved them as being for the benefit of creditors and all concerned. There is surely no difficulty in recognising the co-existence in one transaction of legal and equitable rights and remedies: when the money is advanced, the lender acquires an equitable right to see that it is applied for the primary designated purpose (see *In re Rogers*, 8 Morr. 243 where both Lindley L.J. and Kay L.J. recognised this): when the purpose has been carried out (i.e., the debt paid) the lender has his remedy against the borrower in debt: if the primary purpose cannot be carried out, the question arises if a secondary purpose (i.e., repayment to the lender) has been agreed, expressly or by implication: if it has, the remedies of equity may be invoked to give effect to it, if it has not (and the money is intended to fall within the general fund of the debtor's assets) then there is the appropriate remedy for recovery of a loan. I can appreciate no reason why the flexible interplay of law and equity cannot let in these practical arrangements, and other variations if desired: it would be to the discredit of both systems if they could not. In the present case the intention to create a secondary trust for the benefit of the lender, to arise if the primary trust, to pay the dividend, could not be carried out, is clear and I can find no reason why the law should not give effect to it.

I pass to the second question, that of notice. I can deal with this briefly because I am in agreement with the manner in which it has been disposed of by all three members of the Court of Appeal. I am prepared, for this purpose, to accept, by way of assumption, the position most favorable to the bank, i.e., that it is necessary to show that the bank had notice of the trust or of the circumstances giving rise to the trust, at the time when they received the money, viz., on July 15, 1964, and that notice on a later date, even though they had not in any real sense given value when they received the money or thereafter changed their position, will not do. It is common ground, and I think right, that a mere request to put the money into a separate account is not sufficient to constitute notice. But on July 15, 1964, the bank, when it received the cheque, also received the covering letter of that date which I have set out above: previously there had been the telephone conversation between Mr. Goldbart and Mr. Parker, to which I have also referred. From these there is no doubt that the bank was told that the money had been provided on loan by a third person and was to be used only for the purpose of paying the dividend. This was sufficient to give them notice that it was trust money and not assets of Rolls Razor Ltd.: the fact, if it be so, that they were unaware of the lender's identity (though the respondent's name as drawer was on the cheque) is of no significance. I may add to this, as having some bearing on the merits of the case, that it is quite apparent from earlier documents that the bank were aware that Rolls Razor Ltd. could not provide the money for the dividend and that this would have to come from an outside source and that they never contemplated that the money so provided could be used to reduce the existing overdraft. They were in fact insisting that other or additional arrangements should be made for that purpose. As was appropriately said by Russell L.J., ([1968] Ch. 540, 563F) it would be giving a complete windfall to the bank if they had established a right to retain the money.'

Questions:

When is money simply repayable as a *debt* and when is it impressed with a *trust*? When is it relevant to investigate questions of notice?

3.9.1 Can the 'purpose' of the loan be something other than the payment of certain creditors?

It has been argued that *Quistclose* trusts ought to be restricted on policy grounds by a principle of salvage: they should be available only for attempted rescues of ailing companies. It has also been argued, with more force, that they they should be restricted on legal grounds by the 'human beneficiary' principle and its impact on purpose trusts. The next case shows that the first argument has not been accepted and that the second is not inherently limiting.

[340] *Re EVTR Ltd* [1987] BCLC 647 (CA), (1987) 3 BCC 382, 392–4 *per* Dillon LJ: [The case concerned a loan granted to EVTR for the express purpose of purchasing certain computer equipment. The arrangement was upheld as a *Quistclose* trust.]

> 'In the present case the £60,000 was released by Knapp-Fishers to the company [EVTR] on the appellant's [the lender's] instructions for a specific purpose only, namely the sole purpose of buying new equipment. Accordingly, I have no doubt, in the light of *Quistclose*, that, if the company had gone into liquidation, or the receivers had been appointed, and the scheme had become abortive before the £60,000 had been disbursed by the company, the appellant would have been entitled to recover his full £60,000, as between himself and the company, on the footing that it was impliedly held by the company on a resulting trust for him as the particular purpose of the loan had failed.
>
> At the other end of the spectrum, if after the £60,000 had been expended by the company as it was, the Encore system [the computer equipment] had been duly delivered to, and accepted by, the company, there could be no doubt that the appellant's only right would have been as an unsecured creditor of the company for the £60,000. There would have been no question of the Encore system, or any interest in it, being held on any sort of trust for the appellant, and if, after it had been delivered and installed, the company had sold the system, the appellant could have had no claim whatsoever to the proceeds of sale as trust moneys held in trust for him.
>
> The present case lies on its facts between those two extremes of the spectrum. Other scenarios between the extremes could equally be written. . . .
>
> The deputy judge took the view that the trust concept was spent when the £60,000 was paid out by the company. But he considered that the correctness of that view could be tested by an analogy which, with all respect to him, was false. He considered—rightly on the facts—that, had Concord or Quantel [companies involved in the supply of the computer equipment] gone into liquidation after cashing the cheque or bankers' draft issued by the company, it could not have been argued that the proceeds of the cheque or bankers' draft were other than part of their general assets; but that is a false analogy, in that Concord and Quantel had no notice of any trust in favour of the appellant, whereas the company did have notice, and it was the company and not Concord or Quantel which was bound as to the manner in which the £60,000 could be used.
>
> The deputy judge attached importance to the factor that nobody gave a conscious thought to any possibility that, after the documents had all been signed up and the £60,000 had been paid to Concord or Quantel, the purchase of the Encore system might yet fall through and the £60,000, or a large part of it, might be repaid. That however is not conclusive against the appellant, since a resulting or constructive trust most normally arises by implication of law when circumstances happen to which the parties had not addressed their minds.

On *Quistclose* principles, a resulting trust in favour of the provider of the money arises when money is provided for a particular purpose only, and that purpose fails. In the present case, the purpose for which the £60,000 was provided by the appellant to the company was, as appears from the authority to Knapp-Fishers, the purpose of the company's buying new equipment. But in any realistic sense of the words that purpose has failed in that the company has never acquired any new equipment, whether the Encore system which was then in mind or anything else. True it is that the £60,000 was paid out by the company with a view to the acquisition of new equipment, but that was only at half-time, and I do not see why the final whistle should be blown at half-time. The proposed acquisition proved abortive and a large part of the £60,000 has therefore been repaid by the payees. The repayments were made because of, or on account of, the payments which made up the £60,000 and those were payments of trust moneys. It is a long-established principle of equity that, if a person who is a trustee receives money or property because of, or in respect of, trust property, he will hold what he receives as a constructive trustee on the trusts of the original trust property. An early application of this principle is the well-known case of *Keech v Sandford* (1726) Sel. Cas. t. King 61; 25 E.R. 223, but the instances in the books are legion. (See also *Chelsea Estates Investment Trust Co. Ltd. v Marche & Ors.* [1955] Ch. 328 where somewhat similar reasoning applied to a mortgagee.) It follows, in my judgment, that the repayments made to the receivers are subject to the same trusts as the original £60,000 in the hands of the company. There is now, of course, no question of the £48,536 being applied in the purchase of new equipment for the company, and accordingly, in my judgment, it is now held on a resulting trust for the appellant.

It is irrelevant in my judgment that, if the Encore system for which the £60,000 was paid had been delivered and accepted by the company, the company's interest in that equipment would have been a general asset of the company held by the company free of any proprietary or equitable interest of the appellant by way of trust or otherwise. If that had happened, the purpose of the appellant, and any trust attaching to the money because of that purpose, would indeed have been satisfied, but it did not happen.

The company did of course have the benefit for some months of the loan of the temporary equipment. Therefore, at any rate as between the company and Quantel, there was not a total failure of consideration so far as the company was concerned. But, even assuming (contrary to submissions made by counsel for the appellant) that the appellant was at the material times aware of the loan of the temporary equipment, the loan of the temporary equipment was merely ancillary to the purchase of the Encore system to cover the gap until the Encore system was available to be delivered to the company. On the way matters developed, it was the Encore system, and not the temporary system, that the company was to purchase, and the company never got the Encore system.

In summary there are two factors which to my mind lead to the same conclusion in this case. First, the purpose of the appellant from which any trust is to be implied was, realistically, the purpose of the company's acquiring new equipment, and not the purpose of the company's entering into an abortive contract for the lease-purchase of new equipment. Secondly, on the repayments being made of the £48,536 by the payees of the £60,000, the same trusts must on general principle have attached to the £48,536 as attached to the original £60,000 which were trust moneys.'

3.9.2 Can a debtor create a *Quistclose*-type trust to ensure that certain creditors are paid in priority?

So far the cases considered have all involved situations where the lender/provider of funds specifies the purpose of the loan and, with the borrower's consent, delivers the funds subject to a trust. The advantage to the creditor is that the debtor never, even for an instant, becomes the beneficial owner of the funds which it receives. Can a *debtor* deliver the same advantages to a creditor if the *debtor* unilaterally specifies the purpose for which funds it receives will be used? In a typical case this might be done to ensure that customers sending pre-payments for goods to the debtor are protected until the goods are despatched. Certainly the *creditor* can ensure this by advance specification, by getting the borrower to promise to create a trust, and only advancing the funds on those terms: see *Re Nanwa Gold Mines*, [1955] 1 WLR 1080. But in the next case, below, the debtor was allowed to do this unilaterally. Of course, the debtor is free to create a trust over its *own* assets (assets which it owns legally and beneficially). What is at issue here is the possibility that the debtor can create a trust in such a way that the assets delivered by the creditor are never for an instant owned beneficially by the debtor.

[341] *Re Kayford Ltd* [1975] 1 WLR 279, 281–2 *per* Megarry J:
[Kayford carried on a mail order business. Its solvency was threatened by the possible collapse of its chief supplier. To protect its customers it opened a separate customers' trust deposit account into which all pre-payments from customers were paid. The funds were only released once the goods ordered had been despatched. The customers were unaware of this arrangement. When Kayford did go into liquidation, Megarry J decided that the money in the account was held on trust for the customers and did not form part of the general assets of the company.]

> 'The question for me is whether the money in the bank account (apart from the dormant amount of £47.80 and interest on it) is held on trust for those who paid it, or whether it forms part of the general assets of the company. Mr. Heyman appears for the joint liquidators, one of whom is in fact Mr. Wainwright: and he has contended that there is no trust, so that the money forms part of the general assets of the company and thus will be available for the creditors generally. On the other hand, Mr. Kennedy appears for a Mr. Joels, who on December 12 paid the company £32.20 for goods which have not been delivered; and a representation order is sought on behalf of all others whose moneys have been paid into the bank account, some 700 or 800 in number. I make that order. Mr. Kennedy, of course, argued for the existence of an effective trust. I may say at the outset that on the facts of the case Mr. Heyman was unable to contend that any question of a fraudulent preference arose. If one leaves on one side any case in which an insolvent company seeks to declare a trust in favour of creditors, one is concerned here with the question not of preferring creditors but of preventing those who pay money from becoming creditors, by making them beneficiaries under a trust. I should add that I had some initial doubts about whether Mr. Joels was the most suitable representative beneficiary, in view of the date when he paid his money, and whether Mr. Heyman, in representing Mr. Wainwright (as well as the other joint liquidator), was not to some degree committed to arguing against the efficacy of the course that Mr. Wainwright had advised: but discussion has allayed these doubts.

Now there are clearly some loose ends in the case. Mr. Kay, advised to establish a "Customers' Trust Deposit Account," seems to have thought that it did not matter what the account was called so long as there was a separate account; and so the dormant deposit account suggested by the bank manager was used. The bank statement for this account is before me, and on the first page, for which the title is simply "Deposit account Kayford Ltd.", nearly £26,000 is credited. The second and third pages have the words "Customer Trust Deposit Account" added after the previous title of the account; and Mr. Joels' payment was made after these words had been added. Mr. Kay also left matters resting on a telephone conversation with the bank manager until he wrote his letter of December 12 to the bank. That letter reads: "We confirm our instructions regarding the opening of the deposit account for customer deposits for new orders"; and he then makes some mention of other accounts with the bank. The letter goes on: "Please ensure the reopened deposit account is titled 'Customer Trust Deposit Account'." Then he gives the reference number and asks for confirmation that this has been done. Nevertheless, despite the loose ends, when I take as a whole the affidavits of Mr. Wainwright, Mr. Kay and Mr. Hall (the bank manager) I feel no doubt that the intention was that there should be a trust. There are no formal difficulties. The property concerned is pure personalty, and so writing, though desirable, is not an essential. There is no doubt about the so-called "three certainties" of a trust. The subject-matter to be held on trust is clear, and so are the beneficial interests therein, as well as the beneficiaries. As for the requisite certainty of words, it is well settled that a trust can be created without using the words "trust" or "confidence" or the like: the question is whether in substance a sufficient intention to create a trust has been manifested.

In *In re Nanwa Gold Mines Ltd.* [1955] 1 W.L.R. 1080 the money was sent on the faith of a promise to keep it in a separate account, but there is nothing in that case or in any other authority that I know of to suggest that this is essential. I feel no doubt that here a trust was created. From the outset the advice (which was accepted) was to establish a trust account at the bank. The whole purpose of what was done was to ensure that the moneys remained in the beneficial ownership of those who sent them, and a trust is the obvious means of achieving this. No doubt the general rule is that if you send money to a company for goods which are not delivered, you are merely a creditor of the company unless a trust has been created. The sender may create a trust by using appropriate words when he sends the money (though I wonder how many do this, even if they are equity lawyers), or the company may do it by taking suitable steps on or before receiving the money. If either is done, the obligations in respect of the money are transformed from contract to property, from debt to trust. Payment into a separate bank account is a useful (though by no means conclusive) indication of an intention to create a trust, but of course there is nothing to prevent the company from binding itself by a trust even if there are no effective banking arrangements.

Accordingly, of the alternative declarations sought by the summons, the second, to the effect that the money is held in trust for those who paid it, is in my judgment the declaration that should be made. I understand that questions may be raised as to resorting to the interest on the moneys as a means of discharging the costs of the summons; on that I will, of course, hear argument. I should, however, add one thing. Different considerations may perhaps arise in relation to trade creditors; but here I am concerned only with members of the public, some of whom can ill afford to exchange their money for a claim to a dividend in the liquidation, and all of whom are likely to be anxious to avoid this. In cases concerning the public, it seems to me that where money in advance is being paid to a company in return for the future supply of goods or services, it is an entirely proper and honourable thing for a company to do what this company did, upon skilled advice, namely, to start to pay the money into a trust account as soon as there begin to be doubts as to the company's ability to fulfil its obligations to deliver the goods or provide the services. I wish that, sitting in this court, I had heard of this occurring more frequently; and I can only hope that I shall hear more of it in the future.'

Note:

Certainly a trust had been created by Kayford, but arguably its creation would now constitute a voidable preference under the Insolvency Act 1986 s 239 (a provision which does not require the proof of fraudulent intent).

3.9.3 Can a debtor determine how its own debt payments will be used by a creditor company using this form of trust?

The next case is a difficult one, but it suggests that this is a possibility.

[342] *Carreras Rothmans Ltd v Freeman Matthews Treasure Ltd* [1985] 1 Ch 207, 220–4 *per* Peter Gibson J:

[Rothmans regularly put FMT, an advertising agency, in funds on a monthly basis to enable FMT to meet liabilities which it had incurred on Rothmans' account in the previous month. The payments were made in time for FMT to pay the creditors when each month's debts became due. FMT was in financial difficulties and, at Rothmans' suggestion, FMT opened a special account into which Rothmans paid money to meet invoices due for payment by FMT at the end of July. Cheques were drawn by FMT in favour of the relevant creditors, but on 3 August, FMT went into liquidation and its liquidator had the special account frozen before the cheques were cleared. Peter Gibson J held that the agreement between FMT and Rothmans created a trust which gave Rothmans the right to enforce payment over of the money in the special account to the relevant creditors.]

'(1) Trust

Mr. Millett and Mr. Higham for the plaintiff contended that the language of the contract letter was apt to create a trust and that such trust was fully constituted as to the moneys in the special account when the defendant agreed to the terms of the contract letter and received the moneys from the plaintiff. They relied on the line of cases of which *Quistclose Investments Ltd. v. Rolls Razor Ltd.* [1970] A.C. 567 is the highest authority. Mr. Potts denied that any enforceable trust was created. He submitted that the language of the contract letter was apt to create obligations of a contractual nature only in relation to the moneys to be paid into the special account, that the Quistclose line of cases was distinguishable, that if there were a trust it was an illusory trust and that in any event the court should not order specific performance of the July agreement to perform any trust that was created.

The July agreement was plainly intended to vary the contractual position of the parties as to how, as the contract letter put it, payments made by the plaintiff to the defendant for purely onwards transmission, in effect, to the third party creditors, would be dealt with. If one looks objectively at the genesis of the variation, the plaintiff was concerned about the adverse effect on it if the defendant, which the plaintiff knew to have financial problems, ceased trading and the third party creditors of the defendant were not paid at a time when the defendant had been put in funds by the plaintiff. The objective was accurately described by Mr. Higgs in his informal letter of 19 July as to protect the interests of the plaintiff and the third parties. For this purpose a special account was to be set up with a special designation. The moneys payable by the plaintiff were to be paid not to the defendant beneficially but directly into that account so that the defendant was never free to deal as it pleased with the moneys so paid. The moneys were to be used only for the specific purpose of paying the third parties and as the cheque letter indicated, the amount paid matched the specific invoices presented by the defendant to the plaintiff. The account was intended to be little more than a conduit pipe, but the intention was plain that whilst in the conduit pipe the moneys should be protected. There was even a provision covering the possibility (though what actual situation it was intended to meet it is hard to conceive) that there might be a balance left after payment and in that event the balance was to be paid to the plaintiff and not kept by the defendant. It was thus clearly intended that the moneys once paid would never become the property of the defendant. That was the last thing the plaintiff wanted in view of its concern about the defendant's financial position. As a further precaution the bank was to be put on notice of the conditions and purpose of the account. I infer that this was to prevent the bank attempting to exercise any rights of set off against the moneys in the account.

Only two matters were relied on as indicating that no trust was intended. One was the consideration fee; but the presence of consideration does not negative a trust. The other was the express reference in the penultimate paragraph in relation to placements and forward media options with which was contrasted the absence of the word "trust" in relation to the moneys in the account. But I regard that as of minimal significance when I consider all the other indications as to the capacity in which the defendant was to hold any moneys in the account. In my judgment even in the absence of authority it is manifest that the defendant was intended to act in relation to those moneys in a fiduciary capacity only.

There is of course ample authority that moneys paid by A to B for a specific purpose which has been made known to B are clothed with a trust. In the *Quistclose* case [1970] A.C. 567, 580 Lord Wilberforce referred to the recognition, in a series of cases over some 150 years, that arrangements for the payment of a person's creditors by a third person gives rise to

> "a relationship of a fiduciary character or trust, in favour, as a primary trust, of the creditors, and secondarily, if the primary trust fails, of the third person . . ."

Lord Wilberforce in describing the facts of the *Quistclose* case said a little earlier on p. 580 that the mutual intention of the provider of the moneys and of the recipient of the moneys and the essence of the bargain was that the moneys should not become part of the assets of the recipient but should be used exclusively for payment of a particular class of its creditors. That description seems to me to be apt in relation to the facts of the present case too.

Mr. Potts sought to distinguish the *Quistclose* case in this way. He submitted that for any trust one needed (i) a settlor conveying property to a trustee or declaring a trust of property in his own hands; (ii) trust property and (iii) a beneficiary. He said that in *Quistclose* the settlor was the provider of the moneys, who did so by way of loan. In the present case, he submitted, the settlor was not the plaintiff but the defendant to which the plaintiff owed a debt to reimburse the defendant for the June debts owed to the third parties and he pointed out that the plaintiff made no claim that there was a trust of the book debt. In the *Quistclose* case Lord Wilberforce, in rejecting an argument that the lender only had contractual rights in a transaction of loan, said, at p. 581:

> "There is surely no difficulty in recognising the co-existence in one transaction of legal and equitable rights and remedies: when the money is advanced, the lender acquires an equitable right to see that it is applied for the primary designated purpose."

Mr. Potts submitted that there was no recognition in the *Quistclose* case that anyone else had an enforceable right and that in particular a person in the position of the plaintiff discharging a debt had no right to enforce any trust.

It is of course true that there are factual differences between the *Quistclose* case and the present case. The transaction there was one of loan with no contractual obligation on the part of the lender to make payment prior to the agreement for the loan. In the present case there is no loan but there is an antecedent debt owed by the plaintiff. I doubt if it is helpful to analyse the *Quistclose* type of case in terms of the constituent parts of a conventional settlement, though it may of course be crucial to ascertain in whose favour the secondary trust operates (as in the *Quistclose* case itself) and who has an enforceable right. In my judgment the principle in all these cases is that equity fastens on the conscience of the person who receives from another property transferred for a specific purpose only and not therefore for the recipient's own purposes, so that such person will not be permitted to treat the property as his own or to use it for other than the stated purpose. Most of the cases in this line are cases where there has been an agreement for consideration so that in one sense each party has contributed to providing the property. But if the common intention is that property is transferred for a specific purpose and not so as to become the property of the transferee, the transferee cannot keep the property if for any reason that purpose cannot be fulfilled. I am left in no doubt that the provider of the moneys in the present case was the plaintiff. True it is that its own witnesses said that if the defendant had not agreed to the terms of the contract letter, the plaintiff would not have broken its contract but would have paid its debt to the defendant, but the fact remains that the plaintiff made its payment on the terms of that letter and the defendant received the moneys only for the stipulated purpose. That purpose was expressed to relate only to the moneys in the account. In my judgment therefore the plaintiff can be equated with the lender in *Quistclose* as having an enforceable right to compel the carrying out of the primary trust.

Mr. Potts also submitted that the third party creditors had no enforceable rights and that where the beneficiaries under the primary trust have no enforceable rights, no trust is created. Mr. Millett and Mr. Higham also submitted that the third party creditors had no enforceable rights, though that submission was made primarily with an eye to an argument relevant to the section 95 point that the beneficial interest in the moneys paid into the special account always remained in the plaintiffs. In none of the many reported cases in the *Quistclose* line of cases, so far as I am aware, has any consideration been given to the question whether the person intended to benefit from the carrying out of the specific purpose which created the trust had enforceable rights. Thus the existence of enforceable rights in such persons has not been treated as crucial to the existence of a trust. Further in the one case in which so far as I am aware the question who, in addition to the provider of the property, had enforceable rights was determined by the court, it was held that the persons intended to benefit from the carrying out of the primary trust did have enforceable rights. That case is the decision of Sir Robert Megarry V.-C. in *In re Northern Developments (Holdings) Ltd.* (unreported), 6 October 1978. In that case the eponymous company ("Northern") was the parent company of a group of companies including one ("Kelly") which was in financial straits. Seventeen banks agreed to put up a fund in excess of half a million pounds in an attempt to rescue Kelly.

The banks already had other companies in the group as customers. They paid the moneys into an account in Northern's name for the express purpose of providing moneys for Kelly's unsecured creditors and for no other purpose, the amounts advanced being treated as advances to the banks' other customers in the group. The fund was used to sustain Kelly for a time, but then Kelly was put into receivership at a time when a little over half the fund remained unexpended. One of the questions for the court was who was entitled to that balance. Sir Robert Megarry V.-C. held that there was a *Quistclose* type of trust attaching to the fund, that trust was a purpose trust but enforceable by identifiable individuals, namely the banks as lenders, Kelly, for whose immediate benefit the fund was established, and Kelly's creditors. The reason given by Sir Robert Megarry V.-C. for holding that Kelly's creditors had enforceable rights were the words of Lord Wilberforce in the *Quistclose* case at p. 580 which I have already cited, describing the *Quistclose* type of trust as giving rise to a relationship of a fiduciary character or trust in favour of the creditors. However, Sir Robert Megarry V.-C. went on to describe the interests of the creditors in this way:

> "The fund was established not with the object of vesting the beneficial interest in them, but in order to confer a benefit on Kelly (and so, consequentially, on the rest of the group and the bankers) by ensuring that Kelly's creditors would be paid in an orderly manner. There is perhaps some parallel in the position of a beneficiary entitled to a share of residue under a will. What he has is not a beneficial interest in any asset forming part of residue, but a right to compel the executor to administer the assets of the deceased properly. It seems to me that it is that sort of right which the creditors of Kelly had."

The interest of the banks was held to be under the secondary trust if the primary trust failed. In the light of that authority I cannot accept the joint submission that the third party creditors for the payment of whose debts the plaintiff had paid the moneys into the special account had no enforceable rights. In any event I do not comprehend how a trust, which on no footing could the plaintiff revoke unilaterally, and which was expressed as a trust to pay third parties and was still capable of performance, could nevertheless leave the beneficial interest in the plaintiff which had parted with the moneys. On Sir Robert Megarry V.-C.'s analysis the beneficial interest is in suspense until the payment is made.

I can dispose of Mr. Potts' remaining arguments under this head more briefly. In my judgment the doctrine of illusory trusts has no application to the facts of the present case. That doctrine applies where a debtor for his own convenience settles property in favour of his creditors, the court treating the trust as a revocable one. In the present case although the defendant agreed to the discharge of an asset, its book debt, by payment by its debtor, the plaintiff, in such a way that the moneys paid would be held on trust to pay its creditors, the defendant did not enter into the arrangement for its convenience but for good commercial reasons on the insistence of the plaintiff and the trust was not for its creditors generally but for a particular class of creditor. It cannot be said in the circumstances that the July agreement was intended to be revocable by the defendant alone. Nor can I accept Mr. Potts' argument on specific performance. He submitted that where, as here, the beneficial interest in the moneys in the account has not yet become vested in the third party creditors, the court should not order payment. His argument was based on a suggested analogy with cases like *In re Wiltshire Iron Co.* (1868) L.R. 3 Ch.App. 440 and *In re Oriental Bank Corporation* (1884) 28 Ch.D. 634 in which the court refused to allow the completion of contracts after the commencement of a winding up where the property, the subject of the contracts, remained in the company's ownership at the commencement of the winding up. In the present case the plaintiff seeks an order not for specific performance but for the carrying out of the primary trust in respect of moneys which not only are not the property of the defendant but never have been. At the commencement of the liquidation its previous asset, the book debt, had been discharged. I see no reason why the court should not so order.

In my judgment therefore a trust was created by the July agreement, the trust was completely constituted by the payment of moneys into the special account and the plaintiff as the provider of the moneys has an equitable right to an order for the carrying out by the defendant of the trust.'

Note:

The form of arrangement accepted as legitimate in this case allowed the creditor (FMT)—who had an existing and unqualified right to the proceeds of the debt due from Rothmans—to agree to dispose of its own assets in a particular way: FMT effectively made one of its existing assets (the debt from Rothmans) available exclusively to one class of its creditors (third parties owed money on Rothmans' account). Such an arrangement is now probably a preference (under the Insolvency Act 1986 section 239) or contrary to the principle adopted in *British Eagle International Air Lines Ltd v Cie Nationale Air France* [1975] 1 WLR 758. Do the particular facts of this case nevertheless justify the court's findings?

3.9.4 Policy and principles

[343] P J Millett, 'The *Quistclose* Trust: Who Can Enforce It?' (1985) 101 *LQR* 269, 284–91:

[Footnotes in the original are omitted]

'A Simple and Orthodox Solution

The solution of the problem raised at the beginning of this article is not difficult if basic principles are observed. Two questions are involved: (i) is the so-called "primary trust" truly a trust or is it merely a power, so that B [the borrower] cannot be compelled to exercise it? (ii) if it is a trust, who are the beneficiaries? As in the case of any trust, the answers to both questions depend upon the manifestation of the intentions of the settlor, *i.e.* A [the lender]. In the case of an ordinary express trust the answers depend on the construction of the trust instrument. The *Quistclose* trust, however, arises only partly from the language used. In most cases it arises largely, and in some cases wholly, by implication of law. It is a presumed or implied trust, and the answers to questions such as those raised above have to be inferred from the language and conduct of the parties and the circumstances of the case.

The answer to the first question, it is submitted, is to be found in each case by considering whether A has an interest, separate and distinct from that of B, in seeing that the primary trust is carried out. If the cases down to and including the *Quistclose* case are examined, it will be found that in none of them did A have any such separate interest of his own.

In *Toovey v. Milne*, for example, A had no interest, separate and distinct from any interest of B, in seeing that B's debts were paid. He was B's brother-in-law; his object was to save B from bankruptcy. But this was not something which he could insist on against B's will. His intention, therefore, must be taken to have been to save B from bankruptcy by providing him with the funds with which, *if he chose*, he might pay C, but which otherwise he must return to A. Similarly, in the *Quistclose* case, A had no interest, separate and distinct from any interest of B, in seeing that the dividend was paid. A's object was to prevent the collapse of B which would inevitably follow if the dividend were not paid. Again, A's intention must be taken to have been to benefit B by providing it with funds with which, *if it chose*, it might pay the dividend, but which otherwise it must return to A.

In all the cases down to and including the *Quistclose* case, it is submitted, the purpose of the arrangements would be fulfilled if they were treated as leaving the beneficial interest in the fund in A throughout, but subject to a power in B, revocable by A at any time, to apply the fund for the stated purpose.

In the two more recent cases, however, this would not have been sufficient for A's purpose. In the *Northern Developments* case, as has already been pointed out, the banks had their own interest, separate and distinct from any interest of B or Kelly, in seeing that Kelly's creditors were paid. In the *Carreras Rothmans* case, this was even more obviously true. A was not seeking to enable B to avoid liquidation, but to protect itself from the consequences of B's liquidation. In neither case would A have been content to confer on B a mere power which B should be free to exercise or not as it pleased. In each case, therefore, A must be taken to have intended to subject B to an enforceable obligation to apply the fund for the stated purpose.

It does not follow, however, that the obligation is owed to, or enforceable by, C. Whether this is the case must again depend upon the manifestation of A's intentions, collected from the language used, the conduct of the parties, and the circumstances of the case. If indeed it was his intention to benefit C, there is no difficulty in giving effect to that intention by treating the arrangements as constituting B a trustee of the fund for C. C will have a beneficial interest in the fund, and the trust will in the ordinary way be irrevocable by A, and enforceable by C (but not by A).

If, on the other hand, it was A's intention, not to benefit C except incidentally, but either to benefit B (though without conferring any beneficial interest upon him) or to advance his own commercial interests, then it is submitted the proper way to give effect to that intention is to treat the arrangements as leaving the beneficial interest in the fund in A throughout, subject to an obligation on the part of B, enforceable by A, to apply the fund for the stated purpose. In short, it should make no difference whether B is authorised or required to apply the fund for the stated purpose. In either case he holds the fund as trustee for A alone with, in the one case a power, and in the other a duty, to comply with A's directions. Pending the actual application of the fund by B, A's directions would normally be revocable by him.

If the cases are examined, it will be found that in every case this analysis is the only one which fits the facts. In *Toovey v. Milne*, for example, A had no conceivable reason to be generous to C. His object was to save B from bankruptcy; any benefit which might accrue to C was incidental. He could have achieved his object by paying C himself. Instead, he chose to provide B with the necessary funds. Thus he was simply authorising B to use his (A's) money to pay off his own debts to C. Similarly, in the *Quistclose* case, A had no conceivable reason for being generous to B's shareholders. Its object was to save B from the collapse which would follow a failure to pay the dividend, and any benefit which might accrue to the shareholders from the payment of the dividend was incidental. It was not practicable for A to pay the dividend direct; indeed, this would have given the game away. It had to appear as if dividend was being paid by B in the normal way. Accordingly, A simply provided B with the necessary funds, and authorised it to use its (A's) money to pay the dividend to C. In the *Northern Developments* case, the banks had no reason to be generous to B, or Kelly, or Kelly's unsecured creditors (who included the Revenue). They were acting exclusively in their own commercial interests in the hope of averting the collapse of the group; any benefit which might accrue to B, or Kelly, or Kelly's creditors was incidental. They simply provided B with the necessary funds, and directed it to use their money to pay Kelly's unsecured creditors.

In the *Carreras Rothmans* case the situation was, if anything, even clearer. A had no reason to be generous to C, but had its own commercial reasons for wanting their debts paid. The natural way for A to achieve this was to renegotiate the terms of trade with B so that instead of paying the money to B for onward payment to C, A should pay the money directly to C. This, however, was not commercially practicable, first because B was entitled to trade discounts from C which were not available to A, and secondly (and more importantly) because such an arrangement would have alerted C to B's parlous financial position, and almost certainly have precipitated its collapse. The arrangements which were concluded were designed to achieve essentially the same result; they enabled B to pay C with A's money.

Only in one respect did the *Carreras Rothmans* case differ from earlier cases; for A clearly could not revoke the arrangements without B's consent. A's directions were thus not only mandatory, but irrevocable. This feature led Peter Gibson J. to conclude that the arrangements vested an enforceable beneficial interest in C. "I do not comprehend," he said, "how a trust, which on no footing could [A] revoke unilaterally, and which was still capable of performance, could nevertheless leave the beneficial interest in [A]." But why not? It is not the trust for A which is (normally) revocable, but the directions given by him. There is no conceptual difficulty in constituting B a trustee of a fund for A with an obligation to apply the money in accordance with A's directions, such directions to be irrevocable by A without B's consent. Indeed it is difficult to see any logical reason why a trust to apply money in accordance with A's directions is a trust for A if his directions are revocable by A alone, but a trust for C if revocable by A only with B's consent. The only thing which might give C an enforceable right, surely, would be an agreement by A not to revoke his directions without *C's* consent.

The foregoing analysis is not only in accordance with ordinary trust principles, but solves the two main riddles deriving from the *Quistclose* case which have puzzled commentators. One is the fact, well-established by the authorities, that the primary trust is enforceable by A. But on what basis can A enforce it? If it is taken to be a positive right to see that the money is applied for the stated purpose, then as has been pointed out, A's right is not the right of a beneficiary under the resulting trust, for if the primary purpose is fulfilled there is no resulting trust and A becomes a simple creditor. The precondition of A's claim, *i.e.* that the primary purpose is capable of being carried out, is destructive of his standing to make it. A's true position is comparable to that of a settlor, but it is elementary that a settlor who retains no beneficial interest cannot enforce the trust which he has created. As it is put in Lewin: "A trust being the equitable equivalent of a common law gift, the creator of the trust cannot enforce it, but the beneficiaries can." If Megarry V.-C.'s analysis is accepted, the only remaining character possessed by A is that of lender; and it may be suggested that A's right to enforce execution of the primary trust is, in reality, a right to specific performance of a condition of the contract of loan. There are several objections to this. In the first place, Lord Wilberforce's remarks in the *Quistclose* case were wide enough to embrace cases where the money was provided by A by way of gift or on a non-contractual basis, and there is no reason to confine them to cases of loan; in the second place, it is subversive of the whole basis of Lord Wilberforce's approach, which rests B's obligation firmly on an equitable and not a contractual footing. There is, in fact, only one explanation of A's undoubted right to enforce the primary trust which can be reconciled with basic principles. A can enforce the primary trust *because he is the beneficiary.*

The other puzzle is the basis on which the primary trust is said to have failed in several of the cases, particularly *Toovey v. Milne* and the *Quistclose* case. It has already been suggested that this can only be on the basis that the purpose for which A lent the money was taken to be, not to pay C, but to save B from bankruptcy or collapse. But in itself this is not enough. A trust does not fail merely because the settlor's purpose in creating it has been frustrated; the trust must become illegal or impossible to perform. The settlor's motives must not be confused with the purposes of the trust; the frustration of the former does not by itself cause the failure of the latter. But if the true nature of the trust is that it is a trust to carry out A's revocable directions, and A's purpose in giving those directions is frustrated, revocation is easily inferred. The true reason, it is submitted, why the primary trust to pay the dividend failed in the *Quistclose* case is that A's purpose in directing B to use the money to pay the dividend was to save B from collapse, and when B collapsed anyway A revoked the direction by demanding repayment.

If the foregoing analysis of the *Qustclose* trust is correct, then it is simply an example of what is sometimes called an "illusory trust." The best known example of such a trust is a disposition of property by a debtor to trustees for the benefit of his creditors. This is sometimes said to be an exception to the general rule that a voluntary settlement cannot be revoked by the settlor after it has been fully constituted. But the true view is that the apparent beneficiaries take no beneficial interest at all, the trustees holding the property transferred to them in trust for the debtor exclusively. As Pepys M.R. put it in *Bill v. Cureton*:

> "The character of trustee and cestui que trust never existed between the creditors and the trustees of the trust deeds, but that the settlor himself was the only cestui que trust and, therefore, that he was entitled to direct the application of his own trust fund. . . . A man who without any communication with his creditors, puts property into the hands of his trustees for the purpose of paying his debts, proposes only a benefit to himself by the payment of his debts: his object is not to benefit his creditors."

And as James L.J. said in *John v. James*:

> "such a deed as this is to be construed as a mandate, the same sort of mandate that a man gives when he gives his servant money, with directions to pay it in a particular way: it does not create any legal or equitable right in favour of a particular creditor. The right to the direction of the money is the right of the person who has put the money in the hands of his agent or steward or whoever it may be."

In such a case, the only trust which is created is a trust to comply with A's directions. The trust itself is not revocable, but prima facie A's directions are, so that A is free to change his mind, revoke the directions he has given, and either substitute new directions, allow B to retain the money beneficially, or require repayment to himself. This construction of the deed, however, depends on the intention which the court attributes to A. Thus where the court is able to draw the inference that it was A's intention to benefit his creditors, or where the obvious intention of the transaction would be frustrated if he were to retain a power of revocation, the deed will be held to create an irrevocable trust in favour of the creditors.

In the *Northern Developments* case, Megarry V.-C. rejected an argument that the trust for the payment of Kelly's unsecured creditors was an "illusory trust," apparently on the ground that the banks were parting with their money for the purpose of discharging Kelly's debts and not their own. But a settlement for the payment of the settlor's own debts is only one example of an "illusory trust"; it is not the only possible example. The reason why the trustee of such a settlement holds the fund in trust for the settlor and not for his creditors is that this is the intention which is imputed to the settlor: "he proposes only a benefit to himself—his object is not to benefit his creditors." Where the trust is for payment of A's own debts, it is easy to infer that A's intention is to benefit himself rather than his creditors. Where it is for the payment of B's debts, his intention is less obvious. It may be to benefit B's creditors, though this is unlikely. It is more likely to be to benefit B (though without conferring a beneficial interest upon him) by saving him from bankruptcy, or to promote some private or commercial object of A's own.

All this, of course, depends upon the absence of any communication to C. Where C is a party to the arrangements, or their existence is communicated to him, an irrevocable trust in C's favour is created. It is sometimes suggested that this results from an estoppel, on the ground that there is no other ground upon which a trust, initially revocable, can subsequently become irrevocable. But this would seem to proceed from a misunderstanding of the true nature of the trust at its inception. If, as is here suggested, it is not a revocable trust for C, but a trust for A, then in accordance with ordinary principles communication to C perfects an assignment of A's equitable interest to C, and converts A's revocable mandate into an irrevocable trust for C.

Conclusion

It is submitted that the *Quistclose* trust does not involve any departure from well-settled principles of trust law, and certainly does not call for the recognition of a new kind of enforceable purpose trust, a new kind of trust which the settlor can enforce, or a new situation in which the beneficial interest in the trust fund is in suspense. The answer to the question raised at the beginning of this article depends upon A's intention, to be collected from the language used, the conduct of the parties, and the circumstances of the case. The following, it is suggested, may be regarded as suitable guidelines by which A's intention may be ascertained:

1. If A's intention was to benefit C, or his object would be frustrated if he were to retain a power of revocation, the transaction will create an irrevocable trust in favour of C, enforceable by C but not by A. The beneficial interest in the trust property will be in C.

2. If A's intention was to benefit B (though without vesting a beneficial interest in him), or to benefit himself by furthering some private or commercial interest of his own, and not (except incidentally) to benefit C, then the transaction will create a trust in favour of A alone, and B will hold the trust property in trust to comply with A's directions. The trust will be enforceable by A but not by C. The beneficial interest will remain in A.

3. Where A's object was to save B from bankruptcy by enabling him to pay his creditors, the prima facie inference is that set out in paragraph 2 above. Wherever that is the correct inference:

(i) Where A has an interest of his own, separate and distinct from any interest of B, in seeing that the money is applied for the stated purpose, B will be under a positive obligation enforceable by A, to apply it for that purpose. Where A has no such interest, B will be regarded as having a power, but no duty, to apply it for the stated purpose, and A's remedy will be confined to preventing the misapplication of the money.

(ii) Prima facie, A's directions will be regarded as revocable by him; but he may contract with B not to revoke them without B's consent.

(iii) Communication to C of the arrangements prior to A's revocation will effect an assignment of A's equitable interest to C, and convert A's revocable mandate into an irrevocable trust for C.'

FURTHER READING:

M Bridge, 'Form, Substance and Innovation in Personal Property Security Law' [1992] *JBL* 1.

3.10 The future of security

The UK's insolvency laws are currently under review. Substantial changes could be made, but they are unlikely to eliminate the use of security in all its forms. They are more likely to focus on eliminating some of the more obvious inequities. The next extract summarises the competing 'philosophies' of bankruptcy law.

[344] R Goode, *Principles of Corporate Insolvency Law* (2nd edn, 1997, Sweet & Maxwell: London) pp 35–52:
[Most footnotes in the original are omitted.]

> 'The failure of a corporate enterprise potentially affects a wide range of interests. Those most immediately concerned are, of course, creditors, management, other employees and shareholders. But the failure may have wider repercussions. It may force customers and suppliers into insolvency; it may, in causing job losses, tear the heart out of the local community; in the case of a major bank or industrial company it may even affect the national economy, for example by undermining confidence or by removing a key player from the export market. The community at large may also have an interest in the continued performance of the company's obligations in public law, for example, in the clean-up of environmental pollution caused by the company's activities. So when a company becomes insolvent there are stark choices to be faced: should the sole or primary concern be to maximise returns to creditors? or should it be to preserve the company and its business, even if this can only be done at some expense to creditors' rights? Is the primary concern the protection of private rights or of public interests?
>
> It will be apparent, therefore, that there are serious questions to be addressed as to the legitimate province of corporate insolvency law and as to its philosophical foundations. Given the pragmatic way in which English law in general has developed it is perhaps unsurprising, but nevertheless disconcerting, to discover the lack of a clearly articulated philosophy of law in this field. Scholars in North America have long been interested in the bankruptcy process, and have devoted much time and effort to policy issues and theoretical constructs, if rather less to empirical research.
>
> . . .
>
> (i) The province of corporate insolvency law
>
> **One interest or several?**
>
> How should we mark out the territory that should be occupied by corporate insolvency law? What is its legitimate province? This question has been much debated among scholars in the United States as to the function of corporate insolvency law. Professors Baird, Jackson and Scott are leading proponents of the view that it is not for insolvency law to

concern itself with employment protection or with wider community interests, or to reorder substantive rights acquired under pre-bankruptcy law. Their thesis is that whatever rights and privileges may be conferred in other areas of law, insolvency law has one overriding goal: to allocate the common pool of assets in such a way as to maximise benefits for creditors as a whole. The attainment of this goal is threatened whenever individual creditors take unilateral action to fish in the common pool of assets without regard to the interests of other fishers. Therefore insolvency law must impose a collective procedure for the taking of fish. Two other principles must be strictly observed if the aim of collective asset maximisation is to be fulfilled. First, there must be rigid adherence to the absolute priority rule, *i.e.* that shareholders receive nothing until creditors have been paid in full. Secondly, insolvency law must respect the pre-bankruptcy ordering of entitlements. It is the function of insolvency law to translate pre-bankruptcy assets and liabilities into the bankruptcy forum with minimal dislocation. Among the reasons advanced for this view are (1) that the redistribution of rights on insolvency would create a perverse incentive for a particular creditor who would be advantaged by the change to go for an insolvency proceeding even if this would not be in the general interest of the creditors and (2) that insolvency law should distribute assets in the way in which creditors might have bargained for *ex ante* in order to maximise the collective value of the proceedings and they would have seen this as best achieved, as regards unsecured creditors, by an offer of *pari passu*, distribution and, as regards secured creditors, by an assurance that their priority would be maintained and their participation in the collective process compensated so as not to affect the net value of their pre-bankruptcy entitlements, *i.e.* there would be no transfer of net value from them to unsecured creditors.

These basic propositions, which have been developed into very elegant and sophisticated theories of bankruptcy law, have not passed unchallenged. Powerful attacks have been launched both on the notion that the sole purpose of insolvency proceedings is to maximise returns to creditors and on the assertion that it is not the function of bankruptcy law to alter relative pre-bankruptcy entitlements. Professor Elizabeth Warren has argued convincingly that there are other interests to consider apart from those of creditors, and that to concentrate so exclusively on maximising returns to creditors is a dangerous over-simplification of the nature and purpose of the bankruptcy process. She has also joined with Professor Jay Westbrook in a trenchant criticism of the use of theoretical constructs to reach policy conclusions without any attempt being made to verify by empirical evidence the premises upon which they are based.

The elegance and conceptual clarity of the theories advanced by Jackson and his colleagues have greatly illumined our understanding of the functions of corporate insolvency law. But there is force too in the criticisms that have been made. There are values to be protected that go beyond the interests of existing creditors. One of these is the investigation of the conduct of the directors with a view to sanctions for improper trading and disqualification so as to protect the public against future misconduct, a course of action available in England through the winding up process even where the company has no assets at all. Another is the interest of shareholders in the protection of their financial investment. A third is the interest of the workforce in preserving its investment of labour, expertise and loyalty to the enterprise. To focus so exclusively on maximising returns to creditors is to ignore the fact that there may be different ways of protecting creditors, some of which will also benefit other interests, such as those of employees, shareholders and the local community, and in so doing may even advance creditors' interests.

The answer Professors Baird and Jackson give to all this is that if interests other than those of common pool creditors are to be protected, this should be done outside bankruptcy law and the protection should not be exclusive to bankruptcy but should be slotted into the scheme of relative non-bankruptcy entitlements. So if it is desired to give special rights to employees or tort claimants, that should be done through labour law or tort law and in the latter case should be a protection equally available against closure of a business outside bankruptcy. It is then for bankruptcy law to respect the special non-bankruptcy entitlement given by labour law or tort law, rather than itself to create a new entitlement in the bankruptcy.

The argument is neat but ultimately unpersuasive, for it overlooks the fact that certain problems confronting claimants outside the common pool creditors arise specifically because of the company's insolvency and for no other reason. For example, in England labour [law] already gives rights and remedies to employees who are wrongfully or unfairly dismissed or are made redundant. But in the pursuit of these remedies against a solvent company the former employees are not competing with other creditors, for there are by definition enough assets to meet all claims. It is only on insolvency that the ranking of unsecured claims arises. There is thus no scope for the *general law* to prescribe priority for employees or tort claimants. . . .

This, indeed, is the central problem of law and economics theories of insolvency, that they begin with untested hypotheses of creditor behaviour which, by the end of the argument, have become imperceptibly converted into findings of fact and are thus made the basis for firm conclusions and policy recommendations. A simple example will suffice. It is assumed as an article of faith that a creditor taking security will charge a lower rate of interest than one who lends on an unsecured basis. . . .

But this is simply not how lending works. Banks charge what they consider the market will bear. A bank does not quote a lower rate of interest *because* it is secured; it takes security because of a perceived risk of non-payment and may charge a *higher* rate because of the risk. . . .

Social and economic policy

What is clear from any comparative survey is that the role of corporate insolvency law cannot be constructed in the abstract, and that the extent to which the law of a particular country adheres to or deviates from the principle of collective maximisation of returns for creditors in an insolvency is directly related to its pre-insolvency social and economic policy. Civil law jurisdictions tend to be more debtor-oriented than common law jurisdictions and to place greater emphasis on workers' rights and the importance of preserving the enterprise. This is particularly true of France, which has a long tradition of government paternalism, coupled with strong judicial control over debt collection activity. English law stands at the opposite end of the spectrum, with an extremely liberal attitude towards creditors' rights, self-help and the use of contractual remedies, coupled with a steady erosion of workers' rights and immunities. American law is also strongly pro-creditor, though imposing more restrictions than English law on enforcement both within and outside bankruptcy. . . .

But English law, like other legal systems, does recognise certain types of claim as justifying a priority in bankruptcy that they would not otherwise enjoy. Thus within defined limits the claims of employees rank ahead of other unsecured creditors, reflecting the fact that they lack the opportunities open to other creditors to limit their risk and typically have no source of income other than their wages. The same is true of government taxes, though here there is more controversy. Tax and other government debts have traditionally been accorded priority, on the basis that they are owed to the community and that the government is an involuntary creditor. Both arguments were rejected by the Cork Committee, the first on the ground that there was no reason why the general body of creditors should be made to suffer for the general good and the second on the ground that other classes of involuntary creditor were not given special treatment. But the Report did regard collected taxes as a special case on the ground that these were in substance to be regarded as impressed with a trust and thus ought to be removed from the common pool.

The implications of the rescue culture

Reference has already been made to the growth of the rescue culture and the increasing attention paid to the rehabilitation of the business. The corporate reorganisation which this typically entails cannot readily be achieved without some interference with pre-existing entitlements. So far as possible the legislation seeks to avoid a significant diminution in a creditor's substantive rights. Rather it aims to restrict their enforcement, as by imposing a temporary freeze on remedial measures or by requiring the creditor to accept a monetary equivalent rather than enforcement *in specie*. So rights to non-monetary performance of a contract which the liquidator declines to have performed by the company are converted into a right to prove for damages for the loss suffered through non-performance; the initiation of proceedings for an administration order imposes a freeze on most forms of enforcement, a freeze which continues during the currency of the administration; and the administrator of a company is in certain conditions given power to dispose of charged assets free from the security interest. But in certain cases there is a positive disturbance of the relative entitlements that existed before bankruptcy. For example, even a crystallised floating charge is subordinate to the claims of unsecured preferential creditors. A more significant proposal for interference with pre-bankruptcy entitlements was that put forward by the Cork Committee, that on winding up 10 per cent in value of assets, subject to a floating charge, should be required to be surrendered to form a fund available for distribution among unsecured creditors; and a creditor whose debt was secured by a floating charge would not be allowed to participate in the fund unless he first abandoned his floating charge *in toto*. This, however, proved too controversial to be acceptable to government and was not adopted.

So the redistribution of pre-liquidation rights does feature, albeit in a limited way, in corporate insolvency law. On the other hand, its primary concern has to be with the disposal or closing down of the company's business and the collection and distribution of net realisations. It is not equipped, except in a very small degree, to address wider economic or social problems, such as the maintenance of employment or the protection of the environment. These can only be tackled by measures outside the purview of insolvency law, for example, employment legislation and environmental regulation. . . .

(ii) The recognition and ordering of creditors' rights

Who are to be considered creditors?

. . .

In deciding who qualifies for admission to the insolvency process no distinction is made between voluntary (consensual) and involuntary (non-consensual) claimants. The objection to the admissibility of unliquidated tort claims was on the ground of the perceived difficulty of valuation, not their involuntary character. Indeed, some would argue that involuntary creditors should enjoy a higher status in the priority ranking than voluntary creditors, because they did not intend to assume a risk but had it thrust upon them. A similar argument could be made for Crown preference in relation to taxes and duties. But English insolvency law has not followed this path; on the contrary, under the Insolvency Act 1986 Crown preference has been restricted, while tort claimants rank with other unsecured creditors. The distinction between voluntary and involuntary creditors is in any event less clear than might be supposed. Many debtors delay payment and take credit which was never offered, and many creditors, faced with competition in the market, have little choice but to allow credit to be taken, with or without their prior agreement. So the distinction is not so much between voluntary and involuntary credit as between having and not having a real choice whether to allow the debt to be incurred in the first place.

Priority entitlements and their impact on the insolvency regime

It is a fundamental principle of insolvency law, and one which has many aspects, that the debtor's assets are to be distributed *pari passu*. In the language of the Act of 1542, the proceeds of realisations were to be distributed among creditors "rate and rate alike, according to the quantity of their debts." However, we have already remarked that the expenses of the liquidation have to be deducted in computing the net realisations available for distribution and that no dividends can be paid to ordinary unsecured creditors until the preferential debts have been paid in full. Moreover, with some exceptions it is only those assets in which the company has a beneficial interest that are available to its creditors. So property held by the company as bailee or trustee does not form part of the common pool, nor do goods in the possession of the company under a contract of sale reserving title until payment, if payment has not been completed. Again, property beneficially owned by the company but over which it has given security rights constitutes an asset only to the extent of the company's equity of redemption, measured by the difference between the value of the asset and the amount of the secured indebtedness. Similarly, the liquidator takes control of the company's assets subject to equities, such as rights of set-off and rescission of contracts. All these illustrations of the rule that only assets of the company are available for distribution are manifestations of the broader principle, previously discussed, that corporate insolvency law respects pre-liquidation rights, and in particular property rights and equities.

When bankruptcy was first introduced, property and trust law were much less developed than they are today. . . .

The result of all these developments has been disastrous for the ordinary unsecured creditor. Every new property right, every added security interest, every proprietary restitutionary remedy, every equity, has eroded his or her stake in the insolvency process. Add to this the plethora of debts now given preferential status and it can readily be seen that the lot of the general body of creditors is a very unhappy one.

The justification for protecting ownership and security rights

It is now far too late to turn back the clock and unwind equitable security interests, equities and resulting and constructive trusts, though not too late to change our insolvency law and bring the more extended forms of constructive trust into the ambit of our rules on preferences and transactions at an undervalue or subject them to the exercise of judicial discretion which would take account of the existing or potential interests of unsecured creditors. But if we leave on one side the more doubtful (in policy terms) extensions of equitable proprietary rights, we can see that the protection of ownership and security interests rests on sound principles. Rights of ownership should in principle be respected, for if they are not upheld on insolvency the distinction between property and obligation becomes largely meaningless. The same is true of security interests. To deny recognition of the secured creditor's real rights upon the debtor's insolvency would be to use the very event against which the security interest was designed to give protection as the ground for its destruction. The economic justification for upholding security rights was well put by Professors Jackson and Kronman in a much-cited article published 18 years ago:

> ". . . if the law denied debtors the power to prefer some creditors over others through a system of security agreements, a similar network of priority relationships could be expected to emerge by consensual arrangement between creditors. Permitting debtors to encumber their assets achieves the same result, but in a simpler and more economic fashion. If a debtor has more than two or three creditors, freerider and holdout difficulties are likely to plague any attempt on the part of creditors to work out a set of priority relationships among themselves. These transaction costs can be avoided by allowing the debtor himself to prefer one creditor over another. The rule permitting debtors to encumber their assets by private agreement is therefore justifiable as a cost-saving device that makes it easier and cheaper for the debtor's creditors to do what they would do in any case."[75]

In policy terms, the secured creditor is accorded priority because he bargained for it; other creditors who chose to lend unsecured cannot complain of their subordinated position.'

Questions:

1. What are the critical practical constraints on the creation of effective security?
2. What are the critical policy issues affirming or denying the general right of creditors to take security?
3. Is it possible to devise a perfect formula for the regulation of securities?

FURTHER READING:

D Baird, 'Bankruptcies' Uncontested Axioms' (1998) 108 *Yale LJ* 573.
V Finch, 'The Measures of Insolvency Law' (1997) 17 *OJLS* 227.
E Warren, 'Bankruptcy Policy' (1987) 54 *Univ Chicago L Rev* 775.
A Schwartz, 'Security Interests and Bankruptcy Priorities: A Review of Current Theories' (1981) 10 *J Legal Studies* I.
T Jackson and A T Kronman, 'Secured Financing and Priorities Among Creditors' (1979) 88 *Yale LJ* 1143.

75 "Secured Financing and Priorities Among Creditors", 88 *Yale L.J.* 1143 (1979).

Part III

Transfers of Interests in Personal Property

4

Consensual Transfers of Interests in Property

4.1 Introduction

The previous three chapters have been concerned with defining property and describing the various interests in property. This chapter is about *transferring* property interests from one party to another. Most of the cases considered in this chapter deal with the transfer of *ownership* interests from one party to another. However, these general principles also apply (with only minor modifications[1]) when the interests to be transferred are *security* interests.[2] The aim in these transactions is an outright transfer of one party's property (be it an ownership interest or a security interest) to another. The process which must be adopted to ensure that the transfer is effective depends upon whether the underlying property is legal or equitable, and whether the transfer is effected by gift or by sale.

Of course, it is also possible to transfer *possessory* rights, so as to give the recipient an interest as a lessee or as a bailee (as discussed in Chapter 2). These possibilities are not dealt with in detail in this chapter, because such transfers involve concepts which are either not difficult or not peculiar to personal property. An effective transfer of possessory rights depends upon two things: an effective transfer of possession (either 'actual' or 'constructive'[3]) and an effective imposition of the terms under which possession is taken (either by contract or by tort[4]).

[1] Generally relating to the need for registration.

[2] Although a careful distinction must be drawn between the *transfer* of existing security interests (by means which are described later in this chapter, and which depend upon whether the security interest is legal or equitable) and the *creation* of new security interests (by means which have already been described in Chapter 3).

[3] These are technical terms which refer, respectively, to physical possession and symbolic possession. Symbolic (ie constructive) possession exists where a party has possession of the documents of title to the underlying asset (but not possession of the asset itself) or where a party has the right to give instructions to a warehouseman (or other party) who has custody of goods.

[4] Or by a *sui generis* law of bailment, if the tort categorisation suggested in Chapter 2 is not thought to be compelling.

As already noted, proprietary interests can be transferred from one party to another by gift, by barter or by sale. There are common law rules which govern each mechanism and determine whether the parties' acts have been sufficient to effect a transfer of the property interest at law. This is not the end of the story, however. Equity also has an important role to play. Purported transfers which are ineffective at law are sometimes regarded as effective in equity. The recipient is then deemed to have acquired an equitable interest in the property, even though the parties' acts have been insufficient to transfer a legal interest from one party to another. However, these equitable interests are more precarious than their legal counterparts; as will be seen later, they may be overridden by subsequently created inconsistent legal interests.[5] This chapter considers both the common law rules and their equitable counterparts. The relevance of this chapter is clear. Whether the transaction is one of gift or sale, the intended recipient will be keen to know whether he or she has become a new owner of the property. Other parties, too, may be interested: liability to tax, the application of laws of succession and laws of insolvency may all depend upon a proper assessment of the effectiveness of a purported gift or sale of property.

This chapter must be distinguished from the next. This chapter is concerned with the implementation of the parties' real intentions: given that their intention is to transfer a certain proprietary interest, have their acts been sufficient to effect the desired transfer? The next chapter is concerned with the transfer of proprietary interests by operation of law: the issue then is then whether, regardless of the intentions of the parties, the circumstances are sufficient to warrant the intervention of the law to effect a transfer of property in equity?

4.2 Property which cannot be dealt with: '*nemo dat*' and other rules

4.2.1 The general rule

The basic rule which underpins all forms of transfers—whether by gift, sale, bailment or security—is that a person cannot give what is not his or hers to give. This is summed up in the maxim *nemo dat quod non habet*—or *nemo dat* for short). This rule is subject to several significant statutory and common law exceptions, outlined below,[6] but the importance of the basic rule cannot be over-emphasised, as the next case illustrates. (Also see Section 6.2.1 below.)

[401] *Cundy v Lindsay* (1878) 3 App Cas 459 (HL), 463–6 *per* Lord Cairns LC:
[A rogue named Blenkarn, impersonating a well-known firm named Blenkiron, ordered a quantity of linen by post from Lindsay & Co. When the linen arrived, Blenkarn sold some of it to Messrs Cundy, who purchased in good faith without

[5] See Chapter 6.
[6] See Section 4.2.2.

knowledge of the fraud. The first contract of sale was void (on the grounds of mistaken identity), so that no title to the linen passed to Blenkarn. As a consequence, he could not confer any title on Cundy. Cundy was therefore liable in conversion to Lindsay & Co.]

> 'My Lords, you have in this case to discharge a duty which is always a disagreeable one for any Court, namely, to determine as between two parties, both of whom are perfectly innocent, upon which of the two the consequences of a fraud practised upon both of them must fall. My Lords, in discharging that duty your Lordships can do no more than apply, rigorously, the settled and well known rules of law. Now, with regard to the title to personal property, the settled and well known rules of law may, I take it, be thus expressed: by the law of our country the purchaser of a chattel takes the chattel as a general rule subject to what may turn out to be certain infirmities in the title. If . . . it turns out that the chattel has been found by the person who professed to sell it, the purchaser will not obtain a title good as against the real owner. If it turns out that the chattel has been stolen by the person who has professed to sell it, the purchaser will not obtain a title. If it turns out that the chattel has come into the hands of the person who professed to sell it, by a *de facto* contract [ie a voidable contract], that is to say, a contract which has purported to pass the property to him from the owner of the property, there the purchaser will obtain a good title, even although afterwards it should appear that there were circumstances connected with that contract, which would enable the original owner of the goods to reduce it, and to set it aside, because these circumstances so enabling the original owner of the goods, or of the chattel, to reduce the contract and to set it aside, will not be allowed to interfere with a title for valuable consideration obtained by some third party during the interval while the contract remained unreduced.
>
> My Lords, the question, therefore, in the present case, as your Lordships will observe, really becomes the very short and simple one which I am about to state. Was there any contract which, with regard to the goods in question in this case, had passed the property in the goods from the Messrs. Lindsay to Alfred Blenkarn? If there was any contract passing that property, even although, as I have said, that contract might afterwards be open to a process of reduction, upon the ground of fraud, still, in the meantime, Blenkarn might have conveyed a good title for valuable consideration to the present Appellants.
>
> . . .
>
> Now, my Lords, . . .what the jurors have found is in substance this: it is not necessary to spell out the words, because the substance of it is beyond all doubt. They have found that by the form of the signatures to the letters which were written by Blenkarn, by the mode in which his letters and his applications to the Respondents were made out, and by the way in which he left uncorrected the mode and form in which, in turn, he was addressed by the Respondents; that by all those means he led, and intended to lead, the Respondents to believe, and they did believe, that the person with whom they were communicating was not Blenkarn, the dishonest and irresponsible man, but was a well known and solvent house of Blenkiron & Co., doing business in the same street. My Lords, those things are found as matters of fact, and they are placed beyond the range of dispute and controversy in the case.
>
> If that is so, what is the consequence? It is that Blenkarn—the dishonest man, as I call him—was acting here just in the same way as if he had forged the signature of Blenkiron & Co., the respectable firm, to the applications for goods, and as if, when, in return, the goods were forwarded and letters were sent, accompanying them, he had intercepted the

goods and intercepted the letters, and had taken possession of the goods, and of the letters which were addressed to, and intended for, not himself but, the firm of Blenkiron & Co. Now, my Lords, stating the matter shortly in that way, I ask the question, how is it possible to imagine that in that state of things any contract could have arisen between the Respondents and Blenkarn, the dishonest man? Of him they knew nothing, and of him they never thought. With him they never intended to deal. Their minds never, even for an instant of time rested upon him, and as between him and them there was no *consensus* of mind which could lead to any agreement or any contract whatever. As between him and them there was merely the one side to a contract, where, in order to produce a contract, two sides would be required. With the firm of Blenkiron & Co. of course there was no contract, for as to them the matter was entirely unknown, and therefore the pretence of a contract was a failure.

The result, therefore, my Lords, is this, that your Lordships have not here to deal with one of those cases in which there is *de facto* a contract made which may afterwards be impeached and set aside, on the ground of fraud; but you have to deal with a case which ranges itself under a completely different chapter of law, the case namely in which the contract never comes into existence. My Lords, that being so, it is idle to talk of the property passing. The property remained, as it originally had been, the property of the Respondents, and the title which was attempted to be given to the Appellants was a title which could not be given to them.'

Note:

This common law rule is now also enshrined in the Sale of Goods Act 1979 section 21(1): 'where goods are sold by a person who is not their owner, and who does not sell them under the authority or with the consent of the owner, the buyer acquires no better title to the goods than the seller had'. The statute then provides for certain exceptions to this general rule, as outlined in the next section.

4.2.2 Exceptions to the '*nemo dat*' rule

The *nemo dat* rule reflects a desire to protect the property interests of owners. This protection is delivered by a general rule which says that owners cannot be deprived of their property despite purported dealings with it by strangers. However, this protection of property interests conflicts with the principle which favours the protection of commercial markets. If commercial markets are to be protected, then buyers must be able to rely on the security of receipts; they must know that when they pay money for an asset, the asset will be theirs. In short, to protect commercial transactions it is desirable that a person who takes in good faith, for value and without notice of competing interests should get good title. The conflict between these two principles sets the limits to the general rule of *nemo dat* and explains the common law and statutory exceptions.

The common exceptions to the *nemo dat* rule can be briefly stated, although their application in particular contexts is often far from simple.[7] Note that every excep-

[7] These exceptions are not considered in detail here, but see, eg, M G Bridge, *The Sale of Goods* (1997, Clarendon Press: Oxford), ch IX; L S Sealy and R J A Hooley, *Commercial Law: Text, Cases and Materials* (2nd edn, 1999, Butterworths: London), ch 9.

tion concerns a three-party situation. Invariably an asset is purportedly sold (or otherwise dealt with) by someone who is not its owner and in circumstances where the true owner did not mean to part with the property, although the purchaser certainly intended to acquire it. For example, a hire-car might be sold by the hirer, against the true owner's wishes, to a bona fide party wanting to purchase such an asset. The problem is to devise rules which determine most fairly where the loss should lie.[8] Should the owner's property rights be protected, or should the purchaser's security of commercial dealings be favoured? Usually property rights are preferred, unless the true owner can be seen as somehow responsible for the purchaser's predicament. This might be the case, for example, where the true owner has personally (even if unintentionally) misled the purchaser, or where the true owner has left the asset in another's possession in circumstances where its sale appears legitimate. In those cases the owner, rather than the purchaser, might have to bear the loss.

The eight general exceptions to the *nemo dat* rule are as follows:

1. Estoppel and the related agency doctrine of ostensible authority (these common law exception are also enshrined in the Sale of Goods Act 1979 section 21): ie if the true owner of goods has, by conduct, represented that some third party is authorised to sell the goods, then a buyer in good faith from that third party will take good title to the goods.
2. Sales by mercantile agents[9] (Factors Act 1889 section 2): ie if the true owner has put a mercantile agent in possession of the owner's goods for the purpose of dealing with them, then any dealing by the mercantile agent in the ordinary course of the mercantile agent's business will transfer good title to a buyer who acts in good faith and without notice of the owner's conflicting rights.
3. Sales which are authorised by contractual powers of sale or by court orders (Sale of Goods Act 1979 section 21(2)(b)): eg sales by security holders under the terms of their security or by court order, or sales by a sheriff who has seized goods under a writ of execution.
4. Sales under a voidable title (this common law rule is also enshrined in the Sale of Goods Act 1979 section 23): ie if the seller of goods has voidable title which has not yet been avoided, then a buyer who takes in good faith and without notice of the defect in title acquires good title to the goods. A seller will have voidable title to goods where, for example, title was acquired by the seller pursuant to a contract induced by the seller's misrepresentation, duress or undue influence.

   Note that the consequences for a buyer are quite different depending upon whether the seller has purchased under a void contract (as in *Cundy v*

[8] 'Loss', in this context, refers to one party's failure to acquire, or to keep, title to the asset in dispute. The party who loses *may* have the right to sue the seller for damages, either for unauthorised sale (if it is the true owner who loses title) or for breach of warranty of authority to sell (if it is the intending purchaser who fails to acquire title).

[9] A mercantile agent is a person whose business is to buy and sell goods for other people.

Lindsay, **[401]** above) or under a voidable (but not yet avoided) contract (see, eg, *Lewis v Averay*,[10] **[402]** below, and *Car & Universal Finance Co Ltd v Caldwell*[11]).

5. Sale by a seller who continues in possession (Sale of Goods Act 1979 section 24 and Factors Act 1889 section 8): ie if a seller, having previously sold goods, remains in possession of them, then a subsequent sale to a second buyer who takes in good faith and without notice of the earlier sale will be sufficient to pass good title.
6. Sale by a buyer in possession (Sale of Goods Act 1979 section 25(1) and Factors Act 1889 section 9): ie if a buyer obtains possession of goods with the consent of the seller and then sells those goods to a sub-purchaser who takes in good faith and without notice of any conflicting rights of the seller, the sub-purchaser obtains good title.

   These sections are not effective to deprive the true owner of his property where it is stolen from him and, well after it is out of the thief's hands, certain dealings superficially match the requirements of these sections: see the opinion of Lord Goff in *National Employers' Mutual General Insurance Assocn Ltd v Jones* [1990] 1 AC 24 (HL).

   The risk of this sort of sub-sale is particularly marked where the purchase price is paid in instalments and where, although title does not pass until the final payment is made, the buyer nevertheless takes possession of the goods in the interim.[12]
7. Sale by an unpaid seller in possession (Sale of Goods Act 1979 section 48): ie if an unpaid seller is in possession of the goods *and* has the right to re-sell them (according to the terms of section 48), then a buyer takes good title. Since this section gives the seller a *right* to re-sell, not simply a power to confer good title, the buyer's *bona fides* are irrelevant.
8. Sale to a private purchaser of a motor vehicle held on hire purchase (Hire Purchase Act 1964 Part III). The details of this exception are quite complex, and need not be of concern here.

Question:

Do these eight exceptions reflect a fair and sensible balance between the competing principles of security of property and security of markets (or security of receipts)?

[10] [1972] 1 QB 198 (CA).

[11] [1965] 1 QB 525 (CA).

[12] The modern hire-purchase contract was designed, in part, to overcome this risk. Under a hire-purchase contract, the hirer is not a 'purchaser' in possession; the relationship is simply one of hire until the time comes for the hirer to exercise the option to purchase. Note that now the Sale of Goods Act 1979 s 25(2) treats all conditional sale agreements with *consumers* (ie all those conditional sales covered by the Consumer Credit Act 1974) as equivalent to hire-purchase contracts.

The general principle which underpins exception four—sale under a voidable but not yet avoided contract—is important, and its implications need to be clearly understood. The next extract illustrates the potential practical problems and their resolution.

[402] *Lewis v Averay* [1972] 1 QB 198 (CA), 208 *per* Phillimore J:

[Lewis agreed to sell his car for £450 to a man who claimed to be a well-known actor, Richard Greene, and who showed a Pinewood Studio pass as evidence of his identity. Lewis assumed 'Greene' to be creditworthy, and so allowed him to take the car away, but 'Greene's' cheque for £450 was not honoured by the bank. 'Greene' subsequently sold the car to Averay, a music student, who bought in good faith for £200. The Court of Appeal held that the first sale was voidable for fraud, but not void for mistake of identity. As the first contract had not been avoided before the second contract of sale was entered into, Averay obtained good title to the car.]

> 'I think the law was conveniently stated by Pearce L.J. in the course of his judgment in *Ingram v. Little* [1961] 1 Q.B. 31 to which reference has already been made. He said, at p. 61:
>
> > "Each case must be decided on its own facts. The question in such cases is this. Has it been sufficiently shown in the particular circumstances that, contrary to the prima facie presumption"—and I would emphasise those words—"a party was not contracting with the physical person to whom he uttered the offer, but with another individual whom (as the other party ought to have understood) he believed to be the physical person present. The answer to that question is a finding of fact."
>
> Now, in that particular case the Court of Appeal, by a majority and in the very special and unusual facts of the case, decided that it had been sufficiently shown in the particular circumstances that, contrary to the prima facie presumption, the lady who was selling the motor car was not dealing with the person actually present. But in the present case I am bound to say that I do not think there was anything which could displace the prima facie presumption that Mr. Lewis was dealing with the gentleman present there in the flat—the rogue. It seems to me that when, at the conclusion of the transaction, the car was handed over, the logbook was handed over, the cheque was accepted, and the receipts were given, it is really impossible to say that a contract had not been made. I think this case really is on all fours with *Phillips v. Brooks* [[1919] 2 KB 243], which has been good law for over 50 years. True, the contract was induced by fraud, and Mr. Lewis, when he discovered that he had been defrauded, was entitled to avoid it; but in the meanwhile the rogue had parted with the property in this motor car which he had obtained to Mr. Averay, who bought it bona fide without any notice of the fraud, and accordingly he thereby, as I think, acquired a good title.'

Also see:

Car & Universal Finance Co Ltd v Caldwell [1965] 1 QB 525 (CA) (especially on the steps necessary to avoid a voidable transaction).

Newtons of Wembley Ltd v Williams [1965] 1 QB 560 (CA).

4.2.3 Restrictions on dealing with certain types of property

In addition to the restrictions imposed by the *nemo dat* rule, there are other restrictions which make it impossible to deal with some forms of property. Statutes may prohibit or declare void certain assignments of property. For example, restrictions may be imposed on dealings with currency or with cultural property. The general law, too, prohibits assignments which are deemed contrary to public policy, loosely understood. For example, bare rights to litigate are not assignable. To allow such assignments is seen as encouraging litigation which the assignor is not inclined to prosecute personally.[13] In addition, the benefit of contracts involving personal service or personal confidence cannot be assigned. In these circumstances it is seen as unfair to force one party to perform in favour of someone other than the chosen counter-party.[14] Of course, if the public policy reason underpinning these common law exceptions does not apply in given circumstances, then it is arguable that the assignment is permissible.

Note:

The parties themselves can also provide that certain forms of property are not to be assignable, or are to be assignable only in limited circumstances. This is common with shares, and is becoming increasingly common with rights arising under commercial contracts. The courts, however, tend to interpret these types of provisions restrictively. See, for example, *Don King Productions Inc v Warren* [1999] 3 WLR 276 (CA), where a prohibition on the assignment of certain contractual rights was held not to preclude the holding of those rights on trust for the benefit of the intended assignee.

Also see:

The extracts in Chapters 1 and 8 for further issues surrounding restrictions on the freedom to deal with property.

The potential impact of these basic restrictions must be kept in mind. However, in all of the discussion which follows, it is assumed that the transferor is dealing with his or her own property, and that there is nothing in the surrounding circumstances which would prevent the dealing.

[13] *Trendtex Trading Corp v Crédit Suisse* [1982] AC 679 (HL).

[14] See the discussion in *Tolhurst v Associated Portland Cement Manufacturers* [1903] AC 414.

4.3 Fraud and non-compliance with statutory requirements

As will become apparent from the later sections of this chapter, parties who wish to transfer assets between themselves are often obliged by statute to effect the transfer in writing, or at least to evidence it (either before or after the event) in writing. These writing requirements are generally intended to reduce the incidence of fraud. Because they afford tangible proof of a transaction, neither party will find it easy to deny the arrangement and the resulting changes in ownership. These statutes typically ensure compliance with their demands for writing by providing that non-compliance will render the underlying transaction either void or unenforceable or both.

Generally these demands for formality work well. However, there are some exceptional cases where the result of insisting that parties comply with the necessary formalities seems most unfair. Many of the older examples illustrating this are trusts cases, where land (rather than personal property) has been transferred from A to B, but with the intention that it be held on trust for A. Difficulties arise where the transfer of legal title is evidenced properly, but not the trust relationship. Since all these writing requirements are designed largely to prevent fraud, it would seem particularly unjust if B could assert full legal and beneficial ownership of the land, in defiance of the agreement with A, by asserting non-compliance with the statute. A way around this problem was devised in the Chancery courts and is now a general rule of equity.

The general rule is that 'a statute will not be allowed to cloak a fraud'. What this means is that one party will not be allowed to rely on strict compliance with the terms of a statute where to do so would perpetrate a fraud on another (not necessarily in the strong or intentional common law sense, but in the weaker, 'unconscionable' or 'equitable' sense). In the typical scenario, a statute will require the parties' agreement to be in writing and, relying on this, one party will attempt to deny that another has any interest in the property, notwithstanding their (unwritten) agreement to the contrary. The next case is the one usually cited as authority for the equitable rule that prohibits this.

[403] *Rochefoucauld v Bousted* [1897] 1 Ch 196 (CA), 205–6, 208 *per* Lindley LJ for the Court:

[The case concerned a trust of land where there was insufficient writing to satisfy the Statute of Frauds; the details are immaterial.]

> 'We come, therefore, to the conclusion that the plaintiff [the Comtesse de la Rochefoucauld] has proved that the estates in question [situated in Ceylon] were conveyed to the defendant on May 27, 1873, upon trust for her . . .
>
> This conclusion renders it necessary to consider whether the Statute of Frauds affords a defence to the plaintiff's claim. The section relied upon is s. 7, which . . . .[makes it] necessary to prove by some writing or writings signed by the defendant [the alleged trustee], not only that the conveyance to him was subject to some trust, but also what

that trust was. But it is not necessary that the trust should have been declared by such a writing in the first instance; it is sufficient if the trust can be proved by some writing signed by the defendant, and the date of the writing is immaterial. It is further established by a series of cases, the propriety of which cannot now be questioned, that the Statute of Frauds does not prevent the proof of a fraud; and that it is a fraud on the part of a person to whom land is conveyed as a trustee, and who knows it was so conveyed, to deny the trust and claim the land himself. Consequently, notwithstanding the statute, it is competent for a person claiming land conveyed to another to prove by parol evidence that it was so conveyed upon trust for the claimant, and that the grantee, knowing the facts, is denying the trust and relying upon the form of conveyance and the statute, in order to keep the land himself. . . .

. . .The trust which the plaintiff has established is clearly an express trust within the meaning of that expression as explained in *Soar v. Ashwell* ([1893] 2 Q. B. 390). The trust is one which both plaintiff and defendant intended to create. This case is not one in which an equitable obligation arises although there may have been no intention to create a trust. The intention to create a trust existed from the first.'

Question:

Now that the law of unjust enrichment is better developed, is it more appropriate to see this trust as a resulting trust effecting restitution rather than an express trust which is enforced notwithstanding the absence of writing? The question is important, because a resulting trust will re-deliver the equitable interest to the original settlor, while an express trust will deliver it to the nominated (ie intended) beneficiary. In the case extracted above, the identity of these two parties was the same, but this is not always so.

Also see:

Bannister v Bannister [1948] 2 All ER 133.

FURTHER READING:

T G Youdan, 'Formalities for Trusts of Land, and the Doctrine in *Rochefoucauld* v. *Bousted*' [1984] *CLJ* 306.

This principle has the potential to override all that is said below on consensual transfers of legal and equitable interests. In many of the cases discussed, some statute specifies the requirements which must be met if the transfer is to be effective. In all of those cases, equity will not allow one party to rely on the statute to cloak a fraud. All that follows should be read with that qualification in mind.

4.4 Gifts: general issues

All gifts are premised on the intention of the donor. If a gift is to be effective, either at law or in equity, then the donor must have a present intention to confer an immediate benefit on the donee. If this form of intention does not exist, then there can be no gift of the property. Moreover, the onus of proof lies with the donee. As well as the necessary intention to make a gift, the law prescribes certain formalities (relaxed in some cases by equity) which must be met before the transfer by way of gift can be considered effective to give the donee the intended benefit.

In the discussion which follows, tangible and intangible property are considered separately, since the rules for each form differ. At the end of these sections, the rules relating to conditional gifts are considered. So too are the problems which arise where a donor makes a gift of property by mistake. In both cases the issue is whether the gift is effective notwithstanding the condition or the mistake.

What is being described in these sections is a significant and complicated part of the law of personal property. To understand this area, it helps to have a clear schema in mind before descending into the detailed rules. The diagram at the end of this section may help (*Fig. 2*). In addition, it is important to recognise why this area has generated such interest. After all, if an intended gift is ineffective on the first attempt, then surely the donor can simply 'do it properly' the second time. This is certainly true if the transfer and its timing are a matter affecting only the donor and the donee. However, the legal niceties become crucial when third parties have potential interests. The issue of who owns a particular item of property at a particular moment in time—be it the donor or the donee—becomes critical where taxation, succession or insolvency rules need to be applied to either the donor's or the donee's assets for the benefit of third parties (typically the Inland Revenue, the heirs to the estate, or the creditors of the insolvent). The cases extracted in the next few sections almost invariably involve disputes generated by such third parties.

4.5 Gifts of tangible property (choses in possession)

Gift-giving is common, especially gift-giving of tangible property. Ownership of tangible property is readily transferred from one party to another by gift (ie without consideration). All that is necessary is that the donor deliver the property to the donee with the intention that the donee benefit immediately from the receipt.[15] This—ie delivery with the necessary intention—is all that is needed to effect a transfer of legal title from the donor to the donee. There is no need for writing or formal

[15] Delivery with only a *conditional* intention to benefit the donee is considered later: see Section 4.8, below. Delivery without *any* intention to benefit the donee has quite different consequences: see Chapter 5.

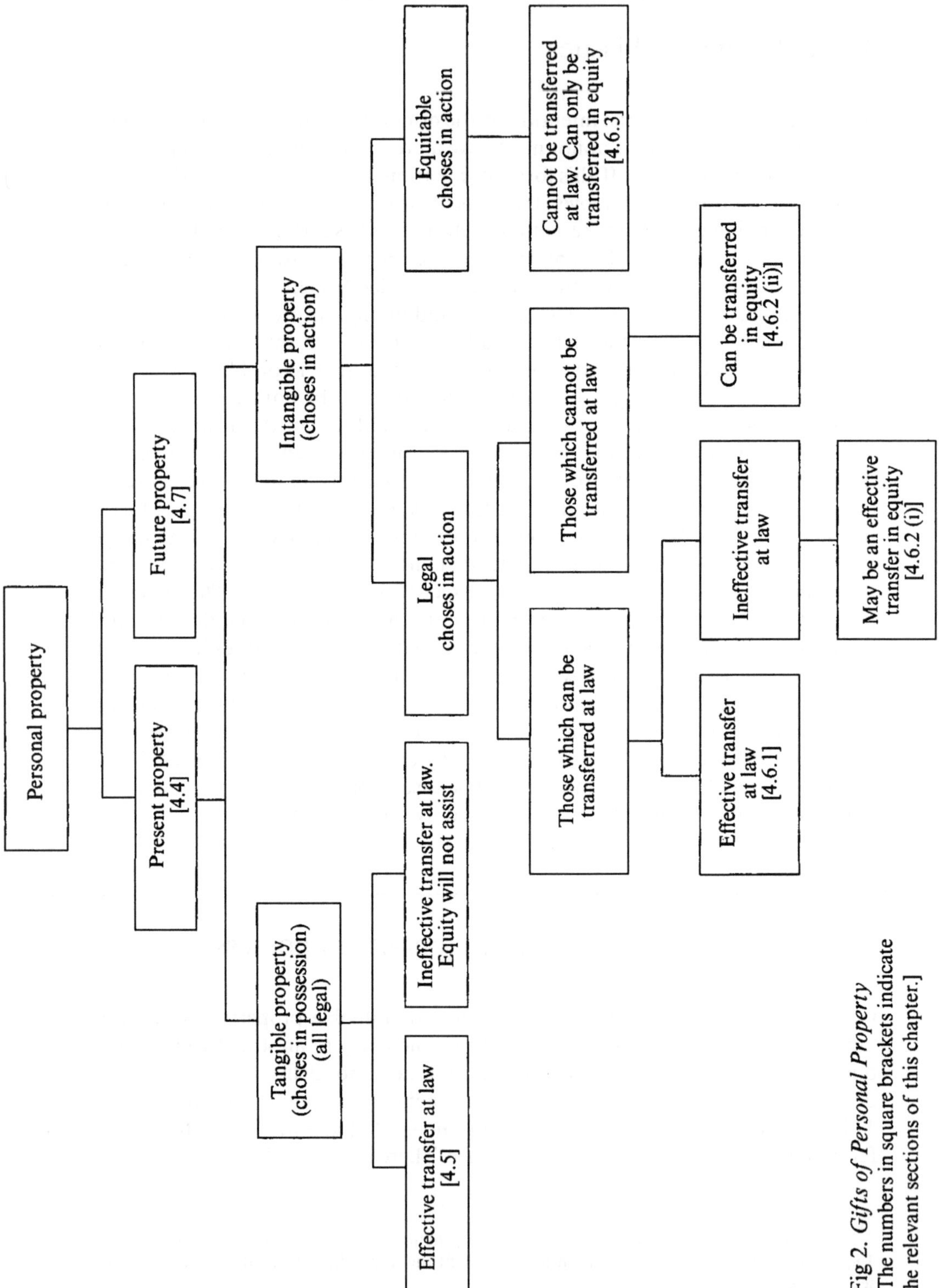

Fig 2. *Gifts of Personal Property*
[The numbers in square brackets indicate the relevant sections of this chapter.]

words or witnesses.[16] However, the common law is rigorous in its insistence on strict compliance with these minimal requirements. The only evident relaxation is that constructive (or symbolic) delivery will suffice in place of actual (or physical) delivery.

Note that in making an effective gift, the intention to benefit the donee immediately is critical. Without this intention, legal *and beneficial* title to the chattel will not pass to the donee.[17] An intention to benefit the donee at some time in the future will not do;[18] nor will an intention to benefit only if certain preconditions are met. When the time comes, or the preconditions are met, a new act of giving will be required by the donor to manifest a present intention to give and so make the gift effective.

The one exception to these rules is a common law exception known as the rule in *Strong v Bird*.[19] The exception applies where a donor evinces a continuing intention to make a gift right up to the time of his or her death, but fails to deliver the property to the intended donee. The normal result is that the gift is ineffective in law. However, if the intention to make a gift continues up to the time of the donor's death and if legal title somehow then legitimately vests in the intended donee (eg because the donee is the executor of the donor's estate), then the law will regard the gift as becoming perfected by the later transfer of legal title notwithstanding that it took place for a different purpose.[20]

At least with gifts of choses in possession, equity does not modify these rules. One of the maxims of equity is that equity will not assist a volunteer. If the gift of the chose in possession is ineffective in law to transfer the legal title, then equity will not come to the aid of the donee to render the gift effective in equity (by deeming the equitable title to the property to have passed in advance of the legal transfer from donor to donee). If the gift of a tangible asset fails at law, it will be completely ineffective; the donee will have nothing. Of course, if the intention of the donor is to create a trust rather than make an outright gift, then the issues are different.[21] In

[16] Alternatively, the donor may achieve the same ends by deed (or 'deed of gift') in place of delivery, but then the arrangement is treated as a contract (for all that a contract to make a gift appears anomalous). A deed is a signed and sealed written legal agreement, not necessarily supported by real consideration moving from the intended donee. However, the formalities of a deed provide notional consideration, and an obligation embodied in a deed is regarded by the common law (although not by equity) as an enforceable contractual obligation. The deed itself provides a substitute for the consideration necessary to support the contract. Moreover, a contract to transfer tangible property can specify the time at which the transfer of title is to be effected. It follows that a 'deed of gift' can be worded so as to create an immediate gift of an asset (with immediate transfer of title, even though there has been no delivery of the asset) or it can create a binding legal obligation on the donor to transfer the property promised by gift at some later time, with the donor obliged to pay common law damages for breach of contract for any failure to do so. In addition, as with any contract, the deed can also specify other terms and conditions upon which the gift will be made. The rules which relate to deeds of gift are therefore different from the rules relating to outright gifts discussed in this section.

[17] Although *legal* title only (ie bare legal title) may pass on delivery: see Chapter 5.

[18] *Re Ridgway* (1885) 15 QBD 447, 449 *per* Cave J.

[19] (1874) LR 18 Eq 318.

[20] See, eg, *Re James* [1935] Ch 449, 451 *per* Farwell J; G Kodilinye, 'A Fresh Look at the Rule in *Strong v Bird*' [1982] *Conv* 14.

[21] The intention is then to give the donee/beneficiary *equitable* ownership of the asset, not legal ownership. Legal ownership will remain in the hands of the donor/trustee. Express trusts of this sort were noted in Chapter 2.

addition, the next section makes it clear that equity does sometimes have a role to play in gift-giving: in certain circumstances it may come to the aid of donees of *intangible* property (choses in action).[22]

The fact that equity will not intervene to save a failed gift can have significant ramifications for both donors and donees. Even when it is clear that the donor intends to benefit the donee, the gift will be ineffective if that intention is not coupled with delivery (or a deed of gift). Equity will not help the parties by construing an intention to benefit the donee by way of gift as an intention to benefit the donee in some other way (eg by trust) simply to save a failed gift.

[404] *Cochrane v Moore* (1890) 25 QBD 57 (CA), 72–3 *per* Fry LJ:
[The case concerned the purported gift of a quarter share in a racehorse. Unsurprisingly, there was no delivery to the donee.]

> 'This review of the authorities leads us to conclude that according to the old law no gift or grant of a chattel was effectual to pass it whether by parol or by deed, and whether with or without consideration unless accompanied by delivery: that on that law two exceptions have been grafted, one in the case of deeds, and the other in that of contracts of sale where the intention of the parties is that the property shall pass before delivery: but that as regards gifts by parol, the old law was in force when *Irons v. Smallpiece* (2 B. & A. 551) was decided: that that case therefore correctly declared the existing law: and that it has not been overruled by the decision of Pollock, B., in 1883, or the subsequent case before Cave, J.
>
> . . .
>
> But assuming delivery to be necessary in the case of the gift of an ordinary chattel, two questions would remain for consideration in the present case—the first, whether the undivided fourth part of the horse admits of delivery, or whether on the other hand it is to be regarded as incorporeal [ie intangible property] and incapable of tradition [ie delivery]; the other, whether the letter written by [the donor] to [the owner of the stable where the horse was stabled] was either a constructive delivery of this undivided fourth part of the horse, or an act perfecting the gift of this incorporeal part so far as the nature of the subject-matter of the gift admits. On these points we do not think it needful to express any decided opinion.'

Questions:

What is the best response to the two questions left unanswered by Fry LJ? If a quarter share in a horse is *intangible* property, how would an effective gift of such property be made (see Section 4.6 below)? If the intending donor had decided to benefit the donee by creating a *trust*, rather than by outright gift, how would the donor effectively constitute such a trust?

[22] As will be seen, this is not because there are inconsistent equitable rules for the different types of property. It is because the circumstances in which equity deems it appropriate to intervene simply cannot arise with transfers of tangible property.

4.6 Gifts of intangible property (choses in action)

Unlike choses in possession (which are all legal interests), choses in action can be either legal (eg debts and shares) or equitable (eg interests under a trust, security interests by way of equitable charge). This complicates the analysis which follows. Legal choses are considered separately from equitable choses.

Legal choses in action can be transferred at law. If this is done effectively, the donor transfers legal title to the chose to the donee. Different statutes specify the formalities which must be complied with in order to transfer the legal title to the chose. But that is not the end of the story. Sometimes an ineffective attempt to transfer legal title is regarded as effective in equity. The transferor retains legal title to the chose (because the transfer of legal title was ineffective), but holds the asset on trust for the intended transferee; the transferee has equitable ownership of the asset. In addition, and just to complicate matters still further, there are certain forms of transfer of legal choses in action which can only be effected in equity. The details of these possibilities are described below. If these transfers are properly effected in equity, then, again, the donor continues to hold the legal title to the chose, but the donee acquires an equitable interest. With legal choses, the transfers which are effective in law and those which are effective in equity are considered separately.

With equitable choses in action, the position is less certain. Such choses are only recognised in equity, so they can only be transferred in equity. Again, statutes impose certain formalities which must be met if the intended transfer is to be recognised as effective. An effective transfer will pass the (equitable) title to the (equitable) chose from the donor to the donee. If these formalities are not met, however, then it is debatable whether equity can nevertheless regard the transferor as holding the equitable chose on trust for the intended transferee (by analogy with ineffective legal transfers of legal choses in action). These issues, too, are considered below.

4.6.1 Gifts of intangible legal property (legal choses in action) effective in law

For a long time all attempted gifts of intangible property were ineffective in law. This is no longer true. Now various statutes prescribe the methods for transfer of legal title to different types of intangible property. For example, the Law of Property Act 1925 section 136 indicates that choses in action are assignable and can be the subject of gifts.

[405] Law of Property Act 1925 section 136

'136. Legal assignments of things in action

(1) Any absolute assignment by writing under the hand of the assignor (not purporting to be by way of charge only) of any debt or other legal thing in action, of which express notice in writing has been given to the debtor, trustee or other person from

whom the assignor would have been entitled to claim such debt or thing in action, is effectual in law (subject to equities having priority over the right of the assignee) to pass and transfer from the date of such notice—

(a) the legal right to such debt or thing in action;

(b) all legal and other remedies for the same; and

(c) the power to give a good discharge for the same without the concurrence of the assignor:

Provided that, if the debtor, trustee or other person liable in respect of such debt or shine in action has notice—

(a) that the assignment is disputed by the assignor or any person claiming under him; or

(b) of any other opposing or conflicting claims to such debt or thing in action;

he may, if he thinks fit, either call upon the persons making claim thereto to interplead concerning the same, or pay the debt or other thing in action into court under the provisions of the Trustee Act, 1925.

(2) This section does not affect the provisions of the Policies of Assurance Act, 1867.

[(3) The county court has jurisdiction (including power to receive payments of money or securities into court) under the proviso to subsection (1) of this section where the amount or value of the debt or thing in action does not exceed [£30,000].]'

Note:

This statute does not apply to every assignment of a chose in action. It does not apply to a conditional assignment, an assignment by way of charge, or an assignment of part of a legal chose in action. Moreover, the wording of the section does not make it clear whether the provisions apply only to the assignment of *legal* choses in action, or whether they also apply to the assignment of equitable choses in action.

A debt is a legal chose in action. The Law of Property Act 1925 section 136 indicates that the benefit of debts owing to a creditor can be given away by gift, provided that the creditor/assignor intends an absolute assignment, that the assignment is in writing signed by the assignor, and that express notice in writing is given to the debtor by either the assignor or the assignee.

With other choses in action (such as company shares, copyright, life policies, bills of exchange and promissory notes), different statutes prescribe specific requirements for effective transfer of the legal title to the property, and the general provisions of the Law of Property Act 1925 section 136 do not apply. With shares, for example, the company's articles of association will, subject to the Companies Act 1985, prescribe the formalities to be satisfied for an effective legal transfer. The company's articles usually require the proper execution of an instrument of transfer followed by registration in the company's share register. The transfer instrument must be accompanied by the relevant share certificates.

All of these formal rules are in addition to the requirement that the donor have the necessary intention to confer an immediate benefit on the donee; the intention to make a gift is vital to all gift-giving.

Given these rules, it is generally a simple matter to determine whether a gift of a chose in action has been effective in law to transfer legal title to the chose from the donor to the donee. Gifts which do not meet these stipulations are simply ineffective in law, although the rule in *Strong v Bird*,[23] considered in the previous section,[24] may sometimes assist a donee who later

[23] (1874) LR 18 Eq 318.

[24] See Section 4.5.

acquires legal title to the intended gift. In addition, equity may sometimes come to the aid of the parties to save attempted gifts of choses in action which are ineffective at law. This is considered next.

4.6.2 Gifts of intangible legal property (legal choses in action) effective in equity

There are two issues to be addressed in this section. The first issue is whether an ineffective, but potentially possible, legal assignment of a legal chose in action can ever be regarded as effective in equity even though it is not effective in law. The second issue is whether there can be an effective assignment in equity of legal choses which are not assignable at law. For example, a part of a debt cannot be assigned at law: the Law of Property Act 1925 section 136 does not cover the possibility. Given this, is it possible to assign part of a debt by way of gift in equity?

(i) legal choses in action which are assignable, but ineffectively assigned, at law

The issue here is whether an ineffective, but potentially possible, legal assignment of a legal chose in action can ever be regarded as effective in equity although not in law. For example, a creditor can *legally* assign a debt to a third party, according to the terms of the Law of Property Act 1925 section 136, provided the assignment is in writing and notice of the assignment is given to the debtor. But will anything less suffice to give the third party *equitable* title to the debt at some earlier stage in the process? The rule established by the cases is that an attempted gift will be effective in equity, even if not at law, if the donor has done all that the donor is *required* to do, notwithstanding that other requirements for an effective legal transfer remain outstanding, so long as those additional matters can be completed by the donee.[25] If the outstanding matters involved in getting in the legal title are all within the control of the donee, then equity (by considering as done all that ought to be done) can regard the parties as being in the same position as if the tasks were already completed. In doing this, equity is not compelling the donor to complete an incomplete gift, for the donor in these circumstances has no further part to play in the transaction. On the other hand, by assuming that the donee has already completed the further tasks, equity effectively sees the donee as the owner of the gift in equity: the donee has the equitable title, although acquiring the legal title will have to await completion of the outstanding tasks. This simple description of the applicable rule disguises some substantial controversies, as the cases below indicate.

[406] ***Milroy v Lord*** **(1862) 4 De GF & J 264 (CA), 274** ***per*** **Turner LJ:**
[Medley executed a deed by which he purported to make a voluntary assignment of 50 shares in the Louisiana Bank to the defendant, Lord, to be held by Lord on trust

[25] This statement makes it obvious that this form of equitable intervention cannot assist a donee when the property being transferred is a tangible asset (a chose in possession). With choses in possession, the gift is effective in law only if the donor has the requisite intention and either delivers the property to the donee or enters into a deed of gift: see section 4.5. Each of these requirements can only be met by the donor; there is nothing left which can be done by the donee.

for the claimants. At law, the bank shares could only be assigned by a transfer entered in the bank's books. Medley had not executed such a transfer, although earlier he had given Lord a power of attorney which authorised Lord to transfer company shares. For three years after the execution of the deed, dividends on the shares were remitted to the claimants. When Medley died, the claimants unsuccessfully sought to compel the executor to hand over the shares to new trustees.]

> 'I take the law of this court to be well settled, that, in order to render a voluntary settlement valid and effectual, the settlor must have done everything which, according to the nature of the property comprised in the settlement, was necessary to be done in order to transfer the property and render the settlement binding upon him. He may of course do this by actually transferring the property to the persons for whom he intends to provide, and the provision will then be effectual, and it will be equally effectual if he transfers the property to a trustee for the purposes of the settlement, or declares that he himself holds it in trust for those purposes; and if the property be personal, the trust may, as I apprehend, be declared either in writing or by parol; but, in order to render the settlement binding, one or other of these modes must, as I understand the law of this court, be resorted to, for there is no equity in this court to perfect an imperfect gift. The cases I think go further to this extent, that if the settlement is intended to be effectuated by one of the modes to which I have referred, the court will not give effect to it by applying another of those modes. If it is intended to take effect by transfer, the court will not hold the intended transfer to operate as a declaration of trust, for then every imperfect instrument would be made effectual by being converted into a perfect trust.'

Questions:

1. Why was the gift of the shares ineffective, given that Lord had power of attorney and so could have signed the transfer forms himself?
2. Was the gift of the dividends effective? Why?

[407] *Re Rose* [1952] Ch 499 (CA), 507–15 *per* Evershed MR, and 518–19 *per* Jenkins LJ:

[On 30 March 1943 Rose executed share transfers in proper form and handed them, with the relevant share certificates, to the transferees or their agent. The transfers were by gift. The transfers were stamped on 12 April and registered on 30 June 1943 (although the directors had power to decline to register transfers). Rose died several years later. Estate duty was payable on the gift unless the it was complete before the 10 April 1943. The Court of Appeal held that no estate duty was payable.]

> ***Evershed MR:***
> 'Now I agree that on the face of the document it was obviously intended (if you take the words used) to operate and operate immediately as a transfer—"I do hereby transfer to the transferee" these shares "to hold unto the said transferee, subject to the several conditions on which I held the same at the time of the execution hereof." It plainly was intended to operate immediately as a transfer of rights. To some extent at least, it is said, it could not possibly do so. To revert to the illustration which has throughout been taken, if the company had declared a dividend during this interregnum, it is not open

to question that the company must have paid that dividend to the deceased. So that vis-à-vis the company, this document did not, and could not, operate to transfer to Mrs. Rose the right against the company to claim and receive that dividend. Shares, Mr. Pennycuick says, are property of a peculiar character consisting, as it is sometimes put, of a bundle of rights—that is, rights against or in the company. It has followed from his argument that if such a dividend had been paid, the deceased could, consistently with the document to which he has set his hand and seal, have retained that dividend, and, if he had handed it over to his wife, it would have been an independent gift. I think myself that such a conclusion is startling. Indeed, I venture to doubt whether to anybody but a lawyer such a conclusion would even be comprehensible—at least without a considerable amount of explanation. That again is not conclusive; but I confess that I approach a matter of this kind with a pre-conceived notion that a conclusion that offends common sense, so much as this would prima facie do, ought not to be the right conclusion.

Jenkins L.J. carried the illustration a stage further. He said: Suppose, on the Crown's view, the deceased, retaining, pending registration, full rights over these shares (for Mr. Pennycuick argued that this document not only did not transfer the legal estate but that it transferred no interest or estate whatever), repented of his generosity and told the company not to register the transfer. Supposing Mrs. Rose went to the company and the directors of the company had nevertheless said that they were willing to register the transfer. Let it be then further supposed that the deceased proceeded to take action to restrain the company by injunction from registering the transfer. If the deceased in truth retained at that time a proprietary interest, the court would be bound to protect it by granting an injunction. That, indeed, was perhaps too startling for Mr. Pennycuick, for he said that he thought the court would not grant an injunction and that, the document having at least operated as a gift of a piece of paper, namely, the share certificate, the deceased could not be heard to claim the court's assistance so as to restrain the company from doing that which possession, as upon gift, of the certificate and of this transfer, enabled the donee to require the company to do.

I do not pursue these examples; but it seems to follow from testing this matter by such extreme cases, that the assertion that nothing whatever passed under this deed except the right to possess, as articles, as physical things, two pieces of paper, is not right. I will now go to the case of *Milroy v. Lord* [see **[406]** above], which is in truth the foundation of the Crown's argument. . . .

. . . the Crown's argument . . . is founded [on] the broad, general proposition that if a document is expressed as, and on the face of it intended to operate as, a transfer, it cannot in any respect take effect by way of trust—so far I understand the argument to go. In my judgment, that statement is too broad and involves too great a simplification of the problem; and is not warranted by authority. I agree that if a man purporting to transfer property executes documents which are not apt to effect that purpose, the court cannot then extract from those documents some quite different transaction and say that they were intended merely to operate as a declaration of trust, which *ex facie* they were not; but if a document is apt and proper to transfer the property—is in truth the appropriate way in which the property must be transferred—then it does not seem to me to follow from the statement of Turner L.J. [in *Milroy v Lord*] that, as a result, either during some limited period or otherwise, a trust may not arise, for the purpose of giving effect to the transfer. . . . And, for my part, I do not think that the case of *Milroy v. Lord* (4 De G.F. & J. 264) is an authority which compels this court to hold that in this case—where, in the terms of Turner L.J.'s judgment, the settlor did everything which, according to the nature of the property comprised in the settlement, was necessary to be done by him in order to transfer the property—the result necessarily negatives the conclusion that, pending registration, the settlor was a trustee of the legal interest for the transferee.

The view of the limitations of *Milroy v. Lord* which I have tried to express, was much better expressed by Jenkins J. in the recent case which also bears the same name of *In re Rose* ([1949] Ch. 78) (though that is a coincidence). It is true that the main point, the essential question to be determined, was whether there had been a transfer *eo nomine* of certain shares within the meaning of a will. The testator in that case, Rose, by his will had given a number of shares to one Hook but the gift was subject to this qualification, "if such shares have not been transferred to him previously to my death." The question was, had the shares been transferred to him in these circumstances? He had executed (as had this Mr. Rose) a transfer in appropriate form and handed the transfer and the certificate to Hook; but, at the time of his death, the transfer had not been registered. It was said, therefore, that there had been no transfer; and (following Mr. Pennycuick's argument) there had been no passing to Hook of any interest, legal or beneficial, whatever, by the time the testator died. If that view were right then, of course, Hook would be entitled to the shares under the will. But my brother went a little more closely into the matter, because it was obvious that on one view of it, if it were held that there was a "transfer" within the terms of the will, though the transfer was inoperative in the eye of the law and not capable of being completed after the death, then Mr. Hook suffered the misfortune of getting the shares neither by gift inter vivos nor by testamentary benefaction. Therefore, my brother considered the case of *Milroy v. Lord* and in regard to it he used this language (at p 89): "I was referred on that to the well known case of *Milroy v. Lord* and also to the recent case of *In re Fry* ([1946] Ch. 312). Those cases, as I understand them, turn on the fact that the deceased donor had not done all in his power, according to the nature of the property given, to vest the legal interest in the property in the donee. In such circumstances it is, of course, well settled that there is no equity to complete the imperfect gift. If any act remained to be done by the donor to complete the gift at the date of the donor's death the court will not compel his personal representatives to do that act and the gift remains incomplete and fails. In *Milroy v. Lord* the imperfection was due to the fact that the wrong form of transfer was used for the purpose of transferring certain bank shares. The document was not the appropriate document to pass any interest in the property at all." Then he refers to *In re Fry*, which is another illustration. "In this case, as I understand it, the testator had done everything in his power to divest himself of the shares in question to Mr. Hook. He had executed a transfer. It is not suggested that the transfer was not in accordance with the company's regulations. He had handed that transfer together with the certificate to Mr. Hook. There was nothing else the testator could do." I venture respectfully to adopt the whole of the passage I have read which, in my judgment, is a correct statement of the law. If that be so, then it seems to me that it cannot be asserted on the authority of *Milroy v. Lord*, and I venture to think it also cannot be asserted as a matter of logic and good sense or principle, that because, by the regulations of the company, there had to be a gap before Mrs. Rose could, as between herself and the company, claim the rights which the shares gave her *vis-à-vis* the company, the deceased was not in the meantime a trustee for her of all his rights and benefits under the shares. That he intended to pass all those rights, as I have said, seems to me too plain for argument. I think the matter might be put perhaps in a somewhat different fashion, though it reaches the same end. Whatever might be the position during the period between the execution of this document and the registration of the shares, the transfers were on June 30, 1943, registered. After registration, the title of Mrs. Rose was beyond doubt complete in every respect; and if the deceased had received a dividend between execution and registration and Mrs. Rose had claimed to have that dividend handed to her, what would have been the the deceased's answer? It could no longer be that the purported gift was imperfect; it had been made perfect. I am not suggesting that the perfection was retroactive. But what else could he say? How could he, in the face of his own statement under seal, deny the proposition that he had, on March 30, 1943, transferred the shares to his wife?—and by the phrase "transfer the shares" surely must be meant transfer to her "the shares and all my right title and interest thereunder." Nothing else could sensibly have been meant. . . .'

Jenkins LJ:

'. . . . In other words, in my view the effect of these transactions, having regard to the form and the operation of the transfers, the nature of the property transferred, and the necessity for registration in order to perfect the legal title, coupled with the discretionary power on the part of the directors to withhold registration, must be that, pending registration, the deceased was in the position of a trustee of the legal title in the shares for the transferees. Thus in the hypothetical case put by the Crown of a dividend being declared and paid (as it would have been paid in accordance with the company's articles) to the deceased as registered holder, he would have been accountable for that dividend to the transferees, on the ground that by virtue of the transfers as between himself and the transferees the owners of the shares were the transferees, to the exclusion of himself.

In my view, in order to arrive at a right conclusion in this case, it is necessary to keep clear and distinct the position as between transferor and transferee and the position as between transferee and the company. It is, no doubt, true that the rights conferred by shares are all rights against the company, and it is no doubt true that, in the case of a company with ordinary regulations, no person can exercise his rights as a shareholder *vis-à-vis* the company or be recognized by the company as member unless and until he is placed on the register of members. But in my view it is a fallacy to adduce from that the conclusion that there can be no complete gift of shares as between transferor and transferee unless and until the transferee is placed on the register. In my view, a transfer under seal in the form appropriate under the company's regulations, coupled with delivery of the transfer and certificate to the transferee, does suffice, as between transferor and transferee, to constitute the transferee the beneficial owner of the shares, and the circumstance that the transferee must do a further act in the form of applying for and obtaining registration in order to get in and perfect his legal title, having been equipped by the transferor with all that is necessary to enable him to do so, does not prevent the transfer from operating, in accordance with its terms as between the transferor and transferee, and making the transferee the beneficial owner. After all, where duty is concerned, the only relevant type of ownership is beneficial ownership, and the situation of the legal estate does not affect the question. . . .'

Question:

If this analysis is correct, then what would happen to any dividend paid out by the company and handed over to the donee if, subsequently, the company legitimately decided to refuse to register the transfer of shares to the donee?

[408] *Olsson v Dyson* (1969) 120 CLR 365 (Aust HCt), 384–6 *per* Windeyer J:

[Dyson was owed £2,000 plus interest. Prior to his death, Dyson purported to make an oral assignment of the debt to his wife by way of gift; he also gave oral instructions to the same effect to the managing director of the debtor company. The Australian High Court was unanimous in its view that this was insufficient to effect either a legal or an equitable assignment of the debt.]

'. . . . The result [of section 136 of the Law of Property Act 1925 and its Australian equivalents] is that a creditor who wishes to give to a donee a debt owed to him must follow the statutory procedure: he must sign a document by which he assigns the debt to the donee; and his gift will be complete in law when express notice in writing of his having done so is given to the debtor. An oral statement to the intended donee that the debt was henceforth to be his will not suffice even if the debtor has notice of it.

This is simply the result of a general rule that to make a gift of any thing the intending donor must actually give it to the donee in a way which the law recognizes. The owner of a thing does not effectively give it away by simply saying "it is yours as a gift". He must not only say it is a gift, he must give it to the donee, who must, by words or conduct, accept it. How a thing can be given away depends on what it is. Since the decision in *Cochrane v. Moore* (1890) 25 QBD 57 [see **[404]**], it is certain that if it be a chattel capable of manual delivery the donor must deliver it to the donee by actually handing it over, or else do some act which in the eye of the law amounts to delivery of possession, as for example handing over some indicia of ownership or the means of obtaining possession. If the donor means to give some thing which is not a chattel, but is an intangible thing such as a share in a company or a debt owing to him or other chose in action, he must give it by some way which the law provides for the transfer of a thing of that kind. In such a case his gift is not of rights of ownership in respect of a visible and tangible thing, but of rights to be asserted against a person or persons natural or artificial.

If there were consideration for an intended, but incomplete, assignment, the Chancellor would compel the assignor to make good his intention and complete the transfer in due form of law. And because this could be compelled in equity, and equity treated as done that which ought to be done, it came to be said that an assignment incomplete in law was valid in equity if supported by some consideration recognized in equity for the purpose. But a gift is, by its very name, an assignment without consideration. So much is I suppose trite. I have said it because, for want of remembering it, arguments were it seems advanced which led the learned trial judge to a conclusion that a pure gift of a debt could be effective although the creditor donor had not executed any written assignment. . . .

There is no equity to perfect an imperfect gift. This sentence, extracted from the well-known judgment of Turner L.J. in *Milroy v. Lord* (1862) 4 De G F & J 264 (45 ER 1185) [see **[406]**] has become an aphorism. People have deplored it and regretted that the Chancery Court did not display a more benevolent attitude in some cases where intended generosity was frustrated because of a failure to give effect to good intentions by doing what law required. But, because equity does not assist a volunteer, the rule stands firm. It would perhaps be better expressed by saying that an intending donor cannot be compelled to perfect his intended gift. To put it in those words rather than in the more brief form commonly used is desirable in the case of an assignment of a debt by way of gift. For if the assignor does all that the statute requires him to do on his part to effect the assignment it will be regarded as effective in equity. He must execute an instrument under his hand which is an absolute assignment in writing. Why? Because the statute so requires. Express notice in writing of the assignment must be given to the debtor to make it effective at law: because the statute so requires. But that notice need not be signed by the assignor or given by him. Why not? Because the statute does not so require. It can be given by the assignee and the gift will then be complete in law. In the meantime the assignor is bound in equity, notwithstanding that the assignment is by way of gift, for he has done all that the law required of him to complete his gift. Equity interposes to prevent his retracting it. But this does not mean that if he omits to do what he must to do make a gift, the omission can be overlooked and the gift take effect. It seems to me that [the trial judge's] view that there was an effective assignment by Dyson of the debt to his wife must be held erroneous. . . .'

Question:

In the case just extracted, the intended gift failed at law because the full complement of statutory requirements for the transfer of a debt had not been satisfied, and it failed in equity because the donor had not completed those particular aspects of the statutory requirements which only the donor could complete. Would the same conclusion necessarily follow if the views of Lord Macnaghten in *William Brandts Sons & Co v Dunlop Rubber Co* [1905] AC 454 (HL) were adopted? In that case, Lord Macnaghten argued that the Judicature Act amendments (now enshrined in the Law of Property Act 1925 section 136) *added* a method of legal assignment to the existing modes of equitable assignment of legal choses in action, but did not impair the efficacy of equitable modes at all. As regards the assignment of debts, the old modes of equitable transfer did not require the transfer to be in writing. Is this approach to the impact of the statutory provisions defensible? Contrast it with the Australian position advanced in *Norman v Federal Commissioner of Taxation* (1963) 109 CLR 9 (Aust HCt), by Windeyer J (see **[416]** below).

Note:

1. Notice that, notwithstanding any demonstrable intention to make a gift, there will be no effective gift in equity if the donor simply places matters (such as completed transfer forms accompanied by the relevant share certificates) in the hands of the *donor's* agent. In those circumstances the donor remains at liberty to recall the gift simply by revoking the instructions previously given to the agent. The donor has not done all that is necessary, and the donee is not in a position to control completion of the transfer. It follows that the intended gift will not be regarded as complete either at law or in equity.
2. From these cases on equitable assignments of legal choses, it might appear that there is no good reason for parties to comply with the more onerous requirements of the Law of Property Act 1925 section 136 so as to effect the *legal* transfer of the chose in action (in particular, by giving notice to the debtor), when an *equitable* transfer can be more easily achieved (without the need for such notice). However, this is not the case. Notice to the debtor is desirable for several reasons: (i) if the debtor pays the donor/assignor before receiving notice of the assignment, then the debtor's liability is discharged and the donee/assignee's only remedy is against the assignor (cf the position if the debtor pays in disregard of the notice of assignment, as in *William Brandt*, then the asignee can require the debtor to pay again); (ii) where there are competing assignees, priority is determined according to the first to give notice to the

debtor (see Chapter 6, below); and (iii) the assignee takes subject to the equities affecting the transaction between the assignor and the debtor, except equities which arise after the debtor has received notice of the assignment (also noted in Chapter 6, below).

FURTHER READING:

L McKay, 'Share Transfers and the Complete and Perfect Rule' [1976] 40 *Conv* 139 (which doubts the correctness of *Re Rose* **[407]**).

(ii) legal choses in action which are unassignable at law

As regards the second issue, which concerns the assignment of legal choses in action which are unassignable at law, the position in England appears to be still unsettled. The following extract, from an Australian High Court case, describes the problem.

[409] *Norman v Federal Commissioner of Taxation* (1963) 109 CLR 9 (Aust HCt), 29–34 *per* Windeyer J:

[The facts and a longer extract appear at **[416]**.]

'*(iii) As to assignments of part of a debt:*

It has been held that the statutory method of assignment is not available for the assignment of parts of debts or choses in action: *Williams v. Atlantic Assurance Co.* ([1933] 1 KB 81); *Re Steel Wing Co Ltd* ([1921] 1 Ch 349). There were some earlier decisions to the contrary; but they must be taken to be overruled. The later decisions should, I consider, be followed by this Court. They are in accordance with general principle. The conclusion does not depend simply on a literal interpretation of the statutory language [of the Australian equivalent of the Law of Property Act 1925 section 136] and of the phrase "absolute assignment". Before the statute an assignee was permitted to bring his action at law in the name of the assignor when he was seeking to recover a whole debt assigned to him. If a debt had been broken into parts this procedure was not appropriate. A creditor cannot recover a debt piecemeal in a court of law. Therefore, when part of a debt was assigned, proceedings to enforce the assignment had to be brought in a court of equity. And the assignee, not the assignor, would be the plaintiff in the suit. The assignor (the creditor) as legal owner, the debtor and any assignees of other parts of the debt were all necessary parties, so that all the obligations of the debtor and the rights of all persons interested in the fund might be established by the decree. This was the rule of the Chancery Court. It is still the law: see *Performing Right Society Ltd. v. London Theatre of Varieties Ltd.* ([1924] AC 1, at pp 14, 20, 30, 31). As an assignment of part of a debt is still necessarily an equitable assignment, the question arises can it be made by way of gift; and, if so, how?

(iv) As to whether consideration is required for the equitable assignment of a chose in action not assignable at law:

One might have expected that this would long ago have been authoritatively settled. But the question is, according to *Halsbury*, 3rd ed. vol. 4 p. 495, "uncertain". Lord Evershed said in *In re McArdle (dec'd)* ([1951] 1 Ch 669) [see **[415]**] that the problem is "vexed and difficult" ([1951] 1 Ch, at p 673). . . .

. . .Turning . . . to assignments [such as assignments of part of a debt] that are equitable because the property assigned is a legal chose in action [which is] not assignable except by the aid of equity: It has been said that historically there could be no equitable assignment of a debt except for value. Whether this be correct or not as a general proposition, it never meant that there must be consideration as now understood in the law of contract. An assignment in satisfaction, or part satisfaction, of an antecedent debt was taken in equity as made for value. And this was what had happened in case after case appearing in the reports in which assignments were upheld in equity before the *Judicature Act*. Whether equity would then give any aid to an assignment of a chose in action made for no value at all, but as a pure gift, is less clear. There are in the reports categorical statements each way, extending over two centuries or more. . . .

. . . The intervention of equity in support of assignments of choses in action has been ascribed historically, in the main, to one or other of two grounds. One is to hold men to agreements and promises which they have made for value; the other is the analogy of a trust . . . . An assignment, of course, differs from a declaration of trust. And it is trite to say that an ineffectual attempt to assign property will not be rescued by equity by being construed as a valid declaration of trust: *Milroy v. Lord* ((1862) 1 De GF & J 264 (45 ER 1185), see **[406]**). Nevertheless, the analogy between the creation of a trust and an equitable assignment of a chose in action, which creates an equitable interest in the assignee, is significant.

An agreement to assign will be effective as an equitable assignment if it be for value; for then equity looks on that as done which ought to be done. But this does not mean that there cannot be in equity an actual assignment of a chose in action as distinct from an agreement to assign. I think there can, and that it can be by way of gift. In such a case equity enforces the assignment, not by compelling the assignor to do something, but by refusing to allow him to act in a way inconsistent with what he has done, that is by restraining him from derogating from his gift. His conscience becomes bound, not by value received, but because, as between him and the assignee, his gift was complete. . . .

. . . Before 1873 a chose in equity [an equitable chose in action] and a [legal] chose in action were both transferable in equity and only in equity. The assignments were alike made effective because of the remedies that a court of equity could provide. To speak of equity not perfecting an imperfect gift seems beside the point where no gift could be made except in equity. To say that the donor must do everything that according to the nature of the property is necessary to transfer it means little when it is in law not transferable; for equity looks to the intent not the form. These considerations have added weight in the case of part of a debt; for a part of debt never was assignable so as to be recoverable at law even in an indirect way. It being necessary for the decision of this case to come to a conclusion on a vexed question, my conclusion is that . . . [t]he whole of a debt being now voluntarily assignable under the statute, it would be a strange anomaly if a part could not be the subject of voluntary equitable assignment. To say, "you can give away the whole, but you cannot give away a part, for a part you must get a price" would seem to contradict common sense. And I do not think it necessary to do so. . . .'

Note:

1. In this extract, Windeyer J appears to proceed by steps: (i) the assignment of part of a debt cannot be effected at law, because the statute does not allow for this possibility; (ii) it follows that if an assignment of part of a debt is to be possible, it must take place in equity; (iii) an assignment for value of part of a debt (ie a sale, even with equity's modified view of what will count as adequate consideration) is possible in equity because a court of equity would, in those circumstances, regard the

transferor's conscience as bound; (iv) an assignment by way of gift is also possible in equity because a court would, in the circumstances, regard the transferor's conscience as bound because the gift is 'complete'; (v) the correctness of this last step is reinforced because otherwise it would be possible to make a gift of all equitable choses in action but only of certain legal choses in action.

2. Whatever the criticisms of Windeyer J's approach, these principles were applied in *Shepherd v Federal Commissioner of Taxation* (1965) 113 CLR 385 (Aust HCt), and are now firmly established as the law in Australia.
3. If these principles are accepted, then part of a debt can be assigned by gift in equity. Moreover, the assignment is not required to be in writing (although writing may well be the easiest way to prove that the donor has an immediate intention to benefit the donee). The writing requirements of the Law of Property Act 1925 section 136 do not apply because the assignment is not absolute, it is of part only of the debt; and the writing requirements of the Law of Property Act 1925 section 53(1)(c) (discussed at Section 4.6.3, below) do not apply because what is being assigned is not a subsisting *equitable* interest, but part of a *legal* interest (although what the donee receives as a result of the transfer is *equitable* title to that part-interest).

Questions:

Is the logic of Windeyer J's approach compelling? In particular, is step (iv) merely a statement of the conclusion which is being argued for? And is step (v) true, or does the Law of Property Act 1925 section 136 (and its Australian equivalent) effectively provide a mechanism for the absolute and unconditional legal transfer of *all* legal choses in action, and deny the propriety of all partial and conditional transfers? If the latter is the case, should equity provide a contrary rule, especially in the absence of consideration? In this context, see the problems which arise with *sales* of part of a specified bulk, a problem which is not limited to legal choses in action: see Section 4.11.4 below.

4.6.3 Gifts of intangible equitable property (equitable choses in action) effective in equity

All of the rules discussed so far relate to gifts of legal choses in action, such as debts and shares. The concern has been to determine whether the purported gift is effective, either at law or in equity. Choses in action can also be equitable (eg an equitable ownership interest under a trust, or a fixed or floating charge security interest). Like legal choses in action, these equitable choses can be transferred by gift. The necessary formalities are laid down in the Law of Property Act 1925 section 53, extracted below.

[410] Law of Property Act 1925 section 53(1)(c), (2):

'**53. Instruments required to be in writing**

(1) . . . . [the earlier sub-sections relate exclusively to land]

(c) a disposition of an equitable interest or trust subsisting at the time of the disposition, must be in writing signed by the person disposing of the same, or by his agent thereunto lawfully authorised in writing or by will.

(2) This section does not affect the creation or operation of resulting, implied or constructive trusts.'

To make an effective gift of an equitable chose, the donor must intend an immediate gift and must comply with these statutory writing requirements. The donee will then become the equitable owner of the chose and the donor will have no further interest in the asset. Problems arise, however, where these writing requirements are not complied with. To what lengths, if any, will equity go to save the gift? The following cases illustrate equity's approach. The analysis depends on distinctions which are not always easy to draw.

[411] *Grey v IRC* [1960] AC 1 (HL), 15–19 *per* Lord Radcliffe:
[The donor dealt with his equitable interest under a trust by directing his trustee to hold the interest on trust for the intended donee. The court held that the disposition had to be in writing to be effective. Hunter transferred shares to the appellants as his nominees (ie as his trustees on trust for himself). Later he orally and irrevocably directed these nominees to hold the shares in five blocks on nominated trusts for his grandchildren, to the exclusion of all rights in himself. The appellants then executed declarations of trust reciting and acknowledging the oral trusts. Hunter signed these written declarations. The House of Lords held that Hunter's oral declaration was ineffective to transfer the equitable interest to the intended beneficiaries. This only happened on execution of the written instruments which met the requirements of the Law of Property Act 1925 section 53(1)(c). Accordingly, the written instruments were assessed to *ad valorem* stamp duty as voluntary dispositions (rather than to nominal stamp duty, which would have reflected the contrary argument that the written document did not effect a transfer of value).].

'My Lords, if there is nothing more in this appeal than the short question whether the oral direction that Mr. Hunter gave to his trustees on February 18, 1955, amounted in any ordinary sense of the words to a "disposition of an equitable interest or trust subsisting at the time of the disposition," I do not feel any doubt as to my answer. I think that it did. Whether we describe what happened in technical or in more general terms the full equitable interest in the 18,000 shares concerned, which at that time was his [Hunter's], was (subject to any statutory invalidity) diverted by his direction from his ownership into the beneficial ownership of the various equitable owners, present and future, entitled under his six existing settlements.

But that is not the question which has led to difference of opinion in the courts below. Where opinions have differed is on the point whether his direction was a "disposition" within the meaning of section 53 (1) (c) of the Law of Property Act, 1925, the argument for giving it a more restricted meaning in that context being that section 53 is to be construed as no more than a consolidation of three sections of the Statute of Frauds, sections 3, 7 and 9. So treated, "disposition," it is said, is merely the equivalent of the former words of section 9, "grants and assignments," except that testamentary disposition has to be covered as well, and a direction to a trustee by the equitable owner of the property prescribing new trusts upon which it is to be held is a declaration of trust but not a grant or assignment. The argument, concludes, therefore, that neither before

January 1, 1926, nor since did such a direction require to be in writing signed by the disponor or his agent in order to be effective.

In my opinion, it is a very nice question whether a parol declaration of trust of this kind was or was not within the mischief of section 9 of the Statute of Frauds. The point has never, I believe, been decided and perhaps it never will be. Certainly it was long established as law that while a declaration of trust respecting land or any interest therein required writing to be effective, a declaration of trust respecting personalty did not. Moreover, there is warrant for saying that a direction to his trustee by the equitable owner of trust property prescribing new trusts of that property was a declaration of trust. But it does not necessarily follow from that that such a direction, if the effect of it was to determine completely or pro tanto the subsisting equitable interest of the maker of the direction, was not also a grant or assignment for the purposes of section 9 and therefore required writing for its validity. Something had to happen to that equitable interest in order to displace it in favour of the new interests created by the direction: and it would be at any rate logical to treat the direction as being an assignment of the subsisting interest to the new beneficiary or beneficiaries or, in other cases, a release or surrender of it to the trustee.

I do not think, however, that that question has to be answered for the purposes of this appeal. It can only be relevant if section 53 (1) of the Law of Property Act, 1925, is treated as a true consolidation of the three sections of the Statute of Frauds concerned and . . . therefore . . . not to be read as effecting changes in the existing law unless the words it employs are too clear in their effect to admit of any other construction. . . . But, in my opinion, it is impossible to regard section 53 of the Law of Property Act, 1925, as a consolidating enactment in this sense.

. . .

. . . For these reasons I think that there is no direct link between section 53 (1) (c) of the Act of 1925 and section 9 of the Statute of Frauds. The link was broken by the changes introduced by the amending Act of 1924, and it was those changes, not the original statute, that section 53 must be taken as consolidating. If so, it is inadmissible to allow the construction of the word "disposition" in the new Act to be limited or controlled by any meaning attributed to the words "grant" or "assignment" in section 9 of the old Act.'

[412] *Vandervell v Inland Revenue Commission* [1967] 2 AC 291 (HL), 310–12 *per* Lord Upjohn, 329–30 *per* Lord Wilberforce:

[The donor (the sole beneficiary under a trust) dealt with his equitable interest under the trust by directing his trustee to transfer *both* the legal and equitable interests to the intended donee. The court held that this disposition did not need to be in writing to be effective. Added features of the disposition make this case a complicated one. Vandervell was the beneficiary of a bare trust of shares in Vandervell Products Ltd. Vandervell's total income was sufficiently high to attract surtax (tax at 98 per cent). Vandervell wished to make a substantial gift to the Royal College of Surgeons, preferably out of his pre-tax income. The scheme designed to achieve this involved a transfer of legal and beneficial interest in the shares to the College, thus enabling the College, as a charity, to receive substantial cash dividends tax free. The transfer of shares was subject to an option for their repurchase, thus ensuring that control of the family company remained with the family. To implement this plan, Vandervell orally directed his trustee, the National Provincial Bank, to transfer the trust shares to the College in return for an option granted to a trustee company associated with Vandervell. Once the transfer was registered, Vandervell Products Ltd declared large dividends and paid them to the College. The trustee company then exercised the option to repurchase the shares. At no stage was there any written disposition of Vandervell's equitable interests.

Vandervell was later assessed to surtax on the dividends. He could challenge the assessment only by showing that the dividends were 'income from property of which the [taxpayer] has divested himself absolutely', that expression carrying a very restrictive meaning. His appeal against the assessment failed. The House of Lords held unanimously that Vandervell *had* divested himself of his beneficial interest in the shares, notwithstanding that there was no writing which complied with Law of Property Act 1925 section 53(1)(c). However, by a bare majority they held that the trustee company held the benefit of the option to repurchase the shares on resulting trust for Vandervell, so he had not 'divested himself absolutely' and was accordingly liable to the surtax. The extract below relates only to the section 53(1)(c) point. (Resulting trusts are discussed in Chapter 5.)]

Lord Upjohn:

'. . . The question is whether notwithstanding the plainly expressed intention of the appellant by himself or his agents the absence of writing prevented any equitable or beneficial interest in the shares passing to the college so that contrary to his wishes and understanding they remained bare trustees for him. This depends entirely upon the true construction of section 53 (1) (c) of the Law of Property Act, 1925, which the Crown maintain makes writing necessary to pass the beneficial interest. This section was generally thought to re-enact section 9 of the Statute of Frauds and that section had never been applied to a trust of an equitable interest of pure personalty. Before the cases of *Grey v. Inland Revenue Commissioners* ([1960] A.C. 1 [**[411]** above]) and *Oughtred v. Inland Revenue Commissioners* ([1960] A.C. 206 **[428]** below]), both in your Lordships' House, this argument would have been quite untenable.

It was shown in those cases that the Law of Property Act, 1925, was not re-enacting section 9 but that it had been amended by the Law of Property Act, 1924. The relevant words of section 53 are:

> ". . .a disposition of an equitable interest or trust subsisting at the time of the disposition, must be in writing signed by the person disposing of the same. . . ."

Those words were applied in *Grey* and *Oughtred* to cases where the legal estate remained outstanding in a trustee and the beneficial owner was dealing and dealing only with the equitable estate. That is understandable; the object of the section, as was the object of the old Statute of Frauds, is to prevent hidden oral transactions in equitable interests in fraud of those truly entitled, and making it difficult, if not impossible, for the trustees to ascertain who are in truth his beneficiaries. But when the beneficial owner owns the whole beneficial estate and is in a position to give directions to his bare trustee with regard to the legal as well as the equitable estate there can be no possible ground for invoking the section where the beneficial owner wants to deal with the legal estate as well as the equitable estate.

I cannot agree with Diplock L.J. [in the court below] that prima facie a transfer of the legal estate carries with it the absolute beneficial interest in the property transferred; this plainly is not so, e.g., the transfer may be on a change of trustee; it is a matter of intention in each case. But if the intention of the beneficial owner in directing the trustee to transfer the legal estate to X is that X should be the beneficial owner I can see no reason for any further document or further words in the document assigning the legal estate also expressly transferring the beneficial interest; the greater includes the less. X may be wise to secure some evidence that the beneficial owner intended him to take the beneficial interest in case his beneficial title is challenged at a later date but it certainly cannot, in my opinion, be a statutory requirement that to effect its passing there must be some writing under section 53 (1) (c).

Counsel for the Crown admitted that where the legal and beneficial estate was vested in the legal owner and he desired to transfer the whole legal and beneficial estate to another he did not have to do more than transfer the legal estate and he did not have to comply with section 53 (1) (c); and I can see no relevant difference between that case and this.

As I have said, that section is, in my opinion, directed to cases where dealings with the equitable estate are divorced from the legal estate and I do not think any of their Lordships in *Grey* and *Oughtred* had in mind the case before your Lordships. To hold the contrary would make assignments unnecessarily complicated; if there had to be assignments in express terms of both legal and equitable interests that would make the section more productive of injustice than the supposed evils it was intended to prevent. . .'

Lord Wilberforce:
'. . . There remains the alternative point taken by the Crown that in any event, by virtue of section 53 (1) (c) of the Law of Property Act, 1925, the appellant never effectively disposed of the beneficial interest in the shares to the Royal College of Surgeons. This argument I cannot accept. Section 53 (1) (c), a successor to the dormant section 9 of the Statute of Frauds, has recently received a new lease of life as an instrument in the hands of the Revenue. The subsection, which has twice recently brought litigants to this House (*Grey v. Inland Revenue Commissioners; Oughtred v. Inland Revenue Commissioners*), is certainly not easy to apply to the varied transactions in equitable interests which now occur. However, in this case no problem arises. The shares in question, the 100,000 "A" shares in Vandervell Products Ltd., were, prior to November 14, 1958, registered in the name of the National Provincial Bank Ltd. upon trust for the appellant absolutely. On November 14, 1958, the appellant's solicitor received from the bank a blank transfer of the shares, executed by the bank, and the share certificate. So at this stage the appellant was the absolute master of the shares and only needed to insert his name as transferee in the transfer and to register it to become the full legal owner. He was also the owner in equity. On November 19, 1958, the solicitor (or Mr. Robins—the case is ambiguous) on behalf of Mr. Vandervell, who intended to make a gift, handed the transfer to the college which, in due course, sealed it and obtained registration of the shares in the college's name. The case should then be regarded as one in which the appellant himself has, with the intention to make a gift, put the college in a position to become the legal owner of the shares, which the college in fact became. If the appellant had died before the college had obtained registration, it is clear on the principle of *In re Rose* [see **[407]**] that the gift would have been complete, on the basis that he had done everything in his power to transfer the legal interest, with an intention to give, to the college. No separate transfer, therefore, of the equitable interest ever came to or needed to be made and there is no room for the operation of the subsection. What the position would have been had there simply been an oral direction to the legal owner (viz. the bank) to transfer the shares to the college, followed by such a transfer, but without any document in writing signed by Mr. Vandervell as equitable owner, is not a matter which calls for consideration here. The Crown's argument on this point fails.'

[413] *Re Vandervell's Trusts (No 2); White v Vandervell Trustees Ltd* [1974] Ch 269 (CA), 320 *per* Lord Denning MR and 324–6 *per* Lawton LJ:

[This cases relates to facts which post-date *Vandervell v IRC* (see **[412]**, above). Vandervell, the donor (and the beneficiary of an option held under a resulting trust), dealt with his equitable interest by permitting his trustees to exercise the option using the donee's funds, not the donor's. The court held that the disposition did not need to be in writing to be effective to transfer to the donee the equitable interest in the property acquired by exercise of the option. Vandervell Trustees Ltd, the trustee company, exercised the option by paying £5,000 out of funds it held on trust for Vandervell's children. Both Vandervell and the trustee company intended that the repurchased shares would be held on trust for the children, although nothing was committed to writing. Later, when Vandervell Products Ltd declared dividends on the shares, these sums were added to the children's trust fund. The IRC claimed that Vandervell had still not divested himself absolutely of the shares, and assessed him to surtax on the dividends. In 1965, Vandervell executed a deed transferring to the trustee company all of his rights (if any) to the option, shares and dividends. Accordingly, the IRC subsequently confined its claims to the period 1961 to 1965. After Vandervell's death, his executors (the claimants) sought a declaration that they were entitled to all the dividends received by the trustee company from 1961 to 1965. The purpose of the proceedings was to test the estate's liability to surtax, although the IRC was not a party to the action.]

Lord Denning MR:

'... Mr. Balcombe for the executors admitted that the intention of Mr. Vandervell and the trustee company was that the shares should be held on trust for the children's settlement. But he said that this intention was of no avail. He said that during the first period, Mr. Vandervell had an equitable interest in the property, namely, a resulting trust; that he never disposed of this equitable interest (because he never knew he had it): and that in any case it was the disposition of an equitable interest which, under section 53 of the Law of Property Act 1925, had to be in writing, signed by him or his agent, lawfully authorised by him in writing (and there was no such writing produced). He cited *Grey v. Inland Revenue Commissioners* [1960] A.C. 1 [**[411]** above] and *Oughtred v. Inland Revenue Commissioners* [1960] A.C. 206 [**[428]** below].

There is a complete fallacy in that argument. A resulting trust for the settlor is born and dies without any writing at all. It comes into existence whenever there is a gap in the beneficial ownership. It ceases to exist whenever that gap is filled by someone becoming beneficially entitled. As soon as the gap is filled by the creation or declaration of a valid trust, the resulting trust comes to an end. In this case, before the option was exercised, there was a gap in the beneficial ownership. So there was a resulting trust for Mr. Vandervell. But, as soon as the option was exercised and the shares registered in the trustees' name, there was created a valid trust of the shares in favour of the children's settlement. Not being a trust of land, it could be created without any writing. A trust of personalty can be created without writing. Both Mr. Vandervell and the trustee company had done everything which needed to be done to make the settlement of these shares binding on them. So there was a valid trust: see *Milroy v. Lord* (1862) 4 De G.F. & J. 264, 274, per Turner L.J.

. . . .

The executors admit that from January 19, 1965, Mr. Vandervell had no interest whatsoever in the shares. The deed of that date operated so as to transfer all his interest thenceforward to the trustee company to be held by them on trust for the children. I asked Mr. Balcombe: What is the difference between the events of October and November 1961, and the event of January 19, 1965? He said that it lay in the writing. In 1965, Mr. Vandervell disposed of his equitable interest in writing: whereas in 1961 there was no writing. There was only conduct or word of mouth. That was insufficient. And, therefore, his executors were not bound by it.

The answer to this argument is what I have said. Mr. Vandervell did not dispose in 1961 of any equitable interest. All that happened was that his resulting trust came to an end—because there was created a new valid trust of the shares for the children's settlement.'

Lawton LJ:
'As to the second of Mr. Balcombe's answers it is pertinent to remember that Mr. Vandervell, who was most anxious not to have any beneficial interest in the shares which he had transferred to the Royal College of Surgeons, was kept fully informed by his solicitor of what was in contemplation and what counsel had advised. He was present at the meeting of the directors of the trustee company held on October 2, 1961, at which they resolved

> "that in view of the advice given by both conveyancing counsel and tax counsel, the trustees should exercise their option to acquire the shares held by the Royal College of Surgeons."

On or about October 10, 1961, the trustee company acquired the shares with money taken by them from the children's settlement. In my judgment the inference from this course of conduct is that Mr. Vandervell intended that to happen which did happen and that when the directors of the trustee company used money from the children's settlement to pay for the shares he intended that company to hold the shares not for himself but for the trusts of the children's settlement. If the trustee company had used this money otherwise than for the benefit of the children they would have been in breach of trust, and as Mr. Vandervell knew what was happening and intended it to happen, he would have been guilty of aiding and abetting them.

The result in law is that after the transfer the trustee company held the shares for the benefit of the children's settlement as Mr. Vandervell had intended it should. This followed from the operation of the rule that if A uses B's money to buy property, in the absence of any evidence to show otherwise, A holds that property for the benefit of B. It follows that once the transfer of the shares had been registered the beneficial interest in them was held by the trustee company on the trusts of the children's settlement so that no declaration of trust was necessary. There is no directors' minute recording the making of a declaration, but there is, in my judgment, ample evidence from which the court is entitled to infer, and I do infer, that a declaration of trust was made by the trustee company with the knowledge and approval of Mr. Vandervell. By letter dated November 2, 1961, the trustee company's solicitor wrote to the special commissioners of income tax informing them, as was the fact, that the option had been exercised out of funds from the children's settlement. This letter ended with these words: "and consequently such shares will henceforth be held by them upon the trusts of that settlement." Thereafter, Mr. Vandervell, knowing what had been done, procured Vandervell Products Ltd., which he controlled, to declare dividends on those shares. Had Mr. Vandervell been alive at the date of trial in this case he would not have sought to submit that after the transfer of the shares to the trustee company he held a beneficial interest in them; and had he tried to do so, he would not have been heard to deny the existence of a beneficial interest for the children which he had done his best to ensure they had. His executors can be in no better position than he would have been.

Estoppel, however, is not the only answer to Mr. Balcombe's submission based on an absence of writing complying with section 53 (1) (c) of the Law of Property Act 1925. The exercise of the option and the transfer of the shares to the trustee company necessarily put an end to the resulting trust of the option. There could not be a resulting trust of a chose in action which was no more. The only reason why there ever had been a resulting trust of the option was the rule that the beneficial interest in property must be held for some one if the legal owner is not entitled to it. The legal, but not the beneficial, interest in the option had vested in the trustee company. The beneficial interest had to be held for some one and as the trustee company had declared no trusts of the option, the only possible beneficiary was Mr. Vandervell. Once the trustee company took a transfer of the shares the position was very different. The legal title to them was vested in the trustee company and by reason of the facts and circumstances to which I have already referred it held the beneficial interest for the trusts of the children's settlement. There was no gap between the legal and beneficial interests and in consequence no need for a resulting trust in favour of Mr. Vandervell to fill it. Neither the extinction of the resulting trust of the option resulting from its exercise nor the creation of a beneficial interest in the shares by the declaration of trust amounted to a disposition of an equitable interest or trust within the meaning of sections 53 (1) (c) and 205 (1) (ii) of the Law of Property Act 1925. . . .'

Questions:

1. What legal propositions do the three previous extracts stand for?
2. The cases considered in the previous section (Section 4.6.2) suggest that an intended gift of a legal chose in action will not be regarded as effective in equity unless the writing requirements imposed by statute on the donor have been satisfied: see, for example, *Olsson v Dyson* (**[408]** above). *If* any of the cases considered in this section supports the view that equitable choses in action can be transferred by gift notwithstanding the absence of writing satisfying the requirements of Law of Property Act 1925 section 53(1)(c), how can the distinction be justified? *Do* the cases considered in this section suggest that writing is not essential?

Note:

Remember that a gift is effective only if the donor intends to confer an *immediate* benefit on the donee (*and* also satisfies any necessary formalities to ensure that the gift is effective, either at law or in equity). If the donor intends a transfer only at some time in the future, then this is, at most, merely a promise to make a gift at some later time. Such a promise is unenforceable since it is not supported by consideration. The outcome is that the donee has neither an interest in property nor any enforceable contractual rights: see *Re McArdle* [1951] 1 Ch 669 (**[415]** below).

4.7 Gifts of future property

As noted earlier (in Section 4.2), the general rule is that a donor cannot give what is not his or hers to give. This means that a donor cannot make an immediate gift of future property (ie property which the donor does not yet own). Any attempt to do so will have no effect on the property interests of the parties concerned. An expressed intention to make such an immediate gift of future property will simply be regarded as a promise to give in the future, a promise which is not binding on the donor because it is not supported by consideration.[26] On the other hand, an expressed intention to make an immediate gift of what the donor already has may be effective either at law or in equity depending upon what else the donor has done. It is therefore crucial to be able to determine whether the subject matter of the intended gift is present or future property. The distinction is not always as easy as might be supposed, as the cases extracted below illustrate.

[414] ***Re Cook's Settlements Trust*** **[1965] Ch 902, 913–14** ***per*** **Buckley J:**
[Under a family settlement arrangement, Sir Francis Cook acquired a large number of valuable pictures. He held these absolutely, not on trust, but he covenanted that if he sold any of the pictures during his lifetime, then he would pay the proceeds of sale to the trustees of the family settlement to be held on the settlement trusts. Cook subsequently gave one of the pictures to his then wife, and she proposed to sell it. The trustees sought directions from the court as to what they ought to do if the picture was sold during Cook's lifetime and if the proceeds were not paid to the trustees. The court held that Cook's covenant was a covenant to settle a fund which did not exist at the time the agreement was made, and might never exist in the future. Accordingly, it effected no immediate transfer of property to the trustees and beneficiaries of the family settlement: there was no immediate trust. It further held, although this is not material here, that if there was a contract obliging Cook to carry out his promise, then it was a contract to which neither the trustees nor the beneficiaries of the family settlement were parties or had provided consideration, so the existence of the contract would not assist them.]

> 'The covenant with which I am concerned did not, in my opinion, create a debt enforceable at law, that is to say, a property right, which, although to bear fruit only in the future and upon a contingency, was capable of being made the subject of an immediate trust. . . . Nor is this covenant associated with property which was the subject of an immediate trust. . . . Nor did the covenant relate to property which then belonged to the covenantor. . . . In contrast to all these cases, this covenant upon its true construction is, in my opinion, an executory contract to settle a particular fund or particular funds of money which at the date of the covenant did not exist and which might never come into existence. It is analogous to a covenant to settle an expectation or to settle after-acquired property. The case, in my judgment, involves the law of contract, not the law of trusts. . . .'

[26] *Re Ellenborough* [1903] 1 Ch. 697, 700 *per* Buckley J. The result may well be quite different if the promise is made for good consideration: see Section 4.12 below.

[415] *Re McArdle* [1951] 1 Ch 669 (CA), 673–4 *per* Evershed MR, 676–7 *per* Jenkins LJ:

[The beneficiaries of a deceased's estate signed a document directed to Mrs McArdle which provided that, in consideration of her carrying out certain alterations to the property, they agreed that the executors would repay her £488 from the estate when it was distributed. The Court of Appeal held that no immediate assignment was intended. Moreover, there was no contract to assign in the future (which might have been enforced in equity) since the consideration was past consideration.]

> ***Evershed MR:***
> '... The real question—and it is by no means easy—is whether this document of 1945 was an effective equitable assignment which passed to Mrs. Marjorie McArdle an indefeasible interest in a proportionate part of the residuary estate; for, if it is not, then I think it is clear, owing to the well-established doctrine of consideration, that it must fail to give her a claim which she can litigate since there was and is no consideration passing from her to support her claim.
>
> The judge came to the conclusion that there was here an equitable assignment, and that it was unnecessary, on the authorities, for such an equitable assignment, in a case in which the subject-matter is existing property, to be supported by valuable consideration. The problem is vexed and difficult. I think it is accurately stated in *Snell's Principles of Equity* (22nd ed.), pp. 57 and 58, as follows: "Whether value is necessary for an equitable assignment is not clearly settled. It has been held that value is not necessary for an assignment of a legal thing in action which complies with the statutory provisions ... and it would seem to be unnecessary also for an assignment of an equitable thing in action, such as a legacy or an interest in trust funds, provided that the assignment is complete and perfect; there is no reason why a man should not be able to give away an equitable interest as freely as he can give away a legal interest. But value appears to be necessary for an equitable assignment of a legal thing in action; ... such an assignment being inoperative at law, the assistance of equity is needed to make it effective, and equity will not assist to make perfect an imperfect gift. Value is certainly necessary for the assignment of rights of property not yet in existence"—for the reason that where the property is not in existence something else has to be done by the giver to give effect to the gift. It can operate only in contract, if there is no subject-matter then capable of being given.
>
> The sentence in that passage, "provided that the assignment is complete and perfect", is important; also the further sentence, "there is no reason why a man should not be able to give away an equitable interest". What the writer is saying there, and I accept it, is this: if what is done amounts to a gift, complete and perfect, of a subject-matter which is an equitable chose in action, then there is no reason in principle or in authority why the donee should not take the benefit just as much as he will if the giver gives him a pound note and puts it in his hand. Since the transaction is thus perfect, the question of consideration becomes irrelevant, for consideration is only necessary to support the assertion of a right to have made perfect something which is not yet perfect—for example, a contractual right.'
>
> ***Jenkins LJ:***
> '... I am further prepared to accept the proposition that an equitable assignment of an existing interest in property of a character capable of being assigned may be a valid and binding assignment notwithstanding that it is made voluntarily—that is to say,

notwithstanding that it has no consideration to support it and is in the nature of a mere gift. . . .

But I accept that last proposition with this reservation: a voluntary equitable assignment, to be valid, must be in all respects complete and perfect so that the assignee is entitled to demand payment from the trustee or holder of the fund, and the trustee is bound to make payment to the assignee, with no further act on the part of the assignor remaining to be done to perfect the assignee's title. Failing these conditions, the voluntary assignment suffers the fate of other incomplete gifts: the donor has a locus poenitentiæ and can change his mind at any time.

No question of conscience enters into the matter, for there is no consideration, and there is nothing dishonest on the part of an intending donor if he chooses to change his mind at any time before the gift is complete.'

This next case is a good one with which to conclude this entire analysis of gifts. Not only does the case deal with future property, but in it Windeyer J sets out the whole of the law of voluntary assignments of both legal and equitable choses in action. His was a dissenting judgment, because he disagreed with the majority's view that the subject matter of the purported assignment was future property, but that does not affect his elucidation of the relevant law. His judgment provides a useful summary of this area of the law.

[416] *Norman v Federal Commissioner of Taxation* (1963) 109 CLR 9 (Aust HCt), 20–32 *per* Menzies J and 23–38 *per* Windeyer J:

[A taxpayer by deed poll purported to assign to his wife by way of gift all the interest derived during the tax year from a sum of £3,000, being part of a sum deposited by him on loan with a firm. This loan was for no fixed term, and the firm was at liberty to repay it, or any part of it, at any time without notice. By the same deed he purported to assign to his wife by way of gift all the interest, dividends, and other income arising from two estates in which he had a beneficial interest in residue. The Australian High Court held that when the deed was executed the future interest was, in each case, merely an expectancy or possibility which could not be effectively assigned without consideration and therefore the interest, when received, was assessable income in the hands of the taxpayer.]

Menzies J:

'. . . In general future property was not assignable at common law: *Lunn v. Thornton* (1845) 1 CB 379 (135 ER 587) but in equity after-acquired property was assignable for value according to the principles stated by Lord Macnaghten in *Tailby v. Official Receiver* (1888) 13 App Cas 523 [**[433]** below] but only for value notwithstanding the assignment was by deed: *In re Ellenborough* (1903) 1 Ch 697. If the interest that may arise under a contract has the character of a future rather than an existing right, the deed, lacking consideration, was not effective to entitle the assignee to the interest in question as and when it became due and payable. I regard interest which may accrue in the future upon an existing loan repayable without notice as having the character of a right to come into existence rather than of a right already in existence and I do not regard *Earle (G. & T.) (1925) Ltd. v. Hemsworth R.D.C.* (1928) 44 TLR 758; (1928) 140 LT 69, upon which Mr. Bright for the taxpayer relied, as any authority to the contrary. In that case no more was decided than that an assignment of a specific fund retained under a building contract which did not become payable until an architect's certificate was given, which happened after the date of the assignment, was a good legal assignment of a chose in action. . . . An accruing debt arising out of contract, though not payable at the date of the assignment, was, it was held, assignable at law. One other observation upon the applicability of that case to the present may be made, that is, it is not to be assumed that every right that can now be assigned at law without consideration pursuant to s. 25(6) of the Judicature Act [now the Law of Property Act 1925 s 136] and corresponding legislation can also be assigned in equity voluntarily. Thus if, as seems to be generally accepted, (see *Halsbury's Laws of England* 3rd ed., vol. 4, par. 1003), the section extends to future debts and not merely debts not presently payable, in equity as distinct from the Judicature Act, the effectiveness of voluntary assignment remains limited to existing rights and interests. See *Tailby v. Official Receiver* (1888) 13 App Cas 523 and *In re McArdle (dec'd)* (1951) 1 Ch. 669, per Jenkins L.J. (1951) 1 Ch, at p 676 [see **[415]** above]. . . .

. . . Under the contract of loan now under consideration, there was no liability for or right to interest until it began to accrue in an annual period and in 1956 the borrowers were under no liability for and the lender had no right to interest for 1958. It is not that interest for 1958 was not payable in 1956; it is that in 1956 interest for 1958 was nothing but an expectancy. It appears to me that the entries which were made in the books of the firm, clearly enough with the approval of both the assignor and the assignee, accorded with the true legal position in that the taxpayer was credited with all interest falling due upon his loan and his account was then debited and his wife's account was then credited with so much of the interest as was interest upon 3,000 pounds of the debt. To put it shortly, there were gifts of interest paid but not a gift of interest to be paid.

The conclusion I have just stated makes it unnecessary for me to consider whether, if at the time of the deed the taxpayer had a right to future interest that was capable of assignment without consideration, the deed constituted a complete and perfect transfer of that right to his wife. . . .'

Windeyer J:
'The ultimate question in this case is whether before 1st July 1957 the taxpayer had effectually assigned his right to receive certain moneys that would otherwise have been receivable by him and been part of his income for the year ending on 30th June 1958. . . . Before examining the transaction in detail, it is as well to consider the legal doctrines around which the argument revolved.

(i) As to attempted assignments of things not yet in existence:
As it is impossible for anyone to own something that does not exist, it is impossible for anyone to make a present gift of such a thing to another person, however sure he may be that it will come into existence and will then be his to give. He can, of course, promise that when the thing is his he will make it over to the intended donee. But in the meantime he may change his mind and when the time comes refuse to carry out his promise, even though it were by deed. A court of law could not compel him to perform it. A court of equity would not. Courts of equity never had the objections to all agreements about future interests that, until the seventeenth century, were deeply rooted in the common law. Equity did not share the view that such agreements were void on the ground of maintenance. But things not yet in existence could only be the subject of agreement, not of present disposition. And, in relation to promises and agreements, equity has been faithful to its maxim that it does not come to the aid of volunteers. For equity a deed does not make good a want of consideration.

If we turn from attempted gifts of future property to purported dispositions of it for value, the picture changes completely. The common law objection remains. But in equity a would-be present assignment of something to be acquired in the future is, when made for value, construed as an agreement to assign the thing when it is acquired. A court of equity will ensure that the would-be assignor performs this agreement, his conscience being bound by the consideration. The purported assignee thus gets an equitable interest in the property immediately the legal ownership of it is acquired by the assignor, assuming it to have been sufficiently described to be then identifiable. The prospective interest of the assignee is in the meantime protected by equity. These principles, which now govern assignments for value of property to be acquired in the future, have been developed and established by a line of well-known cases, of which *Holroyd v. Marshall* (1862) 10 HLC 191 (11 ER 999) [[**432**] below]; *Collyer v Isaacs* (1881) 19 Ch D 342; *Tailby v Official Receiver* (1888) 13 App Cas 523; and *In re Lind; Industrials Finance Syndicate Ltd. v. Lind* (1915) 2 Ch 345 are the most important. "And so", to use Maitland's words, "lawyers easily slipped into the way of saying that in equity one could make an assignment of goods hereafter to be acquired though one could not do so at law. This was a compendious way of putting the matter and was not likely to deceive any equity lawyer": Maitland, *Equity*, 2nd ed. (1936) p. 150. The effect of the decisions was summarized by Dixon J., as he then was, in *Palette Shoes Pty. Ltd. v. Krohn* (1937) 58 CLR 1, at pp 26, 27. These cases, however, are really beside the point in this case. We are concerned here with a purported gift, not with an assignment for value.

Mr. Bright, seeking to get around some of the obstacles that lay in his way if the transaction were held to be a voluntary assignment of future property, referred to one of Lord Chancellor Bacon's Maxims: *Licet dispositio do interesse futuro sit inutilis, tamen fieri potest declaratio praecedens quae sortiatur effectum, interveniente novo actu.* He argued from this that an ineffective assignment of future property could become retrospectively effective as from its date if, on the property coming into existence, the transferor did something to carry the assignment into effect. But that is not the result of the maxim nor of the cases that were cited. . . . The contrast that those cases make between potential property, such as the wool which will grow on my sheep, or the crops which will grow on my land, and future property, which only by a possibility will come to me, is significant in connexion with sales of goods. A purported present sale of future goods operates at law as an agreement to sell the goods. And if when the seller acquires them he delivers them, or in some other way appropriates them to the buyer, the property in them thereupon passes. This is the general rule. If, however, the goods were potentially the goods of the seller at the date of the contract, then the property will pass as soon as they come into existence—"are extant", in the words of the first of the cases mentioned above. The application of these principles to-day is explained in *Benjamin on Sale* 8th ed. (1950), pp. 138–140; *Halsbury* 3rd ed. vol. 34, pp. 64, 65 and illustrated by the cases referred to. They do not support, in fact they contradict, the taxpayer's contention. They show that a purported assignment of a thing before the thing exists can have no effect at law, except as a covenant or contract to assign. The earliest moment at which the property in the thing can actually pass is when it first becomes extant. Moreover the cases deal with sales of chattels, not with purported gifts of choses in action, which is what concerns us in this case.

(ii) As to assignments of choses in action:

In *Lampet's Case* (1612) 10 Rep 46b (77 ER 994), Coke spoke of "the great wisdom and policy of the sages and founders of our law, who have provided that no possibility, right, title, nor thing in action, shall be granted or assigned to strangers, for that would be the occasion of multiplying of contentions and suits" (1612) 10 Rep, at p. 48a (77 E.R., at p. 997). It was a somewhat unsophisticated view of legal rights that led the common lawyers to classify choses in action and debts with mere possibilities, and to condemn all assignments of them as leading to maintenance.

Assignment means the immediate transfer of an existing proprietary right, vested or contingent, from the assignor to the assignee. Anything that in the eye of the law can be regarded as an existing subject of ownership, whether it be a chose in possession or a chose in action, can to-day be assigned, unless it be excepted from the general rule on some ground of public policy or by statute. But a mere expectancy or possibility of becoming entitled in the future to a proprietary right is not an existing chose in action. It is not assignable, except in the inexact sense into which, again to use Maitland's words, lawyers slipped when it is said to be assignable in equity for value.

The distinction between a chose in action, which is an existing legal right, and a mere expectancy or possibility of a future right is of cardinal importance in this case, as will appear. It does not, in my view, depend on whether or not there is a debt presently recoverable by action because presently due and payable. A legal right to be paid money at a future date is, I consider, a present chose in action, at all events when it depends upon an existing contract on the repudiation of which an action could be brought for anticipatory breach.

[Windeyer J then considered the historical developments which led to the possibility of legal and equitable assignments of choses in action.]

. . . .What the provision of the Judicature Act, 1873, did was to render unnecessary the previous circumlocutions. Debts and other legal choses in action were made directly assignable by the statutory method. But this, while it simplified assignments, has not simplified the law surrounding them, as the argument in this case showed.

It is settled that any assignment that satisfies the requirements of the statute [the equivalent of the UK Law of Property Act section 136], is valid and fully effectual although it be voluntary. That is to say the law now provides a means whereby the legal owner of a chose in action may make a complete and perfect gift of it. That being so, and as equity does not perfect an imperfect gift, can there ever now be an effectual voluntary assignment unless all the statutory requirements are met? The question is not an easy one if a purely logical answer be sought. Equity intervened to assist the assignments of choses in action because they were not assignable at law. Now that they are, why, it may be asked, should equity aid imperfect attempts at voluntary assignments of them. On the other hand, it can be urged that the statute provides a method or machinery whereby assignment may be effected, but that it does not detract from the validity of any transaction that would have been effective in equity if it had occurred before the statute came into operation. There is some authority for the latter proposition: see e.g. *German v. Yates* (1915) 32 TLR 52. And Lord Macnaghten's well-known words in *William Brandts' Sons & Co. v. Dunlop Rubber Co.*, (1905) AC 454 are sometimes invoked in support of it: "Why that which would have been a good equitable assignment before the statute should now be invalid and inoperative because it fails to come up to the requirements of the statute, I confess I do not understand. The statute does not forbid or destroy equitable assignments or impair their efficacy in the slightest degree": (1905) AC, at p 461. But this was said in reference to an assignment for value. I do not think that his Lordship's remarks should be read as qualifying the principle that equity does not perfect imperfect voluntary assignments. If an attempt is made to assign, by way of gift, a chose in action assignable under the statute, then, as I see the matter, the requirements of the statute cannot be ignored; for the general rule of equity is that an effective assignment occurs only if the donor does all that, according to the nature of the property, he must do to transfer the property to the donee. But the weight of authority is, I think in favour of the view that in equity there is a valid gift of property transferable at law if the donor, intending to make, then and there, a complete disposition and transfer to the donee, does all that on his part is necessary to give effect to his intention and arms the donee with the means of completing the gift according to the requirements of the law: see *Brunker v. Perpetual Trustee Co. (Ltd.)* (1937) 57 CLR 555 *per* Dixon J. (1937) 57 CLR, at pp. 600–602; *Re Smith* (1901) 84 LT 835; *In re Rose* (1949) Ch 78; *In re Rose* (1952) 1 Ch 499. I think therefore that, if a man, meaning to make an immediate gift of a chose in action that is his, executes an instrument that meets the requirements of the statute and delivers it to the donee, actually or constructively, he has put it out of his power to recall his gift. It is true that until notice is given to the debtor or person against whom the chose is enforceable at law, all the requirements of the statute have not been complied with. But the notice can be given by the donee; and, if the donee has express or implied authority to give it, I think that equity would not allow the donor to deny the right of the donee to do so and so intercept his gift. I reach this conclusion with some hesitation, for it involves some departure from the majority view in *Anning v. Anning* (1907) 4 CLR 1049. But it accords, it seems to me with general principle. For these reasons I consider that, if the debt that the deed in this case purported to assign had been an existing chose in action assignable by the statutory procedure, the only question would be whether the assignor had purported to make an absolute assignment of it, and whether he did all that on his part had to be done to that end. The difficulty is that, as will appear, what it was sought to assign was part only of a prospectively larger debt.

(iii) As to assignments of part of a debt:

. . . .

[see the extract at **[406]**]

(iv) As to whether consideration is required for the equitable assignment of a chose in action not assignable at law:

. . . .

[see the extract at **[406]**]

(v) As to the facts:

. . . . Moreover, quite apart from the absence of a notice in writing [which means that the statutory procedure for assignment has not been followed], this assignment is of a part of a debt. The deed, it is true, speaks of "interest derived from the sum of three thousand pounds deposited." But there was no separate fund of 3,000 pounds in which the taxpayer had an interest; and at all relevant times the amount owing to him by the partnership exceeded 3,000 pounds. . . .

But, said the taxpayer, I do not rely upon the deed as effecting an assignment by virtue of the statute; my case is that there was an effectual assignment in equity. To this the Commissioner made two answers. First that there cannot be a voluntary assignment of an existing legal chose in action. As to that, for the reasons I have given, I do not agree. Secondly it was said a thing which is not yet in existence cannot be the subject of an equitable assignment except for consideration. That, as I have said, is undoubtedly so. It is true too that the interest, to the extent of 450 pounds, that the deed assigned was not due and payable at the date of the deed. But a contract to pay a sum of money on a future day, call it interest or what you will, calculable in amount according to conditions presently agreed, is in my view a presently existing chose in action. As between the parties to a contract of money lent at interest the borrower is simply a debtor who must pay a sum or sums (called interest) that he has, for good consideration (the forbearance of the creditor) contracted to pay to his creditor at the time or times stipulated. Why should not the creditor before the date when this debt becomes due and payable, assign his right to receive payment on the due date? He could assign the whole under the statute: *Walker v. Bradford Old Bank Ltd.* (1884) 12 QBD 511 Why not part in equity? What he assigns is not, it seems to me, a right to arise in the future but a present contractual right to be paid at a future date a sum of money, to be calculated in the agreed manner: cf. *Lett v. Morris* (1831) 4 Sim 607 (58 ER 227). In *Brice v Bannister* (1878) 3 QBD 569, Lord Coleridge CJ said "that a debt to become due is a chose in action, is clear" (1878) 3 QBD, at p 573. Interest on money lent is recoverable by action at law as a debt separate from the principal, as the common *indebitatus* count for interest shows: see *Halsbury* 3rd ed. vol. 27, p. 12.

But it was urged this case is not like a case of a loan for a fixed term. What was owing might, it is pointed out, have been repaid by the partnership, or reduced below 3,000 pounds, after the date of the deed of assignment and before 1st July 1957. As a matter of law, no doubt that is so. But it does not, I think, follow that the taxpayer had for that reason no assignable right. He had a present right to be paid interest at a future date on the money he had lent, unless in the meantime the loan was repaid. The taxpayer assigned the benefit of this contract, to the extent of 450 pounds to become due conditionally in 1958, to his wife by the deed of 1956. I consider that the deed was an effectual equitable assignment. It operated, I think, upon its delivery as a deed. The assignee had notice of it and assented. It was valid and binding as between assignor and assignee. In so far as any notice to the debtor, the partnership, was necessary to perfect it in equity as against the debtor, the companies had sufficient notice of it and acted accordingly.'

Also see:

Williams v Commissioner of Inland Revenue [1965] NZLR 395 (NZ CA).
Shepherd v Commissioner of Taxation (1965) 113 CLR 385 (Aust HCt).
Everett v Federal Commissioner for Taxation (1980) 143 CLR 440 (Aust HCt).

4.8 Conditional gifts

Sometimes a donor does not make an outright gift. Instead, a condition is imposed restricting the donee's entitlement to the gift or else restricting the donee's permitted use of the gift. For example, a gift may be subject to a condition that the donee first reach the age of 30 years, or that the gift itself be used only for the purpose of providing an education for the donee. It is then a little more difficult to decide whether the donee has any immediate proprietary interest in the gift property and, if so, what that interest might be. Proper resolution of the issue depends upon careful interpretation of the imposed condition. The first step is to decide whether the apparent restriction is truly a condition which qualifies the donor's intention to benefit the donee, or whether it merely articulates the motive for making an absolute gift. In two situations courts can be easily persuaded that the donor's intention was to give absolutely. First, many gifts between family members are construed as absolute gifts, notwithstanding an articulated and restricted purpose. This is because it is generally assumed (unless there are clear indications to the contrary) that the donor intends to benefit the donee in any event, and that the specified purpose simply indicates the motive for making the absolute gift. If this is the construction placed on the condition, then it follows that the donee is under no more than a moral obligation to use the gift for those purposes. Another indication that a nominated purpose describes the donor's motive rather than imposes a condition is where there is no 'gift over' to a third party in the event that the condition fails. If the donor does not indicate an alternative person who is to benefit if the nominated condition fails, then the inference is that the initial donee can take absolutely.

[417] *Re Osoba* [1979] 1 WLR 247 (CA), 256–7 *per* Buckley LJ:
[A testator left the residue of his estate to his wife 'for her maintenance and for the training of my daughter Abiola up to University grade and for the maintenance of my aged mother.' This was held to be an absolute gift jointly to his wife, daughter and mother.]

> 'Counsel has submitted that the trusts in favour of the daughter entitles her to no more than the payment of whatever sums might be necessary to pay for her education "to university standard," and that accordingly the trusts for the maintenance of the testator's wife and mother should also be limited to such amounts as might be required for their respective maintenance from time to time during their respective lives.
>
> Such a construction would give rise to some obvious problems. To what standards should the wife and mother be maintained? How far, if at all, would this rest in the discretion of the trustee, who would have a personal interest in the exercise of the discretion? The gift is of course not limited to income, but if the income were insufficient to pay the cost of the daughter's education and to provide for the maintenance of the wife and the mother at suitable standards, at what rate should the trustee have recourse to capital? And should any of the three purposes take priority over the others to any, and what, extent?
>
> Fortunately in my view these problems do not arise, because in my judgment it is erroneous to suppose, notwithstanding the language of the will, that the daughter's interest is limited in the way suggested. Had the trust for the daughter's benefit been the only trust declared in respect of the testator's residue, she would in my judgment have become entitled to the whole residue beneficially upon the testator's death.
>
> . . .
>
> If a testator has given the whole of a fund, whether of capital or income, to a beneficiary, whether directly or through the medium of a trustee, he is regarded, in the absence of any contra indication, as having manifested an intention to benefit that person to the full extent of the subject matter, notwithstanding that he may have expressly stated that the gift is made for a particular purpose, which may prove to be impossible of performance or which may not exhaust the subject matter. This is because the testator has given the whole fund; he has not given so much of the fund as will suffice or be required to achieve the purpose, nor so much of the fund as a trustee or anyone else should determine, but the whole fund. This must be reconciled with the testator's having specified the purpose for which the gift is made. This reconciliation is achieved by treating the reference to the purpose as merely a statement of the testator's motive in making the gift. Any other interpretation of the gift would frustrate the testator's expressed intention that the whole subject matter shall be applied for the benefit of the beneficiary. These considerations have, I think, added force where the subject matter is the testator's residue, so that any failure of the gift would result in intestacy. The specified purpose is regarded as of less significance than the dispositive act of the testator,

which sets the measure of the extent to which the testator intends to benefit the beneficiary.'

Note:

Contrast this case with *Re Sanderson's Trust* (1857) 3 K & J 497, 69 ER 1206. There, a testator left all his property to trustees to apply the whole or any part of the income towards the maintenance of his brother. Page-Wood V-C held that the gift was for the specified purpose only because the trustees had a discretion to apply only part of the income towards it.

Even if the court accepts that the donor truly intends to impose a condition on the gift-giving, the courts may sometimes decline to give effect to the restriction. If the stipulated condition is too uncertain, then the courts will not enforce it. More often, however, the court's refusal is based on policy concerns. On this basis the courts will strike out conditions which offend the rules against perpetuities and accumulations[27] (these are rules which are designed to restrict the donor's ability to control his or her property from the grave); they will also strike out conditions which are illegal or which interfere unacceptably with the donee's life. *Re Piper*[28] illustrates this last category: a gift to four children was made on the condition that they attain the age of 30 years and not reside with their father. The latter condition was held to be invalid because it was calculated to separate the children from their father, and the children were allowed to take the gift free of the condition.

If the court accepts that the donor intended to make a conditional gift, and that the condition is valid, then it becomes necessary to discover the nature of the condition to determine the proprietary interest acquired by the donee. The condition may be either a condition precedent or a condition subsequent. If it is a condition precedent, then the condition must be fulfilled before the donee becomes entitled to the gift; until then, the donee has no proprietary interest in the property. On the other hand, if the condition is a condition subsequent, then the donee will take title to the property but will be liable to lose it upon the happening of the condition subsequent. If the disposition will bear either construction, then the courts are inclined to treat it as a condition subsequent: there is a *prima facie* presumption in favour of early vesting.

Finally, mention should be made of *donationes mortis causa*. These are gifts made in contemplation of the donor's impending death and conditional upon death eventuating. In *Sen v Headley*,[29] Nourse LJ set out the requirements for a valid *donationes mortis causa*:

> 'First, the gift must be made in contemplation, although not necessarily in expectation, of impending death. Secondly, the gift must be made upon the condition that it is to be absolute and perfected only on the donor's death, being revocable until that event occurs and ineffective if it does not. Thirdly, there must be delivery of the subject

[27] Perpetuities and Accumulations Act 1964. Also see F H Lawson and B Rudden, *The Law of Property* (2nd ed, 1982, Clarendon Press: Oxford) pp 176–87.

[28] [1946] 2 All ER 503.

[29] [1991] Ch 425 (CA).

> matter of the gift, or the essential indicia of title thereto, which amounts to a parting with dominion and not mere physical possession over the subject matter of the gift.'[30]

This description makes it clear that the donor will generally retain legal title to the property, even if possession has been transferred to the donee. Legal title will only pass from one party to the other in accordance with the donor's intention—ie on the donor's death. However, even if the donor does transfer legal title to the donee, the donor can recall the gift at any time before death. In the interim it seems that the donee holds the property on trust for the donor: this seems the only way in which it could be said that the gift does not take effect until the donor's death.[31]

FURTHER READING:

R Chambers, 'Conditional Gifts' in N Palmer and E McKendrick (eds), *Interests in Goods* (2nd edn, 1998, Lloyds of London Press: London), ch 18.

4.9 Gifts which may be recalled

Sometimes a donor who has made a gift suffers a change of heart and wishes to recall the gift. Since promises to give cannot be enforced, if the donor acts before *either* legal or equitable title to the property has passed to the donee, then recall is possible. However, if the donor does not act until later, then recall is rarely possible. The policy in favour of security of receipts favours finality. Nevertheless, sometimes the circumstances are such that it would be unconscionable to allow the donee to retain the gift. Then recall is possible. This is generally because the gift was induced by mistake (only certain types of mistake will suffice), fraud, misrepresentation or undue influence. The following cases illustrate the possibilities.

[418] *Lady Hood of Avalon v Mackinnon* [1909] 1 Ch 476, 480–4 *per* Eve J:
[Lady Hood entered into a deed of gift to give £8,600 to her elder daughter, intending that both her daughters be treated equally and forgetting that she had already given half her estate to the elder daughter. The court held that she was entitled to rescind the deed.]

> 'From what I have stated, I think I have made this much clear, that the sole origin of the deed poll of August 4, 1904, was the intention of Lady Hood to bring about equality between her daughters, and that although, in form, the transaction takes the form of appointing a sum of £8600 to the elder daughter, in substance it was to be such an appointment as should give to the elder daughter an interest in the funds subject to

30 [1991] Ch 425 (CA) 431–2.

31 Eg, *Staniland v Willott* (1852) 3 M & G 664, 42 ER 416, where the donor transferred legal title to certain shares to the donee and then successfully reclaimed them when he recovered his health. It seems the trust must have arisen at the time of the transfer, not later when the donor reclaimed the property, because the donor was entitled to an account of the dividends and sale proceeds received by the donee in the interim period.

appointment equal to that which had already been given to the younger daughter. Further, when Lady Hood gave those instructions and when she executed that deed poll she had no recollection of the fact that she had already been party to an appointment to her elder daughter of a moiety of the fund.

Now the question is whether, in that state of facts, I can, consistently with the law, say that such a mistake on the part of the appointor entitles her to have the deed rescinded. . . .

. . . I accept [Lady Hood's] statement that she executed this second deed in entire forgetfulness of the earlier deed. Now is such forgetfulness such a mistake as entitles a party seeking to reform or rescind a deed to relief? Courts of first instance have pointed out, and the Court of Appeal has pointed out, that there is no satisfactory definition of what mistake is. . . . It seems to me that when a person has forgotten the existence of a pre-existing fact, and assumes that such fact did not pre-exist, he is labouring under a mistake, and he acts on the footing that the fact really did not pre-exist; and, . . . I should have thought that a man makes a mistake in forgetting an existing fact quite as much as he does in assuming a state of things to exist which does not in fact exist. . .

. . . [Citing Kay LJ in *Barrow v Isaacs & Son* [1891] 1 QB 420, 425 "The case of *Kelly v. Solari* (9 M. W. 54), however, and the observation of Lord Blackburn in the House of Lords in *Brownlie v. Campbell* (5 App. Cas. 952) establish that, in an action to recover money paid by mistake, it is sufficient to prove that at the time of the payment the person paying was actually ignorant that the money was not due, although he had the means of knowledge, and it was owing to his own carelessness or forgetfulness, that he was in fact ignorant. There undoubtedly forgetfulness of the previous payment is treated as mistake." Then he goes on, as Mr. Whinney has quite properly pointed out, to say that in those cases, that is, the payment over again of money, there was this additional element, that the payee was in possession of money of which he ought not to be allowed to remain in possession, and therefore the Court could not allow him to retain that to which he was not entitled. But, on the other hand, there is the distinct statement by the Lord Justice that forgetfulness of the previous payment is treated as mistake in the cases to which he refers.

Having regard to the facts which I have stated, I must assume that Lady Hood, intending only to bring about equality between her daughters, was labouring under a mistake when she thought that equality would be brought about by the execution of the deed appointing £8600 to her elder daughter. It was obviously a mistake, because the effect of the execution of that deed was to bring about that which Lady Hood never intended and never contemplated. I think she executed the deed under a mistake with regard to the existing facts, and I cannot myself see that it is material whether that mistake arose from her being misinformed as to the true state of things, or from her state of mind being such that she had not, at that moment, knowledge of the true state of things. The absence of knowledge arose from her not bearing in mind, or not appreciating, that she had already appointed to the elder daughter a moiety of the fund, and in these circumstances I feel bound to hold, and, having regard to the evidence, I am glad to be able to hold, that this deed which it is sought to rescind was executed by Lady Hood under a mistake brought about by such circumstances as entitle her to the relief she seeks. Accordingly I make an order that the deed be rescinded and set aside.'

Questions:

What was the basis of this decision? Since this gift was promised by deed, can rescission be justified? Should the sort of mistake which justifies recall of a 'gift' be different from that which allows recall under a 'contract'? Is rescission different from rectification—in particular, is this a case where rectification is possible?

[419] *Allcard v Skinner* (1887) 36 ChD 145 (CA), 185–7 *per* Lindley LJ:
[Allcard became a member of a sisterhood which operated according to rules of poverty, chastity and obedience. The rule of poverty required members to give up all their property, and the rules of obedience required members to look up to the Mother Superior, Skinner, and enjoined them from seeking outside advice without the Superior's leave. On joining the sisterhood, Allcard left all her considerable property to Skinner. Six years after leaving the sisterhood, Allcard attempted to recover it.]

'Two questions are raised by the appeal, namely, 1st, Whether the gifts made by the Plaintiff to the sisterhood were revocable or irrevocable when made? 2nd, Whether, assuming them to have been revocable when made, it was competent for the Plaintiff to revoke them when she did?

The first question is one of great importance and difficulty. Its solution requires a careful consideration of the legal effect of gifts by persons of mature age who feel bound by vows and rules to give away their property, but who have taken the vows and submitted to the rules voluntarily and without pressure, and who are subject to no other coercion or influence than necessarily result from the vows and rules themselves, and from the state of their own mind.

There is no statutory law in this country prohibiting such gifts unless what is given is land or money to be laid out in land. These are provided for by the Mortmain and Charitable Uses Acts. But they have no application to this case. The common law, as distinguished from equity, does not invalidate such gifts as these. There being no duress or fraud, the only ground for impeaching such gifts at law would be want of capacity on the part of the donor; and although the Plaintiff was a religious enthusiast, no one could treat her as in point of law *non compos mentis*. There is no authority whatever for saying that her gifts were invalid at law. It is to the doctrines of equity, then, that recourse must be had to invalidate such gifts, if they are to be invalidated. The doctrine relied upon by the Appellant is the doctrine of undue influence expounded and enforced in *Huguenin v. Baseley* (14 Ves. 273) and other cases of that class. These cases may be subdivided into two groups, which, however, often overlap.

First, there are the cases in which there has been some unfair and improper conduct, some coercion from outside, some overreaching, some form of cheating, and generally, though not always, some personal advantage obtained by a donee placed in some close and confidential relation to the donor. . . .

The second group consists of cases in which the position of the donor to the donee has been such that it has been the duty of the donee to advise the donor, or even to manage his property for him. In such cases the Court throws upon the donee the burden of proving that he has not abused his position, and of proving that the gift made to him has not been brought about by any undue influence on his part. In this class of cases it has been considered necessary to shew that the donor had independent advice, and was removed from the influence of the donee when the gift to him was made. *Huguenin v. Baseley* was a case of this kind. The defendant had not only acquired considerable spiritual influence over the plaintiff, but was intrusted by her with the management of her property. His duty to her was clear, and it was with reference to persons so situated that Lord Eldon used the language so often quoted and so much relied on in this case. He said (14 Ves. 299): "Take it that she (the plaintiff) intended to give it to him (the defendant): it is by no means out of the reach of the principle. The question is, not, whether she knew, what she was doing, had done, or proposed to do, but how the intention was produced: whether all that care and providence was placed round her, as against those, who advised her, which, from their situation and relation with respect to her, they were bound to exert on her behalf." This principle has been constantly recognised and acted upon in subsequent cases, but in all of them, as in *Huguenin v. Baseley* (14 Ves. 273) itself, it was the duty of the donee to advise and take care of the donor. Where there is no such duty the language of Lord Eldon ceases to be applicable.

...

I have not been able to find any case in which a gift has been set aside on the ground of undue influence which does not fall within one or other or both of the groups above mentioned. Nor can I find any authority which actually covers the present case. But it does not follow that it is not reached by the principle on which the Court has proceeded in dealing with the cases which have already called for decision. They illustrate but do not limit the principle applied to them.

The principle must be examined. What then is the principle? Is it that it is right and expedient to save persons from the consequences of their own folly? or is it that it is right and expedient to save them from being victimised by other people? In my opinion the doctrine of undue influence is founded upon the second of these two principles. Courts of Equity have never set aside gifts on the ground of the folly, imprudence, or want of foresight on the part of donors. The Courts have always repudiated any such jurisdiction. *Huguenin v. Baseley* (14 Ves. 273) is itself a clear authority to this effect. It would obviously be to encourage folly, recklessness, extravagance and vice if persons could get back property which they foolishly made away with, whether by giving it to charitable institutions or by bestowing it on less worthy objects. On the other hand, to protect people from being forced, tricked or misled in any way by others into parting with their property is one of the most legitimate objects of all laws; and the equitable doctrine of undue influence has grown out of and been developed by the necessity of grappling with insidious forms of spiritual tyranny and with the infinite varieties of fraud.

As no Court has ever attempted to define fraud so no Court has ever attempted to define undue influence, which includes one of its many varieties. The undue influence which Courts of Equity endeavour to defeat is the undue influence of one person over another; not the influence of enthusiasm on the enthusiast who is carried away by it, unless indeed such enthusiasm is itself the result of external undue influence. But the influence of one mind over another is very subtle, and of all influences religious influence is the most dangerous and the most powerful, and to counteract it Courts of Equity have gone very far. They have not shrunk from setting aside gifts made to persons in a position to exercise undue influence over the donors, although there has been no proof of the actual exercise of such influence; and the Courts have done this on the avowed ground of the necessity of going this length in order to protect persons from the exercise of such influence under circumstances which render proof of it impossible. The Courts have required proof of its non-exercise, and, failing that proof, have set aside gifts otherwise unimpeachable. In this particular case I cannot find any proof that any gift made by the Plaintiff was the result of any actual exercise of power or influence on the part of the lady superior or of Mr. Nihill, apart from the influence necessarily incidental to their position in the sisterhood. Everything that the Plaintiff did is in my opinion referable to her own willing submission to the vows she took and to the rules which she approved, and to her own enthusiastic devotion to the life and work of the sisterhood. This enthusiasm and devotion were nourished, strengthened and intensified by the religious services of the sisterhood and by the example and influence of those about her. But she chose the life and work; such fetters as bound her were voluntarily put upon her by herself; she could shake them off at any time had she thought fit, and had she had the courage so to do; and no unfair advantage whatever was taken of her. Under these circumstances it is going a long way to hold that she can invoke the doctrine of undue influence to save her from the consequences of her own acts, and to entitle her to avoid the gifts she made when in a state of mind different from that in which she now is. I am by no means insensible of the difficulty of going so far.

Nevertheless, consider the position in which the Plaintiff had placed herself. She had vowed poverty and obedience, and she was not at liberty to consult externs without the leave of her superior. She was not a person who treated her vows lightly; she was deeply religious and felt bound by her promise, by her vows, and by the rules of the sisterhood. She was absolutely in the power of the lady superior and Mr. Nihill. A gift made by her under these circumstances to the lady superior cannot in my opinion be retained by the donee. The equitable title of the donee is imperfect by reason of the influence inevitably resulting from her position, and which influence experience has taught the Courts to regard as undue. Whatever doubt I might have had on this point if there had been no rule against consulting externs, that rule in my judgment turns the scale against the Defendant. In the face of that rule the gifts made to the sisterhood cannot be supported in the absence of proof that the Plaintiff could have obtained independent advice if she wished for it, and that she knew that she would have been allowed to obtain such advice if she had desired to do so. I doubt whether the gifts could have been supported if such proof had been given, unless there was also proof that she was free to act on the advice which might be given to her. But the rule itself is so oppressive and so easily abused that any person subject to it is in my opinion brought within the class of those whom it is the duty of the Court to protect from possible imposition. The gifts cannot be supported without proof of more freedom in fact than the Plaintiff can be supposed to have actually enjoyed. . . .

. . .

Where a gift is made to a person standing in a confidential relation to the donor, the Court will not set aside the gift if of a small amount simply on the ground that the donor had no independent advice. In such a case, some proof of the exercise of the influence of the donee must be given. The mere existence of such influence is not enough in such a case; see the observations of Lord Justice Turner in *Rhodes v. Bate* (Law Rep. 1 Ch. 258). But if the gift is so large as not to be reasonably accounted for on the ground of friendship, relationship, charity, or other ordinary motives on which ordinary men act, the burden is upon the donee to support the gift. So, in a case like this, a distinction might well be made between gifts of capital and gifts of income, and between gifts of moderate amount and gifts of large sums, which a person unfettered by vows and oppressive rules would not be likely to wish to make. In this case the

Plaintiff gave away practically all she could, although, having a life interest in other property, she did not reduce herself to a state of poverty.

As I have already stated, I believe that in this case there was in fact no unfair or undue influence brought to bear upon the Plaintiff other than such as inevitably resulted from the training she had received, the promise she had made, the vows she had taken, and the rules to which she had submitted herself. But her gifts were in fact made under a pressure which, whilst it lasted, the Plaintiff could not resist, and were not, in my opinion, past recall when that pressure was removed. When the Plaintiff emancipated herself from the spell by which she was bound, she was entitled to invoke the aid of the Court in order to obtain the restitution from the Defendant of so much of the Plaintiff's property as had not been spent in accordance with the wishes of the Plaintiff, but remained in the hands of the Defendant. The Plaintiff now demands no more. . . .

[The second point, whether it was too late for Allcard to recover the gift, is not material to this chapter, although note the next statement.]

. . . .The case by no means rests on mere lapse of time. There is far more than inactivity and delay on the part of the Plaintiff. There is conduct amounting to confirmation of her gift. Gifts liable to be set aside by the Court on the ground of undue influence have always been treated as voidable and not void.'

Questions:

1. What is the position of third parties to whom the donee has *sold* or *given* the gift property, if the disposition to the third party occurred:
   (i) before the donee was notified of the donor's recall of the gift (see Section 4.2 above)?; or
   (ii) after the donee was notified of the donor's recall of the gift (see Chapter 6, below)?
2. Is the donor's recovery limited to the property still remaining in the donee's hands at the time the gift is recalled?

[420] *Tribe v Tribe* [1996] Ch 107 (CA), 124–5, 128, 132–5 *per* Millett LJ:
[A father transferred shares to his son for no consideration and for the purpose of deceiving his creditors. This illegal purpose was never carried into effect. The son then refused to re-transfer shares. The father successfully claimed that he had an equitable interest in the shares and so was entitled to recover them.]

'There are, in my opinion, two questions of some importance which fall for decision in the present case. The first is whether, once property has been transferred to a transferee for an illegal purpose in circumstances which give rise to the presumption of advancement, it is still open to the transferor to withdraw from the transaction before the purpose has been carried out and, having done so, give evidence of the illegal purpose in order to rebut the presumption of advancement [see Section 5.4.3]. The second is whether, if so, it is sufficient for him to withdraw from the transaction because it is no longer necessary and without repenting of his illegal purpose. I shall deal with these two questions in turn. . . .

. . .

In *Tinsley v. Milligan* [1994] 1 A.C. 340 [**[509]** below], 370 Lord Browne-Wilkinson summarised the common law rules which govern the effect of illegality on the acquisition and enforcement of property rights in three propositions:

> "(1) property in chattels and land can pass under a contract which is illegal and therefore would have been unenforceable as a contract; (2) a plaintiff can at law enforce property rights so acquired provided that he does not need to rely on the illegal contract for any purpose other than providing the basis of his claim to a property right; (3) it is irrelevant that the illegality of the underlying agreement was either pleaded or emerged in evidence: if the plaintiff has acquired legal title under the illegal contract that is enough."

The decision of the majority of their Lordships in that case was that the same principles applied in equity. It is, therefore, now settled that neither at law nor in equity may a party rely on his own fraud or illegality in order to found a claim or rebut a presumption, but that the common law and equity alike will assist him to protect and enforce his property rights if he can do so without relying on the fraud or illegality. This is the primary rule.

It is, however, also settled both at law and in equity that a person who has transferred property for an illegal purpose can nevertheless recover his property provided that he withdraws from the transaction before the illegal purpose has been wholly or partly performed. This is the doctrine of the *locus poenitentiae* and it applies in equity as well as at law: see *Symes v. Hughes* (1870) L.R. 9 Eq. 475 for the former and *Taylor v. Bowers* (1876) 1 Q.B.D. 291 for the latter. The availability of the doctrine in a restitutionary context was expressly confirmed by Lord Browne-Wilkinson in *Tinsley v. Milligan* [1994] 1 A.C. 340, 374.

While both principles are well established, the nature of the relationship between them is unclear. Is the doctrine of the locus poenitentiae coextensive with and by way of general exception to the primary rule? The question in the present case is whether a plaintiff who has made a gratuitous transfer of property to a person in whose favour the presumption of advancement arises can withdraw from the transaction before the illegal purpose has been carried into effect and then recover the property by leading evidence of his illegal purpose in order to rebut the presumption. Closely connected with this question is its converse: is a plaintiff who has made such a transfer in circumstances which give rise to a resulting trust so that he has no need to rely on the illegal purpose, as in *Tinsley v. Milligan* itself, barred from recovering if the illegal purpose has been carried out? If both questions are answered in the negative, then either the *locus poenitentiae* is a common law doctrine which has no counterpart in equity or it is a contractual doctrine which has no place in the law of restitution.

. . . .

Prior to *Tinsley v. Milligan* [1994] 1 A.C. 340 no transferor had ever succeeded in recovering his property by enforcing a resulting trust where he had transferred the property for an illegal purpose and that purpose had been carried out. In *In re Great Berlin Steamboat Co.*, 26 Ch.D. 616 the transferor failed to recover for this very reason; in other cases where the transferor has succeeded he did so only because the illegal purpose had not been carried out.

In *Tinsley v. Milligan* [1994] 1 A.C. 340 the parties, who both contributed to the purchase of a house, arranged for the conveyance to be taken in the name of the plaintiff alone but on the understanding that it was to belong to them jointly. The purpose of this arrangement was to enable the defendant to perpetrate frauds on the Department of Social Security, and over a number of years the defendant, with the connivance of the plaintiff, made false claims for benefit. Despite this the defendant was allowed to recover.

In his dissenting speech Lord Goff of Chieveley refused to draw any distinction between cases where the presumption of advancement applied and cases in which the plaintiff could rely on a resulting trust. From the authorities he derived a single principle: that if one party puts property in the name of another for a fraudulent or illegal purpose neither law nor equity will allow him to recover the property: see p. 356. Even if he can establish a resulting trust in his favour he cannot enforce it. Given Lord Goff's opinion that there was but one principle in play, it was natural for him to describe the doctrine of the *locus poenitentiae* as an exception to that principle. Since the defendant could not bring herself within the exception, he would have allowed the appeal. This was not, however, the view of the majority. Lord Browne-Wilkinson expressly held, at p. 371, that the rule was the same whether the plaintiff founded himself on a legal or an equitable title; he was entitled to succeed if he was not forced to rely on his own illegality, even if it emerged that the title on which he relied was acquired in the course of carrying through an illegal transaction. The defendant had established a resulting trust by showing that she had contributed to the purchase price and that there was a common understanding between her and the plaintiff that they should own the house equally. She had no need to allege or prove why she had allowed the house to be conveyed into the sole name of the plaintiff, since that fact was irrelevant to her claim.

. . .

There is no modern case in which restitution has been denied in circumstances comparable to those of the present case where the illegal purpose has not been carried out. In *Tinsley v. Milligan* Lord Browne-Wilkinson expressly recognised, at p. 374, the availability of the doctrine of the locus poenitentiae in a restitutionary context, and cited *Taylor v. Bowers*, 1 Q.B.D. 291 as well as *Symes v. Hughes*, L.R. 9 Eq. 475 without disapproval. In my opinion the weight of the authorities supports the view that a person who seeks to recover property transferred by him for an illegal purpose can lead evidence of his dishonest intention whenever it is necessary for him to do so provided that he has withdrawn from the transaction before the illegal purpose has been carried out. It is not necessary if he can rely on an express or resulting trust in his favour; but it is necessary (i) if he brings an action at law and (ii) if he brings proceedings in equity and needs to rebut the presumption of advancement. The availability of the *locus poenitentiae* is well documented in the former case. I would not willingly adopt a rule which differentiated between the rule of the common law and that of equity in a restitutionary context.

. . .

At heart the question for decision in the present case is one of legal policy. The primary rule which precludes the court from lending its assistance to a man who founds his cause of action on an illegal or immoral act often leads to a denial of justice. The justification for this is that the rule is not a principle of justice but a principle of policy: see the much quoted statement of Lord Mansfield C.J. in *Holman v. Johnson* (1775) 1 Cowp. 341, 343. The doctrine of the *locus poenitentiae* is an exception which operates to mitigate the harshness of the primary rule. It enables the court to do justice between the parties even though, in order to do so, it must allow a plaintiff to give evidence of his own dishonest intent. But he must have withdrawn from the transaction while his dishonesty still lay in intention only. The law draws the line once the intention has been wholly or partly carried into effect.

Seen in this light the doctrine of the *locus poenitentiae*, although an exception to the primary rule, is not inconsistent with the policy which underlies it. . . .

. . .

In my opinion the following propositions represent the present state of the law. (1) Title to property passes both at law and in equity even if the transfer is made for an illegal purpose. The fact that title has passed to the transferee does not preclude the transferor from bringing an action for restitution. (2) The transferor's action will fail if it would be illegal for him to retain any interest in the property. (3) Subject to (2) the transferor can recover the property if he can do so without relying on the illegal purpose. This will normally be the case where the property was transferred without consideration in circumstances where the transferor can rely on an express declaration of trust or a resulting trust in his favour. (4) It will almost invariably be so where the illegal purpose has not been carried out. It may be otherwise where the illegal purpose has been carried out and the transferee can rely on the transferor's conduct as inconsistent with his retention of a beneficial interest. (5) The transferor can lead evidence of the illegal purpose whenever it is necessary for him to do so provided that he has withdrawn from the transaction before the illegal purpose has been wholly or partly carried into effect. It will be necessary for him to do so (i) if he brings an action at law or (ii) if he brings proceedings in equity and needs to rebut the presumption of advancement. (6) The only way in which a man can protect his property from his creditors is by divesting himself of all beneficial interest in it. Evidence that he transferred the property in order to protect it from his creditors, therefore, does nothing by itself to rebut the presumption of advancement; it reinforces it. To rebut the presumption it is necessary to show that he intended to retain a beneficial interest and conceal it from his creditors. (7) The court should not conclude that this was his intention without compelling circumstantial evidence to this effect. The identity of the transferee and the circumstances in which the transfer was made would be highly relevant. It is unlikely that the court would reach such a conclusion where the transfer was made in the absence of an imminent and perceived threat from known creditors.

[And on the particular issue of when a party can legitimately withdraw from an illegal contract. . .]

It is impossible to reconcile all the authorities on the circumstances in which a party to an illegal contract is permitted to withdraw from it. . . .

The academic articles Grodecki, "In Pari Delicto Potior Est Conditio Defendentis" (1955) 71 L.Q.R. 254, Beatson, "Repudiation of Illegal Purpose as a Ground for Repudiation" (1975) 91 L.Q.R. 313 and Merkin, "Restitution by Withdrawal from Executory Illegal Contracts" (1981) 97 L.Q.R. 420 are required reading for anyone who attempts the difficult task of defining the precise limits of the doctrine. I would draw back from any such attempt. But I would hold that genuine repentance is not required. Justice is not a reward for merit; restitution should not be confined to the penitent. I would also hold that voluntary withdrawal from an illegal transaction when it has ceased to be needed is sufficient. It is true that this is not necessary to encourage withdrawal, but a rule to the opposite effect could lead to bizarre results. . . .

Also see:

Tinsley v Milligan [1994] 1 AC 340 and the discussion of resulting trusts in Chapter 5 below.

Question:

The issue of recalling gifts is a complicated one. An intention to make a gift is an essential component of gift-giving. Because of this it seems sensible for the law to say that a donor who does not truly intend to make a gift, but who acts under pressure (because of duress or undue influence, for example), should be allowed to recall the gift once the pressure is removed. The issue is more difficult when there *is* a genuine intention to make a gift, but the motivation for the gift later turns out to have been unwarranted (as in *Lady Hood*). It is even more difficult where there is no genuine intention to make a gift, but only to create the appearance of a gift so as to mislead or defraud strangers to the transaction (as in *Tribe v Tribe* or *Tinsley v Milligan*). Does the law in this area appropriately balance the rights of the donor, the donee and any third parties dealing with them?

4.10 Sales of goods[32]

The previous sections dealt with gifts of personal property. These next sections deal with sales. The essence of contract of sale is that the seller transfers property to the buyer for a money consideration called the price. As with the discussion on gifts, the important issue for the purposes of this chapter is to determine *when* property passes from the seller to the buyer. Sales of goods must be considered separately from sales of other types of personal property, since the rules on passing of property differ. This difference exists because contracts for the sale of goods are governed by the Sale of Goods Act 1979, which determines many of the proprietary issues with which this section is concerned.

'Goods' are defined in the Sale of Goods Act 1979 section 61(1) as including 'all personal chattels other than things in action and money, and in Scotland all corporeal moveables except money' and specifically as also including 'emblements, industrial growing crops and things attached to or forming part of the land which are agreed to be severed before sale or under the contract of sale'. With only minor exceptions, then, the Sale of Goods Act 1979 is concerned with sales of choses in possession.

The following sections on sales of goods look at the rules which relate to the passing of legal title and equitable title to goods, and the impact on the parties of any failure to pass title as intended by the arrangement between the parties.

[32] This discussion of sales of goods is both issue-specific and rather cursory, although it sufficiently illustrates the points which are relevant to this chapter. For further detail, see any of the leading texts on sales of goods: P S Atiyah and J N Adams, *The Sale of Goods* (9th ed, 1995, Pitman Publishing: London); A G Guest et al (eds), *Benjamin's Sale of Goods* (5th ed, 1997, Sweet & Maxwell: London); R M Goode, *Commercial Law* (2nd ed, 1995, Penguin: Harmondsworth); M G Bridge, *The Sale of Goods* (1997, Clarendon Press: Oxford).

4.10.1 Sale of goods—passing of legal title to the property

Contracts for the sale of goods require no formality (Sale of Goods Act 1979 section 4). There is no need for writing or for formal words. With such contracts, the Sale of Goods Act 1979 sections 16–19 provides rules governing the transfer of legal title to the sale property. The basic rule is that property passes when the parties intend it to pass (section 17). The principal difficulty in applying this basic rule is that the intention of the parties is seldom stated expressly, and the courts are forced to look to the other factors referred to in section 17(2) in an attempt to see what can be implied. If the parties' express or implied intentions are unclear, then section 18 lays down a series of rebuttable presumptions concerning the passing of property. In practice these presumptions generally dominate any consideration of the passing of property. The Sale of Goods Act 1979 section 20(1) provides a further rebuttable presumption, that risk and property pass together. This means that as a general rule the risk of loss, damage or deterioration falls on the owner of the goods.

[421] The Sale of Goods Act 1979 sections 16–18, 20A, 20B:

'16. Goods must be ascertained

Subject to section 20A below, where there is a contract for the sale of unascertained goods no property in the goods is transferred to the buyer unless and until the goods are ascertained.

17. Property passes when intended to pass

(1) Where there is a contract for the sale of specific or ascertained goods the property in them is transferred to the buyer at such time as the parties to the contract intend it to be transferred.

(2) For the purpose of ascertaining the intention of the parties regard shall be had to the terms of the contract, the conduct of the parties and the circumstances of the case.

18. Rules for ascertaining intention

Unless a different intention appears, the following are rules for ascertaining the intention of the parties as to the time at which the property in the goods is to pass to the buyer.

Rule 1.—Where there is an unconditional contract for the sale of specific goods in a deliverable state the property in the goods passes to the buyer when the contract is made, and it is immaterial whether the time of payment or the time of delivery, or both, be postponed.

Rule 2.—Where there is a contract for the sale of specific goods and the seller is bound to do something to the goods for the purpose of putting them into a deliverable state, the property does not pass until the thing is done and the buyer has notice that it has been done.

Rule 3.—Where there is a contract for the sale of specific goods in a deliverable state but the seller is bound to weigh, measure, test, or do some other act or thing with reference to the goods for the purpose of ascertaining the price, the property does not pass until the act or thing is done and the buyer has notice that it has been done.

Rule 4.—When goods arc delivered to the buyer on approval or on sale or return or other similar terms the property in the goods passes to the buyer:—

(a) when he signifies his approval or acceptance to the seller or does any other act adopting the transaction;

(b) if he does not signify his approval or acceptance to the seller but returns the goods without giving notice of rejection, then, if a time has been fixed for the return of the goods, on the expiration of that time, and, if no time has been fixed on the expiration of a reasonable time.

Rule 5.—(1) Where there is a contract for the sale of unascertained or future goods by description, and goods of that description and in a deliverable state are unconditionally appropriated to the contract, either by the seller with the assent of the buyer or by the buyer with the assent of the seller, the property in the goods then passes to the buyer; and the assent may be express or implied, and may be given either before of after the appropriation is made.

(2) Where, in pursuance of the contract, the seller delivers the goods to the buyer or to a carrier or other bailee or custodier (whether named by the buyer or not) for the purpose of transmission to the buyer, and does not reserve the right of disposal, he is to be taken to have unconditionally appropriated the goods to the contract.

(3) Where there is a contract for the sale of a specified quantity of unascertained goods in a deliverable state forming part of a bulk which is identified either in the contract or by subsequent agreement between the parties and the bulk is reduced to (or to less than) that quantity, then, if the buyer under that contract is the only buyer to whom goods are then due out of the bulk—

(a) the remaining goods are to be taken as appropriated to that contract at the time when the bulk is so reduced; and

(b) the property in those goods then passes to that buyer.

(4) Paragraph (3) above applies also (with the necessary modifications) where a bulk is reduced to (or to less than) the aggregate of the quantities due to a single buyer under separate contracts relating to that bulk and he is the only buyer to whom goods are then due out of that bulk.

20A. Undivided shares in goods forming part of a bulk

(1) This section applies to a contract for the sale of a specified quantity of unascertained goods if the following conditions are met—

(a) the goods or some of them form part of a bulk which is identified either in the contract or by subsequent agreement between the parties; and

(b) the buyer has paid the price for some or all of the goods which are the subject of the contract and which form part of the bulk.

(2) Where this section applies, then (unless the parties agree otherwise), as soon as the conditions specified in paragraphs (a) and (b) of subsection (1) above are met or at such later time as the parties may agree—

(a) property in an undivided share in the bulk is transferred to the buyer; and

(b) the buyer becomes an owner in common of the bulk.

(3) Subject to subsection (4) below, for the purposes of this section, the undivided share of a buyer in a bulk at any time shall be such share as the quantity of goods paid for and due to the buyer out of the bulk bears to the quantity of goods in the bulk at that time.

(4) Where the aggregate of the undivided shares of buyers in a bulk determined under subsection (3) above would at any time exceed the whole of the bulk at that time, the undivided share in the bulk of each buyer shall be reduced proportionately so that the aggregate of the undivided shares is equal to the whole bulk.

(5) Where a buyer has paid the price for only some of the goods due to him out of a

bulk, any delivery to the buyer out of the bulk shall, for the purposes of this section, be ascribed in the first place to the goods in respect of which payment has been made.

(6) For the purpose of this section payment of part of the price for any goods shall be treated as payment for a corresponding part of the goods.

20B. Deemed consent by co-owner to dealings in bulk goods

(1) A person who has become an owner in common of a bulk by virtue of section 20A above shall be deemed to have consented to—

(a) any delivery of goods out of the bulk to any other owner in common of the bulk, being goods which are due to him under his contract;

(b) any removal, dealing with, delivery or disposal of goods in the bulk by any other person who is an owner in common of the bulk in so far as the goods fall within that co-owner's undivided share in the bulk at the time of the removal, dealing, delivery or disposal.

(2) No cause of action shall accrue to anyone against a person by reason of that person having acted in accordance with paragraph (a) or (b) of subsection (1) above in reliance on any consent deemed to have been given under that subsection.

(3) Nothing in this section or section 20A above shall—

(a) impose an obligation on a buyer of goods out of a bulk to compensate any other buyer of goods out of that bulk for any shortfall in the goods received by that other buyer;

(b) affects any contractual arrangement between buyers of goods out of a bulk for adjustments between themselves; or

(c) affect the rights of any buyer under his contract.'

These statutory rules make it clear that precise identification of the sale property is crucial if the purchaser is to be able to assert legal title to the sale property. Purchasers can easily be lulled into a false sense of security by the documentation relating to the sale, only to find later that they have no title to goods they intended to purchase. The cases extracted in Section 4.10.3 illustrate some typical problems, and may be contrasted with the next case, where the court adopted a more generous view of what constitutes adequate identification and appropriation of the intended sale property.

[422] *Re Stapylton Fletcher Ltd (in admin rec)* [1994] 1 WLR 1181, 1200–3 *per* Judge Paul Baker QC:

[Two companies sold wine to customers but then held that wine in custody as bailees in return for rentals. In the case of one of the companies, Ellis Son & Vidler Ltd, the customers' wines were stacked by type and vintage, but were not marked with the individual customer's name. A master card index was kept which showed the names of customers and the numbers of cases allotted to each. The index was amended from time to time as delivery of wine was requested by a customer, or additional stocks were bought for customers and added to the stacks. Evidence showed that the card index was virtually 100 per cent accurate. When receivers were appointed to the wine companies, it became necessary to decide who owned these stocks of wine, the customers or the company.]

'The transactions with which I am concerned present the following features.

From the point of view of E.S.V. [Ellis Son & Vidler Ltd], the reserve stocks were completely segregated from the trading stock, and the documentation was in good order. The company did not regard the wine as still belonging to them, even to the extent of refraining from borrowing it. This can be contrasted with the situation revealed as existing at the London Wine Co. [See **[425]** below].

The customers were looking to have their wine properly stored and not unduly disturbed. Further, the nature of the commodity is such that it would be pointless for them to inspect the cases or bottles, and impracticable to inspect their contents. One case of wine of a particular type and vintage is in practice to be regarded as identical with every other case of the same wine, breakages and missing bottles apart. From this two consequences follow. First, it is of secondary importance that the customer's name should be attached to any particular case. Secondly, the customer's assent to any appropriation of specific cases without consultation can be safely inferred. Accordingly, it must seem strange to those not acquainted with the Sale of Goods Act 1979 that a customer's entitlement should differ according to whether a stack of identical cases is allocated to a single customer or is to be shared between two or more.

Having regard to those considerations, the proper legal analysis must begin by recognising that we are not here dealing only with a contract for the sale of goods, but with two separate, if related, contracts, the second with its own consideration being a contract to store wines indefinitely.

Let us assume that each buyer of duty paid wine went to Cliffe [where the warehouses were situated], took delivery of his wine from Unit 13, then handed it back to Mr. Steedman to be added to a stack in Unit 12, knowing that the stack already contained wine belonging to others and that he would not necessarily get the identical cases or bottles back for very good reasons connected with the proper care of his and the other owners' wine. The proper inference there, in my judgment, is that he agreed to become a tenant in common of the entire stack in the proportion that his cases bears to the total number of the cases in the stack for the time being, that total being liable to increase by additions and decrease by removals, where the tenancy in common is determined pro tanto by partition. That such a tenancy in common in goods can exist is not open to doubt, despite the cautionary words of Oliver J., cited above [in the *London Wine* case, **[425]** below]. In fact, in *In re London Wine Co. (Shippers) Ltd.*, at p. 152, Oliver J. referred to *Spence v. Union Marine Insurance Co. Ltd.* (1868) L.R. 3 C.P. 427 [**[623]** below] as a case "when specific goods which undoubtedly were in separate individual ownerships to start with become so mixed as to be indistinguishable." A ship carrying cotton bales was wrecked. Each of the bales had been marked with the name of its consignee. Some of the bales were lost. Others were salvaged, many were damaged, all had lost their distinguishing marks. The remedy for that situation can be taken from the judgment of Bovill C.J., at p. 438:

> "The goods being before they are mixed the separate property of the several owners, unless, which is absurd, they cease to be property by reason of the accidental mixture, when they would not so cease if the mixture were designed, must continue to be the property of the original owners; and, as there would be no means of distinguishing the goods of each, the several owners seem necessarily to become jointly interested, as tenants in common, in the bulk."

Spence's case was one of those cited by Staughton J. in his full survey of the authorities in *Indian Oil Corporation Ltd. v. Greenstone Shipping S.A. (Panama)* [1988] Q.B. 345 [**[625]** below]. In that case shipowners had wrongfully mixed crude oil they had been chartered to transport with their own oil. Thus it was not precisely what had happened here where the goods of a number of innocent claimants have been mixed. Staughton J.'s judgment contains this passage, at pp. 368–369:

> "Two points of significance in my view emerge from the authorities. First, in some cases a decision had to be made 'not upon the notion, that strict justice was done,

> but upon this; that it was the only justice that could be done,' per Lord Eldon L.C. in *Lupton v. White* (1808) 15 Ves. 432, 440. Or as Lord Moulton put it, such cases 'have been little more than instances of cutting the Gordian knot—reasonable adjustments of the rights of the parties in cases where complete justice was impracticable of attainment,' in *Sandeman & Sons v. Tyzack and Branfoot Steamship Co. Ltd.* [1913] A.C. 680, 695."

So one may use the tenancy in common as a tool for remedying an unforeseen mixing, damage or loss. If the creation of a tenancy in common can be brought about by the construction of law, it can equally be brought about by agreement either express or to be inferred from the circumstances.

I now return to the contracts for sale. From the evidence, one can readily infer that the parties intended the property in the goods to pass when they were set aside for storage. In Cliffe that occurred when they were moved from Unit 13 to Unit 12. In the Octavian bond, when they were recorded as belonging to customers and thereafter ceased to be part of the assets of the company in its records. The question remaining is at what point did the goods become "ascertained" for the purposes of section 16. For this one must start from the statute itself. There is no definition of "ascertained." Where, as is normal, the contract is to be performed on the part of the seller by delivery, the goods must be ascertained by the time delivery occurs, but may be ascertained earlier. As we have seen, in the case of goods forming part of a bulk, ascertainment does not occur until they are separated from the bulk, usually immediately prior to delivery. But what if there is to be no delivery, but merely a segregation in the hands of the seller for retention by him? There is no compelling reason why ascertainment should mean the same in such circumstances. A customer orders 20 cases of a particular wine. They are put in a stack which never contains less than 40 cases. Over the next five years the customer takes delivery of a case at a time. It seems absurd that the 20 cases the subject of his contract for sale should thus become ascertained one by one. The sale contract was that 20 cases should be delivered into the customers' reserve. What happened to them thereafter is regulated by the storage contract, whether the terms of that were part of a single contract for sale and storage, or were in a separate contract. It is the segregation of the stock from the company's trading assets, whether done physically or by giving instructions to a bonded warehouse keeper, which causes the goods to be ascertained for the purposes of section 16. The goods are then identified as those to be handed over for storage in performance of the contract for sale. It could not be doubted that if, by agreement with a number of customers, the aggregate number of cases of a specific vintage bought by them were handed over en bloc to another company to hold on their behalf, the cases would be ascertained. The selling company would not be seeking to retain any interest in them. This is quite different from *Healy v. Howlett & Sons* [1917] 1 K.B. 337, where for his own purposes the seller retained control of the appropriation of the goods, and from *Carlos Federspiel & Co. S.A. v. Charles Twigg & Co. Ltd.* [1957] 1 Lloyd's Rep. 240, where he had not completed the arrangements for shipment of the goods and could still withdraw them and replace them with others if it suited him. Where goods were to go to another company for storage there would be an actual delivery. Where the selling company was going to store them and segregated them for that purpose, there will be a constructive delivery. Further at that stage, where the price has been paid in full, there would appear to be nothing to embarrass the ordinary operations of buying and selling goods, and the banking operations which attend them, to which Atkin L.J. referred in *In re Wait* [1927] 1 Ch. 606, 629–630 [**[424]** below].

In summary, on the facts here, I conclude that if a number of cases or bottles of identical wine are held, not mingled with the trading stock, in store for a group of customers, those cases or bottles will be ascertained for the purposes of section 16 of the

Sale of Goods Act 1979 even though they are not immediately appropriated to each individual customer. Property will pass by common intention and not pursuant to section 18 rule (5). They will take as tenants in common.

. . .

[In relation to these ESV claimants, Judge Paul Baker QC thus found that property in the wine passed to them at law. Accordingly, he did not need to consider any of the alternative arguments based in equity. In relation to one of the claimants from Stapylton Fletcher Ltd, however, this was not the case. As the next part of this extract shows, Judge Paul Baker QC was not moved by these alternative arguments.]

. . . There was much discussion of the possibility of a fiduciary relationship or constructive trust existing between the companies and their customers. . . . In the present case we are concerned with the buying and selling of consumables. I am bound by the decision in *In re Wait* [1927] 1 Ch. 606 to hold that a contract for the sale of goods does not of itself create equitable rights. Furthermore, as Gault J. himself commented in *Liggett v. Kensington* [1993] 1 N.Z.L.R. 257, 279, "A contractual obligation to store the goods of another does not give rise to a trust." The respective rights and obligations of the parties are governed exclusively by the terms of the two contracts.

I also cannot accept the submissions based on estoppel and specific performance as creating some kind of equitable interest binding on the bank. On estoppel I respectfully adopt the reasoning of Oliver J. in *In re London Wine Co. (Shippers) Ltd.* [1986] P.C.C. 121. Any estoppel here does no more than provide a defence to some action against the companies under the contracts for sale or storage. Any suggestion of a proprietary estoppel seems quite hopeless. It is notable that Gault J. in *Liggett v. Kensington* [1993] 1 N.Z.L.R. 257, 279 rejected this.

The availability of the remedy of specific performance does not of itself import the existence of some equitable interest. All it imports is the inadequacy of the common law remedy of damages in the particular circumstances. Here, too, I respectfully associate myself with the reasoning of Oliver J.

Equally untenable as leading to an equitable interest are the arguments based on total failure of consideration or what was described as a remedial equitable lien. The former cannot be supported from the facts. Even if it could, it would lead to a personal claim only. Authority for the latter is said to be found in *Lord Napier and Ettrick v. Hunter* [1993] A.C. 713 [**[524]** below]. That case deals with the right of an insurer to claim by subrogation sums recovered by the assured after payment of the claim. I see no way in which that can be extended to give customers a lien as and when their sellers or bailees go into receivership. The court must be very cautious in devising equitable interests and remedies which erode the statutory scheme for distribution on insolvency. It cannot do it because of some perceived injustice arising as a consequence only of the insolvency. Perhaps that is an appropriate note on which to end this judgment.'

Questions:

1. Could the vendor in this case unilaterally resile from the initial appropriation and, instead, satisfy the sale contract from other sources? Is this a criticism of the reasoning in this case?
2. This case was decided prior to the introduction of section 20A into the Sale of Goods Act 1979 (**[421]** above). Would this section now provide a better—or at least an easier—route to the same result?

3. Note the comments of Judge Paul Baker QC in relation to the claims based in equity, and the similar comments made in the cases discussed in Section 4.10.2 below, all relating to choses in possession. Contrast these with the approach adopted in relation to choses in action, whether the transfer is made by gift (Section 4.6 above) or by sale (Section 4.11). Is there a defensible reason for these different approaches?

4.10.2 Sale of goods—passing of equitable title to the property

Because the Sale of Goods Act 1979 presumes that legal title to the sold goods will pass to the purchaser on delivery, or once the goods (or the bulk from which the goods are to be extracted) have been identified and unconditionally appropriated to the contract, there is often little scope for equity to intervene to deem the intending purchaser to have acquired equitable title to the goods in advance of the transfer of legal title: by the time the circumstances warrant equity's intervention, legal title has generally already passed.

Theoretically, equity will only intervene to give the intending purchaser equitable title to the sale property in advance of the legal transfer if the contract of sale is specifically enforceable and unconditional, and the sale property is sufficiently identified (see **[423]** below). There are practical reasons, supported by policy arguments, which suggest that these preconditions will rarely (if ever?) be met in the context of contracts for the sale of goods. The two extracts which follow indicate, respectively, the reason the issue of equitable title is significant and the reason why it is generally denied in the context of contracts for the sale of goods.

[423] S Worthington, *Proprietary Interests in Commercial Transactions* (1996, Clarendon: Oxford), pp 194–7:
[The footnotes in the original are omitted.]

> 'The question at issue is this: if the parties contract to achieve a particular proprietary end, is it possible for either party to acquire an equitable ownership interest in assets belonging to the other party before their agreement is completed? Contracts of sale provide a simple and obvious illustration: before the contract is completed and legal title transferred as planned, can either party assert an equitable ownership interest in the other's property?
>
> The question has obvious practical importance. Its answer defines the parties' respective rights should the transferor's insolvency interrupt the planned execution of the contract; similarly, it determines the equitable allocation of property should third parties assert competing interests in the same asset before the contract is concluded.
>
> So defined, however, the problem is a narrow one. It can only arise where there is some hiatus between the agreement and its eventual completion by transfer of the legal title. Assignments of property which are immediately effective do not raise the same issues: with these, the recipient obtains the intended interest (whether legal or equitable) at the time of the agreement, and the resolution of any competing property interests is relatively straightforward. Given this restriction, the problem appears to be confined exclusively to contracts of sale; moreover, the practicalities of most sale contracts ensure that the equitable rules only operate to benefit purchasers, not vendors.

With contracts for the sale of goods, it is certainly true that the orthodox position is that no equitable interests can arise ahead of the passing of legal title. With other contracts of sale, though, it is possible for a constructive trust to deliver equitable ownership to intending purchasers in advance of the passing of legal property. Contracts for the sale of land illustrate the possibility. In such cases it is clearly not to the point to argue that the parties have only bargained for contractual rights: this is undoubtedly true. The issue is whether, because of the contractual rights agreed, equity will impose by operation of law (not by agreement between the parties) any equitable proprietary interests. It will not do this in every case, but when it does it supplements the purely contractual rights bargained for by the parties.

When the contract is for the sale of land, it is commonly said that the vendor becomes a trustee of the land for the purchaser as soon as there is a binding contract. This happens, it is said, because equity considers that the land ought to be transferred to the purchaser. The purchaser therefore becomes the beneficial owner, although the vendor retains a charge or lien on the estate to secure payment of the price. This description is said to be accurate even if the purchaser has not paid the price and even if the time for completion has not arrived.

Much of this detail might be doubted. Nevertheless, the underlying thesis is clear: the existence and extent of a purchaser's equitable interest in sale property is determined by what equity considers *ought* to be done. The maxim that equity considers as done that which ought to be done is sufficient to describe not only how equity intervenes, but when. This demands a theoretically rigorous approach to the issues: it is not enough to resort to general notions of fairness to determine what ought to be done and when. The analysis is difficult, but arguably it leads to simple rules which can be easily applied to give predictable outcomes.

According to the analysis proposed here, equity only considers that the sale property *ought* to be transferred if the vendor is under a *specifically enforceable* and *unconditional* personal obligation to transfer *identifiable* property to the purchaser. Only then can the purchaser be regarded as the equitable owner of the property, with that ownership interest arising by operation of law. Each of the three italicized pre-conditions merits separate attention. It seems that these requirements are the ones already adopted and applied by the courts, although the comprehensive rule as stated here has never been articulated.

This general rule can be applied to both simple and complicated contracts of sale. In particular, the problems surrounding conditional contracts and contracts for the sale of part of a bulk can be more readily and convincingly resolved. However, perhaps unsurprisingly, the practical result is to afford little assistance to intending purchasers: only rarely are the three essential pre- conditions met. Nevertheless, sympathy for the plight of wronged purchasers, such as those in the *Goldcorp* case, for example, cannot be allowed to defeat a proper application of principles.'

[424] *Re Wait* [1927] 1 Ch 606 (CA), 634–40 *per* Atkin LJ and 641, 644–6, 655–6 *per* Sargant LJ:

[Wait contracted to purchase 1,000 tons of wheat which was due to arrive in port on board the *Challenger*. The following day, he agreed to sell 500 tons of this wheat to Humphries & Bobbett, who paid him the price in advance. A few days before the *Challenger* arrived, Wait went bankrupt. By the time this action came to trial, 530 tons of wheat remained, the rest having been sold to other buyers. Nothing had been done to identify the particular 500 tons which was to be used to fulfil the contract with Humphries & Bobbett. The Court of Appeal by majority (with Sargant

LJ, the only Chancery judge, dissenting) decided that Humphries & Bobbett had no proprietary claim to any of the wheat, but could only prove in Wait's bankruptcy for return of the price.]

Atkin LJ:

'I now proceed to discuss the suggestion that apart from the right to specific performance under s. 52 of the Code [the Sale of Goods Act], there was in this case an equitable assignment to the claimants of 500 tons of flour which entitled them to claim from the trustee delivery of 500 tons out of the 530 tons remaining in his possession, and, indeed, gave the claimants a charge or lien over the whole 1000 tons to which the debtor was entitled under his contract with Balfour Williamson & Co. In the view that I have taken of the facts of this case, I have already said that the goods were never so ascertained that specific performance could have been ordered of them. This consideration would appear to defeat the supposed equitable assignment, and I will not repeat the passages referred to by the Master of the Rolls which establish the test. I have already indicated my own view of the claimants' contract of November 21 and suggested that the debtor does not in fact agree to sell to the claimants any aliquot part of the 1000 tons, which in fact he had agreed to buy from Balfour Williamson & Co [ie in Atkin LJ's view, the contract was not one for the sale of part of a bulk]. But even if he had, I do not think that at any time here there was an equitable assignment which ever gave the claimants a beneficial interest in these goods. It has been difficult to elicit the moment of time at which the beneficial interest came into existence. At various times in the argument it has been the moment when the 1000 tons were shipped; when they were declared to the debtor by Balfour Williamson & Co.; when the bills of lading came into the possession of the bank; when the claimants paid the 5933*l.* 5*s.* to the debtor; when the goods were taken up by the trustee; and when the 530 tons came into the possession of the trustee. The difficulty illustrates the danger of seeking to conduct well established principles into territory where they are trespassers. Without deciding the point, I think that much may be said for the proposition that an agreement for the sale of goods does not import any agreement to transfer property other than in accordance with the terms of the Code, that is, the intention of the parties to be derived from the terms of the contract, the conduct of the parties and the circumstances of the case, and, unless a different intention appears, from the rules set out in s. 18. The Code was passed at a time when the principles of equity and equitable remedies were recognized and given effect to in all our Courts, and the particular equitable remedy of specific performance is specially referred to in s. 52. The total sum of legal relations (meaning by the word "legal" existing in equity as well as in common law) arising out of the contract for the sale of goods may well be regarded as defined by the Code. It would have been futile in a code intended for commercial men to have created an elaborate structure of rules dealing with rights at law, if at the same time it was intended to leave, subsisting with the legal rights, equitable rights inconsistent with, more extensive, and coming into existence earlier than the rights so carefully set out in the various sections of the Code.

The rules for transfer of property as between seller and buyer, performance of the contract, rights of the unpaid seller against the goods, unpaid sellers' lien, remedies of the seller, remedies of the buyer, appear to be complete and exclusive statements of the legal relations both in law and equity. They have, of course, no relevance when one is considering rights, legal or equitable, which may come into existence dehors the contract for sale. A seller or a purchaser may, of course, create any equity he pleases by way of charge, equitable assignment or any other dealing with or disposition of goods, the subject-matter of sale; and he may, of course, create such an equity as one of the terms expressed in the contract of sale. But the mere sale or agreement to sell or the acts in pursuance of such a contract mentioned in the Code will only produce the legal effects which the Code states.

But without deciding this point, we have to apply the words of Lord Westbury in *Holroyd v. Marshall* (10 H. L. C. 191, 209) [**[432]** below]: "In equity it is not necessary for the alienation of property that there should be a formal deed of conveyance. A contract for valuable consideration, by which it is agreed to make a present transfer of property, passes at once the beneficial interest, provided the contract is one of which a Court of equity will decree specific performance. In the language of Lord Hardwicke, the vendor becomes a trustee for the vendee; subject, of course, to the contract being one to be specifically performed. And this is true, not only of contracts relating to real estate, but also of contracts relating to personal property, provided that the latter are such as a Court of equity would direct to be specifically performed." It must be remembered that while Lord Westbury's proposition that a contract for valuable consideration, by which it is agreed to make a present transfer of property, passes at once the beneficial interest, provided the contract is one of which a Court of equity will decree specific performance, may be beyond dispute, the converse that when there is a contract of which the Court of equity will decree specific performance the beneficial interest has passed is not logically true, and is not the law. Nor is it true that in equity when a man agrees in a contract for the sale of goods to sell part of a specified whole, he agrees to make a transfer of property either present or when the property is in fact acquired. Agreements by a farmer to sell a lamb out of his flock, a ton of potatoes out of his crop grown on his farm, a bushel of apples from his orchard, a gallon of milk from this morning's milking, an egg out of the eggs collected yesterday, seem to me not to amount to an equitable assignment of any of the matters sold, or to give an equitable charge or lien over the whole subject-matter to secure the delivery of the part. The doctrine asserted seems to produce the result that in every case of the sale of future goods, as soon as the goods have become identifiable, the beneficial interest in them passes to the buyer, notwithstanding the provision in the Code that, in the absence of express intention, the property only passes when goods of that description and in a deliverable state are appropriated to the contract, either by the seller with the assent of the buyer, or by the buyer with the assent of the seller, and apparently notwithstanding an express agreement that the property shall not pass except on payment. So to hold would be to defeat the intention of the parties, either express or to be implied from their contract being bound by the terms of the Code, and it appears to me not to accord with the principles of equity to impose upon the parties rights which are contrary to their manifest intention.

Does it make any difference that the creditors here paid their purchase money in advance of the due date, and in any case before they could get delivery under the contract? I think not. So far as specific performance is concerned, the right seems to exist, if at all, independently of whether one party or the other has performed his part of the contract; and I have already dealt with the objections to the demand for specific performance under the provisions of s. 52 of the Code.

Lord Westbury in *Holroyd v. Marshall* (10 H. L. C. 191, 211) uses wide words in the passage beginning: "But if a vendor or mortgagor agrees to sell or mortgage property, real or personal, of which he is not possessed at the time, and he receives the consideration for the contract, and afterwards becomes possessed of property answering the description in the contract, there is no doubt that a Court of equity would compel him to perform the contract, and that the contract would, in equity, transfer the beneficial interest to the mortgagee or purchaser immediately on the property being acquired. This, of course, assumes that the supposed contract is one of that class of which a Court of equity would decree the specific performance. If it be so, then immediately on the acquisition of the property described the vendor or mortgagor would hold it in trust for the purchaser or mortgagee, according to the terms of the contract. For if a contract be in other respects good and fit to be performed, and the consideration has been received, incapacity to perform it at the time of its execution will be no answer when the means of doing so are afterwards obtained." I cannot help thinking that in his reference to property real or personal, the learned Lord was not directing his mind to contracts for the sale of goods which ordinarily would not be "of that class of which a Court of equity would decree the specific performance." I cannot believe he intended that in the cases suggested above the farmer, the seller, would hold the lamb, or the potatoes, or the bushel of apples or the egg in trust for the purchaser as soon as they were ascertained, much less, as these words are supposed to mean, as soon as they were acquired by the seller. Similarly, I fail to see how the payment of the price can convert that which was not an equitable assignment before the payment, into an equitable assignment after the payment. Payment of the price has no doubt been material in considering a different question—namely, the right of the purchaser in a contract for the sale of real property, who pays the price or portion of the price before conveyance, to be given a lien on the land for his purchase price. The right is correlative to and appears to be derived from the right of the unpaid vendor of real property to claim a lien on the land after conveyance for the unpaid purchase price. But the latter lien in my judgment does not exist in the case of an ordinary sale of goods. The remedies are defined. The unpaid vendor has a lien which is a possessory lien; and has a right of stoppage in transit; but in my experience no one has ever claimed or been given in the countless cases that have arisen of vendors of goods remaining unpaid after delivery, a right to a lien over the goods in the possession of the purchaser. Similarly, the purchaser who in pursuance of the contract of sale has paid the purchase price or part of it before delivery has never claimed or received a lien over the property which is in the hands of the vendor. I am satisfied that such liens would be quite inconsistent with the provisions of the Code, and do not exist.

It is, however, said, "does not common honesty demand that such a beneficial interest should be created?" The answer is, I think, that the test of honesty is inadequate, it is too narrow or too wide. The sphere of honesty is not confined to dealings with beneficial interests in property. Many would think that deliberately to break a contract for the sale of future goods, where no question of property at law or in equity could arise, would be dishonest; but the law gives only a remedy in damages. In the simple cases suggested, which I hesitate to repeat, the farmer might be acting dishonestly in parting with the whole of his flock, his apples, his potatoes or his eggs to a different purchaser; but I venture to think that if he does the purchaser even with notice acquires a complete title to the property bought.

This brings me to the last subject of this too lengthy judgment. If the contentions put before the Court for the claimants be correct and beneficial interests in property are created as suggested, the whole course of business transactions will be fundamentally affected. Many large business transactions such as this, indeed nearly all import transactions, are financed by banks or financial houses, as this was. It is quite common for the banker to be given information of sub-sales, indeed he often asks for it, or it is proffered voluntarily as some guarantee of the stability of the bank's customer. Such notice was given here. If notice of the sub-sale under a contract which becomes specific when delivery is made, is notice of equitable interests in the sub-purchasers, the bank would be affected even though by taking the bills of lading, or other documents, they acquired the legal title. They would have to satisfy themselves on being paid off that the equitable interests were not being defeated, and their own powers of disposition if their customer made default would be enormously restricted. Presumably they would have to communicate with each sub-purchaser. The effect of the decision below when once appreciated would throw the business world into confusion, for credit would be seriously restricted.

The nett result of this decision is that the buyer of goods in these circumstances is in no better position in bankruptcy than a seller. If a seller of goods delivers them to the buyer before payment, trusting to receive payment in due course, and the buyer becomes bankrupt, the seller is restricted to a proof, and can assert no beneficial interest in the goods. There seems no particular reason why a different principle should prevail where a buyer hands the price to the seller before delivery of the goods trusting to receive delivery in due course. In both cases credit is given to the debtor, and the buyer and the seller respectively take the well known risk of the insolvency of their customer.

I regret to differ from the opinion of the judges below and my brother Sargant. I do not think that there is any difference as to the existence of the principles of equity which are involved. They are well settled, and beyond doubt in their own sphere beneficial. The difference has been as to their application to such facts as appear in this case. . . .'

Sargant LJ:

'I am sorry to find myself in disagreement with the majority of the Court in this case, and the more so because my disagreement is complete and fundamental. In the circumstances of this case, I am of opinion that there had, prior to the bankruptcy, been created in favour of the respondents equitable rights of the nature of equitable lien or equitable assignment in respect of this wheat, which were enforceable against the bankrupt or his trustee in bankruptcy, and which prevented the wheat vesting in the trustee otherwise than subject to those equitable rights.

. . . .

The contract of November 21 was thus obviously not a general contract for the purchase of 500 tons of Western White wheat, but a contract for the purchase of a definite portion of a specific parcel of that wheat to be shipped within a definite period on a named vessel, and the contract would necessarily fail of its own inherent force, should there not be a shipment in accordance with the earlier and larger contract. . . .

The question has to be determined on a consideration of the relative positions of the bankrupt and the respondents just before the commencement of the bankruptcy. At this time the wheat contracted to be purchased by the respondents had been definitely ascertained under their contract and notification and invoice, as 500 tons, or one half, of the particular parcel of 1000 tons then on board the Challenger and comprised in the bill of lading of December 21, 1925. The bankrupt was bound to deliver and the respondents were entitled to receive 500 tons out of that very parcel of 1000 tons. The bankrupt's obligation could not be discharged by the delivery of 500 tons of Western White wheat derived from any other source, not even by the delivery of the whole or a part of the 500 tons shipped on the Challenger by Sanford & Co. under the bill of lading of December 22, 1925; though no doubt if the quality of that wheat were the same, as it would seem to have been through its being shipped partly intermixed with the other wheat, the purchasers might have accepted the substituted wheat or any part thereof that was delivered to them as being equivalent to what they had purchased. But as a matter of strict contract the only wheat which was deliverable under the respondents' contract, and which could be forced on them under that contract, was 500 tons of the wheat bought by the bankrupt from Messrs. Balfour Williamson & Co. and comprised in the bill of lading of December 21, 1925.

Now assume that the respondents, instead of agreeing to buy half of the 1000 tons to be procured from Messrs. Balfour Williamson & Co., had agreed to buy the whole parcel and had paid the bankrupt the whole purchase money therefor less only the 1500*l*. for freight. It is clear to my mind that in such a case the respondents would have been entitled to something much more precise than a mere personal right against the bankrupt to enforce delivery of the 1000 tons; they would have been entitled to an equitable interest in and right to the particular parcel of 1000 tons subject only to the payment of the balance of the purchase money represented by the freight. This right would no doubt be capable of being defeated, should the bankrupt sell the 1000 tons fraudulently to a purchaser for value without notice in such a way as to vest the legal property in the wheat in him. But, subject to that possibility, there would have passed to the respondents the equitable interest in the specific cargo to the extent of the price paid, and they would be entitled to have the 1000 tons delivered to them upon payment of the balance of 1500*l*. And if the bankrupt had threatened to sell or otherwise deal with this 1000 tons cargo in a way inconsistent with the respondents' equitable interest, they would in my judgment have been entitled to obtain an injunction against any such sale or other dealing.

Is there then any real difference in the equitable position of the respondents, because they agreed to buy not the whole 1000 tons parcel but 500 tons or one half only of that parcel? I think not. They became entitled not to the whole 1000 tons, but to have made over to them, subject to the payment of 750*l*., 500 tons out of that definite specific cargo of 1000 tons. It would be a fraud for the bankrupt to sell or deal with the 1000 tons in any manner that would prevent 500 tons part thereof being left available to satisfy the claim of the respondents. He could not justify the making of two fresh contracts to sell 500 tons of wheat out of his parcel of 1000 tons by alleging that he was merely making general contracts to sell that amount of wheat. He would be dishonestly purporting to sell the same wheat twice over. And, on the threat of any such sale or other dealing, the respondents would be entitled to an injunction to restrain it if and so far as it would defeat their equitable right. Or, in other words, they had and were entitled to enforce an equitable lien on the 1000 tons for the purpose of protecting their right to receive out of the 1000 tons the amount of their purchase—namely, 500 tons.

If this is so, no question arises, as was suggested by Mr. Jowitt on opening the appeal, of the particular creditors, the respondents, being paid in priority to the general creditors out of the general assets of the bankrupt, including the 500 tons of wheat agreed to be bought by the respondents. The case is one in which the 1000 tons of wheat, or such part thereof as had not been sold by the bankrupt to other persons, would vest in the trustee in bankruptcy, subject to the equitable right of the respondents to have provided thereout 500 tons upon payment by them of the balance of the purchase price. And it is to be observed that the bankrupt here, so far from acting fraudulently or doing anything which might give a superior title to a subsequent purchaser and so prevent the bankrupt from fulfilling his equitable obligation to deliver 500 tons of the specific parcel of 1000 tons Western White wheat to the respondents, was careful to dispose only of so much of the parcel in question as left a residue of 530 tons of the Western White wheat available to satisfy that equitable obligation.

I will now proceed to examine the cases, some of them of the highest authority, which in my judgment establish conclusively the propositions I have stated. . . .

In the foregoing remarks I have dealt with the question on the basis of what seems to me the well established law in relation to equitable assignments, quite independently of the Sale of Goods Act, 1893. For it is clear that the Act is not exhaustive of the methods by which an equitable title to goods may be acquired, and does not stultify or negative the effect of any transaction which prior to the Act would have amounted to an equitable assignment, or the creation of an equitable lien. Indeed s. 55, and still more s. 61, appear to amount to an express statutory recognition of the possibility of such a title apart from the express provisions of the Act. . . .

Finally, I desire to deal with the contention of the appellant that the decision of the Divisional Court would interfere with the ordinary way in which business is conducted in these matters. I cannot assent to this view. Ordinary business is not conducted dishonestly. It would on any view of the law have been dishonest of the bankrupt after the sale to the respondents of 500 tons of his specific parcel of 1000 tons to have sold more than another 500 tons of this parcel to other buyers; and in fact he acted honestly in the matter and reserved a quantity exceeding 500 tons to satisfy the respondents' claim. Further, when the bank learned the situation, they met it spontaneously and simply by opening separate accounts in respect of the separate portions, though, of course, subject to their overriding rights in respect of their special property as mortgagees of the whole. And if the bankrupt had acted dishonestly and had sold to third parties in the ordinary course of business and so as to pass the general property in portions of the 500 tons which were subject to the equitable claim of the respondents, those third parties would have gained a title superior to the respondents, just as in *Hoare v. Dresser* (7 H. L. C. 290) the defendant's equitable right was displaced by the subsequent superior right of the plaintiff. . . .'

Question:

Which reasoning is more persuasive, that of Atkin LJ or of Sargant LJ, either from the perspective of legal doctrine or from the perspective of commercial policy, or both?

Note:

If the facts in this case had been slightly different, so that at the time of trial only 500 tons of wheat had remained out of the initial bulk of 1,000 tons, then Humphries & Bobbett would have had no difficulty in claiming *legal* title to the wheat, it having been specifically identified (by exhaustion) as the subject matter of the contract: *Wait & James v Midland Bank* (1926) 25 Lloyds LR 313. Moreover, even on the facts as they arose in this case, the outcome now would be different because of the introduction of section 20A into the Sale of Goods Act 1979 (see **[421]** above).

FURTHER READING:

A S Burrows, 'Specific Performance at the Crossroads' [1984] *Legal Studies* 102, especially 102–7.

4.10.3 Sale of goods—failure to pass title

As indicated earlier, many intending purchasers are surprised—and disappointed—when they learn to their cost that they have not acquired title to the goods they thought they had purchased. The reason is invariably a failure sufficiently to identify the goods to be purchased.

[425] ***Re London Wine Company (Shippers) Ltd*** **[1986] PCC 121, 137–8, 146–50, 152–7** ***per*** **Oliver J:**

[The company was in the business of selling and storing fine wines for interested buyers. Each contract of sale between the company and a buyer would specify the type of wine and the quantity purchased and, on full payment of the price, the buyer would receive a 'Certificate of Title' which described the buyer as the 'sole and beneficial owner' of the wine. The company would then charge the buyer for storage and insurance of the wine until the buyer took delivery or re-sold the wine to someone else. The company's stocks of wine were held in various warehouses and, although there was sufficient wine to meet the claims of all buyers, the company had no procedure for identifying or segregating the wine sold to particular individuals.

The court had to decide who owned (beneficially) the company's stocks of wine. The company had granted a floating charge to its bank secured over all its assets. The bank had appointed a receiver, who claimed that all the wine stocks were subject to the charge since no wine had been specifically appropriated to any individual contract of sale. The buyers claimed that the wine was their property, either at law or in equity.

The court considered separately three typical cases: (i) those where the buyer had purchased the company's total stock of a particular wine at the date of purchase (eg Mr Strong); (ii) those where two or more buyers had purchased sufficient quantities of a particular wine to exhaust the whole of the company's stock of that wine (eg Mr Button); and (iii) those where the purchase did not exhaust the particular stock, but where there had been an acknowledgement that the appropriate quantity of the particular wine was being held to the buyer's order (eg Mr Bailey).

Oliver J held that in none of these cases had any legal or equitable proprietary interest in the wine passed to the buyer. The bank's security interest therefore prevailed, and the buyers' were simply unsecured creditors with personal claims for return of the purchase price.]

> 'There, then, are the three categories with which I have to deal and the question which has arisen in each case is whether the wines which have been sold belong to the purchasers and those claiming through or under them or whether on the relevant date they remained the company's property and so became subject to the charge in the debenture which then crystallised. I should perhaps say that there is no question of stocks being insufficient to fulfil all the purchase orders so that there is no competition between purchasers *inter se*.
>
> The question is easier to pose than to answer and I am indebted to counsel for all the respondents for sustained and instructive arguments. It will, I think, be convenient to deal with these in a different order from that in which they were advanced, because there are certain arguments common to all three cases which, if accepted, would render it unnecessary to consider the special features applicable to any particular case.

As regards the case of Mr Strong and Mr Button, Mr Wright's primary submission on their behalf is that the legal title to the goods passed and that, accordingly, the matter ends there. If however, that is wrong, he submits first that the goods became subject to a valid and effective trust before the relevant date, and, as an alternative to this, that each purchaser had, before the relevant date, a right to specific performance of his contract and that, when the floating charge crystallised, the bank took subject to that right. These two submissions apply equally to the third category and have been adopted and expanded by Mr Stamler on behalf of the respondents Vinum and Compass and since they are, therefore, common to all cases, and, if correct, are conclusive of the whole case, they can conveniently be dealt with first.

As regards the creation of a trust, this is put in this way. On the assumption that no property passed in the goods at law—and it is not argued that this could possibly be the case in the third category represented by Mr Bailey and by Mr Stamler's clients—there was, it is submitted, clearly an intention that the property should pass so far as the company had it in its power to make it do so. One has only to look at the terms of its circulars with their references to '*your* wines,' to the purchaser being 'the beneficial owner' and to the company having a lien. This is reinforced when one looks at the terms of the letters of confirmation which list the quantities and types of wine and confirm that the purchaser is 'the sole beneficial owner of these wines,' and is indeed further reinforced in the case of Compass and Vinum when reference is made to the master agreements with Compass and the company where the company joins in to warrant title to the wine. By issuing these documents, the acknowledged purpose of which was to enable the purchasers to deal with their wines by sale or charge, the company, it is said, evinced the clearest possible intention to declare itself a trustee and once you find such an intention, it matters not that the instrument expressing it fails to do so in unequivocal terms or, indeed, that there is no instrument at all. Reliance is placed upon the recent case of *Re Kayford Ltd* ([1975] 1 WLR 279 at 282) where Megarry J said: '. . . [i]t is well settled that a trust can be created without using the words "trust" or "confidence" or the like: the question is whether in substance a sufficient intention to create a trust has been manifested.'

That, of course, is a proposition with which it is impossible to quarrel but I do not find that case, where the evidence of intention to create a trust was exceptionally clear and where the trust property was from the outset specifically set aside and identified, one which assists me very much in ascertaining whether, in the very different circumstances of the instant case, a trust has been effectively declared. Mr Wright, in his reply, put it rather differently. A trust, he said, may be constituted not merely by direct and express declaration but also by the consequences flowing from the acts of the persons themselves to which consequences the law attaches the label 'trust.' A trust, to put it another way, is the technical description of a legal situation; and where you find (i) an intention to create a beneficial interest in someone else, (ii) an acknowledgment of that intention and (iii) property in the ownership of the person making the acknowledgment which answers the description in the acknowledgment, then there is, at the date of the acknowledgment, an effective and completed trust of all the property of the acknowledger answering to that description. This is, I think, in essence the same submission as that made by Mr Stamler—he submits that where one is dealing with a homogeneous mass there is no problem about certainty. So long as the mass can be identified and there is no uncertainty about the quantitative interest of the beneficiary, the court will find no difficulty in administering the trust if it once finds the necessary intention to create an equitable interest in property of the type comprised in the mass. I think, indeed, that if the case is to be made out at all, it must be put in this way, for the submission itself is based on the premise that there are no specific or ascertained goods in which the beneficiary is interested. Were it otherwise there would be no need to invoke the concept of trust for the title would have passed under the Sale of Goods Act (as, indeed, Mr Wright submits in categories 1 and 2, it did). If trust there be, then it must be a trust of the homogeneous *whole* and the terms of the trust must be that the trustee is to hold that whole upon trust to give effect thereout to the proportionate interest of the beneficiary. Thus if we postulate the case of the company having in warehouse 1,000 cases of a particular wine and selling 100 cases to X the circumstances of this case indicate, it is submitted, that the company created an equitable tenancy in common between itself and X in the whole 1,000 cases in the proportions of 9/10ths and 1/10th.

It is with regret that I feel compelled to reject these submissions, for I feel great sympathy with those who paid for their wine and received an assurance that they had title to it. But I find it impossible to spell either out of the acknowledgments signed by the company or out of the circumstances any such trust as is now sought to be set up. Granted that the references to 'beneficial interest' are appropriate words for the creation of a trust; granted, even (although this I think is very difficult to spell out) that that was the company's intention, it seems to me that any such trust must fail on the ground of uncertainty of subject-matter. I appreciate the point taken that the subject-matter is part of a homogeneous mass so that specific identity is of as little importance as it is, for instance, in the case of money. Nevertheless, as it seems to me, to create a trust it must be possible to ascertain with certainty not only what the interest of the beneficiary is to be but to what property it is to attach.

I cannot see how, for instance, a farmer who declares himself to be a trustee of two sheep (without identifying them) can be said to have created a perfect and complete trust whatever rights he may confer by such declaration as a matter of contract. And it would seem to me to be immaterial that at the time he has a flock of sheep out of which he could satisfy the interest. Of course, he could by appropriate words, declare himself to be a trustee of a specified proportion of his whole flock and thus create an equitable tenancy in common between himself and the named beneficiary, so that a proprietary interest would arise in the beneficiary in an undivided share of all the flock and its produce. But the *mere* declaration that a given number of animals would be held upon trust could not, I should have thought, without very clear words pointing to such an intention, result in the creation of an interest in common in the proportion which that number bears to the number of the whole at the time of the declaration. And where the mass from which the numerical interest is to take effect is not itself ascertainable at the date of the declaration such a conclusion becomes impossible.

In the instant case, even if I were satisfied on the evidence that the mass was itself identifiable at the date of the various letters of confirmation I should find the very greatest difficulty in construing the assertion that 'you are the *sole* and beneficial owner of 10 cases of such and such a wine' as meaning or being intended to mean 'you are the owner of such proportion of the total stock of such and such a wine now held by me as 10 bears to the total number of cases comprised in such stock.' All other things apart, such construction would be a total negation of the assertion 'you are the *sole* owner.' But in fact, (leaving aside the first category for the moment) it is far from clear what, at the date of any individual letter of confirmation, was the composition of the mass from which the interest was to take effect. It was suggested in argument that the words 'lying in bond' on the invoice was a reference to the stocks held by the company in bond at that date and that therefore it was possible to predicate of any individual letter of confirmation that it referred to cases forming part of a then existing mass. I do not think that these words signify that, but in any event it does not seem necessarily to have been the case at all that there was an ascertainable existing mass at the time of the individual letter. For example, in the case of Mr Bailey, the exhibited correspondence shows that a quantity of wines of various descriptions was invoiced on August 16th, 1972 and described as 'lying in bond.' At the same time the company wrote to Mr Bailey's bankers undertaking that the wines on the invoice will not be removed from the bond without your written authority. On September 29th, 1972 the bankers wrote to the company asking for the warehouse warrants, and on October 6th Mr Baring replied saying that the wines had 'now just arrived in the country.' The warehouse receipts were actually sent on November 10th, 1972. So that it appears that, at least in this case, the wines described as 'lying in bond' in August were not in fact in the warehouse at all at that date. . . .

I turn now, therefore, to the submissions peculiar to the individual cases. Now in the case of Mr Strong, although the goods were sold by generic description, it happened that at the material time the quantity described was in the company's possession and was the only wine of that description in its possession, although it is not claimed that it could not, without undue difficulty, obtain additional quantities from elsewhere if it required to do so. Mr Wright argues that the result of this was to ascertain the goods and that the property passed; and to make this good he has to rely either upon s 17 or upon an appropriation under s 18, r 5(1) of the Sale of Goods Act. Section 16 states quite clearly that the property is not transferred to the buyer unless and until the goods are ascertained but it is not a necessary corollary of this that the property *does* pass to the buyer when they *are* ascertained. To produce that result one either has had to find an appropriation (from which an intention to pass the property will be inferred) or one has to find an intention manifested in some other way. Mr Wright relies upon what has been referred to as an 'ascertainment by exhaustion' and has drawn my attention to the decision of Roche J in *Wait & James v Midland Bank* ((1926) 31 Com Cas 172).

. . .

The decision in that case was one of obvious common sense because in fact from November 16th onwards there were no goods from which the seller could have fulfilled the contracts except the 850 quarters. They could, no doubt, have delivered 850 quarters of Australian wheat but not 850 quarters of 'ex store Avonmouth ex *Thistleros* [sic].' The instant case seems to me quite different. It is not and cannot be alleged that the sale to Mr Strong was a sale of specific goods. What the company undertook to do was to deliver so many cases and bottles of the specified type of wine 'lying in bond.' This does not in my judgment link the wine sold with any given consignment or warehouse. The fact that the company had at the date of the invoice that amount of wine and that amount only is really irrelevant to the contract. No doubt it could have fulfilled the order from this wine but it could equally have fulfilled it from any other source. It is not contended that there was any act of appropriation and Mr Wright's case is that the property passed under s 17 when the usual title letter mentioning the wine described in the invoice was sent some three months later, by which date, he says, the wine was ascertained. I cannot draw that conclusion from the material before me, for it seems to me clear that the company was, under the contract, at liberty to deliver to the purchaser any bottles of wine which tallied with the description. It never has been, therefore, . . . ascertained what the goods are which are covered by the contract.

The argument in relation to the second category of case is very similar. It will be remembered that in the *Wait & James* case Roche J restricts his remarks to the case of one buyer under several contracts. It is, however, submitted that where you have several buyers under several contracts, then, when you reach a stage where the totality of those contracted quantities exhausts the whole of the mass from which the individual contracts are to be fulfilled, there is no longer any property in the seller but the buyers own the mass as tenants in common. . . .

I think . . . that there are insuperable difficulties in the way of Mr Wright's argument, but even if I am wrong about that, I think that the same objection applies here as in the case of Mr Strong. Even if Mr Wright's argument is correct as a matter of law, its underlying basis must be that there is an identifiable whole which has been appropriated in some way to answer for the quantities which it is said exhaust the entire parcel. That simply does not appear to me to be the case here. I cannot construe the words 'lying in bond' as providing an identifying label for the mass from which the goods were to be selected. In my view, the company remained free to fulfil the contracts to its various purchasers from any source, as, for instance, by importing further wine of the same description. That being so, the mere fact that the company sold quantities of wine which in fact exhausted all the stocks which it held cannot, in my judgment, have had the effect of passing a proprietary interest in those stocks to the various purchasers so that they can now claim the goods collectively and ignore the bank's charge.

In the case of the third category of purchaser, represented by Mr Bailey and by Vinum Ltd and their respective pledgees, the case is put rather differently. It is not contended that any proprietary interest passed at law, but what is said is that an interest by estoppel was vested in the purchasers. . . .

In the case of Mr Bailey, the correspondence exhibited shows how, in very many cases, the company, at the instance of the pledgee from the purchaser, invited the warehouseman to issue warehouse receipts acknowledging that he held wine to the account of the pledgee. The case of Compass is even clearer, for here there was a master agreement to which the company was a party and under which it warranted the validity of the warehouse receipts and that the wine was held by it as a custodian for the pledgor.

There is no doubt that the pledgees were intended to and did alter their position on the faith of these representations by advancing money to Mr Bailey and Vinum Ltd respectively.

In these circumstances Mr Wright on behalf of Mr Bailey and Mr Stamler on behalf of Vinum Ltd and its pledgees submit that both the company and the warehouseman are estopped and that there were created in the purchasers and their pledgees proprietary interests by estoppel created before the bank's charge crystallised and so binding upon it.

None of the warehousemen is a party to these proceedings so that nothing that I say would be binding upon them in any event but in fact I cannot see how an estoppel affecting the warehousemen could affect the bank except in so far as such an estoppel created a proprietary interest in the goods in the warehouse subject to which the bank's charge takes effect. But the authorities to which I have referred above make one thing quite clear and that is that no property *actually* passes, although the estoppel operates to enable the plaintiff to prosecute an action in trover in which he can obtain damages from the warehouseman.

I can find here no estoppel which, in my judgment, can affect the bank or preclude it from asserting its real title to the assets of the company at the relevant date. . . .

Accordingly, I have felt compelled, perhaps rather reluctantly, to the conclusion that I must direct: (1) that all three categories of goods described in the schedule to the summons should be dealt with by the receiver as being the property of the company on the relevant date and so subject to the floating charge and (2) that no such goods are subject to any lien or other interest having priority to the floating charge in favour of the respondent purchasers or their respective assigns or mortgagees.'

[426] ***Re Goldcorp Exchange Ltd (in rec)*** **[1995] 1 AC 74 (PC), 89–91, 95–9** ***per*** **Lord Mustill:**

[The Exchange persuaded thousands of investors to purchase gold bullion as an investment and leave it with the company for storage. As in the *London Wine Case* (**[425]** above), the investors were issued with 'Certificates of Ownership'. In addition, the company's brochures indicated that its stocks of metal were audited monthly to ensure that there were sufficient stocks to meet all commitments. In fact, there were insufficient stocks to meet commitments. Moreover, the small print in the purchase contracts expressly indicated that gold was held only on a 'non-allocated' basis—certainly no gold was ever appropriated to any particular sale contract. When the company collapsed, the bank's secured claims were such that there would be nothing left for unsecured creditors. In particular, the investors could recoup their losses only if they could show that they had a proprietary interest in the gold bullion they had purchased.[33] The Privy Council was of the opinion that no such proprietary claim could be established.]

'II. *The issues*

As already seen, by the time the judgment in the Court of Appeal [1993] 1 N.Z.L.R. 257 had been delivered the proprietary claims of the customers had been widened to comprise not only bullion but also the general assets of the company, to an extent representing the sums originally paid by way of purchase price. The following issues now arise for consideration. (i) Did the property in any bullion pass to the customers immediately upon the making of the purchases—(a) simply by virtue of contract of purchase itself, or (b) by virtue of the written and oral statements made in the brochures and by the company's employees? (Although these were referred to in argument as representations their Lordships believe them to be more in the nature of contractual undertakings, and therefore call them "the collateral promises"). (ii) Did the property in any bullion subsequently acquired by the company pass to the customer upon acquisition? (iii) When the customers paid over the purchase moneys under the contract of sale, did they retain a beneficial interest in them by virtue of an express or constructive trust? (iv) Should the court now grant a restitutionary remedy of a proprietary character in respect of the purchase moneys?

If the answer to any of these questions is in the affirmative it will be necessary to consider the extent to which the customer's rights in the relevant subject matter can be applied to the bullion or other assets now in the possession of the company.

III. *Title to bullion: the sale contracts*

Their Lordships begin with the question whether the customer obtained any form of proprietary interest, legal or equitable, simply by virtue of the contract of sale, independently of the collateral promises. In the opinion of their Lordships the answer is so clearly that he did not that it would be possible simply to quote section 18 of the Sale of Goods Act 1908 (New Zealand) (corresponding to section 16 of the Sale of Goods Act 1893 (56 & 57 Vict. c. 71)) and one reported case, and turn to more difficult issues. It is, however, convenient to pause for a moment to consider why the answer must inevitably be negative, because the reasons for this answer are the same as those which stand in the way of the customers at every point of the case. It is common ground that the contracts in question were for the sale of unascertained goods. For present purposes, two species of unascertained goods may be distinguished. First, there are "generic goods." These are sold on terms which preserve the seller's freedom to decide for himself how and from what source he will obtain goods answering the contractual description. Secondly, there are "goods sold ex-bulk." By this expression their Lordships denote goods which are by express stipulation to be supplied from a fixed and

[33] Or, alternatively, that they had a proprietary interest in the purchase funds they had handed over to the company for their purchase. This claim is dealt with in Chapter 5 (see Section 5.5), but it too failed.

a pre-determined source, from within which the seller may make his own choice (unless the contract requires it to be made in some other way) but outside which he may not go. For example, "I sell you 60 of the 100 sheep now on my farm."

Approaching these situations a priori common sense dictates that the buyer cannot acquire title until it is known to what goods the title relates. Whether the property then passes will depend upon the intention of the parties and in particular on whether there has been a consensual appropriation of particular goods to the contract. On the latter question the law is not straightforward, and if it had been decisive of the present appeal it would have been necessary to examine cases such as *Carlos Federspiel Co. S.A. v. Charles Twigg & Co. Ltd.* [1957] 1 Lloyd's Rep. 240 and other cases cited in argument. In fact, however, the case turns not on appropriation but on ascertainment, and on the latter the law has never been in doubt. It makes no difference what the parties intended if what they intend is impossible: as is the case with an immediate transfer of title to goods whose identity is not yet known.

. . .

Their Lordships have laboured this point, about which there has been no dispute, simply to show that any attempt by the non-allocated claimants to assert that a legal title passed by virtue of the sale would have been defeated, not by some arid legal technicality but by what Lord Blackburn called "the very nature of things." The same conclusion applies, and for the same reason, to any argument that a title in equity was created by the sale, taken in isolation from the collateral promises. It is unnecessary to examine in detail the decision of the Court of Appeal in *In re Wait* [1927] 1 Ch. 606 [**[424]** above] for the facts were crucially different. There, the contract was for a sale ex-bulk. The 500 tons in question formed part of a larger quantity shipped on board a named vessel; the seller could supply from no other source; and once the entire quantity had been landed and warehoused the buyer could point to the bulk and say that his goods were definitely there, although he could not tell which part they were. It was this feature which prompted the dissenting opinion of Sargant L.J. that the sub-purchasers had a sufficient partial equitable interest in the whole to found a claim for measuring out and delivery of 500 tons. No such feature exists here. Nevertheless, the reasoning contained in the judgment of Atkin L.J., at pp. 625–641, which their Lordships' venture to find irresistible, points unequivocally to the conclusion that under a simple contract for the sale of unascertained goods no equitable title can pass merely by virtue of the sale.

This is not, of course, the end of the matter. As Atkin L.J. himself acknowledged, at p. 636:

> "[The rules in the statute] have, of course, no relevance when one is considering rights, legal or equitable, which may come into existence dehors the contract for sale. A seller or a purchaser may, of course, create any equity he pleases by way of charge, equitable assignment or any other dealing with or disposition of goods, the subject matter of sale; and he may, of course, create such an equity as one of the terms expressed in the contract of sale."

Their Lordships therefore turn to consider whether there is anything in the collateral promises which enables the customers to overcome the practical objections to an immediate transfer of title. The most direct route would be to treat the collateral promises as containing a declaration of trust by the company in favour of the customer. The question then immediately arises—What was the subject matter of the trust? The only possible answer, so far as concerns an immediate transfer of title on sale, is that the trust related to the company's current stock of bullion answering the contractual description;

for there was no other bullion to which the trust could relate. Their Lordships do not doubt that the vendor of goods sold ex-bulk can effectively declare himself trustee of the bulk in favour of the buyer, so as to confer pro tanto an equitable title. But the present transaction was not of this type. The company cannot have intended to create an interest in its general stock of gold which would have inhibited any dealings with it otherwise than for the purpose of delivery under the non-allocated sale contracts. Conversely the customer, who is presumed to have intended that somewhere in the bullion held by or on behalf of the company there would be stored a quantity representing "his" bullion, cannot have contemplated that his rights would be fixed by reference to a combination of the quantity of bullion of the relevant description which the company happened to have in stock at the relevant time and the number of purchasers who happened to have open contracts at that time for goods of that description. To understand the transaction in this way would be to make it a sale of bullion ex-bulk, which on the documents and findings of fact it plainly was not.

Nor is the argument improved by reshaping the trust, so as to contemplate that the property in the res vendita did pass to the customer, albeit in the absence of delivery, and then merged in a general equitable title to the pooled stock of bullion. Once again the argument contradicts the transaction. The customer purchased for the physical delivery on demand of the precise quantity of bullion fixed by his contract, not a shifting proportion of a shifting bulk, prior to delivery. . . .

[The Privy Council also considered, and rejected, various arguments based on estoppel.]

. . . .

IV. *Title to after-acquired bullion*

Having for these reasons rejected the submission that the non-allocated claimants acquired an immediate title by reason of the contract of sale and the collateral promises their Lordships turn to the question whether the claimants later achieved a proprietary interest when the company purchased bullion and put it into its own stock. Broadly speaking, there are two forms which such an argument might take.

According to the first, the contracts of sale were agreements for the sale of goods afterwards to be acquired. It might be contended that quite independently of any representation made by the company to the non-allocated claimants, as soon as the company acquired bullion answering the contractual description the purchaser achieved an equitable title, even though the passing of legal title was postponed until the goods were ascertained and appropriated at the time of physical delivery to the purchaser. In the event this argument was not separately pursued, and their Lordships mention it only by way of introduction. They will do so briefly, since it was bound to fail. The line of old cases, founded on *Holroyd v. Marshall* (1862) 10 H.L.Cas. 191 and discussed in *Benjamin's Sale of Goods*, 3rd ed. (1987), pp. 80, 218–219, paras. 106 and 357, which might be said to support it, was concerned with situations where the goods upon acquisition could be unequivocally identified with the individual contract relied upon. As Lord Hanworth M.R. demonstrated in *In re Wait* [1927] 1 Ch. 606, 622, the reasoning of these cases cannot be transferred to a situation like the present where there was no means of knowing to which, if any, of the non-allocated sales a particular purchase by the company was related. Since this objection on its own is fatal, there is no need to discuss the other obstacles which stand in its way.

The second category of argument asserts, in a variety of forms, that the collateral promises operated to impress on the bullion, as and when it was acquired by the company, a trust in favour of each purchaser. Before looking at the arguments in detail it is necessary to mention a problem which is very little discussed in the judgments and arguments. It will be seen that the analysis to date has involved two markedly different assumptions. The first relates to the expectation of the customer in the light of the collateral promises. The customer is assumed to have believed that it would make no difference whether he took immediate delivery of the bullion and put it in a bank, or left it with the company—except that in the latter case he would avoid the trouble, risk and expense of storage. In law this expectation could be fulfilled only by a system under which the company obtained bullion either by an outside purchase or by transfer from its own stock, and immediately stored it separately in the name of the customer, leaving it untouched until the moment of delivery or re-purchase. The second assumption relates to the obligations which the company actually undertook. It has not been suggested that this matched the customer's expectation, for there is nothing in the collateral promises, either written or oral, entitling the customer to separate and individual appropriation of goods. Instead, as shown by the passage already quoted from the judgment of McKay J. [1993] 1 N.Z.L.R. 257, 296–297, the arguments proceed on the basis that the company promised to maintain bullion, separate from its own trading stock, which would in some way stand as security, or reassurance, that the bullion would be available when the customer called for delivery. But what kind of security or reassurance? If the scheme had contemplated that, properly performed, it would have brought about a transfer of title to the individual customer before that customer's appropriated bullion was mixed in the undifferentiated bulk, analogies could have been drawn with decisions such as *Spence v. Union Marine Insurance Co. Ltd.* (1868) L.R. 3 C.P. 427, *South Australian Insurance Co. v. Randell* (1869) L.R. 3 P.C. 101, *Indian Oil Corporation Ltd. v. Greenstone Shipping S.A. (Panama)* [1988] Q.B. 345, and the United States silo cases of which *Savage v. Salem Mills Co.* (1906) 85 P. 69 is an example. Since, however, even if the company had performed its obligations to the full there would have been no transfer of title to the purchaser before admixture, these cases are not in point. The only remaining alternative, consistently with the scheme being designed to give the customer any title at all before delivery, is that the company through the medium of the collateral promises had declared itself a trustee of the constantly changing undifferentiated bulk of bullion which should have been set aside to back the customers' contracts. Such a trust might well be feasible in theory, but their Lordships find it hard to reconcile with the practicalities of the scheme, for it would seem to involve that the separated bulk would become the source from which alone the sale contracts were to be supplied: whereas, as already observed, it is impossible to read the collateral promises as creating a sale ex-bulk.

This being so, whilst it is easy to see how the company's failure to perform the collateral obligations has fuelled the indignation created by its failure to deliver the bullion under the sales to non-allocated purchasers, their Lordships are far from convinced that this particular breach has in fact made any difference.

Let it be assumed, however, as did McKay J. [1993] 1 N.Z.L.R. 257, 284 in his dissenting judgment, that the creation of a separate and sufficient stock would have given the non-allocated purchasers some kind of proprietary interest, the fact remains that the separate and sufficient stock did not exist.

The customers' first response to this objection is that even if the concept of an immediate trust derived from a bailment arising at the time of the original transactions cannot be sustained, the collateral promises created a potential or incomplete or (as it was called in argument) "floating" bailment, which hovered above the continuing relationship between each purchaser and the company, until the company bought and took delivery of bullion corresponding to the claimant's contract, whereupon the company became bailee of the bullion on terms which involved a trust in favour of the purchaser. Their Lordships find it impossible to see how this ingenious notion, even if feasible in principle, could be put into practice here, given that the body of potential beneficiaries was constantly changing as some purchasers called for and took delivery whilst others came newly on the scene, at the same time as the pool of available bullion waxed and waned (sometimes to zero as regards some types of bullion) with fresh deliveries and acquisitions. Even if this is left aside, the concept simply does not fit the facts. True, there is no difficulty with a transaction whereby B promises A that if in the future goods belonging to A come within the physical control of B he will hold them as bailee for A on terms fixed in advance by the agreement. But this has nothing to do with a trust relationship, and it has nothing to do with the present case, since in the example given A has both title to the goods and actual or constructive possession of them before their receipt by B, whereas in the present case the non-allocated claimants had neither. The only escape would be to suggest that every time the company took delivery of bullion of a particular description all the purchasers from the company of the relevant kind of bullion acquired both a higher possessory right than the company (for such would be essential if the company was to be a bailee) and a title to the goods, via some species of estoppel derived from this notional transfer and retransfer of possession. Their Lordships find it impossible to construct such a contorted legal relationship from the contracts of sale and the collateral promises.

Next, the claimants put forward an argument in two stages. First, it is said that because the company held itself out as willing to vest bullion in the customer and to hold it in safe custody on behalf of him in circumstances where he was totally dependent on the company, and trusted the company to do what it had promised without in practice there being any means of verification, the company was a fiduciary. From this it is deduced that the company as fiduciary created an equity by inviting the customer to look on and treat stocks vested in it as his own, which could appropriately be recognised only by treating the customer as entitled to a proprietary interest in the stock.

To describe someone as a fiduciary, without more, is meaningless. As Frankfurter J. said in *S.E.C. v. Chenery Corporation* (1943) 318 U.S. 80, 885–86, cited in Goff and Jones, *The Law of Restitution*, 4th ed. (1993), p. 644:

> "To say that a man is a fiduciary only begins analysis; it gives direction to further inquiry. To whom is he a fiduciary? What obligations does he owe as a fiduciary? In what respect has he failed to discharge these obligations? And what are the consequences of his deviation from duty?"

Here, the argument assumes that the person towards whom the company was fiduciary was the non-allocated claimant. But what kind of fiduciary duties did the company owe to the customer? None have been suggested beyond those which the company assumed under the contracts of sale read with the collateral promises; namely to deliver the goods and meanwhile to keep a separate stock of bullion (or, more accurately, separate stocks of each variety of bullion) to which the customers could look as a safeguard for performance when delivery was called for. No doubt the fact that one person is placed in a particular position vis-à-vis another through the medium of a contract does not necessarily mean that he does not also owe fiduciary duties to that other by virtue of being in that position. But the essence of a fiduciary relationship is that it creates obligations of a different character from those deriving from the contract itself. Their Lordships have not heard in argument any submission which went beyond suggesting that by virtue of being a fiduciary the company was obliged honestly and conscientiously to do what it had by contract promised to do. Many commercial relationships involve just such a reliance by one party on the other, and to introduce the whole new dimension into such relationships which would flow from giving them a fiduciary character would (as it seems to their Lordships) have adverse consequences far exceeding those foreseen by Atkin L.J. in *In re Wait* [1927] 1 Ch. 606. It is possible without misuse of language to say that the customers put faith in the company, and that their trust has not been repaid. But the vocabulary is misleading; high expectations do not necessarily lead to equitable remedies.

Let it be assumed, however, that the company could properly be described as a fiduciary and let it also be assumed that notwithstanding the doubts expressed above the non-allocated claimants would have achieved some kind of proprietary interest if the company had done what it said. This still leaves the problem, to which their Lordships can see no answer, that the company did not do what it said. There never was a separate and sufficient stock of bullion in which a proprietary interest could be created. What the non-allocated claimants are really trying to achieve is to attach the proprietary interest, which they maintain should have been created on the non-existent stock, to wholly different assets. It is understandable that the claimants, having been badly let down in a transaction concerning bullion should believe that they must have rights over whatever bullion the company still happens to possess. Whilst sympathising with this notion their Lordships must reject it, for the remaining stock, having never been separated, is just another asset of the company, like its vehicles and office furniture. If the argument applies to the bullion it must apply to the latter as well, an obviously unsustainable idea.

Finally, it is argued that the court should declare in favour of the claimants a remedial constructive trust, or to use another name a restitutionary proprietary interest, over the bullion in the company's vaults. Such a trust or interest would differ fundamentally from those so far discussed, in that it would not arise directly from the transaction between the individual claimants, the company and the bullion, but would be created by the court as a measure of justice after the event. Their Lordships must return to this topic later when considering the Walker Hall claimants who, the trial judge has held, did acquire a proprietary interest in some bullion, but they are unable to understand how the doctrine in any of its suggested formulations could apply to the facts of the present case. By leaving its stock of bullion in a non-differentiated state the company did not unjustly enrich itself by mixing its own bullion with that of the purchasers: for all the gold belonged to the company. It did not act wrongfully in acquiring, maintaining and using its own stock of bullion, since there was no term of the sale contracts or of the collateral promises, and none could possibly be implied, requiring that all bullion purchased by the company should be set aside to fulfil the unallocated sales. The conduct of the company was wrongful in the sense of being a breach of contract, but it did not involve any injurious dealing with the subject matter of the alleged trust. Nor, if some wider equitable principle is involved, does the case become any stronger. As previously remarked the claimants' argument really comes to this, that because the company broke its contract in a way which had to do with bullion the court should call into existence a proprietary interest in whatever bullion happened to be in the possession and ownership of the company at the time when the competition between the non-allocated claimants and the other secured and unsecured creditors first arose. The company's stock of bullion had no connection with the claimants' purchases, and to enable the claimants to reach out and not only abstract it from the assets available to the body of creditors as a whole, but also to afford a priority over a secured creditor, would give them an adventitious benefit devoid of the foundation in logic and justice which underlies this important new branch of the law.

V. *Conclusion on property in bullion*
For these reasons their Lordships reject, in company with all the judges in New Zealand, the grounds upon which it is said that the customers acquired a proprietary interest in bullion. . .'

[The Privy Council then considered, and rejected, the possibility that the claimants acquired some sort of proprietary interest derived from retaining an interest in the funds paid over as the purchase price for the bullion. This is relevant to the issues discussed in Chapter 5 below.]

Also see:

Mac-Jordan Construction Ltd v Brookmount Erostin Ltd (in rec) [1992] BCLC 350.

Questions:

1. Section 20A was inserted into the Sale of Goods Act 1979 in 1995 (see **[421]** above), *after* the decisions in the cases extracted above. Would it have made any difference to the outcomes?
2. Even if the goods to be purchased *had* been sufficiently identified, could the intending purchaser ever acquire equitable title in advance of the transfer of legal title—in other words, were the relevant contracts of sale specifically enforceable and is this feature necessary?

4.10.4 Sales of future goods

See Section 4.12 below.

4.10.5 Barter

As noted earlier, the essence of contract for the sale of goods is that the seller transfers property in goods to the buyer for a money consideration called the price. Barter, on the other hand, describes a transaction where the consideration (or at least part of the consideration) is not money, but consists of goods, services or other valuable consideration.[34]

Whether the arrangement is a barter or true sale affects when ownership passes and when risk passes. In contracts for the sale of goods, these matters are determined by the Sale of Goods Act 1979. Property often passes at the time the contract

[34] The distinction can be a matter of interpretation. Eg, in *Aldridge v Johnson* (1875) 7 E & B 885, bullocks were exchanged for barley and a cash sum. This agreement was construed as reciprocal sales with the cash sum representing the outstanding balance. However, the court recognised that if the arrangement was simply to exchange the bullocks for the barley and cash without valuing the chattels, then the contract would have been one of barter.

is made, before delivery. With contracts of barter, property in the bartered goods does not pass until delivery.[35] If one party to the agreement does not perform, then old authority suggests that the proper action is in trover or deceit,[36] not an action for the value of the goods transferred.[37] Some aspects of contracts of barter are now governed by the Supply of Goods and Services Act 1982, but not this issue of the passing of property.

FURTHER READING:

E M C Canton, 'Sale of Goods and Barter' (1976) 39 *MLR* 589.

4.11 Sales of choses in action

4.11.1 Sales of legal choses in action

As indicated earlier, choses in action may be either legal or equitable. Sales of legal choses in action will only be effective to transfer legal title to the purchaser once all the requirements for legal transfer have been met. These are the same requirements as considered earlier in relation to gifts of legal choses in action (see Section 4.6.1 above). Generally the determinant is notification of some third party (eg the debtor, if a debt is being transferred), or registration by some third party (eg registration on the company's register of shares if shares are being transferred).

Even if the requirements for legal transfer have not been met, it is nevertheless possible for the intending purchaser to acquire equitable title to the asset in advance of the legal transfer. This will only happen if the contract for the sale of the asset is specifically enforceable and unconditional and the sale property is sufficiently identified (see **[423]** above). The ability of the intending purchaser to assert equitable ownership of the sale property in advance of the transfer of legal title can have important consequences, notably on the vendor's insolvency, but also where the sale property entails valuable interim rights, such as the right to vote shares or the right to dividends on shares.

Many cases where this is an issue concern contracts for the sale of shares. Generally contracts for the sale of shares are specifically enforceable only if the shares are not freely available on the market; only then will damages provide an inadequate remedy. It follows that contracts for the sale of shares in publicly listed

35 *Cochrane v Moore* (1890) 25 QBD 57.
36 *Read v Hutchinson* (1813) 3 Camp 352.
37 Although note that where the agreement is for cash plus part-exchange, then the cash can be recovered by an action for the outstanding price: *Sheldon v Cox* (1824) 3 B & C 420.

companies are not usually specifically enforceable,[38] while contracts for the sale of shares in private companies are.[39]

[427] *Sainsbury plc v O'Connor* [1991] 1 WLR 963 (CA), 977–9 *per* Nourse LJ:
[The case concerned an option, exercisable in five years' time, to purchase certain shares. The court held that prior to the exercise of the option the vendor retained beneficial ownership of the shares. This was important to the vendor, who was claiming tax relief which was dependent upon ownership of the shares in question.]

'The first question is whether, within the meaning of section 532(3) of the Income and Corporation Taxes Act 1970, the "beneficial ownership" in the five per cent. of the shares in Homebase Ltd. which were subject to the unexercised put and call options in favour of G.B. was vested in the taxpayer company or not. . . .

There is no difficulty in ascertaining the legal ownership of shares, which is invariably vested in the registered holder. Equally, it ought not to be difficult to ascertain their beneficial ownership, albeit that it may arise in a variety of ways, for example under a declaration of trust or by operation of law. I therefore approach the construction of section 532(3), a provision having general application for the purposes of the Taxes Acts, in the expectation that the extent to which one company is beneficially owned by another was not intended to depend on fine distinctions between different cases.

Although I might not . . . have gone so far as to think that the expression "beneficial ownership" is a term of art, it is certainly one which has for several centuries had a very well recognised meaning amongst property lawyers. And there can be no doubt that, in enacting a provision such as section 532(3), Parliament must have intended to adopt that meaning. It means ownership for your own benefit as opposed to ownership as trustee for another. It exists either where there is no division of legal and beneficial ownership or where legal ownership is vested in one person and beneficial ownership or, which is the same thing, the equitable interest in the property in another. Thus, to take the simplest case of divided ownership to which section 532(3) can apply, if company A is the registered holder of shares in company B as nominee, i.e. as a bare trustee, for company C, the beneficial ownership of the shares or the equitable interest in them is vested in company C.

Another case to which section 532(3) can apply is where company A enters into an unconditional contract to sell shares in company B to company C. Shares in company B not being readily obtainable in the market, such a contract is specifically enforceable at the suit of company C. By parity with contracts for the sale of land, it has long been held that the right to specific performance gives company C the equitable interest in the shares, company A becoming a qualified trustee in the sense that it must preserve the shares for company C while remaining entitled to any dividends accruing before completion.

In that state of affairs in which of the two companies is the beneficial ownership of the shares vested pending completion of the contract? It cannot be doubted that it is vested in company C. In other words, in this instance at any rate, no distinction is to be drawn between the beneficial ownership and the equitable interest. As appears from the passages in their judgments in *Parway Estates Ltd. v. Inland Revenue Commissioners*, 45

[38] Eg *Cud v Rutter* (1719) 1 P Wms 570; *Re Schwabacher* (1907) 98 LT Rep. 127. Note that specific performance will not be ordered after the company has been wound up since transfer of the shares would be void against the company: *Sullivan v Henderson* [1973] 1 WLR 333.

[39] Eg *Duncuft v Albrecht* (1841) 12 Sim 189; 59 ER 1104. Also see *Harvela Investments Ltd v Royal Trust Co of Canada (CI) Ltd* [1986] AC 207, where a contract for the sale of shares giving a controlling interest in the company was held to be specifically enforceable.

T.C. 135 to which Lloyd L.J. has referred, that is an assumption which has in the past been made by judges as eminent in this field as Lord Jenkins and Lord Upjohn. In the same company I would cite the observations of Sir George Jessel M.R. in relation to a contract for the sale of land in *Lysaght v. Edwards* (1876) 2 Ch.D. 499, 506:

> "It appears to me that the effect of a contract for sale has been settled for more than two centuries; certainly it was completely settled before the time of Lord Hardwicke, who speaks of the settled doctrine of the court as to it. What is that doctrine? It is that the moment you have a valid contract for sale the vendor becomes in equity a trustee for the purchaser of the estate sold, and the beneficial ownership passes to the purchaser . . ."

So far therefore I see no reason to doubt that Parliament intended, in the application of section 532(3) to specifically enforceable contracts for the sale of shares, that there should be no difference between the beneficial ownership of the shares and the equitable interest in them. Nor, in the absence of authority to the contrary, would I be able to grasp the concept of the beneficial ownership being suspended somewhere between the vendor and the purchaser. I would think that it must be vested in the one or in the other and, if it has not passed to the purchaser, that it must remain in the vendor. That is not in any way to cast doubt on the well known examples of a suspension of beneficial ownership to which Lloyd L.J. has referred [ie where legal title is held by a trustee in bankruptcy, or a liquidator, or an administrator of a deceased estate]. They are far removed from contracts for the sale of land or of shares.

Then take the previous example, but suppose that the contract is subject to a condition precedent. Until the condition is satisfied the equitable interest in the shares will not pass to company C. It will remain in company A. What ground is there for thinking that the beneficial ownership of the shares will not also remain in company A? In order to answer that question we must look to *Wood Preservation Ltd. v. Prior* [1969] 1 W.L.R. 1077. That is a difficult decision. Goff J. at first instance did not distinguish between the beneficial ownership of the shares and the equitable interest in them. In my view he was right not to make that distinction. However, he thought that, because the purchaser could obtain specific performance of the contract by waiving the condition precedent at any time, "the beneficial interest had sufficiently passed to the purchaser." I respectfully think that that was an error on the part of the judge. Unless and until the condition was either waived or satisfied there could be no right to specific performance and no passing of the equitable interest.

It seems that Goff J.'s error was perceived by this court who, in the process of correcting it, gave a decision whose effect was to draw a distinction between the beneficial ownership of the shares and the equitable interest in them. Their approach was bound, as the present case demonstrates, to lead to fine distinctions between different cases. . . .

. . . The decision of this court in the *Wood Preservation Ltd.* case is binding on us for what it decided. I would be unwilling to apply it to any case where the vendor retained more than a mere legal shell of ownership. The grantor of an option which has not been exercised retains much more than that.'

Also see:

Michaels v Harley House (Marylebone) Ltd [1999] 3 WLR 229 (CA) (**[801]** below).

Questions:

1. According to this case, if A contracts to sell property to B, when will equitable title to the property pass to B? Once equitable title has passed, what rights does each party have in the sale property? Is it preferable to decide whether A retains an equitable interest in the property by looking at the rights of A (as was done in the *Wood Preservation Ltd* case discussed in the previous extract) or by looking at the rights of B (as was done in the *Sainsbury* case, above)? Is it clear what 'bundle of rights' is essential to the status of an equitable owner, and what rights might be transferred to B without loss of that status?
2. These equitable rules afford more generous protection to intending purchasers than the rules which apply to expectant donees of gifts (see Section 4.6.2 above). Why should this be so?
3. Assume that the effective transfer of legal title to an asset depends upon the contract of transfer being in writing, signed by the transferor. In these circumstances is it possible for the transferee to become the owner in equity of the asset notwithstanding the absence of writing? Note that there are several possible approaches to answering this question. For example, a court might refuse to intervene, on the basis that failure to comply with the legal rule is an absolute bar to beneficial transfer. Alternatively, a court might order specific performance of the agreement simply by ordering the transferor to sign. The effect of this would be that the transferor retains legal and beneficial title to the asset until the time the signature is applied, and in the interim the transferee has only a mere equity, not a proprietary interest in the sale asset. Finally, a court might apply the rule that 'equity regards as done that which ought to be done' and, moreover, it may consider that what ought to be done includes signing by the transferor. The effect of this is that the transferee will have an equitable interest in the asset even before the writing requirements are met. Are there further alternatives? Which approach is preferable? Does the answer depend upon the precise terms of the statute imposing the writing requirement? See Section 4.11.2 below.

4.11.2 Sales of equitable choses in action

Equitable choses can, of course, only be transferred in equity. As indicated earlier, the Law of Property Act 1925 section 53(1)(c) indicates that writing is necessary for the effective transfer of a subsisting equitable interest (see **[410]** above). However, as the cases extracted below indicate, there have been suggestions that this writing requirement can be avoided by recourse to the Law of Property Act 1925 section 53(2): the intending purchaser does not rely on the effective transfer of the equitable chose itself, but on the fact that the contract to transfer is specifically enforceable (even if not in writing) so that the vendor holds the chose on constructive trust for the purchaser.

[428] *Oughtred v IRC* [1960] AC 206 (HL), 227–8 *per* Lord Radcliffe (dissenting), 233 *per* Lord Denning, 238–41 *per* Lord Jenkins:

[Trustees of a settlement held 200,000 shares on trust for Mrs Oughtred for life, remainder to her son, Peter. Mrs Oughtred also owned another 72,700 shares absolutely. The parties agreed orally that Mrs Oughtred would transfer her 72,700 shares to her son, and that he would make her the absolute beneficial owner of the 200,000 shares by giving up his remainder to her. A week later, documents were executed to reflect this agreement. One of these documents was for the transfer of 200,000 shares from the trustees to Mrs Oughtred. If the oral dispositions were effective, this would have attracted nominal stamp duty since it would involve only the transfer of bare legal title to Mrs Oughtred. However, by bare majority the House of Lords considered the document should be assessed to *ad valorem* stamp duty. To a large extent the reasons of the House of Lords relate to the interpretation of taxing statute; however, there are some important observations on the effect of the agreement and the application of the Law of Property Act 1925 section 53.]

Lord Radcliffe (dissenting):

'Yet the law with regard to liability to stamp duty is clear enough. The duty is charged upon instruments, if they exist and come within any of the categories prescribed by the Act. It is not charged upon transactions. Thus property such as chattels, which by law pass on delivery, can be transferred from one owner to another without attracting duty. Again, though an agreement for sale may be chargeable ad valorem, since the Act has so required, an oral agreement for the sale of property involves no charge to duty because no instrument is brought into existence to effect or to record it. The whole point of the present appeal seems to me to turn on the question whether it is open to a court of law to deduce from the documents of this case that Mrs. Oughtred's title to her son's equitable reversionary interest rested upon anything more than the oral agreement which admittedly took place.

My Lords, on this short point my opinion is that such a deduction is not open to a court of law. The materials that would support it are simply not there. . . .

The reasoning of the whole matter, as I see it, is as follows: On June 18, 1956, the son owned an equitable reversionary interest in the settled shares: by his oral agreement of that date he created in his mother an equitable interest in his reversion, since the subject-matter of the agreement was property of which specific performance would normally be decreed by the court. He thus became a trustee for her of that interest sub modo: having regard to subsection (2) of section 53 of the Law of Property Act, 1925, subsection (1) of that section did not operate to prevent that trusteeship arising by operation of law. On June 26 Mrs. Oughtred transferred to her son the shares which were the consideration for her acquisition of his equitable interest: upon this transfer he became in a full sense and without more the trustee of his interest for her. She was the effective owner of all outstanding equitable interests. It was thus correct to recite in the deed of release to the trustees of the settlement, which was to wind up their trust, that the trust fund was by then held upon trust for her absolutely. There was, in fact, no equity to the shares that could be asserted against her, and it was open to her, if she so wished, to let the matter rest without calling for a written assignment from her son. Given that the trustees were apprised of the making of the oral agreement and of Mrs. Oughtred's satisfaction of the consideration to be given by her, the trustees had no more to do than to transfer their legal title to her or as she might direct. This and no more is what they did.

It follows that, in my view, this transfer cannot be treated as a conveyance of the son's equitable reversion at all. The trustees had not got it: he never transferred or released it to them: how then could they convey it? With all respect to those who think otherwise, it is incorrect to say that the trustees' transfer was made either with his authority or at his direction. If the recital as to Mrs. Oughtred's rights was correct, as I think that it was, he had no remaining authority to give or direction to issue. A release is, after all, the normal instrument for winding up a trust when all the equitable rights are vested and the legal estate is called for from the trustees who hold it. What the release gave the trustees from him was acquittance for the trust administration and accounts to date, and the fact that he gave it in consideration of the legal interest in the shares being vested in his mother adds nothing on this point. Nor does it, with respect, advance the matter to say, correctly, that at the end of the day Mrs. Oughtred was the absolute owner of the shares, legal and equitable. I think that she was: but that is description, not analysis. The question that is relevant for the purpose of this appeal is how she came to occupy that position; a position which, under English law, could be reached by more than one road.

Lastly, I ought perhaps to say that I do not myself see any analogy between the operations embraced by the oral agreement and documents and the common case of a sale of shares by an owner for whom they are held by a nominee or bare trustee. What is sold there is the shares themselves, not the owner's equitable interest. What is passed by the transfer executed by his nominee is the shares, according to the contract, without any incumbrance on the title, equitable or legal. It is, I think, a misunderstanding of the law to speak of the nominee as transferring his beneficiary's previous equitable interest to the purchaser.'

[Lord Cohen delivered a dissenting opinion along similar lines]

Lord Denning:
'I do not think it necessary to embark upon a disquisition on constructive trusts: because I take the view that, even if the oral agreement of June 18, 1956, was effective to transfer Peter's reversionary interest to his mother, nevertheless, when that oral agreement was subsequently implemented by the transfer, then the transfer became liable to stamp duty [because, in Lord Denning's opinion, the terms of the statute rendered every conveyance or transfer by which an agreement for sale was implemented liable to stamp duty on the consideration paid]. But I may say that I do not think the oral agreement was effective to transfer Peter's reversionary interest to his mother. I should have thought that the wording of section 53 (1) (c) of the Law of Property Act, 1925, clearly made a writing necessary to effect a transfer: and section 53 (2) does not do away with that necessity.

Lord Jenkins:
'It is said, and said truly, that stamp duty is imposed on instruments, not transactions, and that a transaction of sale carried out without bringing into existence an instrument which has the effect of transferring to or vesting in the purchaser the property sold attracts no duty. . . .

It is said further that in the present case the disputed transfer transferred nothing beyond a bare legal estate, because, in accordance with the well-settled principle applicable to contracts of sale, between contract and completion the appellant became under the oral agreement beneficially entitled in equity to the settled shares, subject to the due satisfaction by her of the purchase consideration, and accordingly the entire beneficial interest in the settled shares had already passed to her at the time of the execution of the disputed transfer, and there was nothing left upon which the disputed transfer could operate except the bare legal estate.

The Commissioners of Inland Revenue seek to meet this argument by reference to section 53 (1) (c) of the Law of Property Act, 1925. They contend that as the agreement of June 18, 1956, was an oral agreement it could not, in view of section 53 (1) (c), effect a disposition of a subsisting equitable interest or trust, and accordingly that Peter's subsisting equitable interest under the trusts of the settlement, in the shape of his reversionary interest, remained vested in him until the execution of the disputed transfer, which in these circumstances operated as a transfer on sale to the appellant of Peter's reversionary interest and additionally as a transfer not on sale to the appellant of the legal interest in the settled shares. It was by this process of reasoning that the Commissioners arrived at the opinion expressed in the case stated that the disputed transfer attracted both the ad valorem duty exigible on a transfer on sale of the reversionary interest and also the fixed duty of 10*s.*

This argument is attacked on the appellant's side by reference to subsection (2) of section 53 of the Act of 1925, which excludes the creation or operation of resulting, implied or constructive trusts from the provisions of subsection (1). It is said that inasmuch as the oral agreement was an agreement of sale and purchase it gave rise, on the principle to which I have already adverted, to a constructive trust of the reversionary interest in favour of the appellant subject to performance by her of her obligation to transfer to Peter the free shares forming the consideration for the sale. It is said that this trust, being constructive, was untouched by section 53 (1) (c) in view of the exemption afforded by section 53 (2), and that the appellant's primary argument still holds good.

I find it unnecessary to decide whether section 53 (2) has the effect of excluding the present transaction from the operation of Section 53 (1) (c), for, assuming in the appellant's favour that the oral contract did have the effect in equity of raising a constructive trust of the settled shares for her untouched by section 53 (1) (c), I am unable to accept the conclusion that the disputed transfer was prevented from being a transfer of the shares to the appellant on sale because the entire beneficial interest in the settled shares was already vested in the appellant under the constructive trust, and there was accordingly nothing left for the disputed transfer to pass to the appellant except the bare legal estate. The constructive trust in favour of a purchaser which arises on the conclusion of a contract for sale is founded upon the purchaser's right to enforce the contract in proceedings for specific performance. In other words, he is treated in equity as entitled by virtue of the contract to the property which the vendor is bound under the contract to convey to him. This interest under the contract is no doubt a proprietary interest of a sort, which arises, so to speak, in anticipation of the execution of the transfer for which the purchaser is entitled to call. But its existence has never (so far as I know) been held to prevent a subsequent transfer, in performance of the contract, of the property contracted to be sold from constituting for stamp duty purposes a transfer on sale of the property in question. Take the simple case of a contract for the sale of land. In such a case a constructive trust in favour of the purchaser arises on the conclusion of the contract for sale, but (so far as I know) it has never been held on this account that a conveyance subsequently executed in performance of the contract is not stampable ad valorem as a transfer on sale. Similarly, in a case like the present one, but uncomplicated by the existence of successive interests, a transfer to a purchaser of the investments comprised in a trust fund could not, in my judgment, be prevented from constituting a transfer on sale for the purposes of stamp duty by reason of the fact that the actual transfer had been preceded by an oral agreement for sale.

In truth, the title secured by a purchaser by means of an actual transfer is different in kind from, and may well be far superior to, the special form of proprietary interest which equity confers on a purchaser in anticipation of such transfer.

This difference is of particular importance in the case of property such as shares in a limited company. Under the contract the purchaser is no doubt entitled in equity as between himself and the vendor to the beneficial interest in the shares, and (subject to due payment of the purchase consideration) to call for a transfer of them from the vendor as trustee for him. But it is only on the execution of the actual transfer that he becomes entitled to be registered as a member, to attend and vote at meetings, to effect transfers on the register, or to receive dividends otherwise than through the vendor as his trustee.

The parties to a transaction of sale and purchase may no doubt choose to let the matter rest in contract. But if the subject-matter of a sale is such that the full title to it can only be transferred by an instrument, then any instrument they execute by way of transfer of the property sold ranks for stamp duty purposes as a conveyance on sale notwithstanding the constructive trust in favour of the purchaser which arose on the conclusion of the contract.'

[Lord Keith concurred in this opinion.]

Question:

Did the House of Lords decide that the oral declaration was effective to transfer Peter's interest to his mother?

Re-read:

Grey v IRC [1960] AC 1 (HL) (**[411]** above).
Vandervell v Inland Revenue Commission [1967] 2 AC 291 (HL) (**[412]** above).
Re Vandervell's Trusts (No 2); White v Vandervell Trustees Ltd [1974] Ch 269 (CA) (**[413]** above).

[429] *Re Holt's Settlement* [1969] 1 Ch 100, 116 *per* Megarry J:
[The facts are immaterial.]

'Where, as here, the arrangement consists of an agreement made for valuable consideration, and that agreement is specifically enforceable, then the beneficial interests pass to the respective purchasers on the making of the agreement. Those interests pass by virtue of the species of constructive trust made familiar by contracts for the sale of land, whereunder the vendor becomes a constructive trustee for the purchaser as soon as the contract is made, albeit the constructive trust has special features about it. . . . Accordingly, because the trust was constructive, section 53(1)(c) is excluded.'

[430] *Neville v Wilson* [1997] Ch 144 (CA), 155–8 *per* Nourse LJ:
[The case concerned an oral agreement to liquidate a company informally and distribute its assets to the shareholders. The court held that the effect of the agreement

was to constitute each shareholder an implied or constructive trustee for the other shareholders, effectively allowing the Law of Property Act 1925 section 53(2) to dispense with the writing requirement demanded by section 53(1)(c).]

'The effect of the agreement, more closely analysed, was that each shareholder agreed to assign his interest in the other shares of J.E.N.'s equitable interest in exchange for the assignment by the other shareholders of their interests in his own aliquot share. Each individual agreement having been a disposition of a subsisting equitable interest not made in writing, there then arises the question whether it was rendered ineffectual by section 53 of the Law of Property Act 1925, which, so far as material, provides:

"(1) Subject to the provisions hereinafter contained with respect to the creation of interests in land by parol . . . (c) a disposition of an equitable interest or trust subsisting at the time of the disposition, must be in writing signed by the person disposing of the same, or by his agent thereunto lawfully authorised in writing or by will. (2) This section does not affect the creation or operation of resulting, implied or constructive trusts."

. . . The question depends on the correct view of a point left open in *Oughtred v. Inland Revenue Commissioners* [1960] A.C. 206.

The simple view of the present case is that the effect of each individual agreement was to constitute the shareholder an implied or constructive trustee for the other shareholders, so that the requirement for writing contained in subsection (1)(c) of section 53 was dispensed with by subsection (2). That was the view taken by Upjohn J. [1958] Ch. 383 at first instance and by Lord Radcliffe in the House of Lords in *Oughtred v. Inland Revenue Commissioners* [1960] A.C. 206. In order to see whether it is open to us to adopt it in this court, we must give careful consideration to those views and to the other speeches in the House of Lords.

[After reciting the facts of *Oughtred* and extracting various parts of the judgments (see **[428]** above), Nourse LJ continued.]

The views of their Lordships as to the effect of section 53 can be summarised as follows. Lord Radcliffe, agreeing with Upjohn J., thought that subsection (2) applied. He gave reasons for that view. Lord Cohen and Lord Denning thought that it did not. Although neither of them gave reasons, they may be taken to have accepted the submissions of Mr. Wilberforce at pp. 220–222. Lord Keith and Lord Jenkins expressed no view either way. We should add that when the case was in this court Lord Evershed M.R., in delivering the judgment of himself, Morris and Ormerod L.JJ., said [1958] Ch. 678, 687:

"In this court the case for the Crown has, we think, been somewhat differently presented, and in the end of all, the question under section 53 of the Law of Property Act 1925, does not, in our judgment, strictly call for a decision. We are not, however, with all respect to the judge, prepared to accept, as we understand it, his conclusion upon the effect of section 53 of the Law of Property Act 1925."

The basis of this court's decision was the same as that adopted by the majority of the House of Lords.

We do not think that there is anything in the speeches in the House of Lords which prevents us from holding that the effect of each individual agreement was to constitute the shareholder an implied or constructive trustee for the other shareholders. In this respect we are of the opinion that the analysis of Lord Radcliffe, based on the proposition that a specifically enforceable agreement to assign an interest in property creates an equitable interest in the assignee, was unquestionably correct; cf. *London and South Western Railway Co. v. Gomm* (1882) 20 Ch.D. 562, 581, per Sir George Jessel M.R. A greater difficulty is caused by Lord Denning's outright rejection of the application of section 53(2), with which Lord Cohen appears to have agreed.

So far as it is material to the present case, what subsection (2) says is that subsection (1)(c) does not affect the creation or operation of implied or constructive trusts. Just as in *Oughtred v. Inland Revenue Commissioners* [1960] A.C. 206 the son's oral agreement created a constructive trust in favour of the mother, so here each shareholder's oral or implied agreement created an implied or constructive trust in favour of the other shareholders. Why then should subsection (2) not apply? No convincing reason was suggested in argument and none has occurred to us since. Moreover, to deny its application in this case would be to restrict the effect of general words when no restriction is called for, and to lay the ground for fine distinctions in the future. With all the respect which is due to those who have thought to the contrary, we hold that subsection (2) applies to an agreement such as we have in this case.

For these reasons we have come to the conclusion that the agreement entered into by the shareholders of J.E.N. in about April 1969 was not rendered ineffectual by section 53 of the Act of 1925.'

Note:

This case has been criticised by R Nolan, 'The Triumph of Technicality' [1996] *CLJ* 436, but supported by M P Thompson, 'Disposition of Equitable Interests' [1996] *Conv* 368. Which view is more convincing?

Questions:

1. Is a contract for the sale of an asset, the disposition of which is required by statute to be in writing, a contract which is specifically enforceable in the absence of such writing?
2. Even if the contract of sale is specifically enforceable, would the order for specific performance simply require the parties to commit their contract to writing, at which time (but not before) the equitable chose would pass to the purchaser; or is it true that the order for specific performance would require the vendor to transfer the chose to the purchaser (so that, before the transfer, equity would regard the vendor as holding the chose on constructive trust for the purchaser, since this is the way equity regards as done that which ought to be done)?
3. *Is* a contract for the sale of an *equitable* interest specifically enforceable?

4.11.3 Sales of future choses in action

See below, Section 4.12.

4.11.4 Sales of part of an identified bulk

It is possible for parties to agree to sell and purchase from an identified bulk. For example, a vendor may agree to sell 10 per cent of her current holding of 100,000 shares in a particular company, or she may agree to sell 10,000 shares out of that same holding (and debate surrounds whether these alternative forms produce the same consequences). With sales of choses in action, there is nothing which is the equivalent of the Sale of Goods Act 1979 section 20A (dealing with the sale of part of a bulk comprising goods) (see **[421]** above). It is left to equity to assist (or not) intending purchasers. The extent to which assistance is provided remains uncertain, as the next extract indicates.

[431] S Worthington, 'Sorting Out Ownership Interests in a Bulk: Gifts, Sales and Trusts' [1999] *JBL* 1, 7–13:
[Footnotes in the original are omitted.]

> 'Again it is helpful to start with the general rule governing acquisition of equitable interests. Where the intended transaction is not a gift but a *sale* of specifically identified property, the general rule is that the purchaser will acquire equitable ownership of the property in advance of the transfer of legal title only if the contract is unconditional and specifically enforceable. Only when these conditions are met can it be said that the sale property *ought* to be transferred. Only when the sale property *ought* to be transferred will equity, treating as done that which ought to be done, regard it as *already* transferred.
>
> The requirement that the contract be specifically enforceable can have unexpected consequences, so it merits some comment. With many contracts of sale, specific enforcement is not available: damages provide an adequate remedy. With contracts for the sale of goods, the availability of specific enforcement is even more restricted: the orthodox view is that specific enforcement is only possible to the extent allowed by the Sale of Goods Act 1979 and, according to section 52, that is limited to contracts "to deliver specific or ascertained goods". The net effect of this is that specific performance is not available in the context of sales of goods which form part of a bulk (and, accordingly, are not "specific or ascertained" goods). It follows that contracts for such sales can never give rise to equitable interests by operation of law (at least in advance of segregation of goods from the bulk), since the prerequisite of a specifically enforceable contract is absent. Had the facts been different in *Re London Wine Company (Shippers) Ltd* or in *Re Goldcorp Exchange Ltd (in rec.)*, so that the contracts of sale could be described as contracts for the sale of goods from an identified bulk, this general rule denying specific enforcability would still have deprived the intending purchasers of an equitable interest in advance of transfer of the legal title to the goods in question.
>
> The matter is simpler with contracts for the sale of personalty other than goods. Then the general equitable rules apply without statutory modification. Consider, for example, a contract for the sale of a specifically identified block of shares. If the shares are in a listed company, then the contract is unlikely to be specifically enforceable; damages will provide an adequate remedy. Describing the contract as not specifically enforceable is

another way of saying that the vendor is not compelled, in equity, to transfer the shares. Since equity only treats as done that which it sees ought to be done, it follows from the absence of specific enforcability that the intending purchaser will *not* acquire an equitable interest in the shares in advance of the transfer of legal title. On the other hand, if the shares are in a private company, then the contract of sale is likely to be specifically enforceable. If that is the case, equity will treat the vendor's obligation to transfer as already effected, and the intending purchaser will acquire equitable ownership of the shares once the purchase price is paid. This requirement that the contract of sale be specifically enforceable operates to ensure that very few intending purchasers acquire equitable interests in advance of the legal transfer, no matter how well identified the sale property.

Surely if the purchaser of an entire block of specifically identified shares in a listed company cannot obtain equitable title to those shares in advance of the transfer of legal title, then the purchaser of part only of the block will be at least equally restricted in obtaining the assistance of equity in advance of the transfer of legal title to the smaller parcel of shares. This impediment was not even adverted to in *Re Harvard.* It is another basis upon which Harvard's clients ought to have been denied an equitable interest in the shares. If, on the other hand, and for the sake of argument, the clients in *Re Harvard* had agreed to purchase small parcels from identified larger blocks of shares in *private* companies, the analysis would necessarily have been more complicated. It would have raised squarely the problem of equitable interests in bulks and whether the subject matter of such a sale is sufficiently well identified.

On these imagined facts, the contract of sale would have been specifically enforceable. Indeed, if the purchaser were to seek a court order for specific performance, the vendor would be obliged to "segregate" the required number of shares and transfer the legal title to the purchaser (by completing the necessary formalities and notifying the company in which the shares were held). The purchaser is thus assured of obtaining eventual legal ownership of the shares. But, *before* legal title is transferred, will the purchaser be regarded as the owner in equity of the parcel of shares? This is the nub of the problem concerning equitable ownership interests in bulks, and is where analytical effort needs to be focused. None of the existing English authorities is definitive; none is concerned with a specifically enforceable contract for the sale of part of an identified bulk. This means that the answer is open to legitimate debate. However, there are sound arguments to suggest that a purchaser in these circumstances ought to be regarded as having an equitable interest in the identified bulk.

The particular arguments in favour of purchasers acquiring such equitable interests have already been presented in detail elsewhere. Here it is sufficient to outline that reasoning and then to answer some of the more obvious criticisms that this suggestion faces. As already noted, equitable interests which arise by operation of law in advance of the agreed transfer of legal title are premised on the notion that equity regards as done that which ought to be done: if specific property ought to be transferred—because the sale contract is specifically enforceable and unconditional—then equity will regard the property as *already transferred* and the intending purchaser will be the owner in equity, although not yet the owner at law. If part of an identified bulk ought to be transferred—again because the sale contract is specifically enforceable and unconditional—then what, if anything, will equity regard as done? Clearly what the vendor ought to do (and what specific performance will compel) is segregate the sale property from the bulk and transfer it to the purchaser. Given this, will equity, considering as done that which ought to be done, assume that the vendor *has segregated* as well as assuming that the vendor *has transferred*? Since equity routinely does this in the context of trusts and tracing exercises—where, in both cases, the principal difference is that the equitable obligation to segregate and to transfer is derived from some source other than a specifically enforceable contract of sale—there would seem to be no practical or theoretical impediment to adopting the same approach with sales. In fact, consistency might be seen as demanding this.

Nevertheless, several arguments are commonly raised to counter this suggestion that a purchaser might acquire an equitable interest in part of a bulk. The first is that such interests—at least in the context of sales of goods—would embarrass the ordinary operations of buying and selling. This argument can no longer stand in the face of recent legislative reforms which deliver *legal* interests to such purchasers precisely because the ordinary operations of buying and selling *demand*, rather than deny, that such interests exist. These recent legislative amendments also give the lie to the suggestion that it is "the very nature of things" (because specific property has not been identified) that such interests cannot possibly exist.

Other arguments are more substantial. They focus on the allegedly unacceptable practical and commercial consequences of finding that the purchaser has an equitable interest in a defined bulk. An example illustrates the imagined difficulties. Suppose that A agrees to sell to B 50 shares out of an identified parcel of 1,000 shares. Suppose, too, that the conditions are such that B is thereby considered to have an equitable interest in 50 of the shares in the parcel. Suppose, further, that A then sells (and legally transfers) 50 shares out of the parcel to another purchaser, C. It is suggested that it would be impossible to determine whether it was A's or B's shares which had been sold to C. This would create all sorts of accounting problems, both between A and B and between either party and the Revenue (in assessing capital gains tax, for example). In particular, if the sale (and any subsequent investment) is advantageous or disadvantageous, is it A or B who will be entitled to or required to take the benefits or burdens? Alternatively, if there is no such problem, then can it really be said that B has any specific proprietary interest which is capable of assignment? Professor Hayton argues not.

This hypothetical problem demands a considered answer. Assume, for the sake of argument, that the purchaser *does* acquire an ownership interest in the bulk. The constructive trust which arises to recognise this interest does not automatically make the vendor a fiduciary, subject to the full rigour of fiduciary duties of self-denial, much less a trustee with powers of investment and duties to maximise the trust property. We readily recognise that fiduciary obligations can exist independently of legal/equitable property splits; conversely, legal/equitable property splits can exist independently of fiduciary obligations (at least when that term is used, as it should be, to suggest obligations of self-denial). The problem is to determine precisely what (non-fiduciary) obligations are imposed on the vendor in these circumstances.

It is important to recognise that even if the obligations imposed on the vendor *were* fiduciary, the beneficiary could only pursue the proceeds or profits derived from dealings with the trust property if those dealings were in breach of the trust. This means that if, for example, the trust required the trustee to sell 100 shares out of the parcel and pay out the proceeds to a particular beneficiary, then the other beneficiaries could not possibly make any claims based upon some purported equitable interest in the shares sold: they would be insulated from both the advantages and the disadvantages of the transaction.

In the context of an enforceable contract of sale, the purchaser with a property interest in the bulk has no possible right to pursue proceeds from dealings with that bulk unless the vendor is in breach of the vendor's obligations. This is notwithstanding the purchaser's proprietary interest in the bulk. If the vendor sells 50 of the 1,000 shares, then the vendor still has 50 shares within the nominated bulk with which to satisfy the contract of sale. This is all that the vendor is obliged to do. This is all the purchaser can demand. It follows that the purchaser cannot lay claim to the proceeds of sale of any of the other shares to a third party. As with express trusts, the purchaser is insulated from the financial advantages and disadvantages of such a sale.

On the other hand, if the *whole* parcel of shares is sold to a third party, then the vendor has clearly breached the contract of sale with the purchaser: the contract was for a sale out of a defined bulk, not a sale from any source. This breach gives the purchaser a choice: either to pursue a personal claim for damages for breach of contract or to pursue a proprietary claim for a lien on the proceeds derived from the sale of the bulk, always assuming those proceeds can be identified. The proprietary remedy is clearly preferable if the vendor is insolvent.

In short, the analysis is premissed on the recognition that the purchaser can only ever claim against the vendor if the vendor is in breach of the obligations assumed. Those obligations are defined solely by the contract of sale. The fact that, on breach, there are personal and proprietary remedial alternatives flows directly from deciding that the particular contract involves a specifically enforceable obligation to transfer sufficiently identified property, not from any super-added fiduciary or trustee duties.

This analysis of the incidence of proprietary interests in bulk in the context of contracts of *sale* is consistent with the accepted analysis of proprietary interests which arise when the contract is for the sale of specifically identified property. In both cases equity's intervention is premised on the fact that equity treats as done that which ought to be done. This means that the purchaser only acquires a proprietary interest if the vendor's obligation to transfer is unconditional and specifically enforceable: this defines what ought to be done. Moreover, equity can only treat the property "as transferred" if the subject matter of the sale can be objectively identified: this means that the sale property must be specifically identified, or it must be part of a fungible bulk. The limitations imposed by these conditions are such that very few purchasers of part of an identified bulk can expect to have an equitable proprietary interest in the bulk in advance of the transfer of legal title.'

4.12 Sale of future property—choses in action and choses in possession

Sometimes a contract of sale does not relate to property which the vendor presently owns, but to property which the vendor will later acquire. Before the vendor acquires the property, it is obvious that the intending purchaser cannot possibly have any sort of proprietary interest in the sale asset, even if it can be clearly identified (eg in the hands of some third party) and even if the purchaser has paid the full purchase price.

But once the vendor acquires the property, matters change. At law it remains true that the purchaser cannot acquire an interest in the asset until the vendor performs some new act designed to transfer legal title to the purchaser (eg by delivering the asset to the purchaser, or by signing transfer forms and having title registered in the purchaser's name). However, in equity it is commonly said that the intending purchaser becomes the owner in equity of the asset at the instant that it is acquired by the vendor, so that at no stage does the vendor have unencumbered title to the property. This simple rule finds support in the leading cases, extracted below.

This is notwithstanding that the cases considered earlier in relation to contracts for the sale of existing property suggest that there must be some limits to this rule. Following those earlier cases, it might be supposed that the contract of sale needs to be specifically enforceable and unconditional, as well as relating to sale property which becomes sufficiently identified once the vendor acquires it. The argument for this approach is considered later (see **[434]** below).

[432] ***Holroyd v Marshall*** **(1862) 10 HLC 191 (HL) at 209–12, 11 ER 999 at 1006–7** ***per*** **Lord Westbury:**

[The case concerned a contract for the mortgage of existing and future property (machinery in a mill). The issue was whether machinery which had been added and substituted since the date of the mortgage was caught by the mortgage. If it was not, then it would be available to the mortgagor's judgment creditors, not the mortgagee.]

> 'The question may be easily decided by the application of a few elementary principles long settled in Courts of Equity. In equity it is not necessary for the alienation of property that there should be a formal deed of conveyance. A contract for valuable consideration, by which it is agree to make a present transfer of property, passes at once the beneficial interest, provided the contract is one of which a Court of Equity will decree specific performance. In the language of Lord Hardwicke, the vendor becomes a trustee for the vendee; subject, of course, to the contract being one to be specifically performed. And this is true, not only of contracts relating to real estate, but also of contracts relating to personal property, provided that the latter are such as a Court of Equity would direct to be specifically performed.
>
> A contract for the sale of goods, as, for example, of five hundred chests of tea, is not a contract which would be specifically performed, because it does not relate to any chests of tea in particular; but a contract to sell five hundred chests of the particular kind of tea which is [210] now in my warehouse in Gloucester, is a contract relating to specific property, and which would be specifically performed. The buyer may maintain a suit in equity for the delivery of a specific chattel when it is the subject of a contract, and for an injunction (if necessary) to restrain the seller from delivering it to any other person. . . .
>
> There can be no doubt, therefore, that if the mortgage deed in the present case had contained nothing but the contract which is involved in the aforesaid covenant of Taylor, the mortgagor, such contract would have amounted to a valid assignment in equity of the whole of the machinery and chattels in question, supposing such machinery and effects to have been in existence and upon the mill at the time of the execution of the deed.
>
> But it is alleged that this is not the effect of the contract, because it relates to machinery not existing at the time, but to be acquired and fixed and placed in the mill at a future time. It is quite true that a deed which professes to convey property which is not in existence at the time is as a conveyance void at law, simply because there [211] is nothing to convey. So in equity a contract which engages to transfer property, which is not in existence, cannot operate as an immediate alienation merely because there is nothing to transfer.
>
> But if a vendor or mortgagor agrees to sell or mortgage property, real or personal, of which he is not possessed at the time, and he receives the consideration for the contract, and afterwards becomes possessed of property answering the description in the contract, there is no doubt that a Court of Equity would compel him to perform the con-

tract, and that the contract would, in equity, transfer the beneficial interest to the mortgagee or purchaser immediately on the property being acquired. This, of course, assumes that the supposed contract is one of that class of which a Court of Equity would decree the specific performance. If it be so, then immediately on the acquisition of the property described the vendor or mortgagor would hold it in trust for the purchaser or mortgagee, according to the terms of the contract. For if a contract be in other respects good and fit to be performed, and the consideration has been received, incapacity to perform it at the time of its execution will be no answer when the means of doing so are afterwards obtained.

Apply these familiar principles to the present case; it follows that immediately on the new machinery and effects being fixed or placed in the mill, they became subject to the operation of the contract, and passed in equity to the mortgagees, to whom Taylor was bound to make a legal conveyance, and for whom he, in the meantime, was a trustee of the property in question.'

[433] *Tailby v Official Receiver* (1888) 13 App Cas 523 (HL), 533–4 *per* Lord Watson, 543, 545–9 *per* Lord Macnaghten:

[The case concerned a bill of sale assigning to a mortgagee all the book debts due and owing to a mortgagor, as well as all those which might later become due and owing. The court held that the assignment of future book debts was sufficiently defined to pass the equitable interest in them to the mortgagee.]

Lord Watson:

'Had there not been such a conflict of judicial opinion, I should have thought that the question thus raised for decision admitted of one answer only. The rule of equity which applies to the assignment of future choses in action is, as I understand it, a very simple one. Choses in action do not come within the scope of the Bills of Sale Acts, and though not yet existing, may nevertheless be the subject of present assignment. As soon as they come into existence, assignees who have given valuable consideration will, if the new chose in action is in the disposal of their assignor, take precisely the same right and interest as if it had actually belonged to him, or had been within his disposition and control at the time when the assignment was made. There is but one condition which must be fulfilled in order to make the assignee's right attach to a future chose in action, which is, that, on its coming into existence, it shall answer the description in the assignment, or, in other words, that it shall be capable of being identified as the thing, or as one of the very things assigned. When there is no uncertainty as to its identification, the beneficial interest will immediately vest in the assignee. Mere difficulty in ascertaining all the things which are included in a general assignment, whether in esse or in posse, will not affect the assignee's right to those things which are capable of ascertainment or are identified. . . .

In the case of book debts, as in the case of choses in action generally, intimation of the assignee's right must be made to the debtor or obligee in order to make it complete. That is the only possession which he can attain, so long as the debt is unpaid, and is sufficient to take it out of the order and disposition of the assignor. In this case the appellant's right, if otherwise valid, was, in any question with the respondent, duly perfected by his notice to Wilson Brothers & Co. before Izon became a bankrupt. . . .'

Lord Macnaghten:

'The claim of the purchaser was rested on well-known principles. It has long been settled that future property, possibilities and expectancies are assignable in equity for value. The mode or form of assignment is absolutely immaterial provided the intention of the parties is clear. To effectuate the intention an assignment for value, in terms present and immediate, has always been regarded in equity as a contract binding on the conscience of the assignor and so binding the subject-matter of the contract when it comes into existence, if it is of such a nature and so described as to be capable of being ascertained and identified.

The position of the purchaser was assailed on one point, and one point only. . . .The contention of the learned counsel for the respondent was this: They asserted as a proposition of law that an assignment of future book debts not limited to any specified business is too vague to have any effect. . . .

. . . . I think your Lordships will come to the conclusion that the proposition on which the respondent relies as the foundation of his case cannot be supported on principle, and that the authorities on which it was supposed to rest may be traced to a decision of the Court of Exchequer which itself is founded on an erroneous view of the principles recognised in this House in *Holroyd v. Marshall* (10 H. L. C. 191) [**[432]** above].

. . .

My Lords, I should wish to say a few words about *Holroyd v. Marshall* (10 H. L. C. 191), because I am inclined to think that *Belding v. Read* (3 H. & C. 955) is not the only case in which Lord Westbury's observations have been misunderstood. To understand Lord Westbury's judgment aright, I think it is necessary to bear in mind the state of the law at the time, and the point to which his Lordship was addressing himself. *Holroyd v. Marshall* laid down no new law, nor did it extend the principles of equity in the slightest degree. Long before *Holroyd v. Marshall* was determined it was well settled that an assignment of future property for value operates in equity by way of agreement, binding the conscience of the assignor, and so binding the property from the moment when the contract becomes capable of being performed, on the principle that equity considers as done that which ought to be done, and in accordance with the maxim which Lord Thurlow said he took to be universal, "that whenever persons agree concerning any particular subject, that, in a Court of Equity, as against the party himself, and any claiming under him, voluntarily or with notice, raises a trust:" *Legard v. Hodges* (1 Ves. Junr. 478). It had also been determined by the highest tribunals in the country, short of this House—by Lord Lyndhurst as Lord Chancellor in England, and by Sir Edward Sugden as Lord Chancellor in Ireland—that an agreement binding property for valuable consideration had precedence over the claim of a judgment creditor. Some confusion, however, had recently been introduced by a decision of a most eminent judge, who was naturally less familiar with the doctrines of equity than with the principles of common law. In that state of things, in *Holroyd v. Marshall*, in a contest between an equitable assignee and an execution creditor, Stuart V.C. decided in favour of the equitable assignee. His decision was reversed by Lord Campbell L.C. in a judgment which seemed to strike at the root of all equitable titles. Lord Campbell did not hold that the equitable assignee obtained no interest in the property the subject of the contract when it came into existence. He held that the equitable assignee did obtain an interest in equity. But at the same time he held that the interest was of such a fugitive character, so shadowy, and so precarious, that it could not stand against the legal title of the execution creditor, without the help of some new act to give it substance and strength.

It was to this view, I think, that Lord Westbury addressed himself; and by way of shewing how real and substantial were equitable interests springing from agreements based on valuable consideration, he referred to the doctrines of specific performance, illustrating his argument by examples. One of the examples, perhaps, requires some qualification. That, however, does not affect the argument. The argument is clear and convincing; but it must not be wrested from its purpose. It is difficult to suppose that Lord Westbury intended to lay down as a rule to guide or perplex the Court, that considerations applicable to cases of specific performance, properly so-called, where the contract is executory, are to be applied to every case of equitable assignment dealing with future property. Lord Selborne has, I think, done good service in pointing out that confusion is sometimes caused by transferring such considerations to questions which arise as to the propriety of the Court requiring something or other to be done in specie (*Wolverhampton and Walsall Railway Company v. London and North Western Railway Company* (Law Rep. 16 Eq. 433)). His Lordship observes that there is some fallacy and ambiguity in the way in which in cases of that kind those words "specific performance," are very frequently used. Greater confusion still, I think, would be caused by transferring considerations applicable to suits for specific performance—involving, as they do, some of the nicest distinctions and most difficult questions that come before the Court—to cases of equitable assignment or specific lien where nothing remains to be done in order to define the rights of the parties, but the Court is merely asked to protect rights completely defined as between the parties to the contract, or to give effect to such rights either by granting an injunction or by appointing a receiver, or by adjudicating on questions between rival claimants.

The truth is that cases of equitable assignment or specific lien, where the consideration has passed, depend on the real meaning of the agreement between the parties. The difficulty, generally speaking, is to ascertain the true scope and effect of the agreement. When that is ascertained you have only to apply the principle that equity considers that done which ought to be done if that principle is applicable under the circumstances of the case. The doctrines relating to specific performance do not, I think, afford a test or a measure of the rights created. There are cases where the rights of the parties may be worked out by means of specific performance, though no specific lien is effected by the agreement itself. More frequently a specific lien is effected though no case of specific performance is contemplated. Take the case of *Mornington v. Keane* (2 D. & J. 292). There Lord Mornington covenanted that he would, on or before a specified day, either by a charge on freehold estates in England or Wales or by an investment in the Funds, or by the best means which might be then in his power, secure the payment of an annuity to a trustee for his wife. The Lord Chancellor did not doubt that the covenant would entitle the covenantee to have it performed in specie, but still it was held by the Court that the covenant of itself created no lien on the covenantor's property. Take the present case. The rights of the parties are completely defined by the bill of sale. Though there is the usual covenant for further assurance, it is plain that no further deed was contemplated. Yet no one can doubt that if Izon had attempted to receive outstanding book debts after the mortgagee had intervened, the Court would at once have lent its assistance by the appointment of a receiver. The case of *Metcalfe v. Archbishop of York* (1 My. & Cr. 547) is, I think, a good illustration of the argument I am presenting to your Lordships. In 1811 an incumbent charged his benefice with an annuity, and covenanted that if he should be preferred to any other benefice he would charge it with the annuity, and that in the meantime it should stand charged therewith, and there was a covenant for further assurance. At the date of the deed the charge was not illegal, for the statute of Elizabeth had been repealed in 1803. In 1814 the incumbent was preferred to another living. In 1817 charges on ecclesiastical benefices were again prohibited by the Act 57 Geo. 3, c. 99. No legal charge upon the new living had been executed before that Act passed. A question afterwards arose between the person entitled to the annuity and judgment creditors in possession under a sequestration. It was argued by Mr. Jacob for the judgment creditors that as specific performance would be in contravention of the statute the equitable title must fail. It was contended that the covenant was all one, and that it amounted only to a covenant for a legal charge which was prohibited by law before any attempt was made to enforce it. But the Lord Chancellor was of opinion that that was not the true construction of thc deed, and that there was an equitable charge independently of the covenant to execute a legal charge. It was then said for the defendants that all equitable charges rest upon specific performance and the right to have a legal charge. Lord Cottenham, however, replied, "This is by no means so," and he affirmed the Vice-Chancellor's judgment giving effect to the equitable charge. There the contract for a legal charge would have raised a case of specific performance. But specific performance of that contract was out of the question. The contract for an equitable charge raised no question of specific performance. A contract for value for an equitable charge is as good an equitable charge as can be. It could not be made any better, though the aid of the Court might be required to protect or to give effect to it. Mr. Jacob's argument (to cite the words of the report, p. 549) was this: "The whole doctrine of equitable charges rests on the right to specific performance, for a person having an equitable charge has no estate or interest." Lord Cottenham summarily rejected the proposition. Lord Westbury demolished the foundation on which it was put. And, oddly enough, the proposition is now supposed to be established by Lord Westbury's authority.

It may be said that this a question of words. To a great extent it is so; most questions are. But I venture to think that the discussion is not out of place, because I observe that Lindley L.J., from whom I differ on a point of equity with much reluctance, was led to disregard the rights of the purchaser in the present case in consequence of the difficulties presented to his mind by the application of the doctrines of specific performance.'

Questions:

1. The rules which determine when an intending purchaser will obtain equitable title to the sale property in advance of the legal transfer are important. Does the conclusion turn on the type of property or on consideration or on specific enforceability? See Sections 4.10–4.12 above and **[434]** below.
2. Three distinct time frames are important. In order of increasing difficulty, first, a purchaser under a specifically enforceable contract for the sale of existing and identified property may obtain equitable title in advance of the legal transfer. When will this happen? Secondly, a purchaser of clearly defined future property may obtain equitable title to that property ahead of other third parties attempting to claim competing interests in the asset when the vendor eventually acquires it. When will this happen? Finally, with contracts for the sale of future property, it seems that even before the vendor acquires the property, the purchaser has something more than a mere contractual right.

   Re Lind [1915] 2 Ch 345 (CA) is a case concerning a transferee's rights *before* the transferor acquired the future property. Lind had an expectancy (ie future property) consisting of a share in the personal estate of his mother should she die intestate. He mortgaged this expectancy. At the time of the mortgage, Lind had no proprietary interest in his mother's estate. It followed that he could not give his mortgagees any immediate interest in that property. Before his expectancy was realised, Lind was adjudicated bankrupt and, shortly afterwards, obtained his discharge. This discharge had the effect of cancelling all Lind's contractual obligations to his existing creditors. If the mortgage contracts rested solely in contract, they too would have been cancelled. On the other hand, any 'proprietary' interests would persist despite the discharge. Lind subsequently assigned his expectancy to the claimants for value and, after his mother died intestate, he executed a further assignment to the claimants. The Court of Appeal held that the claimants took the expectancy *subject* to the rights of the prior mortgagees. How can this be justified? Contrast this with *Collyer v Isaacs* (1881) 19 ChD 342.

[434] S Worthington, *Proprietary Interests in Commercial Transactions* (1996, Clarendon: Oxford), pp 197–201:

[Footnotes in the original have been omitted.]

'8.3.1 The Requirement for a Mandatory (or Specifically Enforceable) Personal Obligation to Transfer Property

A complete discussion of this issue must address two basic themes: first, whether there *is* a need for a specifically enforceable contract before an equitable ownership interest will arise by operation of law; secondly, if so, how frequently this requirement is likely to be satisfied.

In considering the first issue, case law relating to contracts for the sale of land suggests overwhelming support for the requirement; the cases concerning equitable assignments and dealings with future interests are, however, more equivocal. The second issue is superficially more clear-cut: specific performance is ordered when common law damages are inadequate. Nevertheless, even with this straightforward test there are both general and specific difficulties.

8.3.1(i) Whether there is a Need for Specific Enforceability

It is certainly true that specifically enforceable sale contracts do give rise to constructive trusts of the sale property (although the timing may be controversial): contracts for the sale of land provide the prime examples, but the same analysis is applied to sales of personal property. What is less clear is whether other contracts—those which are not specifically enforceable—can give rise to constructive trusts in the same way.

Many cases do suggest that specific enforceability is an essential precondition. With contracts for the sale of land, for example, it is explicitly conceded that the purchaser's equitable ownership interest exists only if (and so far as) specific performance would be granted. This feature is well illustrated by those relatively rare cases where specific performance is refused: then there is no suggestion that the purchaser might be the equitable owner of the property. The same is true of contracts for the sale of personal property.

There are other cases, however, which suggest exactly the opposite. This is seen most strikingly in the analysis of contracts for the sale of future property. With such contracts, payment of the purchase price is apparently all that is necessary to give rise to a constructive trust. If this is true, then it has some startling consequences. Consider a contract for the sale of shares in a public company. Such contracts are not generally specifically enforceable. If a vendor agrees to sell shares he currently owns, then the purchaser does not obtain equitable ownership in advance of transfer of the legal title, notwithstanding payment of the price. If, however, the vendor agrees to sell an expectancy (shares that may become his), then it appears that the paid-up purchaser acquires equitable ownership as soon as the vendor becomes the legal owner of the expectancy. It is difficult to construct a rational argument which justifies this distinction.

The answer, if there is one, must be found in the cases. The starting point in support of the view that payment suffices (and that specific enforceability is not essential) is invariably two House of Lords' decisions, *Holroyd v. Marshall* and *Tailby v. Official Receiver* [**[432]** and **[433]** above]. Both these cases merit re-examination. Both concern security transactions (in the widest sense of that term) and involve future legal property. In *Holroyd v. Marshall* a bill of sale was granted over machinery to be acquired in the future; in *Tailby v. Official Receiver* future book debts were mortgaged. In both cases the transaction was held effective to transfer an equitable interest in the property to the transferee by operation of law as soon as the transferor acquired the property. On its face *Holroyd v. Marshall* suggests that specific enforceability is essential if an equitable interest is to arise by operation of law. However, *Tailby v. Official Receiver* appears to explicitly deny this requirement.

This reading of the latter case is widely, but not universally, accepted. In order to expound general principles, it is clearly necessary to re-examine the decision. A close reading of the judgments themselves, rather than the headnote, suggests that specific enforceability is an issue: the judgments in fact assume it is a requirement and, further, assume that generally a contract of mortgage is specifically enforceable. Attention is then directed to one matter only: whether the general rule that contracts of mortgage are specifically enforceable is ousted if the description of the mortgaged property is "vague", either in the sense of being indefinite or uncertain in its particular terms or in the sense of being too wide in its coverage. The House of Lords concluded that the subject matter of the mortgage (all the mortgagor's book debts, present and future) was not vague in the former sense and that vagueness in the latter sense was not a ground for holding the contract unenforceable. Accordingly, the mortgagee acquired an equitable interest in the book debts, an interest which arose by operation of law. Put this way, specific enforceability was clearly a necessary element in concluding that a proprietary interest arose.

The contrary view comes from the obiter, but well regarded, comments of Lord Macnaghten in describing the principles for which *Holroyd v. Marshall* stands. His discussion suggests that specific enforceability is irrelevant: once the price is paid, he said, the purchaser is entitled to the sale property (or at least to as much of it as the vendor is able to give). However, perhaps this proposition depends upon an unstated but crucial assumption that the relevant contract of sale be specifically enforceable. This is neatly illustrated by the example chosen by Lord Macnaghten himself.

Lord Macnaghten felt his views on the matter were amply confirmed by an old House of Lords' decision, *Bettesworth v. Dean and Chapter of St Paul's*. That case concerned an agreement for a lease. The Dean and Chapter had granted a lease for a long term with a covenant for renewal for ninety-nine years. The grant of a lease for ninety-nine years was prohibited by statute. The House of Lords did *not* find that the plaintiff, having paid, had an equitable proprietary interest which mirrored the legal interest contemplated by the contract. Instead, it held that specific performance could be ordered as far as possible (resulting in a lease for a period of forty years), and that this limited possibility defined the plaintiff's equitable interests. This case is obviously consistent with the view that specific enforceability is crucial in determining ownership interests arising by operation of law; it is not consistent with the contrary viewpoint. Perhaps Lord Macnaghten's comments merit some qualification. That is certainly the view advanced here.

Further support for this approach comes from a general survey of the cases: courts do not appear to have imposed constructive trusts in any cases which are not specifically enforceable. This is so whether the sale property is real or personal, whether it is a chose in possession or in action, and whether the property is present or future.

Logic suggests this is as it should be. Even those who doubt the need for specific enforceability nevertheless assert that the equitable interest which arises by operation of law does so because of the maxim that equity regards as done that which ought to be done. It is axiomatic that the property *ought* to be transferred only if the sale contract is specifically enforceable; if equity will not enforce performance, it has effectively concluded that the vendor need *not* transfer the property.

In summary, part of the proposition advanced here is that specific enforceability is an essential requirement for equitable ownership interests arising by operation of law. This requirement raises the related issue: which contracts of sale are specifically enforceable?

8.3.1(ii) The Factors which Determine whether a Contract is Specifically Enforceable

The fundamental rule is that specific performance of a contract will only be ordered where common law damages would inadequately compensate the plaintiff. Proof that this is so will not automatically guarantee such an order, however: the remedy is discretionary, and other factors might persuade the court that its discretion should not be exercised.

Nevertheless, inadequacy of common law damages is the prime determinant of specific enforceability. This inadequacy is usually assessed by considering the nature of the property agreed to be transferred. Accordingly, contracts for the sale of land are commonly the subject of orders for specific performance but contracts for the sale of personal property are not, even though the rules on discretion which govern both cases are the same. Contracts for the sale of personal property have been specifically enforced where the asset has special value because of its individuality, beauty, or rarity; or where there is no open market for the asset; or where, although there is a market, supplies are limited because of peculiar circumstances. These cases present few theoretical problems. Of more concern are two quite different situations: first, where the defendant's financial position, not the nature of the asset, suggests that damages would inadequately compensate the plaintiff; secondly, where the contract is for the sale of goods and legislation modifies the exercise of the court's discretion. These possibilities are considered below.'

4.13 Flawed contracts to transfer property

It is sometimes the case that a contract intended to operate as a sale or other transfer of property is somehow flawed. Perhaps it is void, because one or other party does not have the capacity to enter into the transaction. Perhaps it is voidable, for mistake or misrepresentation or undue influence, or for some other reason. In these circumstances, the innocent transferor will of course have personal remedies against the transferee. However, the transferor may then be interested to know whether there is any possibility of recovering *in specie* the property transferred—ie whether there is any possibility of asserting a *proprietary* interest in the asset which has been given over to another because of a flawed contract. This form of proprietary remedy is sometimes (but not always) possible: it is considered in Chapter 5.

4.14 Policy considerations

Proprietary interests, even equitable proprietary interests, are given considerable protection by the law. Nowhere is this more apparent than when insolvency intervenes. Then only those assets which are owned beneficially by the insolvent can be distributed to the insolvent's unpaid creditors. Any other assets, notwithstanding that they are in the insolvent's possession or legally owned by the insolvent, must be set aside to meet the particular claims of those able to assert some proprietary interest—whether an ownership interest or a security interest. This priority accorded to those with property interests has come in for considerable criticism: it is seen as upsetting the policy of the insolvency legislation which requires equal sharing of losses amongst the creditors (ie *pari passu* distribution) on insolvency; it is also seen as operating unfairly between different creditors.[40] This criticism of the impact of property interests is most acute where the property interest in question is an equitable interest which arises by operation of law—such as the equitable ownership interests considered in this chapter, which arise in advance of an intended transfer of the legal title because equity sees fit to intervene to assist the intended recipient. The next chapter, too, is concerned with equitable interests which arise by operation of law. The policy arguments surrounding all these proprietary claims can be found in Chapters 3 and 5.

[40] Contracts of sale provide a graphic illustration: the paid-up purchaser of a specifically identified parcel of shares in a private company will acquire equitable ownership of those shares in advance of their legal transfer; the purchaser of a similarly identified parcel of shares in a listed company will not (since the latter contract is not specifically enforceable). On the insolvency of the vendor, the first purchaser will be able to claim the shares *in specie*; the second will have only an unsecured personal claim for a sum of money (either contract damages or restitution of the purchase price).

5

Transfers of Interests in Property by Operation of Law

5.1 Introduction

The previous chapter was concerned with consensual transfers of interests in personal property. Its principal concern was with intended gifts and sales of legal and equitable interests. Even in that chapter, however, there was an extended discussion of the equitable interests which might arise in advance of the intended transfer of legal title to an asset, whether that transfer was designed to take place by gift or by sale. In a sense those equitable interests arose by operation of law rather than in accordance with the intention of the parties. The parties did intend a transfer, it is true, but they intended it to be a transfer of the legal interest and they intended it to take place later.

This chapter pursues that type of equitable intervention further. In this context such intervention can be by means of resulting trust, constructive trust, proprietary estoppel, equitable lien or subrogation. It is commonly said that these forms of intervention arise whenever it would be unconscionable for the legal owner to assert unencumbered title to an asset in the face of another's claims. The response is to give the claimant an equitable interest by operation of law. Despite such generalities, however, these forms of equitable intervention are premised on something more than a loose notion of 'fairness', and most of this chapter is directed at elucidating the doctrinal boundaries. This chapter is a companion to the previous one. The previous chapter was concerned with interests in property transferred by agreement; this one is concerned with interests transferred by operation of law.

Much of this chapter is devoted to equitable forms of intervention. First, however, there is brief consideration of two contexts in which the common law, rather than equity, intervenes to confer legal ownership on another notwithstanding that the parties themselves may have had no intention to confer such benefits. The common law will intervene in cases of intestacy, where the owner of assets has died without leaving a valid will to indicate the desired method of distributing the estate. Then, by operation of law, certain individuals selected by statutory rules will become the new owners of the property. As well, the common law may intervene when property has been transferred under a contract which is voidable at common law. In these circumstances (and in practice these circumstances are very limited), *legal* title may sometimes re-vest in the transferee once the contract is avoided.[1]

For the sake of completeness, it should be noted that the common law may also intervene where one owner's chattels lose their identity because they have been dealt with in an unauthorised manner. For example, if an owner's woodchips are used without authority by another to manufacture chipboard,[2] then the common law may give the owner an interest in the manufactured product. This possibility is dealt with in the next chapter, under the heading of common law tracing. This seems the more appropriate context, since the real motivation for this form of intervention is to protect the owner's original proprietary interest in an asset which has been lost or modified by an unauthorised dealing.

The previous paragraph highlights a common difficulty with this material. It is hard to decide which matters properly belong in this chapter and which are more appropriately sited in Chapters 6 and 7. The division has been made on the basis that Chapters 6 and 7 concern the persistence and protection of the claimant's existing proprietary interests. This chapter concerns the delivery to claimant of an equitable proprietary interest, often for reasons other than the protection of the claimant's property. However, there are many instances where the distinction is rather artificial.

Before turning to the common law methods by which title is transferred by operation of law, it is worth setting out the province of this chapter in a little more detail. An overview helps to make sense of the terrain. The common law section is brief, as reflects its limited practical impact. The potential impact of the equitable rules, on the other hand, is significant, wide-ranging and, currently, unsettled. Much of the jurisprudence underpinning these equitable forms of intervention was developed in the context of family and other close arrangements, and the modern tensions concern the extent to which these rules can and should be applied in more commercial contexts. By definition, these equitable rules are only relevant when the parties have not expressly created a trust to govern their relationship—and the word 'expressly' does not necessarily connote formality; the intention to create a trust can be inferred from the surrounding circumstances, and the terms of a trust often do not need to be in writing. Where there is no express trust relationship, a trust by operation of law should really only be imposed when it can be said that the legal owner 'ought' to hold the property for the benefit of another.[3] This chapter looks at some of the situations where that might be the case. For example:

[1] See Section 1.4.

[2] Recall that if the manufacturer is *authorised* to use the owner's woodchips, then the usual construction placed on the arrangement is that the chipboard belongs to the manufacturer absolutely; at most, the supplier may have a charge on the chipboard to secure payment of the purchase price of the woodchips: see the discussion of retention of title clauses in Chapter 3.

[3] Not only is the law difficult. So, too, is the terminology. Where there is an express trust, there is a division of legal and equitable ownership *and* the trustee owes fiduciary obligations to the beneficiaries. Here, where there is a trust by operation of law, it is assumed that the 'trust' label

1. If X transfers property to a trustee to hold on express trusts, but fails to specify the destination of the entire beneficial interest in the property transferred, *should* the trustee hold those unsettled interests on trust for X? (These are 'automatic resulting trusts': see Section 5.4.)
2. If X transfers property to another for no consideration, but not intending a gift, *should* the transferee hold that property on trust for X? (These are 'presumed resulting trusts': see Section 5.4.)
3. Related to that, if X pays money to another as a contribution to the purchase price of an asset, but not intending to make a loan or a gift, *should* the purchaser hold the asset on trust for X in proportion to X's contribution to the purchase price? (These, too, are presumed resulting trusts, but are commonly called 'purchase money resulting trusts': see Section 5.4.)
4. If a person receives a benefit from X premised on some flawed understanding of the relationship between the two parties (eg that there is a contract when there is not), then *should* that benefit be held on trust for X? (See the discussion of resulting trusts to remedy unjust enrichment in Section 5.5.)
5. If X transfers assets or valuable services to another, on the understanding (not amounting to a contract) that X will be rewarded in some way, *should* the intended reward be held on trust for X? (See the discussion of family homes and equitable estoppel in Sections 5.8 and 5.9.)
6. If a person abuses his or her relationship with X, and thereby makes a profit (eg by taking bribes, breaching confidences, or breaching contractual or tort obligations owed to X), then *should* those profits be held on trust for X? (See the discussion of constructive trusts to effect disgorgement in Section 5.10.)
7. In a three-party situation, where X and Y each have independent relationships with Z, can X ever take the benefit, as against Z, of proprietary interests which Y has acquired against Z? (See the discussion of subrogation in Section 5.12.)

All these questions are difficult to answer, and those lower down the list are even more difficult to answer than the earlier ones. The instinct to give a remedy in one situation must be generalised into a rule which delivers appropriate responses in other situations. This is not easy. Any compelling justification must explain why the law should intervene at all, and why the intervention should be proprietary rather than personal, and why the proprietary remedy should return to X what originally belonged to X or, alternatively, should deliver to X something which X aspired to acquire. The relevant rules have potential application in a wide range of circumstances, and this chapter can probably only hope to convey the flavour of the current debates.

signifies *only* that there is a division of legal and equitable ownership; the label says nothing about the incidence of fiduciary obligations. These must be determined separately. This approach to the terminology (ie using 'trust' to refer to the proprietary incidents and 'fiduciary obligations' to refer to the duty incidents) is common but not universal. For example, it is not the approach adopted by Lord Browne-Wilkinson in the *Westdeutsche Landesbank Case* (**[518]** below). He uses the term 'trust' only when the relationship connotes *both* a division of proprietary interests and the imposition of fiduciary obligations.

5.2 Intestate succession

[501] A P Bell, *Modern Law of Personal Property in England and Ireland* (1989, Butterworths: London), ch 17 , pp 415–16:

> 'A person may die intestate as to the whole of his estate, or he may die leaving a will covering certain amounts but being intestate as to the rest. In either case, the property that has not been provided for is to be distributed according to statutory rules. These rules aim in part to make the distribution that the deceased may be presumed to have intended, but in part they also aim to make provision for those whom he ought to have provided for.'

Note:

The rules governing intestate succession in England can be found in Part IV of the Administration of Estates Act 1925. The specific details are not of particular concern here, but note the policy considerations which favour this form of statutory intervention.

5.3 Revesting of legal title transferred under a contract voidable at common law

The next extract is self-explanatory.

[502] S Worthington, *Proprietary Interests in Commercial Transactions* (1996, Clarendon: Oxford), pp 129–31:
[Footnotes in the original have been omitted.]

> ***'6.1.2(i) Contracts which are Voidable at Law***
>
> If a contract is voidable at law (e.g. for fraudulent misrepresentation or duress), then the aggrieved party can elect whether to rescind or affirm the transaction.
>
> An election to rescind must normally be communicated to the other party. The result is then to avoid the contract *ab initio* rather than merely to discharge the parties from future performance. The operative act is that of the party, and intervention of the court is not a necessary precondition.
>
> When an election to rescind is made, and provided *restitutio in integrum* is possible according to the strict standards of the common law, *dicta* exist suggesting that *legal* title to the property revests in the original owner. Revesting of legal title provides the basis for the common law personal remedies available to the owner, but, as already indicated, it does not give the owner a right to recover the property *in specie*.
>
> Recovery of the property *in specie* is only possible with the intervention of equity. However, if rescission revests legal title in the original owner, then there is no scope for equity. It is otherwise if the rescission cannot revest legal title because the transaction, although voidable at law, involves a formal conveyance. Then, in equity, the transferee

is considered to hold the property on trust for the original owner. With this relationship, the original owner can rely on equity to enable recovery of the property *in specie*. In practice, this equitable avenue is available when the contract concerns land or shares, for example, but not when it concerns goods. Once again, with goods, it is *bona fide* third parties who are put at risk: if they deal with the transferee after rescission, the *nemo dat* rule applies and they will not obtain title to the goods. It is arguable that greater consistency would be preferable.

In any event, since the initial property transfer is effective, the original owner's remedies are particularly prone to being defeated by contrary dealings with the property. The original owner has no proprietary interest until an effective election to rescind is made. Until then the owner has a mere equity, a right not recognized by the common law. Furthermore, when the owner does eventually elect to rescind the contract, no proprietary interest (legal or equitable) can arise unless the asset originally transferred can be identified. If the property can be identified, the original owner's interest will be diminished if the recipient has granted any prior legal or equitable interests in the property to third parties.

6.1.3 Problems with the Rules and Alternative Possibilities

Some aspects of the preceding description are sufficiently undesirable to suggest that there might be a flaw in the analysis adopted. Notably, retention or revesting of legal tide does not give the original owner a right to recover the property *in specie*; and, because the original owner holds both the legal and beneficial title, equity cannot intervene to improve matters. This, of itself, is not cause for concern. What does cause concern is the practical distinctions which follow: the outcome with goods is not the same as with other types of property; moreover, the outcome when the vitiating elements are serious is, in some senses, less favourable to the original owner than when they are less serious. Both matters require some explanation.

With many types of property, goods aside, legal title can only pass on formal conveyance. Then, whatever the problems with the underlying contract, legal title cannot be either retained or revested. The original owner must resort to equity.'

5.4 Automatic and presumed resulting trusts

5.4.1 General principles

The classification of resulting trusts is controversial. This section is concerned with the three principal situations which give rise to resulting trusts:

(a) The first situation is where a settlor transfers property to trustees on trust, but fails to specify the destination of all or part of the beneficial interest. What is not disposed of is said to 'result back' to the settlor, although in one sense it never left him or her. These are *'automatic' resulting trusts*.

(b) The second situation is where a person transfers the legal title to property to another for no consideration and in circumstances where there is no presumption of advancement;[4] then there is a rebuttable presumption that the

[4] Briefly, the presumption of advancement is a rebuttable presumption that the donor intended to make a gift of the equitable interest to the donee. In England, the presumption applies to

transferee holds the property on resulting trust for the transferor. These are *'presumed' resulting trusts*.

(c) The third situation in which resulting trusts arise is a variant of the second. A resulting trust will also be presumed where property is purchased and the legal title to the property is vested in someone other than the provider of the purchase funds. Provided there is no presumption of advancement, there is a rebuttable presumption that the new legal owner holds the property on resulting trust for the provider(s) of the purchase funds. In other words, if there is no evidence that the legal owner was to take beneficially, then the beneficial interest 'results back' to the provider(s) of the purchase funds. Such resulting trusts are also 'presumed' resulting trusts, although they are more commonly called *'purchase money' resulting trusts*. The principle underpinning purchase money resulting trusts applies equally to transfers into joint names (so that there are joint trustees) and to transfers where the purchase money comes from different sources (so that there are several beneficiaries of the presumed 'purchase money' resulting trust). On the other hand, where the presumption of advancement applies, then there is a rebuttable presumption that the provider of the purchase funds intended to make a gift of the equitable title to the holder of the legal title.

In the next extract, Megarry J provides what is now regarded as the classic analysis of automatic and presumed resulting trusts.

[503] ***Re Vandervell's Trusts (No 2)*** **[1974] Ch 269, 288–91** ***per*** **Megarry J:**
[For the facts and extracts from the Court of Appeal decision in this case, see **[413]**.]

> 'I turn to the relevant passages in Lord Upjohn's speech (in *Vandervell v IRC* [1967] 2 AC 291 (HL); see **[412]**). These seem to me to be dealing with two different categories of the doctrine of resulting trusts. The first category arises (see p. 312)
>
> > "Where A transfers, or directs a trustee for him to transfer, the legal estate in property to B otherwise than for valuable consideration." Here, "it is a question of the intention of A in making the transfer whether B was to take beneficially or on trust and, if the latter, on what trusts. If, as a matter of construction of the document transferring the legal estate, it is possible to discern A's intentions, that is an end of the matter and no extraneous evidence is admissible to correct and qualify his intentions so ascertained." But if the document is silent, "then there is said to arise a resulting trust in favour of A. But this is only a presumption and is easily rebutted. All the relevant facts and circumstances can be considered in order to ascertain A's intentions with a view to rebutting this presumption."
>
> Lord Upjohn then considers certain authorities, and concludes by saying, at p. 313, that "In reality the so-called presumption of a resulting trust is no more than a long stop to provide the answer when the relevant facts and circumstances fail to yield a solution." At this stage I need say no more than that Lord Upjohn is obviously assuming that A is not the husband or father of B, and does not stand in loco parentis to him, so that no question of a presumption of advancement arises. I would hesitate even to mention this

transfers from husband to wife (but not vice versa, and not to *de facto* relationships), and to transfers from a man to anyone to whom he is in loco parentis (but not transfers from a woman in the same circumstances).

had not the presumption of advancement entered into the argument in this case at one point in relation to the children's settlement.

Lord Upjohn then turns to consider what I may call the second category of the doctrine of resulting trusts. I think I should read the passage in full. Lord Upjohn says, at p. 313:

> "But the doctrine of resulting trust plays another very important part in our law and, in my opinion, is decisive of this case. If A intends to give away all his beneficial interest in a piece of property and thinks he has done so but, by some mistake or accident or failure to comply with the requirements of the law, he has failed to do so, either wholly or partially, there will, by operation of law, be a resulting trust for him of the beneficial interest of which he had failed effectually to dispose. If the beneficial interest was in A and he fails to give it away effectively to another or others or on charitable trusts it must remain in him. Early references to Equity, like Nature, abhorring a vacuum, are delightful but unnecessary. Let me give an example close to this case. A the beneficial owner informs his trustees that he wants forthwith to get rid of his interest in the property and instructs him to hold the property forthwith upon such trusts as he will hereafter direct; that beneficial interest, notwithstanding the expressed intention and belief of A that he has thereby parted with his whole beneficial interest in the property, will inevitably remain in him for he has not given the property away effectively to or for the benefit of others. As Plowman J. said [1966] Ch. 261, 275: 'As I see it, a man does not cease to own property simply by saying "I don't want it." If he tries to give it away the question must always be, has he succeeded in doing so or not?' "

I pause there. The distinction between the two categories of resulting trusts is important because they operate in different ways. Putting it shortly, in the first category, subject to any provisions in the instrument, the matter is one of intention, with the rebuttable presumption of a resulting trust applying if the intention is not made manifest. For the second category, there is no mention of any expression of intention in any instrument, or of any presumption of a resulting trust: the resulting trust takes effect by operation of law, and so appears to be automatic. What a man fails effectually to dispose of remains automatically vested in him, and no question of any mere presumption can arise. The two categories are thus of presumed resulting trusts and automatic resulting trusts. The first question must therefore be into which category any given case falls; and to determine this one must know what is the distinction between the two categories. I accordingly turn to that.

At first blush it might be thought from reading Lord Upjohn's speech that the two categories consisted of, first, dispositions of the legal estate on the one hand and, second, transactions with the beneficial interest on the other hand. However, I do not think that such a distinction was intended. To take the first category, if what is being transferred is not a legal estate, but a beneficial equitable interest, it seems that the same considerations would apply. Dispositions of equitable interests are by no means uncommon, and if A transfers his equitable interest to B otherwise than for value, it would, I think, equally be a question of construing the instrument of transfer and, in default, applying the presumption of a resulting trust, in order to discover whether B took beneficially or held in trust for A. True, this part of Lord Upjohn's speech is framed in terms merely of a transfer of the legal estate, but I cannot see any reason why he should not have intended what he said to apply equally to transfers of equitable interests.

The principle in the second category is stated in terms of beneficial interests. Nevertheless, it is a principle which seems to apply equally at law. Whether a legal estate, an equitable interest or anything else, what a man fails to dispose of remains his. However, as Lord Upjohn was discussing resulting trusts, he naturally dealt with only that segment of the general principle which runs in equity: if the owner of a legal estate or interest, whether entitled beneficially or merely in a fiduciary capacity, fails to dispose of anything at all, no question of any resulting trust can arise. Nevertheless, it seems to me that the distinction between the two categories cannot have been intended to be that the first is dealing with legal estates and the second with beneficial or equitable interests, for the first is not confined to legal estates and the second is not confined to beneficial or equitable interests. If that is not the distinction, the question is, what is?

A possible answer on a literal reading of the passages in question is that they distinguish between the dynamic and the static. The first category is based on the dynamic. It is in terms concerned with there being a transfer; A transfers a legal estate to B, and so on. That creates no difficulty. But the second category makes no mention of any effective transfer and so appears to be static. A has an animus donandi but by mistake and so on fails to give away anything. "A the beneficial owner informs his trustees that he wants forthwith to get rid of his interest in the property and instructs him"—that must mean "them"—"to hold the property forthwith upon such trusts as he will hereafter direct" (p. 313). A thereby does nothing effective. Of course, everyone would agree that in such a case what A has failed to dispose of remains vested in him; what a man does not dispose of is still his. But what is difficult to see is how this is in any way an example of a resulting trust. The trustees held in trust for A on whatever were the original trusts; A has done nothing effectual to alter that: therefore the trustees continue to hold in trust for A. But how can those trusts be anything save the original trusts which have never been effectually displaced? To say that "there will, by operation of law, be a resulting trust for him of the beneficial interest of which he had failed effectually to dispose" (p. 313) prompts an inquiry as to the process whereby there was some operation of law which replaced the former trusts by the resulting trust. It seems to me that in setting out two categories of resulting trust, Lord Upjohn cannot have intended to distinguish between the dynamic and the static; for the static is no example of a resulting trust.

If the distinction is neither between the legal estate and the equitable interest, nor between the dynamic and the static, what is it? I think the answer may well be that although the second category contains no mention of any transfer of any interest, it must have been founded on an assumption of some transfer. Furthermore, I think the implicit transfer is a transfer on trust. Thus I would read the initial statement of the second category with the insertion of some words such as those which I shall italicise. "If A intends to give away all his beneficial interest, *and transfers the legal estate or bare ownership to trustees*, but by some mistake or accident or failure to comply with the requirements of the law, he has failed to do so, either wholly or partially [that is, give away some or all of his beneficial interest], there will, by operation of law, be a resulting trust for him of the beneficial interest of which he had failed effectually to dispose." In the example that is given, again I think that some such words must be assumed. If A, *the beneficial owner*, transfers property to trustees on trust, and informs his trustees that he wants forthwith to get rid of his interest in the property and instructs them to hold his property forthwith upon such trusts as he shall thereafter direct, the beneficial interest remains vested in A; and so on. In such cases it seems to me that one may properly speak of a resulting trust, and that this is so whether one regards the entire interest as having notionally left A and become vested in the trustees, with some or all of the beneficial interest promptly returning to A, or whether one regards only part of the entire interest as notionally going from A and the rest remaining vested in him throughout. In either case there has been a transaction which has divided the bare ownership from the beneficial interest, and whether A's beneficial interest is something that he keeps back, or whether it is something that he gets back, the result seems substantially the same.'

[504] *Westdeutsche Landesbank Girozentrale v Islington London Borough Council* [1996] AC 669 (HL), 707–9 *per* Lord Browne-Wilkinson:

[This is an important case, which will be referred to at various points in the discussions in this chapter. The facts are given here, although at this stage the focus is simply on Lord Browne-Wilkinson's description of resulting trusts. The claimant bank entered into an interest rate swap agreement with the defendant local authority.[5] This agreement was later held to be void, being beyond the local authority's powers.[6] Both parties had nevertheless made payments under the agreement, the net result being that the bank had paid more than £1 million to the local authority. Both Hobhouse J and the Court of Appeal ([1994] 1 WLR 938) held that the bank was entitled to recover this balance at law as money had and received; they also held that the bank was entitled to recover in equity on the ground that the local authority held the money on resulting trust and was therefore personally liable as a resulting trustee. The Court of Appeal further held that the local authority was liable to pay compound interest on the sum from the date of accrual of the cause of action. The House of Lords (Lords Goff and Woolf dissenting) overturned this final finding, albeit reluctantly, and decided that the bank was entitled to simple interest only. Fundamental to this conclusion was their unanimous finding that an *ultra vires* contract did not give rise to a resulting trust of the funds transferred by the bank. In reaching this conclusion, all the Law Lords bar Lord Goff opted to overrule *Sinclair v Brougham* [1914] AC 398 (HL).]

'Under existing law a resulting trust arises in two sets of circumstances: (A) where A makes a voluntary payment to B or pays (wholly or in part) for the purchase of property which is vested either in B alone or in the joint names of A and B, there is a presumption that A did not intend to make a gift to B: the money or property is held on trust for A (if he is the sole provider of the money) or in the case of a joint purchase by A and B in shares proportionate to their contributions. It is important to stress that this is only a presumption, which presumption is easily rebutted either by the counter-presumption of advancement or by direct evidence of A's intention to make an outright transfer: see *Underhill and Hayton, Law of Trusts and Trustees*, pp. 317 et seq.; *Vandervell v. Inland Revenue Commissioners* [1967] 2 A.C. 291, 312 et seq. [**[412]** above]; *In re Vandervell's Trusts (No. 2)* [1974] Ch. 269, 288 et seq [**[413]** above]. (B) Where A transfers property to B on express trusts, but the trusts declared do not exhaust the whole beneficial interest: *ibid.* and *Quistclose Investments Ltd. v. Rolls Razor Ltd (In Liquidation)* [1970] A.C. 567 [**[339]** above]. Both types of resulting trust are traditionally

[5] At its most basic, an interest rate swap agreement is one where the parties agree to pay each other interest payments calculated on the same notional principal sum, but calculated according to different interest rate indices, one fixed and one floating. In one sense the fixed interest rate payer is 'betting' on the chance that, over time, the nominated fixed rate will be lower than the prevailing floating rate; the floating rate payer, on the other hand, is 'betting' just the opposite. The accuracy of these predictions will determine which party ultimately benefits from the swap transaction. Swap transactions can be entered into in their own right as purely speculative ventures, or in order to 'hedge' the risks associated with other unrelated ventures which require a party to commit to certain interest payments.

[6] *Hazell v Hammersmith and Fulham London BC* [1992] 2 AC 1 (HL).

regarded as examples of trusts giving effect to the common intention of the parties. A resulting trust is not imposed by law against the intentions of the trustee (as is a constructive trust) but gives effect to his presumed intention. Megarry J. in *In re Vandervell's Trusts (No. 2)* suggests that a resulting trust of type (B) does not depend on intention but operates automatically. I am not convinced that this is right. If the settlor has expressly, or by necessary implication, abandoned any beneficial interest in the trust property, there is in my view no resulting trust: the undisposed-of equitable interest vests in the Crown as bona vacantia: see *In re West Sussex Constabulary's Widows, Children and Benevolent (1930) Fund Trusts* [1971] Ch. 1.

Applying these conventional principles of resulting trust to the present case, the bank's claim must fail. There was no transfer of money to the local authority on express trusts: therefore a resulting trust of type (B) above could not arise. As to type (A) above, any presumption of resulting trust is rebutted since it is demonstrated that the bank paid, and the local authority received, the upfront payment with the intention that the moneys so paid should become the absolute property of the local authority. It is true that the parties were under a misapprehension that the payment was made in pursuance of a valid contract. But that does not alter the actual intentions of the parties at the date the payment was made or the moneys were mixed in the bank account. As the article by William Swadling, "A new role for resulting trusts?" 16 *Legal Studies* 133 [**[505]** below] demonstrates the presumption of resulting trust is rebutted by evidence of any intention inconsistent with such a trust, not only by evidence of an intention to make a gift.

Professor Birks, "Restitution and Resulting Trusts" (see *Equity: Contemporary Legal Developments*, p. 335, at p. 360 [the full reference is given in the further reading at the end of this sub-section]), whilst accepting that the principles I have stated represent "a very conservative form" of definition of a resulting trust, argues from restitutionary principles that the definition should be extended so as to cover a perceived gap in the law of "subtractive unjust enrichment" (at p. 368) so as to give a plaintiff a proprietary remedy when he has transferred value under a mistake or under a contract the consideration for which wholly fails. He suggests that a resulting trust should arise wherever the money is paid under a mistake (because such mistake vitiates the actual intention) or when money is paid on a condition which is not subsequently satisfied.

As one would expect, the argument is tightly reasoned but I am not persuaded. The search for a perceived need to strengthen the remedies of a plaintiff claiming in restitution involves, to my mind, a distortion of trust principles. First, the argument elides rights in property (which is the only proper subject matter of a trust) into rights in "the value transferred:" see p. 361. A trust can only arise where there is defined trust property: it is therefore not consistent with trust principles to say that a person is a trustee of property which cannot be defined. Second, Professor Birks's approach appears to assume (for example in the case of a transfer of value made under a contract the consideration for which subsequently fails) that the recipient will be deemed to have been a trustee from the date of his original receipt of money, i.e. the trust arises at a time when the "trustee" does not, and cannot, know that there is going to be a total failure of consideration. This result is incompatible with the basic premise on which all trust law is built, viz. that the conscience of the trustee is affected. Unless and until the trustee is aware of the factors which give rise to the supposed trust, there is nothing which can affect his conscience. Thus neither in the case of a subsequent failure of consideration nor in the case of a payment under a contract subsequently found to be void for mistake or failure of condition will there be circumstances, at the date of receipt, which can impinge on the conscience of the recipient, thereby making him a trustee. Thirdly, Professor Birks has to impose on his wider view an arbitrary and admittedly unprincipled modification so as to ensure that a resulting trust does not arise when there has only been a failure to perform a contract, as opposed to total failure of consideration: see pp. 356–359 and 362. Such arbitrary exclusion is designed to preserve the rights of creditors in the insolvency of the recipient. The fact that it is necessary to exclude artificially one type of case which would logically fall within the wider concept casts doubt on the validity of the concept.

If adopted, Professor Birks's wider concepts would give rise to all the practical consequences and injustices to which I have referred. I do not think it right to make an unprincipled alteration to the law of property (i.e. the law of trusts) so as to produce in the law of unjust enrichment the injustices to third parties which I have mentioned and the consequential commercial uncertainty which any extension of proprietary interests in personal property is bound to produce.'

[505] W J Swadling, 'A New Role for Resulting Trusts?' (1996) 16 *Legal Studies* 110, 130–1:

'Let us first recall Professor Birks's thesis. It is his contention that a transfer of property without consideration between parties who are outside the range of any presumption of advancement will, in the absence of positive evidence of an intention to make a gift, give rise to a resulting trust in favour of the transferor. He then applies it specifically to the case of a mistaken gift and to payments for which the consideration subsequently fails.

In the case of a mistaken gift made to a party to whom the donor does not stand in a relationship generating a presumption of advancement, Birks argues that because the transfer is made without consideration and (by reason of the mistake) with no positive evidence of an intention to give, the donee will hold on resulting trust for the donor. In the case of the payment made for a reason which later fails, he argues for a resulting trust on four grounds: first, that any other result would be inconsistent with his earlier conclusion in respect of mistaken gifts; second, that any other result would be inconsistent with the law relating to transfers on express trust which later fail; third, that the situation is covered by *Barclays Bank Ltd v Quistclose Investments Ltd*; and fourth, that the situation is covered by *Sinclair v Brougham*. I have argued that Professor Birks is wrong in his analysis both of mistaken gifts and payments made for a consideration which later fails.

In the case of mistaken gifts, my objection turns on the implication of a resulting trust in the teeth of evidence which shows that the donee was not intended by the parties to hold on trust for the donor. In the end, it boils down to a debate as to the types of evidence which will rebut the presumption of resulting trust in the case of a gratuitous transfer outside any relationship of advancement. For Professor Birks, only one type of evidence will do, *viz*, evidence of a positive intention to give. My argument has been that the presumed intention resulting trust which arises in the case of a gratuitous transfer is a presumption of actual intent and therefore *any* evidence that the parties intended something other than a transfer on trust will suffice. Evidence of a mistaken intent to give will therefore rebut the presumption of resulting trust in such a case.

If that is right, there would then be no inconsistency between mistaken gifts and failures of consideration. Professor Birks's first reason for finding a resulting trust where property is transferred on a basis which later fails would therefore fall away. As to the other three justifications, the authorities on transfers on express trusts which later fail were shown to be weak, *Quistclose* was shown to be confined to the specific area of fraudulent preferences in bankruptcy and laid down no principle of general application, and *Sinclair v Brougham* was no authority at all, since the question whether property passed was conceded by counsel in the House of Lords and not raised in the courts below.

The article then went on to discuss the implications of Professor Birks's thesis. It put forward three reasons why it must be treated with caution. First, it would elevate most restitutionary plaintiffs from mere claimants *in personam* at law to claimants *in rem* in equity. The essential point which should be borne in mind throughout is the far-reaching effect of Birks's thesis. Although applied by him to two specific areas, mistaken gifts and failures of consideration, if correct it would apply across virtually the whole spectrum of autonomous unjust enrichment. The second reason for caution was that it would destroy much of the substance of the present law since it has no room for the fine-tuning which currently takes place. It can, for example, draw no distinction between the types of pressure or mistake which should or should not give rise to a restitutionary claim. This leads on to the third and final reason for caution. If correct, Professor Birks's thesis would introduce a novel ground of claim, no consideration, and, as the example of the fully executed void contract shows, give restitution to a totally undeserving plaintiff. And at the same time, it would propel us into a system similar to that which prevails in civilian systems, which Professor Birks himself deprecates, where the focus is on the "absence of juristic cause" for an enrichment rather than a "down to earth" enquiry into the reasons for restitution. The argument is that this conclusion can and should be resisted and that the presumed intention resulting trust has little or no role to play in the English law of restitution.'

FURTHER READING:

P Birks, 'Restitution and Resulting Trusts' in S Goldstein (ed), *Equity and Contemporary Legal Problems* (1992, Hamaccabi Press: Jerusalem), p 335.
R Chambers, *Resulting Trusts* (1997, Clarendon: Oxford).

Questions:

1. With 'presumed' resulting trusts, what is presumed? Is there a difference between the approaches taken by Megarry J and Lord Browne-Wilkinson? If there is, what is its significance and which approach is preferable?
2. The answers to these questions are important. Moreover, there appears to be a conflict between the recent opinions of the House of Lords and the Privy Council. The legal position in these circumstances is clear, but what is likely to happen in practice? The current view of the House of Lords was delivered in the *Westdeutsche* case (**[504]** above). In the Privy Council, in *Air Jamaica Ltd v Charlton* [1999] 1 WLR 1399 (PC), 1412 Lord Millett, delivering the opinion of the Committee, stated[7]:

   'In *In re A.B.C. Television Ltd. Pension Scheme* (unreported), 22 May 1973 Foster J. held that a clause similar to clause 4 of the present trust deed "negatives the possibility of implying a resulting trust." This is wrong in principle. Like a constructive trust, a resulting trust arises by operation of law, though unlike a constructive trust it gives effect to intention. But it arises whether or not the transferor intended to retain a beneficial interest—he almost always does not—since it responds to the

[7] The issue was whether a pension fund surplus devolved by way of resulting trust to the employer company and the scheme members.

absence of any intention on his part to pass a beneficial interest to the recipient. It may arise even where the transferor positively wished to part with the beneficial interest, as in *Vandervell v. Inland Revenue Commissioners* [1967] 2 A.C. 291. In that case the retention of a beneficial interest by the transferor destroyed the effectiveness of a tax avoidance scheme which the transferor was seeking to implement. The House of Lords affirmed the principle that a resulting trust is not defeated by evidence that the transferor intended to part with the beneficial interest if he has not in fact succeeded in doing so. As Plowman J. had said in the same case at first instance [1966] Ch. 261, 275: "As I see it, a man does not cease to own property simply by saying 'I don't want it.' If he tries to give it away the question must always be, has he succeeded in doing so or not?" Lord Upjohn [1967] 2 A.C. 291, 314 expressly approved this.'

Automatic resulting trusts, to the extent that they remain a separate category of resulting trusts, are not controversial. Accordingly, the rest of this section focuses on presumed resulting trusts, looking at their impact and at the ways in which the presumption might be rebutted or displaced or reliance on it disallowed. The difficult issue of what, precisely, is presumed in a presumed resulting trust is particularly relevant to the section on rebutting the presumption.

5.4.2 Invoking the presumption of resulting trust

If a transferor can rely on the presumption of a resulting trust, then the consequences for the relevant parties are clear. The transferee will hold the transferred asset on trust (a resulting trust) for the transferor. The size of the transferor's beneficial interest is also clear. It is the entire beneficial interest in the transferred asset. The issue is more complicated when the resulting trust is a purchase money resulting trust, especially if the purchase is made using a secured bank loan. In these circumstances, does the size of a party's interest under a purchase money resulting trust depend upon the initial outright contribution to the purchase price, or on the magnitude of the legal liability incurred under the mortgage, or on the actual sums expended in repaying the mortgage, or simply on the total contribution to the running of the joint enterprise?

These last questions have generally been raised in the context of contributions to the purchase price of real estate in domestic situations, where there is often little likelihood of a formal written agreement setting out entitlements. A strict doctrinal approach to resulting trusts suggests that the relevant contributions to the purchase price must be clear at the time the asset is purchased, and that they must be made by the contributor *as* contributions to the purchase price which are not intended to be either a loan or a gift but which, by implication, are intended to deliver to the contributor an interest in the purchased asset. On this basis, only direct contributions at the time of the purchase and legal obligations to make mortgage repayments incurred at the time of the purchase will count as contributions to the purchase price. The application of such a strict rule in domestic situations, where a home has been purchased (often in the name of the man), usually disadvantages the woman in the relationship. Accordingly, courts have strained to adopt different approaches which better reflect modern perceptions of fairness and justice.

Typically this is done by finding an express or implied agreement between the parties to share the home—often only by dint of straining credibility, it must be said—and then giving effect to the agreement, even though it is not in writing. This is said to be justified on the basis that the woman has relied to her detriment on the existence of the arrangement. Again, the assertion of detrimental reliance is not always well supported by the facts. But the end is seen to justify the means, because the result is that women are better protected when the family breaks down. (See Section 5.8 below.) Nevertheless, it must be conceded that legislative intervention would do less violence to doctrinal coherence. These complications do not seem to have spread beyond the realm of family homes and into the terrain of personal property disputes, and so are treated rather cursorily here.

The next case is a simple application of the doctrine of resulting trusts.

[506] *Jones v Maynard* [1951] Ch 572, 575 *per* Vaisey J:

[A husband and wife operated a joint account. Both parties paid their incomes into it and drew on it as needed. They referred to the account as 'our savings'. The husband's contributions were by far the greater. He withdrew money from time to time to purchase investments in his own name. When the wife left her husband, the husband closed the account and withdrew the balance. The wife successfully claimed to be entitled to half the balance and half the investments purchased in the husband's name. Note that the resolution of this problem is not the same as if one of the parties had died.]

> 'In my judgment, when there is a joint account between husband and wife, and a common pool into which they put all their resources, it is not consistent with that conception that the account should thereafter (in this case in the event of a divorce) be picked apart, and divided up proportionately to the respective contributions of husband and wife, the husband being credited with the whole of his earnings and the wife with the whole of her dividends. I do not believe that, when once the joint pool has been formed, it ought to be, and can be, dissected in any such manner. In my view a husband's earnings or salary, when the spouses have a common purse, and pool their resources, are earnings made on behalf of both; and the idea that years afterwards the contents of the pool can be dissected by taking an elaborate account as to how much was paid in by the husband or the wife, is quite inconsistent with the original fundamental idea of a joint purse or a common pool.
>
> In my view the money which goes into the pool becomes joint property. The husband, if he wants a suit of clothes, draws a cheque to pay for it. The wife, if she wants any housekeeping money, draws a cheque, and there is no disagreement about it.
>
> That being my view, it follows that investments paid for out of the joint account, although made in the name of the husband, were in fact made by him in his own name as a trustee as to a moiety for his wife. If the investments out of the joint account had been made in the name of the wife alone, there is no doubt that the ordinary presumption of law [ie the presumption of advancement] would have applied and she would have been entitled to the investments; but as they were made in the name of the husband, it seems to me that the assumption of half and half is the one which I ought to apply.
>
> I think that the principle which applies here is Plato's definition of equality as a "sort of justice": if you cannot find any other, equality is the proper basis. When moneys were taken out of the joint account for the purpose of making an investment, the [rebuttable]

intention which I attribute to the parties is equality, and not some proportional entitlement to be arrived at by an inquiry as to the amounts contributed respectively by the husband and wife to the common purse. Where one is searching for justice, as one must, and cannot find any other secure and sound basis, I think that equality is the best rule.'

Note:

The decision in this case is based on an express (and presumably written) agreement as to the joint tenancy of the bank account, and then a presumed (purchase money) resulting trust in relation to the investments purchased with funds from the bank account. The resulting trust step involves a *rebuttable* presumption, so it is possible for investments purchased using funds from a joint account to belong entirely (legally and beneficially) to one party.

Questions:

If the investments had been purchased in the wife's name, what would the result have been? Does the answer depend upon who made the purchase? What sort of evidence will rebut the presumption of advancement between husband and wife (see Section 5.4.3 below)?

5.4.3 Overriding the presumption of resulting trust by invoking the presumption of advancement

As noted earlier, the presumption of advancement is a rebuttable presumption that the donor intended to make a gift of the equitable interest to the donee. In England, the presumption applies to transfers from husband to wife (but not vice versa, and not to *de facto* relationships), and it also applies to transfers from a man to anyone to whom he is *in loco parentis* (but not to transfers by a woman in the same circumstances). The following cases illustrate the rules.

(i) ***Shephard v Cartwright* [1955] AC 431 (HL):** a father promoted several private companies and allotted shares to his children. The children later signed documents transferring their shares, but without fully understanding what they were doing. The father credited the proceeds of sale to the children's accounts, but later drew on, and exhausted, the accounts without the children's knowledge. According to Viscount Simonds, at page 445: 'I think that the law is clear that on the one hand where a man purchases shares and they are registered in the name of a stranger there is a resulting trust in favour of the purchaser; on the other hand, if they are registered in the name of a child or one to whom the purchaser then stood in loco parentis, there is no such resulting trust but a presumption of advancement'. On rebutting the presumption of advancement, see *McGrath v Wallis* [1995] 3 FCR 661 (CA).

(ii) ***Bennet v Bennet* (1879) 10 Ch D 474:** the court held that a sum of money borrowed by a widowed mother for her son's benefit was in fact not a gift from her to her son, but a loan to the son provable by her against his estate on his death. According to Jessel MR, at pages 476–7, there is no moral obligation on a mother to provide for her child (ie no presumption of advancement). The position is not the same in other jurisdictions. In Australia, for example, the presumption applies between a mother and her children, although it is easily rebutted: see *Nelson v Nelson* (1995) 184 CLR 538, 547–9 (Aust HCt) (**[510]** below).

5.4.4 Rebutting the presumption of resulting trust by evidence to the contrary

As noted earlier, there is continuing debate about what exactly is presumed in a 'presumed' resulting trust. The House of Lords, in *Westdeutsche Landesbank* (**[504]** above), unanimously adopted the view that it is the intention to create a trust which is presumed. The opposing view is that it is the intention not to make a gift which is presumed. On its face the difference might seem to be a matter of semantics, but it is not. This is pointedly illustrated in the next section, which deals with the possibility of resulting trusts to reverse unjust enrichment (Section 5.5). The extracts below show that it is also crucial in determining what evidence is needed to rebut the presumption.

[507] ***Fowkes v Pascoe* (1875) LR 10 Ch App 343 (CA), 352–3 *per* Mellish LJ:**
[Before her death, a woman of substantial means purchased stock in the joint names of herself and a son of her daughter-in-law. If the presumption of resulting trust operated, the stock would be held on resulting trust for her and would therefore be distributed according to the terms of her will. If, on the other hand, the disposition was a gift, then the boy would take absolutely. The court held that the presumption of a resulting trust was rebutted.]

> 'Now, the presumption must, beyond all question, be of very different weight in different cases. In some cases it would be very strong indeed. If, for instance, a man invested a sum of stock in the name of himself and his solicitor, the inference would be very strong indeed that it was intended solely for the purpose of a trust, and the Court would require very strong evidence on the part of the solicitor to prove that it was intended as a gift; and certainly his own evidence would not be sufficient. On the other hand, a man may make an investment of stock in the name of himself and some person, although not a child or wife, yet in such a position to him as to make it extremely probable that the investment was intended as a gift. In such a case, although the rule of law, if there was no evidence at all, would compel the [353] Court to say that the presumption of trust must prevail, even if the Court might not believe that the fact was in accordance with the presumption, yet, if there is evidence to rebut the presumption, then, in my opinion, the Court must go into the actual facts. And if we are to go into the actual facts, and look at the circumstances of this investment, it appears to me utterly impossible, as the Lord Justice has said, to come to any other conclusion than that the first investment was made for the purpose of gift and not for the purpose of trust. It was either for the purpose of trust or else for the purpose of gift; and therefore any evidence which shews it was not for the purpose of trust is evidence to shew that it was for the

purpose of gift. We find a lady of considerable fortune, having no nearer connections than Mr. Pascoe, who was then a young man living in her house, and for whom she was providing. We find her, manifestly out of her savings, buying a sum of £250 stock in the joint names of herself and him, and at the same time buying another sum of £250 stock, on the very same day, in the joint names of herself and a lady who was living with her as a companion. Then, applying one's common sense to that transaction, what inference is it possible to draw, except that the purchases were intended for the purpose of gifts? If they were intended for the purpose of trusts, what possible reason was there why the two sums were not invested in the same names? Besides, at the very same time the lady had a large sum of stock in her own name, and could anything be more absurd than to suppose that a lady with £4000 or £5000 in her own name at that time in the same stock, and having a sum of £500 to invest out of her savings, should go and invest £250 in the name of herself and a young gentleman who was living in her house, and another £250 in the name of herself and her companion, and yet intend the whole to be for herself? I cannot come to any other conclusion than that it must have been intended by way of a present after her death.'

[508] ***Re Vinogradoff*** **[1935] WN 68, at 68** ***per*** **Farwell J:**

[A woman transferred £800 of War Loan stock into the joint names of herself and her four year old grand-daughter. On her death, the court decided that the child held the stock on resulting trust for the estate.]

'Adjourned summons.

By her will, dated May 14, 1934, the testatrix appointed the plaintiffs to be her executors, and, after bequeathing various legacies, she gave a life interest in her residuary estate to her daughter, the defendant Helen Lee. The testatrix died on May 23, 1934.

In 1926 the testatrix transferred a sum of 800*l*. War Loan, then standing in her name, into the joint names of herself and the defendant, Laura Huth Jackson, a daughter of Helen Lee and then of the age of four years. She lived in the house of and was provided for by her parents. The testatrix continued to receive the income of the War Stock for her own benefit during her lifetime.

This summons, taken out by the plaintiffs, asked for: (1) The determination of the question whether the defendant, Laura Huth Jackson, had any and if so what beneficial interest in the 800*l*. War Loan; (2) an order that the right to call for a transfer of the War Loan should vest in the plaintiffs.

J. H. A. Sparrow for the plaintiffs.

J. V. Nesbitt for Laura Huth Jackson contended that the presumption that the transfer of stock by a beneficial owner into the joint names of himself and another person, the transferor not standing in loco parentis to the transferee, created a resulting trust and the transferee was a trustee for the transferor, either did not arise or was rebutted in the present case by the fact that the transferee was only four years of age at the date of transfer, taken in conjunction with s. 20 of the Law of Property Act, 1925, which provided that the appointment of an infant to be a trustee was void. It must be assumed that at the date of the transfer the transferor knew of the provisions of that section. The transfer must be taken to have been a gift to the transferee.

J. A. Peck for Helen Lee.

FARWELL J. said that it had been argued that by reason of s. 20 of the Law of Property Act, 1925, the presumption had been changed, that the testatrix must be taken in law to have known of the provisions of that section and, knowing that, she could not have intended to transfer the stock into the name of the transferee as trustee, since the result of giving effect to the presumption would be to make the appointment void. In his

Lordship's judgment that would be taking the effect of the section much too far. The section was not intended and did not operate to make any difference to the presumption. The stock was not the property of the infant, but formed part of the estate of the testatrix.'

Re-read:

Westdeutsche Landesbank Girozentrale v Islington London Borough Council [1996] AC 669 (HL), at **[504]**.

Question:

Do any of these later extracts make explicit the answer to the question posed earlier: what, precisely, is being presumed in a 'presumed resulting trust'?

5.4.5 Disallowing reliance on the presumption of resulting trust

In certain circumstances, especially those relating to illegality, public policy suggests that parties' rights to assert an equitable interest in property should be constrained. The followed extract explains the rules. Consider carefully what is being prohibited by the court.

[509] *Tinsley v Milligan* [1994] 1 AC 340 (HL), 354–7 and 362 *per* Lord Goff, 369 and 371–6 *per* Lord Browne-Wilkinson:

[This case concerns real property rather than personal property, but the principles are assumed to have general application. A lesbian couple agreed to purchase a house in one party's name so that the other could misrepresent the extent of her assets to the Department of Social Services and so claim social security benefits to the economic advantage of both of them. Both women were therefore parties to the fraud. When they subsequently fell out, Tinsley (the legal owner) sought to evict Milligan. A bare majority of the House of Lords (Lords Goff and Keith dissenting) allowed Milligan to adduce evidence of her contributions to the purchase price of the house in order to establish a purchase money resulting trust, notwithstanding her part in the fraud, and equity's maxim that 'he who comes to equity must come with clean hands'.]

Lord Goff (dissenting):

'I turn then to the established principles. . . . The basic principle was stated long ago by Lord Mansfield C.J. in *Holman v. Johnson* (1775) 1 Cowp. 341, 343, in the context of the law of contract, when he said:

> "The objection, that a contract is immoral or illegal as between plaintiff and defendant, sounds at all times very ill in the mouth of the defendant. It is not for his sake, however, that the objection is ever allowed; but it is founded in general principles of policy, which the defendant has the advantage of, contrary to the real justice, as between him and the plaintiff, by accident, if I may so say. The principle of public

> policy is this; ex dolo malo non oritur actio. No court will lend its aid to a man who founds his cause of action upon an immoral or an illegal act. If, from the plaintiff's own stating or otherwise, the cause of action appears to arise ex turpi causa, on the transgression of a positive law of this country, there the court says he has no right to be assisted. It is upon that ground the court goes; not for the sake of the defendant, but because they will not lend their aid to such a plaintiff. So if the plaintiff and defendant were to change sides, and the defendant was to bring his action against the [355] plaintiff, the latter would then have the advantage of it; for where both are equally in fault, potior est conditio defendentis."

That principle has been applied again and again, for over 200 years. It is applicable in courts of equity as well as courts of law. . . . It is important to observe that, as Lord Mansfield made clear, the principle is not a principle of justice; it is a principle of policy, whose application is indiscriminate and so can lead to unfair consequences as between the parties to litigation. Moreover the principle allows no room for the exercise of any discretion by the court in favour of one party or the other.

Even so, the mere fact that a transaction is illegal does not have the effect of preventing property, whether general or special, from passing under it. . . .

From these two principles there is to be derived the principle invoked by the appellant in the present case, viz., that if A puts property in the name of B intending to conceal his (A's) interest in the property for a fraudulent or illegal purpose, neither law nor equity will allow A to recover the property, and equity will not assist him in asserting an equitable interest in it. This principle applies whether the transaction takes the form of a transfer of property by A to B, or the purchase by A of property in the name of B. . . .

Furthermore, the existence of the principle has been recognised on numerous occasions, even where it has not been given effect to on the facts of the case in question. In particular, an exception to the principle is to be found in cases in which the illegal purpose has not been carried into effect; but all those cases in which that exception has been recognised have proceeded on the basis that, absent those exceptional circumstances, the principle would have applied. . . .

The reason why the court of equity will not assist the claimant to recover his property or to assert his interest in it has been variously stated. It is sometimes said that it is because he has not come to equity with clean hands. . . .in these cases the requirements necessary to give rise to an equitable interest are present; it is simply that the claimant is precluded from asserting them. This explains why, in cases where the unlawful purpose has not been carried into effect, the court is able to hold that, despite the illegality, there is an equitable interest to which the claimant is entitled. . . .

As I read the authorities, they reveal a consistent application of the principle, subject only to the recognition of a *locus poenitentiae* for the claimant where the illegal purpose has not been carried into effect. . . . This conclusion flows from the nature of the principle itself, which is that a court of equity will not assist a claimant who does not come to equity with clean hands. This equitable maxim is . . . . founded on the principle that he who has committed iniquity shall not have equity; and what is required to invoke the maxim is no more than that the alleged misconduct has "an immediate and necessary relation to the equity sued for:".'

Lord Browne-Wilkinson:
'My Lords, I agree with the speech of my noble and learned friend, Lord Goff of Chieveley, that the consequences of being a party to an illegal transaction cannot

depend, as the majority in the Court of Appeal held, on such an imponderable factor as the extent to which the public conscience would be affronted by recognising rights created by illegal transactions. However, I have the misfortune to disagree with him as to the correct principle to be applied in a case where equitable property rights are acquired as a result of an illegal transaction.

Neither at law nor in equity will the court enforce an illegal contract which has been partially, but not fully, performed. However, it does not follow that all acts done under a partially performed contract are of no effect. In particular it is now clearly established that at law (as opposed to in equity), property in goods or land can pass under, or pursuant to, such a contract. If so, the rights of the owner of the legal title thereby acquired will be enforced, provided that the plaintiff can establish such title without pleading or leading evidence of the illegality. It is said that the property lies where it falls, even though legal title to the property was acquired as a result of the property passing under the illegal contract itself. I will first consider the modern authorities laying down the circumstances under which a legal proprietary interest acquired under an illegal transaction will be enforced by the courts. I will then consider whether the courts adopt a different attitude to equitable proprietary interests so acquired.

. . . .

From these authorities the following propositions emerge: (1) property in chattels and land can pass under a contract which is illegal and therefore would have been unenforceable as a contract; (2) a plaintiff can at law enforce property rights so acquired provided that he does not need to rely on the illegal contract for any purpose other than providing the basis of his claim to a property right; (3) it is irrelevant that the illegality of the underlying agreement was either pleaded or emerged in evidence: if the plaintiff has acquired legal title under the illegal contract that is enough.

. . . .

In my judgment to draw such distinctions between property rights enforceable at law and those which require the intervention of equity would be surprising. More than 100 years has elapsed since the administration of law and equity became fused. The reality of the matter is that, in 1993, English law has one single law of property made up of legal and equitable interests. Although for historical reasons legal estates and equitable estates have differing incidents, the person owning either type of estate has a right of property, a right in rem not merely a right in personam. If the law is that a party is entitled to enforce a property right acquired under an illegal transaction, in my judgment the same rule ought to apply to any property right so acquired, whether such right is legal or equitable.

In the present case, Miss Milligan claims under a resulting or implied trust. The court below have found, and it is not now disputed, that apart from the question of illegality Miss Milligan would have been entitled in equity to a half share in the house in accordance with the principles exemplified in *Gissing v. Gissing* [1971] A.C. 886; *Grant v. Edwards* [1986] Ch. 638 and *Lloyds Bank Plc. v. Rosset* [1991] 1 A.C. 107 [**[527]** below]. The creation of such an equitable interest does not depend upon a contractual obligation but on a common intention acted upon by the parties to their detriment. It is a development of the old law of resulting trust under which, where two parties have provided the purchase money to buy a property which is conveyed into the name of one of them alone, the latter is presumed to hold the property on a resulting trust for both parties in shares proportionate to their contributions to the purchase price. In arguments, no distinction was drawn between strict resulting trusts and a *Gissing v. Gissing* type of trust.

A presumption of resulting trust also arises in equity when A transfers personalty or money to B: see *Snell's Equity*, 29th ed. (1990), pp. 183–184; *Standing v. Bowring* (1885)

31 Ch.D. 282, 287, per Cotton L.J. and *Dewar v. Dewar* [1975] 1 W.L.R. 1532, 1537. Before 1925, there was also a presumption of resulting trust when land was voluntarily transferred by A to B: it is arguable, however, that the position has been altered by the 1925 property legislation: see *Snell's Equity*, p. 182. The presumption of a resulting trust is, in my view, crucial in considering the authorities. On that presumption (and on the contrary presumption of advancement) hinges the answer to the crucial question "does a plaintiff claiming under a resulting trust have to rely on the underlying illegality?" Where the presumption of resulting trust applies, the plaintiff does not have to rely on the illegality. If he proves that the property is vested in the defendant alone but that the plaintiff provided part of the purchase money, or voluntarily transferred the property to the defendant, the plaintiff establishes his claim under a resulting trust unless either the contrary presumption of advancement displaces the presumption of resulting trust or the defendant leads evidence to rebut the presumption of resulting trust. Therefore, in cases where the presumption of advancement does not apply, a plaintiff can establish his equitable interest in the property without relying in any way on the underlying illegal transaction. In this case Miss Milligan as defendant simply pleaded the common intention that the property should belong to both of them and that she contributed to the purchase price: she claimed that in consequence the property belonged to them equally. To the same effect was her evidence in chief. Therefore Miss Milligan was not forced to rely on the illegality to prove her equitable interest. Only in the reply and the course of Miss Milligan's cross-examination did such illegality emerge: it was Miss Tinsley who had to rely on that illegality.

Although the presumption of advancement does not directly arise for consideration in this case, it is important when considering the decided cases to understand its operation. On a transfer from a man to his wife, children or others to whom he stands *in loco parentis*, equity presumes an intention to make a gift. Therefore in such a case, unlike the case where the presumption of resulting trust applies, in order to establish any claim the plaintiff has himself to lead evidence sufficient to rebut the presumption of gift and in so doing will normally have to plead, and give evidence of, the underlying illegal purpose.

Against this background, I turn to consider the authorities dealing with the position in equity where A transferred property to B for an illegal purpose. The earlier authorities, primarily Lord Eldon, support the appellant's proposition that equity will not aid a plaintiff who has transferred property to another for an illegal purpose. . . .

However, in my view, the law was not so firmly established as at first sight it appears to have been. The law on the effect of illegality was developing throughout the 19th century. . . . The principle of *locus poenitentiae* is in my judgment irreconcilable with any rule that where property is transferred for an illegal purpose no equitable proprietary right exists. The equitable right, if any, must arise at the time at which the property was voluntarily transferred to the third party or purchased in the name of the third party. The existence of the equitable interest cannot depend upon events occurring after that date. Therefore if, under the principle of *locus poenitentiae*, the courts recognise that an equitable interest did arise out of the underlying transaction, the same must be true where the illegal purpose was carried through. The carrying out of the illegal purpose cannot, by itself, destroy the pre-existing equitable interest. The doctrine of *locus poenitentiae* therefore demonstrates that the effect of illegality is not to prevent a proprietary interest in equity from arising or to produce a forfeiture of such right: the effect is to render the equitable interest unenforceable in certain circumstances. The effect of illegality is not substantive but procedural. The question therefore is, "In what circumstances will equity refuse to enforce equitable rights which undoubtedly exist."

It is against this background that one has to assess the more recent law. Although in the cases decided during the last 100 years there are frequent references to Lord Eldon's wide principle, with one exception (*Cantor v. Cox*, 239 E.G. 121) none of the English decisions are decided by simply applying that principle. They are all cases where the unsuccessful party was held to be precluded from leading evidence of an illegal situation in order to rebut the presumption of advancement. Lord Eldon's rule would have provided a complete answer whether the transfer was made to a wife or child (where the presumption of advancement would apply) or to a stranger. Yet with one exception none of the cases in this century has been decided on that simple basis.

The majority of cases have been those in which the presumption of advancement applied: in those authorities the rule has been stated as being that a plaintiff cannot rely on evidence of his own illegality to rebut the presumption applicable in such cases that the plaintiff intended to make a gift of the property to the transferee. . . .

In my judgment, the explanation for this departure from Lord Eldon's absolute rule is that the fusion of law and equity has led the courts to adopt a single rule (applicable both at law and in equity) as to the circumstances in which the court will enforce property interests acquired in pursuance of an illegal transaction, viz., the *Bowmakers* rule [1945] K.B. 65. A party to an illegality can recover by virtue of a legal or equitable property interest if, but only if, he can establish his title without relying on his own illegality. In cases where the presumption of advancement applies, the plaintiff is faced with the presumption of gift and therefore cannot claim under a resulting trust unless and until he has rebutted that presumption of gift: for those purposes the plaintiff does have to rely on the underlying illegality and therefore fails.

. . . .

I therefore reach the conclusion that, although there is no case overruling the wide principle stated by Lord Eldon, as the law has developed the equitable principle has become elided into the common law rule. In my judgment the time has come to decide clearly that the rule is the same whether a plaintiff founds himself on a legal or equitable title: he is entitled to recover if he is not forced to plead or rely on the illegality, even if it emerges that the title on which he relied was acquired in the course of carrying through an illegal transaction.

As applied in the present case, that principle would operate as follows. Miss Milligan established a resulting trust by showing that she had contributed to the purchase price of the house and that there was common understanding between her and Miss Tinsley that they owned the house equally. She had no need to allege or prove why the house was conveyed into the name of Miss Tinsley alone, since that fact was irrelevant to her claim: it was enough to show that the house was in fact vested in Miss Tinsley alone. The illegality only emerged at all because Miss Tinsley sought to raise it. Having proved these facts, Miss Milligan had raised a presumption of resulting trust. There was no evidence to rebut that presumption. Therefore Miss Milligan should succeed.'

Also see:

Tribe v Tribe [1996] Ch 107 (CA) (at [420]) and *Rowan v Dann* (1992) 64 P & CR 202.

[510] *Nelson v Nelson* (1995) 184 CLR 538 (Aust HCt), paras 63–8, 83–4, 89, 100–1, 105 *per* Deane and Gummow JJ:

[This case indicates a different approach to the issue of illegality. Again, it is a case concerning real property rather than personal property. Mrs Nelson and her late husband purchased a property in the names of their two children. Later Mrs Nelson obtained a loan on favourable terms under the Defence Service Homes Act 1918, on the basis that she had no interest in any other real estate. Family relationships later broke down, and Mrs Nelson claimed an interest in the proceeds of the sale of the property purchased in her children's names. In Australia, the presumption of advancement applies between a mother and her children, so Mrs Nelson needed to rebut that presumption in order to rely on the purchase money resulting trust to give her an interest in the children's property (and its proceeds). However, any assertion by her that the purchase in the children's name was not intended as a gift to them would be inconsistent with her denial of any interest in other real estate when completing her loan application form for the second property.]

[Not all footnotes in the original are included here.]

> '61. The first respondent's submissions rely upon the apparently pervasive effect of the dictum of Lord Mansfield in *Holman v Johnson* ((1775) 1 Cowp 341 at 343, 98 ER 1120 at 1121) that: "[n]o Court will lend its aid to a man who founds his cause of action upon an immoral or an illegal act." That dictum, as well as the proposition "let the estate lie where it falls", has been applied not only, for example, to actions in tort for damages for conversion as in *Bowmakers Limited v Barnet Instruments Ltd* ([1945] KB 65, 70), and for moneys had and received . . ., but also in suits to enforce resulting trusts,. . . .
>
> 62. We turn to consider these propositions as the first respondent would have them apply to this appeal, commencing with that dealing with reliance upon illegality.
>
> 63. There are several difficulties with the acceptance of such a principle as determinative of a case such as the present. First, it has been held in England that the outcome turns upon whether what immediately is in issue is the rebuttal of a resulting trust by demonstrating that what was intended was a gift, or the rebuttal of a presumption of advancement by demonstrating that a gift was not intended. The distinction may be considered by an example where Blackacre is purchased with the money of A but transferred by the vendor on completion to B, who is the child of A. Authority in England, provided by *Tinsley v Milligan* ([1994] 1 AC 340 at 366, 367, 374–5), is that A cannot rely on evidence of his own illegality to rebut the presumption that a gift in favour of B was intended. On the other hand, if A purchases Blackacre in the name of B, the relationship between them being such that there is no presumption of advancement, A may enforce the resulting trust in A's favour because there is no necessity to prove the reason for the conveyance into the name of B and thus no need to rely on A's illegality (*ibid.* at 367, 368–9, 375–6).
>
> 64. These results depend on the form in which a particular legal proceeding is cast and, unusually for equity, are achieved at the expense of substance. Further, they may operate indiscriminately and thus lead to harsh consequences as between particular parties. It is true, as Lord Mansfield pointed out in *Holman v Johnson* (*supra,* at 343 or 1121) that:
>
> > "if the plaintiff and defendant were to change sides, and the defendant was to bring his action against the plaintiff, the latter would then have the advantage of it".
>
> But that consideration only heightens the lack of attraction of such a proposition in the court of equity. Furthermore, it in turn encourages a quest for mitigation by the drawing of further fine distinctions and exceptions whereby recovery will be permitted.

65. A second approach to the matter is to let the loss lie where it falls, the policy being one to encourage observance of the law by threat of a sharp and broad sword. This view commended itself to the minority in *Tinsley v Milligan*. It was said, again with reference to Lord Mansfield in *Holman v Johnson*, that (*Tinsley* at 355):

> "(i)t is important to observe that, as Lord Mansfield made clear, the principle is not a principle of justice; it is a principle of policy, whose application is indiscriminate and so can lead to unfair consequences as between the parties to litigation. Moreover the principle allows no room for the exercise of any discretion by the court in favour of one party or the other."

Reliance also was placed by the minority upon what was seen as the authoritative source of principle in equity provided by the decision of Lord Eldon LC in *Muckleston v Brown* ((1801) 6 Ves Jun 52). . . .

66. The outcome in *Tinsley v Milligan* indicates that adoption of one approach rather than the other may lead to opposite results. As we have indicated, on this appeal the first respondent relies upon both as operating in her favour. She submits (and the Court of Appeal so decided) that Mrs Nelson can only rebut the presumption of advancement by revealing her purpose of obtaining a subsidised loan by concealment and, further, that the loss should be left to fall upon Mrs Nelson.

67. In our view, neither of these approaches is to be adopted in the present case. Two factors are of paramount importance. First, as the appellants submit and we would accept, the question of illegality is bound up with the view taken of the underlying policy of the Act. To quote a United States scholar, "if illegality consists in the violation of a statute, courts will give or refuse relief depending upon the fundamental purpose of the statute" (Clark, *Equity, An Analysis and Discussion of Modern Equity Problems* (1928 reprint), para 401). Secondly, what is sought are equitable remedies in aid of an alleged trust and equity is equipped to attain a result which eschews harsh extremes.

68. The range and flexibility of equitable remedies assist in achieving an appropriate result in the particular case; this means, in the words of one commentator, "(t)he old common law idea of all or nothing will no longer have to apply" (Wade, 'Restitution of Benefits Acquired Through Illegal Transactions' (1945) 95 *University of Pennsylvania Law Review* 261 at 304). Accordingly, unlike the common law, equity may impose terms upon a party seeking administration of equitable remedies. Further, equity has not subscribed to any absolute proposition that the consequence of illegality, particularly where what is involved is contravention of public policy manifested by statute, is that neither side may obtain any relief, so that the matter lies where it falls. Rather, in various instances equity has taken the view that it may intervene, albeit with the attachment of conditions, lest there be "no redress at all against the fraud nor any body to ask it".

. . . .

Resulting trusts and statutory illegality

83. The intersection between the institution of the resulting trust and the principles of illegality is identified by Scott as follows (Scott and Fratcher, *The Law of Trusts*, 4th ed (1989) par 444):

> "Although a resulting trust ordinarily arises where A purchases property and takes title in the name of B, A may be precluded from enforcing the resulting trust because of the illegality of his purpose. If A cannot recover the property, B keeps it and is thereby enriched. The question in each case is whether the policy against

the unjust enrichment of the grantee is outweighed by the policy against giving relief to the payor who has entered into an illegal transaction."

84. However, where the illegality flows from statute, the matter is not at large in the manner suggested above. Rather it is a question of the impact of the statute itself upon the institution of the resulting trust. As the matter is put by *White and Tudor* . . . :

"There will be no resulting trust if the policy of an Act of Parliament would be thereby defeated."

. . . .

89. Against the background traced above we accept the submission for the appellants that the crucial step is to identify the relevant public policy, beginning with the provisions of the Act. . . .

100. . . . .counsel for the appellants points to these provisions [in the Act] in support of the proposition that the purpose of the Act is sufficiently served by such penalties [as are provided for] and that the denial of the resulting trust would cause prejudice to a person in the position of Mrs Nelson without furthering the objects of the legislation. . . .

101. That submission should be accepted. Further, the relevant provisions of the legislation, before and after the Amendment Act, show its purpose to be the provision of public moneys to facilitate the purchase of housing by eligible persons, but on the footing that the eligible person not own another dwelling. The means by which that purpose has been effected have changed from secured loan to interest subsidy in respect of an advance by the Bank. But it has consistently been the scheme of the legislation that, if the public moneys are misapplied, they are made recoverable by the Corporation or the Commonwealth. However, as the cases on the former s 35 demonstrate, the interest of the Corporation or the Commonwealth in the dwelling or proceeds of sale thereof is co-extensive with the funds provided by it; if they be restored then effect may be given to a trust in respect of the balance of the equitable interest in the dwelling or the proceeds of sale thereof.

105. In our view, as the price of obtaining the relief she seeks for the recognition and enforcement of a resulting trust in respect of the whole of the balance of the proceeds of sale of the Bent Street property, Mrs Nelson must be prepared to do equity according to the requirements of good conscience. That may involve consideration of more than the interests of the parties to the litigation. Here, good conscience calls for the taking by Mrs Nelson of steps sufficient to satisfy the demands of the underlying policy of the Act.'

FURTHER READING:

N Enonchong, 'Title Claims and Illegal Transactions' (1995) 111 *LQR* 135.
F Rose, 'Gratuitous Transfers and Illegal Purposes' (1996) 112 *LQR* 386.

5.5 Resulting trusts which effect restitution for unjust enrichment

Outside the traditional remit of automatic and presumed resulting trusts, there are certain other circumstances which may give rise to resulting trusts. Although a number of cases illustrate the possibilities, these examples might now be regarded as controversial in the light of the House of Lords' decision in *Westdeutsche* (**[504]** above). For example, according to the majority dicta in *Westdeutsche*, no trust will arise as a result of a mistaken (non-contractual) transfer, notwithstanding the contrary conclusion of Goulding J in *Chase Manhattan* (**[511]** below). Similarly, there are cases suggesting that a resulting trust is the means by which title to property is revested in the transferor when a voidable transfer is avoided (see **[513]** below). However, this form of proprietary intervention too might seem distinctly anomalous in the light of the assertion by the House of Lords in *Westdeutsche* that no similar trust arises if the contract between the parties is void, rather than voidable. On the other hand, this 'anomalous' approach to contracts which are voidable in equity is consistent with the common law response to contracts which are voidable at law: see Section 5.2 above.

The following extracts illustrate these different approaches.

5.5.1 Non-contractual situations

[511] ***Chase Manhattan Bank v Israel-British Bank*** **[1981] 1 Ch 105, 115–21** ***per*** **Goulding J:**

[The claimant mistakenly overpaid the defendant more than US$2 million. The court held that the claimant was allowed to trace the overpayment. This right to trace depended upon the court finding that the claimant had a proprietary interest in the over-paid funds, and that there was a fiduciary relationship between the parties. As already noted, this first conclusion might now be doubted in the light of comments made by the House of Lords in *Westdeutsche*. The second conclusion, too, is controversial. Modern scholarship suggests that a fiduciary relationship is not a necessary pre-requisite to the right to trace[8] (despite cases suggesting that it is[9]), and that the mere existence of a split between legal and equitable title does not of itself give rise to such a relationship. In this case, the court did not label the interest as either resulting or constructive, and both types of trust are mentioned in the materials cited.]

> 'The plaintiff's claim, viewed in the first place without reference to any system of positive law, raises problems to which the answers, if not always difficult, are at any rate not obvious. If one party P pays money to another party D by reason of a factual mistake, either common to both parties or made by P alone, few conscientious persons would doubt that D ought to return it. But suppose that D is, or becomes, insolvent before

[8] See L Smith, *The Law of Tracing* (1997, Clarendon Press: Oxford). Also see Section 6.5.

[9] See *Re Diplock's Estate* [1948] Ch 465.

repayment is made, so that P comes into competition with D's general creditors, what then? If the money can still be traced, either in its original form or through successive conversions, and is found among D's remaining assets, ought not P to be able to claim it, or what represents it, as his own? If he ought, and if in a particular case the money has been blended with other assets and is represented by a mixed fund, no longer as valuable as the sum total of its original constituents, what priorities or equalities should govern the distribution of the mixed fund? If the money can no longer be traced, either separate or in mixture, should P have any priority over ordinary creditors of D? In any of these cases, does it make any difference whether the mistake was inevitable, or was caused by P's carelessness, or was contributed to by some fault, short of dishonesty, on the part of D?

At this stage I am asked to take only one step forward, and to answer the initial question of principle, whether the plaintiff is entitled in equity to trace the mistaken payment and to recover what now properly represents the money. The subsequent history of the payment and the rules for ascertaining what now represents it have not been proved or debated before me. They will have to be established in further proceedings if the plaintiff can clear the first hurdle today.

This initial question in the action appears not to be the subject of reported judicial decision in England. Let me read a few lines from Goff and Jones, *The Law of Restitution*, 2nd ed. (1978), p. 89. The authors say:

> "Whether a person who has paid money under a mistake of fact should be granted a restitutionary proprietary claim can arise in a number of contexts. It will be most important when the payee is insolvent and the payer seeks to gain priority over the payee's general creditors. The English courts have never had to consider this question. But in the United States it has arisen on a few occasions. A leading case is *In re Berry* (1906) 147 Fed. 208."

That was a case decided in the Circuit Court of Appeals, Second Circuit. I shall read a passage from the judgment of the court, delivered by Judge Coxe, at p. 210:

> "Stripped of all complications and entanglements we have this naked fact that Raborg Manice by mistake paid Berry & Co. $1,500, which they did not owe and which Berry & Co. could not have retained without losing the respect of every honourable business man. It is conceded on all hands that had not insolvency and bankruptcy intervened Raborg Manice could have recovered the money on an implied assumpsit in the event that Berry & Co. declined to return it after knowledge of the facts—a highly improbable contingency. Of course such an action would lie. On no possible theory could the retention of the money by Berry & Co. be justified; it was paid to them and received by them under mistake, both parties believing that Raborg Manice owed the amount. If $1,500 had been placed in a package by Raborg Manice and delivered to a messenger with instructions to deposit it in their bank, and the messenger, by mistake, had delivered it to Berry & Co., it will hardly be pretended that the latter would acquire any title to the money, and yet the actual transaction in legal effect gave them no better right. It is urged that to compel restitution now will work injustice to the general creditors of the bankrupts, but this contention loses sight of the fact that the money in dispute never belonged to the bankrupts, and their creditors, upon broad principles of equity, have no more right to it than if the transaction of November 25 had never taken place. If the trustees succeed on this appeal the creditors will receive $1,500, the equitable title to which was never in the bankrupts. There can be no doubt of the fact that the payment to Berry & Co. was a mistake and that by reason of this

> mistake the trustees have in their possession $1,500 which, otherwise, they would not have. The proposition that Raborg Manice who have done no wrong, shall be deprived of their property and that it shall be divided among creditors to whom it does not fairly belong, is not one that appeals to the conscience of a court of equity.
>
> "The rule invoked by the District Court is well stated by Judge Story."

Judge Coxe then read a passage from *Story's Commentaries on Equity Jurisprudence*, 2nd ed. (1839), vol. 2, paras. 1255 and 1256. He omitted certain sentences, and I think the extract will be clearer if I read the whole of Story's two paragraphs:

> "1255. One of the most common cases in which a Court of Equity acts upon the ground of implied trusts in invitum, is where a party has received money which he cannot conscientiously withhold from another party. It has been well remarked, that the receiving of money which consistently with conscience cannot be retained is, in Equity, sufficient to raise a trust in favour of the party for whom or on whose account it was received. This is the governing principle in all such cases. And therefore, whenever any controversy arises, the true question is, not whether money has been received by a party of which he could not have compelled the payment, but whether he can now, with a safe conscience, *ex aequo et bono*, retain it. Illustrations of this doctrine are familiar in cases of money paid by accident, or mistake, or fraud. And the difference between the payment of money under a mistake of fact, and a payment under a mistake of law, in its operation upon the conscience of the party, presents the equitable qualifications of the doctrine in a striking manner.
>
> "1256. It is true that courts of law now entertain jurisdiction in many cases of this sort where formerly the remedy was solely in Equity; as, for example, in an action of assumpsit for money had and received, where the money cannot conscientiously be withheld by the party; following out the rule of the Civil Law; *Quod condictio indebiti non datur ultra, quam locupletior factus est, qui accepit*. But this does not oust the general jurisdiction of Courts of Equity over the subject-matter, which had for many ages before been in full exercise, although it renders a resort to them for relief less common, as well as less necessary, than it formerly was. Still, however, there are many cases of this sort where it is indispensable to resort to Courts of Equity for adequate relief, and especially where the transactions are complicated, and a discovery from the defendant is requisite."

Judge Coxe, after citing two reported cases, added, at p. 211:

> "When the money was paid under a plain mistake of fact equity impressed upon it a constructive trust which followed it through the bank and into the hand of the trustees."

The effect of the American case law, developed in a number of different states, as well as in the federal jurisdiction, is summarised as follows in the important book of Professor A. W. Scott, *The Law of Trusts*, 3rd ed. (1967), vol. 5, p. 3428:

> "Similarly where chattels are conveyed or money is paid by mistake, so that the person making the conveyance or payment is entitled to restitution, the transferee or payee holds the chattels or money upon a constructive trust. In such a case, it is true, the remedy at law for the value of the chattels or for the amount of money paid may be an adequate remedy, in which case a court of equity will not ordinarily give specific restitution. If the chattels are of a unique character, however, or if the person to whom the chattels are conveyed or to whom the money is paid is insolvent, the remedy at law is not adequate and a court of equity will enforce the

> constructive trust by decreeing specific restitution. The beneficial interest remains in the person who conveyed the chattel or who paid the money, since the conveyance or payment was made under a mistake."

In my opinion, on the evidence that I have heard, to which I shall have to return later, the foregoing passages correctly represent the law of the State of New York. I believe they are also in accord with the general principles of equity as applied in England, and in the absence of direct English authority I should wish to follow them. Mr. Stubbs for the defendant contends that I am not at liberty to do so, because of the judgment of the Court of Appeal in *In re Diplock* [1948] Ch. 465 [see **[628]**], explaining and developing the earlier decision of the House of Lords in *Sinclair v. Brougham* [1914] A.C. 398 [see **[516]** below]. *In re Diplock* itself went to the House of Lords, sub nom. *Ministry of Health v. Simpson* [1951] A.C. 251, but the appeal did not relate to the question which is material in the present litigation. Mr. Stubbs says that, as stated in *Snell's Principles of Equity* 27th ed. (1973), p. 289, there is no equitable right to trace property unless some initial fiduciary relationship exists, the right being founded on the existence of a beneficial owner with an equitable proprietary interest in property in the hands of a trustee or other fiduciary agent. Mr. Stubbs says further that the essential fiduciary relationship must initially arise from some consensual arrangement.

The facts and decisions in *Sinclair v. Brougham* [1914] A.C. 398 and in *In re Diplock* [1948] Ch. 465 are well known and I shall not take time to recite them. I summarise my view of the *Diplock* judgment as follows: (1) The Court of Appeal's interpretation of *Sinclair v. Brougham* was an essential part of their decision and is binding on me. (2) The court thought that the majority of the House of Lords in *Sinclair v. Brougham* had not accepted Lord Dunedin's opinion in that case, and themselves rejected it. (3) The court (as stated in *Snell*, loc. cit.) held that an initial fiduciary relationship is a necessary foundation of the equitable right of tracing. (4) They also held that the relationship between the building society directors and depositors in *Sinclair v. Brougham* was a sufficient fiduciary relationship for the purpose: [1948] Ch. 465, 529, 540. The latter passage reads, at p. 540: "A sufficient fiduciary relationship was found to exist between the depositors and the directors by reason of the fact that the purposes for which the depositors had handed their money to the directors were by law incapable of fulfilment." It is founded, I think, on the observations of Lord Parker of Waddington at [1914] A.C. 398, 441.

This fourth point shows that the fund to be traced need not (as was the case in *In re Diplock* itself) have been the subject of fiduciary obligations before it got into the wrong hands. It is enough that, as in *Sinclair v. Brougham* [1914] A.C. 398, the payment into wrong hands itself gave rise to a fiduciary relationship. The same point also throws considerable doubt on Mr. Stubbs's submission that the necessary fiduciary relationship must originate in a consensual transaction. It was not the intention of the depositors or of the directors in *Sinclair v. Brougham* to create any relationship at all between the depositors and the directors as principals. Their object, which unfortunately disregarded the statutory limitations of the building society's powers, was to establish contractual relationships between the depositors and the society. In the circumstances, however, the depositors retained an equitable property in the funds they parted with, and fiduciary relationships arose between them and the directors. In the same way, I would suppose, a person who pays money to another under a factual mistake retains an equitable property in it and the conscience of that other is subjected to a fiduciary duty to respect his proprietary right. I am fortified in my opinion by the speech of Viscount Haldane L.C. in *Sinclair v. Brougham* [1914] A.C. 398, 419, 420, who, unlike Lord Dunedin, was not suspected of heresy in *In re Diplock*. Lord Haldane (who spoke for

Lord Atkinson as well as himself) includes money paid under mistake of fact among the cases where money could be followed at common law, and he proceeds, at p. 421, to the auxiliary tracing remedy, available (as he said) wherever money was held to belong in equity to the plaintiff, without making any relevant exception. Thus my problem over *In re Diplock* [1948] Ch. 465 is in the end this: Can I adopt into English equity the passage I have quoted from Professor Scott without making the forbidden transition to the opinion of Lord Dunedin? I have carefully considered the passages, at pp. 541 to 543, in *In re Diplock* where that opinion is criticised. In the end I believe that the whole subject of the Court of Appeal's condemnation was the suggestion that the tracing remedy could be applied wherever the defendant could be shown to have got an unjust enrichment, a superfluity as Lord Dunedin called it. The court insisted on the more precise test of a continuing right of property recognised in equity or of what I think to be its concomitant, "a fiduciary or quasi-fiduciary relationship": [1948] Ch. 465, 520. At the same time they recognised that exactly what relationships were sufficient for the purpose had not yet been precisely laid down: see p. 540.

Thus, in the belief that the point is not expressly covered by English authority and that *In re Diplock* does not conclude it by necessary implication, I hold that the equitable remedy of tracing is in principle available, on the ground of continuing proprietary interest, to a party who has paid money under a mistake of fact. On that prime question, I see no relevant difference between the law of England and the law of New York and there is no conflict of laws to be resolved.'

[512] ***Westdeutsche Landesbank Girozentrale v Islington London Borough Council*** **[1996] AC 669 (HL), 714–15 *per* Lord Browne-Wilkinson:**
[The facts are noted above at **[504]**. This extract is a comment on *Chase Manhattan* (**[511]** above).]

'In that case Chase Manhattan, a New York bank, had by mistake paid the same sum twice to the credit of the defendant, a London bank. Shortly thereafter, the defendant bank went into insolvent liquidation. The question was whether Chase Manhattan had a claim in rem against the assets of the defendant bank to recover the second payment.

Goulding J. was asked to assume that the moneys paid under a mistake were capable of being traced in the assets of the recipient bank: he was only concerned with the question whether there was a proprietary base on which the tracing remedy could be founded: p. 116B. He held that, where money was paid under a mistake, the receipt of such money without more constituted the recipient a trustee: he said that the payer "retains an equitable property in it and the conscience of [the recipient] is subjected to a fiduciary duty to respect his proprietary right:" p. 119.

It will be apparent from what I have already said that I cannot agree with this reasoning. First, it is based on a concept of retaining an equitable property in money where, prior to the payment to the recipient bank, there was no existing equitable interest. [Earlier in his judgment, at p 706, Lord Browne-Wilkinson described as 'fallacious' the argument that the bank could 'retain' equitable title. He noted that '[a] person solely entitled to the full beneficial ownership of money or property, both at law and in equity, does not enjoy an equitable interest in that property. The legal title carries with it all rights. Unless and until there is a separation of the legal and equitable estates, there is no separate equitable title. Therefore to talk about the bank "retaining" its equitable interest is meaningless.'] Further, I cannot understand how the recipient's "conscience" can be affected at a time when he is not aware of any mistake. Finally, the judge found that the law of England and that of New York were in substance the same. I find this a surprising conclusion since the New York law of constructive trusts has for a long time been influenced by the concept of a remedial constructive trust, whereas hitherto English law has for the most part only recognised an institutional constructive trust: see *Metall und Rohstoff A.G. v. Donaldson Lufkin & Jenrette Inc.* [1990] 1 Q.B. 391, 478–480. In the present context, that distinction is of fundamental importance. Under an institutional constructive trust, the trust arises by operation of law as from the date of the circumstances which give rise to it: the function of the court is merely to declare that such trust has arisen in the past. The consequences that flow from such trust having arisen (including the possibly unfair consequences to third parties who in the interim have received the trust property) are also determined by rules of law, not under a discretion. A remedial constructive trust, as I understand it, is different. It is a judicial remedy giving rise to an enforceable equitable obligation: the extent to which it operates retrospectively to the prejudice of third parties lies in the discretion of the court. Thus for the law of New York to hold that there is a remedial constructive trust where a payment has been made under a void contract gives rise to different consequences from holding that an institutional constructive trust arises in English law.

However, although I do not accept the reasoning of Goulding J., *Chase Manhattan* may well have been rightly decided. The defendant bank knew of the mistake made by the paying bank within two days of the receipt of the moneys: see at p. 115A. The judge treated this fact as irrelevant (p. 114F) but in my judgment it may well provide a proper foundation for the decision. Although the mere receipt of the moneys, in ignorance of the mistake, gives rise to no trust, the retention of the moneys after the recipient bank learned of the mistake may well have given rise to a constructive trust: see *Snell's Equity*, p. 193; Pettit, *Equity and the Law of Trusts*, 7th ed. (1993) p. 168; *Metall und Rohstoff A.G. v. Donaldson Lufkin & Jenrette Inc.* [1990] 1 Q.B. 391, 473–474.'

5.5.2 Voidable contracts

[513] *Alati v Kruger* (1955) 94 CLR 216 (Aust HCt), 223–4 *per* Dixon CJ (Webb, Kitto and Taylor JJ agreeing):

[The case concerned a contract for the sale of real property, but the principles are considered to be of general application. The contract was voidable for fraudulent misrepresentation.]

'7. On the footing which must be accepted, that the contract had been induced by a fraudulent representation made by the appellant to the respondent, the latter had a choice of courses open to him. He might sue for damages for breach of the warranty contained in cl. 21, for the statement in that clause clearly formed one of the terms of the contract and was not only a representation; but he could not do this and rescind the contract for misrepresentation. Secondly, he might sue to recover as damages for fraud the difference between the price he had paid and the fair value of the property at the time of the contract . . ., but that again would involve affirming the purchase. Or, thirdly, provided that he was in a position to restore to the appellant substantially that which he had received under the contract, he might avoid the purchase and sue to recover his purchase money back from the appellant, with interest and also with damages for any loss which he may have suffered through carrying on the business in the meantime: cf. *Salmond and Williams on Contracts* (2nd ed.), (1945), p. 269.

. . . .

10. If the case had to be decided according to the principles of the common law, it might have been argued that at the date when the respondent issued his writ he was not entitled to rescind the purchase, because he was not then in a position to return to the appellant *in specie* that which he had received under the contract, in the same plight as that in which he had received it: *Clarke v. Dickson* (1858) EB & E 148 (120 ER 463) . But it is necessary here to apply the doctrines of equity, and equity has always regarded as valid the disaffirmance of a contract induced by fraud even though precise *restitutio in integrum* is not possible, if the situation is such that, by the exercise of its powers, including the power to take accounts of profits and to direct inquiries as to allowances proper to be made for deterioration, it can do what is practically just between the parties, and by so doing restore them substantially to the status quo: *Erlanger v. New Sombrero Phosphate Co.* (1878) 3 App Cas 1218, at pp 1278, 1279 ; *Brown v. Smitt* (1924) 34 CLR 160, at pp 165, 169 ; *Spence v. Crawford* (1939) 3 All ER 271, at pp 279, 280 . It is not that equity asserts a power by its decree to avoid a contract which the defrauded party himself has no right to disaffirm, and to revest property the title to which the party cannot effect. Rescission for misrepresentation is always the act of the party himself : *Reese River Silver Mining Co. v. Smith* (1869) LR 4 HL 64, at p 73 . The function of a court in which proceedings for rescission are taken is to adjudicate upon the validity of a purported disaffirmance as an act avoiding the transaction *ab initio*, and, if it is valid, to give effect to it and make appropriate consequential orders: see *Abram Steamship Co. Ltd. v. Westville Shipping Co. Ltd.* (1923) AC 773 . The difference between the legal and the equitable rules on the subject simply was that equity, having means which the common law lacked to ascertain and provide for the adjustments necessary to be made between the parties in cases where a simple handing back of property or repayment of money would not put them in as good a position as before they entered into their transaction, was able to see the possibility of *restitutio in integrum*, and therefore to concede the right of a defrauded party to rescind, in a much wider variety of cases than those which the common law could recognize as admitting of rescission. Of course, a rescission which the common law courts would not accept as valid cannot of its own force revest the legal title to property which had passed, but if a court of equity would treat it as effectual the equitable title to such property revests upon the rescission.'

Note:

This conclusion was cited with approval in *O'Sullivan v Management Agency and Music Ltd* [1985] QB 428, 457 *per* Dunn LJ.

[514] *Daly v Sydney Stock Exchange Ltd* (1986) 160 CLR 371 (Aust HCt), 387–90 *per* Brennan J:

[Dr Daly consulted a firm of stockbrokers about shares in which he might invest. An employee of the firm, unaware of the firm's parlous financial position, advised Dr Daly that it was not a good time to purchase shares and that he should leave his funds on deposit with the firm. The firm later collapsed and was unable to repay the funds lent by Dr Daly. The High Court accepted that a fiduciary relationship existed between the investor and the firm, and that the firm had breached its fiduciary duty in not disclosing its unsatisfactory financial position. However, these facts did not constitute the firm a constructive trustee of the funds received from Dr Daly, so he was not entitled to compensation from the industry fidelity fund.]

'12. Irrespective of the fairness of its terms, equity regards a contract made between a fiduciary and the person to whom he stands in a fiduciary relationship as voidable if the fiduciary has breached his fiduciary duty in respect of the contract. If property is transferred to the fiduciary pursuant to the contract, the transfer may be set aside in consequence of the avoidance of the contract (*Armstrong v. Jackson*, [1917] 2 KB 822 at pp 825–826). The contract and the transfer are voidable, but not void. If the transfer is set aside, the fiduciary transferee (and, no doubt, a volunteer or a purchaser with notice of the circumstances) holds the property transferred on a constructive trust for the transferor which a court of equity will enforce subject to any accounts or enquiries that may be necessary to do equity to the transferee. The transferor may elect to avoid the contract and to assert his title to the land or other property transferred assuming it still exists in specie or, being money, can be traced. He may invoke the assistance of equity to recover the land or other property in specie or to trace the money.

13. The principles governing the setting aside of contracts of purchase or sale are applicable to contracts of loan. Since equity intervenes to prevent a fiduciary from retaining property acquired under a contract entered into in breach of his fiduciary obligation, equity will intervene to prevent him from retaining money acquired in like circumstances. Of course, the occasions for invoking the assistance of equity to recover money lent may be infrequent, and the remedy of tracing the money lent into hands other than the borrower's—a remedy which the common law does not afford—may frequently be frustrated by dissipation of the money or its payment to another creditor (cf. *In re Diplock, Diplock v. Wintle* [1948] 1 Ch 465, at p 521). Nevertheless, a person lending money to a fiduciary who obtains the loan without discharging his fiduciary duty is entitled in equity to avoid the contract of loan and to recover, by tracing if need be, the money lent.

14. It may be said that a party who elects to avoid a contract and set aside a transfer of property made pursuant to the contract had an equitable interest in the property from the beginning, that the equitable remedies available to him are incidental to that interest and that his equitable interest arose before, and does not depend upon the court's decree: see *Scott on Trusts*, 3rd ed. (1967), Vol.5, §462.4, p 3421. Thus, in *Stump v. Gaby* ((1852) 2 De GM & G 623 (42 ER 1015)), where the plaintiff had conveyed an estate in land to his attorney pursuant to a contract of sale for an undervalue, Lord St Leonards L.C., held the contract to be voidable, saying (at p.630 (p.1018)):

> "In the view of this Court he remains the owner, subject to the repayment of the money which has been advanced by the attorney, and the consequence is that he may devise the estate, not as a legal estate, but as an equitable estate, wholly irrespective of all question as to any rights of entry or action, leaving the conveyance to have its full operation at law, but looking at the equitable right to have it set aside in this Court."

If a decree setting aside the conveyance is made, the plaintiff's equitable title is treated "as having been, from the first, a trustee for the grantor, who, therefore, has an equitable estate, not a mere right of suit". That was the effect, according to Menzies J. in *Latec Investments Ltd. v. Hotel Terrigal Pty.Ltd. (In Liq)* ((1965) 113 CLR 265, at p 290), of the decision of Knight Bruce L.J. in *Gresley v. Mousley* ((1859) 4 De G & J 78 (45 ER 31)). Menzies J. in *Latec Investments* referred to the view that a plaintiff who was entitled to avoid a contract of sale and to have the conveyance set aside had a mere equity and the competing view that he had an equitable interest in the property from the beginning. He said, at pp.290–291:

"If there is a difference between the two lines of authority, that difference seems to me to arise from concentration upon different aspects of what follows from a voidable conveyance. Thus, *Phillips v. Phillips* ((1861) 4 De GF & J 208 (45 ER 1164)), in so far as it says that a person with the right to have a voidable conveyance set aside has but a mere equity, directs attention to the right to have the conveyance set aside as a right to sue which must be successfully exercised as a necessary condition of there being any relation back of the equitable interest established by the suit. *Stump v. Gaby* directs attention to the result of the eventual avoidance of the conveyance upon the position ab initio and throughout of the persons by whom and to whom the conveyance of property was made and says that, in the event of a successful suit (which may be maintained by a devisee), the conveyor had an equitable estate capable of devise and that the conveyee holds, and has always held, as trustee."

15. But where property has been sold and conveyed, the purchaser's beneficial title must be ascertained by reference to the sale so long as it stands; the vendor cannot insist on an equitable interest in the property if he does not choose to enforce his equity to avoid the sale (see per Kitto J. in *Latec Investments* (at pp 277–278); and *In re Sherman dec'd.* ((1954) 1 Ch 653, at p 658). Similarly, until the lender elects to avoid the contract of loan, he cannot assert an equitable title to the money lent. He cannot at once leave the contract on foot and deny the borrowers the title to the money which the contract confers. When, as in the present case, a borrower acquires title to money paid to him under and pursuant to a contract of loan, the borrower cannot be made a trustee of the money without his consent so long as the contract stands. There is no analogy between the present case and one in which a constructive trust is imposed on money or other property which is acquired by a fiduciary in breach of his duty but not pursuant to a voidable contract. In such a case there is no question of avoiding the contract before the constructive trust is imposed. A fortiori, there is no analogy between the present case and one where a constructive trust is imposed on money or other property which is acquired by a non-fiduciary otherwise than by contract (as, for example, in *Chase Manhattan Bank N.A. v. Israel-British Bank (London) Ltd.* ((1981) 1 Ch 105, at pp 118–120).

16. Although Dr Daly was entitled to avoid the contracts of loan for breach of the fiduciary obligation resting on Patrick Partners, there is no evidence that the contracts of loan were avoided. In equity, Patrick Partners' title to the money lent was imperfect from the beginning by reason of their failure to discharge their duty as a fiduciary (cf. *Allcard v. Skinner* (1887) 36 ChD 145, per Lindley L.J. at p 184) and, had the contract of loan been avoided, Mrs Daly's rights as against Patrick Partners might have been determined as though the firm had from the beginning held the money lent on a constructive trust for Dr Daly and then for Mrs Daly.'

Also see:

Latec Investments Ltd v Hotel Terrigal Pty Ltd. (In Liq) (1965) 113 CLR 265 **[[607]** below].

[515] *Lonrho plc v Fayed (No 2)* [1992] 1 WLR 1, 11–12 *per* Millett J:
[The facts are immaterial.]

'A contract obtained by fraudulent misrepresentation is voidable, not void, even in equity. The representee may elect to avoid it, but until he does so the representor is not a constructive trustee of the property transferred pursuant to the contract, and no fiduciary relationship exists between him and the representee: see *Daly v. Sydney Stock Exchange Ltd.* (1986) 160 C.L.R. 371, 387–390, per Brennan J [see **[514]** above]. It may well be that if the representee elects to avoid the contract and set aside a transfer of property made pursuant to it the beneficial interest in the property will be treated as having remained vested in him throughout, at least to the extent necessary to support any tracing claim. But the representee's election cannot retrospectively subject the representor to fiduciary obligations of the kind alleged. It is a mistake to suppose that in every situation in which a constructive trust arises the legal owner is necessarily subject to all the fiduciary obligations and disabilities of an express trustee. Even after the representee has elected to avoid the contract and reclaim the property, the obligations of the representor would in my judgment be analogous to those of a vendor of property contracted to be sold, and would not extend beyond the property actually obtained by the contract and liable to be returned.'

Also see:

El Ajou v Dollar Land Holdings plc [1993] 3 All ER 717, 734 *per* Millett J (rev'd [1994] 2 All ER 685 (CA), but not on this point).

5.5.3 Void contracts

The current position, following the House of Lords' decision in *Westdeutsche Landesbank Girozentrale v Islington London Borough Council* (see **[518]** below), is that a transferee who receives property pursuant to a void contract receives full legal and beneficial title to the property. The transferor does not retain ownership of the property, even in equity.[10] The first two cases extracted below indicate an earlier and contrary approach to this problem.

[516] *Sinclair v Brougham* [1914] AC 398 (HL), 441–2, 444 *per* Lord Parker:
[The Birkbeck Permanent Benefit Building Society operated an *ultra vires* banking business. When the society was wound up, and after the creditors were paid out under a court approved arrangement, there remained insufficient funds to pay all the members of the society and *ultra vires* depositors in full. Neville J held that the *ultra vires* depositors should receive nothing at all until all the members had been paid in full. The majority of the Court of Appeal agreed ([1912] 2 Ch 183), with Fletcher Moulton LJ (dissenting) holding that the depositors should come first. The House of Lords held that the two groups, the members and the *ultra vires* depositors, should share *pari passu*. The judgments of the various Lords are quite different. Only the judgment of Lord Parker is extracted here, since it is this judgment which has subsequently been held best to represent the legal basis of the decision. The House of Lords concluded that the depositors could not succeed in a personal claim against the society to recover their deposits as money had and received, because to do so would be tantamount to the law enforcing a notional contract of

[10] Although the transferor will have a personal claim in unjust enrichment against the transferee. But query whether the result is quite different if the transfer of the property is by virtue of the contract itself, and not by some independent act of transfer (such as delivery or registration).

the same form as the deposit and repayment contract rendered *ultra vires* by statute. This 'implied contract' analysis of restitutionary claims is no longer accepted, and these parts of the judgments from the House of Lords are not extracted. The House of Lords did, however, conclude that the depositors were entitled to assert a proprietary claim to the money they had deposited with the society, and to its traceable proceeds,[11] on the basis that title to money paid over under an *ultra vires* contract did not, at least in equity, pass to the transferee. As already noted, this conclusion, too, has now been overruled by the House of Lords in *Westdeutsche* (see **[518]** below). Nevertheless, a comparison of the analyses adopted in the two cases, and in Hobhouse J's decision at trial in the *Westdeutsche* case (see **[517]** below) is instructive.]

'. . . .it appears to be also well settled that the lender in an ultra vires loan transaction has a right to what is known as a tracing order. A company or other statutory association cannot by itself or through an agent be party to an *ultra vires* act. If its directors or agents affecting to act on its behalf borrow money which it has no power to borrow, the money borrowed is in their hands the property of the lender.

At law, therefore, the lender can recover the money, so long as he can identify it, and even if it has been employed in purchasing property, there may be cases in which, by ratifying the action of those who have so employed it, he may recover the property purchased. Equity, however, treated the matter from a different standpoint. It considered that the relationship between the directors or agents and the lender was a fiduciary relationship, and that the money in their hands was for all practical purposes trust money. Starting from a personal equity, based on the consideration that it would be unconscionable for any one who could not plead purchase for value without notice to retain an advantage derived from the misapplication of trust money, it ended, as was so often the case, in creating what were in effect rights of property, though not recognized as such by the common law.

. . . .

The equity lay in this, that it would be unconscionable for the society to retain the amount by which its assets had been increased by, and in fact still represented, the borrowed money. It would be inequitable for the society to take advantage of the misapplication by its agents of money belonging to others and held by them in a fiduciary capacity.'

[517] ***Westdeutsche Landesbank Girozentrale v Islington London Borough Council*** **[1994] 4 All ER 890, 929–30** ***per*** **Hobhouse J:**

[The facts are noted above at **[504]**.]

'In my judgment, the correct analysis is that any payments made under a contract which is void ab initio, in the way that an ultra vires contract is void, are not contractual payments at all. They are payments in which the legal property in the money passes to the recipient, but in equity the property in the money remains with the payer. The recipient holds the money as a fiduciary for the payer and is bound to recognise his equity and repay the money to him. This relationship and the consequent obligation have been recognised both by courts applying the common law and by Chancery courts. The principle is the same in both cases: it is unconscionable that the recipient should retain the money. Neither mistake nor the contractual principle of total failure of consideration are the basis for the right of recovery.

[11] See Chapter 6.

Where payments both ways have been made the correct view is to treat the later payment as, pro tanto, a repayment of the earlier sum paid by the other party. The character of the remedy, both in law and equity, is restitution, that is to say putting the parties back into the position in which they were before. Accordingly, the remedy is only available to a party on the basis that he gives credit for any benefit which he has received. He must give credit for any payments which have been made by the opposite party to him and, where the court thinks appropriate, pay a quantum meruit or quantum valebat. The same conclusion follows from the application of the principle of unjust enrichment: in so far as the recipient has made cross-payments to the payer, the recipient has ceased to be enriched.

This formulation is explicitly the basis of the decisions in the annuity cases and the decision of the Divisional Court in *Brougham v Dwyer* (1913) 108 LT 504. It is implicit in the decision in *Brailsford*'s case [1962] 1 All ER 502, [1962] 1 WLR 1288. It is also fully consistent with the many judicial statements of the general principle which underlies the law of restitution and unjust enrichment which are typified by the statement, already quoted, of Lord Wright in the *Fibrosa* case [1942] 2 All ER 122 at 135, [1943] AC 32 at 61.

The application of the principle is subject to the requirement that the courts should not grant a remedy which amounts to the direct or indirect enforcement of a contract which the law requires to be treated as ineffective. Since the obligation which law and equity require the conscience of the receiver to recognise is in effect an obligation to repay money, it is hard to think of any situation where this qualification will be relevant save where the void contract was one which purported to create a debtor and creditor relationship, as was the case in *Sinclair v Brougham*. Since *Sinclair v Brougham* was decided on the basis of applying this qualification, it is a decision which tends to confirm the formulation. The existence of the qualification and its relevance in *Sinclair v Brougham* was repeated by Lord Sumner in *R Leslie Ltd v Sheill* [1914] 3 KB 607 at 613, [1914–15] All ER Rep 511 at 515.

The right to recover payments is also subject to any available defences. Generally speaking, those are any defences which affect the equity. This is again either explicit or implicit in the annuity cases and, since the *Lipkin Gorman* case, includes, as an application of that approach, the defence of change of position.

Since the right of recovery, although based on equitable principles, has been recognised by the common law courts and has been held to be capable of founding an action for money had and received, it can form a proper basis for a legally recognised right of recovery in personam in the present cases. If, contrary to my view, there were some distinction to be drawn between the right to restitution as recognised in law and in equity, any such distinction should not now affect the outcome of a case where no question of insolvency arises; the principles of both law and equity should be applied in a unified fashion so as to provide the appropriate remedy.

This decision is sufficient to establish the prima facie right of the plaintiffs to recover in both of the actions which are before me. It also follows from the fact that I consider that the correct analysis is absence of consideration and not failure of consideration that it is not open to Kleinwort Benson to assert an absolute right of recovery on the third and fourth Sandwell swaps on the basis of a right to recover money paid for a contractual consideration that has wholly failed to which there are no defences; it will be open to Sandwell to seek to raise a defence of change of position. Likewise, it follows that it is irrelevant to the existence of a cause of action in connection with the payments made under the first Sandwell swap that the supposed contract was in fact fully performed and there was no failure of consideration at all in the contractual sense.'

[518] *Westdeutsche Landesbank Girozentrale v Islington London Borough Council* [1996] AC 669 (HL), 682–90 *per* Lord Goff, and 702–9 *per* Lord Browne-Wilkinson: [The facts are noted above at **[504]**.]

Lord Goff:
'*The three problems*

There are three reasons why the present case has become so complicated. The first is that, in our law of restitution, there has developed an understanding that money can only be recovered on the ground of failure of consideration if that failure is total. The second is that because, in particular, of the well known but controversial decision of this House in *Sinclair v. Brougham* [**[516]** above], it has come to be understood that a trust may be imposed in cases such as the present where the incapacity of one of the parties has the effect that the transaction is void. The third is that our law of interest has developed in a fragmentary and unsatisfactory manner. . . .

I propose at the outset to devote a little attention to each of these matters.

(1) Total failure of consideration

. . . . The most serious problem which has remained in this connection is the theoretical question whether recovery can here be said to rest upon the ground of failure of consideration. Hobhouse J. thought not. He considered that the true ground in these cases, where the contract is void, is to be found in the absence, rather than the failure, of consideration; and in this he was followed by the Court of Appeal. This had the effect that the courts below were not troubled by the question whether there had been a total failure of consideration.

. . . .

. . . concern has been expressed by a number of restitution lawyers that the approach of Hobhouse J. is contrary to principle and could, if accepted, lead to undesirable consequences: see Professor Birks, "No Consideration: Restitution after Void Contracts" (1993) 23 W.A.L.R. 195; Mr. W. J. Swadling, "Restitution for No Consideration" [1994] R.L.R. 73 and Professor Burrows, "Swaps and the Friction between Common Law and Equity" [1995] R.L.R. 15. However since there is before your Lordships no appeal from the decision that the bank was entitled to recover the balance of the payments so made in a personal claim in restitution, the precise identification of the ground of recovery was not explored in argument before the Appellate Committee. It would therefore be inappropriate to express any concluded view upon it. Even so, I think it right to record that there appears to me to be considerable force in the criticisms which have been expressed. . . .

(2) A proprietary claim in restitution

I have already stated that restitution in these cases can be achieved by means of a personal claim in restitution. The question has however arisen whether the bank should also have the benefit of an equitable proprietary claim in the form of a resulting trust. The immediate reaction must be—why should it? Take the present case. The parties have entered into a commercial transaction. The transaction has, for technical reasons, been held to be void from the beginning. Each party is entitled to recover its money, with the result that the balance must be repaid. But why should the plaintiff bank be given the additional benefits which flow from a proprietary claim, for example the benefit of achieving priority in the event of the defendant's insolvency? After all, it has entered into a commercial transaction, and so taken the risk of the defendant's insolvency, just like the defendant's other creditors who have contracted with it, not to mention other creditors to whom the defendant may be liable to pay damages in tort.

I feel bound to say that I would not at first sight have thought that an equitable proprietary claim in the form of a trust should be made available to the bank in the present case, but for two things. The first is the decision of this House in *Sinclair v. Brougham* [1914] A.C. 398, which appears to provide authority that a resulting trust may indeed arise in a case such as the present. The second is that on the authorities there is an equitable jurisdiction to award the plaintiff compound interest in cases where the defendant is a trustee. . . .

Sinclair v. Brougham

The decision of this House in *Sinclair v. Brougham* . . . . has long been regarded as a controversial decision, and has been the subject of much consideration by scholars, especially those working in the field of restitution.

. . .

It is, I think, apparent from the reasoning of the members of the Appellate Committee that they regarded themselves, not as laying down some broad general principle, but as solving a particular practical problem. In this connection it is, in my opinion, significant that there was a considerable variation in the way in which they approached the problem. Viscount Haldane L.C., with whom Lord Atkinson agreed, did so, at p. 421, on the basis that there arose in the circumstances "a resulting trust, not of an active character." Lord Dunedin based his decision upon a broad equity of restitution, drawn from Roman and French law. He asked himself the question, at p. 435: "Is English equity to retire defeated from the task which other systems of equity have conquered?"—a question which he answered in the negative. Lord Parker of Waddington, at pp. 441–442, attempted to reconcile his decision with the established principles of equity by holding that the depositors' money had been received by the directors of the society as fiduciaries, with the effect that the depositors could thereafter follow their money in equity into the assets of the society. Lord Sumner, at p. 458, considered that the case should be decided on equitable principles on which there was no direct authority. He regarded the question as one of administration, in which "the most just distribution of the whole must be directed, so only that no recognised rule of law or equity be disregarded." Setting on one side the opinion of Lord Parker, whose approach I find very difficult to reconcile with the facts of the case, I do not discern in the speeches of the members of the Appellate Committee any intention to impose a trust carrying with it the personal duties of a trustee.

. . . .

The availability of an equitable proprietary claim in the present case

Having put *Sinclair v. Brougham* on one side as providing no authority that a resulting trust should be imposed in the facts of the present case, I turn to the question whether, as a matter of principle, such a trust should be imposed, the bank's submission being that such a trust arose at the time when the sum of £2.5m. was received by the council from the bank.

As my noble and learned friend, Lord Browne-Wilkinson, observes, it is plain that the present case falls within neither of the situations which are traditionally regarded as giving rise to a resulting trust, viz. (1) voluntary payments by A to B, or for the purchase of property in the name of B or in his and A's joint names, where there is no presumption of advancement or evidence of intention to make an out-and-out gift; or (2) property transferred to B on an express trust which does not exhaust the whole beneficial interest. The question therefore arises whether resulting trusts should be extended beyond such cases to apply in the present case, which I shall treat as a case where money has been paid for a consideration which fails.

In a most interesting and challenging paper, "Restitution and Resulting Trusts," published in *Equity: Contemporary Legal Developments* (1992) (ed. Goldstein), p. 335, Professor Birks has argued for a wider role for the resulting trust in the field of restitution, and specifically for its availability in cases of mistake and failure of consideration. His thesis is avowedly experimental, written to test the temperature of the water. I feel bound to respond that the temperature of the water must be regarded as decidedly cold: see, e.g., Professor Burrows, "Swaps and the Friction between Common Law and Equity" [1995] R.L.R. 15, and Mr. W. J. Swadling, "A new role for resulting trusts?" (1996) 16 Legal Studies 133.

In the first place, as Lord Browne-Wilkinson points out, to impose a resulting trust in such cases is inconsistent with the traditional principles of trust law. For on receipt of the money by the payee it is to be presumed that (as in the present case) the identity of the money is immediately lost by mixing with other assets of the payee, and at that time the payee has no knowledge of the facts giving rise to the failure of consideration. By the time that those facts come to light, and the conscience of the payee may thereby be affected, there will therefore be no identifiable fund to which a trust can attach. But there are other difficulties. First, there is no general rule that the property in money paid under a void contract does not pass to the payee; and it is difficult to escape the conclusion that, as a general rule, the beneficial interest in the money likewise passes to the payee. This must certainly be the case where the consideration for the payment fails after the payment is made, as in cases of frustration or breach of contract; and there appears to be no good reason why the same should not apply in cases where, as in the present case, the contract under which the payment is made is void ab initio and the consideration for the payment therefore fails at the time of payment. It is true that the doctrine of mistake might be invoked where the mistake is fundamental in the orthodox sense of that word. But that is not the position in the present case; moreover the mistake in the present case must be classified as a mistake of law which, as the law at present stands, creates its own special problems. No doubt that much criticised doctrine will fall to be reconsidered when an appropriate case occurs; but I cannot think that the present is such a case, since not only has the point not been argued but (as will appear) it is my opinion that there is [in] any event jurisdiction to award compound interest in the present case. For all of these reasons I conclude, in agreement with my noble and learned friend, that there is no basis for holding that a resulting trust arises in cases where money has been paid under a contract which is ultra vires and therefore void ab initio. This conclusion has the effect that all the practical problems which would flow from the imposition of a resulting trust in a case such as the present, in particular the imposition upon the recipient of the normal duties of trustee, do not arise. The dramatic consequences which would occur are detailed by Professor Burrows in his article on "Swaps and the Friction between Common Law and Equity" [1995] R.L.R. 15, 27: the duty to account for profits accruing from the trust property; the inability of the payee to rely upon the defence of change of position; the absence of any limitation period; and so on. Professor Burrows even goes so far as to conclude that the action for money had and received would be rendered otiose in such cases, and indeed in all cases where the payer seeks restitution of mistaken payments. However, if no resulting trust arises, it also follows that the payer in a case such as the present cannot achieve priority over the payee's general creditors in the event of his insolvency—a conclusion which appears to me to be just.

For all these reasons I conclude that there is no basis for imposing a resulting trust in the present case, and I therefore reject the bank's submission that it was here entitled to proceed by way of an equitable proprietary claim. I need only add that, in reaching that conclusion, I do not find it necessary to review the decision of Goulding J. in *Chase Manhattan Bank N.A. v. Israel-British Bank (London) Ltd.* [1981] Ch. 105 [**[511]** above].'

Lord Browne-Wilkinson:
'*Was there a trust? The argument for the bank in outline*

The bank submitted that, since the contract was void, title did not pass at the date of payment either at law or in equity. The legal title of the bank was extinguished as soon as the money was paid into the mixed account, whereupon the legal title became vested in the local authority. But, it was argued, this did not affect the equitable interest, which remained vested in the bank ("the retention of title point"). It was submitted that whenever the legal interest in property is vested in one person and the equitable interest in another, the owner of the legal interest holds it on trust for the owner of the equitable title: "the separation of the legal from the equitable interest necessarily imports a trust." For this latter proposition ("the separation of title point") the bank, of course, relies on *Sinclair v. Brougham* [1914] A.C. 398 [**[516]** above] and *Chase Manhattan Bank N.A. v. Israel-British Bank (London) Ltd.* [1981] Ch. 105 [**[511]** above].

The generality of these submissions was narrowed by submitting that the trust which arose in this case was a resulting trust "not of an active character:" see per Viscount Haldane L.C. in *Sinclair v. Brougham* [1914] A.C. 398, 421. This submission was reinforced, after completion of the oral argument, by sending to your Lordships Professor Peter Birks's paper "Restitution and Resulting Trusts:" see *Equity: Contemporary Legal Developments*, p. 335. Unfortunately your Lordships have not had the advantage of any submissions from the local authority on this paper, but an article by William Swadling "A new role for resulting trusts?" 16 *Legal Studies* 133 puts forward counter-arguments which I have found persuasive.

It is to be noted that the bank did not found any argument on the basis that the local authority was liable to repay either as a constructive trustee or under the in personam liability of the wrongful recipient of the estate of a deceased person established by *In re Diplock; Diplock v. Wintle* [1948] Ch. 465. I therefore do not further consider those points.

The breadth of the submission

Although the actual question in issue on the appeal is a narrow one, on the arguments presented it is necessary to consider fundamental principles of trust law. Does the recipient of money under a contract subsequently found to be void for mistake or as being ultra vires hold the moneys received on trust even where he had no knowledge at any relevant time that the contract was void? If he does hold on trust, such trust must arise at the date of receipt or, at the latest, at the date the legal title of the payer is extinguished by mixing moneys in a bank account: in the present case it does not matter at which of those dates the legal title was extinguished. If there is a trust two consequences follow: (a) the recipient will be personally liable, regardless of fault, for any subsequent payment away of the moneys to third parties even though, at the date of such payment, the "trustee" was still ignorant of the existence of any trust: see Burrows, "Swaps and the Friction between Common Law and Equity" [1995] R.L.R. 15; (b) as from the date of the establishment of the trust (i.e. receipt or mixing of the moneys by the "trustee") the original payer will have an equitable proprietary interest in the moneys so long as they are traceable into whomsoever's hands they come other than a purchaser for value of the legal interest without notice. Therefore, although in the present case the only question directly in issue is the personal liability of the local authority as a trustee, it is not possible to hold the local authority liable without imposing a trust which, in other cases, will create property rights affecting third parties because moneys received under a void contract are "trust property."

The practical consequences of the bank's argument

Before considering the legal merits of the submission, it is important to appreciate the practical consequences which ensue if the bank's arguments are correct. Those who suggest that a resulting trust should arise in these circumstances accept that the creation of an equitable proprietary interest under the trust can have unfortunate, and adverse, effects if the original recipient of the moneys becomes insolvent: the moneys, if traceable in the hands of the recipient, are trust moneys and not available for the creditors of the recipient. However, the creation of an equitable proprietary interest in moneys received under a void contract is capable of having adverse effects quite apart from insolvency. The proprietary interest under the unknown trust will, quite apart from insolvency, be enforceable against any recipient of the property other than the purchaser for value of a legal interest without notice.

Take the following example. T (the transferor) has entered into a commercial contract with R1 (the first recipient). Both parties believe the contract to be valid but it is in fact void. Pursuant to that contract: (i) T pays £1m. to R1 who pays it into a mixed bank account; (ii) T transfers 100 shares in X company to R1, who is registered as a shareholder. Thereafter R1 deals with the money and shares as follows: (iii) R1 pays £50,000 out of the mixed account to R2 otherwise than for value; R2 then becomes insolvent, having trade creditors who have paid for goods not delivered at the time of the insolvency; (iv) R1 charges the shares in X company to R3 by way of equitable security for a loan from R3.

If the bank's arguments are correct, R1 holds the £1m. on trust for T once the money has become mixed in R1's bank account. Similarly R1 becomes the legal owner of the shares in X company as from the date of his registration as a shareholder but holds such shares on a resulting trust for T. T therefore has an equitable proprietary interest in the moneys in the mixed account and in the shares.

T's equitable interest will enjoy absolute priority as against the creditors in the insolvency of R2 (who was not a purchaser for value) provided that the £50,000 can be traced in the assets of R2 at the date of its insolvency. Moreover, if the separation of title argument is correct, since the equitable interest is in T and the legal interest is vested in R2, R2 also holds as trustee for T. In tracing the £50,000 in the bank account of R2, R2 as trustee will be treated as having drawn out "his own" moneys first, thereby benefiting T at the expense of the secured and unsecured creditors of R2. Therefore in practice one may well reach the position where the moneys in the bank account of R2 in reality reflect the price paid by creditors for goods not delivered by R2: yet, under the tracing rules, those moneys are to be treated as belonging in equity to T.

So far as the shares in the X company are concerned, T can trace his equitable interest into the shares and will take in priority to R3, whose equitable charge to secure his loan even though granted for value will pro tanto be defeated.

All this will have occurred when no one was aware, or could have been aware, of the supposed trust because no one knew that the contract was void.

I can see no moral or legal justification for giving such priority to the right of T to obtain restitution over third parties who have themselves not been enriched, in any real sense, at T's expense and indeed have had no dealings with T. T paid over his money and transferred the shares under a supposed valid contract. If the contract had been valid, he would have had purely personal rights against R1. Why should he be better off because the contract is void?

My Lords, wise judges have often warned against the wholesale importation into commercial law of equitable principles inconsistent with the certainty and speed which are essential requirements for the orderly conduct of business affairs: see *Barnes v. Addy* (1874) L.R. 9 Ch.App. 244, 251 and 255; *Scandinavian Trading Tanker Co. A.B. v. Flota Petrolera Ecuatoriana* [1983] 2 A.C. 694, 703–704. If the bank's arguments are correct, a businessman who has entered into transactions relating to or dependent upon property rights could find that assets which apparently belong to one person in fact belong to another; that there are "off balance sheet" liabilities of which he cannot be aware; that these property rights and liabilities arise from circumstances unknown not only to himself but also to anyone else who has been involved in the transactions. A new area of unmanageable risk will be introduced into commercial dealings. If the due application of equitable principles forced a conclusion leading to these results, your Lordships would be presented with a formidable task in reconciling legal principle with commercial common sense. But in my judgment no such conflict occurs. The resulting trust for which the bank contends is inconsistent not only with the law as it stands but with any principled development of it.

The relevant principles of trust law

(i) Equity operates on the conscience of the owner of the legal interest. In the case of a trust, the conscience of the legal owner requires him to carry out the purposes for which the property was vested in him (express or implied trust) or which the law imposes on him by reason of his unconscionable conduct (constructive trust).

(ii) Since the equitable jurisdiction to enforce trusts depends upon the conscience of the holder of the legal interest being affected, he cannot be a trustee of the property if and so long as he is ignorant of the facts alleged to affect his conscience, i.e. until he is aware that he is intended to hold the property for the benefit of others in the case of an express or implied trust, or, in the case of a constructive trust, of the factors which are alleged to affect his conscience.

(iii) In order to establish a trust there must be identifiable trust property. The only apparent exception to this rule is a constructive trust imposed on a person who dishonestly assists in a breach of trust who may come under fiduciary duties even if he does not receive identifiable trust property.

(iv) Once a trust is established, as from the date of its establishment the beneficiary has, in equity, a proprietary interest in the trust property, which proprietary interest will be enforceable in equity against any subsequent holder of the property (whether the original property or substituted property into which it can be traced) other than a purchaser for value of the legal interest without notice.

These propositions are fundamental to the law of trusts and I would have thought uncontroversial. However, proposition (ii) may call for some expansion. There are cases where property has been put into the name of X without X's knowledge but in circumstances where no gift to X was intended. It has been held that such property is recoverable under a resulting trust: *Birch v. Blagrave* (1755) 1 Amb. 264; *Childers v. Childers* (1857) 1 De G. & J. 482; *In re Vinogradoff; Allen v. Jackson* [1935] W.N. 68; *In re Muller; Cassin v. Mutual Cash Order Co. Ltd.* [1953] N.Z.L.R. 879. These cases are explicable on the ground that, by the time action was brought, X or his successors in title have become aware of the facts which gave rise to a resulting trust; his conscience was affected as from the time of such discovery and thereafter he held on a resulting trust under which the property was recovered from him. There is, so far as I am aware, no authority which decides that X was a trustee, and therefore accountable for his deeds, at any time before he was aware of the circumstances which gave rise to a resulting trust.

Those basic principles are inconsistent with the case being advanced by the bank. The latest time at which there was any possibility of identifying the "trust property" was the date on which the moneys in the mixed bank account of the local authority ceased to be traceable when the local authority's account went into overdraft in June 1987. At that date, the local authority had no knowledge of the invalidity of the contract but regarded the moneys as its own to spend as it thought fit. There was therefore never a time at which both (a) there was defined trust property and (b) the conscience of the local authority in relation to such defined trust property was affected. The basic requirements of a trust were never satisfied.

I turn then to consider the bank's arguments in detail. They were based primarily on principle rather than on authority. I will deal first with the bank's argument from principle and then turn to the main authorities relied upon by the bank, *Sinclair v. Brougham* [1914] A.C. 398 and *Chase Manhattan Bank N.A. v. Israel-British Bank (London) Ltd.* [1981] Ch. 105.

The retention of title point

It is said that, since the bank only intended to part with its beneficial ownership of the moneys in performance of a valid contract, neither the legal nor the equitable title passed to the local authority at the date of payment. The legal title vested in the local authority by operation of law when the moneys became mixed in the bank account but, it is said, the bank "retained" its equitable title.

I think this argument is fallacious. A person solely entitled to the full beneficial ownership of money or property, both at law and in equity, does not enjoy an equitable interest in that property. The legal title carries with it all rights. Unless and until there is a separation of the legal and equitable estates, there is no separate equitable title. Therefore to talk about the bank "retaining" its equitable interest is meaningless. The only question is whether the circumstances under which the money was paid were such as, in equity, to impose a trust on the local authority. If so, an equitable interest arose for the first time under that trust.

This proposition is supported by *In re Cook; Beck v. Grant* [1948] Ch. 212; *Vandervell v. Inland Revenue Commissioners* [1967] 2 A.C. 291, 311G, per Lord Upjohn, and 317F, per Lord Donovan; *Commissioner of Stamp Duties (Queensland) v. Livingston* [1965] A.C. 694, 712B-E; Underhill and Hayton, *Law of Trusts and Trustees*, 15th ed. (1995), p. 866.

The separation of title point

The bank's submission, at its widest, is that if the legal title is in A but the equitable interest in B, A holds as trustee for B.

Again I think this argument is fallacious. There are many cases where B enjoys rights which, in equity, are enforceable against the legal owner, A, without A being a trustee, e.g. an equitable right to redeem a mortgage, equitable easements, restrictive covenants, the right to rectification, an insurer's right by subrogation to receive damages subsequently recovered by the assured: *Lord Napier and Ettrick v. Hunter* [1993] A.C. 713 [**[524]** below]. Even in cases where the whole beneficial interest is vested in B and the bare legal interest is in A, A is not necessarily a trustee, e.g. where title to land is acquired by estoppel as against the legal owner; a mortgagee who has fully discharged his indebtedness enforces his right to recover the mortgaged property in a redemption action, not an action for breach of trust.

The bank contended that where, under a pre-existing trust, B is entitled to an equitable interest in trust property, if the trust property comes into the hands of a third party, X (not being a purchaser for value of the legal interest without notice), B is entitled to enforce his equitable interest against the property in the hands of X because X is a trustee for B. In my view the third party, X, is not necessarily a trustee for B: B's equitable right is enforceable against the property in just the same way as any other specifically enforceable equitable right can be enforced against a third party. Even if the third party, X, is not aware that what he has received is trust property B is entitled to assert his title in that property. If X has the necessary degree of knowledge, X may himself become a constructive trustee for B on the basis of knowing receipt. But unless he has the requisite degree of knowledge he is not personally liable to account as trustee: *In re Diplock; Diplock v. Wintle* [1948] Ch. 465, 478; *In re Montagu's Settlement Trusts* [1987] Ch. 264. Therefore, innocent receipt of property by X subject to an existing equitable interest does not by itself make X a trustee despite the severance of the legal and equitable titles. Underhill and Hayton, *Law of Trusts and Trustees*, pp. 369–370, whilst accepting that X is under no personal liability to account unless and until he becomes aware of B's rights, does describe X as being a constructive trustee. This may only be a question of semantics: on either footing, in the present case the local authority could not have become accountable for profits until it knew that the contract was void.

Resulting trust

This is not a case where the bank had any equitable interest which pre-dated receipt by the local authority of the upfront payment. Therefore, in order to show that the local authority became a trustee, the bank must demonstrate circumstances which raised a trust for the first time either at the date on which the local authority received the money or at the date on which payment into the mixed account was made. Counsel for the bank specifically disavowed any claim based on a constructive trust. This was plainly right because the local authority had no relevant knowledge sufficient to raise a constructive trust at any time before the moneys, upon the bank account going into overdraft, became untraceable. Once there ceased to be an identifiable trust fund, the local authority could not become a trustee: *In re Goldcorp Exchange Ltd.* [1995] 1 A.C. 74. Therefore, as the argument for the bank recognised, the only possible trust which could be established was a resulting trust arising from the circumstances in which the local authority received the upfront payment. . . .'

[Lord Browne-Wilkinson then proceeded with the analysis of resulting trusts already extracted at **[504]** above.]

5.5.4 One final case

[519] ***Nesté Oy v Lloyds Bank Plc*** **[1983] 2 Lloyd's Rep 658, 665–6 *per* Bingham J:** [Shipowners transferred several instalments of funds to their agent to enable the agent to discharge liabilities incurred in respect of their vessels. When the agent went into receivership, the shipowners claimed that what remained of these funds was held on trust for them. Bingham J held that this was true only in the case of the final instalment payment. This payment had been received after the agent resolved to cease trading. It was therefore impossible for the agent to perform its side of the bargain. This situation was held to be materially different from an effective promise to perform which, in the end, was not carried out.]

> 'My conclusion that there was no express trust in respect of the first five payments must, if correct, apply to the last payment also. But Counsel for the plaintiffs contended that PSL were constructive trustees of this last payment, whether or not they were constructive trustees of the earlier payments. He founded this distinction not on a mistake of fact by the plaintiffs (which he was refused leave to amend to allege) but on the fact that this payment was credited to PSL at a time when Peckston Group Ltd. had already resolved that it and its group companies should cease trading immediately (one of the directors supporting that resolution being a director of PSL), at a time when PSL had not paid for the services for which the funds had been remitted and at a time when, in all the circumstances, there was no chance that PSL could pay for the services in question. This, submitted Counsel, was a case falling within the statement of Mr. Justice Cardozo in *Beatty v. Guggenheim Exploration Co.*, 225 N.Y. 380 (1919) at p. 386, and quoted m Snell's Principles of Equity (28th cd.) at p. 192:
>
> > . . . A constructive trust is the formula through which the conscience of equity finds expression. When property has been acquired in such circumstances that the holder of the legal title may not in good conscience retain the beneficial interest, equity converts him into a trustee.
>
> Counsel also relied on the general principles contained in a passage from Story's Commentaries on Equity Jurisprudence, 2nd ed. (1839) vol. 2, par. 1255, accepted as correctly stating the law of England by Mr. Justice Goulding in *Chase Manhattan Bank N.A. v. Israel-British Rank (London) Ltd.*, [1981] Ch. 105 [**[511]** above], at pp. 117C and 118E:
>
> > 1255. One of the most common cases in which a Court of Equity acts upon the ground of implied trusts in invitum, is where a party has received money which he cannot conscientiously withhold from another party. It has been well remarked, that the receiving of money which consistently with conscience cannot be retained is, in Equity, sufficient to raise a trust in favour of the party for whom or on whose account it was received. This is the governing principle in all such cases. And therefore, whenever any controversy arises, the true question is, not whether money has been received by a party of which he could not have compelled the payment, but whether he can now, with a safe conscience, ex aequo et bono, retain it. Illustrations of this doctrine are familiar in cases of money paid by accident, or mistake, or fraud. And the difference between the payment of money under a mistake of fact, and a payment under a mistake of law, in its operation upon the conscience of the party, presents the equitable qualifications of the doctrine in a striking manner.
>
> Counsel for the bank contended that no relevant distinction could he drawn between the first five payments and the last. While naturally diffident at entering seas so little

chart, and regarded with great caution by mariners much more expert than I, it seems to me that there is a relevant distinction. Given the situation of PSL when the last payment was received, any reasonable and honest directors of that company (or the actual directors had they known of it) would, I feel sure, have arranged for the repayment of that sum to the plaintiffs without hesitation or delay. It would have seemed little short of sharp practice for PSL to take any benefit from the payment, and it would have seemed contrary to any ordinary notion of fairness that the general body of creditors should profit from the accident of a payment made at a time when there was bound to be a total failure of consideration. Of course it is true that insolvency always causes loss and perfect fairness is unattainable. The bank, and other creditors, have their legitimate claims. It nonetheless seems to me that at the time of its receipt PSL could not in good conscience retain this payment and that accordingly a constructive trust is to be inferred.'

Question:

The trust in this case was described as a constructive trust. Is it constructive or resulting? Why?

5.5.5 Commentary

[520] S Worthington, 'Backdoor Security Devices' [1999] *Insolvency Lawyer* 153, 157–9:

[The footnotes in the original are omitted.]

'*Chase Manhattan Bank NA v Israel-British Bank (London) Ltd* is the familiar and simple example often used to illustrate the issues at stake. The facts are well known: money which had been mistakenly paid by one bank to another was held to belong in equity to the paying bank, notwithstanding that legal title to the money had passed to the payee. However, that finding would be of no practical benefit to the paying bank if it could not identify its funds (or what remains of them) in the hands of the recipient. So there are two issues: the legitimate assertion of a proprietary claim; and the identification of the assets to which that claim relates. Here only the first issue will be considered. The second raises few theoretical problems, but significant practical ones.

The *Chase Manhattan* case involved a non-contractual mistaken payment. In an insolvency context the transaction at issue will usually be a contract. Then the preferred outcome is generally for each party to obtain all that was initially bargained for. Parties only resort to reclaiming equitable ownership of property originally belonging to them if their commercial dealings fail and they are left with no better security. The reclamation operates by means of a resulting trust imposed by operation of law.

In a typical scenario, the outsider transfers legal title to an asset to the company, as agreed, and then discovers some vitiating element which ensures that the contract will never be completed: the outsider will never get what it bargained for. Then it is important to know whether the outsider can recover the original property in equity, or whether it will be restricted to a personal remedy in contract or restitution. This area of equitable intervention is currently in a state of flux. Equity lawyers often find themselves in policy debates with common law commercial and restitution lawyers who push the view that equitable intervention means unacceptable commercial uncertainty and, in the insolvency context, unacceptable circumvention of the *pari passu* principle. Both groups of lawyers want rigorous and consistent intervention by the courts; however they differ in their views on whether that intervention should have proprietary consequences.

The result is that this area of the law is a mess. There is no consistent theoretical framework to ensure that similar situations are treated in similar ways. It takes only a few examples to illustrate the problems.

First consider voidable transactions. If the transaction between the outsider and the company is voidable, then it is widely accepted that if *restitutio in integrum* can be effected and if the transaction is avoided, then the outsider, on making the election to avoid, immediately has revested in it the equitable title to the asset which was transferred earlier to the company. In fact, if the rescission is effective at law, there are cases suggesting that *legal* title to the asset revests in the original owner (unless, of course, this is simply impossible because, for example, there are registration impediments to automatic revesting). Presumably this result follows because an effective election to avoid the contract renders the contract void *ab initio*: the parties are treated as if there never was a contract between them. This means that both sides have made gratuitous transfers of property in circumstances where a gift is clearly not intended. The resulting trust is equity's response to this, as the cases on presumed resulting trusts confirm. The rationalisation may be disputed, but the law's response in these circumstances is clear.

Next consider cases where the contract between the outsider and the company is not voidable but void. The recent swaps litigation suggests that then the analysis is quite different. In *Westdeutsche Landesbank Girozentrale v Islington London Borough Council*, the House of Lords held that the paying bank did not have any proprietary interest in funds transferred to the local authority pursuant to a void swaps contract. This case has been the subject of considerable analysis and criticism. Nevertheless, even at a superficial level, it is surprising that a contract avoided *ab initio* at the election of one of the parties (ie a voidable contract) can give rise to a proprietary interest in that party, notwithstanding that the original transfer was *intended* to be (and *was*) an effective transfer of the legal and beneficial title to the transferee. Where, however, the *law* (generally on policy grounds) determines that a contract is void *ab initio*, with no discretion to elect given to either party, it is considered fatal to the assertion of a proprietary interest that the transferor *intended* to transfer legal and beneficial title to the transferee. According to the House of Lords it is, it seems, irrelevant that the latter intention was premised (and conditional?) on some corresponding obligation in the transferee. In short, it is irrelevant that most certainly the transfer was not intended as a gift. This is unlikely to be the last word on this issue.

Then, in a third category, there are contracts which are not terminated *ab initio*, but are terminated *de futuro*, either because of frustration, or because the innocent party elects to accept a repudiation. These contacts need to be subjected to careful analysis. It is inappropriate to suggest (as is often done) that they should be regarded in the same manner as contracts which are avoided *ab initio*. This ignores the surely important factor that contractual remedies remain alive as far as they relate to the time before the termination. Parties can claim expectation or reliance damages (a personal remedy). Whether they can, alternatively (or additionally), make a proprietary claim for recovery of an asset is more difficult. Analogy with the voidable contract cases would suggest that such a claim is possible only if the termination has the consequence that the asset in question was transferred gratuitously. This would be the case only if the termination *de futuro* eliminates any obligation on the recipient's part to provide consideration for the transfer. This may be the unarticulated analysis which underpins the orthodox requirement for total failure of consideration (even for personal claims to restitution of money). On the other hand, an analogy with the void contract cases would suggest that even this is not enough, and that any proprietary claim is sure to fail.

Finally, and for the sake of completeness, there are those cases where the contract is not terminated at all, *ab initio* or *de futuro*; it is merely breached, so that the transferor of an asset does not receive what was promised under the contract, notwithstanding that the transferee remains contractually obliged to perform. This class of case presents no problems on the proprietary front. The appropriate remedy is simply damages for breach of contract; there is no basis on which the outsider can argue for proprietary recovery of the asset transferred (although reliance damages, rather than expectation damages, might permit the recovery of its value, but this is a personal claim).

In summary, where resulting trusts are concerned—ie where the claim is to recover assets which the outsider has transferred to a now insolvent company—there is, it seems, a modern drive to clamp down on proprietary claims. The view advanced here is that this move might not be analytically defensible: a lot of the argument depends upon treating as the same situations which clearly are not. Greater regard should be had to the straightforward differences between void, voidable and terminated contracts.'

Questions:

Clearly there are several theoretical ways in which the analysis of resulting trusts might be approached. Is one approach to be preferred over the others?

(i) The most restrictive view of resulting trusts is that they arise only where there is an unrebutted presumption that the transferor intended to create a trust. This would confine resulting trusts to transfers which were not motivated by an actual or purported or imagined contract, nor by some desire (albeit misconceived) to make an absolute gift. Is the result of this approach so restrictive that it confines resulting trusts to circumstances where an actual trust *was* intended? If this is so, and given that the intention necessary to create an express trust need not be explicit, but can be inferred from the circumstances, what policy consideration favours the *presumption* (even a rebuttable one) of an intention to create a trust whenever the transfer is gratuitous? Would it not be preferable to assess the facts and, where appropriate, infer from them an *actual* intention to create a trust? An express trust constituted on this basis need not be defeated by the absence of any necessary writing formalities—equity will not allow a statute to cloak a fraud, so the transferee may not be able to deny the trust: *Rochefoucauld v Bousted* [1897] 1 Ch 196. However, if this approach were adopted, it then becomes a difficult and quite important question to determine whether the 'actual' trust should be enforced, or whether a 'resulting' trust in favour of the settlor is to be preferred. What considerations weigh in favour of either view?

(ii) The wider view of resulting trusts—the view dismissed by the House of Lords in *Westdeutsche Landesbank*—is that they arise whenever there is a gratuitous transfer (ie a transfer for no consideration) and an unrebutted presumption that the transferor did not intend to make a gift to the transferee. On this basis resulting trusts arise whenever the transfer was made in circumstances where there was no obligation on the transferee to provide consideration (ie the transfer was gratuitous) and it cannot be proved (by the transferee) that a gift was intended. The first part of this condition is met if the transfer occurs in a non-contractual context. It is also met where the purported contract is void, or is voidable and has been effectively avoided, since then the contract is terminated *ab initio* and the transferee is therefore under no obligation to provide the nominated consideration. Finally, it may sometimes also be met where the contract is terminated *de futuro*, and where, albeit coincidentally, this has the effect of absolving the transferee from any obligation to provide consideration for the transfer. What policy considerations might conceivably justify this preferential treatment of transferors wishing to recover property they have transferred in ignorance or by mistake or for some other vitiated reason?

(iii) Finally, the widest view of resulting trusts is that they arise—as do other trusts arising by operation of law—whenever it would be unconscionable for the legal owner to assert beneficial ownership of particular property. On this view, resulting trusts might be the *general* means by which unjust enrichment is remedied: if the unjust enrichment can be identified in the transferee's hands, it is held on resulting trust for the transferor.[12] What policy considerations might conceivably favour giving restitutionary claimants such preferential remedies when compared with victims of torts or breaches of contract?

FURTHER READING:

S Stoljar, 'Re-examining Sinclair v Brougham' (1959) 22 *MLR* 21.

P Birks, 'Restitution and Resulting Trusts' in S Goldstein (ed), *Equity and Contemporary Legal Problems* (1992, Hamaccabi Press: Jerusalem), p 335.

A Burrows, 'Swaps and the Friction between Common Law and Equity' [1995] *RLR* 15.

W J Swadling, 'A New Role for Resulting Trusts?' (1996) 16 *Legal Studies* 110.

R Chambers, *Resulting Trusts* (1996, Clarendon: Oxford).

Hon Mr Justice WMC Gummow, 'Unjust Enrichment, Restitution and Proprietary Remedies' in PD Finn (ed), *Essays on Restitution* (1990, Law Book Company: Sydney) ch 3.

[12] If this is an appropriate explanation, should these trusts be called 'resulting' (because they are resulting in form) or 'constructive' (because they are constructive in imposition—see the discussion of constructive trusts in the sections immediately following this)? It must be said that both labels have been applied in different cases.

E McKendrick, 'Total Failure of Consideration and Counter-Restitution: Two Issues or One?' in P Birks (ed), *Laundering and Tracing* (1995, Clarendon Press: Oxford) ch 8.
S Worthington, 'The Proprietary Consequences of Contract Failure' in F Rose (ed), *Failure of Contracts: Contractual, Restitutionary and Proprietary Consequences* (1997, Hart Publishing: Oxford) ch 5.

Further questions:

1. What marks a trust as 'resulting'?
2. What are the similarities and differences between the form of acquisition of ownership by operation of law discussed in this section (Section 5.5) and that discussed in Section 5.3 above?

5.6 Constructive trusts: general issues

Constructive trusts are said to arise where no trust has been directly or indirectly declared, but where, according to the principles of equity, it would be unconscionable for the legal owner to assert beneficial ownership of the property. But this is really no more than vague assertion. The difficult question is *when* is it unconscionable for a legal owner to assert beneficial ownership of property? It has to be said that the cases present a disjointed and unco-ordinated response. Perhaps the answer can be given confidently only in the context of fiduciary relationships, although even here there are compelling and conflicting policy debates. Outside that arena, the classification of constructive trusts and the elucidation of the principles which underpin them appear to be even more controversial than with resulting trusts.

In *Carl-Zeiss Stiftung v Herbert Smith (No 2)*,[13] Edmund Davies LJ noted that 'English law provides no clear and all-embracing definition of a constructive trust. Its boundaries have been left perhaps deliberately vague, so as not to restrict the court by technicalities in deciding what the justice of a particular case may demand.' This sentiment underpins one common view, which is that the rules which govern constructive trusts cannot be rationalised at all, and that there is no coherent general scheme which explains constructive trusts.[14] But others have tried to provide some sort of underlying framework for the area. Donovan Waters, for example, is of the view that all constructive trusts are aimed at effecting restitution.[15] He asserts that they do this by ensuring that any unjust enrichment in a defendant's hands is given up to the deserving claimant. In his view, if a trust does not do this then it should not be classified as a constructive trust. It follows that he

[13] [1969] 2 Ch 276, 300.
[14] See, eg, A J Oakley, *Constructive Trusts* (3rd ed, 1997, Sweet & Maxwell: London).
[15] D Waters, *The Constructive Trust: The Case for a New Approach in English Law* (1964, University of London, Athlone Press: London).

objects to the classification of a vendor under a specifically enforceable contract as a constructive trustee (see Chapter 4). Gbolahan Elias, on the other hand, adopts a wider-ranging rationalisation.[16] He suggests that constructive trusts are designed to further three distinct aims: the first is the perfection aim, which ensures that a person who has chosen to favour another abides by that choice; the second is the restitution aim, which ensures that a person who has gained through another's loss gives up that gain to the other person; the third is the reparation aim, which ensures that a person who has caused loss to another repairs that loss. In reading the materials extracted in the rest of this chapter, consider which, if any, of these theses represents the best analysis of the area.

[521] ***Muschinski v Dodds*** **(1985) 160 CLR 583, 612–17, 620** ***per*** **Deane J:**
[This case concerns real property, not personal property, and the judgment is from the Australian High Court, not an English court. Nevertheless, the discussion of constructive trusts is instructive. An unmarried couple purchased land in their joint names. The purchase price was paid by the woman from her own funds. She agreed to include the man's name on the title if he undertook to renovate a cottage on the property and pay for a pre-fabricated house in which the parties intended to live. The parties separated before the cottage was renovated or the house acquired. The woman claimed sole beneficial ownership of the property on the basis of a purchase money resulting trust. The Australian High Court held that the presumption of resulting trust was rebutted on the facts, and that the parties held the beneficial interest in the property on constructive trust[17] as tenants in common, but subject to the woman being entitled to receive contribution from the man as reimbursement for a half share in the expenditure to purchase the property. Most references in the original are omitted.]

> '6. The nature and function of the constructive trust have been the subject of considerable discussion throughout the common law world for several decades. . . . .At times, disputing factions have tended to polarize the discussion by reference to competing rallying points of "remedy" and "institution". The perceived dichotomy between those two catchwords has, however, largely been the consequence of lack of definition. In a broad sense, the constructive trust is both an institution and a remedy of the law of equity. As a remedy, it can only properly be understood in the context of the history and the persisting distinctness of the principles of equity that enlighten and control the common law. The use or trust of equity, like equity itself, was essentially remedial in its origins. In its basic form it was imposed, as a personal obligation attaching to property, to enforce the equitable principle that a legal owner should not be permitted to use his common law rights as owner to abuse or subvert the intention which underlay his acquisition and possession of those rights. This was consistent with the traditional concern of equity with substance rather than form. In time, the relationships in which the trust was recognized and enforced to protect actual or presumed intention became standardized and were accepted into conveyancing practice (particularly in relation to settlements) and property law as the equitable institutions of the express and implied (including resulting) trust. Like express and implied trusts, the constructive trust developed as a remedial relationship superimposed upon common law rights by order of the Chancery Court. It differs from those other forms of trust, however, in that it arises

[16] G Elias, *Explaining Constructive Trusts* (1990, Clarendon: Oxford).
[17] But only from the date of the Court's judgment. Contrast the UK position: see **[544]** below.

regardless of intention. For that reason, it was not as well suited to development as a conveyancing device or as an instrument of property law. Indeed, whereas the rationale of the institutions of express and implied trust is now usually identified by reference to intention, the rationale of the constructive trust must still be found essentially in its remedial function which it has predominantly retained. . . . The constructive trust shares, however, some of the institutionalized features of express and implied trust. It demands the staple ingredients of those trusts: subject matter, trustee, beneficiary (or, conceivably, purpose), and personal obligation attaching to the property. . . . . When established or imposed, it is a relationship governed by a coherent body of traditional and statute law. Viewed in its modern context, the constructive trust can properly be described as a remedial institution which equity imposes regardless of actual or presumed agreement or intention (and subsequently protects) to preclude the retention or assertion of beneficial ownership of property to the extent that such retention or assertion would be contrary to equitable principle.

7. There is, however, a more limited sense in which there is some superficial plausibility in the notions of "institution" and "remedy" as competing characterizations of the constructive trust. If "institution" is understood as connoting a relationship which arises and exists under the law independently of any order of a court and "remedy" is defined as referring to the actual establishment of a relationship by such an order, the catchwords of "institution" and "remedy" do serve the function of highlighting a conceptual problem that persists about the true nature of a constructive trust. Even in this more limited sense however, any perceived dichotomy between the two notions tends to prove ephemeral upon closer examination. Equity acts consistently and in accordance with principle. The old maxim that equity regards as done that which ought to be done is as applicable to enforce equitable obligations as it is to create them and, notwithstanding that the constructive trust is remedial in both origin and nature, there does not need to have been a curial declaration or order before equity will recognize the prior existence of a constructive trust . . . .Where an equity court would retrospectively impose a constructive trust by way of equitable remedy, its availability as such a remedy provides the basis for, and governs the content of, its existence inter partes independently of any formal order declaring or enforcing it. In this more limited sense, the constructive trust is also properly seen as both "remedy" and "institution". Indeed, for the student of equity, there can be no true dichotomy between the two notions.

8. The acknowledgment of the institutional character of the constructive trust does not involve a denial of its continued flexibility as a remedy. . . . The institutional character of the trust has never completely obliterated its remedial origins even in the case of the more traditional forms of express and implied trust. This is a fortiori in the case of constructive trust where, as has been mentioned, the remedial character remains predominant in that the trust itself either represents, or reflects the availability of, equitable relief in the particular circumstances. Indeed, in this country at least, the constructive trust has not outgrown its formative stages as an equitable remedy and should still be seen as constituting an in personam remedy attaching to property which may be moulded and adjusted to give effect to the application and inter-play of equitable principles in the circumstances of the particular case. In particular, where competing common law or equitable claims are or may be involved, a declaration of constructive trust by way of remedy can properly be so framed that the consequences of its imposition are operative only from the date of judgment or formal court order or from some other specified date. [Contrast this with the UK position: see **[544]** below.] The fact that the constructive trust remains predominantly remedial does not, however, mean that it represents a medium

for the indulgence of idiosyncratic notions of fairness and justice. As an equitable remedy, it is available only when warranted by established equitable principles or by the legitimate processes of legal reasoning, by analogy, induction and deduction, from the starting point of a proper understanding of the conceptual foundation of such principles . . . . Viewed as a remedy, the function of the constructive trust is not to render superfluous, but to reflect and enforce, the principles of the law of equity.

9. Thus it is that there is no place in the law of this country for the notion of "a constructive trust of a new model" which, "(b)y whatever name it is described, . . . is . . . imposed by law whenever justice and good conscience" (in the sense of "fairness" or what "was fair") "require it" (per Lord Denning M.R., *Eves v. Eves* [1975] 1 WLR 1338, at pp 1341, 1342, [1975] 3 All ER 768, at pp 771, 772, and *Hussey v. Palmer* [1972] 1 WLR 1286, at pp 1289–1290, [1972] 3 All ER 744, at p 747). Under the law of this country—as, I venture to think, under the present law of England (cf. *Burns v. Burns* (1984) Ch 317)—proprietary rights fall to be governed by principles of law and not by some mix of judicial discretion . . ., subjective views about which party "ought to win" . . . and "the formless void of individual moral opinion". . . . . Long before Lord Seldon's anachronism identifying the Chancellor's foot as the measure of Chancery relief, undefined notions of "justice" and what was "fair" had given way in the law of equity to the rule of ordered principle which is of the essence of any coherent system of rational law. The mere fact that it would be unjust or unfair in a situation of discord for the owner of a legal estate to assert his ownership against another provides, of itself, no mandate for a judicial declaration that the ownership in whole or in part lies, in equity, in that other. . . . . Such equitable relief by way of constructive trust will only properly be available if applicable principles of the law of equity require that the person in whom the ownership of property is vested should hold it to the use or for the benefit of another. That is not to say that general notions of fairness and justice have become irrelevant to the content and application of equity. They remain relevant to the traditional equitable notion of unconscionable conduct which persists as an operative component of some fundamental rules or principles of modern equity. . . . .

10. The principal operation of the constructive trust in the law of this country has been in the area of breach of fiduciary duty. Some text writers have expressed the view that the constructive trust is confined to cases where some pre-existing fiduciary relationship can be identified. . . . . Neither principle nor authority requires however that it be confined to that or any other category or categories of case. . . . . Once its predominantly remedial character is accepted, there is no reason to deny the availability of the constructive trust in any case where some principle of the law of equity calls for the imposition upon the legal owner of property, regardless of actual or presumed agreement or intention, of the obligation to hold or apply the property for the benefit of another. . . . In the United States of America, a general doctrine of unjust enrichment has long been recognized as providing an acceptable basis in principle for the imposition of a constructive trust. . . .It may well be that the development of the law of this country on a case by case basis will eventually lead to the identification of some overall concept of unjust enrichment as an established principle constituting the basis of decision of past and future cases. Whatever may be the position in relation to the law of other common law countries (cf., as to Canada, *Pettkus v. Becker* (1980) 117 DLR (3d) 257 and, as to New Zealand, *Hayward v. Giordani* (1983) NZLR 140, at p 148) however, no such general principle is as yet established [Note: it now is], . . . It therefore becomes necessary to consider whether there is any narrower and more specific basis on which, independently of the actual intention of the parties, Mrs.

Muschinski can claim to be entitled to relief by way of constructive trust in the particular circumstances of the present case.

....

14. . . . .Those circumstances can be more precisely defined by saying that the principle operates in a case where the substratum of a joint relationship or endeavour is removed without attributable blame and where the benefit of money or other property contributed by one party on the basis and for the purposes of the relationship or endeavour would otherwise be enjoyed by the other party in circumstances in which it was not specifically intended or specially provided that that other party should so enjoy it. The content of the principle is that, in such a case, equity will not permit that other party to assert or retain the benefit of the relevant property to the extent that it would be unconscionable for him so to do (cf. *Atwood v. Maude*, (1868) LR 3 Ch App 369 at pp 374–375 and per Jessel M.R., *Lyon v. Tweddell* (1881) 17 ChD 529, at p 531).

15. The circumstances of the present case provide the necessary context for the operation of that general principle of the law of equity.'

[522] *Re Diplock* [1948] Ch 465, 532 *per* Lord Greene MR:
[The facts are immaterial for present purposes, but are given at **[628]**.]

'the fundamental conception which lies at the root of this equitable jurisdiction [is] that equity intervenes not to do what might be thought to be absolute justice to a claimant but to prevent a defendant from acting in an unconscionable manner. Equity will not restrain a defendant from asserting a claim save to the extent that it would be unconscionable for him to do so. If this limitation on the power of equity results in giving to a plaintiff less than what on some general idea of fairness he might be considered entitled to, that cannot be helped.'

Neither of these extracts advances matters very far. Both suggest that a constructive trust is the method by which the law will 'subtract' from the defendant's dominion any assets which it would be 'unconscionable' for the defendant to retain in the face of the claimant's claims. The imposition of a constructive trust leaves the legal title with the defendant, but effects (by operation of law) a transfer of the beneficial interest in the asset from defendant to claimant. This technique might be used by the law to bring about quite different practical consequences. For example, it could effect a transfer from defendant to claimant of assets which the defendant had agreed to transfer, but had not yet transferred. The result would be to move forward the parties' agreement, and to do this by operation of law rather than by private act of the parties themselves. This use of constructive trusts has already been seen in operation in the context of specifically enforceable contracts of sale (see Chapter 4, especially Sections 4.10–4.13). This technique could also be used to return to the claimant assets which the claimant had transferred to the defendant but which now, for some reason, it would be unconscionable for the defendant to retain. This form of intervention is 'resulting' in pattern, even if it might be considered 'constructive' in imposition, and examples were considered in Section 5.5 above. A constructive trust operating in this way would reverse, or unwind, the parties' agreement, and again would do this by operation of law (although maybe only after the claimant had elected for unwinding of the contract rather than its enforcement).

It is difficult to decide whether an agreement between parties should be specifically enforced or, in different circumstances, unwound. To justify attaching proprietary consequences to that decision complicates matters still further. It is not clear why equity should see fit to intervene and deliver proprietary benefits to claimants in these circumstances. In fact many commentators have suggested that such intervention is unwarranted.[18] On the other hand, the common justification for proprietary consequences in these circumstances is that 'equity treats as done that which ought to be done'. At one level, *every* equitable proprietary interest exists only because equity envisages as 'done' something which in fact has not been done. In this way every equitable proprietary interest involves eliding concepts of obligation and property, so that what starts out as a personal obligation enforceable in equity becomes, for the beneficiary of that obligation, a proprietary right recognised in equity but not at law (ie an equitable proprietary right). This is as true of express trusts (where the obligation being enforced is voluntarily assumed by the trustee) as it is of constructive trusts (where, when they exist, the obligation is imposed by law rather than consensually). Of course, for any obligation to have this proprietary effect, it must relate to specific and identifiable property. This practical limitation frequently denies claimants any possibility of asserting proprietary interests. There can be no proprietary interest if the property to which the interest allegedly relates is uncertain. But, practical constraints aside, the real issue is this: although an obligation in equity which relates to specific property *can* have this proprietary effect, is it the case that *every* obligation in equity which relates to specific property automatically has this effect? The answer is not clear.[19] Many difficulties associated with proprietary remedies would disappear if it were.

But this is not the only cause for concern. The proprietary intervention is avowedly *equitable*, and is premised on an *equitable* obligation relating to specific property. Even ignoring the issue of whether *every* equitable obligation relating to specific property will have proprietary consequences, some assessment has to be made about which obligations are enforceable 'in equity' and which are not. Consider a contract of sale. The vendor is obliged (in contract) to transfer the sale property, or, alternatively, (in unjust enrichment) to return the purchase price or (in contract) to pay damages if no transfer is effected. Consider these obligations in turn.

The obligation to transfer property is agreed between the parties; it is purchased by the provision of consideration. However, interestingly, this obligation to transfer the property *in specie* is rarely enforced at law. The 'common law' never enforces the transfer,[20] and 'equity' enforces it only in limited circumstances (when the contract is said to be 'specifically enforceable').[21] Proprietary consequences attach to the obligation to transfer only in these latter cases. Assessment of whether a case falls on one side of the line or the other may seem somewhat circular, but nevertheless

[18] See, eg, the references already cited in Section 5.5.5 above, and also those cited at the end of this Section and Section 5.10 below.

[19] See especially the debates noted in Section 5.10 below.

[20] Although see the Torts (Interference with Goods) Act 1977.

[21] This segregation of 'common law' and 'equity' creates its own problems in any discussion of legal responses, but the issue opens up an enormous area of debate, and the orthodox division is simply conceded here.

the rule is clear: the obligation to transfer, agreed between the parties, only has equitable proprietary consequences when the law backs its enforcement. The common law never does, and equity rarely does.

Next look at the obligation to return the purchase price, an obligation imposed on a vendor who refuses to transfer the sale property notwithstanding the vendor's receipt of the purchase price. This is not (usually) an obligation agreed by the parties; it is imposed by law (specifically, the law of unjust enrichment). Whether this obligation has proprietary consequences remains controversial. The prevailing view seems to be that it does not. It is said that this obligation, imposed in the law of unjust enrichment, is a common law obligation (derived from the action for money had and received); equity has no role to play. From this it follows that there is no equitable obligation which could possibly support a proprietary interest in the fund representing the purchase price. There is a contrary argument, however. This involves an appreciation that 'equity' is only noticeable when its rules conflict with the common law; otherwise equity's rules 'follow the law'. For example, 'equity' is noticeable when it insists that a contract of sale is specifically enforceable; otherwise it follows the common law, and concedes that the parties' agreed obligation to transfer *in specie* is not supported by the law—the obligation to transfer *in specie* does not exist at law or in equity. Adopting this approach, the common law obligation to return the purchase price is followed by equity: although there is no conflict between the common law and the equitable rules, there *is* an equitable rule. This equitable obligation may then have proprietary consequences *if* the price is identifiable property in the vendor's hands.[22] Predictably, in this difficult area, this approach too has its critics. They are prepared to concede that equity follows the law, but they assert that the common law obligation is not to return the purchase price but to repay its value. Since it is impossible for the latter obligation to relate to identifiable property, it follows that even if equity supported the common law rule, it could not thereby deliver proprietary consequences. Correct assessment of the obligation is therefore critical—and controversial.[23]

Finally, returning to the earlier example of the contract of sale, a vendor who fails to deliver is potentially under an obligation to pay expectation damages for breach of the contract. This is a common law obligation. Even if equity 'follows the law' and imposes a similar obligation, it could never have proprietary consequences: there is no identifiable property representing the damages fund. In these circumstances there is no need for argument about 'law' and 'equity' conflicts—there are none.

[22] As noted earlier, this practical limitation is frequently decisive: only rarely will a purchaser be able to identify purchase funds in the vendor's hands. However, see Section 5.7 below on the possibility of a purchaser's equitable lien on the sale property.

[23] This takes the debate into complicated areas. However, it is worth noting that the common law cannot effect specific restitution of property (aside from the statutory discretion conferred by the Torts (Interference with Goods) Act 1977 s 3); it can *only* provide for the recovery of value (although contrast the cases noted in Section 5.3 above). In equity, the reverse is true. The obligation to repay value is secondary, arising only if the defendant no longer holds the relevant specific property. Moreover, the law of unjust enrichment is concerned with the restitution of an unjust enrichment in the defendant's hands. It is certainly arguable that the obligation is to return (make restitution of) the unjust enrichment, and equity would attach to the enrichment specifically even if the common law could relate to it only by assessing and demanding return of its value.

To recap, two of the problems for legal analysis in this area are, first, whether all equitable obligations have the potential to produce proprietary consequences and, secondly, whether all common law obligations are mirrored by equitable counterparts (assuming that equity does not opt for conflicting rules). These questions need to be answered in order to determine whether, in any given circumstances, a claimant can assert a proprietary interest in specific assets.

The next problem is less difficult. Often the circumstances are such that a potential claimant has a choice of remedial routes. Recall the earlier example of a contract of sale. If the vendor refuses to deliver, the claimant might seek specific performance, or damages, or return of the purchase price. Subject to the uncertainties already indicated, both the first and last options have potential proprietary consequences. Can the claimant select the option most advantageous to the claimant, or will the law restrict the choice? Certainly the general rule is that a claimant can pursue the remedy which is most advantageous to the claimant. But does it automatically follow that a claimant can insist that proprietary consequences attach to the selected option? The position of a purchaser under a specifically enforceable contract of sale suggests that the claimant can. There, the purchaser can assert a constructive trust over the sale property to ensure performance of the contract, or, alternatively, can assert an equitable lien over the sale property to ensure return of the purchase price in an unwinding of the contract. If the extracts cited earlier are to be followed (see **[521]** and **[522]** above), does this available choice best reflect an effort to deny the defendant's unconscionable assertion of an interest in property, or should the choice be restricted?

All of this is only intended as a summary of the difficult issues reflected in the materials which are to follow. But two further matters add to those difficulties. First, all of the preceding discussion of proprietary interests has assumed an obligation to transfer an identified asset. The imposition of a constructive trust—or the *recognition* that a constructive trust exists[24]—acknowledges that, in equity, the asset is to be regarded as already transferred. The asset can be tangible or intangible; it can also be an identified fund of money. This approach has clear advantages for claimants able to advance claims to such assets, but leaves unaided claimants with only general money claims. However, even these claimants sometimes receive the assistance of equity. Sometimes they are entitled to assert an equitable lien (ie an equitable charge arising by operation of law) against specific property in the defendant's hands in order to secure performance by the defendant of the obligation to pay over a sum of money. As with constructive trusts, equitable liens may either secure performance of an agreement (by ensuring that the defendant makes the payment which was promised), or they can secure the unwinding of an agreement (by ensuring that the defendant returns to the claimant a payment received as counter-performance). As with constructive trusts, too, the difficulty is to decide which obligations should be enforced, and which (if any) can and should have proprietary consequences. The next section (Section 5.7) provides a general introduction to equitable liens.

The second matter concerns perhaps the greatest of all the difficulties in this area. So far the discussion has assumed that there is an underlying contract between the

[24] This is probably more accurate, since, in the UK, constructive trusts are 'institutional': see Section 5.11.

parties, or that the defendant is under a clear obligation to perform a trust or to effect restitution for unjust enrichment. In short, the existence of an obligation is not controversial. The difficult issue is simply to determine whether those obligations have proprietary consequences. However, matters are further complicated when the facts do not clearly support the existence of an enforceable obligation (whether in contract, unjust enrichment, or trust). Without an underlying obligation, there should be no proprietary remedy. Notwithstanding this, numerous cases have seen fit to award remedies in these circumstances, and proprietary remedies too, on the basis of 'common intention' constructive trusts, or proprietary estoppel, or rights of subrogation. These 'hard' cases are the focus of the materials extracted in Sections 5.8 and 5.9 below.

Finally, in all of this, one scenario has been ignored. Throughout it has been assumed that the constructive trust or equitable lien will operate either to enforce or to unwind some agreement (or 'pseudo-agreement') between the parties. Clearly that is not the only possibility. This chapter also addresses the possibility that a constructive trust or equitable lien might lend proprietary force to claims in respect of a *breach* of the defendant's obligations, whether those obligations are equitable or contractual or tortious (see Section 5.10 below).

Question:

Reconsider the extracts at **|521|** and **|522|**. In reading the following sections of this chapter on constructive trusts, consider whether the suggested limitations on the operation of equity are observed. The issue is important, if only because there is a growing perception, already articulated in the context of resulting trusts,[25] that these forms of equitable intervention are unfair to third parties, especially third party creditors of an insolvent defendant. In particular, in relation to each case extracted below, consider whether *any* proprietary remedy is warranted, and, if so, whether the *particular* remedy awarded is the best choice or whether some alternative would have been preferable.

This discussion of constructive trusts is not yet complete, although it has traversed the general issues. Now it is necessary to review equitable liens (see Section 5.7 below). Once this is done, it will it be possible to examine the incidence of both constructive trusts and equitable liens in different fact situations. This approach is necessary since these two proprietary interests frequently present as alternatives, and it is then desirable to consider which is preferable in the given circumstances.

FURTHER READING:

E L Sherwin, 'Constructive Trusts in Bankruptcy' (1989) 2 *Uni of Illinois LR* 297.

D M Paccioco, 'The Remedial Constructive Trust: A Principled Basis for Priority Over Creditors' (1989) 68 *Can Bar Rev* 315.

[25] See especially the *Westdeutsche* case at **|518|** above.

R Grantham, 'Doctrinal Bases for the Recognition of Proprietary Rights' (1996) 16 *OJLS* 561.

5.7 Equitable liens: general issues

An equitable lien gives its holder precisely the same rights in property as an equitable charge (see Chapter 3). The difference is that an equitable lien arises by operation of law, while a charge arises by agreement between the parties. Like a charge, an equitable lien secures an obligation imposed on the defendant. If the defendant does not perform, then the claimant can assert rights under the lien.

The most common examples of such liens are vendor's and purchaser's liens on *real* property which is the subject of a contract of sale. A vendor who transfers the property without receiving payment is entitled to a lien on the property now in the purchaser's hands to secure payment by the purchaser of the price. Alternatively, if the purchaser pays for the land before taking a conveyance of it, then the purchaser has a lien on the property (still in the vendor's hands) to secure return of the purchase price should the vendor not perform.[26]

The difficulties in this area are to define and delimit the situations in which equitable liens arise, and to determine their limits. The following extracts illustrate the issues.

[523] J Phillips, 'Equitable Liens—A Search for a Unifying Principle' in N Palmer and E McKendrick (eds), *Interests in Goods* (2nd edn, 1998, Lloyds of London Press: London) ch 39, pp 975–80:

[The footnotes in the original have been omitted.]

'(1) SOME GENERAL CHARACTERISTICS

Some features of the equitable lien are clear enough. Unlike its common law counterpart, the equitable lien does not depend upon possession and it can attach to personalty as well as to land. Enforcement occurs by judicial sale in pursuance of a court order or, where the lien is over a fund, by an order for payment from that fund. Yet, since the equitable lien does not transfer any title to the property on which it is imposed, it cannot be enforced by foreclosure or repossession and thus is quite different from security by way of mortgage.

The equitable lien creates a right *in rem*, so that the holder of the lien can call on the property of another to discharge a monetary obligation. This means that the holder of the lien is also a secured creditor within bankruptcy or winding-up proceedings. The normal rule as to priorities applies so that the interest created by the lien will be defeated by the subsequent acquisition of the legal title to the property by a bona fide purchaser for value. The lien holder's rights may even be postponed to a subsequent equitable

[26] Note that a purchaser in these circumstances will generally also be the equitable owner of the land (ie there will be a constructive trust over the land if the contract is specifically enforceable and unconditional): see Chapter 4. Enforcement of this trust is generally the purchaser's preferred remedy, so that the purchaser obtains the land bargained for. The lien will only be relied upon if, for some reason, the transfer cannot be enforced.

interest where the conduct of the lien holder demands "in fairness and in justice" that the equitable lien should be postponed in priority to that subsequent interest. In *Heid v. Reliance Finance Corp. Pty Ltd* a vendor's equitable lien in respect of the unpaid purchase price of land was postponed in favour of the rights of subsequent equitable mortgagees. In the circumstances, the vendor's conduct in entrusting the transfer documents to an employee of the purchasers, which led to the creation of the subsequent unregistered mortgages, was sufficient to defeat the lien. The general rule that the prior equity in time prevails was thus displaced.

Sometimes the equitable lien is defined as a charge, or at least regarded as a species of a charge. Thus the equitable lien has been described judicially as a "form of equitable charge" or simply as a "charge". *Halsbury's Laws of England* also describes the creation of the equitable lien as arising "from the relationship of the parties, . . . or from a course of conduct or an express contract indicating an intention that such an equitable *charge* shall be created".

This reference to the term "charge", however, both judicially and in legal writing, is at best imprecise because the word lien is more appropriately used to describe a right arising by operation of law rather than by agreement between the parties. As Slade J. explained in *Re Bond Worth*:

> ". . . although the word lien is sometimes used in practice to describe a right which arises by way of express contractual agreement of the interested parties, it is more commonly used, in a narrower sense, to refer to a right arising by operation of law. Liens in this narrow sense may arise by virtue of statute, common law or equity."

The equitable lien, therefore, arises as a result of the application of equitable principles and is distinct from an equitable charge, which arises from a consensual agreement between the relevant parties.

An equitable lien can be excluded by express or implied agreement between the parties. Thus, if there is an express agreement between the parties that the indebtedness is to be secured by a charge, this will usually negate the implication of a lien arising by operation of law. This is so even though the security upon which the parties have agreed is or becomes defective in some way, for example, because of the failure to register the charge. In *Re Bond Worth* [**[332]** above] the parties expressly provided for a retention of title clause to secure the purchase price in respect of goods sold. Slade J. saw "no room for implying any vendor's lien arising by operation of law, after completion of the purchase, *bearing in mind the express agreement of the parties* in the terms embodied in the retention of title clause". The vendor could therefore rely neither on the retention of title clause, which was void for want of registration, nor on the equitable lien which was impliedly excluded by the terms of the parties' own ineffective agreement. The result of such cases is somewhat harsh. A lender who has taken the precaution of obtaining an express charge, albeit one that does not achieve the intended effect, is placed in a worse position than a party who has failed to address its mind to the question of contracting as a secured creditor; only the latter is able to invoke the equitable lien. But the law in this respect is now clearly established.

(2) PROBLEMS OF CLASSIFICATION

It has been correctly said that the list of equitable liens is "something of a themeless rag bag" and within this "rag bag" it is not easy to discern any coherent statements of principle.

Some equitable liens are identifiable because they arise as a consequence of a particular legal relationship. Thus an equitable lien arises between solicitor and client, whereby the solicitor has a lien over property (for example, a fund or the proceeds of a judgment) to secure payment of the costs of litigation; a trustee has a lien on trust property in respect of costs and expenses properly incurred by him in the due performance of his trustee's duties; a receiver or a provisional liquidator appointed by the court has an equitable lien over the assets under his administration; a beneficiary under a trust has a lien over land which a trustee has purchased in breach of trust; and a partner on dissolution of the partnership has a lien on the assets of the partnership.

There is no doubt that some of these liens are commercially significant. For example, the trustee's equitable lien, arising in respect of his costs and expenses, has become increasingly important, at least in the Australian context, in its application to corporate trustees when the trustee company is wound up and issues arise as to whether a payment made by the corporate trustee to a third party amounts to a voidable preference. Yet, from the point of view of discerning any principle in equity, which might give general guidance about when a lien is established, the relevant authorities offer little assistance. Such liens have been held to arise simply because of the status of the parties in that particular legal relationship. The trustee's lien, for instance, is said to be based on the fact that the beneficiaries must pay a "price" for the "gratuitous and onerous services of trustees".

Other equitable liens have been said to arise on a more general basis. Thus it is stated: "a person who has laid out money upon property under a mistaken belief that he is entitled to it or has an interest in it will have a lien for the amount thereof, provided that the owner has, by his conduct in standing by with knowledge of such mistake *estopped* himself from contending to the contrary". But, as the passage indicates, the creation of a lien in this situation arises purely in a remedial way consequent on the successful application of the principles of estoppel. The court, having found an estoppel exists declares that a lien exists over the relevant property, which can be enforced by the plaintiff to recover the expenditure incurred. Cox J. in *Jackson v. Crosby* provides an illustration of this approach: "The principles of equitable estoppel are sufficiently flexible, in my opinion, to allow the relief to be assessed in a suitable case, on a quantum meruit basis—*technically*, as compensation for an equitable lien on the appellant's property for the value of the work done by the respondent."

But sometimes the court may phrase the remedy allowing the recovery of expenditure, in terms of a constructive trust rather than an equitable lien. Indeed, on similar facts, the court may grant the plaintiff not a restitutionary remedy, supported by the equitable lien, but an interest in the land to coincide with his expectations. This flexibility of remedy has been rightly criticised because "it is impossible to say, till after the Court has spoken, whether a restitutionary or a non-restitutionary response will be made". But the crucial point here is that once again the relevant cases reveal nothing about the criteria relevant to the establishment of equitable liens in other contexts aside from the law of estoppel.

It is also said that liens are created by the application of the principles of subrogation. Thus Professors Sykes and Walker in their work, *The Law of Securities*, write that "the vendor's [equitable] lien may in some cases come into existence in favour of persons who are not vendors by virtue of the principle of subrogation". Similarly, Gibbs C.J. in *Hewett v. Court* states that "an equitable lien may arise . . . by reason of subrogation".

. . .

Some well-established categories of equitable liens do operate in a contractual context, namely, the vendor's and purchaser's liens. The vendor's lien has been previously described. A purchaser's lien arises in favour of a purchaser of land who has paid a deposit or instalments of the purchase price to the vendor The purchaser has an equitable lien over the land to be sold for all sums paid by him under the contract which are recoverable by the purchaser because, for example, the contract has been determined otherwise than as a result of the purchaser's default. The purchaser's lien like the vendor's lien also extends to personalty.

Unlike those liens arising from the special relationship of the parties or those said to arise through estoppel or subrogation, it might be thought that the authorities concerning vendor's and purchaser's liens would have generated a fruitful analysis of the circumstances in which liens arise in a contractual context. In particular, there is the central question of whether equitable liens apply to other types of contractual arrangements and, if so, in what circumstances. But, despite no dearth of authority on purchaser's and vendor's liens in the nineteenth century, there has been little exposition of principle. It is true that there has been a recognition that the existence of equitable liens should not be confined within narrow established categories and that "the list" may not be a closed one. But if this is so, it is unacceptable in determining the existence of an equitable lien that the court proceeds "on general notions of justice without regard to settled principles". It was not until the decision of the High Court of Australia in *Hewett v. Court* that we saw some attempt to lay down a unifying principle and isolate some general criteria necessary to establish the existence of the lien in a contractual context.'

[524] *Lord Napier and Ettrick v Hunter* [1993] AC 713, 729–38 *per* Lord Templeman, 743–5 *per* Lord Goff, 752 *per* Lord Browne-Wilkinson:

[Members of a Lloyd's syndicate were insured by stop loss insurers against underwriting losses, and the insurers made payments in respect of certain claims. The syndicate also received sums in respect of the same losses through the settlement of an action by members against the syndicate's managing agents for negligence and breach of duty. The House of Lords was required to determine the extent to which the insurers were subrogated to the members' rights to those settlement sums, and whether the subrogation rights were personal or proprietary. For further details on subrogation, see Section 5.12 below.]

Lord Templeman:

'For purposes of illustration, the arguments in the courts below and in this House assume that for the 1982 year of account a particular hypothetical name suffered a nett underwriting loss of £160,000, that the excess was £25,000, and that the limit was £100,000. On these figures the stop loss insurance paid to the name £100,000 being the fixed amount of the limit (£100,000) which exceeded the excess (£25,000). The names together with other names sued Outhwaite [the managing agent] for damages for negligence and breach of duty in respect of, inter alia, the 1982 year of account. Those proceedings were compromised on payment by Outhwaite of £116m. to the respondents Richards Butler as solicitors for the plaintiffs in the action. For the purposes of the illustration it is assumed that included in the sum of £116m. Richards Butler hold £130,000 attributable to the overall ascertained nett loss of £160,000 suffered by the hypothetical name for the 1982 year of account.

On these assumptions two problems arise. First how much is payable to the stop loss insurers by way of subrogation? Secondly are the stop loss insurers entitled to be paid the amounts found due to them by way of subrogation out of the damages now held by Richards Butler?

[On the first question, the court decided unanimously that the insured had to bear a £25,000 loss (representing the insurance excess), so the insurer was entitled to be subrogated to the extent of £95,000 out of the fund of £130,000 recovered from the managing agent—the insurer being liable for only £5,000 of the unrecovered £30,000 loss.]

The second question is whether the stop loss insurers have an interest in the moneys held by Richards Butler. For this purpose it may be assumed by way of example that the moneys held by Richards Butler include £130,000 paid by Outhwaite as damages for negligence which inflicted a loss of £160,000 on a name in respect of the 1982 year of account; can the stop loss insurers assert an interest in that sum of £130,000 to the extent of the £95,000 which, as I have indicated, is due to them by way of subrogation?

. . . .

In *Yorkshire Insurance Co. Ltd. v. Nisbet Shipping Co. Ltd.* [1962] 2 Q.B. 330 a vessel was insured for £72,000 and became an actual total loss. The insurers paid £72,000. The assured brought proceedings in Canada for the loss of the vessel and the defendants paid to the assured in Canada 336,000-odd Canadian dollars then worth £75,000-odd. The pound was devalued and when the damages were transmitted to London they were worth £127,000.

Diplock J. held that the doctrine of subrogation only entitled the insurers to recoupment of the £72,000 which they had paid. Diplock J. referred to the doctrine of subrogation in these terms, at pp. 339–341:

> "The doctrine of subrogation is not restricted to the law of insurance. Although often referred to as an 'equity' it is not an exclusively equitable doctrine. It was applied by the common law courts in insurance cases long before the fusion of law and equity, although the powers of the common law courts might in some cases require to be supplemented by those of the court of equity in order to give full effect to the doctrine; for example, by compelling an assured to allow his name to be used by the insurer for the purpose of forcing the assured's remedies against third parties in respect of the subject matter of the loss. . . . The expression 'subrogation' in relation to a contract of marine insurance is thus no more than a convenient way of referring to those terms which are to be implied in the contract between the assured and the insurer to give business efficacy to an agreement whereby the assured in the case of a loss against which the policy has been made shall be fully indemnified, and never more than fully indemnified. . . . In my view the doctrine of subrogation in insurance law requires one to imply in contracts of marine insurance only such terms as are necessary to ensure that, notwithstanding that the insurer has made a payment under the policy, the assured shall not be entitled to retain, as against the insurer, a greater sum than what is ultimately shown to be his actual loss. . . . Thus, if after payment by the insurer of a loss that loss, as a result of an act of a third party, is reduced, the insurer can recover from the assured the amount of the reduction because that is the amount which he, the insurer, has overpaid under the contract of insurance. This sum he can recover at common law without recourse to equity, as money had and received . . . the duty of the assured to take proceedings to reduce his loss and the correlative right of the insurer to require him to do so was a contractual duty. The remedy for its breach, by compelling the assured to allow an action to be brought in his name, was an equitable remedy in aid of rights at common law, and was alternative to the common law remedy of recovering damages for the breach of the duty: . . ."

In *Hobbs v. Marlowe* [1978] A.C. 16, 39 Lord Diplock said:

> "For my own part I prefer to regard the doctrine of subrogation in relation to contracts of insurance as having its origin at common law in the implied terms of the

> contract and calling for the aid of a court of equity only where its auxiliary jurisdiction was needed to compel the assured to lend his name to his insurer for the enforcement of rights and remedies to which his insurer was subrogated: see *Yorkshire Insurance Co. Ltd. v. Nisbet Shipping Co. Ltd.* [1962] 2 Q.B. 330. But the practical effects of the doctrine of subrogation upon the rights and remedies of insurer and assured are similar in many respects to the effect of an equitable assignment of a chose in action. . . ."

Thus Lord Diplock, far from deciding that a court of equity could not lend its aid to compel the assured to direct that the insurer be recouped under the doctrine of subrogation out of the damages recovered from the wrongdoer, equated the right of the insurer to that of the assignee of an equitable interest, a right which equity will of course enforce.

It may be that the common law invented and implied in contracts of insurance a promise by the insured person to take proceedings to reduce his loss, a promise by the insured person to account to the insurer for moneys recovered from a third party in respect of the insured loss and a promise by the insured person to allow the insurer to exercise in the name of the insured person rights of action vested in the insured person against third parties for the recovery of the insured loss if the insured person refuses or neglects to enforce those rights of action. There must also be implied a promise by the insured person that in exercising his rights of action against third parties he will act in good faith for the benefit of the insured person so far as he has borne the loss and for the benefit of the insurer so far as he has indemnified the insured person against the insured loss. My Lords, contractual promises may create equitable interests. An express promise by a vendor to convey land on payment of the purchase price confers on the purchaser an equitable interest in the land. In my opinion promises implied in a contract of insurance with regard to rights of action vested in the insured person for the recovery of an insured loss from a third party responsible for the loss confer on the insurer an equitable interest in those rights of action to the extent necessary to recoup the insurer who has indemnified the insured person against the insured loss.

. . . .

The principles which dictated the decisions of our ancestors and inspired their references to the equitable obligations of an insured person towards an insurer entitled to subrogation are discernible and immutable. They establish that such an insurer has an enforceable equitable interest in the damages payable by the wrongdoer. The insured person is guilty of unconscionable conduct if he does not provide for the insurer to be recouped out of the damages awarded against the wrongdoer. Equity will not allow the insured person to insist on his legal rights to all the damages awarded against the wrongdoer and will restrain the insured person from receiving or dealing with those damages so far as they are required to recoup the insurer under the doctrine of subrogation.

Where the insured person has been paid policy moneys by the insurer for a loss in respect of which the insured person recovers damages from a wrongdoer the insured person is guilty of unconscionable conduct if he does not procure and direct that the sum due to the insurer shall by way of subrogation be paid out of the damages.

It is next necessary to consider how equity copes with such unconscionable conduct. Saville J. and the Court of Appeal appear to have thought that equity can only interfere by creating a trust fund held in trust by trustees for different beneficiaries in different shares, the trustees being burdened with administrative and investment duties, the trustees being liable for all the duties imposed on trustees but being free from liability if the trust fund is lost without negligence. I agree that if this were the only method of protecting the rights of an insurer the practical disadvantages would be fearsome. Fortunately, equity is not so inflexible or powerless. In order to protect the rights of the insurer under the doctrine of subrogation equity considers that the damages payable by the wrongdoer to the insured person are subject to an equitable lien or charge in favour of the insurer. The charge is imposed by equity because the insurer, once he has paid under the policy, has an interest in the right of action against the wrongdoer and an interest in the establishment, quantification, recovery and distribution of the damages awarded against the wrongdoer. It would be unconscionable for the insured person, who has received £100,000 from the insurer, to put damages of £130,000 into his own pocket without providing for the recoupment of the insurer who only contracted to indemnify the insured person.'

Lord Goff of Chieveley:

'Despite Saville J.'s reservations on this point, I can discern no inconsistency between the equitable proprietary right recognised by courts of equity in these cases and the personal rights and obligations embodied in the contract of insurance itself. No doubt our task nowadays is to see the two strands of authority, at law and in equity, moulded into a coherent whole; but for my part I cannot see why this amalgamation should lead to the rejection of the equitable proprietary right recognised in the line of cases to which I have referred. Of course, it is proper to start with the contract of insurance, and to see how the common law courts have worked out the mutual rights and obligations of the parties in contractual terms with recourse to implied terms where appropriate. But, with all respect, I am unable to agree with Lord Diplock that subrogation is in this context concerned solely with the mutual rights and obligations of the parties under the contract. In this connection, I observe from the report of *Yorkshire Insurance Co. Ltd. v. Nisbet Shipping Co. Ltd.* [1962] 2 Q.B. 330 that the important case of *White v. Dobinson*, 14 Sim. 273; 116 L.T.O.S. 233 [sub nom. *White v. Dobbinson*] was not cited in argument, and indeed the existence of an equitable proprietary right was not in issue in that case. In these circumstances I cannot derive from Lord Diplock's judgment any justification for sweeping the line of equity cases under the carpet as though it did not exist. In my opinion, this line of authority must be recognised, and appropriate weight should be given to the views expressed in the cases by the distinguished judges who decided them. I wish to add that I do not read section 79 of the Marine Insurance Act 1906 (concerned with the right of subrogation) as in any way detracting from this conclusion.

Even so, an important feature of these cases is that the principle of subrogation in the law of insurance arises in a contractual context. It is true that in some cases at common law it has been described as arising as a matter of equity. Thus in *Burnand v. Rodocanachi Sons & Co.*, 7 App.Cas. 333, 339, Lord Blackburn described it simply as "an equity." Furthermore, it has not been usual to express the principle of subrogation as arising from an implied term in the contract. Even so it has been regarded, both at law and in equity, as giving effect to the underlying nature of a contract of insurance, which is that it is intended to provide an indemnity but no more than an indemnity. Not only does this principle inform the judgments of the Court of Appeal in the leading case of *Castellain v. Preston*, 11 Q.B.D. 380, but it underlies Lord Lyndhurst L.C.'s judgment in *White v. Dobbinson*, 116 L.T.O.S. 233. In so far as the principle requires the payment of money, it could no doubt be formulated as an implied term, to which effect could have been given by the old action for money had and received. But I do not see why the mere fact that the purpose of subrogation in this context is to give effect to the principle of indemnity embodied in the contract should preclude recognition of the equitable proprietary right, if justice so requires. If I search for a parallel, the closest analogy is perhaps to be found in the law of agency in which, although the relationship between principal and agent is governed by a contract, nevertheless the agent may be held in certain circumstances to hold money, which he has received from a third party in his capacity as agent, as trustee for his principal. It is by no means easy to ascertain the circumstances in which a trusteeship exists; but, in a valuable discussion in *Bowstead on Agency*, 15th ed. (1985), pp. 162–163, Professor Francis Reynolds suggests that it is right to inquire

> "whether the trust relationship is appropriate to the commercial relationship in which the parties find themselves; whether it was appropriate that money or property should be, and whether it was, held separately, or whether it was contemplated that the agent should use the money, property or proceeds of the property as part of his normal cash flow in such a way that the relationship of debtor and creditor is more appropriate."

He also suggests that

> "a central question, perhaps too often overlooked (because not directly an issue), is whether the rights of the principal are sufficiently strong, and differentiable from other claims, for him to be entitled to a prior position in respect of them on the agent's bankruptcy."

I have little doubt that the distinguished judges who decided the cases in the line of equity authority to which I have referred must have considered that money received by an assured from a third party in reduction of a loss paid by an insurer should not be treated as available for the assured's normal cash flow, and further that the rights of the insurer to such money were sufficiently strong to entitle the insurer to priority in the event of the assured's bankruptcy, as was indeed held by Wynn-Parry J. in *In re Miller, Gibb & Co. Ltd.* [1957] 1 W.L.R. 703. I for my part can see no good reason to depart from this line of authority. However, since the constitution of the assured as trustee of such money may impose upon him obligations of too onerous a character (a point which troubled Saville J. in the present case), I am very content that the equitable proprietary right of the insurer should be classified as a lien, as proposed by my noble and learned friend, Lord Templeman, and indeed as claimed by the insurer in *White v. Dobinson*, 14 Sim. 273 itself. Indeed a lien is the more appropriate form of proprietary right in circumstances where, as here, its function is to protect the interest of the insurer in an asset only to the extent that its retention by the assured will have the effect that he is more than indemnified under the policy of insurance.'

Lord Browne-Wilkinson:

'In my judgment therefore an insurer who has paid over the insurance moneys does have a proprietary interest in moneys subsequently recovered by an assured from a third party wrongdoer. Although many of the authorities refer to that right as arising under a trust, in my judgment the imposition of a trust is neither necessary nor desirable: to impose fiduciary liabilities on the assured is commercially undesirable and unnecessary to protect the insurers' interests. In my judgment, the correct analysis is as follows. The contract of insurance contains an implied term that the assured will pay to the insurer out of the moneys received in reduction of the loss the amount to which the insurer is entitled by way of subrogation. That contractual obligation is specifically enforceable in equity against the defined fund (i.e., the damages) in just the same way as are other contracts to assign or charge specific property e.g. equitable assignments and equitable charges. Since equity regards as done that which ought to be done under a contract, this specifically enforceable right gives rise to an immediate proprietary interest in the moneys recovered from the third party. In my judgment, this proprietary interest is adequately satisfied in the circumstances of subrogation under an insurance contract by granting the insurers a lien over the moneys recovered by the assured from the third party. This lien will be enforceable against the fund so long as it is traceable and has not been acquired by a bona fide purchaser for value without notice. In addition to the equitable lien, the insurer will have a personal right of action at law to recover the amount received by the assured as moneys had and received to the use of the insurer.'

Questions:

1. Are there any significant differences in the reasoning of the members of the House of Lords extracted above? Does anything turn on these differences?
2. Does the equitable proprietary interest of the insurer attach only to a fund consisting of sums which come into the hands of the assured in reduction of the loss paid by the insurer, or could it also attach to any right of action vested in the assured which, if enforced, would yield such a fund? This question was not answered by the members of the House of Lords in *Lord Napier and Ettrick*. What concerns might suggest a cautious answer?
3. Does *Lord Napier and Ettrick* provide any significant insights into the nature of an equitable lien?

[525] *Hewitt v Court* (1983) 149 CLR 639 (Aust HCt), 664–9 *per* Deane J:

[The case concerned a claim by a purchaser for an equitable lien over a partly completed pre-fabricated house to secure money paid by the purchaser as instalments of the purchase price. The vendor had agreed to construct the house on its premises and, when completed, to transport it to the purchaser's designated site and position it on block foundations. The vendor went into liquidation and was unable to complete the construction.]

'9. An equitable lien is a right against property which arises automatically by implication of equity to secure the discharge of an actual or potential indebtedness. . . . it does not depend upon possession and may, in general, be enforced in the same way as any other equitable charge, namely, by sale in pursuance of court order or, where the lien is over a fund, by an order for payment thereout. . . . While it arises by implication of some equitable doctrine applicable to the circumstances, its implication can be precluded or qualified by express or implied agreement of the parties. . . .

10. Generally speaking, the established examples of equitable lien are between parties in a contractual or quasi-contractual relationship. The best known are the liens which equity recognizes as arising to secure the actual or potential rights of a vendor and purchaser under a contract for the sale of real estate to payment of the balance of purchase price (vendor's lien) or to repayment of instalments of purchase price (purchaser's lien). . . .

11. One finds in some reported cases statements to the effect that an equitable lien can only arise under a contract of which equity would grant specific performance (see, e.g., *In re Bond Worth* (1980) Ch, at p 251). There is, however, no actual decision binding on

this [Australian High Court] which establishes that proposition and, in my view, it should not be accepted. The word "lien" is used somewhat imprecisely in the phrase "equitable lien" to describe not a negative right of retention of some legal or equitable interest but what is essentially a positive right to obtain, in certain circumstances, an order for the sale of the subject property or for actual payment from the subject fund. The peculiar and sometimes discretionary grounds for resisting a decree of specific performance are simply not appropriate to be indiscriminately applied as criteria of exclusion of an equitable interest in the nature of a lien. . . .

12. . . . .In the ordinary case of a purchaser who desires the actual performance of his contract with a defaulting vendor, an equitable lien to secure payment of instalments of purchase price is only of real value if specific performance of the contract would not be decreed. (at p665)

. . . .

15. . . . .It is adequate for present purposes that I identify what I consider to be the circumstances which are sufficient for the implication, independently of agreement, of an equitable lien between parties in a contractual relationship. Those circumstances have, to some extent, been indicated in what has been said above. They are: (i) that there be an actual or potential indebtedness on the part of the party who is the owner of the property to the other party arising from a payment or promise of payment either of consideration in relation to the acquisition of the property or of an expense incurred in relation to it (see *Middleton v. Magnay* (1864) 2 H & M, at p 237 (71 ER, at p 453) ; *Whitbread & Co. Ltd. v. Watt* (1901) 1 Ch 911 ; *Combe v. Lord Swaythling* (1947) Ch 625); (ii) that that property (or arguably property including that property: see Pollock, 'Re Wait', *Law Quarterly Review* (1927), vol. 43, p. 293) be specifically identified and appropriated to the performance of the contract (see per Lord Hanworth M.R., *In re Wait* (1927) 1 Ch [**[424]** above], at pp 622–625); and (iii) that the relationship between the actual or potential indebtedness and the identified and appropriated property be such that the owner would be acting unconscientiously or unfairly if he were to dispose of the property (or, if it be appropriate, more than a particular portion thereof) to a stranger without the consent of the other party or without the actual or potential liability having been discharged. It may be that the above circumstances or tests, particularly (i), would be unduly restrictive if propounded as a statement of exclusion. As has been said however, they are formulated as a statement of what is sufficient rather than what is essential. Whether or not they exist or are satisfied in a particular case should, like most questions involved in the application of equitable doctrines, be determined by reference to the substance of the transaction rather than its form: "the general principle of disregarding the letter for the substance" (*Jamshed Khodaram Irani v. Burjorji Dhunjibhai* (1915) LR 43 Ind App 26, at p 33 ; and see *Hurley v. Atchison, Topeka & Santa Fe Ry.* (1909) 213 US 126, at p 134 (53 Law Ed 729, at p 734) ; *Gage Lumber Co. v. McEldowney* (1913) 207 Fed Rep 255, at p 259). (at p669)

16. In the instant case, the company was the legal owner of the partly completed home. It was a potential debtor of the appellants in that, in the event that it repudiated the contract and the appellants accepted the repudiation, it would be liable to repay the deposit and the first instalment which the appellants had paid to it. That deposit and instalment were paid as part of the price of the work and materials necessary to construct the home and represented consideration in relation to the acquisition by the appellants of the home. The first of the above tests was therefore satisfied. The question whether the home in its partly completed state had been appropriated to the performance of the contract is considered below. Otherwise, the second test was satisfied in that, from the

time construction commenced, the home had been specifically identified as the home being built for the appellants. The relationship between the potential debt and the partly completed home was plain. The potential debt was the potential liability to repay the deposit and the instalment of purchase price which had been paid as the price of work and materials for the construction of that particular home and, in the case of the instalment, on the basis that that particular home had reached the stage where the roof had been pitched. In those circumstances, the company would, adapting the words of the third of the above tests, be acting unconscientiously and unfairly if it were to dispose of that partly completed home to another without the consent of the appellants and without, at the least, repaying to the appellants the money which it had received on the basis that that home would eventually be theirs. Subject to the question whether the partly completed home had been appropriated to the performance of the contract, the circumstances were such that an equitable lien arose in favour of the appellants. (at p669).'

Also see:

Capital Finance Co Ltd v Stokes [1969] 1 Ch 261.
London and Cheshire Insurance Co Ltd v Laplagrene Property Co Ltd [1971] Ch 499.

[526] S Worthington, *Proprietary Interests in Commercial Transactions* (1996, Clarendon: Oxford) pp 237–8, 240:
[Footnotes in the original are omitted.]

'9.3.5 Summary Incidence of Vendors' and Purchasers' Liens

The foregoing discussion presents a complicated picture of the incidence of vendors' and purchasers' liens. Although the analysis is more complicated than with equitable ownership interests, the existence of both types of interest is grounded in the maxim that equity regards as done that which ought to be done, no more and no less.

Applying this maxim, *purchasers' liens on the sale property* are relatively common: they exist whenever the purchaser has paid the price without receiving identified sale property. The sale contract need not be specifically enforceable and, if it is conditional, those conditions need not be satisfied before the lien arises. The lien does not ensure performance; it simply secures the return of the purchase price should performance fail. The mandatory personal obligation which gives rise to this security interest in equity is one imposed by both the common law and equity.

Vendors' liens on the sale property are less common. They arise once the vendor has transferred the sale property without receiving the price, but only if the contract of sale is specifically enforceable. Only then is it possible to subject the purchaser to an obligation to pay the price or return the property. Without such an obligation to deal with property, there is no foundation for the imposition of an equitable proprietary interest.

In contrast, it seems that *vendors' liens on the purchase fund* are non- existent. If the parties intend to restrict the purchaser's dealings with the nominated fund so that payment of the purchase price is secured, then the vendor will have a charge on the fund. This is an interest arising by agreement between the parties, not by operation of law. If the parties have a different reason for nominating the purchase fund, then there is no charge and, it seems, no basis for a lien to arise by operation of law: the agreement does not impose a mandatory obligation on the purchaser restricting the purchaser's dealings with the fund until the vendor's rights are satisfied. Without such an obligation, there is no basis for a lien.

Similarly with *purchasers' liens on the purchase fund*: they, too, appear to be non-existent. If the vendor is to be restricted in using the funds received from the purchaser, then those restrictions must be agreed by the parties. They will not be presumed. The purchaser can, perhaps, assert an *ownership* interest in the purchase funds, but that is quite a separate issue.

The ambit of these liens is defined by what equity considers *ought to* be done: the obligation imposed on one party is the source of the proprietary interest in the other. This obligation cannot be described fully without considering the particular circumstances surrounding the sale contract. Accordingly, all these general statements are subject to revision if the particular agreement between the parties alters equity's view of what ought to be done. This possibility is considered next.

. . .

9.5 Equitable Liens and Contracts for the Sale of Goods

The issue of equitable liens and contracts for the sale of goods deserves separate, but brief, attention. As the law stands, there seems to be no possibility of either the vendor or the purchaser asserting an equitable lien on goods contracted to be sold. This conclusion follows from acceptance of the *dictum* of Atkin LJ in *Re Wait* [**[424]** above], discussed earlier. It must be added, however, that there would be very little scope for the operation of such liens in any event.

If the sale property is not specifically identified, then clearly there can be no lien. On the other hand, if there is identified property, then legal title generally passes to the purchaser at the time of the contract. The purchaser, as legal owner, does not need the protection of a purchaser's lien; the seller in possession may be content simply to rely on the statutory possessory lien. This does leave unprotected the vendor who transfers the property without receiving the price. But even if a vendor's lien were possible, such a lien would only arise, on the analysis proposed here, if the sale contract were specifically enforceable. This is rarely the case with contracts for the sale of goods. These factors combine to account for the frequent resort to retention of title agreements.'

Questions:

1. These extracts suggest that equitable liens sometimes advance a party's interest in having a contract performed (eg a vendor's lien). At other times they effect an unwinding of the contract (eg a purchaser's lien). In either case, what determines whether a claimant will be successful in asserting rights under an equitable lien?
2. Can an equitable lien arise in non-contractual circumstances?
3. Is there any evident relationship between these cases on equitable liens and the cases dealing with constructive trusts which are considered in the next section (Section 5.8 below)?

5.8 Constructive trusts and agreements for the transfer of property

In Chapter 4 some consideration was given to constructive trusts which effect the transfer of equitable title to a purchaser in advance of the anticipated transfer of legal title to the property. Such constructive trusts are uncommon. They arise only when the underlying contract of sale is specifically enforceable and unconditional (see Sections 4.10–4.13). In addition, that chapter also discussed gifts. Certain promises to make gifts which are incompletely implemented at law may be regarded as complete in equity, so that the donee is regarded as the equitable owner of the gift (see Section 4.5–4.7). These constructive trusts, too, are relatively uncommon.

By contrast, at least in the context of family homes—although not, so far, in the context of personal property[27]—courts have been prepared to recognise the possibility of constructive trusts to enforce informal and often imprecise arrangements in respect of land which are unenforceable for want of writing. Moreover, in some of these cases it might be thought that the 'arrangement' between the parties is one constructed by the courts rather than by the parties themselves. This is a controversial and growing area of the law. Its treatment here is cursory, since all the cases to date concern real property. Nevertheless, there appears to be nothing in the reasoning adopted by the court which would deny its application to family property which is 'personal' rather than 'real'.[28] The following extracts indicate the approach adopted by the courts. The concern is to attempt to define the circumstances in which a court will impose an obligation on one party to transfer property to another, being an obligation which gives rise to an equitable proprietary interest in the intended recipient.

[527] *Lloyds Bank plc v Rosset* [1991] 1 AC 107 (HL), 129–34 *per* Lord Bridge (for the Court):

[A husband and wife purchased a semi-derelict property in the husband's name only (as demanded by the trustee of the husband's family trust in Switzerland). The wife made no financial contribution to either the purchase price of the property or the cost of its renovation, although she did do some of the renovation work herself and managed the site during the proceedings. She was unsuccessful in her claim to a proprietary interest in the house.]

> '[129] . . . Even if there had been the clearest oral agreement between Mr. and Mrs. Rosset that Mr. Rosset was to hold the property in trust for them both as tenants in common, this would, of course, have been ineffective since a valid declaration of trust by way of gift of a beneficial interest in land is required by section 53(1) of the Law of Property Act 1925 to be in writing. But if Mrs. Rosset had, as pleaded, altered her position in reliance on the agreement this could have given rise to an enforceable interest in her favour by way either of a constructive trust or of a proprietary estoppel.
>
> . . .

[27] Although see the further reading noted at the end of this section.

[28] Eg, pension or business investment assets.

[132] . . . The first and fundamental question which must always be resolved is whether, independently of any inference to be drawn from the conduct of the parties in the course of sharing the house as their home and managing their joint affairs, there has at any time prior to acquisition, or exceptionally at some later date, been any agreement, arrangement or understanding reached between them that the property is to be shared beneficially. The finding of an agreement or arrangement to share in this sense can only, I think, be based on evidence of express discussions between the partners, however imperfectly remembered and however imprecise their terms may have been. Once a finding to this effect is made it will only be necessary for the partner asserting a claim to a beneficial interest against the partner entitled to the legal estate to show that he or she has acted to his or her detriment or significantly altered his or her position in reliance on the agreement in order to give rise to a constructive trust or a proprietary estoppel.

In sharp contrast with this situation is the very different one where there is no evidence to support a finding of an agreement or arrangement to share, however reasonable it might have been for the parties to reach such an arrangement if they had applied their minds to the question, and where the court must rely entirely on the conduct of the parties both as the basis from which to infer a common intention to share the property beneficially and as the conduct relied on to give rise to a [133] constructive trust. In this situation direct contributions to the purchase price by the partner who is not the legal owner, whether initially or by payment of mortgage instalments, will readily justify the inference necessary to the creation of a constructive trust. But, as I read the authorities, it is at least extremely doubtful whether anything less will do.

The leading cases in your Lordships' House are *Pettitt v. Pettitt* [1970] A.C. 777 and *Gissing v. Gissing* [1971] A.C. 886. Both demonstrate situations in the second category to which I have referred and their Lordships discuss at great length the difficulties to which these situations give rise. The effect of these two decisions is very helpfully analysed in the judgment of Lord MacDermott L.C.J. in *McFarlane v. McFarlane* [1972] N.I. 59.

Outstanding examples on the other hand of cases giving rise to situations in the first category are *Eves v. Eves* [1975] 1 W.L.R. 1338 and *Grant v. Edwards* [1986] Ch. 638. In both these cases, where the parties who had cohabited were unmarried, the female partner had been clearly led by the male partner to believe, when they set up home together, that the property would belong to them jointly. In *Eves v. Eves* the male partner had told the female partner that the only reason why the property was to be acquired in his name alone was because she was under 21 and that, but for her age, he would have had the house put into their joint names. He admitted in evidence that this was simply an "excuse." Similarly in *Grant v. Edwards* the female partner was told by the male partner that the only reason for not acquiring the property in joint names was because she was involved in divorce proceedings and that, if the property were acquired jointly, this might operate to her prejudice in those proceedings. As Nourse L.J. put it, at p. 649:

> "Just as in *Eves v. Eves* [1975] 1 W.L.R. 1338, these facts appear to me to raise a clear inference that there was an understanding between the plaintiff and the defendant, or a common intention, that the plaintiff was to have some sort of proprietary interest in the house; otherwise no excuse for not putting her name on to the title would have been needed."

The subsequent conduct of the female partner in each of these cases, which the court rightly held sufficient to give rise to a constructive trust or proprietary estoppel supporting her claim to an interest in the property, fell far short of such conduct as would by itself have supported the claim in the absence of an express representation by the male partner that she was to have such an interest. It is significant to note that the share to which the female partners in *Eves v. Eves* and *Grant v. Edwards* were held entitled were one quarter and one half respectively. In no sense could these shares have been regarded as proportionate to what the judge in the instant case described as a "qualifying contribution" in terms of the indirect contributions to the acquisition or enhancement of the value of the houses made by the female partners.

I cannot help thinking that the judge in the instant case would not have fallen into error if he had kept clearly in mind the distinction between the effect of evidence on the one hand which was capable of [134] establishing an express agreement or an express representation that Mrs. Rosset was to have an interest in the property and evidence on the other hand of conduct alone as a basis for an inference of the necessary common intention.'

Questions:

1. Could this reasoning ever apply in the context of personal property? What preconditions would need to be met? Could these preconditions ever be met outside a domestic arrangement?
2. An unwritten agreement between the parties which purports to dispose of interests in real property does not satisfy the writing requirement of the Law of Property Act 1925 section 53 or the Law of Property (Miscellaneous Provisions) Act 1989 section 2. *Prima facie* such an agreement will not be enforced. Notwithstanding this, the judgment extracted above suggest that such agreements (whether express or implied from the surrounding circumstances) can be enforced in equity. Is the reasoning defensible? In determining enforceability, what significance, if any, attaches to contributions to the purchase price? Would the court have been on firmer ground in declining to enforce the purported agreement, but instead awarding a remedy which effected restitution for unjust enrichment (see Section 5.5 above, especially 5.5.1 and 5.5.3) or which implemented the doctrine of presumed (purchase money) resulting trusts (see Section 5.4 above)? Is either of these alternative approaches more in line with the sentiments expressed by Lord Greene in *Re Diplock* (see **[522]** above)?
3. Is it defensible to elide the principles of constructive trusts and proprietary estoppel (see Section 5.9 below) as Lord Bridge seems to in the first paragraph of this extract? Do the principles suggest identical outcomes on the same facts?
4. *Lloyds Bank plc v Rosset* (at **[527]** above) suggests that constructive trusts in the UK are underpinned by 'common intentions'. On the other hand, *Muschinski v Dodds* (at **[521]** above), indicates that in Australia they are underpinned by 'unconscionability'. In Canada, this role is played by 'unjust enrichment' principles (see *Pettkus v Becker* (1980) 117 DLR (3d) 257), and in New Zealand by 'reasonable expectations' (see *Gillies v Keogh* [1989] 2 NZLR 327). Do these different approaches suggest different outcomes? In particular, do certain approaches support enforcement of the collapsed arrangement and others the unwinding (or reversal) of it? Which is preferable?

Also see:

(i) UK: the cases cited by Lord Bridge in *Rosset* (ie *Pettitt v Pettitt* [1970] AC 777; *Gissing v Gissing* [1971] AC 886; *Eves v Eves* [1975] 1 WLR 1338; *Grant v Edwards* [1986] Ch 638.
(ii) Australia: *Muschinski v Dodds* (1985) 160 CLR 583, 612–17, 620 *per* Deane J at **[521]** above; *Baumgartner v Baumgartner* (1987) 164 CLR 137 (Aust HCt).
(iii) Canada: *Pettkus v Becker* (1980) 117 DLR (3d) 257).
(iv) New Zealand: *Gillies v Keogh* [1989] 2 NZLR 327

FURTHER READING:

There is an enormous literature in this area. Given the focus of this chapter, the following are good starting points:
G Moffat, *Trusts Law: Text and Materials* (2nd ed, 1999, Butterworths: London), ch 12.
S Gardner, 'Rethinking Family Property' (1993) 109 *LQR* 263.

FURTHER CASES:

Pallant v Morgan [1953] Ch 43.
Banner Homes Group plc v Luff Developments Ltd, *The Times*, 17 February 2000 (CA).
Are these cases also based upon on the principles described above, or upon some wider (or narrower) doctrine?

5.9 Proprietary estoppel

As in the previous section, the concern here is with situations where an orthodox approach would find no obligations imposed on the parties by virtue of contract, tort or unjust enrichment which could give rise to proprietary interests. Nevertheless, in some of these situations the courts somehow construe the facts to find such an interest, asserting reliance on 'the doctrine of proprietary estoppel'. The circumstances in which courts are prepared to do this are tightly circumscribed—proprietary estoppel provides a limited exception to the general rule (see **[528]** below).

The doctrine of proprietary estoppel[29] applies in two related circumstances, both premised on one party expending money to improve another's property in the expectation of receiving some reciprocal benefit by way of an interest in the property. If (and only if) it would be unconscionable for the owner to deny the expected benefit to the improver, then proprietary estoppel will operate to give the improver

[29] Proprietary estoppel is now regarded merely as a particular example of equitable estoppel: *Amalgamated Investment & Property Co Ltd v Texas Commerce International Bank Ltd* [1982] QB 84 (CA), 103 *per* Robert Goff J, and 109 *per* Goff LJ; *Crabb v Arun District Council* [1976] Ch 179 (CA) [**[530]** below], 193. Here, however, the focus is exclusively on proprietary consequences, and the description of the circumstances in which an estoppel arises relate exclusively to proprietary estoppel.

a remedy. In one class of cases, the expectation of benefit is encouraged by express representations made by the owner[30]; in the other class of cases, the owner simply stands by in the knowledge that the improver is mistaken about his or her legal rights to the subject property.[31] The representation or expectation may be of fact or intention, but it must relate to the subject property. Moreover, there need not be any pre-existing relationship or contract between the parties. Earlier cases suggested that the claimant's equity in the first class of case was to have the representation made good (much like specific enforcement of a contract, although the facts were regarded as not sufficient to support the finding of a contract). In the second class of case the remedy was to strip the defendant of any unjust enrichment. However, more modern cases do not adhere to this classification, and these rules may now be seen simply as a *prima facie* guide to the relief which is merited.[32]

Most of the authorities on proprietary estoppel concern real property. It is still not clear that the doctrine applies to personal property, although both principle and authority[33] supports a wider application even though the facts may be less likely to arise in practice.

As noted earlier, the general rule is *against* proprietary estoppel, as the next extract indicates. It is important to remember this. Although the other cases extracted here deal with proprietary estoppel, they represent the exception, not the rule.

[528] *Falcke v Scottish Imperial Insurance Co* (1886) 36 Ch D 243 (CA), 248 *per* Bowen LJ:

> 'The general principle is, beyond all question, that work and labour done or money expended by one man to preserve or benefit the property of another do not according to English law create any lien upon the property saved or benefited, nor, even if standing alone, create any obligation to repay the expenditure. Liabilities are not to be forced upon people behind their backs any more than you can confer a benefit upon a man against his will.'

[529] *Ramsden v Dyson* (1865) LR 1 HL 129, 170–1 *per* Lord Kingsdown (dissenting on the facts):

[The case concerned a tenant from year to year who built on the tenanted land, allegedly in the expectation that a long lease would be forthcoming. The tenant was given no interest in the land.]

> 'The rule of law applicable to the case appears to me to be this: If a man, under a verbal agreement with a landlord for a certain interest in land, or, what amounts to the same thing, under an expectation, created or encouraged by the landlord, that he shall have a certain interest, takes possession of such land, with the consent of the landlord,

[30] *Dillwyn v Llewelyn* (1862) 4 De GF & J 517, [1861–73] All ER Rep 384 (see the note following *Ramsden v Dyson* (1865) LR 1 HL 129, at **[529]** below).

[31] *Ramsden v Dyson* (1865) LR 1 HL 129, at **[529]** below, although, on the facts, the rule was not applied. So much were the two categories considered separate, that *Dillwyn v Llewelyn* was not cited in *Ramsden v Dyson*, even though Lord Westbury was involved in both cases.

[32] The doctrine of proprietary estoppel may give the representee either a personal remedy (so that the label, 'proprietary' estoppel, is somewhat misleading) or a proprietary interest in the subject property. Only the latter is of interest here.

[33] *Crabb v Arun District Council* [1976] Ch 179, 187 [**[530]** below]; *Olsson v Dyson* (1969) 120 CLR 365 (Aust HCt) [**[408]** above], but cf *Western Fish Products v Penwith District Council* [1981] 2 All ER 204, 218.

> and upon the faith of such promise or expectation, with the knowledge of the landlord, and without objection by him, lays out money upon the land, a Court of equity will compel the landlord to give effect to such promise or expectation.
>
> . . . .
>
> . . . . [The relief would be] either in the form of a specific interest in the land, or in the shape of compensation for the expenditure, . . . and protect[ion] in the meantime [of] the possession of the tenant.
>
> If, on the other hand, a tenant being in possession of land, and knowing the nature and extent of his interest, lays out money upon it in the hope or expectation of an extended term or an allowance for expenditure, then, if such hope or expectation has not been created or encouraged by the landlord, the tenant has no claim which any Court of law or equity can enforce. . . .'
>
> The whole question, I think, in this case, is, within which class does the present claim fall; a point which, of course, depends entirely on the effect of the evidence. The evidence, in my opinion, shews that it falls under the former.'

Also see:

Dillwyn v Llewelyn (1862) 4 De GF & J 517, [1861–73] All ER Rep 384. This was a case where a father promised to make a gift of a farm to his son. The father had not put anything in writing, so he had certainly not done 'all that the donor was required to do' to make the gift effective in equity. Nevertheless, the court enforced the promise. It seems the court did this because the son had detrimentally relied on the father's assurance, and it would be unconscionable for the father to go back on his word. Although this is the conventional assessment of the case, a closer examination of the judgments renders the inference of compulsory gift-giving less certain. It is not clear whether the decision rests on an analogy with part performance and the enforcement of unenforceable contracts (unenforceable for lack of writing), or on some equity to perfect an imperfect gift, or on a separate doctrine which was inherent in the estoppel cases cited to the court. Lord Westbury (at p 521) said, 'I cannot doubt that the donee acquires a right from the subsequent transaction to call on the donor to perform that contract and complete the imperfect donation which was made. The case is somewhat analogous to [part performance].'

Questions:

> Do the above cases suggest that the doctrine of proprietary estoppel is an independent equitable doctrine, or do they suggest that equity is somehow modifying the law of contract (or the law of gifts)? Does the independence (or otherwise) of the doctrine have any implications for the remedy which ought to be awarded on given facts?

[530] *Crabb v Arun District Council* [1976] Ch 179, 187–8 *per* Lord Denning MR: [Council workers assured Mr Crabb that the council would grant him a right of way over their land. They had no authority to make such assurances, but both parties acted as though these intentions would be carried out. In particular, Mr Crabb sold part of his land without retaining a right of way over it, on the assumption that he would have a right of way over the council land. When the council subsequently declined to give him a right of way, his land was land-locked. The council did not know about his earlier sale (ie it was not aware of his detrimental reliance), but it was nevertheless ordered, by injunction, to make its representations good.]

> 'The basis of this proprietary estoppel—as indeed of promissory estoppel—is the interposition of equity. Equity comes in, true to form, to mitigate the rigours of strict law. The early cases did not speak of it as "estoppel." They spoke of it as "raising an equity." If I may expand what Lord Cairns L.C. said in *Hughes v. Metropolitan Railway Co.* (1877) 2 App.Cas. 439, 448: "it is the first principle upon which all courts of equity proceed," that it will prevent a person from insisting on his strict legal rights—whether arising under a contract, or on his title deeds, or by statute—when it would be inequitable for him to do so having regard to the dealings which have taken place between the parties.
>
> What then are the dealings which will preclude him from insisting on his strict legal rights? If he makes a binding contract that he will not insist on the strict legal position, a court of equity will hold him to his contract. Short of a binding contract, if he makes a promise that he will not insist upon his strict legal rights—then, even though that promise may be unenforceable in point of law for want of consideration or want of writing—then, if he makes the promise knowing or intending that the other will act upon it, and he does act upon it, then again a court of equity will not allow him to go back on that promise: see *Central London Property Trust Ltd. v. High Trees House Ltd.* [1947] K.B. 130 and *Charles Rickards Ltd. v. Oppenhaim* [1950] 1 K.B. 616, 623. Short of an actual promise, if he, by his words or conduct, so behaves as to lead another to believe that he will not insist on his strict legal rights—knowing or intending that the other will act on that belief—and he does so act, that again will raise an equity in favour of the other; and it is for a court of equity to say in what way the equity may be satisfied. The cases show that this equity does not depend on agreement but on words or conduct. In *Ramsden v. Dyson* (1866) L.R. 1 H.L. 129, 170 Lord Kingsdown spoke of a verbal agreement "or what amounts to the same thing, an expectation, created or encouraged." In *Birmingham and District Land Co. v. London and North Western Railway Co.* (1888) 40 Ch.D. 268, 277, Cotton L.J. said that ". . . what passed did not make a new agreement, but . . . what took place . . . raised an equity against him." And it was the Privy Council in *Plimmer v. Wellington Corporation* (1884) 9 App.Cas. 699, 713–714 who said that ". . . the court must look at the circumstances in each case to decide in what way the equity can be satisfied" giving instances.'

[531] ***Re Basham (dec'd)*** **[1986] 1 WLR 1498, 1503–4** ***per*** **Mr Edward Nudgee QC:** [The facts are irrelevant.]

> 'I turn then to the law. The plaintiff relies on proprietary estoppel, the principle of which, in its broadest form, may be stated as follows: where one person, A, has acted to his detriment on the faith of a belief, which was known to and encouraged by another person, B, that he either has or is going to be given a right in or over B's property, B cannot insist on his strict legal rights if to do so would be inconsistent with A's belief. The principle is commonly known as proprietary estoppel, and since the effect of it is that B is prevented from asserting his strict legal rights it has something in common with estoppel. But in my judgment, at all events where the belief is that A is going to be given a right in the future, it is properly to be regarded as giving rise to a species of constructive trust, which is the concept employed by a court of equity to prevent a person from relying on his legal rights where it would be unconscionable for him to do so. The rights

to which proprietary estoppel gives rise, and the machinery by which effect is given to them, are similar in many respects to those involved in cases of secret trusts, mutual wills and other comparable cases in which property is vested in B on the faith of an understanding that it will be dealt with in a particular manner, of which Nourse J. said in *In re Cleaver, decd.* [1981] 1 WLR 939, 947:

> "The principle of all these cases is that a court of equity will not permit a person to whom property is transferred by way of gift, but on the faith of an agreement or clear understanding that it is to be dealt with in a particular way for the benefit of a third person, to deal with that property inconsistently with that agreement or understanding. If he attempts to do so after having received the benefit of the gift equity will intervene by imposing a constructive trust on the property which is the subject matter of the agreement or understanding."

The factor which gives rise to the equitable obligation in the cases to which Nourse J. referred is B's receipt of the property on the faith of an understanding. In cases of proprietary estoppel the factor which gives rise to the equitable obligation is A's alteration of his position on the faith of a similar understanding. A third situation in which the court imposes a constructive trust is where A and B set up house together in a property which is in the name of B alone, and A establishes a common intention between A and B, acted on by A to his (or more usually her) detriment, that A should have a beneficial interest in the property: see the statements of principle by Nourse LJ and Browne-Wilkinson V.-C. in *Grant v. Edwards* [1986] 3 WLR 114. Here too, if the two elements of common understanding or intention and detrimental acts on the part of A are established, they give rise to an equitable obligation enforceable against B which is in the nature of a constructive trust. A common theme can be discerned in each of these classes of case; and although different situations may give rise to differences of detail in the manner in which the court will give effect to the equity which arises in favour of A, one would expect the general principles applicable in the different situations to be the same unless there is a sound reason to the contrary.'

Note:

This assessment of the law has been criticised as providing too generous and general a statement of the rules: see *Taylor v Dickens* [1998] 1 FLR 806.

Also see:

Giumelli v Giumelli (2000) 196 CLR 101 (Aust HCt) (the remedy was not enforcement of the representation, but an equitable lien on the property to secure repayment of the wasted expenditure incurred in reliance on the representation).

Olsson v Dyson (1969) 120 CLR 365 (Aust HCt) (at **[408]** above).

FURTHER READING:

R Smith, 'How Proprietary is Proprietary Estoppel?' in F Rose (ed), *Consensus ad Idem* (1996, Clarendon: Oxford) 235.

A Robertson, 'Reliance and Expectation in Estoppel Remedies' (1998) 18 *Legal Studies* 360.
S Gardner, 'The Remedial Discretion in Proprietary Estoppel' (1999) 115 *LQR* 438.

Questions:

1. What is the justification for a proprietary response, rather than a personal one, in these equitable estoppel cases? Does the claimant deserve to be better protected than the defendant's general creditors should the defendant become insolvent?
2. What is the justification for enforcing the representation or expectation rather than restricting the claimant to a claim for recovery of wasted expenditure? (See *Giumelli v Giumelli* (2000) 196 CLR 101 (Aust HCt) for an example of the latter approach.)
3. How, if at all, does the doctrine of proprietary estoppel differ from the principles of constructive trusts that were considered in Section 5.8 above?
4. What reasons favour generalising the basis of equitable intervention in the way that Mr Edward Nudgee QC does (in *Re Basham (dec'd)*, **[531]** above), and what reasons tell against it?
5. If the generalised approach were adopted, would it be better to see all of these cases concerning constructive trusts and equitable estoppel as cases where equity modifies the rigours of the common law in its approach to contract and unjust enrichment, or do these cases suggest that equity is imposing *sui generis* obligations on defendants?

5.10 Constructive trusts arising on breach of obligation

So far the discussion of constructive trusts (and equitable liens) has focused on proprietary interests which arise by operation of law to reflect some agreement or arrangement between the parties or, alternatively, to reflect the need to effect restitution for unjust enrichment when the agreement or arrangement between the parties breaks down or was never effectively constituted. This section considers a further possibility. Constructive trusts (and equitable liens) may also arise to remedy the breach of an obligation owed by the defendant to the claimant.

This possibility is subject to one significant limitation. Any proprietary interest must relate to an identified asset. For a proprietary interest to arise by operation of law, there must be an obligation imposed on the defendant to transfer an identified asset to the claimant (or otherwise deal with the asset for the benefit of the claimant). In the context of a breach of the defendant's obligations, this will only ever be the case if the remedy for the breach obliges the defendant to transfer a specific asset to the claimant (or otherwise deal with the asset for the benefit of the claimant). An award of expectation damages for breach of contractual obligations, or compensatory damages for breach of tort obligations, is not of this form: there is no identified fund of money representing the damages which must be paid over to the claimant. It follows that these damages claims can never have proprietary consequences. On the other hand, if the remedy is to pay over profits derived from the defendant's breach of obligation, the answer may be different. The profits may constitute an identified fund and, if the obligation is to pay over this fund *in specie*, then the remedy will be proprietary. Equity, considering as done that which ought to be done, will consider the claimant to be the owner in equity of the fund. The defendant will hold the fund on constructive trust for the claimant.

The two difficulties which bedevil this analysis are, first, when will breach of an obligation give rise to a remedy requiring disgorgement of the profits (rather than expectation or compensatory damages)? Secondly, even if the remedy is disgorgement, is this remedy properly characterised as an obligation to pay over the profits *themselves* (ie *in specie*, so that proprietary consequences are possible) or only to pay over the *value* of those profits (so that the remedy is personal)? Both issues are controversial, and the controversy has both doctrinal and policy aspects. The extracts below and the further reading indicate the scope of the debate.

5.10.1 Constructive trusts which arise on breach of fiduciary obligations

A fiduciary obligation requires one party (the fiduciary) to act in the interests of another party (the principal, or the beneficiary of the fiduciary obligation) rather than in the fiduciary's own interests. In imposing this requirement, the law is effectively demanding self-denial of the fiduciary: where there is a choice, the fiduciary must favour the principal's interests over those of the fiduciary. The situations in which it would be appropriate for the law to demand this form of disinterested altruism, and to impose legal sanctions to ensure compliance, are limited. The classic situation attracting this response is the relationship between trustee and beneficiary—that relationship is fiduciary. So too is the relationship between a director and the company being managed, and between the several partners in a partnership. These situations are often termed 'status-based' fiduciary relationships. The fiduciary obligation is imposed because of the form of the relationship. 'Fact-based' fiduciary relationships are also possible. Sometimes the particular facts of the relationship between two parties are seen as sufficient to warrant imposing on one party fiduciary obligations in respect of the other. When this should be so is controversial, but it is not the concern of this discussion.[34] This discussion is concerned solely with the remedies—the proprietary remedies—which may arise upon breach of an established fiduciary obligation.

Fiduciary obligations are commonly said to comprise two distinct but overlapping rules. The first, the 'conflict of duty and interest rule', prohibits fiduciaries from favouring their own interests where they conflict with the duties owed to their principal. The second, the 'no secret profit rule', prohibits fiduciaries from making secret profits from their positions. If breach of either of these rules results in a

[34] See, eg, J C Shepherd, 'Towards a Unified Concept of Fiduciary Relationships' (1981) 97 *LQR* 51; S Worthington, 'Fiduciaries: When is Self-Denial Obligatory?' [1999] *CLJ* 500, and the references cited there.

benefit to the fiduciary, then the principal can demand, as a remedy, either an account of the profits made from the breach or a constructive trust of those profits.[35] The first is a personal remedy; the second is proprietary. The issue for this section is whether the choice between the personal and the proprietary remedy is one for the principal, or whether the law discriminates between different fiduciary breaches so that only certain breaches give rise to proprietary remedies.

The cases in this area often contain detailed consideration of whether the relationship between the parties is fiduciary, and whether, if it is, the facts suggest that the fiduciary obligation has been breached. These are interesting and difficult issues, but not of primary concern here. The extracts below concentrate on the *form* of the remedy which the courts award once they are satisfied that an established fiduciary obligation has been breached.

[532] *Boardman v Phipps* [1967] 2 AC 46 (HL), 100–4 *per* Lord Cohen, 105–11 *per* Lord Hodson, 115–17 *per* Lord Guest, 123–9 *per* Lord Upjohn (dissenting):
[The respondent, John Phipps, was a residuary legatee under the fully administered will of his father. The appellants were Boardman, the solicitor to the trustees of the will, and Thomas Phipps, a beneficiary. The appellants had made a successful takeover bid for a company in which the trustees held a minority shareholding. Before the takeover the appellants had, as representatives of the trust, acquired information which enabled them to realise the opportunities which might be gained from effective reorganisation of the company. After the takeover, this reorganisation was implemented and the shareholders, including the trust and the appellants personally, received substantial distributions.

John Phipps alleged that the appellants' acquisition of the shares and the consequential dividends was in breach of their fiduciary obligations and that, because of this, they held the shares on constructive trust for the family trust and had to account for the profits (in the form of distributions) acquired as a result of the shareholding. The House of Lords agreed. This finding was made notwithstanding that the trust had benefited from the breach; that the trust itself could not have acquired the benefit[36]; and that the appellants had acted in good faith throughout.[37]]

Lord Cohen:
'[100] In the case before your Lordships it seems to me clear that the appellants throughout were obtaining information from the company . . . but it does not necessarily follow that the appellants were thereby debarred from acquiring shares in the company for themselves. They were bound to give the information to the trustees but they could not exclude it from their own minds. . . . . [T]he mere use of any knowledge or opportunity which comes to the trustee or agent in the course of his trusteeship or agency does not necessarily make him liable to account. In the present case had the company been a

[35] And this is true even if the fiduciary acted in good faith, and even though the principal would never have obtained the benefit in the absence of a breach by the fiduciary.

[36] The will establishing the trust was drafted so that acquisition of further shares in the company would have been an unauthorised investment which would have required the sanction of the court. In any event, the trustees did not want to acquire further shares, and any decision to do so would have to have been unanimous.

[37] Although technically they had neither made full disclosure to the trust beneficiaries, nor obtained the informed consent of all the trustees to their proposals.

public company and had the appellants bought the shares on the market, they would not, I think, have been accountable. But the company is a private company and not only the information but the opportunity to purchase these shares came to them through [their fiduciary roles]. . . .

. . . .

Wilberforce J. and, in the Court of Appeal, both Lord Denning M.R. and Pearson L.J. based their decision in favour of the respondent on the decision of your Lordships' House in *Regal (Hastings) Ltd. v. Gulliver* ([1967] 2 AC 134). I turn, therefore, to consider that case. Mr. Walton relied upon a number of passages in the judgments of the learned Lords who heard the appeal: in particular on (1) a passage in the speech of Lord Russell of Killowen where he says (at p 144G-145A):

> "The rule of equity which insists on those, who by use of a fiduciary position make a profit, being liable to account for that profit, in no way depends on fraud, or absence of bona fides, or upon such questions or considerations as whether the profit would or should otherwise have gone to the plaintiff, or whether the profiteer was under a duty to obtain the source of the profit for the plaintiff, or whether he took a risk or acted as he did for the benefit of the plaintiff, or whether the plaintiff has in fact been damaged or benefited by his action. The liability arises from the mere fact of a profit having, in the stated circumstances, been made."

(2) a passage in the speech of Lord Wright, where he says (at p 154B-C):

> "That question can be briefly stated to be whether an agent, a director, a trustee or other person in an analogous fiduciary position, when a demand is made upon him by the person to whom he stands in the fiduciary relationship to account for profits acquired by him by reason of his fiduciary position, and by reason of the opportunity and the knowledge, or either, resulting from it, is entitled to defeat the claim upon any ground save that he made profits with the knowledge and assent of the other person. The most usual [102] and typical case of this nature is that of principal and agent. The rule in such cases is compendiously expressed to be that an agent must account for net profits secretly (that is, without the knowledge of his principal) acquired by him in the course of his agency. The authorities show how manifold and various are the applications of the rule. It does not depend on fraud or corruption."

. . . [Here] . . . the appellants obtained both the information which satisfied them that the purchase of the shares would be a good investment and the opportunity of acquiring them as a result of acting for certain purposes on behalf of the trustees. Information is, of course, not property in the strict sense of that word and, as I have already stated, it does not necessarily follow that because an agent acquired information and opportunity while acting in a fiduciary capacity he is accountable to his principals for any profit that comes his way as the [103] result of the use he makes of that information and opportunity. His liability to account must depend on the facts of the case. . . .

[Lord Cohen concluded on the facts that liability did arise.]

. . . .

That is enough to dispose of the case but I would add that an agent is, in my opinion, liable to account for profits he makes out of trust property if there is a possibility of conflict between his interest and his duty to his principal. Mr. Boardman and Tom Phipps were not general agents of the trustees but they were their agents for certain limited purposes. The information they had obtained and the opportunity to purchase the 21,986 shares afforded them by their relations with the directors of the company—an opportunity they got as the result of their introduction to the directors by Mr. Fox—were not property in the strict sense but that information and that opportunity they owed to their representing themselves as agents for the holders of the 8,000 shares held by the trustees. In these circumstances they could not, I think, use that information and that opportunity to purchase the shares for themselves if there was any possibility that the trustees might wish to acquire them for the trust. Mr. Boardman was the solicitor whom the trustees were in the habit of consulting if they wanted legal advice. Granted that he would not be bound to advise on any point unless he is consulted, he would still be the person they would consult if they wanted advice . . . in my opinion, Mr. Boardman would not have been able to give unprejudiced advice if he had been consulted by the trustees and was at the same time negotiating for the purchase of the shares [104] on behalf of himself and Tom Phipps. In other words, there was, in my opinion, at the crucial date (March, 1959), a possibility of a conflict between his interest and his duty.'

[Accordingly, Lord Cohen also found the appellants liable on the basis of a breach of the conflict of duty and interest rule.]

Lord Hodson:

'[105] The proposition of law involved in this case is that no person standing in a fiduciary position, when a demand is made upon him by the person to whom he stands in the fiduciary relationship to account for profits acquired by him by reason of his fiduciary position and by reason of the opportunity and the knowledge, or either, resulting from it, is entitled to defeat the claim upon any ground save that he made profits with the knowledge and assent of the other person.

I take the above proposition from the opening words of the speech of Lord Wright in *Regal (Hastings) Ltd. v. Gulliver* where he states the proposition in the form of the question which he answered as had all the members of your Lordships' House in such a way as to affirm the proposition.

It is obviously of importance to maintain the proposition in all cases and to do nothing to whittle away its scope or the absolute responsibility which it imposes.

. . . .

[107] As to this it is said on behalf of the appellants that information as such is not necessarily property and it is only trust property which is relevant. I agree, but it is nothing to the point to say that in these times corporate trustees, e.g., the Public Trustee and others, necessarily acquire a mass of information in their capacity of trustees for a particular trust and cannot be held liable to account if knowledge so acquired enables them to operate to their own advantage, or to that of other trusts. Each case must depend on its own facts and I dissent from the view that information is of its nature something which is not properly to be described as property. We are aware that what is called "know-how" in the commercial sense is property which may be very valuable as an asset. I agree with the learned judge and with the Court of Appeal that the confidential information acquired in this case which was capable of being and was turned to account can be properly regarded as the property of the trust. It was obtained by Mr. Boardman by reason of the opportunity which he was given as solicitor acting for the trustees in the negotiations with the chairman of the company, as the correspondence demonstrates. The end result was that out of the special position in which they were standing in the course of the negotiations the appellants got the opportunity to make a profit and the knowledge that it was there to be made.

. . .

[110] The confidential information which the appellants obtained at a time when Mr. Boardman was admittedly holding himself out as solicitor for the trustees was obtained by him as representing the trustees, the holders of 8,000 shares of Lester & Harris. As Russell L.J. put it ([1965] Ch. 992, 1031):

> "The substantial trust share holding was an asset of which one aspect was its potential use as a means of acquiring knowledge of the company's affairs, or of negotiating allocations of the company's assets, or of inducing other shareholders to part with their shares."

[111] Whether this aspect is properly to be regarded as part of the trust assets is, in my judgment, immaterial. The appellants obtained knowledge by reason of their fiduciary position and they cannot escape liability by saying that they were acting for themselves and not as agents of the trustees. Whether or not the trust or the beneficiaries in their stead could have taken advantage of the information is immaterial, as the authorities clearly show. No doubt it was but a remote possibility that Mr. Boardman would ever be asked by the trustees to advise on the desirability of an application to the court in order that the trustees might avail themselves of the information obtained. Nevertheless, even if the possibility of conflict is present between personal interest and the fiduciary position the rule of equity must be applied. . . .'

Lord Guest:
'[115] I do not for one moment suggest that there was anything dishonest or underhand in what Boardman did. He has obtained a clean certificate below and I do not wish to sully it. But the law has a strict regard for principle in ensuring that a person in a fiduciary capacity is not allowed to benefit from any transactions into which he has entered with trust property. If Boardman was acting on behalf of the trust, then all the information he obtained . . . became trust property. The weapon which he used to obtain this information was the trust holding. And I see no reason why information and knowledge cannot be trust property. . . .

The position of a person in a fiduciary capacity is referred to in *Regal (Hastings) Ltd. v. Gulliver* by Lord Russell of Killowen ([1967] 2 AC 134, 144A-145B) where he said:

> "My Lords, with all respect I think there is a misapprehension here. The rule of equity which insists on those, who by use of a fiduciary position make a profit. being liable to account for that profit, in no way depends on fraud, or absence of bona fides; or upon such questions or considerations as whether the profit would or should otherwise have gone to the plaintiff, or whether the profiteer was under a duty to obtain the source of the profit for the plaintiff, or whether he took a risk or acted as he did for the benefit of the plaintiff, or whether the plaintiff has in fact been damaged or benefited by his action. The liability arises from the mere fact of a profit having, in the stated circumstances, been made. The profiteer, however honest and well-intentioned, cannot escape the risk of being called upon to account."

. . . .

[117] Applying these principles to the present case I have no hesitation in coming to the conclusion that the appellants hold the Lester & Harris shares as constructive trustees and are bound to account to the respondent.'

Lord Upjohn (dissenting):
'[123] In these circumstances the respondent rather surprisingly seeks to hold the appellants accountable to him for his 5/18ths share of the 21,986 shares so purchased, on the footing that the appellants are constructive trustees of these shares for and on behalf of

the trust. So I turn to the relevant law upon which this claim is based, but start by stating what is not in dispute, that the conduct of the appellants and each of them has never been anything except utterly honest and above board in every way. If they or either of them are accountable it is because of the operation of some harsh doctrine of equity upon consciences completely innocent in every way.

Rules of equity have to be applied to such a great diversity of circumstances that they can be stated only in the most general terms and applied with particular attention to the exact circumstances of each case. The relevant rule for the decision of this case is the fundamental rule of equity that a person in a fiduciary capacity must not make a profit out of his trust which is part of the wider rule that a trustee must not place himself in a position where his duty and his interest may conflict. I believe the rule is best stated in *Bray v. Ford* ([1896] AC 44, 51) by Lord Herschell, who plainly recognised its limitations:

> "It is an inflexible rule of a Court of Equity that a person in a fiduciary position, such as the respondent's, is not, unless otherwise expressly provided, entitled to make a profit; he is not allowed to put himself in a position where his interest and duty conflict. It does not appear to me that this rule is, as has been said, founded upon principles of morality. I regard it rather as based on the consideration that, human nature being what it is, there is danger, in such circumstances, of the person holding a fiduciary position being swayed by interest rather than by duty, and thus prejudicing those whom he was bound to protect. It has, therefore, been deemed expedient to lay down this positive rule. But I am satisfied that it might be departed from in many cases, without any breach of morality, without any wrong being inflicted, and without any consciousness of wrong-doing. Indeed, it is obvious that it might sometimes be to the advantage of the beneficiaries that their trustee should act for them professionally rather than a stranger, even though the trustee were paid for his services."

[124] It is perhaps stated most highly against trustees or directors in the celebrated speech of Lord Cranworth L.C. in *Aberdeen Railway v. Blaikie* (1 Macq. 461, 471), where he said:

> "And it is a rule of universal application, that no one, having such duties to discharge, shall be allowed to enter into engagements in which he has, or can have, a personal interest conflicting, or which possibly may conflict, with the interests of those whom he is bound to protect."

The phrase "possibly may conflict" requires consideration. In my view it means that the reasonable man looking at the relevant facts and circumstances of the particular case would think that there was a real sensible possibility of conflict; not that you could imagine some situation arising which might, in some conceivable possibility in events not contemplated as real sensible possibilities by any reasonable person, result in a conflict.

Your Lordships were referred at length to the decision of this House in *Regal (Hastings) Ltd. v. Gulliver* ([1967] 2 AC 134). That is a helpful case for its restatement of the well-known principles but the case itself bears no relation to the one before your Lordships. The facts were very different and I summarise them from the opinion of Lord Russell of Killowen (at p 140). The plaintiff company (Regal), the owner of a cinema, was contemplating the purchase of the leases of two other cinemas which were to be transferred to a subsidiary company formed by Regal called Amalgamated. Concurrently Regal was contemplating the sale of all three cinemas to a third party. The intention of the directors was that Regal should subscribe for shares in Amalgamated and then Regal would sell those shares to the third party. There was some trouble over providing a guarantee; the transaction was changed so that the directors of Regal subscribed for shares in Amalgamated instead of Regal itself and then those directors sold those shares to the third party, thereby making an immediate and handsome profit of £2 16s 1d per share. That was an obvious case where duty of the director and his interest conflicted. The scheme had been that Regal would make the profit, in fact its directors did. It was a clear case and does not really assist in the present case. It had long been settled in *Keech v. Sandford* (Sel.Cas.Ch. 61) that the inability of a beneficiary to obtain the renewal of a lease which was trust property and a renewal of which has always been considered to be [125] trust property did not permit the purchase of that property by the trustee himself. That bears no relation to this case. This case, if I may emphasise it again, is one concerned not with trust property or with property which the persons to whom the fiduciary duty was owed were contemplating a purchase but in contrast to the facts in *Regal* with property which was not trust property nor property which was ever contemplated as the subject-matter of a possible purchase by the trust.

. . . .

[127] This analysis [of fiduciary liability] requires detailed consideration:

1. The facts and circumstances must be carefully examined to see whether in fact a purported agent and even a confidential agent is in a fiduciary relationship to his principal. It does not necessarily follow that he is in such a position (see *In re Coomber* ([1911] 1 Ch 723, CA).
2. Once it is established that there is such a relationship, that relationship must be examined to see what duties are thereby imposed upon the agent, to see what is the scope and ambit of the duties charged upon him.
3. Having defined the scope of those duties one must see whether he has committed some breach thereof and by placing himself within the scope and ambit of those duties in a position where his duty and interest may possibly conflict. It is only at this stage that any question of accountability arises.
4. Finally, having established accountability it only goes so far as to render the agent accountable for profits made within the scope and ambit of his duty.

Before applying these principles to the facts, however, I shall refer to the judgment of Russell L.J., which proceeded on a rather different basis. He said ([1965] Ch. 992, 1031):

> "The substantial trust share holding was an asset of which one aspect was its potential use as a means of acquiring knowledge of the company's affairs, or of negotiating allocations of the company's assets, or of inducing other shareholders to part with their shares. That aspect was part of the trust assets."

My Lords, I regard that proposition as untenable.

In general, information is not property at all. It is normally open to all who have eyes to read and ears to hear. The true test is to determine in what circumstances the information has been acquired. If it has been acquired in such circumstances that it would be a breach of confidence to disclose it to another then courts of equity will restrain the recipient from communicating it to another. In such cases such confidential information is often and for many years has been described as the property of the donor, the books of authority are full of such references; knowledge of secret processes, "know-how," confidential information as to the prospects of a company or of someone's intention or the [128] expected results of some horse race based on stable or other confidential information. But in the end the real truth is that it is not property in any normal sense but equity will restrain its transmission to another if in breach of some confidential relationship.

With all respect to the views of Russell L.J. I protest at the idea that information acquired by trustees in the course of their duties as such is necessarily part of the assets of the trust which cannot be used by the trustees except for benefit of the trust. Russell L.J. referred to the fact that two out of three of the trustees could have no authority to turn over this aspect of trust property to the appellants except for the benefit of the trust; this I do not understand, for if such information is trust property not all the trustees acting together could do it for they cannot give away trust property.

. . . .

There is, in my view, and I know of no authority to the contrary, no general rule that information learnt by a trustee during the course of his duties is property of the trust and cannot be used by him. If that were to be the rule it would put the Public Trustee and other corporate trustees out of business and make it difficult for private trustees to be trustees of more than one trust. This would be the greatest possible pity for corporate trustees and others may have much information which they may initially acquire in connection with some particular trust but without prejudice to that trust can make it readily available to other trusts to the great advantage of those other trusts.

The real rule is, in my view, that knowledge learnt by a trustee in the course of his duties as such is not in the least property of [129] the trust and in general may be used by him for his own benefit or for the benefit of other trusts unless it is confidential information which is given to him (1) in circumstances which, regardless of his position as a trustee, would make it a breach of confidence for him to communicate to anyone for it has been given to him expressly or impliedly as confidential, or (2) in a fiduciary capacity, and its use would place him in a position where his duty and his interest might possibly conflict. Let me give one or two simple examples. A, as trustee of two settlements X and Y holding shares in the same small company, learns facts as trustee of X about the company which are encouraging. In the absence of special circumstances (such, for example, that X wants to buy more shares) I can see nothing whatever which would make it improper for him to tell his co-trustees of Y who feel inclined to sell that he has information that this would be a bad thing to do. Another example: A as trustee of X learns facts that make him and his co-trustees want to sell. Clearly he could not communicate this knowledge to his co-trustees of Y until at all events the holdings of X have been sold for there would be a plain conflict, reflected in the prices that might or might possibly be obtained.

My Lords, I do not think for one moment that Lord Brougham in *Hamilton v. Wright* (9 Cl. & F. 111, 124), quoted in the speech of my noble and learned friend Lord Guest, was saying anything to the contrary; you have to look and see whether the knowledge acquired was capable of being used for his own benefit *to injure* the trust (my italics). That test can have no application to the present. There was no possibility of the information being used to injure the trust. The knowledge obtained was used not in connection with trust property but to enhance the value of the trust property by the purchase of other property in which the trustees were not interested.

With these general observations on the applicable principles of law let me apply them to the facts of this case.'

Questions:

In *Boardman v Phipps*, **[532]** above, the majority of the House of Lords found that the appellants held the newly-purchased shares on constructive trust for the trust beneficiaries either on the basis that they had been acquired using trust property (the trust property being the information which had suggested that the share acquisition was desirable), or on the basis that their acquisition involved a conflict of duty and interest (because of the remote possibility that Boardman might be required to advise the trust on related matters). Lord Upjohn disagreed that information was trust property, or that a conflict of duty and interest included remote possibilities of such conflicts. His views have now become mainstream.

1. In this case, in rejecting the appeal, it seems that the House of Lords restored an order which imposed a constructive trust over the purchased shares. This is a proprietary remedy. Do any of the judgments extracted above explain why the remedy of 'a duty to account for profits' should involve proprietary consequences rather than merely personal ones?
2. Does the answer depend upon whether the fiduciary breach involved a use of trust property or only a conflict of duty and interest? *Should* the answer depend upon this distinction?

Also see:

Regal (Hastings) Ltd v Gulliver [1942] 1 All ER 378 (HL), noted [1967] 2 AC 134.

[533] ***Hospital Products Ltd v United States Surgical Corporation*** **(1984) 156 CLR 41 (Aust HCt), 99–100, 107–10** ***per*** **Mason J, 124–5** ***per*** **Deane J:**

[The claimant manufactured surgical products in the USA. It granted the defendant an exclusive licence to distribute these products in Australia. In clear breach of contract, the defendant used its position to set up in direct competition with the claimant as a manufacturer and distributor of similar products. The claimant alleged that the relationship between the parties was not only contractual but also fiduciary, and that, consequently, the defendant was not simply liable in damages for breach of contract but also held its competing business on constructive trust for the claimant. The imposition of such a constructive trust would have enabled the claimant to recover the past and future profits made by the defendant from selling its own (not the claimant's) products, a measure of recovery which was not available for breach of contract. In addition, in the likely event that the defendant became insolvent, the constructive trust would give the claimant priority over the defendant's other creditors. A majority of the High Court held that the relationship was not fiduciary and that therefore there could be no constructive trust remedy. Mason and Deane JJ dissented from this conclusion, and the segments of their judgments extracted below concentrate on the remedy had their views been accepted (views which differ markedly from each other). Mason J's assessment of the law is regarded as orthodox; he simply dissented on its application to the facts. Deane J's assessment, on the other hand, does not reflect the current approach, although see Section 5.10.3 and 5.11 below.]

Mason J (dissenting):
[*On the existence of a fiduciary relationship*:]
'77. There has been an understandable reluctance to subject commercial transactions to the equitable doctrine of constructive trust and constructive notice. But it is altogether too simplistic, if not superficial, to suggest that commercial transactions stand outside the fiduciary regime as though in some way commercial transactions do not lend themselves to the creation of a relationship in which one person comes under an obligation to act in the interests of another. The fact that in the great majority of commercial transactions the parties stand at arms' length does not enable us to make a generalization that is universally true in relation to every commercial transaction. In truth, every such transaction must be examined on its merits with a view to ascertaining whether it manifests the characteristics of a fiduciary relationship.

78. The disadvantages of introducing equitable doctrine into the field of commerce, which may be less formidable than they were, now that the techniques of commerce are far more sophisticated, must be balanced against the need in appropriate cases to do justice by making available relief in specie through the constructive trust, the fiduciary relationship being a means to that end. If, in order to make relief in specie available in appropriate cases it is necessary to allow equitable doctrine to penetrate commercial transactions, then so be it. See, for example, *Barclays Bank Ltd. v. Quistclose Investments Ltd.* (1970) AC 567 [at **[339]** above] and *Swiss Bank Corporation v. Lloyds Bank Ltd.* (1982) AC 584 [at **[307]** above]. A preferable approach to an artificial narrowing of the fiduciary relationship—the gateway to relief in specie—is to define and delimit more precisely the circumstances in which the remedy by way of constructive trust will be granted. . . . .

Relief for Breach of Fiduciary Duty

(a) General Principle Governing Liability to Account
95. The principle, accepted by the courts below, is that the fiduciary cannot be permitted to retain a profit or benefit which he has obtained by reason of his breach of fiduciary duty (*Consul Development Pty Ltd v DPC Estates Pty Ltd*, (1975) 132 CLR 373, at p.393; *Queensland Mines Ltd v Hudson* (1978) 52 ALJR 399, at p.401). A fiduciary is liable to account for a profit or benefit if it was obtained (1) in circumstances where there was a conflict, or possible conflict of interest and duty or (2) by reason of the fiduciary position or by reason of the fiduciary taking advantage of opportunity or knowledge which he derived in consequence of his occupation of the fiduciary position.

(b) Constructive Trust
96. Any profit or benefit obtained by a fiduciary in either of the two situations already described is held by him as a constructive trustee (*Keith Henry & Co. Pty. Ltd. v. Stuart Walker & Co. Pty. Ltd.* (1958) 100 CLR 342, at p 350). Neither principle nor authority provide any support for the proposition that relief by way of constructive trust is available only in the case where a profit or benefit obtained by the fiduciary was one which it was an incident of his duty to obtain for the person to whom he owed the fiduciary duty. Once it is established that the fiduciary is liable to account for a profit or benefit which he has obtained there can be no objection to his being held to account as a constructive trustee of that profit or benefit. It can make no difference that it was not his

duty to obtain the profit or benefit for the person to whom the duty was owed. What is important is that the advantage has accrued to him in breach of his fiduciary duty or by his misuse of his fiduciary position. The consequence is that he must account for it and in equity the appropriate remedy is by means of a constructive trust.

97. In *Beatty v. Guggenheim Exploration Co.* (1919) 225 NY 380, Cardozo J. observed (at p 386) that an agent or a partner who promised or covenanted not to engage in some other business does not, as a matter of course, become chargeable as a trustee for the profits of the forbidden venture. For this proposition he cited well-known authorities which included *Dean v. MacDowell* (1878) 8 ChD 345, and *Aas v. Benham* (1891) 2 Ch 244. He went on to say (at p 386):

> "A constructive trust is the formula through which the conscience of equity finds expression. When property has been acquired in such circumstances that the holder of the legal title may not in good conscience retain the beneficial interest, equity converts him into a trustee."

Later he said (at p.389):

> "A court of equity in decreeing a constructive trust is bound by no unyielding formula. The equity of the transaction must shape the measure of relief."

98. The decided cases provide many illustrations of the fiduciary who has been held to be accountable as a constructive trustee of a profit or benefit which he has obtained for himself, notwithstanding that it was not his duty to acquire that profit or benefit as an incident of his fiduciary duty. See, for example, *Regal (Hastings) Ltd. v. Gulliver* (1967) 2 AC 134; *Phipps v. Boardman* [at **[532]** above]; *Prebble v. Reeves* (1910) VLR 88; *Industrial Development Consultants Ltd. v. Cooley* (1972) 1 WLR 443, at p 453; and *Pre-Cam Exploration & Development Ltd. v. McTavish* (1966) 57 DLR (2d) 557. The principle and the policy which underlie the cases was comprehensively expressed by Rich, Dixon and Evatt JJ. in *Furs Ltd. v. Tomkies* (1936) 54 CLR 583. Their Honours, after pointing out the rule that an undisclosed profit derived by a director from the execution of his fiduciary duties belongs in equity to the company, observed (at p.592):

> "It is no answer to the application of the rule that the profit is of a kind which the company could not itself have obtained, or that no loss is caused to the company by the gain of the director. It is a principle resting upon the impossibility of allowing the conflict of duty and interest which is involved in the pursuit of private advantage in the course of dealing in a fiduciary capacity with the affairs of the company. If, when it is his duty to safeguard and further the interests of the company, he uses the occasion as a means of profit to himself, he raises an opposition between the duty he has undertaken and his own self interest, beyond which it is neither wise nor practicable for the law to look for a criterion of liability. The consequences of such a conflict are not discoverable. Both justice and policy are against their investigation."

99. However, there is authority for the proposition that equity does not assume jurisdiction to punish a fiduciary for misconduct by making him account for more than he actually received as a result of his breach of fiduciary duty. In *Vyse v. Foster* (1872) LR 8 Ch App 309, James L.J. said (at p 333):

> "This Court is not a Court of penal jurisdiction. It compels restitution of property unconscientiously withheld; it gives full compensation for any loss or damage through failure of some equitable duty; but it has no power of punishing any one.

> In fact, it is not by way of punishment that the Court ever charges a trustee with more than he actually received, or ought to have received, and the appropriate interest thereon. It is simply on the ground that the Court finds that he actually made more, constituting moneys in his hands 'had and received to the use' of the cestui que trust."

The decision of the Court of Appeal was affirmed by the House of Lords ((1874) L.R. 7 H.L. 318) without their Lordships reflecting on the passage which I have quoted.

100. The proposition which I have stated based on the observations of James L.J. needs to be modified in order to take account of the situation where the fiduciary has so mixed an indeterminate profit with his own property as to render the identification of the gain impossible. There "... the whole will be treated as trust property, except so far as he may be able to distinguish what is his own." (*Brady v. Stapleton* (1952) 88 CLR 322, at p 336, quoting Page Wood V-C. in *Frith v. Cartland* (1865) 2 H & M 417, at p 418 (71 ER 525, at p 526)). The proposition may also need to be modified to take account of a profit acquired by a fraudulent fiduciary through a combination of trust property and his own property or efforts. It may well be that equity in such circumstances will not seek to apportion the gain.

101. The propriety of granting relief by way of constructive trust is therefore closely associated with the answers to two questions: (1) What is the breach of fiduciary duty? and (2) What is the profit or benefit which the fiduciary has made in consequence of that breach? Before proceeding to answer the second question, which is the outstanding question, I should mention that a particular problem has arisen with respect to the declaration of a constructive trust of a competing business established and carried on by a fiduciary in breach of his duty. One approach, more favourable to the fiduciary, is that he should be held liable to account as constructive trustee not of the entire business but of the particular benefits which flowed to him in breach of his duty. Another approach, less favourable to the fiduciary, is that he should be held accountable for the entire business and its profits, due allowance being made for the time, energy, skill and financial contribution that he has expended or made. In *In re Jarvis* (1958) 1 WLR 815, Upjohn J. observed (at p 820), correctly in my opinion, that it is not possible to say that one approach is universally to be preferred to the other, for each case depends on its own facts and the form of inquiry which ought to be directed must vary according to the circumstances. In each case the form of inquiry to be directed is that which will reflect as accurately as possible the true measure of the profit or benefit obtained by the fiduciary in breach of his duty.'

Deane J (dissenting):
'*Constructive Trust*

. . .

11. In these circumstances, I agree with the conclusion reached by McLelland J. at first instance and Mason J. in this Court that USSC was entitled to an order that HPI account, as constructive trustee, for any profits it derived from the business of distributing within Australia its own re-packaged or manufactured products up until November 1980 when it ceased to distribute in this country. The reasoning which leads me to that conclusion diverges however from that accepted by McLelland J. at first instance and by Mason J. in this Court in that I am not persuaded that a "fiduciary relationship" existed between USSC and HPI in respect of the local products goodwill. Provided that it did not act in breach of the terms of the contract, HPI was, as I see the

matter, entitled to exploit that local goodwill for its own benefit not only as regards its profit from sales of USSC's products but also, for example, by taking advantage of the "flow on" advantage which it might derive in marketing any non-competing products to the existing customers for USSC's products. If it had not acted in breach of its contractual obligations, it would have subsequently been free to exploit the advantage of its previous association with USSC's products to build up the goodwill of its own. In my view, the constructive trust pursuant to which HPI is liable to account for the profits arising from the sale in Australia of its own re-packaged or manufactured competing products should properly be seen as imposed as equitable relief appropriate to the particular circumstances of the case rather than as arising from a breach of some fiduciary duty flowing from an identified fiduciary relationship. HPI's business of distributing those competing products in Australia was founded upon and incorporated the appropriation to itself, by a course of conduct which involved calculated breach of its contractual obligations to USSC, of the local goodwill for USSC's products. In all the circumstances, USSC was entitled to a declaration that HPI was liable to account as a constructive trustee for the profits of that Australian business in accordance with the principles under which a constructive trust may be imposed as the appropriate form of equitable relief in circumstances where a person could not in good conscience retain for himself a benefit, or the proceeds of a benefit, which he has appropriated to himself in breach of his contractual or other legal or equitable obligations to another. Since this particular aspect of the matter was not explored in argument and a majority of the Court is of the view that there is no basis for any finding of constructive trust however, it is preferable that I defer until some subsequent occasion a more precise identification of the principles governing the imposition of a constructive trust in such circumstances.'

Questions:

What is the difference between the approach of Mason J and that of Deane J? In what circumstances would each see a constructive trust as legitimately imposed? Is the constructive trust one imposed on the facts of the breach (and at the time the breach occurs), or is it one imposed by order of the court once the issues have been resolved? What justifications are offered by each judge for this proprietary response to a breach of obligation by the defendant? Are the justifications compelling? Will the third party creditors of the defendant be *unfairly* disadvantaged should the defendant become insolvent?

[534] *Lister & Co v Stubbs* (1890) 45 Ch D 1 (CA), 14–15 *per* Lindley LJ:
[The authority of this case is now in doubt. It has been overruled by the Privy Council (see **[535]** below), but not by the House of Lords. The claimant company carried on business as a silk-spinner, dyer and manufacturer. The defendant was employed as a foreman, and was responsible for the purchase of dyestuffs for the company. He took bribes from one of the company's suppliers, and successfully invested the sums received. The Court of Appeal held that the claimant's remedies were personal only; the company had no proprietary interest in either the bribes or their investment proceeds.]

'If we were to accede to this application, I do not think that *Stubbs* could complain; but the question is, whether, having regard to the rules by which we are governed, we can properly make the order. I am clearly of opinion that we cannot. The real state of the case as between *Lister & Co.* and Messrs. *Varley* and *Stubbs* is this: *Lister & Co.*, through their agent *Stubbs*, buy goods of Messrs. *Varley* at certain prices, and pay for them. The ownership of the goods of course is in *Lister & Co.*; the ownership of the money is in Messrs. *Varley*. Then Messrs. *Varley* have entered into an arrangement with *Stubbs*, who ordered the goods of them, to give *Stubbs* a commission. That is what it comes to. What is the legal position between Messrs. *Varley* and *Stubbs*? They owe him the money. He can recover it from them by an action, unless the illegality of the transaction afford them a defence; but the Appellants have asked us to go further, and to say that Messrs. *Varley* were *Stubbs*' agents in getting his commission from *Lister & Co.* That appears to me to be an entire mistake. The relation between Messrs. *Varley* and *Stubbs* is that of debtor and creditor—they pay him. Then comes the question, as between *Lister & Co.* and *Stubbs*, whether *Stubbs* can keep the money he has received without accounting for it? Obviously not. I apprehend that he is liable to account for it the moment that he gets it. It is an obligation to pay and account to Messrs. *Lister & Co.*, with or without interest, as the case may be. I say nothing at all about that. But the relation between them is that of debtor and creditor; it is not that of trustee and *cestui que trust*. We are asked to hold that it is—which would involve consequences which, I confess, startle me. One consequence, of course, would be that, if *Stubbs* were to become bankrupt, this property acquired by him with the money paid to him by Messrs. *Varley* would be withdrawn from the mass of his creditors and be handed over bodily to *Lister & Co.* Can that be right? Another consequence would be that, if the Appellants are right, *Lister & Co.* could compel *Stubbs* to account to them, not only for the money with interest, but for all the profits which he might have made by embarking in trade with it. Can that be right? It appears to me that those consequences shew that there is some flaw in the argument. If by logical reasoning from the premises conclusions are arrived at which are opposed to good sense, it is necessary to go back and look again at the premises and see if they are sound. I am satisfied that they are not sound—the unsoundness consisting in confounding ownership with obligation.'

[535] *Att-Gen for Hong Kong v Reid* [1994] 1 AC 324 (PC), 330–8 *per* Lord Templeman for their Lordships:

[Reid was a Hong Kong Public Prosecutor who was convicted of accepting bribes as an inducement to obstruct the prosecution of certain criminals. He was ordered to pay the Crown the sum of HK$12.4 million, being the value of assets then controlled by him which could only have been derived from the bribes. No payment was forthcoming, so the Attorney-General for Hong Kong brought proceedings in New Zealand claiming that three freehold houses, which the bribes had been used to purchase, were held on constructive trust for the Crown. The New Zealand Court of Appeal applied *Lister & Co v Stubbs* (**[534]** above), and dismissed the claim. The Privy Council reversed this decision, holding that *Lister & Co v Stubbs* was wrongly decided.]

'A bribe is a gift accepted by a fiduciary as an inducement to him to betray his trust. A secret benefit, which may or may not constitute a bribe, is a benefit which the fiduciary derives from trust property or obtains from knowledge which he acquires in the course of acting as a fiduciary. A fiduciary is not always accountable for a secret benefit but he is undoubtedly accountable for a secret benefit which consists of a bribe. In addition a person who provides the bribe and the fiduciary who accepts the bribe may each be guilty of a criminal offence. . . ..

When a bribe is offered and accepted in money or in kind, the money or property constituting the bribe belongs in law to the recipient. Money paid to the false fiduciary belongs to him. The legal estate in freehold property conveyed to the false fiduciary by way of bribe vests in him. Equity, however, which acts in personam, insists that it is unconscionable for a fiduciary to obtain and retain a benefit in breach of duty. The provider of a bribe cannot recover it because he committed a criminal offence when he paid the bribe. The false fiduciary who received the bribe in breach of duty must pay and account for the bribe to the person to whom that duty was owed. In the present case, as soon as the first respondent received a bribe in breach of the duties he owed to the Government of Hong Kong, he became a debtor in equity to the Crown for the amount of that bribe. So much is admitted. But if the bribe consists of property which increases in value or if a cash bribe is invested advantageously, the false fiduciary will receive a benefit from his breach of duty unless he is accountable not only for the original amount or value of the bribe but also for the increased value of the property representing the bribe. As soon as the bribe was received it should have been paid or transferred instanter to the person who suffered from the breach of duty. Equity considers as done that which ought to have been done. As soon as the bribe was received, whether in cash or in kind, the false fiduciary held the bribe on a constructive trust for the person injured. Two objections have been raised to this analysis. First it is said that if the fiduciary is in equity a debtor to the person injured, he cannot also be a trustee of the bribe. But there is no reason why equity should not provide two remedies, so long as they do not result in double recovery. If the property representing the bribe exceeds the original bribe in value, the fiduciary cannot retain the benefit of the increase in value which he obtained solely as a result of his breach of duty. Secondly, it is said that if the false fiduciary holds property representing the bribe in trust for the person injured, and if the false fiduciary is or becomes insolvent, the unsecured creditors of the false fiduciary will be deprived of their right to share in the proceeds of that property. But the unsecured creditors cannot be in a better position than their debtor. The authorities show that property acquired by a trustee innocently but in breach of trust and the property from time to time representing the same belong in equity to the cestui que trust and not to the trustee personally whether he is solvent or insolvent. Property acquired by a trustee as a result of a criminal breach of trust and the property from time to time representing the same must also belong in equity to his cestui que trust and not to the trustee whether he is solvent or insolvent.

When a bribe is accepted by a fiduciary in breach of his duty then he holds that bribe in trust for the person to whom the duty was owed. If the property representing the bribe decreases in value the fiduciary must pay the difference between that value and the initial amount of the bribe because he should not have accepted the bribe or incurred the risk of loss. If the property increases in value, the fiduciary is not entitled to any surplus in excess of the initial value of the bribe because he is not allowed by any means to make a profit out of a breach of duty.

The courts of New Zealand were constrained by a number of precedents of the New Zealand, English and other common law courts which established a settled principle of law inconsistent with the foregoing analysis. That settled principle is open to review by the Board in the light of the foregoing analysis of the consequences in equity of the receipt of a bribe by a fiduciary. . . .

[Lord Templeman then proceeded to discuss the authorities.]

It has always been assumed and asserted that the law on the subject of bribes was definitively settled by the decision of the Court of Appeal in *Lister & Co. v. Stubbs* (1890) 45 Ch.D. 1. . . .

[Lord Templeman outlined the facts, the Court of Appeal's conclusions, and then quoted the paragraph from the judgment of Lindley LJ in which he questioned two 'startling consequences' which were suggested by a proprietary response and asked 'Can that be right?': see **[534]** above.]

For the reasons which have already been advanced their Lordships would respectfully answer both these questions in the affirmative. If a trustee mistakenly invests moneys which he ought to pay over to his cestui que trust and then becomes bankrupt, the moneys together with any profit which has accrued from the investment are withdrawn from the unsecured creditors as soon as the mistake is discovered. A fortiori if a trustee commits a crime by accepting a bribe which he ought to pay over to his cestui que trust, the bribe and any profit made therefrom should be withdrawn from the unsecured creditors as soon as the crime is discovered.

The decision in *Lister & Co. v. Stubbs* is not consistent with the principles that a fiduciary must not be allowed to benefit from his own breach of duty, that the fiduciary should account for the bribe as soon as he receives it and that equity regards as done that which ought to be done. From these principles it would appear to follow that the bribe and the property from time to time representing the bribe are held on a constructive trust for the person injured. A fiduciary remains personally liable for the amount of the bribe if, in the event, the value of the property then recovered by the injured person proved to be less than that amount.

. . .

Their Lordships are also much indebted for the fruits of research and the careful discussion of the present topic in the address entitled "Bribes and Secret Commissions" [1993] R.L.R. 7 delivered by Sir Peter Millett to a meeting of the Society of Public Teachers of Law at Oxford in 1993. The following passage, at p. 20, elegantly sums up the views of Sir Peter Millett:

> "[The fiduciary] must not place himself in a position where his interest may conflict with his duty. If he has done so, equity insists on treating him as having acted in accordance with his duty; he will not be allowed to say that he preferred his own interest to that of his principal. He must not obtain a profit for himself out of his fiduciary position. If he has done so, equity insists on treating him as having obtained it for his principal; he will not be allowed to say that he obtained it for himself. He must not accept a bribe. If he has done so, equity insists on treating it as a legitimate payment intended for the benefit of the principal; he will not be allowed to say that it was a bribe."

The conclusions reached by Lai Kew Chai J. in *Sumitomo Bank Ltd. v. Kartika Ratna Thahir* [1993] 1 S.L.R. 735 [declining to follow *Lister v Stubbs*] and the views expressed by Sir Peter Millett were influenced by the decision of the House of Lords in *Phipps v. Boardman* [1967] 2 A.C. 46 [see **[532]** above] which demonstrates the strictness with which equity regards the conduct of a fiduciary and the extent to which equity is willing to impose a constructive trust on property obtained by a fiduciary by virtue of his office. . . . If a fiduciary acting honestly and in good faith and making a profit which his principal could not make for himself becomes a constructive trustee of that profit then it seems to their Lordships that a fiduciary acting dishonestly and criminally who accepts a bribe and thereby causes loss and damage to his principal must also be a constructive trustee and must not be allowed by any means to make any profit from his wrongdoing.'

FURTHER READING:

Sir Peter Millett, 'Bribes and Secret Commissions' [1993] *RLR* 7.
W M C Gummow, 'Unjust Enrichment, Restitution and Proprietary Remedies' in P D Finn (ed), *Essays on Restitution* (1990, Law Book Co: Sydney) ch 3, pp 71 ff.
R P Austin, 'Fiduciary Accountability for Business Opportunities' in P D Finn (ed), *Equity and Commercial Relationships* (1987, Law Book Co: Sydney) ch 6.

[536] R Goode, 'Proprietary Restitutionary Claims' in WR Cornish, R Nolan, J O'Sullivan and G Virgo (eds), *Restitution: Past, Present and Future* (1998, Hart Publishing: Oxford) ch 5, pp
[Footnotes in the original are omitted.]

'*Bribes*

There is now a serious division of judicial authority on the correct treatment of bribes. English case law clearly establishes that where D is paid a bribe by T to secure business from P, P is entitled to recover the amount or value of the bribe but is not entitled to recover the bribe *in specie* or its proceeds. This was decided by two decisions of the Court of Appeal, *Metropolitan Bank v. Heiron* and *Lister & Co. v. Stubbs*, which have remained authority for well over a century. A contrary view was taken by the Privy Council in *Attorney-General for Hong Kong v. Reid*, and though technically all courts below the House of Lords remain bound by the Court of Appeal decisions, the ruling in *Reid* is plainly of great persuasive authority.

The question is highly controversial. At the root of the problem lies the assumption that where D obtains an identified benefit in breach of his duty to P he automatically incurs an obligation to transfer to P not merely the amount or value of that benefit at the time of its receipt but the very benefit itself in *specie* or, in the case of money, as a money fund. For this purpose, it is said, no distinction should be drawn between enrichment by subtraction from P's estate and enrichment by improper receipt from T of money or property in which P had no prior legal or equitable interest. But the award of a proprietary remedy in the latter case has the effect of excluding from D's estate an asset which would otherwise be available for its general creditors. How is this sought to be justified? There are two possible approaches, the conceptual approach and the policy approach.

The conceptual approach

The conceptual approach is based on two alternative lines of argument. The first is the maxim that equity treats as done that which ought to be done. The second is that D's creditors cannot stand in any better position than D himself. As I hope to show, both lines of argument are circular and presuppose the very question in issue.

Let me begin with the principle that equity treats as done that which ought to be done. D has received a bribe. He has a duty to make over the bribe to P; therefore he holds the bribe and its proceeds on trust for P. D's general creditors cannot complain, for since the bribe and its proceeds never belonged in equity to D, their recovery by P does not reduce D's estate.

In . . . *Proprietary Interests in Commercial Transactions*, Dr Sarah Worthington offers by way of a general formulation the proposition that one party will become the equitable owner of property belonging to another if, but only if, that other party is under a mandatory and unconditional personal obligation to transfer identifiable property to the first party. These three conditions are said to be both necessary and sufficient requirements for establishing the existence of new equitable interests by operation of law and to be grounded in equity's cardinal rule, that equity treats as done that which ought to be done. This unifying principle, it is argued, explains why a bribee holds the bribe or its proceeds on constructive trust. For present purposes I am happy to accept Sarah Worthington's proposition as one of normal application, though I would point out that there is at least one major exception, in that the proposition does nor hold good in relation to the contract for sale of goods. [Arguably it does: such contracts are rarely specifically enforceable, even when they relate to identifiable property. In these circumstances application of the proposed general rule would suggest that no equitable proprietary interest will arise.] But assuming the general truth of the proposition, does it explain the constructive trust of a bribe? Certainly Lord Templeman thought so in *Attorney-General for Hong Kong v. Reid*, where, in giving the opinion of the Privy Council upholding a claim to trace a bribe into property purchased with the bribe, he likewise invoked the principle that equity treats as done that which ought to be done. However, this, with respect, assumes that the bribee has a duty not merely to pay the injured party the amount or value of the bribe, as was held to be the case in *Metropolitan Bank v. Heiron* and *Lister & Co. v. Stubbs*, but to transfer the bribe itself *in specie* or, in the case of money, as an identified money fund. Such an assumption presupposes the very question in issue and thereby inevitably leads to the result which the opponents of those cases desire. The point to be addressed is whether the bribee *does* have a duty to transfer the identical property improperly received and where this duty comes from. Why should it be assumed that such a duty exists? At the conceptual level all the arguments are against it. Not only did P not bargain for the bribe, he had no expectation of receiving it, for if D had honoured his obligations it would never have been paid in the first place. It is thus impossible to say that D received the bribe for the account of P. For his part, T, the party paying the bribe, did not intend that it should be held for P, quite the reverse. We can all agree that P should be entitled to recover the amount or value of the bribe, but why should he be given a proprietary remedy?

The other way of putting the argument in favour of a proprietary remedy is that D's creditors cannot stand in a better position than D himself. But this is true only if, again, we assume the very point in issue, namely that P's claim is proprietary. It is inherent in the *pari passu* principle that upon D's bankruptcy creditors holding purely personal claims *are* in a better position than D himself in that the assets comprising the estate cease to be attachable by any one unsecured creditor, whether by way of execution or otherwise, and become available to creditors *pro rata*. Thus the burden of the common misfortune is borne equally. Hence to say that D's creditors stand in D's shoes is simply to assert, without reasoned argument, that P's claim is proprietary, not personal. D's creditors do, of course, take D's estate as they find it, subject to proprietary claims and to equities. But what is lacking is any explanation why P's claim should he proprietary and should thus rank ahead of, rather than *pari passu* with, the claims of other creditors. If a claimant with no preexisting proprietary base or equity for his claim is nevertheless to be elevated above other creditors and to have his claim characterised as proprietary, that requires justification. This is not furnished by question-begging appeals to the maxim that equity treat as done that which ought to be done or the equally question-begging assertion that D's creditors stand in his shoes. At the end of the day the issue is one of policy.

The policy approach

What, then, is the policy that demands that P be given a proprietary right over the bribe itself and, in consequence, of its proceeds and of any enhancement in the value of the bribe or proceeds? At this level the appeal is to moral indignation, never more fervently expressed than in relation to bribes:

> "Bribery is an evil practice which threatens the foundations of any civilised society. In particular bribery of policemen and prosecutors brings the administration of justice into disrepute. Where bribes are accepted by a trustee, servant, agent or other fiduciary, loss and damage are caused to the beneficiaries, master or principal whose interests are betrayed".

Thus Lord Templeman in *Attorney-General for Hong Kong v. Reid.* One can only agree with these sentiments. Bribery is indeed a deeply corrosive force. But how does that get us to the recognition of P's claim as proprietary? The answer given is that the delinquent fiduciary must not be allowed to profit from his wrongdoing, and he will so profit if he is allowed to retain for himself any enhancement in the value of what he received. This can be avoided only by treating P as beneficial owner of the money or other asset given by way of a bribe, thereby giving him the proprietary base he needs to capture the added value. This rule is not confined to bribes but applies to any benefit received by D in breach of his fiduciary duty to his principal. The most powerful and elegant exponent of this argument is Sir Peter Millett:

> "the principal is given a remedy because this is considered necessary to enforce the high standards which equity demands of a fiduciary. A fiduciary who fails to observe them must be stripped of every advantage which he has obtained thereby; better that the principal should receive a windfall than that the fiduciary (or his creditors) should benefit".

Now one can see the argument for stripping the fiduciary himself of benefits attributable to his wrongdoing, as an inducement to future fiduciaries to observe the requisite standards of behaviour, or, to quote Sir Peter Millett again, "*pour encourager les autres*". It is less clear that the fiduciary's general creditors should be similarly deprived. They have done nothing wrong. Why, then, should they be expected to suffer for the fiduciary's delinquency? They are not the fiduciary's legal representatives but independent third parties. Why should they not rank on an equal footing with the principal? Moreover, they are parties who by definition have given value to the fiduciary, swelling his estate. What considerations of policy dictate that they should be subordinated to a claimant who had no pre-existing property interest, who has given no value, who may have suffered no loss, and who cannot even invoke a reliance interest? The policy "*pour encourager les autres*" has no relevance to the creditors, for their own conduct cannot be affected by it.

. . .

The preference thus given to the principal is all the more extraordinary when we consider that the proprietary right is accorded not only in cases of bribes but in all cases of receipt of benefit in breach of fiduciary obligation, even where the fiduciary has acted in good faith. The decision of the House of Lords in *Boardman v. Phipps* provides an example. What is the moral justification for a rule under which money received in breach of fiduciary duty by a fiduciary acting honestly is impressed with a trust in favour of his principal and removed from the reach of his general creditors when a person who was induced to part with his money by fraud is left to prove in competition with other creditors in the fraudster's bankruptcy?

The outcome is also objectionable in terms of principles of insolvency law. P's proprietary right, lacking any proprietary base, derives in substance from a transfer by operation of law from D's estate, a transfer which, moreover, is retrospective in its effect and which, if taking effect by agreement, would be struck down under the Insolvency Act as a transaction at an undervalue. If our avoidance rules in insolvency law were properly fashioned, they would catch all transfers not for value, whether consensual or non-consensual, as is the case under the American federal Bankruptcy Code.

In the light of these considerations, and subject to the special case of deemed agency gains to which I shall now turn, the case for denying proprietary rights for enrichment by a wrong is surely overwhelming. I am happy to find powerful support for this position from Professor Andrew Burrows, who has presented the case for such denial with his customary penetration and elegance.

Deemed agency gains

Special considerations apply to deemed agency gains, that is, gains which D receives through improperly engaging in dealings on his own account which, if he entered into them at all, should have been engaged in for the benefit of P. The typical case is that of the company director who uses his position to pursue for himself in dealings with T business opportunities which should have been pursued on behalf of his company. For this purpose the assumption is that P had no direct claim against T to the money or property paid or transferred to D, so that there is no question of D intercepting P's asset. In this case there has been no diminution in P's estate. All that has happened is that D has broken a fiduciary obligation to subordinate his own interests to those of P and perhaps also the separate obligation not to make a secret profit.

This distinction, which I drew in my earlier paper, between deemed agency gains and what I would call true interceptive subtraction has been criticised as unnecessary, unrealistic and unworkable. [P.J. Millett, "The Error in *Lister v. Stubbs*" in P. Birks (ed.) *The Frontiers of Liability* (Vol. 1) (1994, OUP: Oxford) ch 5, p. 56.] In particular, it has been objected that this is a distinction without a difference and that where the facts are disputed and the evidence is unreliable it may be difficult to determine whether D's receipt came at a time when P had already acquired a contractual right against T or whether it came when the acquisition of this right was merely in prospect. But I remain unrepentant. There is all the difference in the world between D's misappropriation of P's contract rights on the one hand and D's diversion to himself of a contract not yet concluded between P and T. In the former case P's estate is diminished by D's improper act; in the latter, D's breach does not involve any subtraction from P's estate but simply intercepts a potential augmentation of it. As for the evidential difficulties, these are no different in kind or degree from those which regularly confront the courts when having to decide whether negotiations between a plaintiff and a defendant had or had not crystallised into a contract.

In short, deemed agency gains do not erode P's existing proprietary base; they represent a particular form of enrichment by a wrong, and in principle the allocation of a proprietary right to P in respect of such gains confronts the same objections as to other forms of enrichment by wrong. However, given that the gain is one which, if pursued at all, should have been pursued for P's benefit, not for that of D, and is therefore necessarily associated with activity relevant to P's business, there is a case for allowing P to obtain the gain *in specie* as an accretion to his business, so long as this can be done without detriment to general creditors and intervening security interests or other proprietary rights. There are different ways of achieving this objective. One of them, advocated in my earlier paper, is for the court to impose a remedial constructive trust operating *pro nunc* rather than *pro tunc* or to order conditions for proprietary relief which in some other way protect intervening rights. Another is to recognise that the allocation of deemed agency gains to P is in substance a transfer by operation of law from D's estate and to subject this involuntary transfer to the same rules of avoidance in insolvency as apply to consensual transfers.'

[Professor Goode then considers failure of consideration: see section 5.5 above.]

Question:

The issue of proprietary remedies for breach of fiduciary obligations is clearly controversial. To the extent that the proprietary remedy exists, it provides a further mechanism by which one party can acquire assets in equity by operation of law. The judiciary appears to favour a proprietary response; many commentators do not. In the light of the materials above, which is the better view?

5.10.2 Constructive trusts which arise on breach of obligations of confidence

The previous section considered proprietary interests which arose on breach of fiduciary obligations. The controversy surrounding these fiduciary cases centred on the policy justification for delivering proprietary remedies to parties who did not have a 'proprietary base' (see Roy Goode at **[536]** above). In the context of fiduciary breaches, a claimant will be able to assert a proprietary base in some circumstances (eg when a fiduciary/trustee misappropriates trust assets, then the trust assets provide the 'proprietary base') but not in others (eg when a fiduciary receives a bribe). Whatever the policy considerations, it is not clear that the distinction has any impact on the remedy: *AG v Reid* (at **[535]** above) would suggest that it does not. This debate is also important in the context of breaches of obligations of confidence.

In particular, if a proprietary remedy depends upon the existence of a proprietary base, then breaches of confidence should not give rise to proprietary remedies unless 'confidential information' is classed as property (as to which see Lord Upjohn in *Boardman v Phipps* at **[532]** above). On the other hand, if a proprietary remedy does not depend on the existence of a proprietary base, then breaches of confidence may give rise to proprietary remedies. The conventional view is that remedies for breach of confidence are personal, but more recent judicial statements suggest that this view may be under reconsideration. The following extracts illustrate the issues.

[537] ***Seager v Copydex Ltd* [1967] 2 All ER 415 (CA), 417 *per* Lord Denning MR:**
[The facts are immaterial. They concern misuse of an invention for a carpet grip.]

'I start with one sentence in the judgment of Lord Greene MR in *Saltman Engineering Co Ltd v Campbell Engineering Co Ltd* [1963] 3 All ER 413 at 414:

> "If a defendant is proved to have used confidential information, directly or indirectly obtained from the plaintiff, without the consent, express or implied, of the plaintiff, he will be guilty of an infringement of the plaintiff's rights.'

To this I add a sentence from the judgment of Roxburgh J in *Terrapin Ltd v Builders' Supply Co (Hayes) Ltd, Taylor Woodrow Ltd & Swiftplan Ltd* [1960] RPC 128 at 130 which was quoted and adopted as correct by Roskill J in *Cranleigh Precision Engineering Co Ltd v Bryant* [1964] 3 All ER 298 at 301:

> "As I understand it, the essence of this branch of the law, whatever the origin of it may be, is that a person who has obtained information in confidence is not allowed to use it as a springboard for activities detrimental to the person who made the confidential communication . . . ."

The law on this subject does not depend on any implied contract. It depends on the broad principle of equity that he who has received information in confidence shall not take unfair advantage of it. He must not make use of it to the prejudice of him who gave it without obtaining his consent. . . . . He should not get a start over others [a commercial head-start] by using the information which he received in confidence. At any rate, he should not get a start without paying for it. It may not be a case for injunction but only for damages, depending on the worth of the confidential information to him in saving him time and trouble. . . .

The court grants neither an account of profits, nor an injunction, but only damages . . . to be assessed on the basis of reasonable compensation for the use of the confidential information.'

Questions:

1. If Lord Denning MR was referring to common law damages as awarded in tort, then his judgment can be criticised as providing an inappropriate remedy (a common law remedy) for breach of a purely equitable obligation. However, later cases have suggested that Lord Denning was referring (more appropriately) to damages in lieu of an injunction (ie damages under Lord Cairns's Act): see Slade J in *English v Dedham Vale Properties Ltd* [1978] 1 All ER 382, 389. Is there any good reason to maintain this doctrinal purity in the award of remedies? [Note that obligations of confidence may arise in contract or by virtue of statute—see **[538]** below—and then the 'appropriate' remedy must be assessed differently.]
2. If proof of detriment to the claimant is an essential part of breach of confidence, then breach of the obligation of confidence is unlike the breaches of fiduciary obligations discussed in the previous section. Where causing detriment is a necessary part of the breach, one sensible remedy (although not necessarily the only one) is 'damages' or equitable compensation. Is such a 'damages' remedy ever proprietary?
3. Given the various statements of the obligation of confidence adopted by Lord Denning in the previous extract, are there any analogies with breach

of fiduciary obligations which might suggest that disgorgement is the appropriate remedy? If disgorgement is an appropriate remedy, should it be a proprietary or a personal remedy?

4. If there is a choice of remedy—damages or disgorgement—how should the choice be made?

[538] *A-G v Guardian Newspapers (No 2)* [1990] 1 AC 109, 255–7, 262–3 *per* Lord Keith, 281–9 *per* Lord Goff:

[Peter Wright was a former member of the British Security Service, MI5. He retired to Tasmania and wrote a book, *Spycatcher*, based on his experiences. This was in breach of both his contract of service with the Crown and the provisions of the Official Secrets Act 1911. It followed that the book could not be published in the UK. However, Wright entered into an agreement with the Australian subsidiary of an English publishing company for the book's publication in Australia. The Crown obtained interim relief preventing publication in Australia, but this did not extend to other overseas jurisdictions. The publishers therefore took steps to have the book published in the United States, where injunctive relief could not be obtained to prevent publication. In the UK, the *Observer* and the *Guardian* newspapers each published articles on the Australian legal proceedings, including controversial details from Wright's book. They were then enjoined from publishing further details. The following year, the *Sunday Times* purchased the British newspaper serialisation right to *Spycatcher* from the Australian publisher, and published the first instalment of extracts from the book two days before the book's publication in the United States. An injunction was issued preventing publication of further extracts. The House of Lords held that all the injunctions against the newspapers should be lifted, that further publication by them would not be in breach of confidence since the information was now in the public domain, but that the one-issue serialisation by the *Sunday Times* had been a breach of confidence for which the newspaper was liable to an account of profits. The majority held that these conclusions followed notwithstanding that Peter Wright owed a lifelong duty of confidence and would continue to be in breach if he persisted in publication (although if he remained in Australia he would continue to be beyond the jurisdiction of the court).]

Lord Keith:

'The Crown's case upon all the issues which arise invokes the law about confidentiality. So it is convenient to start by considering the nature and scope of that law. The law has long recognised that an obligation of confidence can arise out of particular relationships. Examples are the relationships of doctor and patient, priest and penitent, solicitor and client, banker and customer. The obligation may be imposed by an express or implied term in a contract but it may also exist independently of any contract on the basis of an independent equitable principle of confidence: *Saltman Engineering Co. Ltd. v. Campbell Engineering Co. Ltd.* (1948) 65 R.P.C. 203. It is worthy of some examination whether or not detriment to the confider of confidential information is an essential ingredient of his cause of action in seeking to restrain by injunction a breach of confidence. Presumably that may be so as regards an action for damages in respect of a past breach of confidence. If the confider has suffered no detriment thereby he can hardly be in a position to recover compensatory damages. However, the true view may be that he would be entitled to nominal damages. Most of the cases have arisen in circumstances where there has been a threatened or actual breach of confidence by an employee or ex-employee of the plaintiff, or where information about the plaintiff's business affairs has been given in confidence to someone who has proceeded to exploit it for his own benefit: an example of the latter type of case is *Seager v. Copydex Ltd.* [1967] 1 W.L.R. 923. In such cases the detriment to the confider is clear. In other cases there may be no financial detriment to the confider, since the breach of confidence involves no more than an invasion of personal privacy. Thus in *Duchess of Argyll v. Duke of Argyll* [1967] Ch. 302 an injunction was granted against the revelation of marital confidences. The right to personal privacy is clearly one which the law should in this field seek to protect. If a profit has been made through the revelation in breach of confidence of details of a person's private life it is appropriate that the profit should [256] be accounted for to that person. Further, as a general rule, it is in the public interest that confidences should be respected, and the encouragement of such respect may in itself constitute a sufficient ground for recognising and enforcing the obligation of confidence even where the confider can point to no specific detriment to himself. Information about a person's private and personal affairs may be of a nature which shows him up in a favourable light and would by no means expose him to criticism. The anonymous donor of a very large sum to a very worthy cause has his own reasons for wishing to remain anonymous, which are unlikely to be discreditable. He should surely be in a position to restrain disclosure in breach of confidence of his identity in connection with the donation. So I would think it a sufficient detriment to the confider that information given in confidence is to be disclosed to persons whom he would prefer not to know of it, even though the disclosure would not be harmful to him in any positive way.

The position of the Crown, as representing the continuing government of the country may, however, be regarded as being special. In some instances disclosure of confidential information entrusted to a servant of the Crown may result in a financial loss to the public. In other instances such disclosure may tend to harm the public interest by impeding the efficient attainment of proper governmental ends, and the revelation of defence or intelligence secrets certainly falls into that category. The Crown, however, as representing the nation as a whole, has no private life or personal feelings capable of being hurt by the disclosure of confidential information. In so far as the Crown acts to prevent such disclosure or to seek redress for it on confidentiality grounds, it must necessarily, in my opinion, be in a position to show that the disclosure is likely to damage or has damaged the public interest. How far the Crown has to go in order to show this must depend on the circumstances of each case. In a question with a Crown servant himself, or others acting as his agents, the general public interest in the preservation of confidentiality, and in encouraging other Crown servants to preserve it, may suffice. But where the publication is proposed to be made by third parties unconnected with the particular confidant, the position may be different. The Crown's argument in the present case would go to the length that in all circumstances where the original disclosure has been made by a Crown servant in breach of his obligation of confidence any person to whose knowledge the information comes and who is aware of the breach comes under an equitable duty binding his conscience not to communicate the information to anyone else irrespective of the circumstances under which he acquired the knowledge. In my opinion that general proposition is untenable and impracticable, in addition to being unsupported by any authority. The general rule is that anyone is entitled to communicate anything he pleases to anyone else, by speech or in writing or in any other way. That rule is limited by the law of defamation and other restrictions similar to these mentioned in article 10 of the Convention for the Protection of

Human Rights and Fundamental Freedoms (1953) (Cmd. 8969). All those restrictions are imposed in the light of considerations of public interest such as to countervail the public interest in freedom of expression. A communication about some aspect [257] of government activity which does no harm to the interests of the nation cannot, even where the original disclosure has been made in breach of confidence, be restrained on the ground of a nebulous equitable duty of conscience serving no useful practical purpose.

. . . .

This leads on to consideration of the question whether "The Sunday Times" should be held liable to account to the Crown for profits made from past and future serialisation of Spycatcher. An account of profits made through breach of confidence is a recognised form of remedy available to a claimant: *Peter Pan Manufacturing Corporation v. Corsets Silhouette Ltd.* [1969] 1 W.L.R. 96; cf. *Reading v. Attorney-General* [1951] A.C. 507. In cases where the information disclosed is of a commercial character an account of profits may provide some compensation to the claimant for loss which he has suffered through the disclosure, but damages are the main remedy for such loss. The remedy is, in my opinion, more satisfactorily to be attributed to the principle that no one should be permitted to gain from his own wrongdoing. Its availability may also, in general, serve a useful purpose in lessening the temptation for recipients of confidential information to misuse it for financial gain. In the present case "The Sunday Times" did misuse confidential information and it would be naive to suppose that the prospect of financial gain was not one of the reasons why it did so. I can perceive no good ground why the remedy should not be made available to the Crown in the circumstances of this case, and I would therefore hold the Crown entitled to an account of profits in respect of the publication on 12 July 1987. I would add that in my opinion "The Sunday Times," in the taking of the account, is not entitled to deduct in computing any gain the sums paid to Mr. Wright's publishers as consideration for the licence granted by the latter, since neither Mr. Wright nor his publishers were or would in the future be in a position to maintain an action in England for recovery of such payments. Nor would the courts of this country enforce a claim by them to the copyright in a work the publication of which they had brought about contrary to the public interest: cf. *Glyn v. Weston Feature Film Co.* [1916] 1 Ch. 261, 269. Mr Wright is powerless to prevent anyone who chooses to do so from publishing Spycatcher in whole or in part in this country, or to obtain any other remedy against them. There remains of [263] course, the question whether the Crown might successfully maintain a claim that it is in equity the owner of the copyright in the book. Such a claim has not yet been advanced, but might well succeed if it were to be.'

Lord Goff of Chieveley:

'I start with the broad general principle (which I do not intend in any way to be definitive) that a duty of confidence arises when confidential information comes to the knowledge of a person (the confidant) in circumstances where he has notice, or is held to have agreed, that the information is confidential, with the effect that it would be just in all the circumstances that he should be precluded from disclosing the information to others. I have used the word "notice" advisedly, in order to avoid the (here unnecessary) question of the extent to which actual knowledge is necessary; though I of course understand knowledge to include circumstances where the confidant has deliberately closed his eyes to the obvious. The existence of this broad general principle reflects the fact that there is such a public interest in the maintenance of confidences, that the law will provide remedies for their protection.

I realise that, in the vast majority of cases, in particular those concerned with trade secrets, the duty of confidence will arise from a transaction or relationship between the parties—often a contract, in which event the duty may arise by reason of either an express or an implied term of that contract. It is in such cases as these that the expressions "confider" and "confidant" are perhaps most aptly employed. But it is well settled that a duty of confidence may arise in equity independently of such cases; and I have expressed the circumstances in which the duty arises in broad terms, not merely to embrace those cases where a third party receives information from a person who is under a duty of confidence in respect of it, knowing that it has been disclosed by that person to him in breach of his duty of confidence, but also to include certain situations, beloved of law teachers—where an obviously confidential document is wafted by an electric fan out of a window into a crowded street, or where an obviously confidential document, such as a private diary, is dropped in a public place, and is then picked up by a passer-by. I also have in mind the situations where secrets of importance to national security come into the possession of members of the public—a point to which I shall refer in a moment. I have however deliberately avoided the fundamental question whether, contract apart, the duty lies simply "in the notion of an obligation of conscience arising from the circumstances in or through which the information was communicated or obtained" (see *Moorgate Tobacco Co. Ltd. v. Philip Morris Ltd. (No. 2)* (1984) 156 C.L.R. 414, 438, per Deane J., and see also *Seager v. Copydex Ltd.* [1967] 1 W.L.R. 923, 931, per Lord Denning M.R.), or whether confidential information may also be regarded as property (as to which see Dr Francis Gurry's valuable monograph on *Breach of Confidence* (1984), pp. 46–56 and Professors Birks' *An Introduction to the Law of Restitution* (1985), pp. 343–344). I would also, like Megarry J. in *Coco v. A. N. Clark (Engineers) Ltd.* [1969] R.P.C. 41, 48, wish to keep open the question whether detriment to the plaintiff is an essential ingredient of an action for breach of confidence. Obviously, detriment [282] or potential detriment to the plaintiff will nearly always form part of his case; but this may not always be necessary. Some possible cases where there need be no detriment are mentioned in the judgment of Megarry J. to which I have just referred (at p. 48), and in Gurry, *Breach of Confidence*, at pp. 407–408. In the present case the point is immaterial, since it is established that in cases of Government secrets the Crown has to establish not only that the information is confidential, but also that publication would be to its "detriment" in the sense that the public interest requires that it should not be published. That the word "detriment" should be extended so far as to include such a case perhaps indicates that everything depends upon how wide a meaning can be given to the word "detriment" in this context.

To this broad general principle, there are three limiting principles to which I wish to refer. The first limiting principle (which is rather an expression of the scope of the duty) is highly relevant to this appeal. It is that the principle of confidentiality only applies to information to the extent that it is confidential. In particular, once it has entered what is usually called the public domain (which means no more than that the information in question is so generally accessible that, in all the circumstances, it cannot be regarded as confidential) then, as a general rule, the principle of confidentiality can have no application to it. I shall revert to this limiting principle at a later stage.

The second limiting principle is that the duty of confidence applies neither to useless information, nor to trivia. There is no need for me to develop this point.

The third limiting principle is of far greater importance. It is that, although the basis of the law's protection of confidence is that there is a public interest that confidences should be preserved and protected by the law, nevertheless that public interest may be outweighed by some other countervailing public interest which favours disclosure. This limitation may apply, as the learned judge pointed out, to all types of confidential information. It is this limiting principle which may require a court to carry out a balancing operation, weighing the public interest in maintaining confidence against a countervailing public interest favouring disclosure.

. . . .

In cases concerned with Government secrets . . . . it is incumbent upon the Crown, in order to restrain disclosure of Government secrets, not only to show that the information is confidential, but also to show that it is in the public interest that it should not be published. . . . The reason for this additional requirement in cases concerned with Government secrets appears to be that, although in the case of private citizens there is a public interest that confidential information should as such be protected, in the case of Government secrets the mere fact of confidentiality does not alone support such a conclusion, because in a free society there is a continuing public interest that the workings of government should be open to scrutiny and criticism. From this it follows that, in such cases, there must be demonstrated some other public interest which requires that publication should be restrained.

. . . .

[285] As I have already indicated, it is well established that a duty of confidence can only apply in respect of information which is confidential: see *Saltman Engineering Co. Ltd. v. Campbell Engineering Co. Ltd.*, 65 R.P.C. 203, 215, per Lord Greene M.R. From this it should logically follow that, if confidential information which is the subject of a duty of confidence ceases to be confidential, then the duty of confidence should cease to bind the confidant. . . . [Lord Goff concluded that this rule did not depend upon whether the information had been revealed by the confider or by some other person.] . . .

Even so, it has been held by the learned judge, and by all members of the Court of Appeal in the present case, that Peter Wright cannot be released from his duty of confidence by his own publication of the confidential information, apparently on the basis that he cannot be allowed to profit from his own wrong. I feel bound to say that, in my opinion, this proposition calls for careful examination.

The statement that a man shall not be allowed to profit from his own wrong is in very general terms, and does not of itself provide any sure guidance to the solution of a problem in any particular case. That there are groups of cases in which a man is not allowed to profit from his own wrong, is certainly true. An important section of the law of restitution is concerned with cases in which a defendant is required to make restitution in respect of benefits acquired through his own wrongful act—notably cases of waiver of tort; of benefits acquired by certain criminal acts; of benefits acquired in breach of a fiduciary relationship; and, of course, of benefits acquired in breach of confidence. The plaintiff's claim to restitution is usually enforced by an account of profits made by the defendant through his wrong at the plaintiff's expense. This remedy of an account is alternative to the remedy of damages, which in cases of breach of confidence is now available, despite the equitable nature of the wrong, through a beneficent interpretation of the Chancery Amendment Act 1858 (Lord Cairns' Act), and which by reason of the difficulties attending the taking of an account is often regarded as a more satisfactory remedy, at least in cases where the confidential information is of a commercial nature, and quantifiable damage may therefore have been suffered.

I have to say, however, that I know of no case (apart from the present) in which the maxim has been invoked in order to hold that a person under an obligation is not released from that obligation by the destruction of the subject matter of the obligation, on the ground that that destruction was the result of his own wrongful act. To take an obvious case, a bailee who by his own wrongful, even deliberately wrongful, act destroys the goods entrusted to him, is obviously relieved of his obligation as bailee, though he is of course liable in damages for his tort. Likewise a nightwatchman who deliberately sets fire to and destroys the building he is employed to watch; and likewise also the keeper at a zoo who turns out to be an animal rights campaigner and releases rare birds or animals which escape irretrievably into the countryside. On this approach, it is difficult to see how a confidant who publishes the relevant confidential information to the whole world can be under any further obligation not to disclose the information, simply because it was he who wrongfully destroyed its confidentiality. The information has, after all, already been so fully disclosed that it is in the public domain: how, therefore, can he thereafter be sensibly restrained from disclosing it? Is he not even to be permitted to mention in public what is now common knowledge? For his wrongful act, he may be held [287] liable in damages, or may be required to make restitution; but, to adapt the words of Lord Buckmaster, the confidential information, as confidential information, has ceased to exist, and with it should go, as a matter of principle, the obligation of confidence. . . .

. . . .

I have naturally been concerned by the fact that so far in this case it appears to have been accepted on all sides that Peter Wright should not be released from his obligation of confidence. I cannot help thinking that this assumption may have been induced, in part at least, by three factors—first, the fact that Peter Wright himself is not a party to the litigation, with the result that no representations have been made on his behalf; second, the wholly unacceptable nature of his conduct; and third, the fact that he appears now to be able, with impunity, to reap vast sums from his disloyalty. Certainly, the prospect of Peter Wright, safe in his Australian haven, reaping further profits from the sale of his book in this country is most unattractive. The purpose of perpetuating Peter Wright's duty of confidence appears to be, in part to deter others, and in part to ensure that a man who has committed so flagrant a breach of his duty should not be enabled freely to exploit the formerly confidential information, placed by him in the public domain, with impunity. Yet the real reason why he is able to exploit it is because he has found a safe place to do so. If within the jurisdiction of the English courts, he would be held liable to account for any profits made by him from his wrongful disclosure, which might properly include profits accruing to him from any subsequent exploitation of the confidential information after its disclosure: and, in cases where damages were regarded as the appropriate remedy, the confidant would be liable to compensate the confider for any damage, present or future, suffered by him by reason of his wrong. So far as I can see, the confider must be content with remedies such as these.

I have considered whether the confidant who, in breach of duty, places confidential information in the public domain, might remain at least under a duty thereafter not to exploit the information, so disclosed, for his own benefit. . . . To me, however, it is doubtful whether the answer to this question lies in artificially prolonging the duty of confidence in information which is no longer confidential. Indeed, there is some ground for saying that the true answer is that the copyright in the book, including the film rights, are held by him on constructive trust for the confider—so that the remedy lies not in breach of confidence, but in restitution or in property, whichever way you care to look at it: see, in this connection, ante, pp. 210D—211C, per Dillon L.J.'

Questions:

Does this case suggest that the courts are moving towards a view that the obligation of confidence depends upon the proprietary nature of the confidential information (ie a view that the claimant's has property which merits protection)? If this approach becomes the prevailing view, should the appropriate remedy be proprietary or personal? Should the remedy effect disgorgement or repair damage? Is the answer to each of these questions different if the basis of the obligation is, for example, the protection of socially valuable relationships?

The next case is usually regarded as exceptional. Remedies for breach of the equitable obligation of confidence are generally personal, not proprietary. The claimant is entitled to an account of profits, or to (equitable) damages, but not to a constructive trust. This may be changing, so the next case has added importance in revealing justifications which have been found persuasive in other jurisdictions.

[539] *Lac Minerals Ltd v International Corona Resources Ltd* (1989) 61 DLR (4th) 14 (Canadian SCt), 17 *per* Wilson J, 44–57 *per* La Forest J, 74–5 *per* Sopinka J:
[The claimant, a junior mining company, entered into negotiations with the defendant, a senior mining company, with a view to exploiting the mineral rights on certain land. During the course of those negotiations, the claimant company revealed that its drilling results indicated that the adjoining land also contained substantial gold deposits, and that the claimant company was therefore seeking to acquire this land. While negotiations were still in progress, the defendant company put in a successful competing offer for this adjoining land. Negotiations then broke down and the defendant company developed the adjoining land for its own benefit. Although the claimant company was unsuccessful in asserting that the defendant owed the claimant fiduciary obligations, it successfully argued that the defendant was in breach of its equitable obligations of confidence and that the adjoining land was therefore held on constructive trust for the claimant.]

Wilson J:
'I believe that the remedy of constructive trust is available for breach of confidence as well as for breach of fiduciary duty. The distinction between the two causes of action as they arise on the facts of this case is a very fine one. Inherent in both causes of action are concepts of good conscience and vulnerability. It would be strange indeed if the law accorded them widely disparate remedies. In his article on "The Role of Proprietary Relief in the Modern Law of Restitution", John D. McCamus, Cambridge Lecture (1987) 141 at p. 150, Professor McCamus poses the rhetorical question:

> Would it not be anomalous to allow more sophisticated forms of relief for breach of fiduciary duty than for those forms of wrongdoing recognized by the law of torts, some of which, at least, would commonly be more offensive from the point of view of either public policy or our moral sensibilities than some breaches of fiduciary duty?

. . .'

La Forest J:

'The appropriate remedy in this case can not be divorced from the findings of fact made by the courts below. As I indicated earlier, there is no doubt in my mind that but for the actions of LAC in misusing confidential information and thereby acquiring the Williams property, that property would have been acquired by Corona. That finding is fundamental to the determination of the appropriate remedy.

. . .

The issue then is this. If it is established that one party (here LAC) has been enriched by the acquisition of an asset, the Williams property, that would have, but for the actions of that party been acquired by the plaintiff (here Corona), and if the acquisition of that asset amounts to a breach of duty to the plaintiff, here either a breach of fiduciary obligation or a breach of a duty of confidence, what remedy is available to the party deprived of the benefit? In my view the constructive trust is one available remedy, and in this case it is the only appropriate remedy.

In my view the facts present in this case make out a restitutionary claim, or what is the same thing, a claim for unjust enrichment. When one talks of restitution, one normally talks of giving back to someone something that has been taken from them (a restitutionary proprietary award), or its equivalent value (a personal restitutionary award). As the Court of Appeal noted in this case, Corona never in fact owned the Williams property, and so it cannot be "given back" to them. However, there are concurrent findings below that but for its interception by LAC, Corona would have acquired the property.

. . .

That enrichment is also unjust, or unjustified, so that the plaintiff is entitled to a remedy. There is, in the words of Dickson J. in *Pettkus v. Becker* (1980), 117 D.L.R. (3d) 257 at p. 274, [1980] 2 S.C.R. 834, 19 R.F.L. (2d) 165, "an absence of any juristic reason for the enrichment". The determination that the enrichment is "unjust" does not refer to abstract notions of morality and justice, but flows directly from the finding that there was a breach of a legally recognized duty for which the courts will grant relief. Restitution is a distinct body of law governed by its own developing system of rules. Breaches of fiduciary duties and breaches of confidence are both wrongs for which restitutionary relief is often appropriate.

. . .

In breach of confidence cases as well, there is considerable flexibility in remedy. Injunctions preventing the continued use of the confidential information are commonly awarded. Obviously that remedy would be of no use in this case where the total benefit accrues to the defendant through a single misuse of information. An account of profits is also often available. Indeed in both courts below an account of profits to the date of transfer of the mine was awarded. Usually an accounting is not a restitutionary measure of damages. Thus, while it is measured according to the defendant's gain, it is not measured by the defendant's gain at the plaintiff's expense. Occasionally, as in this case, the measures coincide. In a case quite relevant here, this court unanimously imposed a constructive trust over property obtained from the misuse of confidential information: *Pre-Cam Exploration & Development Ltd v. McTavish* (1966), 57 D.L.R. (2d) 557, 50 C.P.R. 299, [1966] S.C.R. 551. More recently, a compensatory remedy has been introduced into the law of confidential relations. Thus in *Seager v. Copydex Ltd. (No. 2)*, [1969] 2 All E.R. 718 (C.A.), an inquiry was directed concerning the market value of the information between a willing buyer and a willing seller. The defendant had unconsciously plagiarized the plaintiff's design. In those circumstances it would obviously have been unjust to exclude the defendant from the market when there was room for more than one participant.

I noted earlier that the jurisdictional base for the law of confidence is a matter of some dispute. In the case at bar however, it is not suggested that either the contractual or property origins of the doctrine can be used to found the remedy. Thus while there can be considerable remedial flexibility for such claims, it was not argued that the court may not have jurisdiction to award damages as compensation and not merely in lieu of an injunction in the exercise of its equitable jurisdiction, and since I am of the view that a constructive trust is in any event the appropriate remedy, I need not consider the question of jurisdiction further.

In view of this remedial flexibility, detailed consideration must be given to the reasons a remedy measured by LAC's gain at Corona's expense is more appropriate than a remedy compensating the plaintiff for the loss suffered.

. . .

The essence of the imposition of fiduciary obligations is its utility in the promotion and preservation of desired social behaviour and institutions. Likewise with the protection of confidences. In the modern world the exchange of confidential information is both necessary and expected. Evidence of an accepted business morality in the mining industry was given by the defendant, and the Court of Appeal found that the practice was not only reasonable, but that it would foster the exploration and development of our natural resources. The institution of bargaining in good faith is one that is worthy of legal protection in those circumstances where that protection accords with the expectations of the parties.

. . .

The imposition of a remedy which restores an asset to the party who would have acquired it but for a breach of fiduciary duties or duties of confidence acts as a deterrent to the breach of duty and strengthens the social fabric those duties are imposed to protect. The elements of a claim in unjust enrichment having been made out, I have found no reason why the imposition of a restitutionary remedy should not be granted.

. . .

There is no unanimous agreement on the circumstances in which a constructive trust will be imposed. Some guidelines can, however, be suggested. First, no special relationship between the parties is necessary.

. . .

Secondly, it is not the case that a constructive trust should be reserved for situations where a right of property is recognized. That would limit the constructive trust to its institutional function, and deny to it the status of a remedy, its more important role. Thus, it is not in all cases that a pre-existing right of property will exist when a constructive trust is ordered. The imposition of a constructive trust can both recognize and create a right of property.

. . .

It is not the recognition of a right of property that leads to a constructive trust. It is not necessary, therefore, to determine whether confidential information is property, though a finding that it was would only strengthen the conclusion that a constructive trust is appropriate. This is the view of Fridman and McLeod, *Restitution* (1982), at p. 539, where they say:

> . . . there appears to be no doubt that a fiduciary who has consciously, made use of confidential information for private gain will be forced to account for the entire profits by holding such profits made from the use of the confidential information on a constructive trust for the beneficiary-estate. The proprietary remedy flows naturally from the conclusion that the information itself belonged to the beneficiary, and there has been no transaction effective to divest his rights over the property.

I do not countenance the view that a proprietary remedy can be imposed whenever it is "just" to do so, unless further guidance can be given as to what those situations may be. To allow such a result would be to leave the determination of proprietary rights to "some mix of judicial discretion . . . subjective views about which party 'ought to win' . . . and 'the formless void of individual moral opinion'", *per* Deane J. in *Muschinski v. Dodds* (1985), 160 C.L.R. 583 at p. 616.

As Deane J. further noted, at p. 616:

> Long before Lord Seldon's anachronism identifying the Chancellor's foot as the measure of Chancery relief, undefined notions of "justice" and what was "fair" had given way in the law of equity to the rule of ordered principle which is of the essence of any coherent system of rational law. The mere fact that it would be unjust or unfair in a situation of discord for the owner of a legal estate to assert his ownership against another provides, of itself, no mandate for a judicial declaration that the ownership in whole or in part lies, in equity, in that other.

Much of the difficulty disappears if it is recognized that in this context the issue of the appropriate remedy only arises once a valid restitutionary claim has been made out. The constructive trust awards a right in property, but that right can only arise once a right to relief has been established. In the vast majority of cases a constructive trust will not be the appropriate remedy. Thus, in *Hunter, supra*, had the restitutionary claim been made out, there would have been no reason to award a constructive trust, as the plaintiff's claim could have been satisfied simply by a personal monetary award; a constructive trust should only be awarded if there is reason to grant to the plaintiff the additional rights that flow from recognition of a right of property. Among the most important of these will be that it is appropriate that the plaintiff receive the priority accorded to the holder of a right of property in a bankruptcy. More important in this case is the right of the property holder to have changes in value accrue to his account rather than to the account of the wrongdoer. Here as well it is justified to grant a right of property since the concurrent findings below are that the defendant intercepted the plaintiff and thereby frustrated its efforts to obtain a specific and unique property that the courts below held would otherwise have been acquired. The recognition of a constructive trust simply redirects the title of the Williams property to its original course. The moral quality of the defendants' act may also be another consideration in determining whether a proprietary remedy is appropriate. Allowing the defendant to retain a specific asset when it was obtained through conscious wrongdoing may so offend a court that it would deny to the defendant the right to retain the property. This situation will be more rare, since the focus of the inquiry should be upon the reasons for recognizing a right of property in the plaintiff, not on the reasons for denying it to the defendant.

Having specific regard to the uniqueness of the Williams property, to the fact that but for LAC's breaches of duty Corona would have acquired it, and recognizing the virtual impossibility of accurately valuing the property, I am of the view that it is appropriate to award Corona a constructive trust over that land.'

Sopinka J (dissenting on the remedy):

'The foundation of action for breach of confidence does not rest solely on one of the traditional jurisdictional bases for action of contract, equity or property. The action is *sui generis* relying on all three to enforce the policy of the law that confidences be respected: see Gurry, *Breach of Confidence* (Clarendon Press, Oxford, 1984), at pp. 25–6, and Goff & Jones, *The Law of Restitution*, 3rd ed. (Sweet & Maxwell, 1986) at pp. 664–7.

> This multi-faceted jurisdictional basis for the action provides the court with considerable flexibility in fashioning a remedy. The jurisdictional basis supporting the particular claim is relevant in determining the appropriate remedy: . . . . A constructive trust is ordinarily reserved for those situations where a right of property is recognized.
>
> . . .
>
> Although confidential information has some of the characteristics of property, its foothold as such is tenuous.
>
> . . .
>
> As a result, there is virtually no support in the cases for the imposition of a constructive trust over property acquired as a result of the use of confidential information.'

5.10.3 Constructive trusts and breaches of common law obligations

So far the focus has been on equitable obligations and the possibility that their breach might be remedied by the imposition of a constructive trust. It remains a moot point whether breach of common law obligations might also be remedied by disgorgement (rather than by damages orders) and, moreover, whether the requirement to disgorge would be effected by constructive trust or by personal obligation. The idea of disgorgement remedies for breach of common law obligations is finding increasing favour;[38] the idea that the remedy might be proprietary is, as already noted, increasingly disputed.

The appeal of disgorgement remedies, and their common justification, is that 'no man should be allowed to profit from his wrong'. A disgorgement remedy would strip the wrongdoer of the profits of the wrongdoing. Attempts to justify this high-minded response often call on cases such as *Cleaver v Mutual Reserve Fund Life Association*,[39] where Fry LJ said: 'It appears to me that no system of jurisprudence can with reason include among the rights which it enforces rights directly resulting to the person asserting them from the crime of that person. If no action can arise from fraud, it seems impossible to suppose that it can arise from felony or misdemeanor. The principle of public policy, like all such principles, must be applied to all cases to which it can be applied without reference to the particular character of the right asserted or the form of its assertion.' This principle operates to ensure that a thief does not benefit from the theft, or that a murderer does not benefit from the unlawful killing.[40] However, this principle does not go so far as to compel disgorgement. Rather, it denies the wrongdoer the assistance of the law in claiming the fruits of the wrongdoing. The further step which the disgorgement remedy represents requires more considered justification.

Even if the disgorgement remedy can be justified, its potential proprietary consequences remain controversial. 'Disgorgement' bears no necessary relationship to the loss suffered by the victims of the breach, and reflects no express or implied agreement between the parties to deliver such a reward. This, added to the usual

[38] See, eg, Law Commission Report (No. 247): *Aggravated, Exemplary and Restitutionary Damages* (1997), recommendations 7–9 and Draft Bill, clause 12, suggesting that the common law ought to be allowed to develop unimpeded, but that, in addition, restitutionary damages (their preferred term) ought to be available where the defendant's wrong (other than a breach of contract) was committed with 'deliberate and outrageous disregard of the claimant's rights'.

[39] [1892] 1 QB 147, 156.

[40] *In the Estate of Crippen* [1911] P 108; *Re Sigsworth* [1935] 1 Ch 89.

arguments already encountered in relation to proprietary remedies, is used by many commentators to deny the remedy proprietary consequences. The cases, on the other hand, reflect a more ambivalent response.

The scope of the discussion would be enormous were it to include the availability of personal remedies against wrongdoers to ensure that they are stripped of the profits of their wrongdoing. Here, however, we are concerned only with the (still difficult) question of the availability of proprietary remedies to compel disgorgement of the profits of wrongdoing.[41]

[540] *Brown v Litton* (1711) 1 P Wms 140, 24 ER 329, at 329 *per* Lord Keeper Harcourt:

[Footnotes in the original are omitted.]

> 'But Lord Keeper said, that the case of an executor's putting out money without the indemnity of a decree if it were on a real security, and one that there was no ground at that time to suspect, had not been settled; though it was his opinion, that the executor under such circumstances, was not liable to answer for the loss, and so should account for the interest.
>
> But that he took the defendant, in this case, to be more like a trustee than an executor, and if so, he ought clearly to account for the profits made of the money; that the primary intent in carrying abroad this money was, to invest it in trade, and not to return with it home again; and therefore, the defendant having observed the intent of the testator in trading therewith, and having taken such a prudent care in the management of it, as (it might be presumed) he would have taken of his own money, his Lordship apprehended the defendant would not have been liable to answer for any loss that might have happened; and compared it to the case of two joint traders, where, if one dies, and the survivor carries on the trade after the death of the partner, the survivor shall answer for the gain made by this trade. . . . But that, to recompense the defendant for his care in trading with it, the Master should settle a proper salary for the pains and trouble he had been at in the management thereof . . .'

Question:

> Does the previous extract suggest that a constructive trust will be imposed whenever a defendant makes a profit trading with another's property, or is the rule limited to particular types of defendants, or to particular types of property, or to particular claimant's interests in that property?

[541] *Halifax Building Society v Thomas* [1996] Ch 217 (CA), 224, 226–9 *per* Peter Gibson LJ:

[The defendant obtained a mortgage advance from the claimant by fraudulently misrepresenting his identity and earnings. He purchased a property which increased

[41] As a result, there is no discussion here of the difficult area of personal liability (confusingly, termed personal liability 'as a constructive trustee') for 'knowing assistance' in a breach of trust and 'knowing receipt' of trust property disposed of in breach of trust. These are considered in Sections 7.2.4 and 7.4.

substantially in value. The defendant could not maintain his mortgage repayments, and the property was repossessed and sold. The building society unsuccessfully sought to retain not just the sums due to it under the mortgage, but also the profit which the defendant had made from his fraud.]

'Mr. Waters puts the society's case in each of two ways: that Mr. Thomas should be required to account to the society on the basis of the application of the doctrine of waiver of tort, alternatively as the beneficiary of a constructive trust of the surplus.... He lays emphasis on the fact that the surplus represents a profit from a fraud. He submits that it would be offensive to basic concepts of justice if a fraudster were to be allowed to take that profit....

.... Mr. Waters .... accepts that there is no English authority to support the proposition that a wrongdoing defendant will be required to account for a profit which is not based on the use of the property of the wronged plaintiff. Cases where a fiduciary is required to account for a profit are plainly distinguishable from the facts of the present case. So too is the one authority cited by Mr. Waters of an action for an account which was not based on the use of the property of the plaintiff, the decision of the U.S. District Court for the Southern District of New York, *Federal Sugar Refining Co. v. United States Sugar Equalization Board* (1920) 268 F. 575. In that case a buyer contracted to purchase from the plaintiff, the defendant procured the buyer to break that contract and purchase from itself instead, and the plaintiff's claim to recover from the defendant the profit made on the sale was upheld on demurrer.

Mr. Waters's difficulty is that the society's only interest was that of a secured creditor who has fully recovered all that it was entitled to recover under the mortgage. When it discovered the fraud, it could and did affirm the mortgage and proceed to enforce its rights as mortgagee..... [It did not adopt its alternative course of action, which was to set aside the mortgage], obtained as it was by fraud. It might then have claimed in equity that it remained the owner of the moneys advanced and traced those moneys into the flat and the sale proceeds, or it might have made a common law claim for money had and received to the society's use. Mr. Waters accepts that the mortgage was voidable by the fraud, not void, and, absent avoidance, it cannot assert a property right.

Mr. Waters submits that there were two further remedies available to the society, neither of them inconsistent with the affirmation of the mortgage. One was to sue in tort, claiming damages for deceit.... The other, he says, was to waive the tort, in the sense that that term has been explained in *United Australia Ltd. v. Barclays Bank Ltd.* [1941] A.C. 1 as meaning that the plaintiff chooses not to sue in tort for damages but sues instead in restitution for the recovery of the benefit taken by the wrongdoer. In the *United Australia* case the House of Lords did away with the fiction that the restitutionary claim was dependent on an implied promise by the wrongdoer. So, Mr. Waters says, there is no inconsistency between the affirmation of the mortgage and the recovery thereunder on the one hand and the restitutionary claim on the other, and there is no dispute but that deceit is a tort that is waivable.

Attractively though Mr. Waters has argued the point, I remain wholly unpersuaded that in the circumstances of the present case the law should accord a restitutionary remedy to a secured creditor who has elected not to avoid the mortgage but to affirm it and has received full satisfaction thereunder. To my mind there is an inconsistency between a person being such a creditor and yet claiming more than that to which he is contractually entitled and which he has already fully recovered. Once the creditor has so elected and recovered in full, I do not see why the law should come to his aid to allow him to make a further claim. In *In re Simms; Ex parte Trustee* [1934] Ch. 1 this court refused to allow a trustee in bankruptcy, who had elected to treat a receiver as a tortfeasor for converting to his own use the chattels of a bankrupt, to recover the profits made by the receiver as money had and received. The authority of that case is weakened by the reliance by this court on the now exploded implied promise theory, but I note that it is still cited in text-books: see, for example, *Chitty on Contracts*, 27th ed. (1994), vol. 1, p. 1437, para. 29–052) and it serves to illustrate that not every action for an account of profits from a wrongdoer, even where there has been use of the plaintiff's property, will be allowed, and that it may be barred when there has been an election for another remedy.

Further I am not satisfied that in the circumstances of the present case it would be right to treat the unjust enrichment of Mr. Thomas as having been gained "at the expense of" the society, even allowing for the possibility of an extended meaning for those words to apply to cases of non-subtractive restitution for a wrong. There is no decided authority that comes anywhere near to covering the present circumstances. I do not overlook the fact that the policy of law is to view with disfavour a wrongdoer benefiting from his wrong, the more so when the wrong amounts to fraud, but it cannot be suggested that there is a universally applicable principle that in every case there will be restitution of benefit from a wrong. As Professor Birks says (*An Introduction to the Law of Restitution*, p. 24): "there are some circumstances in which enrichment by wrongdoing has to be given up. That is, the wrong itself is not always in itself a sufficient factor to call for restitution." On the facts of the present case, in my judgment, the fraud is not in itself a sufficient factor to allow the society to require Mr. Thomas to account to it.

I would add that, in so far as the society relies on the submission that to allow a fraudster to take a profit derived from his fraud would be offensive to concepts of justice, the House of Lords in *Tinsley v. Milligan* [1994] 1 A.C. 340 [see **[509]** above], although divided in their decision, were unanimous in rejecting the "public conscience" test as determinative of the extent to which rights created by illegal transactions should be recognised. It is not appropriate to ask whether the allowance of a claim would be an affront to the public conscience. The correct test is whether a claimant to an interest in property must plead or rely on an illegality. If so, he will not be entitled to recover. That question does not arise in the present case where it is the society which is claiming a declaration.

For these reasons I conclude that section 105 required the society to hold the surplus in trust for Mr. Thomas, unless a constructive trust operated in its own favour. To that question I now turn.

Mr. Waters again relies on the fact that the surplus represents a profit derived from a fraud, which, he submits, justifies allowing the society the benefits of a proprietary claim to the surplus. Again Mr. Waters is unable to cite any English authority that lends direct support to this claim. He referred us to the statement of Lord Westbury in *McCormick v. Grogan* (1869) L.R. 4 H.L. 82, 97:

> "the jurisdiction which is invoked here by the appellant is founded altogether on personal fraud. It is a jurisdiction by which a court of equity, proceeding on the ground of fraud, converts the party who has committed it into a trustee for the party who is injured by that fraud."

But that statement must be read in the context in which it was made, namely the jurisdiction where a secret trust is alleged. It cannot be elevated into a universal principle that wherever there is personal fraud the fraudster will become a trustee for the party injured by the fraud.

Again in the present case there is the difficulty that the society, having affirmed the mortgage, remained only a secured creditor. I cannot accept that the wrongdoing of the mortgagor can translate the mortgagee into the owner of the entire beneficial interest in the property when the mortgage has not been set aside. That appears to have been the view too of Hoffmann J. in another case of mortgage fraud, *Chief Constable of Leicestershire v. M.* [1989] 1 W.L.R. 20, 21, where he said:

> "None of the lenders have made any claim by way of constructive trust or otherwise to the profits made on the houses bought with their money. They have preferred to affirm the advances and enforce their rights under the mortgages."

In *Lister & Co. v. Stubbs* (1890) 45 Ch.D. 1 this court considered the case of a servant who received a bribe. Lindley L.J. said, at p. 15, that the relationship between the plaintiff employers and the defendant servant in respect of that bribe

> "is that of debtor and creditor; it is not that of trustee and cestui que trust. We are asked to hold that it is—which would involve consequences which, I confess, startle me."

That decision has been subjected to much criticism and was disapproved by the Privy Council in *Attorney-General for Hong Kong v. Reid* [1994] 1 A.C. 324 [see **[535]** above] on the basis that it was inconsistent with basic principles of equity affecting the conduct of a fiduciary. In *Daly v. Sydney Stock Exchange Ltd.* (1986) 160 C.L.R. 371[see **[514]** above], 379 Gibbs C.J. refused to accept that money lent by an investor to a firm in a fiduciary relationship with him should be treated as subject to a constructive trust. He said that the reasons of Lindley L.J. in the *Lister* case, 45 Ch.D. 1 appeared to him to be "impeccable when applied to the case in which the person claiming the money has simply made an outright loan to the defendant." In the present case there was no fiduciary relationship between Mr. Thomas and the society in respect of the mortgage but merely that of debtor and secured creditor.

English law has not followed other jurisdictions where the constructive trust has become a remedy for unjust enrichment. As is said in *Snell's Equity*, 29th ed. (1990), p. 197:

> "In England the constructive trust has in general remained essentially a substantive institution; ownership must not be confused with obligation, nor must the relationship of debtor and creditor be converted into one of trustee and cestui que trust."

In considering whether to extend the law of constructive trusts in order to prevent a fraudster benefiting from his wrong, it is also appropriate to bear in mind that Parliament has acted in recent years (notably in Part VI of the Criminal Justice Act 1988) on the footing that without statutory intervention the criminal might keep the benefit of his crime. Moreover, Parliament has given the courts the power in specific circumstances to confiscate the benefit rather than reward the person against whom the crime has been committed. I bear in mind the wise comment of Hoffmann J. in *Chief Constable of Leicestershire v. M.* [1989] 1 W.L.R. 20, 23:

> "The recent and detailed interventions of Parliament in this field suggest that the courts should not indulge in parallel creativity by the extension of general common law principles."

Accordingly I would reject the argument based on constructive trust.'

[542] *Rochefoucauld v Bousted* [1897] 1 Ch 196, 206 *per* Lindley LJ:
[Re-read the extract at **[403]** above.]

Questions:

1. The trust in *Rochefoucauld v Bousted* was classified as an express trust. Is this appropriate, or is it better classified as a constructive trust? (Note that prior to the enactment of the Limitation Act 1939, express trustees were unable to rely on the Statute of Limitation; constructive trustees, however, were protected by its provisions. This feature encouraged courts to find express, rather than constructive, trusts when it wished to make trustees liable.)
2. Although the courts have never directly considered whether a third party beneficiary could enforce such a constructive trust, cases such as *Binions v Evans* [1972] Ch 359 suggest this would be allowed. What does this say about the enforcement of statutory writing requirements? Contrast this with the approach advocated in Section 4.3.

[543] *A-G v Blake* [1998] Ch 439 (CA), 455–9 *per* Lord Woolf MR for the Court and *per* Lord Nicholls (HL, unreported 27 July 2000):
[The Crown successfully sought to intercept the royalties payable in respect of an autobiography by George Blake, a former member of the Secret Intelligence Service. Blake became a Russian spy and was later caught and imprisoned for breach of the Official Secrets Act. He escaped from prison and fled to Moscow. The Court of Appeal agreed that Blake was no longer subject to fiduciary obligations as an employee (since his employment with the Crown had long ceased), nor to equitable obligations of confidence (since the material in issue was not confidential). He did, however, owe a lifelong contractual obligation not to disclose matters related to his employment. The extract below relates to the availability of a disgorgement remedy for breach of this contractual obligation. However, since the Attorney-General declined to press the argument, the comments are dicta only. The point was argued on appeal to the House of Lords. Their decision is still pending.]

Lord Woolf MR:

'The general rule is that damages for breach of contract are compensatory not restitutionary, that is to say, they are measured by the loss to the plaintiff and not by the gain to the defendant. It is unnecessary to cite authority for this proposition, since it is beyond dispute. It is accepted to be the general position by the Law Commission in its Consultation Paper No. 132, *Aggravated, Exemplary and Restitutionary Damages* (1993), p. 159, para. 7.7. Its elevation into a fundamental principle which admits of no exceptions, however, has been disputed, attributed to inertia and has attracted widespread (though not universal) academic criticism. [See, Further Reading below.] Even its proponents recognise that some flexibility is desirable, Jackman (for example) suggesting that the moral calibre of the defendant's conduct might justify an award of restitutionary damages for a cynical breach of contract.

Judicial opinion is also divided. The exclusively compensatory basis of damages for breach of contract does not lack judicial critics, and there are signs that the traditional view that the rule admits of no exceptions may not long survive. In *Hospital Products Ltd. v. United States Surgical Corporation* (1984) 156 C.L.R. 41 [see **[533]** above], Deane J. indicated that he regarded the question as deserving of reconsideration; and in *Jaggard v. Sawyer* [1995] 1 W.L.R. 269, 281 Sir Thomas Bingham M.R. expressed the view that the judgments in *Surrey County Council v. Bredero Homes Ltd.* [1993] 1 W.L.R. 1361 [**[709]** below] (in which the court refused to countenance the possibility of awarding restitutionary damages for breach of contract) might "not be the last word on the subject."

In reality the doctrine is already subject to exceptions, for the gain (or saving of expense) made by the defendant is sometimes used as the measure of the plaintiff's loss. *Wrotham Park Estate Co. Ltd. v. Parkside Homes Ltd.* [1974] 1 W.L.R. 798 and the cases which followed it are examples of this. In such cases the measure of damages is the same, whether they are calculated by reference to the loss sustained by the plaintiff or to the saving of expense by the defendant, with the result that their classification as compensatory or restitutionary has been controversial. Those who insist that they are restitutionary, but reject any further departure from the general rule, justify them by reference to the proprietary nature of a claim to enforce restrictive covenants annexed to land. This is hardly convincing, seeing that the measure of damages cannot depend on whether the proceedings are between the original parties to the contract or their successors in title.

If the court is unable to award restitutionary damages for breach of contract, then the law of contract is seriously defective. It means that in many situations the plaintiff is deprived of any effective remedy for breach of contract, because of a failure to attach a value to the plaintiff's legitimate interest in having the contract duly performed: see Professor Coote, "Contract Damages, *Ruxley*, and the Performance Interest" [1997] C.L.J. 537. In our opinion, the time has come to accept Professor Jones's view, expressed as long ago as 1983 in "The Recovery of Benefits Gained from a Breach of Contract," 99 L.Q.R. 443, 452, that the law is now sufficiently mature to recognise a restitutionary claim for profits made from a breach of contract in appropriate circumstances. The difficult question is not whether restitutionary damages should ever be available for breach of contract, but in what circumstances they should be made available. In *Surrey County Council v. Bredero Homes Ltd.* [1993] 1 W.L.R. 1361 Steyn L.J. gave persuasive reasons why such circumstances should remain exceptional.

We do not think that the basis on which damages are awarded should depend on the defendant's moral culpability alone. The fact that his breach of contract is deliberate and cynical is not by itself a good ground for departing from the normal basis on which damages are awarded. It is not only that the line cannot easily be drawn in practice; it is rather that the defendant's motives will normally be irrelevant. To adapt an observation of Lord Keith of Kinkel made in a different context in *Attorney-General v. Guardian Newspapers Ltd. (No. 2)* [1990] 1 A.C. 109 [see **[538]** above], 261, a natural desire to deprive a deliberate wrongdoer of profit is not a valid ground for departing from the normal measure of damages for breach of contract.

The mere fact that the defendant's breach of his contract with the plaintiff has enabled him to enter into a more profitable contract with someone else should also not be sufficient: *Teacher v. Calder* [1899] A.C. 451 is sound law. Nor should it suffice that, by entering into the later and more profitable contract, the defendant has put it out of his power to perform his contract with the plaintiff: the distinction between the two cases is not one of substance. But we think that there are at least two situations in which justice requires the award of restitutionary damages where compensatory damages would be inadequate.

The first may be described as the case of skimped performance. This is where the defendant fails to provide the full extent of the services which he has contracted to provide and for which he has charged the plaintiff. Professor Jones cites the Louisiana case of *City of New Orleans v. Firemen's Charitable Association* (1891) 9 So. 486 as an example. The defendant contracted with the plaintiff to provide a firefighting service and was paid the full contract price. After the expiry of the contract the plaintiff discovered that the defendant had not provided the stipulated number of firemen or horses or the promised length of hosepipe. The defendant had saved itself substantial expense by the breach, but had not failed to put out any fires in consequence. The court ruled that the plaintiff had not proved that it had suffered any loss and was unable to recover more than nominal damages. Justice surely demands an award of substantial damages in such a case, and the amount of expenditure which the defendant has saved by the breach provides an appropriate measure of damages. This could be achieved by presuming that the plaintiff has suffered a loss of an amount corresponding to the amount by which he has been overcharged for the service actually provided; and the presumption could be justified by invoking the notion of the "consumer surplus." But it would surely be preferable, as well as simpler and more open, to award restitutionary damages.

The second case is where the defendant has obtained his profit by doing the very thing which he contracted not to do. In his article "Restitutionary Damages for Breach of Contract: *Snepp* and the Fusion of Law and Equity" [1987] L.M.C.L.Q. 421, 434 Professor Birks observed: "If you promise not to pursue a particular profit-making activity and then do pursue it, nothing is more apt than that you should make restitution of your profits."

This covers the present case exactly. The defendant's breach of contract in submitting the book for publication did not merely provide him with an opportunity for profit; nor did his contract with the publishers merely put it out of his power to perform his contractual obligations to the Crown. The connection between the breach and the profit is far more direct. He promised not to disclose official information and he did so for profit. He earned the profits by doing the very thing which he had promised not to do.

The two cases have this in common: that in both the profits in question are occasioned directly by the breach, which does not merely provide the defendant with the opportunity to make them; and in both compensatory damages are an inadequate remedy if regard is paid to the objects which the plaintiff sought to achieve by the contract. They do not precisely coincide with the provisional conclusion of the Law Commission in the consultation paper referred to above. However, the present case falls squarely within the two conditions they identify for the existence of such a claim: see pp. 170–171, para. 7.20. There was "deliberate wrongdoing" which could have been restrained by injunction. In addition, the gains which would be made by the defendant are "attributable to the interest infringed," in the sense that they are referable to the disclosure of official information the defendant contracted not to disclose.

Only time will tell whether these distinctions are tenable. They may not hold. But it appears to us that the general rule that damages for breach of contract are compensatory can safely be maintained without denying the availability of restitutionary damages in exceptional cases.'

Lord Nicholls:
[Extract taken from
www.publications.parliament.uk/pa/ld199900/ldjudgmt/jd000727/ blake-2.htm.]
'An account of profits [as a remedy for breach of contract] will be appropriate only in exceptional circumstances. Normally the remedies of damages, specific performance and injunction, coupled with the characterisation of some contractual obligations as fiduciary,

will provide an adequate response to a breach of contract. It will be only in exceptional cases, where those remedies are inadequate, that any question of accounting for profits will arise. No fixed rules can be prescribed. The court will have regard to all the circumstances, including the subject matter of the contract, the purpose of the contractual provision which has been breached, the circumstances in which the breach occurred, the consequences of the breach and the circumstances in which relief is being sought. A useful general guide, although not exhaustive, is whether the plaintiff had a legitimate interest in preventing the defendant's profit-making activity and, hence, in depriving him of his profit.

It would be difficult, and unwise, to attempt to be more specific. [He continued, disagreeing with the Court of Appeal's categories of 'skimped performance' and 'negative obligations', holding the first to be more appropriately remedied by other means, and the second to be too broad. He did, however, agree with their comments on cynical breaches and breaches which enabled the defendant to enter into alternative more profitable ventures.]

The present case

The present case is exceptional. . . .

. . . When he joined the Secret Intelligence Service Blake expressly agreed in writing that he would not disclose official information, during or after his service, in book form or otherwise. He was employed on that basis. That was the basis on which he acquired official information. The Crown had and has a legitimate interest in preventing Blake profiting from the disclosure of official information, whether classified or not, while a member of the service and thereafter. Neither he, nor any other member of the service, should have a financial incentive to break his undertaking. It is of paramount importance that members of the service should have complete confidence in all their dealings with each other, and that those recruited as informers should have the like confidence. Undermining the willingness of prospective informers to co-operate with the services, or undermining the morale and trust between members of the services when engaged on secret and dangerous operations, would jeopardise the effectiveness of the service. An absolute rule against disclosure, visible to all, makes good sense.

In considering what would be a just response to a breach of Blake's undertaking the court has to take these considerations into account. The undertaking, if not a fiduciary obligation, was closely akin to a fiduciary obligation, where an account of profits is a standard remedy in the event of breach. Had the information which Blake has now disclosed still been confidential, an account of profits would have been ordered, almost as a matter of course. In the special circumstances of the intelligence services, the same conclusion should follow even though the information is no longer confidential. That would be just response to the breach. . . .'

[Lords Goff, Browne-Wilkinson and Steyn agreed, making few additional comments, but see Lord Hobhouse's dissenting opinion.]

Questions:

1. Does this case provide compelling justification for disgorgement remedies for breach of contract? Are the suggested limitations defensible? Why, historically, have such disgorgement remedies been confined to 'proprietary torts' (such as *Wrotham Park Estate Co Ltd* v *Parkside Homes Ltd* [1974] 1 WLR 798)?
2. Can and should such disgorgement remedies be proprietary?

FURTHER READING:

S Worthington and R Goode, 'Commercial Law: Confining the Remedial Boundaries' in D Hayton (ed), *Law's Future(s): British Legal Developments in the 21st Century* (2000, Hart Publishing: Oxford), ch 15.

S Worthington, 'Reconsidering Disgorgement for Wrongs' (1999) 62 *MLR* 218.

J Beatson, *The Use and Abuse of Unjust Enrichment* (1991, Clarendon: Oxford) ch 8.

I M Jackman, 'Restitution for Wrongs' [1989] *CLJ* 302.

D Friedmann, 'The Efficient Breach Fallacy' (1989) 18 *J Legal Studies* 1.

G Jones, 'The Recovery of Benefits Gained from a Breach of Contract' (1983) 99 *LQR* 443.

R Sharpe and S M Waddams, 'Damages for Lost Opportunity to Bargain' (1982) 2 *OJLS* 290.

5.11 The possibility of a 'remedial' constructive trust

In English law, the constructive trust is said to be 'institutional' rather than 'remedial'. Broadly speaking, what this means[42] is that the trust arises upon the occurrence of certain fact patterns (such as those discussed in the Sections above). The court's role is simply to declare that a trust exists, and that it did so from the time the relevant facts occurred. If the facts fall within the relevant class, then a trust exists. The court has no discretion to affirm or deny its genesis. A 'remedial' constructive trust, on the other hand, is a remedy delivered by the court, and at the court's discretion. The court determines that the facts call for a remedy and, moreover, that the most appropriate remedy is a proprietary one. Their order 'creates' a remedial constructive trust. Note that, as described, such a remedial trust might arise at the time of the court's order or at some earlier date; all depends upon the exercise of the court's discretion. 'Remedial' constructive trusts are well accepted in the United States, but seem unlikely to take hold in the UK if the views expressed in the following extract continue to hold sway.

[544] ***Re Polly Peck International Plc (in admin); Marangos Hotel Ltd v Stone (Re Polly Peck International Plc (No 2))*** **[1998] 3 All ER 812 (CA), 827 *per* Mummery LJ:** [The facts are immaterial.]

> 'If the asset is the absolute beneficial property of the company there is no general power in the liquidator, the administrators or the court to amend or modify the statutory scheme [implemented by the Insolvency Act 1986] so as to transfer that asset or to declare it to be held for the benefit of another person. To do that would be to give a preference to another person who enjoys no preference under the statutory scheme. . . .
>
> [It was] submitted that 'the law moves'. That is true. But it cannot be legitimately moved by a judicial decision down a road signed 'No Entry' by Parliament. The insolvency road is blocked off to remedial constructive trusts, at least when judge driven in a vehicle of discretion.

[42] See *Westdeutsche Landesbank Girozentrale v Islington London Borough Council* [1996] AC 669, 714–15 *per* Lord Browne-Wilkinson (see **[518]** above).

For these reasons alone, I would refuse leave to the applicants to commence these proceedings. To a trust lawyer, and even more so to an insolvency lawyer, the prospect of a court imposing such a trust is inconceivable and, in my judgement, even the most enthusiastic student of the law of restitution would be forced to recognise that the scheme imposed by the statute for the fair distribution of the assets of an insolvent company precludes the application of the equitable principles manifested in the remedial constructive trust developed by such courts as the Supreme Court of Canada.'

[Also see the judgment of Nourse LJ.]

Also see:

Fortex Group Ltd v MacIntosh [1998] 3 NZLR 171.
D Wright, 'Professor Birks and the Demise of the Remedial Constructive Trust' [1999] *RLR* 128.

Question:

In the light of all the preceding discussion on constructive trusts, are there convincing reasons to deny the possibility of a remedial constructive trust? Is this the best point at which the decision should be made, or would it be preferable to amend the Insolvency Act 1986 (eg so that all constructive and resulting trusts were liable to be defeated as preferences, as are other gratuitous or undervalue transfers[43])?

FURTHER READING:

C E F Rickett and R Grantham, 'Towards a More Constructive Classification of Trusts' [1999] *LMCLQ* 111.
Sir Peter Millett, 'Restitution and Constructive Trusts' (1998) 114 *LQR* 399.
A J Oakley, 'The Precise Effect of the Imposition of a Constructive Trust' in S Goldstein (ed), *Equity and Contemporary Legal Developments* (1992, Hamaccabi Press: Jerusalem) p 427ff.

5.12 Subrogation

So far all the discussion has concerned proprietary interests which arise by operation of law in two-party situations. Subrogation is concerned with three-party situations. As Lord Diplock notes in the next extract, subrogation 'is a convenient way

[43] This will work only *if* the facts suggest that the constructive or resulting trust is the result of a gratuitous or undervalue transfer. This is not always the case. In addition, the Insolvency Act 1986 preference provisions would have to be amended so that they catch transactions which have the *effect* of delivering a preference, not just those *intended* by the debtor to deliver a preference.

of describing a transfer of rights from one person to another, without assignment or assent of the person from whom the rights are transferred and which takes place by operation of law in a whole variety of widely different circumstances.'

Subrogation is frequently encountered in cases of insurers and sureties. An insurer under a contract of indemnity insurance is entitled to 'stand in the shoes of the insured' for the purpose of exercising any rights the insured may have which could diminish the loss insured against. A surety is in the same position in relation to the rights of the creditor against the principal debtor. If this is how subrogation works, then clearly it need not have proprietary consequences. For example, an insurer is subrogated to the insured's right to claim against any tortfeasor who caused the insurable damage. This subrogated claim is not proprietary. On the other hand, a surety subrogated to a charge granted by the creditor in favour of the principal debtor will obtain a proprietary interest by subrogation.

The extracts below are concerned exclusively with subrogation which gives third parties a proprietary interest; the focus of this chapter is on the acquisition of proprietary interests by operation of law. Note, however, that the proprietary interest may be qualified. Subrogation is not the same as assignment (see Chapter 4). With subrogation, the subrogated claimant 'stands in the shoes' of the principal claimant. This means that any defects in the principal claimant's rights will affect the subrogated claimant to the same extent. Moreover, the court itself may limit the scope of the rights granted to the subrogated claimant (see the *Parc (Battersea)* case at **[546]** below).

[545] *Orakpo v Manson Investments Ltd* [1978] AC 95, 104–5 *per* Lord Diplock:
[A lender's secured loan was unenforceable because the formalities required by the Moneylenders Act 1927 had not been observed. The House of Lords refused to allow the lender to be subrogated to the unpaid vendor's liens on the properties purchased by the borrower with the borrowed funds.]

> '[Subrogation] embraces more than a single concept in English law. It is a convenient way of describing a transfer of rights from one person to another, without assignment or assent of the person from whom the rights are transferred and which takes place by operation of law in a whole variety of widely different circumstances. Some rights by subrogation are contractual in their origin, as in the case of contracts of insurance. Others, such as the right of an innocent lender to recover from a company moneys borrowed ultra vires to the extent that these have been expended on discharging the company's lawful debts, are in no way based on contract and appear to defeat classification except as an empirical remedy to prevent a particular kind of unjust enrichment.
>
> This makes particularly perilous any attempt to rely upon analogy to justify applying to one set of circumstances which would otherwise result in unjust enrichment a remedy of subrogation which has been held to be available for that purpose in another and different set of circumstances.
>
> One of the sets of circumstances in which a right of subrogation arises is when a liability of a borrower B to an existing creditor C secured on the property of B is discharged out of moneys provided by the lender L and paid to C either by L himself at B's request and on B's behalf or directly by B pursuant to his agreement with L. In these circumstances L is prima facie entitled to be treated as if he were the transferee of the benefit of C's security on the property to the extent that the moneys lent by L to B were applied

to the discharge of B's liability to C. This subrogation of L to the security upon the property of B is based upon the presumed mutual intentions of L and B; in other words where a contract of loan provides that moneys lent by L to B are to be applied in discharging a liability of B to C secured on property, it is an implied term of that contract that L is to be subrogated to C's security.

The mere fact that money lent has been expended upon discharging a secured liability of the borrower does not give rise to any implication of subrogation unless the contract under which the money was borrowed provides that the money is to be applied for this purpose: *Wylie v. Carlyon* [1922] 1 Ch. 51. Furthermore, even where the contract does so provide, the implication may be displaced by the presence in the contract of express terms which are inconsistent with the acquisition or retention by the lender of a right of subrogation. An express provision that the borrower shall create a legal charge upon the property in favour of the lender as security for the money lent does not necessarily displace the implication that pending the execution of the legal charge the lender is to be subrogated to any equitable security on the property in discharge of which his loan is to be applied. On the execution of the legal charge, however, the equitable charge-by-subrogation will merge in the higher ranking legal charge in favour of the same chargee.

Much as I should like to be able to do so, there seem to me to be insuperable obstacles to relying upon this particular kind of subrogation to mitigate the harshness to the moneylender and the undeserved enrichment of the borrower which would otherwise follow from a technical failure to observe the provision of section 6 of the Moneylenders Act 1927.

In the first place the origin of the right of subrogation is the contract between the borrower and the moneylender for the loan of money by the moneylender to the borrower. The contract either will or will not incorporate a term that the moneys lent shall be applied in discharging a security on the property of the borrower in favour of a third party. If it does, the term that the moneys shall be so applied must be included in the note or memorandum under section 6. If it does not and there is no contractual obligation upon the borrower to apply the moneys in this way (as was held to be the case in *Hanyet Securities Ltd. v. Mallett* [1968] 1 W.L.R. 1265), the expectation of the parties that the money will in fact be used by the borrower for this purposes does not give rise to any right of subrogation in the moneylender even if the money is so applied.'

Also see:

Lord Napier & Ettrick v Hunter [1993] AC 713, 728–31 *per* Lord Templeman, at **[524]** above.

[546] ***Banque Financière de la Cité v Parc (Battersea) Ltd*** **[1999] 1 AC 221 (HL), 228–9, 231–7 *per* Lord Hoffmann:**

[The facts are rather complicated. Parc and Omnicorp Overseas Ltd (OOL) were members of the Omni Group of companies. To finance the purchase of property in London, Parc borrowed money from Royal Trust Bank (Switzerland) (RTB) and from OOL and secured those loans by first and second charges, respectively, over the property. Later on, Parc wished to repay part of its debt to RTB using funds borrowed from the claimant, also a Swiss bank (Banque Financière de la Cité, BFC). To avoid the need to have the transaction approved by the Swiss regulatory authorities, the £10 million loan from BFC was not made directly to Parc. Instead, the funds were lent to Mr Herzig, the general manager of the Swiss holding company of the Omni Group, who then lent them to Parc on the security of a promissory note, which Mr Herzig subsequently assigned to BFC. Unknown to Parc and OOL, Mr Herzig also gave BFC a 'postponement letter', on the holding company's letterhead, which confirmed that none of the companies in the Omni Group would demand repayment of any loans granted to Parc until the loan to Mr Herzig had been fully repaid. The £10 million was paid by BFC directly to RTB. The balance of Parc's debt to RTB was later repaid using further loan funds from OOL. Parc's charge in favour of RTB was thereby extinguished. Parc then defaulted in its repayments and BFC, as the assignee of the promissory note specifying the terms of repayment, sought to enforce its rights. It wanted to rank ahead of OOL's charge (on the basis of the postponement letter or by subrogation to RTB's earlier rights as first charge holder), and to do this notwithstanding that the creation of a charge over Parc's property to secure the loan had been considered and specifically rejected so as to avoid disclosure of the transaction to the Swiss authorities. The House of Lords held unanimously that (i) the postponement letter was not binding on either Parc or OOL; but that (ii) BFC was entitled to be treated as though it had been subrogated to a proportionate share of RTB's rights against Parc, to the extent that this would enable it to acquire priority over OOL in Parc's insolvency, but no further than that. As far as Parc and its other creditors were concerned, BFC's status was that of an unsecured creditor.]

'My Lords, this appeal raises, in unusual circumstances, a question on the scope of the equitable remedy of subrogation. The appellant, the Banque Financière de la Cité, made an advance of DM30m. for the purpose of enabling Parc (Battersea) Ltd. to repay part of a loan from another bank secured by a first charge upon its property. The transaction did not contemplate that Parc would provide any security. It was however an express condition of the advance that other companies in the group to which Parc belonged would not demand repayment of their loans until B.F.C. had been repaid. One such company was Omnicorp Overseas Ltd. which was owed £26.25m. secured by a second charge over the property. Unfortunately the persons who negotiated the transaction had no authority to commit O.O.L. to such an undertaking and it was not binding upon it. Parc is insolvent and if B.F.C. has no priority over O.O.L.'s second charge, it is unlikely to be repaid. The question is whether, as against O.O.L., B.F.C. is entitled to be subrogated to the first charge to the extent that its money was used to repay the debt which it secured. The judge, Robert Walker J., decided that the remedy was available. The Court of Appeal, in a judgment delivered by Morritt L.J., decided that it was not. Against that decision B.F.C. appeals to your Lordships' House.

The striking feature of this case, which distinguishes it from familiar cases on subrogation to which it bears a partial resemblance such as *Butler v. Rice* [1910] 2 Ch. 277 and *Ghana Commercial Bank v. Chandiram* [1960] A.C. 732 is that B.F.C. did not contemplate that Parc would provide it with any security at all. As against Parc, it was content to be an unsecured creditor. What was contemplated was a negative form of protection from certain of Parc's other creditors, namely the other companies in the group, in the form of an undertaking that they would not enforce any claims they might have against Parc in priority to B.F.C. It is this distinction which is principally relied upon by the respondents for their submission, which found favour in the Court of Appeal, that subrogation is not available. To allow B.F.C. to be subrogated to the first charge would mean, it is said, giving it far greater security than it ever bargained for. But there are also other distinctions and for this purpose it is necessary to set out the facts in rather more detail.

. . .

My Lords, the subject of subrogation is bedevilled by problems of terminology and classification which are calculated to cause confusion. For example, it is often said that subrogation may arise either from the express or implied agreement of the parties or by operation of law in a number of different situations: see, for example, Lord Keith of Kinkel in *Orakpo v. Manson Investments Ltd.* [1978] A.C. 95, 119. As a matter of current terminology, this is true. Lord Diplock, for example, was of the view that the doctrine of subrogation in contracts of insurance operated entirely by virtue of an implied term of the contract of insurance (*Hobbs v. Marlowe* [1978] A.C. 16, 39) and although in *Lord Napier and Ettrick v. Hunter* [1993] A.C. 713 [see **[524]** above] your Lordships rejected the exclusivity of this claim for the common law and assigned a larger role to equitable principles, there was no dispute that the doctrine of subrogation in insurance rests upon the common intention of the parties and gives effect to the principle of indemnity embodied in the contract. Furthermore, your Lordships drew attention to the fact that it is customary for the assured, on payment of the loss, to provide the insurer with a letter of subrogation, being no more nor less than an express assignment of his rights of recovery against any third party. Subrogation in this sense is a contractual arrangement for the transfer of rights against third parties and is founded upon the common intention of the parties. But the term is also used to describe an equitable remedy to reverse or prevent unjust enrichment which is not based upon any agreement or common intention of the party enriched and the party deprived. The fact that contractual subrogation and subrogation to prevent unjust enrichment both involve transfers of rights or something resembling transfers of rights should not be allowed to obscure the fact that one is dealing with radically different institutions. One is part of the law of contract and the other part of the law of restitution. Unless this distinction is borne clearly in mind, there is a danger that the contractual requirement of mutual consent will be imported into the conditions for the grant of the restitutionary remedy or that the absence of such a requirement will be disguised by references to a presumed intention which is wholly fictitious. There is an obvious parallel with the confusion caused by classifying certain restitutionary remedies as quasi-contractual and importing into them features of the law of contract.

In this case there was plainly no common intention as between O.O.L., the party enriched, and B.F.C., the party deprived. O.O.L. had no knowledge of the postponement letter or reason to believe that the advance to Parc of the money provided by B.F.C. was otherwise than unsecured. But why should this necessarily exclude subrogation as a restitutionary remedy? I shall refer to five authorities which in my view demonstrate the contrary.

. . .

In *Chetwynd v. Allen* [1899] 1 Ch. 353 one Terrell had in 1891 lent Mr. Chetwynd £2,000 secured upon mortgages over two properties: a house called Cedars, which belonged to his wife, and a riding school, which was his own. Mrs. Chetwynd had consented to the mortgage over her property. In 1892 Mr. Chetwynd borrowed £1,200 from one Mynors, saying that it was to pay off Terrell's mortgage on Cedars and promising him a transfer of that mortgage. He did not disclose that Cedars belonged to his wife or that Terrell's mortgage was for a larger sum and was over the riding school as well. Mr. Chetwynd applied £1,000 of Mynor's money in part repayment to Terrell. Mrs. Chetwynd, who had known nothing of the transaction with Mynors, claimed that she was entitled to

Cedars with the benefit of the part repayment to Terrell but free of any claim by Mynors. Romer J. held, at p. 357, that the charge over Cedars and the riding school was, to the extent of £1,000, "kept alive in equity in favour of Mynors." I shall have to return to the question of what that expression means, but the case shows that the remedy of subrogation does not depend upon any common intention between the plaintiff and the party enriched.

In *Butler v. Rice* [1910] 2 Ch. 277, Mrs. Rice owned properties in Bristol and Cardiff which were equitably mortgaged to a bank (by deposit of title deeds) to secure a loan of £450. Mr. Rice asked Mr. Butler to lend him £450 to pay off the mortgage on the Bristol property, not mentioning the Cardiff property or the fact that both belonged to his wife. Mr. Butler agreed to lend on a mortgage for £300 over the Bristol property and a guarantee for the rest from Mr. Rice's solicitor. The money was used to pay off the bank but Mrs. Rice refused to execute a mortgage over the Bristol property. She too had known nothing about the transaction before the bank's mortgage was paid off. Warrington J. said, at p. 282 that the question was whether the bank's charge had been "paid off or kept alive" and on that question "the concurrence of the mortgagor is immaterial." He followed *Chetwynd v. Allen* [1899] 1 Ch. 353 in holding that Mr. Butler was entitled to the benefit of the mortgage over the Bristol property to secure the £450 he had advanced.

In *Ghana Commercial Bank v. Chandiram* [1960] A.C. 732 the bank made an advance to the owner of property in Accra which was used to pay off his indebtedness to Barclays (D.C.O.) Ltd., secured by an [233] equitable mortgage. The owner executed a legal mortgage in favour of the Ghana Bank, but this was invalidated by a previous attachment of the property by a creditor. The Privy Council, following *Butler v. Rice* and *Chetwynd v. Allen* held that the Ghana Bank was entitled to be subrogated to the equitable mortgage which had been paid off. Lord Jenkins said, at p. 745:

> "It is not open to doubt that where a third party pays off a mortgage he is presumed, unless the contrary appears, to intend that the mortgage shall be kept alive for his own benefit . . ."

In *Paul v. Speirway Ltd.* [1976] Ch. 220 the plaintiff made a loan to a company in which he had a joint interest in order to enable it to pay the price due under a contract for the purchase of development land. When the company failed, he claimed to be a secured creditor by subrogation to the vendor's lien. Oliver J. found on the facts that the advance to the company was intended to be an unsecured loan and held that this excluded any remedy by way of subrogation, which would give the plaintiff more than he had bargained for. The learned judge rejected the proposition, advanced by counsel for the company, that the remedy of subrogation was available only when the common intention of the parties was (as in the three earlier cases to which I have referred) that the plaintiff should have some security which, for one reason or another, he did not get. He confined himself to the much narrower proposition, at p. 232 that:

> "where on all the facts the court is satisfied that the true nature of the transaction between the payer of the money and the person at whose instigation it is paid is simply the creation of an unsecured loan, this in itself will be sufficient to dispose of any question of subrogation."

In formulating this proposition, the judge was clearly confining himself to cases in which the claim was to subrogation to security and not referring to subrogation to a mere debt, as in cases of ultra vires borrowings.

The wisdom of the caution shown by Oliver J. was demonstrated by the facts in *Boscawen v. Bajwa* [1996] 1 W.L.R. 328 [see **[608]** below], which contains a valuable and illuminating analysis of the remedy of subrogation by Millett L.J. The Abbey National Building Society agreed to make an advance on mortgage to a purchaser of property and paid the money to the solicitors acting for them and the purchaser to hold on behalf of the Abbey National until paid over against a first legal charge on the property. The solicitors paid it over to the vendor's solicitors to hold to their order pending completion but the latter used the money in advance of completion to pay off the vendor's mortgage to the Halifax Building Society. In fact completion never took place: the vendor failed to convey to the purchaser and the Abbey National accordingly obtained no legal charge or other security. It claimed to be subrogated to the Halifax mortgage. It will be seen at once that there was no common intention that the vendor, whose mortgage had been paid off, should grant any security to the Abbey National. As Millett L.J. pointed out, at p. 339, the Abbey National expected to obtain a charge from the purchaser as legal owner after completion of the sale, and, in the event which happened of there being [234] no such completion, did not intend its money to be used at all. This meant that:

> "The factual context in which the claim to subrogation arises is a novel one which does not appear to have arisen before but the justice of its claim cannot be denied."

These cases seem to me to show that it is a mistake to regard the availability of subrogation as a remedy to prevent unjust enrichment as turning entirely upon the question of intention, whether common or unilateral. Such an analysis has inevitably to be propped up by presumptions which can verge upon outright fictions, more appropriate to a less developed legal system than we now have. I would venture to suggest that the reason why intention has played so prominent a part in the earlier cases is because of the influence of cases on contractual subrogation. But I think it should be recognised that one is here concerned with a restitutionary remedy and that the appropriate questions are therefore, first, whether the defendant would be enriched at the plaintiff's expense; secondly, whether such enrichment would be unjust; and thirdly, whether there are nevertheless reasons of policy for denying a remedy. An example of a case which failed on the third ground is *Orakpo v. Manson Investments Ltd.* [1978] A.C. 95 [**[545]** above], in which it was considered that restitution would be contrary to the terms and policy of the Moneylenders Acts.

This does not of course mean that questions of intention may not be highly relevant to the question of whether or not enrichment has been unjust. I would certainly not wish to question the proposition of Oliver J. in *Paul v. Speirway Ltd.* [1976] Ch. 220 that, as against a borrower, subrogation to security will not be available where the transaction was intended merely to create an unsecured loan. I do not express a view on the question of where the burden of proof lies in these matters. Oliver J., following the dictum of Lord Jenkins in *Ghana Commercial Bank v. Chandiram* [1960] A.C. 732, 745 which I have quoted, held that if the plaintiff's money was used to discharge a secured liability, he was presumed to "intend that the mortgage shall be kept alive for his own benefit" and this presumption was applied by Nicholls J. in *Boodle, Hatfield Co. v. British Films Ltd.*, 1986 P.C.C. 176. However, if it is recognised that the use of the plaintiff's money to pay off a secured debt and the intentions of the parties about whether or not the plaintiff should have security are only materials upon which a court may decide that the defendant's enrichment would be unjust, it could be argued that on general principles it is for the plaintiff to make out a case of unjust enrichment.

In this case, I think that in the absence of subrogation, O.O.L. would be enriched at B.F.C.'s expense and that prima facie such enrichment would be unjust. The bank advanced the DM30m. upon the mistaken assumption that it was obtaining a postponement letter which would be effective to give it priority over any intra-group indebtedness. It would not otherwise have done so. On the construction of the letter adopted by Robert Walker J., namely that Holdings was purporting to contract on behalf of all companies in the Omni Group, the payment was made under a mistake as to Holdings's authority. On the construction adopted by the Court of Appeal the mistake was as to the power of Holdings to ensure [235] that other group companies would postpone their claims. For my part, I prefer the construction adopted by the judge. But I do not think that for present purposes it matters which view one takes. In either case, B.F.C. failed to obtain that priority over intra-group indebtedness which was an essential part of the transaction under which it paid the money. It may have attached more importance to the pledge of the shares but the provision of the postponement letter was a condition of completion. The result of the transaction is that B.F.C.'s DM30m. has been used to reduce the debt secured by R.T.B.'s first charge and that this reduction will, by reason of O.O.L.'s second charge, enure wholly to the latter's advantage.

I turn, therefore, to the grounds upon which the Court of Appeal decided that the enrichment of O.O.L. would not be unjust. The first four seem to me to carry little weight. It is true that the transaction was structured to pass the money through the hands of Mr. Herzig in order to avoid disclosure under Swiss banking law. But there is no difficulty in tracing B.F.C.'s money into the discharge of the debt due to R.T.B.: the payment to R.T.B. was direct. In this respect, the case is stronger than in *Boscawen v. Bajwa* [1996] 1 W.L.R. 328. Since the money can be traced, the differences in the terms of the loans by B.F.C. to Mr. Herzig and by Mr. Herzig to Parc do not seem to me to matter, although of course on the principle of *Paul v. Speirway Ltd.* [1976] Ch. 220, B.F.C. could not, on the basis of any terms agreed between Mr. Herzig and Parc, assert by way of subrogation greater rights than they bargained for. As for the avoidance of Swiss banking law, it seems to me that there was no evidence that this amounted to an illegality which would disqualify B.F.C. from obtaining equitable relief and I do not think that Morritt L.J. suggested this to be the case.

The second ground was that B.F.C. did not take proper precautions to ensure that Mr. Herzig had authority to execute the postponement letter. But there is, so far as I know, no case in which it has been held that carelessness is a ground for holding that a consequent enrichment is not unjust. No doubt Mr. Mynors (in *Chetwynd v. Allen* [1899] 1 Ch. 353) and Mr. Butler (in *Butler v. Rice* [1910] 2 Ch. 277) were careless in parting with their money without bothering to inspect the borrower's title deeds. They relied upon Mr. Chetwynd and Mr. Rice as B.F.C. relied upon Mr. Herzig. But that did not entitle Mrs. Chetwynd or Mrs. Rice to be enriched as a result of their mistakes. As a third ground, Morritt L.J. said that there had been no misrepresentation or sharp practice on the part of the recipient of the enrichment. But neither had there been on the part of Mrs. Chetwynd or Mrs. Rice. Both were found to have known nothing about the transactions which resulted in their indebtedness being paid off. All that could be said against them was that they, in common with O.O.L., wanted to retain the benefit of their enrichment.

Fourthly, there is the "conceptual problem" about B.F.C. and R.T.B. appearing to share the same security. In my view this is not a real problem. B.F.C. does not claim any priority over R.T.B. It accepts that R.T.B. was entitled to rely upon its first charge, in priority to B.F.C., in respect of the whole of its outstanding indebtedness. B.F.C. claims only to be able to rely upon that security against O.O.L. after R.T.B. has been paid. In this respect the case is in my view no different from *Chetwynd v. Allen* [1899] 1 Ch. 353,

357 in which Romer J. said that the unpaid balance of Terrell's debt would take priority over Mynors's claim by way of subrogation to his security. Morritt L.J. regarded this authority as of no assistance because "Romer J. made it plain that his decision was not based on any principle of subrogation." It is true that Romer J., following the submissions of counsel, appeared to distinguish between "keeping the charge alive," or what would now be called subrogation to the security, and "subrogation," by which he seems to have meant subrogation to the debt (and, presumably, the security). But subrogation to the security is precisely the remedy sought in this case and *Chetwynd v. Allen* therefore seems to me very much in point. In any case, the priority of R.T.B. over B.F.C. can be explained on a wider ground which I shall in due course discuss.

This brings me to the fifth reason relied upon by the Court of Appeal and what I regard as the main question in the case, namely the fact that "keeping the charge alive" for the benefit of B.F.C. would give it more than it was entitled to expect. The transaction contemplated that B.F.C. would be an unsecured creditor of Parc; "keeping the charge alive" would give it the benefit of a first charge. This makes it necessary, as I earlier foreshadowed, to examine more closely what is involved in subrogation to a security.

In my view, the phrase "keeping the charge alive" needs to be handled with some care. It is not a literal truth but rather a metaphor or analogy: see Birks, *An Introduction to the Law of Restitution*, pp. 93–97. In a case in which the whole of the secured debt is repaid, the charge is not kept alive at all. It is discharged and ceases to exist. In a case like the present, in which part of the secured debt is repaid, the charge remains alive only to secure the remainder of the debt for the benefit of the original chargee. Nothing can affect his rights and there is no question of competition between him and the party claiming subrogation. It is important to remember that, as Millett L.J. pointed out in *Boscawen v. Bajwa* [1996] 1 W.L.R. 328, 335, subrogation is not a right or a cause of action but an equitable remedy against a party who would otherwise be unjustly enriched. It is a means by which the court regulates the legal relationships between a plaintiff and a defendant or defendants in order to prevent unjust enrichment. When judges say that the charge is "kept alive" for the benefit of the plaintiff, what they mean is that his legal relations with a defendant who would otherwise be unjustly enriched are regulated as if the benefit of the charge had been assigned to him. It does not by any means follow that the plaintiff must for all purposes be treated as an actual assignee of the benefit of the charge and, in particular, that he would be so treated in relation to someone who would not be unjustly enriched.

This, I interpose, is the real reason why there is no "conceptual problem" about treating B.F.C. as subrogated to part of the R.T.B. secured debt. The equitable remedy is available only against O.O.L., which is the only party which would be unjustly enriched. As between R.T.B. and B.F.C., subrogation has no part to play. R.T.B. is entitled to its security and B.F.C. is no more than an unsecured creditor. The same is true as between B.F.C. and any secured or unsecured creditor of Parc other than the members of the Omni Group. The transaction contemplated that as against non-group creditors, B.F.C. would incur no more than an unsecured [237] liability, evidenced by the promissory note issued to Mr. Herzig and assigned by him to B.F.C. As against such creditors, therefore, the remedy of subrogation is not available. Nor is it available against Parc itself, so as to give B.F.C. the rights of sale, foreclosure etc. which would normally follow from B.F.C. being treated as if it were an assignee of the R.T.B. charge.

It follows that subrogation as against O.O.L., which is all that B.F.C. claims in the action, would not give it greater rights than it bargained for. All that would happen is that O.O.L. would be prevented from being able to enrich itself to the extent that B.F.C.'s money paid off the R.T.B. charge. This is fully within the scope of the equitable remedy. I would therefore allow the appeal. Robert Walker J. made a declaration that B.F.C. "is and has since 28 September 1990 been entitled to the benefit of" the R.T.B. charge and the priority agreement of 13 February 1990. I think that this declaration goes further than is justified. As against Parc, B.F.C. is not entitled to such a declaration. I would therefore insert after the words "entitled to" the words "be treated as against O.O.L. as if it had." Subject to that amendment, I would restore the declaration made by the judge.'

Questions:

1. Note the very different concepts of subrogation advanced by Lord Diplock in *Orakpo* and Lord Hoffmann in *Banque Financière*. Which, if either, better clarifies the incidence of proprietary rights arising as a result of subrogation? Which, if either, is preferable from a doctrinal perspective and from a commercial markets perspective?
2. *Was* Parc unjustly enriched at OOL's expense? Is it possible to implement the remedy ordered by the House of Lords, or does the order create a circular priorities problem?

FURTHER READING:

C Mitchell, *The Law of Subrogation* (1994, Clarendon: Oxford).
S Worthington, 'Subrogation Claims on Insolvency' in F Rose (ed), *Restitution and Insolvency* (2000, LLP: London).

5.13 Policy considerations

All of the proprietary interests discussed in this chapter arise by operation of law. These interests are felt most profoundly when the potential defendant is insolvent. Then the defendant's unsecured creditors lose out to those who can assert proprietary interests in the defendant's assets, whether these are interests arising by agreement or interests arising by operation of law. Is there any justification for giving priority to the holders of interests arising by operation of law? This is one of the most controversial issues in this area of the law.

Re-read:

Westdeutsche Landesbank Girozentrale v Islington London Borough Council [1996] AC 669 (HL) at **[518]** above.

R Goode, 'Proprietary Restitutionary Claims' in W R Cornish, R Nolan, J O'Sullivan and G Virgo (eds), *Restitution: Past, Present and Future* (1998, Hart Publishing: Oxford) ch 5 at **[536]** above.

FURTHER READING:

D Milman, 'Priority Rights on Corporate Insolvency' in A Clarke (ed), *Current Issues in Insolvency Law* (1991, Stevens & Sons: London) p 57.

Part IV

Persistence and Protection of Interests in Property

6

Persistence of Interests in Property

6.1 Introduction

The previous two chapters were concerned with the acquisition of property rights, whether by agreement or by operation of law. The next two chapters are concerned with the extent to which the law affords protection to those acquired property rights. One mode of protection is for the law to assert that the holder of a property right continues to enjoy such a right notwithstanding that there are others who also assert property rights in the same property. This involves either the resolution of title conflicts (ie identical and therefore inconsistent claims to the same property, for example where both parties claim legal ownership) or the resolution of priority disputes (ie different and competing claims to the same property, for example where both parties claim security interests which must be prioritised). Note that the different and competing claims may also be totally inconsistent, so that resolution of the priority dispute also involves the assertion that only one party can enjoy the rights claimed. This is the case, for example, where one party claims full legal ownership and the other claims beneficial ownership: if the claims of the legal owner are conceded to have priority, then the claims of the beneficial owner are necessarily simply overridden.

A second mode of protection is for the law to assert that the holder of a property right continues to enjoy some sort of property right (perhaps the same sort, perhaps a different sort) notwithstanding that the original property has been changed into—or exchanged for—other property. For example, an owner's woodchips may be mixed with resin to produce chipboard, or an owner's painting sold for cash, or an owner's cash used to purchase shares. This second mode of protection involves tracing property into its substitutes and allowing the tracer to claim some sort of proprietary interest in the substitute property. This mechanism for protecting property interests is particularly valuable where an owner's property has been dealt with without the owner's authority so that the owner can no longer lay claim to the original asset (either because it has been consumed or destroyed, or because it has been sold to a *bona fide* purchaser for value who takes unencumbered title).

Both of these modes of protection are considered in this chapter. The next chapter is also concerned with protection of proprietary interests, but it is devoted exclusively to personal (money) remedies which the law might award when one party's property is interfered with in some way by another.

Before turning to the detail, something more needs to be said about terminology. Title conflicts and priority disputes involve the claimant and the defendant pointing to property which they identify as 'theirs' (in the sense that they have some sort of interest in it, although not necessarily an ownership interest). The function of the law is to resolve their dispute. The way that the claimant and the defendant identify property as 'theirs' is by a process called '*following*' (to distinguish it from '*tracing*'). A claimant '*follows*' the property from one person's hand to another, so that at the end of the process the claimant can point to an asset as being the very property which is the subject of competing claims by different parties. Note that the property being claimed is precisely the same at the start as at the end of the exercise; it is simply *followed* from hand to hand to establish its new whereabouts. This is not the case with *tracing*, which brings no new person into the picture, but traces the original property as it is changed from one form to another in the hands of one person (the defendant) against whom the claimant is attempting to assert proprietary rights. Of course, in practice the facts are rarely so neat; a problem will commonly involve both following and tracing as a claimant who has been deprived of property attempts to recover the very property (by *following*) or its substitutes (by *tracing*) in the hands of third parties.

For example, A's car may be stolen by B, who then sells it to C for £2,000 and uses the funds to purchase shares. A can focus on the car: A can *follow* the car through B's hands into C's, and then attempt to assert ownership of the car notwithstanding C's competing claim (ie there is a *title conflict* between A and C in respect of the car). Alternatively, A can focus on the thief: A can *trace* the car into its substitutes in B's hands, first into the £2,000 and then into the shares purchased with those funds. A can then attempt to assert some sort of proprietary interest in the shares, by way either of equitable ownership or equitable lien. Notice that *if* the shares increase in value, and *if* A is entitled to assert equitable ownership rather than a lien, then A will benefit from their increase in value. Assuming that A can establish a clear proprietary right at the start of the story, the function of the law in these tracing cases is to determine, first, whether the original asset is still represented in the substitute asset[1] and, secondly, whether the claimant is entitled to claim ownership of that substitute asset or merely an equitable lien.

[1] For example, if a horse eats hay, the law is unlikely to say that the hay is 'represented' in the horse, it being the 'substitute asset'. In other words, the hay cannot be 'traced' into the horse; it simply disappears—it is 'consumed' without producing an end-product. A purely economic analysis might suggest a different answer, but the law remains preoccupied with the 'thing' rather than its value. This is perhaps as it should be when the goal at the end of the exercise is to assert a *proprietary* right in some asset.

6.2 Title conflicts and priority disputes

In this section the concern is with disputes over property which is clearly identified,[2] but where two or more parties are alleging inconsistent or competing claims to it. The function of the law is to resolve the dispute between the parties.

6.2.1 Protection of legal ownership: the '*nemo dat*' principle

Legal ownership is carefully protected. The general common law rule is designed to safeguard legal owners against involuntary loss of their ownership rights. For example, Chapter 4 dealt with the various means by which one party might acquire ownership from another. Clearly theft was not such a means. A thief certainly obtains (illegitimate) possession of the stolen property, but this does not carry with it either legal or beneficial ownership, or title to possession The original owner (the victim of the theft) remains the legal and beneficial owner of the stolen property. Moreover, if the thief attempts to give away, or even to sell, the stolen property, the purported transferee obtains no title. The original owner remains the owner, and can assert ownership rights against the transferee. In any priority dispute between the original owner and the transferee, the original owner will 'win'. This may leave the innocent transferee out of pocket, since the only available remedies are those against the thief, and these will be of little comfort if the thief has disappeared without trace. See Section 4.2 above.

This state of affairs is encapsulated by the Latin maxim, *nemo dat quod non habet*: no one can give what he does not have; and, in particular, no one can give a better title than he himself possesses. In applying this maxim, the law is protecting the property rights of owners, but at a cost to the security of commercial bargains. A person who takes property in good faith and for value will not necessarily receive good title. As Lord Denning observed in *Bishopsgate Motor Finance Corp v Transport Brakes Ltd*,[3] 'In the development of our law, two principles have striven for mastery. The first is for the protection of property: no one can give a better title than he himself possesses. The second is for the protection of commercial transactions: the person who takes in good faith and for value without notice should get a good title. The first principle has held sway for a long time, but it has been modified by the common law itself and by statute so as to meet the needs of our own times.'

The following extracts illustrate the operation of the *nemo dat* principle.

[601] *Rowland v Divall* [1923] 2 KB 500 (CA), 506–7 *per* Atkin LJ:
[The claimant, a car dealer, purchased a car from the defendant for £334. He kept it for two months, painted it, and re-sold it to a third party. Two months later, the police reclaimed the car as stolen property. It had been stolen before the defendant purported to sell it, and so he had no title to pass to the claimant. The claimant successfully sued the defendant for return of the purchase price on the basis of a total

[2] By a process of 'following'.
[3] [1949] 1 KB 322, 336–7.

failure of consideration. (The claimant had, in turn, refunded the purchase price paid by the third party sub-purchaser.)]

> '. . .It seems to me that in this case there has been a total failure of consideration, that is to say that the buyer has not got any part of that for which he paid the purchase money. He paid the money in order that he might get the property, and he has not got it. It is true that the seller delivered to him the de facto possession, but the seller had not got the right to possession and consequently could not give it to the buyer. Therefore the buyer, during the time that he had the car in his actual possession had no right to it, and was at all times liable to the true owner for its conversion. Now there is no doubt that what the buyer had a right to get was the property in the car, for the Sale of Goods Act expressly provides that in every contract of sale there is an implied condition that the seller has a right to sell; and the only difficulty that I have felt in this case arises out of the wording of s. 11, sub-s. 1 (c), which says that: "Where a contract of sale is not severable, and the buyer has accepted the goods . . . the breach of any condition to be fulfilled by the seller can only be treated as a breach of warranty, and not as a ground for rejecting the goods and treating the contract as repudiated, unless there be a term of the contract, express or implied, to that effect." It is said that this case falls within that provision, for the contract of sale was not severable and the buyer had accepted the car. But I think that the answer is that there can be no sale at all of goods which the seller has no right to sell. The whole object of a sale is to transfer property from one person to another. And I think that in every contract of sale of goods there is an implied term to the effect that a breach of the condition that the seller has a right to sell the goods may be treated as a ground for rejecting the goods and repudiating the contract notwithstanding the acceptance, within the meaning of the concluding words of sub-s. (c); or in other words that the sub-section has no application to a breach of that particular condition. It seems to me that in this case there must be a right to reject, and also a right to sue for the price paid as money had and received on failure of the consideration, and further that there is no obligation on the part of the buyer to return the car, for ex hypothesi the seller had no right to receive it. Under those circumstances can it make any difference that the buyer has used the ear before he found out that there was a breach of the condition? To my mind it makes no difference at all. The buyer accepted the car on the representation of the seller that he had a right to sell it, and inasmuch as the seller had no such right he is not entitled to say that the buyer has enjoyed a benefit under the contract. In fact the buyer has not received any part of that which he contracted to receive—namely, the property and right to possession—and, that being so, there has been a total failure of consideration. The plaintiff is entitled to recover the £334 which he paid.'

Questions:

On its face, this result seems defensible. It reflects the law's decision to favour the true owner's property rights over security of transactions between those who derive their rights from a thief. But should the true owner of the car have to reimburse or otherwise compensate the claimant for the enhanced value of the car as a result of his repainting it? And should the claimant have to account to the true owner for the period of use of the car, even though he does not have to account to the defendant seller for such use? Unwinding a transaction which breaches the *nemo dat* rules often involves subtle unjust enrichment issues, not simply the return of property to its rightful owner. This case has generated significant debate amongst restitution lawyers about the proper working out of these issues as between the true owner, the claimant, the defendant and the third party sub-purchaser. Here the principal concern is with the proprietary consequences of such scenarios, but it is important to appreciate the potential impact of these subtle complications.[4]

Also see:

Cundy v Lindsay (1878) 3 App Cas 459 (HL), extracted at **[401]** above.

The nemo dat principle finds statutory expression in the Sale of Goods Act 1979:

[602] Sale of Goods Act 1979, section 21(1):

> 'Subject to this Act, where goods are sold by a person who is not their owner, and who does not sell them under the authority or with the consent of the owner, the buyer acquires no better title to the goods than the seller had, unless the owner of the goods is by his conduct precluded from denying the seller's authority to sell.'

Note:

Clearly this statutory provision has exceptions, as suggested by the words '[s]ubject to this Act' and 'unless the owner is . . . precluded'. The general law rule, too, has exceptions. These are considered below.

Question:

Does the *nemo dat* principle apply to equitable title, or just to legal title?

6.2.2. Exceptions to the *nemo dat* principle

The most important common law exception to the *nemo dat* rule arises with currency. The transfer of coins or banknotes as *currency*[5] to a person taking in good

[4] The law of unjust enrichment requires A to make restitution to B of any unjust enrichment in A's hands which was gained at the expense of B. In the example posed by this case, the enrichment in the true owner's (A's) hands is the repainted car rather than the car in its original state. The argument for restitution is then as follows. The enrichment is clearly at B's (the dealer's) expense, since B provided the repainting. Moreover, it would be 'unjust' for A to retain the enrichment because it was provided by mistake, B thinking the car was his to repaint as he wished for his own benefit. However, A only has to make restitution of the enrichment which it would be unjust for A to retain. A, provided he acts *bona fide*, can 'subjectively devalue' the enrichment; he can quite reasonably say that he did not want the car repainted, and that it is of little (or no) value to him. The precise limits of subjective devaluation are unsettled.

[5] And not, for example, as valuable objects in their own right, such as antique coins.

faith and for valuable consideration confers good title on the transferee (*Miller v Race* (1758) 1 Burr 452). It follows that a bona fide sale to a thief who uses stolen coins to make the purchase will be effective to give the vendor title to the coins which is good against the whole world. The purpose of this rule is simple; it is to facilitate trade.

The most important statutory exceptions to the *nemo dat* principle are contained in the Sale of Goods Act 1925. They are not dealt with in detail here. They were outlined briefly in Section 4.2.2 and the detail can be found in most textbooks on sales of goods. Recall that the Act displaces the *nemo dat* principle in circumstances of (i) estoppel (section 21(1)); (ii) sale under a voidable title (section 23); (iii) sale by a mercantile agent (section 62(2)); (iv) sale by a seller in possession (section 24); and (v) sale by a buyer in possession (section 25(1)). Other statutes deal with specific types of property, rather than with the particular circumstances of the transaction. For example, the *nemo dat* principle is displaced when the property being sold is a motor vehicle which is subject to a hire purchase agreement (Hire Purchase Agreement Act 1964, Part III).

6.2.3 Conditional protection of security interests: registration or 'perfection' requirements

Certain types of legal and equitable interests are not protected *at all* in title or priority disputes if they are not registered (or 'perfected') as required by statute. For example, certain charges granted by companies are not protected in disputes between competing claimants to the property unless they are registered in accordance with the Companies Act 1985.[6] This rule reflects a policy choice. That choice is to allow parties to take security to protect their own interests, but only on the condition that other prospective lenders, sellers or buyers are put on notice of the fact. This is done so that these latter parties are not unwittingly seduced by the chargor's apparent wealth, but can properly assess the risks associated with their proposed dealing.

[603] Companies Act 1985 sections 395, 396:

> **'395 Certain charges void if not registered**
> (1) Subject to the provisions of this Chapter, a charge created by a company registered in England and Wales and being a charge to which this section applies is, so far as any security on the company's property or undertaking is conferred by the charge, void against the liquidator or administrator and any creditor of the company, unless the prescribed particulars of the charge together with the instrument (if any) by which the charge is created or evidenced, are delivered to or received by the registrar of companies for registration in the manner required by this Chapter within 21 days after the date of the charge's creation.
> (2) Subsection (1) is without prejudice to any contract or obligation for repayment of the money secured by the charge; and when a charge becomes void under this section, the money secured by it immediately becomes payable.

[6] Note that the provision only avoids the *security*; it does not invalidate the underlying debt.

396 Charges which have to be registered

(1) Section 395 applies to the following charges—

(a) a charge for the purpose of securing any issue of debentures,
(b) a charge on uncalled share capital of the company,
(c) a charge created or evidenced by an instrument which, if executed by an individual, would require registration as a bill of sale,
(d) a charge on land (wherever situated) or any interest in it, but not including a charge for any rent or other periodical sum issuing out of the land,
(e) a charge on book debts of the company,
(f) a floating charge on the company's undertaking or property,
(g) a charge on calls made but not paid,
(h) a charge on a ship or aircraft, or any share in a ship,
(i) a charge on goodwill, on a patent or a licence under a patent, on a trademark or on a copyright or a licence under a copyright.

(2) Where a negotiable instrument has been given to secure the payment of any book debts of a company, the deposit of the instrument for the purpose of securing an advance to the company is not, for the purposes of section 395, to be treated as a charge on those book debts.

(3) The holding of debentures entitling the holder to a charge on land is not for the purposes of this section deemed to be an interest in land.

(4) In this Chapter, "charge" includes mortgage.'

Re-read:

Siebe Gorman & Co Ltd v Barclays Bank Ltd [1979] 2 Lloyd's Rep 142, 164 *per* Slade J at **[309]** above.

Also see:

Chapter 3, Section 3.8, on retention of title clauses which have been construed by the courts as registrable but unregistered floating charges.

FURTHER READING:

J S Ziegel, 'Canadian Perspectives on Chattel Security Law Reform in the United Kingdom' [1995] *CLJ* 430.

I Davies, 'The Reform of Personal Property Security Law: Can Article 9 of the US Uniform Commercial Code be a Precedent?' (1988) 37 *ICLQ* 465.

6.2.4 Priority disputes: A's earlier legal interest v. B's later equitable interest

If the owner of property grants A an interest in the property and then, later, grants B an interest in the same property, it is necessary to know how those interests should be ranked. In deciding who has priority, several factors are relevant: the nature of the property (whether it is tangible or intangible), the nature of the competing interests (legal or equitable), and the conduct of the parties themselves.

Where A has been granted a legal interest and, later, B has been granted an equitable interest, the resolution of any dispute is relatively simple. The basic rule, here and in other circumstances,[7] is that the first in time prevails. This means that A's legal interest takes priority over B's equitable interest. If A's legal interest is full ownership, then B's interest will be extinguished—there is nothing left for B to claim once A asserts his or her prior and prioritised interest. This general rule, that the first in time prevails, is subject to a very limited number of exceptions in this context. A may lose priority if A is somehow responsible for B's predicament, usually because A has somehow represented that the interest is available to B.

6.2.5 Priority disputes: A's earlier equitable interest v. B's later legal interest

If the picture is reversed, so that the owner of property first grants A an equitable interest in the property and later grants B a legal interest, then the first in time rule does *not* apply, at least not where B is a *bona fide* purchaser for value without notice of A's prior equitable interest. Where B is in this fortunate position, B is especially protected: B is then referred to as 'equity's darling', and takes free of A's prior equitable interest.

In these circumstances the rule is that 'where the equities are equal, the legal title prevails', displacing the usual rule that 'where the equities are equal, the first in time prevails'.[8] No compelling justification exists for such a rule, although it has been described as founded on jurisdictional politics between the common law and Chancery courts or, alternatively, as based on the need to make (legal) transfers of property secure.

This rule is often called into play in cases of money laundering, and then entitlement to large sums of money will turn on the outcome of the priority dispute. For example, P's funds may be diverted (ie stolen) by a fraudster. These funds may then pass through several hands—and probably several jurisdictions—before reaching D. When P attempts to recover the funds, the fraudster has often disappeared or is insolvent, and P's attention turns to D. *If* P can assert equitable ownership of the very funds which D received,[9] then the dispute will come down to a priority dispute between P's earlier equitable interest and D's later legal interest.[10] The priority rule asserts that P's interest will prevail unless D is a *bona fide* purchaser for value. The next extract illustrates the court's approach to this '*bona fide* purchaser for value' qualification.

[7] Except where 'equity's darling' is concerned (ie where B's later interest is a legal title which has been acquired by B *bona fide* and for value): see Section 6.2.5 below.

[8] But if B is not a *bona fide* purchaser for value without notice, then the general 'first in time' rule applies, and B will take subject to A's interest, which will have priority.

[9] To do this, P will need to establish equitable title to the funds in the fraudster's hands and then either *follow* or, more usually, *trace* those funds into D's hands, ensuring that P has an unbroken chain of proprietary interests from start to finish. In this way, the facts often demand application of both the priority and the tracing rules discussed in this chapter.

[10] It is not usually in dispute that the legal title to the funds will pass along the chain to D, although see the case of *F C Jones & Sons (Trustee in Bankruptcy) v Jones* [1997] Ch 159 at **|619|** below.

[604] *Polly Peck International plc v Nadir (No. 2)* [1992] 4 All ER 769 (CA), 782 *per* Scott LJ:

[Asil Nadir was the chief executive of Polly Peck International (PPI), which was in insolvent administration. Nadir, as chief executive, owed the company fiduciary obligations. Nadir also controlled IBK Bank, which was both PPI's and Nadir's personal bank. PPI's administrators alleged that IBK Bank had misappropriated sterling funds which were the property of PPI and had exchanged them for Turkish lira in IBK's account with the Central Bank of Cyprus (CBC). This currency exchange gave CBC legal title to the sterling funds. The administrators argued that PPI could trace its funds into CBC's hands and assert a (prior) equitable interest.[11] Notwithstanding this, CBC successfully argued that it was protected in the resulting priority dispute because it was a *bona fide* purchaser for value without notice of PPI's earlier equitable interest.]

> 'Mr. Potts submitted that, in order to defeat PPI's claim, the Central Bank must discharge the onus of proving that it received the funds without notice of PPI's equitable interest. I disagree. The Central Bank is the legal owner of the money. It is for PPI to raise a case that places the mantle of constructive trustee on the Central Bank's shoulders. Nothing, however, for present interlocutory purposes turns on onus.
>
> The question, for the purposes of the tracing remedy,[12] is whether the Central Bank had notice or constructive notice of PPI's equitable interest. "Notice" and "constructive notice", as Sir Robert Megarry, V.-C., pointed out in *Montagu's Settlement Trusts*, [1987] Ch 264, are not synonyms for "knowledge" and "constructive knowledge" (see p 277). Mr. Justice Vinelott in *Eagle Trust v S.B.C. Securities* [[1991] BCLC 438] commented at p. 447 that—
>
>> . . . notice is often used in a sense or in contexts where the facts do not support the inference of knowledge. A man may have actual notice of a fact and yet not know it. He may have been supplied . . . with a document and so have actual notice of its content, but he may not in fact have read it; or he may have read it some time ago and have forgotten its content.
>
> The present case, however, does not concern land, or some valuable chattel, the title to which can be traced, but concerns money paid to the Central Bank on a foreign currency exchange transaction. In my judgment, for the purposes of the proprietary tracing claim, as for the in personam constructive trust claim, PPI must prove knowledge on the part of the Central Bank, actual or constructive as the case may be. I think this is the type of case to which Lord Justice Lindley's remarks in *Manchester Trust v Furness*, [1895] 2 QB 539 at 545, cited also by Mr. Justice Vinelott in *Eagle Trust v S.B.C. Securities* at p. 458 are applicable. Lord Justice Lindley said this:
>
>> . . . as regards the extension of the equitable doctrines of constructive notice to commercial transactions, the Courts have always set their face resolutely against it. The equitable doctrines of constructive notice are common enough in dealings with land and estates, with which the Court is familiar; but there have been repeated protests against the introduction into commercial transactions of

[11] The initial assertion of an equitable interest in the diverted funds is easy here. It is based on misapplication by a fiduciary (Nadir) of funds belonging to his principal (PPI). The next stage, asserting an equitable interest in funds in CBC's hands, is more difficult. 'Following' is impossible in banking transactions involving electronic transfers and mixed funds. 'Tracing' is often both factually and doctrinally complicated: see especially Section 6.5 below.

[12] This terminology is no longer favoured: see Section 6.3 below.

> anything like an extension of those doctrines, and the protest is founded on perfect good sense. In dealing with estates in land title is everything, and it can be leisurely investigated: in commercial transactions possession is everything and there is not time to investigate title; and if we were to extend the doctrine of constructive notice to commercial transactions we should be doing infinite mischief and paralyzing the trade of the country.

In the *Eagle Trust* case Mr. Justice Vinelott, after citing the above passage, went on to observe that "The courts have been particularly reluctant to extend the doctrine of constructive notice to cases where monies are paid in the ordinary course of business . . . [p 459]".

I respectfully agree with these comments.'

[And so, since Scott LJ had found earlier that there was nothing in the nature of the transactions or their size which was such as to put the bank on inquiry as to whether there was any impropriety in the dealings, the CBC was not fixed with notice and therefore took unencumbered legal title to the sterling funds.]

Note:

1. PPI had two potential claims against CBC. The first was the proprietary claim discussed here. The second was a *personal* claim against CBC based on 'knowing receipt',[13] requiring CBC to repay the value of the funds it had received on the basis that it knew that their receipt was in breach of trust or fiduciary obligations owed to PPI. This claim failed too, since (as the above extract makes clear) Scott LJ was of the view that the notice and knowledge requirements in each claim amounted to the same thing.
2. In these complicated commercial cases, it is usually a company which must have knowledge or notice of the relevant facts. Whether a director's knowledge ought to be attributed to a company is often a difficult matter: see *Meridian Global Funds Management Asia Ltd v Securities Commission* [1995] 2 AC 500 (PC); *El Ajou v Dollar Land Holdings plc* [1994] 2 All ER 685 (CA).

Question:

Consider the following chronology of events. A beneficiary, A, has an equitable interest in certain shares held on express trust. An equitable mortgagee, B, later acquires an equitable interest in the same shares from their legal owner (the trustee), for value and without notice of A's interest. B's equitable mortgage has been created by putting B in possession of the share certificates and signed instruments of transfer. B then discovers A's interest, and, notwithstanding this, exercises his rights to obtain legal title to the shares by submitting the necessary documentation to the company to effect a change on the company's register of share owners. This B can do without the assistance of A. A and B both claim beneficial ownership of the shares. B claims that the dispute is between a prior equitable interest (A's) and a subsequent legal

[13] Discussed in Chapter 7, Sections 7.4.2 and 7.6.1.

interest (B's) acquired *bona fide* and for value without notice of A's competing interest. How should the dispute be resolved? See *Macmillan Inc v Bishopsgate Investment Trust plc* (No 3) [1995] 1 WLR 978 (Millett J) (aff'd on different grounds by the CA: [1996] 1 WLR 387); and *MCC Proceeds Inc v Lehman Bros International (Europe)* [1998] 4 All ER 675 (CA).

6.2.6 Priority disputes: A's earlier equitable interest v. B's later equitable interest

Consider the position if the scenario is altered yet again, so that the property owner first transfers an equitable interest in the property to A, and then later transfers an equitable interest in the same property to B. For example, the owner might grant equitable charges over the same property first to A and then to B. In these circumstances the general rule applies: 'where the equities are equal, the first in time prevails'. This is in truth only a rule of last resort.[14] It says no more than that if nothing in the facts compels a more appropriate resolution, then A's prior interest will prevail over B's later one. On the other hand, if A's conduct has contributed to B's predicament, then the equities will not be equal, and A may find the earlier interest postponed to the later one.

Note, however, that where the property is intangible, the applicable rule is slightly more complicated. The concern is still with the competition between two people who are successive assignees of an equitable interest in certain property, but property which is intangible. For example, a creditor may assign a debt in equity to A and then later attempt to assign the same debt to B. Alternatively, the beneficiary under a trust may attempt to assign the beneficial interest first to A and later to B. In these circumstances, although the 'first in time' rule is the primary rule, this rule will give way to 'the rule in *Dearle v Hall*'.[15] This rule gives priority to the first assignee to give notice of the assignment to the person required to pay out a fund in respect of the interest assigned. In the first example of an assignment of a debt, the rule would give priority to the first assignee to give notice to the debtor who owes the assigned debt. This is the person who is required to make a payment, either to the creditor or to the creditor's assignee. In the second example, it would require the assignee to give notice to the trustee of the trust fund, since that is the person responsible for distributing the trust assets to the beneficiary or the beneficiary's assignee.

On its face the rule appears designed to protect the party in the position of debtor or trustee in the examples cited. Such people, if they make a payment to someone who is not entitled, remain liable to make a second payment to the proper person. In the preceding examples, this would be a payment to the proper creditor or assignee, or to the proper beneficiary or assignee. Unless notified of the assignments which have been effected, they have no way of knowing who is the proper assignee entitled to the fund. Moreover, the assignee is the person best able (and most motivated) to give notice. The rule might thus be seen to rest on the assumption that an

[14] *Rice v Rice* (1853) 2 Drew 73.
[15] (1828) 3 Russ 1; 38 ER 475.

assignee who does not give such notice cannot later be heard to complain if a second assignment is purportedly made and if the debtor or trustee pays out on the assumption that it is proper.

However, this apparent justification is not consistent with the qualifications which apply to the rule. These qualifications indicate, instead, that the rule is based on the assumption that a first assignee who fails to give the appropriate notice is thereby responsible for the fact that the original assignor continues to appear in possession of the beneficial interest in the fund. It follows that the first assignee is therefore partly responsible for enabling a fraud to be committed on the second assignee by the purported second assignment. Because of this, equity sees it as only fair that the first assignee should be postponed to the second to preserve the second from harm. But this justification for postponement only applies where the first assignee's failure to give notice has in fact worked to cause a detriment to the second assignee. This means it will only apply if the second assignee could have been deceived by appearances because he or she had no actual or constructive notice of the earlier assignment. Furthermore, the rule favouring the second assignee only apples where the second assignee has given value for the assignment, and so has in fact suffered a detriment which can be seen as being a result of the earlier assignee's failure. So the rule in *Dearle v Hall* only allows second assignees to obtain priority by being the first to give notice if they are assignees for value without notice of the earlier assignment. A second assignee who does not meet these criteria, either because of notice of the earlier assignment or because the assignment was gratuitous, will not be protected by the rule; the first assignee will take in priority (under the 'first in time' rule) notwithstanding the second assignee's earlier notice.

[605] *E Pfeiffer Weinkellerei-Weineinkauf GmbH & Co v Arbuthnot Factors Ltd* [1988] 1 WLR 150, 161–3 *per* Phillips J:

[The claimant, a German company, sold wine to an English importer, X, under a retention of title agreement which expressly gave the claimant an interest in the proceeds of sub-sales of the wine. X sold the wine on credit terms, and entered into a factoring arrangement with the defendant whereby the invoices relating to the sub-sales were assigned to the defendant, who notified the debtors and collected the debts as they fell due. When X failed to meet its obligations to the claimant, the claimant claimed to be beneficially entitled to the proceeds of sub-sales in priority to the defendant's claims on them. The defendant successfully argued that (i) the retention of title clause created a registrable but unregistered charge over the proceeds, which was therefore void against the defendant (as to which see Chapter 3); and (ii) in any event, regardless of the nature of the claimant's equitable interest, the defendant's interest took priority under the rule in *Dearle v Hall*. Note that, for the purpose of determining priorities, the defendant was not treated as a *bona fide* purchaser for value of the *legal* title to the debts, notwithstanding that the assignment (the factoring agreement) complied with the requirements of the Law of Property Act 1925 section 136(1). Had the defendant been in such a position, the priority rule discussed in Section 6.2.5 would have applied.]

> 'Such equitable rights as the plaintiff enjoyed in the proceeds of sale of wine sub-sold by Springfield [X] were acquired prior to the rights that the defendant acquired under the factoring agreement and the assignments pursuant thereto. Mr. Hapgood con-

tended that on the facts of this case the plaintiff was entitled to invoke the rule "*Qui prior est tempore potior est jure*," which I shall call the "first in time rule," and thereby established a superior title to that of the defendant. To this Mr. Potts raised two alternative answers: (i) The rule does not apply where the competition is between the holder of an equitable title and the holder of a legal title who has purchased it bona fide for value without notice of the prior equitable title. The defendant was a bona fide purchaser of the legal title for value. (ii) Mr. Hapgood contended, for reasons I shall shortly explain, that the defendant must be treated for purposes of priorities as holders of equitable, not legal, title. In that event Mr. Potts submitted that the "first in time" rule gave way to the rule in *Dearle v. Hall* (1828) 3 Russ. 1 and that, in consequence, the defendant still had priority.

The defendant as bona fide purchaser for value

The debate between counsel proceeded on the premise that the competition was between the plaintiff's equitable rights in the debts owed to Springfield, whatsoever the true nature of those rights might be, and the defendant's rights as assignee of the legal title to those debts by virtue of a statutory assignment under the provisions of section 136(1) of the Law of Property Act 1925. That section provides:

> "(1) Any absolute assignment by writing under the hand of the assignor (not purporting to be by way of charge only) of any debt or other legal thing in action, of which express notice in writing has been given to the debtor, trustee or other person from whom the assignor would have been entitled to claim such debt or thing in action, is effectual in law (subject to equities having priority over the right of the assignee) to pass and transfer from the date of such notice—(a) the legal right to such debt or thing in action; (b) all legal and other remedies for the same; and (c) the power to give a good discharge for the same without the concurrence of the assignor:. . ."

Section 136 replaced section 25(6) of the Supreme Court of Judicature Act 1873 which provided:

> "Any absolute assignment, by writing under the hand of the assignor (not purporting to be by way of charge only), of any debt or other legal chose in action, of which express notice in writing shall have been given to the debtor, trustee, or other person from whom the assignor would have been entitled to receive or claim such debt or chose in action, shall be, and be deemed to have been effectual in law (subject to all equities which would have been entitled to priority over the right of the assignee if this Act had not passed), to pass and transfer the legal right to such debt or chose in action from the date of such notice, and all legal and other remedies for the same, and the power to give a good discharge for the same, without the concurrence of the assignor:. . ."

Mr. Hapgood submitted that the effect of section 136(1) of the Act of 1925 is clear and that of section 25(6) of the Act of 1873 even more clear. The section enables the assignee to acquire a title that has all the procedural advantages of legal title, but so far as priorities are concerned his position is no better than if the assignment had been effected prior to the Acts. It follows that, even if the assignment is effected for value without notice of a prior equity, priorities fall to be determined as if the assignment had been effected in equity, not in law.

Mr. Potts challenged this contention and referred me to *Stoddart v. Union Trust Ltd.* [1912] 1 KB 181 in support of the proposition that a bona fide purchaser of legal title to a chose in action under the statute acquires a title free of equities of which he has no notice. I do not think that *Stoddart v. Union Trust Ltd.* supports the proposition for which it was cited. In that case a debtor was seeking to raise by way of defence to an action by a statutory assignee of the debt a claim for damages for fraud on the part of the assignor which had induced the transaction out of which the debt arose. It is not easy to glean a common ratio decidendi from the judgments of the court but the case appears to me to have turned essentially upon a finding that a claim for damages for fraud by the assignor of a chose in action is not an equity which can be set up against an assignee: see, in particular, the judgment of Kennedy LJ at p. 194.

Mr. Hapgood's submissions appear to me to be soundly based upon the natural meaning of the statutory wording. They gain support from a note in *Halsbury's Statutes of England*, 3rd ed., vol. 27 (1971), p. 549, and from a passage in *Snell's Principles of Equity*, 28th ed. (1982), p. 82. They also echo the view expressed by Channell J. in respect of section 25(6) of the Act of 1873 in *Marchant v. Morton, Down & Co.* [1901] 2 KB 829, 832. I accept Mr. Hapgood's interpretation of section 136(1) and, accordingly, it is necessary to consider priorities as if the assignments of the debts to the defendant were no more than equitable assignments. It is at this point that Mr. Potts places reliance on the rule in *Dearle v. Hall*, 3 Russ. 1.

The rule in *Dearle v. Hall* is an exception to the general principle that equitable interests take priority in the order in which they are created. The rule applies to dealings with equitable interests in any property and, in particular, to equitable assignments of legal choses in action. Under the rule priority depends upon the order in which notice of the interest created by the dealing is given to the person affected by it, i.e., in the case of assignments of a debt, the debtor. Mr. Hapgood cited a number of authorities that were critical of the rule in support of his contention that the application of the rule should not be extended and, in particular, that the rule should not be applied to a competition between an equitable right to trace and an equitable assignment. He conceded, however, that if the rights asserted by the plaintiff were rights conferred by equitable assignment, the rule in *Dearle v. Hall* must apply. I have held that such security rights as were conferred upon the plaintiff by clause 5 were conferred by equitable assignment. Accordingly the rule in *Dearle v. Hall* governs and the defendant, which was the first to give notice of its rights to the sub-purchasers, enjoys priority over the plaintiff. Thus the second preliminary issue falls to be answered "Yes."

This finding makes it unnecessary for me to determine a further point that arose late in argument. Assuming that the plaintiff's equitable interest in the debts owed by the sub-purchasers enjoyed priority to that of the defendant as statutory assignee, does the fact that the defendant has actually been paid the debts enable it to claim precedence as a bona fide purchaser for value of the legal title in the payments received? *Taylor v. Blakelock* (1886) 32 Ch.D. 560 would seem to favour the defendant in relation to this question, but the point is not an easy one and it is with some relief that I leave it to be determined on another occasion.'

Questions:

1. Would it be inappropriate to extend the rule in *Dearle v Hall* to equitable interests acquired by virtue of the party's ability to rely on a tracing claim? Why?
2. What is the answer to the final unanswered question in this extract—can the defendant claim unencumbered legal title to the payments actually received from the sub-purchasers without accounting to the claimant?

6.2.7 Priority disputes: A's earlier mere equity v. B's later equitable interest

If the earlier right given to A is not an equitable interest but a mere equity, then the rule is that B's later interest prevails, whether it is legal or equitable, provided it was acquired *bona fide*, for value, and without notice of A's rights. A mere equity is not itself a proprietary interest (although note the attributes ascribed to it by Menzies J in the *Latec Investments* case at **[607]** below), but it gives its holder the right to take action which may subsequently deliver a proprietary interest to the holder. Two common examples of mere equities are the right to rescind a contract (for fraud, or for some other reason),[16] and the right to rectification for mistake.

[606] ***Phillips v Phillips*** **(1862) 4 De G F & J 208, 215–8; 45 ER 1164, 1166–7** ***per*** **Lord Westbury:**

[This is the first statement of the general principle. The facts are immaterial.]

> 'Hence grantees and incumbrancers claiming in equity take and are ranked according to the dates of their securities; and the maxim applies, '*Qui prior est tempore potior est jure*'. The first grantee is *potior*—that is, *potentior*. He has a better and superior—because a prior—equity. The first grantee has a right to be paid first, and it is quite immaterial whether the subsequent incumbrancers at the time when they took their securities and paid their money had notice of the first incumbrance or not. . . . Now, the defence of a purchaser for valuable consideration is the creature of a Court of Equity, and it can never be used in a manner at variance with the elementary rules which have already been stated. . . . But there appear to be three cases in which the use of this defence is most familiar: – . . . Thirdly, where there are circumstances that give rise to an equity as distinguished from an equitable estate—as for example, an equity to set aside a deed for fraud, or to correct it for mistake—and the purchaser under the instrument maintains the plea of purchase for valuable consideration without notice, the Court will not interfere.'

[607] ***Latec Investments Ltd v Hotel Terrigal Pty Ltd*** **(1965) 113 CLR 265 (Aust HCt), 276–8** ***per*** **Kitto J, 289–91** ***per*** **Menzies J:**

[This case concerns real property, but the principles are of general application. Latec Investments was the mortgagee of registered land (under the Australian Torrens title system of registration). When the mortgagor defaulted, Latec Investments exercised its power of sale by selling the land to its wholly owned subsidiary. The subsidiary then charged the land to a trustee for debenture holders (MLC Nominees). The trustee had no notice of the circumstances of the earlier sale. Five years after the sale, the mortgagor sought to set aside the sale as a fraudulent exercise of the mortgagee's power of sale. This involved a competition between the mortgagor's alleged interest and the equitable security interest of the trustee. The Australian High Court held that although the mortgagor was entitled, as against the mortgagee and the purchaser, to an order setting aside the sale, the interest of the mortgagor which resulted from this would be subject to the charge of the trustee.]

[16] See Section 5.5.2, above.

Kitto J:

'In all cases where a claim to enforce an equitable interest in property is opposed on the ground that after the interest is said to have arisen a third party innocently acquired an equitable interest in the same property, the problem, if the facts relied upon as having given rise to the interests be established, is to determine where the better equity lies. If the merits are equal, priority in time of creation is considered to give the better equity. This is the true meaning of the maxim *qui prior est tempore potior est jure*: *Rice v. Rice* (1853) 2 Drew 73, at p 78 (61 ER 646, at p 648). But where the merits are unequal, as for instance where conduct on the part of the owner of the earlier interest has led the other to acquire his interest on the supposition that the earlier did not exist, the maxim may be displaced and priority accorded to the later interest. In the present case it seems to me that there is much to be said for holding that, since during the long period of the mortgagor's delay in setting up the invalidity of the purchaser's title persons were induced to lend money on debentures in the belief that an unencumbered fee simple in the subject property formed part of the security under the trustee's floating charge, the mortgagor ought not to be allowed to insist upon its equity of redemption as against the equitable interest of the trustee. (at p276)

9. But apart altogether from any question of estoppel by conduct, in my opinion the equitable charge of the trustee for the debenture holders stands in the way of the mortgagor's success because it was acquired for value and without any notice either of the existence of the mortgagor's right to set aside the sale or of any facts from which such a right might be inferred. The trustee, of course, has not the legal estate; its rights are purely equitable; but the case falls within one of the categories described in the judgment of Lord Westbury in *Phillips v. Phillips* (1861) 4 De GF & J 208, at p 218 (45 ER 1164, at p 1167) . . . .

[See **[606]** above.]

. . . . it seems to me, that the cases to which [Lord Westbury] was referring were not only those in which there is an assertion of an equity unaccompanied by an equitable interest (as was held to be the case in *Westminster Bank Ltd. v. Lee* (1956) Ch 7 and *National Provincial Bank Ltd. v. Hastings Car Mart Ltd.* (1964) Ch 9)—indeed he may not have had them in mind at all—but those in which an equity is asserted which must be made good before an equitable interest can be held to exist. In the latter class of cases the equity is distinct from, because logically antecedent to, the equitable interest, and it is against the equity and not the consequential equitable interest that the defence must be set up. That the defence of purchase for value without notice (in the absence of the legal estate) is a good defence against the assertion of the equity in such a case had been established long before Lord Westbury's time. . . . The reason of the matter, as I understand it, is that the purchaser who has relied upon the instrument as taking effect according to its terms and the party whose rights depend upon the instrument being denied that effect have equal merits, and the court, finding no reason for binding the conscience of either in favour of the other, declines to interfere between them. Consequently the party complaining of the fraud or mistake finds himself unable to set up as against the other the equitable interest he asserts; but the fact remains that it is against the preliminary equity, and not against the equitable interest itself, that the defence of purchase for value without notice has succeeded. The maxim *qui prior est tempore* is not applicable, for it applies only as between equitable interests, the logical basis of it being that in a competition between equitable interests the conveyance in virtue of which the later interest is claimed is considered, as Lord Westbury pointed out, to be innocent, in the sense of being intended to pass that which the conveyor is justly entitled to and no more: (1861) 4 De G F & J 208, at p 215 (45 ER 1164, at p 1166). Where a claim to an earlier equitable interest is dependent for its success upon the setting aside or rectification of an instrument, and the court, notwithstanding that the fraud or mistake (or other cause) is established, leaves the instrument to take effect according to its terms in favour of a third party whose rights have intervened, the alleged earlier equitable interest is unprovable against the third party, and consequently, so far as the case against him discloses, there is no prior equitable interest to which his conveyance can be held to be subject. (at p278)

Menzies J:
'4. The second question—that is, the question of priority between Terrigal's and M.L.C. Nominees' equitable rights—I find one of substantial difficulty. If the maxim "*Qui prior est tempore potior est jure*" applies, Terrigal's right to have the conveyance set aside and to be restored to the register, without regard to M.L.C. Nominees' equitable interest, prevails, but the appellants' contention is that this right is a mere equity and the maxim has no application when the contest is between such an equity and an equitable interest of the character held by M.L.C. Nominees. This contention rests upon the line of authority based upon *Phillips v. Phillips* (1861) 4 De GF & J 208 (45 ER 1164) . Lord Westbury there said. . . .

[See **[606]** above.]

. . . .

5. There is, however, . . . another line of cases, the authority of which is beyond question, establishing that where there is an equity to have the voidable conveyance of an estate set aside, there remains in the conveyor, notwithstanding the conveyance, an equitable estate which may be devised or transferred. Thus, in *Stump v. Gaby* (1852) 2 De GM & G 623 (42 ER 1015) , Lord St. Leonards, speaking of a conveyance by an heir at law to his solicitor, said: "I do not deny that a deed may be so fraudulent as to be set aside at law; this, however, is not such a case; but I will assume that the conveyance might have been set aside in equity for fraud: what then is the interest of a party in an estate which he has conveyed to his attorney under circumstances which would give a right in this Court to have the conveyance set aside? In the view of this Court he remains the owner, subject to the repayment of the money which has been advanced by the attorney, and the consequence is that he may devise the estate, not as a legal estate, but as an equitable estate, wholly irrespective of all question as to any rights of entry or action, leaving the conveyance to have its full operation at law, but looking at the equitable right to have it set aside in this Court. The testator therefore had a devisable interest. My strong impression is that this very point is concluded upon authority, but if not I am ready to make an authority on the present occasion, and to decide that, assuming the conveyance to have been voidable, the grantor had an equitable estate which he might have devised" (1852) 2 De G M & G, at p 630 (42 ER, at p 1018). . . .

6. If there is a difference between the two lines of authority, that difference seems to me to arise from concentration upon different aspects of what follows from a voidable conveyance. Thus, *Phillips v. Phillips* (1861) 4 De G F & J 208 (45 ER 1164), in so far as it says that a person with the right to have a voidable conveyance set aside has but a mere equity, directs attention to the right to have the conveyance set aside as a right to sue which must be successfully exercised as a necessary condition of there being any relation back of the equitable interest established by the suit. *Stump v. Gaby* (1852) 2 De G M & G 623 (42 ER 1015) directs attention to the result of the eventual avoidance of the

> conveyance upon the position *ab initio* and throughout of the persons by whom and to whom the conveyance of property was made and says that, in the event of a successful suit (which may be maintained by a devisee), the conveyor had an equitable estate capable of devise and that the conveyee holds, and has always held, as trustee. (at p291)
>
> 7. There is no doubt that the two lines of authority are well established. See, for instance, Halsbury's Laws of England, 3rd ed., vol. 14, pars. 1009 and 1030. Furthermore, there is room for the application of each in appropriate circumstances. Thus, if Terrigal were a person instead of a company and the question were whether, in the circumstances here, that person had a devisable interest in the hotel property by virtue of his equity to have the conveyance to Southern set aside, *Stump v. Gaby* (1852) 2 De G M & G 623 (42 ER 1015) would require an affirmative answer on the footing that, in the circumstances, Terrigal had an equitable interest in the hotel property. Where, however, the question arises in a contest between Terrigal and M.L.C. Nominees, the holders of an equitable interest in the hotel property acquired without notice of Terrigal's rights, the authority of *Phillips v. Phillips* (1861) 4 De G F & J 208 (45 ER 1164) is (i) that the contest is between Terrigal's equity to have the conveyance set aside and the equitable interest of M.L.C. Nominees and (ii) that in that contest, Terrigal's equity is not entitled to priority merely because it came into existence at an earlier time than the equitable interest of M.L.C. Nominees. In the circumstances here, therefore, the maxim "*Qui prior est tempore potior est jure*" has no application. (at p291)

Questions:

On the basis of this extract, what rights does the holder of a mere equity have? Is there any significance in allowing broad freedom to alienate the right, but limiting enforcement against third parties? Does the distinction say anything about the essential attributes of 'property'?

6.3 Tracing and claiming: conceptual issues

The previous section concerned disputes over property which was clearly identified, but where two or more parties were asserting inconsistent or competing claims to it. The function of the law was to resolve the dispute between the parties. Here, the problem is different. Here the concern is with situations where property loses its identity (because it is irretrievably mixed with other similar property) or property is exchanged or transformed without authority (whether the act is innocent or intentional) and afterwards, as a consequence, the person who exchanged or transformed it only has possession of unidentifiable original property, or its exchanged or transformed product, not the identifiable original property. The function of the law in these circumstances is to determine whether the owner, who cannot reclaim the original property, can instead assert some sort of claim to its exchanged or transformed product. This involves two steps. First the owner must show that it is his or her property which was transformed, and must specifically identify the product of the transformation. Secondly, the owner must show that the circumstances are such that they entitle the owner assert some claim (personal or proprietary) to that product. These two steps are termed '*tracing*' and '*claiming*' respectively. The rules and their consequences differ at common law and in equity.[17]

[608] *Boscawen v Bajwa* [1996] 1 WLR 328 (CA), 334 *per* Millett LJ:
[The facts are outlined at **[629]** below.]

> 'Equity lawyers habitually use the expressions "the tracing claim" and "the tracing remedy" to describe the proprietary claim and the proprietary remedy which equity makes available to the beneficial owner who seeks to recover his property in specie from those into whose hands it has come. Tracing properly so-called, however, is neither a claim nor a remedy but a process. Moreover, it is not confined to the case where the plaintiff seeks a proprietary remedy; it is equally necessary where he seeks a personal remedy against the knowing recipient or knowing assistant. It is the process by which the plaintiff traces what has happened to his property, identifies the persons who have handled or received it, and justifies his claim that the money which they handled or received (and, if necessary, which they still retain) can properly be regarded as representing his property. He needs to do this because his claim is based on the retention by him of a beneficial interest in the property which the defendant handled or received. Unless he can prove this he cannot (in the traditional language of equity) raise an equity against the defendant or (in the modern language of restitution) show that the defendant's unjust enrichment was at his expense.'

Questions:

> This quotation is often cited in support of the need for a distinction between tracing and claiming, but does it fail to distinguish adequately between tracing and following? What misconceptions, if any, might result from this?

[609] L D Smith, *The Law of Tracing* (1997, Clarendon: Oxford), p 399:

> 'The process of tracing is simply the proof of a series of exchanges. This process cannot create rights ex nihilo. What it can do is allow rights to be transmitted from one asset to another. If a claimant held some rights in the form of Asset A, and Asset B is the traceable proceeds of Asset A, then it may well be that the claimant will be able to assert rights in Asset B. But the rights in Asset A must be established without any regard to the exercise of tracing.'

[610] P Birks, 'On Taking Seriously the Difference Between Tracing and Claiming' (1997) 12 *Trust Law International* 2, 8:

> 'It is necessary to underline at this point the independence of tracing and the claims which are contingent on tracing. Tracing is neutral as to rights. Successful tracing

[17] This is certainly true as regards claiming; there are, however, suggestions that the tracing process should follow the same rules at law and in equity.

confers no rights, though it is often a precondition of the exercise of rights. The tracing exercise being successfully completed, there always remains a separate inquiry as to what, if any, rights the facts of the case give rise to in respect of the assets found at the end of the tracing claim. The form of the inquiry will often be whether on the given facts the plaintiff is entitled to a proprietary claim.'

6.3.1 Tracing at common law and in equity

'The exercise of tracing allows one asset to stand in the place of another for certain legal purposes.'[18] In the following extract, the Court of Appeal compares the common law and equitable doctrines of tracing.

[611] Re Diplock [1948] 1 Ch 465 (CA), 518–23 *per* Lord Greene MR for the Court: [The facts are irrelevant here, but are detailed below at **[628]**.]

'Before passing to a consideration of the case of *Sinclair v. Brougham* ([1914] A. C. 398) we may usefully make some observations of our own as to the distinction between the attitude of the common law and that of equity to these questions [of tracing].

The common law approached them in a strictly materialistic way. It could only appreciate what might almost be called the "physical" identity of one thing with another. It could treat a person's money as identifiable so long as it had not become mixed with other money. It could treat as identifiable with the money other kinds of property acquired by means of it, provided that there was no admixture of other money. It is noticeable that in this latter case the common law did not base itself on any known theory of tracing such as that adopted in equity. It proceeded on the basis that the unauthorized act of purchasing was one capable of ratification by the owner of the money (see per Lord Parker in *Sinclair v. Brougham* (at p 441).) Certain words of Lord Haldane in *Sinclair v. Brougham* may appear to suggest a further limitation, i.e., that "money" as we have used that word was not regarded at common law as identifiable once it had been paid into a banking account (at p 419) [**[615]** below]. We do not, however, think it necessary to discuss this point at length. We agree with the comments of Wynn-Parry J. upon it ([1947] Ch. 716, 745–6) and those of Atkin L.J. (as he then was) in *Banque Belge v. Hambrouck* ([1921] 1 K. B. 321, 335 [**[616]** below]). If it is possible to identify a principal's money with an asset purchased exclusively by means of it we see no reason for drawing a distinction between a chose in action such as a banker's debt to his customer and any other asset. If the principal can ratify the acquisition of the one, we see no reason for supposing that he cannot ratify the acquisition of the other.

We may mention three several matters which we think are helpful in understanding the limitation of the common law doctrine and the reasons why equity was able to take a more liberal view. They are as follows:

(i) The common law did not recognize equitable claims to property, whether money or any other form of property. Sovereigns in A's pocket either belonged in law to A or they belonged in law to B. The idea that they could belong in law to A and that they should nevertheless be treated as belonging to B was entirely foreign to the common law. This is the reason why the common law doctrine finds its typical exemplification in cases of principal and agent. If B, a principal, hands cash to A, his agent, in order that it may be applied in a particular manner, the cash, in the eyes of the common law, remains the

[18] L D Smith, *The Law of Tracing* (1997, Clarendon: Oxford) p 17.

property of B. If, therefore, A, instead of applying it in the authorized manner, buries it in a sack in his garden or uses it for an unauthorized purchase, B can, in the former case, recover the cash as being still his own property and, in the latter case, affirm the purchase of something bought with his money by his agent. If, however, the relationship of A and B was not one which left the property in the cash in B but merely constituted a relationship of debtor and creditor between them, there could, of course, have been no remedy at law under this head, since the property in the cash would have passed out of B into A.

(ii) The narrowness of the limits within which the common law operated may be linked with the limited nature of the remedies available to it. Specific relief as distinct from damages (the normal remedy at common law) was confined to a very limited range of claims as compared with the extensive uses of specific relief developed by equity. In particular, the device of a declaration of charge was unknown to the common law and it was the availability of that device which enabled equity to give effect to its wider conception of equitable rights.

(iii) It was the materialistic approach of the common law coupled with and encouraged by the limited range of remedies available to it that prevented the common law from identifying money in a mixed fund. Once the money of B became mixed with the money of A its identification in a physical sense became impossible. Owing to the fact of mixture there could be no question of ratification of an unauthorized act; and the only remedy of B, if any, lay in a claim for damages.

Equity adopted a more metaphysical approach. It found no difficulty in regarding a composite fund as an amalgam constituted by the mixture of two or more funds each of which could be regarded as having, for certain purposes, a continued separate existence. Putting it in another way, equity regarded the amalgam as capable, in proper circumstances, of being resolved into its component parts.

Adapting, for the sake of contrast, the phraseology which we have used in relation to the common law, it was the metaphysical approach of equity coupled with and encouraged by the far-reaching remedy of a declaration of charge that enabled equity to identify money in a mixed fund. Equity, so to speak, is able to draw up a balance sheet on the right-hand side of which appears the composite fund and on its left-hand side the two or more funds of which it is to be deemed to be made up.

Regarded as a pure piece of machinery for the purpose of tracing money into a mixed fund or into property acquired by means of a mixed fund, a declaration of charge might be thought to be a suitable means of dealing with any case where one person has, without legal title, acquired some benefit by the use of the money of another—in other words, any case of what is often called "unjust enrichment." The opinion of Lord Dunedin in *Sinclair v. Brougham* ([1914] AC 398, 437) appears to us to come very nearly to this, for he appears to treat the equitable remedy as applicable in any case where a superfluity, expressed or capable of being expressed in terms of money, is found to exist. Such a view would dispense with the necessity of establishing as a starting point the existence of a fiduciary or quasi-fiduciary relationship or of a continuing right of property recognized in equity. We may say at once that, apart from the possible case of Lord Dunedin's speech, we cannot find that any principle so wide in its operation is to be found enunciated in English law. The conditions which must exist before the equitable form of relief becomes available will be considered later in this judgment. But one truism may be stated here in order to get it out of the way. The equitable form of relief whether it takes the form of an order to restore an unmixed sum of money (or property acquired by means of such a sum) or a declaration of charge upon a mixed fund (or upon property acquired by means of such a fund) is, of course, personal in the sense that its efficacy is founded upon the jurisdiction of equity to enforce its rules by acting upon the individual. But it is not personal in the sense that the person against whom an order of this nature is sought can be made personally liable to repay the amount claimed to have belonged to the claimant. The equitable remedies pre-suppose the continued existence of the money either as a separate fund or as part of a mixed fund or as latent in property acquired by means of such a fund. If, on the facts of any individual case, such continued existence is not established, equity is as helpless as the common law itself. If the fund, mixed or unmixed, is spent upon a dinner, equity, which dealt only in specific relief and not in damages, could do nothing. If the case was one which at common law involved breach of contract the common law could, of course, award damages but specific relief would be out of the question. It is, therefore, a necessary matter for consideration in each case where it is sought to trace money in equity, whether it has such a continued existence, actual or notional, as will enable equity to grant specific relief.

To turn to another preliminary matter: We do not think that confusion can be avoided unless the meaning of the word "money" as used in connexion with this class of question is kept in mind. It is tempting to use the illustration of sovereigns in a bag or, to use an expression of Lord Dunedin's, a strong box. But this must not blind us to the fact that such an illustration has little or no likeness to actual facts in present day conditions. We can explain what we mean by a reference to the present cases. The plaintiffs claim that "money" forming part of the residuary estate of the testator and, therefore, divisible among his next-of-kin, has been improperly paid to a charity. This "money" when "paid" was in the form of a cheque on the executorship account, i.e., a negotiable instrument. This negotiable instrument at the moment preceding its delivery to the charity belonged to the residuary estate of the testator and any of the next-of-kin, if he had known of the situation, could have secured an injunction restraining the executors from delivering it to the charity. As in that event the cheque would never have been presented for payment, the "money" representing the relevant portion of the residuary estate would have remained in its existing state, i.e., as part of the chose in action constituted by the banker's debt to the executors in respect of the executorship account.

The charity accepted the cheque; and on the assumption that it was not a purchaser for value and is not to be charged with such notice as to make it a constructive trustee, it accepted the cheque as a volunteer. The first stage, therefore, was that the charity had in its possession a negotiable instrument which in origin belonged to the residuary estate and in which the next-of-kin were, in the eyes of equity, interested.

If the next-of-kin had been in a position to interfere at that stage they could, in our view, clearly (and the contrary was not argued) have recovered the cheque from the charity whom, as a volunteer, equity would have compelled to recognize the equitable interest of the next-of-kin in it. But the cheque was in fact paid into a banking account in the name of the charity. The next-of-kin claim to follow their "money." What really happened was that when the cheque was cleared, a credit was passed by the paying bank to the collecting bank for the benefit of the charity who thus, without handling any "money" in the sense of cash, became possessed of "money" in the sense of credit in its banking account, i.e., a chose in action. Now, if the "money" in the form of the cheque was "paid in" to a separate account so that the "money" in the form of a chose in action which resulted from the operation remained "unmixed" (i.e., was identifiable as a chose in action having a separate existence) it is not disputed that the "money" will be specifically recoverable from the charity. It is not suggested in that case that the title to the "money" of the charity as a volunteer can defeat the claim of the next-of-kin to recover it for the benefit of the estate. The appropriate equitable relief would be by way of specific order for restoration of what, in the eyes of equity, never ceased to belong in equity to the estate; the reason, of course, being that the charity, which took the cheque not as a purchaser for value without notice but merely as a volunteer, could not set up a title adverse to the estate in respect of "money" (i.e., on those facts a separate and identifiable chose in action) obtained by means of "money" in the form of a cheque, i.e., an order by the executors on their bankers to transfer from "money" belonging to the estate in the form of a chose in action an aliquot sum of "money" in the form of a credit in favour of the charity, as payee of the cheque, in its account with its bankers.

When the various senses in which the word "money" is used are appreciated, the conceptions of "purchaser for value without notice" and of "volunteer" which are common currency in the language of equity, do not appear inappropriate, as they might perhaps have done (at any rate at first sight) in the case of current coins which pass by delivery: and one of the apparent difficulties in the way of tracing, identifying and locating "money" does, we think, disappear.'

Note:

This analysis has been criticised on the basis that it underestimates the common law. See M Scott, 'The Right to "Trace" at Common Law' (1966) 7 *UWALR* 463; R Goode, 'The Right to Trace and its Impact in Commercial Transactions' (1976) 92 *LQR* 360, 528.

[612] *F C Jones & Sons (Trustee in Bankruptcy) v Jones* [1997] Ch 159, 169–70 *per* Millett LJ:

[The facts are given below at **[619]**.]

'In *Agip (Africa) Ltd. v. Jackson* [1990] Ch. 265 [**[617]** below], 285 I said that the ability of the common law to trace an asset into a changed form in the same hands was established in *Taylor v. Plumer* (1815) 3 M. & S. 562 [**[613]** below]. Lord Ellenborough C.J. in that case had said, at p. 575:

> "the product of or substitute for the original thing still follows the nature of the thing itself, as long as it can be ascertained to be such, and the right only ceases when the means of ascertainment fail, which is the case when the subject is turned into money, and mixed and confounded in a general mass of the same description."

In this it appears that I fell into a common error, for it has since been convincingly demonstrated that, although *Taylor v. Plumer* was decided by a common law court, the court was in fact applying the rules of equity: see Lionel Smith, "Tracing in *Taylor v. Plumer*: Equity in the Court of King's Bench" [1995] L.M.C.L.Q. 240.

But this is no reason for concluding that the common law does not recognise claims to substitute assets or their products. Such claims were upheld by this court in *Banque Belge pour l'Etranger v. Hambrouck* [1921] 1 K.B. 321 [**[616]** below] and by the House of Lords in *Lipkin Gorman v. Karpnale Ltd.* [1991] 2 A.C. 548 [**[618]** below]. It has been suggested by commentators that these cases are undermined by their misunderstanding of *Taylor v. Plumer*, 3 M. & S. 562, but that is not how the English doctrine of *stare decisis* operates. It would be more consistent with that doctrine to say that, in recognising claims to substituted assets, equity must be taken to have followed the law, even though the law was not declared until later. Lord Ellenborough C.J. gave no indication that, in following assets into their exchange products, equity had adopted a rule which was peculiar to itself or which went further than the common law.

There is no merit in having distinct and differing tracing rules at law and in equity, given that tracing is neither a right nor a remedy but merely the process by which the plaintiff establishes what has happened to his property and makes good his claim that the assets which he claims can properly be regarded as representing his property. The fact that there are different tracing rules at law and in equity is unfortunate though probably inevitable, but unnecessary differences should not be created where they are not required by the different nature of legal and equitable doctrines and remedies. There is, in my view, even less merit in the present rule which precludes the invocation of the equitable tracing rules to support a common law claim; until that rule is swept away unnecessary obstacles to the development of a rational and coherent law of restitution will remain.'

Also see:

L D Smith, *The Law of Tracing* (1997, Clarendon: Oxford) pp 278–9 which summarises and defends the view that the rules of tracing are the same at common law and in equity. But contrast P Millett, 'Tracing the Proceeds of Fraud' (1991) 107 *LQR* 71, (before his judgment in *F C Jones*) suggesting that the common law rules are inadequate and its jurisprudence defective.

6.3.2 Further comments on following, tracing and claiming at common law and in equity

To return to the issues considered at the start of this chapter, it is clear that the exercise of following is quite separate from that of claiming. For example, a car originally owned by A might, during the course of six months, pass through B's hands and into C's. 'Following' tells the story of the car's changing physical location. However, it does not indicate whether A still owns the car and can reclaim it from C. If A had sold the car to B, who had in turn given or sold it to C, then A would have no claim to the car; the contrary is true, however, if the car had been stolen from A. Following shows where the car is; but conflict and priority rules are needed to determine whether A still has an interest in the car. The 'following' exercise is easy (in legal terms, even if not in practical terms); the 'claiming' exercise is more difficult.

Now turn to tracing. The purpose of tracing is not to locate the original asset, but to identify a substitute asset which can be seen as representing the value which was inherent in the original asset. Following focuses on the original asset, and monitors its movements from recipient to recipient; tracing focuses on one particular recipient, and monitors dealings with the original asset and then with its products and proceeds. For example, A might give a painting to B which B then sells to C for £5,000. 'Following' indicates that the painting is now in C's possession. 'Tracing' indicates that, in B's hands, the value inherent in the painting is now represented by £5,000 cash. In this simple example, the distinction between tracing and claiming, and the parallels between tracing and following seem clear: tracing determines that the painting's value is now represented by £5,000 cash, and claiming determines whether A has any claim to the painting—or to the cash—in B's hands.

But consider a slightly more complicated—and more realistic—example: A gives £1,000 in cash to B; B deposits this amount in her bank account, which is already £1,000 in credit; B then spends £1,000 on a skiing holiday and £1,000 on blue chip shares. If the aim is to trace through dealings with this £1,000 to identify an asset in B's hands which represents its value, the difficulty is clear. Will the rules of tracing allow A to say that the value of the notes is represented by the shares, or will the rules compel A to accept that the £1,000 was spent on a skiing holiday, so that there is no longer any asset which continues to represent the value inherent in the £1,000? Does the answer depend upon whether B is innocent or a wrongdoer? Does it depend on the type of wrongdoing? If the tracing rules depend upon the circumstances, then, notwithstanding the earlier extracts, it appears difficult to draw a clear distinction between tracing and claiming: the tracing exercise may be inextricably linked with the particular claiming impetus which motivates it.

Question:

The extracts below illustrate the particular rules of tracing. Do they suggest that the rules of tracing differ depending upon the particular claim being advanced?

FURTHER READING:

R H Maudsley, 'Proprietary Remedies for the Recovery of Money' (1959) 75 *LQR* 234.
M Scott, 'The Right to "Trace" at Common Law' (1966) 7 *UWALR* 63.
F O B Babafemi, 'Tracing Assets: A Case for the Fusion of Common Law and Equity in English Law' (1971) 34 *MLR* 12.
R Pearce, 'A Tracing Paper' [1976] *Conv* 277.
R M Goode, 'The Right to Trace and its Impact on Commercial Transactions' (1976) 92 *LQR* 360, 528.
R M Goode, 'Ownership and Obligation in Commercial Transactions' (1987) 103 *LQR* 433.

6.4 Tracing: the common law rules

As noted earlier, the exercise of tracing allows one asset to stand in the place of another for certain legal purposes. Before investigating the common law rules of tracing, it is important to know when application of such rules might prove advantageous in pursuing a common law claim. It seems there are two situations where this could be the case.

6.4.1 Tort claims

The first situation concerns claims which are dependent on the claimant's assertion of legal title to an asset which is now in the hands of another. Claims in trespass and conversion (under the Torts (Interference with Goods) Act 1977) are of this type; they depend upon the claimant having a right to possession of the asset. Such common law claims give the claimant a right to monetary damages (a personal remedy), but not—perhaps surprisingly—a right to have the asset returned. Instead, the Torts (Interference with Goods) Act 1977 section 3 gives the court a statutory discretion to order specific recovery of the goods, and it will do this if damages are inadequate.[19] Because of this limitation, specific recovery is rarely ordered. Moreover, damages are recoverable even if the defendant no longer has possession of the claimant's asset, provided unauthorised interference at an earlier date can be proved. Given these two features of claims in trespass and conversion, it would seem that common law tracing will afford little assistance to claimants.

However, there are two situations where tracing might improve the claimant's lot. The first is when the defendant is insolvent. It has been suggested that in some circumstances these common law tort claims will afford the claimant full protection on the defendant's insolvency.[20] In an action for trespass to goods, for example, the general rule is that wrongdoing defendant must return either the goods or their full value. This is true whether or not the defendant still has the goods. If the defendant *has* the goods, however, then it seems that the defendant's liquidator or trustee in bankruptcy cannot elect to return only their value (rather than the goods *in specie*) and then allow that value claim to abate as a result of the operation of the *pari passu* principle of insolvency distribution. The defendant must return either the goods or their *full* value. This suggests that tracing could assist a claimant *if* the defendant is insolvent and *if* substitutions for the original asset are allowed to stand in the place of the original asset for the purpose of this rule. Use of tracing in this way does not increase the quantum of the claimant's claim; it simply protects that claim against abatement on the defendant's insolvency.

The second and separate advantage which tracing might deliver is to increase the quantum of the claimant's claim. Argument from first principles suggest that this could only be the case where the original property is converted into a more valuable substitute asset *and* the claimant is entitled to assert legal title to that substitute asset. The claimant could then demand damages for trespass or conversion in respect of the substitute asset. The law suggests that this is possible, but rarely so. The issue is controversial, and is taken up later.

Note that these problems only arise when the dealing with the original asset is unauthorised. When it is authorised, ownership of any products or proceeds will follow the parties' express or implied agreement.[21] Unauthorised dealing with the original asset may produce a number of different consequences, not all of which are treated in the same way by the law. Consider the case where the original asset is a quantity of oil owned by A. Different scenarios can be imagined. For example, A's

[19] *Whiteley v Hill* [1918] 2 KB 808.

[20] M Scott, 'The Right to "Trace" at Common Law' (1966) 7 *UWALR* 463, 480.

[21] Although see Chapter 3, Section 3.8, for examples of the difficulties which can arise.

oil may be filtered to remove sediments; the purified oil is not the same as the unpurified oil (so this is not a case of 'following'), but might A nevertheless assert ownership of the purified form? Alternatively, A's oil may be mixed with oil belonging to other parties, so that it is impossible to isolate the very oil which originally belonged to A. Can A nevertheless assert some sort of ownership of the oil mixture? A further alternative is that A's oil may be used to manufacture plastics. Can A then assert part-ownership of the newly manufactured product? Some of the extracts below indicate the courts' approaches to these problems.

Question:

Do the cases extracted below (especially those concerning common law tracing into mixtures, substitutions and products) suggest that the claimant acquires legal *title* to (ie ownership of) the new end product, or do they simply suggest that the original claim is fully preserved and protected notwithstanding any changes to the original property? The distinction is critical in determining whether the claimant can ever benefit from the increased value of the substitute asset, as discussed in the previous paragraph.

6.4.2 Unjust enrichment claims

The second situation where common law tracing may prove useful is with claims which depend upon proof that, in the circumstances, the defendant's receipt of the claimant's asset is an unjust enrichment obtained at the claimant's expense. The claimant then has a common law right to restitution of the value of the unjust enrichment. For example, if the claimant pays money to the defendant as a result of a mistake, the claimant may be entitled to recover an equivalent sum from the defendant. The common law restitutionary remedy is personal,[22] although in certain circumstances it is supported by an equitable proprietary claim.[23] The remedy does not depend upon the defendant's continued holding of the asset which constitutes the unjust enrichment, but (whether or not the asset is still held) the quantum of the claim will abate if the defendant has a defence of change of position. This suggests that there are two classes of case where tracing might prove useful in pursuing these claims.

The first is where the claimant uses tracing to establish a proprietary claim to a substitute asset in the defendant's hands in order to protect the claimant on the defendant's insolvency. The aim is not to alter the quantum of the claim; it is merely to preserve its proprietary status. It is clear that this process will be effective if the claimant starts the process with an equitable proprietary interest in assets in the

[22] Although again it has been suggested that it affords the claimant protection on the defendant's insolvency: see *Scott v Surman* (1742) Willes 400, 405 (125 ER 1235).

[23] It remains difficult to say what divides cases of proprietary and non-proprietary restitution, but see Chapter 5, especially Sections 5.5 and 5.10, for some insights into the debate.

defendant's hands and traces that interest in equity into the substitutes. It is less clear whether the same consequences follow at common law. At the end of the common law tracing exercise, the common law claim is personal, not proprietary, but it may nevertheless be protected on the defendant's insolvency, as indicated in the discussion of claims in trespass and conversion.

The second class of case is where the claimant with a restitutionary claim does wish to increase the quantum of the claim. For example, if a claimant with a restitutionary claim to £1,000 in the defendant's hands can prove that the original £1,000 was spent on shares which are now worth £2,000, can the claimant recover the shares (a proprietary claim) or their value (a personal claim) on the basis that the defendant has been unjustly enriched to that extent, not merely to the extent of £1,000? The answer is not at all clear. Does it depend upon whether the claimant can assert legal or equitable title to the original £1,000? If the claimant can assert legal title, then arguably the claim is not in unjust enrichment—the defendant is no richer and the claimant no poorer as a result of the initial transfer; the claim is perhaps in conversion, and then the issues discussed earlier will apply. If the claimant can assert equitable title to the £1,000, then it seems sensible for the equitable rules of tracing (not the common law rules) to apply. Although these equitable rules may allow the money to be traced into the shares, on what basis can the claimant assert a claim to *ownership* of those shares? This is even more the case where the claimant has no proprietary interest at all in the original £1,000, merely an unjust enrichment claim to that value. And yet, where the defendant is a wrongdoer, there is a strong sense of moral outrage at the suggestion that the defendant might be able to profit from the wrong. The cases extracted below indicate the courts' responses. These cases need to be read in conjunction with the later cases on equitable tracing.

Question:

As the foregoing comments suggest, the application of the common law rules in these different circumstances is controversial. Do the cases extracted below suggest that the rules differ depending upon whether the claim is in tort or in unjust enrichment?

6.4.3 Substitutions: the common law tracing rules

[613] ***Taylor v Plumer*** **(1815) 3 M & S 562, 575 (105 ER 721)** ***per*** **Lord Ellenborough:** [The defendant handed money to his stockbroker, Walsh, to purchase exchequer bonds. Instead, Walsh purchased American investments and bullion and tried to abscond to America. He was apprehended, and his investments and bullion seized and delivered to the defendant. His assignees in bankruptcy sought to recover the property, on the basis that it belonged to Walsh and hence to them, but they failed.]

'The plaintiff . . . is not entitled to recover if the defendant has succeeded in maintaining these propositions in point of law — viz., that the property of a principal entrusted by him to his factor for any special purpose belongs to the principal, notwithstanding any change which that property may have undergone in point of form, so long as such property is capable of being identified, and distinguished from all other property. . . . It makes no difference in reason or in law into what other form different from the original, the change may have been made . . . for the product of or substitute for the original thing still follows the nature of the thing itself, as long as it can be ascertained to be such, and the right only ceases when the means of ascertainment fail, which is the case when the subject is turned into money, and mixed and confounded in a general mass of the same description.'

[And see the further excerpts in the next extract, **[614]** below.]

Note:

This case used to be regarded as showing that common law tracing into direct *substitutes* was possible, but not into a *mixed* fund. However, Lionel Smith, in 'Tracing in *Taylor v Plumer*: Equity in the Court of King's Bench' [1995] *LMCLQ* 240, argues that the decision was based on the assertion of equitable proprietary rights to the proceeds of a wrongful disposition by a defaulting fiduciary, and so says nothing about common law tracing. A similar conclusion had been advanced earlier by the S Kurshid and P Matthews (see **[614]** below).[24] But also see M Scott, 'The Right to "Trace" at Common Law' (1966) 7 *UWALR* 463, 470.

[614] S Kurshid and P Matthews, 'Tracing Confusion' (1979) 95 *LQR* 78, 79–83:

[Footnotes in the original are omitted.]

'The exchange-product theory asserts that, where A owns property which B without authority exchanges for cash or other property from C, A can claim that cash or property (the "exchange product") either as owner or at least as having a sufficient right to immediate possession to enable him to maintain conversion. This theory is accepted conventionally by textbook writers and is usually based on the dicta of Lord Ellenborough in *Taylor v Plumer*: . . .

[see **[613]** above.]

. . . The problem as we see it is that not enough attention is paid to the context of the dicta or the facts of the case.

The facts are well known. The defendant gave his stockbroker a banker's draft to buy exchequer bills for him, but the stockbroker misapplied part of the proceeds of the draft in buying other securities and bullion for his own personal benefit. Having become insolvent he attempted to flee the country, but was caught by the defendant at Falmouth and forced to surrender the securities and bullion. The assigness in bankruptcy of the stockbroker thereafter sued the defendant in trover. Now, to maintain trover the plaintiffs had to show a better right to possession than the defendant's. Their right to possession came from their title as assignees in bankruptcy, vested in them under the Bankruptcy Act 1623. But as Lord Ellenborough pointed out: "trust property in the possession of a factor empowered to dispose of it for his principal does not pass to his assignees under the statute . . . upon his becoming bankrupt."

Thus because the defendant had retained the beneficial interest in the property (which a court of equity would allow him to trace *in rem*) the legal title vested in his

[24] And perhaps earlier still by Roy Goode, 'The Right to Trace and its Impact in Commercial Transactions—I' (1976) 92 *LQR* 360, 369 n 36.

agent stockbroker did not pass to the plaintiffs on the agent's bankruptcy and they had no other basis for a right to immediate possession to challenge the defendant's actual possession.

Michael Scott asserts [(1966) 7 UWALR 463, 481] that "the principal was allowed to retain the property as against the assignees," which is perfectly correct, but he then goes on:

> "Suppose the case had been otherwise, and it had been the assignees who caught up with the broker and seized the property. The result would have been the same. They would not have been allowed to retain it as against the principal; and had they refused to deliver it to him, would have been *personally* liable in detinue or conversion."

We contend that this is mistaken and that the defendant, in order to become plaintiff in trover or detinue would have had to invoke the name of his trustee, the bankrupt stockbroker, in whom the legal title was, despite the bankruptcy, still vested. Of course it is true that Lord Ellenborough at a later stage in his judgment says that "the assignees cannot in this action recover that which, if an action were brought against them the assignees by the defendant, they could not have effectually retained against him," but this is heavily qualified by the rest of the sentence: ". . . inasmuch as it was trust property of the defendant, which, as such, did not pass to them under the commission. . . ."

Thus the defendant could have sued the plaintiffs in his own name, if they had had the possession of the bullion, but not at law—in equity. To maintain an action in trover, a plaintiff had to show a common law right, and if Sir Thomas Plumer had such a right, why was Lord Ellenborough throughout his judgment talking about trust property?

> "[I]ndeed, upon a view of the authorities, and consideration of the arguments, it should seem that if the property in its original state and form was covered with a trust in favour of the principal, no change of that state and form can divest it of such trust, or give the factor, or those who represent him in right, any other more valid claim in respect to it, than they respectively had before such change. An abuse of trust can confer no rights on the party abusing it, nor on those who claim in privity with him. The argument which has been advanced in favour of the plaintiffs, that the property of the principal continues only so long as the authority of the principal is pursued in respect to the order and disposition of it, and that it ceases when the property is tortiously converted into another form for the use of the factor himself, is mischievous in principle and supported by no authorities of law."

It is quite clear that Lord Ellenborough's words here are devoted to one thing and one thing only, *viz*.: meeting head-on the only possible argument for the plaintiffs. Their title as assignees depended on the Statute of James I. But, it having been previously held that it did not operate on trust property held by the bankrupt, and *it having been conceded* that the defendant retained (at least) a beneficial interest in the original banker's draft, the plaintiffs were forced to contend that the bankrupt's abuse of authority terminated that beneficial interest and prevented it passing in equity into the exchange product, leaving the bankrupt sole owner both at law and in equity, and the defendant nothing more than his creditor. This argument, as we saw above, was rejected as "mischievous in principle and supported by no authorities of law."

The problem was fairly and squarely within equity's general jurisdiction over fiduciaries. Though there is in English law no general doctrine of the remedial constructive trust, in circumstances such as those in *Taylor v. Plumer* where money or property is entrusted to a fiduciary for a particular purpose equity binds the conscience of the wrongdoing fiduciary regarding the product acquired through the breach of his duty. Really there seems no reason why extra protection should not be extended to a principal who parts with something he owns as contrasted with another who is wrongfully deprived of a benefit that should have come to him. In the latter case any attempt to go further than the existing tortious or quasi-contractual actions conflicts with policy considerations regarding the interests of ordinary creditors.

One further point which supports the equitable basis of the decision in *Taylor v. Plumer* seems worth mentioning. Many commentators cite the words of Lord Ellenborough, that the right to trace "only ceases when the means of ascertainment fail, which is the case when the subject is turned into money and mixed and confounded in a general mass of the same description," as showing the limitation of common law as opposed to equitable tracing. We submit that the limitation there mentioned was not that of common law but (as Lord Ellenborough supposed) of *equity*. Actions at common law such as the common law tracing theory requires never suffered from any such limitation. In *Jackson v. Anderson* [(1811) 4 Taunt 24] a plaintiff was held entitled to maintain trover for his gold coins mixed in a barrelful of the same description after the defendant had disposed of the whole barrel. This case was decided only four years before *Taylor v. Plumer*. If Lord Ellenborough was really concerned with common law tracing what he said about the limitation would be patently wrong. As it was, he was in the passage quoted dealing exclusively with equity. In fact Sir George Jessel M.R. in *Re Hallet's Estate* [13 ChD 696, 717 [**[627]** below]] pointed out that Lord Ellenborough was mistaken in that supposition of such a limitation on tracing in equity, and he did so in a passage which makes it quite clear that it was equity and not the common law that was under discussion in the earlier case. Quoting Lord Ellenborough, he said:

> ". . . 'and the right only ceases when the means of ascertainment fail.' That is correct. Now there comes a point which is not correct, but which I am afraid only ceases to be correct because Lord Ellenborough's knowledge of the rules of Equity was not quite commensurate with his knowledge of the rules of Common Law, 'which is the case when the subject is turned into money, and mixed and confounded in a general mass of the same description.' He was not aware of the rule of Equity that gave you a charge—that if you lent £1,000 of your own and £1,000 trust money on a bond for £2,000 . . . Equity could follow it, and create a charge; but he gives that, not as law—the law is that it only fails when the means of ascertainment fail—he gives it as a case in which the means of ascertainment fail, not being aware of this refinement of Equity by which the means of ascertainment still remain. . . ."

Consequently we would suggest that this distinction relied on by commentators, that the equity lawyer's tracing horizon was superbly unbounded, whilst, on the other side, there was that "poor mutt, the common lawyer, able to grasp the identity of specific coins, but retiring mouth agape in baffled amazement once they were mixed with other coins" is so far as it is based on *Taylor v. Plumer*, erroneous. Further, if the exchange-product theory has any validity at law it cannot be by virtue of anything in that case.'

[615] ***Sinclair v Brougham* [1914] AC 398 (HL), 418–420 *per* Viscount Haldane LC:** [The facts are outlined at **[516]** above. Recall from Chapter 5 that, to the extent that this case decides that the ultra vires depositors were entitled to a proprietary claim to the funds initially deposited, it has been overruled by the House of Lords in *Westdeutsche Landesbank Girozentrale v Islington London Borough Council* [1996] AC 669 (see **[504]** for the facts, and **[518]** for the law). However, the judgments make some potentially important general comments on the common law (and equitable) right to trace.]

***Viscount Haldane LC*:**
'It follows that the depositors in the present case will not succeed unless they are able to trace their money into the hands of the society or its agents as actually existing assets. The question is whether they are able to establish enough to succeed upon this footing. Their claim cannot be in personam and must be in rem, a claim to follow and recover property with which, in equity at all events, they had never really parted.

I proceed, therefore, to consider the case on this restricted footing. The evidence is very scanty, but it must be taken that the depositors' money was used on a large scale in acquiring the assets now in the liquidator's hands; for the value of these assets is far in excess of the contributions of the shareholders, and much of it can be due to the money of the depositors alone. The difficulty of establishing a title in rem in this case arises from the apparent difficulty of following money. [What is being referred to would now be termed 'tracing', rather than 'following'; in many early cases these two words were used interchangeably.] In most cases money cannot be followed. When sovereigns or bank notes are paid over as currency, so far as the payer is concerned, they cease ipso facto to be the subjects of specific title as chattels. If a sovereign or bank note be offered in payment it is, under ordinary circumstances, no part of the duty of the person receiving it to inquire into title. The reason of this is that chattels of such a kind form part of what the law recognizes as currency, and treats as passing from hand to hand in point, not merely of possession, but of property. It would cause great inconvenience to commerce if in this class of chattel an exception were not made to the general requirement of the law as to title.

But the exception is not extended beyond the limits which necessity imposes. If money in a bag is stolen, and can be identified in the form in which it was stolen, it can be recovered in specie. Even if it has been expended by the person who has wrongfully taken it in purchasing some particular asset, that asset, if capable of being earmarked as purchased with the money, can be claimed by the true owner of the money. This is a principle not [419] merely of equity, but of the common law. It is explained in the judgment of Lord Ellenborough in *Taylor v. Plumer* ((1815) 3 M. & S. 562) [**[613]** above], who pointed out that there was no reason why the doctrine that money could not be followed should apply to circumstances in which a broker had wrongfully invested money of his principal in purchasing securities into which it could be traced. The reason of this is plain. The broker could not in these circumstances set up as against his principal the rule which applies to what has been paid over as currency, that ordinarily transfer of possession is transfer of property. So long as the money which the principal has handed to his agent to be applied specifically, and not on a debtor and creditor account, can be traced into what has been procured with it, the principal can waive his right of action for damages for tort, and, affirming the proceeding of the broker, claim that his money is invested in a specific thing, which is his. But Lord Ellenborough laid down, as a limit to this proposition, that if the money had become incapable of being traced, as, for instance, when it had been paid into the broker's general account with his banker, the principal had no remedy excepting to prove as a creditor for money had and received. The explanation was, of course, that a relation of debtor and creditor had arisen between the banker and his client, the broker, which precluded the notion of following the money.

That seems to be, so far as the doctrine of the common law is concerned, the limit to which the exception to the rule about currency was carried; whether the case be that of a thief or of a fraudulent broker, or of money paid under mistake of fact, you can, even at law, follow, but only so long as the relation of debtor and creditor has not superseded the right in rem. This is well put by Bramwell L.J. in *Ex parte Cooke* ((1876) 4 Ch. D. 123), who explains why the principal in *Taylor v. Plumer* could claim the money: "Because the money was paid to the broker, not as a trustee in the strict sense of the word, so that no action at law could be maintained against him, and he would only be liable to have a bill filed against him, but was handed to him in a fiduciary character, so as not to create the mere relation of debtor and creditor between him and his principal." Thesiger L.J. in *In* [420] *re Hallett's Estate* (13 Ch. D. 696 [**[627]** below], at p. 723) states the principle in other words, but to the same effect: "All cases where it has been held that moneys mixed and confounded, but still existing in a mass, cannot be followed, may, I think, be resolved into cases where, although there may have been a trust with reference to the disposition of the particular chattel which those moneys subsequently represented, there was no trust, no duty, in reference to the moneys themselves beyond the ordinary duty of a man to pay his debts; in other words, that they were cases where the relationship of debtor and creditor had been constituted, instead of the relation either of trustee and cestui que trust, or principal and agent."

My Lords, it is, in my opinion, impossible to confine the right at law to follow to cases where there was a fiduciary relationship. The principle appears to me to cover all cases where the property in the money has not passed, and the money itself can be earmarked in the hands of the person who has wrongfully obtained it. A person standing in a fiduciary relation may be in this position, but it is not because of his trust or fiduciary duty. The common law, which we are now considering, did not take cognizance of such duties. It looked simply to the question whether the property had passed, and if it had not, for instance, where no relationship of debtor and creditor had intervened, the money could be followed, notwithstanding its normal character as currency, provided it could be earmarked or traced into assets acquired with it. And this appears to me to be, on ground of principle, as true of money paid under mistake of fact or on an ultra vires contract, under which no property could pass or relation of debtor be constituted, as it is true in the case of a broker or bailee. [To what extent does this final statement remain true after the *Westdeutsche* case (see **[518]** above)?]

But while the common law gave the remedy I have stated, it gave no remedy when the money had been paid by the wrong-doer into his account with his banker, who simply owed him a debt, so that no money was or could be, in the contemplation of a Court of law, earmarked. Here equity, which had so far exercised a concurrent jurisdiction based upon trust, gave a further remedy.'

[616] ***Banque Belge Pour l'Etranger v Hambrouck*** **[1921] 1 KB 321 (CA), 333–6** ***per*** **Atkin LJ:**

[A clerk fraudulently obtained cheques from his employer, drawn on the claimant bank. The clerk paid the cheques into his own bank, which collected payment from the claimant. The clerk then drew cheques on his own account and paid them to his mistress, Mlle Spanoghe. She paid them into her account, where the funds remained. The claimant successfully brought an action against the clerk, his mistress and her bank for a declaration that the money paid into her account was the claimant's property.]

'The appellant however contends that the plaintiffs cannot assert their title to the sum of money which was on a deposit account: 1. because it has passed through one if not two bank accounts and therefore cannot be identified as the plaintiffs' money; 2. because in any case a transfer to an innocent donee defeats the original owner's claim. The course of the proceedings in this case is not quite clear. The statement of claim alleges specifically that the money is the property of the plaintiffs which they are entitled to follow, and the relief asked is not for a money judgment against the defendants, but an order that the sum paid into Court, by the defendant Bank should be paid out to the plaintiffs. In giving judgment however, the learned judge has treated the claim as one for money had and received, and the judgment entered is an ordinary judgment against the appellant on a money claim for £315 together with an order that the sum in Court should be paid out to the plaintiffs in part satisfaction. The two forms of relief are different, and though in this case there is no substantial difference in the result, the grounds upon which relief is based might have been material. . . .

[On the first issue, Atkin LJ considered that the proprietary claim, based on a entitlement to trace in equity, could be maintained.]

The question whether they are entitled to a common law judgment for money had and received may involve other considerations. I am not without further consideration prepared to say that every person who can in equity establish a right to have his money or the proceeds of his property restored to him, can, as an alternative, bring an action against the person who has been in possession of such money or proceeds for money had and received; still less that he can always bring trover or detinue. But the common law rights are large and are admirably stated in *Taylor v. Plumer* (3 M & S 562, 574) . . . [**[613]** above] . . . I notice that in *Sinclair v. Brougham* ([1914] AC 398, 419, **[615]** above) Lord Haldane L.C. in dealing with this decision says: "Lord Ellenborough laid down, as a limit to this proposition, that if the money had become incapable of being traced, as, for instance, when it had been paid into the broker's general account with his banker, the principal had no remedy excepting to prove as a creditor for money had and received," and proceeds to say "you can, even at law, follow, but only so long as the relation of debtor and creditor has not superseded the right in rem." The words above "as for instance" et seq. do not represent and doubtless do not purport to represent Lord Ellenborough's actual words; and I venture to doubt whether the common law ever so restricted the right as to hold that the money became incapable of being traced, merely because paid into the broker's general account with his banker. The question always was, Had the means of ascertainment failed? But if in 1815 the common law halted outside the bankers' door, by 1879 equity had had the courage to lift the latch, walk in and examine the books: *In re Hallett's Estate.* (13 Ch D 696, [**[627]** below]) I see no reason why the means of ascertainment so provided should not now be available both for common law and equity proceedings. If, following the principles laid down in *In re Hallett's Estate*, it can be ascertained either that the money in the bank, or the commodity which it has bought, is "the product of, or substitute for, the original thing," then it still follows "the nature of the thing itself." On these principles it would follow that as the money paid into the bank can be identified as the product of the original money, the plaintiffs have the common law right to claim it, and can sue for money had and received. In the present case less difficulty than usual is experienced in tracing the descent of the money, for substantially no other money has ever been mixed with the proceeds of the fraud.'

[Bankes and Scrutton LJJ agreed. Bankes LJ said that the bank could follow the money at common law, without needing to have recourse to the equitable doctrine, because there had been no mixing in the account. Scrutton LJ though that the plaintiff could not trace at common law, but could do so in equity.]

Note:

See the criticism of the breadth of this approach by Fox LJ in the *Agip* case, below at [617].

Question:

Given that this was a common law action for money had and received, was it proper for Atkin and Scrutton LJJ to allow the claimant to rely on equitable tracing rules to prove the necessary ingredients of the claim?

[617] *Agip (Africa) Ltd v Jackson* [1990] Ch 265, 285–6 *per* Millett J; [1991] Ch 547 (CA), 563–6 *per* Fox LJ:

[Zdiri, an employee of the claimant company, fraudulently altered the name of the payee on payment orders of over £0.5 million from the claimant. This money was transferred from the claimant's account with the Banque du Sud, in Tunisia, to Baker Oil Services Ltd's account with Lloyds Bank in London. Baker Oil was a puppet company set up and controlled by the defendants, who were chartered accountants. These funds were then transferred to accounts of the defendant's accountancy firm and all but £43,000 was paid out to unknown parties. Throughout these dealings the defendants were acting on the instructions of their clients. Both Millett J and the Court of Appeal held that the claimant had an equitable proprietary claim to the remaining £43,000 and a personal claim against the defendants for equitable compensation for their dishonest assistance in a breach of trust. Millett J held, further, that the defendants were not personally liable for knowing receipt of the £0.5 million because they had received these funds as agents and not for their own benefit. Moreover, both Millett J and the Court of Appeal held that the claimant's common law action for money had and received failed because the claimant's money could not be traced at common law into the Baker Oil account. According to Millett J, this was because it had been transferred electronically rather than physically; according to the Court of Appeal, it was because it had been mixed in the New York clearing system.]

Millett J:

'*Tracing at common law*

The next question is whether the plaintiffs can follow the payment into the hands of Jackson & Co; for the fact that it was the plaintiffs' money which left the Banque du Sud does not mean that it was the plaintiffs' money which reached Baker Oil or Jackson & Co. Tracing at common law, unlike its counterpart in equity, is neither a cause of action nor a remedy but serves an evidential purpose. The cause of action is for money had and received. Tracing at common law enables the defendant to be identified as the recipient of the plaintiff's money and the measure of his liability to be determined by the amount of the plaintiff's money he is shown to have received.

The common law has always been able to follow a physical asset from one recipient to another. Its ability to follow an asset in the same hands into a changed form was established in *Taylor v. Plumer*, 3 M. & S. 562. In following the plaintiff's money into an asset purchased exclusively with it, no distinction is drawn between a chose in action such as the debt of a bank to its customer and any other asset: *In re Diplock* [1948] Ch. 466 [**[611]** above], 519. But it can only follow a physical asset, such as a cheque or its proceeds, from one person to another. It can follow money but not a chose in action. Money can be followed at common law into and out of a bank account and into the hands of a subsequent transferee, provided that it does not cease to be identifiable by being mixed with other money in the bank account derived from some other source: *Banque Belge pour l'Etranger v. Hambrouck* [1921] 1 K.B. 321 [**[616]** above]. Applying these principles, the plaintiffs claim to follow their money through Baker Oil's account where it was not mixed with any other money and into Jackson & Co.'s account at Lloyds Bank.

The defendants deny this. They contend that tracing is not possible at common law because the money was mixed, first when it was handled in New York, and secondly in Jackson & Co.'s own account at Lloyds Bank.

The latter objection is easily disposed of. The cause of action for money had and received is complete when the plaintiff's money is received by the defendant. It does not depend on the continued retention of the money by the defendant. Save in strictly limited circumstances it is no defence that he has parted with it. A fortiori it can be no defence for him to show that he has so mixed it with his own money that he cannot tell whether he still has it or not. Mixing by the defendant himself must, therefore, be distinguished from mixing by a prior recipient. The former is irrelevant, but the latter will destroy the claim, for it will prevent proof that the money received by the defendant was the money paid by the plaintiff.

In my judgment, however, the former objection is insuperable. The money cannot be followed by treating it as the proceeds of a cheque presented by the collecting bank in exchange for payment by the paying bank. The money was transmitted by telegraphic transfer. There was no cheque or any equivalent. The payment order was not a cheque or its equivalent. It remained throughout in the possession of the Banque du Sud. No copy was sent to Lloyds Bank or Baker Oil or presented to the Banque du Sud in exchange for the money. It was normally the plaintiffs' practice to forward a copy of the payment order to the supplier when paying an invoice but this was for information only. It did not authorise or enable the supplier to obtain payment. There is no evidence that this practice was followed in the case of forged payment orders and it is exceedingly unlikely that it was.

Nothing passed between Tunisia and London but a stream of electrons. It is not possible to treat the money received by Lloyds Bank in London or its correspondent bank in New York as representing the proceeds of the payment order or of any other physical asset previously in its hands and delivered by it in exchange for the money. The Banque du Sud merely telexed a request to Lloyds Bank to make a payment to Baker Oil against its own undertaking to reimburse Lloyds Bank in New York. Lloyds Bank complied with the request by paying Baker Oil with its own money. It thereby took a delivery risk. In due course it was no doubt reimbursed, but it is not possible to identify the source of the money with which it was reimbursed without attempting to follow the money through the New York clearing system. Unless Lloyds Bank's correspondent bank in New York was also Citibank, this involves tracing the money through the accounts of Citibank and Lloyds Bank's correspondent bank with the Federal Reserve Bank, where it must have been mixed with other money. The money with which Lloyds Bank was reimbursed cannot therefore, without recourse to equity, be identified as being that of the Banque du Sud. There is no evidence that Lloyds Bank's correspondent bank in

New York was Citibank, and accordingly the plaintiffs' attempt to trace the money at common law must fail.

This is, however, not the only objection to the plaintiffs' claim to recover the money from Jackson & Co. at common law and without proof of dishonesty or want of probity on their part'

Fox LJ:
'*Tracing at common law*

The judge [Millett J] held that Agip was not entitled to trace at law. Tracing at law does not depend upon the establishment of an initial fiduciary relationship. Liability depends upon receipt by the defendant of the plaintiff's money and the extent of the liability depends on the amount received. Since liability depends upon receipt the fact that a recipient has not retained the asset is irrelevant. For the same reason dishonesty or lack of inquiry on the part of the recipient are irrelevant. Identification in the defendant's hands of the plaintiff's asset is, however, necessary. It must be shown that the money received by the defendant was the money of the plaintiff. Further, the very limited common law remedies make it difficult to follow at law into mixed funds. The judge's view [1990] Ch. 265, 286 of the present case was that the common law remedy was not available. . . . [See the excerpt above. Fry LJ also referred to *Taylor v Plumer* and *Banque Belge*—see **[613]** and **[616]** above]. . . .

Now, in the present case, the course of events was as follows. (1) The original payment order was in December signed by an authorised signatory. (2) The name of the payee was then altered to Baker Oil. (3) The altered order was then taken to Banque du Sud who complied with it by debiting the account of Agip with $518,822.92 and then instructing Lloyds Bank to pay Baker Oil. Banque du Sud also instructed Citibank in New York to debit its account with Citibank and credit Lloyds Bank with the amount of the order. (4) Lloyds Bank credited the money to Baker Oil's account on the morning of 7 January. (5) On 8 January, Lloyds Bank in pursuance of instructions from Baker Oil transferred the $518,822.92, which was the only sum standing to the credit of Baker Oil's account, to an account in the name of Jackson & Co. (6) Immediately before the transfer from Baker Oil, Jackson & Co.'s account was $7,911.80 in credit. In consequence of the transfer it became $526,734.72 in credit.

The inquiry which has to be made is whether the money paid to Jackson & Co.'s account "was the product of, or substitute for, the original thing." In answering that question I do not think that it matters that the order was not a cheque. It was a direction by the account holder to the bank. When Atkin L.J. referred in the *Banque Belge* case to the "original money" he was, I assume, referring to the money credited by Banque Belge (the plaintiff) to Hambrouck's account. Money from that account was the only money in Mlle. Spanoghe's deposit account. It was not, therefore, difficult to say that the money in issue (i.e. the residue of Mlle. Spanoghe's account) could be identified as the product of the original money. There were no complexities of tracing at all. Everything in Mlle. Spanoghe's account came from Hambrouck's account and everything in Hambrouck's account came from the credit in respect of the fraudulent cheque.

The position in the present case is much more difficult. Banque du Sud can be regarded as having paid with Agip's money but Lloyds Bank, acting as directed by Banque du Sud, paid Baker Oil with its own money. It had no other and, accordingly, took a delivery risk. It was, in the end, put in funds, but it is difficult to see how the origin of those funds can be identified without tracing the money through the New York clearing system. The money in the present case did get mixed on two occasions. The first was in the New York clearing system and the second was in Jackson & Co.'s own account. The judge held that the latter was of no consequence. I agree. The common law remedy attached to the recipient of the money and its subsequent transposition does not alter his liability. The problem arises at an earlier stage. What did Jackson & Co. receive which was the product of Agip's asset? Baker Oil was controlled for present purposes by Jackson & Co. but Baker Oil was paid by Lloyds Bank which had not been put in funds from New York. It was subsequently recouped. But it is not possible to show the source from which it was recouped without tracing the money through the New York clearing system. The judge said ([1990] Ch. 265, 286):

> "Unless Lloyds Bank's correspondent bank in New York was also Citibank, this involves tracing the money through the accounts of Citibank and Lloyds Bank's correspondent bank with the Federal Reserve Bank, where it must have been mixed with other money. The money with which Lloyds Bank was reimbursed cannot therefore, without recourse to equity, be identified as being that of the Banque du Sud."

I respectfully agree with that view. Accordingly, it seems to me that the common law remedy is not available.

I should add this. Atkin L.J.'s approach in the *Banque Belge* case amounts virtually to saying that there is now no difference between the common law and equitable remedies. Indeed, the common law remedy might be wider because of the absence of any requirement of a fiduciary relationship. There may be a good deal to be said for that view but it goes well beyond any other case and well beyond the views of Bankes and Scrutton L.JJ. And in the 70 years since the *Banque Belge* decision it has not been applied. Whether, short of the House of Lords, it is now open to the courts to adopt it I need not consider. I would in any event feel difficulty in doing so in the present case where, as I indicate later, it seems to me that the established equitable rules provide an adequate remedy in relation to this action.'

Question:

Are *Banque Belge* ([616]) and *Agip* ([617]) irreconcilable? See E McKendrick, 'Tracing Misdirected Funds' [1991] *LMCLQ* 378.

[618] *Lipkin Gorman (a firm) v Karpnale Ltd* [1991] 2 AC 548 (HL), 572–4 *per* Lord Goff:

[Cass was a partner in the claimant firm of solicitors. He was an authorised signatory on the firm's account at Lloyds Bank, and had drawn money from this account which he used to fund gambling sprees at the defendant Playboy Club. As a result of this fraud, the firm had lost £220,000 and (taking into account the winnings paid out to Cass) the Playboy Club had gained £154,695. The claimant firm successfully recovered £154,695 from the Club (£150,960 as money had and received, and £3,735 as damages for conversion of a banker's draft).]

'*Title to the money*

The first ground is concerned with the solicitors' title to the money received by Cass (through Chapman) from the bank. It is to be observed that the present action, like the action in *Clarke v. Shee and Johnson* [(1774) 1 Cowp 197], is concerned with a common law claim to money, where the money in question has not been paid by the appellant directly to the respondents—as is usually the case where money is, for example, recoverable as having been paid under a mistake of fact, or for a consideration which has failed. On the contrary, here the money had been paid to the respondents by a third party, Cass; and in such a case the appellant has to establish a basis on which he is entitled to the money. This (at least, as a general rule) he does by showing that the money is his legal property, as appears from Lord Mansfield's judgment in *Clarke v. Shee and Johnson*. If he can do so, he may be entitled to succeed in a claim against the third party for money had and received to his use, though not if the third party has received the money in good faith and for a valuable consideration. The cases in which such a claim has succeeded are, I believe, very rare: see the cases, including *Clarke v. Shee and Johnson*, collected in Goff and Jones, *The Law of Restitution*, 3rd ed. (1986), p. 64, note 29. This is probably because, at common law, property in money, like other fungibles, is lost as such when it is mixed with other money. Furthermore, it appears that in these cases the action for money had and received is not usually founded upon any wrong by the third party, such as conversion; nor is it said to be a case of waiver of tort. It is founded simply on the fact that, as Lord Mansfield said, the third party cannot in conscience retain the money—or, as we say nowadays, for the third party to retain the money would result in his unjust enrichment at the expense of the owner of the money.

So, in the present case, the solicitors seek to show that the money in question was their property at common law. But their claim in the present case for money had and received is nevertheless a personal claim; it is not a proprietary claim, advanced on the basis that money remaining in the hands of the respondents is their property. Of course there is no doubt that, even if legal title to the money did vest in Cass immediately on receipt, nevertheless he would have held it on trust for his partners, who would accordingly have been entitled to trace it in equity into the hands of the respondents. However, your Lordships are not concerned with an equitable tracing claim in the present case, since no such case is advanced by the solicitors, who have been content to proceed at common law by a personal action, viz. an action for money had and received. I should add that, in the present case, we are not concerned with the fact that money drawn by Cass from the solicitors' client account at the bank may have become mixed by Cass with his own money before he gambled it away at the club. For the respondents have conceded that, if the solicitors can establish legal title to the money in the hands of Cass, that title was not defeated by mixing of the money with other money of Cass while in his hands. On this aspect of the case, therefore, the only question is whether the solicitors can establish legal title to the money when received by Cass from the bank by drawing cheques on the client account without authority.

Before your Lordships, and no doubt before the courts below, elaborate argument was advanced by counsel upon this issue. The respondents relied in particular upon two decisions of the Privy Council as showing that where a partner obtains money by drawing on a partnership bank account without authority, he alone and not the partnership obtains legal title to the money so obtained. These cases, *Union Bank of Australia Ltd. v. McClintock* [1922] 1 A.C. 240 and *Commercial Banking Co. of Sydney Ltd. v. Mann* [1961] A.C. 1, were in fact concerned with bankers' cheques; but for the respondents it was submitted that the same principle was applicable in the case of cash. The solicitors argued that these cases were wrongly decided, or alternatively sought to distinguish them on a number of grounds. I shall have to examine these cases in some detail when I come to consider the respondents' cross-appeal in respect of the banker's draft; and, as will then appear, I am not prepared to depart from decisions of such high authority as these. They show that, where a banker's cheque payable to a third party or bearer is obtained by a partner from a bank which has received the authority of the partnership to pay the partner in question who has, however, unknown to the bank, acted beyond the authority of his partners in so operating the account, the legal property in the banker's cheque thereupon vests in the partner. The same must a fortiori be true when it is not such a banker's cheque but cash which is so drawn from the bank by the partner in question. Even so, I am satisfied that the solicitors are able to surmount this difficulty, as follows.

It is well established that a legal owner is entitled to trace his property into its product, provided that the latter is indeed identifiable as the product of his property. Thus, in *Taylor v. Plumer* (1815) 3 M. & S. 562 [**[613]** above], where Sir Thomas Plumer gave a draft to a stockbroker for the purpose of buying exchequer bills, and the stockbroker instead used the draft for buying American securities and doubloons for his own purposes, Sir Thomas was able to trace his property into the securities and doubloons in the hands of the stockbroker, and so defeat a claim made to them by the stockbroker's assignees in bankruptcy. Of course, "tracing" or "following" property into its product involves a decision by the owner of the original property to assert his title to the product in place of his original property. This is sometimes referred to as ratification. I myself would not so describe it, but it has, in my opinion, at least one feature in common with ratification, that it cannot be relied upon so as to render an innocent recipient a wrongdoer (cf. *Bolton Partners v. Lambert* (1889) 41 Ch.D. 295, 307, per Cotton L.J.: "an act lawful at the time of its performance [cannot] be rendered unlawful, by the application of the doctrine of ratification.")

I return to the present case. Before Cass drew upon the solicitors' client account at the bank, there was of course no question of the solicitors having any legal property in any cash lying at the bank. The relationship of the bank with the solicitors was essentially that of debtor and creditor; and since the client account was at all material times in credit, the bank was the debtor and the solicitors were its creditors. Such a debt constitutes a chose in action, which is a species of property; and since the debt was enforceable at common law, the chose in action was legal property belonging to the solicitors at common law.

There is in my opinion no reason why the solicitors should not be able to trace their property at common law in that chose in action, or in any part of it, into its product, i.e. cash drawn by Cass from their client account at the bank. Such a claim is consistent with their assertion that the money so obtained by Cass was their property at common law. Further, in claiming the money as money had and received, the solicitors have not sought to make the respondents liable on the basis of any wrong, a point which will be of relevance at a later stage, when I come to consider the defence of change of position.

Authority for the solicitors' right to trace their property in this way is to be found in the decision of your Lordships' House in *Marsh v. Keating* (1834) 1 Bing. (N.C.) 198. Mrs. Keating was the proprietor of £12,000 interest or share in joint stock reduced 3 per cent. annuities, standing to her credit in the books of the Bank of England, where the accounts were entered in the form of debtor and creditor accounts in the ledgers of the bank. Under what purported to be a power of attorney given by Mrs. Keating to the firm of Marsh, Sibbard & Co., on which Mrs. Keating's signature was in fact forged by

Henry Fauntleroy, a partner in Marsh, Sibbard & Co., an entry was made in the books of the Bank of England purporting to transfer £9,000 of Mrs. Keating's interest or share in the stock to William Tarbutt, to whom, on the instructions of Henry Fauntleroy, the stock had been sold for the sum of £6,018 15s. In due course, the broker who conducted the sale accounted for £6,013 2s. 6d. (being the sale price less commission) by a cheque payable to Marsh & Co. Upon the discovery of the forgery, Mrs. Keating made a claim upon the Bank of England; and the bank requested Mrs. Keating to prove in the bankruptcy of the partners in Marsh & Co. in respect of the sum so received by them. Mrs. Keating then commenced an action, pursuant to an order of the Lord Chancellor, for the purpose of trying the question whether the partners in Marsh & Co. were indebted to her, in which she claimed the sum so received by Marsh & Co. as money had and received to her use. The opinion of the judges was taken, and their opinion was to the effect that Mrs. Keating was entitled to succeed in her claim. Your Lordships' House ruled accordingly. It must follow a fortiori that the solicitors, as owners of the chose in action constituted by the indebtedness of the bank to them in respect of the sums paid into the client account, could trace their property in that chose in action into its direct product, the money drawn from the account by Cass. It further follows, from the concession made by the respondents, that the solicitors can follow their property into the hands of the respondents when it was paid to them at the club.'

Questions:

Lord Goff said that, to succeed in their claim for money had and received (ie their claim in unjust enrichment), the solicitors needed to show that the money was their legal property. This they could do, it seems, because of the common law tracing rules. Is this assertion consistent with the other assertion, that Cass obtained legal title to the money and held it on trust for the solicitors? Did the solicitors need to show that the money was their legal property before they could pursue a claim for money had and received? Such a claim was based on the defendant's unjust enrichment. Arguably there is no enrichment at all (regardless of whether it is an unjust enrichment) unless the defendant, not the solicitors, had title to the money. What, then, is the real purpose—and the real effect—of common law tracing in this case?

[619] *F C Jones & Sons (Trustee in Bankruptcy) v Jones* [1997] Ch 159 (CA), 169 *per* Millett LJ:

[F C Jones & Sons was a potato-growing firm which became bankrupt. After the relevant act of bankruptcy, one of the partners withdrew over £11,000 from the partnership account and paid the money to his wife. She invested the funds in potato futures, making a profit of over £50,000 which she deposited with Raphaels & Sons plc. The court held that these profits belonged to the trustee in bankruptcy, and not to Mrs Jones.]

'The trustee's case, as presently formulated, is simplicity itself. The money in court represents the proceeds of the defendant's successful speculation with the £11,700 which she received from her husband. The £11,700, in turn, was paid to her out of the joint account of two of the partners, who were afterwards adjudicated bankrupt. The money was drawn from the joint account after the date of the act of bankruptcy on which the receiving order was made. All this is undisputed. But, says the trustee, the money in the joint account had already vested in him, for under section 37 of the Bankruptcy Act 1914 his title to the assets of the bankrupts related back to the date of the act of bankruptcy. Accordingly, the defendant never acquired any title to the money. The money which she received from her husband belonged to the trustee, and the money in court represents the proceeds of her successful speculation with his money.

. . .

It is . . . in my view [and contrary to the findings of the trial judge] plain that the defendant did not receive the money in a fiduciary capacity and that she did not become a constructive trustee. The deputy judge's conclusion presupposes that A, who in this case is the bankrupt, had a legal title to transfer. In the present case, however, the bankrupts had been divested of all title by statute. Mr. F. W. J. Jones had no title at all at law or in equity to the money in the joint account at Midland Bank, and could confer no title on the defendant. While, however, I accept the submissions of counsel for the defendant that she did not become a constructive trustee, I do not accept the proposition that the trustee in bankruptcy is unable to recover the profits which the defendant made by the use of his money unless she can be shown to have received it in one or other of the two capacities mentioned; nor do I consider it necessary for him to invoke the assistance of equity in order to maintain his claim. In short, I do not accept the main submission of counsel that the only action at law which was available to the trustee was an action against the defendant for money had and received.

It is, in my view, unhelpful to categorise the payment of the £11,700 to the defendant as either "void" or "voidable." Neither term is strictly accurate. In order to see why this is so it is necessary to consider the effect of the doctrine of relation back under the old bankruptcy law. I recently [165] had occasion to examine this in detail in *In re Dennis (A Bankrupt)* [1996] Ch. 80. I said, at p. 104:

> "It is clear from the authorities that the relation back of the trustee's title did not merely make the title of the debtor himself or any person claiming through the debtor defeasible in the event of adjudication. If the debtor was adjudicated bankrupt, then as from the date of the act of bankruptcy neither the debtor nor any such person claiming under him who could not bring himself within the protective provisions of the Bankruptcy Acts had any title at all; as from that date title was vested in the trustee. The position of the debtor and persons who claimed under him during the intermediate period was extremely curious. They did not possess a defeasible title, but either an indefeasible title if the act of bankruptcy was not followed by adjudication or no title at all if it was. Outside the law of bankruptcy no similar ambulatory title was known to the law."

In saying this I was summarising the law expounded by this court in *In re Gunsbourg* [1920] 2 K.B. 426. . . .

Accordingly, as from the date of the act of bankruptcy the money in the bankrupts' joint account at Midland Bank belonged to the trustee. The account holders had no title to it at law or in equity. The cheques which they drew in favour of the defendant were not "void" or "voidable" but, in the events which happened, they were incapable of passing any [167] legal or equitable title. They were not, however, without legal effect, for the bank honoured them. The result was to affect the identity of the debtor but not the creditor and to put the defendant in possession of funds to which she had no title.

A debt formally owed by Midland Bank apparently to Mr. F. W. J. Jones and Mr. A. C. Jones but in reality to their trustee ultimately became a debt owed by Raphaels apparently to the defendant but in reality to the trustee.

What is the result? If the cheques had passed the legal title to the defendant but not the beneficial ownership, she would have received the money as constructive trustee and be liable to a proprietary restitutionary claim in equity (sometimes, though inaccurately, described as a tracing claim). The defendant would have been obliged, not merely to account for the £11,700 which she had received, but to hand over the £11,700 in specie to the trustee. Her position would have been no different from that of an express trustee who held the money in trust for the trustee; or from that of Mr. Reid in *Attorney-General for Hong Kong v. Reid* [1994] 1 A.C. 324 [**[535]** above], whose liability to account for the profits which he made from investing a bribe was based on his obligation to pay it over to his principal as soon as he received it. The existence of any such obligation has been disputed by commentators, but no one disputes that, if the obligation exists, it carries with it the duty to pay over or account for any profits made by the use of the money.

But the defendant was not a constructive trustee. She had no legal title to the money. She had no title to it at all. She was merely in possession; that is to say, in a position to deal with it even though it did not belong to her. Counsel for the defendant says that it follows that she cannot be made liable to any kind of proprietary claim. . . .

. . . . [but here] [t]he defendant had no title [168] at all, at law or in equity. If she became bankrupt, the money would not vest in her trustee. But this would not be because it was trust property; it would be because it was not her property at all. If she made a profit, how could she have any claim to the profit made by the use of someone else's money? In my judgment she could not. If she were to retain the profit made by the use of the trustee's money, then, in the language of the modern law of restitution, she would be unjustly enriched at the expense of the trustee. If she were a constructive trustee of the money, a court of equity, as a court of conscience, would say that it was unconscionable for her to lay claim to the profit made by the use of her beneficiary's money. It would, however, be a mistake to suppose that the common law courts disregarded considerations of conscience. Lord Mansfield C.J., who did much to develop the early law of restitution at common law, founded it firmly on the basis of good conscience and unjust enrichment. It would, in my judgment, be absurd if a person with no title at all were in a stronger position to resist a proprietary claim by the true owner than one with a bare legal title. In the present case equity has no role to play. The trustee must bring his claim at common law. It follows that, if he has to trace his money, he must rely on common law tracing rules, and that he has no proprietary remedy. But it does not follow that he has no proprietary claim. His claim is exclusively proprietary. He claims the money because it belongs to him at law or represents profits made by the use of money which belonged to him at law.

The trustee submits that he has no need to trace, since the facts are clear and undisputed. The defendant did not mix the money with her own. The trustee's money remained identifiable as such throughout. But, of course, he does have to trace it in order to establish that the money which he claims represents his money. Counsel for the defendant acknowledges that the trustee can successfully trace his money into her account at Raphaels, for his concession in respect of the £11,700 acknowledges this. I do not understand how his concession that the trustee is entitled to £11,700 of the money in court is reconcilable with his submission that the only cause of action available to the trustee is an action for money had and received. I say this for two reasons. In the first place, the trustee has never brought such an action, and any such action would now be long out of time. In the second place, in an action for money had and received it would be irrelevant what the defendant had done with the money after she received it. Her liability would be based on her receipt of the money, and she would be personally liable to a money judgment for £11,700. But, while the trustee would be entitled to a money judgment for that sum, he would not be entitled to any particular sum of £11,700 such as the money in court in specie.

But in my judgment the concession that the trustee can trace the money at common law is rightly made. There are no factual difficulties of the kind which proved fatal in this court to the common law claim in *Agip (Africa) Ltd. v. Jackson* [1991] Ch. 547 [**[617]** above]. It is not necessary to trace the passage of the money through the clearing system or the London potato futures market. The money which the defendant paid into her account with the commodity brokers represented the proceeds of cheques which she received from her husband. Those cheques represented money [169] in the bankrupts' joint account at Midland Bank which belonged to the trustee.

In *Lipkin Gorman v. Karpnale Ltd.* [1991] 2 A.C. 548 [**[618]** above], 573 Lord Goff of Chieveley held that the plaintiffs could trace or follow their "property into its product" for this "involves a decision by the owner of the original property to assert his title to the product in place of his original property." In that case the original property was the plaintiffs' chose in action, a debt owed by the bank to the plaintiffs. Lord Goff held, at p. 574, that the plaintiffs could "trace their property at common law in that chose in action, or in any part of it, into its product, i.e. cash drawn by Cass from their client account at the bank."

Accordingly, the trustee can follow the money in the joint account at Midland Bank, which had been vested by statute in him, into the proceeds of the three cheques which the defendant received from her husband. The trustee does not need to follow the money from one recipient to another or follow it through the clearing system; he can follow the cheques as they pass from hand to hand. It is sufficient for him to be able to trace the money into the cheques and the cheques into their proceeds.

In *Agip (Africa) Ltd. v. Jackson* [1990] Ch. 265, 285 I said that the ability of the common law to trace an asset into a changed form in the same hands was established in *Taylor v. Plumer* (1815) 3 M. & S. 562. Lord Ellenborough C.J. . . . [see the excerpt at **[613]** above] . . .

Given that the trustee can trace his money at Midland Bank into the money in the defendant's account with the commodity brokers, can he successfully assert a claim to that part of the money which represents the profit made by the use of his money? I have no doubt that, in the particular circumstances of this case, he can. There is no need to trace through the dealings on the London potato futures market. If the defendant, as the nominal account holder, had any entitlement to demand payment from the brokers, this was because of the terms of the contract which she made with them. Under the terms of that contract it is reasonable to infer that the brokers were authorised to deal in potato futures on her account, to debit her account with losses and to credit it with profits, and to pay her only the balance standing to her account. It is, in my opinion, impossible to separate the chose in action constituted by the deposit of the trustee's money on those terms from the terms upon which it was deposited. The chose in action, which was vested in the defendant's name but which in reality belonged to the trustee, was not a right to payment from the brokers of the original amount deposited but a right to claim the balance, whether greater or less than the amounted deposited; and it is to that chose in action that the trustee now lays claim.

Given, then, that the trustee has established his legal claim to the £11,700 and the profits earned by the use of his money, and has located the money, first, in the defendant's account with the commodity brokers and, later, in the defendant's account at Raphaels, I am satisfied that the common law has adequate remedies to enable him to recover his property. He did not need to sue the defendant; and he did not do so. He was entitled to bring an action for debt against Raphaels and obtain an order for payment. When he threatened to do so, Raphaels interpleaded, and the issue between the trustee and the defendant was which of them could give a good receipt to Raphaels. That depended upon which of them had the legal title to the chose in action. The money now being in court, the court can grant an appropriate declaration and make an order for payment.

In my judgment the trustee was entitled at law to the money in the joint account of the bankrupts at Midland Bank, which had vested in him by statute. He was similarly entitled to the balance of the money in the defendant's account with the commodity brokers, and the fact that it included profits made by the use of that money is immaterial. He was similarly entitled to the money in the defendant's account at Raphaels and able to give them a good receipt for the money. The defendant never had any interest, legal or equitable, in any of those moneys. The trustee is plainly entitled to the money in court and the judge was right to order that it be paid out to him.

Questions:

1. Is it the case that the beneficial owner of property (whether that person also has the legal title or not) is always entitled to any profits derived from the use of the property? (See Chapter 7, especially Section 7.4.3.)
2. Does a positive response to the previous question involve an unacceptable elision of the concepts of *tracing* and *claiming*? Or does it depend upon general principles of unjust enrichment? Or on some special application of the law of property?
3. *Should* the answer to this question of automatic disgorgement of the profits be yes? (See, for example, the policy arguments surrounding proprietary remedies detailed in Sections 5.5, 5.10, 5.13 above.)

Contrast the above cases with the approach taken in the next case.

[620] *R v Preddy* [1996] AC 815 (HL), 833, 834–5, 837 *per* Lord Goff:
[The case concerned mortgage frauds. The issue was whether the perpetrators of the frauds were guilty of theft from the banks concerned.]

'I now turn to the first question which your Lordships have to consider, which is whether the debiting of a bank account and the corresponding crediting of another's bank account brought about by dishonest misrepresentation amount to the obtaining of property within section 15 of the [Theft] Act of 1968.

. . .

[834] The crucial question, as I see it, is whether the defendant obtained (or attempted to obtain) property belonging to another. Let it be assumed that the lending institution's bank account is in credit, and that there is therefore no difficulty in identifying a credit

balance standing in the account as representing property, i.e. a chose in action, belonging to the lending institution. The question remains however whether the debiting of the lending institution's bank account, and the corresponding crediting of the bank account of the defendant or his solicitor, constitutes obtaining of that property. The difficulty in the way of that conclusion is simply that, when the bank account of the defendant (or his solicitor) is credited, he does not obtain the lending institution's chose in action. On the contrary that chose in action is extinguished or reduced pro tanto, and a chose in action is brought into existence representing a debt in an equivalent sum owed by a different bank to the defendant or his solicitor. In these circumstances, it is difficult to see how the defendant thereby obtained property belonging to another, i.e. to the lending institution.

Professor Sir John Smith, in his commentary on the decision of the Court of Appeal in the present case [1995] Crim. L.R. 564, 565–566, has suggested that "Effectively, the victim's property has been changed into another form and now belongs to the defendant. There is the gain and equivalent loss which is characteristic of, and perhaps the substance of, obtaining." But even if this were right, I do not for myself see how this can properly be described as obtaining property belonging to another. In truth the property which the defendant has obtained is the new chose in action constituted by the debt now owed to him by his bank, and represented by the credit entry in his own bank account. This did not come into existence until the debt so created was owed to him by his bank, and so never belonged to anyone else. True, it corresponded to the debit entered in the lending institution's bank account; but it does not follow that the property which the defendant acquired can be identified with the property which the lending institution lost when its account was debited. In truth, section 15(1) is here being invoked for a purpose for which it was never designed, and for which it does not legislate.

I should add that, throughout the above discussion, I have proceeded on the assumption that the bank accounts of the lending institution and the defendant (or his solicitor) are both sufficiently in credit to allow for choses in action of equivalent value to be extinguished in the one case, and created in the other. But this may well not be the case; and in that [835] event further problems would be created, since it is difficult to see how an increase in borrowing can constitute an extinction of a chose in action owned by the lending institution, or a reduction in borrowing can constitute the creation of a chose in action owned by the defendant. It may be that it could be argued that in such circumstances it was the lending institution's bank whose property was "obtained" by the defendant; but, quite apart from other problems, that argument would in any event fail for the reasons which I have already given. For these reasons, I would answer the first question in the negative.

. . .

[837] [And] cases where the advance was made by cheque would have been equally flawed if the appellants had been charged with obtaining the cheque in question by deception as they were when the appellants were charged with obtaining the advance itself by deception, contrary to section 15(1).'

Questions:

Is this analysis consistent with the earlier extracts? Does it help to clarify the function and effect of common law tracing?

Also see:

Black v Freedman & Co (1910) 12 CLR 105: is this a quite different treatment of a similar problem?

FURTHER READING:

D Fox, 'Common Law Claims to Substituted Assets' [1999] *RLR* 55.
R Goode, 'The Right to Trace and its Impact in Commercial Transactions—I' (1976) 92 *LQR* 360. (This is a classic and deserves to be read in full.)

6.4.4 Alteration (*accessio*): the common law tracing rules

The next extract describes the problems addressed by common law tracing into altered products, or into mixtures, or into manufactured products. It therefore summarises the issues dealt with in the next three sub-sections, but it is useful to see the problem in its entirety before addressing the details.

[621] S Worthington, *Proprietary Interests in Commercial Transactions* (1996, Clarendon: Oxford), pp 135–43:
[Footnotes in the original are omitted.]

> '[Here the first concern is with cases] where the original owner's property does not lose its physical integrity, although it is somehow combined with another's property. The practical compass of the problem is broad. The original owner's property might simply be joined to other property but still be visibly identifiable: for example, car parts may be used to effect repairs. On the other hand, the owner's property might no longer be identifiable even though it remains physically intact: the owner's wheat or oil might, for example, be mixed with that of another. Common notions of justice suggest that no owner should automatically have the entire mass. Rules for sharing are needed.
>
> Crucial though the practical problem is, its common law solutions have been largely ignored, considered irrelevant to many claims in contract and tort and certainly less functional than the corresponding equitable proprietary remedies. This creates a vicious circle. Because there is little modern authority on the problem, the first resort of both judges and commentators, if they do not simply ignore the problem, is frequently to Roman law doctrines.
>
> The Roman analysis does at least provide a useful starting point for dividing the problem into manageable components. Moreover, since the Roman law divisions are so frequently a starting point in the cases, it is useful to define the terminology. According to Roman analysis, there are three typical scenarios which might result in an original owner's property losing its identity. First, that property might become attached to the property of another owner (*accessio*) [see this Section]; secondly, the original owner's property might become confused or mingled with property belonging to other owners, although not thereby losing its physical identity (*confusio* (dry mixtures) and *commixtio* (fluid mixtures)) [see Section 6.4.5 below]; and, finally, the original owner's property might lose its physical identity because it is used in some manufcturing process (*specificatio*) [see Section 6.4.6. below]. The last of these three situations (*specificatio*) is the only category in which the original owner's property loses its physical identity: accordingly, here it is discussed separately from the other categories just described.

In Roman law each of these possibilities was subject to its own rules determining the eventual allocation of proprietary interests. This is notwithstanding that it can sometimes be very difficult to determine which category best describes a particular set of facts. When resin and woodchips are mixed to make chipboard, for example, has the resin simply been inextricably mixed with the woodchips, although without losing its own physical identity, or has it undergone a change of identity as a result of a manufacturing process? Correct categorization determines the appropriate legal response, yet Roman categorization does not necessarily accord with modern chemical analysis. Furthermore, the Roman law solutions do not always accord with those of the common law. In both legal systems, however, cases of accession are treated differently from those of confusion and commingling, and so are usefully treated separately here.

(i) Accession

Accession (when it is authorized) is rarely encountered in practice. Contracting parties usually provide expressly for the event or else it can be readily inferred that the end product is to belong exclusively to one party. In either case the problem is then removed from the realm of rules as to ownership arising by operation of law.

When this is not the case, and only then, the Roman rule is that accessions belong exclusively to the owner of the dominant chattel. The problems with this rule are obvious: the degree of annexation necessary to constitute an accession must be defined; so must the dominant chattel.

There are suggestions that the common law offers a slightly different solution, at least with accessions to goods. Once again, the rules of accession are not applied when individual components can be returned to their original owners. If that is not possible, however, some cases defend the view that accessions belong to the owner of the dominant chattel only when it impossible to apportion the respective shares of the parties. In other words, they favour co-ownership over automatic application of the Roman solution. This divergence from Roman law can be defended both on principle and in terms of the justice of the solution. Moreover, it has the advantage of being consistent with the common law's treatment of other types of 'mixtures'. Nevertheless, it must be said that the few relevant cases offer little real support for either approach.

If it is true that the common law resolution of the problem is via co-ownership so long as the parties' respective contributions can be assessed, then arguably this ought to be the rule in every instance, even when assessment is impossible. Any evidential difficulties in valuing the parties' contributions ought not to result in the denial of co-ownership: the common law, like equity, can *assume* equality of co-ownership or apply a penal rule to the disavantage of the wrongdoer who made assessment of the respective contributions impossible. Either approach would produce results more consistent with the policies supporting co-ownership (assuming these are favoured), rather than adopting the opposite approach by falling back on Roman rules.

(ii) Confusion or Commingling without Loss of Physical Identity

Goods belonging to different owners are frequently mixed so that they can no longer be identified and separated, even though their physical identity has not been altered. This happens, for example, when bulk supplies of wheat or oil (perhaps of varying grades) are combined and either shipped or stored for several owners.

Roman law distinguishes between *confusio* (wet mixtures) and *commixtio* (dry mixtures). The Romans viewed the constituent elements as losing their physical integrity in wet mixtures but not in dry mixtures. For wet mixtures, Roman law provided for ownership in common of the bulk; for dry mixtures, however, each party remained the owner of the original components notwithstanding that they could not be identified and separated from the bulk. This dividing line is not supported by current scientific knowledge: even a wet mixture can be seen as granular, or 'dry', at the molecular level. The distinction was rejected centuries ago by the Scots, notwithstanding their civilian bias: in their view the same rules apply to all mixtures once the components cease to be identifiable.

The Scottish view is in line with the common law position described below, which, except in the case of money, has settled on co-ownership of both wet and dry mixtures, not continued ownership of the original components. The common law solution appears to be both a more just and a more commercially acceptable resolution of the problem.

When mixing happens without the consent of the original owners, the common law rule is that the bulk mixture is owned in common in proportion to the value of the original owners' contributions. Of course, the precise contributions are not always known. Then the common law retreats from strict justice and, like equity, resorts to a solution which delivers the only possible justice in the circumstances. If all the contributing owners are innocent, then the bulk is deemed to be owned in equal proportions. If, on the other hand, one of the contributing owners carried out the unauthorized mixing, thereby creating the problem, another solution is called for: any uncertainties as to quantum are then resolved in favour of the innocent parties. This might involve denying the mixer *any* interest in the bulk. More frequently, though, it will simply involve a diminution in the mixer's interest to the advantage of the innocent parties. This does not render the rules of law defining property interests unacceptably uncertain; it simply recognizes the practicalities, and does that in a manner most consistent with principle.

Nevertheless, these common law rules are sometimes the subject of some unexpected difficulties in their application. If the question before the court is simply a dispute between the contributing owners, then strict application of the common law rules provides a workable and acceptable solution. However, if the question involves other parties, the courts sometimes appear to deny the rule of law its full application.

Two cases illustrate the problem. In *Jones v. Moore*, oil casks leaked and the owners of the oil agreed that they were (legally) tenants in common of the resulting mixture in proportion to their respective losses. Nevertheless, the court held that the individual consignees could not set off the share of the money due from the shipowner's sale of the mixed oil against the freight due. However, all the owners could join for an account and equitable set off. This finding appears to deny that the consignees were legally tenants in common of the oil mixture: they were not simply viewed as such for the purposes of any division among themselves.

Sandeman & Sons v. Tyzack & Branfoot Steamship Co. Ltd [see **[624]** below] provides another example. When a consignment of jute bales finally arrived at its destination, fourteen bales were missing and eleven had lost their markings. One consignee was six bales short of his quota. The shipowner claimed freight for the consignee's notional share of the unmarked bales. The claim was successfully defended. The House of Lords held that, in order to claim freight, the shipowner was required to prove that the consignee's bales of jute were *delivered*, whether unmarked or not. This the shipowner could not do, for the consignee's six bales might be among the fourteen missing.

Obviously this case turns on the strict rules governing entitlement to freight. It also appears to turn on the assumption that fourteen bales were first lost, and then eleven were 'mixed' (by losing their markings). This scenario permits the consignee to assert that his bales are not necessarily included in the mixture. If, contrary to this, the bales were mixed first and then lost, the analysis is different: the consignee is then legally the co-owner of the unmarked bales (and of the missing bales) in proportion to his total losses. It is a moot point whether the facts should necessarily be presumed in favour of the consignee.

Notwithstanding all these difficulties, the common law rules applying to mixtures, as just described, are undoubtedly simpler and better understood than those applying to products.

Products

This is the final category in the classification describing how the original owner's property might cease to be identifiable in the defendant's hands. In this category the property ceases to be identifiable because the defendant makes unauthorized use of it to manufacture a new product. The owner, deprived of the original property, no doubt expects to be able to assert at least some degree of legal ownership in the product. The law remains unclear, but the owner's prospects are less than promising.

Given our industrial society, it is surprising that this problem is the subject of such little and inconsistent authority. Goods continually lose their identity as the result of manufacturing processes, and not all these processes occur with the consent of the original owners. The Roman solution was to give the manufacturer ownership of the new product subject to an obligation to compensate the original owner for the constituent materials. This is seen by some as the common law solution too. If it is, it patently conflicts with the results and the rationale underlying the common law rules which apply in the other categories.

This conflict might be tolerated if the practical distinctions separating one category from another were not so marginal. If categorization is difficult and the resulting consequences for the original owner are completely at odds, the rules are, rightly it seems, perceived as unjust. For example, according to the Roman rule, grapes converted to wine, or olives to oil, are examples of *specificatio* (manufacture of a product), with the product belonging to the manufacturer; leather made into shoes, cloth into a coat, or timber into a plank, on the other hand, are considered by some to be examples where the original goods have not lost their physical identity and so continue to belong to the original owner (the rules of law then having no application).

Professor Goode suggests a more tenable solution, asserting that the parties become tenants in common in proportion to their respective contributions to the manufactured product. This has the advantage of consistency with the other common law rules, but the only authority cited is one of mixing, not manufacture. Moreover, even Professor Goode accepts the rule that the manufacturer becomes the owner of the product if the manufacturer supplies all the labour but no materials. Commercial sensibilities would arguably see this as the *least* acceptable resolution of the problem.

The rule that the manufacturer becomes the owner of the product if the labour is supplied, but not the materials, illustrates another difficulty peculiar to cases of manufacture. Although labour is expended in cases of accession and mixing, it generally contributes little to the value of the product, which remains largely the sum of its parts. With manufacturer, on the other hand, the product can be immensely more valuable than the components simply because of the labour input. The Roman solution, amounting to an enforced sale of the original goods to the manufacturer, gave the manufacturer proprietary rights in return for a non-proprietary input. It is not at all clear that the common law would, or should, follow suit. The common law might best adopt a solution which denies a property interest unless property has been contributed to the product: restitution for the costs of labour, fuel and so on are, it seems, best satisfied by personal remedies.'

[622] ***Hendy Lennox (Industrial Engines) Ltd v Grahame Puttick Ltd*** **[1984] 1 WLR 485, 493–4** ***per*** **Staughton J:**

[The sellers supplied diesel engines to the buyers under contracts containing retention of title clauses reserving the sellers' title to the engines until full payment of the price (see Section 3.8 above). The sellers successfully claimed that the clause allowed the sellers to recover certain engines notwithstanding that they had been incorporated into generating sets. (Of course, they could only do this before the generating sets had been sold to sub-purchasers. A sub-sale would pass title to the engines to the sub-purchasers).]

> 'I have already stated the facts as to how incorporation would be effected. It was a question of doing up bolts and other connections, which could later be undone. Indeed there was evidence, which I accept, that the engine in a generator set may in practice be changed from time to time—for example if it is worn out or has broken down. In an emergency, removal and replacement may have to be effected quickly and efficiently.
>
> Some guidance on the law is to be found in *Crossley Vaines on Personal Property*, 5th ed. (1973). . . .
>
> On p. 430 there is this passage:
>
> > "According to Bracton and Blackstone when a thing is changed into a different species, as by making wine, oil, bread or malt out of the grapes, olives, wheat or barley of another, the operator becomes the new owner thereof and is only liable (in damages) to the former proprietor for the value of the materials he has so converted. Similarly, says *Halsbury* (e), when the goods of one man are affixed to the land or chattel, e.g., a ship, of another, they may become part of it and so accrue to the owner of the principal thing."
>
> Then there is a footnote:
>
> > "(e) *Halsbury's Laws of England*, 3rd. ed., vol. 29 (1960), p. 378. But this statement has been discounted in so far as it applies to attachment to chattels; (1935) 9 A.L.J. p. 50 (G. Sawer), approved in *Lewis v. Andrew and Rowley Pty. Ltd.* (1937) 73 W.N.(N.S.W.) 670, 671; (1960) 39 A.L.J., p. 408 (J. A. Nicholson)."
>
> None of the authorities there mentioned have been available to me. I am aware that until very recently the radio and radar apparatus on a ship was commonly hired by the shipowner rather than bought by him. No doubt it was attached to the ship; but I do not suppose that it hereby became the property of the shipowner or his mortgagee. Nor in my judgment would an engine which was the property of A become the property of B merely because B incorporated it in a generator set otherwise composed of his own materials.
>
> Those reflections and the facts of this case persuade me that the proprietary rights of the sellers in the engines were not affected when the engines were wholly or partially incorporated into generator sets. They were not like the Acrilan which became the yarn and then carpet (the *Bond Worth* case [**[332]** above]), or the resin which became chipboard (*Borden's* case [**[334]** above]), or the leather which became handbags (the *Peachdart* case), or the grapes, olives, wheat and barley mentioned by *Crossley Vaines*. They just remained engines, albeit connected to other things.'

Question:

Does this analysis depend upon the intention of the parties, or does it describe a rule of law? For example, does the question whether a chattel becomes a fixture depend upon the intention of the parties in affixing the chattel?

Also see:

Greenwood v Bennett [1973] QB 195, 202 *per* Lord Denning MR (see **[708]** below). This case illustrates the problems which can arise when repairs, for example, are made in good faith to property which turns out not to belong to the repairer. The improvements belong to the true owner of the property, but it seems the repairer can recover monetary compensation (restitution) for the improvements. However, if the remedy is to remain consistent with the doctrinal framework of the law of unjust enrichment, then the appropriate method for valuing the repairs is difficult. Why is this so?

6.4.5 Mixtures (*confusio* and *commixtio*): common law tracing rules

The potential problems faced by owners whose property is mixed, without their consent, with the property of others have already been highlighted in earlier extracts: see **[621]** above. The likely common law response has also been suggested: see *Taylor v Plumer* (1815) 3 M & S 562 (105 ER 721), 575 *per* Lord Ellenborough (see **[613]** above). The picture suggests that the common law is relatively helpless. But the cases extracted below show that, so long as the property mixed without authority is not money, the common law can intervene to provide a solution. Consider whether there is anything in the approach adopted in these cases which could not be applied to mixtures of money.

[623] ***Spence v Union Marine Insurance Co*** **(1868) LR 2 CP 427, 436–9** ***per*** **Bovill CJ:** [This is a case of accidental mixing. Bales of cotton shipped for different owners were either lost or damaged in a shipwreck. A few bales remained identifiable as the property of particular consignees, but 231 bales were lost and 1,645 bales arrived without any distinguishing marks. Because the price of cotton had dropped dramatically, the claimant claimed that *all* 41 of his bales were amongst those lost, thus entitling him to claim under his insurance policy for 'total loss'. The issue for the court was therefore to determine who owned the lost and the surviving bales.]

> 'It is manifest that the plaintiffs' argument would equally apply if not a single bale of cotton had been lost or damaged out of the whole cargo, and if the marks only had been obliterated from this and other cotton by the same vessel; and it would lead to the strange anomaly that, although all the goods which had been put on board arrived safely at their destination, there would, according to the plaintiffs' contention, be a total loss, for the purpose of insurance law, of the whole of them. . . . [A]nd this strange conclusion would also follow, that, if the cargo all belonged to one owner, it might be said to be entirely safe and uninjured, under circumstances in which, if there were two own-

ers, however small the proportion of one of them, it must be said to be totally lost; so that, if one shipper owned ninety-nine bales, and another, one, of the same description, . . . each owner would have wholly lost all he had, because neither could affirm as to any given bale that it belonged to him. . . .

In our own law there are not many authorities to be found upon this subject; but, as far as they go, they are in favour of the view, that, when goods of different owners become by accident so mixed together as to be undistinguishable, the owners of the goods so mixed become tenants in common of the whole, in the proportions which they have severally contributed to it. The passage cited from the judgment of Blackburn, J., in the case of the tallow which was melted and flowed into the sewers, is to that effect: *Buckley v. Gross*. (3 B. & S. 574.) And a similar view was adopted by Lord Abinger in the case of the mixture of oil by leakage on board ship, in *Jones v. Moore* (4 Y. & C. 351).

It has been long settled in our law, that, where goods are mixed so as to become undistinguishable, by the wrongful act or default of one owner, he cannot recover, and will not be entitled to his proportion, or any part of the property, from the other owner: but no authority has been cited to shew that any such principle has ever been applied, nor indeed could it be applied, to the case of an accidental mixing of the goods of two owners; and there is no authority nor sound reason for saying that the goods of several persons which are accidentally mixed together thereby absolutely cease to be the property of their several owners, and become bona vacantia.

The goods being before they are mixed the separate property of the several owners, unless, which is absurd, they cease to be property by reason of the accidental mixture, when they would not so cease if the mixture were designed, must continue to be the property of the original owners; and, as there would be no means of distinguishing the goods of each, the several owners seem necessarily to become jointly interested, as tenants in common, in the bulk.

[Bovill CJ also noted that this was the rule under both Roman and French law.]

. . .

We are thus, by authorities in our own law, by the reason of the thing, and by the concurrence of foreign writers, justified in adopting the conclusion that, by our own law, the property in the cotton of which the marks were obliterated did not cease to belong to the respective owners; and that, by the mixture of the bales, and their becoming undistinguishable by reason of the action of the sea, and without the fault of the respective owners, these parties became tenants in common of the cotton, in proportion to their respective interests. This result would follow only in those cases where, after the adoption of all reasonable means and exertions to identify or separate the goods, it was found impracticable to do so.'

[624] ***F S Sandeman & Sons v Tyzack & Branfoot Steamship Co Ltd*** **[1913] AC 680, 694–9** ***per*** **Lord Moulton:**

[Bales of jute consigned to various consignees and specifically marked were shipped under bills of lading. On the discharge of the ship, 14 bales were missing and 11 bales could not be identified from their markings as belonging to any particular consignment. All the consignees received their full consignments except four, who refused to accept any of the 11 bales. In an action for freight by the shipowner against one of the four consignees, who had received six bales fewer than his full consignment, the consignee counterclaimed for shortage. The shipowner was willing to account to the four consignees for the value of the 14 missing bales in proportion to their respective shortages, but claimed that the 11 bales ought to be allocated amongst them in the same proportion.]

'My Lords, if we proceed upon the principles of English law, I do not think it a matter of difficulty to define the legal consequences of the goods of "A." becoming indistinguishably and inseparably mixed with the goods of "B." If the mixing has arisen from the fault of "B.," "A." can claim the goods. He is guilty of no wrongful act, and therefore the possession by him of his own goods cannot be interfered with, and if by the wrongful act of "B." that possession necessarily implies the possession of the intruding goods of "B.," he is entitled to it (2 *Kent's Commentaries*, 10th ed., 465). But if the mixing has taken place by accident or other cause, for which neither of the owners is responsible, a different state of things arises. Neither owner has done anything to forfeit his right to the possession of his own property, and if neither party is willing to abandon that right the only equitable solution of the difficulty, and the one accepted by the law, is that "A." and "B." become owners in common of the mixed property.

Farther than this I do not think that it is safe to go. That the whole matter is far from being within the domain of settled law is shewn by the divergence of opinions as to the relative shares of the participating parties in the case of an accidental *commixtio*. Blackburn J. in *Buckley v. Gross* ((1863) 3 B. & S. 566, at p. 575) (following *Kent's Commentaries*) considers that they would be tenants in common in equal shares. In *Spence v. Union Marine Insurance Co.* (L. R. 3 C. P. 427 [**[623]** above]) they were judged to possess the mixed mass in proportion to the probable amounts of their contributions to it. The fact is that the conclusions of the Courts in such cases, though influenced by certain fundamental principles, have been little more than instances of cutting the Gordian knot—reasonable adjustments of the rights of parties in cases where complete justice was impracticable of attainment. I doubt whether even the fundamental principles enunciated above would be strictly adhered to in extreme cases where they would lead to substantial injustice. For instance, if a small portion of the goods of "B." became mixed with the goods of "A." by a negligent act for which "A." alone was liable, I think it quite possible that the law would prefer to view it as a conversion by "A." of this small amount of "B.'s" goods rather than do the substantial injustice of treating "B." as the owner of the whole of the mixed mass.

It is from these propositions of law that the pursuers in this case attempt to spell out a right to compel the defenders to accept a proportion of the unidentified bales as a good delivery under the bills of lading. My Lords, there are, to my mind, two fatal objections to this—the one of fact and the other of law. In the first place, before any such principles can be applied it is necessary that it should be proved or admitted that the goods of the owners in question have in fact contributed to form the mixed mass. If the goods of "A." and "B." have become mixed, and it is possible, but not proved or admitted, that some of "C.'s" goods are in the mixture, there cannot possibly be a presumption of law that they are or are not to be found there, and accordingly "C." cannot be compelled to take up the position of being a co-owner with "A." and "B.," nor is he entitled to insist on being regarded as such co-owner if "A." or "B." objects thereto. Whether his goods are to be found therein is a question of fact, which must be proved by the party asserting it. Now, in the present case there is not the slightest proof that any of the goods shipped under the bills of lading issued to the defenders are to be found in the unidentifiable bales. Everything, indeed, points the other way, because they are of a wholly different quality to any of the jute purported to be shipped by the defenders. But it is not necessary to discuss this question, or to do more than say that it is admitted that fourteen bales must be taken to have been lost, and there is no evidence, and there can be no presumption of fact, that the six bales belonging to the defenders were not among these missing bales. It follows, therefore, that, accepting to the full the above doctrines as to the effect of a confusion of goods, they afford no ground for requiring the defenders to accept the position of co-owners of the unidentifiable bales.

But, my Lords, there is, in my opinion, an objection of law which is equally serious. The doctrines to which I have referred deal with property, and not with contract. To illustrate my meaning, let me take a case where the circumstances are such as would justify in the strongest manner the application of these doctrines in the case of goods shipped under bills of lading. Let me assume that "A." and "B." were the owners of two separate parcels of cargo which have become inseparably and indistinguishably mixed, without loss and without deterioration.

It may well be that they could assert the position of joint owners in the mixed cargo, and as such take action against any person who sought to get possession of it or convert it to his own use. But it does not follow that the shipowners would have performed their contract of carriage. Their duty is to deliver the goods entrusted to them for carriage, and they do not perform that duty if all that the consignee obtains is a right to claim as tenant in common a mixture of those goods with the goods of other people. No doubt, if such a right is of some value, and the consignee avails himself of it, the shipowners are entitled to the benefit of what he receives in reduction of damages for their breach of contract, just in the same way as they would be entitled to credit for whatever value the goods possessed if they were delivered mixed up with some extraneous substance which lessened their value or compelled the consignee to go to expense in separating it out. In the present instance, therefore, the defenders were, under the bills of lading, entitled to the delivery of their goods, and even if the pursuers could compel them to take up the position of co-owners of the mixed mass, it would not be a defence to their claim for breach of contract to deliver, nor would it affect the damages recoverable thereunder, except so far as they had received or could receive payment representing the value of that co-ownership. The pursuers would have no right to claim that the right of the shippers to the proceeds of the goods as co-owners was a fulfilment of their own contract of carriage. They could only claim that any payment so received or receivable would be pro tanto a reduction of their liability in damages by reason of the defenders having received or being in a position to receive payment to that extent, so that the damages which they would suffer from the breach of contract would be diminished by a like amount. In the present case the defenders have received no payment of this kind, and for all that appears in the case the unidentifiable bales may possess no appreciable value, so that (apart from all other grounds) the pursuers are not on this account in a position to claim any reduction of the damages prima facie due from them to the defenders for their breach of contract to deliver.

. . . .

I now turn to the decisions which it is contended establish doctrines inconsistent with the above conclusions. The chief, and in fact the only decision to which we are referred, is that of *Spence v. Union Marine Insurance Co.* [see **|623|** above]. . . .

[In the *Spence* case there] was no question of breach of contract to deliver. It was, therefore, open to the Court to regard the case as one in which, by reason of the perils of the sea and from no other cause, it came about, first, that the goods became indistinguishably mixed, and, secondly, that a portion of this mixed mass was lost. Under those circumstances the owners of the goods were clearly entitled to take up the position of having become co-owners of the mixed mass, and of every part of it, and therefore of the surviving portion of it, and seeing that the goods were all of the same quality, this was the only position they could take up in fairness to the underwriters. Everything had been done consistently with this view, and all that the Court decided was that this was the proper view to take of the matter; and if the judgment be carefully read, it will, in my opinion, appear that the Court arrived at its decision from the considerations that I have enumerated above, and did not purport or intend to make any addition to the law as to the effect of commixtio as previously enunciated by recognized authority.'

Questions:

Are these last two cases (**[623]** and **[624]**) consistent with each other? Are they internally consistent in their treatment of lost and unmarked bales? Is the rationalisation of the two cases proposed by Lord Moulton convincing? How would Lord Moulton deal with a case where several bales were washed overboard *before* the markings on the remaining bales were obliterated? How would Bovill CJ treat such a case?

[625] ***Indian Oil Co Ltd v Greenstone Shipping SA (Panama) (The Ypatianna)*** **[1988] 1 QB 345, 360, 368–71** ***per*** **Staughton J:**

[This was a case of wrongful mixing. An owner's crude oil was mixed with some of the shipowner's crude oil which was already on board the vessel. The mixture could not be separated, and the owner unsuccessfully claimed delivery of all the oil on board.]

'Mr. Rokison's submission is as follows: where B wrongfully mixes the goods of A with goods of his own, so that the original goods cannot be separated or identified, the whole of the mixture becomes the property of A. So it is a case of "happy undeserving A," if not also of "wretched meritorious B."

Mr. Pollock's submission is this: where a wilful admixture occurs without consent, both parties have a joint interest in the whole and the innocent party is entitled to receive his full contribution from the mixture even if it has been diminished by subsequent accidental loss. Alternatively, he submits that the general rule is as above, but that the innocent party is entitled to the whole if (1) the admixture was deliberately brought about for the purpose of depriving the innocent party of his rights, or making them difficult of enforcement, and (2) it is impossible to tell with any certainty what the contributing proportions had been.

There are numerous and very distinguished authorities. But it is agreed on both sides that none of them is binding on me. In the circumstances, I do not see that I can refrain from citing all those which were put before me, even if the result is an inordinately long judgment for a case where the argument lasted rather less than two days.

. . . .

Two points of significance in my view emerge from the authorities. First, in some cases a decision had to be made "not upon the notion, that strict justice was done, but upon this; that it was the only justice, that could be done," per Lord Eldon L.C. in *Lupton v. White*, 15 Ves. Jun. 432, 440. Or as Lord Moulton put it, such cases "have been little more than instances of cutting the Gordian knot—reasonable adjustments of the rights of the parties in cases where complete justice was impracticable of attainment," in *Sandeman Sons v. Tyzack and Branfoot Steamship Co. Ltd.* [1913] A.C. 680 [**[624]** above], 695. Secondly, if the wrongdoer has destroyed or impaired the evidence by which the innocent party could show how much he has lost, the wrongdoer must suffer from the resulting uncertainty. Thus the jury in *Armory v. Delamirie*, 1 Str. 505 were directed by Pratt C.J. to award the plaintiff the value of the finest jewel which the socket would hold, not the finest jewel that had ever been known.

The combined effect of those principles would justify and require that where it is totally unknown how much of the innocent party's goods went into the mixture, the whole should belong to him. But I do not see that they require or justify the same result where it is known how much was contributed by the innocent party, or even what the maximum quantity is that he can have contributed, being something less than the whole. That would not be the only justice that could be done; it would be injustice.

As for the reason given by Blackstone—"to guard against fraud"—in my opinion that will be sufficiently achieved if the principle in *Armory v. Delamirie*, 1 Str. 505 is followed. I do not see that it is the function of civil justice to punish or discourage crime by awarding the victim more than he has lost, unless it be in the special case of an award of exemplary damages. There is the allied principle that the courts will not enforce an illegal contract or one that is tainted with illegality. But that has its limits. See the judgment of Devlin J. in *St. John Shipping Corporation v. Joseph Rank Ltd.* [1957] 1 Q.B. 267, 279–280:

> "When the master of the plaintiff's ship St. John was prosecuted at Birkenhead under the [Merchant Shipping (Safety and Loadline Conventions) Act 1932] and, on 28 November 1955, found to have overloaded his ship by more than 11 inches, he was fined the maximum of £1,200; but the amount of cargo by which the ship was overloaded was 427 tons and the extra freight earned was £2,295. So the ship came very well out of this situation; and she and other ships will doubtless continue to come very well out of similar situations until the Act of 1932 is amended. I can see that it is a situation that must cause some concern to cargo owners whose property is at risk. The ship was carrying a cargo of about 10,000 tons of grain from Mobile, Alabama, U.S.A., to Birkenhead. The defendants held a bill of lading for about 3,500 tons of this quantity on which the freight due was nearly £19,000. The defendants, apparently in association with the charterers, decided that some additional punishment should be inflicted on the plaintiffs, and that it should take the form of withholding the £2,295 extra freight. The defendants have withheld £2,000, for which sum they are being sued in this action, and another cargo owner has withheld £295 and is being sued for it in an action that depends on this one. This is the explanation of how this dispute has arisen. But I, of course, have not got to decide whether the defendants are morally justified in trying to make good deficiencies in the criminal law; nor is any justification of that sort put forward in the case."

In the present case there is, as I have said, a hint that the owners were engaged in wrong doing, but on the award as a whole I do not conclude that they mixed the cargo with their own oil for some commercial motive. It would be a severe penalty to impose on them a fine of U.S. $342,000 for their conduct (that being the difference between the receivers' larger claim of U.S. $388,000 and the award in respect of the shortage of some U.S. $46,000). The arbitrators, who know a great deal about the business of carriage by sea, did not perceive justice in that; and neither do I. But in any event, the rule cannot, unless Lord Moulton's qualification in the *Sandeman & Sons* case [1913] A.C. 680, 695, represents the existing law, be altered to suit the circumstances of each particular case. It must be one rule for all cases. Those may vary between one where the shipowner deliberately mixes property with a view to stealing it, to another where he does so purely for convenience of carriage without any intention to harm anybody.

The other motive to be found in the cases is that of Coke C.J. in *Warde v. Aeyre*, 2 Bulst. 323, 324, "otherwise, a man should be made to be a trespasser, volens nolens, by the taking of his goods again. . ." In theory there may still be cases where that reasoning is sound, for example, if a farmer wished to retake his hay from a heap where it had been wrongly mixed with that of somebody else. In practice, it is not likely to arise often and certainly not in the present case: the notion of the Indian receivers boarding the owners' vessel after the conclusion of discharge at Madras in order to retake their oil is implausible. I would not regard that argument as justification for a rule which may work substantial injustice.

In the days when corn and hay were to be found in heaps which could not be measured accurately, when such disputes were tried by jury and witnesses might be illiterate or ignorant, a rough and ready rule which *Goff and Jones*, p. 66, describe as punitive may have been the best that the law could find. But a primitive rule is no longer appropriate when modern and sophisticated methods of measurement are available. The measurement of cargoes of oil is, as I learnt in *Amoco Oil Co. v. Parpada Shipping Co. Ltd.* [1987] 2 Lloyd's Rep. 69, conducted with care and precision. It will not, of course, achieve absolute accuracy. What method of measurement ever does? But for all practical purposes the quantity of the innocent party's goods which have gone into the mixture can often be ascertained with a sufficient degree of precision, as it can be in this case. Similarly, there are methods of sampling and analysis which should enable the quality of the innocent party's goods, and of the mixture, to be assessed. If doubt remains as to either quantity or quality, the principle of *Armory v. Delamirie*, 1 Str. 505 provides a solution.

Seeing that none of the authorities is binding on me, although many are certainly persuasive, I consider that I am free to apply the rule which justice requires. This is that, where B wrongfully mixes the goods of A with goods of his own, which are substantially of the same nature and quality, and they cannot in practice be separated, the mixture is held in common and A is entitled to receive out of it a quantity equal to that of his goods which went into the mixture, any doubt as to that quantity being resolved in favour of A. He is also entitled to claim damages from B in respect of any loss he may have suffered, in respect of quality or otherwise, by reason of the admixture.

Whether the same rule would apply when the goods of A and B are not substantially of the same nature and quality must be left to another case. It does not arise here. The claim based on a rule of law that the mixture became the property of the receivers fails.'

Note:

If the dealings with property are authorised, then the question of legal ownership will be determined on the basis of the parties' contract, not by operation of law. The process is easy if the contract is explicit (although see Section 3.8 above), but more difficult if intention has to be inferred: see, for example, *Coleman v Harvey* [1989] 1 NZLR 723.

Questions:

Is the focus in all these cases on *actual* ownership, or is it on extending the rights (or obligations) of ownership via common law tracing? Is this a distinction without a difference? If it is, then is the modern assertion that tracing is a process, not a remedy, misplaced?

6.4.6 Manufacture of a new product (*specificatio*): common law tracing rules

The next case concerns equitable tracing, rather than common law tracing, but it provides a good modern example of the approach the courts are likely to take to these problems. In circumstances where tracing in equity is impossible for the reasons articulated in the case below, it is most improbable that courts would allow the possibility of tracing at common law.

[626] *Borden (UK) Ltd v Scottish Timber Products Ltd* [1981] 1 Ch 25, 41 *per* Bridge LJ, 44 *per* Templeman LJ:
[The facts are outlined at **[334]**.]

> ***Bridge LJ:***
> [See the extract at **[334]**.]
>
> ***Templeman LJ:***
> 'On behalf of the plaintiffs it was submitted that the retention of title condition, which reserved to the plaintiffs the property in the resin, imposed on the defendants fiduciary duties and enables the plaintiffs to trace the resin [in equity] through all its transformations. In my judgment, when resin was sold and delivered the property in the resin could be retained by the plaintiffs, and was retained only as security for the payment of the purchase price and other debts incurred, and to be incurred, by the defendants to the plaintiffs in respect of supplies of resin. If the defendants repudiated one contract the plaintiffs could accept that repudiation and recover possession of the resin. If the plaintiffs did not accept repudiation, or if the defendants failed to make payment due under any other contract, the plaintiffs could enforce their security by selling the resin, for which purpose they had reserved the title to themselves. When resin was sold and delivered, the defendants admittedly took possession subject to the title and rights of the plaintiffs; but the defendants did not receive the resin in any fiduciary capacity, but for themselves as purchasers. They could not sell and make title to the resin, because the title had been retained by the plaintiffs. But the defendants were free to employ the resin in the manufacture of chipboard.
>
> When the resin was incorporated in the chipboard, the resin ceased to exist, the plaintiffs' title to the resin became meaningless and their security vanished. There was no provision in the contract for the defendants to provide substituted or additional security. The chipboard belonged to the defendants.'

Also see:

Borden (UK) Ltd v Scottish Timber Products Ltd [1979] 2 Lloyd's Rep 168, 170–1 (ie this same case at first instance).

Question:

Reconsider all these cases on common law tracing. What are the purposes and effects of common law tracing? Are all these cases best described as 'tracing' cases, or is some other classification more apt?

FURTHER READING:

A S Guest, 'Accession and Confusion in the Law of Hire-Purchase' (1964) 27 *MLR* 505.
P Matthews, 'Proprietary Claims at Common Law for Mixed and Improved Goods' [1981] *CLP* 159.
P J Millett, 'Tracing the Proceeds of Fraud' (1991) 107 *LQR* 71.
P Birks, 'Mixing and Tracing: Property and Restitution' (1992) 45 *CLP* 69.
P Birks, 'Mixtures' in N Palmer and E McKendrick (eds), *Interests in Goods* (2nd ed, 1998, LLP: London), ch 9.

6.5 Tracing: the equitable rules

Again, before looking at the rules in detail, it is useful to consider why a claimant might wish to trace in equity. More often than not it is because the claimant wants to establish an equitable proprietary interest in an asset in the defendant's hands. A claimant who can establish an initial equitable proprietary interest in some asset in the defendant's hands *and* can trace that asset in equity into its substitutions, mixtures or products in the hands of the same person is generally allowed an equitable proprietary claim of some sort to those traceable proceeds. Whether that claim takes the form of a constructive trust (with an associated order for conveyance) or an equitable lien is discussed later in this chapter.

But why should a claimant be so concerned to establish a proprietary interest, rather than to pursue personal claims against the defendant? Two advantages motivate most attempts to assert proprietary interests. The first is the priority thereby accorded to the claimant on the defendant's insolvency. If a defendant becomes insolvent, the assets available for distribution to the defendant's creditors are confined to assets beneficially owned by the defendant. To the extent that a claimant can show that assets in the defendant's hands belong beneficially to the claimant, not to the defendant, the claimant can isolate those assets from the liquidation or bankruptcy of the defendant. This often allows a claimant to recover in full, leaving the other unsecured creditors with an even smaller estate to be distributed *pari passu*.

The second advantage often seen as associated with a tracing claim is that it has the potential to enlarge the quantum of the claim. If the traceable proceeds are worth more than the original asset being traced, then it is often assumed that the claimant is entitled to claim the more valuable traced asset. As with the common law cases, it is not at all clear that this assumption, however common, is correct. Suppose, for example, that a trustee misappropriates £1,000 of trust funds and, as in the example cited earlier, purchases shares which increase in value to £2,000. The rules about equitable tracing into substitutes confirm that the money can be traced into the shares and, at least where the defendant is a trustee, the trust beneficiary can assert equitable ownership of the shares. It is then sometimes assumed that this is a general rule, and that, even where the defendant is not a trustee but an innocent volunteer in receipt of misdirected trust funds, the claimant will be entitled to assert equitable ownership of the profitable investment. This is doubtful. The reason a trust beneficiary can claim the proceeds of the profitable investment from the trustee is not because ownership of the money *ipso facto* entitles the beneficiary to ownership of the shares, but because either the beneficiary can adopt the unauthorised investment made with the trust funds or the beneficiary can insist that the trustee is not entitled to make a secret personal profit from the trust. Tracing, it is true, may assist the claimant to determine what profits arise from either of these breaches of trust; but ownership of those profits arises because of a direct claim to them, not because tracing enlarges the claim to the initial sum of money. If this is true, then an innocent volunteer who makes a profit from investing funds which belong in equity to a claimant will, it is true, have to cede to the claimant an equitable lien on those traceable profits to secure the return of the initial funds; this is the protective function of tracing. But some basis other than tracing must be found to justify the claimant's entitlement to equitable ownership of the entire investment proceeds.

Question:

Do the cases extracted below support or deny the validity of the distinction articulated in the previous paragraph? *Should* an innocent volunteer be allowed to keep proceeds gained from the successful investment of money which belongs beneficially to another? (See *F C Jones & Sons (Trustee in Bankruptcy) v Jones* at **[619]** for the common law position.)

One further introductory point is necessary. It is often said that equitable tracing is also necessary to support certain personal claims in equity, especially against those who might be liable in knowing receipt or dishonest assistance. This is not exactly true. Personal liability in knowing receipt depends upon the knowing recipient receiving trust property—so clearly trust property (or its traceable product) must be *followed* into the hands of the knowing recipient and then the recipient's (personal) liability must be established (by confirming the necessary degree of knowledge). With dishonest assistance, the accessory's (or assistant's) liability does not depend upon receipt of trust property, but merely on the dishonest provision of assistance to the fiduciary acting in a breach of trust; it follows that tracing is not strictly necessary, although it may help to prove a particular case.[25]

With equitable tracing, the original property is often money and the factual dealings involve a combination of mixing, substitution and the creation of new products. This makes tidy categorisation of the cases difficult.

6.5.1 General principles: equitable tracing

In the extracts below, the focus is on the conditions which must be met before a claimant can use the technique of equitable tracing. The later sub-sections then consider the particular rules which govern the tracing process. *Re Diplock* [1948] 1 Ch 465 (see **[628]** below) is seen as demanding that a claimant wishing to trace in equity must establish an initial fiduciary relationship the breach of which enables the claimant to trace, and an equitable proprietary interest. These preconditions mean that equitable proprietary remedies based on tracing are not available in the auxiliary jurisdiction, in aid of common law rights.[26] The justification for these requirements is increasingly the subject of debate. It is suggested that equitable tracing should be available to protect equitable proprietary interests, whether or not there is a fiduciary relationship associated with (or pre-dating) such proprietary interests. On this basis, the fiduciary relationship limitation should go. It is further suggested that if tracing is simply a process, and says nothing about the claims which might be asserted at the end of the exercise, then perhaps the starting point need only be property (whether legal or equitable) in the hands of the claimant. This position can be reached either by asserting that the common law and equitable tracing rules are the same, or by conceding that the equitable rules can be used to further common law claims. What limitations do the following extracts suggest ought to apply to equitable tracing?

[627] *Re Hallett's Estate* (1880) 13 Ch D 696 (CA), 708–11 and 727–8 *per* Jessel MR, 733 *per* Baggallay LJ, 722–4 *per* Thesiger LJ:

[Mrs Cotterill engaged Hallett as her solicitor and either gave him custody of, or instructed him to purchase, some Russian bonds. He then sold them, together with some bonds held in trust under his marriage settlement, and deposited the proceeds in his bank account which contained money of his own. He used the account, making deposits and withdrawals, but at no stage did the balance fall below the proceeds of sale of the bonds. He died insolvent. Mrs Cotterill and the trustees of the marriage settlement sought to trace into the account. The Court of Appeal refused to apply the rule in *Clayton's case*[27] (a common law 'first in, first out' rule, which would have treated a substantial portion of the relevant sale proceeds as withdrawn and dissipated), and instead allowed both claimants a charge over the account for the

[25] These are *personal* claims and are discussed in Chapter 7.

[26] Recall the 'fudge' in finding a fiduciary relationship which would support equitable tracing in *Chase Manhattan Bank NA v Israel British Bank (London) Ltd* [1981] Ch 105 (see **[511]** above).

[27] (1817) 1 Mer 575; 35 ER 781.

entire proceeds of the sale of the bonds. Mr Hallett was unanimously seen as a fiduciary, although not as a trustee of the assets entrusted to him.]

Sir George Jessel MR:

'[708] The modern doctrine of Equity as regards property disposed of by persons in a fiduciary position is a very clear and well-established doctrine. You can, if the sale was rightful, take the proceeds of the sale, if you can identify them. If the sale was wrongful, you can still take the proceeds of the sale, in a sense adopting the sale for the purpose of [709] taking the proceeds, if you can identify them. There is no distinction, therefore, between a rightful and a wrongful disposition of the property, so far as regards the right of the beneficial owner to follow the proceeds. But it very often happens that you cannot identify the proceeds. The proceeds may have been invested together with money belonging to the person in a fiduciary position, in a purchase. He may have bought land with it, for instance, or he may have bought chattels with it. Now, what is the position of the beneficial owner as regards such purchases? I will, first of all, take his position when the purchase is clearly made with what I will call, for shortness, the trust money, although it is not confined, as I will shew presently, to express trusts. In that case, according to the now well-established doctrine of Equity, the beneficial owner has a right to elect either to take the property purchased, or to hold it as a security for the amount of the trust money laid out in the purchase; or, as we generally express it, he is entitled at his election either to take the property, or to have a charge on the property for the amount of the trust money. But in the second case, where a trustee has mixed the money with his own, there is this distinction, that the *cestui que trust*, or beneficial owner, can no longer elect to take the property, because it is no longer bought with the trust-money simply and purely, but with a mixed fund. He is, however, still entitled to a charge on the property purchased, for the amount of the trust-money laid out in the purchase; and that charge is quite independent of the fact of the amount laid out by the trustee. The moment you get a substantial portion of it furnished by the trustee, using the word "trustee" in the sense I have mentioned, as including all persons in a fiduciary relation, the right to the charge follows. That is the modern doctrine of Equity. Has it ever been suggested, until very recently, that there is any distinction between an express trustee, or an agent, or a bailee, or a collector of rents, or anybody else in a fiduciary position? I have never heard, until quite recently, such a distinction suggested. It cannot, as far as I am aware (and since this Court sat last to hear this case, I have taken the trouble to look for authority), be found in any reported case even suggested, except in the recent decision of Mr. Justice Fry, to which I shall draw attention presently. It can have no foundation in principle, [710] because the beneficial ownership is the same, wherever the legal ownership may be. If you have goods bargained and sold to a man upon trust to sell and hand over the net proceeds to another, that other is the beneficial owner; but if instead of being bargained and sold, so as to vest the legal ownership in the trustee, they are deposited with him to sell as agent, so that the legal ownership remains in the beneficial owner, can it be supposed, in a Court of Equity, that the rights of the beneficial owner are different, he being entire beneficial owner in both cases? I say on principle it is impossible to imagine there can be any difference. In practice we know there is no difference, because the moment you get into a Court of Equity, where a principal can sue an agent as well as a *cestui que trust* can sue a trustee, no such distinction was ever suggested, as far as I am aware. Therefore, the moment you establish the fiduciary relation, the modern rules of Equity, as regards following trust money, apply. I intentionally say modern rules, because it must not be forgotten that the rules of Courts of Equity are not, like the rules of the Common Law, supposed to have been established from time immemorial. It is perfectly well known that they have been established from time to time—altered, improved, and refined from time to time. In many cases we know the names of the Chancellors who invented them. No doubt they were invented for the purpose of securing the better administration of justice, but still they were invented. . . . We can name the Chancellors who first invented them, and state the date when they were first introduced into Equity jurisprudence; and, therefore, in cases of this kind, the older precedents in Equity are of very little value. The doctrines are progressive, refined, and improved; and if we want to know what the rules of Equity are, we must look, of course, rather to the more modern than the more ancient cases.

Now that being the established doctrine of Equity on this point, I will take the case of the pure bailee. If the bailee sells the goods bailed, the bailor can in Equity follow the proceeds, and can follow the proceeds wherever they can be distinguished, either being actually kept separate, or being mixed up with other [711] moneys. I have only to advert to one other point, and that is this—supposing, instead of being invested in the purchase of land or goods, the moneys were simply mixed with other moneys of the trustee, using the term again in its full sense as including every person in a fiduciary relation, does it make any difference according to the modern doctrine of Equity? I say none. It would be very remarkable if it were to do so. Supposing the trust money was 1000 sovereigns, and the trustee put them into a bag, and by mistake, or accident, or otherwise, dropped a sovereign of his own into the bag. Could anybody suppose that a Judge in Equity would find any difficulty in saying that the *cestui que trust* has a right to take 1000 sovereigns out of that bag? I do not like to call it a charge of 1000 sovereigns on the 1001 sovereigns, but that is the effect of it. I have no doubt of it. It would make no difference if, instead of one sovereign, it was another 1000 sovereigns; but if instead of putting it into his bag, or after putting it into his bag, he carries the bag to his bankers, what then? According to law, the bankers are his debtors for the total amount; but if you lend the trust money to a third person, you can follow it. If in the case supposed the trustee had lent the £1000 to a man without security, you could follow the debt, and take it from the debtor. If he lent it on a promissory note, you could take the promissory note; or the bond, if it were a bond. If, instead of lending the whole amount in one sum simply, he had added a sovereign, or had added £500 of his own to the £1000, the only difference is this, that instead of taking the bond or the promissory note, the *cestui que trust* would have a charge for the amount of the trust money on the bond or promissory note. So it would be on the simple contract debt; that is, if the debt were of such a nature as that, between the creditor and the debtor, you could not sever the debt into two, so as to shew what part was trust money, then the *cestui que trust* would have a right to a charge upon the whole. Therefore, there is no difficulty in following out the rules of Equity and deciding that in a case of a mere bailee, as Mr. Justice Fry has decided, you can follow the money. . . .

[727] Now, first upon principle, nothing can be better settled, either in our own law, or, I suppose, the law of all civilised countries, than this, that where a man does an act which may be rightfully performed, he cannot say that that act was intentionally and in fact done wrongly. A man who has a right of entry cannot say he committed a trespass in entering. A man who sells the goods of another as agent for the owner cannot prevent the owner adopting the sale, and deny that he acted as agent for the owner. It runs throughout our law, and we are familiar with numerous instances in the law of real property. A man who grants a lease believing he has sufficient estate to grant it, although it turns out that he has not, but has a power which enables him to grant it, is not allowed to say he did not grant it under the power. Wherever it can be done rightfully, he is not allowed to say, against the person entitled to the property or the right, that he has done it wrongfully. That is the universal law.

When we come to apply that principle to the case of a trustee who has blended trust moneys with his own, it seems to me perfectly plain that he cannot be heard to say that he took away the trust money when he had a right to take away his own money. The simplest case put is the mingling of trust moneys in a bag with money of the trustee's own. Suppose he has a hundred sovereigns in a bag, and he adds to them another hundred sovereigns of his own, so that they are commingled in such a way that they cannot bc distinguished, and the next day he draws out for his own purposes £100, is it tolerable for anybody to allege that what he drew out was the first £100, the trust money, and that he misappropriated it, and left his own £100 in the bag? It is obvious he must have taken away that which he had a right to take away, his own £100. What difference does it make if, instead of being in a hag, he deposits it with his banker, and then pays in other money of his own, and draws out some money for his own purposes? Could he say that he had actually drawn out anything but his own money? His money was there, and he had a right to draw it out, and why should the natural act of simply drawing [728] out the money be attributed to anything except to his ownership of money which was at his bankers.

It is said, no doubt, that according to the modern theory of banking, the deposit banker is a debtor for the money. So he is, and not a trustee in the strict sense of the word. At the same time one must recollect that the position of a deposit banker is different from that of an ordinary debtor. Still he is for some purposes a debtor, and it is said if a debt of this kind is paid by a banker, although the total balance is the amount owing by the banker, yet considering the repayments and the sums paid in by the depositor, you attribute the first sum drawn out to the first sum paid in. That was a rule first established by Sir William Grant in *Clayton's Case* (1 Mer. 572); a very convenient rule, and I have nothing to say against it unless there is evidence either of agreement to the contrary or of circumstances from which a contrary intention must be presumed, and then of course that which is a mere presumption of law gives way to those other considerations. Therefore, it does appear to me there is nothing in the world laid down by Sir William Grant in *Clayton's Case*, or in the numerous cases which follow it, which in the slightest degree affects the principle, which I consider to be clearly established.'

Baggallay LJ:
'[Citing from the decision of the Court of Appeal in *Pennell v Deffell* (4 D. M. & G. 372)] Lord Justice Turner in the course of his judgment [at p. 388] expressed himself as follows: "It is, I apprehend, an undoubted principle of this Court that as between *cestui que trust and trustee*, and all parties claiming under the trustee otherwise than by purchase for valuable consideration without notice, all property belonging to a trust, however much it may be changed or altered in its nature or character, and all the fruit of such property, whether in its original or in its altered state, continues to be subject to or affected by the trust." And after illustrating this principle by a reference to the way in which the Court was in the habit of dealing with cases in which trust property had been invested in trade, the Lord Justice proceeded as follows: "But of course in those cases as in other cases the property which is the subject of the trust must in some manner be ascertained." [It is this process which relies on the equitable rules of tracing.]'

Thesiger LJ:
'[722] The principle of law may be stated, as it appears to me, in the form of a very simple, although at the same time very wide and general proposition. I would state that proposition in these [723] terms, namely, that wherever a specific chattel is intrusted by one man to another, either for the purposes of safe custody or for the purpose of being disposed of for the benefit of the person intrusting the chattel; then, either the chattel

itself, or the proceeds of the chattel, whether the chattel has been rightfully or wrongfully disposed of, may be followed at any time, although either the chattel itself, or the money constituting the proceeds of that chattel, may have been mixed and confounded in a mass of the like material. . . . As far as I can judge, the only exception to the general proposition which I have stated is not a real exception, but an apparent exception, for all cases where it has been held that moneys mixed and confounded, but still existing, in a mass cannot be followed, may, I think, be resolved into cases where, although there may have been a trust with reference to the disposition of the particular chattel which those moneys subsequently represented, there was no trust, no [724] duty in reference to the moneys themselves beyond the ordinary duty of a man to pay his debts; in other words, that they were cases where the relationship of debtor and creditor had been constituted, instead of the relation either of trustee and cestui que trust, or principal and agent. [Thesiger LJ then dissented in the practical application of these principles, holding that the rule in *Clayton's Case* should apply.]'

Questions:

Does this case permit a *legal* owner of property to trace that property in equity into its substitutions? Mrs Cotterill was the legal owner of the Russian bonds. Was it simply equitable tracing which allowed her to trace those bonds into Mr Hallett's bank account? Or did Mrs Cotterill first have to 'ratify' her (fiduciary) agent's unauthorised dealing with the bonds, and *that* step constituted Mr Hallett a trustee of the proceeds of sale, so that Mr Hallett then held the legal title to the funds on trust for Mrs Cotterill. Mrs Cotterill could then use equitable tracing to identify the present location of those funds. Does this difference in approach entail any significantly different consequences?

Note:

The principles described in *Re Hallett's Estate* are not confined to mixtures of money. They also apply to mixtures of other fungibles: see *Brady v Stapleton* (1952) 88 CLR 322 (Aust HCt), a case concerning shares.

[628] *Re Diplock* [1948] 1 Ch 465 (CA), 516–7, 518–26, 539–40, 544–53 *per* Lord Greene MR for the Court:

[Caleb Diplock's will directed his executors to apply his large residuary estate to 'charitable or benevolent' objects selected by his executors. The '*or*' proved fatal. The trustees, acting in good faith, paid out over £200,000 to 139 different charitable institutions, including hospitals and schools for the disabled. However, the House of Lords in *Chichester Dioscesan Fund v Simpson* [1944] AC 431 then held the clause to be wholly invalid because it permitted distributions for purposes which were not, at law, charitable. The next of kin thus became entitled to the residuary estate. They compromised their claims against the executors for breach of duty, and then sought to recover the balance owing to them from the recipient charities. The next of kin's claims were based on either a personal right of recovery (upheld by both the Court of Appeal and the House of Lords ([1951] AC 251)) or a proprietary right to trace (upheld by the Court of Appeal, as extracted below, and not dealt with by the House of Lords). Strictly speaking, the Court of Appeal did not need to discuss the proprietary claim since it had found in favour of the next of kin on the personal claim. However, three circumstances persuaded the Court to deliver its views: the issues had been fully argued before the Court, the personal claim might have been overruled by the House of Lords (it was not), and the proprietary claim could carry interest in some circumstances whereas the personal claim could not.]

[See the extract at **[611]** above for comments on the difference between common law and equitable tracing and on some of the fundamental attributes of equitable tracing.]

'The first question which appears to us to fall for decision on this part of the present appeals may, we think, be thus formulated: Did the power of equity to treat Diplock "money" as recoverable from the charity, which undoubtedly existed down to the moment when the cheque was paid by the bank on which it was drawn, cease the moment that the "money" by the process of "mixture" came to be represented by an accretion to or an enlargement of the chose in action consisting of a debt already owing to the charity by its own bankers? Wynn-Parry J. [at first instance], in effect, decided that it did. His reason for taking this view, shortly stated, was as follows: The principle applicable was to be extracted from the decision in *Hallett's* case [**[627]** above] and that principle was in no way extended by the decision in *Sinclair v. Brougham* ([1914] AC 398). The principle can operate only in cases where the mixing takes place in breach of a trust, actual or constructive, or in breach of some other fiduciary relationship and in proceedings against the trustee or fiduciary agent: here the mixing was not of this character, since it was effected by an innocent volunteer: there is no ground on which, according to principle, the conscience of such a volunteer can be held in equity to be precluded from setting up a title adverse to the claim: in every case, therefore, where a "mixture" has been carried out by the charity, the claim, whether it be against a mixed monetary fund or against investments made by means of such a mixed fund, must fail in limine.

Now we may say at once that this view of the inability of equity to deal with the case of the volunteer appears to us, with all respect to Wynn-Parry J., to be in conflict with the principles expounded, particularly by Lord Parker, in *Sinclair v. Brougham*. . . . We shall deal further with Lord Parker's observations on this topic when we come to them in our examination of *Sinclair v. Brougham*. But here we may conveniently summarize what we consider to be the effect of them as follows: Where an innocent volunteer (as distinct from a purchaser for value without notice) mixes "money" of his own with "money" which in equity belongs to another person, or is found in possession of such a mixture, although that other person cannot claim a charge on the mass superior to the claim of the volunteer he is entitled, nevertheless, to a charge ranking *pari passu* with the claim of the volunteer. And Lord Parker's reasons for taking this view appear to have been on the following lines: Equity regards the rights of the equitable owner as being "in effect rights of property" though not recognized as such by the common law. Just as a volunteer is not allowed by equity in the case, e.g., of a conveyance of the legal estate in land, to set up his legal title adversely to the claim of a person having an equitable interest in the land, so in the case of a mixed fund of money the volunteer must give such recognition as equity considers him in conscience (as a volunteer) bound to give to the interest of the equitable owner of the money which has been mixed with the volunteer's own. But this burden on the conscience of the volunteer is not such as to compel him to treat the claim of the equitable owner as paramount. That would be to treat the volunteer as strictly as if he himself stood in a fiduciary relationship to the equitable owner which ex hypothesi he does not. The volunteer is under no greater duty of conscience to recognize the interest of the equitable owner than that which lies upon a person having an equitable interest in one of two trust funds of "money" which have become mixed towards the equitable owner of the other. Such a person is not in conscience bound to give precedence to the equitable owner of the other of the two funds.

We may enlarge upon the implications which appear to us to be contained in Lord Parker's reasoning. First of all, it appears to us to be wrong to treat the principle which underlies *Hallett's* case as coming into operation only where the person who does the mixing is not only in a fiduciary position but is also a party to the tracing action. If he is a party to the action he is, of course, precluded from setting up a case inconsistent with the obligations of his fiduciary position. But supposing that he is not a party? The result cannot surely depend on what equity would or would not have allowed him to say if he had been a party. Suppose that the sole trustee of (say) five separate trusts draws £100 out of each of the trust banking accounts, pays the resulting £500 into an account which he opens in his own name, draws a cheque for £500 on that account and gives it as a present to his son. A claim by the five sets of beneficiaries to follow the money of their respective trusts would be a claim against the son. He would stand in no fiduciary relationship to any of them. We recoil from the conclusion that all five beneficiaries would be dismissed empty handed by a court of equity and the son left to enjoy what in equity was originally their money. Yet that is the conclusion to which the reasoning of the learned judge would lead us. Lord Parker's reasoning, on the other hand, seems to us to lead to the conclusion that each set of beneficiaries could set up its equitable interest which would prevail against the bare legal title of the son as a volunteer and that they would be entitled to share pari passu in so much of the fund or its proceeds as remained identifiable.

An even more striking example was admitted by Mr. Pennycuick to be the result of his argument, and he vigorously maintained that it followed inevitably from the principles of equity involved. If a fiduciary agent takes cash belonging to his principal and gives it to his son, who takes it innocently, then so long as the son keeps it unmixed with other cash in one trouser pocket, the principal can follow it and claim it back. Once, however, the son, being under no fiduciary duty to the principal, transfers it to his other trouser pocket in which there are reposing a coin or two of his own of the same denomination, the son, by a sort of process of accretion, acquires an indefeasible title to what the moment before the transfer he could not have claimed as his own. This result appears to us to stultify the beneficent powers of equity to protect and enforce what it recognizes as equitable rights of property which subsist until they are destroyed by the operation of a purchase for value without notice.

The error into which, we respectfully suggest, the learned judge has fallen is in thinking that what, in *Hallett's* case was only the method (there appropriate) of bringing a much wider-based principle of equity into operation—*viz.*, the method by which a fiduciary agent, who has himself wrongfully mixed the funds, is prohibited from asserting a breach of his duty—is an element which must necessarily be present before equity can afford protection to the equitable rights which it has brought into existence. We are not prepared to see the arm of equity thus shortened.

. . . .

From the foregoing study of Lord Parker's speech [in *Sinclair v Brougham*], it would appear that in his opinion there is an equitable principle common to all these cases of mixed funds. It operates in different ways according to the circumstances. In some cases it results in a priority to one or other of the claimants, in other cases the claimants rank pari passu. Where one claimant is a person in a fiduciary relationship to another and has mixed moneys of that other with moneys of his own, that other takes priority. The same result follows where a person taking that other claimant's money from the person in a fiduciary relationship, with notice that it is money held in a fiduciary capacity, proceeds to mix it with money of his own. Where the contest is between two claimants to a mixed fund made up entirely of moneys held on behalf of the two of them respectively and mixed together by the fiduciary agent, they share pari passu, each being innocent. Where the moneys are handed by way of transfer to a person who takes for value without notice, the claim of the owner of the moneys is extinguished just as all other equitable estates or interests are extinguished by a purchase for value without notice. In the case, however, of a volunteer who takes without notice, e.g., by way of gift from the fiduciary agent, if there is no question of mixing, he holds the money on behalf of the true owner whose equitable right to the money still persists as against him. On the other hand, if the volunteer mixes the money with money of his own, or receives it mixed from the fiduciary agent, he must admit the claim of the true owner, but is not precluded from setting up his own claim in respect of the moneys of his own which have been contributed to the mixed fund. The result is that they share *pari passu*. It would be inequitable for the volunteer to claim priority for the reason that he is a volunteer: it would be equally inequitable for the true owner of the money to claim priority over the volunteer for the reason that the volunteer is innocent and cannot be said to act unconscionably if he claims equal treatment for himself. The mutual recognition of one another's rights is what equity insists upon as a condition of giving relief.

. . .

It is to be observed that neither Lord Parker nor Lord Haldane [in *Sinclair v Brougham*] suggests that the equitable remedy extends to cover all cases where A becomes possessed of money belonging to B, a view which Lord Dunedin seemed inclined to accept if he did not actually do so. Lord Parker and Lord Haldane both predicate the existence of a right of property recognized by equity which depends upon there having existed at some stage a fiduciary relationship of some kind (though not necessarily a positive duty of trusteeship) sufficient to give rise to the equitable right of property. Exactly what relationships are sufficient to bring such an equitable right into existence for the purposes of the rule which we are considering is a matter which has not been precisely laid down. Certain relationships are clearly included, e.g., trustee (actual or constructive) and cestui que trust; and "fiduciary" relationships such as that of principal and agent. *Sinclair v. Brougham* ([1914] A. C. 398, 418, 419) itself affords another example. There, a sufficient fiduciary relationship was found to exist between the depositors and the directors by reason of the fact that the purposes for which the depositors had handed their money to the directors were by law incapable of fulfilment. [This is now overruled by the *Westdeutsche* case: see **[518]** above.]

. . .

In the analysis we have made of the speeches in Sin*clair v. Brougham*, and of the principle which underlies them, it has been made clear that though the equity may operate upon the conscience of a volunteer, it will not operate upon the conscience of a purchaser for value without notice. Some attempt was made on the part of the respondents to establish that they or some of them might properly be described as falling within the latter category, e.g., by reason of the fact that moneys which certain of them had received were paid upon the terms that such moneys were applied in a particular way. The argument was not strenuously stressed before us and was rejected by Wynn-Parry J. We entirely agree with the learned judge on this point and do not find it necessary to add anything to the reasons which he gave for his conclusion.

We have now to consider how the principles which we have outlined are to be applied to the facts of the individual cases which are before us.'

[The practical application of these rules is extracted at **[636]** below.]

[629] ***Boscawen v Bajwa*** **[1996] 1 WLR 328 (CA), 334–8, 341–2 *per* Millett LJ:**
[A building society advanced funds for the purchase of a property, the advance to be secured by a first legal charge. Although the purchase had fallen through, the vendor's solicitors, who had received these funds from the purchaser, used them to discharge a mortgage over the property. Other creditors of the vendor then obtained a charging order over the property, and sought possession and sale of the property. The building society successfully sought to be subrogated to the mortgagee's rights, and to assert a charge over the proceeds of sale of the property in priority to the other creditors of the vendor.]

[Millett LJ referred to the possibility that the defendant might attempt to challenge the validity of the tracing exercise, or raise a priority dispute (eg by claiming to be a bona fide purchaser for value), or raise the defence of innocent change of position. He then continued.]

'[334] If the plaintiff succeeds in tracing his property, whether in its original or in some changed form, into the hands of the defendant, and overcomes any defences which are put forward on the defendant's behalf, he is entitled to a remedy. The remedy will be fashioned to the circumstances. The plaintiff will generally be entitled to a personal remedy; if he seeks a proprietary remedy he must usually prove that the property to which he lays claim is still in the ownership of the defendant. If he succeeds in doing this the court will treat the defendant as holding the property on a [335] constructive trust for the plaintiff and will order the defendant to transfer it in specie to the plaintiff. But this is only one of the proprietary remedies which are available to a court of equity. If the plaintiff's money has been applied by the defendant, for example, not in the acquisition of a landed property but in its improvement, then the court may treat the land as charged with the payment to the plaintiff of a sum representing the amount by which the value of the defendant's land has been enhanced by the use of the plaintiff's money. And if the plaintiff's money has been used to discharge a mortgage on the defendant's land, then the court may achieve a similar result by treating the land as subject to a charge by way of subrogation in favour of the plaintiff. . . .

It is still a prerequisite of the right to trace in equity that there must be a fiduciary relationship which calls the equitable jurisdiction into being: see *Agip (Africa) Ltd. v. Jackson* [1991] Ch. 547 [**[617]** above], 566, per Fox L.J. That requirement is satisfied in the present case by the fact that from the first moment of its receipt by Dave [the purchaser's solicitor] in their general client account the £140,000 was trust money held in trust for the Abbey National [the building society]. The appellants do not dispute that the Abbey National can successfully trace £137,405 of its money into Hill Lawson's [the vendor's solicitors'] client account. But they do dispute the judge's finding that it can trace the sum further into the payment to the Halifax [the original mortgagee].

The £137,405 was paid into Hill Lawson's general client account at the bank because it was only intended to be kept for a short time. Funds which were held for clients for any length of time were held in separate designated accounts. Hill Lawson's ledger cards showed Mr. Bajwa [the vendor] as the relevant client. According to Mr. Duckney, Hill Lawson also held other funds for Mr. Bajwa which were the result of an inheritance which he had received. These were the source from which Hill Lawson made good the shortfall of £2,595 which arose when Dave's cheque was dishonoured. The amount of these other funds is unknown, though it was certainly nothing like £140,000. The evidence does not show whether they were held in Hill Lawson's general client account or whether they were held in a separate designated account. If they were held in the general client account the £137,405 received from Dave was (quite properly) mixed not only with moneys belonging to other clients but also with money belonging to Mr. Bajwa. Hill Lawson can be presumed not to have committed a breach of trust by resorting to moneys belonging to other clients but they were perfectly entitled to use Mr. Bajwa's own money to discharge the Halifax's charge on his property. Whether they did so or not cannot be determined in the absence of any evidence of the amount involved. Accordingly, it is submitted, the Abbey National has failed to establish how much of its money was applied in the discharge of the Halifax's charge and how much of the money which was applied for this purpose was Mr. Bajwa's own money.

The Abbey National answers this submission in two ways. First, it submits that Hill Lawson's ledger cards show that Hill Lawson appropriated the £137,405, which they had received from Dave, towards the payment of the sum of £140,000 to the Halifax, and resorted to Mr. Bajwa's other funds only when Dave's cheque for the balance was dishonoured. The ledger cards were, of course, made up after the event, though long before any litigation ensued, so they are not primary evidence of actual appropriation; but they are reliable evidence of the appropriation which Hill Lawson believed that they had made.

I accept this submission. It is not necessary to apply artificial tracing rules where there has been an actual appropriation. A trustee will not be allowed to defeat the claim of his beneficiary by saying that he has resorted to trust money when he could have made use of his own; but if the beneficiary asserts that the trustee has made use of the trust money there is no reason why he should not be allowed to prove it.

The second way in which the Abbey National answers the appellants' submission is by reliance on equity's ability to follow money through a bank account where it has been mixed with other moneys by treating the money in the account as charged with the repayment of his money. As against a wrongdoer the claimant is not obliged to appropriate debits to credits in order to ascertain where his money has gone. Equity's power to charge a mixed fund with the repayment of trust moneys enables the claimant to follow the money, not because it is his, but because it is derived from a fund which is treated as if it were subject to a charge in his favour: see *In re Hallett's Estate; Knatchbull v. Hallett* (1880) 13 Ch.D. 696 [**[627]** above]; *In re Oatway; Hertslet v. Oatway* [1903] 2 Ch. 356 [**[630]** below] and *El Ajou v. Dollar Land Holdings Plc.* [1993] 3 All E.R. 717.

The appellants accept this but submit that for this purpose Mr. Bajwa was not a wrongdoer. He was, as I have said, not guilty of any impropriety or want of probity. He relied on his solicitors and they acted unwisely, perhaps negligently, and certainly precipitately, but not dishonestly. Mr. Bajwa, it is submitted, was an innocent volunteer who mixed trust money with his own. As such, he was not bound to give priority to the Abbey National, but could claim parity with it. Accordingly, Mr. Bajwa and the Abbey National, must be treated as having contributed pari passu to the discharge of the

Halifax's charge; and in the absence of the necessary evidence the amounts which were provided by Mr. Bajwa and the Abbey National respectively cannot be ascertained. (In fact, on this footing, the Abbey National would be entitled to succeed to the extent of one half of its claim, but that is by the way.) For this proposition the appellants rely on a passage in *In re Diplock; Diplock v. Wintle* [1948] Ch. 465 [**[628]** above], 524:

> "Where an innocent volunteer (as distinct from a purchaser for value without notice) mixes 'money' of his own with 'money' which in equity belongs to another person, or is found in possession of such a mixture, although that other person cannot claim a charge on the mass superior to the claim of the volunteer he is entitled, nevertheless, to a charge ranking pari passu with the claim of the volunteer. . . . But this burden on the conscience of the volunteer is not such as to compel him to treat the claim of the equitable owner as paramount. That would be to treat the volunteer as strictly as if he himself stood in a fiduciary relationship to the equitable owner which ex hypothesi he does not. The volunteer is under no greater duty of conscience to recognise the interest of the equitable owner than that which lies upon a person having an equitable interest in one of two trust funds of 'money' which have become mixed towards the equitable owner of the other. Such a person is not in conscience bound to give precedence to the equitable owner of the other of the two funds."

This would be highly relevant if the distinction which the court was there making was between the honest and the dishonest recipient. But it was not. The distinction was between the innocent recipient who had no reason to suspect that the money was not his own to dispose of as he pleased and the recipient who knew or ought to have known that the money belonged to another. In *In re Diplock* the defendants were the recipients of grants made to them by the personal representatives of a deceased testator in accordance with the terms of the residuary gift in his will. The gift was afterwards held by the House of Lords to be ineffective, with the result that the testator's residue passed on intestacy. The next of kin then brought proceedings to recover the moneys paid away. The defendants found themselves in an unenviable position. Not only had they received the money honestly and in good faith but they had had no reason to think that it was not theirs. There was no question of their having consciously mixed money which belonged to another with their own.

But the present case is very different. Neither Mr. Bajwa nor his solicitors acted dishonestly, but nor were they innocent volunteers. Hill Lawson knew that the money was trust money held to Dave's order pending completion and that it would become available for use on behalf of their client only on completion. They were manifestly fiduciaries. Mr. Bajwa, who was plainly intending to redeem the Halifax's mortgage out of the proceeds of sale of the property, must be taken to have known that any money which his solicitors might receive from the purchasers or their mortgagees would represent the balance of the proceeds of sale due on completion and that, since he had made no arrangement with the purchasers to be advanced any part of that amount before completion, it would be available to him only on completion. He cannot possibly have thought that he could keep both the property and the proceeds of sale. Had he thought about the matter at all, he would have realised that the money was not his to mix with his own and dispose of as he saw fit. The only reason that he and his solicitors can be acquitted of dishonesty is that he relied on his solicitors and they acted in the mistaken belief that, save for the tidying up of some loose ends, they were on the point of completing.

It follows that Mr. Bajwa cannot avail himself of the more favourable tracing rules which are available to the innocent volunteer who unconsciously mixes trust money with his own. . . .

The appellants' submissions on adoption and ratification are misconceived. The short answer to them is that the right to follow an asset, whether at common law or in equity, does not depend on adoption or ratification. In the leading case of *Taylor v. Plumer* (1815) 3 M. & S. 562 [**[613]** above] Lord Ellenborough C.J. pointed out that, had the successful party's case depended on ratification, it must fail; in *United Australia Ltd. v. Barclay's Bank Ltd.* [1941] A.C. 1, 27–29 Lord Atkin exposed the doctrine as a fiction; and in *Lipkin Gorman v. Karpnale Ltd.* [1991] A.C. 548 [**[618]** above], 573, after pointing out that tracing or following property into its product involves a decision by the original owner to assert his title to the product in place of his original property, Lord Goff said that this was sometimes referred to as ratification but that he himself would not so describe it. In *Agip (Africa) Ltd. v. Jackson* [1990] Ch. 265 [**[617]** above] the money was paid away by the bank in reliance on a forged payment order. It was argued that a forgery was a nullity and that the plaintiffs could not ratify it. It was pointed out that the plaintiffs did not rely on the forgery but on the bank's want of authority. They did not seek to ratify the payment or treat it as made with their authority; on the contrary, they pleaded that it was made without their authority and sought to recover it on that very ground.

In my view counsel for the Abbey National was correct in analysing the doctrine in play as one of election between remedies. The beneficiary who complains that his trustee has committed a breach of trust by using trust money to acquire an asset for himself may either reject the asset and insist that the trustee replace the money or assert his title to the asset. In the latter case the breach of trust of which he complains is the trustee's retention of the asset for his own benefit. The fact that he does not also complain of the acquisition of the asset but seeks to take advantage of it does not mean that he adopts or ratifies it—he will almost certainly plead that it was a breach of trust—it means only that he does not seek a remedy in respect of it. There is no justification for the proposition that the Abbey National's right to be subrogated to the Halifax's charge did not arise until the Abbey National elected to seek that remedy.

Nor, in my judgment, is there any justification for the proposition that the Abbey National's right to be subrogated to the Halifax's charge did not arise until the court made the necessary order. The order merely satisfied a pre-existing equity. The Abbey National's equity arose from the conduct of the parties. It arose at the very moment that the Halifax's charge was discharged, in whole or in part, with the Abbey National's money. It arose because, having regard to the circumstances in which the Halifax's charge was discharged, it would have been unconscionable for Mr. Bajwa to assert that it had been discharged for his benefit. At law, Mr. Bajwa became the owner of an unincumbered freehold interest in the property; but he never did, even for an instant, in equity.'

Questions:

As noted at the outset, it is often said that equitable tracing depends upon the establishment of an equitable proprietary base and a fiduciary relationship. Do the previous extracts support that view? On this basis, is it possible to trace the proceeds of theft? (See the comments of Lord Browne-Wilkinson in *Westdeutsche Landesbank Girozentrale v Islington London Borough Council* [1996] AC 669, 715–16; Lord Denning MR in *Bankers Trust Co v Shapira* [1980] 1 WLR 1274, 1282. Also see *Black v Freedman & Co* (1910) 12 CLR 105; and *Zobory v Federal Commissioner of Taxation* (1995) 129 ALR 485.)

FURTHER READING:

R Goode, 'The Right to Trace and its Impact in Commercial Transactions—II' (1976) 92 *LQR* 528 (This is the second part of the article referred to in the earlier section on common law tracing. This, too, deserves to be read in full.)

R H Maudsley, 'Proprietary Remedies for the Recovery of Money' (1959) 75 *LQR* 234.

6.5.2 Mixed funds: the equitable tracing rules

The previous sub-section was concerned with general concepts which are important to equitable tracing. This sub-section and the next two are concerned with the practical applications of the particular rules.

Re-read:

Re Hallett's Estate (1880) 13 Ch D 696 (CA), at **[627]** above.

[630] ***Re Oatway* [1903] 2 Ch 356, 359–61 *per* Joyce J:**

[Oatway, a solicitor and trustee of the relevant trust, paid £3,000 of trust money into his own account, which already stood in credit. He continued to operate the account, and at one stage withdrew £2,137 for the purchase of Oceana shares, leaving a balance of more than £3,000 which he later dissipated. He died insolvent. The court declined to apply *Re Hallett's Estate* (**[627]** above), and instead allowed an application to have the proceeds of the sale of the shares paid into the trust fund.]

> 'It is a principle settled as far back as the time of the Year Books that, whatever alteration of form any property may undergo, the true owner is entitled to seize it in its new shape if he can prove the identity of the original material: see Blackstone, vol. ii. p. 405, and *Lupton v. White*. ((1808) 15 Ves. 432) But this rule is carried no farther than necessity requires, and is applied only to cases where the compound is such as to render it impossible to apportion the respective shares of the parties. Thus, if the quality of the articles that are mixed be uniform, and the original quantities known, as in the case of so many pounds of trust money mixed with so many pounds of the trustee's own money, the person by whose act the confusion took place is still entitled to claim his proper quantity, but subject to the quantity of the other proprietor being first made good out of the whole mass: 2 *Stephen's Commentaries* (13th ed.), 20. Trust money may be followed into land or any other property in which it has been invested; and when a trustee has, in making any purchase or investment, applied trust money together with his own, the cestuis que trust are entitled to a charge on the property purchased for the amount of the trust money laid out in the purchase or investment. Similarly, if money held by any person in a fiduciary capacity be paid into his own banking account, it may be followed by the equitable owner, who, as against the trustee, will have a charge for what belongs to him upon the balance to the credit of the account. If, then, the trustee pays in further sums, and from time to time draws out money by cheques, but leaves a balance to the credit of the account, it is settled that he is not entitled to have the rule in *Clayton's Case* ((1816) 1 Mer. 572) applied so as to maintain that the sums which have been drawn out and paid away so as to be incapable of being recovered represented pro tanto the trust money, and that the balance remaining is not trust money, but represents

only his own moneys paid into the account. *Brown v. Adams* (L. R. 4 Ch. 764) to the contrary ought not to be followed since the decision in *In re Hallett's Estate.* (13 Ch. D. 696) It is, in my opinion, equally clear that when any of the money drawn out has been invested, and the investment remains in the name or under the control of the trustee, the rest of the balance having been afterwards dissipated by him, he cannot maintain that the investment which remains represents his own money alone, and that what has been spent and can no longer be traced and recovered was the money belonging to the trust. In other words, when the private money of the trustee and that which he held in a fiduciary capacity have been mixed in the same banking account, from which various payments have from time to time been made, then, in order to determine to whom any remaining balance or any investment that may have been paid for out of the account ought to be deemed to belong, the trustee must be debited with all the sums that have been withdrawn and applied to his own use so as to be no longer recoverable, and the trust money in like manner be debited with any sums taken out and duly invested in the names of the proper trustees. The order of priority in which the various withdrawals and investments may have been respectively made is wholly immaterial. I have been referring, of course, to cases where there is only one fiduciary owner or set of cestuis que trust claiming whatever may be left as against the trustee. In the present case there is no balance left. The only investment or property remaining which represents any part of the mixed moneys paid into the banking account is the Oceana shares purchased for £2137. Upon these, therefore, the trust had a charge for the £3000 trust money paid into the account. That is to say, those shares and the proceeds thereof [amounting to a little over £2473] belong to the trust.

It was objected that the investment in the Oceana shares was made at a time when Oatway's own share of the balance to the credit of the account (if the whole had been then justly distributed) would have exceeded £2137, the price of the shares; that he was therefore entitled to withdraw that sum, and might rightly apply it for his own purposes; and that consequently the shares should be held to belong to his estate. To this I answer that he never was entitled to withdraw the £2137 from the account, or, at all events, that he could not be entitled to take that sum from the account and hold it or the investment made therewith, freed from the charge in favour of the trust, unless or until the trust money paid into the account had been first restored, and the trust fund reinstated by due investment of the money in the joint names of the proper trustees, which never was done.'

Questions:

In this case, why was it necessary for the trust to pursue a proprietary rather than a personal claim against the trustee? Why was the trust entitled to the full proceeds from the sale of the shares (ie £2,474), rather than being confined to a lien against those proceeds to secure the maximum possible contribution the trust funds could have made to their purchase (ie £2,137)? Would the response have been different had Oatway not been a trustee of the trust, but instead an innocent volunteer?

In both *Re Hallett's Estate* (**[627]**) and *Re Oatway* (**[630]**), the court did not apply the rule in Clayton's Case (the 'first in, first out' rule re running accounts). In both of these cases its application was seen to work an injustice to the principal as against the defaulting fiduciary. The next extract indicates that the rule will also not be applied as between innocent beneficiaries when to do so would work an injustice. This suggests that the rule in *Clayton's Case* might now require positive justification before it will be applied.

[631] *Barlow Clowes International Ltd (in liq) v Vaughan* [1992] 4 All ER 22, 35–6, 38–9, 42–3 *per* Woolf LJ:

[The issue was to determine the appropriate method for apportioning the assets salvaged after the collapse of Barlow Clowes International Ltd (BCI) amongst the investors with a claim to those assets.]

> 'Mr Walker QC submitted that there are three possible solutions for resolving the competing claims of the investors to the assets which have been recovered. The first solution, which is the one which was adopted by the judge, depends on the rule in *Clayton's Case, Devaynes v Noble* (1816) 1 Mer 572, [1814–23] All ER Rep 1. That case was authority for the principle that, when sums are mixed in a bank account as a result of a series of deposits, withdrawals are treated as withdrawing the money in the same order as the money was deposited. It is accepted that normally the rule in *Clayton's Case* has to be applied to govern the respective interests of a banker and his customer in a bank account, but it is submitted by Mr Walker that the rule should not be applied to the different situation which he submits is at the heart of this appeal. Mr Walker contends that in a case of this sort the application of the *Clayton* rule can and would produce results of a highly arbitrary nature. It could enable a particular group of investors to establish an entitlement to a particular asset . . . to the exclusion of other investors just because they invested on one day of the week rather than another.
>
> . . .
>
> In addition to relying upon the arbitrary results which follow from the 'mechanistic' application of the rule Mr Walker relies upon the expense and time which will be involved in having to apply the rule. With the advent of computer technology it cannot be said the task is impossible but it is clearly complex. The costs involved will result in a depletion of the assets available to the investors. In determining the appropriateness of the machinery used for resolving the claims of the investors among themselves, surely this should be a relevant consideration.
>
> The second solution for resolving the claims of the investors among themselves is the rolling charge or North American solution ('North American' because it is the solution adopted or favoured in preference to the rule in *Clayton's Case* in certain decisions of the courts in the United States and Canada because it is regarded as being manifestly fairer). This solution involves treating credits to a bank account made at different times and from different sources as a blend or cocktail with the result that when a withdrawal is made from the account it is treated as a withdrawal in the same proportions as the different interests in the account (here of the investors) bear to each other at the moment before the withdrawal is made. This solution should produce the most just result, but in this case, as counsel accept, it is not a live contender, since while it might just be possible to perform the exercise the costs involved would be out of all proportion even to the sizeable sums which are here involved.
>
> The third solution (and the only other solution canvassed in argument) is the pari passu ex post facto solution. This involves establishing the total quantum of the assets available and sharing them on a proportionate basis among all the investors who could be said to have contributed to the acquisition of those assets, ignoring the dates on which they made their investment. Mr Walker submits this is the solution which is

appropriate in this case. It has the virtue of relative simplicity and therefore relative economy and also the virtue of being in this case more just than the first solution. It would have the effect of sharing the pool of assets available proportionately among the thousands of investors in a way which reflected the fact that they were all the victims of a 'common misfortune'.

On the evidence which is available to this court as to the circumstances of this case, I have no doubt that, if, as a matter of principle, this court is in a position to adopt the third solution, then that is the solution which is the most appropriate. It is therefore necessary to turn to the authorities to see whether they prevent this court adopting what I would see as being the correct result.

...

The decision in *Re Diplock's Estate* must be considered together with the other judgments to which I have referred. When this is done, short of the House of Lords, it is settled law that the rule in *Clayton's Case can* be applied to determine the extent to which, as between each other, equally innocent claimants are entitled in equity to moneys which have been paid into a bank account and then subject to the movements within that account. However, it does not, having regard to the passages from the judgments in the other authorities cited, follow that the rule has always to be applied for this purpose. In a number of different circumstances the rule has not been applied. The rule need only be applied when it is convenient to do so and when its application can be said to do broad justice having regard to the nature of the competing claims. *Re Hallett's Estate* shows that the rule is displaced where its application would unjustly assist the trustee to the disadvantage of the beneficiaries. In *Re Diplock's Estate* the rule would have been displaced by the trustee subsequently earmarking the beneficiary's funds. It is not applied if this is the intention or presumed intention of the beneficiaries. The rule is sensibly not applied when the cost of applying it is likely to exhaust the fund available for the beneficiaries.

...

For the reasons I have expressed, the approach, in summary, which I would adopt to resolving the issues raised by this appeal are as follows.

(1) While the rule in *Clayton's Case* is prima facie available to determine the interests of investors in a fund into which their investments have been paid, the use of the rule is a matter of convenience and if its application in particular circumstances would be impracticable or result in injustice between the investors it will not be applied if there is a preferable alternative.

(2) Here the rule will not be applied because this would be contrary to either the express or inferred or presumed intention of the investors. If the investments were required by the terms of the investment contract to be paid into a common pool this indicates that the investors did not intend to apply the rule. If the investments were intended to be separately invested, as a result of the investments being collectively misapplied by BCI a common pool of the investments was created. Because of their shared misfortune, the investors will be presumed to have intended the rule not to apply.

(3) As the rule is inapplicable the approach which should be adopted by the court depends on which of the possible alternative solutions is the most satisfactory in the circumstances. If the North American solution is practical this would probably have advantages over the pari passu solution. However, the complications of applying the North American solution in this case make the third solution the most satisfactory.

(4) It must however be remembered that any solution depends on the ability to trace and if the fund had been exhausted (ie the account became overdrawn) the investors whose moneys were in the fund prior to the fund being exhausted will not be able to claim against moneys which were subsequently paid into the fund.

Their claims will be limited to following, if this is possible, any of the moneys paid out of the fund into other assets before it was exhausted.'

Questions:

1. What composite rule encapsulates the approach adopted in both *Re Hallett's Estate* (**[627]**) and *Re Oatway* (**[630]**)? Contrast the application of this composite rule with the application of the 'first in, first out' rule in *Clayton's Case* (1817) 1 Mer 572, 605 (35 ER 781) to the facts of those two cases. Was this composite rule applied in *Barlow Clowes* (**[631]**), or did Woolf LJ 'invent' a further rule?
2. What sort of proprietary interest (if it *is* proprietary) does a claimant have who can elect whether to trace out of a mixture into *either* asset A *or* asset B purchased using the mixed funds? See Millett J in *El Ajou v Dollar Land Holdings plc* [1993] 3 All ER 717, especially 735, 737 (unaffected by the appeal: [1994] 2 All ER 685).

6.5.3 Entitlement to profits: the equitable tracing rules

As noted earlier (see the introduction to Section 6.5, above), one of the advantages commonly thought to be associated with equitable tracing is the consequential ability to assert an equitable proprietary claim to any profits derived from dealings with the original asset or its traceable proceeds. In short, the value of the claim to the traceable proceeds (should it be possible to establish such a claim) may be greater than the value of the claim to the original property.

Re Oatway (**[630]** above) illustrates the potential. There, the beneficiaries of the trust fund were found to be entitled to equitable ownership of the proceeds of sale of shares which had been purchased without authority using their trust funds. It was irrelevant that the sum of money misappropriated by the trustee for the share purchase was less than the proceeds derived from the subsequent sale of the shares.

In reading the next series of extracts, the crucial issue is to determine when and why this result might be appropriate. There are a number of possible reasons:

(i) The result may follow only when the defendant is expressly or impliedly authorised to deal (or refrain from dealing) with the original asset on behalf of the claimant, so that—because of the pre-existing relationship between the parties[28]—the claimant can ratify any unauthorised dealings, and only then can claim any profits derived from such dealings. (Although see the comments of Millett LJ in *Boscawen v Bajwa* (**[629]** above).)

(ii) Alternatively, and more broadly, the result may follow automatically from the law of property. The claimant's equitable ownership of the original asset may

[28] This can be a relationship which is unilaterally assumed by one party, as, for example, might be the case with a trustee. It remains a moot point whether a thief or a fraudster might fall into this category.

entail that any profits derived from that asset inevitably belong to the claimant.[29] If that is the case, then tracing is not simply a process designed to preserve the attributes of the initial claim, but has the additional consequence that it automatically determines ownership of the proceeds of the tracing exercise. This approach has the attraction of simplicity, but arguably it misconceives the nature of equitable ownership and, in particular, the inter-relationship between equitable property rights and the obligations owed to the beneficiary of these rights by the legal owner of the property. (Although see the common law approach adopted in *F C Jones & Sons (Trustee in Bankruptcy) v Jones* at **[619]** above.)

(iii) Finally, and more broadly still, the result may follow from the law of unjust enrichment. Any profit made from the use of another person's property may constitute an unjust enrichment which must be returned to the owner of the property. The equitable tracing rules may then permit the claimant to claim a proprietary remedy rather than a personal one. This is probably instinctively the most attractive approach, yet it might perhaps lead to some strange results. Certainly the deliberate use of another's property for profit-making ought to be remedied, but the laws of unjust enrichment operate without the need for fault on the part of the defendant. If the unjust enrichment analysis is appropriate,[30] then an innocent defendant who profits from the use of another's property will be liable to make restitution of the benefits. Consider a case where an innocent defendant receives £100 which belongs in equity to the claimant. If, as a result of the receipt, the defendant donates £50 to charity, then it is generally conceded that the change of position defence will cause the proprietary claim to abate to £50. This is so even if the £100 remains identifiable in the defendant's hands (as might be the case if the donation to charity was made from the defendant's other resources). In short, the unjust enrichment claim is distinct from the physical identification of the property, although if the property representing the enrichment can be identified, then the claim may sometimes[31] be proprietary rather than merely personal. Now if the defendant, instead of donating the fund, invests it in shares which increase in value to £200, what are the unjust enrichment consequences? If the defendant spends his own funds on the shares, even if the expenditure is motivated by the initial receipt, there is never any suggestion that the claimant should be entitled to the shares. But if the defendant fortuitously spends the claimant's £100 on the shares, then the unjust enrichment approach would see the claimant as entitled to them. The more appropriate response may be simply to give the claimant a *lien* on the (traceable) shares to secure repayment of the £100 due under the unjust enrichment claim, not to give the claimant equitable ownership of the shares.

The extracts below illustrate the approach taken by the courts to these issues.

[29] To what extent are purchase money resulting trusts based on this idea? (See Chapter 5, especially Section 5.4.)

[30] ie if the unjust factor is simply use of another's property.

[31] Precisely when is a most difficult issue: see Chapter 5.

[632] ***Re Tilley's Will Trusts*** **[1967] 1 Ch 1179, 1188–9, 1192–4** ***per*** **Ungoed-Thomas J:**

[Mrs Tilley received £2,237 on trust for her daughter and son. In breach of trust she mixed this fund with her private funds in a bank account which also provided her with substantial overdraft facilities. She used funds from this account to purchase houses which substantially increased in value over time, so that at her death the fund stood at £94,000. The court decided that the beneficiaries were only entitled to a charge on the mixed fund to secure return of £2,237 plus interest; they were not entitled to a proportionate share of the profits of the investments.]

'It seems to me that when Lord Parker says [in *Sinclair v Brougham* [1914] AC 398, 442] . . . that "In such a case [where an asset is purchased with a mixed fund] the beneficiary can only claim a charge on the property for the amount of the trust money expended in the purchase" he is merely contrasting the charge with the right to take the whole property which is the matter he had just been dealing with; Lord Parker is not, as I see it, addressing his mind to the question of whether the beneficiary could claim a proportion of the property corresponding to his own contribution to its purchase. This interpretation of the passage seems to me to be the only interpretation which in principle is consistent with Lord Parker's view expressed at the end of the passage which I quoted, and to which I drew particular attention, where the purchase is made by the trustee wholly out of moneys of two different beneficiaries. In that case he says that they are not limited to charges for their respective amounts, but are together entitled to the whole property. But if each of two beneficiaries can, in co-operation with the other, take the whole property which has resulted in profit from the trustee's action in buying it with their money, why can they not do so if the trustee himself has also paid some part of the purchase price? And if two beneficiaries can do so, why not one? Indeed, it was conceded in argument that the passage should be so interpreted as suggested.

In Snell's Principles of Equity, 26th ed. (1966), the law is thus stated at page 315:

"Where the trustee mixes trust money with his own, the equities are clearly unequal. Accordingly, the beneficiaries are entitled to a first charge on the mixed fund, or on any land, securities or other assets purchased with it. Thus if the trustee purchases shares with part of the mixed fund, leaving enough of it to repay the trust moneys, and then dissipates the balance, the beneficiaries' charge binds the shares; for although under the rule in *In re Hallett's Estate* (13 Ch D 696, [**[627]** above]) the trustee is presumed to have bought the shares out of his own money, the charge attached to the entire fund, and could be discharged only by restoring the trust moneys. Where the property purchased has increased in value, the charge will be not merely for the amount of the trust moneys but for a proportionate part of the increased value. Thus if the trustee purchases land with £500 of his own money and £1,000 of trust moneys, and the land doubles in value, he would be profiting from his breach of trust if he were entitled to all except £1,000; the beneficiaries are accordingly entitled to a charge on the land for £2,000."

For the defendants it has been rightly admitted that if a trustee wrongly uses trust money to pay the whole of the purchase price in respect of the purchase of an asset a beneficiary can elect either to treat the purchased asset as trust property or to treat the purchased asset as security for the recouping of the trust money. It was further conceded that this right of election by a beneficiary also applies where the asset is purchased by a trustee in part out of his own money and in part out of the trust moneys, so that he may, if he wishes, require the asset to be treated as trust property with regard to that proportion of it which the trust moneys contributed to its purchase.

Does this case fall within that principle? . . .

In the circumstances of this case there would be a charge on the properties purchased by Mrs. Tilley out of the bank account as security for repayment of the £2,237 trust moneys paid into her bank account in accordance with the principle in *In re Oatway*, ([1903] 2 Ch 356, [**[630]** above]) but that would be immaterial as the £2,237 is readily available out of Mrs. Tilley's estate.

But can the beneficiary claim the proportion of the proceeds of sale of [the two properties which the figures indicated were part-funded by trust monies]. . ., plus costs? These trust moneys bore a small proportion to the purchase price of the properties. Mrs. Tilley had ample overdraft facilities to pay the price without relying on these trust sums at the time of the . . . purchase, for she had an overdraft of over £22,000 apparently within her own overdraft facilities, and presumably properly secured, and this would make any contribution of [trust monies] negligible. She had throughout mixed her personal finances and those of her husband's estate, whether paying that estate's debts when it was without ready money or paying its proceeds of sale into her account. The £179 and the £82 10 were clearly not trust moneys deliberately taken by Mrs. Tilley out of the trust fund for the purpose of investing in property in her name. They merely avoided, to the extent of their amount, the use of Mrs. Tilley's ample overdraft facilities, and in the case of the £179 that advantage was lost after two months by her bank account showing a credit, although it went into debit again 17 months later. And no interest in these trust sums was lost to any other beneficiary as Mrs. Tilley was herself the life-tenant.

All these considerations appear to me to indicate overwhelmingly that Mrs. Tilley was not deliberately using trust moneys to invest in or contribute towards or otherwise buy properties in her own name and the whole course of dealing with the trust funds and the bank accounts and the properties purchased and their history, which I have mentioned, indicate that what happened was that Mrs. Tilley mixed the trust moneys and her own in the bank account but did not rely on the trust moneys for any of the purchases. If, as it was suggested for the defendants, the correct test whether a beneficiary is entitled to adopt a purchase by a trustee to which his trust moneys have contributed and thus claim a due proportion of its profits, is a subjective test, depending on the trustee's intention to use the trust moneys to contribute to the purchase then in my view there was no such intention and the beneficiary is not so entitled. But my conclusion about the trustee's intention is based not on any direct evidence but on the circumstantial evidence which I have mentioned. If, of course, a trustee deliberately uses trust money to contribute with his own money to buy property in his own name, then I would see no difficulty in enabling a beneficiary to adopt the purchase and claim a share of any resulting profits. But the subjective test does not appear to me to be exclusive, or indeed adequate, if it is the only test.

It seems to me that if, having regard to all the circumstances of the case objectively considered, it appears that the trustee has in fact, whatever his intention, laid out trust moneys in or towards a purchase, then the beneficiaries are entitled to the property purchased and any profits which it produces to the extent to which it has been paid for out of the trust moneys. But, even by this objective test, it appears to me that the trust moneys were not in this case so laid out. It seems to me, on a proper appraisal of all the facts of this particular case, that Mrs. Tilley's breach halted at the mixing of the funds in her bank account. Although properties bought out of those funds would, like the bank account itself, at any rate if the moneys in the bank account were inadequate, be charged with repayment of the trust moneys which then would stand in the same position as the bank account, yet the trust moneys were not invested in properties at all but merely went in reduction of Mrs. Tilley's overdraft which was in reality the source of the purchase-moneys.

The plaintiff's claim therefore fails and he is entitled to no more than repayment of the half of the £2,237, interest not being in issue. £2,237 is readily available, which makes the existence of any charge for its security immaterial.'

[633] *Scott v Scott* (1963) 109 CLR 649 (Aust HCt), 660–4 *per* McTiernan, Taylor and Owen JJ (in a joint judgment of the Court):

[W H Scott was one of the trustees of his deceased wife's estate. In breach of trust, although with the consent of all the of-age beneficiaries and the other trustees, the family home was sold and a new property purchased. The new property was purchased by W H Scott absolutely, subject to a mortgage to the trust and to one of the trustees to secure loans of £1,014 and £500 respectively. W H Scott provided the balance of the purchase price, less than £200. More than 15 years later, W H Scott took out a new mortgage over the property from an independent source, and repaid the trust estate and the other trustee. He did not pay interest to the trust estate, claiming that as life tenant of the estate he was not required to do so. After his death, the trustees sought a declaration that, subject to the existing mortgage, the house was held on trust for the wife's estate.]

'What must be borne in mind in the case is that the order appealed from rests upon a twofold basis and it is on this basis that the respondents' argument primarily attempts to support it. It rests upon the liability of W.H. Scott to make good a breach of trust and also upon his liability to account for a profit which accrued to him, or to his estate, as the result of his misuse of trust funds. These are two different and distinct notions. A trustee's liability to account for profits accruing to him may arise without any positive breach of trust; on the other hand, a trustee may become liable to make good a misapplication of trust moneys with interest even though he has made no profit by the misapplication. But where the expenditure of moneys constitutes a breach of trust the remedies may overlap for the beneficiaries may have both a proprietary and personal remedy and, of course, if they choose to pursue the former this will be the full measure of the relief available to them.

There is, of course, abundant authority for the proposition that if trust moneys have been exclusively used in the purchase of property the beneficiary may elect to take the property itself. There is also authority for the proposition that if trust funds from two different estates are exclusively used by a common trustee in the purchase of land in his name which has increased in value each estate will be held entitled to a proportionate part of the increase: *The Lord Provost etc. of Edinburgh v. Lord Advocate* (1879) 4 App Cas 823 . In such a case it would be unthinkable that each estate should be entitled merely to a charge for the amount misapplied with, perhaps, some allowance for interest, and the trustee left with a residual profit. Why, then, should a trustee who has mixed moneys of his own with trust moneys for the purpose of purchasing lands which have greatly increased in value be held entitled, upon repayment of the trust moneys misapplied, to retain the whole of any profit which has resulted, at least in part, from the misuse of the trust moneys?

Considerations such as these carried considerable weight with the learned trial judge and in a careful and learned judgment he discussed the classic cases of *Docker v. Somes* (1834) 2 My & K 655 (39 ER 1095) and *Vyse v. Foster* (1874) 7 HL 318 not only for the purpose of emphasizing that a trustee may not make a profit out of the trust, but also to show that his duty to account is not necessarily confined to cases where trust funds have been wrongly embarked in the trustee's business but extends to "all profits received by a trustee who deals with the trust fund for his own advantage". It is, we think, important to observe that the liability of a trustee to account in such cases is not confined to a limited group of categories but extends to all cases where such a profit has, in fact, been made. We agree with his Honour's analysis of the cases to which he referred and we agree with his conclusion. The argument to the contrary is, we think, based upon an erroneous conception of the true principle. No doubt it is true to say that in this case the estate was entitled to assert a lien upon the property purchased with the mixed fund to secure the amount misapplied. But it is erroneous to say that in the circumstances of this case this was the full measure of the relief to which the estate was entitled. It was, of course, conceded that where property is, in breach of trust, bought exclusively with trust moneys the beneficiaries may, instead of pursuing their personal right against the trustee, elect to take the property. Again it was conceded that where property is purchased, in breach of trust, with a "mixed fund" the beneficiaries may, if the property is "specifically severable", elect to take such part thereof as bears the same proportion to the whole as the misapplied trust moneys bore to the purchase price. Property may be thought to be "specifically severable" where it consists of bonds or a parcel of shares: *Brady v. Stapleton* (1952) 88 CLR 322. This may also be the position if the property purchased consists of a flock of sheep or a herd of cattle or so many bales of wool and so on though difficulties might arise where the severance could not be made at a point precisely commensurate with the amount of trust moneys misapplied. This, however, is by the way. In its final analysis the appellant's argument on this branch of the case seems to rest upon the assertion that it cannot be said that there was any liability to account for any part of the profit which accrued to the trustee or, ultimately, to his estate, unless it can be established that the estate of the testatrix became entitled to a beneficial interest in the property which W.H. Scott purchased. This, it was said, could not upon the authorities be established. Upon this latter proposition we will make some observations presently. But for the moment we are content to assume that this could not be established for the basic contention finds no support in the innumerable and varied cases in which trustees have been held liable to account for profits arising from the misapplication of trust moneys.

Nevertheless it is asserted that in cases such as the present where the breach of trust is said to have been constituted by the application of trust moneys together with other moneys in the purchase of property which is not "specifically severable", there is no liability to account for profit made on a resale. This is so, it is said, because equity provides the beneficiaries only with a lien to secure the amount of trust moneys applied in breach of trust and denies them the right to claim a proportionate interest in the property. But even if these propositions should be fully accepted what have they to say concerning the liability of a trustee to account for profits made by the improper application of trust funds for the trustee's own advantage? We may, for instance, take the case of a trustee who, in breach of trust, purchases shares for £2,000 by the use of £1,000 of trust moneys together with £1,000 of his own. There is no doubt that the beneficiaries might elect, either, to take one-half of the shares or, alternatively, to claim a lien on the shares for £1,000. But they may not know of the purchase and do neither. Then suppose that prior to any election by the beneficiaries the trustee sells the shares for £3,000 and retains the proceeds in his hands. Is it to be thought that the right of the beneficiaries at this stage will be limited to a claim on those moneys for the specific sum of £1,000? The case, of course, would be one where the beneficiaries had never become entitled to any proprietary interest in the shares and where the proceeds of sale were not attributable in any measure to the sale of property to which they had become beneficially entitled. But there can be no doubt that they would be entitled not only to have the sum originally misapplied made good but also to obtain one-half of the resultant profit. We think the same conclusion must inevitably follow even if the property purchased with the mixed fund is property which is not "specifically severable" and that the argument to the contrary must be rejected.

We have spoken of the profit which accrued to the trustee but it is said that if there was a profit in his lifetime it was an unrealized profit and that no obligation could arise until he had sold the property at an enhanced price and so realized a profit. But we think that this argument is without substance. Clearly enough the estate was entitled as against W. H. Scott to seek an order for sale to enforce its lien and upon any such sale the profit would have been realized. It is true, no doubt, that if the property had not increased in value the trustee, in his lifetime, might have chosen to avoid a sale by repayment of the amount for which the lien subsisted. But no such choice can be said to have been open to him in this case for he could not be allowed to escape his liability to account merely by repayment of the amount of trust moneys misapplied. Accordingly, we take the view that repayment of the sum of £1,014 in 1959 did not operate to defeat the beneficiaries' right to a sale; this, we think, could have been defeated only by an accounting for profits as on a notional sale. For this purpose the learned judge of first instance took the value of the property as at the commencement of the suit. As it was then worth somewhat less than it was at the date of W. H. Scott's death and there is no cross-appeal it is unnecessary for us to express any opinion concerning the time at which the value of the property should be ascertained.

. . .

The matter which we reserved for subsequent comment was concerned with the second ground upon which the respondent sought to support the order. It was, in effect, that, notwithstanding the fact that the property which W. H. Scott purchased could not be said to be "specifically severable" property, the estate, nevertheless, became entitled to claim a proportionate interest in it. We think, in principle, that there is much to be said for this proposition. Some support may, perhaps, be found for it in *Lord Provost, etc. of Edinburgh v. Lord Advocate* (1879) 4 App Cas 823 and we observe that equity has had no difficulty in holding parties beneficially entitled to proportionate shares in property where they have jointly provided the purchase money and title is taken in the name of one only: *The Venture* [1908] P 218, at p 229 ; *Diwell v. Farnes* [1959] 2 All ER 379 ; *Bull v. Bull* [1955] 1 QB 234 ; and *Gravesend Corporation v. Kent County Council* [1935] 1 KB 339. It was said in argument that the principle applied in these cases rests upon the intention, or the presumed intention, of the parties. But if this be a fundamental distinction it introduces a curious anomaly into the law as will appear from the following illustration. If A. contributes one-half of the purchase price for the purpose of purchasing Blackacre and B., providing the other one-half, takes Blackacre in his own name they will each be beneficially entitled to a one-half interest. But if B. in breach of trust, purchases, not Blackacre, but Whiteacre, A. will be denied any right to a like proportionate interest in that property. This, of course, would follow from the appellant's argument and we confess to some difficulty in seeing why this should be so. It is, however, unnecessary for us to pronounce upon the respondents' alternative argument but we cannot fail to observe that the Courts of the United States have carried the matter to its logical conclusion. In effect, they have held that where trust moneys are mixed with moneys of the trustee and the mixed fund is used in acquiring other property which is not "specifically severable", the beneficiaries are, nevertheless, entitled to claim a proportionate interest in the property. The matter is dealt with at length in *Scott on*

Trusts 2nd ed. p. 3289 et seq. and a number of cases are cited in support of the proposition. We think it necessary to refer, however, only to passages in the *Restatement of the Law, Trusts*, vol. 1, (1935) pp. 540, 541 and the *Corpus Juris Secundum* vol. 90, pp. 844–849 and an interesting judgment of Learned Hand J. in *Primeau v. Granfield* (1911) 184 Fed R 480 in which he rejects the contention that the proposition in question is in conflict with observations made in *In re Hallett's Estate* (1880) 13 Ch D 696 . However, as we have already said, it is unnecessary to express any concluded view on the point and it may well be left for further consideration.'

Questions:

The trust was held to be entitled to a proportionate share of the unauthorised investment, thereby benefiting proportionately from the increase in property values over the period of the investment. Does the Australian High Court's analysis suggest that the trust might have successfully argued for recovery of *all* the investment gains?[32] Is this desirable? How can this case be reconciled with *Re Tilley's Will Trusts* (**[632]**)?

The next extract concerns a defendant who is not an express trustee, but a constructive trustee.

[634] ***Lake v Bayliss* [1974] 1 WLR 1073, 1074–6 *per* Walton J:**

[The case concerns real property, not personal property, but (apart from the establishment of the initial constructive trust) nothing in the reasoning seems to turn on that fact. The facts are rather unusual. Miss Bayliss entered into a written agreement to sell a certain parcel of land to Dr Mullen. The consideration for the transfer was that Dr Mullen withdraw two writs which he had issued against Miss Bayliss, and that he assume certain liability in respect of a planning application. Miss Bayliss then proceeded to dispose of the land to a third party for £50,000, notwithstanding that Dr Mullen had issued a writ for specific performance of his agreement. The third party purchaser appeared totally innocent in all this. Miss Bayliss' solicitor received the purchase price from the third party and then sought directions from the court as to how it should be applied.]

'I take first the way it is presented from the point of view of Dr Mullen. On his behalf Mr. Millett has urged that although the relief which he is seeking is unusual, one has to go back to first principles, and if one goes back to first principles there is really no difficulty in the matter. He says that it is one of the standing doctrines of the court that upon a contract for the transfer of property being entered into the vendor or intending transferor becomes a trustee for the purchaser or transferee. Admittedly, it is a qualified trusteeship. It does not have all the usual incidence of a bare trusteeship for a cestui que trust, and of course the most glaring and obvious departure from such normal incidence is that the trustee has his own interest, in the shape of the receipt of the purchase money, to protect. Of course he has a lien on the property until he has been paid his

[32] In its judgment, the court expressly noted that it was not asked to consider this possibility, and so it did not.

purchase money in the normal course of events. But, says Mr. Millett, as to the basic relationship in regard to the land contracted to be sold or transferred, no matter what may be the case in relation to other collateral matters, such as moneys paid under a contract of insurance or receipts under derequisitioning procedures, there is no doubt at all that the property itself is held as by a trustee. That being the case, he says, if in fact before the contract comes to be completed the vendor wrongfully—as is the allegation here—sells the property then the purchaser is entitled, if he is so minded, to say that what has happened is that the vendor has sold trust property, and he is entitled under those circumstances to follow the trust property and say when it comes to the final performance of the contract that he will take the proceeds of sale instead of the property.

There is certainly a dearth of authority in the books on this point, and Mr. Millett points out that the reason is, in his view, that no less than four matters must concur before it is worthwhile for a purchaser to pursue this remedy. The first is that the vendor must have sold the property twice over, and that in itself is rare because most people honourably fulfil their obligations. Secondly, for some reason the registration of an estate contract by the purchaser must either not have taken place, or if it has taken place it must have been for some rare reason, such as an error in searching, of no effect. Thirdly—and of course this is most vital—the purchaser must be in time to intercept the purchase money, to trace the purchase money. Once it has been paid into an overdrawn bank account or something of that nature, which is the only likely occasion on which these prior circumstances would concur, it is too late to follow it. Lastly, for some reason the purchaser must prefer to pursue the tracing of the purchase money rather than to pursue his remedy in damages. Where the vendor is solvent, of course there is really very little in it. Again, where the vendor has a lien on the trust property for a purchase price, which will normally be very roughly the amount of the sale price, there is not much in it, and probably it is hardly worthwhile in these days seeking to trace the proceeds of sale rather than simply taking the remedy in damages. But of course in the present case the consideration to be provided by Dr. Mullen is rather special, and if he cannot in fact trace the purchase money in the way suggested, he will of necessity be forced into a completely different contract from the one which he intended to enter into, because he will be left with the rights which he was going to give up in exchange for the land, and he will get nothing but damages. That will be a very extraordinary result as far as he is concerned.

Authority appears to be silent on this save for one case which the industry of Mr. Millett has unearthed, a decision of Lord Eldon L.C. in *Daniels v. Davison* (1809) 16 Ves. Jun. 249. I can go straight away to the passage in the judgment of Lord Eldon L.C. on this point where he says, at p. 254:

> "My judgment on that point"—after dealing with other points in the case—"lays out of consideration the question, whether, taking Cole not to be affected with notice, Davison, the vendor, is to be considered in equity as holding the money, derived from the second purchase, viz. the difference between the prices, in trust for the person, to whom he had first agreed to sell the estate. The estate by the first contract becoming the property of the vendee, the effect is, that the vendor was seised as a trustee for him; and the question then would be, whether the vendor should be permitted to sell for his own advantage the estate, of which he was so seised in trust; or should not be considered as selling it for the benefit of that person, for whom by the first agreement he became trustee; and therefore liable to account. It is not however necessary to decide that point; . . ."

It is perfectly true that Lord Eldon L.C. there puts it in the form of a query, but I think that it is to be understood in the sense that he would have given, if pressed, the answer to that query that that indeed represented the law.

Again, the industry of Mr. Millett has found out that Sir George Jessel, when Solicitor-General, arguing the leading case of *Shaw v. Foster* (1872) L.R. 5 H.L. 321, 327, stated flatly that

> "*Daniels v. Davison* shews that after a contract for the sale of an estate, if the vendor sells to another person for valuable consideration he is accountable for the money as a trust."

In my opinion that is absolutely in line with authority, and entirely represents the law.

. . .

Miss Cockburn did raise a very good point, that is to say, how far does this concept of trusteeship go? Does it follow, for example, if Mr. Millett was right, that if a vendor obtained better offers for the property after having entered into a contract for sale, he would be under an obligation to pass them on? If so, she said, that would be an extraordinary result. I do not think it is such an extraordinary result, but I do not think that that is the sort of question—good question though it is—that can be asked in vacuo. I think one must have a concrete case in which that sort of thing happens before one knows what the duty of the vendor is. After all, in most cases one will know that the purchaser is purchasing the property for his own occupation. Under those circumstances, quite clearly, unless the subsequent offer was astronomical, there would be no real reason for thinking that it would be of any interest to the purchaser. In other cases it may be that the vendor well knows that the purchaser is merely buying for speculation and, although I do not say that it will necessarily be the case, I can see that under certain circumstances it might very well be the case that the vendor ought to pass the offers on.'

Also see:

Tang Man Sit v Capacious Investments Ltd [1996] AC 514 (PC).

Questions:

1. Does it appear to make any difference that the defendant is not an express trustee, but a constructive trustee?
2. What *should* be the outcome if the defendant resells the property at a substantial profit?

This final extract is a long one, but it highlights the issues at stake.

[635] *Foskett v McKeown* [2000] 2 WLR 1299 (HL), 1302, 1304–1307 *per* Lord Browne-Wilkinson, 1308, 1310 *per* Lord Steyn, 1311–12 *per* Lord Hoffmann, 1315–16, 1320 *per* Lord Hope, 1322–37, 1340 *per* Lord Millett:

[A trustee misappropriated trust funds to pay part of the premiums on a policy of life insurance which was held on another trust for the trustee's own children. When the trustee committed suicide, the insurance payout amounted to over £1million. The House of Lords, by a 3:2 majority, decided that the beneficiaries of the defrauded trust were entitled to trace their misappropriated funds into the life insurance payout and claim a proportionate interest in it. The Court of Appeal decision, which was overturned, is reported at [1998] Ch 265 (CA). The detailed facts are summarised in Lord Browne-Wilkinson's judgment.]

Lord Browne-Wilkinson:

'There are many cases in which the court has to decide which of two innocent parties is to suffer from the activities of a fraudster. This case, unusually, raises the converse question: which of two innocent parties is to benefit from the activities of the fraudster. In my judgment, in the context of this case the two types of case fall to be decided on exactly the same principles, viz. by determining who enjoys the ownership of the property in which the loss or the unexpected benefit is reflected.

On 6 November 1986, Mr. Murphy effected a whole-life policy ("the policy") with Barclays Life Assurance Co. Ltd. ("the insurers") in the sum of £1m. at an annual premium of £10,220. The policy (which was issued on 27 January 1987) provided that on the death of Mr. Murphy a specified death benefit became payable, such benefit being the greater of (1) the sum assured (£1m.) and (2) the aggregate value of units notionally allocated under the terms of the policy to the policy at their bid price on the day of the receipt by the Insurers of a written notice of death. The policy stated that "in consideration of the first premium already paid and of the further premiums payable and subject to the conditions of this policy the company will on the death of the life assured pay to the policy holder or his successors in title ("the policy holder") the benefits specified." [Mr. Murphy later appointed the policy and all moneys payable thereunder upon trust (in the events which happened) as to one-tenth for Mrs. Brigette Murphy and as to nine-tenths for his three children equally.]

Although primarily a whole-life policy assuring the sum assured of £1m., the policy had an additional feature, viz. a notional investment content which served three purposes. First, it determined the surrender value of the policy. Second, it determined the alternative calculation of the death benefit if the value of the notionally allocated units exceeded the sum assured of £1m. Third, the investment element was used to pay for the cost of life cover after the payment of the second premium in November 1987. By condition 4 of the policy, units were notionally allocated to the policy upon receipt of the second and all subsequent premiums. By condition 6 of the policy, upon receipt of each premium resulting in the notional allocation of units under condition 4, the Insurers cancelled sufficient units to meet the cost of life cover for the next year. Condition 10 provided for conversion of the policy into a paid-up policy: units would thereafter continue to be cancelled under condition 6 so long as there were units available for that purpose. As soon as there were no units available, no death benefit or surrender value was to be available under the policy. Sir Richard Scott V.-C., [1998] Ch. 265, 275, summarised the position as follows:

> "if a premium is not paid, then (provided at least two years' premiums have been paid) the policy is converted into a paid-up policy and units that have been allocated to the policy are applied annually in meeting the cost of life insurance until all the allocated units have been used up. Only at that point will the policy lapse."

Five premiums were paid, in November 1986, 1987, 1988, 1989 and 1990. The 1986 and 1987 premiums were paid by Mr. Murphy out of his own resources. The 1989 and 1990 premiums were paid out of [trust] moneys misappropriated by Mr. Murphy [as trustee] from the plaintiffs [as beneficiaries under the trust]. The source of the 1988 premium is disputed: unconditional leave to defend on issues relating to this premium has been granted.

. . . .

As to the appeal, at the conclusion of the hearing I considered that the majority of the Court of Appeal were correct and would have dismissed the appeal. However, having read the draft speech of Lord Millett I have changed my mind and for the reasons which he gives I would allow the appeal. But, as we are differing from the majority of the Court of Appeal I will say a word or two about the substance of the case and then deal with one minor matter on which I do not agree with my noble and learned friend Lord Millett.

The crucial factor in this case is to appreciate that the purchasers are claiming a proprietary interest in the policy moneys and that such proprietary interest is not dependent on any discretion vested in the court. Nor is the purchasers' claim based on unjust enrichment. It is based on the assertion by the purchasers of their equitable proprietary interest in identified property.

The first step is to identify the interest of the purchasers: it is their absolute equitable interest in the moneys originally held by Mr. Deasy on the express trusts of the purchasers trust deed. This case does not involve any question of resulting or constructive trusts. The only trusts at issue are the express trusts of the purchasers trust deed. Under those express trusts the purchasers were entitled to equitable interests in the original moneys paid to Mr. Deasy by the purchasers. Like any other equitable proprietary interest, those equitable proprietary interests under the purchasers trust deed which originally existed in the moneys paid to Mr. Deasy now exist in any other property which, in law, now represents the original trust assets. Those equitable interests under the purchasers trust deed are also enforceable against whoever for the time being holds those assets other than someone who is a bona fide purchaser for value of the legal interest without notice or a person who claims through such a purchaser. No question of a bona fide purchaser arises in the present case: the children are mere volunteers under the policy Trust. Therefore the critical question is whether the assets now subject to the express trusts of the purchasers trust deed comprise any part of the policy moneys, a question which depends on the rules of tracing. If, as a result of tracing, it can be said that certain of the policy moneys are what now represent part of the assets subject to the trusts of the purchasers trust deed, then as a matter of English property law the purchasers have an absolute interest in such moneys. There is no discretion vested in the court. There is no room for any consideration whether, in the circumstances of this particular case, it is in a moral sense "equitable" for the purchasers to be so entitled. The rules establishing equitable proprietary interests and their enforceability against certain parties have been developed over the centuries and are an integral part of the property law of England. It is a fundamental error to think that, because certain property rights are equitable rather than legal, such rights are in some way discretionary. This case does not depend on whether it is fair, just and reasonable to give the purchasers an interest as a result of which the court in its discretion provides a remedy. It is a case of hard-nosed property rights.

Can then the sums improperly used from the purchaser's moneys be traced into the policy moneys? Tracing is a process whereby assets are identified. I do not now want to enter into the dispute whether the legal and equitable rules of tracing are the same or differ. The question does not arise in this case. The question of tracing which does arise is whether the rules of tracing are those regulating tracing through a mixed fund or those regulating the position when moneys of one person have been innocently expended on the property of another. In the former case (mixing of funds) it is established law that the mixed fund belongs proportionately to those whose moneys were mixed. In the latter case it is equally clear that money expended on maintaining or improving the property of another normally gives rise, at the most, to a proprietary lien to recover the moneys so expended. In certain cases the rules of tracing in such a case may give rise to no proprietary interest at all if to give such interest would be unfair: see *In re Diplock; Diplock v Wintle* [1948] Ch. 465, 548.

Both Sir Richard Scott V.-C. and Hobhouse L.J. considered that the payment of a premium on someone else's policy was more akin to an improvement to land than to the mixing of separate trust moneys in one account. Hobhouse L.J. was additionally influenced by the fact that the payment of the fourth and fifth premiums out of the purchasers' moneys conferred no benefit on the children: the policy was theirs and, since the first two premiums had already been paid, the policy would not have lapsed even if the fourth and fifth premiums had not been paid.

Cases where the money of one person has been expended on improving or maintaining the physical property of another raise special problems. The property left at the end of the day is incapable of being physically divided into its separate constituent assets, i.e. the land and the money spent on it. Nor can the rules for tracing moneys through a mixed fund apply: the essence of tracing through a mixed fund is the ability to re-divide the mixed fund into its constituent parts pro rata according to the value of the contributions made to it. The question which arises in this case is whether, for tracing purposes, the payments of the fourth and fifth premiums on a policy which, up to that date, had been the sole property of the children for tracing purposes fall to be treated as analogous to the expenditure of cash on the physical property of another or as analogous to the mixture of moneys in a bank account. If the former analogy is to be preferred, the maximum amount recoverable by the purchasers will be the amount of the fourth and fifth premiums plus interest: if the latter analogy is preferred the children and the other purchasers will share the policy moneys pro rata.

The speech of my noble and learned friend Lord Millett demonstrates why the analogy with moneys mixed in an account is the correct one. Where a trustee in breach of trust mixes money in his own bank account with trust moneys, the moneys in the account belong to the trustee personally and to the beneficiaries under the trust rateably according to the amounts respectively provided. On a proper analysis, there are "no moneys in the account" in the sense of physical cash. Immediately before the improper mixture, the trustee had a chose in action being his right against the bank to demand a payment of the credit balance on his account. Immediately after the mixture, the trustee had the same chose in action (i.e. the right of action against the bank) but its value reflected in part the amount of the beneficiaries' moneys wrongly paid in. There is no doubt that in such a case of moneys mixed in a bank account the credit balance on the account belongs to the trustee and the beneficiaries rateably according to their respective contributions.

So in the present case. Immediately before the payment of the fourth premium, the trust property held in trust for the children was a chose in action i.e. the bundle of rights enforceable under the policy against the insurers. The trustee, by paying the fourth premium out of the moneys subject to the purchasers trust deed, wrongly mixed the value of the premium with the value of the policy. Thereafter, the trustee for the children held the same chose in action (i.e. the policy) but it reflected the value of both contributions. The case, therefore, is wholly analogous to that where moneys are mixed in a bank account. It follows that, in my judgment, both the policy and the policy moneys belong to the children and the trust fund subject to the purchasers trust deed rateably according to their respective contributions to the premiums paid.

The contrary view appears to be based primarily on the ground that to give the purchasers a rateable share of the policy moneys is not to reverse an unjust enrichment but to give the purchasers a wholly unwarranted windfall. I do not myself quibble at the description of it being "a windfall" on the facts of this case. But this windfall is enjoyed because of the rights which the purchasers enjoy under the law of property. A man under whose land oil is discovered enjoys a very valuable windfall but no one suggests that he, as owner of the property, is not entitled to the windfall which goes with his property right. We are not dealing with a claim in unjust enrichment.

Moreover the argument based on windfall can be, and is, much over-stated. It is said that the fourth and fifth premiums paid out of the purchasers' moneys did not increase the value of the policy in any way: the first and second premiums were, by themselves, sufficient under the unusual terms of the policy to pay all the premiums falling due without any assistance from the fourth and fifth premiums: even if the fourth and fifth premiums had not been paid the policy would have been in force at the time of Mr. Murphy's death. Therefore, it is asked, what value has been derived from the fourth and fifth premiums which can justify giving the purchasers a pro rata share. In my judgment this argument does not reflect the true position. It is true that, *in the events which have happened*, the fourth and fifth premiums were not required to keep the policy on foot until the death of Mr. Murphy. But at the times the fourth and fifth premiums were paid (which must be the dates at which the beneficial interests in the policy were established) it was wholly uncertain what the future would bring. What if Mr. Murphy had not died when he did? Say he had survived for another five years? The premiums paid in the fourth and fifth years would in those events have been directly responsible for keeping the policy in force until his death since the first and second premiums would long since have been exhausted in keeping the policy on foot. In those circumstances, would it be said that the purchasers were entitled to 100 per cent. of the policy moneys? In my judgment, the beneficial ownership of the policy, and therefore the policy moneys, cannot depend upon how events turn out. The rights of the parties in the policy, one way or another, were fixed when the relevant premiums were paid when the future was unknown.

For these reasons and the much fuller reasons given by Lord Millett, I would allow the appeal and declare that the policy moneys were held in trust for the children and the purchasers in proportion to the contributions which they respectively made to the five premiums paid.

There is one small point on which my noble and learned friends Lord Millett and Lord Hoffmann disagree, namely, whether the pro rata division should take account of the notional allocation of units to the policy and to the fact that contributions were made at different times, i.e. when the various premiums were paid. I agree that, for the reasons given by Lord Hoffmann, it is not necessary to complicate the calculation of the pro rata shares by taking account of these factors and would therefore simply divide the policy moneys pro rata according to the contributions made to the payment of the premiums.'

Lord Steyn (dissenting):

'. . . . I will explain my reasons for concluding that the purchasers have no rights to the policy moneys. . . . .

There are four considerations which materially affect my approach to the claim of the purchasers. First the relative moral claims of the purchasers and the children must be considered. The purchasers emphasise that their claim is the result of the deliberate wrongdoing of Mr. Murphy. This is a point in favour of the purchasers. Moreover the case for the children is not assisted by the fact that Mr. Murphy sought to make provision for his family. The legal question would be the same if the beneficiary under the express trust was a business associate of Mr. Murphy. On the other hand, it is an important fact that the children were wholly unaware of any wrongdoing by their father. Secondly, it is clear that in the event the premiums paid in 1989 and 1990 added

nothing of value to the policy. The policy was established and the children acquired vested interests (subject to defeasance) before Mr. Murphy pursuant to the rights acquired by the children before 1989. The entitlement of the children was not in any way improved by payment of the 1989 and 1990 premiums. Thirdly, the purchasers have no claim in unjust enrichment in a substantive sense against the children because the payment of the 1989 and 1990 premiums conferred no additional benefit on the children. They were not enriched by the payment of those premiums: they merely received their shares of the sum assured in accordance with their pre-existing entitlement. The fourth point is that the children, as wholly innocent parties, can cogently say that, if they had become aware that Mr. Murphy planned to use trust money to pay the fourth and fifth premiums, they would have insisted that he did not so pay those premiums, with the result that they would still have received the same death benefit. (The relevance of such a factor is helpfully explained by Professor Hayton, "Equity's Identification Rules", Chapter 1 in P. Birks (ed) *Laundering and Tracing* (Oxford, 1995), p. 11–12 and Charles Mitchell, "Tracing Trust Funds Into Insurance Proceeds", [1997] L.M.C.L.Q. 465, 472.)
. . . .

There is in principle no difficulty about allowing a proprietary claim in respect of the proceeds of an insurance policy. If in the circumstances of the present case the stolen moneys had been wholly or partly causative of the production of the death benefit received by the children there would have been no obstacle to admitting such a proprietary claim. But those are not the material facts of the case. I am not influenced by hindsight. The fact is that the rights of the children had crystallised by 1989 before any money was stolen and used to pay the 1989 and 1990 premiums. . . . . the stolen moneys were not causally relevant to any benefit received by the children. The 1989 and 1990 premiums did not contribute to a mixed fund in which the purchasers have an equitable interest entitling them to a rateable division. It would be an innovation to create a proprietary remedy in respect of an asset (the death benefit) which had already been acquired at the date of the use of the stolen moneys. Far from assisting the case of the purchasers the impact of wider considerations of policy in truth tend to undermine the case of the purchasers. One needs to consider the implication of a holding in favour of the purchasers in other cases. Suppose Mr. Murphy had surrendered the policy before going bankrupt. Assume Mr. Murphy had partly used his own money and partly used money stolen from the purchasers to pay premiums. The hypothesis is that the stolen money did not in any way increase the surrender value of the policy. Justice does not support the creation to the prejudice of trade creditors of a new proprietary right in the surrender value of the policy: compare Roy Goode, "Proprietary Restitutionary Claims", essay in *Restitution: Past Present and Future*, ed. Cornish, Nolan, O'Sullivan, and Virgo [**[536]** above], p. 63 et seq. For these reasons I differ from the analysis of Morritt L.J. and reject the argument of the purchasers. . . . .'

Lord Hoffmann:

'My Lords, I have had the advantage of reading in draft the speech of my noble and learned friend Lord Millett. I agree with him that this is a straightforward case of mixed substitution (what the Roman lawyers, if they had had an economy which required tracing through bank accounts, would have called confusio). I agree with his conclusion that Mr. Murphy's children, claiming through him, and the trust beneficiaries whose money he used, are entitled to share in the proceeds of the insurance policy in proportion to the value which they respectively contributed to the policy. This is not based upon unjust enrichment except in the most trivial sense of that expression. It is, as my noble and learned friend says, a vindication of proprietary right.

The only point on which I differ from my noble and learned friend is the calculation of the proportions. . . . . The policy was a single chose in action under which some amount would fall due for payment in consideration of the premiums which had been paid. Immediately before Mr. Murphy's suicide, it was owned by the children and the beneficiaries in proportion to the value of their contributions to that consideration. The fact that the contingency which made the money payable was the death of Mr. Murphy cannot affect the proprietary interests in the chose in action and therefore in its proceeds: see *D'Avigdor-Goldsmid v. Inland Revenue Commissioners* [1953] A.C. 347.
In the case of contributions which are made at different times to the consideration for a single item of property such as the chose in action in this case, I can see an argument for saying that the value of earlier payments is greater than that of later payments. A pound today is worth more than the promise of a pound in a year's time. So there may be a case for applying some discount according to the date of payment. But no such argument was advanced in this case and I do not think that your Lordships should impose it upon the parties. I therefore agree with Morritt L.J. that the fund should be held simply in proportion to the contributions which the parties made to the five premiums.'

Lord Hope of Craighead (dissenting):
'. . . . The purchasers' [first] argument was . . . . that they were entitled as a result of the tracing exercise to a proprietary right of part ownership in the proceeds which, on the application of common justice, enabled them to claim a share of them proportionate to the contribution which their money had made to the total sum paid to the insurers by way of premium. [Their second, subsidiary, argument was based on the law of unjust enrichment.] . . . .

It seems to me that two quite separate questions arise in regard to the first of these two arguments. The first question is simply one of evidence. This is whether, if the purchasers can show that their money was used to pay any of the premiums, they can trace their money into the proceeds obtained by the trustees from the insurers in virtue of their rights under the policy. The second question is more difficult, and I think that it is the crucial question in this case. As I understand the question, it is whether it is equitable, in all the circumstances, that the purchasers should recover from the trustees a share of the proceeds calculated by reference to the contribution which their money made to the total amount paid to the insurers by way of premium.

I believe that I have already said almost all that needs to be said on the first question. . . . . at least to the extent of the last two premiums the purchasers can trace their money into the policy. The terms of the policy provide a sufficient basis for tracing their money one step further. They show that this money can be followed into the proceeds received by the trustees of the policy by way of death benefit. It is clearly stated in the policy document that the benefits specified are to be made in consideration of the payment to the insurer of all the premiums. This is enough to show that the tracing exercise does not end with the receipt of the premiums by the insurers. . . . .

But the result of the tracing exercise cannot solve the remaining question, which relates to the extent of the purchasers' entitlement. It is the fact that this is a case of mixed substitution which creates the difficulty. If the purchasers' money had been used to pay all the premiums there would have been no mixture of value with that contributed by others. Their claim would have been to the whole of the proceeds of the policy. As it is, there are competing claims on the same fund. In the absence of any other basis for division in principle or on authority—and no other basis has been suggested—it must be divided between the competitors in such proportions as can be shown to be equitable. In my opinion the answer to the question as to what is equitable does not depend solely on the terms of the policy. The equities affecting each party must be examined. They must be balanced against each other. The conduct of the parties so far as this may be relevant, and the consequences to them of allowing and rejecting the purchasers' claim, must be analysed and weighed up. It may be helpful to refer to what would be done in other situations by way of analogy. But it seems to me that in the end a judgment requires to be made as to what is fair, just and reasonable.

My noble and learned friend Lord Hoffmann states that this is a straightforward case of mixed substitution, which the Roman lawyers (if they had an economy which required tracing through bank accounts) would have called confusio. I confess that I have great difficulty in following this observation, as the relevant texts seem to me to indicate that they would have found the case far from straightforward and that it is quite uncertain what they would have made of it. [Lord Hope also thought that, in any event, the Romans would have resorted to the law of obligations (and some appropriate condictio) since the property was incorporeal, and therefore fell to be dealt with differently from things corporeal.]

. . . .

In the present case the purchasers are, in my opinion, unable to demonstrate that the value of the entitlement of the trustees of the policy to death benefit was increased to any extent at all as a result of the use of their money to keep the policy on foot, as the entitlement had already been fixed before their money was misappropriated. In these circumstances the equities lie with the children and not with the purchasers. I do not need to attach any weight to the fact that the purchasers have already been compensated by the successful pursuit of other remedies. Even without that fact I would hold that it is fair, just and reasonable that the children should be allowed to receive the whole of the sum now in the hands of the trustees after the purchasers have been reimbursed, with interest, for the amount of their money which was used to pay the premiums. . . .'

Lord Millett:

'My Lords this is a textbook example of tracing through mixed substitutions. At the beginning of the story the plaintiffs were beneficially entitled under an express trust to a sum standing in the name of Mr. Murphy in a bank account. From there the money moved into and out of various bank accounts where in breach of trust it was inextricably mixed by Mr. Murphy with his own money. After each transaction was completed the plaintiffs' money formed an indistinguishable part of the balance standing to Mr. Murphy's credit in his bank account. The amount of that balance represented a debt due from the bank to Mr. Murphy, that is to say a chose in action. At the penultimate stage the plaintiffs' money was represented by an indistinguishable part of a different chose in action, viz. the debt prospectively and contingently due from an insurance company to its policyholders, being the trustees of a settlement made by Mr. Murphy for the benefit of his children. At the present and final stage it forms an indistinguishable part of the balance standing to the credit of the respondent trustees in their bank account.

Tracing and following

The process of ascertaining what happened to the plaintiffs' money involves both tracing and following. These are both exercises in locating assets which are or may be taken to represent an asset belonging to the plaintiffs and to which they assert ownership. The processes of following and tracing are, however, distinct. Following is the process of following the same asset as it moves from hand to hand. Tracing is the process of identifying a new asset as the substitute for the old. Where one asset is exchanged for another, a claimant can elect whether to follow the original asset into the hands of the new owner or to trace its value into the new asset in the hands of the same owner. In practice his choice is often dictated by the circumstances. In the present case the plaintiffs do not seek to follow the money any further once it reached the bank or insurance company, since its identity was lost in the hands of the recipient (which in any case obtained an unassailable title as a bona fide purchaser for value without notice of the plaintiffs' beneficial interest). Instead the plaintiffs have chosen at each stage to trace the money into its proceeds, viz. the debt presently due from the bank to the account holder or the debt prospectively and contingently due from the insurance company to the policy holders.

Having completed this exercise, the plaintiffs claim a continuing beneficial interest in the insurance money. Since this represents the product of Mr. Murphy's own money as well as theirs, which Mr. Murphy mingled indistinguishably in a single chose in action, they claim a beneficial interest in a proportionate part of the money only. The transmission of a claimant's property rights from one asset to its traceable proceeds is part of our law of property, not of the law of unjust enrichment. There is no "unjust factor" to justify restitution (unless "want of title" be one, which makes the point). The claimant succeeds if at all by virtue of his own title, not to reverse unjust enrichment. Property rights are determined by fixed rules and settled principles. They are not discretionary. They do not depend upon ideas of what is "fair, just and reasonable." Such concepts, which in reality mask decisions of legal policy, have no place in the law of property.

A beneficiary of a trust is entitled to a continuing beneficial interest not merely in the trust property but in its traceable proceeds also, and his interest binds every one who takes the property or its traceable proceeds except a bona fide purchaser for value without notice. In the present case the plaintiffs' beneficial interest plainly bound Mr. Murphy, a trustee who wrongfully mixed the trust money with his own and whose every dealing with the money (including the payment of the premiums) was in breach of trust. It similarly binds his successors, the trustees of the children's settlement, who claim no beneficial interest of their own, and Mr. Murphy's children, who are volunteers. They gave no value for what they received and derive their interest from Mr. Murphy by way of gift.

Tracing

We speak of money at the bank, and of money passing into and out of a bank account. But of course the account holder has no money at the bank. Money paid into a bank account belongs legally and beneficially to the bank and not to the account holder. The bank gives value for it, and it is accordingly not usually possible to make the money itself the subject of an adverse claim. Instead a claimant normally sues the account holder rather than the bank and lays claim to the proceeds of the money in his hands. These consist of the debt or part of the debt due to him from the bank. We speak of tracing money into and out of the account, but there is no money in the account. There is merely a single debt of an amount equal to the final balance standing to the credit of the account holder. No money passes from paying bank to receiving bank or through the clearing system (where the money flows may be in the opposite direction). There is simply a series of debits and credits which are causally and transactionally linked. We also speak of tracing one asset into another, but this too is inaccurate. The original asset still exists in the hands of the new owner, or it may have become untraceable. The claimant claims the new asset because it was acquired in whole or in part with the original asset. What he traces, therefore, is not the physical asset itself but the value inherent in it.

Tracing is thus neither a claim nor a remedy. It is merely the process by which a claimant demonstrates what has happened to his property, identifies its proceeds and the persons who have handled or received them, and justifies his claim that the proceeds can properly be regarded as representing his property. Tracing is also distinct from claiming. It identifies the traceable proceeds of the claimant's property. It enables the claimant to substitute the traceable proceeds for the original asset as the subject matter of his claim. But it does not affect or establish his claim. That will depend on a number of factors including the nature of his interest in the original asset. He will normally be able to maintain the same claim to the substituted asset as he could have maintained to the original asset. If he held only a security interest in the original asset, he cannot claim more than a security interest in its proceeds. But his claim may also be exposed to potential defences as a result of intervening transactions. Even if the plaintiffs could demonstrate what the bank had done with their money, for example, and could thus identify its traceable proceeds in the hands of the bank, any claim by them to assert ownership of those proceeds would be defeated by the bona fide purchaser defence. The successful completion of a tracing exercise may be preliminary to a personal claim (as in *El Ajou v. Dollar Land Holdings* [1993] 3 All E.R. 717) or a proprietary one, to the enforcement of a legal right (as in *Trustees of the Property of F.C. Jones & Sons v. Jones* [1997] Ch. 159 [see **[619]** above]) or an equitable one.

Given its nature, there is nothing inherently legal or equitable about the tracing exercise. There is thus no sense in maintaining different rules for tracing at law and in equity. One set of tracing rules is enough. The existence of two has never formed part of the law in the United States: see *Scott The Law of Trusts* 4th. ed. (1989), pp. 605–609. There is certainly no logical justification for allowing any distinction between them to produce capricious results in cases of mixed substitutions by insisting on the existence of a fiduciary relationship as a precondition for applying equity's tracing rules. The existence of such a relationship may be relevant to the nature of the claim which the plaintiff can maintain, whether personal or proprietary, but that is a different matter. I agree with the passages which my noble and learned friend Lord Steyn has cited from Professor Birks' essay "The Necessity of a Unitary Law of Tracing", and with Dr. Lionel Smith's exposition in his comprehensive monograph *The Law of Tracing* (1997) see particularly pp. 120–130, 277–9 and 342–347.

This is not, however, the occasion to explore these matters further, for the present is a straightforward case of a trustee who wrongfully misappropriated trust money, mixed it with his own, and used it to pay for an asset for the benefit of his children. Even on the traditional approach, the equitable tracing rules are available to the plaintiffs. There are only two complicating factors. The first is that the wrongdoer used their money to pay premiums on an equity linked policy of life assurance on his own life. The nature of the policy should make no difference in principle, though it may complicate the accounting. The second is that he had previously settled the policy for the benefit of his children. This should also make no difference. The claimant's rights cannot depend on whether the wrongdoer gave the policy to his children during his lifetime or left the proceeds to them by his will; or if during his lifetime whether he did so before or after he had recourse to the claimant's money to pay the premiums. The order of events does not affect the fact that the children are not contributors but volunteers who have received the gift of an asset paid for in part with misappropriated trust moneys.

The cause of action

As I have already pointed out, the plaintiffs seek to vindicate their property rights, not to reverse unjust enrichment. The correct classification of the plaintiffs' cause of action may appear to be academic, but it has important consequences. The two causes of action have different requirements and may attract different defences.

A plaintiff who brings an action in unjust enrichment must show that the defendant has been enriched at the plaintiff's expense, for he cannot have been unjustly enriched if he has not been enriched at all. But the plaintiff is not concerned to show that the defendant is in receipt of property belonging beneficially to the plaintiff or its traceable proceeds. The fact that the beneficial ownership of the property has passed to the defendant provides no defence; indeed, it is usually the very fact which founds the claim. Conversely, a plaintiff who brings an action like the present must show that the defendant is in receipt of property which belongs beneficially to him or its traceable proceeds, but he need not show that the defendant has been enriched by its receipt. He may, for example, have paid full value for the property, but he is still required to disgorge it if he received it with notice of the plaintiff's interest.

Furthermore, a claim in unjust enrichment is subject to a change of position defence, which usually operates by reducing or extinguishing the element of enrichment. An action like the present is subject to the bona fide purchaser for value defence, which operates to clear the defendant's title.

The tracing rules

The insurance policy in the present case is a very sophisticated financial instrument. Tracing into the rights conferred by such an instrument raises a number of important issues. It is therefore desirable to set out the basic principles before turning to deal with the particular problems to which policies of life assurance give rise.

The simplest case is where a trustee wrongfully misappropriates trust property and uses it exclusively to acquire other property for his own benefit. In such a case the beneficiary is entitled *at his option* either to assert his beneficial ownership of the proceeds or to bring a personal claim against the trustee for breach of trust and enforce an equitable lien or charge on the proceeds to secure restoration of the trust fund. He will normally exercise the option in the way most advantageous to himself. If the traceable proceeds have increased in value and are worth more than the original asset, he will assert his beneficial ownership and obtain the profit for himself. There is nothing unfair in this. The trustee cannot be permitted to keep any profit resulting from his misappropriation for himself, and his donees cannot obtain a better title than their donor. If the traceable proceeds are worth less than the original asset, it does not usually matter how the beneficiary exercises his option. He will take the whole of the proceeds on either basis. This is why it is not possible to identify the basis on which the claim succeeded in some of the cases.

Both remedies are proprietary and depend on successfully tracing the trust property into its proceeds. A beneficiary's claim against a trustee for breach of trust is a personal claim. It does not entitle him to priority over the trustee's general creditors unless he can trace the trust property into its product and establish a proprietary interest in the proceeds. If the beneficiary is unable to trace the trust property into its proceeds, he still has a personal claim against the trustee, but his claim will be unsecured. The beneficiary's proprietary claims to the trust property or its traceable proceeds can be maintained against the wrongdoer and anyone who derives title from him except a bona fide purchaser for value without notice of the breach of trust. The same rules apply even where there have been numerous successive transactions, so long as the tracing exercise is successful and no bona fide purchaser for value without notice has intervened.

A more complicated case is where there is a mixed substitution. This occurs where the trust money represents only part of the cost of acquiring the new asset. As

James Barr Ames pointed out in "Following Misappropriated Property into its Product" (1906) Harv.L.Rev. 511, consistency requires that, if a trustee buys property partly with his own money and partly with trust money, the beneficiary should have the option of taking a proportionate part of the new property or a lien upon it, as may be most for his advantage. In principle it should not matter (and it has never previously been suggested that it does) whether the trustee mixes the trust money with his own and buys the new asset with the mixed fund or makes separate payments of the purchase price (whether simultaneously or sequentially) out of the different funds. In every case the value formerly inherent in the trust property has become located within the value inherent in the new asset.

The rule, and its rationale, were stated by Samuel Williston in "The Right to Follow Trust Property when Confused with Other Property" (1880) 2 Harv.L.Rev. 28, p. 29:

> "If the trust fund is traceable as having furnished in part the money with which a certain investment was made, and the proportion it formed of the whole money so invested is known or ascertainable, the cestui que trust should be allowed to regard the acts of the trustee as done for his benefit, in the same way that he would if all the money so invested had been his; that is, he should be entitled in equity to an undivided share of the property which the trust money contributed to purchase—such a proportion of the whole as the trust money bore to the whole money invested. The reason in the one case as in the other is that the trustee cannot be allowed to make a profit from the use of the trust money, and if the property which he wrongfully purchased were held subject only to a lien for the amount invested, any appreciation in value would go to the trustee."

If this correctly states the underlying basis of the rule (as I believe it does), then it is impossible to distinguish between the case where mixing precedes the investment and the case where it arises on and in consequence of the investment. It is also impossible to distinguish between the case where the investment is retained by the trustee and the case where it is given away to a gratuitous donee. The donee cannot obtain a better title than his donor, and a donor who is a trustee cannot be allowed to profit from his trust.

In *In re Hallett's Estate; Knatchbull v. Hallett* (1880) 13 Ch. D. 696 [see **[627]** above], 709 Sir George Jessel M.R. acknowledged that where an asset was acquired exclusively with trust money, the beneficiary could either assert equitable ownership of the asset or enforce a lien or charge over it to recover the trust money. But he appeared to suggest that in the case of a mixed substitution the beneficiary is confined to a lien. Any authority that this dictum might otherwise have is weakened by the fact that Jessel M.R. gave no reason for the existence of any such rule, and none is readily apparent. The dictum was plainly *obiter*, for the fund was deficient and the plaintiff was only claiming a lien. It has usually been cited only to be explained away: see for example *In re Tilley's Will Trusts* [1967] Ch. 1179 [see **[632]** above], 1186 per Ungoed-Thomas J.; *Burrows, The Law of Restitution* (1993) p. 368. It was rejected by the High Court of Australia in *Scott v. Scott* (1963) 109 C.L.R. 649 [see **[633]** above]: see the passage at pp. 661–2 cited by Morritt L.J. below at [1998] Ch. 265, 300–301). It has not been adopted in the United States: see the *American Law Institute, Restatement of the Law, Trusts*, 2d (1959) at section 202(h). In *Primeau v. Granfield* (1911) 184 F. 480, 184 Learned Hand J. expressed himself in forthright terms: "On principle there can be no excuse for such a rule."

In my view the time has come to state unequivocally that English law has no such rule. It conflicts with the rule that a trustee must not benefit from his trust. I agree with Burrows that the beneficiary's right to elect to have a proportionate share of a mixed substitution necessarily follows once one accepts, as English law does, (i) that a claimant can trace in equity into a mixed fund and (ii) that he can trace unmixed money into its proceeds and assert ownership of the proceeds.

Accordingly, I would state the basic rule as follows. Where a trustee wrongfully uses trust money to provide part of the cost of acquiring an asset, the beneficiary is entitled *at his option* either to claim a proportionate share of the asset or to enforce a lien upon it to secure his personal claim against the trustee for the amount of the misapplied money. It does not matter whether the trustee mixed the trust money with his own in a single fund before using it to acquire the asset, or made separate payments (whether simultaneously or sequentially) out of the differently owned funds to acquire a single asset.

Two observations are necessary at this point. First, there is a mixed substitution (with the results already described) whenever the claimant's property has contributed in part only towards the acquisition of the new asset. It is not necessary for the claimant to show in addition that his property has contributed to any increase in the *value* of the new asset. This is because, as I have already pointed out, this branch of the law is concerned with vindicating rights of property and not with reversing unjust enrichment. Secondly, the beneficiary's right to claim a lien is available only against a wrongdoer and those deriving title under him otherwise than for value. It is not available against competing contributors who are innocent of any wrongdoing. The tracing rules are not the result of any presumption or principle peculiar to equity. They correspond to the common law rules for following into physical mixtures (though the consequences may not be identical). Common to both is the principle that the interests of the wrongdoer who was responsible for the mixing and those who derive title under him otherwise than for value are subordinated to those of innocent contributors. As against the wrongdoer and his successors, the beneficiary is entitled to locate his contribution in any part of the mixture and to subordinate their claims to share in the mixture until his own contribution has been satisfied. This has the effect of giving the beneficiary a lien for his contribution if the mixture is deficient.

Innocent contributors, however, must be treated equally inter se. Where the beneficiary's claim is in competition with the claims of other innocent contributors, there is no basis upon which any of the claims can be subordinated to any of the others. Where the fund is deficient, the beneficiary is not entitled to enforce a lien for his contributions; all must share rateably in the fund.

The primary rule in regard to a mixed fund, therefore, is that gains and losses are borne by the contributors rateably. The beneficiary's right to elect instead to enforce a lien to obtain repayment is an exception to the primary rule, exercisable where the fund is deficient and the claim is made against the wrongdoer and those claiming through him. It is not necessary to consider whether there are any circumstances in which the beneficiary is confined to a lien in cases where the fund is more than sufficient to repay the contributions of all parties. It is sufficient to say that he is not so confined in a case like the present. It is not enough that those defending the claim are innocent of any wrongdoing if they are not themselves contributors but, like the trustees and Mr. Murphy's children in the present case, are volunteers who derive title under the wrongdoer otherwise than for value. On ordinary principles such persons are in no better position than the wrongdoer, and are liable to suffer the same subordination of their interests to those of the claimant as the wrongdoer would have been. They certainly cannot do better than the claimant by confining him to a lien and keeping any profit for themselves.

. . . .

Insurance policies

. . . .

It is, however, of critical importance in the present case to appreciate that the plaintiffs do not trace the premiums directly into the insurance money. They trace them first into the policy and thence into the proceeds of the policy. It is essential not to elide the two steps. In this context, of course, the word "policy" does not mean the contract of insurance. You do not trace the payment of a premium into the insurance contract any more than you trace a payment into a bank account into the banking contract. The word "policy" is here used to describe the bundle of rights to which the policyholder is entitled in return for the premiums. These rights, which may be very complex, together constitute a chose in action, viz. the right to payment of a debt payable on a future event and contingent upon the continued payment of further premiums until the happening of the event. That chose in action represents the traceable proceeds of the premiums; its current value fluctuates from time to time. When the policy matures, the insurance money represents the traceable proceeds of the policy and hence indirectly of the premiums.

It follows that, if a claimant can show that premiums were paid with his money, he can claim a proportionate share of the policy. His interest arises by reason of and immediately upon the payment of the premiums, and the extent of his share is ascertainable at once. He does not have to wait until the policy matures in order to claim his property. His share in the policy and its proceeds may increase or decrease as further premiums are paid; but it is not affected by the realisation of the policy. His share remains the same whether the policy is sold or surrendered or held until maturity; these are merely different methods of realising the policy. They may affect the amount of the proceeds received on realisation but they cannot affect the extent of his share in the proceeds. In principle the plaintiffs are entitled to the insurance money which was paid on Mr. Murphy's death in the same shares and proportions as they were entitled in the policy immediately before his death.

Since the manner in which an asset is realised does not affect its ownership, and since it cannot matter whether the claimant discovers what has happened before or after it is realised, the question of ownership can be answered by ascertaining the shares in which it is owned immediately before it is realised. Where A misappropriates B's money and uses it to buy a winning ticket in the lottery, B is entitled to the winnings. Since A is a wrongdoer, it is irrelevant that he could have used his own money if in fact he used B's. This may seem to give B an undeserved windfall, but the result is not unjust. Had B discovered the fraud before the draw, he could have decided whether to keep the ticket or demand his money back. He alone has the right to decide whether to gamble with his own money. If A keeps him in ignorance until after the draw, he suffers the consequence. He cannot deprive B of his right to choose what to do with his own money; but he can give him an informed choice.

The application of these principles ought not to depend on the nature of the chose in action. They should apply to a policy of life assurance as they apply to a bank account or a lottery ticket. It has not been suggested in argument that they do not apply to a policy of life assurance. This question has not been discussed in the English authorities, but it has been considered in the United States. . . . .

. . . .

The reasoning of the Court of Appeal

The majority of the Court of Appeal (Sir Richard Scott V.-C. and Hobhouse L.J.) held that the plaintiffs could trace their money into the premiums but not into the policy, and were accordingly not entitled to a proportionate share in the proceeds. They did so, however, for different and, in my view, inconsistent reasons which cannot both be correct and which only coincidentally led to the same result in the present case.

Sir Richard Scott V.-C. considered that Mr. Murphy's children acquired vested interests in the policy at its inception. They had a vested interest (subject to defeasance) in the death benefit at the outset and before any of the plaintiffs' money was used to pay the premiums. The use of the plaintiffs' money gave the plaintiffs a lien on the proceeds of the policy for the return of the premiums paid with their money, but could not have the effect of divesting the children of their existing interest. The children owned the policy; the plaintiffs' money was merely used to maintain it. The position was analogous to that where trust money was used to maintain or improve property of a third party.

. . . .

In my opinion there is no reason to differentiate between the first premium or premiums and later premiums. Such a distinction is not based on any principle. Why should the policy belong to the party who paid the first premium, without which there would have been no policy, rather than to the party who paid the last premium, without which it would normally have lapsed? Moreover, any such distinction would lead to the most capricious results. If only four annual premiums are paid, why should it matter whether A paid the first two premiums and B the second two, or B paid the first two and A the second two, or they each paid half of each of the four premiums? Why should the children obtain the whole of the sum assured if Mr. Murphy used his own money before he began to use the plaintiffs' money, and only a return of the premiums if Mr. Murphy happened to use the plaintiffs' money first? Why should the proceeds of the policy be attributed to the first premium when the policy itself is expressed to be in consideration of all the premiums? There is no analogy with the case where trust money is used to maintain or improve property of a third party. The nearest analogy is with an instalment purchase.

Hobhouse L.J. adopted a different approach. He concentrated on the detailed terms of the policy, and in particular on the fact that in the event the payment of the fourth and fifth premiums with the plaintiffs' money made no difference to the amount of the death benefit. Once the third premium had been paid, there was sufficient surrender value in the policy, built up by the use of Mr. Murphy's own money, to keep the policy on foot for the next few years, and as it happened Mr. Murphy's death occurred during those few years. But this was adventitious and unpredictable at the time the premiums were paid. The argument is based on causation and as I have explained is a category mistake derived from the law of unjust enrichment. It is an example of the same fallacy that gives rise to the idea that the proceeds of an ordinary life policy belong to the party who paid the last premium without which the policy would have lapsed. But the question is one of attribution not causation. The question is not whether the same death benefit would have been payable if the last premium or last few premiums had not been paid. It is whether the death benefit is attributable to all the premiums or only to some of them. The answer is that death benefit is attributable to all of them because it represents the proceeds of realising the policy, and the policy in turn represents the product of all the premiums.

In any case, Hobhouse L.J.'s analysis of the terms of the policy does not go far enough. It is not correct that the last two premiums contributed nothing to the sum payable on Mr. Murphy's death but merely reduced the cost to the insurers of providing it. Life cover was provided in return for a series of internal premiums paid for by the cancellation of units previously allocated to the policy. Units were allocated to the policy in return for the annual premiums. Prior to their cancellation the cancelled units formed part of a mixed fund of units which was the product of all the premiums paid by Mr. Murphy, including those paid with the plaintiffs' money. On ordinary principles, the plaintiffs can trace the last two premiums into and out of the mixed fund and into the internal premiums used to provide the death benefit.

It is true that the last two premiums were not needed to provide the death benefit in the sense that in the events which happened the same amount would have been payable even if those premiums had not been paid. In other words, with the benefit of hindsight it can be seen that Mr. Murphy made a bad investment when he paid the last two premiums. It is, therefore, superficially attractive to say that the plaintiffs' money contributed nothing of value. But the argument proves too much, for if the plaintiffs cannot trace their money into the proceeds of the policy, they should have no proprietary remedy at all, not even a lien for the return of their money. But the fact is that Mr. Murphy, who could not foresee the future, did choose to pay the last two premiums, and to pay them with the plaintiffs' money; and they were applied by the insurer towards the payment of the internal premiums needed to fund the death benefit. It should not avail his donees that he need not have paid the premiums, and that if he had not then (in the events which happened) the insurers would have provided the same death benefit and funded it differently.

In the case of an ordinary life policy which lapses if the premiums are not paid, the Vice-Chancellor's approach gives the death benefit to the party whose money was used to pay the first premium, and Hobhouse L.J.'s approach gives it to the party whose money was used to pay the last premium. In the case of a policy like the present, Hobhouse L.J.'s approach also produces unacceptable and capricious results. The claimant must wait to see whether the life assured lives long enough to exhaust the amount of the policy's surrender value as at the date immediately before the claimant's money was first used. If the life assured dies the day before it would have been exhausted, the claimant is confined to his lien to recover the premiums; if he dies the day after, then the claimant's premiums were needed to maintain the life cover. In the latter case he takes at least a proportionate share of the proceeds or, if the argument is pressed to its logical conclusion, the whole of the proceeds subject to a lien in favour of the trustees of the children's settlement. This simply cannot be right.

Hobhouse L.J.'s approach is also open to objection on purely practical grounds. It must, I think, be unworkable if there is an eccentric pattern of payment; or if there is a fall in the value of the units at a critical moment. Like the Vice-Chancellor's approach, it prompts the question: why should the order of payments matter? It is true that the premiums paid with the plaintiff's money did not in the event increase the amount payable on Mr. Murphy's death, but they increased the surrender value of the policy and postponed the date at which it would lapse if no further premiums were paid. Why should it be necessary to identify the premium the payment of which (in the events which happened) prevented the policy from lapsing? Above all, this approach makes it impossible for the ownership of the policy to be determined until the policy matures or is realised. This too cannot be right.

The trustees argued that such considerations are beside the point. It is not necessary, they submitted, to consider what the plaintiffs' rights would have been if the policy had been surrendered, or if Mr. Murphy had lived longer. It is sufficient to take account of what actually happened. I do not agree. A principled approach must yield a coherent solution in all eventualities. The ownership of the policy must be ascertainable at every moment from inception to maturity; it cannot be made to await events. In my view the only way to achieve this is to hold firm to the principle that the manner in which an asset is converted into money does not affect its ownership. The parties' respective rights to the proceeds of the policy depend on their rights to the policy immediately before it was realised on Mr. Murphy's death, and this depends on the shares in which they contributed to the premiums and nothing else. They do not depend on the date at which or the manner in which the chose in action was realised. Of course, Mr. Murphy's early death greatly increased the value of the policy and made the bargain a good one. But the idea that the parties' entitlements to the policy and its proceeds are altered by the death of the life assured is contrary to principle and to the decision of your Lordships' House in *D'Avigdor-Goldsmid v. Inland Revenue Commissioners* [1953] A.C. 347. That case establishes that no fresh beneficial interest in a policy of life assurance accrues or arises on the death of the life assured. The sum assured belongs to the person or persons who were beneficial owners of the policy immediately before the death.

In the course of argument it was submitted that if the children, who were innocent of any wrongdoing themselves, had been aware that their father was using stolen funds to pay the premiums, they could have insisted that the premiums should not be paid, and in the events which happened would still have received the same death benefit. But the fact is that Mr. Murphy concealed his wrongdoing from both parties. The proper response is to treat them both alike, that is to say rateably. It is morally offensive as well as contrary to principle to subordinate the claims of the victims of a fraud to those of the objects of the fraudster's bounty on the ground that he concealed his wrongdoing from both of them.

The submission is not (as has been suggested) supported by Professor David Hayton's article "Equity's Identification Rules" in *Laundering and Tracing* (1995), edited by Peter Birks, at pp. 11–12. Professor Hayton is dealing with the very different case of the party who decides to purchase an asset and has the means to pay for it, but who happens to use trust money which he has received innocently, not knowing it to belong to a third party and believing himself to be entitled to it. In such a case his decision to use the trust money rather than his own is independent of the breach of trust; it is a matter of pure chance. This is a problem about tracing, not claiming, and has nothing to do with mixtures, as Professor Hayton's article itself makes clear. It is a difficult problem on the solution to which academic writers are not agreed. But it does not arise in the present case. It was Mr. Murphy's decision to use the plaintiffs' money to pay the later premiums. The children are merely passive recipients of an asset acquired in part by the use of misappropriated trust money. They are innocent of any personal wrongdoing, but they are not contributors. They are volunteers who derive their interest from the wrongdoer otherwise than for value and are in no better position than he would have been if he had retained the policy for the benefit of his estate. It is not, with respect to those who think otherwise, a case where there are competing claimants to a fund who are both innocent victims of a fraud and where the equities are equal. But if it were such a case, the parties would share rateably, which is all that the plaintiffs claim.

[Lord Millett then dealt with the finding of all the members of the Court of Appeal that the plaintiffs were entitled to enforce a lien on the proceeds of the policy to secure repayment of the premiums paid with their money.]

The relevant proportions

Accordingly, I agree with Morritt L.J. in the Court of Appeal that, on well established principles, the parties are entitled to the proceeds of the policy in the proportions in which those proceeds represent their respective contributions. It should not, however, be too readily assumed that this means in the proportions in which the insurance premiums were paid with their money. These represent the *cost* of the contributions, not necessarily their *value*.

A mixed fund, like a physical mixture, is divisible between the parties who contributed to it rateably in proportion to the value of their respective contributions, and this must be ascertained at the time they are added to the mixture. Where the mixed fund consists of sterling or a sterling account or where both parties make their contributions to the mixture at the same time, there is no difference between the cost of the contributions and their sterling value. But where there is a physical mixture or the mixture consists of an account maintained in other units of account and the parties make their contributions at different times, it is essential to value the contributions of *both* parties at the same time. If this is not done, the resulting proportions will not reflect a comparison of like with like. The appropriate time for valuing the parties' respective contributions is when successive contributions are added to the mixture.

This is certainly what happens with physical mixtures. If 20 gallons of A's oil are mixed with 40 gallons of B's oil to produce a uniform mixture of 60 gallons, A and B are entitled to share in the mixture in the proportions of 1 to 2. It makes no difference if A's oil, being purchased later, cost £2 a gallon and B's oil cost only £1 a gallon, so that they each paid out £40. This is because the mixture is divisible between the parties rateably in proportion to the *value* of their respective contributions and not in proportion to their respective *cost*. B's contribution to the mixture was made when A's oil was added to his, and *both* parties' contributions should be valued at that date. Should a further 20 gallons of A's oil be added to the mixture to produce a uniform mixture of 80 gallons at a time when the oil was worth £3 a gallon, the oil would be divisible equally between them. (A's further 20 gallons are worth £3 a gallon—but so are the 60 gallons belonging to both of them to which they have been added). It is not of course necessary to go through the laborious task of valuing every successive contribution separately in sterling. It is simpler to take the account by measuring the contributions in gallons rather than sterling. This is merely a short cut which produces the same result.

In my opinion the same principle operates whenever the mixture consists of fungibles, whether these be physical assets like oil, grain or wine or intangibles like money in an account. Take the case where a trustee misappropriates trust money in a sterling bank account and pays it into his personal dollar account which also contains funds of his own. The dollars are, of course, merely units of account; the account holder has no proprietary interest in them. But no one, I think, would doubt that the beneficiary could claim the dollar value of the contributions made with trust money. Most people would explain this by saying that it is because the account is kept in dollars. But the correct explanation is that it is because the contributions are made in dollars. In order to allocate the fund between the parties rateably in proportion to the value of their respective contributions, it is necessary to identify the point at which the trust money becomes mixed with the trustee's own money. This does not occur when the trustee pays in a sterling cheque drawn on the trust account. At that stage the trust money is still identifiable. It occurs when the bank credits the dollar equivalent of the sterling cheque to the trustee's personal account. Those dollars represent the contribution made by the trust. The sterling value of the trust's contribution must be valued at that time; and it follows that the trustee's contributions, which were also made in dollars, must be valued at the same time. Otherwise one or other party will suffer the injustice of having his contributions undervalued.

Calculating the plaintiffs' share

I finally come to the difficult question: how should the parties' contributions, and therefore their respective shares in the proceeds, be calculated in the case of a unit-linked policy of the present kind? This makes it necessary to examine the terms of the policy in some detail.

[There then followed a long discussion of the appropriate approach.]

This approach is substantially more favourable to the children than a crude allocation by reference to the premiums. By taking account of the value of the units, it automatically weights the earlier premiums which should have bought more units than the later ones. And it gives effect to the fact that, under the terms of the policy, both parties contributed to the later internal premiums which produced the greater part of the death benefit.

It is, of course, always open to the parties in any case to dispense with complex calculations and agree upon a simpler method of apportionment. But in my opinion the court ought not to do so without the parties' consent. If it does, anomalies and inconsistencies will inevitably follow. . . . . Cutting corners in the interest of simplicity is tempting, but in my opinion the temptation ought to be resisted.

Conclusion

Accordingly I would allow the appeal. In my opinion the insurance money ought to be divided between the parties in the proportions I have indicated. But I am alone in adopting this approach, and as the question was not argued before us I am content that your Lordships should declare that the money should be divided between the parties in proportions in which they contributed to the premiums. . . ..'

Questions:

1. What divides the different analyses? Which analysis is more persuasive? Which is more consistent with the cases extracted earlier? *Is* tracing treated as a 'remedy' or a 'process'?
2. What difference, if any, does it make that the claimant is 'vindicating a property right' rather than, for example, claiming a remedy in unjust enrichment?
3. To what extent does the outcome in this case turn on the fact that Mr Murphy was a defaulting trustee?
4. Compare this case with *F C Jones & Sons (Trustee in Bankruptcy) v Jones* (**[619]** above). What distinctions exist between these two cases?
5. Suppose a mixed fund is used to purchase shares. (i) If the shares increase in value, when will a claimant be entitled to claim equitable ownership of a proportion of the shares (and so share in the benefit of the profitable investment)? (ii) On the other hand, if the shares decrease in value, when (if ever) will a claimant be entitled to a charge *over the whole mass* of the shares to secure return of the full amount of the original input in the mixed fund (and so perhaps avoid sharing the loss inherent in the investment)?
6. Is it possible to deduce from these cases the governing principles in relation to claims to profits? Is the legal result satisfactory from a policy perspective? (See the readings cited in Sections 5.5, 5.10 and 5.13, and at the end of this Chapter.)

6.5.4 The end of the tracing trail: constraints on the equitable tracing rules

The focus of this final section is plain: when will the tracing trail go cold? The previous extracts make it plain that equitable tracing is grounded on the physical existence of some asset which can be said to be derived from (or partly derived from) the original asset which belonged in equity to the claimant. This means that a claimant wishing to trace in equity must be able to say, 'This asset, asset 1, was mine (in equity) at the start, and the defendant has used it to acquire or produce asset 2, and then used that asset to acquire or produce asset 3, and so on, and so I am now entitled to assert a claim against the final asset in the chain'.[33]

From this it is clear that the tracing trail will go cold if the claimant cannot prove that asset 1 *was* used to acquire or produce asset 2. The easiest cases for the claimant are those of direct exchange: for example, the claimant's £100 is used to purchase shares. Most cases are more complicated. Certain assumptions are allowed. If the claimant's property has been mixed in a fungible mixture with the defendant's property so that it is impossible to say with certainty whether the claimant's or the defendant's property was used in subsequent dealings with parts of the mixture, the rules of equity allow the claimant to assume, against a wrongdoing defendant,[34] whatever particular allocation of property is best for the claimant's case. But, in allowing this, it must at least be physically *possible* (even if not certain) for the claimant's property to have been used in the dealing. The tracing trail goes cold if this is not the case. (See **[637]** and **[638]** below.)

More controversially, the initial proposition has been taken as suggesting that the tracing trail will go cold if the claimant cannot prove that asset 1 contributed *value* to asset 2. This could be the case if the claimant's money were used to effect idiosyncratic renovations to a house, for example: the value of the defendant's house *after* the expenditure may be less than it was before. *Re Diplock* (**[636]** below) illustrates the issue, but also see *Foskett v McKeown* [**[635]** above].

Still more controversially, it is also suggested that the tracing trail will go cold if asset 1 is not somehow *physically* present in asset 2: ***re-read** Borden (UK) Ltd v Scottish Timber Products Ltd* [1981] Ch 25 (CA) (**[626]** above). It might be more correct to say that the *following* trail will go cold in these circumstances.

[636] *Re Diplock* [1948] 1 Ch 465 (CA), 545–8 *per* Lord Greene MR:

[The facts and an earlier part of the decision are extracted at **[628]** above.]

> 'We deal first of all with what appear to be the most important claims from the point of view of amount. They are cases in which the money received from the Diplock executors was used in the execution of works upon land or buildings already belonging to the charities. The appellants claim in each case declarations of charge on land of the charity in respect of these amounts. . . .
>
> Where the contribution of a volunteer to a mixed fund or the acquisition of what we may call a "mixed asset" is in the form of money, it is, as we hope to have shown, inequitable for him to claim the whole fund or the whole asset. The equitable charge given to the other claimant in respect of the money contributed by him results merely

33 The precise nature of the claim which can be made is difficult, as has been seen.

34 But not otherwise.

in the division of the mixed fund between the two of them or the reduction of the asset by sale to its original components, *i.e.*, money which is then divisible in the same manner. The volunteer gets back what he put in, *i.e.*, money. On this basis, if a charity had used a mixed fund, consisting in part of its own money and in part of Diplock money, in the acquisition of property, whether (for example) land or stock, the application of the equitable remedy would have presented no particular difficulty. The Diplock money and the charity money could each have been traced. A charge enforced by sale and distribution would have been effective as well as fair to both parties. The charity would not, as the result of the mixture, have been deprived of anything that it had before.

In the present cases, however, the charities have used the Diplock money, not in combination with money of their own to acquire new assets, but in the alteration and improvement of assets which they already owned. The altered and improved asset owes its existence, therefore, to a combination of land belonging to the charity and money belonging to the Diplock estate. The question whether tracing is possible and if so to what extent, and also the question whether an effective remedy by way of declaration of charge can be granted consistently with an equitable treatment of the charity as an innocent volunteer, present quite different problems from those arising in the simple case above stated. In the case of the purchase of an asset out of a mixed fund, both categories of money are, as we have said, necessarily present throughout the existence of the asset in an identifiable form. In the case of adaptation of property of the volunteer by means of trust money, it by no means necessarily follows that the money can be said to be present in the adapted property. The beneficial owner of the trust money seeks to follow and recover that money and claims to use the machinery of a charge on the adapted property in order to enable him to do so. But in the first place the money may not be capable of being followed. In every true sense, the money may have disappeared. A simple example suggests itself. The owner of a house who, as an innocent volunteer, has trust money in his hands given to him by a trustee uses that money in making an alteration to his house so as to fit it better to his own personal needs. The result may add not one penny to the value of the house. Indeed, the alteration may well lower its value; for the alteration, though convenient to the owner, may be highly inconvenient in the eyes of a purchaser. Can it be said in such cases that the trust money can be traced and extracted from the altered asset? Clearly not, for the money will have disappeared leaving no monetary trace behind: the asset will not have increased (or may even have depreciated) in value through its use.

But the matter does not end here. What, for the purposes of the inquiry, is to be treated as "the charity property"? Is it to be the whole of the land belonging to the charity? or is it to be only that part of it which was altered or reconstructed or on which a building has been erected by means of Diplock money? If the latter, the result may well be that the property, both in its original state and as altered or improved, will, when taken in isolation, have little or no value. What would be the value of a building in the middle of Guy's hospital without any means of access through other parts of the hospital property? If, on the other hand, the charge is to be on the whole of the charity land, it might well be thought an extravagant result if the Diplock estate, because Diplock money had been used to reconstruct a corner of it, were to be entitled to a charge on the entirety.

But it is not merely a question of locating and identifying the Diplock money. The result of a declaration of charge is to disentangle trust money and enable it to be withdrawn in the shape of money from the complex in which it has become involved. This can only be done by sale under the charge. But the equitable owner of the trust money must in this process submit to equality of treatment with the innocent volunteer. The latter too, is entitled to disentangle his money and to withdraw it from the complex. Where the complex originates in money on both sides there is no difficulty and no inequity. Each is entitled to a charge. But if what the volunteer has contributed is not money but other property of his own such as land, what then? You cannot have a charge for land. You can, it is true, have a charge for the value of land, an entirely different thing. Is it equitable to compel the innocent volunteer to take a charge merely for the value of the land when what he has contributed is the land itself? In other words, can equity, by the machinery of a charge, give to the innocent volunteer that which he has contributed so as to place him in a position comparable with that of the owner of the trust fund? In our opinion it cannot.

In the absence of authority to the contrary our conclusion is that as regards the Diplock money used in these cases it cannot be traced in any true sense; and, further, that even if this were not so, the only remedy available to equity, viz., that of a declaration of charge would not produce an equitable result and is inapplicable accordingly.'

Question:

Is this the only means of resolving this type of problem? See *Boscawen v Bajwa* [1996] 1 WLR 328 (CA) (**[715]** below) for Millett LJ's comments on this case.

[637] ***James Roscoe (Bolton) Ltd v Winder*** **[1915] 1 Ch 62, 68–9 *per* Sargant J:** [This case describes what is commonly termed the 'lowest intermediate balance rule'. The defendant had agreed to purchase the claimant company and to pay over to the claimant all moneys received up until a certain date on account of book debts owing to the claimant. The defendant collected £455 of such book debts but, in breach of the agreement, put the money into his personal account. He then dissipated all but £25 of the mixed fund. Still later he made further deposits into the account so that at his death the balance stood at £358. Sargant J held that the claimant could only trace through to the £25 (the 'lowest intermediate balance'), and could lay no claim to the full £358.]

'It appears that after the payment in by the debtor of a portion of the book debts which he had received the balance at the bank on May 19, 1913, was reduced by his drawings to a sum of £25 18*s* only on May 21. So that, although the ultimate balance at the debtor's death was about £358 there had been an intermediate balance of only £25 18*s*. The result of that seems to me to be that the trust moneys cannot possibly be traced into this common fund, which was standing to the debtor's credit at his death, to an extent of more than £25 18*s*, because, although prima facie under the second rule in *In re Hallett's Estate* (13 Ch. D. 696 [**[627]** above]) any drawings out by the debtor ought to be attributed to the private moneys which he had at the bank and not to the trust moneys, yet, when the drawings out had reached such an amount that the whole of his private money part had been exhausted, it necessarily followed that the rest of the drawings must have been against trust moneys. There being on May 21, 1913, only £25 18*s*, in all, standing to the credit of the debtor's account, it is quite clear that on that day he must have denuded his account of all the trust moneys there—the whole £455 18*s* 11*d*—except to the extent of £25 18*s*.

Practically, what Mr. Martelli and Mr. Hansell have been asking me to do—although I think Mr. Hansell in particular rather disguised the claim by the phraseology he used—is to say that the debtor, by paying further moneys after May 21 into this common account, was impressing upon those further moneys so paid in the like trust or obligation, or charge of the nature of a trust, which had formerly been impressed upon the previous balances to the credit of that account. No doubt, Mr. Hansell did say "No. I am only asking you to treat the account as a whole, and to consider the balance from time to time standing to the credit of that account as subject to one continual charge or trust." But I think that really is using words which are not appropriate to the facts. You must, for the purpose of tracing, which was the process adopted in *In re Hallett's Estate* (13 Ch. D. 696), put your finger on some definite fund which either remains in its original state or can be found in another shape. That is tracing, and tracing, by the very facts of this case, seems to be absolutely excluded except as to the £25 18*s*.

Then, apart from tracing, it seems to me possible to establish this claim against the ultimate balance of £358 5*s* 5*d* only by saying that something was done, with regard to the additional moneys which are needed to make up that balance, by the person to whom those moneys belonged, the debtor, to substitute those moneys for the purpose of, or to impose upon those moneys a trust equivalent to, the trust which rested on the previous balance. Of course, if there was anything like a separate trust account, the payment of the further moneys into that account would, in itself, have been quite a sufficient indication of the intention of the debtor to substitute those additional moneys for the original trust moneys, and accordingly to impose, by way of substitution, the old trusts upon those additional moneys. But, in a case where the account into which the moneys are paid is the general trading account of the debtor on which he has been accustomed to draw both in the ordinary course and in breach of trust when there were trust funds standing to the credit of that account which were convenient for that purpose, I think it is impossible to attribute to him that by the mere payment into the account of further moneys, which to a large extent he subsequently used for purposes of his own, he intended to clothe those moneys with a trust in favour of the plaintiffs.'

[638] *Bishopsgate Investment Management Ltd v Homan* [1995] Ch 211 (CA), 216–21 *per* Dillon LJ, 221–2 *per* Leggatt LJ:

[Money from pension funds belonging to Bishopsgate Investment Management Ltd (BIM) (the trustee) was wrongly transferred to Maxwell Communications Corporation Plc (MCC) by Robert Maxwell. BIM claimed that this breach entitled BIM to an equitable charge over all of MCC's assets to secure recovery of the sum wrongly transferred. This would have given BIM priority over all of the unsecured creditors of MCC. The claim was rejected by the Court of Appeal (upholding Vinelott J's decision) on the grounds that the misappropriated money had been paid into an account that was overdrawn, or subsequently became so, and that tracing out of an exhausted mixed fund was impossible.]

Dillon LJ:

'In essence the judge [Vinelott J at first instance] held that B.I.M. could only claim an equitable charge on any assets of M.C.C. in accordance with the recognised principles of equitable tracing and these principles do not permit tracing through an overdrawn bank account—whether an account which was already overdrawn at the time the relevant moneys were paid into it or an account which was then in credit, but subsequently became overdrawn by subsequent drawings.

The judge reserved, however, the position if it were shown that there was a connection between a particular misappropriation of B.I.M.'s moneys and the acquisition by M.C.C. of a particular asset. The judge gave as an instance of such a case what he called "backward tracing"—where an asset was acquired by M.C.C. with moneys borrowed from an overdrawn or loan account and there was an inference that when the borrowing was incurred it was the intention that it should be repaid by misappropriations of B.I.M.'s moneys. Another possibility was that moneys misappropriated from B.I.M. were paid into an overdrawn account of M.C.C. in order to reduce the overdraft and so make finance available within the overdraft limits for M.C.C. to purchase some particular asset.

By a respondent's notice by way of cross-appeal, the administrators ask us to overrule these reservations of the judge, and hold that even if the possible facts which the judge envisages were clearly proved that could not in law give B.I.M. any equitable charge on the particular asset acquired. For my part I would not interfere at all with this aspect of the judge's exercise of his discretion. In my judgment, if the connection he postulates between the particular misappropriation of B.I.M.'s money and the acquisition by M.C.C. of a particular asset is sufficiently clearly proved, it is at least arguable, depending on the facts, that there ought to be an equitable charge in favour of B.I.M. on the asset in question of M.C.C.

But the main claims of B.I.M. are put much more widely as claims to an equitable charge on all the assets of M.C.C. These claims are not founded on proving any particular intention of Robert Maxwell or others in charge of M.C.C. but on general principles which it is said that the court ought to apply. They are founded primarily on certain observations of Lord Templeman in giving the judgment of the Privy Council in *Space Investments Ltd. v. Canadian Imperial Bank of Commerce Trust Co. (Bahamas) Ltd.* [1986] 1 W.L.R. 1072. In particular, in that case Lord Templeman said, at p. 1074:

> "In these circumstances it is impossible for the beneficiaries interested in trust money misappropriated from their trust to trace their money to any particular asset belonging to the trustee bank. But equity allows the beneficiaries, or a new trustee appointed in place of an insolvent bank trustee . . . to trace the trust money to all the assets of the bank and to recover the trust money by the exercise of an equitable charge over all the assets of the bank. . . that equitable charge secures for the beneficiaries and the trust priority over the claims of the customers . . . and . . . all other unsecured creditors."

What Lord Templeman there said was strictly obiter, in that on the facts the Privy Council held that the bank trustee was authorised by the trust instruments to deposit trust money with itself as banker and so there had been no misappropriation. The beneficiaries or their new trustee therefore could merely prove with the other general creditors of the insolvent bank trustee for a dividend in respect of the moneys so deposited.

Vinelott J. rejected the submissions of B.I.M. founded on the *Space Investments* case. He considered that Lord Templeman could not have intended to effect such a fundamental change to the well-understood limitations to equitable tracing; Lord Templeman was only considering the position of an insolvent bank which had been taking deposits and lending money.

. . .

As I read the judgment of the Privy Council in *In re Goldcorp Exchange Ltd.* [[1995] 1 AC 74] delivered by Lord Mustill, it makes it clear that Lord Templeman's observations in the *Space Investments* case [1986] 1 W.L.R. 1072 were not concerned at all with the situation we have in the present case where trust moneys have been paid into an overdrawn bank account, or an account which has become overdrawn. Lord Mustill said in the clearest terms, [1995] 1 A.C. 74, 104:

> "Their Lordships should, however, say that they find it difficult to understand how the judgment of the Board in *Space Investments Ltd. v. Canadian Imperial Bank of Commerce Trust Co. (Bahamas) Ltd.* [1986] 1 W.L.R. 1072, on which the claimants leaned heavily in argument, would enable them to overcome the difficulty that the moneys said to be impressed with the trust were paid into an overdrawn account and thereupon ceased to exist: see, for example, *In re Diplock* [1948] Ch. 465. The observations of the Board in the *Space Investments* case were concerned with a mixed, not a non-existent, fund."

. . .

Thus the wide interpretation of those observations put forward by Cooke P., which is the basis of the first ground of appeal in the present case, is rejected. Instead the decision of the Court of Appeal in *In re Diplock; Diplock v. Wintle* [1948] Ch. 465 [**[628]** above] is endorsed. There it was said, at p. 521:

> "The equitable remedies presuppose the continued existence of the money either as a separate fund or as part of a mixed fund or as latent in property acquired by means of such a fund. If, on the facts of any individual case, such continued existence is not established, equity is as helpless as the common law itself."

Also endorsed, in my judgment, in the decision of the Board delivered by Lord Mustill is the long-standing first instance decision in *James Roscoe (Bolton) Ltd. v. Winder* [1915] 1 Ch. 62 [**[637]** above], which Mr. Heslop for B.I.M., in his submissions in March, invited us to overrule. . . .

[In conclusion] . . . [i]t is not open to us to say that because the moneys were trust moneys the fact that they were paid into an overdrawn account or have otherwise been dissipated presents no difficulty to raising an equitable charge on assets of M.C.C. for their amount in favour of B.I.M. The difficulty Lord Mustill referred to is not displaced.'

Leggatt LJ:

'. . . as this court asserted in *In re Diplock* [1948] 1 Ch. 465, . . . it is only possible to trace in equity money which has continued existence, actual or notional. That was why in *James Roscoe (Bolton) Ltd. v. Winder* [1915] 1 Ch. 62, where trust funds had been mixed with private moneys in a bank account and the credit balance reduced at one point to £25 18s. 0d. before being replenished, Sargant J. held that the beneficiary's charge extended only to that sum. As Buckley L.J. said in *Borden (U.K.) Ltd. v. Scottish Timber Products Ltd.* [1981] Ch. 25 [**[626]** above], 46: "it is a fundamental feature of the doctrine of tracing that the property to be traced can be identified at every stage of its journey through life. . . ."

For the same reason there can be no equitable remedy against an asset acquired before misappropriation of money takes place, since ex hypothesi it cannot be followed into something which existed and so had been acquired before the money was received and therefore without its aid.

The concept of a "composite transaction" is in my judgment fallacious. What is envisaged is (a) the purchase of an asset by means of an overdraft, that is, a loan from a bank, and (b) the discharge of the loan by means of misappropriated trust money. The judge thought that the money could be regarded as having been used to acquire the asset. His conclusion was that "It is sufficient to say that proof that trust moneys were paid into an overdrawn account of the defaulting trustee may not always be sufficient to bar a claim to an equitable charge."

I see the force of Mr. Kosmin's submission that, if an asset were used as security for an overdraft which was then discharged by means of misappropriated money, the beneficiary might obtain priority by subrogation. But there can ordinarily be no tracing into an asset which is already in the hands of the defaulting trustee when the misappropriation occurs.'

[639] ***Foskett v McKeown* [1998] Ch 265 (CA), 283–4 *per* Sir Richard Scott V-C:** [The facts are outlined at **[635]** above.]

'[283] It has been argued on behalf of the purchasers that not simply the £596.74 but the whole of the 1988 premium ought to be treated as having been paid out of the purchasers' money. Put shortly, the £10,220 premium appears to have been paid out of an account which was in credit when the payment was made to the tune only of £596.74. This is the £596.74 which the judge concluded had derived from the purchasers' money. The balance of the £10,220 premium was raised by use of the overdraft facilities allowed on the account. That being so, the balance of the premium would appear to have been provided not by the purchasers' money but by the bank. The judge, relying on such authorities as *James Roscoe (Bolton) Ltd. v. Winder* [1915] 1 Ch. 62 [**[637]** above]; *In re Goldcorp Exchange Ltd.* [1995] 1 A.C. 74 and *Bishopsgate Investment Management Ltd. v. Homan* [1995] Ch. 211 [**[638]** above], 221, per Leggatt L.J., concluded that, save for the £596.74, the purchasers could not, therefore, trace their money into the 1988 premium. However, very shortly after the 1988 premium was paid, there was a transfer into the overdrawn account of a sum of money sufficient in amount to repay the borrowing. It is contended by Mr. Cooper that this sum of money, as well as the £596.74, derived from the purchasers' money. A conclusion in the purchasers' favour on this point cannot be made at this summary judgment stage. It may be, however, that at trial the purchasers will succeed in establishing that not only the £594.76 but also the money used to repay the overdrawing was their money. And it may be, indeed as at present advised I regard it as likely, that they will establish that it was Mr. Murphy's intention throughout to use purchasers' money to pay the 1988 premium. If that is the case, it does not seem to me at all obvious that the circumstance that the payment into the account of the purchasers' money was made very shortly after the payment of the premium, rather than before or at the same time as the payment, should be regarded as fatal to the purchasers' equitable tracing claim. The availability of equitable remedies ought, in my view, to depend upon the substance of the transaction in question and not upon the strict order in which associated events happen. Moreover, there is at least some authority which the purchasers could pray in aid: see *Agricultural Credit Corporation of Saskatchewan v. Pettyjohn* (1991) 79 D.L.R. (4th) 22 and [L Smith] "Tracing into the Payment of a Debt" [1995] C.L.J. 290, 292–295. I would wish, for my part, to make it clear that I regard the point as still open and, in particular, that I do not regard the fact that an asset is paid for out of borrowed money with the borrowing subsequently repaid out of trust [284] money as being necessarily fatal to an equitable tracing claim by the trust beneficiaries. If, in such a case, it can be shown that it was always the intention to use the trust money to acquire the asset, I do not see why the order in which the events happen should be regarded as critical to the claim. I am of the opinion, however, that the purchasers have not, in respect of any part of the 1988 premium, shown a case that justifies summary judgment.'

Question:

Do these last two cases indicate a potential role for 'backwards tracing'? If so, is the role truly 'tracing', or is it some other legal mechanism?

Also see:

Re Goldcorp Exchange Ltd [1995] 1 AC 74 (PC) and contrast this case and the previous two case extracts with the 'swollen assets' theory advanced in *Space Investments Ltd v Canadian Imperial Bank of Commerce Trust Co. (Bahamas) Ltd* [1986] 1 WLR 1072, 1074 *per* Lord Templeman (cited in the extract at **[638]**).

FURTHER READING:

S Evans, 'Rethinking Tracing and the Law of Restitution' (1999) 115 *LQR* 469.
L Smith, 'Tracing in Bank Accounts: The Lowest Intermediate Balance Rule on Trial' (2000) 33 *Can Bus LJ* 75.

FURTHER GENERAL READING:

D A McConville, 'Tracing and the Rule in Clayton's Case' (1963) 79 *LQR* 388.
A J Oakley, 'The Prerequisites of an Equitable Tracing Claim' (1975) 28 *CLP* 64.
R Goode, 'The Right to Trace and its Impact in Commercial Transactions' (1976) 92 *LQR* 360, 528.
P Millett, 'Tracing the Proceeds of Fraud' (1991) 107 *LQR* 71.
D Hayton, 'Equity's Identification Rules' in P Birks (ed), *Laundering and Tracing* (1995, Clarendon: Oxford), pp 1–21.
S Moriarty, 'Tracing, Mixing and Laundering' in P Birks (ed), *Laundering and Tracing* (1995, Clarendon: Oxford), pp 73–94.
L D Smith, 'Tracing into the Payment of a Debt' [1995] *CLJ* 290.
P Oliver, 'The Extent of Equitable Tracing' (1995) 9 *Trust Law International* 78.
L D Smith, *The Law of Tracing* (1997, Clarendon: Oxford).
C Band, 'The Development of Tracing Rules in Commercial Cases' [1997] *LMCLQ* 65.
NH Andrews and J Beatson, 'Common Law Tracing: Springboard or Swansong?' (1997) 113 *LQR* 21.

7

Protection of Interests in Property

7.1 Introduction

The previous chapter indicated the ways in which the law protects proprietary interests by allowing or deeming them to persist despite unauthorised dealings with the claimant's property. That chapter examined proprietary interests which might persist in the original property, notwithstanding the purported granting of conflicting interests in the same property to third parties. It also considered the possibility of asserting new proprietary interests (whether ownership interests or something less) in alternative property in order to preserve and protect some of the rights inherent in ownership of the original property where that ownership had been lost. The focus was on remedies which were proprietary.

This chapter is concerned with the *personal* remedies which the law provides to protect holders of proprietary interests. Protection is provided under the rubric of tort law, contract law, the law of unjust enrichment and, either in an independent or a supplementary role, equity. This chapter cannot detail the law in all these areas. All that it aims to do is outline the strategy with underpins certain aspects of each of these areas, so as to indicate in very broad terms how such intervention can be used to advantage by holders of proprietary interests. While the other chapters could hope to provide some degree of detail, this chapter is more in the nature of a signpost, indicating potential avenues for the protection of proprietary interests.

It will be apparent that the extracts included in this chapter tend to focus on the margins of contract, tort, unjust enrichment and trust. It is assumed that the general remedial principles associated with these various branches of the law are familiar—damages for breach of contract, compensation for tort (especially the tort of negligence), restitution for subtractive unjust enrichment, or equitable compensation for breach of trust. Instead, this chapter focuses on specific issues within these branches of the law which seem particularly relevant to the protection of personal property, or particularly relevant to a proper understanding of the issues discussed in earlier chapters. The collection of extracts is therefore selective, rather than representative of the usual routes to personal remedies for the protection of proprietary interests.

7.2 Remedies in tort

7.2.1 Introduction

The most common route in tort for the protection of interests in personal property is by an action in negligence alleging damage to the claimant's property which occasions loss to the claimant. The general principles of the law of negligence apply in determining both the existence of the breach of tortious duty and the quantum of the remedy. These principles are well known, and are not examined here. Alternatively, the claimant may be able to obtain an injunction (an equitable remedy) to prevent a threatened breach or to compel reinstatement of the property damaged by a past breach: the relevant principles are considered in Section 7.6.2 below.

Apart from alleging negligent damage to property, a claimant may also rely on the law relating to trespass and conversion. These options, which afford special protection to choses in possession, are considered below. Both actions are directed at remedying wrongful interference with the claimant's *possession* of the chattels; they are based on the claimant's right to possession, not on rights of ownership.[1] The protection is statutory, delivered by the Torts (Interference with Goods) Act 1977. This Act applies to all personal property *other than* money and choses in action (see section 14(1)). The difference between trespass and conversion was described by Atkin LJ in *Sanderson v Marsden & Jones* (1922) 10 Lloyd's LR 467, 472, as follows:

> 'An act of conversion differs from mere trespass inasmuch as the former must amount to a deprivation of possession to such an extent as to be inconsistent with the right of the owner and [must] evidence an intention to deprive him of that right, whereas the latter includes every direct forcible injury or act disturbing the possession of the owner, however slight the act may be.'

7.2.2 Trespass to goods

The tort of trespass to goods protects individuals against direct interference with their possession of the chattel. This includes taking away the chattel, as well as any unauthorised contact with the chattel. The claimant must be in possession of the chattel at the time of the interference,[2] and the interference must be negligent or wilful, not merely accidental (see **[701]** below).

A claimant who can prove trespass to goods is entitled to recover damages for the destruction or depreciation of the goods, and damages for losses (including loss of

[1] Although often the claimant will have both rights of ownership and rights to possession.

[2] Although an exception is made in favour of a trustee not yet in possession if the beneficiary has possession of the chattel.

profits) which result from the claimant being deprived of the use of the asset. In some circumstances the claimant may also (or as an alternative) be able to obtain an injunction in support of these rights (see Section 7.6.2 below). A claimant can also rely on the Torts (Interference with Goods) Act 1977 sections 3 and 4, which expands upon these common law remedies by providing that in certain circumstances the defendant can be required to re-deliver the asset to the claimant rather than simply paying damages. This possibility may make it advantageous for a claimant to claim in trespass rather than in negligence.

[701] *National Coal Board v JE Evans & Co (Cardiff) Ltd* [1951] 2 KB 861 (CA), 880–1 *per* Morris LJ:

[The claimants laid an electric cable under the land of a county council without its knowledge or consent. The council contracted with the first defendants to dig a trench on the land, the proposed line of which crossed the cable, but the cable was not visible on the plan given to the first defendants by the council. The first defendants sub-contracted with the second defendants to dig the trench, and in the course of doing so their driver hit the cable and it was damaged. The Court of Appeal held that there was no liability in trespass, since the act was involuntary and accidental and neither negligent nor wilful.]

> 'I am of the same opinion. *Weaver v. Ward* (Hob. 134), to which my Lords have referred, was decided in 1607 and has been much referred to in the later authorities. The words cited by my Lords: "Therefore, no man shall be excused of a trespass . . . except it may be judged utterly without his fault", show . . . that there clearly may be such cases. Illustrations of the types of such cases were given in the concluding words of the report in *Weaver v. Ward.* The words are: "As if a man by force take my hand and strike you, or if here the defendant had said that the plaintiff ran cross his piece when it was discharging, or had set forth the case with the circumstances, so as it had appeared to the court that it had been inevitable, and that the defendant had committed no negligence to give occasion to the hurt".
>
> The first of those illustrations would be a case in which the act was not in reality that of the defendant at all. The second illustration given is that "the plaintiff ran cross his piece when it was discharging". That illustration may, perhaps, be comparable with the facts of this case. In my judgment, the position of the two defendants in this action must be judged on the same footing as the conduct of Glamorgan County Council would have been judged if the county council had themselves done the work on their own land, instead of employing others to do it. If somebody is lawfully digging on his own land and someone else comes and interposes an article between the spade as it is descending and the ground, so that the article is damaged, and damaged without any intention on the part of the person digging, it cannot, in my judgment, be said that the latter was guilty of a trespass. It would be a case within the illustration given in *Weaver v. Ward.* The position, in my judgment, would be no different if someone, without the permission or knowledge of the owner of the land, buried an article under the soil in a place where the owner would be perfectly entitled to dig. If he did so dig and unintentionally damaged the thing which had been buried without his knowledge or permission, it could not, in my judgment, be said that the occurrence was the fault of the owner of the land rather than the fault of the owner of the thing. Those really are the facts of this case, which, on its own facts, affords an illustration of what was referred to as an act that might be "judged utterly without his fault". There was, in my judgment, no fault at all in either of the defendants.'

As well as showing that the alleged trespass was without the defendant's fault (ie neither wilful nor negligent), a defendant may have a defence to an act of trespass (or any other tort) if the act was *necessary* to protect third parties or their property from immediate and serious danger (the defence of 'necessity'). However, this defence will apply only in exceptional circumstances. For example, in *Monsanto v Tilly & Ors*[3] the defendants were protesting against the growing of genetically modified crops by Monsanto. They visited a farm in Oxfordshire and pulled up many of Monsanto's GM plants. They then unsuccessfully sought to justify their actions (which would otherwise constitute trespass to both goods and land) on the basis that they were necessary to protect third parties and their property, or were in the public interest. The Court of Appeal found that the special circumstances necessary to justify the defence of necessity were not present in this case. Moreover, that defence is available only if the defendant acts reasonably, and private action where there is a responsible public authority could rarely qualify as reasonable.[4]

The *Monsanto* case also rejected the existence of the wider defence of 'public interest', which might often be used to excuse all sorts of wrongdoing.[5] It reiterated the statement in *Blackstone's Commentaries* Volume 1 134–140: 'So great moreover is the regard of the Law for private property that it will not authorise the least violation of it; no, not even for the general good of the whole community.'

7.2.3 Conversion

(a) The claimant's right to bring an action

Conversion is any deliberate dealing with a chattel in a manner inconsistent with the claimant's right to possession. It follows that a claimant wishing to sue in conversion must have the right to possession at the time the conversion takes place.[6] If the claimant cannot show this, then the action will fail. However, the claimant does not have to show that he has the ultimate or best right to possession; all he has to show is that he has a better right than the defendant. The dispute is one purely between claimant and defendant. It follows that bailees and 'finders' may be able to sue in conversion if the bailed or found property is taken from them by someone with no better right to it than they have.[7]

[3] Court of Appeal, 25 November 1999, unreported (New Law Online case no. 2991120505). See the judgment of Mummery LJ, pp. 16–18 of the transcript.

[4] See *Burmah Oil Co Ltd v Lord Advocate* [1965] AC 75, 164 *per* Lord Upjohn.

[5] See *Southwark LBC v Williams* [1971] Ch 734, 744 *per* Lord Denning, 747 *per* Megaw LJ.

[6] *The Future Express* [1993] 2 Lloyd's Rep 542.

[7] Where there are competing rights to the goods, the Torts (Interference with Goods) Act 1977 s 8 requires the claimant to identify any other person known to have an interest in the goods; the defendant may then apply to have such interested parties joined in the action.

Re-read:

Parker v British Airways Board [1982] QB 1004, at **[212]** above.

Difficulties can arise if the claimant relies on an immediate right to possession which exists because the claimant has *equitable* title to the property. On one view, the precondition to an action in conversion is met no matter how the immediate right to possession arises. The next extract illustrates that approach. The other view, however, is that if the legal owner could not have sued the defendant in conversion (eg because he consented to the defendant's act) then there is no basis upon which the equitable owner can recover.[8] Which approach is preferable?

[702] *International Factors Ltd v Rodriguez* [1979] QB 351, 356–9 *per* Sir David Cairns:

[The claimants entered into a factoring agreement with X Ltd, whereby X Ltd would hold all cheques received on trust for the claimants. The defendant was a director of X Ltd and was held liable in conversion when he paid cheques made out to X Ltd into that company's own account. Note the way in which damages for conversion were assessed. Although the claimants could have sued X Ltd in contract, the company was in dire financial straits. This explains the focus on the personal liability of one of its directors.]

> 'As to whether this was a conversion, counsel for the defendant says that the plaintiffs here had no more than a contractual right to receive these cheques; they had no proprietary right so as to enable them to sue in conversion. On the issue of damages, Mr. Steinfeld's proposition is that in this case, because the debts had been assigned, because notice of the assignment had been given to the debtors, their payment of the debts to the company did not discharge them from liability; that accordingly the plaintiffs are in a position to recover the full amount of those debts from the original debtors and that their damages should be limited to any trouble, inconvenience and expense to which they might be put in recovering the debts from the debtors and, no doubt, to any amount that proved to be irrecoverable if it so happened that any of the debtors were not able to pay.
>
> . . .
>
> In support of his contention that the plaintiffs were not entitled to sue in conversion, counsel relies, first, on a passage in *Clerk & Lindsell on Torts*, 14th ed. (1975), para. 1108, indicating that to have a right to sue in conversion, a plaintiff must have a right to possession; that a mere contractual right is not sufficient, but that a cestui qui trust would have a right to sue for conversion of property the legal ownership of which was in a bare trustee.
>
> It is clear law that a contractual right to have goods handed to him by another person is not in itself sufficient to clothe the person who has that right with power to sue in conversion. That was the decision of this court in *Jarvis v. Williams* [1955] 1 W.L.R. 71. . . .
>
> In my view, however, there was here something more than a contractual right. Clause 11 (e) of the agreement provided both that the company was to hold any debt paid direct

[8] In *The Future Express* [993] 2 Lloyd's Rep 542, it was accepted that the bank, as equitable pledgee of the goods, could not sue the carrier in conversion: see p 548 *per* Lloyd LJ.

to the company in trust for the plaintiffs and immediately after receipt of a cheque, in the case of payment by cheque, to hand over that cheque to the plaintiffs. Taking together the trust which was thereby set up and the obligation immediately on receipt to hand over the cheque to the plaintiffs, I am satisfied that the plaintiffs had here a sufficient proprietary right to sue in conversion.

For the proposition that a person with an equitable title to goods can sue in conversion assistance is derived from the decision of Shearman J. in *Healey v. Healey* [1915] 1 K.B. 938. That was a case where by a marriage settlement a husband assigned to trustees certain chattels upon trust to allow them to be used by the wife during her life; the wife brought an action against the husband for wrongful detention of the chattels and it was held that the action could be maintained by the wife without joining the trustees of the settlement as parties. It is perhaps curious that that is the only decision that counsel has been able to discover of a cestui qui trust being entitled to sue in conversion, but it seems to me that since the fusion of law and equity that is sound law.

. . . It is further contended that *Healey v. Healey* is no authority for the proposition that the trustee himself can be sued in conversion. It would be surprising to me if the trustee could not be sued in conversion; certainly before the Theft Act 1968 there was a specific crime of conversion by trustee; probably under the Theft Act a disposal for his own purposes of goods held in trust by the trustee would constitute theft, and I find it difficult to suppose that a trustee making away for his own benefit with trust property, or for the benefit of some person other than the equitable owner of it, would not be liable in conversion. But however that may be, the defendant himself was not the trustee; the defendant himself disposed of the cheques in such a way as to take them away from the plaintiffs, who were entitled to have them, and put them into the company's bank account; that was a disposition which I am quite satisfied amounted to a conversion.

The judge in the court below derived assistance in reaching his decision from the judgment of McNair J. in *Marquess of Bute v. Barclays Bank Ltd.* [1955] 1 Q.B. 202. That was a case of conversion of certain warrants by a farm manager, who had received the warrants in connection with his occupation as farm manager with the intention that the money should go to his employer, the Marquess of Bute; the defendant used the warrants for his own purposes and it was held that notwithstanding the fact that the warrants were made out in the name of the defendant his act constituted a conversion of them. That decision is of some assistance to the plaintiffs in this case, inasmuch as it shows that the fact that the cheques were made out in favour of the company is no sufficient answer to the claim of the plaintiffs that they were the persons who owned the cheques in equity and were entitled to have them handed directly to them. I am accordingly satisfied that conversion was established here.

So far as damages are concerned, in my view, the general position in relation to the conversion of a cheque is that the conversion gives the person entitled to the cheque a right to damages measured by the face value of the cheque. That, as the judge stated, has been established by a whole series of cases in some of which the defendants were banks. The damages may, of course, be mitigated by special circumstances; for example, to take the case which Mr. Steinfeld suggested to us, if the cheque were stopped before payment into his bank by the wrongdoer and a fresh cheque given in substitution for it which was duly met. But it would be for the defendant to establish that there were circumstances of that kind which relieved him of his full liability in damages.

It is said here that the plaintiffs are not shown to have suffered any damage and certainly not the amount of damages which they claim, because they still have a right of action against the debtors. That seems to me to be no ground upon which the defendant can escape from paying damages in full. The position simply is that, assuming, as I will, that there is a right of action against the debtors, a plaintiff who has two causes of action cannot be met when he makes a claim against one defendant by the answer: "Oh, no; you've suffered nothing by my tort because you have a cause of action against somebody else." That clearly cannot be right. To take an example, if X wrongfully converted Y's motor car and handed it to Z, an auctioneer, who innocently sold it, Y could recover full damages from Z and it would be no answer to his claim to say that he had an equal claim against X. This is an a fortiori case, because here it is the defendant who is the wrongdoer, and, in my judgment, he cannot set up against the plaintiffs' claim to the full value of the cheques the contention that the plaintiffs could call upon the debtors to pay over again for goods that they have already paid for, though unfortunately they made the mistake of paying them to the wrong person at the time.'

Questions:

1. Was it critical in this case that the trust was an express trust? Would the same result have followed if the trust had been a constructive trust arising because the underlying contract to transfer was specifically enforceable? *Should* there be any difference in the treatment of these two situations?
2. When, precisely, will a contractual right to have the goods handed over be an insufficient basis for an action in conversion? In *Moorgate Mercantile Co Ltd v Finch and Read* [1962] 1 QB 701 (CA) (see **[705]** below), the court considered that a term in a hire-purchase agreement which provided that, on certain breaches, 'the owners shall forthwith without notice or demand become entitled immediately to recover possession of the vehicle', was sufficient to give the hirers the right to sue in conversion after such a breach and without recovering actual possession of the car (which had in any event become impossible).

(b) Property which can be converted

Since conversion is premised on interference with the claimant's right to possession, only property which can be possessed can be converted. It follows that choses in possession can be converted, but not choses in action. Moreover, an action may lie for conversion in respect of dealings with money but only so long as it has not passed into currency.[9] Once the money has passed into currency no action in conversion will lie, although it may be possible to recover the money in a restitutionary action for money had and received.[10]

[9] This happens when it passes to a *bona fide* purchaser for value. Such a person takes full legal title (ie the rights to legal ownership and possession) regardless of any defects in the title of the transferor of the money.

[10] See *Lipkin Gorman v Karpnale Ltd* [1991] 2 AC 548, 559 *per* Lord Templeman (see **[618]** above and **[713]** below).

(c) Dealings which may constitute conversion

Many forms of dealing can constitute conversion. A defendant who wrongfully takes the claimant's property, or keeps it, or sells it, or loses it, or destroys it, or gives it away may be liable to the claimant in conversion. However, the defendant will be liable only if the act was carried out with an intention to assert some sort of dominion over the asset inconsistent with the claimant's (see **[703]** and **[704]** below). Still, this condition is not as limiting as it seems. In particular, the convertor need not 'know' that the claimant has any inconsistent rights. A purchaser from a thief, for example, may think that his rights of ownership and possession are exclusive; nevertheless, if he sells the goods, or refuses to give them up to the true owner, he will commit an act of conversion.

[703] ***Fouldes v Willoughby*** **(1841) 5 M & W 540, 547** ***per*** **Lord Abinger:**
[The claimant had paid for the transportation of 2 horses on the defendant's ferry. The defendant wrongfully refused to carry them, took them from the claimant and turned them loose on the landing-place. It was held that this did not constitute a conversion.]

> 'It has never yet been held that the single act of removal of a chattel independent of any claim over it, either in favour of the party himself or anyone else, amounts to a conversion of a chattel. In the present case, therefore, the simple removal of the horses by the defendant for a purpose wholly unconnected with any least denial of the right of the plaintiff to the possession and enjoyment of them is no conversion.'

[704] ***Ashby v Tolhurst*** **[1937] 2 KB 242, 256–7** ***per*** **Romer LJ:**
[The facts are outlined at **[215]** above. Of interest here is the finding that the defendant car park owners were not liable in conversion for allowing an imposter to take away the claimant's car.]

> '[256] It only remains to deal with the suggestion that there was a conversion of the car by the servant of the defendants. Although the car was not delivered to the defendants [ie the defendants never acquired the right to possession of the car under a contract of bailment], I apprehend that the servant acting within his authority might have bound the defendants by an act of conversion if he had purported to deal with the car as the owner. All that is said is that the attendant told the plaintiff, when he came back for his car and found it was not there, that he, the attendant, had given the car to somebody else. It is quite plain that the attendant did not use the word "given" in its ordinary sense, because the car was not his to give and he knew it. But it is said by Mr. Cloutman that what the word "given" shows is that the attendant purported to deal with the car in some way inconsistent with the rights of the plaintiff, who was the true owner. The circumstances in which such a dealing [257] amounts to conversion have been stated by Atkin J., as he then was, in *Lancashire and Yorkshire Ry. Co. v. MacNicoll* (118 L.T. 596, 598): "It appears to me plain that dealing with goods in a manner inconsistent with the right of the true owner amounts to a conversion." Then he adds these words: "providing it is also established that there is an intention on the part of the defendant in so doing to deny the owner's right or to assert a right which is inconsistent with the owner's right." It is perfectly plain that this attendant did neither the one nor the other.'

These extracts suggest that an act will only count as conversion if it is consciously adverse to the claimant's rights.[11] However, as the next extract shows, this does not mean that the act must carry with it an actual intention to deprive the claimant of rights. It need only be a deliberate (including negligent) act which has that consequence.

[705] ***Moorgate Mercantile Co Ltd v Finch & Read*** **[1962] 1 QB 701 (CA), 705–6** ***per*** **Dankwerts LJ:**

[The Court of Appeal held that it was conversion when the defendant used a hire purchase car for smuggling, and it was then confiscated by H.M. Customs and Excise.]

> 'The first question to decide is whether what the second defendant did constituted a conversion. What he did, of course, was to go to the place where the car happened to be, to borrow it and then fill it up with the uncustomed goods, which conduct was likely to result in the consequence which indeed in fact happened, that the car was seized by the customs authorities and sold. I think it is clear, and it seems to me to be an irresistible inference, that when he went to borrow the car, he had already in his mind the intention of using it for the illegal purposes for which he did in fact use it, and I think that if he had not deceived the persons who were concerned with the car about his intentions, that is to say, the hirer and the garage owner, they would not have allowed him to take it. In any case it seems to me that the consequences of what he did resulted in a conversion of the car in question.
>
> The county court judge cited a passage from *Salmond on Torts*, 13th ed. (1961), p. 262:
>
>> "Conversion Defined: A conversion is an act of wilful interference, without lawful justification, with any chattel in a manner inconsistent with the right of another, whereby that other is deprived of the use and possession of it. Two elements are combined in such interference: (1) a dealing with the chattel in a manner inconsistent with the right of the person entitled to it, and (2) an intention in so doing to deny that person's right or to assert a right which is in fact inconsistent with such right."
>
> What the second defendant did in fact was to take the car and use it in a way which necessarily, or might, at any rate, in all probability, result in the owners being deprived of the car for ever, because he had placed the watches in the car, and that, if it was found out, would inevitably give the customs authorities a right to confiscate the car with, of course, a final loss of it to the plaintiffs if that event occurred. It seems to me that whether the second defendant intended that consequence to follow or not—presumably he did not intend it, but hoped he would not be found out—nonetheless, he must be taken to intend the consequences which were likely to happen from the conduct of which he was guilty, and which did in fact result in the loss of the car to the plaintiffs. To my mind, there is no doubt whatever that there was a conversion by the second defendant.'

(d) Forms of relief

The usual form of relief is damages. The claimant can recover damages for all the losses which are the natural and direct result of the conversion. These may include

[11] It follows that simply keeping goods will not count as conversion unless the act is consciously adverse to the claimant's rights (eg a refusal to give up the goods on demand).

damages for non-pecuniary interests, such as the inconvenience and distress of being deprived of the property. The general rule, as for other torts, is that damages are assessed at the date of the conversion. This is so even if the value of the goods falls after the date of the conversion (see **[706]** below). This rule ensures that the converter bears the loss. However, if the value of the goods *rises* after the date of the conversion, so that the converter stands to profit from the conversion, it is sometimes possible for the claimant to recover the rise in value of the goods as consequential damages.[12]

As indicated earlier, the Torts (Interference with Goods) Act 1977 adds to these remedies. It gives the court the discretion to order re-delivery of the converted property. In practice, the claimant can safely assume that a court would make such an order where damages would provide an inadequate remedy. But equally, in other cases such an order may be unlikely. In the absence of such an order, the claimant is only entitled to damages; the *defendant* has the discretion to elect whether to return the good or pay damages.[13]

Finally, both the common law and the 1977 Act provide some protection for 'innocent' converters. If the defendant has improved the converted goods in the honest but mistaken belief that he had a good title to them, then both the general law and section 6(1) provide that the assessment of damages due to the claimant should make allowance for any resulting increase in the value of the goods. The statutory provision is effectively an enactment of the judgment of Lord Denning in *Greenwood v Bennett* (see **[708]** below).

[706] ***BBMB Finance (Hong Kong) Ltd v EDA Holdings Ltd*** **[1990] 1 WLR 409 (PC), 412–3 *per* Lord Templeman for the Board:**

[A bonus issue of shares was held on trust for the claimants. The share certificate and executed blank transfers were deposited with the defendant as security for a loan from the defendant. The defendant then irreversibly converted the certificate and shares by selling them to a third party in return for a postdated cheque representing the market value of the shares at that time (HK$90 million). The cheque was never presented for payment. The defendant subsequently purchased replacement shares, but at a much lower price (approximately HK$21.5 million). The claimants sued in conversion and were awarded the difference between the value of the shares at the date of conversion and the value of the replacement shares at the date of replacement (ie approximately HK$28.5 million).]

> 'In this appeal the defendant contends that the plaintiffs suffered no damage; they were entitled to 10,886,855 E.I.L. shares and they have received 10,886,855 E.I.L. shares.
>
> The general rule is that a plaintiff whose property is irreversibly converted has vested in him a right to damages for conversion measured by the value of the property at the date of conversion. For this rule, there is clear authority. In *Solloway v. McLaughlin* [1938] A.C. 247 a company of brokers unlawfully sold shares deposited with them by a client for $65,320 and later replaced the shareholding with identical shares at a cost of $32,000. The client was awarded the difference between the sums by way of damages for conversion. Lord Atkin, delivering the advice of the Board, said, at pp. 257–258:

12 Eg, *The Playa Larga* [1983] 2 Lloyd's Rep. 171 (CA), 181–2 *per* Ackner LJ.

13 It seems that the claimant would be protected on the defendant's insolvency: the defendant could not elect to keep the goods and pay damages unless the damages claim was paid in full.

> "As to the deposited shares, in the circumstances of the case the company never had any right to deal with them. . . . Their disposal of the deposited shares amounted to nothing short of conversion, and the client on each occasion on which the shares were sold had vested in him a right to damages for conversion which would be measured by the value of the shares at the date of the conversion . . . not knowing of the conversion, he received from the wrongdoer, and has retained, the very goods converted or their equivalent . . . the only effect is that he must give credit for the value of what he has received at the time he received it, and . . . the damages are reduced by this amount."

[On the other hand] Mr. Evans-Lombe, who appeared for the defendant, submitted, correctly, that there is a line of authority which establishes the basic principle that, in the assessment of damages, a plaintiff can recover the loss he has suffered, no more and no less. This principle and some of its exceptions are indicated in the judgment of Denning L.J. in *Strand Electric and Engineering Co. Ltd. v. Brisford Entertainments Ltd.* [1952] 2 Q.B. 246, 253.

Mr. Evans-Lombe pointed out that damages for conversion may exceed the value of the property at the date of conversion if, for example, the property increases in value between the date of conversion and the date when the plaintiff discovers the conversion: see *Sachs v. Miklos* [1948] 2 K.B. 23. And where in conversion or in detinue, the plaintiff has only suffered temporary deprivation of his property, the appropriate measure of damages may be assessed by reference to the value at the date when the plaintiff demanded the return of the property (*Williams v. Archer* (1847) 5 C.B. 318) or the date when the plaintiff was prevented from reselling the property (*Barrow v. Arnaud* (1846) 8 Q.B. 595). In *Brandeis Goldschmidt Co. Ltd. v. Western Transport Ltd.* [1981] Q.B. 864 the plaintiffs' cargo of copper had been wrongfully detained for a period of nine months. The plaintiffs had never intended to resell the copper and failed to prove that they had suffered any damage by reason of the delay in delivery up. Brandon L.J. rejected, at p. 872,

> "the proposition that there is some universal rule of law governing the assessment of damages in cases of detention, which can be applied by rule of thumb . . ."

Brandon L.J. cited, and in the present case Mr. Evans-Lombe relied upon, the judgment of Bowen L.J. in *Williams v. Peel River Land and Mineral Co. Ltd.* (1886) 55 L.T. 689, 692–693, where it was said, inter alia:

> "If, in an action for wrongful detention by one man of that which belongs to another, there be no substantial loss at all sustained, but the mere denial of the right, which right is vindicated in the course of the action, in such a case, there being no pecuniary damage sustained, no pecuniary compensation is given, and nominal damages will be enough; but, if a substantial loss has been suffered in consequence of the wrongful act, what those who have to redress the wrong ought to do is to give compensation for the loss. You do not give damages in an action for detention *in poenam*; it is not a paternal correction inflicted by the court, but simply compensation for the loss . . . I cannot think that the law would really lay down anything so ridiculous as that a man should be compensated whether he suffered damages or not."

Both the *Brandeis* case [1981] Q.B. 864 and the *Peel River* case (1886) 55 L.T. 689 were concerned with damages caused by temporary deprivation of possession and use of property. A different consideration will apply when the property is irreversibly converted and the plaintiff loses that property. The plaintiff loses the value of the property at the date of conversion and the general rule is that the measure of damages is the value thus lost. To depart from that rule in the present case would be inconsistent with *Solloway v. McLaughlin* [1938] A.C. 247. Mr. Evans-Lombe submitted that in that case Lord Atkin was only concerned to deprive the defendant of a profit. But Lord Atkin's judgment is inconsistent with this submission. Mr. Evans-Lombe also sought to argue that the effect of *Solloway v. McLaughlin* has in some way been modified by the Torts (Interference with Goods) Act 1977, joined with the decision in the *Brandeis* case [1981] Q.B. 864. Their Lordships do not consider that the decision in *Solloway v. McLaughlin* can be affected by the *Brandeis* case or by the Act of 1977 which only came into force after the *Brandeis* case had been decided.

In the present case, on the findings of the trial judge, the defendant sold and irreversibly converted the Etek certificate, receiving in return the cheque for $90 million, and the plaintiffs thereupon became entitled to damages for conversion equal to the market price which was also the sale price. The inexplicable failure by the defendant to collect the sale price cannot mitigate or reduce the damages recoverable by the plaintiffs and cannot alter the measure of damages.'

[707] *Solloway v McLaughlin* [1938] AC 247 (PC), 259 *per* Lord Atkin for the Committee:

[The facts and outcome are indicated in the previous extract.]

'It is objected that this will be to put him [the plaintiff] in a better position than if he had not been defrauded at all, and this appears to have influenced the decision of the majority of the Court of Appeal in Ontario. All that this amounts to is to recognize that fraudulent brokers have often sounder judgment than their clients as to the future course of markets. If the shares had been converted and not returned, there can be no question that the client would have been entitled to receive the proceeds of the conversion though he himself had planned to hold and thought he had succeeded in holding the shares until a time when the value was nothing. Fortunately for the commercial community the law has many effective forms of relief against dishonest agents, and no injustice is done if the principal benefits, as he occasionally may, by the superior astuteness of an unjust steward in carrying out a fraud.'

Questions:

Is it sensible to distinguish between a conversion which permanently deprives the claimant of the property and a conversion which does not (see **[706]**)? Why should a defendant have to disgorge profits in one case but not in the other? *Does* the defendant have to disgorge profits in one case but not in the other, or is the measure compensatory in both cases?

[708] *Greenwood v Bennett* [1973] QB 195 (CA), 201–2 *per* Lord Denning MR:

[B's company was the legal owner of a second hand Jaguar car (although the case was argued as if B were the legal owner). B left the car with S to do specified repairs. S did not do the repairs, but used the car and wrecked it in an accident. S then sold the car for £75 to H, who honestly believed that S was the owner. H spent £226 on repairs, and sold the car to a finance company, which let it on hire purchase to P.

The police took possession of the car and sought directions from the court to determine who was entitled to it. The Court of Appeal held that B could have specific restitution of the car,[14] on the condition that he repay H the £226 spent improving its value.]

'To decide this case, I think it helpful to consider the legal position as if the police had not taken possession of the car, but it had remained in Mr. Prattle's possession.

In the first place, if Mr. Bennett's company had brought an action against Mr. Harper for conversion of the car (relying on his purchase of it from Mr. Searle for £75 as the act of conversion), then the damages would be £75 as its value at that time: whereas, if they had brought an action for conversion (relying on his sale of it to the finance company as the act of conversion) the damages would be its improved value at the time of sale, but the company would have to give credit for the work which Mr. Harper had done on it: see *Munro v. Willmott* [1949] 1 K.B. 295. So I suppose they would recover again about £75.

. . .

[Alternatively] if Mr. Bennett's company had brought an action against Mr. Prattle for specific delivery of the car, it is very unlikely that an order for specific delivery of the car would be made. But if it had been, no court would order its delivery unless compensation was made for the improvements. There is a valuable judgment by Lord Macnaghten in *Peruvian Guano Co. v. Dreyfus Brothers Co.* [1892] A.C. 166, 176, where he said:

> "I am not aware of any authority upon the point, but I should doubt whether it was incumbent upon the court to order the defendant to return the goods in specie where the plaintiff refused to make a fair and just allowance,"

So if this car was ordered to be returned to Mr. Bennett's company, I am quite clear the court in equity would insist upon a condition that payment should be made to Mr. Harper for the value of the improvements which he put on it.

Applying the principles stated by Lord Macnaghten, I should have thought that the county court judge here should have imposed a condition on the plaintiffs. He should have required them to pay Mr. Harper the £226 as a condition of being given delivery of the car.

But the judge did not impose such a condition. The plaintiffs have regained the car, and sold it. What then is to be done? It seems to me that we must order the plaintiffs to pay Mr. Harper the £226; for that is the only way of putting the position right.

Upon what principle is this to be done? Mr. Rawlins has referred us to the familiar cases which say that a man is not entitled to compensation for work done on the goods or property of another unless there is a contract express or implied, to pay for it. We all remember the saying of Pollock C.B.: "One cleans another's shoes; what can the other do but put them on?": *Taylor v. Laird* (1856) 25 L.J.Ex. 329, 332. That is undoubtedly the law when the person who does the work knows, or ought to know, that the property does not belong to him. He takes the risk of not being paid for his work on it. But it is very different when he honestly believes himself to be the owner of the property and does the work in that belief. (That distinction is drawn in the mining cases such as *Wood v. Morewood* (1841) 3 Q.B. 440 and *Livingstone v. Rawyards Coal Co.* (1880) 5 App.Cas. 25). Here we have an innocent purchaser who bought the car in good faith and without

[14] In fact, B had already taken unconditional delivery under the original order of the county court, and had resold the car for £400. H then appealed to the Court of Appeal.

notice of any defect in the title to it. He did work on it to the value of £226. The law is hard enough on him when it makes him give up the car itself. It would be most unjust if the company could not only take the car from him, but also the value of the improvements he has done to it—without paying for them. There is a principle at hand to meet the case. It derives from the law of restitution. The plaintiffs should not be allowed unjustly to enrich themselves at his expense. The court will order the plaintiffs, if they recover the car, or its improved value, to recompense the innocent purchaser for the work he has done on it. No matter whether the plaintiffs recover it with the aid of the courts, or without it, the innocent purchaser will recover the value of the improvements he has done to it.

In my opinion, therefore, the judge ought not to have released the car to the plaintiffs except on condition that the plaintiffs paid Mr. Harper the £226. But now that it has been released to them and they have sold it, we should order Mr. Bennett's company to pay Mr. Harper £226 in respect of the improvements he made to the car. I would allow the appeal accordingly.'

Question:

Did Lord Denning *need* to rely on principles of unjust enrichment? Does the unjust enrichment approach leave it open to the enriched party to rely on the defence of 'subjective devaluation'? For example, in the above case, would it be open to B to assert that, to B, the improvements made by H are worth less than £226, so B is only 'enriched' by some lesser sum, and only has to make restitution of that lesser sum to H? Is the remedy of 'damages' in conversion subject to the same problem, at least if it is effected by specific restitution of the chattel with an allowance for alterations or improvements?

7.2.4 Equity's contribution

Equity's contribution to the law of tort, and in particular to tort's protection of personal property, is usually seen as confined to the issuing of injunctions to prevent or to repair damage caused by acts regarded as common law torts. Injunctions are discussed in Section 7.6.2 below.

Only recently has equity been seen as adding to tort law in another way. It adds to the law on 'accessory liability' with its action for 'dishonest assistance'[15] in a breach of trust. An individual who dishonestly assists a trustee or fiduciary in the breach of fiduciary obligations owed by the fiduciary will be personally liable to the same extent as the fiduciary to make equitable compensation[16] to remedy any resulting losses to the trust fund or the fiduciary's property. This form of liability is still confusingly called 'liability as a constructive trustee'. That label is intended to suggest that the individual is liable in the same way as a trustee, although he is not a

[15] A term preferred to the older 'knowing assistance'.

[16] This is traditionally regarded as assessed differently from common law damages, although it seems that parallels are being increasingly recognised.

trustee. Moreover, there is no possibility of a 'trust', or any proprietary consequences, since no trust property need ever have come into the hands of the assister in the course of his assistance. The Privy Council decision in *Royal Brunei Airlines Sdn Bhd v Tan* [1995] 2 AC 378 effected a fundamental change of focus in these actions, recognising that the gist of the action is accessory liability, not some sort of (constructive) trusteeship. This route is now more clearly recognised as protecting the property of beneficiaries and principals (of fiduciaries) against unauthorised dealings by providing remedies against those who assist in such dealings.

7.3 Remedies in contract

7.3.1 Introduction

Property owners frequently enter into contracts in respect of their property. If things go wrong, they are protected by the remedies available in the law of contract. It is generally recognised that the right to claim damages protects a threefold division of interests, namely expectation, reliance and restitutionary interests. The claims in the expectation and reliance measures are alternatives.[17]

The general rules on assessment of damages are not considered in detail here. These rules are familiar.[18] However, something specific needs to be said about the possibility of disgorgement for breach of contract. This possibility relates to the situation where a defendant profits from a breach of contract, but where the payment of expectation damages to the claimant does not work to strip the defendant of those profits. The claimant may then seek disgorgement of those profits. The orthodox view is that such a remedy is not available for breach of contract, although in some circumstances a claimant can achieve the same ends by non-contractual routes. For example, a claimant may allege that the defendant has not only breached a contract, but has also engaged in a profitable breach of fiduciary duty; this latter breach is conventionally remedied by demanding disgorgement of the profits. However, the orthodox contractual view is under challenge. The reasons are explained in the extracts which follow (see **[709]** and **[710]** below).

The other focus of this section is on the equitable remedy of relief against forfeiture. In addition, equity can also provide a remedy by way of injunction (see Section 7.6.2). Both of these equitable remedies can provide valuable assistance to claimants in the protection of their property interests.

7.3.2 Disgorgement of profits for breach of contract

The central issue has already been explained. The next two extracts make clear the arguments on both sides.

[17] *Cullinane v British 'Rema' Manufacturing Co Ltd* [1954] 1 QB 292.

[18] That does not mean that the rules escape criticism. See, eg, E McKendrick, 'Breach of Contract and the Meaning of Loss' [1999] *CLP* 37.

[709] *Surrey CC v Bredero Homes Ltd* [1993] 1 WLR 1361 (CA), 1364–8 *per* Dillon LJ, 1368–70 *per* Steyn LJ:

[The case concerns real property, but the judgments articulate the general issues. The claimants sold their registered land to the defendant, subject to a covenant by the defendant to develop the land in accordance with a planning permission which the defendant had obtained. That planning permission provided for the building of only 72 dwelling houses, but the defendant, in accordance with a later planning permission, built 77 dwelling houses on the land. The court awarded only nominal damages for the breach of covenant.[19]]

Dillon LJ:

'[1364] The starting point, however, in my judgment is that the remedy at common law for a breach of contract is an award of damages, and damages at common law are intended to compensate the victim for his loss, not to transfer to the victim if he has suffered no loss the benefit which the wrongdoer has gained by his breach of contract. Thus it is stated in *Chitty on Contracts*, 26th ed. (1989), vol. 1. p. 1116, para. 1771:

> "Damages for a breach of contract committed by the defendant are a compensation to the plaintiff for the damage, loss or injury he has suffered through that breach."

Similarly, Viscount Haldane L.C. in *British Westinghouse Electric and Manufacturing Co. Ltd. v. Underground Electric Railways Co. of London Ltd.* [1912] A.C. 673, 689, said: "The fundamental basis is thus compensation for pecuniary loss naturally flowing from the breach; . . ." Lord Wilberforce in *Johnson v. Agnew* [1980] A.C. 367, 400, said: "The general principle for the assessment of damages is compensatory . . ."

[1365] Each of these three statements is accompanied by a statement to the effect that the innocent party is to be placed, so far as money can do so, in the same position as if the contract had been performed. That follows the wording of the statement of the rule of the common law by Parke B. in *Robinson v. Harman* (1848) 1 Ex. 850, 855. That rule has been referred to in argument in the present case as the "conventional" rule.

Sir William Goodhart, for the plaintiffs, pointed out that the conventional rule is not of universal application in that there are cases in which the plaintiff is awarded not what is required to place him in the same situation as if the contract had been performed, but what is required to recoup to him the expenditure which he has incurred and which has been wasted because the contract has not been performed: see, for instance, *Wallington v. Townsend* [1939] Ch. 588 and *Anglia Television Ltd. v. Reed* [1972] 1 Q.B. 60. The principle is still compensation for loss. The difference is merely that there are cases where the contract has so palpably not been performed at all that it would be unreal to assume that it has been performed and impossible to calculate damages on such an unreal assumption. Every student is taught that the basis of assessing damages for breach of contract is the rule in *Hadley v. Baxendale* (1854) 9 Ex. 341, which is wholly concerned with the losses which can be compensated by damages. Such damages may, in an appropriate case, cover profit which the injured plaintiff has lost, but they do not cover an award, to a plaintiff who has himself suffered no loss, of the profit which the defendant has gained for himself by his breach of contract.

In the field of tort there are areas where the law is different and the plaintiff can recover in respect of the defendant's gain. Thus in the field of trespass it is well established that if one person has, without leave of another, been using that other's land for his own pur-

[19] Contrast *Wrotham Park Estate Co Ltd v. Parkside Homes Ltd* [1974] 1 WLR 798.

poses he ought to pay for such user. Thus even if he had done no actual harm to the land he was charged for the user of the land. This was applied originally in wayleave cases where a person had without authority used his neighbour's land for passage: see, for instance, *Jegon v. Vivian* (1871) L.R. 6. Ch. App. 742 and *Phillips v. Homfray* (1871) L.R. 6 Ch. App. 770. The same principle was applied where the defendant had trespassed by tipping spoil on the plaintiff's land: *Whitwham v. Westminster Brymbo Coal and Coke Co.* [1896] 2 Ch. 538. The same principle was applied to patent infringement by the House of Lords in *Watson, Laidlaw Co. Ltd. v. Pott, Cassels and Williamson* (1914) 31 R.P.C. 104. The infringer was ordered to pay by way of damages a royalty for every infringing article because the infringement damaged the plaintiff's property right, that is to say, his patent monopoly. So in a case of detinue the defendant was ordered to pay a hire for chattels he had detained: *Strand Electric and Engineering Co. Ltd. v. Brisford Entertainments Ltd.* [1952] 2 Q.B. 246. Those cases do not apply in the present case as the defendant has made no use of any property of either plaintiff.

The cases have been taken still further in some fields of tort particularly concerned with intellectual property, where it is well established that the plaintiff can choose to have either damages or an account of profits made by the defendant by his wrongful acts: see, for instance, *Lever v. Goodwin* (1887) 36 Ch. D. 1, 7, per Cotton L.J. This is in line with the long-established common law doctrine of waiving the tort. The liability in the present case is solely in contract and not in tort.

[1366] I come then to the *Wrotham Park* case [1974] 1 W.L.R. 798. In that case the predecessor in title of the plaintiffs had in 1935 sold some land to a predecessor in title of the defendants, subject to a restrictive covenant restricting building to a particular layout. That covenant was duly registered under the Land Charges Act 1925. In 1971 the land was sold to the defendants, who had no actual knowledge of the restrictive covenant and proceeded to build 14 houses on the land in breach of the covenant. In early 1972 the plaintiffs, as successors in title to the benefit of the covenant, issued their writ against the defendants claiming an injunction to restrain building in breach of the covenant, and demolition of anything built in breach. The plaintiffs made no application for an interim injunction. By the time the action came on for trial in July 1973, the 14 houses had all been completed and sold to purchasers with the benefit of indemnity insurance policies. At the trial Brightman J. held that the plaintiffs were indeed entitled to the benefit of the covenant and the defendants were bound by it. For obvious reasons however—he could not shut his eyes to the fact that the houses existed and it would be an unpardonable waste of much needed houses to direct that they be pulled down—he refused to grant a mandatory injunction. He commented that no damage of a financial nature had been done to the plaintiffs by the breach of the covenant and proceeded to consider what damages, if any, he should award under the jurisdiction which had originated under Lord Cairns's Act to award damages in substitution for an injunction.

It was submitted to him that the damages should be nil or purely nominal because the value of the Wrotham Park estate was not diminished by one farthing in consequence of the breach of covenant. But the judge concluded that such a result would be of questionable fairness. He said, at p. 812:

> "If, for social and economic reasons, the court does not see fit in the exercise of its discretion, to order demolition of the 14 houses, is it just that the plaintiffs should receive no compensation and that the defendants should be left in undisturbed possession of the fruits of their wrongdoing?"

He then referred to the wayleave cases and *Whitwham v. Westminster Brymbo Coal and Coke Co.* [1896] 2 Ch. 538 and the other cases which I have mentioned where the same principle has been applied. He concluded that the appropriate course was that the defendants should pay by way of damages the sum which the plaintiffs might hypothetically have been willing to accept—though actually they would never have been willing to relax the covenant—to permit the defendants to do what they wanted to do on the land. He fixed that at a small percentage of the defendants' anticipated profit from building the 14 houses on the land.

The difficulty about the decision in the *Wrotham Park* case is that in *Johnson v. Agnew* [1980] A.C. 367, 400G, Lord Wilberforce, after citing certain decisions on the scope and basis of Lord Cairns's Act which were not cited to Brightman J., stated in the clearest terms that on the balance of those authorities and on principle he found in the Act no warrant for the court awarding damages differently from common law damages. Sir William Goodhart submits that it follows from that analysis by Lord Wilberforce in *Johnson v. Agnew* that the damages awarded by Brightman J. in the *Wrotham Park* case were indeed damages assessed on recognised common law principles which should, so he says, be applied in the present case.

[1367] I doubt, however, whether that does follow from Lord Wilberforce's analysis in *Johnson v. Agnew*. As I read his judgment, Brightman J. was not seeking to analyse the scope or basis of the court's jurisdiction under Lord Cairns's Act. He merely concluded that, as Parliament had expressly empowered the court to grant damages in lieu of an injunction, Parliament must have intended that in every case the court must be able to award such damages as would achieve a fair result between the parties and would not be limited to awarding nominal damages only. He sought to apply that conclusion. That involves a conclusion by the judge that Lord Cairns's Act effected a substantive change in the law of damages and was not a merely procedural statute as *Johnson v. Agnew* has held. It is unnecessary to refer further in this judgment to the *Wrotham Park* case since that was under Lord Cairns's Act and stands or falls by that; whereas, the present case is not, and makes no pretence of being, under that Act.

I should however mention in passing that we were referred to a number of cases where the measure of damages chosen by Brightman J. in the *Wrotham Park* case was applied by other judges, for instance, *Bracewell v. Appleby* [1975] Ch. 408; *Carr-Saunders v. Dick McNeil Associates Ltd.* [1986] 1 W.L.R. 922 and *Griffiths v. Kingsley-Stubbs* (unreported), 3 June 1986; Court of Appeal (Civil Division) Transcript No. 506 of 1986. All those were cases where the plaintiff's cause of action lay in tort, either trespass or nuisance, and the defendant had interfered with the plaintiff's property rights. The decisions and awards of damages are amply justified by the common law principles in tort of the wayleave cases and *Whitwham v. Westminster Brymbo Coal and Coke Co.* [1896] 2 Ch. 538 already mentioned.

Given that the established basis of an award of damages in contract is compensation for the plaintiff's loss, as indicated above, I have difficulty in seeing how Sir William Goodhart's suggested common law principle of awarding the plaintiff who has suffered no loss the gain which the defendant has made by the breach of contract is intended to go. Is it to apply, for instance, to shipping contracts or contracts of employment or contracts for building works?

Sir William suggested, in his and Mr. Weatherill's skeleton argument, that the conventional measure fails to do justice and a different measure should be applied where the following conditions are satisfied. (a) The breach is deliberate, in the sense that the defendant is deliberately doing an act which he knows or should know is plainly or arguably in breach of contract. (b) The defendant, as a result of the breach, has profited by making a gain or reducing a loss. (c) At the date of the breach it is clear or probable that damages under the conventional measure will either be nominal or much smaller than the profit to the defendant from the breach. (d) If the profit results from the avoidance of expenditure, the expenditure would not have been economically wasteful or grossly disproportionate to the benefit which would have resulted from it. He suggested in the skeleton argument that the underlying principle might be that the conventional measure of damages might be overridden in certain circumstances by the rule that no one should benefit from his deliberate wrongdoing.

In the course of his submissions Sir William limited his formulation and, while retaining conditions (a), (b) and (c), substituted for condition (d): "Damages for loss of bargaining power can be awarded if, but only if, the party in breach could have been restrained by injunction from committing the breach of contract or compelled by specific performance [1368] to perform the contract. Where no such possibility existed there was no bargaining power in reality and no right to damages for loss of it. Hence damages for loss of bargaining power cannot be awarded where there is, for example, a contract for the sale of goods or generally a contract of employment."

I find difficulty with that because in theory every time there is a breach of contract the injured party is deprived of his "bargaining power" to negotiate for a financial consideration a variation of the contract which would enable the party who wants to depart from its terms to do what he wants to do. In addition it has been held in *Walford v. Miles* [1992] 2 A.C. 128 that an agreement to negotiate is not an animal known to the law and a duty to negotiate in good faith is unworkable in practice, and so I find it difficult to see why loss of bargaining or negotiating power should become an established factor in the assessment of damages for breach of contract.

Beyond that, since we are looking for the measure of damages at common law for breach of contract apart from Lord Cairns's Act, I do not see why that should vary, depending on whether the party in breach could or could not have been restrained by injunction from committing the breach or compelled by specific performance to perform the contract. Injunction and specific performance were not remedies in the common law courts and were granted by the court of chancery, which, before Lord Cairns's Act, had no power to award damages, just because the common law remedy of damages was not an adequate remedy.

We were referred, in the course of Sir William's argument, to a number of other cases and, in particular, to passages in the judgment of Sir Robert Megarry V.-C. in *Tito v. Waddell (No.2)* [1977] Ch. 106 and to the decision of this court in *Stoke on Trent City Council v. W. J. Wass Ltd.* [1988] 1 W.L.R. 1406. In the latter case this court upheld the general principle that in tort a plaintiff recovered damages equivalent to the loss he had suffered and held also that the "user" principle in the wayleave cases and *Whitwham v. Westminster Brymbo Coal and Coke Co.* [1896] Ch. 538 should not be extended to cover infringement of a market right of the plaintiff council by the holding by the defendant of an unauthorised market where the plaintiff could not show he had suffered any actual loss by the infringement. What was sought in that case was damages calculated by reference to a notional licence fee that the plaintiff council might have charged for permitting the defendant's infringement but that was refused. I need not refer to the cases further.

As I see it, therefore, there never was in the present case, even before the writ was issued, any possibility of the court granting an injunction to restrain the defendant from implementing the later planning permission. The plaintiffs' only possible claim from the outset was for damages only, damages at common law. The plaintiffs have suffered no damage. Therefore on basic principles, as damages are awarded to compensate loss, the damages must be merely nominal. For these reasons, which substantially accord with those of Ferris J, I would dismiss this appeal.'

Steyn LJ:

'I agree. The issue in this appeal was defined by Sir William Goodhart, appearing for the plaintiffs, as the correct measure of damages in a case where the following three circumstances are satisfied. (a) There has been a deliberate breach of contract, (b) the party in breach has made a profit from that breach and (c) the innocent party is [1369] in financial terms in the same position as if the contract had been fully performed. It is an important issue with considerable implications for the shape of our law of obligations, and I therefore add a few remarks of my own.

Dillon L.J. has reviewed the relevant case law. It would not be a useful exercise for me to try to navigate through those much travelled waters again. Instead, it seems to me that it may possibly be useful to consider the question from the point of view of the application of first principles.

An award of compensation for breach of contract serves to protect three separate interests. The starting principle is that the aggrieved party ought to be compensated for loss of his positive or expectation interests. In other words, the object is to put the aggrieved party in the same financial position as if the contract had been fully performed. But the law also protects the negative interest of the aggrieved party. If the aggrieved party is unable to establish the value of a loss of bargain he may seek compensation in respect of his reliance losses. The object of such an award is to compensate the aggrieved party for expenses incurred and losses suffered in reliance on the contract. These two complementary principles share one feature. Both are pure compensatory principles. If the aggrieved party has suffered no loss he is not entitled to be compensated by invoking these principles. The application of these principles to the present case would result in an award of nominal damages only.

There is, however, a third principle which protects the aggrieved party's restitutionary interest. The object of such an award is not to compensate the plaintiff for a loss, but to deprive the defendant of the benefit he gained by the breach of contract. The classic illustration is a claim for the return of goods sold and delivered where the buyer has repudiated his obligation to pay the price. It is not traditional to describe a claim for restitution following a breach of contract as damages. What matters is that a coherent law of obligations must inevitably extend its protection to cover certain restitutionary interests. How far that protection should extend is the essence of the problem before us. In my view *Wrotham Park Estate Co. Ltd. v. Parkside Homes Ltd.* [1974] 1 W.L.R. 798 is only defensible on the basis of the third or restitutionary principle: see *MacGregor on Damages*, 15th ed. (1988), pp. 12–13, para. 18 and Professor P. B. H. Birks, "Civil Wrongs: A New World," *Butterworth Lectures* (1990–1991), pp. 55, 71.

The plaintiffs' argument that the *Wrotham Park* case can be justified on the basis of a loss of bargaining opportunity is a fiction. The object of the award in the *Wrotham Park* case was not to compensate the plaintiffs for financial injury, but to deprive the defendants of an unjustly acquired gain. Whilst it must be acknowledged that the *Wrotham Park* case represented a new development, it seems to me that it was based on a principled legal theory, justice and sound policy. In the defendant's skeleton argument some doubt was cast, by way of alternative submission, on the correctness of the award of damages for breach of covenant in the *Wrotham Park* case. In my respectful view, it was rightly decided and represents a useful development in our law. In *Tito v. Waddell (No. 2)* [1977] Ch. 106, 335C–336C, Sir Robert Megarry V.-C. interpreted the *Wrotham Park* case and *Bracewell v. Appleby* [1975] Ch. 408, which followed the *Wrotham Park* case, as cases of invasion of property rights. I respectfully agree. The *Wrotham Park* case is analogous to cases where [1370] a defendant has made use of the aggrieved party's property and thereby saved expense: see *Penarth Dock Engineering Co. Ltd. v. Pounds* [1963] 1 Lloyd's Rep. 359. I readily accept that "property" in this context must be interpreted in a wide sense. I would also not suggest that there is no scope for further development in this branch of the law.

But, in the present case, we are asked to extend considerably the availability of restitutionary remedies for breach of contract. I question the desirability of any such development. The acceptance of the plaintiffs' primary or alternative submission, as outlined by Dillon L.J., will have a wide-ranging impact on our commercial law. Even the alternative and narrower submission will, for example, cover charterparties and contracts of affreightment where the remedy of a negative injunction may be available. Moreover, so far as the narrower submission restricts the principle to cases where the remedies of specific performance and injunction would have been available, I must confess that that seems to me a bromide formula without any rationale in logic or common sense. Given a breach of contract, why should the availability of a restitutionary remedy, as a matter of legal entitlement, be dependent on the availability of the wholly different and discretionary remedies of injunction and specific performance? If there is merit in the argument I cannot see any sense in restricting a compensatory remedy which serves to protect restitutionary interests to cases where there would be separate remedies of specific performance and injunction designed directly and indirectly to enforce payment.

For my part I would hold that if Sir William Goodhart's wider proposition fails the narrower one must equally fail. Both submissions hinge on the defendant's breach being deliberate. Sir William invoked the principle that a party is not entitled to take advantage of his own wrongdoing. Despite Sir William's disclaimer it seems to me that the acceptance of the propositions formulated by him will inevitably mean that the focus will be on the motive of the party who committed the breach of contract. That is contrary to the general approach of our law of contract and, in particular, to rules governing the assessment of damages.

In my view there are also other policy reasons which militate against adopting Sir William's primary or narrower submission. The introduction of restitutionary remedies to deprive cynical contract breakers of the fruits of their breaches of contract will lead to greater uncertainty in the assessment of damages in commercial and consumer disputes. It is of paramount importance that the way in which disputes are likely to be resolved by the courts must be readily predictable. Given the premise that the aggrieved party has suffered no loss, is such a dramatic extension of restitutionary remedies justified in order [to] confer a windfall in each case on the aggrieved party? I think not. In any event such a widespread availability of restitutionary remedies will have a tendency to discourage economic activity in relevant situations. In a range of cases such liability would fall on underwriters who have insured relevant liability risks. Inevitably underwriters would have to be compensated for the new species of potential claims. Insurance premiums would have to go up. That, too, is a consequence which mitigates against the proposed extension. The recognition of the proposed extension will in my view not serve the public interest. It is sound policy to guard against extending the protection of the law of obligations too widely. For these substantive and policy reasons I regard it as undesirable that the range of restitutionary remedies should be extended in the way in which we have been invited to do so.'

Question:

Is there an important difference in reasoning in these two judgments?

[710] *AG v Blake* [1998] Ch 439, 456–9 *per* Lord Woolf MR and *per* Lord Nicholls (HL, unreported 27 July 2000):
[Re-read the extract at **[543]**.]

Question:

Which approach to disgorgement is more persuasive?

FURTHER READING:

See the articles cited after extract **[543]**.

7.3.3 Relief against forfeiture provisions in contracts

Equity has a tightly circumscribed jurisdiction to provide occasional relief against the operation of contractual terms which provide for the forfeiture of one party's ownership or possessory interests in personal property upon that party's breach of a term of the contract. The jurisdiction is exercised in a more liberal fashion in relation to rights over real property. It was this jurisdiction which gave rise to the mortgagor's 'equity of redemption'.

This form of relief is only available (and even then it is by no means guaranteed) where the rights being 'forfeited' are proprietary, so this initial classification is important: see *Scandinavian Trading Tanker Co AB v Petrolera Ecuatoriana (The Scaptrade)* [1983] 2 AC 694 (HL) (time charter of a ship); *Sports International Bussum v. Inter-Footwear Ltd* [1984] 1 WLR 776 (HL), 793 *per* Lord Templeman (licence to use trade marks), both cases where the rights in issue were not proprietary. The equitable jurisdiction to relieve against penalty clauses may sometimes help in these latter circumstances, but this is a much more tightly circumscribed jurisdiction: in some respects it involves re-making contracts, and the courts are reluctant to do this.

[711] *BICC plc v Burndy Corp* [1985] Ch 232 (CA), 251–2 *per* Dillon LJ:
[The parties held joint interests in certain patents. Their agreement contained a clause providing for the forfeiture of a party's interest on failure to pay half the costs of maintaining the patents. The facts raised other issues which are not relevant here.]

> 'Even though . . . I take the view that [the] clause . . . is not a penalty clause, it is a forfeiture clause in that its enforcement would involve the forfeiture to B.I.C.C. of Burndy's half share in the relevant patent or other joint rights.

There are here two questions, viz.: has the court jurisdiction to grant Burndy relief against forfeiture by an extension of time; and, if so, is it appropriate that the court should exercise that jurisdiction in Burndy's favour?

The judge decided, in reliance especially on the judgment of the Court of Appeal in *Scandinavian Trading Tanker Co. A.B. v. Flota Petrolera Ecuatoriana (The Scaptrade)* [1983] Q.B. 529, that the court had no such jurisdiction, because the assignment was a commercial agreement between commercial parties. The decision of the Court of Appeal in *The Scaptrade* was, as the judge noted, affirmed by the House of Lords [1983] 2 A.C. 694. As I understand the decision of the House of Lords, however, and the decision of the House of Lords in the subsequent case of *Sport International Bussum B.V. v. Inter-Footwear Ltd.* [1984] 1 W.L.R. 776, their effect was to confine the court's jurisdiction to grant relief against forfeiture to contracts concerning the transfer of proprietary or possessory rights: see the speech of Lord Templeman in the latter case at p. 794. The present case, however, is distinguishable from those cases in that clause 10(iii) of the assignment is concerned with a transfer of property rights.

In *Shiloh Spinners Ltd. v. Harding* [1973] A.C. 691, the House of Lords held that the court had jurisdiction to grant relief against forfeiture of proprietary rights in circumstances outside the ordinary landlord and tenant relationship; but the case was concerned with a claim for relief against a right of re-entry on land, and the speeches do not cast light on the extent to which jurisdiction exists to grant relief against forfeiture of property other than an interest in land. In *Barton Thompson Co. Ltd. v. Stapling Machines Co.* [1966] Ch. 499, 509, Pennycuick J. considered it to be arguable that relief could be granted against forfeiture of a lease of chattels. That view seems to have been approved by Edmund Davies L.J. in *Starside Properties Ltd. v. Mustapha* [1974] 1 W.L.R. 816, 822; and in *Stockloser v. Johnson* [1954] 1 Q.B. 476 [**[712]** below], 502, Romer L.J. apparently considered that the court would have power in an appropriate case to grant relief by way of extension of time to a purchaser of a diamond necklace who had failed to pay the final instalment of the price in due time.

There is no clear authority, but for my part I find it difficult to see why the jurisdiction of equity to grant relief against forfeiture should only be available where what is liable to forfeiture is an interest in land and not an interest in personal property. Relief is only available where what is in question is forfeiture of proprietary or possessory rights, but I see no reason in principle for drawing a distinction as to the type of property in which the rights subsist. The fact that the right to forfeiture arises under a commercial agreement is highly relevant to the question whether relief against forfeiture should be granted, but I do not see that it can preclude the existence of the jurisdiction to grant relief, if forfeiture of proprietary or possessory rights, as opposed to merely contractual rights, is in question. I hold, therefore, that the court has jurisdiction to grant Burndy relief.

The judge was of the view that, even if there was jurisdiction, relief should not be granted. . . .

In my judgment, it is necessary to consider all the circumstances, including what was happening on B.I.C.C.'s side. I remind myself that there is not, and has never been, any plea against B.I.C.C. of waiver or equitable estoppel, on the basis of *Hughes v. Metropolitan Railway Co.* (1877) 2 App.Cas. 439, in respect of B.I.C.C.'s exercise of its right under clause 10(iii). The facts remain, however, that B.I.C.C., having initially sent in ordinary commercial invoices for the half-share of the costs and fees, and having plainly not insisted on the 30 days time limit when the invoices were rendered, invoked clause 10(iii) out of the blue on 18 October 1982, when there had been no relevant correspondence between the parties for two months, and at a time when a meeting had been set up between Mr. Reiter and Mr. Ross-Gower to resolve outstanding billing questions, and at a time when B.I.C.C. in truth owed Burndy more under the commercial agreement than Burndy owed B.I.C.C. under the assignment. In my judgment, the case for relief is made out and, if I had not taken the view that Burndy had a good defence to the action on the ground of set off, I would grant Burndy relief, by way of an extension of time, against forfeiture of its rights under clause 10(iii).'

Note:

The previous extract, short though it is, suggests that relief against forfeiture may be available—although only rarely—to a claimant who can show that he has an interest in property (whether an ownership or a possessory interest) which he is in danger of losing if the terms of the contract are enforced to the letter. The relief provided by the court ('relief against forfeiture') is to give the claimant more time to perform the contract according to its terms. This gives the defendant what was promised while saving the claimant from the effects of forfeiture of his property. The proprietary precondition and the form of relief operate as limiting conditions on the equitable doctrine. It is important, in ordering relief, that the defendant obtain what was promised. It seems that equity will not intervene in this fashion unless the intervention causes no detriment to the defendant, or no detriment which cannot be compensated for by the payment of costs or interest on an overdue sum. *If* this is possible, then it also seems to be the case that the discretion to intervene will not be exercised unless the claimant would otherwise suffer substatial detriment. This limited remit of equity's jurisdiction in relation to forfeiture clauses is reiterated in *Shiloh Spinners Ltd v Harding* [1973] AC 691 (HL), 724 *per* Lord Wiberforce (a case concerning a right of re-entry onto real property):

> 'it remains true today that equity expects men to carry out their bargains and will not let them buy their way out by uncovenanted payment. But it is consistent with these principles that we should reaffirm the right of courts of equity in appropriate and limited cases to relieve against forfeiture for breach of covenant or condition where the primary object of the bargain is to secure a stated result which can effectively be attained when the matter comes before the court, and where the forfeiture provision is added by way of security for the production of that result. The word "appropriate" involves consideration of the conduct of the applicant for relief, in particular whether his default was wilful, of the gravity of the breaches, and of the disparity between the value of the property of which forfeiture is claimed as compared with the damage caused by the breach.'

In the light of these limitations, consider the next extract.

[712] *Stockloser v Johnson* [1954] 1 QB 476 (CA), 488–92 *per* Denning LJ, 495–502 *per* Romer LJ:

[A purchaser contracted to purchase plant and machinery and pay the purchase price by instalments. The contract provided that if the purchaser was in default in paying any instalment for a period exceeding 28 days, the vendor was entitled to rescind the contract, forfeit the instalments already paid and retake possession of the plant and machinery. The purchaser defaulted and the vendor exercised these rights. The purchaser was financially unable or unwilling to complete the contracts, but claimed the return of the paid instalments on the grounds that the effect of the contractual forfeiture clause was penal and unconscionable and that in equity he was entitled to relief. The court declined to grant relief.]

Denning LJ:

'There was acute contest as to the proper legal principles to apply in this case. On the one hand, Mr. Neil Lawson urged us to hold that the buyer was entitled to recover the instalments at law. He said that the forfeiture clause should be ignored because it was of a penal character; and once it was ignored, it meant that the buyer was left with a simple right to repayment of his money on the lines of *Dies v. British and International Mining and Finance Corporation* ([1939] 1 K.B. 724), subject only to a cross-claim for damages. In asking us to ignore the forfeiture clause, Mr. Lawson relied on the familiar tests which are used to distinguish between penalties and liquidated damages, and said that these tests had been applied in cases for the repayment of money, citing *Barton v. Capewell* ((1893) 68 L.T. 857) and *Commissioner of Public Works v. Hills* ([1906] A.C. 368). In neither of those cases, however, was the point argued or discussed, and I do not think they warrant Mr. Lawson's proposition. There is, I think, a plain distinction between penalty cases, strictly so called, and cases like the present.

It is this: when one party seeks to exact a penalty from the other, he is seeking to exact payment of an extravagant sum either by action at law or by appropriating to himself moneys belonging to the other party, as in *Commissioner of Public Works v. Hills*. The claimant invariably relies, like Shylock, on the letter of the contract to support his demand, but the courts decline to give him their aid because they will not assist him in [489] an act of oppression: see the valuable judgments of Somervell and Hodson L.JJ. in *Cooden Engineering Co. v. Stanford* ([1953] 1 Q.B. 86).

In the present case, however, the seller is not seeking to exact a penalty. He only wants to keep money which already belongs to him. The money was handed to him in part payment of the purchase price and, as soon as it was paid, it belonged to him absolutely. He did not obtain it by extortion or oppression or anything of that sort, and there is an express clause—a forfeiture clause, if you please—permitting him to keep it. It is not the case of a seller seeking to enforce a penalty, but a buyer seeking restitution of money paid. If the buyer is to recover it, he must, I think, have recourse to somewhat different principles from those applicable to penalties, strictly so called.

On the other hand, Mr. Beney urged us to hold that the buyer could only recover the money if he was able and willing to perform the contract, and for this purpose he ought to pay or offer to pay the instalments which were in arrear and be willing to pay the future instalments as they became due; and he relied on *Mussen v. Van Dieman's Land Co* ([1938] Ch. 253). I think that this contention goes too far in the opposite direction. If the buyer was seeking to re-establish the contract, he would of course have to pay up the arrears and to show himself willing to perform the contract in the future, just as a lessee, who has suffered a forfeiture, has to do when he seeks to re-establish the lease. So, also, if the buyer were seeking specific performance he would have to show himself able and willing to perform his part. But the buyer's object here is not to re-establish the contract. It is to get his money back, and to do this I do not think that it is necessary for him to go so far as to show that he is ready and willing to perform the contract.

I reject, therefore, the arguments of counsel at each extreme. It seems to me that the cases show the law to be this: (1) When there is no forfeiture clause. If money is handed over in part payment of the purchase price, and then the buyer makes default as to the balance, then, so long as the seller keeps the contract open and available for performance, the buyer cannot recover the money; but once the seller rescinds the contract or treats it as at an end owing to the buyer's default, then the buyer is entitled to recover his money by action at law, subject to a cross-claim by the seller for damages: see *Palmer v. Temple* ((1839) 9 Ad. & El. 508); *Mayson v. Clouet* ([1924] A.C. 980); *Dies v. British and International Co.* ([1939] 1 K.B. 724); *Williams on Vendor and Purchaser*, 4th ed., p. 1006. (2) But when there is a forfeiture clause or the money is expressly paid as a deposit (which is equivalent to a forfeiture clause), then the buyer who is in default cannot recover the money at law at all. He may, however, have a remedy in equity, for, despite the express stipulation in the contract, equity can relieve the buyer from forfeiture of the money and order the seller to repay it on such terms as the court thinks fit. That is, I think, shown clearly by the decision of the Privy Council in *Steedman v. Drinkle* ([1916] 1 A.C. 275), where the Board consisted of a strong three, Viscount Haldane, Lord Parker and Lord Sumner.

The difficulty is to know what are the circumstances which give rise to this equity, but I must say that I agree with all that Somervell L.J. has said about it, differing herein from the view of Romer L.J. Two things are necessary: first, the forfeiture clause must be of a penal nature, in this sense, that the sum forfeited must be out of all proportion to the damage, and, secondly, it must be unconscionable for the seller to retain the money. Inasmuch as the only case in which this jurisdiction has been exercised is *Steedman v. Drinkle*, I have examined the record and would draw attention to the circumstances of that case. The agreement was in effect a hire-purchase agreement of land. The purchase-money was payable by instalments over six years, completion to be at the end of the six years, and meanwhile the purchasers were to be let into possession of the land as tenants with the instalments ranking as rent. In case of default the vendor was at liberty to cancel the contract and retain the payments which had been made. The purchasers paid the first instalment and went into possession, but they failed to pay the second instalment which was due at the end of the first year. The value of the land had risen greatly during that year and the vendor seized upon the purchaser's default as giving him the opportunity to rescind the contract. Without previous warning, the vendor gave notice cancelling the contract. The purchasers at once tendered the amount due but the vendor refused to accept it. The purchasers issued a writ for specific performance and meanwhile remained in possession of the land taking the crops off it. They failed to get specific performance in the first court, then succeeded in the Court of Appeal, but failed again in the [491] Privy Council on the ground that time was expressly of the essence of the contract. Nevertheless, the Privy Council relieved the purchasers from forfeiture of the sums already paid. The purchasers would no doubt have to give credit for the crops they had taken from the land during the three years or more that they had been in possession, but subject to that credit they would get their money back.

In the later case of *Mussen v. Van Dieman's Land Co.* ([1938] Ch. 253) Farwell J. said that the whole basis of the decision in *Steedman v. Drinkle* was that the purchasers were ready and willing to perform the contract; but I think that that is much too narrow an explanation. Readiness and willingness is essential in specific performance, and in relief from forfeiture of leases, but not in relief from forfeiture of sums paid. The basis of the decision in *Steedman v. Drinkle* was, I think, that the vendor had somewhat sharply exercised his right to rescind the contract and retake the land, and it was unconscionable for him also to forfeit the sums already paid. Equity could not specifically enforce the contract, but it could and would relieve against the forfeiture.

In the course of the argument before us Somervell L.J. put an illustration which shows the necessity for this equity even though the buyer is not ready and willing to perform the contract. Suppose a buyer has agreed to buy a necklace by instalments, and the contract provides that, on default in payment of any one instalment, the seller is entitled to rescind the contract and forfeit the instalments already paid. The buyer pays 90 per cent. of the price but fails to pay the last instalment. He is not able to perform the contract because he simply cannot find the money. The seller thereupon rescinds the contract and retakes the necklace and resells it at a higher price. Surely equity will relieve the buyer against forfeiture of the money on such terms as may be just.

Again, suppose that a vendor of property, in lieu of the usual 10 per cent. deposit, stipulates for an initial payment of 50 per cent. of the price as a deposit and a part payment; and later, when the purchaser fails to complete, the vendor resells the property at a profit and in addition claims to forfeit the 50 per cent. deposit. Surely the court will relieve against the forfeiture. The vendor cannot forestall this equity by describing an extravagant sum as a deposit, any more than he can recover a penalty by calling it liquidated damages.

[492] These illustrations convince me that in a proper case there is an equity of restitution which a party in default does not lose simply because he is not able and willing to perform the contract. Nay, that is the very reason why he needs the equity. The equity operates, not because of the plaintiff's default, but because it is in the particular case unconscionable for the seller to retain the money. In short, he ought not unjustly to enrich himself at the plaintiff's expense. This equity of restitution is to be tested, I think, not at the time of the contract, but by the conditions existing when it is invoked. Suppose, for instance, that in the instance of the necklace, the first instalment was only 5 per cent. of the price; and the buyer made default on the second instalment. There would be no equity by which he could ask for the first instalment to be repaid to him any more than he could claim repayment of a deposit. But it is very different after 90 per cent. has been paid. Again, delay may be very material. Thus in *Mussen's* case ([1938] Ch. 253) the court was much influenced by the fact that the purchaser had allowed nearly six years to elapse before claiming restitution. He had already had a good deal of land conveyed to him and, during his six years delay, values had so greatly changed that it may be that he had had his money's worth. At any rate, it was not unconscionable for the defendant to retain the money.

Applying these principles to the present case, even if one regards the forfeiture clause as of a penal nature—as the judge did and I am prepared to do—nevertheless I do not think that it was unconscionable for the seller to retain the money. The buyer seems to have gambled on the royalties [obtained by the buyer for the lime he was quarrying using the equipment he was purchasing] being higher than they were. He thought that they would go a long way to enable him to pay the instalments; but owing to bad weather they turned out to be smaller than he had hoped and he could not find the additional amount necessary to pay the instalments. The judge summarized the position neatly when he said that the purchaser "is in the position of a gambler who has lost his stake and is now saying that it is for the court of equity to get it back for him." He said, "if it is a question of what is unconscionable, or, to use a word with a less legal flavour, unfair, I can see nothing whatever unfair in the defendant retaining the money." With that finding of the judge I entirely agree and think that it disposes of the purchaser's claim to restitution.'

Romer LJ (agreeing in the result, but taking a stricter view of the relevant law):
'Generally speaking, courts of equity have never interfered with contracts merely by reason of their being improvident. "The Chancery," as Lord Nottingham said in *Maynard v. Moseley* ((1676) 3 Swanst. 651, 655), "mends no man's bargain." To this rule exceptions were made, notably in favour of expectant heirs and borrowers, to whom equity manifested some tenderness, on the supposition that the sale or mortgaging of their inheritances or properties was usually induced by the pressure of financial need.

Such persons were regarded as being to some extent at the mercy of persons who were willing, on terms, to enter into financial relations with them, and the court frequently intervened so as to relieve them from the strict letter of their obligations upon such conditions as it considered fair and just. The equity of redemption which mortgagors have enjoyed for over 300 years had its origin in this exceptional jurisdiction and may be taken as an example of it.

In general, however, as I have said, people were expected to abide by their contracts, and if a man made a foolish or improvident one so much the worse for him. The question, then, is whether a purchaser who freely and voluntarily negotiates and executes a contract of sale upon terms that the price is to be paid by instalments and that, on default by him of payment of any instalment, the vendor may rescind the contract and retain any instalments previously paid, is entitled to relief in equity if he finds himself unable to comply with his bargain. It is to be observed that, in such a case, no element of pressure or duress exists and no question of the purchaser acting under the stress of economic necessity; both parties to the contract are on terms of bargaining equality with each other, the one desiring to exchange cash for property, the other desiring to exchange property for cash. I confess that, in these circumstances, I am unable to see what ground there is for interference by a court of equity if it ultimately turns out that the terms on which these exchanges are mutually agreed operate hardly on either vendor or purchaser. If one of the terms which the vendor requires is disagreeable to the purchaser he is under no compulsion to accept it; he can either keep his money and forgo the property or he can purchase a similar property from some other vendor who is more tolerant in his approach to the conditions of sale.

If a man agrees to buy property by instalments which he will [496] forfeit to the vendor if he cannot continue them to completion, he knows perfectly well the risk which he is taking and I do not know what right he has to appeal to equity if that risk does in fact ripen into actuality. That was the view which Farwell J. expressed without hesitation in *Mussen's* case ([1938] Ch. 253), and I respectfully and entirely agree with it. There are, however, reported cases in which equity has given partial and conditional relief to purchasers who default in their payments on the footing that such a forfeiture clause amounts to something in the nature of a penalty. In *In re Dagenham (Thames) Dock Co.* (L.R. 8 Ch. 1022) a statutory company agreed to purchase certain land for the purposes of its undertaking. The contract provided for an immediate payment of £2,000 and that the balance of the price should be paid on a subsequent date (time to be of the essence), and it was stipulated that on default by the company in making punctual payment of that balance the vendors should recover possession of the entire property and the original £2,000 should be forfeited to them. The company did in fact make default in payment of the balance. . . . [The court] did not declare that the stipulation for forfeiture was void as against the company as being a penalty or something in the nature of a penalty; all that the Lords Justices did was to relieve the company from its operation on payment of the residue of the purchase-money with interest. In other words, they, in effect, extended [497] the time for payment of the balance in spite of the provision that time was to be of the essence of the contract—a course which was plainly justifiable if only by reason of the fact that the plaintiffs themselves had twice postponed the date which had been originally agreed for the payment. . . .

Kilmer v. British Columbia Orchard Lands Ld.([1913] A.C. 319) was another case in which similar relief was given to a purchaser who was in default but desired further time to complete his obligations. . . .

[498] In *Kilmer's* case, therefore, as in the *Dagenham Dock* case, the court intervened by giving a purchaser who, although in default in punctual payment, desired a further chance of completing his purchase, an opportunity of doing so. So far as I can see, in neither of those cases did the court declare, or even intimate, that the purchaser should be relieved from the forfeiture if he failed through want of funds to take advantage of the limited relief which was extended to him—although admittedly there was little reason to deal with this point in *Kilmer's* case as the purchaser had brought the whole of the unpaid purchase-money and interest into court.

Apart from *Steedman v. Drinkle* ([1916] 1 A.C. 275) (to which I will return) two other cases require mention, though I do not think that either of them has much bearing on the present question. The first is *Commissioner of Public Works v. Hills* ([1906] A.C. 368). In that case a railway contractor was relieved from the forfeiture of certain sums of money notwithstanding that he became contractually liable to forfeit them, but (as was pointed out by Lord Dunedin in the *Dunlop Pneumatic Tyre Co.* case ([1915] A.C. 79) the question there was whether those sums were penalties (in the strict sense) or liquidated damages, and the Judicial Committee held that they were the former. The second is *Mayson v. Clouet* ([1924] A.C. 980) where a defaulting purchaser, although adjudged liable to forfeit his deposit, was held entitled to recover, on rescission by the vendor, subsequent instalments of purchase-money which he had paid. Lord Dunedin, in delivering the judgment of the Privy Council, said that questions such as that which was before them must always depend on the terms of the particular contract and that on the construction of the agreement between Mayson and Clouet only the deposit was forfeitable. The purchaser does not appear to have contended, as an alternative to his submission on construction which succeeded, that if in fact the forfeiture clause operated on the subsequent instalments as well as on the initial deposit it should be regarded pro tanto as being a penalty, and the Board did not expressly deal with the matter from that aspect, though Lord [499] Dunedin said ([1924] A.C. 987): "The truth is that the (vendors') contention really amounts to a claim to keep the instalments as liquidated damages for the breach of contract for which they are entitled to sue."

Pausing then at this point, it appears to me that the cases establish that if a purchaser defaults in punctual payment of instalments of purchase-money the court will, in a proper case, relieve the purchaser from his contractual liability to forfeit instalments (apart from the deposit) already paid to the extent of giving him a further chance and further time to pay the money which is in arrear if he is able and willing to do so; but the cases do not, in my judgment, show that the court will relieve such a purchaser to any further extent than this.

The decision of the Privy Council in *Steedman v. Drinkle* would at first sight appear to have gone further than this and to have relieved a defaulting purchaser from forfeiting past instalments notwithstanding that the vendor had already validly rescinded the sale agreement so that there was no question of the purchaser, by being given further time, being able to complete the purchase. So far, however, as one can gather, this point was not really in issue, nor could it be having regard to the pleadings in the case. . . .

[500] In *Mussen's* case ([1938] Ch. 253) Farwell J. was obviously a little puzzled by *Steedman v. Drinkle.* After considering the case he said that in his judgment it turned upon its own particular circumstances and was of no general application; he then said (at p. 266): "In [501] my judgment the whole basis of that decision turns upon the fact that the appellant was ready and willing to perform the contract and the only reason why performance was impossible was that the respondents refused to agree and the terms of the contract made it impossible for the court to decree specific performance.

The court appears to have thought that it was unconscionable for the respondents to take up the attitude of saying: 'We will not complete but we will retain the money' and on that ground relief could be granted." Whether that be the true explanation, or whether the explanation is that the point was assumed or conceded, I am certainly in agreement with Farwell J. that the case was a special one and cannot be treated as of general application. In my judgment the decision cannot be regarded as a satisfactory authority for the view that an equity exists in a purchaser, as against a vendor who has validly rescinded the agreement by reason of the purchaser's default, to recover instalments of purchase-money which the vendor is contractually entitled to retain. Farwell J. in *Mussen's* case expressed the opinion that there is no such equity and I agree with him.

There is, in my judgment, nothing inequitable per se in a vendor, whose conduct is not open to criticism in other respects, insisting upon his contractual right to retain instalments of purchase-money already paid. In my judgment, there is no sufficient ground for interfering with the contractual rights of a vendor under forfeiture clauses of the nature which are now under consideration, while the contract is still subsisting, beyond giving a purchaser who is in default, but who is able and willing to proceed with the contract, a further opportunity of doing so; and no relief of any other nature can properly be given, in the absence of some special circumstances such as fraud, sharp practice or other unconscionable conduct of the vendor, to a purchaser after the vendor has rescinded the contract.

My brother Denning in his judgment has referred to the hypothetical case which was suggested during the argument of a purchaser who buys a pearl necklace on terms that the purchase price is to be payable by instalments and that the vendor is to be entitled to get the necklace back and retain all previous payments if the purchaser makes default in the punctual payment of any instalment, even the final one. It would certainly seem hard that the purchaser should lose both the necklace and all previous [502] instalments owing to his inability to pay the last one. But that is the bargain into which the purchaser freely entered and the risk which he voluntarily accepted. The court would doubtless, as I have already indicated, give him further time to find the money if he could establish some probability of his being able to do so, but I do not know why it should interfere further; nor would it be easy to determine at what point in his failure to pay the agreed instalments the suggested equity would arise. In any event I venture to suggest that it is extremely unlikely that such a case would occur in practice; for a purchaser who had paid, say, nine-tenths of the agreed price for the necklace would have little difficulty in borrowing the remaining one-tenth on the security of his interest therein.

It will appear from what I have already said that in my opinion *Mussen's* case was rightly decided and that I agree with the grounds and reasoning upon which the decision was based, namely, that subject to the exceptions or qualifications to which I have referred (and which Farwell J. in terms recognized), there is no "equity . . . in favour of a purchaser who has failed to complete his contract through no fault of the vendor." For my part I share the reluctance which Farwell J. expressed to sponsor such an equity; it seems to me that in the long run it is much better that people who freely negotiate and conclude a contract of sale should be held to their bargain rather than that the judges should intervene by substituting, each according to his own individual sense of fairness, terms which are contrary to those which the parties have agreed upon for themselves. Agreeing as I do with Farwell J.'s judgment, no useful purpose would be served by further considering the case beyond emphasizing (possibly *ex abundanti cautela*) that the decision of Farwell J. was not directed to relief from penalties in the strict sense, but from the forfeiture of sums which the purchaser had paid in pursuance of the contract and in part payment of the purchase-money for the property agreed to be sold.

I have dealt with this question at, I am afraid, some length because it is an important one and because we heard considerable argument on at least some aspects of it. It does not in truth arise in the present case because, on the facts and on the true construction of the agreements between the plaintiff and the defendant, nothing in the nature of a penalty (or indeed of a forfeiture in any real sense) enters into the picture.'

Also see:

Union Eagle Ltd v Golden Achievement Ltd [1997] AC 514 (PC), a case concerning real property, but nevertheless one which is illustrative of the limits of the jurisdiction.

Questions:

1. In *Stockloser v Johnson* ([712] above), did the judges decide the case on the basis that the clause effected a forfeiture or that it imposed a penalty? What difference does the distinction make in the matters to be proved by the claimant and the remedy to be awarded? (On penalty clauses, see *Jobson v Johnson* [1989] 1 WLR 1026.)
2. If the claimant in the *Stockloser* case *was* claiming forfeiture, what proprietary interest was being forfeited: his interest in the plant being purchased, or his interest in the purchase price instalments? *Does* the claimant have a proprietary interest in either of these assets? Why?
3. What policy is the law trying to implement in these cases? Would a more direct approach be better, or would that necessarily leave courts with an unacceptably wide discretion to exercise?
4. Unless the facts are very special, courts seem disinclined in commercial dealings to order relief against forfeiture of proprietary interests in personal property. What alternative arguments might have a better chance of success?

7.3.4 Injunctions in aid of contractual arrangements

See Section 7.6.2 below.

7.4 Remedies in unjust enrichment

Earlier discussion in Chapters 5 and 6 included quite extensive consideration of issues often regarded as falling within the ambit of the law of unjust enrichment. In broad terms, the law of unjust enrichment aims to take from a defendant and return to a claimant any enrichment received by the defendant at the expense of the claimant which it would be unjust for the defendant to retain. This somewhat convoluted statement emphasises that not all enrichments are reversed: the law looks to the defendant, and determines whether justice demands that the enrichment (or some part of it) should be given up; it looks to the claimant, as the person at whose expense the enrichment was obtained, to determine the person to whom the enrichment should be ceded. There are several typical 'unjust factors' which may have motivated the initial transfer and, when those facts are discovered, entitle a transferor[20] to recover some or all of the value transferred. These include mistake, duress, undue influence and total failure of consideration. These claims are of particular importance here because a successful claim in unjust enrichment for restitution of the value[21] of an asset transferred to the defendant provides a further means by which the law protects the claimant's interests in personal property.

7.4.1 Simple unjust enrichment claims ('subtractive unjust enrichment')

The particular circumstances which will support a claim in unjust enrichment remain controversial,[22] and are beyond the scope of this Section. Nevertheless, since the basis of unjust enrichment claims is generally less well known than the basis of claims in tort and contract, something more needs to be said. As already indicated, the successful assertion of a claim in unjust enrichment depends upon proof that (i) the defendant was enriched, (ii) at the claimant's expense, (iii) in circumstances where it would be unjust for the defendant to retain the benefit, and (iv) the defendant can raise no defences which alter the *prima facie* conclusion that the defendant is obliged to make restitution of the value of the enrichment received. The term 'subtractive' unjust enrichment reflects the idea that in these cases there is a subtraction of wealth from the claimant and an addition to the defendant.[23] Two points of particular relevance to this Section should be noted. They relate to the evaluation of the enrichment (in (i)), and the potential defences which might be raised (in (iv)).

First, the defendant is only required to make restitution of the enrichment unjustly received. If the claim is personal, then that enrichment needs to be valued so that the court can make a money order. If the asset received is money, then valuation is easy. But if the asset is not money, then valuation can be problematic. For example, if the defendant receives a £50 bottle of wine and drinks it in circum-

[20] Or sometimes the person at whose expense the transferor acted. For example, a bank (as transferor) may transfer a client's funds to a payee. Whether the payee's 'enrichment' is at the client's expense or at the bank's expense depends upon whether the bank is entitled to deduct the payment from the client's account. Whether the payee's enrichment is 'unjust' is a separate matter.

[21] Restitution of the asset itself, or its traceable proceeds, is more controversial (ie proprietary restitution). Many of the relevant issues have already been considered in Chapters 5 and 6. This chapter is concerned with personal remedies only.

[22] The jurisdiction was only formally recognised in England in 1991 by the House of Lords in *Lipkin Gorman (a firm) v Karpnale Ltd* [1991] 2 AC 549 (see **[713]** below).

[23] But see Section 7.4.3 below.

stances giving rise to a claim in unjust enrichment, what sum of money ought to be paid as restitution to the claimant? Quite different values may be placed on an asset by the market, the claimant and the defendant. Moreover, an unjust enrichment claim can arise without fault or wrongdoing on the defendant's part. The remedy is designed solely to make a defendant give up enrichments which it would be unjust for the defendant to keep. It follows that an innocent defendant who no longer has the wine, and who has not realised its value in money, ought to be able to say the bottle was not worth £50 to the defendant: for example, she would not have drunk it had she realised that it was not a gift, or that it was not the £10 bottle ordered. This process is termed 'subjective devaluation' of the enrichment. It may limit the protection which unjust enrichment claims provide to a claimant.

FURTHER READING:

J Beatson, 'Benefit, Reliance and the Structure of Unjust Enrichment' (1987) 40 *CLP* 71, revised in *Use and Abuse of Unjust Enrichment* (1991, Clarendon: Oxford) ch 2.

A S Burrows, 'Free Acceptance and the Law of Restitution' (1988) 104 *LQR* 576.

M Garner, 'The Role of Subjective Benefit in the Law of Unjust Enrichment' (1990) 10 *OJLS* 42.

P Birks, 'In Defence of Free Acceptance' in A Burrows (ed), *Essays on the Law of Restitution* (1991, Clarendon: Oxford) ch 5, especially pp 105–9 and 127–46.

The second point to note is that the defendant may have defences to a claim in unjust enrichment. There are several well known defences. First, a defendant who receives the asset as a *bona fide* purchaser for value is fully entitled to keep the asset, and does not have to make restitution. Again, a defendant who receives the asset for another, and not beneficially for himself, is also not required to make restitution. This is 'ministerial receipt'.[24] Restitution is not required because the defendant is not in fact enriched by the receipt. Finally,[25] and most importantly, the defendant in an unjust enrichment claim can rely on a special defence known as 'change of position'. This defence is available if the defendant has so acted upon receipt of the benefit that it would no longer be just to require restitution. Take the case of a defendant who receives £100 by mistake, and so *prima facie* is obliged to make restitution of £100 to the claimant. If, in reliance on the receipt and before the defendant becomes aware of the mistake, the defendant donates £80 to charity, then the change of position defence will allow the defendant to reduce the unjust enrichment claim to £20, the 'true' enrichment received. The extract at **[713]** illustrates the prima facie claim and the change of position defence.

FURTHER READING:

G H Jones, 'Change of Circumstances in Quasi-Contract' (1957) 73 *LQR* 273.

W J Swadling, 'The Nature of Ministerial Receipt' in P Birks (ed), *Laundering and Tracing* (1995, Clarendon: Oxford) ch 9.

[24] eg *Agip (Africa) Ltd v Jackson* [1990] Ch 265, 291–3 *per* Millett J.

[25] There is one further important defence, based on illegality. It is not considered here.

P Birks, 'Change of Position and Surviving Enrichment', in W J Swadling (ed), *The Limits of Restitutionary Claims—A Comparative Analysis* (1997, UKNCCL: London).

W J Swadling, 'Property, Restitution and the Defence of Bona Fide Purchase', in W J Swadling (ed), *The Limits of Restitutionary Claims—A Comparative Analysis* (1997, UKNCCL: London).

D Fox, 'Bona Fide Purchase and the Currency of Money' (1996) 16 *OJLS* 561.

[713] *Lipkin Gorman v Karpnale Ltd* [1991] 2 AC 548, 577–83 *per* Lord Goff:

[The facts are outlined at **[618]** above. The House of Lords found that, because gaming contracts are void, the Playboy club had given no consideration for the money and so was unjustly enriched at the expense of the firm of solicitors. The claimant firm succeeded in its common law action to recover the money as money had and received, subject to a partial defence of change of position.]

> 'However, contracts by way of gaming or wagering are void in English law. What is the effect of this? It is obvious that each time a bet is placed by the gambler, the agreement under which the bet is placed is an agreement by way of gaming or wagering, and so is rendered null and void. It follows, as I have said, that the casino, by accepting the bet, does not thereby give valuable consideration for the money which has been wagered by the gambler, because the casino is under no legal obligation to honour the bet. Of course, the gambler cannot recover the money from the casino on the ground of failure of consideration; for he has relied upon the casino to honour the wager—he has in law given the money to the casino, trusting that the casino will fulfil the obligation binding in honour upon it and pay him if he wins his bet—though if the casino does so its payment to the gambler will likewise be in law a gift. But suppose it is not the gambler but the true owner of the money (from whom the gambler has perhaps, as in the present case, stolen the money) who is claiming it from the casino. What then? In those circumstances the casino cannot, in my opinion, say that it has given valuable consideration for the money, whether or not the gambler's bet is successful. It has given no consideration if the bet is unsuccessful, because its promise to pay on a successful bet is void; nor has it done so if the gambler's bet is successful and the casino has paid him his winnings, because that payment is in law a gift to the gambler by the casino.
>
> For these reasons I conclude, in agreement with Nicholls L.J., that the respondents did not give valuable consideration for the money. But the matter does not stop there; because there remains the question whether the respondents can rely upon the defence of change of position.
>
> . . .
>
> I accept that the solicitors' claim in the present case is founded upon the unjust enrichment of the club, and can only succeed if, in accordance with the principles of the law of restitution, the club was indeed unjustly enriched at the expense of the solicitors. The claim for money had and received is not, as I have previously mentioned, founded upon any wrong committed by the club against the solicitors. But it does not, in my opinion, follow that the court has carte blanche to reject the solicitors' claim simply because it thinks it unfair or unjust in the circumstances to grant recovery. The recovery of money in restitution is not, as a general rule, a matter of discretion for the court. A claim to recover money at common law is made as a matter of right; and even though the underlying principle of recovery is the principle of unjust enrichment, nevertheless, where recovery is denied, it is denied on the basis of legal principle.

It is therefore necessary to consider whether Mr. Lightman's submission can be upheld on the basis of legal principle. In my opinion it is plain, from the nature of his submission, that he is in fact seeking to invoke a principle of change of position, asserting that recovery should be denied because of the change in position of the respondents, who acted in good faith throughout.

Whether change of position is, or should be, recognised as a defence to claims in restitution is a subject which has been much debated in the books. It is however a matter on which there is a remarkable unanimity of view, the consensus being to the effect that such a defence should be recognised in English law. I myself am under no doubt that this is right.

Historically, despite broad statements of Lord Mansfield to the effect that an action for money had and received will only lie where it is inequitable for the defendant to retain the money (see in particular *Moses v. Macferlan* (1760) 2 Burr. 1005), the defence has received at most only partial recognition in English law. I refer to two groups of cases which can arguably be said to rest upon change of position: (1) where an agent can defeat a claim to restitution on the ground that, before learning of the plaintiff's claim, he has paid the money over to his principal or otherwise altered his position in relation to his principal on the faith of the payment; and (2) certain cases concerned with bills of exchange, in which money paid under forged bills has been held irrecoverable on grounds which may, on one possible view, be rationalised in terms of change of position: see, e.g. *Price v. Neal* (1762) 3 Burr. 1355, and *London and River Plate Bank Ltd. v. Bank of Liverpool* [1896] 1 Q.B. 7. There has however been no general recognition of any defence of change of position as such; indeed any such defence is inconsistent with the decisions of the Exchequer Division in *Durrant v. Ecclesiastical Commissioners for England and Wales* (1880) 6 Q.B.D. 234, and of the Court of Appeal in *Baylis v. Bishop of London* [1913] 1 Ch. 127. Instead, where change of position has been relied upon by the defendant, it has been usual to approach the problem as one of estoppel: see, e.g. *R. E. Jones Ltd. v. Waring and Gillow Ltd.* [1926] A.C. 670 and *Avon County Council v. Howlett* [1983] 1 W.L.R. 605. But it is difficult to see the justification for such a rationalisation. First, estoppel normally depends upon the existence of a representation by one party, in reliance upon which the representee has so changed his position that it is inequitable for the representor to go back upon his representation. But, in cases of restitution, the requirement of a representation appears to be unnecessary. It is true that, in cases where the plaintiff has paid money directly to the defendant, it has been argued (though with difficulty) that the plaintiff has represented to the defendant that he is entitled to the money; but in a case such as the present, in which the money is paid to an innocent donee by a thief, the true owner has made no representation whatever to the defendant. Again, it was held by the Court of Appeal in *Avon County Council v. Howlett* that estoppel cannot operate pro tanto, with the effect that if, for example, the defendant has innocently changed his position by disposing of part of the money, a defence of estoppel would provide him with a defence to the whole of the claim. Considerations such as these provide a strong indication that, in many cases, estoppel is not an appropriate concept to deal with the problem.

In these circumstances, it is right that we should ask ourselves: why do we feel that it would be unjust to allow restitution in cases such as these? The answer must be that, where an innocent defendant's position is so changed that he will suffer an injustice if called upon to repay or to repay in full, the injustice of requiring him so to repay outweighs the injustice of denying the plaintiff restitution. If the plaintiff pays money to the defendant under a mistake of fact, and the defendant then, acting in good faith, pays the money or part of it to charity, it is unjust to require the defendant to make restitution to the extent that he has so changed his position. Likewise, on facts such as those in the present case, if a thief steals my money and pays it to a third party who gives it away to charity, that third party should have a good defence to an action for money had and received. In other words, bona fide change of position should of itself be a good defence in such cases as these. The principle is widely recognised throughout the common law world. It is recognised in the United States of America (see American Law Institute, *Restatement of the Law, Restitution* (1937), section 142, pp. 567–578 and Palmer, *The Law of Restitution* (1978), vol. III, para. 16.8); it has been judicially recognised by the Supreme Court of Canada (see *Rural Municipality of Storthoaks v. Mobil Oil Canada Ltd.* (1975) 55 D.L.R. (3d) 1); it has been introduced by statute in New Zealand (Judicature Act 1908, section 94B (as amended)), and in Western Australia (see Western Australia Law Reform (Property, Perpetuities and Succession) Act 1962, section 24, and Western Australia Trustee Act 1962, section 65(8)), and it has been judicially recognised by the Supreme Court of Victoria: see *Bank of New South Wales v. Murphett* [1983] 1 V.R. 489. In the important case of *Australia and New Zealand Banking Group Ltd. v. Westpac Banking Corporation* (1988) 78 A.L.R. 157, there are strong indications that the High Court of Australia may be moving towards the same destination (see especially at pp. 162 and 168, per curiam). The time for its recognition in this country is, in my opinion, long overdue.

I am most anxious that, in recognising this defence to actions of restitution, nothing should be said at this stage to inhibit the development of the defence on a case by case basis, in the usual way. It is, of course, plain that the defence is not open to one who has changed his position in bad faith, as where the defendant has paid away the money with knowledge of the facts entitling the plaintiff to restitution; and it is commonly accepted that the defence should not be open to a wrongdoer. These are matters which can, in due course, be considered in depth in cases where they arise for consideration. They do not arise in the present case. Here there is no doubt that the respondents have acted in good faith throughout, and the action is not founded upon any wrongdoing of the respondents. It is not however appropriate in the present case to attempt to identify all those actions in restitution to which change of position may be a defence. A prominent example will, no doubt, be found in those cases where the plaintiff is seeking repayment of money paid under a mistake of fact; but I can see no reason why the defence should not also be available in principle in a case such as the present, where the plaintiff's money has been paid by a thief to an innocent donee, and the plaintiff then seeks repayment from the donee in an action for money had and received. At present I do not wish to state the principle any less broadly than this: that the defence is available to a person whose position has so changed that it would be inequitable in all the circumstances to require him to make restitution, or alternatively to make restitution in full. I wish to stress however that the mere fact that the defendant has spent the money, in whole or in part, does not of itself render it inequitable that he should be called upon to repay, because the expenditure might in any event have been incurred by him in the ordinary course of things. I fear that the mistaken assumption that mere expenditure of money may be regarded as amounting to a change of position for present purposes has led in the past to opposition by some to recognition of a defence which in fact is likely to be available only on comparatively rare occasions. In this connection I have particularly in mind the speech of Lord Simonds in *Ministry of Health v. Simpson* [1951] A.C. 251, 276.

I wish to add two further footnotes. The defence of change of position is akin to the defence of bona fide purchase; but we cannot simply say that bona fide purchase is a species of change of position. This is because change of position will only avail a defendant to the extent that his position has been changed; whereas, where bona fide purchase is invoked, no inquiry is made (in most cases) into the adequacy of the consideration. Even so, the recognition of change of position as a defence should be doubly beneficial. It will enable a more generous approach to be taken to the recognition of the right to restitution, in the knowledge that the defence is, in appropriate cases, available; and while recognising the different functions of property at law and in equity, there may also in due course develop a more consistent approach to tracing claims, in which common defences are recognised as available to such claims, whether advanced at law or in equity.

I turn to the application of this principle to the present case. In doing so, I think it right to stress at the outset that the respondents, by running a casino at the club, were conducting a perfectly lawful business. There is nothing unlawful about accepting bets at a casino; the only relevant consequence of the transactions being gambling transactions is that they are void. In other words, the transactions as such give rise to no legal obligations. Neither the gambler, nor the casino, can go to court to enforce a gaming transaction. That is the legal position. But the practical or business position is that, if a casino does not pay winnings when they are due, it will simply go out of business. So the obligation in honour to pay winnings is an obligation which, in business terms, the casino has to comply with. It is also relevant to bear in mind that, in the present case, there is no question of Cass having gambled on credit. In each case, the money was put up front, not paid to discharge the balance of an account kept for gambling debts. It was because the money was paid over, that the casino accepted the bets at all.

In the course of argument before your Lordships, attention was focused upon the overall position of the respondents. From this it emerged, that, on the basis I have indicated (but excluding the banker's draft), at least £150,960 derived from money stolen by Cass from the solicitors was won by the club and lost by Cass. On this approach, the possibility arose that the effect of change of position should be to limit the amount recoverable by the solicitors to that sum. But there are difficulties in the way of this approach. Let us suppose that a gambler places two bets with a casino, using money stolen from a third party. The gambler wins the first bet and loses the second. So far as the winning bet is concerned, it is readily understandable that the casino should be able to say that it is not liable to the true owner for money had and received, on the ground that it has changed its position in good faith. But at first sight it is not easy to see how it can aggregate the two bets together and say that, by paying winnings on the first bet in excess of both, it should be able to deny liability in respect of the money received in respect of the second.

There are other ways in which the problem might be approached, the first narrower and the second broader than that which I have just described. The narrower approach is to limit the impact of the winnings to the winning bet itself, so that the amount of all other bets placed with the plantiff's money would be recoverable by him regardless of the substantial winnings paid by the casino to the gambler on the winning bet. On the broader approach, it could be said that, each time a bet is accepted by the casino, with the money up front, the casino, by accepting the bet, so changes its position in good faith that it would inequitable to require it to pay the money back to the true owner. This would be because, by accepting the bet, the casino has committed itself, in business terms, to pay the gambler his winnings if successful. In such circumstances, the bookmaker could say that, acting in good faith, he had changed his position, by incurring the risk of having to pay a sum of money substantially larger than the amount of the stake. On this basis, it would be irrelevant whether the gambler won the bet or not, or, if he did win the bet, how much he won.

I must confess that I have not found the point an easy one. But in the end I have come to the conclusion that on the facts of the present case the first of these three solutions is appropriate. Let us suppose that only one bet was placed by a gambler at a casino with the plaintiff's money, and that he lost it. In that simple case, although it is true that the casino will have changed its position to the extent that it has incurred the risk, it will in the result have paid out nothing to the gambler, and so prima facie it would not be inequitable to require it to repay the amount of the bet to the plaintiff. The same would, of course, be equally true if the gambler placed a hundred bets with the plaintiff's money and lost them all; the plaintiff should be entitled to recover the amount of all the bets. This conclusion has the merit of consistency with the decision of the Court of King's Bench in *Clarke v. Shee and Johnson*, 1 Cowp. 197. But then, let us suppose that the gambler has won one or more out of one hundred bets placed by him with the plaintiff's money at a casino over a certain period of time, and that the casino has paid him a substantial sum in winnings, equal, let us assume, to one half of the amount of all the bets. Given that it is not inequitable to require the casino to repay to the plaintiff the amount of the bets in full where no winnings have been paid, it would, in the circumstances I have just described, be inequitable, in my opinion, to require the casino to repay to the plaintiff more than one half of his money. The inequity, as I perceive it, arises from the nature of gambling itself. In gambling only an occasional bet is won, but when the gambler wins he will receive much more than the stake placed for his winning bet. True, there may be no immediate connection between the bets. They may be placed on different occasions, and each one is a separate gaming contract. But the point is that there has been a series of transactions under which all the bets have been placed by paying the plaintiff's money to the casino, and on each occasion the casino has incurred the risk that the gambler will win. It is the totality of the bets which yields, by the laws of chance, the occasional winning bet; and the occasional winning bet is therefore, in practical terms, the result of the casino changing its position by incurring the risk of losing on each occasion when a bet is placed with it by the gambler. So, when in such circumstances the plaintiff seeks to recover from the casino the amount of several bets placed with it by a gambler with his money, it would be inequitable to require the casino to repay in full without bringing into account winnings paid by it to the gambler on any one or more of the bets so placed with it. The result may not be entirely logical; but it is surely just.'

Questions:

In relation to the unjust enrichment claim, if Cass had stolen a painting (rather than money) from the firm of solicitors, and passed it on to the Playboy Club, would the firm have been able to sue the Club in conversion, or in unjust enrichment, or both? If both actions are available, is there any difference in the remedies they provide? Would it make any difference that each partner had authority to deal with the partnership assets without obtaining the prior consent of the other partners? Is it legitimate—or useful—to try to distinguish between claims based on interference with property (including claims in conversion) and claims in unjust enrichment?

FURTHER READING:

A Tettenborn, 'Conversion, Tort and Restitution' in N Palmer and E McKendrick, *Interests in Goods* (2nd edn, 1998, Lloyds of London Press: London) ch 32.

Also see:

Boscawen v Bajwa [1996] 1 WLR 328 (CA) (**[715]** below).
Macmillan Inc v Bishopsgate Investment Trust plc (No 3) [1996] 1 WLR 387 (CA).

There are a few special complications in the law of unjust enrichment which need to be noted in this discussion of personal property. They are the focus of the next two sub-sections.

7.4.2 Subtractive unjust enrichment when the claimant relies on equitable ownership

As already noted, the simplest cases of unjust enrichment ('subtractive' unjust enrichment) involve a transfer of assets from the claimant to the defendant; there is a subtraction from the claimant's wealth and an addition to the defendant's. The appropriate unjust enrichment analysis is relatively simple when the claimant relies on a pre-existing *legal* title. Then the most difficult aspect is often to determine the 'unjust factor' which makes restitution compulsory. However, when the dealing is with the claimant's *equitable* title, the rules are more confused.

Consider how the problem might arise. In the simplest case, a trustee with legal title to the trust property might make an unauthorised transfer of the claimant beneficiary's trust property to a defendant. If the defendant recipient is a *bona fide* purchaser for value without notice of the claimant's equitable interest, then the defendant takes free of any claims of the claimant (see Section 6.2.5 above). The claimant's only recourse will be a personal claim against the defaulting trustee (see Section 7.6.1 below). The same would be true if the dealing between the claimant and the defendant had been a direct dealing with the claimant's legal (and beneficial) title: a *bona fide* purchaser for value would take free of any potential claim by the claimant in unjust enrichment (see Section 7.4.1 above).

But the defendant may not be a *bona fide* purchaser for value without notice of the claimant's interests. The defendant might be a volunteer (with or without notice), or a purchaser with notice. In either of these cases, the rule is that, where the equities are equal, the first in time prevails (see Sections 6.2.5 and 6.2.6 above). In both cases, the claimant's equitable title is likely to prevail over the defendant's title; the defendant will hold the legal title on trust for the claimant. If the property is still in the defendant's hands, then the claimant can rely on the trust and call for an outright transfer of the property to the claimant. If the property is no longer identifiable, but its traceable proceeds are, then the claimant may still be able to assert a proprietary claim (see Section 6.5 above). All of this is routine and orthodox analysis.

The difficulty arises if neither the property nor its traceable proceeds are identifiable in the defendant's hands. Then the claimant will want to know if there is a personal claim against the defendant for recovery of its value (either in full, or subject to abatement on the basis of the defendant's change of position defence).

It seems clear that recovery *is* possible, and slowly the grounds are being recognised as based on unjust enrichment rather than on some special equitable rule conventionally termed 'personal liability as a constructive trustee in knowing receipt', or, in short, 'knowing receipt'.[26] But *when* recovery is possible remains controversial. If the claim is analysed along conventional equitable lines, then personal liability is said to be imposed on a person who 'has received trust property with actual or constructive notice that it is trust property transferred in breach of trust, or because (not being a *bona fide* purchaser for value without notice), he acquires notice subsequent to such receipt and then deals with the property in a manner inconsistent with the trust'.[27] On the other hand, if the claim is analysed using unjust enrichment principles, then the fault of the defendant is irrelevant. In this context, all that is necessary is proof that the defendant received the claimant's property, being property to which the defendant is not entitled. Subject to any defences, it would then be unjust for the defendant to keep the enrichment.

Adopting an unjust enrichment analysis, a claimant should automatically have a personal claim against a defendant who is a volunteer. Regardless of the innocence of such a defendant, the property received is, in equity, the claimant's.[28] Support for this result can be found in *Re Diplock's Estate* (see **[714]** below).[29] However, that case expressly restricted its conclusions to claims in relation to the maladministration of a deceased's estate. Moreover, the remedy did not carry interest and was sub-

[26] Different categories of knowledge were defined by Peter Gibson J in *Baden v Société Générale pour Favoriser le Développement du Commerce et de l'Industrie en France SA* (1983) BCLC 325, [1993] 1 WLR 509n, 575–6:

(i) actual knowledge;
(ii) wilfully shutting one's eyes to the obvious [Nelsonian knowledge];
(iii) wilfully and recklessly failing to make such enquiries as an honest and reasonable person would make ['naughty' knowledge];

[All of these are forms of *actual* knowledge: ie in the assessment of a party's knowledge, fraud is not allowed.]

(iv) knowledge of circumstances which would indicate the facts to an honest and reasonable person;
(v) knowledge of circumstances which would put an honest and reasonable person on inquiry.

[These last two categories are classed as *constructive* knowledge.]

If personal liability is based on '*knowing* receipt', then it becomes a matter of some importance to determine what sort of knowledge counts as 'knowing'. It seems that different standards are imposed on volunteers and purchasers, but even within those classes the cases are not consistent. Moreover, as the text immediately following this footnote indicates, the courts also alternate between concepts of 'knowledge' and 'notice' in their discussion of these issues. ('Notice' is familiar concept in relation to priority disputes in proprietary claims—see Section 6.2 above.) In any event, the categories of knowledge are not watertight, and it can often be difficult to determine where in the hierarchy the facts would place a defendant. The Privy Council in *Royal Brunei Airlines Sdn Bhd v Tan* [1995] 2 AC 378 (a 'dishonest assistance' case—see Section 7.2.4 above) suggested the list was unhelpful and should be discarded.

[27] *Karak Rubber Co Ltd v Burden (No 2)* [1972] 1 WLR 602, 632 *per* Brightman J.

[28] This is the approach favoured by P J Millett, 'Tracing the Proceeds of Fraud' (1991) 107 *LQR* 71, 80–2.

[29] [1948] Ch 465 (CA), aff'd sub nom *Ministry of Health v Simpson* [1952] AC 251 (HL). Although the analogy is not strong: the claimants in this case had no equitable proprietary interest in the maladministered estate. See the comments following extract **[714]**.

ject to the claimants first exhausting their primary claims against the administrator of the deceased estate. Other cases, adopting the conventional 'knowing receipt' analysis in relation to *inter vivos* trusts, suggest that a volunteer who receives an unauthorised distribution from the trust will only be liable to make restitution if the property was received with actual knowledge of the trust (or perhaps even the *breach* of trust): see the dicta of Sir Robert Megarry VC in *Re Montagu's Settlement Trusts* [1987] Ch 264. The theoretical unjust enrichment analysis and the existing equitable precedents are not in accord.

The situation is only a little better with claims against purchasers who cannot profess to be 'equity's darlings' (ie those who are not *bona fide* purchasers for value without notice of the claimant's interests). With them, as with volunteer recipients, conventional unjust enrichment analysis would see them as obliged to make restitution once they are shown to have received property to which the claimant remains entitled. This qualifying condition does, of course, raise the question of notice. A defendant purchaser without notice of the claimant's interests receives the property absolutely; it is not property to which the claimant remains entitled. Such a defendant will not have to make restitution. All other defendants should have to make restitution. In this context, both actual and constructive notice will count against the defendant: either form will operate to defeat the defendant's claim against the claimant (see Section 6.2.5, and note the special meaning of constructive notice in the context of personal property). This is perhaps where the more modern authorities on 'knowing receipt' seem to be heading, but their analysis still leaves much to be desired.[30]

Proper resolution of these issues is important. Often large sums of money are at stake. Modern situations raising these issues frequently concern fiduciaries rather than trustees, and the context is not mistaken distributions of trust assets, but complex money laundering frauds or illegal share purchase schemes. Claims against the defaulting fiduciary are often worthless because the individual has absconded or is insolvent, or both. The defrauded claimant then turns to the 'deep pockets'—often accountants, lawyers and banks—who have received the funds at some stage along their trail. Whether or not these deep pockets are personally liable to the claimant is vital to both parties.

[714] *Re Diplock* [1948] Ch 465, 475, 477–9, 488–90, 502–4, 506–7 *per* Lord Greene MR:

[For the facts, see **[628]**.]

> 'Against this general background of fact it is now possible to state the nature of the appellants' claims in these appeals. These claims fall broadly under two heads which have been compendiously described as claims in personam and claims in rem. The former (which, as will be seen, must be sub-divided) are personal claims which it is said the

[30] See *Agip (Africa) Ltd v Jackson* [1990] Ch 265 (Millett J) (not dealt with by the Court of Appeal in [1991] Ch 547); *El Ajou v Dollar Land Holdings plc* [1993] 3 All ER 717, 739 *per* Millett J, rev'd on other grounds [1994] 2 All ER 685, both requiring either actual or constructive knowledge. But cf *Polly Peck International plc v Nadir (No 2)* [1992] 4 All ER 769 (CA), where Scott LJ appears to require actual knowledge (although on the facts there may be little in the distinction). See A J Oakley, *Parker and Mellows: The Modern Law of Trusts* (7th edn, 1998, Sweet & Maxwell: London) pp 341–8 for a discussion of the relevant authorities in favour of both views.

appellants are able to make in equity against each of the respondents. If it be held that, in accordance with this argument, there is a good foundation for such equitable claims, then further questions will arise whether and to what extent the Statutes of Limitation—particularly the Limitation Act of 1939—directly or by analogy apply to defeat such claims. . . .

As already indicated, the appellants' claims in personam must be sub-divided and fall under two quite distinct heads. First, it is argued that by the terms of the letters which accompanied all the executors' payments, the respondents were given notice of the invalidity of the trusts declared of the testator's residuary estate, or at least were put upon inquiry as regards their validity so that the respondents (who were in any event pure volunteers) were subjected to a constructive trust of the moneys they received in favour of the next-of-kin. Secondly, it is argued that apart from any notice which the respondents may have had of the true effect of the testator's will, they had in truth no right to receive any of the moneys paid to them and that in the circumstances of the case already set forth the unpaid next-of-kin have a direct claim, recognized and established by the courts of equity, to recover from the respondents the sums improperly paid to the respondents and properly belonging to the next-of-kin.

The first of these claims was not argued in the court below and has been somewhat faintly argued in this court. . . .

The argument has, it must be confessed, some attraction. For to the eye of the lawyer, particularly one made wise after the event of the decision of the House of Lords in *Diocesan Fund and Board of Finance (Inc.) v. Simpson* ([1944] AC 341) it may seem plain enough that the executors had embarked upon an entirely irregular execution of their duties. But we have come to the conclusion that this branch of the appellants' claim ought not to succeed. As we have already stated each of the respondents in fact accepted the moneys paid to them in good faith and in the belief that they were properly entitled to receive what the executors handed to them. As a matter of general principle the appellants' argument would indeed lead to startling results. For if the respondents can be said to be put upon inquiry then they must have been under some duty to inquire. What, on the basis of this contention on the part of the appellants (which is, of course, wholly distinct from the other branch of their personal claim, later dealt with), would be the duty of one who is told by executors that he is a legatee under a testator's will and paid that which he is told he has been given? Must he call for and examine the will to satisfy himself of its validity? Must he inquire whether all claims ranking in priority to his own have been satisfied? . . . In our judgment persons in the position of the respondents, themselves unversed in the law, are entitled in such circumstances as existed in the present case to assume that the executors are properly administering their estate: and if, as is admitted in this case, they took the money bona fide believing themselves to be entitled to it, they should not have imposed upon them the heavy obligations of trusteeship. . . .

But the second branch of the appellants' personal claim is one of far greater difficulty and complexity. It has involved considerable research into cases over a period of more than two hundred and fifty years and we have been much indebted to counsel for the help which their industry and argument have given to the court. . . .

Before dealing with the later cases which were cited to the learned judge below it may be convenient to make some observations on the effect of the authorities to which we have referred from *Noel v. Robinson* (1 Vern. 90) in 1682 to *Walcott v. Hall* ((1788) 29 E. R. 167 (n); 2 Br. C. C. 305), in 1788.

First it is in our judgment impossible to find in any of them any trace of such an underlying principle or ratio decidendi as that contended for by the respondents in this court. It is no doubt true that an equitable claim predicates that the conscience of the defendant must be affected. But we have failed to observe any justification, in the judgments cited, for the suggestion that the state of the defendant's conscience depends upon his knowledge or assumed knowledge that his title to the money paid to him may or may not be defeasible in favour of other interested persons. The test as regards conscience seems rather to be whether at the time when the payment was made the legatee received anything more than, at the time, he was properly entitled to receive.

Second, there is equally in our judgment no trace of any such limitation to the right of action as Wynn-Parry J. thought to be discernible from the later cases, namely, that there must be or have been administration of the estate by the court, and that the mistake made by the executor in paying the first legatee in full must be a mistake of fact. As regards the latter, it is no doubt true that so far as can be gathered from the reports, the overpayments that had been made arose from nothing more than a miscalculation of the assets available and might therefore fairly be regarded as due to mistakes of fact. But so far from suggesting that the nature of the mistake made was a relevant consideration, the reports do not for the most part even indicate how it came about that the payments were made in fact. As regards the suggested qualification that there was or had been an administration by the court of the estate of the testator, the reports of the cited cases seem to us wholly to negative any such requirement. There are frequent references to the effect of payment by the executor voluntarily, that is, in the absence of any decree sanctioning or ordering the payment. It is nowhere suggested that the right of the unpaid legatee to claim from the fully or overpaid legatee depends upon there being or having been an administration of the estate by the court.

Thirdly, it is in our view of the first importance to bear in mind the circumstances in which the equitable cause of action arose and the reason for which it came into existence, namely, the aim and desire of the chancery court, in the course of its struggle with the spiritual court, to provide some means of relief which would render unnecessary and take the place of the requirement of the spiritual court for the giving of security by the first paid legatee.

On the other hand it is, finally, to be noted that, so far, no case had arisen in which the plaintiffs were not legatees under a will but next-of-kin either claiming to share in the distribution with other next-of-kin or claiming to be entitled to the estate against other persons in whose favour distribution had been made as the persons supposedly entitled under the terms of a will or under an intestacy.

. . .

What then is the conclusion to be drawn on this part of the appellants' claim from what we fear has been a long citation of the authorities? It is not, we think, necessary or desirable that we should attempt any exhaustive formulation of the nature of the equity invoked which will be applicable to every class of case. But it seems to us, first, to be established and that the equity may be available equally to an unpaid or underpaid creditor, legatee, or next-of-kin. Second, it seems to us that a claim by a next-of-kin will not be liable to be defeated merely (a) in the absence of administration by the court: or (b) because the mistake under which the original payment was made was one of law rather than fact; or (c) because the original recipient, as things turn out, had no title at all and was a stranger to the estate; though the effect of the refund in the last case will be to dispossess the original recipient altogether rather than to produce equality between him and the claimant and other persons having a like title to that of the recipient. In our judgment there is no authority either in logic or in the decided cases for such limitations to the equitable right of action. In our judgment also there is no justification for such limitations to be found in the circumstances which gave rise to the equity. And as regards the conscience of the defendant upon which in this as in other jurisdictions equity is said to act, it is prima facie at least a sufficient circumstance that the defendant, as events have proved, has received some share of the estate to which he was not entitled. "A party" said Sir John Leach in *David v. Frowd* (1 My. & K. 200, 211) "claiming under such circumstances has no great reason to complain that he is called upon to replace what he has received against his right."

On the other hand, to such a claim by an unpaid beneficiary, there is, in our judgment, at least in circumstances such as the present, one important qualification. Since the original wrong payment was attributable to the blunder of the personal representatives, the right of the unpaid beneficiary is in the first instance against the wrongdoing executor or administrator: and the beneficiary's direct claim in equity against those overpaid or wrongly paid should be limited to the amount which he cannot recover from the party responsible. In some cases the amount will be the whole amount of the payment wrongly made, e.g., where the executor or administrator is shown to be wholly without assets or is protected from attack by having acted under an order of the court.

Authority for this qualification is to be found in the judgment of Sir J. Strange in the case of *Orr v. Kaines* (2 Ves. Sen. 194), where he observed that, if the executor is insolvent, an unpaid legatee is admitted to claim direct from the wrongly paid recipient because "there is no other way." See also the note to *Hodges v. Waddington* ((1684) 2 Ventris. 360), "the principal case went upon the insolvency of the executor." It is true that no direct authority for the qualification is to be found in any of the other decided cases; but in none of those cases where the direct claim was allowed, did it appear in fact that there was an executor or administrator against whom a claim might have been made or successfully made. Roper in the passage which we have cited from his text book treats the qualification as established by the authority of *Orr v. Kaines* (2 Ves. Sen. 194): where the unpaid legatee "can have no redress against" the personal representative the direct claim is justified since otherwise "he would be without a remedy." In our judgment the absence or exhaustion of the beneficiary's right to go against the wrongdoing executor or administrator ought properly to be regarded as the justification for calling upon equity to come to the aid of the law by providing a remedy which would otherwise be denied to the party who has been deprived of that which justly is his.

. . .

We should add that, as already indicated, in our judgment the respondents are liable under this head of their claim for the principal claimed only and not for any interest. This last result appears to follow from the case of *Gittins v. Steele* ((1818) 1 Swanst. 200) cited in Roper (*Roper on Legacies*) at p. 461, where the language of Lord Eldon in the case is cited: "If a legacy has been erroneously paid to a legatee, who has no farther property in the estate, in recalling that payment, I apprehend that the rule of the court is, not to charge interest; but if the legatee is entitled to another fund making interest in the hands of the court, justice must be done out of his share."

. . .'

The House of Lord confirmed this assessment of the law: see *Ministry of Health v Simpson* [1951] AC 251. Lord Simonds described the reasoning and conclusions of the Court of Appeal as 'unimpeachable'. However, in doing so he was perhaps even more cautious than the Court of Appeal in confining this form of response to the remedying of problems in the administration of deceased estates. The judgments in both the Court of Appeal and the House of Lords indicate that the remedy is supported by authority, but it is (or, more accurately, *was*) nevertheless quite exceptional. As already noted, it is subject to the conditions that it carries no interest and is available only after remedies against the administrator have been exhausted.[31] Moreover, it was available to creditors, legatees and next of kin (none of whom hold any proprietary interest in the unadministered assets of a deceased estate)[32] in circumstances where a beneficiary under an *inter vivos* trust (with an undoubted proprietary interest) would have had no claim against third parties receiving unauthorised distributions. Prior to *Re Diplock*, it was generally believed that the beneficiary of an *inter vivos* trust could only claim against such third parties where the mistaken distribution resulted from a mistake of fact, rather than a mistake of law. In short, it was thought that the equitable action was based on an analogy with the common law action for money had and received. Of course, the mistake of law bar has now been lifted,[33] but the point to note is simply that the '*Re Diplock*-type' claim was unusual.

The position now that the mistake of law bar has been lifted must be different. Both the administrator and the trustee under an *inter vivos* trust could now recover from an overpaid beneficiary in a common law action for money had and received (or, if the distribution was specific, in a *quantum valebat*). *If* the rights of a beneficiary under an *inter vivos* trust are analogous to these common law rights, then a deprived beneficiary should also be able to recover in the same manner. The restrictions associated with the *Re Diplock*-type claim then look most anomalous. Although such a claimant could not base his or her claim on any pre-distribution proprietary interest in the deceased estate, there it would seem to be nothing to prevent a normal (and unrestricted) common law restitutionary claim based on mistake.[34] The wrongly paid recipient is thus potentially liable to claims from two parties—the trustee/administrator and the beneficiary/legatee—but of course will only have to pay out once.[35]

Lord Simonds also confirmed that the defendants in these *Re Diplock*-type circumstances are strictly liable (after the claimants have exhausted their primary remedy against the administrator)—in short, he leaves no opening for the operation of a change of position defence. Contrast this with the extract at **[715]** where Millett J suggests that the change of position defence would now be used in *Re Diplock*-type situations in relation to the *proprietary* claim. Does his argument also apply to personal claims?

[31] Note that the *administrator* could not have recovered from the overpaid legatees, because of the mistake of law bar. Moreover, there would be no value in an administrator claiming to be subrogated to the claimant beneficiary's rights against the defendant: the claimant's rights do not compel the defendant to pay out sums already recouped from the administrator. However, if the present legal position is now as suggested in the next paragraph, then this claim to subrogation would have value.

[32] *Commissioner of Stamp Duties (Qld) v Livingston* [1965] AC 694 (PC).

[33] *Kleinwort Benson Ltd v Lincoln City Council* [1998] 3 WLR 1095.

[34] Eg, by analogy with the claim of a bank customer against a payee wrongly paid by the bank.

[35] This potential for two different claimants seems insufficient reason to deny the trust beneficiary a claim (or, more oddly still, to make the beneficiary's claim depend upon 'knowing receipt' or some sort of moral turpitude on the defendant's part). Others disagree.

[715] ***Boscawen v Bajwa*** **[1996] 1 WLR 328 (CA), 340–1** ***per*** **Millett LJ:**
[The facts are outlined at **[629]** above.]

'The appellants place much reliance on a passage in *In re Diplock* [1948] Ch. 465, 549–550, where the court was dealing with the claim against the Leaf Homoeopathic Hospital. The hospital received a grant for the specific purpose of enabling it to pay off a secured bank loan. The passage in question reads:

> "Here, too, we think that the effect of the payment to the bank was to extinguish the debt and the charge held by the bank ceased to exist. The case cannot, we think, be regarded as one of subrogation, and if the appellants were entitled to a charge it would have to be a new charge created by the court. The position in this respect does not appear to us to be affected by the fact that the payment off of this debt was one of the objects for which the grant was made. The effect of the payment off was that the charity, which had previously held only an equity of redemption, became the owners of unincumbered property. That unincumbered property derived from a combination of two things, the equity of redemption contributed by the charity and the effect of the Diplock money in getting rid of the incumbrance. If equity is now to create a charge (and we say 'create' because there is no survival of the original charge) in favour of the judicial trustee, it will be placing him in a position to insist upon a sale of what was contributed by the charity. The case, as it appears to us, is in effect analogous to the cases where Diplock money is expended on improvements on charity land. The money was in this case used to remove a blot on the title; to give the judicial trustee a charge in respect of the money so used would, we think, be equally unjust to the charity who, as the result of such a charge, would have to submit to a sale of the interest in the property which it brought in. We may point out that if the relief claimed were to be accepted as a correct application of the equitable principle, insoluble problems might arise in a case where in the meanwhile fresh charges on the property had been created or money had been expended upon it."

The passage is not without its difficulties and is in need of reappraisal in the light of the significant developments in the law of restitution which have taken place in the last 50 years. The second sentence is puzzling. The discharge of the creditor's security at law is certainly not a bar to subrogation in equity; it is rather a precondition. But the court was probably doing no more than equate the remedy to the creation of a new charge for the purpose of considering whether this was justified.

It is also unclear what conclusion was thought to follow from the observation that the unincumbered property derived from two sources, the equity of redemption contributed by the charity and the money belonging to the next of kin which was used to redeem the mortgage. If the money had been used to buy the property without any contribution from the charity, the next of kin would have sought a declaration that they were solely and beneficially entitled to the property under a constructive trust. Their claim to be subrogated to the security which had been discharged with their money reflected the respective contributions which they and the charity had made, and did not encroach upon the charity's equity of redemption at all.

Nor is it clear to me why insoluble problems would arise in a case where there had been fresh charges created on the property in the meantime. The next of kin would obtain a charge by subrogation with the same priority as the charge which had been redeemed except that it would not enjoy the paramountcy of the legal estate. A subsequent incumbrancer who obtained a legal estate for value without notice of the interest of the next of kin would take free from it. It is not necessary to decide whether a subsequent incumbrancer who took an equitable charge only would take free from the interest of the next of kin; the question has not yet arisen for decision, but it is not insoluble.

Taken as a whole, however, the passage cited is an explanation of the reasons why, in the particular circumstances of that case, it was considered unjust to grant the remedy of subrogation. The hospital had changed its position to its detriment. It had in all innocence used the money to redeem a mortgage held by its bank, which, no doubt, was willing to allow its advance to remain outstanding indefinitely so long as it was well secured and the interest was paid punctually. The next of kin were seeking to be subrogated to the bank's security in order to enforce it and enable a proper distribution of the estate to be made. This would have been unjust to the hospital. It may be doubted whether in its anxiety to avoid injustice to the hospital the court may not have done an even greater injustice to the next of kin, who were denied even the interest on their money. Justice did not require the withholding of any remedy, but only that the charge by subrogation should not be enforceable until the hospital had had a reasonable opportunity to obtain a fresh advance on suitable terms from a willing lender, perhaps from the bank which had held the original security.

Today, considerations of this kind would be regarded as relevant to a change of position defence rather than as going to liability. They do not call for further consideration in the present case.'

FURTHER READING:

Lord Nicholls, 'Knowing Receipt: The Need for a New Landmark' in W Cornish *et al*, *Restitution: Past, Present and Future* (1998, Hart Publishing: Oxford) p 231.
L Smith, 'W(h)ither Knowing Receipt?' (1998) 114 *LQR* 398.
C Harpum, 'The Stranger as Constructive Trustee' (1986) 102 *LQR* 267.

7.4.3 Unjust enrichment and use of the claimant's property

The other complication in this area arises where the claimant's assets are not transferred to the defendant, but are *used*, profitably, by the defendant. Early restitutionary analysis postulated two classes of restitutionary claims: restitution for subtractive unjust enrichment, and restitution for wrongdoing. On this approach, the defendant's unauthorised use of the claimant's asset is a wrong and, because of this, so the analysis asserted, the enrichment derived from it could be classed as an enrichment gained at the claimant's expense. The basic restitutionary framework would then require the defendant to make restitution of all the ill-gotten profits. The restitutionary claim was thus parasitic on the wrong, but was nevertheless regarded as a claim in unjust enrichment. An alternative approach leads to the same result, but on a different basis. This alternative argument concedes that the defendant's wrong is fundamental, but that the remedy for the wrong (the tort) is not restricted to compensatory damages, but might also in some circumstances require disgorgement of the defendant's ill-gotten gains (ie 'restitutionary damages'). It is left to common law case development to define the wrongs for which restitutionary damages are appropriate.

Opposed to both of these approaches is the view which sees *use* of the claimant's property by the defendant as amenable to analysis as a case of simple *subtractive* unjust enrichment, independent of any associated tort. The difficulty with this approach is said to be that subtractive unjust enrichment is grounded in a loss to the claimant and a gain to the defendant. In these 'use' cases, it is often hard to see that the claimant has suffered a loss. However, this misconceives subtractive unjust enrichment. The claimant's loss is in fact irrelevant to such a claim, so long as the defendant's gain comes *from* the claimant—which, arguably, it does when it is derived from use of the claimant's asset. If this is true, then the 'unjust factor' calling for restitution is the claimant's absence of consent, not any tort committed by the defendant (although the defendant's conduct may also constitute a tort for which the defendant is required to make compensation). This approach would require the defendant to make restitution of the 'use value' of the asset, that being the benefit received by the defendant from the claimant. This measure is *not* measured by the profits secured by the defendant as a result of the breach. It is not a disgorgement remedy. It may amount to either less or more than those profits, depending upon whether the defendant's use has been commercially successful. On this analysis, disgorgement is not seen as the function of the law of unjust enrichment, or even the law of tort. On the other hand, with many obligations imposed in equity (eg fiduciary obligations and obligations of confidence) and their statutory counterparts (especially those relating to intellectual property), such remedies are common (see Section 5.10 above).

[716] ***Strand Electric & Engineering Co Ltd v Brisford Entertainments Ltd*** **[1952] 2 QB 246 (CA), 253–5** ***per*** **Lord Denning MR:**

[The defendants were negotiating the sale of a theatre. A prospective purchaser went into possession and hired portable switchboards for theatre lighting from the claimants. When the defendants re-took possession of the theatre, they gave instructions that nothing (including the switchboards) should be removed. Presumably the lights would make the theatre more saleable, if only to indicate possibilities to prospective purchasers. The claimants successfully claimed the return of their equipment or its value and recovered the full market rate of hire for as long as the switchboards were retained by the defendants.]

> 'In assessing damages, whether for a breach of contract or for a tort, the general rule is that the plaintiff recovers the loss he has suffered, no more and no less. This rule is, however, often departed from. Thus in cases where the damage claimed is too remote in law the plaintiff recovers less than his real loss . . . In other cases the plaintiff may get more than his real loss. Thus, where the damage suffered by the plaintiff is recouped or lessened owing to some reason with which the defendant is not concerned, the plaintiff gets full damages without any deduction on that account . . . Again, in cases where the defendant has obtained a benefit from his wrongdoing he is often made liable to account for it, even though the plaintiff has lost nothing and suffered no damage: *Reading v. Attorney-General* ([1951] A.C. 507).
>
> The question in this case is: What is the proper measure of damages for the wrongful detention of goods? Does it fall within the general rule that the plaintiff only recovers for the loss he has suffered or within some other, and if so what, rule? It is strange that there is no authority upon this point in English law; but there is plenty on the analogous

case of detention of land. The rule there is that a wrongdoer, who keeps the owner out of his land, must pay a fair rental value for it, even though the owner would not have been able to use it himself or to let it to anyone else. So also a wrongdoer who uses land for his own purposes without the owner's consent, as, for instance, for a fair ground, or as a wayleave, must pay a reasonable hire for it, even though he has done no damage to the land at all: *Whitwham v. Westminster Brymbo Coal Company* ([1896] 2 Ch. 538). I see no reason why the same principle should not apply to detention of goods.

If a wrongdoer has made use of goods for his own purposes, then he must pay a reasonable hire for them, even though the owner has in fact suffered no loss. It may be that the owner would not have used the goods himself, or that he had a substitute readily available, which he used without extra cost to himself. Nevertheless the owner is entitled to a reasonable hire. If the wrongdoer had asked the owner for permission to use the goods, the owner would be entitled to ask for a reasonable remuneration as the price of his permission. The wrongdoer cannot be better off because he did not ask permission. He cannot be better off by doing wrong than he would be by doing right. He must therefore pay a reasonable hire. This will cover, of course, the wear and tear which is ordinarily included in a hiring charge; but for any further damage the wrongdoer must pay extra. I do not mean to suggest that an owner who has suffered greater loss will not be able to recover it. Suppose that a man used a car in his business, and owing to its detention he had to hire a substitute at an increased cost, he would clearly be able to recover the cost of the substitute. In such cases the plaintiff recovers his actual loss. I am not concerned with those cases.

I am here concerned with the cases where the owner has in fact suffered no loss, or less loss than is represented by a hiring charge. In such cases if the wrongdoer has in fact used the goods he must pay a reasonable hire for them. Nor do I mean to suggest that a wrongdoer who has merely detained the goods and not used them would have to pay a hiring charge. The damages for detention recoverable against a carrier or a warehouseman have never been measured by a hiring charge. They are measured by the loss actually sustained by the plaintiff, subject, of course, to questions of remoteness. They are like cases of injury to a ship or a car by negligence. If it is put out of action during repair the wrongdoer is only liable for the loss suffered by the plaintiff. (See the principles set out in *The Susquehanna* ([1926] A.C. 655) and many other cases.) The claim for a hiring charge is therefore not based on the loss to the plaintiff, but on the fact that the defendant has used the goods for his own purposes. It is an action against him because he has had the benefit of the goods. It resembles, therefore, an action for restitution rather than an action of tort. But it is unnecessary to place it into any formal category. The plaintiffs are entitled to a hiring charge for the period of detention, and that is all that matters. I can imagine cases where an owner might be entitled to the profits made by a wrongdoer by the use of a chattel, but I do not think this is such a case.'

[Somervell and Romer LJJ concurred in the result, but expressly based their decisions on compensatory damages for the tort, their difficulty simply being in quantifying those damages. Parts of their judgments are cited in the next extract, at **[717]**.]

Question:

What are the potential differences in the quantum of damages recoverable by the claimant in contract (had there been a contract of hire between claimants and defendants, which there was not), tort and unjust enrichment (restitution)? With an unjust enrichment claim, what are the alternative measures of recovery? Which route provides a claimant with the best protection of his or her proprietary interests?

[717] *Stoke-on-Trent Council v W & J Wass Ltd* [1988] 1 WLR 1406 (CA), 1410–15 *per* Nourse LJ, 1416–7 *per* Nicholls LJ:

[The defendant set up an unauthorised market in competition with the Council's statutory market. The Council successfully sought an injunction restraining the defendant from holding the market. It also sought general damages, alleging that its right to operate its own market was being infringed. The Court of Appeal held that the Council had suffered no loss as a result of the defendant's unauthorised market, so it was entitled to nominal damages only. The defendant's wrong was nuisance only, not unauthorised use of any property belonging to the claimant. This approach seems entirely defensible, although it has generated considerable criticism from restitution scholars.]

> ***Nourse LJ:***
>
> 'The levying of an unlawful rival market is a tort. Whether it should properly be categorised as a nuisance or a trespass is probably not a question of importance. The better view must be that it is a nuisance. The general rule is that a successful plaintiff in an action in tort recovers damages equivalent to the loss which he has suffered, no more and no less. If he has suffered no loss, the most he can recover are nominal damages. A second general rule is that where the plaintiff has suffered loss to his property or some proprietary right, he recovers damages equivalent to the diminution in value of the property or right. The authorities establish that both these rules are subject to exceptions. These must be closely examined, in order to see whether a further exception ought to be made in this case.
>
> The first and best established exception is in trespass to land. It originated in the way-leave cases, where the defendant trespassed by [1411] carrying coals along an underground way through the plaintiff's mine. Although the value of his land had not been diminished by the trespass, the plaintiff recovered damages equivalent to what he would have received if he had been paid for a way-leave: see *Martin v. Porter* (1839) 5 M. & W. 351; *Jegon v. Vivian* (1871) L.R. 6 Ch. App. 742 and *Phillips v. Homfray* (1871) L.R. 6 Ch. App. 770. The principle of those cases was applied in *Whitwham v. Westminster Brymbo Coal and Coke Co.* [1896] 2 Ch. 538, where for six years the defendants had trespassed by tipping refuse from their colliery onto part of the plaintiffs' land. The official referee found that the defendants had thereby rendered the whole of the land valueless for any but tipping purposes and he assessed its diminution in value at £200. But the plaintiffs contended that the proper measure was the reasonable value to the defendants of the land for tipping purposes and the official referee found that on that footing the damages were £963. It was held by Chitty J. and this court that as to that part of the land which had been used for tipping the defendants must pay on the footing of the

value of the land to them for tipping purposes, but without interest; and as to the rest of the land that they ought to pay on the footing of the diminished value of the land to the plaintiffs. That decision was applied by Lord Denning M.R., sitting as a judge of the Queen's Bench Division, in *Penarth Dock Engineering Co. Ltd. v. Pounds* [1963] 1 Lloyd's Rep. 359 and by this court in *Swordheath Properties Ltd. v. Tabet* [1979] 1 W.L.R. 285. In the latter case it was held that a defendant who had occupied residential premises as a trespasser was liable to pay damages calculated by reference to the ordinary letting value of the premises even where there was no evidence that the plaintiff could or would have let the premises to someone else. With the partial exception of *Whitwham's* case, all those were cases where the plaintiff had suffered no loss.

The second exception is in detinue. In *Strand Electric and Engineering Co. Ltd. v. Brisford Entertainments Ltd.* [1952] 2 Q.B. 246 [**[716]** above] the defendants, wrongfully and in furtherance of their own ends, detained some portable electric switchboards which were owned by the plaintiffs and were normally hired out by them in the course of their business. It was held by this court that the plaintiffs were entitled to recover as damages the full market rate of hire for the switchboards during the period of their wrongful detention. Although Denning L.J. proceeded on a broad application of the principle established in *Whitwham's* case to the wrongful detention of goods, the judgments of Somervell and Romer L.JJ. were more narrowly based. Thus Somervell L.J. said, at p. 252:

> "The nearest analogy is a claim for mesne profits. The measure there is a reasonable sum in the nature of rent for the user during the period of the defendant's trespass. In other words the defendant must pay what the plaintiff would have obtained if the defendant had lawfully been in possession. In principle the same measure should, I think, apply where a defendant has detained and used a chattel of the plaintiff which the plaintiff, as part of his business, hires out to users. I have added these latter words because I do not wish in this so far uncharted field to go beyond the facts of the case. We were referred to statements as to the law in the United States of America. . . It would appear from the statements in these books that the principle may be more widely applied in the United States [1412] of America and would cover, for example, detention and use of a private motorcar. I am not saying this is wrong. There may be no distinction in principle. The question had, however, better be left till it arises."

Romer L.J. said, at p. 256:

> "In my judgment the three salient facts on which the assessment of damages in this case depends are, first, that the equipment of the plaintiffs which the defendants detained was profit-earning property; secondly, that the plaintiffs normally hired out the equipment in the course of their business; and, thirdly, that the defendants during the period of wrongful detention applied the property to the furtherance of their own ends."

Later, at p. 257, he said that he expressed no opinion as to what the position would have been had the property detained been of a non-profit earning character, or if, although profit-earning, the plaintiffs had never applied it to remunerative purposes. The majority judgments in that case assume that the plaintiffs had suffered loss through being unable to hire out the switchboards to other users.

The third exception is in infringement of patents: see *Meters Ltd. v. Metropolitan Gas Meters Ltd.* (1911) 28 R.P.C. 157; *Watson, Laidlaw & Co. Ltd. v. Pott, Cassels & Williamson* (1914) 31 R.P.C. 104 and *General Tire & Rubber Co. v. Firestone Tyre &*

Rubber Co. Ltd. [1975] 1 W.L.R. 819. In the first of these cases the principle was stated by Fletcher Moulton L.J., 28 R.P.C. 157, 164–165:

> "It is the duty of the defendant to respect the monopoly rights of the plaintiff. The reward to a patentee for his invention is that he shall have the exclusive right to use the invention, and if you want to use it your duty is to obtain his permission. I am inclined to think that it would be right for the court to consider what would have been the price which—although no price was actually quoted—could have reasonably been charged for that permission, and estimate the damage in that way. Indeed, I think that in many cases that would be the safest and best way to arrive at a sound conclusion as to the proper figure."

That statement, although expressed in somewhat tentative terms, was expressly approved by the House of Lords in the two later cases. It undoubtedly represents the basis on which damages are usually awarded in patent infringement cases where the patentee permits, or could permit, others to use his invention under licence. In all such cases the plaintiff is readily proved or assumed to have suffered loss. I do not therefore think that they can, as a class, be regarded, like the trespass cases, as cases where the plaintiff has suffered no loss.

To these exceptions to the general rules in tort must be added the decision of Brightman J. in *Wrotham Park Estate Co. Ltd. v. Parkside Homes Ltd.* [1974] 1 W.L.R. 798. In that case the first defendants had erected houses and constructed roads in breach of a restrictive covenant which was binding on them and other defendants who had purchased houses from them. The writ was issued shortly after building works were begun, but the plaintiffs did not seek an interlocutory injunction to restrain them. By the date of the trial the works had been finished, the purchases completed and the purchasers had moved in. The plaintiffs [1413] sought a mandatory injunction for the demolition of the buildings. Brightman J. held that there was jurisdiction to grant such an injunction, against the first defendants in respect of the roads and against the defendant purchasers in respect of the houses. But he declined to do so. He then considered what damages should be awarded in substitution for injunctions under the Chancery Amendment Act 1858 (Lord Cairns's Act). Notwithstanding the fact that there had been no diminution in the value of the plaintiffs' land to which the benefit of the covenant was annexed, and founding himself on the trespass, detinue and patent infringement cases, he awarded the plaintiffs damages equivalent to the sum which they might reasonably have demanded as a quid pro quo for relaxing the covenant had the first defendants applied to them for relaxation. Before embarking on his consideration of those cases, the judge, in answer to the defendants' submission that no damages ought to be awarded, said, at p. 812:

> "That would seem, on the face of it, a result of questionable fairness on the facts of this case. Had the offending development been the erection of an advertisement hoarding in defiance of protest and writ, I apprehend (assuming my conclusions on other points to be correct) that the court would not have hesitated to grant a mandatory injunction for its removal. If, for social and economic reasons the court does not see fit in the exercise of its discretion to order demolition of the 14 houses, is it just that the plaintiffs should receive no compensation and that the defendants should be left in undisturbed possession of the fruits of their wrongdoing?"

Later he said, at p. 815:

> "In the present case I am faced with the problem what damages ought to be awarded to the plaintiffs in the place of mandatory injunctions which would have

> restored the plaintiffs' rights. If the plaintiffs are merely given a nominal sum, or no sum, in substitution for injunctions, it seems to me that justice will manifestly not have been done."

That was a case where the plaintiffs had suffered no loss.

The same approach to the assessment of damages awarded in lieu of a final injunction was adopted by Graham J. in *Bracewell v. Appleby* [1975] Ch. 408 (where the burden of an easement was wrongfully increased) and by Millett J. in *Carr-Saunders v. Dick McNeil Associates Ltd.* [1986] 1 W.L.R. 922 (where a right to light was wrongfully obstructed). In each of those cases the plaintiff's claim lay in nuisance, of which tort damage is an essential ingredient. Indeed, it is clear that in each case the plaintiff had suffered loss and was therefore entitled to substantial damages.

As I understand these authorities, their broad effect is this. In cases of trespass to land and patent infringement and in some cases of detinue and nuisance the court will award damages in accordance with what Nicholls L.J. has aptly termed "the user principle." On an analogous principle, in a case where there was a breach of a restrictive covenant the court has, in lieu of a permanent mandatory injunction to restore the breach, awarded damages equivalent to the sum which the plaintiffs might reasonably have demanded for a relaxation of the covenant. But it is only in the last-mentioned case and in the trespass cases that damages [1414] have been awarded in accordance with either principle without proof of loss to the plaintiff. In all the other cases, the plaintiff having established his loss, the real question has not been whether substantial damages should be awarded at all, but whether they should be assessed in accordance with the user principle or by reference to the diminution in value of the property or right. In other words, those other cases are exceptions to the second, but not to the first, of the general rules stated above.

Do the authorities support an award of damages in accordance with the user principle where an unlawful rival market has caused no loss to the market owner? In other words, is this case to be governed by the principle of the trespass cases and that of the *Wrotham Park* case?

The latter decision is in my opinion one which stands very much on its own. The conclusion of Brightman J. may, I think, be more fully explained as follows. An injunction is frequently granted to enforce an express negative covenant, especially a restrictive covenant affecting land, without proof of loss to the plaintiff. Injunctions could therefore and would have been granted in that case but for the social and economic reasons against ordering the demolition of 14 houses. If injunctions had been granted, the loss to the defendant purchasers would have been enormous. If, on the other hand, injunctions were not granted and no damages were awarded, the purchasers would have been left in undisturbed possession of the correspondingly enormous fruits of their wrongdoing. Accordingly, if the plaintiffs had not been awarded substantial damages, justice manifestly would not have been done. If this analysis is correct, the practical result of the *Wrotham Park* decision was something akin to an award of exemplary damages for breach of contract, albeit that their amount bore no relation to the loss which would have been suffered by the defendant purchasers if they had had to demolish their houses. In saying this, I do not wish to suggest that that case was wrongly decided. Indeed, I regard the result as having been entirely appropriate and I see no reason why it should not serve as a precedent for other cases of the same kind. I merely wish to emphasise that it stands a long way away from the present problem and does not assist in its solution.

On a superficial view, the trespass cases present a greater difficulty. In trespass the defendant makes an unlawful use of the plaintiff's land. Similarly, it can be said that in levying an unlawful rival market the defendant makes an unlawful use of the plaintiff's right to hold his own market, which, at any rate in the case of a franchise market, is an incorporeal hereditament. Ought it to make all the difference that in the first case the unlawful use is a physical one? This is a formidable line of argument, but I think that it is unsound. If the way-leave cases are put on one side, it seems to me that the trespass cases really depend on the fact that the defendant's use of the plaintiff's land deprives the plaintiff of any opportunity of using it himself. And even on the assumption, which may be correct, that the broad view of Denning L.J. in the *Strand Electric* case [1952] 2 Q.B. 246 is a correct view of the law, the same can be said of an unlawful detention of the plaintiff's chattel. On the other hand, an unlawful use of the plaintiff's right to hold his own market does not deprive him of the opportunity of holding one himself. Such indeed has been the state of affairs in the present case. If of course the plaintiff can show that he has thereby suffered loss, nobody would suggest that he ought not to receive substantial damages. But why [1415] should he receive them when he has been able to hold his own market and has suffered no loss from the defendant's?

It is characteristic of the development of the common law that the invention and increasingly extended application of the user principle should appear to have come about by accident rather than by design. Thus it seems from the interlocutory observations of the members of this court in *Whitwham's* case [1896] 2 Ch. 538, 539, 540, 541 that they were initially resistant to the principle of the way-leave cases. But they saw in it a basis for the just decision of that case, and once it had been so decided the application of the principle to analogous states of affairs, for example the wrongful detention of chattels, seems to have been a perfectly natural development. However, in a process of development it is sometimes necessary to stand back from the authorities and to ask not simply where they have come to, but where, if a further extension is made, they may go next.

Although I would accept that there may be a logical difficulty in making a distinction between the present case and the way-leave cases, I think that if the user principle were to be applied here there would be an equal difficulty in distinguishing other cases of more common occurrence, particularly in nuisance. Suppose a case where a right to light or a right of way had been obstructed to the profit of the servient owner but at no loss to the dominant owner. It would be difficult, in the application of the user principle, to make a logical distinction between such an obstruction and the infringement of a right to hold a market. And yet the application of that principle to such cases would not only give a right to substantial damages where no loss had been suffered but would revolutionise the tort of nuisance by making it unnecessary to prove loss. Moreover, if the principle were to be applied in nuisance, why not in other torts where the defendant's wrong can work to his own profit, for example in defamation? As progenitors of the rule in trespass and some other areas, the way-leave cases have done good service. But just as their genus is peculiar, so ought their procreative powers to be exhausted.

These considerations have led me to conclude that the user principle ought not to be applied to the infringement of a right to hold a market where no loss has been suffered by the market owner. If loss caused by the diversion of custom from one market to the other had been proved, I would have agreed with Nicholls L.J. that the general rule ought to apply, so that the council would have recovered damages equivalent to the diminution in value of their right through the loss of stallage, tolls and so forth. But I rest my decision in this case on the simple ground that where no loss has been suffered no substantial damages of any kind can be recovered. Otherwise we would have to allow that the right to recover nominal damages for disturbance of a same day market without proof of loss had become one to receive substantial damages on top. If we had to allow that, why not also in the case of an other day market where no loss had been proved? It is possible that the English law of tort, more especially of the so-called "proprietary torts," will in due course make a more deliberate move towards recovery based not on loss suffered by the plaintiff but on the unjust enrichment of the defendant: see Goff and Jones, *The Law of Restitution*, 3rd ed. (1986), pp. 612–614. But I do not think that that process can begin in this case and I doubt whether it can begin at all at this level of decision.'

Nicholls LJ:

'It is an established principle concerning the assessment of damages that a person who has wrongfully used another's property without causing the latter any pecuniary loss may still be liable to that other for more than nominal damages. In general, he is liable to pay, as damages, a reasonable sum for the wrongful use he has made of the other's property. The law has reached this conclusion by giving to the concept of loss or damage in such a case a wider meaning than merely financial loss calculated by comparing the property owner's financial position after the wrongdoing with what it would have been had the wrongdoing never occurred. Furthermore, in such a case it is no answer for the wrongdoer to show that the property owner would probably not have used the property himself had the wrongdoer not done so. In *The Mediana* [1900] A.C. 113, 117, Earl of Halsbury L.C. made the famous observation that a defendant who had deprived the plaintiff of one of the chairs in his room for 12 months could not diminish the damages by showing that the plaintiff did not usually sit upon that chair or that there were plenty of other chairs in the room.

What is in issue on this appeal is a novel application of this principle (which, for convenience, I shall call "the user principle"). Heretofore that principle has been applied to the use of land. In 1896 Lindley L.J. in *Whitwham v. Westminster Brymbo Coal and Coke Co.* [1896] 2 Ch. 538, 542, observed that if one man trucks on rails over another man's land it does not do any harm whatever, and there is no pecuniary damage, but that the law was "now settled." He stated the principle thus, at pp. 541–542: "if one person has without leave of another been using that other's land for his own purposes, he ought to pay for such user."

Rigby L.J., at pp. 543–544, noted that there was nothing special in the nature of a way-leave, which was the subject matter of the earlier cases, starting with *Martin v. Porter*, 5 M. & W. 351, in which the principle had been established:

> "There is nothing special in the nature of a way-leave, and there is nothing special for this purpose in an underground way. The principle is that a trespasser shall not be allowed to make use of another person's land without in some way compensating that other person for that user. Where the trespass consists in using a way over the plaintiff's land, a convenient way of assessing damages may be an inquiry as to way-leave, which, when there is a customary rate of charge for way-leave in the locality, may furnish a convenient measure of damages; but the principle is that in some way or other, if you can do nothing better then by rule of thumb, the trespasser must be charged for the use of the land."

The user principle has also been applied to chattels: *Strand Electric and Engineering Co. Ltd. v. Brisford Entertainments Ltd.* [1952] 2 Q.B. 246. But the principle is not confined to the physical use of another's property. The same principle has been applied in relation to incorporeal property, in particular patents. In *Meters Ltd. v. Metropolitan Gas Meters Ltd.*, 28 R.P.C. 157 the Court of Appeal rejected an argument that if the customers for the goods which infringed the plaintiff's patent [1417] would in any event not have bought from the plaintiff, the plaintiff can recover no damages in respect of those infringements.

. . .

In the present case the council seeks to extend the user principle by applying it to a case of disturbance of market rights. Market rights have existed for centuries, but we have been referred to no case where such a claim has previously been made or considered. . . .

The common law, however, is constantly being developed and adapted as social conditions change, and novelty by itself is not an answer to the present claim. Indeed, for some time I was attracted by the analogy between infringement of a patent and infringement of a market right. The argument is to the following effect. The owner of a market right has a legal monopoly in respect of the holding of a market within a certain area. If, for the purpose of assessment of damages on the user principle, infringement of a patent is to be regarded as the invasion and abstraction by the infringer of the property which consists of the monopoly of the patented articles granted to the patentee, as Lord Shaw observed in the passage I have cited from the *Watson, Laidlaw* case, so also is the disturbance of a market right to be regarded as the invasion and abstraction of the property which consists of the monopoly of the holding of a market in the place in question. In other words, if the infringement of a patent is to be regarded as the wrongful user of the property comprised in the patent, then by parity of reasoning the disturbance of a market right may properly be regarded as the wrongful user of the property comprised in the market right. If, in the one instance, damages may be awarded on the user principle in a suitable case, so may they be in the other instance.

I have, however, concluded that the analogy is unsound and that the application of the user principle in the case of the disturbance of a market right would not accord with the basic principles applicable to that cause of action. A market right confers a monopoly, as does a patent, but the protection which the law affords to the owner of a market right is limited to protecting him against being disturbed in the enjoyment of his right. If an unauthorised market is held without disturbing the lawful market, the owner of the lawful market has no remedy, either for damages or otherwise. In such an event there is no place for an award of damages to be assessed on the user principle. Thus, for example, if and so long as the owner of the market right is currently not exercising or seeking to exercise his right, and is not holding a market at all, he has no cause of action against a person holding an unauthorised market, for in such a case he is not being disturbed in the enjoyment of his market right: cf. Channell B. in *Dorchester Corporation v. Ensor* (1869) L.R. 4 Ex. 335, 339, where a market was not being held on one of the material days.'

Questions:

Is there a material difference between these two judgments and their analysis of precedents? *Is* a market right a property right, or is it a licence/personal (contractual) right? Is this categorisation important? What statement of principle can be drawn from these cases?

These cases support the existence of a 'use value' remedy when the claimant's property has been used without the claimant's consent. There is still debate surrounding the characterisation of this remedy—is it in tort or in unjust enrichment? But, whatever the characterisation, the remedy is not available unless the defendant makes use of the *claimant's* property. This qualification is material, especially in relation to circumstances which give rise to unjust enrichment claims. A claimant with an unjust enrichment claim against a defendant does not necessarily own the property which is the subject of the claim. If the claimant does not own the property, then there would seem to be no basis for a 'use value' claim.

One further issue needs to be noted. If 'use value' claims were available when a defendant uses property which is the claimant's in *equity* rather than in law, then the potential scope of the remedy would be much increased—especially if the debates over proprietary restitution were resolved in favour of proprietary claims rather than against them.[36] The next extract, concerning equity's treatment of money, is instructive.

[718] *Westdeutsche Landesbank Girozentrale v Islington London BC* [1996] AC 669, 701–2 *per* Lord Browne-Wilkinson:

[The facts appear at **[504]** above.]

> 'In the absence of fraud courts of equity have never awarded compound interest except against a trustee or other person owing fiduciary duties who is accountable for profits made from his position. Equity awarded simple interest at a time when courts of law had no right under common law or statute to award any interest. The award of compound interest was restricted to cases where the award was in lieu of an account of profits improperly made by the trustee. We were not referred to any case where compound interest had been awarded in the absence of fiduciary accountability for a profit. The principle is clearly stated by Lord Hatherley L.C. in *Burdick v. Garrick*, L.R. 5 Ch.App. 233, 241:
>
>> "the court does not proceed against an accounting party by way of punishing him for making use of the plaintiff's money by directing rests, or payment of compound interest, but proceeds upon this principle, either that he has made, or has put himself into such a position as that he is to be presumed to have made, 5 per cent., or compound interest, as the case may be."
>
> The principle was more fully stated by Buckley L.J. in *Wallersteiner v. Moir (No. 2)* [1975] Q.B. 373, 397:
>
>> "Where a trustee has retained trust money in his own hands, he will be accountable for the profit which he has made or which he is assumed to have made from the use of the money. In *Attorney-General v. Alford*, 4 De G.M. & G. 843, 851 Lord Cranworth L.C. said: 'What the court ought to do, I think, is to charge him only with the interest which he has received, or which it is justly entitled to say he ought to have received, or which it is so fairly to be presumed that he did receive that he is estopped from saying that he did not receive it.' This is an application of the doctrine that the court will not allow a trustee to make any profit from his trust. The defaulting trustee is normally charged with simple interest only, but if it is established that he has used the money in trade he may be charged compound interest...
>>
>> The justification for charging compound interest normally lies in the fact that

[36] See Sections 5.5 and 5.10 above.

profits earned in trade would be likely to be used as working capital for earning further profits. Precisely similar equitable principles apply to an agent who has retained moneys of his principal in his hands and used them for his own purposes: *Burdick v. Garrick*."

In *President of India v. La Pintada Compania Navigacion S.A.* [1985] A.C. 104, 116 Lord Brandon of Oakbrook (with whose speech the rest of their Lordships agreed) considered the law as to the award of interest as at that date in four separate areas. His third area was equity, as to which he said:

"Thirdly, the area of equity. The Chancery courts, again differing from the common law courts, had regularly awarded simple interest as ancillary relief in respect of equitable remedies, such as specific performance, rescission and the taking of an account. Chancery courts had further regularly awarded interest, including not only simple interest but also compound interest, when they thought that justice so demanded, that is to say in cases where money had been obtained and retained by fraud, or where it had been withheld or misapplied by a trustee or anyone else in a fiduciary position. . . . Courts of Chancery only in two special classes of case, awarded compound, as distinct from simple, interest."

These authorities establish that in the absence of fraud equity only awards compound (as opposed to simple) interest against a defendant who is a trustee or otherwise in a fiduciary position by way of recouping from such a defendant an improper profit made by him. It is unnecessary to decide whether in such a case compound interest can only be paid where the defendant has used trust moneys in his own trade or (as I tend to think) extends to all cases where a fiduciary has improperly profited from his trust. Unless the local authority owed fiduciary duties to the bank in relation to the upfront payment, compound interest cannot be awarded.'

Questions:

Is Lord Browne-Wilkinson's statement in the last sentence of this extract an absolute rule? Would it be preferable to say that the rationale underpinning the distinction between awards of simple and compound interest reflect a distinction between circumstances where the claimant is entitled only to the use value of the money (assessed as simple interest on the sum)[37] and circumstances where the claimant is entitled to disgorgement of the defaulting fiduciary's profits (assessed as compound interest on the sum if the facts so warrant)? If this is the case, then would modern financial markets now assess the use value of money as compound interest on the sum?

[37] The suggestion that this might represent equity's assessment of the 'use value' of money is reinforced when considered in conjunction with equity's provision of allowances for the use value of chattels in cases of rescission. All this was done before the common law provided for interest on damages awards.

FURTHER READING:

D Friedmann, 'Restitution for Wrongs: The Basis of Liability' in W R Cornish *et al* (eds), *Restitution Past, Present and Future* (Oxford: Hart Publishing, 1998) ch 9.
S Worthington, 'Reconsidering Disgorgement for Wrongs' (1999) 62 *MLR* 218.
J W Harris, *Property and Justice* (1996, Clarendon: Oxford) ch 17, especially pp 336–41.
J Beatson, *The Use and Abuse of Unjust Enrichment* (1991, Clarendon: Oxford) ch 8.

7.5 Remedies in bailment

The indicia of a bailment and its associated rights and obligations were considered in Chapter 2 (see Section 2.5). Here the focus is on the remedies which are available when there has been a breach of the obligations imposed by the bailment arrangement. In Chapter 2, the issue of the appropriate categorisation of bailment obligations was raised. Consider to what extent the cases extracted below support the notion of *sui generis* remedies in bailment, rather than reliance on the general remedies available in tort and contract.

There are two issues of particular significance which need to be addressed. The first concerns the ability of a bailee to sue a sub-bailee or other third parties, rather than have the bailor take the action. The second concerns the extent to which bailees and sub-bailees can rely on exclusion clauses.

7.5.1 Onus of proof in bailment actions

At the outset it is important to recall that the onus of proof in bailment cases is reversed. A defendant bailee is liable for any loss or damage to the claimant bailor's goods while they are in the bailee's possession unless he can show that this occurred without any neglect or default or misconduct on his own part or on the part of any servants or agents to whom he delegated his duty: *Morris v C W Martin & Sons Ltd* [1966] 1 QB 716 (CA), 726 *per* Lord Denning MR (see **[217]** above). This, at least, distinguishes bailment claims from general tort and contract claims, although the practical significance of the distinction may be minimal.

7.5.2 Actions by a bailee against third parties

[719] *The Winkfield* [1902] P 42 (CA), 54–6, 58–61 *per* Collins MR:
[A ship collided and sank off the coast of South Africa, with the loss of letters and parcels. The Postmaster General, as bailee of the mail, successfully claimed damages against the other ship, notwithstanding that he would have had a good answer to an action by the bailors. It was assumed by both sides that the Potmaster General was the bailee in possession at the time of the collision.]

> 'It seems to me that the position, that possession is good against a wrongdoer and that the latter cannot set up the *jus tertii* unless he claims under it, is well established in our

law, and really concludes this case against the respondents. As I shall shew presently, a long series of authorities establishes this in actions of trover and trespass at the suit of a possessor. And the principle being the same, it follows that he can equally recover the whole value of the goods in an action on the case for their loss through the tortious conduct of the defendant. I think it involves this also, that the wrongdoer who is not defending under the title of the bailor is quite unconcerned with what the rights are between the bailor and bailee, and must treat the possessor as the owner of the goods for all purposes quite irrespective of the rights and obligations as between him and the bailor.

I think this position is well established in our law, though it may be that reasons for its existence have been given in some of the cases which are not quite satisfactory. I think also that the obligation of the bailee to the bailor to account for what he has received in respect of the destruction or conversion of the thing bailed has been admitted so often in decided cases that it cannot now be questioned; and, further, I think it can be shewn that the right of the bailee to recover cannot be rested on the ground suggested in some of the cases, namely, that he was liable over to the bailor for the loss of the goods converted or destroyed. It cannot be denied that since the case of *Armory v. Delamirie* (1 Stra. 504), not to mention earlier cases from the Year Books onward, a mere finder may recover against a wrongdoer the full value of the thing converted. That decision involves the principle that as between possessor and wrongdoer the presumption of law is, in the words of Lord Campbell in *Jeffries v. Great Western Ry. Co.* (5 E. & B. 802, at p. 806), "that the person who has possession has the property." In the same case he says (at p. 805): "I am of opinion that the law is that a person possessed of goods as his property has a good title as against every stranger, and that one who takes them from him, having no title in himself, is a wrongdoer, and cannot defend himself by shewing that there was title in some third person, for against a wrongdoer possession is title. The law is so stated by the very learned annotator in his note to *Wilbraham v. Snow*." (2 Wms. Saund. 47 f.) Therefore it is not open to the defendant, being a wrongdoer, to inquire into the nature or limitation of the possessor's right, and unless it is competent for him to do so the question of his relation to, or liability towards, the true owner cannot come into the discussion at all; and, therefore, as between those two parties full damages have to be paid without any further inquiry. The extent of the liability of the finder to the true owner not being relevant to the discussion between him and the wrongdoer, the facts which would ascertain it would not have been admissible in evidence, and therefore the right of the finder to recover full damages cannot be made to depend upon the extent of his liability over to the true owner. To hold otherwise would, it seems to me, be in effect to permit a wrongdoer to set up a *jus tertii* under which he cannot claim. But, if this be the fact in the case of a finder, why should it not be equally the fact in the case of a bailee? Why, as against a wrongdoer, should the nature of the plaintiff's interest in the thing converted be any more relevant to the inquiry, and therefore admissible in evidence, than in the case of a finder? It seems to me that neither in one case nor the other ought it to be competent for the defendant to go into evidence on that matter.

I think this view is borne out by authority. . . .

Holmes C.J. in his admirable lectures on the Common Law, in the chapter devoted to bailments, traces the origin of the bailee's right to sue and recover the whole value of chattels converted, and arrives at the clear conclusion that the bailee's obligation to account arose from the fact that he was originally the only person who could sue, though afterwards by an extension, not perhaps quite logical, the right to sue was conceded to the bailor also. He says at p. 167: "At first the bailee was answerable to the owner because he was the only person who could sue; now it was said he could sue because he was answerable to the owner." And again at p. 170: "The inverted explanation of *Beaumanoir* will be remembered, that the bailee could sue because he was answerable over, in place of the original rule that he was answerable over so strictly because only he could sue." This inversion, as he points out, is traceable through the Year Books, and has survived into modern times, though, as he shews, it has not been acted upon. *Pollock and Maitland's History of English Law*, vol. 2, p. 170, puts the position thus:— "Perhaps we come nearest to historical truth if we say that between the two old rules there was no logical priority. The bailee had the action because he was liable, and was liable because he had the action." It may be that in early times the obligation of the bailee to the bailor was absolute, that is to say, he was an insurer. But long after the decision of *Coggs v. Bernard* ((1704) 2 Ld. Raym. 909), which classified the obligations of bailees, the bailee has, nevertheless, been allowed to recover full damages against a wrongdoer, where the facts would have afforded a complete answer for him against his bailor. The cases above cited are instances of this. In each of them the bailee would have had a good answer to an action by his bailor; for in none of them was it suggested that the act of the wrongdoer was traceable to negligence on the part of the bailee. . . .

. . . Therefore, as I said at the outset, and as I think I have now shewn by authority, the root principle of the whole discussion is that, as against a wrongdoer, possession is title. The chattel that has been converted or damaged is deemed to be the chattel of the possessor and of no other, and therefore its loss or deterioration is his loss, and to him, if he demands it, it must be recouped. His obligation to account to the bailor is really not *ad rem* in the discussion. It only comes in after he has carried his legal position to its logical consequence against a wrongdoer, and serves to soothe a mind disconcerted by the notion that a person who is not himself the complete owner should be entitled to receive back the full value of the chattel converted or destroyed. There is no inconsistency between the two positions; the one is the complement of the other. As between bailee and stranger possession gives title—that is, not a limited interest, but absolute and complete ownership, and he is entitled to receive back a complete equivalent for the whole loss or deterioration of the thing itself. As between bailor and bailee the real interests of each must be inquired into, and, as the bailee has to account for the thing bailed, so he must account for that which has become its equivalent and now represents it. What he has received above his own interest he has received to the use of his bailor. The wrongdoer, having once paid full damages to the bailee, has an answer to any action by the bailor.'

Questions:

On the facts of this case, the bailee is not liable to the bailor. However, the third party is liable to both bailor and bailee to the full extent of the loss (although only one of them will be able to recover).[38] What would motivate a bailee to sue in these circumstances? Are the damages recovered by the bailee held *on trust* for the bailor? When would the answer to this question be important?

[38] Note that both bailor and bailee will not inevitably be entitled to sue. The right to sue may depend upon an immediate right to possession. The bailor may have this (as in *O'Sullivan v Williams* [1992] 3 All ER 385 (CA)), but may not, depending upon the terms of the bailment.

Also see:

Torts (Interference with Goods) Act 1977 sections 7, 8.
The Jag Shakti [1986] 1 AC 337 (PC) (**[207]** above).
O'Sullivan v Williams [1992] 3 All ER 385 (CA).

7.5.3 Exclusion clauses

The next two extracts indicate the limitations imposed on bailees and sub-bailees wishing to rely on exclusion clauses. Some of the law on the incorporation of exclusion clauses into contracts is no doubt relevant, but the law in relation to bailment is not so tightly circumscribed.

[720] ***Morris v C W Martin & Sons Ltd*** **[1966] 1 QB 716 (CA), 729–30** ***per*** **Lord Denning MR:**
[The facts are summarised at **[217]** above. Since the court decided that in any event the exclusion clause did not cover the facts, these comments are obiter.]

> 'Now comes the question: Can the defendants rely, as against the plaintiff, on the exempting conditions although there was no contract directly between them and her? There is much to be said on each side. On the one hand, it is hard on the plaintiff if her just claim is defeated by exempting conditions of which she knew nothing and to which she was not a party. On the other hand, it is hard on the defendants if they are held liable to a greater responsibility than they agreed to undertake. As long ago as 1601 Lord Coke advised a bailee to stipulate specially that he would not be responsible for theft, see *Southcote's* case ((1601) 4 Co.Rep. 83b), a case of theft by a servant. It would be strange if his stipulation was of no avail to him. The answer to the problem lies, I think, in this: the owner is bound by the conditions if he has expressly or impliedly consented to the bailee making a sub-bailment containing those conditions, but not otherwise. Suppose the owner of goods lets them out on hire, and the hirer sends them for repair, and the repairer holds them for a lien. The owner is bound by the lien because he impliedly consented to the repairs being done, since they were reasonably incidental to use of the car. . . . So also if the owner of a ship accepts goods for carriage on a bill of lading containing exempting conditions (i.e., a "bailment upon terms") the owner of the goods (although not a party to the contract) is bound by those conditions if he impliedly consented to them as being in "the known and contemplated form," see the words of Lord Sumner in *Elder, Dempster & Co. v. Paterson, Zochonis & Co. Ltd.* ([1924] A.C, 522, 564(HL)) which were regarded by Dixon C.J. and Fullagar J. as stating the ratio decidendi, see *Wilson v. Darling Island Stevedoring & Lighterage Co. Ltd.* ((1956) 95 C.L.R. 43 (Aust HCt)) with whose judgment Viscount Simonds entirely agreed in *Midland Silicones Ltd. v. Scruttons Ltd.* ([1962] A.C. 446, 472 (HL)) and also the cases to which I referred in that case ([1962] A.C. 446, 489, 491).'

[721] ***The Pioneer Container*** **[1994] 2 AC 324 (PC), 334–6, 337–40, 345–6** ***per*** **Lord Goff:**
[The claimants engaged carriers to ship goods under bills of lading which gave the carriers authority to sub-contract the carriage 'on any terms'. The carriers sub-bailed the goods to the defendant shipowners for carriage on their ship from Taiwan to Hong Kong under feeder bills of lading which contained an exclusive jurisdiction

clause requiring any claim or dispute to be determined in Taiwan. The vessel sank with all her cargo off the coast of Taiwan. The claimants were held bound by the exclusive jurisdiction clause notwithstanding that they had not dealt directly with the sub-bailees and that their claims were now out of time in Taiwan.]

'*The central problem*

Their Lordships turn immediately to the central problem in the case, which is whether the shipowners can rely, as against the Scandutch and Hanjin plaintiffs, on the exclusive jurisdiction clause (clause 26) in the feeder bills of lading to which these plaintiffs were not parties. They think it right to observe, at the outset, that in commercial terms it would be most inconvenient if these two groups of plaintiffs were not so bound. Here is a ship, upon which goods are loaded in a large number of containers; indeed, one container may contain goods belonging to a number of cargo owners. One incident may affect goods owned by several cargo owners, or even (as here) all the cargo owners with goods on board. Common sense and practical convenience combine to demand that all of [335] these claims should be dealt with in one jurisdiction, in accordance with one system of law. If this cannot be achieved, there may be chaos. Much expense may be wasted on litigation in a number of different jurisdictions, as indeed happened in the present case, where there was litigation in eight other countries as well as Hong Kong and Taiwan. . . .

However, so far as English law and the law of Hong Kong are concerned, a technical problem faces shipowners who carry goods, for example under the feeder bills of lading in the present case, where there is no contractual relationship between the shipowners and certain cargo owners. This is because English law still maintains, though subject to increasing criticism, a strict principle of privity of contract, under which as a matter of general principle only a person who is a party to a contract may sue upon it. The force of this principle is supported and enhanced by the doctrine of consideration, under which as a general rule only a promise supported by consideration will be enforceable at common law. How long these principles will continue to be maintained in all their strictness is now open to question. But, in the middle of this century, judges of great authority and distinction were in no doubt that they should be so maintained. Their Lordships refer in particular to the speech of Viscount Simonds in *Midland Silicones Ltd. v. Scruttons Ltd.* [1962] A.C. 446, 467–468. The present case is concerned with the question whether the law of bailment can here be invoked by the shipowners to circumvent this difficulty.

. . .

[336] In approaching the central problem in the present case, their Lordships wish to observe that they are here concerned with two related questions. The first question relates to the identification of the relationship between the owner and the sub-bailee. Once that question is answered [see the extract at **[218]**], it is possible to address the second question, which is whether, given that relationship, it is open to the sub-bailee to invoke as against the owner the terms upon which he received the goods from the bailee.

. . .

[Turning to the second question.]

[338] In *Morris v. C. W. Martin & Sons Ltd.* Lord Denning M.R. expressed his opinion on this point in clear terms, though on the facts of the case his opinion was obiter. He said, at p. 729:

> "The answer to the problem lies, I think, in this: the owner is bound by the conditions if he has expressly or impliedly consented to the bailee making a sub-bailment containing those conditions, but not otherwise."

. . .

[339] In order to decide whether, like Steyn J., to accept the principle so stated by Lord Denning M.R., it is necessary to consider the relevance of the concept of "consent" in this context. It must be assumed that, on the facts of the case, no direct contractual relationship has been created between the owner and the sub-bailee, the only contract created by the sub-bailment being that between the bailee and the sub-bailee. Even so, if the effect of the sub-bailment is that the sub-bailee voluntarily receives into his custody the goods of the owner and so assumes towards the owner the responsibility of a bailee, then to the extent that the terms of the sub-bailment are consented to by the owner, it can properly be said that the owner has authorised the bailee so to regulate the duties of the sub-bailee in respect of the goods entrusted to him, not only towards the bailee but also towards the owner. (Their Lordships add in parenthesis that for this purpose it is not, in their opinion, necessary to have recourse to the doctrine of estoppel: cf. *Hispanica de Petroleos S.A. v. Vencedora Oceanica Navegacion S.A. (No. 2) (Note)* [1987] 2 Lloyd's Rep. 321, 336, 340, *per* Nicholls and Dillon L.JJ. Even where there is express or implied consent to the relevant terms by the owner of the goods, there can be no estoppel without some holding out on his part. Estoppel may, however, be relevant if recourse is to be had to the doctrine of ostensible authority).

Such a conclusion, finding its origin in the law of bailment rather than the law of contract, does not depend for its efficacy either on the doctrine of privity of contract or on the doctrine of consideration. That this may be so appears from the decision of the House of Lords in *Elder, Dempster & Co. Ltd. v. Paterson, Zochonis & Co. Ltd.* [1924] A.C. 522. In that case, shippers of cargo on a chartered ship brought an action against the shipowners for damage caused to the cargo by bad stowage, for which the shipowners were responsible. It is crucial to observe that the cargo was shipped under charterers' bills of lading, so that the contract of carriage contained in or evidenced by the bills of lading was between the shippers and the charterers. The shipowners nevertheless sought to rely, as against the shippers, upon an exception in the bill of lading which protected the charterers from liability for damage due to bad stowage. It was held that the shipowners were entitled to do so, the preferred reason upon which the House so held (see *Midland Silicones Ltd. v. Scruttons Ltd.* [1962] A.C. 446, 470, *per* Viscount Simonds, following the opinion of Fullagar J. in *Wilson v. Darling Island Stevedoring and Lighterage Co. Ltd.* [1956] 1 Lloyd's Rep. 346, 364; 95 C.L.R. 43, 78) being found in the speech of Lord Sumner [1924] A.C. 522, 564:

> "in the circumstances of this case the obligations to be inferred from the reception of the cargo for carriage to the United Kingdom amount to a bailment upon terms, which include the exceptions and limitations of liability stipulated in the known and contemplated form of bill of lading."

Of course, there was in that case a bailment by the shippers direct to the shipowners, so that it was not necessary to have recourse to the concept of sub-bailment. Even so, notwithstanding the absence of any contract between the shippers and the shipowners, the shipowners' obligations as bailees were effectively subject to the terms upon which the shipowners implicitly received the goods into their possession. Their Lordships do not imagine that a different conclusion would have been reached in the *Elder, Dempster* case if the shippers had delivered the goods, not directly to the ship, but into the possession of agents of the charterers who had, in their turn, loaded the goods on board;

because in such circumstances, by parity of reasoning, the shippers may be held to have impliedly consented that the sub-bailment to the shipowners should be on terms which included the exemption from liability for bad storage.

. . .

[345] Having disposed of these three threshold points, their Lordships turn to the basic question which arises on this aspect of the case which is whether, in the case of a sub-bailment, the owners of the goods who seek to hold the sub-bailee liable to them as a bailee will be bound by an exclusive jurisdiction clause which forms part of the contract governing the sub-bailment. Their Lordships start, of course, with the position that, under clauses 6 and 4(1) of the Hanjin and Scandutch bills of lading respectively, there was vested in both Hanjin and Scandutch a very wide authority to sub-contract the whole or any part of the carriage of the goods "on any terms." Since the sub-contracting of any part of the carriage to another will ordinarily involve a bailment (or sub-bailment) to that carrier, it must follow that both the Hanjin and Scandutch plaintiffs had expressly consented to the sub-bailment of their goods to another carrier on any terms. It further follows that no question arises in the present case of implied consent, the only question relating to the scope of the express consent so given.

At first sight, the words used are wide enough to authorise consent to the application of an exclusive jurisdiction clause to the sub-bailment. However, it was the submission of the plaintiffs that this was not so. They submitted that the exclusive jurisdiction clause should be excluded from such incorporation because it was not a clause directly germane to the subject matter of the bill of lading, viz. the shipment, carriage and delivery of the relevant goods. . . . [346] Here, however, the question is whether consent given by the owner of goods to his bailee to bail the goods to a sub-bailee on any terms is wide enough to embrace an exclusive jurisdiction clause in the contract governing the sub-bailment; and their Lordships do not perceive a similar [commercial] need to limit the terms so consented to. Nor do their Lordships consider that the mere fact that the relevant clause may (as here) be regarded as, in a sense, imposing a positive obligation on the owner is of itself sufficient to exclude it from the scope of the consent so given. In such a case, it seems to them, the element of control must be derived from the scope of the owner's consent; and where, as here, the consent is very wide in its terms, only terms which are so unusual or so unreasonable that they could not reasonably be understood to fall within such consent are likely to be held to be excluded. Bearing this in mind, their Lordships perceive a number of considerations which militate in favour of the incorporation of the exclusive jurisdiction clause in the present case. First, by way of introduction, it is common in the present context for an exclusive jurisdiction clause to be coupled with an express choice of law clause, often contained (as here) in the same contractual provision, and usually providing for the law of the chosen forum to be the law governing the contract. Second, a provision in this form is by no means uncommon in shipowners' standard forms of bill of lading; indeed such a provision must, their Lordships imagine, be very common in the case of shipowners engaged in the container trade. Third, their Lordships do not consider that it can possibly be said that the incorporation of such a clause in a bill of lading is per se unreasonable. In this connection, they refer again to the difficulties, described earlier, which may arise if bill of lading holders are free to pursue their claims in various jurisdictions throughout the world; and they do not overlook the fact that, in common law countries, a stay of proceedings to enforce an exclusive jurisdiction clause is a matter for the court's discretion.'

Question:

This situation is not covered by the Contracts (Rights of Third Parties) Act 1999. Why not? Which situations would be covered by this Act?

7.5.4 Quantifying damages

The normal tort measure of damages applies. If the property cannot be returned to the bailor, then the measure of damages is usually the market value of the goods.[39] Sometimes this has to be assessed sensitively, as the next extract indicates.

[722] ***Building & Civil Engineering Ltd v Post Office*** **[1966] 1 AC 247 (HL), 261–3** ***per*** **Lord Denning MR:**

[The facts are immaterial. The case concerned the loss of 'holiday stamps' in the post, and was a claim under statute, not under the common law of bailment.]

> 'At common law in a case of bailment, the general principle is *restitutio in integrum*, which means that the party damnified is entitled to such a sum of money as will put him in as good a position as if the goods had not been lost or damaged. This is subject, however, to the qualification that the damages must not be too remote, that is, they must be such damages as flow directly and in the usual course of things from the loss or damage, see *The Argentino* ((1888) 13 P.D. 191, 196, 200, C.A.). If the party damnified suffers damage of a special kind, he is entitled to recover it, subject to the qualification that the damages must not exceed such damages as would be produced in the ordinary course of things by the act complained of, see *Cory v. Thames Ironworks* ((1868) L.R. 3 Q.B. 181). When goods are lost or damaged in transit, the damage ordinarily produced is, in the case of loss, the cost of replacement; or in the case of damage, the cost of repair. That is the amount which, in the absence of contract, the bailor can recover. He cannot recover indirect or consequential damages (such as loss of profits on a business) because those can only be recovered in cases on contracts proper, where notice of special circumstances is brought home, see *British Columbia Saw-Mill Co. v. Nettleship* ((1868) L.R. 3 C.P. 499, 506).
>
> It seems to me that the measure of damages, thus ascertained by the common law of bailment, is applicable in cases under section 9 (2) of the [Crown Proceedings Act 1947]: subject, however, to two maxima provided by the section itself, namely the amount recoverable shall not exceed (i) the market value of the package, see section 9 (2) (b); and (ii) the maximum amount for the fee paid.
>
> It remains to apply these principles to the loss of holiday stamps. In the ordinary way, I should think it clear that when a book of stamps is sent by registered post, and then stolen in transit, the owner can recover from the Post Office the face value of the stamps. Take the simple case where a contractor buys a book of stamps from the plaintiffs, pays for them and keeps them in his head office. He then sends them by registered post to a branch office where his men are working. If they are stolen in transit, the contractor can clearly recover the face value from the Post Office: for the simple reason that, in order to replace them, he has to buy another book from the plaintiffs. Take next the case

[39] *Chubb Cash Ltd v John Crilley & Son* [1983] 1 WLR 599.

where the plaintiffs sell the book of stamps to a contractor; and despatch it to him by registered post; and it is stolen. If it were not for the special arrangement (by which the plaintiffs replace the book free) the contractor would himself have suffered the loss and would have had to replace it by buying a fresh book of stamps from the plaintiffs.

The Post Office now seek to get out of this ordinary liability. They take advantage of the special arrangement whereby the plaintiffs replace the stamps free, and say that on that account the plaintiffs have suffered no loss. They say that it costs the plaintiffs very little to replace the stamps. The plaintiffs simply take another book out of their stock and send it to the contractor. It only costs the plaintiffs the amount they paid to the printers, i.e., the cost of the paper and printing.

That argument would be legitimate if the books of stamps had been destroyed by fire in transit: and could never be re-presented. But these books were not destroyed. They were stolen in transit. And, being stolen, there was a good chance that they would be sold in the thieves' market and be presented for payment: and paid at face value. Every stolen stamp that was so presented and paid, meant a loss to the plaintiffs of the money paid.

Even so, Mr. Ashton Roskill asked the question: What loss have the plaintiffs suffered? Or rather, proved that they have suffered? He says they have not proved any damage. The stolen stamps might never be used by anyone. The thief might have thrown them into the fire. No damage would be suffered, he said, by the plaintiffs unless the thief disposed of them to an employer (who stuck them on a card and got money back on them) or to an employee (who stuck them on his card and presented it). There was no evidence, he said, of any of the stolen stamps being presented to the plaintiffs for payment. Unless and until they were presented, no damage would be suffered. So said Mr. Ashton Roskill. I pressed him on this point to say, when did the cause of action arise? Only, he said, when the stolen stamps were presented for payment. That is palpably wrong. The cause of action arises as soon as the goods are lost or damaged in transit. Indeed the period of limitation (which is only one year) begins to run as soon as the packet is posted: see section 5 (3) of the Law Reform (Limitation of Actions) Act, 1954. If the plaintiffs had to wait until the stolen stamps were presented and paid, they might lose their action before they had it: which is absurd. The truth is that they have not to wait until the stolen stamps are presented. They can bring their action for the loss at once: and their damages will be reckoned on the probability that the stolen stamps may sooner or later be presented for payment, and they will then have to pay. It is trite law that damages can be recovered for the probability that loss will be suffered in the future owing to the wrongful act of the defendant, no matter whether it be a breach of contract (see *Chaplin v. Hicks* [1911] 2 K.B. 786 (CA)) or a tort (see *Domine v. Grimsdall* [1937] 2 All E.R. 119, 125). Every day when a plaintiff brings an action for personal injuries, he is entitled to damages for the probability that some future ill may befall him, such as arthritis supervening. So here, the plaintiffs are entitled to damages for the probable future loss. It is a matter of guesswork, but I should put it at 75 per cent. of the face value (£27) of the stamps.'

Question:

Do any of these cases help to clarify the true nature of a bailment?

7.6 Remedies in equity

In almost every chapter in this book there has been some reference to the role of equity. Its impact in the context of personal property is enormous. It defines certain proprietary interests (such as equitable ownership and security interests) and allows parties to confer such interests on each other; it creates proprietary interests by operation of law, accelerating or counteracting the parties' own intentions; it provides a tracing process to protect existing interests; it modifies the impact of common law rules of contract and expands the list of circumstances which will found a claim in unjust enrichment. In this chapter, the influence of equity has already been noted in the context of actions in tort (accessory liability), in contract (relief against forfeiture clauses) and in unjust enrichment (recipient liability).

In the following extracts the focus is exclusively on two further areas of equity's intervention: the liability of trustees to reinstate trust funds, and the remedy of injunctive relief (which can be granted in aid of either common law or equitable rights). There is no discussion of a fiduciary's personal liability to account for profits made in breach of the duty of loyalty, or a confidant's liability for breach of confidence. These liabilities are not controversial—unlike their proprietary corollaries, discussed in Section 5.10 above.

7.6.1 Trustees' liability to reinstate the trust fund

A trustee is strictly liable to the trust beneficiaries to reinstate the trust fund if losses are caused, directly or indirectly, by the trustee's failure to obey the terms of the trust in dealing with the trust assets. This is not an obligation in tort, contract or unjust enrichment. It does not depend upon the trustee's negligence, or any contract between the trustee and the beneficiaries, or any enrichment flowing to the trustee from the breach.[40] Trustees are subject to this form of liability even if when they act in good faith, in ignorance, and for no reward.

Many types of breaches can give rise to this form of liability. The breach may be a positive act, such as making an unauthorised investment; it may be a failure to act, such as a failure to convert an investment when the trust instrument so requires. Two points need to be noted. First, if the unauthorised investment is profitable then, instead of claiming reinstatement, the beneficiaries may adopt the unauthorised investment as part of the trust property.[41] Alternatively, the beneficiaries may sue the trustee for breach of fiduciary duty, claiming either a constructive trust (a proprietary remedy)[42] or an account of profits (a personal remedy) of the unau-

[40] It follows that this liability cannot be a liability in either subtractive unjust enrichment or unjust enrichment for wrongs (if there is such a category, distinct from restitutionary damages for the wrong). The remedy is not disgorgement.

[41] Such adoption depends upon all the beneficiaries being *sui juris*, unanimous, and together absolutely entitled to the trust property.

[42] See Section 5.10 above.

thorised profits made in breach of trust.[43] Provided the beneficiaries do not claim double recovery, it seems they can also require the trustee to make good any losses.[44] Although both routes can lead to much the same practical end, the first depends upon ratification of the breach which consists in failure to comply with the terms of the trust, the second on pursuit of remedies for breach of the trustee's fiduciary duty of loyalty. The second point to note is that this remedy, compelling reinstatement of the trust fund, is available only when the breach consists in a mis-dealing with the trust assets in breach of the terms of the trust deed. It is not the appropriate remedy when the trustee complies with the trust deed but, for example, causes losses through negligence[45] or fraud.[46] Then the appropriate remedies lie in tort.

The difficulty with this remedy is to determine precisely what 'reinstatement' requires of the trustee. The next extract illustrates the advantages and the limitations inherent in the remedial obligation to reinstate the trust fund.

[723] *Target Holdings Ltd v Redferns (a firm)* [1996] 1 AC 421 (HL), 431, 432, 434–7 *per* Lord Browne-Wilkinson:

[Target Holdings Ltd, the claimant finance company, agreed to lend £1,706,000 to Crowngate Developments Ltd, secured on property to be purchased by Crowngate for £2 million. The loan application was supported by a professional valuation of the property at £2 million. Redferns, a firm of solicitors, acted for both lender and mortgagor. In fact Crowngate had negotiated for the purchase of the property for £775,000. It devised a scheme whereby the property would be purchased for that price by a Jersey company associated with Crowngate, and then would pass through a series of sub-sales to Crowngate, who would pay £2 million. Target Holdings gave the solicitors a total of £1,525,000 to be held on a bare trust and transferred to the mortgagor once the property had been purchased and charged to the claimant. In breach of trust and before the mortgagor bought the property, the solicitors paid away £1,490,000 without having received any charge on the property. The solicitors lied and told the claimant that the purchase and charges had been completed. The charges were eventually completed as originally envisaged, although after the breach of trust. Crowngate subsequently went insolvent, and Target Holdings sold the mortgaged property for £500,000. In an unsuccessful attempt to recoup its massive losses, it brought an action alleging breach of trust by the solicitors and seeking restitution of the entire sum paid over.]

> 'Before considering the technical issues of law which arise, it is appropriate to look at the case more generally. Target allege, and it is probably the case, that they were defrauded by third parties (Mr. Kohli and Mr. Musafir and possibly their associates) to advance money on the security of the property. If there had been no breach by Redferns of their instructions and the transaction had gone through, Target would have suffered a loss in round figures of £1.2m. (i.e. £1.7m. advanced less £500,000 recovered on the realisation of the security). Such loss would have been wholly caused by the fraud of the

[43] The remedy is designed to strip the trustee of unauthorised profits, not to be penal, so the beneficiaries must give allowance for the trustee's contribution (whether in money or labour).

[44] *Re Lake* [1903] 1 KB 439, but cf *Thornton v Stokhill* (1855) 1 Jur NS 751.

[45] *Henderson v Merrett Syndicates Ltd.*[1995] 2 AC 145 (HL), 205 *per* Lord Browne-Wilkinson; *White v Jones* [1995] 2 AC 207 (HL), 270–1 *per* Lord Browne-Wilkinson; *Bristol & West BS v Mothew* [1998] 1 Ch 1 (CA), 16–17 *per* Millett LJ (although referring to an equitable duty of care).

[46] *Paragon Finance plc v D B Thakerar & Co (a firm)* [1999] 1 All ER 400 (CA).

third parties. The breach of trust committed by Redferns left Target in exactly the same position as it would have been if there had been no such breach: Target advanced the same amount of money, obtained the same security and received the same amount on the realisation of that security. In any ordinary use of words, the breach of trust by Redferns cannot be said to have caused the actual loss ultimately suffered by Target unless it can be shown that, but for the breach of trust, the transaction would not have gone through, e.g. if Panther [the Jersey company] could not have obtained a conveyance from Mirage [the vendor of the property] otherwise than by paying the purchase money to Mirage out of the moneys paid out, in breach of trust, by Redferns to Panther on 29 June. If that fact can be demonstrated, it can be said that Redferns' breach of trust was a cause of Target's loss: if the transaction had not gone through, Target would not have advanced the money at all and therefore Target would not have suffered any loss. . . .

[This may significantly qualify what follows, especially in cases such as this which are 'redolent of fraud and negligence' (p 432).]

. . .

At common law there are two principles fundamental to the award of damages. First, that the defendant's wrongful act must cause the damage complained of. Second, that the plaintiff is to be put "in the same position as he would have been in if he had not sustained the wrong for which he is now getting his compensation or reparation:" *Livingstone v. Rawyards Coal Co.* (1880) 5 App.Cas. 25, 39, per Lord Blackburn. Although, as will appear, in many ways equity approaches liability for making good a breach of trust from a different starting point, in my judgment those two principles are applicable as much in equity as at common law. Under both systems liability is fault-based: the defendant is only liable for the consequences of the legal wrong he has done to the plaintiff and to make good the damage caused by such wrong. He is not responsible for damage not caused by his wrong or to pay by way of compensation more than the loss suffered from such wrong. The detailed rules of equity as to causation and the quantification of loss differ, at least ostensibly, from those applicable at common law. But the principles underlying both systems are the same. . . .

The basic right of a beneficiary is to have the trust duly administered in accordance with the provisions of the trust instrument, if any, and the general law. Thus, in relation to a traditional trust where the fund is held in trust for a number of beneficiaries having different, usually successive, equitable interests, (e.g. A for life with remainder to B), the right of each beneficiary is to have the whole fund vested in the trustees so as to be available to satisfy his equitable interest when, and if, it falls into possession. Accordingly, in the case of a breach of such a trust involving the wrongful paying away of trust assets, the liability of the trustee is to restore to the trust fund, often called "the trust estate," what ought to have been there.

The equitable rules of compensation for breach of trust have been largely developed in relation to such traditional trusts, where the only way in which all the beneficiaries' rights can be protected is to restore to the trust fund what ought to be there. In such a case the basic rule is that a trustee in breach of trust must restore or pay to the trust estate either the assets which have been lost to the estate by reason of the breach or compensation for such loss. Courts of Equity did not award damages but, acting in personam, ordered the defaulting trustee to restore the trust estate: see *Nocton v. Lord Ashburton* [1914] A.C. 932, 952, 958, per Viscount Haldane L.C. If specific restitution of the trust property is not possible, then the liability of the trustee is to pay sufficient compensation to the trust estate to put it back to what it would have been had the breach not been committed: *Caffrey v. Darby* (1801) 6 Ves. 488; *Clough v. Bond* (1838) 3 M. & C. 490. Even if the immediate cause of the loss is the dishonesty or failure of a third party, the trustee is liable to make good that loss to the trust estate if, but for the breach, such loss would not have occurred: see *Underhill and Hayton, Law of Trusts & Trustees* 14th ed. (1987), pp. 734–736; *In re Dawson, decd.; Union Fidelity Trustee Co. Ltd. v. Perpetual Trustee Co. Ltd.* [1966] 2 N.S.W.R. 211; *Bartlett v. Barclays Bank Trust Co. Ltd. (Nos. 1 and 2)* [1980] Ch. 515. Thus the common law rules of remoteness of damage and causation do not apply. However there does have to be some causal connection between the breach of trust and the loss to the trust estate for which compensation is recoverable, viz. the fact that the loss would not have occurred but for the breach: see also *In re Miller's Deed Trusts* (1978) 75 L.S.G. 454; *Nestlé v. National Westminster Bank Plc.* [1993] 1 W.L.R. 1260.

Hitherto I have been considering the rights of beneficiaries under traditional trusts where the trusts are still subsisting and therefore the right of each beneficiary, and his only right, is to have the trust fund reconstituted as it should be. But what if at the time of the action claiming compensation for breach of trust those trusts have come to an end? Take as an example again the trust for A for life with remainder to B. During A's lifetime B's only right is to have the trust duly administered and, in the event of a breach, to have the trust fund restored. After A's death, B becomes absolutely entitled. He of course has the right to have the trust assets retained by the trustees until they have fully accounted for them to him. But if the trustees commit a breach of trust, there is no reason for compensating the breach of trust by way of an order for restitution and compensation to the trust fund as opposed to the beneficiary himself. The beneficiary's right is no longer simply to have the trust duly administered: he is, in equity, the sole owner of the trust estate. Nor, for the same reason, is restitution to the trust fund necessary to protect other beneficiaries. Therefore, although I do not wholly rule out the possibility that even in those circumstances an order to reconstitute the fund may be appropriate, in the ordinary case where a beneficiary becomes absolutely entitled to the trust fund the court orders, not restitution to the trust estate, but the payment of compensation directly to the beneficiary. The measure of such compensation is the same, i.e. the difference between what the beneficiary has in fact received and the amount he would have received but for the breach of trust.

Thus in *Bartlett v. Barclays Bank Trust Co. Ltd. (Nos. 1 and 2)* [1980] Ch. 515 by the date of judgment some of the shares settled by the trust deed had become absolutely vested in possession: see at p. 543A. The compensation for breach of trust, though quantified by reference to what the fund would have been but for the breach of trust, was payable directly to the persons who were absolutely entitled to their shares of the trust fund: see at p. 544. Accordingly, in traditional trusts for persons by way of succession, in my judgment once those trusts have been exhausted and the fund has become absolutely vested in possession, the beneficiary is not normally entitled to have the exhausted trust reconstituted. His right is to be compensated for the loss he has suffered by reason of the breach.

I turn then to the two arguments urged before your Lordships.

Argument (A)

As I have said, the critical step in this argument is that Target is now entitled to an order for reconstitution of the trust fund by the repayment into client account of the moneys wrongly paid away, so that Target can now demand immediate repayment of the whole of such moneys without regard to the real loss it has suffered by reason of the breach.

Even if the equitable rules developed in relation to traditional trusts were directly applicable to such a case as this, as I have sought to show a beneficiary becoming absolutely entitled to a trust fund has no automatic right to have the fund reconstituted in all circumstances. Thus, even applying the strict rules so developed in relation to traditional trusts, it seems to me very doubtful whether Target is now entitled to have the trust fund reconstituted. But in my judgment it is in any event wrong to lift wholesale the detailed rules developed in the context of traditional trusts and then seek to apply them to trusts of quite a different kind. In the modern world the trust has become a valuable device in commercial and financial dealings. The fundamental principles of equity apply as much to such trusts as they do to the traditional trusts in relation to which those principles were originally formulated. But in my judgment it is important, if the trust is not to be rendered commercially useless, to distinguish between the basic principles of trust law and those specialist rules developed in relation to traditional trusts which are applicable only to such trusts and the rationale of which has no application to trusts of quite a different kind.

This case is concerned with a trust which has at all times been a bare trust. Bare trusts arise in a number of different contexts: e.g. by the ultimate vesting of the property under a traditional trust, nominee shareholdings and, as in the present case, as but one incident of a wider commercial transaction involving agency. In the case of moneys paid to a solicitor by a client as part of a conveyancing transaction, the purpose of that transaction is to achieve the commercial objective of the client, be it the acquisition of property or the lending of money on security. . . . the basic equitable principle applicable to breach of trust is that the beneficiary is entitled to be compensated for any loss he would not have suffered but for the breach. I have no doubt that, until the underlying commercial transaction has been completed, the solicitor can be required to restore to client account moneys wrongly paid away. But to import into such trust an obligation to restore the trust fund once the transaction has been completed would be entirely artificial. The obligation to reconstitute the trust fund applicable in the case of traditional trusts reflects the fact that no one beneficiary is entitled to the trust property and the need to compensate all beneficiaries for the breach. That rationale has no application to a case such as the present. To impose such an obligation in order to enable the beneficiary solely entitled (i.e. the client) to recover from the solicitor more than the client has in fact lost flies in the face of common sense and is in direct conflict with the basic principles of equitable compensation. In my judgment, once a conveyancing transaction has been completed the client has no right to have the solicitor's client account reconstituted as a "trust fund."

Argument (B)

. . . The key point in the reasoning of the Court of Appeal is that where moneys are paid away to a stranger in breach of trust, an immediate loss is suffered by the trust estate: as a result, subsequent events reducing that loss are irrelevant. . . .

A trustee who wrongly pays away trust money, like a trustee who makes an unauthorised investment, commits a breach of trust and comes under an immediate duty to remedy such breach. If immediate proceedings are brought, the court will make an immediate order requiring restoration to the trust fund of the assets wrongly distributed or, in the case of an unauthorised investment, will order the sale of the unauthorised investment and the payment of compensation for any loss suffered. But the fact that there is an accrued cause of action as soon as the breach is committed does not in my judgment mean that the quantum of the compensation payable is ultimately fixed as at the date when the breach occurred. The quantum is fixed at the date of judgment at which date, according to the circumstances then pertaining, the compensation is assessed at the figure then necessary to put the trust estate or the beneficiary back into the position it would have been in had there been no breach. I can see no justification for "stopping the clock" immediately in some cases but not in others: to do so may, as in this case, lead to compensating the trust estate or the beneficiary for a loss which, on the facts known at trial, it has never suffered.'

Also see:

Bartlett v Barclays Bank Trust Co Ltd (Nos 1 and 2) [1980] Ch 515.
In re Dawson, dec'd [1966] 2 NSWR 211 (SCt NSW).
Canson Enterprises Ltd v Boughton & Co (1991) 85 DLR (4th) 129 (SCt Canada).

Questions:

Does this form of liability apply to constructive or resulting trustees? Should it? See the earlier discussion of 'knowing receipt' (Section 7.4.2 above). How, if at all, is that form of liability related to the liability to reinstate the trust fund?

FURTHER READING:

I E Davidson, 'The Equitable Remedy of Compensation' (1982) 13 *Melbourne University Law Review* 349.

7.6.2 Injunctions

Injunctions are discretionary orders issued by a court to prevent or reverse some wrongful activity. The discretion is wide; the Supreme Court Act 1981 section 37(1) allows for injunctions 'in all cases where it appears to the court to be just and convenient'.[47] Injunctions are not limited to restraining defendants from acting (*prohibitory* injunctions). They may also compel activity (*mandatory* injunctions). One of their great values, however, lies in the fact that they can be ordered *before* the claimant's rights are infringed, in order to prevent a threatened infringement (*quia timet* injunctions).[48] Injunctions can also be issued on either a permanent or a

[47] Despite the apparent breadth of these words, the claimant must show the infringement (or potential infringement) of some *legal or equitable* right: *Gouriet v Union of Post Office Workers* [1978] AC 435; *Paton v Trustees of the British Pregnancy Advisory Service* [1979] QB 276.

[48] In *Redland Bricks Ltd v Morris* [1970] AC 652 (HL), Lord Upjohn listed the four principles governing the award of such injunctions. Only the first seems specific to *quia timet* injunctions, and that is that the jurisdiction should be exercised sparingly and with caution, and only in circumstances where the claimant can prove that there is a strong probability of serious damage occurring in the future.

temporary basis, and they can be *interlocutory* (ie granted pending trial) or *final* (ie granted after full determination of the legal issues). All of this makes injunctions powerful legal tools. Moreover, failure to comply with their conditions is a contempt of court.

(i) Equitable discretion in ordering injunctions

An injunction is a discretionary remedy. This means that, whether interlocutory or final, it is subject to all the usual equitable considerations. In particular, a claimant cannot obtain an injunction unless common law damages are inadequate.[49] *If* this is the case, then a claimant who can show that his or her legal rights are being (or will be) violated by the defendant's conduct is *prima facie* entitled to a final *prohibitory* injunction. Only rarely will a court in these circumstances order damages in lieu of an injunction (although see *Jaggard v Sawyer* [1995] 1 WLR 269, **[726]** below). However, this *prima facie* entitlement is further circumscribed if the injunction requested is *mandatory* rather than prohibitory. Then the courts are concerned to see that the injunction does not cause undue hardship to the defendant (again, see *Jaggard v Sawyer* [1995] 1 WLR 269, **[726]** below). Even further special considerations operate where the claimant seeks an interlocutory injunction rather than a final injunction. Interlocutory injunctions are discussed in more detail below.

In addition to this fundamental constraint that common law damages must be inadequate, it is also true that the claimant must come to court with 'clean hands',[50] in good time,[51] in circumstances which do not suggest that the claimant has acquiesced in the defendant's behaviour.[52] Furthermore, equity will not act in vain, so an injunction will not be ordered where it would achieve no useful purpose. A typical illustration is the courts' denial of an injunction to restrain a breach of confidence once the information is in the public domain.[53] Nor will equity act contrary to the public interest, even when the claimant has satisfactorily proved all the other elements of his case.

(ii) Interlocutory injunctions

All the various forms of injunctions have enormous potential to protect a claimant's interests in personal property. However, interlocutory injunctions provide an especially valuable means of protection. These are short term injunctions granted, pending trial, in order to maintain the *status quo* by preserving the claimant from further harm. For example, an interlocutory injunction may prevent assets being removed from premises, or a fund being dissipated, or shares being allotted, pending final resolution of the legal dispute in court. By their very nature these injunctions create special difficulties for courts in deciding whether to exercise their discretion to

[49] This rule cannot inhibit the award of an injunction to protect an *equitable* right, since common law damages are not then available.

[50] *Argyll v Argyll* [1967] Ch 302.

[51] This is because of the equitable doctrine (or defence) of laches. See, eg, *Jaggard v Sawyer* [1995] 1 WLR 269 (**[726]** below). However, long delays will not necessarily warrant denial of an injunction unless the delay has destroyed the legal right or prejudiced the defendant: *HP Bulmer Ltd & Showerings Ltd v J Bollinger SA* [1977] 2 CMLR 625 (CA).

[52] *Shaw v Applegate* [1977] 1 WLR 970.

[53] *AG v Observer Ltd (Spycatcher case)* [1990] 1 AC 109 (HL).

make such orders. The object of legal proceedings is to reach a just resolution of a dispute between the parties. If, pending final determination of the issues, there is ongoing and irreparable harm to the claimant's interests, the eventual resolution of the issues may come too late to provide the claimant with a remedy of any value. On the other hand, the defendant may be right in denying that any legal wrong is being committed. An order maintaining the *status quo* may therefore obstruct the defendant's exercise of his legitimate rights. The courts have therefore developed a test that looks to the 'balance of convenience' between the parties. This involves assessing the harm each side is likely to incur if the injunction is granted and if it is not, and whether that harm could be compensated for in money when the issues are finally determined at trial. To maintain fairness between the parties, such injunctions are often supported by cross-undertakings in damages, whereby the claimant promises to compensate the defendant for any consequential losses should the injunction turn out not to have been warranted. The next extract illustrates this balancing process.

[724] *American Cyanamid Co v Ethicon Ltd* [1975] AC 396 (HL), 406–10 *per* Lord Diplock:

[The claimant, an American company, owned a patent covering certain sterile absorbable surgical sutures. The defendant, also an American company, was about to launch on the British market a suture which the claimant claimed infringed its patent. The defendants contested the validity of the patent and also denied that it covered their product. The claimant successfully applied for an interlocutory injunction restraining the defendant from distributing its sutures.]

> '[406] My Lords, when an application for an interlocutory injunction to restrain a defendant from doing acts alleged to be in violation of the plaintiff's legal right is made upon contested facts, the decision whether or not to grant an interlocutory injunction has to be taken at a time when ex hypothesi the existence of the right or the violation of it, or both, is uncertain and will remain uncertain until final judgment is given in the action. It was to mitigate the risk of injustice to the plaintiff during the period before that uncertainty could be resolved that the practice arose of granting him relief by way of interlocutory injunction; but since the middle of the 19th century this has been made subject to his undertaking to pay damages to the defendant for any loss sustained by reason of the injunction if it should be held at the trial that the plaintiff had not been entitled to restrain the defendant from doing what he was threatening to do. The object of the interlocutory injunction is to protect the plaintiff against injury by violation of his right for which he could not be adequately compensated in damages recoverable in the action if the uncertainty were resolved in his favour at the trial; but the plaintiff's need for such protection must be weighed against the corresponding need of the defendant to be protected against injury resulting from his having been prevented from exercising his own legal rights for which he could not be adequately compensated under the plaintiff's undertaking in damages if the uncertainty were resolved in the defendant's favour at the trial. The court must weigh one need against another and determine where "the balance of convenience" lies.
>
> In those cases where the legal rights of the parties depend upon facts that are in dispute between them, the evidence available to the court at the hearing of the application for an interlocutory injunction is incomplete. It is given on affidavit and has not been tested by oral cross-examination. The purpose sought to be achieved by giving to the court

discretion to grant such injunctions would be stultified if the discretion were clogged by a technical rule forbidding its exercise if upon that incomplete untested evidence the court evaluated the chances of the plaintiff's ultimate success in the action at 50 per cent. or less, but permitting its exercise if the court evaluated his chances at more than 50 per cent.

The notion that it is incumbent upon the court to undertake what is in effect a preliminary trial of the action upon evidential material different from that upon which the actual trial will be conducted, is, I think, of comparatively recent origin, though it can be supported by references in [407] earlier cases. . . .

Your Lordships should in my view take this opportunity of declaring that there is no such rule. The use of such expressions as "a probability," "a prima facie case," or "a strong prima facie case" in the context of the exercise of a discretionary power to grant an interlocutory injunction leads to confusion as to the object sought to be achieved by this form of temporary relief. The court no doubt must be satisfied that the claim is not frivolous or vexatious, in other words, that there is a serious question to be tried.

It is no part of the court's function at this stage of the litigation to try to resolve conflicts of evidence on affidavit as to facts on which the claims of either party may ultimately depend nor to decide difficult questions of law which call for detailed argument and mature considerations. These are matters to be dealt with at the trial. One of the reasons for the introduction of the practice of requiring an undertaking as to damages upon the [408] grant of an interlocutory injunction was that "it aided the court in doing that which was its great object, viz. abstaining from expressing any opinion upon the merits of the case until the hearing": *Wakefield v. Duke of Buccleugh* (1865) 12 L.T. 628, 629. So unless the material available to the court at the hearing of the application for an interlocutory injunction fails to disclose that the plaintiff has any real prospect of succeeding in his claim for a permanent injunction at the trial, the court should go on to consider whether the balance of convenience lies in favour of granting or refusing the interlocutory relief that is sought.

As to that, the governing principle is that the court should first consider whether, if the plaintiff were to succeed at the trial in establishing his right to a permanent injunction, he would be adequately compensated by an award of damages for the loss he would have sustained as a result of the defendant's continuing to do what was sought to be enjoined between the time of the application and the time of the trial. If damages in the measure recoverable at common law would be adequate remedy and the defendant would be in a financial position to pay them, no interlocutory injunction should normally be granted, however strong the plaintiff's claim appeared to be at that stage. If, on the other hand, damages would not provide an adequate remedy for the plaintiff in the event of his succeeding at the trial, the court should then consider whether, on the contrary hypothesis that the defendant were to succeed at the trial in establishing his right to do that which was sought to be enjoined, he would be adequately compensated under the plaintiff's undertaking as to damages for the loss he would have sustained by being prevented from doing so between the time of the application and the time of the trial. If damages in the measure recoverable under such an undertaking would be an adequate remedy and the plaintiff would be in a financial position to pay them, there would be no reason upon this ground to refuse an interlocutory injunction.

It is where there is doubt as to the adequacy of the respective remedies in damages available to either party or to both, that the question of balance of convenience arises. It would be unwise to attempt even to list all the various matters which may need to be taken into consideration in deciding where the balance lies, let alone to suggest the relative weight to be attached to them. These will vary from case to case.

Where other factors appear to be evenly balanced it is a counsel of prudence to take such measures as are calculated to preserve the status quo. If the defendant is enjoined temporarily from doing something that he has not done before, the only effect of the interlocutory injunction in the event of his succeeding at the trial is to postpone the date at which he is able to embark upon a course of action which he has not previously found it necessary to undertake; whereas to interrupt him in the conduct of an established enterprise would cause much greater inconvenience to him since he would have to start again to establish it in the event of his succeeding at the trial.

Save in the simplest cases, the decision to grant or to refuse an interlocutory injunction will cause to whichever party is unsuccessful on the application some disadvantages which his ultimate success at the trial may [409] show he ought to have been spared and the disadvantages may be such that the recovery of damages to which he would then be entitled either in the action or under the plaintiff's undertaking would not be sufficient to compensate him fully for all of them. The extent to which the disadvantages to each party would be incapable of being compensated in damages in the event of his succeeding at the trial is always a significant factor in assessing where the balance of convenience lies, and if the extent of the uncompensatable disadvantage to each party would not differ widely, it may not be improper to take into account in tipping the balance the relative strength of each party's case as revealed by the affidavit evidence adduced on the hearing of the application. This, however, should be done only where it is apparent upon the facts disclosed by evidence as to which there is no credible dispute that the strength of one party's case is disproportionate to that of the other party. The court is not justified in embarking upon anything resembling a trial of the action upon conflicting affidavits in order to evaluate the strength of either party's case.

I would reiterate that, in addition to those to which I have referred, there may be many other special factors to be taken into consideration in the particular circumstances of individual cases. The instant appeal affords one example of this.

Returning, therefore, to the instant appeal, it cannot be doubted that the affidavit evidence shows that there are serious questions to be tried. Graham J. and the Court of Appeal have already tried the question of infringement on such affidavit evidence as was available and have come to contrary conclusions. . . .

The factors which he [Graham J, the trial judge with significant patent experience] took into consideration, and in my view properly, were that Ethicon's sutures XLG were not yet on the market, so they had no business which would be brought to a stop by the injunction, no factories would be closed and no work-people would be thrown out of work. They held a dominant position in the United Kingdom market for absorbent surgical sutures and adopted an aggressive sales policy. Cyanamid on the other hand were in the course of establishing a growing market in PHAE surgical sutures which competed with the natural catgut sutures marketed by Ethicon. If Ethicon were entitled also to establish themselves in the market for PHAE absorbable surgical sutures until the action is tried, which may not be for two or three years yet, and possibly thereafter until the case is finally disposed of on appeal, Cyanamid, even though ultimately successful in proving infringement, would have lost its chance of continuing to increase [410] its share in the total market in absorbent surgical sutures which the continuation of an uninterrupted monopoly of PHAE sutures would have gained for it by the time of the expiry of the patent in 1980. It is notorious that new pharmaceutical products used exclusively by doctors or available only on prescription take a long time to become established in the market, that much of the benefit of the monopoly granted by the patent derives from the fact that the patented product is given the opportunity of becoming established and this benefit continues to be reaped after the patent has expired.

In addition there was a special factor to which Graham J. attached importance. This was that, once doctors and patients had got used to Ethicon's product XLG in the period prior to the trial, it might well be commercially impracticable for Cyanamid to deprive the public of it by insisting on a permanent injunction at the trial, owing to the damaging effect which this would have upon its goodwill in this specialised market and thus upon the sale of its other pharmaceutical products.

I can see no ground for interfering in the learned judge's assessment of the balance of convenience or for interfering with the discretion that he exercised by granting the injunction.'

[725] *Hoffmann-La Roche (F) & Co AG v Secretary of State for Trade and Industry* [1975] AC 295 (HL), 360–1 *per* Lord Diplock:

[This case concerned the Trade Secretary's application for an interlocutory injunction against drug companies which refused to reduce prices in compliance with a government order. The drug companies claimed the legislation was *ultra vires*. The injunction was eventually ordered without requiring the Crown to give an undertaking as to damages, notwithstanding that the potential loss to the defendants was of the order of £8 million. The following extract describes the nature and purpose of these cross-undertakings.]

'By the end of the [nineteenth] century the insertion of such an undertaking in all orders for interim injunctions granted in litigation between subject and subject had become a matter of course.

The advantages of this practice in any suit for the protection or enforcement of personal or proprietary rights are plain enough. An interim injunction is a temporary and exceptional remedy which is available before the rights of the parties have been finally determined and, in the case of an ex parte injunction, even before the court has been apprised of the nature of the defendant's case. To justify the grant of such a remedy the plaintiff must satisfy the court, first, that there is a strong prima facie case that he will be entitled to a final order restraining the defendant from doing what he is threatening to do, and, secondly, that he will suffer irreparable injury which cannot be compensated by a subsequent award of damages in the action if the defendant is not prevented from doing it between the date of the application for the interim injunction and the [361] date of the final order made on trial of the action. Nevertheless, at the time of the application it is not possible for the court to be absolutely certain that the plaintiff will succeed at the trial in establishing his legal right to restrain the defendant from doing what he is threatening to do. If he should fail to do so the defendant may have suffered loss as a result of having been prevented from doing it while the interim injunction was in force; and any loss is likely to be damnum absque injuria for which he could not recover damages from the plaintiff at common law. So unless some other means is provided in this event for compensating the defendant for his loss there is a risk that injustice may be done.

. . .

The court has no power to compel an applicant for an interim injunction to furnish an undertaking as to damages. All it can do is to refuse the application if he declines to do so. The undertaking is not given to the defendant but to the court itself. Non-performance of it is contempt of court, not breach of contract, and attracts the remedies available for contempts, but the court exacts the undertaking for the defendant's benefit. It retains a discretion not to enforce the undertaking if it considers that the conduct of the defendant in relation to the obtaining or continuing of the injunction or the enforcement of the undertaking makes it inequitable to do so, but if the undertaking is enforced the measure of the damages payable under it is not discretionary. It is assessed on an inquiry into damages at which principles to be applied are fixed and clear. The assessment is made upon the same basis as that upon which damages for breach of contract would be assessed if the undertaking had been a contract between the plaintiff and the defendant that the plaintiff would not prevent the defendant from doing that which he was restrained from doing by the terms of the injunction: see *Smith v. Day* (1882) 21 Ch.D. 421, per Brett L.J., at p. 427.

Besides mitigating the risk of injustice to the defendant the practice of exacting an undertaking as to damages facilitates the conduct of the business of the courts. It relieves the court of the necessity of embarking at an interlocutory stage upon an inquiry as to the likelihood of the defendant being able to establish facts to destroy the strong prima facie case which ex hypothesi will have been made out by the plaintiff. The procedure on motions is unsuited to inquiries into disputed facts. This is best left to the trial of the action, and if the plaintiff then succeeds in establishing his claim he suffers no harm from having given the undertaking, while if he fails to do so the defendant is compensated for any loss which he may have suffered by being temporarily prevented from doing what he was legally entitled to do.'

[Lord Diplock then considered the position of the Crown in relation to such undertakings. He concluded that only in exceptional circumstances should the Crown be excused from the obligation to give an undertaking in damages, but that this was such an exceptional case.]

Questions:

1. The *Hoffmann-La Roche* case (**[725]** above) was decided four months earlier than the *Cyanamid* case (**[724]** above). Has Lord Diplock changed his mind? (Laddie J in *Series 5 Software Ltd v Clarke* [1996] 1 All ER 853 thinks he has not.)
2. Often the parties do not take their case to trial after obtaining an interlocutory injunction. The *Cyanamid* case indicates that the grant of an interlocutory injunction can often mean victory (or defeat) for one party without the need for further proceedings. Does this mean that the principles upon which interlocutory injunctions are awarded should be changed? Also see *Kirklees Borough Council v Wickes Building Supplies Ltd* [1993] AC 227 (HL).

(iii) Damages in lieu of or in addition to injunctive relief

The Supreme Court Act 1981 section 50 gives courts the power to award damages in addition to or in substitution for an injunction.[54] In *Shelfer v City of London Electric Lighting Co*,[55] A L Smith LJ considered that damages should only be awarded in substitution for an injunction where the injuries to the claimant's rights were small, and able to be estimated in money, and adequately compensable by a small sum, and where it would be oppressive to the defendant to grant the injunction requested. The first three conditions suggest that, on the principles already discussed, the claimant would not succeed in obtaining an injunction. Whether a claimant should be able to obtain damages in lieu in these circumstances is open to debate. The other complaint about the four conditions proposed by A L Smith LJ is the implication that in cases of trespass and nuisance damages should often be awarded in lieu of an injunction. In many of these cases the burden of remedying the situation is out of all proportion to the damage to the claimant. Nevertheless, courts should be reluctant to allow a defendant to buy his way out of the breach. The next extract illustrates a modern application of these rules.

[726] *Jaggard v Sawyer* [1995] 1 WLR 269 (CA), 283–9, 291–2 *per* Millett LJ:
[The case concerns real property, but the principles discussed apply generally. The claimant owned a house which was part of a residential development of 10 houses served by a private road which was a cul de sac. Each plot, together with the area of roadway immediately in front of the plot up to the centre of the roadway, had been conveyed subject to covenants binding on successive owners not to use any part of the unbuilt land other than as a private garden and to keep the relevant portion of roadway in good repair. The defendants owned a house at the opposite end of the cul de sac from the claimant's property. They purchased a plot of land contiguous with their property, without access to the cul de sac and lying parallel to it. They obtained planning permission to build a dwelling house on the plot and, in the belief that the cul de sac was a public road, they proposed that access should be provided by use of the cul de sac and a driveway which would be constructed over part of their garden. The claimant threatened to bring proceedings for an injunction to restrain such user, but did not proceed. Eventually, when the building was at an advanced stage, the claimant did commence proceedings for an injunction. Thereafter the house was completed and occupied by the defendants for a short time before being let. The Court of Appeal refused the application for an injunction and awarded damages in lieu.]

> 'This appeal raises yet again the questions: what approach should the court adopt when invited to exercise its statutory jurisdiction to award damages instead of granting an injunction to restrain a threatened or continuing trespass or breach of a restrictive covenant? [284] And if the court accedes to the invitation on what basis should damages be assessed?
>
> Before considering these questions, it is desirable to state some general propositions which are established by the authorities and which are, or at least ought to be, uncontroversial.

[54] And also in addition to or in substitution for an order for specific performance.
[55] [1895] 1 Ch 287, 322–3.

(1) The jurisdiction was originally conferred by section 2 of the Chancery Amendment Act 1858, commonly known as Lord Cairns's Act. It is now to be found in section 50 of the Supreme Court Act 1981. It is a jurisdiction to award damages "in addition to or in substitution for such injunction or specific performance."

(2) The principal object of Lord Cairns's Act is well known. . . . It was to enable the Court of Chancery, when declining to grant equitable relief and leaving the plaintiff to his remedy at law, to award the plaintiff damages itself instead of sending him to the common law courts to obtain them. From the very first, however, it was recognised that the Act did more than this. The jurisdiction of the Court of Chancery was wider than that of the common law courts, for it could give relief where there was no cause of action at law. . . . Damages at common law are recoverable only in respect of causes of action which are complete at the date of the writ; damages for future or repeated wrongs must be made the subject of fresh proceedings. Damages in substitution for an injunction, however, relate to the future, not the past. They inevitably extend beyond the damages to which the plaintiff may be entitled at law. In *Leeds Industrial Co-operative Society Ltd. v. Slack* [1924] A.C. 851 the House of Lords confirmed the jurisdiction of the courts to award damages under the Act in respect of an injury which was threatened but had not yet occurred. No such damages could have been awarded at common law.

(3) The nature of the cause of action is immaterial; it may be in contract or tort. . . .

(4) The power to award damages under Lord Cairns's Act arises whenever the court "has jurisdiction to entertain an application" for an injunction or specific performance. This question must be determined as at the date of the writ. If the court would then have had jurisdiction to [285] grant an injunction, it has jurisdiction to award damages instead. When the court comes to consider whether to grant an injunction or award damages instead, of course, it must do so by reference to the circumstances as they exist at the date of the hearing.

(5) The former question is effectively one of jurisdiction. The question is whether, at the date of the writ, the court could have granted an injunction, not whether it would have done: *City of London Brewery Co. v. Tennant* (1873) L.R. 9 Ch.App. 212. . . .

(6) It is not necessary for the plaintiff to include a claim for damages in his writ. As long ago as 1868 Lord Chelmsford L.C. held that damages may be awarded under Lord Cairns's Act

> "though not specifically prayed for by the bill, the statute having vested a discretion in the judge, which he may exercise when he thinks the case fitting without the prayer of the party:" see *Betts v. Neilson* (1868) L.R. 3 Ch.App. 429, 441.

It would be absurd as well as misleading to insist on the plaintiff including a claim for damages in his writ when he is insisting on his right to an injunction and opposing the defendant's claim that he should be content to receive damages instead. By a parity of reasoning it is not in my opinion necessary for a plaintiff to include a claim for an injunction in order to found a claim for damages under the Act. It would be absurd to require him to include a claim for an injunction if he is sufficiently realistic to recognise that in the circumstances he is unlikely to obtain one and intends from the first to ask the court for damages instead. But he ought to make it clear whether he is claiming damages for past injury at common law or under the Act in substitution for an injunction.

(7) . . . [M]any judges . . . from the very first have recognised that, while the Act does not enable the court to license future wrongs, this may be the practical result . . . it is not the

award of damages which has the practical effect of licensing the defendant to commit the wrong, [286] but the refusal of injunctive relief. Thereafter the defendant may have no right to act in the manner complained of, but he cannot be prevented from doing so. The court can in my judgment properly award damages "once and for all" in respect of future wrongs because it awards them in substitution for an injunction and to compensate for those future wrongs which an injunction would have prevented. The doctrine of res judicata operates to prevent the plaintiff and his successors in title from bringing proceedings thereafter to recover even nominal damages in respect of further wrongs for which the plaintiff has been fully compensated.

It has always been recognised that the practical consequence of withholding injunctive relief is to authorise the continuance of an unlawful state of affairs. If, for example, the defendant threatens to build in such a way that the plaintiff's light will be obstructed and he is not restrained, then the plaintiff will inevitably be deprived of his legal right. This was the very basis upon which before 1858 the Court of Chancery had made the remedy of injunction available in such cases. After the passing of Lord Cairns's Act many of the judges warned that the jurisdiction to award damages instead of an injunction should not be exercised as a matter of course so as to legalise the commission of a tort by any defendant who was willing and able to pay compensation. In *Shelfer v. City of London Electric Lighting Co.* [1895] 1 Ch. 287, 315–316 Lindley L.J. said:

> "But in exercising the jurisdiction thus given attention ought to be paid to well settled principles; and ever since Lord Cairns's Act was passed the Court of Chancery has repudiated the notion that the legislature intended to turn that court into a tribunal for legalizing wrongful acts; or in other words, the court has always protested against the notion that it ought to allow a wrong to continue simply because the wrongdoer is able and willing to pay for the injury he may inflict."

. . .

Lord Cairns's Act did not worsen the plaintiff's position but improved it. Thenceforth, if injunctive relief was withheld, the plaintiff was not compelled to wait until further wrongs were committed and then [287] bring successive actions for damages; he could be compensated by a once and for all payment to cover future as well as past wrongs. Of course, the ability to do "complete justice" in this way made it easier for the courts to withhold the remedy of an injunction, and it was therefore necessary for the judges to remind themselves from time to time that the discretion to withhold it, which had existed as well before 1858 as after it, was to be exercised in accordance with settled principles; that a plaintiff who had established both a legal right and a threat to infringe it was prima facie entitled to an injunction to protect it; and that special circumstances were needed to justify withholding the injunction.

Nevertheless references to the "expropriation" of the plaintiff's property are somewhat overdone, not because that is not the practical effect of withholding an injunction, but because the grant of an injunction, like all equitable remedies, is discretionary. Many proprietary rights cannot be protected at all by the common law. The owner must submit to unlawful interference with his rights and be content with damages. If he wants to be protected he must seek equitable relief, and he has no absolute right to that. In many cases, it is true, an injunction will be granted almost as of course; but this is not always the case, and it will never be granted if this would cause injustice to the defendant. Citation of passages in the cases warning of the danger of "expropriating" the plaintiff needs to be balanced by reference to statements like that of Lord Westbury L.C. in *Isenberg v. East India House Estate Co. Ltd.* (1863) 3 De G. J. & S. 263, 273 where he held that it was the duty of the court not

> "by granting a mandatory injunction, to deliver over the defendants to the plaintiff bound hand and foot, in order to be made subject to any extortionate demand that he may by possibility make, but to substitute for such mandatory injunction an inquiry before itself, in order to ascertain the measure of damage that has been actually sustained."

When the plaintiff claims an injunction and the defendant asks the court to award damages instead, the proper approach for the court to adopt cannot be in doubt. Clearly the plaintiff must first establish a case for equitable relief, not only by proving his legal right and an actual or threatened infringement by the defendant, but also by overcoming all equitable defences such as laches, acquiescence or estoppel. If he succeeds in doing this, he is prima facie entitled to an injunction. The court may nevertheless in its discretion withhold injunctive relief and award damages instead. How is this discretion to be exercised? In a well known passage in *Shelfer v. City of London Electric Lighting Co.* [1895] 1 Ch. 287, 322–323, A. L. Smith L.J. set out what he described as "a good working rule" that

> "(1) If the injury to the plaintiff's legal right is small, (2) And is one which is capable of being estimated in money, (3) And is one which can be adequately compensated by a small money payment, (4) And the case is one in which it would be oppressive to the defendant to grant an injunction:—then damages in substitution for an injunction may be given."

Laid down just 100 years ago, A. L. Smith L.J.'s check-list has stood the test of time; but it needs to be remembered that it is only a working rule and does not purport to be an exhaustive statement of the circumstances in which damages may be awarded instead of an injunction.

. . .

[288] The outcome of any particular case usually turns on the question: would it in all the circumstances be oppressive to the defendant to grant the injunction to which the plaintiff is prima facie entitled? Most of the cases in which the injunction has been refused are cases where the plaintiff has sought a mandatory injunction to pull down a building which infringes his right to light or which has been built in breach of a restrictive covenant. In such cases the court is faced with a fait accompli. The jurisdiction to grant a mandatory injunction in those circumstances cannot be doubted, but to grant it would subject the defendant to a loss out of all proportion to that which would be suffered by the plaintiff if it were refused, and would indeed deliver him to the plaintiff bound hand and foot to be subjected to any extortionate demands the plaintiff might make. In the present case, as in the closely similar case of *Bracewell v. Appleby* [1975] Ch. 408, the plaintiff sought a prohibitory injunction to restrain the use of a road giving access to the defendants' house. The result of granting the injunction would be much the same; the house would not have to be pulled down, but it would be rendered landlocked and incapable of beneficial enjoyment.

. . .

In considering whether the grant of an injunction would be oppressive to the defendant, all the circumstances of the case have to be considered. At one extreme, the defendant may have acted openly and in good faith and in ignorance of the plaintiff's rights, and thereby inadvertently placed himself in a position where the grant of an injunction would either force him to yield to the plaintiff's extortionate demands or expose him to substantial loss. At the other extreme, the defendant may have acted with [289] his eyes open and in full knowledge that he was invading the plaintiff's rights, and hurried on his work in the hope that by presenting the court with a fait accompli he could compel the plaintiff to accept monetary compensation. Most cases, like the present, fall somewhere in between.

. . .

Having decided to refuse an injunction and to award the plaintiff damages instead, the [trial] judge had to consider the measure of damages. He based them on her share of the amount which, in his opinion, the plaintiff and the other residents of Ashleigh Avenue could reasonably have demanded as the price of waiving their rights. In this he applied the measure of damages which had been adopted by Brightman J. in *Wrotham Park Estate Co. Ltd. v. Parkside Homes Ltd.* [1974] 1 W.L.R. 798, a case which has frequently been followed. It would not be necessary to consider this matter further but for the fact that in the recent case in this court of *Surrey County Council v. Bredero Homes Ltd.* [1993] 1 W.L.R. 1361 [**[709]** above] doubts were expressed as to the basis on which this measure of damages could be justified and whether it was consistent with the reasoning of Lord Wilberforce in *Johnson v. Agnew* [1980] A.C. 367. It is, therefore, necessary to examine those cases further.

. . .

[291] In my view Lord Wilberforce's statement [in *Johnson v. Agnew*] that the measure of damages is the same whether damages are recoverable at common law or under the Act must be taken to be limited to the case where they are recoverable in respect of the same cause of action. It cannot sensibly have any application where the claim at common law is in respect of a past trespass or breach of covenant and that under the Act is in respect of future trespasses or continuing breaches of covenant.

Accordingly I am of opinion that the [trial judge in this case] was not precluded by the decision of the House of Lords in *Johnson v. Agnew* from adopting the measure of damages which he did. It is, however, necessary to notice the observations of Steyn L.J. in *Surrey County Council v. Bredero Homes Ltd.* [1993] 1 W.L.R. 1361, 1369:

> "In my view *Wrotham Park Estate Co. Ltd. v. Parkside Homes Ltd.* [1974] 1 W.L.R. 798 is only defensible on the basis of the third or restitutionary principle . . . The plaintiffs' argument that the *Wrotham Park* case can be justified on the basis of a loss of bargaining opportunity is a fiction."

I find these remarks puzzling. It is plain from his judgment in the *Wrotham Park* case that Brightman J.'s approach was compensatory, not restitutionary. He sought to measure the damages by reference to what the plaintiff had lost, not by reference to what the defendant had gained. He did not award the plaintiff the profit which the defendant had made by the breach, but the amount which he judged the plaintiff might have obtained as the price of giving its consent. The amount of the profit which the defendant expected to make was a relevant factor in that assessment, but that was all.

. . . .

[292] In the present case the plaintiff brought proceedings at a time when her rights were still capable of being protected by injunction. She has accordingly been able to invoke the court's jurisdiction to award in substitution for an injunction damages which take account of the future as well as the past. In my view there is no reason why compensatory damages for future trespasses and continuing breaches of covenant should not reflect the value of the rights which she has lost, or why such damages should not be measured by the amount which she could reasonably have expected to receive for their release.'

Question:

In what situations are the courts likely to award damages in lieu of an injunction in respect of a claimant's interests in *personal* property? How will such damages be assessed?

(iv) Freezing orders ('Mareva *injunctions'*[56]*)*

A freezing order is a special and powerful form of interlocutory injunction granted on somewhat different principles from normal interlocutory injunctions. The aim of a freezing order is, as the name indicates, to prevent a defendant from dissipating his assets. The order is made if the claimant can show a good arguable case, a real risk that the defendant will dissipate his assets and so frustrate any judgment order eventually made against him, and—as with all interlocutory injunctions—that the balance of convenience favours the order.[57] These orders are somewhat surprising, especially in view of the fact that the threatened dispersal of assets is not a wrongful act. Subject to any special rules relating to insolvency, a defendant can usually do what he likes with his own assets.[58] The orders are said to be justified on the basis that they are necessary to enable a claimant to obtain satisfaction at law, and that they preserve the credibility of the legal process.

By their very nature, applications for these injunctions are usually heard *ex parte* (in the absence of the other party) and quickly. These features are sufficient to warrant imposing additional demands on the claimant applicant in the interests of doing justice to the defendant. In addition to meeting the criteria already indicated, a claimant must make full and frank disclosure of all the material facts which are or should reasonably be known to him, and must give particulars of the claim, the amount in dispute, and the defendant's likely answers to the claim. Moreover, as might be expected, the claimant must give an undertaking as to damages.

The potential disadvantages for the defendant, if an order is made, are enormous. Before his dispute has been tried, his assets are frozen. This may be sufficient to put the defendant out of business—at a time when the courts avowedly presume innocence until guilt is proven. This factor is an element in assessing the 'balance of convenience', but it is not determinative.

The order does not give the claimant any proprietary interest in the defendant's assets. It merely 'freezes' the assets so that the defendant cannot deal with them except according to the terms of the order. The order is a personal order against the defendant, so it cannot be made unless the defendant is amenable to the jurisdiction

[56] So called after the second case in which this form of relief was granted: *Mareva Compania Naviera SA v International Bulkcarriers SA* [1975] 2 Lloyd's Rep 509 (CA). The order now has statutory backing: Supreme Court Act 1981 s 37(3). These freezing orders, and search orders ('*Anton Piller*' orders) discussed in the next section, have been described as 'law's two "nuclear" weapons': *Bank Mellat v Nikpour* [1985] FSR 87 (CA), 92 *per* Donaldson LJ.

[57] *Derby & Co Ltd v Weldon* [1990] Ch 48; *Polly Peck International v Nadir (No 2)* [1992] 2 All ER 769. Also see Practice Direction CPR 1999 25PD–003ff.

[58] *Mercedes Benz v Leiduck* [1996] AC 284.

of the court.[59] However, provided this is the case, the order can relate to the defendant's worldwide assets, both legal and equitable, including any future acquisitions. Breach of the order is a contempt of court for both the defendant and any party (such as a bank) who is aware of the order.

Also see:

Re Bank of Credit and Commerce International SA (No 9) [1994] 3 All ER 764.
Polly Peck International v Nadir (No 2) [1992] 2 All ER 769.
Derby & Co v Weldon (Nos 3 and 4) [1990] Ch 65.
Derby & Co Ltd v Weldon [1990] Ch 48.

*(v) Search orders ('*Anton Piller *orders'*[60]*)*

Like freezing orders, search orders are *ex parte* interlocutory injunctions. They are mandatory, not prohibitory, injunctions designed to prevent the removal or destruction of evidence which is essential to the effective prosecution of the claimant's claim. Also like freezing orders, they are awarded in the interests of justice.

These orders were initially designed as a means of aiding the bringing of cases to prevent the pirating of records. The offence of pirating was easily discovered, but by the time the claimant had served a writ and obtained an interlocutory hearing or an order for discovery, the pirated copies—which were essential evidence—would have been destroyed or removed from the jurisdiction. This gave rise to the practice of *ex parte* interlocutory injunctions allowing the claimant to inspect the defendant's premises and list or remove documents or objects. The jurisdictional basis is clear: it was to preserve the property which was the subject of an impending trial or was genuinely ancillary to the vindication of a recognised legal or equitable claim. The advantage to the claimant was that the trial could proceed with the necessary proof which might otherwise be removed or destroyed.

Equally obviously, the defendant must be protected: the injunction should only be ordered if the defendant is likely to remove or destroy the evidence; also, the defendant's rights against self-incrimination[61] and the right to continue carrying on business must be protected. This protective factor is even more important with search orders than with freezing orders, because search orders cannot be 'undone'. The defendant's business is particularly at risk because of the tendency of claimants to take the defendant's goods and hold them pending trial, which is delayed for as long as possible—so that the defendant's business closes down, thus achieving the claimant's aims without trial.

These search orders are regarded as less controversial than freezing orders, but they too have come in for considerable criticism. The protective features adopted with freezing orders also apply in relation to search orders. The claimant must show a strong *prima facie* case, a substantial risk of serious potential or actual damage to the claimant's interests if the order is not made, clear evidence that the defendant

[59] *Siskina v Distos Compania Naveira SA* [1979] AC 210 (HL).
[60] After *Anton Piller KG v Manufacturing Processes Ltd* [1976] Ch 55 (CA).
[61] The Supreme Court Act ensures that the evidence is not used in criminal prosecutions.

has in his possession incriminating documents or property and a serious possibility that he will destroy them before an application *inter partes* can be made, and, finally, a clear assessment that the harm that execution of the order is likely to cause the defendant and his business affairs is not excessive or out of proportion to the legitimate objects of the order itself. As with freezing orders, the claimant is obliged to make full disclosure of material facts, and to give an undertaking as to damages. In addition, the terms of the order are generally framed so as to protect as far as possible the defendant's civil liberties: reasonable constraints are imposed on matters such as the time at which the order is to be executed, the parties to be present, the premises to be searched, the materials to be searched for and whether or not they are to be removed or merely copied.

Also see:

Lock International plc v Beswick [1989] 1 WLR 1268.
Columbia Pictures Inc v Robinson [1987] Ch 38.
Anton Pillar KG v Manufacturing Process [1976] Ch 55 (CA).

FURTHER READING:

I C F Spry, *Equitable Remedies* (4th edn, 1990, Law Book Company: Sydney).
J E Martin, 'Equitable and Inequitable Remedies' (1990) 20 *UWALRev* 143.

FURTHER GENERAL READING:

Rt Hon Sir Peter Millett, 'Equity's Place in the Law of Commerce' (1998) 114 *LQR* 214.
A Mason, 'The Place of Equity and Equitable Remedies in the Contemporary Common Law World' (1994) 110 *LQR* 238.
J E Martin, 'Fusion Fallacy and Confusion' [1994] *Conv* 13.
G Hammond, 'Equity and Abortive Commercial Transactions' (1990) 106 *LQR* 207.

7.7 Limitation periods

The operation of limitation periods in respect of a claimant's claims can sometimes severely circumscribe the practical value of the claimant's rights. The subject is therefore of great importance, although its treatment here is necessarily superficial. A claimant's ability to bring an action can be lost either by the operation of statutory limitation periods, or, where an equitable remedy is sought, by the operation of the equitable doctrines of acquiescence or laches. Sometimes loss of the right to take action is, of itself, sufficient to destroy the practical value of the claimant's proprietary interest. At other times, loss of the right to take action is formally associated with loss of the right to the property too.

What follows is a brief survey of particular aspects of the law of limitation which are particularly relevant to interests in personal property.

7.7.1 Limitation periods and legal choses in possession

The usual limitation period in respect of most personal actions is six years. In addition, time generally starts to run from the date of the breach. These time limitations restrict a claimant's ability to take action to remedy interference with or damage to interests in personal property, but they will not usually deprive the claimant of those interests. For example, a claimant's property may be damaged by a trespasser. The claimant then has six years in which to take action to recover damages for the trespass. However, failure to proceed will not affect the claimant's status as owner of the asset.

However, this is not always the case. If the interference amounts to total denial of the claimant's ownership interests, as when an asset is converted, then the six year limitation period operates to deny both the ability to take action[62] *and* the ownership right itself. [63] This result is justified on policy grounds. To allow an owner to reassert ownership after many years would lead to unacceptable uncertainty in dealings with personal property. On the other hand, the rule would seem unfair if it prevented an owner from pursuing a thief. Where the interference with goods is not merely tortious but also criminal (as when goods are obtained by theft or deception or blackmail), then there is *no* time limit for bringing an action against the thief, and no question of the owner's title being extinguished as against the thief.[64] This protective provision has its limits, however. If the thief sells[65] the property to a *bona fide* purchaser for value then, as against that person,[66] time will start to run from the date of the thief's further conversion.[67] Of course, the owner remains able to sue the thief.

7.7.2 Limitation periods and legal choses in action

For many choses in action, such as shares, there are no limitation periods which operate to deny the property in the chose. Nevertheless, the general limitation periods will restrict an owner's ability to pursue any claims in contract or tort, for example, in relation to the chose.

Debts, however, are different. Debts are created by simple contract or by deed, and so the underlying property (the debt itself) is affected by the limitation periods applying to those forms of contract. The general limitation period for simple con-

62 Limitation Act 1980 s 2. The 6-year limitation period starts to run from the date of the conversion, irrespective of when the claimant discovers that the property has been converted: *Granger v George* (1826) 5 B & C 149, 108 ER 56; *R B Policies at Lloyds v Butler* [1950] 1 KB 76.

63 Limitation Act 1980 s 3(2).

64 Limitation Act 1980 s 4(5).

65 For some reason this is the only form of transaction protected in this way.

66 The *nemo dat* rule prevents transfer of good title to the property. The innocent purchaser will only obtain such title after limitation periods have run against the true owner.

67 Limitation Act 1980 s 4(2) and 4(4).

tracts is six years,[68] and for contracts created by deed it is 12 years.[69] However, if, after a debt has fallen due, the debtor pays part of it or acknowledges that he owes the money, then time begins to run afresh from that date.[70] If the owner of the debt fails to take action to recover the debt within the appropriate time frame, then the debt is extinguished.

The rules are different, and more complicated, for secured debts. If the debt is secured by a mortgage or a charge, then, in general, the limitation period in respect of the principal sum is 12 years,[71] and in respect of the interest arrears is six years.[72] Importantly, however, these limitation periods do not start to run so long as the mortgaged or charged property includes a future interest in property.[73] This means that time will not start to run in respect of most debts secured by a floating charge, and even in respect of debts secured by a fixed charge provided the charge is worded to include future assets falling within the description of the charge. If, despite these relaxed rules, the debt does become barred by time, then it seems that the security too will lapse.[74] However, given the practical management of most commercial debts and the effect of part payment or acknowledgement, this position is unlikely to arise.

If the debt is secured by a possessory security—a pledge or a common law lien—then barring of the debt by effluxion of time still leaves the creditor in possession of the security, and his rights in respect of that security remain intact. He can retain or sell the property, depending upon the nature of the possessory security (see Sections 3.1–3.3 above).

7.7.3 Limitation periods and equitable interests

(a) Trust property

[727] Limitation Act 1980 section 21:

> **'21. Time limit for actions in respect of trust property**
>
> (1) No period of limitation prescribed by this Act shall apply to an action by a beneficiary under a trust, being an action—
>
> (a) in respect of any fraud or fraudulent breach of trust to which the trustee was a party or privy; or
>
> (b) to recover from the trustee trust property or the proceeds of trust property in the possession of the trustee, or previously received by the trustee and converted to his use.
>
> . . .

[68] Limitation Act 1980 s 5.

[69] Limitation Act 1980 s 8.

[70] Limitation Act 1980 s 29(5). So, too, with time for enforcing certain rights associated with any security: s 29(3).

[71] Limitation Act 1980 s 20(1).

[72] Limitation Act 1980 s 20(5), although if the parties agree that the arrears of interest are to be treated as part of the principal, then a 12 year period applies to them too (s 20(7)(b)).

[73] Limitation Act 1980 s 20(3), 20(7)(a).

[74] Although see the doubts expressed in A P Bell, *Modern Law of Personal Property in England and Ireland* (1989, Butterworths: London), pp 542–3. See Limitation Act 1980 s 20.

> (3) Subject to the preceding provisions of this section, an action by a beneficiary to recover trust property or in respect of any breach of trust, not being an action for which a period of limitation is prescribed by any other provision of this Act, shall not be brought after the expiration of six years from the date on which the right of action accrued.'[75]

This section has wide application. This is because the Limitation Act 1980 section 38 provides that the expressions 'trust' and 'trustee' have the same meanings as in the Trustee Act 1925 section 68(17). This extends the meaning of these expressions to include 'implied, resulting and constructive trusts'.

The basic rule—provided by section 21(3)—is that a six year limitation period applies to actions by a beneficiary to recover trust property or sue for breach of trust. An exception is made if there is fraud,[76] or a fraudulent breach of trust, to which the trustee is a party or privy. On one interpretation, this sub-section is wide enough to mean that, provided there has been a fraud or a fraudulent breach of trust to which the trustee was party or privy, the claimant beneficiary can take action without the prejudice of limitation periods against *any* person who subsequently receives the trust property from the fraudulent trustee.[77] The only defence for such parties would then seem to be that they are *bona fide* purchasers for value without notice of the beneficiary's interest. An alternative, and narrower, construction of the Act would instead apply the general provisions relating to fraud as against these third parties, so that time was merely suspended until the fraud was, or could reasonably have been, discovered.[78]

In relation to the second limb of section 21(1), the wide definition of 'trust' and 'trustee' ensures that a beneficiary under a resulting or constructive trust, as well as under an express trust, can proceed against the trustee for recovery of the trust property (or its value) without being prejudiced by limitation periods.[79]

FURTHER READING:

Paragon Finance plc v D B Thakerar & Co (a firm) [1999] 1 All ER 400 (CA): Millett LJ explains the operation of the Limitation Act 1980 section 21 and the meaning of 'constructive trust' and 'constructive trustee'.

(b) Acquiescence and laches

Equity has long exercised a general discretion to refuse a remedy to a claimant whose acquiescence or laches in asserting his rights has prejudiced the defendant.

[75] The cause of action will accrue on the date of the commission of the breach of trust and not the date when the beneficiary suffers the loss: *Thorne v Heard* [1894] 1 Ch 599. However, it is also the case that time only starts to run when the beneficiary's interest vests in possession.

[76] Defined quite widely, it seems: *Re Sale Hotel and Botanical Gardens Ltd* (1897) 77 LT 681, rev'd on other grounds (1898) 78 LT 368 (CA).

[77] *G L Baker Ltd v Medway Building & Supplies Ltd* [1958] 1 WLR 1216, rev'd on other grounds *ibid.*

[78] Limitation Act 1980 s 32, with innocent disponees for value being expressly excluded from the rule. Also see A P Bell, *Modern Law of Personal Property in England and Ireland* (1989, Butterworths: London), pp 541.

[79] *Soar v Ashwell* [1893] 2 QB 390. Also see *Re Sharp* [1906] 1 Ch 793.

The two doctrines are closely related. Acquiescence is conduct, usually delay, which suggests that the claimant has waived his rights. Laches is delay in circumstances which would make it inequitable for the claimant to enforce the right. In either case, the lapse of time which constitutes the delay only starts to run from the moment when the claimant is aware of his rights, or is at least aware of facts which reasonably suggest such rights.[80]

These equitable doctrines have been preserved in the Limitation Act 1980,[81] although with significant differences. The statutory rules impose fixed time periods which, on the whole, run against a claimant whether or not he knows, or has the means of knowing, that he has a cause of action.

7.7.4 Limitation periods and deceased's estates

Where the personal estate of a deceased person has been wrongfully disposed of, the basic limitation period applying to claimants claiming an interest, whether under a will or an intestacy, is 12 years.[82] However, where there is fraud involved, no limitation period applies.[83]

7.7.5 General grounds for extending limitation periods

There are two principal grounds for extending the normal statutory limitation periods. The first is where the action is based on the defendant's fraud, or where any matter relevant to the claimant's action has been deliberately concealed from the claimant by the defendant, or where the action is for relief from the consequences of a mistake. Time then runs only from the date on which the claimant actually discovered, or with reasonable diligence could have discovered, the fraud, concealment or mistake.[84] This extended limitation period also protects the claimant in any actions against third party recipients,[85] other than third parties who take innocently and for value.[86]

The other ground for extending limitation periods is to protect claimants who are subject to some form of legal disability. For them, a special limitation period of six years applies to all actions, but time only starts to run from the date the disability ceases or the person dies.[87]

[80] See *Allcard v Skinner* (1887) 36 Ch D 145; *Leaf v International Galleries* [1950] 2 KB 86 (CA).
[81] S 36(2).
[82] Limitation Act 1980 s 22.
[83] The Limitation Act 1980 s 22 is expressly subject to s 21(1) (see above).
[84] Limitation Act 1980 s 32(1).
[85] *Ibid.*
[86] Or parties claiming through such third parties: Limitation Act 1980 s 32(3).
[87] Limitation Act 1980 s 28(1).

Part V

Conclusions

8

Future Horizons

8.1 Introduction

This is a chapter for summing up. At the end of all the readings in this book, it is necessary to ask what is really meant by the word 'property'. Is it simply a label which the law attaches to achieve a desired end? Is it a word which describes a unified concept, or does it have different meanings in different contexts? The extracts in this chapter will not necessarily provide answers; they may add uncertainty rather than remove it.

8.2 The boundary between personal and proprietary rights

Much of this book might suggest that there is little debate about the classification of rights as either personal or proprietary (bar the heated debate surrounding remedies: see especially Chapter 5). But this perception does not reflect the reality. The following sub-sections reveal three particular concerns. First, assuming a claimant *can* assert a proprietary interest is certain property, how far should the law go in protecting that interest by imposing personal obligations on a third party property holder to 'look after' the property for the claimant? Secondly, is every physical object to be regarded as 'property' in law? And, finally, which intangible 'rights', or bundles of rights, should be classed as 'proprietary' rather than personal? At the margins, the answers to each of these questions are unclear.

8.2.1 The interaction between personal and proprietary rights

Before turning to the more difficult and controversial issues, it is worth recalling some of the fundamental features of property. They may have become lost in the detail of the earlier chapters. An interest in property is a 'bundle of rights', a bundle of *proprietary* rights. The inference is that these rights can be asserted against the world at large (although not necessarily every individual in the world). This is what distinguishes proprietary rights from rights which are merely personal. But vindication of a proprietary *right* does not inevitably deliver a proprietary *remedy*. The assertion of a proprietary right can lead to either a proprietary remedy (a remedy entitling the claimant to specific property—and so a *remedy* which the claimant can assert against the world) or a personal remedy (a remedy entitling the claimant to the benefit of a specific obligation from the defendant, usually an obligation to pay money).[1] Constructive trusts, resulting trusts and equitable liens are all proprietary remedies. Common law damages, equitable compensation and accounts of profits are all personal remedies. All of this is elementary.

One further point should be noted. A personal obligation associated with property can often be of enormous protective value to the property owner. For example, a legal owner has added protection because third parties in possession of his property owe him a common law duty of care. Similarly, a beneficiary under an express trust has added protection because the trustee owes her common law and equitable duties in the management of the trust property.

The ideas underlying the two previous paragraphs can be combined to pose a question. If a claimant is entitled to a proprietary *remedy*, is the claimant also entitled to the added protection provided by personal obligations imposed on the defendant property holder in relation to *that* property? The question is difficult to answer in the abstract. A concrete example does not make matters much easier. For example, given an appropriate mix of facts, a claimant beneficiary under an express trust may be able to assert a proprietary remedy against a defendant volunteer who has received the traceable proceeds of that trust property. In addition to the liability imposed by the proprietary remedy,[2] should the volunteer also be subjected to personal obligations in relation to the management of that property and fiduciary obligations of loyalty? It is easy to fall into the trap of assuming that, since the proprietary remedy is a trust (ie a split of legal and equitable ownership between two parties), it should therefore automatically have associated with it all the attributes of an *express* trust. However, an obligation to hand over property is not necessarily associated with a personal obligation to manage the property for the claimant's benefit in the interim, or obligations of loyalty requiring the defendant to put the claimant's interests ahead of his own. These personal obligations of trusteeship are usually imposed only when the trustee has knowledge that the property belongs to another—only then can equity act on the conscience of the volunteer defendant. It seems important to separate the property aspects of the relationship (which can be labelled with the familiar *trust* terminology) from the personal obligations (especially fiduciary obligations, since it is often the remedies

[1] Looked at from a different perspective, a *remedy* is merely another *right*: if a constructive trust arises to remedy a wrong, its effect is to give the plaintiff a right to an equitable interest in the underlying property; if money damages are ordered as compensation for a wrong, the order gives the plaintiff a personal right against the defendant to have the sum paid.

[2] If the defendant volunteer no longer had the property or its traceable proceeds, the plaintiff *may* be able to claim a personal remedy against the defendant volunteer requiring him to pay over the value of the property received: see Section 7.4.2. This form of liability is not of concern here.

associated with these obligations which drives the claimant to assert their inevitable association with the trust). This issue remains controversial.

Re-read:

Westdeutsche Landesbank Girozentrale v Islington London Borough Council [1996] AC 669 (HL), especially the opinion of Lord Browne-Wilkinson: see **[518]** above.

Question:

Does Lord Browne-Wilkinson think it is possible to have a 'trust' without the legal owner being subject to 'trustee-type' obligations?

The next extract indicates the potential advantages which can be delivered by associated personal obligations imposed on the defendant. It also indicates their limits.

[801] ***Michaels v Harley House (Marylebone) Ltd*** **[1999] 3 WLR 229, 236–42** ***per*** **Robert Walker LJ:**
[The detailed facts are irrelevant. The case concerned a scheme to sell property in a way which would disentitle the tenants from exercising their statutory right to enfranchise the lease. However, the extract below deals with the specific issue of whether a vendor of shares under a contract which is specifically enforceable can be compelled to vote the shares in the purchaser's interests or at the purchaser's direction.]

> 'The starting-point, on which both sides agree, is that a contract for the sale of shares (at any rate in a company whose shares are not quoted and readily obtainable on the market) is, like a contract for the sale of land, at first sight enforceable by specific performance; and that the effect of specific performance being available is to make the vendor under an uncompleted contract of sale a trustee of some sort for the purchaser.
>
> In relation to sales of land the principles and the leading authorities are set out in Megarry & Wade, *The Law of Real Property*, 5th ed. (1984) pp. 602–603. The authorities are well-known and lengthy citation is [237] unnecessary but I will refer briefly to *Rayner v. Preston* (1881) 18 Ch.D. 1, 6, where Cotton L.J. said:
>
> > "An unpaid vendor is a trustee in a qualified sense only, and is so only because he has made a contract which a court of equity will give effect to by transferring the property sold to the purchaser, and so far as he is a trustee he is so only in respect of the property contracted to be sold . . ."
>
> —and to *Clarke v. Ramuz* [1891] 2 Q.B. 456, 459–460, where Lord Coleridge C.J. said:
>
> > "It appears to be well established in equity that, in the case of a contract for the sale and purchase of land, although the legal property does not pass until the execution of the conveyance, during the interval prior to completion the vendor in possession is a trustee for the purchaser, and as such has duties to perform towards

> him, not exactly the same as in the case of other trustees, but certain duties, one of which is to use reasonable care to preserve the property in a reasonable state of preservation, and, so far as may be, as it was when the contract was made."

The company accepts that general principle but contends, first, that it does not apply to voting rights attached to shares pending completion of a contract for sale of the shares; and secondly, that the principle does not in any case apply to a contract which is (in the relevant sense) conditional, as the company submits the agreement for sale of the company's shares was. . . . The [trial] judge dealt with the significance of the sale agreement being, in some sense, conditional before he dealt with the issue of fiduciary capacity. That is plainly the more logical order, since if the conditionality of a contract prevents any sort of trusteeship arising, the second point does not arise, and I will follow the same order. . . .

In considering the effect of a conditional contract the judge referred first to observations of Nourse L.J. in a tax case concerned with the meaning of "beneficial ownership" in provisions relating to group relief from corporation tax, *J. Sainsbury Plc. v. O'Connor* [1991] 1 W.L.R. 963 [**[427]** above], 978–979. In that case Sainsbury's and a Belgian company held 75 per cent. and 25 per cent. respectively of a joint-venture company. Sainsbury had an option, not exercised for five years, to acquire the 25 per cent. holding. The option was never exercised and was cancelled. The case is therefore very distant on the facts: an option can be regarded as a sort of conditional contract, but unless and until the option is exercised there is no contract of which specific performance can be claimed or ordered. Another type of condition precedent is where the principal obligation under the contract (for instance, to sell land) arises only on fulfilment of a condition which is not within the control of the parties (for instance the grant of planning permission). In such a case there may be a contract with [238] some unconditional obligations of a preliminary character (for instance, to seek planning permission and to appeal if necessary) but the contract is properly classified as being subject to a condition precedent as regards its principal obligation.

However, there are other contracts which appear to contain conditions but which are not properly regarded as conditional contracts. The judge referred to, and decided this point in favour of the plaintiffs in reliance on, the decision of this court in *Eastham v. Leigh London and Provincial Properties Ltd.* [1971] Ch. 871. That was another tax case. . . . This court held, upholding Goff J. at first instance, that the contract was not, in the relevant sense, conditional. Buckley L.J. read clause 4 and said, at p. 891:

> ". . . . Although clause 4 is couched in conditional language, in my view, it amounts to no more than this: it provides that if the tenants perform their part of the contract, then the landlords will perform their part of the contract; in other words, it is a recognition of the fact that the obligations of the parties are mutual and that the granting of the lease will, in fact, follow completion of performance of the obligations of the tenants. That is not, in my judgment, a condition precedent to the contract at all, it is part of the terms of the contract. You may call it a condition if you please, but it does not make it a condition precedent to the existence of a contract."

Cairns L.J. agreed and the judgment of Russell L.J., which treated it as a short and simple point, reached the same conclusion. The same principle appears in the judgment of Jenkins L.J., with whom Parker L.J. and Pearce L.J. concurred, in *Parway Estates Ltd. v. Inland Revenue Commissioners* (1957) 45 T.C. 135, 147–148.

Lloyd J. [the trial judge] applied this principle to the share sale agreement between [the parties in this dispute], and in my judgment he was right to do so. He recognised the important difference (mentioned by Goff J. in *Eastham v. Leigh London and Provincial Properties Ltd.* [1971] Ch. 871, 880–881) between a true condition precedent which it is not within a contracting party's power to bring about, even though he may undertake to use his best endeavours to bring it about, and a promissory condition which the party does have power to fulfil or to cause to be fulfilled. In this case the share sale agreement was said to be conditional on completion of the sale of the freehold to the company. But T.W.D. had control over the freehold, T.W.P.'s capacity being merely that of a nominee; moreover the company was T.W.D.'s wholly-owned subsidiary, and T.W.D. [668] had already put in place the loan notes arrangement enabling the company to complete its purchase. In clause 10.3 of the share sale agreement T.W.D. covenanted with Frogmore in the clearest terms to procure completion of the sale and purchase of the freehold. In short, completion of the sale and purchase of the freehold was something that T.W.D. had power to bring about, and which it undertook to bring about.

. . .

[For the purposes of this dispute it was] the voting rights attached to the company's shares which had to be shown to be held in a fiduciary capacity. The judge then referred to the decision of Russell J. in *Musselwhite v. C. H. Musselwhite & Son Ltd.* [1962] Ch. 964 and, in reliance on that decision, resolved this second part of the first issue against the plaintiffs. He referred to Russell J.'s conclusion that the vendor under an uncompleted contract for the sale of shares is prima facie entitled to exercise the voting rights, even though he could no doubt be restrained by injunction from exercising the rights in a way inconsistent with the terms of the contract. Lloyd J. then said [1997] 1 W.L.R. 967, 980:

> "it seems to me that it is impossible to say, in those circumstances, that he holds the voting rights in a fiduciary capacity for the purchaser even if, because of the doctrines of equity, he holds the shares themselves in a fiduciary capacity. This is consistent with the proposition that the vendor's trusteeship of the property agreed to be sold does not extend to the pre-completion fruits of the property, or give the purchaser a right to possession."

So the judge made a clear distinction between the shares themselves and the voting rights, which he seems to have regarded as equivalent or analogous to "fruits" of the shares, or to a right to possession of the shares.

As I have already noted, the judge regarded this result as "fortuitous," and at first blush I find it surprising. The legal nature of a share in a company is frequently (and not inaptly) described as a "bundle of rights" and if the bundle is held in a fiduciary capacity by the registered shareholder it might be thought that each constituent part of the bundle must also be held in the same way. It is therefore necessary to look with some care at *Musselwhite v. C. H. Musselwhite & Son Ltd.* [1962] Ch. 964, and also at *J. R. R. T. (Investments) Ltd. v. Haycraft* [1993] B.C.L.C. 401 in which the *Musselwhite* case was followed by Chadwick J. In the *Musselwhite* case there was a small family company. Exactly half of the issued shares belonged to one brother, Ross, and his wife, and the other half belonged to the other brother, Kenneth, and his wife. In May 1958 Ross (on behalf of himself and his wife) agreed to sell their shares to Kenneth for an immediate payment of £2,500 with the balance to be paid by quarterly instalments over five years, without interest. Ross and his wife executed transfers of their shares and the transfers and share certificates were lodged with the company's solicitors, but Ross and his wife remained on the register. In December 1958 no notice of the company's annual general meeting was given to Ross and his wife. In October 1959 a small number of additional shares was issued to Kenneth's wife. Instalments of the purchase price continued to be paid promptly.

In January 1960 Ross and his wife issued a writ against Kenneth and his wife claiming that the annual general meeting in 1958 had not been validly convened, and seeking an order for a new meeting to be convened. The defendants counterclaimed for an injunction to restrain the plaintiffs from voting at any annual general meeting or exercising any other rights in respect of the shares registered in their names otherwise than in accordance with Kenneth's directions. There appears to have been no allegation on the pleadings that Ross and his wife had been guilty of, or were threatening, any breach of fiduciary duty.

The counterclaim did therefore put the defendants' case very high: not that Ross and his wife owed general fiduciary duties to the defendants in exercising any rights attached to the shares still registered in the plaintiffs' names, but that they owed a specific duty to comply with Kenneth's directions, unless it happened that their lien as partly-unpaid vendors was [241] improperly prejudiced: [1962] Ch. 964, 980. That far-reaching claim was rejected by Russell J. But it is in my view important to see how the case was argued. Counsel for the plaintiffs is reported as having argued, at p. 969:

> "Where vendors retain the legal title to the property, that legal title is part of their security for the unpaid part of the purchase price. The plaintiffs can, therefore, vote in respect of the shares as they think fit and, if the male defendant objects to anything they do, he can sue them for breach of trust, but he cannot, as he is attempting to do, control the exercise of their voting right in advance, unless they are threatening to commit a breach of trust."

So the existence of a fiduciary relationship, and the possibility of its inhibiting the vendor in the exercise of his voting rights, were conceded, and Russell J. seems to have regarded the concession as rightly made. At pp. 985–987 he cited some well-known statements of principle (Lord Cairns and Lord O'Hagan in *Shaw v. Foster* (1872) L.R. 5 H.L. 321, 338, 349 and Jessel M.R. in *Lysaght v. Edwards* (1876) 2 Ch.D. 499, 505) and he also referred to the decision of this court in *Parway Estates Ltd. v. Inland Revenue Commissioners*, 45 T.C. 135. He did not express any sort of dissent from those principles, which were binding on him. He referred several times in the *Musselwhite* case, and most notably in his conclusion, to what he called the vendors' "prima facie right" to vote in respect of the shares in his name: [1962] Ch. 964, 987. Mr. Lewison submitted that that referred to his right in the absence of contractual provisions ousting or qualifying it, and that seems to be the view which Lloyd J. took of the *Musselwhite* case. Certainly Russell J. had, at pp. 981–984, cited extensively from the decision of this court in *Seimen Bros. & Co. v. Burns* [1918] 2 Ch. 324 in which it was recognised that the rights of mortgagees of shares, registered in their names, might be qualified by contractual provisions (the fact that the mortgagees in that case were trustees for debenture-holders is an irrelevance which should not cause confusion). But Russell J. then went on to cite *Shaw v. Foster*, *Lysaght v. Edwards* and the *Parway Estates* case, and I cannot accept that it was not the inhibition of a fiduciary obligation which he had in mind in speaking of a "prima facie right."

The "prima facie right" of Ross and his wife was sufficient, in the *Musselwhite* case, for them to resist the defendants' high-pitched counterclaim, not founded on any pleading of breach of fiduciary duty, seeking to prevent them making any exercise whatever of their voting rights except at Kenneth's direction. I do not accept Mr. Lewison's submission that this court cannot decide this point in favour of the plaintiffs without overruling the *Musselwhite* case. Chadwick J. followed the *Musselwhite* case in *J.R.R.T.*

(Investments) Ltd. v. Haycraft [1993] B.C.L.C. 401 but that was another case in which a purchaser of shares (under an agreement which Chadwick J. described as ineptly drawn) had pitched his claim very high. The summons under R.S.C., Ord. 14A raised the single issue of whether the purchaser was entitled to direct the vendor to vote the shares. I do not differ in any way from what Chadwick J. said in the *J.J.R.T. (Investments)* case.

The new section 736A of the Companies Act 1985, as amended, may raise some problems but the provisions in its subsections (5), (6) and (7) do seem to me to fit together, and to fit in with the authorities, reasonably coherently. A registered shareholder who is absolute beneficial owner can vote as he pleases, subject only to rather imprecise constraints imposed by [242] company law: see *Smith v. Croft (No. 2)* [1988] Ch. 114, 186. A registered shareholder who is a nominee must vote in accordance with the directions of the absolute beneficial owner, to whom his voting rights are attributed. A registered shareholder who is vendor under an uncompleted contract is in an intermediate position, a fiduciary but not a nominee, and his voting rights are for the purposes of section 736 in abeyance. Mr. Lewison submitted that it cannot have been the intention of Parliament to produce that result in a commercial context such as a sale, but I am not persuaded of that. The only qualification that I would express about the *Musselwhite* case is that the special provision about voting rights attached to mortgaged shares in section 736A(7) suggests that the analogy which Russell J. drew in the *Musselwhite* case between a vendor and a mortgagee may no longer be helpful for the purposes of applying section 736A.

Mr. Lewison put forward and developed some further arguments, all aimed at restricting the scope of "fiduciary capacity" in section 736A(5). He pointed out that not all contracts for the sale of shares are specifically enforceable. If the shares are quoted shares then (apart, possibly from some special market situation) damages would be an adequate remedy and specific performance would not be available. Parliament cannot, Mr. Lewison submitted, have intended that the test for status as a subsidiary should vary depending on whether a company's shares were quoted or unquoted. But the situation in which the shares of a subsidiary company are quoted is very rare indeed, and I cannot attach much importance to this supposed anomaly. Mr. Lewison cited *Bristol and West Building Society v. Mothew* [1998] Ch. 1, 16, for Millett L.J.'s salutary reminder that not every breach of duty by a fiduciary is a breach of fiduciary duty. He cited *Kelly v. Cooper* [1993] A.C. 205, 215 in which Lord Browne-Wilkinson, delivering the opinion of the Privy Council, referred to the judgment of Mason J. in *Hospital Products Ltd. v. United States Surgical Corporation* (1984) 156 C.L.R. 41, 97:

> "That contractual and fiduciary relationships may co-exist between the same parties has never been doubted. Indeed, the existence of a basic contractual relationship has in many situations provided a foundation for the erection of a fiduciary relationship. In these situations it is the contractual foundation which is all important because it is the contract that regulates the basic rights and liabilities of the parties. The fiduciary relationship, if it is to exist at all, must accommodate itself to the terms of the contract so that it is consistent with, and conforms to, them. The fiduciary relationship cannot be superimposed upon the contract in such a way as to alter the operation which the contract was intended to have according its true construction."

These citations show that claims for breach of fiduciary obligations must not be extended outside their proper limits, and even within those limits they may be influenced and restrained by contractual terms. But they do not in my judgment displace the existence of the fiduciary relationship (or in the words of section 736A(5), fiduciary capacity); nor do they cast doubt on the proposition that in the *Musselwhite* case the vendor's right to vote as he pleased was inhibited by a fiduciary, rather than a contractual obligation.'

Note:

This case suggests that the purchaser under a specifically enforceable and unconditional contract for the sale of shares has equitable ownership of the shares; the vendor holds the legal title on trust for the purchaser. This gives the purchaser certain *proprietary rights*. *If* the vendor also owes the purchaser fiduciary obligations in relation to that property, then orthodox fiduciary law would suggest that the principal (the purchaser) cannot compel the fiduciary to exercise his discretion in any particular fashion, but can seek either injunctive relief to prevent a threatened abuse of power by the fiduciary, or, after the event, equitable compensation to remedy any damage caused by the defaulting fiduciary's abuse of his powers. These are the purchaser's associated *personal rights*.[3]

Questions:

1. What aspects of a sale relationship suggest that a purchaser should have the benefit of both proprietary and personal (fiduciary) rights against a vendor?
2. Should these benefits also apply to a person claiming against a volunteer?
3. What, precisely, are the personal and proprietary benefits which cause concern? (See *Westdeutsche Landesbank Girozentrale v Islington London Borough Council* [1996] AC 669 (HL), **[518]** above.)

8.2.2 The classification of 'things' as property

It is usually assumed without argument that every physical object is property, and that any uncertainties in classification are concerned solely with intangibles. The next extract indicates that even this simplification is not entirely accurate.

[802] ***R v Kelly*** **[1999] QB 621 (CA), 630–1** ***per*** **Rose LJ:**
[Kelly, an artist, was accused of the theft of human medical specimens from the Royal College of Surgeons. His taking of the specimens would not constitute theft unless the specimens were 'property'. The Court of Appeal held that they were.]

'We return to the first question, that is to say whether or not a corpse or part of a corpse is property. We accept that, however questionable the historical origins of the principle, it has now been the common law for 150 years at least that neither a corpse nor parts of a corpse are in themselves and without more capable of being property protected by rights: see, for example, Erle J., delivering the judgment of a powerful Court for Crown

[3] The purchaser also has personal rights under the contract of sale which can be enforced against the vendor.

Cases Reserved in *Reg. v. Sharpe* (1857) Dears. B. 160, 163, where he said: "Our law recognises no property in a corpse, and the protection of the grave at common law as contradistinguished from ecclesiastic protection to consecrated ground depends on this form of indictment." He was there referring to an indictment which charged not theft of a corpse but removal of a corpse from a grave.

If that principle is now to be changed, in our view, it must be by Parliament, because it has been express or implicit in all the subsequent [631] authorities and writings to which we have been referred that a corpse or part of it cannot be stolen.

To address the point as it was addressed before the trial judge and to which his certificate relates, in our judgment, parts of a corpse are capable of being property within section 4 of the Theft Act 1968 if they have acquired different attributes by virtue of the application of skill, such as dissection or preservation techniques, for exhibition or teaching purposes: see *Doodeward v. Spence*, 6 C.L.R. 406, 413, 414 in the judgment of Griffith C.J. to which we have already referred and *Dobson v. North Tyneside Health Authority* [1997] 1 W.L.R. 596, 601 where this proposition is not dissented from and appears, in the judgment of this court, to have been accepted by Peter Gibson L.J.; otherwise, his analysis of the facts of *Dobson's* case, which appears at that page in the judgment, would have been, as it seems to us, otiose. Accordingly the trial judge was correct to rule as he did.

Furthermore, the common law does not stand still. It may be that if, on some future occasion, the question arises, the courts will hold that human body parts are capable of being property for the purposes of section 4, even without the acquisition of different attributes, if they have a use or significance beyond their mere existence. This may be so if, for example, they are intended for use in an organ transplant operation, for the extraction of DNA or, for that matter, as an exhibit in a trial. It is to be noted that in *Dobson's* case, there was no legal or other requirement for the brain, which was then the subject of litigation, to be preserved: see the judgment of Peter Gibson L.J., at p. 601.'

Also see:

Moore v Regents of University of California 249 Cal Rptr 494 (1988).

Question:

How is this 'property/not property' decision being made? Would the same considerations be appropriate in dealing with eggs, sperm and embryos held by hospitals involved in IVF programmes?

8.2.3 The classification of rights as proprietary

Although there is some concern over the classification of physical 'things' as property, the real debate centres on whether intangible rights should be classed as property. Much of the interest in the past has centred on whether 'information' and 'privacy' involve rights (or not) which might be protected by conceding to them a proprietary status. These issues continue to be important. Added to them there is now the growing problem of wealth represented by financial instruments traded electronically. Should the rights associated with these dealings be classed as 'property'? The extracts below outline the concerns.

[803] K Gray, 'Property in Thin Air' [1991] *CLJ* 252, 264–9:

[Footnotes in the original are omitted. Another part of this article is extracted at **[103]**.]

'All of which draws us inescapably to the pivotal case of *Victoria Park Racing and Recreation Grounds Co. Ltd.* v. *Taylor* [(1937) 58 CLR 479]. Even after more than half a century this decision of the High Court of Australia still holds an uncanny fascination for anyone who confesses an interest in the legal phenomenon of property. The case embodies one of the last great problems of property law and reverberates with a significance which has outlived its particular facts. With justification it may be said that the concept of property cannot be entirely satisfactorily explained without accounting, in some way or other, for the ruling in *Victoria Park Racing*.

As is well known, the plaintiff company in *Victoria Park Racing* owned a racecourse on which it frequently held what Rich J. was to describe as "competitions in the comparative merits of racehorses". The ground was enclosed by a fence and the plaintiff charged members of the public for admission. One of the defendants, Taylor, owned a cottage opposite the racecourse and on his own land he erected a raised wooden platform. From this vantage point he commanded a view of the entire racecourse including, significantly, the boards and semaphores by means of which starting prices were displayed. He was also clearly within earshot of other information announced to members of the race-going public within the ground. Taylor then arranged with another of the defendants, the Commonwealth Broadcasting Corporation, that a commentator should, from a position on Taylor's platform, broadcast live radio reports on the races to listeners in the Sydney area. The instant popularity of these transmissions stimulated an illicit off-course betting industry in Sydney, and there was unchallenged evidence that punters who would otherwise have attended the race meetings in person now preferred to follow those proceedings either from the comfort of their own homes or, even better, from their local hostelry. The plaintiff, perturbed by the catastrophic loss of business, sued for an injunction on the footing of nuisance and breach of copyright. (It was common ground that the mere construction and use of the raised platform constituted no breach of building or zoning regulations or of the betting and gaming legislation or indeed of the regulations governing broadcasting.)

By the narrowest of majorities the High Court of Australia decided that the facts disclosed no wrong known to the law. Latham C.J. relied heavily on the 19th century cases on "overlooking" of property, and insisted that "[a]ny person is entitled to look over the plaintiff's fences and to see what goes on in the plaintiff's land". If the plaintiff desired to prevent this, the plaintiff could erect a higher fence; the law would not by means of injunction "in effect erect fences which the plaintiff is not prepared to provide". In the meantime, and notwithstanding the defendants' activities, the racecourse remained "as suitable as ever it was for use as a racecourse". Latham C.J. also rejected the allegation that broadcasting the numbers of the placings as notified on boards within the ground constituted a breach of copyright. Dixon and McTiernan JJ. entered strong supporting judgments in favour of the Chief Justice's conclusions.

It was left to Rich and Evatt JJ. to argue in the minority that a justiciable wrong had been inflicted upon the plaintiff company and that this wrong was remediable in the law of nuisance. Rich J. thought that the right of view or observation from adjacent land had never been "absolute . . . and exercisable at all hazards notwithstanding its destructive effect upon the enjoyment of the land overlooked". Evatt J. agreed and, seeing the matter as one involving unfair commercial competition by the defendants, was minded to award damages to the plaintiff even though no damages claim had in fact been made.

III. The "Propertiness" of Property

Perhaps the lasting significance of *Victoria Park Racing* lies in the fact that the conflict between the majority and minority views in this case throws up critical clues to the identification of the "propertiness" of property. True it is that much of the discussion in *Victoria Park Racing* was conducted obliquely in terms of the law of nuisance. But the central issue—so central that it lay largely unspoken—was whether the defendants had taken anything that might be regarded as the plaintiff's "property". (We must always be ready to hear the resonance of property in the dialogue of trespass and nuisance.)

There can be no doubt—and there was certainly none in the High Court—that in *Victoria Park Racing* the defendants had exploited a competitive commercial opportunity, in circumstances of no great credit to themselves, in order to profit from a market of horseracing enthusiasts.

For property lawyers by far the most interesting feature of *Victoria Park Racing* is the High Court majority's unanimous rejection of the plaintiff's claim that there could be "property" or even "quasi-property" in a spectacle. Latham C.J. declared in his usual acerbic style that he could attach no precise meaning to the phrase "property in a spectacle", and that the phrase functioned if at all only as an extra-legal metaphor. A spectacle, he said, "cannot be 'owned' in any ordinary sense of that word".

At this point, of course, we are again confronted by a stern refusal to propertise a particular resource—always an occasion of some moment in the jurisprudence of property. The enduring significance of *Victoria Park Racing* is that in this decision we are offered a rare opportunity to learn something of the tacit rules which govern the propertisation of resources.

Unpropertised resources remain in the commons, available for use and exploitation by all. The primordial principle which emerges from the majority judgments in *Victoria Park Racing* is that a resource can be propertised only if it is—to use another ugly but effective word—"excludable". A resource is "excludable" only if it is feasible for a legal person to exercise regulatory control over the access of strangers to the various benefits inherent in the resource. A classic example of a non-excludable resource is the beam of light thrown out by a lighthouse. To be sure, the lighthouse-keeper may control access to the benefits of the light by the simple action or inaction of never switching on the light. But if the light is allowed to operate at all, it is necessarily on terms that its benefits are distributed indiscriminately. The light cannot be artificially confined to a subset of the seafarers within its broad sweep. In this sense the beam of light—if it exists at all—is non-excludable, and non-excludable resources are retained in the commons. Somebody may have "property" in the lighthouse, but nobody can have "property" in light.

The notion of excludability thus imports a hidden structure of rules which critically define the legal phenomenon of private property. Excludability is, however, a more complex idea than is indicated by the example of the lighthouse. A resource may remain non-excludable for reasons which go far beyond the essentially factual and distributional contingencies which govern a beam of light. It is here that *Victoria Park Racing* comes into its own, for quietly but persistently the majority judgments press home the message that a resource may be non-excludable for any or all of three different sorts of reason. These three bases may broadly be described as physical, legal and moral. A resource cannot be propertised if, on any of these grounds, it lacks the quality of excludability. Non-excludable resources thus lie outside the field of private property; they remain in the common.'

Also see:

Sports and General Press Agency Ltd v "Our Dogs" Publishing Co Ltd [1916] 2 KB 880 (Horridge J), [1917] 2 KB 125 (CA).
International News Service v Associated Press 248 US 215 (1918) (US S Ct).
Victoria Park Racing and Recreational Ground Co Ltd v Taylor (1937) 58 CLR 479 (Aust H Ct).
Davis v Commonwealth of Australia (1988) 166 CLR 79 (Aust HCt).

FURTHER READING:

There is an enormous literature in this area. Two of the classics are:
P H Winfield, 'Privacy' (1931) 47 *LQR* 23.
S D Warren and L D Brandeis, 'The Right to Privacy' (1890–1) 4 *Harvard Law Review* 193.

Classification of rights as 'proprietary' may not be necessary. From very early on, particular rights were conceded to have characteristics which made classification difficult. For example, the general rule suggests that proprietary rights bind third parties, personal rights do not. And yet there is a line of cases from *De Mattos v Gibson* (1858) 4 De G & J 276 suggesting that certain personal rights can have a similar impact. In that case, the owner of a ship entered into a charterparty and then later mortgaged the ship to a mortgagee who was aware at all times of the charterparty and its terms. When the mortgagee tried to enforce the mortgage, the charterer successfully applied for an interlocutory injunction (see Section 7.6.2) to prevent him doing anything which would interfere with the performance of the charterparty.[4] Knight Bruce LJ (at p 282) said:

> 'Reason and justice seem to prescribe that, at least as a general rule, where a man, by gift or purchase, acquires property from another, with knowledge of a previous contract, lawfully and for valuable consideration made by him with a third person, to use and employ the property for a particular purpose in a specified manner, the acquirer shall not, to the material damage of the third person, in opposition to the contract and inconsistently with it, use and employ the property in a manner not allowable to the giver or seller. This rule, applicable alike in general as I conceive to moveable and immoveable property, and recognised and adopted, as I apprehend, by the English law, may, like other general rules, be liable to exceptions arising from special circumstances; but I see at present no room for any exception in the instance before us.'

The full reach of the *De Mattos* principle remains surrounded by confusion and uncertainty,[5] but it does at least indicate the potential for personal rights to have an impact beyond the immediate parties to the contract.

[4] The final injunction was subsequently refused on other grounds.
[5] See S Worthington, *Proprietary Interests in Commercial Transactions* (1996, Clarendon: Oxford) ch 5 and the references there cited for various explanations.

Question:

Does this extended reach make the rights 'proprietary'? What makes a right proprietary?

Again, the general rule suggests that proprietary rights are assignable at will,[6] and personal rights are not. Yet it is very common for rights which are clearly proprietary to have restrictions imposed on alienability. Many shares in private companies are not assignable, or only assignable with the consent of certain third parties. And it is also common for rights which are not usually regarded as proprietary to be assigned. Rights under contracts can often be assigned; on the transfer of a business, 'interests' in confidential information may be assigned.

All of this does no more than indicate that the margins are not as clearly defined as might be expected. That throws into sharp relief the problem of definition. For example, it used to be the case that a debt was regarded at common law simply as a personal right between debtor and creditor. Equity later permitted such rights to be assigned by the creditor. Later still, the common law adopted the same stance by providing a statutory mechanism for assignment. The current position is that a debt remains a personal obligation imposed on the debtor, but, both at common law and in equity, a debt is now property in the hands of the creditor.

The same evolutionary process can be expected to occur with other rights now regarded as personal. The impetus to do so is no doubt being escalated by the information age. Information is a valuable commodity; commercial parties want to trade in it—they want to treat it as property. They may well expect the law to move to keep up with the practice. The next extract questions whether this is either appropriate or necessary.

[804] P Kohler and N Palmer, 'Information as Property' in N Palmer and E McKendrick (eds), *Interests in Goods* (2nd edn, 1998, Lloyd's of London Press: London) ch 1, pp 21–4:

[Footnotes in the original are omitted.]

'CRITERIA FOR A PROPRIETARY ANALYSIS

> Cornish once suggested three specific tests for establishing the proprietary quality of confidential information. He maintained that such information would acquire the characteristics of property only when rights are given against third parties in the circumstances outlined by him. The tests were: (i) does possession of the information in private *per se* generate rights against those who misappropriate it? (ii) if know-how is assigned, does the assignee acquire the assignor's rights to sue both direct and indirect recipients who are breaking the confidence? and (iii) in the case of two licences or assignments to different parties by way of inconsistent dealings, does one of them attain priority over the other, and if so on what principle? On the latter point, Cornish cited *De Beer v. Graham* (where it was held that neither recipient had more than a personal right against

[6] This distinguishes them from many contractual rights, for example, which are assignable with the consent of the original parties to the contract, but not necessarily otherwise.

his source) as tending to negate the proprietary quality of information. He pointed out, however, that under modern law an undertaking that the provider of the information will not dispose of it to anyone else may generate an obligation of confidence binding on a later recipient.

Austin is more critical of the categorisation of information as property, and advances four reasons against it. First, he contends that such an approach gives no guidance as to the direction the law should take; ridiculous results would ensue if all information were treated as property, but it is difficult to separate those categories which should be so treated from those which should not. Secondly, he argues that it can produce wrong results: a volunteer receiving from a fiduciary would be liable as a constructive trustee, whereas a bona fide purchaser of the information for value would not be. Thirdly, it would prevent trustees or other fiduciaries from disclosing information even if they resolved unanimously to do so in the best interests of their beneficiaries or principals, for if information is property its disclosure would necessarily amount to a wrongful disposal thereof. (This would also create great problems for professional trustees.) Fourthly, it would make for inflexibility of remedies, because strictly speaking no allowance could be made to account for the fiduciary's skill or effort in turning the information into gain.

These assertions are not beyond question. In relation to the second, for example, it may still be legitimate (at least in special cases) to recognise a common law property in information, producing the reservation of a legal interest in favour of the claimant; such characterisation would render immaterial questions of notice and purchase for value. Austin's fourth criticism arguably describes the precise sort of situation in which adaptation from the law of personal property would be desirable, and in which analogies based, for example, on the doctrines of accession and improvement have a beneficial function. Such comparisons might be derived from statute (see section 6 of the Torts (Interference with Goods) Act 1977) or even from the law of real property, arriving via the law of personalty (as, for instance, with the notion of proprietary estoppel).

CONCLUSION

At the very least, Austin's analysis reminds us of the need to conduct future classifications of information more sensitively and selectively, and with a sharper awareness of the limitations of juridical labels, than has hitherto been the case. It is unacceptable merely to attach the property label as an afterthought, in a decision which is amply justifiable by reference to some other analysis (such as the discovery of a fiduciary relationship between the parties). It is equally unacceptable to impose some unnecessarily universal characterisation upon a particular category of information, purely to attain a desired result in a single case.

The point to be made is that the property label is a conclusion not a premise. If some aspects of the law's treatment of confidential information display a proprietary parallel, that does not mean that confidential information is property *per se* but that in that regard it displays a proprietary characteristic. As Gummow J. noted in *Smith Kline and French Laboratories v. Secretary to the Department of Community Services and Health*:

> "The degree of protection afforded by equitable doctrine and remedies to what equity considers confidential information makes it appropriate to describe it as having a proprietary character. This is not because property is the basis upon which that protection is given, but because of the effect of that protection."

. . .

The property analysis is not, therefore, without its resources. But one cannot overstate the need for a complete awareness of its implications before pursuing each application to its final conclusion. Former judicial classifications of information as property have arguably done as much to obscure the essential questions of policy and principle at issue as to elucidate them; future tribunals may be better advised to confront specific issues directly and individually, without invoking all-purpose solutions of marginal conceptual value. But in confronting the particular issues, the courts should remain alive to the value of analogy; for as Gurry has remarked, although the status of the property analysis remains uncertain, its confirmation would have the desirable effect of providing the courts with a valuable additional jurisdiction by which confidential information could be protected. Only then can the courts effectively address Finn's description of the proprietary controversy as "Perhaps the most sterile of the debates which have arisen around the subject of information received in confidence", and mount a decisive endeavour to comprehend issues of confidentiality "in the round".'

[805] J W Harris, *Property and Justice* (1996, Clarendon: Oxford) pp 332–6, 341–2, 347–8:

[This extract is from chapter 17 ('The Limits of Property'). The footnotes in the original are omitted.]

'(a) Conceptual Limits

Any plausible account of human well-being will include features which are not susceptible to specific trespassory protection or participation in which cannot be guided by the organizing idea of ownership. In either case, they are, conceptually, beyond the scope of property institutions. For an entity to be a proprietary subject matter, a human subject must be distanced from it in two ways. It must be something others could be accused of 'taking' and something the subject himself could be seen to control or use as 'owner'.

Specific trespassory protection is not possible in the case of abstract features of well-being such as friendship, joy, passion, curiosity, a sense of beauty, faith, hope, and charity. We may condemn individual conduct or public programmes for neglecting, under-valuing, or even 'interfering with' these things; but we could not devise concrete rules which would mark out behaviour as amounting to their theft or invasion. 'Property' may be invoked, rhetorically, in relation to such things. 'Jane's childhood sense of beauty was stolen from her by the Philistines who controlled her education.' Such rhetoric builds, appropriately, on our familiarity with resources which everywhere are the subject of specific trespassory protection. But in the case of such abstract facets of well-being, no social or legal code could be devised according to which X's conduct constituted precisely, and no more than, a trespass against them.

The necessary distancing between subject and resource may also be absent even where specific trespassory protection exists. That which others are banned from meddling with may be something as to which I do not have the open-ended set of use-privileges and control-powers constitutive of mere property, let alone the transmission powers incident to full-blooded ownership.

Defamation law protects people's reputations. Yet our judgements about conduct are not guided by the notion that reputation is something one owns. If Jones scribbles in his book or paints his drawing-room in garish colours and his conduct is questioned, it will usually be a sufficient answer that his book or his house belongs to him and a man may do what he likes with his own. If Smith behaves disreputably, it could hardly be an adequate response for him to say: 'I can do what I like with my own reputation.' There are a panoply of uses of his book or of his house which Jones may authorize Brown to make as to which no third party may gainsay him, because Jones owns these things. It would be odd to say of a range of corrupt dealings between Smith and Brown that all complaints must be off-side since the reputation could be used by Brown in any way its owner, Smith, chose to authorize. And, of course, no-one can transfer his reputation to someone else. Reputations are not sufficiently distanced from their subjects such that dealings with them can be described, otherwise than rhetorically, in terms of the exercise of ownership privileges or powers.

All just legal systems prohibit torture as a means of extracting information. It does not follow from the fact that this trespassory protection is in place that the information, so long as it exists only within the skull of a potential victim, is something he "owns". Depending on the context, we may suppose that he has obligations to pass on, or to withhold, the information. These may be difficult moral questions, but they will not be guided by the idea that he has a set of use-privileges or control-powers somewhere along the ownership spectrum. Information once communicated may be, as we shall see later in this Chapter, a propertizable resource. So long as it is known only to a single individual, it lacks that distancing which is a pre-condition of an ownership interest.

The most flagrant instance in which the requisite distancing has been overlooked in the history of speculative thought about property relates to 'self-ownership'. As we have seen, the uses to which a person may put his own body, or which he may permit others to make of it, are, notwithstanding frequent invocations of property rhetoric, actually guided by what we have called the 'bodily-use freedom principle'. We shall return to this topic later in this Chapter when we consider property in separated bodily parts.

The distancing between subject and resource which is a conceptual limit on property may be summarized as follows. Before any entity, material or ideational, can be subjected to a property institution it must be (1) susceptible of specific trespassory protection; and (2) a potential subject of an ownership or quasi-ownership interest; so that it is (3) reifiable as a person-independent resource.

(b) Practical Limits

We have seen that the outer perimeter of ownership interests is fixed by their trespassory protection. There are uses of resources which it would be impracticable to ban, such as passers-by looking at an attractive house; and consequently such uses do not come within ownership control-powers. It is sometimes suggested that there are resources of which it would be impracticable to prohibit any uses, so that there are physical limits to property institutions. An example which has been suggested is that of a lighthouse beam, since vessels sailing nearby could not be prevented from using it.

Such claims should be viewed with caution. Even if specific trespassory protection (whilst not conceptually impossible) cannot be practicably enforced, a resource may be treated as though it were the subject of an ownership interest for particular purposes. In the example of the lighthouse beam, ship-owners could be taxed on the basis that they had used a coastal State's property because they had, wittingly or not, seen the beam of light.

A parallel situation actually confronted English courts. BBC Enterprises wanted to make a profit from television programmes beamed to Western Europe. They were transmitted in encrypted form so that special decoders were needed to receive them. BBC Enterprises made arrangements for a company to manufacture the decoders and to pay to BBC Enterprises £100 on each decoder that was sold. The defendants upset this arrangement by manufacturing and selling cheaper decoders to the European market. BBC Enterprises sought an injunction to stop this. The issue turned on the interpretation of section 298 of the Copyright Designs and Patents Act 1988, which provided a remedy against any person making apparatus designed to enable people to receive transmissions when the recipients 'are not entitled to do so'.

Scott J, at first instance, held that, since reception was not prohibited, the plaintiffs could have no property rights in the waves in the ether, and he dismissed the action. The Court of Appeal reversed his decision, and the House of Lords upheld the Court of Appeal. The judgments of the appellate courts lack lucidity. They held, in effect, that since Parliament must have supposed that creator-incentives warranted moral protection of the programmes, its language must be interpreted as if reception on the continent without the plaintiff's consent was not allowed—that is, as though ether waves were the subject of a protected ownership interest.

There may be many reasons, having to do with the content of the necessary trespassory rules, why an otherwise arguable case for creating an ownership or quasi-ownership interest is overridden. It may be that the restraints run counter to some valued freedom. Or perhaps they would entail excessive policing costs. Literal impossibility will, however, be rare.

We have seen that a resource must normally be scarce before there is any point in introducing trespassory protection. However, it is always possible to create artificial scarcity, as intellectual property regimes do in the case of published ideas. Seawater and sunlight are not scarce, but a lunatic tyrant might seek to establish a monopoly of these things by attempting to ban their use without his permission. He could make no progress if he sought to extend the prohibition to atmospheric oxygen. Yet, even here, he could impose a tax on breathing premised on the assumption that oxygen belonged exclusively to him.

(c) Justice Limits

Genuine problems concerning the limits of property are unlikely to raise the conceptual and practical issues so far considered. No-one will suggest placing abstract features of human well-being on the property agenda; and the tyrannical regimes we encounter have easier ways of despoiling their subjects without instituting impracticable trespassory rules. The limits are met, in practice, when some category of resource is encountered as to which we presently lack any clear guidance, from social convention or juristic doctrine, as to how the mix of property justice reasons is to be applied. It is not now, as it once was, a matter of public debate whether human beings should be the subject of proprietary interests. But persistent controversy surrounds the question whether patents should be granted in respect of animals created in the furtherance of biotechnological research.

It may be clear enough that a resource should be allocated to someone, but who that is to be is a wide open question. Or it may be that the resource could be subjected to ownership protection, but might better be left as common property. Or it may be that the alternatives include ownership interests, quasi-ownership interests, or protected non-property holdings. We shall in the rest of this Chapter consider three kinds of resource which illustrate these problems: the fruits of wrong-doing; information; and separated bodily parts. These topics raise very different issues at the margins of property. In each case, however, the difficulties have to do with assessing the strength of applicable property-specific justice reasons. No other conceptual or practical problems are involved.

. . .

(iii) INFORMATION

A person who creates or gathers information which, but for his initiative, would not have been collated ought to be regarded as its owner.

Few things are more distinctive of the modern world than the explosion in what is often called the 'information industry'. Gathered information is the subject of much piecemeal legal protection. It is encompassed within various forms of intellectual property. It is the subject of criminal prohibitions against 'insider dealing', or 'hacking' of computerized data. Might we not, as a matter of property-institutional design, achieve conceptual sublimation and normative consistency by recognizing a broad principle such as that set out above?

Would not that be a worthy contribution of modern juristic doctrine to Weberian 'logically formal' rationality?

In assessing how far the law implicitly already recognizes property in information, the basic question of ownership has to be disentangled from other issues. There are many instances in which duties are imposed against communicating information where the information has been acquired in the course of a contractual or fiduciary relationship. Courts have, in addition, been prepared to grant *prima facie* injunctive relief (or damages in lieu) against those who knowingly receive such information in breach of contract or confidence, subject to a 'public interest' defence. Sometimes this extension of the obligation is spoken of as a recognition of 'property' in the information. We mentioned in the last section the rule that a fiduciary who makes a profit from his fiduciary role is expropriated of it in favour of his principal. The normal justification for that rule is deterrence against fiduciaries preferring their interest to their duty of loyalty. But sometimes an alternative 'fruits' rationale is floated, by suggesting that the information acquired in the course of such a relationship is 'property' already belonging to the principal.

The principle set out at the beginning of this section affirms that, quite apart from such special relationships and remedies, a person who creates or gathers information should be regarded as its owner. He should be granted generalized trespassory protection, civil and criminal, in respect of uses of it against all-comers; and he himself should be accorded an open-ended set of use-privileges, control-powers, and powers of transmission over it, at some point along the ownership spectrum. That is what is meant by 'owning' gathered information.

It is sometimes suggested that the conceptual objection examined in the last section applies. Information cannot be distanced from the minds of individuals and so is intrinsically non-propertizable. Latham CJ said in a tax case heard by the High Court of Australia: 'knowledge is neither real nor personal property. A man with a richly stored mind is not for that reason a man of property.'

There is no force in this objection. It is true that the contents of the human memory fail the distancing test which is a necessary, conceptual precondition of property. Nevertheless, information, once communicated, can be regarded as a distinct ideational entity whose use by all except some favoured 'owner' could be banned.

The use-policing and use-channelling advantages of mere-property freedoms which apply to tangible assets have no bearing on information, any more than on any other ideational entities. All may use information simultaneously. The vast majority of indicative propositions are, and always have been, in the public domain—'common property'. What we have to consider is whether there are property-specific justice reasons sufficient to warrant the creation of artificial scarcity, as with other forms of intellectual property, by the enactment of specialized trespassory rules in the case of collated information.

...

The only argument which can be invoked for ownership of commercial information is, as with other forms of property in ideational entities, the instrumental one from creator-incentives. It may be obvious in particular contexts that a person or enterprise will not create or gather information unless its exploitation of the information is protected against commercial rivals. That instrumental argument will, as we have seen, enter into the mix of property-specific justice reasons if the item so created and marketed increases social wealth in such a way that justice costs can be more fully discharged. In the case of information it may also be that what is created contributes directly to human well-being on the ground that knowledge has value for its own sake. That was the principal ground relied on in the *International News* case. Pitney J said that the complainant association was providing a valuable service in bringing information about the daily events of the world to the breakfast table of the millions. The trifling payments made by its ultimate customers were sufficient in the aggregate to afford compensation for the cost of gathering and distributing the news 'with the added profit so necessary as an incentive to effective action in the commercial world'.

That being the sole reason for recognizing an ownership interest in commercial information, it follows that the kind of interest in question and the degree of trespassory protection need to be tailored precisely to what is required, and no more than is required, to provide the necessary incentive. The requisite ownership interest will, in one sense, be high on the ownership spectrum since it must carry powers of transmission for value. Without marketability the incentive will almost certainly be absent. On the other hand, it need not include ordinary control-powers associated with ownership of tangible resources. So long as the 'owner' can control commercial exploitation, he will have the incentive to create or gather the information even if he is not armed with control over many non-commercial uses. It will still be 'ownership' of a sort, since ownership will play the role of an organizing idea from which an open-ended set of exploitation powers may be inferred. Similarly, trespassory protection need extend only to prohibitions against competing commercial uses. There may be a case for criminal prohibitions in particular contexts, where certain kinds of data misuse ought to be excluded as a background to ownership interests over many kinds of information and leaving each owner to seek a civil remedy might be wasteful. The vandal who spreads computer viruses is a menace to everyone. But there need be no *a priori* assumption that, wherever the incentive argument supports a limited ownership interest, civil infringements must always be accompanied by criminal offences.

Thus, the principle stated at the beginning of this section can be accepted, in the case of commercial information where the incentive argument applies, only if 'owning' is understood in a special sense peculiar to the subject matter—as the Supreme Court recognized in the *International News* case. It is a mistake to assume that either we must align property in information with property in other resources, or else we must exclude information from the property agenda. Property-institutional design may be and should be much more flexible than these alternatives allow.'

FURTHER READING:

P Eleftheriadis, 'The Analysis of Property Rights' (1996) 16 *OJLS* 31.
S Munzer, *A Theory of Property* (1990, Cambridge University Press: Cambridge).

Question:

What defines property? How, if at all, will the introduction of the Human Rights Act 1999 affect the classification of rights as proprietary? It provides, in Article 1 of the First Protocol, that:

'Every natural or legal person is entitled to the peaceful enjoyment of his possessions. No one shall be deprived of his possessions except in the public interest and subject to conditions provided for by law and by the general principles of international law.

The preceding provisions shall not, however, in any way impair the right of a state to enforce such laws as it deems necessary to control the use of property in accordance with the general interest or to secure the payment of taxes or other contributions or penalties.'

8.3 The need for a concept of property

As might be expected, views differ dramatically on the utility and function of the concept of property. The following extracts illustrate some of the different perspectives.

[806] W T Murphy and S Roberts, *Understanding Property Law* (3rd edn, 1998, Sweet & Maxwell: London), pp 1–5:

'If any social group is to exist as such, there have to be some shared understandings as to how access to things in general, and to scarce valued resources in particular, is to be arranged. To use the lawyer's distinction, there is always a difference between a person's acquisition of physical control over resources and the common recognition, the shared understanding, that he or she rather than anyone else *should* control these resources. This much is true of even the most remote groups of hunter-gatherers, where relations between people and things are primarily geared towards consumption. Observers detect clear understandings how food, once gathered, should be consumed, about how the larger game animals should be divided up. Among the Hadza of what is now Tanzania, for example, only adult males may consume certain parts of game animals; and a hunter is expected to provide meat for the mother of the woman with whom he lives (Woodburn, 1972). In even the simplest societies, therefore, a set of norms surrounds the consumption of valued scarce resources, norms concerned not just with what kinds of things should or should not be consumed, but with who can consume particular things over which control has been assumed.

A general human and social condition, then, is being delineated. In any culture, there must be some conception of right ways to allocate resources. There must be ideas about who can properly act in a given way in relation to a particular resource. In other words, there must be ideas about relations between persons, as well as ideas about the relations between persons and things, and these requirements tend to force other, sometimes very important, questions. Over which resources are persons to be permitted to assume control? In what sense, if any, are persons to count as or to be treated as resources? Perhaps most fundamental, if not always explicit, in any culture is the question of how the difference between a person and a thing is to be specified, which already presupposes that answers of some kind are available to the questions "What is a person?" and "What is a thing?".

Possession among hunter-gatherers of the most important resources—food—is of necessity transient and geared to regimes of consumption. In groups that are organised around stock-herding, the position is transformed. The accent is no longer confined to the distribution and closely connected consumption of valued things, but shifts to their conservation and management through time. The element of time is decisive here, since the time span over which people remain in control of certain things is greatly increased, and with it the degree of control which is required increases. The bush from which hunter-gatherers have picked today's nuts or berries can be forgotten until, with the cycle of the seasons, a new growth appears. A herd of goats, by contrast, demands closer and most constant attention. Assembling a herd of animals makes people think and reach understandings about what it means to have things in a way that a regime geared exclusively to distribution and consumption does not. Who shall assume managerial responsibility for the herd? Who should enjoy the resources which the herd represents? What should be done with the increased resources to the herd as contemporary managers grow old and die? All of these questions also point to the fact that the herd may represent a source of social power, more extensive in its contemporary implications, and more enduring in time, than the resources available to any hunter-gatherer.

. . .

The need in any society for common understandings about management of and access to resources does not say anything about what those understandings might be. It does not mean that in any society there will be a conception of ownership in the sense that "This goat is mine" or "This is my field" means that I have exclusive access to it. It is possible for no one to think in terms of "my goat" or "my field" at all. But in all societies the different normative problems which the existence of the goat and the field presents for the members must be resolved. Who can manage the goat undisturbed, who can have its milk, its offspring, or the goat itself to eat, and what is to happen when the present holder dies? The same is true of land: who is responsible for its management, who may cultivate it, who can take the harvest and what difference will the death of human beings make to the answers to these questions? All of these questions flow from the very nature of the relation between people in society and goats or land, and answers to these questions are invariably found.

This general condition does not necessarily imply any explicit agreement, consciously arrived at, about these matters. Understandings about allocation may develop slowly over time, with their origins and content remaining unexamined by members of the group. Nor does anything that has been said require the presence of "government" in the sense of self-conscious efforts to provide rules about allocation or attempts to police those rules, let alone the presence of differentiated agencies established for that purpose. Ethnography abounds with examples of communities which clearly have shared ideas about how resources should be allocated, and where people appear to act regularly in conformity to those ideas, but where there are no specialised agencies to oversee how resources are managed or controlled.

While the presence of common understandings about management of, and access to, animals and land does not in any sense imply the need for government, the social power represented by the accumulation of a herd or the exercise of control over land does bring with it the possibility of sustained domination, and creates the conditions under which government may come into being. Stock-herding and settlement may provide both the resources on the basis of which it becomes possible to support a following and the means for rewarding loyal support.

Where the state does exist, this must have implications for the common understandings about resource management. First, these are likely to become progressively more articulate and explicit. Among the means through which sovereigns invariably seek to consolidate and extend control over their subjects are getting to know the local rules and offering facilities for dispute resolution. This necessarily implicates the state in recognising at least parts of the social repertoires of norms already in place, even in areas where the state does not actively become involved in rule-making. Where the state exists, the spontaneous, unconscious reproduction of norms within social groups will thus be supplemented by the conscious, often calculated, recognition and production of "law" within agencies of the state. So as the state assumes responsibility for handling disputes about resource allocation, at least some of the understandings relating to these matters are likely to be transformed into explicit, ultimately written, rules.

The evolution of specific royal or state machinery for dispute settlement is closely associated with taxation. This is perhaps the primordial form of the relation between a state and its citizens or subjects, in which resources are exacted for the waging of war or the staging of spectacles, or to pay for the costs of dispute settlement itself. Many of the earliest pressures to establish good government and to define property rights are rooted in royal searches for revenue and the resistance of loyal subjects. Some of the oldest conceptions of law and legality solidify around this set of problems. If the emergence of state-based adjudication presses in the direction of an ideal of judicial impartiality, how can that objective be sustained when the legal questions at stake concern the state's own rights to exact resources from its subjects? Institutional solutions adopted with varying degrees of success by different states—such as the separation of powers—went some way to managing this tension; the very recognition of property rights should also be seen as an outcome of the struggles and conflicts engendered in this situation.

A second major function assumed by states has been to police the circulation of things. Governments of the past often sought to control the movement of things within, or in and out of, the territories they claimed to control, to maximise the amount of wealth within the territory and thus the resources available for fighting wars. (For a different view, see Ekelund and Tollison, 1981.) Within this logic, the ideal of every state was to aim at a net inflow, through trade, of resources (and therefore the underlying assumption was that only some states could be winners in the game). For related reasons, governments in the past also sought to regulate consumption, by enacting "sumptuary legislation", to regulate, for example, the wearing of certain types of clothing (see Hunt, 1997). Such forms of regulation also sought to preserve gradations of rank in a stratified society, to regulate the signification or communication of status through things, through the clothes which people wore. Even the once common prohibition upon aliens owning land, which survives in some countries even today, has been a consequence of this way of thinking about the relation between people and things. Perhaps only the modern world has experienced a purely economic, rational approach to the planned regulation of consumption, in the form, for example, of war rationing.'

[807] R A Posner, *Economic Analysis of Law* (4th edn, 1992, Little, Brown & Co: Boston) pp 32–8:

[Footnotes in the original are omitted.]

'§3.1 The Economic Theory of Property Rights; Static and Dynamic Aspects

To understand the economics of property rights, it is first necessary to grasp the economist's distinction between *static* and *dynamic* analysis. Static analysis suppresses the time dimension of economic activity: All adjustments to change are assumed to occur instantaneously. The assumption is unrealistic but often fruitful; the attentive reader of Chapter 1 will not be too disturbed by a lack of realism in assumptions.

Dynamic analysis, in which the assumption of instantaneous adjustment to change is relaxed, is usually more complex than static analysis. So it is surprising that the economic basis of property rights was first perceived in dynamic terms. Imagine a society in which all property rights have been abolished. A farmer plants corn, fertilizes it, and erects scarecrows, but when the corn is ripe his neighbor reaps it and takes it away for his own use. The farmer has no legal remedy against his neighbor's conduct since he owns neither the land that he sowed nor the crop. Unless defensive measures are feasible (and let us assume for the moment that they are not), after a few such incidents the cultivation of land will be abandoned and society will shift to methods of subsistence (such as hunting) that involve less preparatory investment.

As this example suggests, legal protection of property rights creates incentives to use resources efficiently. Although the value of the crop in our example, as measured by consumers' willingness to pay, may have greatly exceeded its cost in labor, materials, and forgone alternative uses of the land, without property rights there is no incentive to incur these costs because there is no reasonably assured reward for incurring them. The proper incentives are created by parceling out mutually exclusive rights to the use of particular resources among the members of society. If every piece of land is owned by someone—if there is always someone who can exclude all others from access to any given area—then individuals will endeavor by cultivation or other improvements to maximize the value of land. Of course, land is just an example. The principle applies to all valuable resources.

All this has been well known for hundreds of years. In contrast, the static analysis of property rights is little more than 50 years old. Imagine that a number of farmers own a pasture in common; that is, none has the right to exclude any of the others and hence none can charge the others for the use of the pasture. We can abstract from the dynamic aspects of the problem by assuming that the pasture is a natural (uncultivated) one. Even so, pasturing additional cows will impose a cost on all the farmers. The cows will have to graze more in order to eat the same amount of grass, and this will reduce their weight. But because none of the farmers pays for the use of the pasture, none will take this cost into account in deciding how many additional cows to pasture, with the result that more cows will be pastured than would be efficient. (Can you see an analogy to highway congestion?)

The problem would disappear if someone owned the pasture and charged each farmer for its use (for purposes of this analysis, disregard the cost of levying such a charge). The charge to each farmer would include the cost he imposes on the other farmers by pasturing additional cows, because that cost reduces the value of the pasture to the other farmers and hence the price they are willing to pay the owner for the right to graze.

The creation of exclusive rights is a necessary rather than a sufficient condition for the efficient use of resources: The rights must be transferable. Suppose the farmer in our first example owns the land that he sows but is a bad farmer; his land would be more productive in someone else's hands. Efficiency requires a mechanism by which the farmer can be induced to transfer the property to someone who can work it more productively. A transferable property right is such a mechanism. Suppose Farmer A owns a piece of land that he anticipates will yield him $100 a year above his labor and other costs, indefinitely. Just as the price of a share of common stock is equal to the present value of the anticipated earnings to which the shareholder will be entitled, so the present value of a parcel of land that is expected to yield an annual net income of $100 can be calculated and is the minimum price that A will accept in exchange for his property right. Suppose Farmer B believes that he can use A's land more productively than A. The present value of B's expected earnings stream will therefore exceed the present value calculated by A. Suppose the present value calculated by A is $1,000 and by B $1,500. Then at any price between $1,000 and $1,500 both A and B will be made better off by a sale. Thus there are strong incentives for a voluntary exchange of A's land for B's money.

This discussion implies that if every valuable (meaning scarce as well as desired) resource were owned by someone (the criterion of universality), ownership connoted the unqualified power to exclude everybody else from using the resource (exclusivity) as well as to use it oneself, and ownership rights were freely transferable, or as lawyers say alienable (transferability), value would be maximized. This leaves out of account, however, the costs of a property-rights system, both the obvious and the subtle ones. Those costs are a particular focus of this chapter.

An example will illustrate a subtle cost of exclusivity. Suppose our farmer estimates that he can raise a hog with a market value of $100 at a cost of only $50 in labor and materials and that no alternative use of the land would yield a greater net value—in the next best use, his income from the land would be only $20. He will want to raise the hog. But now suppose his property right is qualified in two respects: He has no right to prevent an adjacent railroad from accidentally emitting engine sparks that may set fire to the hog's pen, killing the hog prematurely; and a court may decide that his raising a hog on this land is a nuisance, in which event he will have to sell the hog at disadvantageous (why disadvantageous?) terms before it is grown. In light of these contingencies he must reevaluate the yield of his land: He must discount the $100 to reflect the probability that the yield may be much less, perhaps zero. Suppose that, after this discounting, the expected revenue from raising the hog (market value times the probability that it will reach the market) is only $60. He will not raise the hog. He will put the land to another use, which we said was less valuable; the value of the land will fall.

But the analysis is incomplete. Removing the hog may increase the value of surrounding residential land by more than the fall in the value of the farmer's parcel; or the cost of preventing the emission of engine sparks may exceed the reduction in the value of the farmer's land when he switches from raising hogs to growing, say, fireproof radishes. But, the alert reader may interject, if the increase in value to others from a different use of the farmer's land exceeds the decrease to him, let them buy his right: The railroad can purchase an easement to emit sparks; the surrounding homeowners can purchase a covenant from the farmer not to raise hogs; there is no need to limit the farmer's property right. But as we shall see (in §3.8 *infra*), the costs of effecting a transfer of rights—transaction costs—are often prohibitive, and when this is so, giving someone the exclusive right to a resource may reduce rather than increase efficiency.

We could, of course, preserve exclusivity in a purely notional sense by regarding the property right in a given thing as a bundle of distinct rights, each exclusive; that is in fact the legal position. The economic point however is that the nominal property owner will rarely have exclusive power over his property.

§3.2 Problems in the Creation and Enforcement of Property Rights

Property rights are not only less exclusive but less universal than they would be if they were not costly to enforce. Imagine a primitive society in which the principal use of land is for grazing. The population of the society is small relative to the amount of land, and its flocks are small too. No technology exists for increasing the value of the land by fertilizer, irrigation, or other techniques. The cost of wood or other materials for fencing is very high and, the society being illiterate, a system for publicly recording land ownership is out of the question. In these circumstances the costs would be the costs of fencing to keep out other people's grazing animals, and would be substantial. The benefits might be zero. Since there is no crowding problem, property rights would confer no static benefits, and since there is no way of improving the land, there would be no dynamic benefits either. It is therefore not surprising that property rights are less extensive in primitive than in advanced societies and that the pattern by which property rights emerge and grow in a society is related to increases in the ratio of the benefits of property rights to their costs.

The common law distinction between domestic and wild animals illustrates the general point. Domestic animals are owned like any other personal property; wild animals are not owned until killed or put under actual restraint (as in a zoo). Thus, if your cow wanders off your land, it is still your cow; but if a gopher whose burrow is on your land wanders off, he is not your property, and anyone who wants can capture or kill him, unless he is tame—unless he has an *animus revertendi* (the habit of returning to your land). (Can you think of an economic argument for the doctrine of *animus revertendi*?)

The reason for the difference in legal treatment between domestic and wild animals is that it would be both difficult to enforce a property right in a wild animal and pretty useless; most wild animals, as in our gopher illustration, are not valuable, so there is nothing to be gained from creating incentives to invest in them. But suppose the animals are valuable. If there are no property rights in valuable fur-bearing animals such as sable and beaver, hunters will hunt them down to extinction, even though the present value of the resource will be diminished by doing so. The hunter who spares a mother beaver so that it can reproduce knows that the beavers born to her will almost certainly be caught by someone other than him (so long as there are many hunters), and he will not forgo a present benefit to confer a future benefit on someone else. Property rights would be desirable in these circumstances but it is hard to imagine a feasible scheme for giving the hunter who decided to spare the mother beaver a property right in her unborn litter. The costs of enforcing such a property right would still exceed the benefits, though the benefits would now be substantial.

There are two possible solutions. The more common is to use the regulatory powers of the state to reduce hunting to the approximate level it would be at if the animals were hunted at an optimal rate; this is an example of how regulation can be a substitute for property rights in correcting a divergence between private and social costs or benefits. The other solution is for one person to buy up the entire habitat of the animals; he will then regulate hunting on his property optimally because he will obtain all the gains from doing so.

Another example of the correlation between property rights and scarcity is the difference in the water law systems of the eastern and western states of the United States. In the eastern states, where water is plentiful, water rights are communalized to a significant extent, the basic rule being that riparian owners (i.e., the owners of the shore of a body of water) are each entitled to make reasonable use of the water—a use that does not interfere unduly with the uses of the other riparians. In the western states, where water is scarce, exclusive rights can be obtained, by appropriation (use).

Now consider the example of things, often very valuable things such as the treasure in a shipwreck, which were once owned but have been abandoned. Here the general rule is finders keepers. In a sense this is the same rule as for wild animals and for water in western states. Ownership of the thing is obtained by reducing it to actual possession. Until then the thing is unowned (the unborn beavers, the abandoned ship), and it is this gap in ownership—this interval when no one has a property right—that is the source of the economic problem.

But the problem is slightly different in the animal and treasure cases. In the case of wild animals the problem is too rapid exploitation; in the case of abandoned property it is too costly exploitation. Suppose the treasure in the shipwreck is worth $1 million and it will cost $250,000 to hire a team of divers to salvage it. Because the expected profit of the venture is so high, someone else may decide to hire his own team and try to beat the first team to it. A third and even a fourth may try, too, for if each one has the same chance (25 percent) of reaching the treasure first, then the expected value of the venture to each one ($1 million × .25) will still cover each one's expected cost. If four try, however, the cost of obtaining the treasure, $1 million, will be four times what it would have been if only one had tried. Actually the net social loss from this competition will be less than $750,000, because the competition probably will result in the treasure's being found sooner (thus increasing its present value) than if only one were trying. But the gain in time may be modest and not worth the additional expenditures that accelerated the search.

There would be no problem of excessive cost if the treasure had not been abandoned; for then the owner would simply have hired one of the four salvagers for $250,000. But when we call property abandoned in the legal sense, we mean that the cost of revesting the property in the original owner is prohibitive, either because he cannot be found at reasonable cost or he considers the property (perhaps incorrectly) to be worth less than the cost of finding or using it. The problem of too costly exploitation of a valuable resource, like the problem of too rapid exploitation, is rooted ultimately in the sometimes prohibitive costs of enforcing property rights.

The law can do something about the abandonment problem and to some extent has done so. The common law sometimes gives the first committed searcher for abandoned property a right to prevent others from searching so long as his search is conscientiously pursued. Another common law rule makes abandoned treasure trove (currency and bullion), if found, escheat to the government rather than becoming the property of the finder. This rule reduces the investment in finding to whatever level the government thinks proper; the government determines that level by determining how much reward to give the finder. In the case of currency (as distinct from treasure that has historical, aesthetic, or collectors' value), the optimal level is very low, perhaps zero. Finding money does not increase the wealth of society; it just enables the finder to have more of society's goods than someone else. The optimal reward may therefore be very low—maybe zero. The trend in the common law is to expand the escheat principle of treasure trove into other areas of found property and thus give the finder a reward rather than the property itself; this makes economic sense.

It might appear that nothing could be more remote from the sunken treasure than patented inventions, and yet the economic problem created by patents is remarkably like that of abandoned property. Ideas are in a sense created but in another sense found. Suppose that whoever invents the widget will, if allowed to exclude others from its use by being granted a patent, be able to sell the patent to a manufacturer for $1 million. And suppose that the cost of invention is $250,000. Others will try to be first to invent the widget. This competition will cause it to be invented sooner. but suppose it is invented only one day sooner; the value of having the widget a day earlier will be less than the cost of duplicating the entire investment in invention.'

Also see:

B Rudden, 'Economic Theory v. Property Law: The *Numerus Clausus* Problem' in J Eekelaar and J Bell (eds), *Oxford Essays in Jurisprudence (Third Series)* (1987, Clarendon: Oxford) ch 11. (This paper asks why the law imposes rigid constraints on the types of property rights it will recognise, when it would seem economically efficient to recognise as wide a variety as possible.)

[808] R Cotterrell, 'The Law of Property and Legal Theory' in W Twining (ed), *Legal Theory and Common Law* (1986, Blackwell: Oxford) ch 5, pp 94–6:
[Footnotes in the original are omitted.]

'The concept of property in law is a device by which law guarantees relations of power while disguising their nature. In private law, power is not normally recognized directly in legal doctrine as an attribute of an individual which he can wield over another. This is because the fundamental principle of general equality before the law of all citizens is inconsistent with any such general recognition. The property form allows the attributes which give an individual power over another to be *separated* from him in legal doctrine as an asset which he owns. The attributes, facilities, capacities and resources which give some persons power over others become "things"—objects of property—which can be conceptualized in law as distinct from their holder. In property law, therefore, the situation is not that persons are recognized as having power over others but that power resides in the property which they own—in the things which are conceived by law as distinct from them and to which they are connected by legal rights acquired in various possible ways which, as far as legal doctrine is concerned, are equally available to all. Looking at matters in this way suggests why the problem of defining modern types of property-asset in legally convincing ways may be more than just a minor technical problem for legal doctrine. If the property form provides a particular framework for the exercise of power which is ideologically significant, changes both in the kinds of assets recognized by law and in the kinds of property rights so recognized may have very important consequences for legal ideology.

. . .

Thus if, as suggested above, the property form disguises and guarantees power by mean of the specific relationship established in ideology between the person, on the one hand, and the thing owned, on the other, the thing-ownership conception of property cannot be dismissed as insignificant quite as easily as modern Hohfeldian legal analysis suggests. The conception may be of great social or ideological significance, even if of limited value as an aid to lawyers in solving technical problems in doctrine. Ackerman argues that the thing-ownership conception is, indeed, fundamental to lay conceptions of property. If this is so it may well be that ideology sets important limitations on the scope of legal doctrinal innovation in the property law field.

Analysis of the ideological significance of the property form may help in understanding the persistence of two distinct and apparently competing doctrinal traditions in Western property law: the continental Romanist conception of property as *dominium* over things (single owner having absolute entitlement to a distinct asset) and the common law conception of fragmentation of ownership (no *dominus* but many possible kinds of property entitlement held by different people in relation to a single material source of wealth). It may be suggested that *technically* the common law conception is more appropriate to encompass the changing forms of wealth which have emerged in Western societies since the beginnings of capitalist development, and to provide extremely flexible and sophisticated devices for their deployment and protection. On the other hand, the Romanist conception of *dominium* which serves to crystallize ownership in terms of a distinct, identifiable asset owned (*res*) and a distinct, more or less absolute owner (*dominus*) provides a means of clearly distinguishing property rights from personal rights. In this way it creates the clear separation of owner and owned which, it has been suggested above, is perhaps fundamental to some major *ideological* effects of the property form. That continental systems have sought to modify Romanist tradition in many ways to create considerable flexibility in property conceptions reflects the problem of meeting technical demands on legal doctrine. Equally, the tensions in common law property doctrine identified in this paper suggest that ideological aspects of law may set limits on its technical capabilities.

. . .

The idea of property has often been associated, not only in a long tradition of political theory but also in popular conceptions, with broad notions of liberty. The orthodox conception of property as the unfettered freedom to do as one will with lawfully held objects of wealth, whatever the social effects of so doing and irrespective of the claims of the property-less to a share in the resources of life, supports a conception of liberty as the freedom to exercise property-power for the accumulation of profit without any limits except those created by the opposed property-power of others. One consequence of the extensive challenges to the orthodox legal conception of property which this paper has discussed may be a more widespread recognition that liberty as an ideal in contemporary conditions must mean not the liberty of property-power but the liberty of *property-security* in which the diffusion of guaranteed entitlements to the use of resources necessary for personal welfare is recognized as the basis of genuine freedom. Thus tensions in legal doctrine in this area may promote ideological change in various ways as well as reflecting it.'

[809] C M Rose, 'Property as the Keystone Right' (1996) 71 *Notre Dame Law Review* 329, 351–5:

[Footnotes in the original are omitted. Other parts of this article are extracted at **[105]** above.]

'V. THE CIVILIZING ARGUMENT

Property is the keystone right because the acquisition and management of property inculcates the moral and civil behavior on which rights depend.

The Civilizing Argument sounds rather peculiar to modern ears. In our own time, the common-sense picture of property's relation to morality is probably closer to a Marxist view. On that depiction, property is at best a concession to the flawed character of human beings, and at worst an open gate to insufferable egocentrism, through which people grasp more, more, more for me, me, me.

Much medieval and early-modern culture was especially hostile to commercially-acquired property and regarded commerce as an activity of a largely despised class—despised precisely because commercial dealers supposedly acquired the habits of avarice and mean-spiritedness..

. . . .

But some eighteenth century economic thinkers—particularly those associated with the Scottish Enlightenment—tried to alter attitudes about the commercial pursuit of property, by transforming the singularly unattractive sin of avarice into the sociable sense of "interest." On this account, commerce was a moral antidote to the pride, violence and vainglory of aristocrats. In contrast to highstrung aristocratic bellicosity, they said, commerce was calm and above all "gentle." Would businessmen dream of fighting duels? Of course not. That is because commerce requires one to focus not on others' slights to one's own honor, but rather on satisfying the others' wants and interests. Commerce thus inculcates sociability and consideration, softening and civilizing rough manners instead of exacerbating them. In this intellectual turnabout, the interdependency of commercial dealings, once considered cause for suspicion, turns out to be a fount of virtue.

Marx and Engels were soon to ridicule the notion of "gentle commerce," of course, and even earlier, Alexander Hamilton suggested that the notion was preposterous, at least insofar as it predicted that a widening commerce would foster peace among nations. Commercial nations, he said, are just as driven as any others by jealousy and fear—and they had better prepare themselves for the attacks of those who hope to plunder them.

But recent historical scholarship suggests that there may indeed have been some truth in the old thesis about "gentle commerce." Although the issue is certainly contested, some historians of the last generation have linked the early nineteenth century's burgeoning commerce to the right of new and vastly expanded forms of philanthropy. One thesis has it that through trade, commercial dealers became interested in people who were very distant from themselves, both socially and geographically. The traders felt some sympathy for the situation of those distant others, and perhaps most importantly, felt that they could make some difference in righting the wrongs that afflicted them. And interestingly enough, some modern game theory experiments appear to confirm that complete strangers can develop strong social and moral bonds simply through the cultivation of trading relationships, especially when those relationships depend on mutual commitment and trust.

Perhaps the most interesting depiction of the way that the pursuit of property influences the "moral sentiments" lies in Alexis de Tocqueville's portrait of mid-nineteenth century Americans. Tocqueville thought that Americans were intoxicated by trade and commerce, even with respect to that most aristocratic if possessions—land—which Americans seemed to regard as just one more commodity. How did this ubiquitous commercial buzz affect personality? Tocqueville's picture shows a people whose prodigious commercial activities left them restless and impelled them to even greater levels of commotion; but those activities also left them largely unconcerned with social distinctions, sympathetic to all kinds of people, generally respectful of other peoples' rights, and infused with a kind of can-do attitude and capacity to work with others to get things done. These traits, if true, seemed to confirm the thesis that commercial pursuits help to instill sociable qualities—though Tocqueville clearly thought that they also corresponded to a platitudinous and shallow intellectual life.

Do we have a modern version of the Civilizing Argument? Perhaps, but only a somewhat muted and contested one, appearing indirectly, for example, in recent historians' debates about whether capitalist growth advanced or impeded the global antislavery movement of the nineteenth century. If there is a modern version, it may be best represented in literature. Here the commercial, property-pursuing person has been the subject of a number of fictional personifications as a moral type: George Babbitt, Sammy Glick, Rabbit Angstrom, Scrooge McDuck. These fictional characters are not entirely admirable types, but on the whole they are not so terrible either. They share with Tocqueville's Americans the tendency to an unfulfilled restlessness, but also, to a greater or lesser extent, most also share the Tocquevillian Americans' sociability, egalitarianism, pragmatism—and their platitudes as well. Taken together, they are of a type that I have described elsewhere not as Athenian, and certainly not Spartan, but rather Babylonian.

The newly transformed republics of the post-socialist age are another intriguing modern showcase for the relationship between capitalism and what Tocqueville might have called morals or *moeurs*. Small facts about these countries tell volumes: some sales clerks have to be taught to smile at the newly-opened McDonalds; others have to learn to pay attention to customers rather than lounging around and insulting them; new businesses have to learn that they cannot bait and switch the same partners twice. These events suggest that capitalist property has a kind of moral and cultural infrastructure that we may have mistakenly thought was simply natural, whereas in fact it is learned through sustained commercial practice, and lost when those practices deteriorate. The content of this infrastructure includes the attitudes that Tocqueville noticed: confidence about one's ability to get things done, either individually or by joining with others; and accompanying that confidence, a certain absence of covetousness even amidst the mad scramble for more material things. In the commercial society, well-being is not a zero-sum game, and apparently the citizenry is aware of that fact.

But how successful is this property-pursuing moral type in attending to other kinds of rights, and in shielding those from depredation? In the America that Tocqueville saw, property did appear to be a kind of school for self-restraint, perhaps most strikingly evident in the annals of the migrant trails west across the continent, where even the most desperate travellers showed a mind-boggling respect for the property of others. Indeed, the Americans' dealings with property and commerce must have borne a striking resemblance to the "self-interest rightly understood" that Tocqueville found so impressive in American political life.

But Tocqueville himself was famously pessimistic about the Americans' ability to respect rights and liberties beyond property, due to their egalitarian propensity to give in to majority opinion. Whatever Tocqueville thought of the "gentle commerce" thesis—or of the evidence that commerce could inculcate confidence, cooperativeness, or respect for others—when he discussed institutions that might dam the egalitarian floodwaters of majoritarianism, he focused on local government, voluntary associations and the legal profession, far more than on property and commerce. Indeed, he often appeared to think that commercial pursuits were part and parcel of American egalitarianism and striving. Commerce seemed clearly as vulgar as those other egalitarian traits, and possibly even subtly dangerous to liberty.

Tocqueville's picture certainly leaves some ambiguity about whether the pursuit of property makes people more civil, and hence more capable of supporting and respecting rights generally. The haunting fear is that commerce and property may indeed have these civilizing qualities to some degree, but that they remain vulnerable to the sudden, irresistible blows of envy and majoritarian passions.'

[810] J Waldron, *The Right to Private Property* (1988, Clarendon: Oxford), pp 423–6: [Footnotes in the original are omitted.]

'Could private property be the subject of a general right? Is it something we could plausibly provide *for everyone* in the way we try to provide political rights, civil liberty, health, education and welfare? Or—to put it another way—is the ideal of a "property-owning democracy" anything more than a *petit-bourgeois* utopian pipe-dream?

In this final chapter, I want to consider two negative answers to these questions which amount to quite radical challenges to the idea that private property could be one of the general rights of man. The challenges come from utterly different political perspectives.

(i) Nozick

The first comes from the Right and is most lucidly expressed in an argument adapted from Nozick's work.

A principle of justice requiring private property for everyone would, if implemented, soon be frustrated by the exercise of the very property rights that were distributed. Suppose access to and control of resources were distributed so that everyone was the owner of at least the share deemed necessary for liberty or ethical development by whatever GR-based argument we favoured. What would happen subsequently when someone lost his shirt in a poker game or invested his share imprudently in an enterprise that went bust? The required pattern of distribution of private property would be disrupted by these events and the GR-based case for a distribution of private property would no longer be satisfied on a universal scale. But yet that would have happened as a result of the free exercise of the rights which it was the whole point of the argument to make available. As Nozick puts it:

> Any favored pattern would be transformed into one unfavored by the principle, by people choosing to act in various ways; for example, by people exchanging goods and services with other people, or giving things to other people, things the transferrers are entitled to under the favored distributional pattern. To maintain a pattern one must either continually interfere to stop people from transferring resources as they wish to, or continually (or periodically) interfere to take from some persons resources that others for some reason chose to transfer to them. (But if some time limit is to be set on how long people may keep resources others voluntarily transfer to them, why let them keep resources for *any* period of time? Why not have immediate confiscation?)

(The answer to the last question, I suppose, will refer to difficulties of administration.) The point of Nozick's challenge in the present context is that the only way to ensure that everyone has a specified amount of private property seems to involve prohibiting or frustrating the exercise of the very rights which constitute the private property that we want everybody to have.

. . .

(ii) Marx

The second attack comes from the opposite direction. It is the challenge laid down by Karl Marx in a furious response to bourgeois critics of the socialist programme outlined in *The Communist Manifesto*:

> You are horrified at our intending to do away with private property. But in your existing society, private property is already done away with for nine tenths of the population; its existence for the few is solely due to its nonexistence in the hands of these nine-tenths. You reproach us, therefore, with intending to do away with a form of property the necessary condition for whose existence is the nonexistence of any property for the immense majority of society. In one word, you reproach us for intending to do away with your property. Precisely so; that is just what we intend.

Throughout his work, Marx is adamant that the indictment against capitalism is not merely the fact that private property happens to be distributed unequally or in a way that leaves millions without any guaranteed access to the means of production; the problem is that private ownership is a form of property that has this characteristic *necessarily*. No matter how noble your egalitarian intentions, the existence of any distribution of private property rights in the means of production will lead quickly to their concentration in the hands of a few. Thus egalitarian intentions, so far as private property is concerned are hopelessly utopian, for they underestimate the dynamic tendencies of the system they are interested in: "for us the issue cannot be the alteration of private property but its annihilation". GR-based arguments for private property therefore would stand condemned on this approach just to the extent that they have egalitarian or quasi-egalitarian implications.'

FURTHER READING:

J E Penner, *The Idea of Property in Law* (1997, Clarendon: Oxford).

B Rudden, 'Things as Things and Things as Wealth' (1994) 14 *OJLS* 82, and a revised version in J W Harris, *Property Problems: From Genes to Pension Funds* (1997, Kluwer: London) ch 12.

G Calabresi and A D Melamed, 'Property Rules, Liability Rules, and Inalienability: One View of the Cathedral' (1972) 85 *Harvard Law Rev* 1089.

F Snare, 'The Concept of Property' (1972) 9 *American Philosophical Quarterly* 200.

C Reich, 'The New Property' (1964) 73 *Yale Law Journal* 733. (The central thesis in this paper is regarded as path-breaking—notwithstanding that the ideas are not all new, and their practical impact is, as yet, unclear.)

8.4 The future

[811] K Gray, 'Equitable Property' [1994] *CLP* 157, 181–7, 207–10:

[The footnotes in the original are omitted. In addition, the later pages appear first: they provide a statement of the general thesis. The earlier pages then provide an illustration of its application.]

> 'The task of the immediate future is, in part, to reconceive the law of property for the 21st century. It must be highly improbable that our current perceptions of property will retain a wholly undiminished relevance in the days to come. This paper has therefore tried to suggest some ways in which wider notions of 'equitable property' are in the process of being impressed on a number of resources to which increasing community value is attached. In a number of legal regimes across the world a more socially oriented vision of entitlement is starting to emerge from the dialectic of property. This new equitable property constitutes a sort of 'meta-property', arising in the historic pattern of equity in order to supplement and fulfil the rules of the law. The new equity seeks exactly what the old equity achieved, and aims to engraft a different or corrective image of entitlement on to pre-existing legal estates. As always equity operates in response to demands of conscience, the sole difference being that the doctrinal force which drives equity here is more palpably the conscience of *community*. Although its full scope has yet to be elaborated, the new equitable property is more heavily committed to the articulation of a civic or social morality relating to the goods of life. In respect of certain publicly defined goods it strongly endorses claims of access in preference to those of exclusion.
>
> The move towards this communitarian vision of property relationships is, of course, both controversial and far from complete. By imposing collectively perceived limitations on the exclusory control exercised over important resources, the regime of equitable property points up the intensely correlative nature of rights and responsibilities as incidents of 'property'. The language of 'property' begins to disclose a deep subtext of social 'propriety' in opposition to its once more common connotation of appetitive economic power. The concept of 'property' reveals an inner morality founded upon what, in another context, Paul Finn has called 'two characteristic and inter-related concerns: the first, respect for self; the second, regard for others.' When entitlement and duty intersect, property ceases to operate merely as a vehicle for individual preference-

satisfaction and begins to carry 'the authority, but also the responsibility, of a trust to the larger community.'

There is nevertheless nothing quite so dangerous as a vested right, since *any* subsequent contraction of its scope—however justified—inevitably appears as unlawful deprivation. The proposal of any social curbs on private autonomy in the control and exploitation of resources is often apt to be considered an unpleasant communist perversion. There is, accordingly, a need for constant reminder that the operation of equitable property is distributive rather than *re*distributive. The claims of civic property endorsed by the new equity comprise merely the assertion of latent human entitlements which have long been submerged by superficial allocations of formal title. Charles Reich wrote recently of the new property that it does not represent 'value transferred to the needy from another group in society', but represents instead the 'birthright of every individual' and is, as such, 'inseparable from citizenship and personhood'. Those who entertain dark fears of left wing subversion lack the clarity of vision—or perhaps the wit—to realise that the truly conservative option is in fact the more radical and that, ironically, it is only the more radical vision of property which will preserve the conventional *desiderata* of an ordered society characterised by justice, tolerance and the rule of law.

It is, moreover, a constant of communitarian philosophy that the reinforcement of collectively oriented perceptions of 'property' promotes, rather than inhibits, the preconditions of personal autonomy and individual fulfilment. The controlled dispersal of access to a range of socially valued opportunities and life chances has, almost paradoxically, the effect of enhancing personal liberty. In so far as 'equitable property' contributes to a process of distributive justice, it consolidates both the dignity of the individual and some sense of the reciprocal responsibility which each citizen owes to his or her community. The best path for the future thus lies in a wider recognition of the heavily interdependent nature of our social and economic arrangements.

. . .

It may, of course, be asked why the interests represented in the new equitable property are not merely urged as human or civic rights. The answer must be the one given by Professor Macpherson: 'We have made property so central to our society that any thing and any rights that are not property are very apt to take second place'. In adopting the terminology of equitable property we lock into the insidiously powerful leverage of the primal claim, 'it's mine', and we harness this claim for more constructive social purposes. When important assets of the human community are threatened, we are able to say, with collective force, 'You can't do that: these assets are ours.' When you pollute our air or our rivers or exclude us unreasonably from wild and open spaces, we can mobilise the enormous symbolic and emotional impact of the property attribution by asserting that you are taking away some of our 'property'.

. . . .

[And at pp. 181–7:]

(2) EQUITABLE PROPERTY IN TRADITIONAL COUNTRY

A second (and rather different) example of the recognition of the 'access dimension' of property is to be found in recent attempts to resolve claims of original or aboriginal title made by the historically dispossessed native peoples of Canada, the United States and Australia. The Australian experience is particularly informative. Blackburn J.'s well-known decision in *Milirrpum* v. *Nabalco Pty Ltd* [(1971) 17 FLR 141, 272 ff] expressly (albeit reluctantly) denied that the Australian Aboriginal's customary intimate relationship with his land—based upon the personal usufructuary right to go walkabout and forage over traditional tracts of country—could ever conform to the essential indicia of proprietary ownership in its common law sense. The standard ingredients of conventional proprietary ownership were notably absent not least because the Aboriginal nomad had no concept of a right to exclude others, still less to alienate lands to a stranger. At the heart of the Aboriginal concept of land has always been the notion of access not of exclusion. Its fundamental feature has been the acknowledgement of a duty to care for the land—to 'look after country'—in the discharge of which responsibility Aboriginal people 'see themselves as caretakers of a relationship of trust deriving from The Dreaming and passed on to them by their immediate forebears.'

As Brennan J was to emphasise in *R.* v. *Toohey; Ex parte Meneling Station Pty Ltd*, [(1982) 158 CLR 327, 357 f] the connection of the Aboriginal group with the land 'does not consist in the communal holding of rights with respect to the land, but in the group's spiritual affiliations to a site on the land and the group's spiritual responsibility for the site and for the land.' Aboriginal ownership, said Brennan J., is 'primarily a spiritual affair rather than a bundle of rights.' Paradoxically, it is the performance of an amalgam of symbolic, organic and ritual duties which, for the Aboriginal, constitutes the closest approximation to 'land rights' known to his community. Right and responsibility emerge not only as correlatives but as deeply interpenetrating images of the 'proper' association with the resources of the earth. Here 'property' has more in common with 'propriety' than entitlement and the notion of 'right' has more to do with perceptions of 'rightness' than with any understanding of enforceable exclusory title.

It was in the context of this intensely symbiotic relationship with the natural environment that in *Milirrpum* Blackburn J. found that the Aboriginals had 'a more cogent feeling of obligation to the land than of ownership of it'. It was, he declared, 'easier . . . to say that the clan belongs to the land than that the land belongs to the clan'. It thus followed, with brutal clarity, that native claims were incompatible with, were not accommodated within, and were indeed extinguished by, the common law system of property brought by the white settler two hundred years earlier. The Aboriginal relationship with land being essentially religious, the spiritual or ritual evocation of The Dreaming could simply not be comprehended within the impoverished common law notion of property.

It has taken virtually two centuries for the Australian conscience to catch up the inequity that customary native title throughout Australia (as indeed elsewhere in the New World) should be wholly swallowed up by the process of colonisation. During the 1970s and 1980s suggestions began to emerge—and the language is significant—that government owed some fiduciary obligation to the indigenous peoples, even that there was an element of trust (public or otherwise) in the relationship between government and Aboriginal in respect of native land. This infusion of equitable terminology was given significant support by Canadian courts which slowly recognised that native Indians might collectively have a beneficial interest in their reserved lands. In *Guerin v. The Queen* [(1984) 13 DLR (4th) 321, 339] Dickson J. considered there to be 'no real conflict between the cases which characterise Indian title as a beneficial interest of some sort, and those which characterise it a personal, usufructuary right. Any apparent inconsistency derives from the fact that in describing what constitutes a unique interest in land the courts have almost inevitably found themselves applying a somewhat inappropriate terminology drawn from general property law.' In the view of Dickson J. and the Supreme Court, the *sui generis* character of native title, hovering between 'beneficial ownership' and 'personal right', was capable of giving rise to a 'distinctive fiduciary obligation on the part of the Crown to deal with land for the benefit of the . . . Indians.'

Precisely this fiduciary theme has been taken up in Australia, most famously in the controversial ruling of the High Court in 1992 in the second *Mabo* case (*Mabo v.*

Queensland (No 2)) [(1992) 175 CLR 1]. Here a strong majority in the High Court conceded that Australia, on first colonisation, was not *terra nullius*, and that the settlers' law of property must recognise pre-existing customary native rights in respect of the land. Brennan J. had earlier spoken of the 'sadly familiar' phenomenon of 'landless, rootless Aboriginal peoples'. In dealing in *Mabo (No 2)* with the land rights of the Meriam people of the Murray Islands, Brennan J. forthrightly condemned as 'discriminatory denigration' the theory that indigenous inhabitants of a 'settled' colony lost all 'proprietary interest' in the land which they continued to occupy. Brennan J. was therefore prepared to regard customary claims as comprising a 'proprietary community title' which could be recognised as 'a burden on the Crown's radical title when the Crown acquires sovereignty over that territory.' According to Brennan J. it was 'only the fallacy of equating sovereignty and beneficial ownership of land that gives rise to the notion that native title is extinguished by the acquisition of sovereignty.' Some form of beneficial ownership thus remained vested in the indigenous peoples at least in relation to lands occupied by them at the date of the Crown's assumption of sovereign control.

In *Mabo*'s case Toohey J., another member of the High Court majority, was happy to adopt the reasoning in the parallel Canadian case law in pointing to the existence of a fiduciary obligation in the Crown to protect the integrity of native title. Toohey J. openly admitted that, in the present context, recognition of a fiduciary relationship 'may be tantamount to saying that the legal interest in traditional rights is in the Crown whereas the beneficial interest in the rights is in the indigenous owners.' Although viewing as 'fruitless' and 'unnecessarily complex' any further inquiry as to whether native title is 'personal' or 'proprietary', Toohey J. had no doubt that, for present purposes, 'the kind of fiduciary obligation imposed on the Crown is that of a constructive trustee.' Deane and Gaudron JJ likewise recognised the inappropriateness of forcing native title within conventional common law classifications, but acknowledged nonetheless that the rights of occupation or use conferred by native title 'can themselves constitute valuable property'.

FURTHER READING:

C B MacPherson (ed), *Property: Mainstream and Critical Positions* (1978, Basil Blackwell: Oxford).

A Ryan, *Property and Political Theory* (1984, Basil Blackwell: Oxford).

J Waldron, *The Right to Private Property* (1988, Clarendon Press: Oxford).

Questions:

Is the concept of personal property essential? If it is, what social, moral and commercial functions must it perform? What changes to existing personal property law would see these ends more readily achieved?

Index

9 781901 362435

Printed by Libri Plureos GmbH in Hamburg,
Germany